Literature

Structure, Sound, and Sense

FOURTH EDITION

Literature

Structure, Sound, and Sense

FOURTH EDITION

Laurence Perrine
With the assistance of
Thomas R. Arp

SOUTHERN METHODIST UNIVERSITY

HBJ HARCOURT BRACE JOVANOVICH, PUBLISHERS
SAN DIEGO   NEW YORK   CHICAGO   ATLANTA   WASHINGTON D.C.
LONDON   SYDNEY   TORONTO

ISBN: 0-15-551106-8

Library of Congress Catalog Card Number: 82-083236

Printed in the United States of America

COPYRIGHTS AND ACKNOWLEDGMENTS

FICTION

BILL ADAMS "God Rest You Merry, Gentlemen" reprinted from *The Atlantic Monthly* (162: 758–66, Dec. 1945) by permission of the author.

JAMES AGEE "A Mother's Tale" from *The Collected Short Prose of James Agee*. Copyright © 1968 and 1969 by The James Agee Trust. Reprinted by permission of Houghton Mifflin Company.

SHERWOOD ANDERSON "I'm a Fool" reprinted by permission of Harold Ober Associates Incorporated. Copyright © 1922 by The Dial Publishing Company, Inc. Renewed 1949 by Eleanor Copenhaver Anderson.

MARGARET ATWOOD "Rape Fantasies" from *Dancing Girls and Other Stories* by Margaret Atwood. Reprinted by permission of The Canadian Publishers, McClelland and Stewart Limited, Toronto.

DONALD BARTHELME "Some of Us Had Been Threatening Our Friend Colby" from *Amateurs* by Donald Barthelme. Copyright © 1973, 1976 by Donald Barthelme. Reprinted by permission of Farrar, Straus and Giroux, Inc. This story originally appeared in *The New Yorker*.

ALBERT CAMUS "The Guest" from *Exile and the Kingdom* by Albert Camus, translated by Justin O'Brien. Copyright © 1957, 1958 by Alfred A. Knopf, Inc. Reprinted by permission of the publisher.

TRUMAN CAPOTE "A Christmas Memory" copyright © 1956 by Truman Capote. Reprinted from *Selected Writings of Truman Capote*, by Truman Capote, by permission of Random House, Inc. Originally appeared in *Madamoiselle*.

WILLA CATHER "Paul's Case" reprinted from *Youth and the Bright Medusa*, by Willa Cather, by courtesy of Alfred A. Knopf, Inc.

JOHN CHEEVER "The Pot of Gold" copyright 1950 and renewed 1978 by John Cheever. Reprinted from *The Stories of John Cheever*, by John Cheever, by permission of Alfred A. Knopf, Inc.

Copyrights and acknowledgments continue on pages 1467–76.

Preface

Literature: Structure, Sound, and Sense is intended for the student who is beginning a serious study of imaginative literature. It provides a comprehensive introduction to the principal forms of fiction, poetry, and drama. Each section begins with a simple discussion of the elements of the form and is illustrated, throughout, by carefully chosen stories, poems, and plays. Each section also includes additional selections for further reading. The book seeks to give the student a sufficient grasp of the nature and variety of literary works, some reasonable means for reading them with appreciative understanding, and some basic principles for making literary judgments. Its objective is to help the student understand, enjoy, and prefer good works of literature.

Each of the three sections has been revised for this fourth edition: thirteen of the forty stories, about twenty-eight percent of the two-hundred-seventy-seven poems, and five of the twelve plays are new. Canadian authors have been included for the first time. More glosses have been provided than in previous editions. Each story and play is provided with an introductory footnote giving the date of its first publication, background information necessary for understanding it, and information locating the author in time, place, and circumstance *in relation to* the selection. In the poetry section the chapter on rhythm and meter has been rewritten using a different illustrative poem. Finally, an appendix on writing about literature has been added.

The fiction section is the same as the sixth edition of *Story and Structure*; the poetry section is the same as the sixth edition of *Sound and Sense*. For each of the three sections a glossary of technical terms is included.

A book of this kind inevitably owes something to all who have thought or written about literature. It would be impossible to express all indebtedness, but for personal advice, criticism, and assistance I wish especially to thank my wife, Catherine Perrine; Marshall Terry, Daniel T. Orlovsky, and the late Margaret Morton Blum, Southern Methodist University; Maynard Mack, Yale University; David Thorburn, Massachusetts Institute of Technology; the late Mark Schorer, University of California; the late Charles S. Holmes, Pomona College; Donald Peet, Indiana University; James W. Byrd, East Texas State University; Calvin L. Skaggs, Drew University; Willis Glover, Mercer University; Paul T. Hopper, Washington, D.C.; and Margaret Rusk White, Keene State College.

I would also like to thank the following instructors, who have sent me helpful reactions and suggestions for this fourth edition of *Literature: Structure, Sound, and Sense*: John Adair, Cumberland Community College; Louise Adams, Blue Ridge Community College; Carl Adkins, Buena Vista College; Anne Agee, Anne Arundel Community College; Carolyn R. Allison, Essex Community College; Dora Jena Ashe, Lynchburg College; Leroy Earl Ater, Los Angeles Pierce College; Verdon Ballantyne, Brigham Young University; Ronald Ballard, Hagerstown Junior College; Joseph Barba, College of the Sequoias; James Barreca, Chaffey College; Donna Bauerly, Loras College; Ronald E. Becht, Marquette University; Meredith Bedell, Virginia Military Institute; Hazel M. Benn, Northern State College; Mark Bernheim, Miami University; Gerard Bevan, County College of Morris; Manuel B. Blanco, Laredo Junior College; John Boggs, University of Richmond; Jill Bohlander, Los Angeles Pierce College; Paul Borgman, Northwestern College; Wilson Boyton, Holyoke Community College; Phillip E. Bozek, Illinois Benedictine College; Arnold J. Bradford, Northern Virginia Community College; Vivian Brown, Laredo Junior College; Robert Bruce, Los Angeles Pierce College; Peter Brunette, George Mason University; Mary Jane Burns, Johnson County Community College; Stuart Burns, Drake University; Jon C. Burton, Northern Virginia Community College; Ronald W. Butler, Henderson Community College; Mary Cane, Mississippi University for Women; John Canuteson, William Jewell College; Mary Casper, West Valley College; Helen G. Chapin, Hawaii Pacific College; M. G. Cheney, Weber State College; Penelope Choy, Los Angeles City College; Edward Cifelli, County College of Morris; Tony Clark, Paris Junior College; Doris Clatanoff, Concordia College; Lawrence Clayton, Hardin-Simmons University; Thomas Clayton, Los Angeles Valley College; Betty C. Clement, Paris Junior College; Burt Collins, Kankakee Community College; Lynne M. Constantine, James Madison University; E. Wayne Cook, Mt. View College; Ethel F. Cornwell, Shepherd College; Lynn

Cox, Lincoln Land Community College; G. B. Crump, Central Missouri State College; Joan Cunningham, Meridian Junior College; Gordon Curzon, California Polytechnic State University; Daniel Dalton, John Tyler Community College; R. W. Danielson, Grossmont College; James Davis, Virginia Military Institute; William R. Day, County College of Morris; William J. Deegan, Roanoke College; Francine De France, Cerritos College; Brian J. Delaney, Blue Ridge Community College; John W. Dickinson, San Diego State University; James Dighera, Cerritos College; Sister Mary Colleen Dillon, Thomas More College; Anne B. Dobie, University of Southwestern Louisiana; Pauline Douglas, Prairie State College; Walter Dudek, Fullerton College; Margaret Duggar, Chicago State University; Marianne Duty, John Tyler Community College; Janet E. Eber, County College of Morris; C. H. Edgren, North Park College; David Eggebrecht, Concordia College; Robert A. Elderdice, Salisbury State College; Fiona I. Emde, West Valley College; Toni Empringham, El Camino College; Thomas Evans, North Carolina Central University; Gabriel Fagan, St. Mary's College; Gene Fehler, Kishwaukee College; Charles E. Ferguson, Alvin Community College; Virginia G. Fick, Davidson Community College; John W. Fields, Weatherford College; Frank M. Flack, Los Angeles Pierce College; Robert Foxworthy, Fullerton College; William L. Frank, Longwood College; Don Fraser, De Anza College; J. L. Funston, James Madison University; K. Gabrielson, County College of Morris; Maryanne Garbowsky, County College of Morris; Dennis Gendron, St. Paul's College; Peter Gillett, University of Wisconsin; Michael Glaser, St. Mary's College; William Glassman, Fullerton College; Bill Gracie, Miami University; William Grady, Middlesex Community College; Gary Grassinger, Community College of Allegheny County; Jane Grissinger, Shepherd College; Garland Gunter, University of Richmond; William Gutherie, Wilmington College; John Hall, Bergen Community College; Frank Hanenkraf, Lynchburg College; John K. Hanes, Duquesne University; T. Hanley, Glendale College; Nikki Hansen, Weber State College; James J. Harcharik, Kishwaukee College; Harold Harp, Johnson County Community College; Marvin Harris, East Texas Baptist College; Carol T. Hayes, Holyoke Community College; Mary Dell Heathington, Cooke County Junior College; Neva Herrington, Northern Virginia Community College; Iris Hill, Durham Technical Institute; Dennis Hoilman, Ball State University; Anne Holbrooks, Davidson County Community College; Julia Hornbostel, University of Wisconsin; James E. Horner, National Business College; Ann Hostetler, Golden West College; Thomas R. Howerton, Jr., Johnston Technical Institute; Wayne Hubert, Chaffey College;

Betty Hughes, Beaufort County Community College; Gerald Hunt, Miami University; Darrel W. Hurst, Blue Ridge Community College; Sandra T. Jackson, County College of Morris; Irene O. Jacobs, Frederick Community College; Leonard Jellema, Moraine Valley Community College; Kenneth G. Johnston, Kansas State University; Dan Jones, Wytheville Community College; Mary Jane Kearney, National College of Education; John Keeler, County College of Morris; John Kelly, South Dakota School of Mines and Technology; Kathryn Kenkins, Chaffey Community College; Michael Ketcham, Texas A & M University; Jeannette E. Kinyon, South Dakota School of Mines and Technology; Audrey S. Kirby, Forsyth Technical Institute; Paul Kistel, Los Angeles Pierce College; William Klink, Charles County Community College; Patricia C. Knight, Amarillo College; Allen J. Koppenhaver, Wittenberg University; Sister Mary Conrad Kraus, Viterbo College; Sara E. Kreps, Tidewater Community College; Reverend Laurence Kriegshauser, OSB, St. Louis Priory School; Alexander Kucsma, County College of Morris; Donald Kummings, University of Wisconsin, Parkside; William Landau, Los Angeles Pierce College; Lyle Larsen, Santa Monica College; Dixie LeHardy, Hagerstown Junior College; Scott Loughton, Weber State College; Carolyn V. Luce, Columbia Union College; Katherine Lyle, Southern Seminary Junior College; Joanne H. McCarthy, Tacoma Community College; E. Carole McClanahan, Danville Community College; Allison McCormack, Miami University; Jo Ray McCuen, Glendale College; Virginia McGovern, Charles County Community College; Emily Madden, Virginia State University; Gretchen Marlotte, West Los Angeles College; T. Marshall, Robert Morris College; Margo Matarese, John Tyler Community College; Joan Mathis, Paris Junior College; Nancy Mellman, County College of Morris; Robert Meredith, Chicago State University; Don Meyer, Ventura College; Sara M. Miller, Northern Virginia Community College; Virginia R. Mollenkott, William Paterson College of New Jersey; George E. Montag, Longview Community College; T. D. Nostwich, Iowa State University; Jean O'Donnell, Holyoke Community College; Judith A. Oliver, Robert Morris College; Larry Olpin, Central Missouri State University; Alice Omelia, Essex Community College; Luz Maria Orozer, Marycrest College; Robert J. Owens, Los Angeles City College; Tom Padgett, Southwest Baptist College; John Peters, Los Angeles Valley College; Gloria Dibble Pond, Mattatuck Community College; Dale Porter, West Los Angeles College; Nancy C. Potts, Davidson County Community College; Kurt V. Rachwitz, Bellevue College; Thomas D. Ragan, Ventura College; Noel Peter Robinson, County College of Morris; Jack Rollow, Bergen Community College; Robert Sather, College of Lake County; Marilyn Satlof, Columbus College; Jerry Sattin, Bergen Community College; John Scanlon, Quinsigamond Community College; James C. Schaap, Dordt College; Gloria Schleimer, Compton College; Robert Schultz, El Camino College; Kent Seltman, Pacific Union College; Robert V. Shaven, Danville Community College; William Sheehan, West Valley College; Beth B. Shelton, Paris Junior College; Gerald Siegel, York College of Pennsylvania; Carole Slaugh, North Harris County College; Keith Slocum, Montclair State College; William F. Smith, Fullerton College; Mary S. Spangler, Los Angeles Valley College; Patricia Spano, Columbus College; Jacqueline K. Stark, Los Angeles Valley College; Maurine Stein, Prairie State College; Eric Steinbaugh, U.S. Naval Academy; J. E. Stewart, U.S. Naval Academy; J. M. Stiker, Lewis University; Massie Stinson, Longwood College; Harryette Stover, Eastfield College; J. Richard Stracke, University of Wisconsin; Marianne W. Strong, Prince George's Community College; Donald Stuart, Longwood College; Maureen Townsend, Kankakee Community College; Peter J. Ulisse, Housatonic Regional Community College; James Vanden Bosch, Dordt College; Charles L. Van Hof, Dordt College; Sandra C. Vekasy, Evangel College; Mary Waldrop, Tyler Junior College; Robert K. Wallace, Northern Kentucky University; Martha Waller, Butler University; Thomas C. Ware, University of Tennessee; Clifford Warren, Prince George's Community College; Jean Weber, Cerritos College; John P. Weber, Cypress College; Ray Weinstein, West Los Angeles College; J. L. Wheeler, Southwestern Adventist College; Jack H. White, Mississippi State University; Richard W. White, Edison Community College; John H. Whiting, Orange County Community College; J. Peter Williams, County College of Morris; Marianne Wilpiszewski, Prince George's Community College; Virginia S. Wilson, New River Community College; Ken Wolfskill, Chowan College; Joyce Wszalek, James Madison University; Robert W. Wylie, Amarillo College; Clemewell Young, Manchester Community College; John Young, Villa Maria College; Sander Zulauf, County College of Morris.

L. P.

Southern Methodist University
Dallas, Texas

Contents

Poetry

THE ELEMENTS OF POETRY

6.   Figurative Language 2: Symbol, Allegory   589

7.   Figurative Language 3: Paradox, Overstatement, Understatement, Irony   609

8. Allusion   629

9. Meaning and Idea   640

15.   Bad Poetry and Good   736

16.   Good Poetry and Great   752

POEMS FOR FURTHER READING

Drama

THE ELEMENTS OF DRAMA

1. The Nature of Drama   837

2. Realistic and Nonrealistic Drama   877

3. Tragedy and Comedy   1051

PLAYS FOR FURTHER READING

Literature

Structure, Sound, and Sense

FOURTH EDITION

Fiction

The Elements
of Fiction

1. Escape and Interpretation

The first question to ask about fiction is, Why bother to read it? With life as short as it is, with so many pressing demands on our time, with books of information, instruction, and discussion waiting to be read, why should we spend precious time on works of imagination? The eternal answers to this question are two: enjoyment and understanding.

Since the invention of language, men have taken pleasure in following and participating in the imaginary adventures and imaginary experiences of imaginary people. Whatever—without causing harm—serves to make life less tedious, to make the hours pass more quickly and pleasurably, surely needs nothing else to recommend it. Enjoyment—and ever more enjoyment—is the first aim and justification of reading fiction.

But, unless fiction gives something more than pleasure, it hardly justifies itself as a subject of college study. Unless it expands or refines our minds or quickens our sense of life, its value is not appreciably greater than that of video games, bridge, or ping-pong. To have a compelling claim on our attention, it must yield not only enjoyment but understanding.

The experience of humankind through the ages is that literature may furnish such understanding and do so effectively—that the depiction of imagined experiences can provide authentic insights. "The truest history," said Diderot of the novels of Samuel Richardson, "is full of falsehoods, and your romance is full of truths." But the bulk of fiction does not present such insights. Only some does. Initially, therefore, fiction may be classified into two broad categories: literature of escape and literature of interpretation.

ESCAPE LITERATURE is that written purely for entertainment—to help us pass the time agreeably. INTERPRETIVE LITERATURE is written to broaden and deepen and sharpen our awareness of life. Escape literature takes us *away* from the real world: it enables us temporarily to forget our troubles. Interpretive literature takes us, through the imagination, deeper *into* the real world: it enables us to understand our troubles. Escape literature has as its only object pleasure. Interpretive literature has as its object pleasure *plus* understanding.

Having established a distinction, however, we must not exaggerate or oversimplify it. Escape and interpretation are not two great bins, into one or the other of which we can toss any given story. Rather, they are opposite ends of a scale, the two poles between which the world of fiction spins. The difference between them does not lie in the absence or presence of a "moral." The story which in all of its incidents and characters is shallow may have an unimpeachable moral, while the interpretive story may have no moral at all in any conventional sense. The difference does not lie in the absence or presence of "facts." The historical romance may be full of historical information and yet be pure escape in its depiction of human behavior. The difference does not lie in the presence or absence of an element of fantasy. The escape story may have a surface appearance of everyday reality, while the tale of seeming wildest fancy may press home on us some sudden truth. The difference between the two kinds of literature is deeper and more subtle than any of these distinctions. A story becomes interpretive as it illuminates some aspect of human life or behavior. An interpretive story presents us with an insight—large or small—into the nature and conditions of our existence. It gives us a keener awareness of what it is to be a human being in a universe sometimes friendly, sometimes hostile. It helps us to understand our world, our neighbors, and ourselves.

Perhaps we can clarify the difference by suggestion. Escape writers are like inventors who devise a contrivance for our diversion. When we push the button, lights flash, bells ring, and cardboard figures move jerkily across a painted horizon. Interpretive writers are discoverers: they take us out into the midst of life and say, "Look, here is the world!" Escape writers are full of tricks and surprises: they pull rabbits out of hats, saw a beautiful woman in two, and snatch brightly colored balls out of the air. Interpretive writers take us behind the scenes, where they show us the props and mirrors and seek to make clear the illusions. This is not to say that interpretive writers are merely reporters. More surely than escape writers they shape and give form to their materials. But they shape and form them always with the intent that we may see and feel and understand them better, not for the primary purpose of furnishing entertainment.

Now, just as there are two kinds of fiction, there are also two kinds of readers. Immature readers seek only escape.* Even when they think they are reading for interpretation or some useful moral, they insist that what they read return them always some pleasant or exciting image of the world or some flattering image of themselves. We all begin with fairy tales. Our early reading experiences are likely to be with stories such as that of Cinderella, whose fairy godmother transforms a pumpkin and mice into a coach-and-four, whose slim foot is the only one that fits the crystal slipper, who rises superior to her cruel stepmother and taunting stepsisters to marry and "live happily ever after" with the charming prince, and who, never for a moment anything but sweet and virtuous, forgives her former tormenters who tried to keep her a cinder girl.

Though most people move on from fairy tales into a seemingly more adult kind of reading, they may well be mistaken in thinking that they have progressed. The element of unreality does not lie primarily in magic wands and fairy godmothers but in a superficial treatment of life. The story of a shopgirl who is lifted from the painful conditions of her work and home life by a handsome young suitor from the upper classes may be as truly a Cinderella story as the one we read in childhood, though its setting is Hoboken rather than a kingdom by the sea. Unfortunately many readers never grow beyond the fairy tale except in the most elementary of senses. In some ways, perhaps, their movement is backward, for it involves a loss of that sense of wonder that marks the child's vision.

There are many signs of immature readers. They make fixed demands of every story and feel frustrated and disappointed unless these demands are satisfied. Often they stick to one type of subject matter. Instead of being receptive to any story that puts human beings in human situations, they read only sports stories, western stories, love stories, crime stories, or science fiction. If they are willing to accept a wider range of experience, they still wish every story to conform at bottom to several strict

---

*The distinction made in this book between "mature" and "immature" readers is based not on age or status, but only on the possession of literary perception, judgment, and taste. Young people may often be more "mature" in this respect than their elders, and students sometimes more so than their teachers. Like the distinction between escape literature and interpretive literature, that between "mature" and "immature" readers is relative, not absolute. The terms do not represent two categories into which all readers may be classified, but simply the opposed ends of a graduated scale. No sharp line divides one class from the other: some students may be more mature than others in one aspect of their reading and less mature in another.

though perhaps unconsciously formulated expectations. Among the most common of these expectations are (1) a sympathetic hero or heroine—one with whom the reader can in imagination identify while reading and whose adventures and triumphs the reader can share; (2) a plot in which something exciting is always happening and in which there is a strong element of suspense; (3) a happy outcome, that sends the reader away undisturbed and optimistic about the world; (4) a theme—if the story has a theme—that confirms the reader's already-held opinions of the world.

There is nothing wrong with any of these characteristics as story elements. Significant fiction has been written with them all. The error lies in elevating these characteristics into a set of rigid requirements that a story must meet to be enjoyed. Such limitations restrict drastically the opportunity for expanding one's experience or broadening one's insights. They reduce one's demands on literature to a formula.*

Immature readers want the essentially familiar combined with super-ficial novelty. Each story must have a slightly new setting or twist or "gimmick," though the fundamental features of the characters and situa-tions remain the same. They evaluate a story not by its truth but by its twists, turns, and surprises, by its suspense or its love interest. They want stories to be mainly pleasant. Evil, danger, and misery may appear in them, but not in such a way that they need be taken really seriously or are felt to be oppressive or permanent. Immature readers want reading that slips easily and smoothly through the mind, requiring little mental effort.

---

*Fiction is sometimes roughly divided into COMMERCIAL fiction—that written for wide popular consumption—and QUALITY fiction—that written with a more serious artistic in-tent. In commercial fiction, the most general formula is: a sympathetic hero is faced with obstacles that he finally overcomes to achieve his goal. Most frequently, the hero's goal is to win the hand of the heroine; therefore, the most common subtype of the formula is: boy meets girl, boy loses girl, boy wins girl. The hero is usually ruggedly handsome, and the heroine is beautiful or at least winsomely attractive. Even when the hero's primary objective is something other than love, commercial writers usually toss in a beautiful girl in order to supply their stories with some element of "love interest." The cheaper types of commercial fiction are generally characterized by a good deal of physical conflict—fistfights and gun-fights—and by crude contrasts between good and evil. Although its more sophisticated forms use less obvious contrasts between good and evil and put less emphasis on physical conflict, they still cling to the happy ending. These forms are often concerned with marital problems that find a happy solution or with sentimental treatments of children or old people, in which the "innocent wisdom" of childhood or the "mellow wisdom" of old age is shown to be superior to the "practical wisdom" of the years between. In contrast, quality fiction does not rely upon tested formulas, is more original—sometimes experimental—and seeks to be interpretive. All of the classifications made in this chapter are meant to be suggestive rather than rigid: absolute distinctions between commercial and quality fiction, between escape and interpretation, or between immature and mature readers cannot be made. One blends into the other.

Most of all, they want something that helps sustain their fantasy life, providing ready-made daydreams in which they overcome their limitations, thwart their enemies, and win success or fame or the desired mate.

Discriminating readers, in contrast, take deeper pleasure in fiction that deals significantly with life than in fiction based on the formulations of escape. They do not reject escape literature, for escape literature need not be cheap or trite. It may be original, witty, absorbing, beautifully written, and artistically constructed. Some of literature's most enduring masterpieces are essentially escape—Barrie's *Peter Pan* and Stevenson's *Treasure Island,* for instance. Such reading may be a refreshment for the mind and spirit. For a steady diet, however, they prefer interpretive literature. They know, moreover, that an exclusive diet of escape, especially of the cruder sorts, has two dangers: (1) it may leave us with merely superficial attitudes toward life; (2) it may actually distort our view of reality and give us false concepts and false expectations.

Fiction, like food, is of different nutritive values. Some is rich in protein and vitamins; it builds bone and sinew. Some is highly agreeable to the taste but not permanently sustaining. Some may be adulterated and actually harmful to our health. Escape fiction is of the latter two sorts. The harmless kind bears frankly on the face of it what it is. It pretends to be nothing else than pleasant diversion and never asks to be taken seriously. The second kind masquerades under the appearance of interpretation. It pretends to give a faithful treatment of life as it is, perhaps even thinks that it does so, but through its shallowness it subtly falsifies life in every line. Such fiction, taken seriously and without corrective, may give us false notions of reality and lead us to expect from experience what experience does not provide.

When we enter a library and glance at the books on the shelves, we are at first likely to be bewildered by their variety and profusion. Thousands of books sit there, each making its claim on our attention, each seeming to cry out "Read me! Read me! Read me!" or "No, read *me!*" We have time to read only a fraction of them. If we are wise, we shall read as many as we can without neglecting the other claims of life. Our problem is how to get the most out of what time we have. To make the richest use of our portion, we need to know two things: (1) how to get the most out of any book we read; (2) how to choose the books that will best repay the time and attention we devote to them. The assumption of this book is that a proper selection will include both fiction and nonfiction—nonfiction as an indispensable fund of information and ideas, of one kind of knowledge of the world; fiction as an equally indispensable source of a different kind of knowledge, a knowledge of experience, felt in the emotions as well as apprehended by the mind. The aim of this book is to aid in the growth of understanding and judgment.

Richard Connell

THE MOST DANGEROUS GAME

"Off there to the right—somewhere—is a large island," said Whitney. "It's rather a mystery—"

"What island is it?" Rainsford asked.

"The old charts call it 'Ship-Trap Island,'" Whitney replied. "A suggestive name, isn't it? Sailors have a curious dread of the place. I don't know why. Some superstition—"

"Can't see it," remarked Rainsford, trying to peer through the dank tropical night that was palpable as it pressed its thick warm blackness in upon the yacht.

"You've good eyes," said Whitney, with a laugh, "and I've seen you pick off a moose moving in the brown fall bush at four hundred yards, but even you can't see four miles or so through a moonless Caribbean night."

"Nor four yards," admitted Rainsford. "Ugh! It's like moist black velvet."

"It will be light in Rio," promised Whitney. "We should make it in a few days. I hope the jaguar guns have come from Purdey's. We should have some good hunting up the Amazon. Great sport, hunting."

"The best sport in the world," agreed Rainsford.

"For the hunter," amended Whitney. "Not for the jaguar."

"Don't talk rot, Whitney," said Rainsford. "You're a big-game hunter, not a philosopher. Who cares how a jaguar feels?"

"Perhaps the jaguar does," observed Whitney.

"Bah! They've no understanding."

"Even so, I rather think they understand one thing—fear. The fear of pain and the fear of death."

"Nonsense," laughed Rainsford. "This hot weather is making you soft, Whitney. Be a realist. The world is made up of two classes—the hunters and the huntees. Luckily, you and I are the hunters. Do you think we've passed that island yet?"

"I can't tell in the dark. I hope so."

"Why?" asked Rainsford.

"The place has a reputation—a bad one."

"Cannibals?" suggested Rainsford.

THE MOST DANGEROUS GAME   First published in 1924. Richard Connell (1893–1949) was a native of New York state, graduated from Harvard, and served a year in France with the United States army during World War I.

"Hardly. Even cannibals wouldn't live in such a God-forsaken place. But it's gotten into sailor lore, somehow. Didn't you notice that the crew's nerves seemed a bit jumpy to-day?"

"They were a bit strange, now you mention it. Even Captain Nielsen—"

"Yes, even that tough-minded old Swede, who'd go up to the devil himself and ask him for a light. Those fishy blue eyes held a look I never saw there before. All I could get out of him was: 'This place has an evil name among seafaring men, sir.' Then he said to me, very gravely: 'Don't you feel anything?'—as if the air about us was actually poisonous. Now, you mustn't laugh when I tell you this—I did feel something like a sudden chill.

"There was no breeze. The sea was as flat as a plate-glass window. We were drawing near the island then. What I felt was a—a mental chill; a sort of sudden dread."

"Pure imagination," said Rainsford. "One superstitious sailor can taint the whole ship's company with his fear."

"Maybe. But sometimes I think sailors have an extra sense that tells them when they are in danger. Sometimes I think evil is a tangible thing—with wave lengths, just as sound and light have. An evil place can, so to speak, broadcast vibrations of evil. Anyhow, I'm glad we're getting out of this zone. Well, I think I'll turn in now, Rainsford."

"I'm not sleepy," said Rainsford. "I'm going to smoke another pipe on the after deck."

"Good night, then, Rainsford. See you at breakfast."

"Right. Good night, Whitney."

There was no sound in the night as Rainsford sat there, but the muffled throb of the engine that drove the yacht swiftly through the darkness, and the swish and ripple of the wash of the propeller.

Rainsford, reclining in a steamer chair, indolently puffed on his favorite brier. The sensuous drowsiness of the night was on him. "It's so dark," he thought, "that I could sleep without closing my eyes; the night would be my eyelids—"

An abrupt sound startled him. Off to the right he heard it, and his ears, expert in such matters, could not be mistaken. Again he heard the sound, and again. Somewhere, off in the blackness, some one had fired a gun three times.

Rainsford sprang up and moved quickly to the rail, mystified. He strained his eyes in the direction from which the reports had come, but it was like trying to see through a blanket. He leaped upon the rail and balanced himself there, to get greater elevation; his pipe, striking a rope, was knocked from his mouth. He lunged for it; a short, hoarse cry came from his lips as he realized he had reached too far and had lost his balance. The cry was pinched off short as the blood-warm waters of the Caribbean Sea closed over his head.

He struggled up to the surface and tried to cry out, but the wash from the speeding yacht slapped him in the face and the salt water in his open mouth made him gag and strangle. Desperately he struck out with strong strokes after the receding lights of the yacht, but he stopped before he had swum fifty feet. A certain cool-headedness had come to him; it was not the first time he had been in a tight place. There was a chance that his cries could be heard by some one aboard the yacht, but that chance was slender, and grew more slender as the yacht raced on. He wrestled himself out of his clothes, and shouted with all his power. The lights of the yacht became faint and ever-vanishing fireflies; then they were blotted out entirely by the night.

Rainsford remembered the shots. They had come from the right, and doggedly he swam in that direction, swimming with slow, deliberate strokes, conserving his strength. For a seemingly endless time he fought the sea. He began to count his strokes; he could do possibly a hundred more and then—

Rainsford heard a sound. It came out of the darkness, a high screaming sound, the sound of an animal in an extremity of anguish and terror.

He did not recognize the animal that made the sound; he did not try to; with fresh vitality he swam toward the sound. He heard it again; then it was cut short by another noise, crisp, staccato.

"Pistol shot," muttered Rainsford, swimming on.

Ten minutes of determined effort brought another sound to his ears—the most welcome he had ever heard—the muttering and growling of the sea breaking on a rocky shore. He was almost on the rocks before he saw them; on a night less calm he would have been shattered against them. With his remaining strength he dragged himself from the swirling waters. Jagged crags appeared to jut into the opaqueness, he forced himself upward, hand over hand. Gasping, his hands raw, he reached a flat place at the top. Dense jungle came down to the very edge of the cliffs. What perils that tangle of trees and underbrush might hold for him did not concern Rainsford just then. All he knew was that he was safe from his enemy, the sea, and that utter weariness was on him. He flung himself down at the jungle edge and tumbled headlong into the deepest sleep of his life.

When he opened his eyes he knew from the position of the sun that it was late in the afternoon. Sleep had given him new vigor; a sharp hunger was picking at him. He looked about him, almost cheerfully.

"Where there are pistol shots, there are men. Where there are men, there is food," he thought. But what kind of men, he wondered, in so forbidding a place? An unbroken front of snarled and ragged jungle fringed the shore.

He saw no sign of a trail through the closely knit web of weeds and trees; it was easier to go along the shore, and Rainsford floundered along by the water. Not far from where he had landed, he stopped.

Some wounded thing, by the evidence a large animal, had thrashed about in the underbrush; the jungle weeds were crushed down and the moss was lacerated; one patch of weeds was stained crimson. A small, glittering object not far away caught Rainsford's eye and he picked it up. It was an empty cartridge.

"A twenty-two," he remarked. "That's odd. It must have been a fairly large animal too. The hunter had his nerve with him to tackle it with a light gun. It's clear that the brute put up a fight. I suppose the first three shots I heard was when the hunter flushed his quarry and wounded it. The last shot was when he trailed it here and finished it."

He examined the ground closely and found what he had hoped to find—the print of hunting boots. They pointed along the cliff in the direction he had been going. Eagerly he hurried along, now slipping on a rotten log or a loose stone, but making headway; night was beginning to settle down on the island.

Bleak darkness was blacking out the sea and jungle when Rainsford sighted the lights. He came upon them as he turned a crook in the coast line, and his first thought was that he had come upon a village, for there were many lights. But as he forged along he saw to his great astonishment that all the lights were in one enormous building—a lofty structure with pointed towers plunging upward into the gloom. His eyes made out the shadowy outlines of a palatial château; it was set on a high bluff, and on three sides of it cliffs dived down to where the sea licked greedy lips in the shadows.

"Mirage," thought Rainsford. But it was no mirage, he found, when he opened the tall spiked iron gate. The stone steps were real enough; the massive door with a leering gargoyle for a knocker was real enough; yet about it all hung an air of unreality.

He lifted the knocker, and it creaked up stiffly, as if it had never before been used. He let it fall, and it startled him with its booming loudness. He thought he heard steps within; the door remained closed. Again Rainsford lifted the heavy knocker, and let it fall. The door opened then, opened as suddenly as if it were on a spring, and Rainsford stood blinking in the river of glaring gold light that poured out. The first thing Rainsford's eyes discerned was the largest man Rainsford had ever seen—a gigantic creature, solidly made and black-bearded to the waist. In his hand the man held a long-barreled revolver, and he was pointing it straight at Rainsford's heart.

Out of the snarl of beard two small eyes regarded Rainsford.

"Don't be alarmed," said Rainsford, with a smile which he hoped was disarming. "I'm no robber. I fell off a yacht. My name is Sanger Rainsford of New York City."

The menacing look in the eyes did not change. The revolver pointed as rigidly as if the giant were a statue. He gave no sign that he understood Rainsford's words, or that he had even heard them. He was dressed in uniform, a black uniform trimmed with gray astrakhan.

"I'm Sanger Rainsford of New York," Rainsford began again. "I fell off a yacht. I am hungry."

The man's only answer was to raise with his thumb the hammer of his revolver. Then Rainsford saw the man's free hand go to his forehead in a military salute, and he saw him click his heels together and stand at attention. Another man was coming down the broad marble steps, an erect, slender man in evening clothes. He advanced to Rainsford and held out his hand.

In a cultivated voice marked by a slight accent that gave it added precision and deliberateness, he said: "It is a very great pleasure and honor to welcome Mr. Sanger Rainsford, the celebrated hunter, to my home."

Automatically Rainsford shook the man's hand.

"I've read your book about hunting snow leopards in Tibet, you see," explained the man. "I am General Zaroff."

Rainsford's first impression was that the man was singularly handsome; his second was that there was an original, almost bizarre quality about the general's face. He was a tall man past middle age, for his hair was a vivid white; but his thick eyebrows and pointed military mustache were as black as the night from which Rainsford had come. His eyes, too, were black and very bright. He had high cheek bones, a sharp-cut nose, a spare, dark face, the face of a man used to giving orders, the face of an aristocrat. Turning to the giant in uniform, the general made a sign. The giant put away his pistol, saluted, withdrew.

"Ivan is an incredibly strong fellow," remarked the general, "but he has the misfortune to be deaf and dumb. A simple fellow, but, I'm afraid, like all his race, a bit of a savage."

"Is he Russian?"

"He is a Cossack," said the general, and his smile showed red lips and pointed teeth. "So am I."

"Come," he said, "we shouldn't be chatting here. We can talk later. Now you want clothes, food, rest. You shall have them. This is a most restful spot."

Ivan had reappeared, and the general spoke to him with lips that moved but gave forth no sound.

"Follow Ivan, if you please, Mr. Rainsford," said the general. "I was about to have my dinner when you came. I'll wait for you. You'll find that my clothes will fit you, I think."

It was to a huge, beam-ceilinged bedroom with a canopied bed big enough for six men that Rainsford followed the silent giant. Ivan laid out an evening suit, and Rainsford, as he put it on, noticed that it came from a London tailor who ordinarily cut and sewed for none below the rank of duke.

The dining room to which Ivan conducted him was in many ways remarkable. There was a medieval magnificence about it; it suggested a baronial hall of feudal times with its oaken panels, its high ceiling, its vast refectory table where twoscore men could sit down to eat. About the hall were the mounted heads of many animals—lions, tigers, elephants, moose, bears; larger or more perfect specimens Rainsford had never seen. At the great table the general was sitting, alone.

"You'll have a cocktail, Mr. Rainsford," he suggested. The cocktail was surpassingly good; and, Rainsford noted, the table appointments were of the finest—the linen, the crystal, the silver, the china.

They were eating *borsch*, the rich, red soup with whipped cream so dear to Russian palates. Half apologetically General Zaroff said: "We do our best to preserve the amenities of civilization here. Please forgive any lapses. We are well off the beaten track, you know. Do you think the champagne has suffered from its long ocean trip?"

"Not in the least," declared Rainsford. He was finding the general a most thoughtful and affable host, a true cosmopolite. But there was one small trait of the general's that made Rainsford uncomfortable. Whenever he looked up from his plate he found the general studying him, appraising him narrowly.

"Perhaps," said General Zaroff, "you were surprised that I recognized your name. You see, I read all books on hunting published in English, French, and Russian. I have but one passion in my life, Mr. Rainsford, and it is the hunt."

"You have some wonderful heads here," said Rainsford as he ate a particularly well cooked filet mignon. "That Cape buffalo is the largest I ever saw."

"Oh, that fellow. Yes, he was a monster."

"Did he charge you?"

"Hurled me against a tree," said the general. "Fractured my skull. But I got the brute."

"I've always thought," said Rainsford, "that the Cape buffalo is the most dangerous of all big game."

For a moment the general did not reply; he was smiling his curious red-lipped smile. Then he said slowly: "No. You are wrong, sir. The Cape buffalo is not the most dangerous big game." He sipped his wine. "Here in my preserve on this island," he said in the same slow tone, "I hunt more dangerous game."

Rainsford expressed his surprise. "Is there big game on this island?"

The general nodded. "The biggest."

"Really?"

"Oh, it isn't here naturally, of course. I have to stock the island."

"What have you imported, general?" Rainsford asked. "Tigers?"

The general smiled. "No," he said. "Hunting tigers ceased to interest me some years ago. I exhausted their possibilities, you see. No thrill left in tigers, no real danger. I live for danger, Mr. Rainsford."

The general took from his pocket a gold cigaret case and offered his guest a long black cigaret with a silver tip; it was perfumed and gave off a smell like incense.

"We will have some capital hunting, you and I," said the general. "I shall be most glad to have your society."

"But what game—" began Rainsford.

"I'll tell you," said the general. "You will be amused, I know. I think I may say, in all modesty, that I have done a rare thing. I have invented a new sensation. May I pour you another glass of port, Mr. Rainsford?"

"Thank you, general."

The general filled both glasses, and said: "God makes some men poets. Some He makes kings, some beggars. Me He made a hunter. My hand was made for the trigger, my father said. He was a very rich man with a quarter of a million acres in the Crimea, and he was an ardent sportsman. When I was only five years old he gave me a little gun, specially made in Moscow for me, to shoot sparrows with. When I shot some of his prize turkeys with it, he did not punish me; he complimented me on my marksmanship. I killed my first bear in the Caucasus when I was ten. My whole life has been one prolonged hunt. I went into the army—it was expected of noblemen's sons—and for a time commanded a division of Cossack cavalry, but my real interest was always the hunt. I have hunted every kind of game in every land. It would be impossible for me to tell you how many animals I have killed."

The general puffed at his cigaret.

"After the debacle in Russia I left the country, for it was imprudent for an officer of the Czar to stay there. Many noble Russians lost everything. I, luckily, had invested heavily in American securities, so I shall never have to open a tea room in Monte Carlo or drive a taxi in Paris. Naturally, I continued to hunt—grizzlies in your Rockies, crocodiles in the Ganges, rhinoceroses in East Africa. It was in Africa that the Cape buffalo hit me and laid me up for six months. As soon as I recovered I started for the Amazon to hunt jaguars, for I had heard they were unusually cunning. They weren't." The Cossack sighed. "They were no match at all for a hunter with his wits about him, and a high-powered rifle. I was bitterly disappointed. I was lying in my tent with a splitting headache one night when a terrible thought pushed its way into my mind. Hunting was beginning to bore me! And hunting, remember, had been my life. I have heard that in America business men often go to pieces when they give up the business that has been their life."

"Yes, that's so," said Rainsford.

The general smiled. "I had no wish to go to pieces," he said. "I must do something. Now, mine is an analytical mind, Mr. Rainsford. Doubtless that is why I enjoy the problems of the chase."

"No doubt, General Zaroff."

"So," continued the general, "I asked myself why the hunt no longer fascinated me. You are much younger than I am, Mr. Rainsford, and have not hunted as much, but you perhaps can guess the answer."

"What was it?"

"Simply this: hunting had ceased to be what you call 'a sporting proposition.' It had become too easy. I always got my quarry. Always. There is no greater bore than perfection."

The general lit a fresh cigaret.

"No animal had a chance with me any more. That is no boast; it is a mathematical certainty. The animal had nothing but his legs and his instinct. Instinct is no match for reason. When I thought of this it was a tragic moment for me, I can tell you."

Rainsford leaned across the table, absorbed in what his host was saying.

"It came to me as an inspiration what I must do," the general went on.

"And that was?"

The general smiled the quiet smile of one who has faced an obstacle and surmounted it with success. "I had to invent a new animal to hunt," he said.

"A new animal? You're joking."

"Not at all," said the general. "I never joke about hunting. I needed a new animal. I found one. So I bought this island, built this house, and here I do my hunting. The island is perfect for my purposes—there are jungles with a maze of trails in them, hills, swamps—"

"But the animal, General Zaroff?"

"Oh," said the general, "it supplies me with the most exciting hunting in the world. No other hunting compares with it for an instant. Every day I hunt, and I never grow bored now, for I have a quarry with which I can match my wits."

Rainsford's bewilderment showed in his face.

"I wanted the ideal animal to hunt," explained the general. "So I said: 'What are the attributes of an ideal quarry?' And the answer was, of course: 'it must have courage, cunning, and, above all, it must be able to reason.'"

"But no animal can reason," objected Rainsford.

"My dear fellow," said the general, "there is one that can."

"But you can't mean—" gasped Rainsford.

"And why not?"

"I can't believe you are serious, General Zaroff. This is a grisly joke."

"Why should I not be serious? I am speaking of hunting."

"Hunting? Good God, General Zaroff, what you speak of is murder."

The general laughed with entire good nature. He regarded Rainsford quizzically. "I refuse to believe that so modern and civilized a young man as you seem to be harbors romantic ideas about the value of human life. Surely your experiences in the war—"

"Did not make me condone cold-blooded murder," finished Rainsford stiffly.

Laughter shook the general. "How extraordinarily droll you are!" he said. "One does not expect nowadays to find a young man of the educated class, even in America, with such a naive, and, if I may say so, mid-Victorian point of view. It's like finding a snuff-box in a limousine. Ah, well, doubtless you had Puritan ancestors. So many Americans appear to have had. I'll wager you'll forget your notions when you go hunting with me. You've a genuine new thrill in store for you, Mr. Rainsford."

"Thank you, I'm a hunter, not a murderer."

"Dear me," said the general, quite unruffled, "again that unpleasant word. But I think I can show you that your scruples are quite ill founded."

"Yes?"

"Life is for the strong, to be lived by the strong, and, if need be, taken by the strong. The weak of the world were put here to give the strong pleasure. I am strong. Why should I not use my gift? If I wish to hunt, why should I not? I hunt the scum of the earth—sailors from tramp ships—lascars, blacks,

Chinese, whites, mongrels—a thoroughbred horse or hound is worth more than a score of them."

"But they are men," said Rainsford hotly.

"Precisely," said the general. "That is why I use them. It gives me pleasure. They can reason, after a fashion. So they are dangerous."

"But where do you get them?"

The general's left eyelid fluttered down in a wink. "This island is called Ship-Trap," he answered. "Sometimes an angry god of the high seas sends them to me. Sometimes, when Providence is not so kind, I help Providence a bit. Come to the window with me."

Rainsford went to the window and looked out toward the sea.

"Watch! Out there!" exclaimed the general, pointing into the night. Rainsford's eyes saw only blackness, and then, as the general pressed a button, far out to sea Rainsford saw the flash of lights.

The general chuckled. "They indicate a channel," he said, "where there's none: giant rocks with razor edges crouch like a sea monster with wide-open jaws. They can crush a ship as easily as I crush this nut." He dropped a walnut on the hardwood floor and brought his heel grinding down on it. "Oh, yes," he said, casually, as if in answer to a question, "I have electricity. We try to be civilized here."

"Civilized? And you shoot down men?"

A trace of anger was in the general's black eyes, but it was there for but a second, and he said, in his most pleasant manner: "Dear me, what a righteous young man you are! I assure you I do not do the thing you suggest. That would be barbarous. I treat these visitors with every consideration. They get plenty of good food and exercise. They get into spendid physical condition. You shall see for yourself to-morrow."

"What do you mean?"

"We'll visit my training school," smiled the general. "It's in the cellar. I have about a dozen pupils down there now. They're from the Spanish bark San Lucar that had the bad luck to go on the rocks out there. A very inferior lot, I regret to say. Poor specimens and more accustomed to the deck than to the jungle."

He raised his hand, and Ivan, who served as waiter, brought thick Turkish coffee. Rainsford, with an effort, held his tongue in check.

"It's a game, you see," pursued the general blandly. "I suggest to one of them that we go hunting. I give him a supply of food and an excellent hunting knife. I give him three hours' start. I am to follow, armed only with a pistol of the smallest caliber and range. If my quarry eludes me for three whole days, he wins the game. If I find him"—the general smiled—"he loses."

"Suppose he refuses to be hunted?"

"Oh," said the general, "I give him his option, of course. He need not play that game if he doesn't wish to. If he does not wish to hunt, I turn him over to Ivan. Ivan once had the honor of serving as official knouter to the

Great White Czar, and he has his own ideas of sport. Invariably, Mr. Rainsford, invariably they choose the hunt."

"And if they win?"

The smile on the general's face widened. "To date I have not lost," he said.

Then he added, hastily: "I don't wish you to think me a braggart, Mr. Rainsford. Many of them afford only the most elementary sort of problem. Occasionally I strike a tartar. One almost did win. I eventually had to use the dogs."

"The dogs?"

"This way, please. I'll show you."

The general steered Rainsford to a window. The lights from the windows sent a flickering illumination that made grotesque patterns on the courtyard below, and Rainsford could see moving about there a dozen or so huge black shapes; as they turned toward him, their eyes glittered greenly.

"A rather good lot, I think," observed the general. "They are let out at seven every night. If anyone should try to get into my house—or out of it— something extremely regrettable would occur to him." He hummed a snatch of song from the Folies Bergère.

"And now," said the general, "I want to show you my new collection of heads. Will you come with me to the library?"

"I hope," said Rainsford, "that you will excuse me tonight, General Zaroff. I'm really not feeling at all well."

"Ah, indeed?" the general inquired solicitously. "Well, I suppose that's only natural, after your long swim. You need a good, restful night's sleep. Tomorrow you'll feel like a new man, I'll wager. Then we'll hunt, eh? I've one rather promising prospect—"

Rainsford was hurrying from the room.

"Sorry you can't go with me tonight," called the general. "I expect rather fair sport—a big, strong black. He looks resourceful—Well, good night, Mr. Rainsford; I hope you have a good night's rest."

The bed was good, and the pajamas of the softest silk, and he was tired in every fiber of his being, but nevertheless Rainsford could not quiet his brain with the opiate of sleep. He lay, eyes wide open. Once he thought he heard stealthy steps in the corridor outside his room. He sought to throw open the door; it would not open. He went to the window and looked out. His room was high up in one of the towers. The lights of the château were out now, and it was dark and silent, but there was a fragment of sallow moon, and by its wan light he could see, dimly, the courtyard; there, weaving in and out in the pattern of shadow, were black, noiseless forms; the hounds heard him at the window and looked up, expectantly, with their green eyes. Rainsford went back to the bed and lay down. By many methods he tried to put himself to sleep. He had achieved a doze when, just as morning began to come, he heard, far off in the jungle, the faint report of a pistol.

General Zaroff did not appear until luncheon. He was dressed faultlessly in the tweeds of a country squire. He was solicitous about the state of Rainsford's health.

"As for me," sighed the general, "I do not feel so well. I am worried, Mr. Rainsford. Last night I detected traces of my old complaint."

To Rainsford's questioning glance the general said: "Ennui. Boredom."

Then, taking a second helping of Crêpes Suzette, the general explained: "The hunting was not good last night. The fellow lost his head. He made a straight trail that offered no problems at all. That's the trouble with these sailors; they have dull brains to begin with, and they do not know how to get about in the woods. They do excessively stupid and obvious things. It's most annoying. Will you have another glass of Chablis, Mr. Rainsford?"

"General," said Rainsford firmly, "I wish to leave this island at once."

The general raised his thickets of eyebrows; he seemed hurt. "But, my dear fellow," the general protested, "you've only just come. You've had no hunting—"

"I wish to go today," said Rainsford. He saw the dead black eyes of the general on him, studying him. General Zaroff's face suddenly brightened.

He filled Rainsford's glass with venerable Chablis from a dusty bottle.

"Tonight," said the general, "we will hunt—you and I."

Rainsford shook his head. "No, general," he said. "I will not hunt."

The general shrugged his shoulders and delicately ate a hothouse grape. "As you wish, my friend," he said. "The choice rests entirely with you. But may I not venture to suggest that you will find my idea of sport more diverting than Ivan's?"

He nodded toward the corner to where the giant stood, scowling, his thick arms crossed on his hogshead of chest.

"You don't mean—" cried Rainsford.

"My dear fellow," said the general, "have I not told you I always mean what I say about hunting? This is really an inspiration. I drink to a foeman worthy of my steel—at last."

The general raised his glass, but Rainsford sat staring at him.

"You'll find this game worth playing," the general said enthusiastically. "Your brain against mine. Your woodcraft against mine. Your strength and stamina against mine. Outdoor chess! And the stake is not without value, eh?"

"And if I win—" began Rainsford huskily.

"I'll cheerfully acknowledge myself defeated if I do not find you by midnight of the third day," said General Zaroff. "My sloop will place you on the mainland near a town."

The general read what Rainsford was thinking.

"Oh, you can trust me," said the Cossack. "I will give you my word as a gentleman and a sportsman. Of course you, in turn, must agree to say nothing of your visit here."

"I'll agree to nothing of the kind," said Rainsford.

"Oh," said the general, "in that case—But why discuss that now? Three days hence we can discuss it over a bottle of Veuve Cliquot, unless—" The general sipped his wine.

Then a businesslike air animated him. "Ivan," he said to Rainsford, "will supply you with hunting clothes, food, a knife. I suggest you wear moccasins; they leave a poorer trail. I suggest too that you avoid the big swamp in the southeast corner of the island. We call it Death Swamp. There's quicksand there. One foolish fellow tried it. The deplorable part of it was that Lazarus followed him. You can imagine my feelings, Mr. Rainsford. I loved Lazarus; he was the finest hound in my pack. Well, I must beg you to excuse me now. I always take a siesta after lunch. You'll hardly have time for a nap, I fear. You'll want to start, no doubt. I shall not follow till dusk. Hunting at night is so much more exciting than by day, don't you think? Au revoir, Mr. Rainsford, au revoir."

General Zaroff, with a deep, courtly bow, strolled from the room.

From another door came Ivan. Under one arm he carried khaki hunting clothes, a haversack of food, a leather sheath containing a long-bladed hunting knife; his right hand rested on a cocked revolver thrust in the crimson sash about his waist. . . .

Rainsford had fought his way through the bush for two hours. "I must keep my nerve. I must keep my nerve," he said through tight teeth.

He had not been entirely clear-headed when the château gates snapped shut behind him. His whole idea at first was to put distance between himself and General Zaroff, and, to this end, he had plunged along, spurred on by the sharp rowels of something very like panic. Now he had got a grip on himself, had stopped, and was taking stock of himself and the situation.

He saw that straight flight was futile; inevitably it would bring him face to face with the sea. He was in a picture with a frame of water, and his operations, clearly, must take place within that frame.

"I'll give him a trail to follow," muttered Rainsford, and he struck off from the rude paths he had been following into the trackless wilderness. He executed a series of intricate loops; he doubled on his trail again and again, recalling all the lore of the fox hunt, and all the dodges of the fox. Night found him leg-weary, with hands and face lashed by the branches, on a thickly wooded ridge. He knew it would be insane to blunder on through the dark, even if he had the strength. His need for rest was imperative and he thought: "I have played the fox, now I must play the cat of the fable." A big tree with a thick trunk and outspread branches was nearby, and, taking care to leave not the slightest mark, he climbed up into the crotch, and stretching out on one of the broad limbs, after a fashion, rested. Rest brought him new confidence and almost a feeling of security. Even so zealous a hunter as General Zaroff could not trace him there, he told himself; only the devil himself could follow that complicated trail through the jungle after dark. But, perhaps, the general was a devil—

An apprehensive night crawled slowly by like a wounded snake, and sleep did not visit Rainsford, although the silence of a dead world was on the jungle. Toward morning when a dingy gray was varnishing the sky, the cry of some startled bird focused Rainsford's attention in that direction. Something was coming through the bush, coming slowly, carefully, coming by the same winding way Rainsford had come. He flattened himself down on the limb, and through a screen of leaves almost as thick as tapestry, he watched. The thing that was approaching was a man.

It was General Zaroff. He made his way along with his eyes fixed in utmost concentration on the ground before him. He paused, almost beneath the tree, dropped to his knees and studied the ground. Rainsford's impulse was to hurl himself down like a panther, but he saw the general's right hand held something metallic—a small automatic pistol.

The hunter shook his head several times, as if he were puzzled. Then he straightened up and took from his case one of his black cigarets; its pungent incense-like smoke floated up to Rainsford's nostrils.

Rainsford held his breath. The general's eyes had left the ground and were traveling inch by inch up the tree. Rainsford froze there, every muscle tensed for a spring. But the sharp eyes of the hunter stopped before they reached the limb where Rainsford lay; a smile spread over his brown face. Very deliberately he blew a smoke ring into the air; then he turned his back on the tree and walked carelessly away, back along the trail he had come. The swish of the underbrush against his hunting boots grew fainter and fainter.

The pent-up air burst hotly from Rainsford's lungs. His first thought made him feel sick and numb. The general could follow a trail through the woods at night; he could follow an extremely difficult trail; he must have uncanny powers; only by the merest chance had the Cossack failed to see his quarry.

Rainsford's second thought was even more terrible. It sent a shudder of cold horror through his whole being. Why had the general smiled? Why had he turned back?

Rainsford did not want to believe what his reason told him was true, but the truth was as evident as the sun that had by now pushed through the morning mists. The general was playing with him! The general was saving him for another day's sport! The Cossack was the cat; he was the mouse. Then it was that Rainsford knew the full meaning of terror.

"I will not lose my nerve. I will not."

He slid down from the tree, and struck off again into the woods. His face was set and he forced the machinery of his mind to function. Three hundred yards from his hiding place he stopped where a huge dead tree leaned precariously on a smaller, living one. Throwing off his sack of food, Rainsford took his knife from its sheath and began to work with all his energy.

The job was finished at last, and he threw himself down behind a fallen log a hundred feet away. He did not have to wait long. The cat was coming again to play with the mouse.

Following the trail with the sureness of a bloodhound, came General Zaroff. Nothing escaped those searching black eyes, no crushed blade of grass, no bent twig, no mark, no matter how faint, in the moss. So intent was the Cossack on his stalking that he was upon the thing Rainsford had made before he saw it. His foot touched the protruding bough that was the trigger. Even as he touched it, the general sensed his danger and leaped back with the agility of an ape. But he was not quite quick enough; the dead tree, delicately adjusted to rest on the cut living one, crashed down and struck the general a glancing blow on the shoulder as it fell; but for his alertness, he must have been smashed beneath it. He staggered, but he did not fall; nor did he drop his revolver. He stood there, rubbing his injured shoulder, and Rainsford, with fear again gripping his heart, heard the general's mocking laugh ring through the jungle.

"Rainsford," called the general, "if you are within the sound of my voice, as I suppose you are, let me congratulate you. Not many men know how to make a Malay man-catcher. Luckily, for me, I too have hunted in Malacca. You are proving interesting, Mr. Rainsford. I am going now to have my wound dressed; it's only a slight one. But I shall be back. I shall be back."

When the general, nursing his bruised shoulder, had gone, Rainsford took up his flight again. It was flight now, a desperate, hopeless flight, that carried him on for some hours. Dusk came, then darkness, and still he pressed on. The ground grew softer under his moccasins; the vegetation grew ranker, denser; insects bit him savagely. Then, as he stepped forward, his foot sank into the ooze. He tried to wrench it back, but the muck sucked viciously at his foot as if it were a giant leech. With a violent effort, he tore loose. He knew where he was now. Death Swamp and its quicksand.

His hands were tight closed as if his nerve were something tangible that some one in the darkness was trying to tear from his grip. The softness of the earth had given him an idea. He stepped back from the quicksand a dozen feet or so, and, like some huge prehistoric beaver, he began to dig.

Rainsford had dug himself in in France when a second's delay meant death. That had been a placid pastime compared to his digging now. The pit grew deeper; when it was above his shoulders, he climbed out and from some hard saplings cut stakes and sharpened them to a fine point. These stakes he planted in the bottom of the pit with the points sticking up. With flying fingers he wove a rough carpet of weeds and branches and with it he covered the mouth of the pit. Then, wet with sweat and aching with tiredness, he crouched behind the stump of a lightning-charred tree.

He knew his pursuer was coming; he heard the padding sound of feet on the soft earth, and the night breeze brought him the perfume of the general's cigaret. It seemed to Rainsford that the general was coming with unusual swiftness; he was not feeling his way along, foot by foot. Rainsford, crouching there, could not see the general, nor could he see the pit. He lived a year in a minute. Then he felt an impulse to cry aloud with joy, for he heard the sharp crackle of the breaking branches as the cover of the pit gave way; he heard the sharp scream of pain as the pointed stakes found their mark. He leaped up from his place of concealment. Then he cowered back. Three feet from the pit a man was standing, with an electric torch in his hand.

"You've done well, Rainsford," the voice of the general called. "Your Burmese tiger pit has claimed one of my best dogs. Again you score. I think, Mr. Rainsford, I'll see what you can do against my whole pack. I'm going home for a rest now. Thank you for a most amusing evening."

At daybreak Rainsford, lying near the swamp, was awakened by the sound that made him know that he had new things to learn about fear. It was a distant sound, faint and wavering, but he knew it. It was the baying of a pack of hounds.

Rainsford knew he could do one of two things. He could stay where he was and wait. That was suicide. He could flee. That was postponing the inevitable. For a moment he stood there, thinking. An idea that held a wild chance came to him, and, tightening his belt, he headed away from the swamp.

The baying of the hounds drew nearer, then still nearer, nearer, ever nearer. On a ridge Rainsford climbed a tree. Down a watercourse, not a quarter of a mile away, he could see the bush moving. Straining his eyes, he saw the lean figure of General Zaroff; just ahead of him Rainsford made out another figure whose wide shoulders surged through the tall jungle weeds; it was the giant Ivan, and he seemed pulled forward by some unseen force; Rainsford knew that Ivan must be holding the pack in leash.

They would be on him any minute now. His mind worked frantically. He thought of a native trick he had learned in Uganda. He slid down the tree. He caught hold of a springy young sapling and to it he fastened his hunting knife, with the blade pointing down the trail; with a bit of wild grapevine he tied back the sapling. Then he ran for his life. The hounds raised their voices as they hit the fresh scent. Rainsford knew now how an animal at bay feels.

He had to stop to get his breath. The baying of the hounds stopped abruptly, and Rainsford's heart stopped too. They must have reached the knife.

He shinnied excitedly up a tree and looked back. His pursuers had stopped. But the hope that was in Rainsford's brain when he climbed died, for he saw in the shallow valley that General Zaroff was still on his feet. But Ivan was not. The knife, driven by the recoil of the springing tree, had not wholly failed.

"Nerve, nerve, nerve!" he panted, as he dashed along. A blue gap showed between the trees dead ahead. Ever nearer drew the hounds. Rainsford forced himself on toward that gap. He reached it. It was the shore of the sea. Across a cove he could see the gloomy gray stone of the château. Twenty feet below him the sea rumbled and hissed. Rainsford hesitated. He heard the hounds. Then he leaped far out into the sea. . . .

When the general and his pack reached the place by the sea, the Cossack stopped. For some minutes he stood regarding the blue-green expanse of water. He shrugged his shoulders. Then he sat down, took a drink of brandy from a silver flask, lit a perfumed cigaret, and hummed a bit from *Madame Butterfly*.

General Zaroff had an exceedingly good dinner in his great paneled dining hall that evening. With it he had a bottle of Pol Roger and half a bottle of Chambertin. Two slight annoyances kept him from perfect enjoyment. One was the thought that it would be difficult to replace Ivan; the other was that his quarry had escaped him; of course the American hadn't played the game—so thought the general as he tasted his after-dinner liqueur. In his library he read, to soothe himself, from the works of Marcus Aurelius. At ten he went up to his bedroom. He was deliciously tired, he said to himself, as he locked himself in. There was a little moonlight, so, before turning on his light, he went to the window and looked down at the courtyard. He could see the great hounds, and he called: "Better luck another time," to them. Then he switched on the light.

A man, who had been hiding in the curtains of the bed, was standing there.

"Rainsford!" screamed the general. "How in God's name did you get here?"

"Swam," said Rainsford. "I found it quicker than walking through the jungle."

The general sucked in his breath and smiled. "I congratulate you," he said. "You have won the game."

Rainsford did not smile. "I am still a beast at bay," he said, in a low, hoarse voice. "Get ready, General Zaroff."

The general made one of his deepest bows. "I see," he said. "Splendid! One of us is to furnish a repast for the hounds. The other will sleep in this very excellent bed. On guard, Rainsford. . . ."

He had never slept in a better bed, Rainsford decided.

QUESTIONS

1. On what simple ironical reversal is the plot of the story based? What two meanings has the title?
2. How important is suspense in the story? In what ways is it aroused and sustained? What part do chance and coincidence play in the story?
3. Discuss the characterizations of Rainsford and General Zaroff. Which one is more fully characterized? Are both characters plausible?
4. What purpose is served by the "philosophical" discussion between Whitney and Rainsford at the beginning of the story (page 8)? What limitation does

it show Rainsford to have? To what extent is his character illuminated during the course of the story? Does he change his ideas?

5. In what ways is the discussion between Whitney and Rainsford paralleled by the after-dinner discussion between Rainsford and Zaroff (pages 14–16)? In these discussions, is Rainsford more like Whitney or Zaroff? How does he differ from Zaroff? Does the end of the story resolve that difference?

6. Is the principal emphasis of the story on plot, character, or theme? On escape or interpretation? Support your answer.

Thomas Wolfe

THE CHILD BY TIGER

> Tiger, tiger, burning bright
> In the forests of the night,
> What immortal hand or eye
> Could frame thy fearful symmetry?

One day after school, twenty-five years ago, several of us were playing with a football in the yard at Randy Shepperton's. Randy was calling signals and handling the ball. Nebraska Crane was kicking it. Augustus Potterham was too clumsy to run or kick or pass, so we put him at center, where all he'd have to do would be to pass the ball back to Randy when he got the signal.

It was late in October and there was a smell of smoke, of leaves, of burning in the air. Nebraska had just kicked to us. It was a good kick, too—a high, soaring punt that spiraled out above my head, behind me. I ran back and tried to get it, but it was far and away "over the goal line"—that is to say, out in the street. It hit the street and bounded back and forth with that peculiarly erratic bounce a football has.

The ball rolled away from me down toward the corner. I was running out to get it when Dick Prosser, Shepperton's new Negro man, came along, gathered it up neatly in his great black paw and tossed it to me. He turned in then, and came on down the alleyway, greeting us as he did. He called all of us "Mister" except Randy, and Randy was always "Cap'n"—"Cap'n Shepperton." This formal address—"Mr." Crane, "Mr." Potterham, "Mr." Spangler, "Cap'n" Shepperton—pleased us immensely, gave us a feeling of mature importance and authority.

"Cap'n Shepperton" was splendid! It had a delightful military association, particularly when Dick Prosser said it. Dick had served a long enlistment in the United States Army. He had been a member of a regiment of crack Negro troops upon the Texas border, and the stamp of the military man was evident in everything he did. It was a joy, for example, just to watch him

THE CHILD BY TIGER First published in 1937. Thomas Wolfe (1900–1938) was born and grew up in Asheville, North Carolina. An altered, expanded version of this story was included in chapter 8 of his novel *The Web and the Rock* (1939).

split up kindling. He did it with a power, a kind of military order, that was astounding. Every stick he cut seemed to be exactly the same length and shape as every other one. He had all of them neatly stacked against the walls of the Shepperton basement with such regimented faultlessness that it almost seemed a pity to disturb their symmetry for the use for which they were intended.

It was the same with everything else he did. His little whitewashed basement room was as spotless as a barracks room. The bare board floor was always cleanly swept, a plain bare table and a plain straight chair were stationed exactly in the center of the room. On the table there was always just one object: an old Bible almost worn out by constant use, for Dick was a deeply religious man. There was a little cast-iron stove and a little wooden box with a few lumps of coal and a neat stack of kindling in it. And against the wall, to the left, there was an iron cot, always precisely made and covered cleanly with a coarse gray blanket.

The Sheppertons were delighted with him. He had come there looking for work just a month or two before, and modestly presented his qualifications. He had, he said, only recently received his discharge from the Army and was eager to get employment, at no matter what wage. He could cook, he could tend the furnace, he knew how to drive a car—in fact, it seemed to us boys that there was very little that Dick Prosser could not do. He could certainly shoot. He gave a modest demonstration of his prowess one afternoon, with Randy's .22, that left us gasping. He just lifted that little rifle in his powerful black hands as if it were a toy, without seeming to take aim, pointed it toward a strip of tin on which we had crudely marked out some bull's-eye circles, and he simply peppered the center of the bull's-eye, putting twelve holes through a space one inch square, so fast we could not even count the shots.

He knew how to box too. I think he had been a regimental champion. At any rate, he was as cunning and crafty as a cat. He never boxed with us, of course, but Randy had two sets of gloves, and Dick used to coach us while we sparred. There was something amazingly tender and watchful about him. He taught us many things—how to lead, to hook, to counter and to block—but he was careful to see that we did not hurt each other.

He knew about football, too, and today he paused, a powerful, respectable-looking Negro man of thirty years or more, and watched us for a moment as we played.

Randy took the ball and went up to him. "How do you hold it, Dick?" he said. "Is this right?"

Dick watched him attentively as he gripped the ball, and held it back above his shoulder. The Negro nodded approvingly and said, "That's right, Cap'n Shepperton. You've got it. Only," he said gently, and now took the ball in his own powerful hand, "when you gits a little oldah yo' handses gits biggah and you gits a bettah grip."

His own great hand, in fact, seemed to hold the ball as easily as if it were an apple. And, holding it so a moment, he brought it back, aimed over his outstretched left hand as if he were pointing a gun, and rifled it in a beautiful, whizzing spiral thirty yards or more to Gus. He then showed us how to kick, how to get the ball off of the toe in such a way that it would rise and spiral cleanly. He knew how to do this too. He must have got off kicks there, in the yard at Shepperton's, that traveled fifty yards.

He showed us how to make a fire, how to pile the kindling so that the flames shot up cone-wise, cleanly, without smoke or waste. He showed us how to strike a match with the thumbnail of one hand and keep and hold the flame in the strongest wind. He showed us how to lift a weight, how to tote a burden on our shoulders in the easiest way. There was nothing that he did not know. We were all so proud of him. Mr. Shepperton himself declared that Dick was the best man he'd ever had, the smartest darky that he'd ever known.

And yet? He went too softly, at too swift a pace. He was there upon you sometimes like a cat. Looking before us, sometimes, seeing nothing but the world before us, suddenly we felt a shadow at our backs and, looking up, would find that Dick was there. And there was something moving in the night. We never saw him come or go. Sometimes we would waken, startled, and feel that we had heard a board creak, and the soft clicking of a latch, a shadow passing swiftly. All was still.

"Young white fokes, oh, young white gent'mun,"—his soft voice ending in a moan, a kind of rhythm in his hips—"oh, young white fokes, Ise tellin' *you*"—that soft low moan again—"you gotta love each othah like a brothah." He was deeply religious and went to church three times a week. He read his Bible every night. It was the only object on his square board table.

Sometimes Dick would come out of his little basement room, and his eyes would be red, as if he had been weeping. We would know, then, that he had been reading his Bible. There would be times when he would almost moan when he talked to us, a kind of hymnal chant that came from some deep and fathomless intoxication of the spirit, and that transported him. For us, it was a troubling and bewildering experience. We tried to laugh it off and make jokes about it. But there was something in it so dark and strange and full of a feeling that we could not fathom that our jokes were hollow, and the trouble in our minds and in our hearts remained.

Sometimes on these occasions his speech would be made up of some weird jargon of Biblical phrases, of which he seemed to have hundreds, and which he wove together in this strange pattern of his emotion in a sequence that was meaningless to us, but to which he himself had the coherent clue. "Oh, young white fokes," he would begin, moaning gently, "de dry bones in de valley. I tell you, white fokes, de day is comin' when He's comin' on dis earth again to sit in judgment. He'll put de sheep upon de right hand and de goats upon de left. Oh, white fokes, white fokes, de Armageddon day's a-comin', white fokes, an' de dry bones in de valley."

Or again, we could hear him singing as he went about his work, in his deep rich voice, so full of warmth and strength, so full of Africa, singing hymns that were not only of his own race but familiar to us all. I don't know where he learned them. Perhaps they were remembered from his Army days. Perhaps he had learned them in the service of former masters. He drove the Sheppertons to church on Sunday morning, and would wait for them throughout the morning service. He would come up to the side door of the church while the service was going on, neatly dressed in his good dark suit, holding his chauffeur's hat respectfully in his hand, and stand there humbly and listen during the course of the entire sermon.

And then, when the hymns were sung and the great rich sound would swell and roll out into the quiet air of Sunday, Dick would stand and listen, and sometimes he would join in quietly in the song. A number of these favorite Presbyterian hymns we heard him singing many times in a low rich voice as he went about his work around the house. He would sing Who Follows in His Train? or Alexander's Glory Song, or Rock of Ages, or Onward, Christian Soldiers!

And yet? Well, nothing happened—there was just "a flying hint from here and there," and the sense of something passing in the night. Turning into the square one day as Dick was driving Mr. Shepperton to town, Lon Everett skidded murderously around the corner, sideswiped Dick and took the fender off. The Negro was out of the car like a cat and got his master out. Shepperton was unhurt. Lon Everett climbed out and reeled across the street, drunk as a sot at three o'clock. He swung viciously, clumsily, at the Negro, smashed him in the face. Blood trickled from the flat black nostrils and from the thick liver-colored lips. Dick did not move. But suddenly the whites of his eyes were shot with red, his bleeding lips bared for a moment over the white ivory of his teeth. Lon smashed at him again. The Negro took it full in the face again; his hands twitched slightly, but he did not move. They collared the drunken sot and hauled him off and locked him up. Dick stood there for a moment, then he wiped his face and turned to see what damage had been done the car. No more now, but there were those who saw it who remembered later how the eyes went red.

Another thing: Sheppertons had a cook named Pansy Harris. She was a comely Negro wench, young, plump, black as the ace of spades, a good-hearted girl with a deep dimple in her cheeks and faultless teeth, bared in the most engaging smile. No one ever saw Dick speak to her. No one ever saw her glance at him, or him at her, and yet that smilingly good-natured wench became as mournful-silent and as silent-sullen as midnight pitch. She went about her work as mournfully as if she were going to a funeral. The gloom deepened all about her. She answered sullenly now when spoken to.

One night toward Christmas she announced that she was leaving. In response to all entreaties, all efforts to find the reason for her sudden and unreasonable decision, she had no answer except a sullen repetition of the assertion that she had to leave. Repeated questionings did finally wring from her a sullen statement that her husband needed her at home. More than this she would not say, and even this excuse was highly suspect, because her husband was a Pullman porter, only home two days a week and well accustomed to do himself such housekeeping tasks as she might do for him.

The Sheppertons were fond of her. They tried again to find the reason for her leaving. Was she dissatisfied? "No'm"—an implacable monosyllable, mournful, unrevealing as the night. Had she been offered a better job elsewhere? "No'm"—as untelling as before. If they offered her more wages, would she stay with them? "No'm," again and again, sullen and unyielding, until finally the exasperated mistress threw her hands up in a gesture of defeat and said, "All right then, Pansy. Have it your own way, if that's the way you feel. Only for heaven's sake don't leave us in the lurch until we get another cook."

This, at length, with obvious reluctance, the girl agreed to. Then, putting on her hat and coat and taking the paper bag of "leavings" she was allowed to take home with her at night, she went out the kitchen door and made her sullen and morose departure.

This was on Saturday night, a little after eight o'clock. That afternoon Randy and I had been fooling around the basement and, seeing that Dick's door was slightly ajar, we looked in to see if he was there. The little room was empty, swept and spotless, as it had always been.

But we did not notice that! We saw it! At the same moment, our breaths caught sharply in a gasp of startled wonderment. Randy was the first to speak. "Look!" he whispered. "Do you see it?"

See it! My eyes were glued upon it. Squarely across the bare board table, blue-dull, deadly in its murderous efficiency, lay a modern repeating rifle. Beside it was a box containing one hundred rounds of ammunition, and behind it, squarely in the center, face downward on the table, was the familiar cover of Dick's worn old Bible.

Then he was on us like a cat. He was there like a great dark shadow before we knew it. We turned, terrified. He was there above us, his thick lips bared above his gums, his eyes gone small and red as rodents'.

"Dick!" Randy gasped, and moistened his dry lips. "Dick!" he fairly cried now.

It was all over like a flash. Dick's mouth closed. We could see the whites of his eyes again. He smiled and said softly, affably, "Yes, suh, Cap'n Shepperton. Yes, suh! You gent'mun lookin' at my rifle?" he said, and moved into the room.

I gulped and nodded my head and couldn't say a word, and Randy whispered, "Yes." And both of us still stared at him, with an expression of appalled and fascinated interest.

Dick shook his head and chuckled. "Can't do without my rifle, white fokes. No, suh!" he shook his head good-naturedly again. "Ole Dick, he's—he's—he's an ole Ahmy man, you know. If they take his rifle away from him, why, that's jest lak takin' candy from a little baby. Yes, suh!" he chuckled, and picked the weapon up affectionately. "Ole Dick felt Christmas comin' on—he-he—I reckon he must have felt it in his bones"—he chuckled—"so I been savin' up my money. I just thought I'd hide this heah and keep it as a big supprise fo' the young white fokes untwil Christmas morning. Then I was gonna take the young white fokes out and show 'em how to shoot."

We had begun to breathe more easily now and, almost as if we had been under the spell of the Pied Piper of Hamelin, we had followed him, step by step, into the room.

"Yes, suh," Dick chuckled, "I was just fixin' to hide this gun away twill Christmas Day, but Cap'n Shepperton—hee!" He chuckled heartily and slapped his thigh. "You can't fool ole Cap'n Shepperton. He just must've smelled this ole gun right out. He comes right in and sees it befo' I has a chance to tu'n around. . . . Now, white fokes"—Dick's voice fell to a tone of low and winning confidence—"now that you's found out, I'll tell you what I'll do. If you'll just keep it a supprise from the other white fokes twill Christmas Day, I'll take all you gent'mun out and let you shoot it. Now, cose," he went on quietly, with a shade of resignation, "if you want to tell on me, you can, but"—here his voice fell again, with just the faintest, yet most eloquent shade of sorrowful regret—"ole Dick was looking fahwad to this; hopin' to give all the white fokes a supprise Christmas Day."

We promised earnestly that we would keep his secret as if it were our own. We fairly whispered our solemn vow. We tiptoed away out of the little basement room as if we were afraid our very footsteps might betray the partner of our confidence.

This was four o'clock on Saturday afternoon. Already, there was a somber moaning of the wind, gray storm clouds sweeping over. The threat of snow was in the air.

Snow fell that night. It came howling down across the hills. It swept in on us from the Smokies. By seven o'clock the air was blind with sweeping snow, the earth was carpeted, the streets were numb. The storm howled on, around houses warm with crackling fires and shaded light. All life seemed to have withdrawn into thrilling isolation. A horse went by upon the streets with muffled hoofs. Storm shook the houses. The world was numb. I went to sleep upon this mystery, lying in the darkness, listening to that exultancy of storm, to that dumb wonder, that enormous and attentive quietness of snow, with something dark and jubilant in my soul I could not utter.

A little after one o'clock that morning I was awakened by the ringing of a bell. It was the fire bell of the city hall, and it was beating an alarm—a hard fast stroke that I had never heard before. Bronze with peril, clangorous through the snow-numbed silence of the air, it had a quality of instancy and menace I had never known before. I leaped up and ran to the window to look for the telltale glow against the sky. But almost before I looked, those deadly strokes beat in upon my brain the message that this was no alarm for fire. It was a savage clangorous alarm to the whole town, a brazen tongue to warn mankind against the menace of some peril, secret, dark, unknown, greater than fire or flood could ever be.

I got instantly, in the most overwhelming and electric way, the sense that the whole town had come to life. All up and down the street the houses were beginning to light up. Next door, the Shepperton house was ablaze with light from top to bottom. Even as I looked, Mr. Shepperton, wearing an overcoat over his pajamas, ran down the snow-covered steps and padded out across the snow-covered walk toward the street.

People were beginning to run out of doors. I heard excited shouts and questions everywhere. I saw Nebraska Crane come pounding down the middle of the street. I knew that he was coming for me and Randy. As he ran by Shepperton's, he put his fingers to his mouth and whistled piercingly. It was a signal we all knew.

I was all ready by the time he came running down the alley toward our cottage. He hammered at the door; I was already there.

"Come on!" he said, panting with excitement, his black eyes burning with an intensity I'd never seen before. "Come on!" he cried. We were halfway out across the yard by now. "It's that nigger. He's gone crazy and is running wild."

"Wh-wh-what nigger?" I gasped, pounding at his heels.

Even before he spoke, I had the answer. Mr. Crane had already come out of his house, buttoning his heavy policeman's overcoat as he came. He had paused to speak for a moment to Mr. Shepperton, and I heard Shepperton say quickly, in a low voice, "Which way did he go?"

Then I heard somebody cry, "It's that nigger of Shepperton's!"

Mr. Shepperton turned and went quickly back across his yard toward the house. His wife and two girls stood huddled in the open doorway, white, trembling, holding themselves together, their arms thrust into the wide sleeves of their kimonos.

The telephone in Shepperton's house was ringing like mad, but no one was paying any attention to it. I heard Mrs. Shepperton say quickly, as he ran up the steps, "Is it Dick?" He nodded and passed her brusquely, going toward the phone.

At this moment, Nebraska whistled piercingly again upon his fingers and Randy Shepperton ran past his mother and down the steps. She called sharply to him. He paid no attention to her. When he came up, I saw that his fine thin face was white as a sheet. He looked at me and whispered, "It's—it's Dick!" And in a moment, "They say he's killed four people."

"With—" I couldn't finish.

Randy nodded dumbly, and we both stared there for a minute, aware now of the murderous significance of the secret we had kept, with a sudden sense of guilt and fear, as if somehow the crime lay on our shoulders.

Across the street a window banged up in the parlor of Suggs' house, and Old Man Suggs appeared in the window, clad only in his nightgown, his brutal old face inflamed with excitement, his shock of silvery white hair awry, his powerful shoulders, and his thick hands gripping his crutches.

"He's coming this way!" he bawled to the world in general. "They say he lit out across the square! He's heading out in this direction!"

Mr. Crane paused to yell back impatiently over his shoulder, "No, he went down South Dean Street! He's heading for Wilton and the river! I've already heard from headquarters!"

Automobiles were beginning to roar and sputter all along the street. Across the street I could hear Mr. Potterham sweating over his. He would whirl the crank a dozen times or more; the engine would catch for a moment, cough and sputter, and then die again. Gus ran out-of-doors with a kettle of boiling water and began to pour it feverishly down the radiator spout.

Mr. Shepperton was already dressed. We saw him run down the back steps toward the carriage house. All three of us, Randy, Nebraska, and myself, streaked down the alleyway to help him. We got the old wooden doors open. He went in and cranked the car. It was a new one, and started up at once. Mr. Shepperton backed out into the snowy drive. We all clambered up on the running board. He spoke absently, saying, "You boys stay here. . . . Randy, your mother's calling you," but we all tumbled in and he didn't say a word.

He came backing down the alleyway at top speed. We turned into the street and picked up Mr. Crane at the corner. We lit out for town, going at top speed. Cars were coming out of alleys everywhere. We could hear people shouting questions and replies at one another. I heard one man shout, "He's killed six men!"

I don't think it took us over five minutes to reach the square, but when we got there, it seemed as if the whole town was there ahead of us. Mr. Shepperton pulled the car up and parked in front of the city hall. Mr. Crane leaped out and went pounding away across the square without another word to us.

From every corner, every street that led into the square, people were streaking in. One could see the dark figures of running men across the white carpet of the square. They were all rushing in to one focal point.

The southwest corner of the square where South Dean Street came into it was like a dog fight. Those running figures streaking toward that dense crowd gathered there made me think of nothing else so much as a fight between two boys upon the playgrounds of the school at recess time. The way the crowd was swarming in was just the same.

But then I *heard* a difference. From that crowd came a low and growing mutter, an ugly and insistent growl, of a tone and quality I had never heard before. But I knew instantly what it meant. There was no mistaking the blood note in that foggy growl. And we looked at one another with the same question in the eyes of all.

Only Nebraska's coal-black eyes were shining now with a savage sparkle even they had never had before. "Come on," he said in a low tone, exultantly.

"They mean business this time, sure. Let's go." And he darted away toward the dense and sinister darkness of the crowd.

Even as we followed him we heard coming toward us now, growing, swelling at every instant, one of the most savagely mournful and terrifying sounds that night can know. It was the baying of the hounds as they came up upon the leash from Niggertown. Full-throated, howling deep, the savagery of blood was in it, and the savagery of man's guilty doom was in it too.

They came up swiftly, fairly baying at our heels as we sped across the snow-white darkness of the square. As we got up to the crowd, we saw that it had gathered at the corner where my uncle's hardware store stood. Cash Eager had not yet arrived, but, facing the crowd which pressed in on them so close and menacing that they were almost flattened out against the glass, three or four men were standing with arms stretched out in a kind of chain, as if trying to protect with the last resistance of their strength and eloquence the sanctity of private property.

Will Hendershot was mayor at that time, and he was standing there, arm to arm with Hugh McNair. I could see Hugh, taller by half a foot than anyone around him, his long gaunt figure, the gaunt passion of his face, even the attitude of his outstretched bony arms, strangely, movingly Lincolnesque, his one good eye blazing in the cold glare of the corner lamp with a kind of cold inspired Scotch passion.

"Wait a minute! You men wait a minute!" he cried. His words cut out above the clamor of the mob like an electric spark. "You'll gain nothing, you'll help nothing if you do this thing!"

They tried to drown him out with an angry and derisive roar. He shot his big fist up into the air and shouted at them, blazed at them with that cold single eye, until they had to hear. "Listen to me!" he cried. "This is no time for mob law! This is no case for lynch law! This is a time for law and order! Wait till the sheriff swears you in! Wait until Cash Eager comes! Wait—"

He got no farther. "Wait, hell!" cried someone. "We've waited long enough! We're going to get that nigger!"

The mob took up the cry. The whole crowd was writhing angrily now, like a tormented snake. Suddenly there was a flurry in the crowd, a scattering. Somebody yelled a warning at Hugh McNair. He ducked quickly, just in time. A brick whizzed past him, smashing the plate-glass window into fragments.

And instantly a bloody roar went up. The crowd surged forward, kicked the fragments of jagged glass away. In a moment the whole mob was storming into the dark store. Cash Eager got there just too late. He arrived in time to take out his keys and open the front doors, but as he grimly remarked it was like closing the barn doors after the horse had been stolen.

The mob was in and helped themselves to every rifle they could find. They smashed open cartridge boxes and filled their pockets with the loose cartridges. Within ten minutes they had looted the store of every rifle, every cartridge in the stock. The whole place looked as if a hurricane had hit it. The mob was streaming out into the street, was already gathering round the dogs a hundred feet or so away, who were picking up the scent at that point, the place where Dick had halted last before he had turned and headed south, downhill along South Dean Street toward the river.

The hounds were scampering about, tugging at the leash, moaning softly with their noses pointed to the snow, their long ears flattened down. But in that light and in that snow it almost seemed no hounds were needed to follow Dick. Straight as a string right down the center of the sheeted car tracks, the Negro's footsteps led away until they vanished downhill in the darkness.

But now, although the snow had stopped, the wind was swirling through the street and making drifts and eddies in the snow. The footprints were fading rapidly. Soon they would be gone.

The dogs were given their head. They went straining on softly, sniffing at the snow; behind them the dark masses of the mob closed in and followed. We stood there watching while they went. We saw them go on down the street and vanish. But from below, over the snow-numbed stillness of the air, the vast low mutter of the mob came back to us.

Men were clustered now in groups. Cash Eager stood before his shattered window, ruefully surveying the ruin. Other men were gathered around the big telephone pole at the corner, pointing out two bullet holes that had been drilled cleanly through it.

And swiftly, like a flash, running from group to group, like a powder train of fire, the full detail of that bloody chronicle of night was pieced together.

This was what had happened. Somewhere between nine and ten o'clock that night, Dick Prosser had gone to Pansy Harris' shack in Niggertown. Some said he had been drinking when he went there. At any rate, the police had later found the remnants of a gallon jug of raw corn whisky in the room. What happened, what passed between them, was never known. And, besides, no one was greatly interested. It was a crazy nigger with "another nigger's woman."

Shortly after ten o'clock that night, the woman's husband appeared upon the scene. The fight did not start then. According to the woman, the real trouble did not come until an hour or more after his return.

The men drank together. Each was in an ugly temper. Shortly before midnight, they got into a fight. Harris slashed at Dick with a razor. In a second they were locked together, rolling about and fighting like two madmen on the floor. Pansy Harris went screaming out-of-doors and across the street into a dingy little grocery store.

A riot call was telephoned at once to police headquarters on the public square. The news came in that a crazy nigger had broken loose on Gulley Street in Niggertown, and to send help at once. Pansy Harris ran back across the street toward her little shack.

As she got there, her husband, with blood streaming from his face, staggered out into the street, with his hands held up protectively behind his head in a gesture of instinctive terror. At the same moment, Dick Prosser appeared in the doorway of the shack, deliberately took aim with his rifle and shot the fleeing Negro squarely through the back of the head. Harris dropped forward on his face into the snow. He was dead before he hit the ground. A huge dark stain of blood-soaked snow widened out around him. Dick Prosser seized the terrified Negress by the arm, hurled her into the shack, bolted the door, pulled down the shades, blew out the lamp and waited.

A few minutes later, two policemen arrived from town. They were a young constable named Willis, and John Grady, a lieutenant of police. The policemen took one look at the bloody figure in the snow, questioned the frightened keeper of the grocery store and, after consulting briefly, produced their weapons and walked out into the street.

Young Willis stepped softly down on to the snow-covered porch of the shack, flattened himself against the wall between the window and the door, and waited. Grady went around to the side and flashed his light through the window, which, on this side, was shadeless. Grady said in a loud tone: "Come out of there!"

Dick's answer was to shoot him cleanly through the wrist. At the same moment Willis kicked the door in and, without waiting, started in with pointed revolver. Dick shot him just above the eyes. The policeman fell forward on his face.

Grady came running out around the house, rushed into the grocery store, pulled the receiver of the old-fashioned telephone off the hook, rang frantically for headquarters and yelled out across the wire that a crazy nigger had killed Sam Willis and a Negro man, and to send help.

At this moment Dick stepped out across the porch into the street, aimed swiftly through the dirty window of the little store and shot John Grady as he stood there at the phone. Grady fell dead with a bullet that entered just below his left temple and went out on the other side.

Dick, now moving in a long, unhurried stride that covered the ground with catlike speed, turned up the long snow-covered slope of Gulley Street and began his march toward town. He moved right up the center of the street, shooting cleanly from left to right as he went. Halfway up the hill, the second-story window of a two-story Negro tenement flew open. An old Negro man stuck out his ancient head of cotton wool. Dick swiveled and shot casually from his hip. The shot tore the top of the old Negro's head off.

By the time Dick reached the head of Gulley Street, they knew he was coming. He moved steadily along, leaving his big tread cleanly in the middle of the sheeted street, shifting a little as he walked, swinging his gun crosswise before him. This was the Negro Broadway of the town, but where those poolrooms, barbershops, drugstores and fried-fish places had been loud with dusky life ten minutes before, they were now silent as the ruins of Egypt. The word was flaming through the town that a crazy nigger was on the way. No one showed his head.

Dick moved on steadily, always in the middle of the street, reached the end of Gulley Street and turned into South Dean—turned right, uphill, in the middle of the car tracks, and started toward the square. As he passed the lunchroom on the left, he took a swift shot through the window at the counter man. The fellow ducked behind the counter. The bullet crashed into the wall above his head.

Meanwhile, at police headquarters, the sergeant had sent John Chapman out across the square to head Dick off. Mr. Chapman was perhaps the best-liked man upon the force. He was a pleasant florid-faced man of forty-five, with curling brown mustaches, congenial and good-humored, devoted to his family, courageous, but perhaps too kindly and too gentle for a good policeman.

John Chapman heard the shots and ran. He came up to the corner by Eager's hardware store just as Dick's last shot went crashing through the lunchroom window. Mr. Chapman took up his post there at the corner behind the telephone post that stood there at that time. Mr. Chapman, from his vantage point behind this post, took out his revolver and shot directly at Dick Prosser as he came up the street.

By this time Dick was not more than thirty yards away. He dropped quietly upon one knee and aimed. Mr. Chapman shot again and missed. Dick fired. The high-velocity bullet bored through the post a little to one side. It grazed the shoulder of John Chapman's uniform and knocked a chip out of the monument sixty yards or more behind him in the center of the square.

Mr. Chapman fired again and missed. And Dick, still coolly poised upon his knee, as calm and steady as if he were engaging in a rifle practice, fired again, drilled squarely through the center of the post and shot John Chapman through the heart. Then Dick rose, pivoted like a soldier in his tracks and started down the street, straight as a string, right out of town.

This was the story as we got it, pieced together like a train of fire among the excited groups of men that clustered there in trampled snow before the shattered glass of Eager's store.

But now, save for these groups of talking men, the town again was silent. Far off in the direction of the river, we could hear the mournful baying of the hounds. There was nothing more to see or do. Cash Eager stooped, picked up some fragments of the shattered glass and threw them in the window. A policeman was left on guard, and presently all five of us—Mr. Shepperton, Cash Eager and we three boys—walked back across the square and got into the car and drove home again.

But there was no more sleep, I think, for anyone that night. Black Dick had murdered sleep. Toward daybreak, snow began to fall again. The snow continued through the morning. It was piled deep in gusting drifts by noon. All footprints were obliterated; the town waited, eager, tense, wondering if the man could get away.

They did not capture him that day, but they were on his trail. From time to time throughout the day, news would drift back to us. Dick had turned east along the river and gone out for some miles along the Fairchilds road. There, a mile or two from Fairchilds, he crossed the river at the Rocky Shallows. Shortly after daybreak, a farmer from the Fairchilds section had seen him cross a field. They picked the trail up there again and followed it across the field and through a wood. He had come out on the other side and got down into the Cane Creek section, and there, for several hours, they lost him. Dick had gone right down into the icy water of the creek and walked upstream a mile or so. They brought the dogs down to the creek, to where he broke the trail, took them over to the other side and scented up and down.

Toward five o'clock that afternoon they picked the trail up on the other side, a mile or more upstream. From that point on, they began to close in on him. The dogs followed him across the fields, across the Lester road, into a wood. One arm of the posse swept around the wood to head him off. They knew they had him. Dick, freezing, hungry and unsheltered, was hiding in that wood. They knew he couldn't get away. The posse ringed the wood and waited until morning.

At 7:30 the next morning he made a break for it. He got through the line without being seen, crossed the Lester road and headed back across the field in the direction of Cane Creek. And there they caught him. They saw him plunging through the snowdrift of a field. A cry went up. The posse started after him.

Part of the posse were on horseback. The men rode in across the field. Dick halted at the edge of the wood, dropped deliberately upon one knee and for some minutes held them off with rapid fire. At two hundred yards he dropped Doc Lavender, a deputy, with a bullet through the throat.

The posse came in slowly, in an encircling, flankwise movement. Dick got two more of them as they closed in, and then, as deliberately as a trained soldier retreating in good order, still firing as he went, he fell back through the wood. At the other side he turned and ran down through a sloping field that bordered on Cane Creek. At the creek edge, he turned again, knelt once more in the snow and aimed.

It was Dick's last shot. He didn't miss. The bullet struck Wayne Foraker, a deputy, dead center in the forehead and killed him in his saddle. Then the posse saw the Negro aim again, and nothing happened. Dick snapped the breech open savagely, then hurled the gun away. A cheer went up. The posse came charging forward. Dick turned, stumblingly, and ran the few remaining yards that separated him from the cold and rock-bright waters of the creek.

And here he did a curious thing—a thing that no one ever wholly understood. It was thought that he would make one final break for freedom, that he would wade the creek and try to get away before they got to him. Instead, he sat down calmly on the bank and, as quietly as if he were seated on his cot in an Army barracks, he unlaced his shoes, took them off, placed them together neatly at his side, and then stood up like a soldier, erect, in his bare bleeding feet, and faced the mob.

The men on horseback reached him first. They rode up around him and discharged their guns into him. He fell forward in the snow, riddled with bullets. The men dismounted, turned him over on his back, and all the other men came in and riddled him. They took his lifeless body, put a rope around his neck and hung him to a tree. Then the mob exhausted all their ammunition on the riddled carcass.

By nine o'clock that morning the news had reached town. Around eleven o'clock, the mob came back along the river road. A good crowd had gone out to meet it at the Wilton Bottoms. The sheriff rode ahead. Dick's body had been thrown like a sack and tied across the saddle of the horse of one of the deputies he had killed.

It was in this way, bullet-riddled, shot to pieces, open to the vengeful and the morbid gaze of all, that Dick came back to town. The mob came back right to its starting point in South Dean Street. They halted there before an undertaking parlor, not twenty yards away from where Dick knelt to kill John Chapman. They took that ghastly mutilated thing and hung it in the window of the undertaker's place, for every woman, man, and child in town to see.

And it was so we saw him last. We said we wouldn't look. But in the end we went. And I think it has always been the same with people. They protest. They shudder. And they say they will not go. But in the end they always have their look.

At length we went. We saw it, tried wretchedly to make ourselves believe that once this thing had spoken to us gently, had been partner to our confidence, object of our affection and respect. And we were sick with nausea and fear, for something had come into our lives we could not understand.

We looked and whitened to the lips, craned our necks and looked away, and brought unwilling, fascinated eyes back to the horror once again, and craned and turned again, and shuffled in the slush uneasily, but could not go. And we looked up at the leaden reek of day, the dreary vapor of the sky, and, bleakly, at these forms and faces all around us—the people come to gape and stare, the poolroom loafers, the town toughs, the mongrel conquerors of earth—and yet, familiar to our lives and to the body of our whole experience, all known to our landscape, all living men.

And something had come into life—into our lives—that we had never known about before. It was a kind of shadow, a poisonous blackness filled with bewildered loathing. The snow would go, we knew; the reeking vapors of the sky would clear away. The leaf, the blade, the bud, the bird, then April, would come back again, and all of this would be as it had ever been. The homely light of day would shine again familiarly. And all of this would vanish as an evil dream. And yet not wholly so. For we would still remember the old dark doubt and loathing of our kind, of something hateful and unspeakable in the souls of men. We knew that we should not forget.

Beside us, a man was telling the story of his own heroic accomplishments to a little group of fascinated listeners. I turned and looked at him. It was Ben Pounders of the ferret face, the furtive and uneasy eye, Ben Pounders of the mongrel mouth, the wiry muscles of the jaw, Ben Pounders, the collector of usurious lendings to the blacks, the nigger hunter. And now Ben Pounders boasted of another triumph. He was the proud possessor of another scalp.

"I was the first one to git in a shot," he said. "You see that hole there?" He pointed with a dirty finger. "That big hole right above the eye?" They turned and goggled with a drugged and feeding stare.

"That's mine," the hero said, turned briefly to the side and spat tobacco juice into the slush. "That 's where I got him. Hell, after that he didn't know what hit him. He was dead before he hit the ground. We all shot him full of holes then. We sure did fill him full of lead. Why, hell, yes," he declared, with a decisive movement of his head, "we counted up to two hundred and eighty-seven. We must have put three hundred holes in him."

And Nebraska, fearless, blunt, outspoken as he always was, turned abruptly, put two fingers to his lips and spat between them, widely and contemptuously.

"Yeah—*we!*" he grunted. "*We* killed a big one! We—we killed a b'ar, we did! . . . Come on, boys," he said gruffly. "Let's be on our way!"

And, fearless and unshaken, untouched by any terror or any doubt, he moved away. And two white-faced, nauseated boys went with him.

A day or two went by before anyone could go into Dick's room again. I went in with Randy and his father. The little room was spotless, bare and tidy as it had always been. But even the very austerity of that little room now seemed terribly alive with the presence of its black tenant. It was Dick's room. We all knew that. And somehow we all knew that no one else could ever live there again.

Mr. Shepperton went over to the table, picked up Dick's old Bible that still lay there, open and face downward, held it up to the light and looked at it, at the place that Dick had marked when he last read in it. And in a moment, without speaking to us, he began to read in a quiet voice:

"The Lord is my shepherd; I shall not want.

"2. He maketh me to lie down in green pastures: he leadeth me beside the still waters.

"3. He restoreth my soul: he leadeth me in the paths of righteousness for his name's sake.

"4. Yea, though I walk through the valley of the shadow of death, I will fear no evil: for thou art with me—"

Then Mr. Shepperton closed the book and put it down upon the table, the place where Dick had left it. And we went out the door, he locked it, and we went back into that room no more forever.

The years passed, and all of us were given unto time. We went our ways. But often they would turn and come again, these faces and these voices of the past, and burn there in my memory again, upon the muted and immortal geography of time.

And all would come again—the shout of the young voices, the hard thud of the kicked ball, and Dick moving, moving steadily, Dick moving, moving silently, a storm-white world and silence, and something moving, moving in the night. Then I would hear the furious bell, the crowd a-clamor and the baying of the dogs, and feel the shadow coming that would never disappear. Then I would see again the little room that we would see no more, the table and the book. And the pastoral holiness of that old psalm came back to me and my heart would wonder with perplexity and doubt.

For I had heard another song since then, and one that Dick, I know, had never heard, and one perhaps he might not have understood, but one whose phrases and whose imagery it seemed to me would suit him better:

What the hammer? What the chain?
In what furnace was thy brain?
What the anvil? What dread grasp
Dare its deadly terrors clasp?

When the stars threw down their spears,
And water'd heaven with their tears,
Did He smile His work to see?
Did He who made the lamb make thee?

"*What* the hammer? *What* the chain?" No one ever knew. It was a mystery and a wonder. There were a dozen stories, a hundred clues and rumors; all came to nothing in the end. Some said that Dick had come from Texas, others that his home had been in Georgia. Some said that it was true that he had been enlisted in the Army, but that he had killed a man while there and served a term at Leavenworth. Some said he had served in the Army and had received an honorable discharge, but had later killed a man and had served a term in a state prison in Louisiana. Others said that he had been an Army man, but that he had gone crazy, that he had served a period in an asylum when it was found that he was insane, that he had escaped from an asylum, that he had escaped from prison, that he was a fugitive from justice at the time he came to us.

But all these stories came to nothing. Nothing was ever proved. Men debated and discussed these things a thousand times—who and what he had been, what he had done, where he had come from—and all of it came to nothing. No one knew the answer. But I think that I have found the answer. I think I know from where he came.

He came from darkness. He came out of the heart of darkness, from the dark heart of the secret and undiscovered South. He came by night, just as he passed by night. He was night's child and partner, a token of the other side of man's dark soul, a symbol of those things that pass by darkness and that still remain, a symbol of man's evil innocence, and the token of his mystery, a projection of his own unfathomed quality, a friend, a brother and a mortal enemy, an unknown demon, two worlds together—a tiger and a child.

QUESTIONS

1. Discuss the setting of the story. How important is it? How much do we learn about the town and its people? On what implicit premise are the black-white relationships in this town based?
2. The story begins and ends with stanzas from William Blake's poem, "The Tiger" (see page 778 for the complete poem). How does this poem relate to the theme of the story? If you are not familiar with it, look it up and read the whole poem. How is it related to the passage in the Bible to which Dick's Bible is left open (page 38)?
3. The second sentence in "The Most Dangerous Game" is, "It's rather a mystery" (page 8). Are there any "mysteries" in this story? With what kind of mystery is each story concerned? To what extent is the mystery in each resolved?
4. Dick Prosser's character, like that of General Zaroff, consists of many contradictions. Discuss. In his contradictions, is Dick completely unlike the people of the white community? Why does he "go crazy"? Is his character more or less plausible than General Zaroff's?
5. Compare the man-hunt in this story with that in "The Most Dangerous Game." How is it similar? How is it different?
6. What feelings and considerations motivate the whites in tracking Dick down? What meaning has Dick's final gesture of removing his shoes and awaiting the posse? How does this action contrast with the way his body is treated by the whites?
7. "The Most Dangerous Game" ends with General Zaroff's death. "The Child by Tiger" continues for several pages after Dick Prosser's death. Why? In what element of the story is each author most interested?
8. The narrator tells this story twenty-five years after its events took place. What importance does this removal in time have for the meaning of the story?
9. Discuss the conflict of good and evil as it is presented in this story and in "The Most Dangerous Game." Which story has greater moral significance? Why?

2. Plot

Plot is the sequence of incidents or events of which a story is composed. When recounted by itself, it bears about the same relationship to a story that a map does to a journey. Just as a map may be drawn on a finer or grosser scale, so a plot may be recounted with lesser or greater detail. It may include what a character says or thinks, as well as what he does, but it leaves out description and analysis and concentrates ordinarily on major happenings.

Because plot is the easiest element in fiction to comprehend and put into words, beginning readers tend to equate it with the content of the work. When asked what a story is about, they will say that it is about a person to whom particular events happen, not that it is about a certain kind of person or that it presents a particular insight into life. Immature readers read chiefly for plot; mature readers read for whatever revelations of character or life may be presented by means of plot. Because they read chiefly for plot, immature readers may put a high valuation on intricacy of plot or on violent physical action. On the one hand, they may want schemes and intrigues, mixed identities, disguises, secret letters, hidden passages and similar paraphernalia. On the other, they may demand fights by land and sea, dangerous missions, hazardous journeys, hair-breadth escapes. There is nothing improper in liking such things, of course, and sometimes the greatest fiction provides them. But, if readers can be satisfied *only* with stories having these elements, they are like persons who can enjoy only highly spiced foods. Physical action by itself, after all, is meaningless. In a good story a minimum of physical action may be used to yield a maximum of insight. Every story has *some* action, but for a worthwhile story it must be *significant* action. For a superior writer there may be as much significant action in the way a man greets a friend as in how he handles a sword.

Conceivably a plot might consist merely of a sequence of related actions. Ordinarily, however, both the excitement craved by immature readers and the meaningfulness demanded by mature readers arise out of some sort of CONFLICT—a clash of actions, ideas, desires, or wills. The main character may be pitted against some other person or group of persons (man against man); he may be in conflict with some external force—physical nature, society, or "fate" (man against environment); or he may be in conflict with some element in his own nature (man against himself). The conflict may be physical, mental, emotional, or moral. There is conflict in a chess game, where the competitors sit quite still for hours, as surely as in a wrestling match; emotional conflict may be raging within a person sitting quietly in an empty room. The central character in the conflict, whether he be a sympathetic or an unsympathetic person, is referred to as the PROTAGONIST; the forces arrayed against him, whether persons, things, conventions of society, or traits of his own character, are the ANTAGONISTS.* In some stories the conflict is single, clear-cut, and easily identifiable. In others it is multiple, various, and subtle. A person may be in conflict with other persons, with society or nature, and with himself, all at the same time, and sometimes he may be involved in conflict without being aware of it.

"The Most Dangerous Game" illustrates most of these kinds of conflict. Rainsford, the protagonist, is pitted first against other men—against Zaroff and Whitney in the discussions preceding the manhunt and against General Zaroff and Ivan during the manhunt. Near the beginning of the story, he is pitted against nature when he falls into the sea and is unable to get back to the yacht. At the beginning of the manhunt, he is in conflict with himself when he tries to fight off his panic by saying to himself, over and over, "I must keep my nerve. I must keep my nerve." The various conflicts illuminated in this story are physical (Rainsford against the sea and Zaroff), mental (Rainsford's initial conflict of ideas with Whitney and his battle-of-wits with Zaroff during the manhunt, which Zaroff refers to as "outdoor chess"), emotional (Rainsford's efforts

---

*The technical term PROTAGONIST is preferable to the popular term "hero" because it is less ambiguous. The protagonist is simply the central character, the one whose struggles we follow with interest, whether he or she be good or bad, sympathetic or repulsive. A "hero" or "heroine" may be *either* a person of heroic qualities *or* simply the main character, heroic or unheroic.

to control his terror), and moral (Rainsford's refusal to "condone cold-blooded murder" in contrast with Zaroff's contempt for "romantic ideas about the value of human life").

Excellent interpretive fiction has been written utilizing all four of these major kinds of conflict. The cheaper varieties of commercial fiction, however, emphasize the conflict between man and man, depending on the element of physical conflict to supply the main part of their excitement. It is hard to conceive of a western story without a fistfight or a gunfight. Even in the crudest kinds of fiction, however, something more will be found than mere physical combat. Good men will be arrayed against bad men, and thus the conflct will also be between moral values. In cheap fiction this conflict is usually clearly defined in terms of moral absolutes, hero versus villain. In interpretive fiction, the contrasts are likely to be less marked. Good may be opposed to good or half-truth to half-truth. There may be difficulty in determining what *is* the good, and internal conflict tends therefore to be more frequent than physical conflict. In the world in which we live, significant moral issues are seldom sharply defined, judgments are difficult, and choices are complex rather than simple. Interpretive writers are aware of this complexity and are more concerned with displaying its various shadings of moral values than with presenting glaring contrasts of good and evil, right and wrong.

SUSPENSE is the quality in a story that makes readers ask "What's going to happen next?" or "How will this turn out?" and impels them to read on to find the answers to these questions. Suspense is greatest when the readers' curiosity is combined with anxiety about the fate of some sympathetic character. Thus in the old serial movies—often appropriately called "cliffhangers"—a strong element of suspense was created at the end of each episode by leaving the hero hanging from the edge of a cliff or the heroine tied to the railroad tracks with the express train rapidly approaching. In murder mysteries—often called "who-dun-its"—suspense is created by the question of who committed the murder. In love stories it is created by the question "Will the boy win the girl?" or "Will the lovers be re-united, and how?" In more sophisticated forms of fiction the suspense often involves not so much the question *what* as the question *why*—not "What will happen next?" but "How is the protagonist's behavior to be explained in terms of human personality and character?" The forms of suspense range from crude to subtle and may concern not only actions but psychological considerations and moral issues. Two common devices for achieving suspense are to introduce an element of MYS-TERY—an unusual set of circumstances for which the readers crave an explanation, or to place the protagonist in a DILEMMA—a position in which he or she must choose between two courses of action, both undesirable. But suspense can be readily created for most readers by placing *anybody* on a seventeenth-story window ledge or simply by bringing together two physically attractive young people.

In "The Most Dangerous Game," suspense is initiated in the opening sentences with Whitney's account of the mystery of "Ship-Trap Island," of which sailors "have a curious dread"— a place that seems to emanate evil. The mystery grows when, in this out-of-the-way spot, Rainsford discovers an enormous château with a leering gargoyle knocker on its massive door and is confronted by a bearded giant pointing a long-barreled revolver straight at his heart. A second mystery is introduced when General Zaroff tells Rainsford that he hunts "more dangerous game" on this island than the Cape buffalo. He then puts off Rainsford's (and the reader's) curiosity for some thirty-six paragraphs before revealing what the game is. Meanwhile, by placing the hero in physical danger, a second kind of suspense is introduced. Initiated by Rainsford's fall into the sea and his confrontation with Ivan, this kind of suspense becomes the principal suspense device in the second half of the story. Will Rainsford escape—and how?—are the questions that keep the reader going. The manhunt itself begins with a dilemma. Rainsford must choose between three undesirable courses of action: he can hunt men with Zaroff; he can let himself be hunted; or he can submit to being tortured by Ivan. During the hunt, he is faced with other lesser dilemmas. For instance, on the third day, pursued by Zaroff's hounds, "Rainsford knew he could do one of two things. He could stay where he was and wait. That was suicide. He could flee. That was postponing the inevitable."

Suspense is usually the first quality mentioned by immature readers when asked what makes a good story—and, indeed, unless a story makes us eager to keep on reading it, it can have little merit at all. Nevertheless, the importance of suspense is often overrated. After all, we don't listen to a Beethoven symphony to discover how it will turn out. A good story, like a good dinner, should furnish its pleasure as it goes, because it is amusing or well-written or morally penetrating or because the characters are interesting to live with. One test of a story is whether it creates a desire to read it again. Like a Beethoven symphony, a good story should be as good or better on a second or third encounter—when we already know what is going to happen—as on the first. Discriminating readers, therefore, while they do not *disvalue* suspense, may be suspicious of stories in which suspense is artificially created—by the simple withholding of vital information, for instance—or in which suspense is all there is. They will ask whether the author's purpose has been merely to keep them guessing what will happen next or to reveal something about experience. They will be less interested in whether the man on the seventeenth-story window ledge will jump than in the reasons that impel him to jump. When the readers' primary interest is shifted from "What happens next?" to "*Why* do things happen as they do?" or "What is the significance of this series of events?" they have taken their most important step forward.

Closely connected with the element of suspense in a short story is the element of SURPRISE. If we know ahead of time exactly what is going to happen in a story and why, there can be no suspense; as long as we do not know, whatever happens comes with an element of surprise. The surprise is proportional to the unexpectedness of what happens; it becomes pronounced when the story departs radically from our expectation. In the short story such radical departure is most often found in a surprise ending: one that reveals a sudden new turn or twist.

As with physical action and suspense, inexperienced readers make a heavier demand for surprise than do experienced readers. The escape story supplies a surprise ending more frequently than does the interpretive. There are two ways by which the legitimacy and value of a surprise ending may be judged: (1) by the fairness with which it is achieved; (2) by the purpose that it serves. If the surprise is brought about as a result of an improbable coincidence or an unlikely series of small coincidences or by the planting of false clues—details whose only purpose is to mislead the readers—or through the withholding of information that the readers ought to have been given earlier in the story or by manipulation of the point of view (see Chapter 5), then we may well dismiss it as a cheap trick. If, on the other hand, the ending that comes at first as a surprise seems perfectly logical and natural as we look back over the story, we may grant it as fairly achieved. Again, a surprise ending may be judged as trivial if it exists simply for its own sake—to shock or to titillate the reader. We may judge it as a fraud if it serves, as it does in much routine commercial fiction, to conceal earlier weaknesses in the story by giving the readers a shiny bauble at the end to absorb and concentrate their attention. Its justification comes when it serves to open up or to reinforce the meaning of the story. The worthwhile surprise is one that furnishes illumination, not just a reversal of expectation.

Whether or not a story has a surprise ending, immature readers usually demand that it have a HAPPY ENDING: the protagonist must solve his problems, defeat the villain, win the girl, "live happily ever after." A common obstacle confronting readers who are making their first attempts to enjoy interpretive fiction is that such fiction often, though by no means always, ends unhappily. They are likely to label such stories as "depressing" and to complain that "real life has troubles enough of its own" or, conversely, that "real life is seldom as unhappy as all that."

Two justifications may be made for the UNHAPPY ENDING. First, many situations in real life have unhappy endings; therefore, if fiction is to illuminate life, it must present defeat as well as triumph. Commercial sports-story writers usually write of how an individual or a team achieves victory against odds. Yet, if one teams wins the pennant, thirteen others must lose it, and if a golfer wins a tournament, fifty or a hundred others must fail to win it. In situations like these, at least, success is much less frequent than failure. Sometimes sports writers, for a variant, will tell how an individual lost the game but learned some important moral lesson— good sportsmanship, perhaps, or the importance of fair play. But here again, in real life, such compensations are gained only occasionally. Defeat, in fact, sometimes embitters people and makes them less able to cope with life than before. Thus we need to understand and perhaps expect defeat as well as victory.

Second, the unhappy ending has a peculiar value for writers who wish us to ponder life. The story with a happy ending has been "wrapped up" for us: readers are sent away feeling pleasantly if vaguely satisfied with the world and cease to think about the story searchingly. The unhappy ending, on the other hand, may cause them to brood over the results, to go over the story in their minds, and thus by searching out its implications to get more from it. Just as we can judge individuals better when we see how they behave in trouble, so we can see deeper into life when it is pried open for inspection. The unhappy endings are more likely to raise significant issues. Shakespeare's tragedies reverberate longer and more resonantly than his comedies. The ending of "The Most Dangerous Game" is designed to resolve all our anxieties. The ending of "Child by Tiger" is designed to make us brood over the mysteries and contradictions of human nature—that is, of our own natures.

Discriminating readers evaluate an ending not by whether it is happy or unhappy but by whether it is logical in terms of what precedes it* and by the fullness of revelation it affords. They have learned that an ending that meets these tests can be profoundly satisfying, whether happy or unhappy. They have learned also that a story, to be artistically satisfying, need have no ending at all in the sense that its central conflict is resolved in favor of protagonist or antagonist. In real life some problems are

---

*The movies or television frequently make a book with an unhappy ending into a film with a happy ending. Such an operation, if the book was artistically successful, sets aside the laws of logic and the expectations we naturally build on them.

never solved and some contests never permanently won. A story, therefore, may have an INDETERMINATE ENDING, one in which no definitive conclusion is arrived at. Conclusion of some kind there must of course be: the story, if it is to be an artistic unit, cannot simply stop. But the conclusion need not be in terms of a resolved conflict. We never learn in Faulkner's "That Evening Sun" (page 254) the outcome of the conflict between Nancy and Jesus. But the story is more effective without a resolution, for this individual conflict merely symptomizes a larger social conflict that has no easy solution.

ARTISTIC UNITY is essential to a good plot. There must be nothing in the story that is irrelevant, that does not contribute to the total meaning, nothing that is there only for its own sake or its own excitement. Good writers exercise rigorous selection: they include nothing that does not advance the central intention of the story. But they must not only select; they must also arrange. The incidents and episodes should be placed in the most effective order, which is not necessarily the chronological order, and when rearranged in chronological order, should make a logical progression. In a highly unified story each event grows out of the preceding one in time and leads logically to the next. The various stages of the story are linked together in a chain of cause and effect. With such a story one seldom feels that events might as easily have taken one turn as another. One feels not that the author is managing the plot but rather that the plot has a quality of inevitability, given a certain set of characters and an initial situation.

An author who gives his story a turn unjustified by the situation or the characters involved is guilty of PLOT MANIPULATION. Any unmotivated action furnishes an instance of plot manipulation. We suspect authors of plot manipulation also if they rely too heavily on chance or on coincidence to bring about a solution to a story. In Poe's famous story "The Pit and the Pendulum," when the victim of the Spanish Inquisition is rescued by the outstretched arm of the commanding general of the invading French army just at the moment when the converging fiery walls of his torture chamber have caused him to fall fainting into the abyss, we have a famous example of such a manipulated ending.*

Chance cannot be barred from fiction, of course, any more than it can be barred from life. But, if an author uses an improbable chance to effect a

---

*This kind of coincidental resolution is sometimes referred to as *deus ex machina* ("god from the machine") after the practice of some ancient Greek dramatists in having a god descend from heaven (in the theater by means of a stage machine) to rescue their protagonist at the last minute from some impossible situation. The general in Poe's story is clearly the modern counterpart of such a supernatural deliverer.

resolution to a story, the story loses its sense of conviction and inevitability. The objections to such a use of coincidence* are even more forcible, for coincidence is chance compounded. Coincidence may be justifiably used to initiate a story, and occasionally to complicate it, but not to resolve it. It is objectionable in proportion to its improbability, its importance to the story, and its nearness to the end. If two characters in a story both start talking of the same topic at once, it may be a coincidence but hardly an objectionable one. If they both decide suddenly to kill their mothers at the same time, we may find the coincidence less acceptable. But the use of even a highly improbable coincidence may be perfectly appropriate at the start of a story. Just as a chemist may wonder what will happen if certain chemical elements are placed together in a test tube, an author may wonder what will happen if two former lovers accidentally meet long after they have married and in Majorca where they longed as young lovers to go. The improbable initial situation is justified because it offers a chance to observe human nature in conditions that may be particularly revealing, and good readers demand only that the author develop a story logically from that initial situation. But the writer who uses a similar coincidence to resolve a story is avoiding the logic of life rather than revealing it. It is often said that fact is stranger than fiction: it *should* be stranger than fiction. In life almost any concatenation of events is possible; in a story the sequence of events should be probable.

There are various approaches to the analysis of plot. We may, if we wish, draw diagrams of different kinds of plots or trace the development of rising action, climax, and falling action. Such procedures, however, if they are concerned with the examination of plot *per se*, are not likely to take us far into the story. Better questions will concern themselves with the *function* of plot—with the relationship of each incident to the total meaning of the story. Plot is important, in interpretive fiction, for what it reveals. The analysis of a story through its central conflict is likely to be especially fruitful, for it rapidly takes us to what is truly at issue in the story. In testing a story for quality, it is useful to examine how the incidents and episodes are connected, for such an examination is a test of the story's probability and unity. We can never get very far, however, by

---

*CHANCE is the occurrence of an event that has no apparent cause in antecedent events or in predisposition of character. In an automobile accident in which a drunk, coming home from a party, crashes into a sober driver from behind, we say that the accident was a chance event in the life of the sober driver but that it was a logical consequence in the life of the drunk. COINCIDENCE is the chance concurrence of *two* events that have a peculiar correspondence. If the two drivers involved in the accident had been brothers and were coming from different places, it would be coincidence.

analysis of plot alone. In any good story, plot is inextricable from character and total meaning. Plot by itself gives little more indication of the total story than a map gives of the quality of a journey.

Graham Greene
THE DESTRUCTORS

1

It was the eve of August Bank Holiday that the latest recruit became the leader of the Wormsley Common Gang. No one was surprised except Mike, but Mike at the age of nine was surprised by everything. "If you don't shut your mouth," somebody once said to him, "you'll get a frog down it." After that Mike had kept his teeth tightly clamped except when the surprise was too great.

The new recruit had been with the gang since the beginning of the summer holidays, and there were possibilities about his brooding silence that all recognized. He never wasted a word even to tell his name until that was required of him by the rules. When he said "Trevor" it was a statement of fact, not as it would have been with the others a statement of shame or defiance. Nor did anyone laugh except Mike, who finding himself without support and meeting the dark gaze of the newcomer opened his mouth and was quiet again. There was every reason why T., as he was afterwards referred to, should have been an object of mockery—there was his name (and they substituted the initial because otherwise they had no excuse not to laugh at it), the fact that his father, a former architect and present clerk, had "come down in the world" and that his mother considered herself better than the neighbors. What but an odd quality of danger, of the unpredictable, established him in the gang without any ignoble ceremony of initiation?

The gang met every morning in an impromptu car-park, the site of the last bomb of the first blitz. The leader, who was known as Blackie, claimed to have heard it fall, and no one was precise enough in his dates to point out that he would have been one year old and fast asleep on the down platform of Wormsley Common Underground Station. On one side of the car-park leant

THE DESTRUCTORS First published in 1954. The setting is London nine years after the conclusion of World War II (1939–1945). During the first sustained bombing attacks on London ("the first blitz") from September 1940 to May 1941, many families slept in the Underground (i.e., subway) stations, which were used as bomb shelters. "Trevor" was typically an upper-class English name. Sir Christopher Wren (1632–1723), England's most famous architect, designed St. Paul's Cathedral and many other late seventeenth- and early eighteenth-century buildings. Graham Greene, an Englishman and a Roman Catholic convert, was born in 1904 and has lived in London at various stages of his life.

the first occupied house, No. 3, of the shattered Northwood Terrace—literally leant, for it had suffered from the blast of the bomb and the side walls were supported on wooden struts. A smaller bomb and some incendiaries had fallen beyond, so that the house stuck up like a jagged tooth and carried on the further wall relics of its neighbor, a dado, the remains of a fireplace. T., whose words were almost confined to voting "Yes" or "No" to the plan of operations proposed each day by Blackie, once startled the whole gang by saying broodingly, "Wren built that house, father says."

"Who's Wren?"

"The man who built St. Paul's."

"Who cares?" Blackie said. "It's only Old Misery's."

Old Misery—whose real name was Thomas— had once been a builder and decorator. He lived alone in the crippled house, doing for himself: once a week you could see him coming back across the common with bread and vegetables, and once as the boys played in the car-park he put his head over the smashed wall of his garden and looked at them.

"Been to the lav," one of the boys said, for it was common knowledge that since the bombs fell something had gone wrong with the pipes of the house and Old Misery was too mean to spend money on the property. He could do the redecorating himself at cost price, but he had never learnt plumbing. The lav was a wooden shed at the bottom of the narrow garden with a star-shaped hole in the door: it had escaped the blast which had smashed the house next door and sucked out the window-frames of No. 3.

The next time the gang became aware of Mr. Thomas was more surprising. Blackie, Mike and a thin yellow boy, who for some reason was called by his surname Summers, met him on the common coming back from the market. Mr. Thomas stopped them. He said glumly, "You belong to the lot that play in the car-park?"

Mike was about to answer when Blackie stopped him. As the leader he had responsibilities. "Suppose we are?" he said ambiguously.

"I got some chocolates," Mr. Thomas said. "Don't like 'em myself. Here you are. Not enough to go round, I don't suppose. There never is," he added with somber conviction. He handed over three packets of Smarties.

The gang were puzzled and perturbed by this action and tried to explain it away. "Bet someone dropped them and he picked 'em up," somebody suggested.

"Pinched 'em and then got in a bleeding funk," another thought aloud.

"It's a bribe," Summers said. "He wants us to stop bouncing balls on his wall."

"We'll show him we don't take bribes," Blackie said, and they sacrificed the whole morning to the game of bouncing that only Mike was young enough to enjoy. There was no sign from Mr. Thomas.

Next day T. astonished them all. He was late at the rendezvous, and the voting for the day's exploit took place without him. At Blackie's suggestion the gang was to disperse in pairs, take buses at random and see how many free rides could be snatched from unwary conductors (the operation was to be carried out in pairs to avoid cheating). They were drawing lots for their companions when T. arrived.

"Where you been, T.?" Blackie asked. "You can't vote now. You know the rules."

"I've been *there,*" T. said. He looked at the ground, as though he had thoughts to hide.

"Where?"

"At Old Misery's." Mike's mouth opened and then hurriedly closed again with a click. He had remembered the frog.

"At Old Misery's?" Blackie said. There was nothing in the rules against it, but he had a sensation that T. was treading on dangerous ground. He asked hopefully, "Did you break in?"

"No. I rang the bell."

"And what did you say?"

"I said I wanted to see his house."

"What did he do?"

"He showed it to me."

"Pinch anything?"

"No."

"What did you do it for then?"

The gang had gathered round: it was as though an impromptu court were about to form and to try some case of deviation. T. said, "It's a beautiful house," and still watching the ground, meeting no one's eyes, he licked his lips first one way, then the other.

"What do you mean, a beautiful house?" Blackie asked with scorn.

"It's got a staircase two hundred years old like a corkscrew. Nothing holds it up."

"What do you mean, nothing holds it up. Does it float?"

"It's to do with opposite forces, Old Misery said."

"What else?"

"There's paneling."

"Like in the Blue Boar?"

"Two hundred years old."

"Is Old Misery two hundred years old?"

Mike laughed suddenly and then was quiet again. The meeting was in a serious mood. For the first time since T. had strolled into the car-park on the first day of the holidays his position was in danger. It only needed a single use of his real name and the gang would be at his heels.

"What did you do it for?" Blackie asked. He was just, he had no jealousy, he was anxious to retain T. in the gang if he could. It was the word "beautiful" that worried him—that belonged to a class world that you could still see parodied at the Wormsley Common Empire° by a man wearing a top hat and a monocle, with a haw-haw accent. He was tempted to say, "My dear Trevor,

---

Wormsley Common Empire: a music hall for revues and popular entertainments

old chap," and unleash his hell hounds. "If you'd broken in," he said sadly—
that indeed would have been an exploit worthy of the gang.

"This was better," T. said. "I found out things." He continued to stare at
his feet, not meeting anybody's eye, as though he were absorbed in some
dream he was unwilling—or ashamed—to share.

"What things?"

"Old Misery's going to be away all tomorrow and Bank Holiday."

Blackie said with relief, "You mean we could break in?"

"And pinch things?" somebody asked.

Blackie said, "Nobody's going to pinch things. Breaking in—that's good
enough, isn't it? We don't want any court stuff."

"I don't want to pinch anything," T. said. "I've got a better idea."

"What is it?"

T. raised eyes, as grey and disturbed as the drab August day. "We'll pull it
down," he said. "We'll destroy it."

Blackie gave a single hoot of laughter and then, like Mike, fell quiet,
daunted by the serious implacable gaze. "What'd the police be doing all the
time?" he asked.

"They'd never know. We'd do it from inside. I've found a way in." He
said with a sort of intensity, "We'd be like worms, don't you see, in an apple.
When we came out again there'd be nothing there, no staircase, no panels,
nothing but just walls, and then we'd make the walls fall down—somehow."

"We'd go to jug," Blackie said.

"Who's to prove? And anyway we wouldn't have pinched anything." He
added without the smallest flicker of glee, "There wouldn't be anything to
pinch after we'd finished."

"I've never heard of going to prison for breaking things," Summers said.

"There wouldn't be time," Blackie said. "I've seen housebreakers at
work."

"There are twelve of us," T. said. "We'd organize."

"None of us know how . . ."

"I know," T. said. He looked across at Blackie, "Have you got a better
plan?"

"Today," Mike said tactlessly, "we're pinching free rides . . ."

"Free rides," T. said. "You can stand down, Blackie, if you'd rather . . ."

"The gang's got to vote."

"Put it up then."

Blackie said uneasily, "It's proposed that tomorrow and Monday we destroy Old Misery's house."

"Here, here," said a fat boy called Joe.

"Who's in favor?"

T. said, "It's carried."

"How do we start?" Summers asked.

"He'll tell you," Blackie said. It was the end of his leadership. He went
away to the back of the car-park and began to kick a stone, dribbling it this

way and that. There was only one old Morris in the park, for few cars were left there except lorries: without an attendant there was no safety. He took a flying kick at the car and scraped a little paint off the rear mudguard. Beyond, paying no more attention to him than to a stranger, the gang had gathered round T.; Blackie was dimly aware of the fickleness of favor. He thought of going home, of never returning, of letting them all discover the hollowness of T.'s leadership, but suppose after all what T. proposed was possible—nothing like it had ever been done before. The fame of the Wormsley Common car-park gang would surely reach around London. There would be headlines in the papers. Even the grown-up gangs who ran the betting at the all-in wrestling and the barrow-boys would hear with respect of how Old Misery's house had been destroyed. Driven by the pure, simple and altruistic ambition of fame for the gang, Blackie came back to where T. stood in the shadow of Misery's wall.

T. was giving his orders with decision: it was as though this plan had been with him all his life, pondered through the seasons, now in his fifteenth year crystalized with the pain of puberty. "You," he said to Mike, "bring some big nails, the biggest you can find, and a hammer. Anyone else who can better bring a hammer and a screwdriver. We'll need plenty of them. Chisels too. We can't have too many chisels. Can anybody bring a saw?"

"I can," Mike said.

"Not a child's saw," T. said. "A real saw."

Blackie realized he had raised his hand like any ordinary member of the gang.

"Right, you bring one, Blackie. But now there's a difficulty. We want a hacksaw."

"What's a hacksaw?" someone asked.

"You can get 'em at Woolworth's," Summers said.

The fat boy called Joe said gloomily, "I knew it would end in a collection."

"I'll get one myself," T. said. "I don't want your money. But I can't buy a sledge-hammer."

Blackie said, "They are working on No. 15. I know where they'll leave their stuff for Bank Holiday."

"Then that's all," T. said. "We meet here at nine sharp."

"I've got to go to church," Mike said.

"Come over the wall and whistle. We'll let you in."

2

On Sunday morning all were punctual except Blackie, even Mike. Mike had had a stroke of luck. His mother felt ill, his father was tired after Saturday night, and he was told to go to church alone with many warnings of what would happen if he strayed. Blackie had had difficulty in smuggling out the saw, and then in finding the sledge-hammer at the back of No. 15. He approached the house from a lane at the rear of the garden, for fear of the policeman's beat along the main road. The tired evergreens kept off a stormy sun: another wet Bank Holiday was being prepared over the Atlantic, beginning in swirls of dust under the trees. Blackie climbed the wall into Misery's garden.

There was no sign of anybody anywhere. The lav stood like a tomb in a neglected graveyard. The curtains were drawn. The house slept. Blackie lumbered nearer with the saw and the sledge-hammer. Perhaps after all nobody had turned up: the plan had been a wild invention: they had woken wiser. But when he came close to the back door he could hear a confusion of sound hardly louder than a hive in swarm: a clickety-clack, a bang bang, a scraping, a creaking, a sudden painful crack. He thought: it's true, and whistled.

They opened the back door to him and he came in. He had at once the impression of organization, very different from the old happy-go-lucky ways under his leadership. For a while he wandered up and down stairs looking for T. Nobody addressed him: he had a sense of great urgency, and already he could begin to see the plan. The interior of the house was being carefully demolished without touching the outer walls. Summers with hammer and chisel was ripping out the skirting-boards in the ground floor dining-room: he had already smashed the panels of the door. In the same room Joe was heaving up the parquet blocks, exposing the soft wood floor-boards over the cellar. Coils of wire came out of the damaged skirting and Mike sat happily on the floor clipping the wires.

On the curved stairs two of the gang were working hard with an inadequate child's saw on the banisters—when they saw Blackie's big saw they signaled for it wordlessly. When he next saw them a quarter of the banisters had been dropped into the hall. He found T. at last in the bathroom—he sat moodily in the least cared-for room in the house, listening to the sounds coming up from below.

"You've really done it," Blackie said with awe. "What's going to happen?"

"We've only just begun," T. said. He looked at the sledge-hammer and gave his instructions. "You stay here and break the bath and the wash-basin. Don't bother about the pipes. They come later."

Mike appeared at the door. "I've finished the wires, T.," he said.

"Good. You've just got to go wandering round now. The kitchen's in the basement. Smash all the china and glass and bottles you can lay hold of. Don't turn on the taps—we don't want a flood—yet. Then go into all the rooms and turn out drawers. If they are locked get one of the others to break them open. Tear up any papers you find and smash all the ornaments. Better take a carving-knife with you from the kitchen. The bedroom's opposite here. Open the pillows and tear up the sheets. That's enough for the moment. And you, Blackie, when you've finished in here crack the plaster in the passage up with your sledge-hammer."

"What are you going to do?" Blackie asked.

"I'm looking for something special," T. said.

It was nearly lunch-time before Blackie had finished and went in search of T. Chaos had advanced. The kitchen was a shambles of broken glass and china. The dining-room was stripped of parquet, the skirting was up, the door had been taken off its hinges, and the destroyers had moved up a floor. Streaks of light came in through the closed shutters where they worked with the seriousness of creators—and destruction after all is a form of creation. A kind of imagination had seen this house as it had now become.

Mike said, "I've got to go home for dinner."

"Who else?" T. asked, but all the others on one excuse or another had brought provisions with them.

They squatted in the ruins of the room and swapped unwanted sandwiches. Half an hour for lunch and they were at work again. By the time Mike returned, they were on the top floor, and by six the superficial damage was completed. The doors were all off, all the skirtings raised, the furniture pillaged and ripped and smashed—no one could have slept in the house except on a bed of broken plaster. T. gave his orders—eight o'clock next morning, and to escape notice they climbed singly over the garden wall, into the car-park. Only Blackie and T. were left: the light had nearly gone, and when they touched a switch, nothing worked—Mike had done his job thoroughly.

"Did you find anything special?" Blackie asked.

T. nodded. "Come over here," he said, "and look." Out of both pockets he drew bundles of pound notes. "Old Misery's savings," he said. "Mike ripped out the mattress, but he missed them."

"What are you going to do? Share them?"

"We aren't thieves," T. said. "Nobody's going to steal anything from this house. I kept these for you and me—a celebration." He knelt down on the floor and counted them out— there were seventy in all. "We'll burn them," he said, "one by one," and taking it in turns they held a note upwards and lit the top corner, so that the flame burnt slowly towards their fingers. The grey ash floated above them and fell on their heads like age. "I'd like to see Old Misery's face when we are through," T. said.

"You hate him a lot?" Blackie asked.

"Of course I don't hate him," T. said. "There'd be no fun if I hated him." The last burning note illuminated his brooding face. "All this hate and love," he said, "it's soft, it's hooey. There's only things, Blackie," and he looked round the room crowded with the unfamiliar shadows of half things, broken things, former things. "I'll race you home, Blackie," he said.

3

Next morning the serious destruction started. Two were missing—Mike and another boy whose parents were off to Southend and Brighton in spite of the slow warm drops that had begun to fall and the rumble of thunder in the estuary like the first guns of the old blitz. "We've got to hurry," T. said.

Summers was restive. "Haven't we done enough?" he said. "I've been given a bob for slot machines. This is like work."

"We've hardly started," T. said. "Why, there's all the floor left, and the stairs. We haven't taken out a single window. You voted like the others. We are going to *destroy* this house. There won't be anything left when we've finished."

They began again on the first floor picking up the top floor-boards next the outer wall, leaving the joists exposed. Then they sawed through the joists and retreated into the hall, as what was left of the floor heeled and sank. They had learnt with practice, and the second floor collapsed more easily. By the evening an odd exhilaration seized them as they looked down the great hollow of the house. They ran risks and made mistakes: when they thought of the windows it was too late to reach them. "Cor," Joe said, and dropped a penny down into the dry rubble-filled well. It cracked and span among the broken glass.

"Why did we start this?" Summers asked with astonishment; T. was already on the ground, digging at the rubble, clearing a space along the outer wall. "Turn on the taps," he said. "It's too dark for anyone to see now, and in the morning it won't matter." The water overtook them on the stairs and fell through the floorless rooms.

It was then they heard Mike's whistle at the back. "Something's wrong," Blackie said. They could hear his urgent breathing as they unlocked the door.

"The bogies?"° Summers asked.

"Old Misery," Mike said. "He's on his way." He put his head between his knees and retched. "Ran all the way," he said with pride.

"But why?" T. said "He told me . . ." He protested with the fury of the child he had never been, "It isn't fair."

"He was down at Southend," Mike said, "and he was on the train coming back. Said it was too cold and wet." He paused and gazed at the water. "My, you've had a storm here. Is the roof leaking?"

"How long will he be?"

"Five minutes. I gave Ma the slip and ran."

"We better clear," Summers said. "We've done enough, anyway."

"Oh no, we haven't. Anybody could do this—" "this" was the shattered hollowed house with nothing left but the walls. Yet the walls could be preserved. Façades were valuable. They could build inside again more beautifully than before. This could again be a home. He said angrily, "We've got to finish. Don't move. Let me think."

"There's no time," a boy said.

"There's got to be a way," T. said. "We couldn't have got this far . . ."

"We've done a lot," Blackie said.

"No. No, we haven't. Somebody watch the front."

"We can't do any more."

"He may come in at the back."

"Watch the back too." T. began to plead. "Just give me a minute and I'll

bogies: police

fix it. I swear I'll fix it." But his authority had gone with his ambiguity. He was only one of the gang. "Please," he said.

"Please," Summers mimicked him, and then suddenly struck home with the fatal name. "Run along home, Trevor."

T. stood with his back to the rubble like a boxer knocked groggy against the ropes. He had no words as his dreams shook and slid. Then Blackie acted before the gang had time to laugh, pushing Summers backward. "I'll watch the front, T.," he said, and cautiously he opened the shutters of the hall. The grey wet common stretched ahead, and the lamps gleamed in the puddles. "Someone's coming, T. No, it's not him. What's your plan, T.?"

"Tell Mike to go out to the lav and hide close beside it. When he hears me whistle he's got to count ten and start to shout."

"Shout what?"

"Oh, 'Help,' anything."

"You hear, Mike," Blackie said. He was the leader again. He took a quick look between the shutters. "He's coming, T."

"Quick, Mike. The lav. Stay here, Blackie, all of you till I yell."

"Where are you going, T.?"

"Don't worry. I'll see to this. I said I would, didn't I?"

Old Misery came limping off the common. He had mud on his shoes and he stopped to scrape them on the pavement's edge. He didn't want to soil his house, which stood jagged and dark between the bomb-sites, saved so narrowly, as he believed, from destruction. Even the fanlight had been left unbroken by the bomb's blast. Somewhere somebody whistled. Old Misery looked sharply round. He didn't trust whistles. A child was shouting: it seemed to come from his own garden. Then a boy ran into the road from the car-park. "Mr. Thomas," he called, "Mr. Thomas."

"What is it?"

"I'm terribly sorry, Mr. Thomas. One of us got taken short, and we thought you wouldn't mind, and now he can't get out."

"What do you mean, boy?"

"He's got stuck in your lav."

"He'd no business . . . Haven't I seen you before?"

"You showed me your house."

"So I did. So I did. That doesn't give you the right to . . ."

"Do hurry, Mr. Thomas. He'll suffocate."

"Nonsense. He can't suffocate. Wait till I put my bag in."

"I'll carry your bag."

"Oh no, you don't. I carry my own."

"This way, Mr. Thomas."

"I can't get in the garden that way. I've got to go through the house."

"But you *can* get in the garden this way, Mr. Thomas. We often do."

"You often do?" He followed the boy with a scandalized fascination. "When? What right? . . ."

"Do you see . . . ? The wall's low."

"I'm not going to climb walls into my own garden. It's absurd."

"This is how we do it. One foot here, one foot there, and over." The boy's face peered down, an arm shot out, and Mr. Thomas found his bag taken and deposited on the other side of the wall.

"Give me back my bag," Mr. Thomas said. From the loo° a boy yelled and yelled. "I'll call the police."

"Your bag's all right, Mr. Thomas. Look. One foot there. On your right. Now just above. To your left." Mr. Thomas climbed over his own garden wall. "Here's your bag, Mr. Thomas."

"I'll have the wall built up," Mr. Thomas said, "I'll not have you boys coming over here, using my loo." He stumbled on the path, but the boy caught his elbow and supported him. "Thank you, thank you, my boy," he murmured automatically. Somebody shouted again through the dark. "I'm coming, I'm coming," Mr. Thomas called. He said to the boy beside him, "I'm not unreasonable. Been a boy myself. As long as things are done regular. I don't mind you playing round the place Saturday mornings. Sometimes I like company. Only it's got to be regular. One of you asks leave and I say Yes. Sometimes I'll say No. Won't feel like it. And you come in at the front door and out at the back. No garden walls."

"Do get him out, Mr. Thomas."

"He won't come to any harm in my loo," Mr. Thomas said, stumbling slowly down the garden. "Oh, my rheumatics," he said. "Always get 'em on Bank Holiday. I've got to go careful. There's loose stones here. Give me your hand. Do you know what my horoscope said yesterday? 'Abstain from any dealings in first half of week. Danger of serious crash.' That might be on this path," Mr. Thomas said. "They speak in parables and double meanings." He paused at the door of the loo. "What's the matter in there?" he called. There was no reply.

"Perhaps he's fainted," the boy said.

"Not in my loo. Here, you come out," Mr. Thomas said, and giving a great jerk at the door he nearly fell on his back when it swung easily open. A hand first supported him and then pushed him hard. His head hit the opposite wall and he sat heavily down. His bag hit his feet. A hand whipped the key out of the lock and the door slammed. "Let me out," he called, and heard the key turn in the lock. "A serious crash," he thought, and felt dithery and confused and old.

A voice spoke to him softly through the star-shaped hole in the door. "Don't worry, Mr. Thomas," it said, "we won't hurt you, not if you stay quiet."

Mr. Thomas put his head between his hands and pondered. He had noticed that there was only one lorry in the car-park, and he felt certain that the driver would not come for it before the morning. Nobody could hear him from the road in front, and the lane at the back was seldom used. Anyone who

loo: outdoor toilet (an older term for "lav")

passed there would be hurrying home and would not pause for what they would certainly take to be drunken cries. And if he did call "Help," who, on a lonely Bank Holiday evening, would have the courage to investigate? Mr. Thomas sat on the loo and pondered with the wisdom of age.

After a while it seemed to him that there were sounds in the silence—they were faint and came from the direction of his house. He stood up and peered through the ventilation-hole—between the cracks in one of the shutters he saw a light, not the light of a lamp, but the wavering light that a candle might give. Then he thought he heard the sound of hammering and scraping and chipping. He thought of burglars—perhaps they had employed the boy as a scout, but why should burglars engage in what sounded more and more like a stealthy form of carpentry? Mr. Thomas let out an experimental yell, but nobody answered. The noise could not even have reached his enemies.

4

Mike had gone home to bed, but the rest stayed. The question of leadership no longer concerned the gang. With nails, chisels, screwdrivers, anything that was sharp and penetrating, they moved around the inner walls worrying at the mortar between the bricks. They started too high, and it was Blackie who hit on the damp course and realized the work could be halved if they weakened the joints immediately above. It was a long, tiring, unamusing job, but at last it was finished. The gutted house stood there balanced on a few inches of mortar between the damp course and the bricks.

There remained the most dangerous task of all, out in the open at the edge of the bomb-site. Summers was sent to watch the road for passers-by, and Mr. Thomas, sitting on the loo, heard clearly now the sound of sawing. It no longer came from his house, and that a little reassured him. He felt less concerned. Perhaps the other noises too had no significance.

A voice spoke to him through the hole. "Mr. Thomas."

"Let me out," Mr. Thomas said sternly.

"Here's a blanket," the voice said, and a long grey sausage was worked through the hole and fell in swathes over Mr. Thomas' head.

"There's nothing personal," the voice said. "We want you to be comfortable tonight."

"Tonight," Mr. Thomas repeated incredulously.

"Catch," the voice said. "Penny buns—we've buttered them, and sausage-rolls. We don't want you to starve, Mr. Thomas."

Mr. Thomas pleaded desperately. "A joke's a joke, boy. Let me out and I won't say a thing. I've got rheumatics. I got to sleep comfortable."

"You wouldn't be comfortable, not in your house, you wouldn't. Not now."

"What do you mean, boy?" but the footsteps receded. There was only the silence of night: no sound of sawing. Mr. Thomas tried one more yell, but he was daunted and rebuked by the silence—a long way off an owl hooted and made away again on its muffled flight through the soundless world.

At seven next morning the driver came to fetch his lorry. He climbed into the seat and tried to start the engine. He was vaguely aware of a voice shouting, but it didn't concern him. At last the engine responded and he backed the lorry until it touched the great wooden shore that supported Mr. Thomas' house. That way he could drive right out and down the street without reversing. The lorry moved forward, was momentarily checked as though something were pulling it from behind, and then went on to the sound of a long rumbling crash. The driver was astonished to see bricks bouncing ahead of him, while stones hit the roof of his cab. He put on his brakes. When he climbed out the whole landscape had suddenly altered. There was no house beside the car-park, only a hill of rubble. He went round and examined the back of his car for damage, and found a rope tied there that was still twisted at the other end round part of a wooden strut.

The driver again became aware of somebody shouting. It came from the wooden erection which was the nearest thing to a house in that desolation of broken brick. The driver climbed the smashed wall and unlocked the door. Mr. Thomas came out of the loo. He was wearing a grey blanket to which flakes of pastry adhered. He gave a sobbing cry. "My house," he said. "Where's my house?"

"Search me," the driver said. His eye lit on the remains of a bath and what had once been a dresser and he began to laugh. There wasn't anything left anywhere.

"How dare you laugh," Mr. Thomas said. "It was my house. My house."

"I'm sorry," the driver said, making heroic efforts, but when he remembered the sudden check to his lorry, the crash of bricks falling, he became convulsed again. One moment the house had stood there with such dignity between the bomb-sites like a man in a top hat, and then, bang, crash, there wasn't anything left—not anything. He said, "I'm sorry. I can't help it, Mr. Thomas. There's nothing personal, but you got to admit it's funny."

QUESTIONS

1. Who is the protagonist in this story—Trevor, Blackie, or the gang? Who or what is the antagonist? Identify the conflicts of the story.
2. How is suspense created?
3. This story uses the most common basic formula of commercial fiction: protagonist aims at a goal, is confronted with various obstacles between himself and his goal, overcomes the obstacles and achieves his goal. Comment on the differences. Does this story have a happy ending?
4. Discuss the gang's motivations, taking into account (a) the age and beauty of the house, (b) Blackie's reasons for not going home after losing his position of leadership, (c) the seriousness with which the gang work at their task, and their loss of concern over their leadership, (d) the burning of the banknotes, (e) their consideration for Old Misery, (f) the lorry driver's reaction. What

characteristics do the gang's two named exploits—pinching free rides and destroying the house—have in common?

5. Of what significance, if any, is the setting of this story in blitzed London? Does the story have anything to say about the consequences of war? about the causes of war?

6. Explain as fully as you can the causes of the gang's delinquency, taking into account (a) their reaction to the name Trevor, (b) their reaction to Old Misery's gift of chocolates, (c) Blackie's reaction to the word "beautiful," (d) Trevor's comments on "hate and love," (e) Summers' reaction to the word "Please," (f) the setting.

7. What good qualities do the delinquents in this story have? Do they differ as a group from other delinquent gangs you have read or know about? If so, account for the differences.

8. On the surface this is a story of action, suspense, and adventure. At a deeper level it is about delinquency, war, and human nature. Try to sum up what the story says about human nature in general.

John Galsworthy
THE JAPANESE QUINCE

As Mr. Nilson, well known in the City, opened the window of his dressing room on Campden Hill, he experienced a peculiar sweetish sensation in the back of his throat, and a feeling of emptiness just under his fifth rib. Hooking the window back, he noticed that a little tree in the Square Gardens had come out in blossom, and that the thermometer stood at sixty. "Perfect morning," he thought; "spring at last!"

Resuming some meditations on the price of Tintos, he took up an ivory-backed handglass and scrutinized his face. His firm, well-colored cheeks, with their neat brown mustaches, and his round, well-opened, clear grey eyes, wore a reassuring appearance of good health. Putting on his black frock coat, he went downstairs.

In the dining room his morning paper was laid out on the sideboard. Mr. Nilson had scarcely taken it in his hand when he again became aware of that queer feeling. Somewhat concerned, he went to the French window and descended the scrolled iron steps into the fresh air. A cuckoo clock struck eight.

"Half an hour to breakfast," he thought; "I'll take a turn in the Gardens."

He had them to himself, and proceeded to pace the circular path with his morning paper clasped behind him. He had scarcely made two revolutions,

THE JAPANESE QUINCE   First published in 1910. "The City" is the financial and commercial center of London: the term has roughly the meaning for Englishmen that "Wall Street" has for Americans. "Tintos" are stock shares, probably in the Rio Tinto Mining Company. John Galsworthy (1867-1933) was born in London, educated at Harrow and Oxford, and graduated with honors in law, but, after a period of travel, turned to writing as a career.

however, when it was borne in on him that, instead of going away in the fresh air, the feeling had increased. He drew several deep breaths, having heard deep breathing recommended by his wife's doctor; but they augmented rather than diminished the sensation—as of some sweetish liquor in course within him, together with a faint aching just above his heart. Running over what he had eaten the night before, he could recollect no unusual dish, and it occurred to him that it might possibly be some smell affecting him. But he could detect nothing except a faint sweet lemony scent, rather agreeable than otherwise, which evidently emanated from the bushes budding in the sunshine. He was on the point of resuming his promenade, when a blackbird close by burst into song, and, looking up, Mr. Nilson saw at a distance of perhaps five yards a little tree, in the heart of whose branches the bird was perched. He stood staring curiously at this tree, recognizing it for that which he had noticed from his window. It was covered with young blossoms, pink and white, and little bright green leaves both round and spiky; and on all this blossom and these leaves the sunlight glistened. Mr. Nilson smiled; the little tree was so alive and pretty! And instead of passing on, he stayed there smiling at the tree.

"Morning like this!" he thought; "and here I am the only person in the Square who has the—to come out and—!" But he had no sooner conceived this thought than he saw quite near him a man with his hands behind him, who was also staring up and smiling at the little tree. Rather taken aback, Mr. Nilson ceased to smile, and looked furtively at the stranger. It was his next-door neighbor, Mr. Tandram, well known in the City, who had occupied the adjoining house for some five years. Mr. Nilson perceived at once the awkwardness of his position, for, being married, they had not yet had occasion to speak to one another. Doubtful as to his proper conduct, he decided at last to murmur: "Fine morning!" and was passing on, when Mr. Tandram answered: "Beautiful, for the time of year!" Detecting a slight nervousness in his neighbor's voice, Mr. Nilson was emboldened to regard him openly. He was of about Mr. Nilson's own height, with firm, well-colored cheeks, neat brown mustaches, and round, well-opened, clear grey eyes; and he was wearing a black frock coat. Mr. Nilson noticed that he had his morning paper clasped behind him as he looked up at the little tree. And, visited somehow by the feeling that he had been caught out, he said abruptly:

"Er—can you give me the name of that tree?"

Mr. Tandram answered:

"I was about to ask you that," and stepped towards it. Mr. Nilson also approached the tree.

"Sure to have its name on, I should think," he said.

Mr. Tandram was the first to see the little label, close to where the blackbird had been sitting. He read it out.

"Japanese quince!"

"Ah!" said Mr. Nilson, "thought so. Early flowerers."

"Very," assented Mr. Tandram, and added: "Quite a feelin' in the air today."

Mr. Nilson nodded.

"It was a blackbird singin'," he said.

"Blackbirds," answered Mr. Tandram. "I prefer them to thrushes myself; more body in the note." And he looked at Mr. Nilson in an almost friendly way.

"Quite," murmured Mr. Nilson. "These exotics, they don't bear fruit. Pretty blossoms!" and he again glanced up at the blossom, thinking: "Nice fellow, this, I rather like him."

Mr. Tandram also gazed at the blossom. And the little tree, as if appreciating their attention, quivered and glowed. From a distance the blackbird gave a loud, clear call. Mr. Nilson dropped his eyes. It struck him suddenly that Mr. Tandram looked a little foolish; and, as if he had seen himself, he said: "I must be going in. Good morning!"

A shade passed over Mr. Tandram's face, as if he, too, had suddenly noticed something about Mr. Nilson.

"Good morning," he replied, and clasping their journals to their backs they separated.

Mr. Nilson retraced his steps toward his garden window, walking slowly so as to avoid arriving at the same time as his neighbor. Having seen Mr. Tandram mount his scrolled iron steps, he ascended his own in turn. On the top step he paused.

With the slanting spring sunlight darting and quivering into it, the Japanese quince seemed more living than a tree. The blackbird had returned to it, and was chanting out his heart.

Mr. Nilson sighed; again he felt that queer sensation, that choky feeling in his throat.

The sound of a cough or sigh attracted his attention. There, in the shadow of his French window, stood Mr. Tandram, also looking forth across the Gardens at the little quince tree.

Unaccountably upset, Mr. Nilson turned abruptly into the house, and opened his morning paper.

QUESTIONS

1. Although we are given only a brief glimpse of Mr. Nilson's life, there are many clues as to what the whole of his life is like. What kind of house and district does he live in? To what social class does he belong? What kind of existence does he lead? What clues enable us to answer these questions?

2. Mr. Nilson at first thinks something is wrong with his health. What really is troubling him? How do the terms in which his symptoms are described (paragraphs 1 and 5) help to define his "ailment"?

3. In what ways might Mr. Nilson's fragmentary sentence at the beginning of paragraph 6 be completed? Why doesn't Mr. Nilson complete it?

4. How are Mr. Nilson and Mr. Tandram alike in appearance, manner, and situation? Of what significance are these similarities?

5. Mr. Nilson's meeting of Mr. Tandram at the tree might be described as a coincidence. Is it pure coincidence or does it have antecedent causes? Is it a legitimate device in terms of the story? Why or why not?
6. The quince tree is what we shall later refer to as a *symbol* (see Chapter 6). What qualities or abstractions does it seem to you to represent?
7. Although this story contains little action, it dramatizes a significant conflict. What are the opposed forces? How can the conflict be stated in terms of protagonist and antagonist? Is the conflict external or internal? How is it resolved—that is, which force wins?
8. This story demonstrates how a very slight plot may be used to provide a considerable illumination of life. How would you describe, in a sentence, the purpose of the story?

3. Character

In the preceding chapter plot was considered apart from character, as if the two were separable. Actually, like the ends of a seesaw, the two are one substance; there can be no movement at one end without movement at the other. The two ends of the seesaw may be talked about separately, however, and we can determine which element in any story is being emphasized—which end is up and which is down. As fiction passes from escape to interpretive, the character end is likely to go up. Good readers are less interested in actions done by characters than in characters doing actions.

Reading for character is more difficult than reading for plot, for character is much more complex, variable, and ambiguous. Anyone can repeat what a person has done in a story, but considerable skill may be needed to describe what a person *is*. Even the puzzles posed by the detective story are less complex and put less strain on comprehension than does human nature. Hence, escape fiction tends to emphasize plot and to present characters that are relatively simple and easy to understand. Limited readers demand that the characters be easily identifiable and clearly labeled as good or bad; they must not be so complex as to tax the readers' understanding.

Limited readers also demand that the main character always be an attractive one. If the main character is male, he need not be perfect, but he must ordinarily be fundamentally decent—honest, good-hearted, and preferably good-looking. If he is not virtuous, he must have strong compensatory qualities—he must be daring, dashing, or gallant. He may defy law and order only if he has a tender heart, a great love, or a gentleman's code. Readers who make these demands do so because for them the story is not a vehicle for understanding but material for a daydream. Identifying with the main character as they read, they vicariously share that character's adventures, escapes, and triumphs. The main character must therefore return them a pleasing image of self, must be someone such as they imagine themselves to be or such as they would like to be. In this way the story subtly flatters the readers, who forget their own inadequacies and satisfy their egos. If the hero or heroine has vices, these vices must be such as the readers themselves would not mind or would enjoy having. Some escape fiction has been about the man or woman who is appealing but sexually easy. Readers have thus been able to indulge imaginatively in forbidden pleasures without losing a flattering self-image.

Interpretive fiction does not necessarily renounce the attractive central character. It simply furnishes a greater variety of central characters, characters that are less easily labeled and pigeonholed, characters that are sometimes unsympathetic. Human nature is not often entirely bad or perfectly good, and interpretive fiction deals usually with characters that are neither.

Once we get past the need of a mechanical opposition between hero and villain, we discover that fiction offers an unparalleled opportunity to observe human nature in all its complexity and multiplicity. It enables us to know people, to understand them, and to learn compassion for them, as we might not otherwise do. In some respects we can know fictional characters even better than we know real people. For one thing, we are enabled to observe them in situations that are always significant and that serve to bring forth their character as the ordinary situations of life only occasionally do. For another, we can view their inner life in a way that is impossible to us in ordinary life. Authors can tell us, if they wish, exactly what is going on in a character's mind and exactly what the character feels. In real life we can only guess at these inner thoughts and feelings from a person's external behavior, which may be designed to conceal what is going on inside. In limited ways, therefore, we can know people in fiction more thoroughly than we can know them in real life, and by knowing fictional characters we can also understand people in real life better than we otherwise could.

Authors may present their characters either directly or indirectly. In DIRECT PRESENTATION they tell us straight out, by exposition or analysis, what the characters are like, or have someone else in the story tell us what they are like. In INDIRECT PRESENTATION the authors *show* us the characters in action; we infer what they are like from what they think or say or do. Graham Greene uses direct presentation when he tells us about Blackie: "He was just, he had no jealousy." He uses indirect presentation when he shows Blackie allowing the gang to vote on Trevor's project, accepting the end of his leadership fairly calmly, taking orders from Trevor without resentment, burning banknotes with Trevor, and racing him home. In this story, of course, the word "just" has a slight ironical twist—it applies only to behavior within the gang—and Greene presents this indirectly. John Galsworthy relies entirely on indirect presentation to show us that Mr. Nilson is a man of regulated habit who lives a life that is ordered and convention-bound.

The method of direct presentation has the advantages of being clear and economical, but it can scarcely ever be used alone. The characters must act, if there is to be a story; when they do not act, the story approaches the condition of an essay. The direct method, moreover, unless supported by the indirect, will not be emotionally convincing. It will give us not a character but an explanation. Readers must be shown as well as told. They need to see and hear and overhear. A story is successful when the characters are DRAMATIZED—shown speaking and acting, as in a drama. If we are really to believe in the selfishness of a character, we must see the character acting selfishly. Successful writers therefore rely mainly on indirect presentation and may use it entirely.

When most convincing, characterization also observes three other principles. First, the characters are CONSISTENT in their behavior: they do not behave one way on one occasion and a different way on another unless there is a clearly sufficient reason for the change. Second, the characters are clearly MOTIVATED in whatever they do, especially when there is any change in their behavior: we must be able to understand the reasons for what they do, if not immediately, at least by the end of the story. Third, the characters are PLAUSIBLE or lifelike. They must be neither paragons of virtue nor monsters of evil nor an impossible combination of contradictory traits. Whether we have observed anyone like them in our own experience or not, we must feel that they have come from the author's experience—that they could appear somewhere in the normal course of events.

In proportion to the fullness of their development, the characters in a story are relatively flat or round.* FLAT CHARACTERS are characterized by one or two traits; they can be summed up in a sentence. ROUND CHARACTERS are complex and many-sided; they might require an essay for full analysis. Both types of character may be given the vitality that good

---

*These terms were originated by the novelist E. M. Forster, who discussed them in *Aspects of the Novel* (New York: Harcourt Brace Jovanovich, 1927), pp. 103-18.

fiction demands. Round characters live by their very roundness, by the many points at which they touch life. Huck Finn, in all respects an individual, lives vigorously in the imagination of the reader, while scholars and critics debate his moral development. Flat characters, though they touch life at only one or two points, may be made memorable in the hands of an expert author through some individualizing detail of appearance, gesture, or speech. Ebenezer Scrooge, in Dickens' "Christmas Carol," can be summed up and fully expressed in the two words "miserly misanthropy," but his "Bah! Humbug!" makes him live vividly in every reader's memory.

The requirement of good fiction is that all characters be characterized fully enough to justify their roles in the story and make them convincing. Most short stories will hardly have room for more than one or two very fully developed characters. Minor characters must necessarily remain flat. If the primary intention of a story is something other than the exhibition of character, none of the characters need be fully developed. Inferior fiction, however, is often developed with characters who are insufficiently characterized to justify their roles. The essential nature and motivations of the protagonist may be so vaguely indicated that we are neither shocked nor convinced by any unusual action he performs or change of nature he undergoes. If a thief suddenly reforms and becomes an honest man, we must obviously know a great deal about him if the change is to be truly convincing. It is easier, however, for writers to leave the characterization shadowy and hope that this weakness will slip by their readers unnoticed—as with uncritical readers it well may do.

A special kind of flat character is the STOCK CHARACTER—the stereotyped figure who has occurred so often in fiction that his nature is immediately known: the strong silent sheriff, the brilliant detective of eccentric habits, the mad scientist who performs fiendish experiments on living human beings, the beautiful international spy of mysterious background, the comic Englishman with a monocle and an exaggerated Oxford accent, the handsome brave hero, the beautiful modest heroine, the cruel stepmother, the sinister villain with a waxed black mustache. Such stock characters are found very often in inferior fiction because they require neither imagination nor observation on the part of the writer and are instantly recognizable to the reader. Like interchangeable parts, they might be transferred from one story to another with little loss of efficiency. Really good writers, however, may take a conventional type and by individualizing touches create a new and memorable figure. Conan Doyle's Sherlock Holmes is constructed on a pattern often imitated since, but he outlives the imitations and remains in our imaginations long after we have forgotten the details of his adventures. To the degree that authors give their characters such individualizing touches, they become less flat and accordingly less stock.

All fictional characters may be classified as static or developing. The STATIC CHARACTER is the same sort of person at the end of the story as at the beginning. The DEVELOPING (or dynamic) CHARACTER undergoes a permanent change in some aspect of character, personality, or outlook. The change may be a large or a small one; it may be for better or for worse; but it is something important and basic: it is more than a change in condition or a minor change in opinion. Cinderella is a static character, though she rises from cinder girl to princess. Dick Prosser in "The Child by Tiger" (page 24) is a dynamic character, for he changes from a gentle, "amazingly tender," "deeply religious" man (who tells the white boys, "you gotta love each othah like a brothah") into a "crazy" killer. Paul in "Paul's Case" (page 176) is likewise dynamic, for his need to escape from everyday reality grows progressively stronger.

Obviously, we must not expect many developing characters in *any* piece of fiction: in a short story there is not usually room for more than one. A not infrequent basic plan of short stories, however, is to show change in the protagonist as the result of a crucial situation in his life. When this is done in an interpretive story, the change is likely to be the surest clue to the story's meaning. To state and explain the change will be the best way to get at the point of the story. In escape fiction, changes in character are likely to be more superficial, intended merely to ensure a happy ending. Such changes will necessarily be less believable. To be convincing, a change must meet three conditions: (1) it must be within the possibilities of the character who makes it, (2) it must be sufficiently motivated by the circumstances in which the character is placed, and (3) it must be allowed sufficient time for a change of its magnitude believably to take place. Basic changes in human character seldom occur suddenly. Interpretive writers do not present bad people who suddenly reform at the end of the story and become good or drunkards who jump on the wagon at a moment's notice. They are satisfied with smaller changes that are carefully prepared for.

Human life began, we are told, when God breathed life into a handful of dust and created Adam. Fictional life begins when an author breathes life into his characters and convinces us of their reality. Though fullness of characterization need not be the ultimate aim, soundness of characterization is a test by which the author stands or falls. The reader of good fiction lives in a world where the initial act of creation is repeated again and again by the miracle of imagination.

Sherwood Anderson

I'M A FOOL

It was a hard jolt for me, one of the most bitterest I ever had to face. And it all came about through my own foolishness, too. Even yet sometimes, when I think of it, I want to cry or swear or kick myself. Perhaps, even now, after all this time, there will be a kind of satisfaction in making myself look cheap by telling of it.

It began at three o'clock one October afternoon as I sat in the grand stand at the fall trotting and pacing meet at Sandusky, Ohio.

To tell the truth, I felt a little foolish that I should be sitting in the grand stand at all. During the summer before I had left my home town with Harry Whitehead and, with a nigger named Burt, had taken a job as swipe with one of the two horses Harry was campaigning through the fall race meets that year. Mother cried and my sister Mildred, who wanted to get a job as a schoolteacher in our town that fall, stormed and scolded about the house all during the week before I left. They both thought it something disgraceful that one of our family should take a place as a swipe with race horses. I've an idea Mildred thought my taking the place would stand in the way of her getting the job she'd been working so long for.

But after all I had to work, and there was no other work to be got. A big lumbering fellow of nineteen couldn't just hang around the house and I had got too big to mow people's lawns and sell newspapers. Little chaps who could get next to people's sympathies by their sizes were always getting jobs away from me. There was one fellow who kept saying to everyone who wanted a lawn mowed or a cistern cleaned that he was saving money to work his way through college, and I used to lay awake nights thinking up ways to injure him without being found out. I kept thinking of wagons running over him and bricks falling on his head as he walked along the street. But never mind him.

I got the place with Harry and I liked Burt fine. We got along splendid together. He was a big nigger with a lazy sprawling body and soft, kind eyes, and when it came to a fight he could hit like Jack Johnson.° He had Bucephalus, a big black pacing stallion that could do 2.09 or 2.10 if he had to, and I had a little gelding named Doctor Fritz that never lost a race all fall when Harry wanted him to win.

I'M A FOOL First published in 1922. The time of the story ("before Prohibition") is probably well before 1919, when the Eighteenth Amendment was passed. The racing in the story is harness racing, in which the horse draws a light two-wheeled vehicle seating the driver. Dan Patch, mentioned near the story's end, was one of the fastest harness horses in history. Sherwood Anderson (1876-1941) grew up in northern Ohio near Sandusky.

Jack Johnson: world heavyweight boxing champion, 1908-1915, black.

We set out from home late in July, in a box car with the two horses and after that, until late November, we kept moving along to the race meets and the fairs. It was a peachy time for me, I'll say that. Sometimes now I think that boys who are raised regular in houses, and never have a fine nigger like Burt for best friend, and go to high schools and college, and never steal anything, or get drunk a little, or learn to swear from fellows who know how, or come walking up in front of a grand stand in their shirt sleeves and with dirty horsy pants on when the races are going on and the grand stand is full of people all dressed up—What's the use of talking about it? Such fellows don't know nothing at all. They've never had no opportunity.

But I did. Burt taught me how to rub down a horse and put the bandages on after a race and steam a horse out and a lot of valuable things for any man to know. He could wrap a bandage on a horse's leg so smooth that if it had been the same color you would think it was his skin, and I guess he'd have been a big driver, too, and got to the top like Murphy and Walter Cox and the others if he hadn't been black.

Gee whizz! it was fun. You got to a county-seat town, maybe say on a Saturday or Sunday, and the fair began the next Tuesday and lasted until Friday afternoon. Doctor Fritz would be, say, in the 2.25 trot on Tuesday afternoon and on Thursday afternoon Bucephalus would knock 'em cold in the "free-for-all" pace. It left you a lot of time to hang around and listen to horse talk, and see Burt knock some yap cold that got too gay, and you'd find out about horses and men and pick up a lot of stuff you could use all the rest of your life, if you had some sense and salted down what you heard and felt and saw.

And then at the end of the week when the race meet was over, and Harry had run home to tend up to his livery-stable business, you and Burt hitched the two horses to carts and drove slow and steady across country, to the place for the next meeting, so as to not overheat the horses, etc., etc., you know.

Gee whizz! Gosh amighty! the nice hickory-nut and beechnut and oaks and other kinds of trees along the roads, all brown and red, and the good smells, and Burt singing a song called "Deep River," and the country girls at the windows of houses and everything. You can stick your colleges up your nose for all me. I guess I know where I got my education.

Why, one of those little burgs of towns you came to on the way, say now on a Saturday afternoon, and Burt says, "Let's lay up here." And you did.

And you took the horses to a livery stable and fed them, and you got your good clothes out of a box and put them on.

And the town was full of farmers gaping, because they could see you were racehorse people, and the kids maybe never see a nigger before and was afraid and run away when the two of us walked down their main street.

And that was before prohibition and all that foolishness, and so you went into a saloon, the two of you, and all the yaps come and stood around, and there was always some one pretended he was horsy and knew things and spoke up and began asking questions, and all you did was to lie and lie all you could about what horses you had, and I said I owned them, and then some fellow said, "Will you have a drink of whisky?" and Burt knocked his eye out the way he could say, offhand like, "Oh, well, all right, I'm agreeable to a little nip. I'll split a quart with you." Gee whizz!

But that isn't what I want to tell my story about. We got home late in November and I promised mother I'd quit the race horses for good. There's a lot of things you've got to promise a mother because she don't know any better.

And so, there not being any work in our town any more than when I left there to go to the races, I went off to Sandusky and got a pretty good place taking care of horses for a man who owned a teaming and delivery and storage and coal and real-estate business there. It was a pretty good place with good eats, and a day off each week, and sleeping on a cot in a big barn, and mostly just shoveling in hay and oats to a lot of big good-enough skates of horses that couldn't have trotted a race with a toad. I wasn't dissatisfied and I could send money home.

And then, as I started to tell you, the fall races come to Sandusky and I got the day off and I went. I left the job at noon and had on my good clothes and my new brown derby hat I'd bought the Saturday before, and a stand-up collar.

First of all I went downtown and walked about with the dudes. I've always thought to myself, "Put up a good front," and so I did it. I had forty dollars in my pockets and so I went into the West House, a big hotel, and walked up to the cigar stand. "Give me three twenty-five cent cigars," I said. There was a lot of horsemen and strangers and dressed-up people from other towns standing around in the lobby and in the bar, and I mingled amongst them. In the bar there was a fellow with a cane and a Windsor tie on, that it made me sick to look at him. I like a man to be a man and dressed up, but not to go put on that kind of airs. So I pushed him aside, kind of rough, and had me a drink of whisky. And then he looked at me, as though he thought maybe he'd get gay, but he changed his mind and didn't say anything. And then I had another drink of whisky, just to show him something, and went out and had a hack out to the races, all to myself, and when I got there I bought myself the best seat I could get up in the grand stand, but didn't go in for any of these boxes. That's putting on too many airs.

And so there I was, sitting up in the grand stand as gay as you please and looking down on the swipes coming out with their horses, and with their dirty horsy pants on and the horseblankets swung over their shoulders, same as I had been doing all the year before. I liked one thing about the same as the other, sitting up there and feeling grand and being down there and looking up at the yaps and feeling grander and more important, too.

One thing's about as good as another, if you take it just right. I've often said that.

Well, right in front of me, in the grand stand that day, there was a fellow with a couple of girls and they was about my age. The young fellow was a nice guy, all right. He was the kind maybe that goes to college and then comes to be a lawyer or maybe a newspaper editor or something like that, but he wasn't stuck on himself. There are some of that kind are all right and he was one of the ones.

He had his sister with him and another girl and the sister looked around over his shoulder, accidental at first, not intending to start anything—she wasn't that kind—and her eyes and mine happened to meet.

You know how it is. Gee, she was a peach! She had on a soft dress, kind of a blue stuff and it looked carelessly made, but was well sewed and made and everything. I knew that much. I blushed when she looked right at me and so did she. She was the nicest girl I've ever seen in my life. She wasn't stuck on herself and she could talk proper grammar without being like a schoolteacher or something like that. What I mean is, she was O.K. I think maybe her father was well-to-do, but not rich to make her chesty because she was his daughter, as some are. Maybe he owned a drug store or a dry-goods store in their home town, or something like that. She never told me and I never asked.

My own people are all O.K. too, when you come to that. My grandfather was Welsh and over in the old country, in Wales he was— But never mind that.

The first heat of the first race come off and the young fellow setting there with the two girls left them and went down to make a bet. I knew what he was up to, but he didn't talk big and noisy and let everyone around know he was a sport, as some do. He wasn't that kind. Well, he come back and I heard him tell the two girls what horse he'd bet on, and when the heat trotted they all half got to their feet and acted in the excited, sweaty way people do when they've got money down on a race, and the horse they bet on is up there pretty close at the end, and they think maybe he'll come on with a rush, but he never does because he hasn't got the old juice in him, come right down to it.

And then, pretty soon, the horses came out for the 2.18 pace and there was a horse in it I knew. He was a horse Bob French had in his string but Bob didn't own him. He was a horse owned by a Mr. Mathers down at Marietta, Ohio.

This Mr. Mathers had a lot of money and owned some coal mines or something and he had a swell place out in the country, and he was stuck on race horses, but was a Presbyterian or something, and I think more than likely his wife was one, too, maybe a stiffer one than himself. So he never raced his horses hisself, and the story round the Ohio race tracks was that when one of his horses got ready to go to the races he turned him over to Bob French and pretended to his wife he was sold.

So Bob had the horses and he did pretty much as he pleased and you can't blame Bob, at least, I never did. Sometimes he was out to win and sometimes he wasn't. I never cared much about that when I was swiping a horse. What I did want to know was that my horse had the speed and could go out in front, if you wanted him to.

And, as I'm telling you, there was Bob in this race with one of Mr.

Mathers' horses, was named "About Ben Ahem"° or something like that, and was fast as a streak. He was a gelding and had a mark of 2.21, but could step in .08 or .09.

Because when Burt and I were out, as I've told you, the year before, there was a nigger Burt knew, worked for Mr. Mathers and we went out there one day when we didn't have no race on at the Marietta Fair and our boss Harry was gone home.

And so everyone was gone to the fair but just this one nigger and he took us all through Mr. Mathers' swell house and he and Burt tapped a bottle of wine Mr. Mathers had hid in his bedroom, back in a closet, without his wife knowing, and he showed us this Ahem horse. Burt was always stuck on being a driver but didn't have much chance to get to the top, being a nigger, and he and the other nigger gulped the whole bottle of wine and Burt got a little lit up.

So the nigger let Burt take this About Ben Ahem and step him a mile in a track Mr. Mathers had all to himself, right there on the farm. And Mr. Mathers had one child, a daughter, kinda sick and not very good looking, and she came home and we had to hustle to get About Ben Ahem stuck back in the barn.

I'm only telling you to get everything straight. At Sandusky, that afternoon I was at the fair, this young fellow with the two girls was fussed, being with the girls and losing his bet. You know how a fellow is that way. One of them was his girl and the other his sister. I had figured that out.

"Gee whizz," I says to myself, "I'm going to give him the dope."

He was mighty nice when I touched him on the shoulder. He and the girls were nice to me right from the start and clear to the end. I'm not blaming them.

And so he leaned back and I give him the dope on About Ben Ahem. "Don't bet a cent on this first heat because he'll go like an oxen hitched to a plow, but when the first heat is over go right down and lay on your pile." That's what I told him.

Well, I never saw a fellow treat any one sweller. There was a fat man sitting beside the little girl, that had looked at me twice by this time, and I at her, and both blushing, and what did he do but have the nerve to turn and ask the fat man to get up and change places with me so I could set with his crowd.

Gee whizz, craps amighty. There I was. What a chump I was to go and get gay up there in the West House bar, and just because that dude was standing there with a cane and that kind of a necktie on, to go and get all balled up and drink that whisky, just to show off.

Of course she would know, me setting right beside her and letting her

"About Ben Ahem": Abou Ben Adhem is the title character of a well-known poem by Leigh Hunt.

smell of my breath. I could have kicked myself right down out of that grand stand and all around that race track and made a faster record than most of the skates of horses they had there that year.

Because that girl wasn't any mutt of a girl. What wouldn't I have give right then for a stick of chewing gum to chew, or a lozenger, or some licorice, or most anything. I was glad I had those twenty-five cent cigars in my pocket and right away I gave that fellow one and lit one myself. Then that fat man got up and we changed places and there I was, plunked right down beside her.

They introduced themselves and the fellow's best girl, he had with him, was named Miss Elinor Woodbury, and her father was a manufacturer of barrels from a place called Tiffin, Ohio. And the fellow himself was named Wilbur Wessen and his sister was Miss Lucy Wessen.

I suppose it was their having such swell names that got me off my trolley. A fellow, just because he has been a swipe with a race horse, and works taking care of horses for a man in the teaming, delivery, and storage business isn't any better or worse than any one else. I've often thought that, and said it too.

But you know how a fellow is. There's something in that kind of nice clothes, and the kind of nice eyes she had, and the way she had looked at me, awhile before, over her brother's shoulder, and me looking back at her, and both of us blushing.

I couldn't show her up for a boob, could I?

I made a fool of myself, that's what I did. I said my name was Walter Mathers from Marietta, Ohio, and then I told all three of them the smashingest lie you ever heard. What I said was that my father owned the horse About Ben Ahem and that he had let him out to this Bob French for racing purposes, because our family was proud and had never gone into racing that way, in our own name, I mean, and Miss Lucy Wessen's eyes were shining, and I went the whole hog.

I told about our place down at Marietta, and about the big stables and the grand brick house we had on a hill, up above the Ohio River, but I knew enough not to do it in no bragging way. What I did was to start things and then let them drag the rest out of me. I acted just as reluctant to tell as I could. Our family hasn't got any barrel factory, and since I've known us, we've always been pretty poor, but not asking anything of any one at that, and my grandfather, over in Wales—but never mind that.

We sat there talking like we had known each other for years and years, and I went and told them that my father had been expecting maybe this Bob French wasn't on the square, and had sent me up to Sandusky on the sly to find out what I could.

And I bluffed it through I had found out all about the 2.18 pace, in which About Ben Ahem was to start.

I said he would lose the first heat by pacing like a lame cow and then he would come back and skin 'em alive after that. And to back up what I said I took thirty dollars out of my pocket and handed it to Mr. Wilbur Wessen and asked him, would he mind, after the first heat, to go down and place it on About Ben Ahem for whatever odds he could get. What I said was that I didn't want Bob French to see me and none of the swipes.

Sure enough the first heat come off and About Ben Ahem went off his stride, up the back stretch, and looked like a wooden horse or a sick one, and come in to be last. Then this Wilbur Wessen went down to the betting place under the grand stand and there I was with the two girls, and when that Miss Woodbury was looking the other way once, Lucy Wessen kinda, with her shoulder you know, kinda touched me. Not just tucking down, I don't mean. You know how a woman can do. They get close, but not getting gay either. You know what they do. Gee whizz.

And then they give me a jolt. What they had done, when I didn't know, was to get together, and they had decided Wilbur Wessen would bet fifty dollars, and the two girls had gone and put in ten dollars each, of their own money, too. I was sick then, but I was sicker later.

About the gelding, About Ben Ahem, and their winning their money, I wasn't worried a lot about that. It came out O.K. Ahem stepped the next three heats like a bushel of spoiled eggs going to market before they could be found out, and Wilbur Wessen had got nine to two for the money. There was something else eating at me.

Because Wilbur come back, after he had bet the money, and after that he spent most of his time talking to that Miss Woodbury, and Lucy Wessen and I was left alone together like on a desert island. Gee, if I'd only been on the square or if there had been any way of getting myself on the square. There ain't any Walter Mathers, like I said to her and them, and there hasn't ever been one, but if there was, I bet I'd go to Marietta, Ohio, and shoot him tomorrow.

There I was, big boob that I am. Pretty soon the race was over, and Wilbur had gone down and collected our money, and we had a hack downtown, and he stood us a swell supper at the West House, and a bottle of champagne beside.

And I was with the girl and she wasn't saying much, and I wasn't saying much either. One thing I know. She wasn't stuck on me because of the lie about my father being rich and all that. There's a way you know . . . Craps amighty. There's a kind of girl you see just once in your life, and if you don't get busy and make hay, then you're gone for good and all, and might as well go jump off a bridge. They give you a look from inside of them somewhere, and it ain't no vamping, and what it means is—you want that girl to be your wife, and you want nice things around her like flowers and swell clothes, and you want her to have the kids you're going to have, and you want good music played and no ragtime. Gee whizz.

There's a place over near Sandusky, across a kind of bay, and it's called Cedar Point. And after we had supper we went over to it in a launch, all by ourselves. Wilbur and Miss Lucy and that Miss Woodbury had to catch a ten o'clock train back to Tiffin, Ohio, because, when you're out with girls like that you can't get careless and miss any trains and stay out all night, like you can with some kinds of Janes.

And Wilbur blowed himself to the launch and it cost him fifteen cold plunks, but I wouldn't never have knew if I hadn't listened. He wasn't no tin horn kind of a sport.

Over at the Cedar Point place, we didn't stay around where there was a gang of common kind of cattle at all.

There was big dance halls and dining places for yaps, and there was a beach you could walk along and get where it was dark, and we went there.

She didn't talk hardly at all and neither did I, and I was thinking how glad I was my mother was all right, and always made us kids learn to eat with a fork at the table, and not swill soup, and not be noisy and rough like a gang you see around a race track that way.

Then Wilbur and his girl went away up the beach and Lucy and I sat down in a dark place, where there was some roots of old trees the water had washed up, and after that the time, till we had to go back in the launch and they had to catch their trains, wasn't nothing at all. It went like winking your eye.

Here's how it was. The place we were setting in was dark, like I said, and there was the roots from that old stump sticking up like arms, and there was a watery smell, and the night was like—as if you could put your hand out and feel it—so warm and soft and dark and sweet like an orange.

I most cried and I most swore and I most jumped up and danced, I was so mad and happy and sad.

When Wilbur come back from being alone with his girl, and she saw him coming, Lucy she says, "We got to go to the train now," and she was most crying too, but she never knew nothing I knew, and she couldn't be so all busted up. And then, before Wilbur and Miss Woodbury got up to where we was, she put her face up and kissed me quick and put her head up against me and she was all quivering and—Gee whizz.

Sometimes I hope I have cancer and die. I guess you know what I mean. We went in the launch across the bay to the train like that, and it was dark, too. She whispered and said it was like she and I could get out of the boat and walk on water, and it sounded foolish, but I knew what she meant.

And then quick we were right at the depot, and there was a big gang of yaps, the kind that goes to the fairs, and crowded and milling around like cattle, and how could I tell her? "It won't be long because you'll write and I'll write to you." That's all she said.

I got a chance like a hay barn afire. A swell chance I got.

And maybe she would write me, down at Marietta that way, and the letter would come back, and stamped on the front of it by the U.S.A. "there ain't any such guy," or something like that, whatever they stamp on a letter that way.

And me trying to pass myself off for a big-bug and a swell—to her, as decent a little body as God ever made. Craps amighty—swell chance I got!

And then the train come in, and she got on it, and Wilbur Wessen, he come and shook hands with me, and that Miss Woodbury was nice too and bowed to me, and I at her, and the train went and I busted out and cried like a kid.

Gee, I could have run after the train and made Dan Patch look like a freight train after a wreck but, socks amighty, what was the use? Did you ever see such a fool?

I'll bet you what—if I had an arm broke right now or a train had run over my foot—I wouldn't go to no doctor at all. I'd go set down and let her hurt and hurt—that's what I'd do.

I'll bet you what—if I hadn't a drunk that booze I'd never been such a boob as to go tell such a lie—that couldn't never be made straight to a lady like her.

I wish I had that fellow right here that had on a Windsor tie and carried a cane. I'd smash him for fair. Gosh darn his eyes. He's a big fool—that's what he is.

And if I'm not another you just go find me one and I'll quit working and be a bum and give him my job. I don't care nothing for working, and earning money, and saving it for no such boob as myself.

QUESTIONS

1. This story is told by an uneducated boy who is handicapped in the telling by bad grammar, an inadequate vocabulary, ignorance, and a digressive story-telling method. Find a good exemplification of each. Why do these handicaps advance rather than hinder the story? What is the story's main purpose?

2. What kind of moral standards does the swipe have? Is he mean? Where does he get his moral standards?

3. What is the swipe's attitude toward education? Can you reconcile "You can stick your colleges up your nose for all me" with "The young fellow was a nice guy, all right. He was the kind maybe that goes to college and then comes to be a lawyer . . ."? What is an *ambivalent* attitude? What is *rationalization?* Explain the swipe's attitude.

4. The main tenet of the swipe's rather rudimentary philosophy of life is "Put up a good front." On what occasions in the story does the swipe put up a good front? Is this the philosophy of a mature individual? What is the difference between "putting up a good front" and "putting on airs"?

5. Another tenet of the swipe's philosophy is that "A fellow, just because he has been a swipe with a race horse, and works taking care of horses for a man in the teaming, delivery, and storage business, isn't any better or worse than any one else." Why has the swipe "often thought that, and said it too"? Why is he so impressed by the "swell names" and good clothes of the Wessens and Miss Woodbury? What is his attitude toward being a swipe? What does he like about being a swipe?

6. Why does the swipe resent the man in the Windsor tie? Why does he like Burt and the Wessens and Miss Woodbury? Why does he refer to most people as "yaps"?

7. Evaluate the swipe's emotional maturity in the light of his reactions to the little chap who got jobs away from him, what he would do to the real Walter Mathers if there were one, his behavior toward the man in the Windsor tie, what he would like to happen to himself at the end of the story.
8. What psychological term might be used to explain the swipe? Account for his behavior in terms of his size, his social and economic background, his success in school, his earning ability.
9. The swipe blames his whopper at the race track on the whisky, and he blames the whisky on the man in the Windsor tie. What is the real reason for his behavior?
10. How is your attitude toward the swipe affected by the fact that you hear his story from himself? How would it be different if you had heard it from, say, a high school principal?

Doris Lessing
THE BLACK MADONNA

There are some countries in which the arts, let alone Art, cannot be said to flourish. Why this should be so it is hard to say, although of course we all have our theories about it. For sometimes it is the most barren soil that sends up gardens of those flowers which we all agree are the crown and justification of life, and it is this fact which makes it hard to say, finally, why the soil of Zambesia should produce such reluctant plants.

Zambesia is a tough, sunburnt, virile, positive country contemptuous of subtleties and sensibility: yet there have been States with these qualities which have produced art, though perhaps with the left hand. Zambesia is, to put it mildly, unsympathetic to those ideas so long taken for granted in other parts of the world, to do with liberty, fraternity and the rest. Yet there are those, and some of the finest souls among them, who maintain that art is impossible without a minority whose leisure is guaranteed by a hardworking majority. And whatever Zambesia's comfortable minority may lack, it is not leisure.

Zambesia—but enough; out of respect for ourselves and for scientific accuracy, we should refrain from jumping to conclusions. Particularly when one remembers the almost wistful respect Zambesians show when an artist does appear in their midst.

Consider, for instance, the case of Michele.

THE BLACK MADONNA First published in 1957. Zambesia was a name once applied to British territories in the Zambezi river basin, including the southern part of Rhodesia, at the time of the story a British colony, now the republic of Zimbabwe. The British established P.O.W. camps there during World War II (1939–45). Italy, at the beginning of the war one of the Axis countries (with Nazi Germany), surrendered to the Allies in 1943, two years before the Germans. Doris Lessing, born in 1919 of British parents, lived in southern Rhodesia from 1924 to 1949.

He came out of the internment camp at the time when Italy was made a sort of honorary ally, during the Second World War. It was a time of strain for the authorities, because it is one thing to be responsible for thousands of prisoners of war whom one must treat according to certain recognized standards; it is another to be faced, and from one day to the next, with these same thousands transformed by some international legerdemain into comrades in arms. Some of the thousands stayed where they were in the camps; they were fed and housed there at least. Others went as farm laborers, though not many; for while the farmers were as always short of labor, they did not know how to handle farm laborers who were also white men: such a phenomenon had never happened in Zambesia before. Some did odd jobs around the towns, keeping a sharp eye out for the trade unions, who would neither admit them as members nor agree to their working.

Hard, hard, the lot of these men, but fortunately not for long, for soon the war ended and they were able to go home.

Hard, too, the lot of the authorities, as has been pointed out; and for that reason they were doubly willing to take what advantages they could from the situation; and that Michele was such an advantage there could be no doubt.

His talents were first discovered when he was still a prisoner of war. A church was built in the camp, and Michele decorated its interior. It became a show-place, that little tin-roofed church in the prisoners' camp, with its whitewashed walls covered all over with frescoes depicting swarthy peasants gathering grapes for the vintage, beautiful Italian girls dancing, plump dark-eyed children. Amid crowded scenes of Italian life, appeared the Virgin and her Child, smiling and beneficent, happy to move familiarly among her people.

Culture-loving ladies who had bribed the authorities to be taken inside the camp would say, "Poor thing, how homesick he must be." And they would beg to be allowed to leave half a crown for the artist. Some were indignant. He was a prisoner, after all, captured in the very act of fighting against justice and democracy, and what right had he to protest?—for they felt these paintings as a sort of protest. What was there in Italy that we did not have right here in Westonville, which was the capital and hub of Zambesia? Were there not sunshine and mountains and fat babies and pretty girls here? Did we not grow—if not grapes, at least lemons and oranges and flowers in plenty?

People were upset—the desperation of nostalgia came from the painted white walls of that simple church, and affected everyone according to his temperament.

But when Michele was free, his talent was remembered. He was spoken of as "that Italian artist." As a matter of fact, he was a bricklayer. And the virtues of those frescoes might very well have been exaggerated. It is possible they would have been overlooked altogether in a country where picture-covered walls were more common.

When one of the visiting ladies came rushing out to the camp in her own car, to ask him to paint her children, he said he was not qualified to do so. But at last he agreed. He took a room in the town and made some nice likenesses of the children. Then he painted the children of a great number of the first lady's friends. He charged ten shillings a time. Then one of the ladies wanted a portrait of herself. He asked ten pounds for it; it had taken him a month to do. She was annoyed, but paid.

And Michele went off to his room with a friend and stayed there drinking red wine from the Cape and talking about home. While the money lasted he could not be persuaded to do any more portraits.

There was a good deal of talk among the ladies about the dignity of labor, a subject in which they were well versed; and one felt they might almost go so far as to compare a white man with a kaffir, who did not understand the dignity of labor either.

He was felt to lack gratitude. One of the ladies tracked him down, found him lying on a camp-bed under a tree with a bottle of wine, and spoke to him severely about the barbarity of Mussolini and the fecklessness of the Italian temperament. Then she demanded that he should instantly paint a picture of herself in her new evening dress. He refused, and she went home very angry.

It happened that she was the wife of one of our most important citizens, a General or something of that kind, who was at that time engaged in planning a military tattoo or show for the benefit of the civilian population. The whole of Westonville had been discussing this show for weeks. We were all bored to extinction by dances, fancy-dress balls, fairs, lotteries and other charitable entertainments. It is not too much to say that while some were dying for freedom, others were dancing for it. There comes a limit to everything. Though, of course, when the end of the war actually came and the thousands of troops stationed in the country had to go home—in short, when enjoying ourselves would no longer be a duty, many were heard to exclaim that life would never be the same again.

In the meantime, the Tattoo would make a nice change for us all. The military gentlemen responsible for the idea did not think of it in these terms. They thought to improve morale by giving us some idea of what war was really like. Headlines in the newspaper were not enough. And in order to bring it all home to us, they planned to destroy a village by shell-fire before our very eyes.

First, the village had to be built.

It appears that the General and his subordinates stood around in the red dust of the parade-ground under a burning sun for the whole of one day, surrounded by building materials, while hordes of African laborers ran around with boards and nails, trying to make something that looked like a village. It became evident that they would have to build a proper village in order to destroy it; and this would cost more than was allowed for the whole entertainment. The General went home in a bad temper, and his wife said what they needed was an artist, they needed Michele. This was not because she wanted to do Michele a good turn; she could not endure the thought of him lying around singing while there was work to be done. She refused to undertake any delicate diplomatic missions when her husband said he would be damned if he would ask favors of any little Wop. She solved the problem for him in her own way: a certain Captain Stocker was sent out to fetch him.

The Captain found him on the same camp-bed under the same tree, in rolled-up trousers, and an uncollared shirt; unshaven, mildly drunk, with a bottle of wine standing beside him on the earth. He was singing an air so wild, so sad, that the Captain was uneasy. He stood at ten paces from the disreputable fellow and felt the indignities of his position. A year ago, this man had been a mortal enemy to be shot at sight. Six months ago, he had been an enemy prisoner. Now he lay with his knees up, in an untidy shirt that had certainly once been military. For the Captain, the situation crystalized in a desire that Michele should salute him.

"Piselli!" he said sharply.

Michele turned his head and looked at the Captain from the horizontal. "Good morning," he said affably.

"You are wanted," said the Captain.

"Who?" said Michele. He sat up, a fattish, olive-skinned little man. His eyes were resentful.

"The authorities."

"The war is over?"

The Captain, who was already stiff and shiny enough in his laundered khaki, jerked his head back frowning, chin out. He was a large man, blond, and wherever his flesh showed, it was brick-red. His eyes were small and blue and angry. His red hands, covered all over with fine yellow bristles, clenched by his side. Then he saw the disappointment in Michele's eyes, and the hands unclenched. "No it is not over," he said. "Your assistance is required."

"For the war?"

"For the war effort. I take it you are interested in defeating the Germans?"

Michele looked at the Captain. The little dark-eyed artisan looked at the great blond officer with his cold blue eyes, his narrow mouth, his hands like bristle-covered steaks. He looked and said: "I am very interested in the end of the war."

"*Well?*" said the Captain between his teeth.

"The pay?" said Michele.

"You will be paid."

Michele stood up. He lifted the bottle against the sun, then took a gulp. He rinsed his mouth out with wine and spat. Then he poured what was left on to the red earth, where it made a bubbling purple stain.

"I am ready," he said. He went with the Captain to the waiting lorry, where he climbed in beside the driver's seat and not, as the Captain had expected, into the back of the lorry. When they had arrived at the parade-ground the officers had left a message that the Captain would be personally responsible for Michele and for the village. Also for the hundred or so laborers who were sitting around on the grass verges waiting for orders.

The Captain explained what was wanted. Michele nodded. Then he waved his hand at the Africans. "I do not want these," he said.

"You will do it yourself—a village?"

"Yes."

"With no help?"

Michele smiled for the first time. "I will do it."

The Captain hesitated. He disapproved on principle of white men doing heavy manual labor. He said: "I will keep six to do the heavy work."

Michele shrugged; and the Captain went over and dismissed all but six of the Africans. He came back with them to Michele.

"It is hot," said Michele.

"Very," said the Captain. They were standing in the middle of the parade-ground. Around its edge trees, grass, gulfs of shadow. Here, nothing but reddish dust, drifting and lifting in a low hot breeze.

"I am thirsty," said Michele. He grinned. The Captain felt his stiff lips loosen unwillingly in reply. The two pairs of eyes met. It was a moment of understanding. For the Captain, the little Italian had suddenly become human. "I will arrange it," he said, and went off down-town. By the time he had explained the position to the right people, filled in forms and made arrangements, it was late afternoon. He returned to the parade-ground with a case of Cape brandy, to find Michele and the six black men seated together under a tree. Michele was singing an Italian song to them, and they were harmonizing with him. The sight affected the Captain like an attack of nausea. He came up, and the Africans stood to attention. Michele continued to sit.

"You said you would do the work yourself?"

"Yes, I said so."

The Captain then dismissed the Africans. They departed, with friendly looks towards Michele, who waved at them. The Captain was beef-red with anger. "You have not started yet?"

"How long have I?"

"Three weeks."

"Then there is plenty of time," said Michele, looking at the bottle of brandy in the Captain's hand. In the other were two glasses. "It is evening," he pointed out. The Captain stood frowning for a moment. Then he sat down on the grass, and poured out two brandies.

"Ciao," ° said Michele.

"Cheers," said the Captain. Three weeks, he was thinking. Three weeks with this damned little Itie! He drained his glass and refilled it, and set it in

Ciao: cheers!

the grass. The grass was cool and soft. A tree was flowering somewhere close—hot waves of perfume came on the breeze.

"It is nice here," said Michele. "We will have a good time together. Even in a war, there are times of happiness. And of friendship. I drink to the end of the war."

Next day, the Captain did not arrive at the parade-ground until after lunch. He found Michele under the trees with a bottle. Sheets of ceiling board had been erected at one end of the parade-ground in such a way that they formed two walls and part of a third, and a slant of steep roof supported on struts.

"What's that?" said the Captain, furious.

"The church," said Michele.

"Wha-at?"

"You will see. Later. It is very hot." He looked at the brandy bottle that lay on its side on the ground. The Captain went to the lorry and returned with the case of brandy. They drank. Time passed. It was a long time since the Captain had sat on grass under a tree. It was a long time, for that matter, since he had drunk so much. He always drank a great deal, but it was regulated to the times and seasons. He was a disciplined man. Here, sitting on the grass beside this little man whom he still could not help thinking of as an enemy, it was not that he let his self-discipline go, but that he felt himself to be something different: he was temporarily set outside his normal behavior. Michele did not count. He listened to Michele talking about Italy, and it seemed to him he was listening to a savage speaking: as if he heard tales from the mythical South Sea islands where a man like himself might very well go just once in his life. He found himself saying he would like to make a trip to Italy after the war. Actually, he was attracted only by the North and by Northern people. He had visited Germany, under Hitler, and though it was not the time to say so, had found it very satisfactory. Then Michele sang him some Italian songs. He sang Michele some English songs. Then Michele took out photographs of his wife and children, who lived in a village in the mountains of North Italy. He asked the Captain if he were married. The Captain never spoke about his private affairs.

He had spent all his life in one or other of the African colonies as a policeman, magistrate, native commissioner, or in some other useful capacity. When the war started, military life came easily to him. But he hated city life, and had his own reasons for wishing the war over. Mostly, he had been in bush-stations with one or two other white men, or by himself, far from the rigors of civilization. He had relations with native women; and from time to time visited the city where his wife lived with her parents and the children. He was always tormented by the idea that she was unfaithful to him. Recently he had even appointed a private detective to watch her; he was convinced the detective was inefficient. Army friends coming from L——— where his wife was, spoke of her at parties, enjoying herself. When the war ended, she would not find it so easy to have a good time. And why did he not simply live with her and be done with it? The fact was, he could not. And his long exile to remote bush-stations was because he needed the excuse not to. He could not bear to think of his wife for too long; she was that part of his life he had never been able, so to speak, to bring to heel.

Yet he spoke of her now to Michele, and of his favorite bushwife, Nadya. He told Michele the story of his life, until he realized that the shadows from the trees they sat under had stretched right across the parade-ground to the grandstand. He got unsteadily to his feet, and said: "There is work to be done. You are being paid to work."

"I will show you my church when the light goes."

The sun dropped, darkness fell, and Michele made the Captain drive his lorry on to the parade-ground a couple of hundred yards away and switch on his lights. Instantly, a white church sprang up from the shapes and shadows of the bits of board.

"Tomorrow, some houses," said Michele cheerfully.

At the end of a week, the space at the end of the parade-ground had crazy gawky constructions of lath and board over it, that looked in the sunlight like nothing on this earth. Privately, it upset the Captain; it was like a nightmare that these skeleton-like shapes should be able to persuade him, with the illusions of light and dark, that they were a village. At night, the Captain drove up his lorry, switched on the lights, and there it was, the village, solid and real against a background of full green trees. Then, in the morning sunlight, there was nothing there, just bits of board stuck in the sand.

"It is finished," said Michele.

"You were engaged for three weeks," said the Captain. He did not want it to end, this holiday from himself.

Michele shrugged. "The army is rich," he said. Now, to avoid curious eyes, they sat inside the shade of the church, with the case of brandy between them. The Captain talked, talked endlessly, about his wife, about women. He could not stop talking.

Michele listened. Once he said: "When I go home—when I go home—I shall open my arms . . ." He opened them, wide. He closed his eyes. Tears ran down his cheeks. "I shall take my wife in my arms, and I shall ask nothing, nothing. I do not care. It is enough to be together. That is what the war has taught me. It is enough, it is enough. I shall ask no questions and I shall be happy."

The Captain stared before him, suffering. He thought how he dreaded his wife. She was a scornful creature, gay and hard, who laughed at him. She had been laughing at him ever since they married. Since the war, she had taken to calling him names like Little Hitler, and Storm-trooper. "Go ahead, my little Hitler," she had cried last time they met. "Go ahead, my Storm-trooper. If you want to waste your money on private detectives, go ahead. But don't think I don't know what *you* do when you're in the bush. I don't care what you do, but remember that I know it . . ."

The Captain remembered her saying it. And there sat Michele on his packing-case, saying: "It's a pleasure for the rich, my friend, detectives and the law. Even jealousy is a pleasure I don't want any more. Ah, my friend, to be together with my wife again, and the children, that is all I ask of life. That and wine and food and singing in the evenings." And the tears wetted his cheeks and splashed on to his shirt.

That a man should cry, good lord! thought the Captain. And without shame! He seized the bottle and drank.

Three days before the great occasion, some high-ranking officers came strolling through the dust, and found Michele and the Captain sitting together on the packing-case, singing. The Captain's shirt was open down the front, and there were stains on it.

The Captain stood to attention with the bottle in his hand, and Michele stood to attention too, out of sympathy with his friend. Then the officers drew the Captain aside—they were all cronies of his—and said, what the hell did he think he was doing? And why wasn't the village finished?

Then they went away.

"Tell them it is finished," said Michele. "Tell them I want to go."

"No," said the Captain, "no. Michele, what would you do if your wife . . ."

"This world is a good place. We should be happy—that is all."

"Michele . . ."

"I want to go. There is nothing to do. They paid me yesterday."

"Sit down, Michele. Three more days, and then it's finished."

"Then I shall paint the inside of the church as I painted the one in the camp."

The Captain laid himself down on some boards and went to sleep. When he woke, Michele was surrounded by the pots of paint he had used on the outside of the village. Just in front of the Captain was a picture of a black girl. She was young and plump. She wore a patterned blue dress and her shoulders came soft and bare out of it. On her back was a baby slung in a band of red stuff. Her face was turned towards the Captain and she was smiling.

"That's Nadya," said the Captain. "Nadya . . ." He groaned loudly. He looked at the black child and shut his eyes. He opened them, and mother and child were still there. Michele was very carefully drawing thin yellow circles around the heads of the black girl and her child.

"Good God," said the Captain, "you can't do that."

"Why not?"

"You can't have a black Madonna."

"She was a peasant. This is a peasant. Black peasant Madonna for black country."

"This is a German village," said the Captain.

"This is my Madonna," said Michele angrily. "Your German village and my Madonna. I paint this picture as an offering to the Madonna. She is pleased—I feel it."

The Captain lay down again. He was feeling ill. He went back to sleep.

When he woke for the second time it was dark. Michele had brought in a flaring paraffin lamp, and by its light was working on the long wall. A bottle of brandy stood beside him. He painted until long after midnight, and the Captain lay on his side and watched, as passive as a man suffering a dream. Then they both went to sleep on the boards. The whole of the next day Michele stood painting black Madonnas, black saints, black angels. Outside, troops were practicing in the sunlight, bands were blaring and motorcyclists roared up and down. But Michele painted on, drunk and oblivious. The Captain lay on his back, drinking and muttering about his wife. Then he would say "Nadya, Nadya," and burst into sobs.

Towards nightfall the troops went away. The officers came back, and the Captain went off with them to show how the village sprang into being when the great lights at the end of the parade-ground were switched on. They all looked at the village in silence. They switched the lights off, and there were only the tall and angular boards leaning like gravestones in the moonlight. On went the lights—and there was the village. They were silent, as if suspicious. Like the Captain, they seemed to feel it was not right. Uncanny it certainly was, but *that* was not it. Unfair—that was the word. It was cheating. And profoundly disturbing.

"Clever chap, that Italian of yours," said the General.

The Captain, who had been woodenly correct until this moment, suddenly came rocking up to the General, and steadied himself by laying his hand on the august shoulder. "Bloody Wops," he said. "Bloody kaffirs. Bloody . . . Tell you what, though, there's one Itie that's some good. Yes, there is. I'm telling you. He's a friend of mine, actually."

The General looked at him. Then he nodded at his underlings. The Captain was taken away for disciplinary purposes. It was decided, however, that he must be ill, nothing else could account for such behavior. He was put to bed in his own room with a nurse to watch him.

He woke twenty-four hours later, sober for the first time in weeks. He slowly remembered what had happened. Then he sprang out of bed and rushed into his clothes. The nurse was just in time to see him run down the path and leap into his lorry.

He drove at top speed to the parade-ground, which was flooded with light in such a way that the village did not exist. Everything was in full swing. The cars were three deep around the square, with people on the running-boards and even the roofs. The grandstand was packed. Women dressed up as gipsies, country girls, Elizabethan court dames, and so on, wandered about with trays of ginger beer and sausage-rolls and programs at five shillings each in aid of the war effort. On the square, troops deployed, obsolete machine-guns were being dragged up and down, bands played, and motorcyclists roared through flames.

As the Captain parked the lorry, all this activity ceased, and the lights went out. The Captain began running around the outside of the square to reach the place where the guns were hidden in a mess of net and branches. He was sobbing with the effort. He was a big man, and unused to exercise, and sodden with brandy. He had only one idea in his mind—to stop the guns firing, to stop them at all costs.

Luckily, there seemed to be a hitch. The lights were still out. The unearthly graveyard at the end of the square glittered white in the moonlight. Then the lights briefly switched on, and the village sprang into existence for just long enough to show large red crosses all over a white building beside the church. Then moonlight flooded everything again, and the crosses vanished. "Oh, the bloody fool!" sobbed the Captain, running, running as if for his life. He was no longer trying to reach the guns. He was cutting across a corner of the square direct to the church. He could hear some officers cursing behind him: "Who put those red crosses there? Who? We can't fire on the Red Cross."

The Captain reached the church as the searchlights burst on. Inside, Michele was kneeling on the earth looking at his first Madonna. "They are going to kill my Madonna," he said miserably.

"Come away, Michele, come away."

"They're going to . . ."

The Captain grabbed his arm and pulled. Michele wrenched himself free and grabbed a saw. He began hacking at the ceiling board. There was a dead silence outside. They heard a voice booming through the loudspeakers: "The village that is about to be shelled is an English village, not as represented on the program, a German village. Repeat, the village that is about to be shelled is . . ."

Michele had cut through two sides of a square around the Madonna.

"Michele," sobbed the Captain, *"get out of here."*

Michele dropped the saw, took hold of the raw edges of the board and tugged. As he did so, the church began to quiver and lean. An irregular patch of board ripped out and Michele staggered back into the Captain's arms. There was a roar. The church seemed to dissolve around them into flames. Then they were running away from it, the Captain holding Michele tight by the arm. "Get down," he shouted suddenly, and threw Michele to the earth. He flung himself down beside him. Looking from under the crook of his arm, he heard the explosion, saw a great pillar of smoke and flame, and the village disintegrated in a flying mass of debris. Michele was on his knees gazing at his Madonna in the light from the flames. She was unrecognizable, blotted out with dust. He looked horrible, quite white, and a trickle of blood soaked from his hair down one cheek.

"They shelled my Madonna," he said.

"Oh, damn it, you can paint another one," said the Captain. His own voice seemed to him strange, like a dream voice. He was certainly crazy, as mad as Michele himself . . . He got up, pulled Michele to his feet, and marched him towards the edge of the field. There they were met by the ambulance people. Michele was taken off to hospital, and the Captain was sent back to bed.

A week passed. The Captain was in a darkened room. That he was having some kind of a breakdown was clear, and two nurses stood guard over him.

Sometimes he lay quiet. Sometimes he muttered to himself. Sometimes he sang in a thick clumsy voice bits out of opera, fragments from Italian songs, and—over and over again—"There's a Long Long Trail." He was not thinking of anything at all. He shied away from the thought of Michele as if it were dangerous. When, therefore, a cheerful female voice announced that a friend had come to cheer him up, and it would do him good to have some company, and he saw a white bandage moving towards him in the gloom, he turned sharp over on to his side, face to the wall.

"Go away," he said. "Go away, Michele."

"I have come to see you," said Michele. "I have brought you a present."

The Captain slowly turned over. There was Michele, a cheerful ghost in the dark room. "You fool," he said. "You messed everything up. What did you paint those crosses for?"

"It was a hospital," said Michele. "In a village there is a hospital, and on the hospital the Red Cross, the beautiful Red Cross—no?"

"I was nearly court-martialed."

"It was my fault," said Michele. "I was drunk."

"I was responsible."

"How could you be responsible when I did it? But it is all over. Are you better?"

"Well, I suppose those crosses saved your life."

"I did not think," said Michele. "I was remembering the kindness of the Red Cross people when we were prisoners."

"Oh shut up, shut up, shut up."

"I have brought you a present."

The Captain peered through the dark. Michele was holding up a picture. It was of a native woman with a baby on her back smiling sideways out of the frame.

Michele said: "You did not like the haloes. So this time, no haloes. For the Captain—no Madonna." He laughed. "You like it? It is for you. I painted it for you."

"God damn you!" said the Captain.

"You do not like it?" said Michele, very hurt.

The Captain closed his eyes. "What are you going to do next?" he asked tiredly.

Michele laughed again. "Mrs. Pannerhurst, the lady of the General, she wants me to paint her picture in her white dress. So I paint it."

"You should be proud to."

"Silly bitch. She thinks I am good. They know nothing—savages. Barbarians. Not you, Captain, you are my friend. But these people they know nothing."

The Captain lay quiet. Fury was gathering in him. He thought of the General's wife. He disliked her, but he had known her well enough.

"These people," said Michele. "They do not know a good picture from a bad picture. I paint, I paint, this way, that way. There is the picture—I look at it and laugh inside myself." Michele laughed out loud. "They say, he is a

Michelangelo, this one, and try to cheat me out of my price. Michele—Michelangelo—that is a joke, no?"

The Captain said nothing.

"But for you I painted this picture to remind you of our good times with the village. You are my friend. I will always remember you."

The Captain turned his eyes sideways in his head and stared at the black girl. Her smile at him was half innocence, half malice.

"Get out," he said suddenly.

Michele came closer and bent to see the Captain's face. "You wish me to go?" He sounded unhappy. "You saved my life. I was a fool that night. But I was thinking of my offering to the Madonna—I was a fool, I say to myself. I was drunk, we are fools when we get drunk."

"Get out of here," said the Captain again.

For a moment the white bandage remained motionless. Then it swept downwards in a bow.

Michele turned towards the door.

"And take that bloody picture with you."

Silence. Then, in the dim light, the Captain saw Michele reach out for the picture, his white head bowed in profound obeisance. He straightened himself and stood to attention, holding the picture with one hand, and keeping the other stiff down his side. Then he saluted the Captain.

"Yes, *sir*," he said, and he turned and went out of the door with the picture.

The Captain lay still. He felt—what did he feel? There was a pain under his ribs. It hurt to breathe. He realized he was unhappy. Yes, a terrible unhappiness was filling him slowly, slowly. He was unhappy because Michele had gone. Nothing had ever hurt the Captain in all his life as much as that mocking *Yes, sir*. Nothing. He turned his face to the wall and wept. But silently. Not a sound escaped him, for the fear the nurses might hear.

QUESTIONS

1. The first nineteen paragraphs of the story, while they introduce Michele, are chiefly devoted to portraying Zambesia. What is its social structure? Who are its "comfortable minority"? What are their attitudes toward (a) Art, (b) liberty/freedom, (c) fraternity, (d) leisure, (e) democracy, (f) foreigners, (g) Michele's painting? What division of interest and concern marks off the women from the men?

2. In paragraphs 1, 3, 9, 16, and 17, the narrator uses the first person plural pronoun in its various forms (*we, our, ourselves, us*). To whom does this pronoun refer in the earlier two paragraphs? in the latter three? To what extent does the narrator include herself in each group? What is her attitude toward the "culture-loving ladies" and the "military gentlemen," and how is it conveyed? Explain the meaning and tone of paragraphs 14 (on "the dignity of labor") and 16 (on "charitable entertainments").

3. What does Michele express in his art? Discuss his feelings and attitudes, and those of the British characters, toward each of the following: (a) the painting in the P.O.W. camp, (b) the commissioned portraits of children—and of women, (c) the Black Madonna, (d) the "village," (e) the painting for Stocker with "no haloes."

4. Contrast the characters of Michele and Captain Stocker. In what respects are they opposites? Compare their attitudes toward work, war, the native population, the sexes, jealousy, drink, self-discipline, duty, men weeping, friendship, happiness.

5. Trace the progress of Captain Stocker's association with Michele from their first meeting until his rescue of Michele from the bombarded village. How does his attitude toward Michele change during this time? What effect does the association have on his behavior? Is Michele's influence on him good or bad? Why does Stocker not want the three weeks to end? Is his drunken assertion to the General of his friendship for Michele (page 87) sincere? What causes Stocker's breakdown after his rescue of Michele? Why does he reject Michele's present and turn Michele away?

6. Why is the village suddenly changed from "a German village" to "an English village"? Discuss the ironies involved in this climax of the attempt to improve morale by giving the ladies "some idea of what war was actually like."

7. Who is the protagonist of this story?

8. Defend one of the following propositions: (a) Captain Stocker has undergone a small but permanent change in character as a result of his association with Michele. He will never be quite the same again. (b) Although Captain Stocker undergoes a large change in his characteristic behavior during his association with Michele, it is only temporary. At the end of the story he is reverting to type and will soon be the same Captain Stocker as before.

John Cheever
THE POT OF GOLD

You could not say fairly of Ralph and Laura Whittemore that they had the failings and the characteristics of incorrigible treasure hunters, but you could say truthfully of them that the shimmer and the smell, the peculiar force of money, the promise of it, had an untoward influence on their lives. They were always at the threshold of fortune; they always seemed to have something on the fire. Ralph was a fair young man with a tireless commercial imagination and an evangelical credence in the romance and sorcery of business success, and although he held an obscure job with a clothing manufacturer, this never seemed to him anything more than a point of departure.

The Whittemores were not importunate or overbearing people, and they had an uncompromising loyalty to the gentle manners of the middle class.

THE POT OF GOLD First published in 1951. John Cheever (1912–1982) was born in Quincy, Massachusetts, and resided in various parts of New England, in New York State, and in New York City.

Laura was a pleasant girl of no particular beauty who had come to New York from Wisconsin at about the same time that Ralph had reached the city from Illinois, but it had taken two years of comings and goings before they had been brought together, late one afternoon, in the lobby of a lower Fifth Avenue office building. So true was Ralph's heart, so well did it serve him then, that the moment he saw Laura's light hair and her pretty and sullen face he was enraptured. He followed her out of the lobby, pushing his way through the crowd, and since she had dropped nothing, since there was no legitimate excuse to speak to her, he shouted after her, *"Louise! Louise! Louise!"* and the urgency in his voice made her stop. He said he'd made a mistake. He said he was sorry. He said she looked just like a girl named Louise Hatcher. It was a January night and the dark air tasted of smoke, and because she was a sensible and a lonely girl, she let him buy her a drink.

This was in the thirties, and their courtship was hasty. They were married three months later. Laura moved her belongings into a walk-up on Madison Avenue, above a pants presser's and a florist's, where Ralph was living. She worked as a secretary, and her salary, added to what he brought home from the clothing business, was little more than enough to keep them going, but they never seemed touched by the monotony of a saving and gainless life. They ate dinners in drugstores. She hung a reproduction of van Gogh's "Sunflowers" above the sofa she had bought with some of the small sum of money her parents had left her. When their aunts and uncles came to town— their parents were dead—they had dinner at the Ritz and went to the theater. She sewed curtains and shined his shoes, and on Sundays they stayed in bed until noon. They seemed to be standing at the threshold of plenty; and Laura often told people that she was terribly excited because of this wonderful job that Ralph had lined up.

In the first year of their marriage, Ralph worked nights on a plan that promised him a well-paying job in Texas, but through no fault of his own this promise was never realized. There was an opening in Syracuse a year later, but an older man was decided upon. There were many other profitable but elusive openings and projects between these two. In the third year of their marriage, a firm that was almost identical in size and character with the firm Ralph worked for underwent a change of ownership, and Ralph was approached and asked if he would be interested in joining the overhauled firm. His own job promised only meager security after a series of slow promotions and he was glad of the chance to escape. He met the new owners, and their enthusiasm for him seemed intense. They were prepared to put him in charge of a department and pay him twice what he was getting then. The arrangement was to remain tacit for a month or two, until the new owners had secured their position, but they shook hands warmly and had a drink on the deal, and that night Ralph took Laura out to dinner at an expensive restaurant.

They decided, across the table, to look for a larger apartment, to have a child, and to buy a secondhand car. They faced their good fortune with perfect calm, for it was what they had expected all along. The city seemed to them a generous place, where people were rewarded either by a sudden and deserved development like this or by the capricious bounty of lawsuits, eccentric and peripheral business ventures, unexpected legacies, and other windfalls. After dinner, they walked in Central Park in the moonlight while Ralph smoked a cigar. Later, when Laura had fallen asleep, he sat in the open bedroom window in his pajamas.

The peculiar excitement with which the air of the city seems charged after midnight, when its life falls into the hands of watchmen and drunks, had always pleased him. He knew intimately the sounds of the night street: the bus brakes, the remote sirens, and the sound of water turning high in the air—the sound of water turning a mill wheel—the sum, he supposed, of many echoes, although, often as he had heard the sound, he had never decided on its source. Now he heard all this more keenly because the night seemed to him portentous.

He was twenty-eight years old; poverty and youth were inseparable in his experience, and one was ending with the other. The life they were about to leave had not been hard, and he thought with sentiment of the soiled tablecloth in the Italian restaurant where they usually went for their celebrations, and the high spirits with which Laura on a wet night ran from the subway to the bus stop. But they were drawing away from all this. Shirt sales in department-store basements, lines at meat counters, weak drinks, the roses he brought her up from the subway in the spring, when roses were cheap—these were all unmistakably the souvenirs of the poor, and while they seemed to him good and gentle, he was glad that they would soon be memories.

Laura resigned from her job when she got pregnant. The reorganization and Ralph's new position hung fire, but the Whittemores talked about it freely when they were with friends. "We're *terribly* pleased with the way things are going," Laura would say. "All we need is patience." There were many delays and postponements, and they waited with the patience of people expecting justice. The time came when they both needed clothes, and one evening Ralph suggested that they spend some of the money they had put aside. Laura refused. When he brought up the subject, she didn't answer him and seemed not to hear him. He raised his voice and lost his temper. He shouted. She cried. He thought of all the other girls he could have married— the dark blonde, the worshipful Cuban, the rich and pretty one with a cast in her right eye. All his desires seemed to lie outside the small apartment Laura had arranged. They were still not speaking in the morning, and in order to strengthen his position he telephoned his potential employers. Their secretary told him they were both out. This made him apprehensive. He called several times from the telephone booth in the lobby of the building he worked in and was told that they were busy, they were out, they were in conference with lawyers, or they were talking long-distance. This variety of excuses frightened him. He said nothing to Laura that evening and tried to call them the next day. Late in the afternoon, after many tries, one of them came to the phone. "We gave the job to somebody else, sonny," he said. Like a saddened father, he spoke to Ralph in a hoarse and gentle voice. "Don't try and get us on the telephone any more. We've got other things to do besides answer the telephone. This other fellow seemed better suited, sonny. That's all I can tell you, and don't try to get me on the telephone any more."

Ralph walked the miles from his office to his apartment that night, hoping to free himself in this way from some of the weight of his disappointment. He was so unprepared for the shock that it affected him like vertigo, and he walked with an odd, high step, as if the paving were quicksand. He stood downstairs in front of the building he lived in, trying to decide how to describe the disaster to Laura, but when he went in, he told her bluntly. "Oh, I'm sorry, darling," she said softly and kissed him. "I'm terribly sorry." She wandered away from him and began to straighten the sofa cushions. His frustration was so ardent, he was such a prisoner of his own schemes and expectations, that he was astonished at the serenity with which she regarded the failure. There was nothing to worry about, she said. She still had a few hundred dollars in the bank, from the money her parents had left her. There was nothing to worry about.

When the child, a girl, was born, they named her Rachel, and a week after the delivery Laura returned to the Madison Avenue walk-up. She took all the care of the baby and continued to do the cooking and the housework.

Ralph's imagination remained resilient and fertile, but he couldn't seem to hit on a scheme that fit into his lack of time and capital. He and Laura, like the hosts of the poor everywhere, lived a simple life. They still went to the theater with visiting relatives and occasionally they went to parties, but Laura's only continuous contact with the bright lights that surrounded them was vicarious and came to her through a friend she made in Central Park.

She spent many afternoons on a park bench during the first years of Rachel's life. It was a tyranny and a pleasure. She resented her enchainment but enjoyed the open sky and the air. One winter afternoon, she recognized a woman she had met at a party, and a little before dark, as Laura and the other mothers were gathering their stuffed animals and preparing their children for the cold journey home, the woman came across the playground and spoke to her. She was Alice Holinshed, she said. They had met at the Galvins'. She was pretty and friendly, and walked with Laura to the edge of the Park. She had a boy of about Rachel's age. The two women met again the following day. They became friends.

Mrs. Holinshed was older than Laura, but she had a more youthful and precise beauty. Her hair and her eyes were black, her pale and perfectly oval face was delicately colored, and her voice was pure. She lighted her cigarettes with Stork Club matches and spoke of the inconvenience of living with a child in a hotel. If Laura had any regrets about her life, they were expressed in her friendship for this pretty woman, who moved so freely through expensive stores and restaurants.

It was a friendship circumscribed, with the exception of the Galvins', by the sorry and touching countryside of Central Park. The women talked principally about their husbands, and this was a game that Laura could play with an empty purse. Vaguely, boastfully, the two women discussed the irons their men had in the fire. They sat together with their children through the sooty twilights, when the city to the south burns like a Bessemer furnace, and the air smells of coal, and the wet boulders shine like slag, and the Park itself seems like a strip of woods on the edge of a coal town. Then Mrs. Holinshed would remember that she was late—she was always late for something mysterious and splendid—and the two women would walk together to the edge of the woods. This vicarious contact with comfort pleased Laura, and the pleasure would stay with her as she pushed the baby carriage over to Madison Avenue and then began to cook supper, hearing the thump of the steam iron and smelling the cleaning fluid from the pants presser's below.

One night, when Rachel was about two years old, the frustration of Ralph's search for the goat track that would let him lead his family to a realm of reasonable contentment kept him awake. He needed sleep urgently, and when this blessing eluded him, he got out of bed and sat in the dark. The charm and excitement of the street after midnight escaped him. The explosive brakes of a Madison Avenue bus made him jump. He shut the window, but the noise of traffic continued to pass through it. It seemed to him that the penetrating voice of the city had a mortal effect on the precious lives of the city's inhabitants and that it should be muffled.

He thought of a Venetian blind whose outer surface would be treated with a substance that would deflect or absorb sound waves. With such a blind, friends paying a call on a spring evening would not have to shout to be heard above the noise of trucks in the street below. Bedrooms could be silenced that way—bedrooms, above all, for it seemed to him then that sleep was what everyone in the city sought and only half captured. All the harried faces on the streets at dusk, when even the pretty girls talk to themselves, were looking for sleep. Night-club singers and their amiable customers, the people waiting for taxis in front of the Waldorf on a wet night, policemen, cashiers, window washers—sleep eluded them all.

He talked over this Venetian blind with Laura the following night, and the idea seemed sensible to her. He bought a blind that would fit their bedroom window, and experimented with various paint mixtures. At last he stumbled on the one that dried to the consistency of felt and was porous. The paint had a sickening smell, which filled their apartment during the four days it took him to coat and recoat the outer surface of the slats. When the paint had dried, he hung the blind, and they opened the window for a test. Silence—a relative silence—charmed their ears. He wrote down his formula, and took it during his lunch hour to a patent attorney. It took the lawyer several weeks to discover that a similar formula had been patented some years earlier. The patent owner—a man named Fellows—had a New York address, and the lawyer suggested that Ralph get in touch with him and try to reach some agreement.

The search for Mr. Fellows began one evening when Ralph had finished work, and took him first to the attic of a Hudson Street rooming house, where the landlady showed Ralph a pair of socks that Mr. Fellows had left behind when he moved out. Ralph went south from there to another rooming house and west to the neighborhood of ship chandlers and marine boarding houses. The nocturnal search went on for a week. He followed the thread of Mr. Fellows' goings south to the Bowery and then to the upper West Side. He climbed stairs past the open doors of rooms where lessons in Spanish dancing were going on, past whores, past women practicing the "Emperor" Concerto, and one evening he found Mr. Fellows sitting on the edge of his bed in an attic room, rubbing the spots out of his necktie with a rag soaked in gasoline.

Mr. Fellows was greedy. He wanted a hundred dollars in cash and fifty percent of the royalties. Ralph got him to agree to twenty percent of the royalties, but he could not get him to reduce the initial payment. The lawyer drew up a paper defining Ralph's and Mr. Fellows' interests, and a few nights later Ralph went over to Brooklyn and got to a Venetian-blind factory after its doors had closed but while the lights of the office were still burning. The manager agreed to manufacture some blinds to Ralph's specifications, but would not take an order of less than a hundred dollars. Ralph agreed to this and to furnish the compound for the outer surface of the slats. These expenditures had taken more than three-fourths of the Whittemores' capital, and now the problem of money was joined by the element of time. They put a small advertisement in the paper for a housewares salesman, and for a week Ralph interviewed candidates in the living room after supper. He chose a young man who was leaving at the end of the week for the Midwest. He wanted a fifty-dollar advance, and pointed out to them that Pittsburgh and Chicago were just as noisy as New York. A department-store collection agency was threatening to bring them into the small-claims court at this time, and they had come to a place where any illness, any fall, any damage to themselves or to the few clothes they owned would be critical. Their salesman promised to write them from Chicago at the end of the week, and they counted on good news, but there was no news from Chicago at all. Ralph wired the salesman twice, and the wires must have been forwarded, for he replied to them from Pittsburgh: "Can't merchandise blinds. Returning samples express." They put another advertisement for a salesman in the paper and took the first one who rang their bell, an old gentleman with a cornflower in his buttonhole. He had a number of other lines—mirror wastebaskets, orange-juicers—and he said that he knew all the Manhattan housewares buyers intimately. He was garrulous, and when he was unable to sell the blinds, he came to the Whittemores' apartment and discussed their product at length, and with a blend of criticism and charity that we usually reserve for human beings.

Ralph was to borrow money, but neither his salary nor his patent was considered adequate collateral for a loan at anything but ruinous rates, and one day, at his office, he was served a summons by the department-store collection agency. He went out to Brooklyn and offered to sell the Venetian blinds back to the manufacturer. The man gave him sixty dollars for what had cost a hundred, and Ralph was able to pay the collection agency. They hung the samples in their windows and tried to put the venture out of their minds.

Now they were poorer than ever, and they ate lentils for dinner every Monday and sometimes again on Tuesday. Laura washed the dishes after dinner while Ralph read to Rachel. When the girl had fallen asleep, he would go to his desk in the living room and work on one of his projects. There was always something coming. There were the plastic arch preserver, the automatic closing device for icebox doors, and the scheme to pirate marine specifications and undersell Jane's. For a month, he was going to buy some fallow acreage in upstate New York and plant Christmas trees on it, and then, with one of his friends, he projected a luxury mail-order business, for which they could never get backing. When the Whittemores met Uncle George and Aunt Helen at the Ritz, they seemed delighted with the way things were going. They were terribly excited, Laura said, about a sales agency in Paris that had been offered to Ralph but that they had decided against, because of the threat of war.

The Whittemores were apart for two years during the war. Laura took a job. She walked Rachel to school in the morning and met her at the end of the day. Working and saving, Laura was able to buy herself and Rachel some clothes. When Ralph returned at the end of the war, their affairs were in good order. The experience seemed to have refreshed him, and while he took up his old job as an anchor to windward, as an ace in the hole, there had never been more talk about jobs—jobs in Venezuela and jobs in Iran. They resumed all their old habits and economies. They remained poor.

Laura gave up her job and returned to the afternoons with Rachel in Central Park. Alice Holinshed was there. The talk was the same. The Holinsheds were living in a hotel. Mr. Holinshed was vice-president of a new firm manufacturing a soft drink, but the dress that Mrs. Holinshed wore day after day was one that Laura recognized from before the war. Her son was thin and bad-tempered. He was dressed in serge, like an English schoolboy, but his serge, like his mother's dress, looked worn and outgrown. One afternoon when Mrs. Holinshed and her son came into the Park, the boy was crying. "I've done a dreadful thing," Mrs. Holinshed told Laura. "We've been to the doctor's and I forgot to bring any money, and I wonder if you could lend me a few dollars, so I can take a taxi back to the hotel." Laura said she would be glad to. She had only a five-dollar bill with her, and she gave Mrs. Holinshed this. The boy continued to cry, and his mother dragged him off toward Fifth Avenue. Laura never saw them in the Park again.

Ralph's life was, as it had always been, dominated by anticipation. In the years directly after the war, the city appeared to be immensely rich. There seemed to be money everywhere, and the Whittemores, who slept under their worn overcoats in the winter to keep themselves warm, seemed separated from their enjoyment of this prosperity by only a little patience, resourcefulness, and luck. On Sunday, when the weather was fine, they walked with the prosperous crowds on upper Fifth Avenue. It seemed to Ralph that it might only be another month, at the most another year, before he found the key to the prosperity they deserved. They would walk on Fifth Avenue until the afternoon was ended and then go home and eat a can of beans for dinner and, in order to balance the meal, an apple for dessert.

They were returning from such a walk one Sunday when, as they climbed the stairs to their apartment, the telephone began to ring. Ralph went on ahead and answered it.

He heard the voice of his Uncle George, a man of the generation that remains conscious of distance, who spoke into the telephone as if he were calling from shore to a passing boat. "This is Uncle George, Ralphie!" he shouted, and Ralph supposed that he and Aunt Helen were paying a surprise visit to the city, until he realized that his uncle was calling from Illinois. "Can you hear me?" Uncle George shouted. "Can you hear me, Ralphie? . . . I'm calling you about a job, Ralphie. Just in case you're looking for a job. Paul Hadaam came through—can you hear me, Ralphie?—Paul Hadaam came through here on his way East last week and he stopped off to pay me a visit. He's got a lot of money, Ralphie—he's rich—and he's starting this business out in the West to manufacture synthetic wool. Can you hear me, Ralphie? . . . I told him about you, and he's staying at the Waldorf, so you go and see him. I saved his life once. I pulled him out of Lake Erie. You go and see him tomorrow at the Waldorf, Ralphie. You know where that is? The Waldorf Hotel. . . . Wait a minute, here's Aunt Helen. She wants to talk with you."

Now the voice was a woman's, and it came to him faintly. All his cousins had been there for dinner, she told him. They had had a turkey for dinner. All the grandchildren were there and they behaved very well. George took them all for a walk after dinner. It was hot, but they sat on the porch, so they didn't feel the heat. She was interrupted in her account of Sunday by her husband, who must have seized the instrument from her to continue his refrain about going to see Mr. Hadaam at the Waldorf. "You go see him tomorrow, Ralphie—the nineteenth—at the Waldorf. He's expecting you. Can you hear me? . . . The Waldorf Hotel. He's a millionaire. I'll say goodbye now."

Mr. Hadaam had a parlor and a bedroom in the Waldorf Towers, and when Ralph went to see him, late the next afternoon, on his way home from work, Mr. Hadaam was alone. He seemed to Ralph a very old man, but an obdurate one, and in the way he shook hands, pulled at his earlobes, stretched himself, and padded around the parlor on his bandy legs Ralph recognized a spirit that was unimpaired, independent, and canine. He poured Ralph a strong drink and himself a weak one. He was undertaking the manufacture of synthetic wool on the West Coast, he explained, and had come East to find men who were experienced in merchandising wool. George had given him Ralph's name, and he wanted a man with Ralph's experience. He would find the Whittemores a suitable house, arrange for their transportation, and begin Ralph at a salary of fifteen thousand. It was the size of the salary that made Ralph realize that the proposition was an oblique attempt to repay his uncle for having saved Mr. Hadaam's life, and the old man seemed to sense what he was feeling. "This hasn't got anything to do with your uncle's saving my life," he said roughly. "I'm grateful to him—who wouldn't be?—but this hasn't got anything to do with your uncle, if that's what you're thinking. When you get to be as old and as rich as I am, it's hard to meet people. All my old friends are dead—all of them but George. I'm surrounded by a cordon of associates and relatives that's damned near impenetrable, and if it wasn't for George giving me a name now and then, I'd never get to see a new face. Last year, I got into an automobile accident. It was my fault. I'm a terrible driver. I hit this young fellow's car and I got right out and went over to him and introduced myself. We had to wait about twenty minutes for the wreckers and we got to talking. Well, he's working for me today and he's one of the best friends I've got, and if I hadn't run into him, I'd never have met him. When you get to be as old as me, that's the only way you can meet people— automobile accidents, fires, things like that."

He straightened up against the back of his chair and tasted his drink. His rooms were well above the noise of traffic and it was quiet there. Mr. Hadaam's breath was loud and steady, and it sounded, in a pause, like the heavy breath of someone sleeping. "Well, I don't want to rush you into this," he said. "I'm going back to the Coast the day after tomorrow. You think it over and I'll telephone you." He took out an engagement book and wrote down Ralph's name and telephone number. "I'll call you on Tuesday evening, the twenty-seventh, about nine o'clock—nine o'clock your time. George tells me you've got a nice wife, but I haven't got time to meet her now. I'll see her on the Coast." He started talking about baseball and then brought the conversation back to Uncle George. "He saved my life. My damned boat capsized and then righted herself and sunk right from underneath me. I can still feel her going down under my feet. I couldn't swim. Can't swim today. Well, goodbye." They shook hands, and as soon as the door closed, Ralph heard Mr. Hadaam begin to cough. It was the profane, hammering cough of an old man, full of bitter complaints and distempers, and it hit him pitilessly for all the time that Ralph was waiting in the hallway for the elevator to take him down.

On the walk home, Ralph felt that this might be it, that this preposterous chain of contingencies that had begun with his uncle's pulling a friend out of Lake Erie might be the one that would save them. Nothing in his experience made it seem unlikely. He recognized that the proposition was the vagary of an old man and that it originated in the indebtedness Mr. Hadaam felt to his uncle—an indebtedness that age seemed to have deepened. He gave Laura the details of the interview when he came in, and his own views on Mr. Hadaam's conduct, and, to his mild surprise, Laura said that it looked to her like the bonanza. They were both remarkably calm, considering the change that confronted them. There was no talk of celebrating, and he helped her wash the dishes. He looked up the site of Mr. Hadaam's factory in an atlas, and the Spanish place name on the coast north of San Francisco gave them a glimpse of a life of reasonable contentment.

Eight days lay between Ralph's interview and the telephone call, and he realized that nothing would be definite until Tuesday, and that there was a possibility that old Mr. Hadaam, while crossing the country, might, under the subtle influence of travel, suffer a change of heart. He might be poisoned by a fish sandwich and be taken off the train in Chicago, to die in a nursing home there. Among the people meeting him in San Francisco might be his lawyer, with the news that he was ruined or that his wife had run away. But eventually Ralph was unable to invent any new disasters or to believe in the ones he had invented.

This inability to persevere in doubting his luck showed some weakening of character. There had hardly been a day when he had not been made to feel the power of money, but he found that the force of money was most irresistible when it took the guise of a promise, and that years of resolute self-denial, instead of rewarding him with reserves of fortitude, had left him more than ordinarily susceptible to temptation. Since the change in their lives still depended upon a telephone call, he refrained from talking—from thinking, so far as possible—about the life they might have in California. He would go so far as to say that he would like some white shirts, but he would not go beyond this deliberately contrite wish, and here, where he thought he was exercising restraint and intelligence, he was, instead, beginning to respect the bulk of superstition that is supposed to attend good fortune, and when he wished for white shirts, it was not a genuinely modest wish so much as it was a memory—he could not have put it into words himself—that the gods of fortune are jealous and easily deceived by false modesty. He had never been a superstitious man, but on Tuesday he scooped the money off his coffee table and was elated when he saw a ladybug on the bathroom window sill. He could not remember when he had heard money and this insect associated, but neither could he have explained any of the other portents that he had begun to let govern his movements.

Laura watched this subtle change that anticipation worked on her husband, but there was nothing she could say. He did not mention Mr. Hadaam or California. He was quiet; he was gentle with Rachel; he actually grew pale. He had his hair cut on Wednesday. He wore his best suit. On Saturday, he had his hair cut again and his nails manicured. He took two baths a day, put on a fresh shirt for dinner, and frequently went into the bathroom to wash his hands, brush his teeth, and wet down his cowlick. The preternatural care he gave his body and his appearance reminded her of an adolescent surprised by early love.

The Whittemores were invited to a party for Monday night and Laura insisted that they go. The guests at the party were the survivors of a group that had coalesced ten years before, and if anyone had called the roll of the earliest parties in the same room, like the retreat ceremony of a breached and decimated regiment, "Missing. . . . Missing. . . . Missing" would have been answered for the squad that had gone into Westchester;° "Missing. . . . Missing. . . . Missing" would have been spoken for the platoon that divorce, drink, nervous disorders, and adversity had slain or wounded. Because Laura had gone to the party in indifferent spirits, she was conscious of the missing.

She had been at the party less than an hour when she heard some people coming in, and, looking over her shoulder, saw Alice Holinshed and her husband. The room was crowded and she put off speaking to Alice until later. Much later in the evening, Laura went into the toilet, and when she came out of it into the bedroom, she found Alice sitting on the bed. She seemed to be waiting for Laura. Laura sat down at the dressing table to straighten her hair. She looked at the image of her friend in the glass.

"I hear you're going to California," Alice said.

"We hope to. We'll know tomorrow."

"Is it true Ralph's uncle saved his life?"

"That's true."

"You're lucky."

"I suppose we are."

"You're lucky, all right." Alice got up from the bed and crossed the room and closed the door, and came back across the room again and sat on the bed. Laura watched her in the glass, but she was not watching Laura. She was stooped. She seemed nervous. "You're lucky," she said. "You're so lucky. Do you know how lucky you are? Let me tell you about this cake of soap," she said. "I have this cake of soap. I mean I had this cake of soap. Somebody gave it to me when I was married, fifteen years ago. I don't know who. Some maid, some music teacher—somebody like that. It was good soap, good English soap, the kind I like, and I decided to save it for the big day when Larry made a killing, when he took me to Bermuda. First, I was going to use it when he got the job in Bound Brook. Then I thought I could use it when we were going to Boston, and then Washington, and then when he got this new job, I thought maybe this is it, maybe *this* is the time when I get to take the boy out of that rotten school and pay the bills and move out of those bum hotels we've been living in. For fifteen years I've been planning to use this cake of soap. Well, last week I was looking through my bureau drawers and I saw this cake of soap. It was all cracked. I threw it out. I threw it out because I knew I was never going to have a chance to use it. Do you realize what that means? Do you know what that feels like? To live for fifteen years on promises and expectations and loans and credits in hotels that aren't fit to live in, never for a single day to be out of debt, and yet to pretend, to feel that every year, every winter, every job, every meeting is going to be the one. To live like this for fifteen years and then to realize that it's never going to end. Do you know what that feels like?" She got up and went over to the dressing table and stood in

Westchester: a prosperous and fashionable residential county near New York City.

front of Laura. Tears had risen into her large eyes, and her voice was harsh and loud. "I'm never going to get to Bermuda," she said. "I'm never even going to get to Florida. I'm never going to get out of hock, ever, ever, *ever*. I know that I'm never going to have a decent home and that everything I own that is worn and torn and no good is going to stay that way. I know that for the rest of my life, for the rest of my life, I'm going to wear ragged slips and torn nightgowns and torn underclothes and shoes that hurt me. I know that for the rest of my life nobody is going to come up to me and tell me that I've got on a pretty dress, because I'm not going to be able to afford that kind of a dress. I know that for the rest of my life every taxi driver and doorman and headwaiter in this town is going to know in a minute that I haven't got five bucks in that black imitation-suede purse that I've been brushing and brushing and brushing and carrying around for ten years. How do you get it? How do you rate it? What's so wonderful about you that you get a break like this?" She ran her fingers down Laura's bare arm. The dress she was wearing smelled of benzine. "Can I rub it off you? Will that make me lucky? I swear to Jesus I'd murder somebody if I thought it would bring us in any money. I'd wring somebody's neck—yours, anybody's—I swear to Jesus I would—"

Someone began knocking on the door. Alice strode to the door, opened it, and went out. A woman came in, a stranger looking for the toilet. Laura lighted a cigarette and waited in the bedroom for about ten minutes before she went back to the party. The Holinsheds had gone. She got a drink and sat down and tried to talk, but she couldn't keep her mind on what she was saying.

The hunt, the search for money that had seemed to her natural, amiable, and fair when they first committed themselves to it, now seemed like a hazardous and piratical voyage. She had thought, earlier in the evening, of the missing. She thought now of the missing again. Adversity and failure accounted for more than half of them, as if beneath the amenities in the pretty room a keen race were in progress, in which the loser's forfeits were extreme. Laura felt cold. She picked the ice out of her drink with her fingers and put it in a flower vase, but the whiskey didn't warm her. She asked Ralph to take her home.

After dinner on Tuesday, Laura washed the dishes and Ralph dried them. He read the paper and she took up some sewing. At a quarter after eight, the telephone, in the bedroom, rang, and he went to it calmly. It was someone with two theater tickets for a show that was closing. The telephone didn't ring again, and at half past nine he told Laura that he was going to call California. It didn't take long for the connection to be made, and the fresh voice of a young woman spoke to him from Mr. Hadaam's number. "Oh, yes, Mr. Whittemore," she said. "We tried to get you earlier in the evening but your line was busy."

"Could I speak to Mr. Hadaam?"

"No, Mr. Whittemore. This is Mr. Hadaam's secretary. I know he meant to call you, because he had entered this in his engagement book. Mrs. Hadaam has asked me to disappoint as few people as possible, and I've tried to take care of all the calls and appointments in his engagement book. Mr. Hadaam had a stroke on Sunday. We don't expect him to recover. I imagine he made you some kind of promise, but I'm afraid he won't be able to keep it."

"I'm very sorry," Ralph said. He hung up.

Laura had come into the bedroom while the secretary was talking. "Oh, darling!" she said. She put her sewing basket on the bureau and went toward the closet. Then she went back and looked for something in the sewing basket and left the basket on her dressing table. Then she took off her shoes, treed them, slipped her dress over her head and hung it up neatly. The she went to the bureau, looking for her sewing basket, found it on the dressing table, and took it into the closet, where she put it on a shelf. Then she took her brush and comb into the bathroom and began to run the water for a bath.

The lash of frustration was laid on and the pain stunned Ralph. He sat by the telephone for he did not know how long. He heard Laura come out of the bathroom. He turned when he heard her speak.

"I feel dreadfully about old Mr. Hadaam," she said. "I wish there were something we could do." She was in her nightgown, and she sat down at the dressing table like a skillful and patient woman establishing herself in front of a loom, and she picked up and put down pins and bottles and combs and brushes with the thoughtless dexterity of an experienced weaver, as if the time she spent there were all part of a continuous operation. "It did look like the treasure. . ."

The word surprised him, and for a moment he saw the chimera, the pot of gold, the fleece, the treasure buried in the faint lights of a rainbow, and the primitivism of his hunt struck him. Armed with a sharp spade and a home-made divining rod, he had climbed over hill and dale, through droughts and rain squalls, digging wherever the maps he had drawn himself promised gold. Six paces east of the dead pine, five panels in from the library door, underneath the creaking step, in the roots of the pear tree, beneath the grape arbor lay the bean pot full of doubloons and bullion.

She turned on the stool and held her thin arms toward him, as she had done more than a thousand times. She was no longer young, and more wan, thinner than she might have been if he had found the doubloons to save her anxiety and unremitting work. Her smile, her naked shoulders had begun to trouble the indecipherable shapes and symbols that are the touchstones of desire, and the light from the lamp seemed to brighten and give off heat and shed that unaccountable complacency, that benevolence, that the spring sunlight brings to all kinds of fatigue and despair. Desire for her delighted and confused him. Here it was, here it all was, and the shine of the gold seemed to him then to be all around her arms.

QUESTIONS

1. The first two paragraphs present the characters of the Whittemores directly. Are the qualities ascribed to them, individually and collectively, dramatized in the story? Discuss and illustrate.

2. How good a marriage do Ralph and Laura have, as exhibited before the climax of the story? What is shown about them and their marriage by the account of their courtship, their domestic life, their recreations, their relationships with uncles and aunts, the stability of their address as compared with that of the owner of the Venetian blind formula patent, the account of the "Missing" at the Monday night party?

3. Three of Ralph's many prospects and "adventures" are described in detail. Why? Why three? Why these three? Do they support the narrator's statement (page 92) that Ralph's failures were "not his own fault"? How do Ralph and Laura handle their anticipations and their disappointment in each? How does the first foreshadow the last?

4. Discuss the three stages of Laura's relationship with Alice Holinshed. What is Laura's initial reaction to Alice? How are the two women alike? How are they different? What is changed when they resume their friendship after the war? How does their last meeting affect Laura? Why? Is Alice a developing character?

5. How is Laura changed by her experiences at the Monday night party? How is Ralph changed by Laura's words and actions after his last disappointment? What is meant by the final sentence of the story? Is the change in Ralph and Laura large or small? significant or insignificant? How do they contrast as developing characters with Alice Holinshed?

6. How does the New York setting support the theme of the story? Why have Ralph and Laura each come there? Point out passages in which Cheever exhibits an especially keen sense of setting, and show how that setting is used for more than mere background.

7. Discuss the title of the story. Why is it better than, say, "The Golden Fleece" or "The Treasure " or "The Buried Gold"?

4. Theme

"Daddy, the man next door kisses his wife every morning when he leaves for work. Why don't you do that?"

"Gracious, little one, I don't even know the woman."

"Daughter, your young man stays until a very late hour. Hasn't your mother said anything to you about this habit of his?"

"Yes, father. Mother says men haven't altered a bit."

For readers who contemplate the two jokes above, a significant difference emerges between them. The first joke depends only upon a reversal of expectation. We expect the man to explain why he doesn't kiss his wife; instead he explains why he doesn't kiss his neighbor's wife. The second joke, though it contains a reversal of expectation, depends as much or more for its effectiveness on a truth about human life; namely, that *men tend to grow more conservative as they grow older,* or that *fathers often scold their children for doing exactly what they did themselves when young.* This truth, which might be stated in different ways, is the *theme* of the joke.

The THEME of a piece of fiction is its controlling idea or its central insight. It is the unifying generalization about life stated or implied by the story. To derive the theme of a story, we must ask what its central *purpose* is: what view of life it supports or what insight into life it reveals.

Not all stories have theme. The purpose of a horror story may be simply to scare readers, to give them gooseflesh. The purpose of an adventure story may be simply to carry readers through a series of exciting escapades. The purpose of a murder mystery may be simply to pose a problem for readers to try to solve (and to prevent them from solving it, if possible, until the last paragraph). The purpose of some stories may be simply to provide suspense or to make readers laugh or to surprise them with a sudden twist at the end. Theme exists only (1) when an author has seriously attempted to record life accurately or to reveal some truth about it or (2) when an author has deliberately introduced as a unifying element some concept or theory of life that the story is meant to illustrate. Theme exists in all interpretive fiction but only in some escape fiction. In interpretive fiction it is the purpose of the story; in escape fiction, when it exists, it is merely an excuse, a peg to hang the story from.

In many stories the theme may be equivalent to the revelation of human character. If a story has as its central purpose to exhibit a certain kind of human being, our statement of theme may be no more than a concentrated description of the person revealed, with the addition, "Some people are like this." Frequently, however, a story through its portrayal of specific persons in specific situations will have something to say about the nature of all human beings or about their relationship to each other or to the universe. Whatever central generalization about life arises from the specifics of the story constitutes theme.

The theme of a story, like its plot, may be stated very briefly or at greater length. With a simple or very brief story, we may be satisfied to sum up the theme in a single sentence. With a more complex story, if it is successfully unified, we can still state the theme in a single sentence, but we may feel that a paragraph—or occasionally even an essay—is needed to state it adequately. A rich story will give us many and complex insights into life. In stating the theme in a sentence, we must pick the *central* insight, the one that explains the greatest number of elements in the story and relates them to each other. For theme is what gives a story its unity. In any story at all complex, however, we are likely to feel that a one-sentence statement of theme leaves out a great part of the story's meaning. Though the theme of *Othello* may be expressed as "Jealousy exacts a terrible cost," such a statement does not begin to suggest the range and depth of Shakespeare's play. Any successful story is a good deal more and means a good deal more than any one-sentence statement of theme that we may extract from it, for the story will modify and expand this statement in various and subtle ways.

We must never think, once we have stated the theme of a story, that the whole purpose of the story has been to yield up this abstract statement. If this were so, there would be no reason for the story: we could stop with the abstract statement. The function of interpretive writers is not to state a theme but to vivify it. They wish to deliver it not simply to our intellects but to our emotions, our senses, and our imaginations. The theme of a story may be little or nothing except as it is embodied and vitalized by the story. Unembodied, it is a dry backbone, without flesh or life.

Sometimes the theme of a story is explicitly stated somewhere in the story, either by the author or by one of the characters. In "The Black Madonna" the opening line of the second paragraph might serve as a very broad statement of theme: "Zambesia is a tough, sunburnt, virile, positive country contemptuous of subtleties and sensibility." The story of Captain Stocker, though it may slightly modify that statement, is essentially a confirmation of it. More often, however, the theme is implied. Story writers, after all, are story writers, not essayists or philosophers. Their first business is to reveal life, not to comment on it. They may well feel that unless the story somehow expresses its own meaning, without their having to point it out, they have not told the story well. Or they may feel that if the story is to have its maximum emotional effect, they must refrain from interrupting it or making remarks about it. They are also wary of spoiling a story for perceptive readers by "explaining" it as some people ruin jokes by explaining them. For these reasons theme is more often left implicit than stated explicitly. Good writers do not ordinarily write a story to "illustrate" a theme, as do the writers of parables or fables. They write stories to bring alive some segment of human existence. When they do so searchingly and coherently, theme arises naturally out of what they have written. Good readers may state the generalizations for themselves.

Some readers—especially student readers—look for a "moral" in everything they read—some rule of conduct that they regard as applicable to their lives. They consider the words "theme" and "moral" to be interchangeable. Sometimes the words are interchangeable. Occasionally the theme of a story may be expressed as a moral principle without doing violence to the story. More frequently, however, the word "moral" is too narrow to fit the kind of illumination provided by a first-rate story. It is hardly suitable, for instance, for the kind of story that simply displays human character. Such terms as "moral" and "lesson" and "message" are therefore best avoided in the discussion of fiction. The critical term THEME is preferable for several reasons. First, it is less likely to obscure the fact that a story is not a preachment or a sermon: a story's *first* object is enjoyment. Second, it should keep us from trying to wring from every story a didactic pronouncement about life. The person who seeks a moral in every story is likely to oversimplify and conventionalize it—to reduce it to some dusty platitude like "Be kind to animals" or "Look before you leap" or "Crime does not pay." The purpose of interpretive story writers is to give us a greater awareness and a greater understanding of life, not to inculcate a code of moral rules for regulating daily conduct. In getting at the theme of the story it is better to ask not *What does this story teach?* but *What does this story reveal?* Readers who interpret Anderson's "I'm a Fool" as being merely a warning against lying have missed nine-tenths of the story. It is really a marvelously penetrating exploration of a complex personality. The theme is *not* "Honesty is the best policy" but something more like this: "A young man of respectable background who fails in various enterprises may develop ambivalent or contradictory values as well as feelings of inferiority. Consciously or unconsciously he will adopt various stratagems to compensate for these feelings by magnifying his importance both in his own eyes and in the eyes of others. If these stratagems backfire, he may recognize his folly but not the underlying reasons for it." Obviously, this dry statement is a poor thing beside the living reality of the story. But it is a more faithful abstracting of the content of the story than any "moral."

The revelation offered by a good story may be something fresh or something old. The story may bring us some insight into life that we had not had before, and thus expand our horizons, or it may make us *feel* or *feel again* some truth of which we have long been merely intellectually aware. We may know in our minds, for instance, that "War is horrible" or that "Old age is often pathetic and in need of understanding," but these are insights that need to be periodically renewed. *Emotionally* we may forget them, and if we do, we are less alive and complete as human beings. Story writers perform a service for us—interpret life for us—whether they give us new insights or refresh and extend old ones.

The themes of commercial and quality stories may be identical, but frequently they are different. Commercial stories, for the most part, confirm their readers' prejudices, endorse their opinions, ratify their feelings, and satisfy their wishes. Usually, therefore, the themes of such stories are widely accepted platitudes of experience that may or may not be supported by the life around us. They represent life as we would like it to be, not always as it is. We should certainly like to believe, for instance, that "Motherhood is sacred," that "True love always wins through," that "Virtue and hard work are rewarded in the end," that "Cheaters never win," that "Old age brings a mellow wisdom that compensates for its infirmity," and that "Every human being has a soft spot in him somewhere." Interpretive writers, however, being thoughtful observers of life, are likely to question these beliefs and often to challenge them. Their ideas about life are not simply taken over ready-made from what they were taught in Sunday school or from the books they read as children; they are the formulations of sensitive and independent observers who have collated all that they have read and been taught with life itself. The themes of their stories therefore do not often correspond to the pretty little sentiments we find inscribed on candy valentines. They may sometimes represent rather somber truths. Much of the process of maturing as a reader lies in the discovery that there may be more nourishment and deeper enjoyment in assimilating these somber truths than in licking the sugar off of candy valentines.

We do not, however, have to accept the theme of an interpretive story any more than we do that of a commercial story. Though we should never summarily dismiss it without reflection, we may find that the theme of a story represents a judgment on life with which, on examination, we cannot agree. If it is the reasoned view of a seasoned and serious artist, nevertheless, it cannot be without value to us. There is value in knowing what the world looks like to others, and we can thus use a judgment to expand our knowledge of human experience even though we cannot ourselves accept it. Genuine artists and thoughtful observers, moreover, can hardly fail to present us with partial insights along the way although we disagree with the total view. Good readers, therefore, will not reject a story because they reject its theme. They can enjoy any story that arises from sufficient depth of observation and reflection and is artistically composed, though they disagree with its theme; and they will prefer it to a shallower, less thoughtful, or less successfully integrated story that presents a theme they endorse.

Discovering and stating the theme of a story is often a delicate task. Sometimes we will *feel* what the story is about strongly enough and yet find it difficult to put this feeling into words. If we are skilled readers, it is perhaps unnecessary that we do so. The bare statement of the theme, so lifeless and impoverished when abstracted from the story, may seem to diminish the story to something less than it is. Often, however, the attempt to state a theme will reveal to us aspects of a story that we should otherwise not have noticed and will thereby lead to more thorough understanding. The ability to state theme, moreover, is a test of our understanding of a story. Beginning readers often think they understand a story when in actuality they have misunderstood it. They understand the events but not what the events add up to. Or, in adding up the events, they arrive at an erroneous total. People sometimes miss the point of a joke. It is not surprising that they should frequently miss the point of a good piece of fiction, which is many times more complex than a joke.

There is no prescribed method for discovering theme. Sometimes we can best get at it by asking in what way the main character has changed in the course of the story and what, if anything, the character has learned before its end. Sometimes the best approach is to explore the nature of the central conflict and its outcome. Sometimes the title will provide an important clue. At all times we should keep in mind the following principles:

1. Theme must be expressible in the form of a statement with a subject and a predicate. It is insufficient to say that the theme of a story is motherhood or loyalty to country. Motherhood and loyalty are simply subjects. Theme must be a statement *about* the subject. For instance, "Motherhood sometimes has more frustrations than rewards" or "Loyalty to country often inspires heroic self-sacrifice." If we express the theme in the form of a phrase, the phrase must be convertible to sentence form. A phrase such as "the futility of envy," for instance, may be converted to the statement "Envy is futile": it may therefore serve as a statement of theme.

2. The theme must be stated as a *generalization* about life. In stating theme we do not use the names of the characters or refer to precise places or events, for to do so is to make a specific rather than a general statement. The theme of "The Destructors" is not that "The Wormsley Common Gang of London, in the aftermath of World War II, found a creative outlet in destroying a beautiful two-hundred-year-old house designed by Sir Christopher Wren." Rather, it is something like this: "The dislocations caused by a devastating war may produce among the young a conscious or unconscious rebellion against all the values of the reigning society—a rebellion in which the creative instincts are channeled into destructive enterprises."

3. We must be careful not to make the generalization larger than is justified by the terms of the story. Terms like *every, all, always* should be used very cautiously; terms like *some, sometimes, may* are often more accurate. The theme of "The Japanese Quince" is not that "Spring stirs vague longings in the hearts of all people," for we are presented with only two instances in the story. In this particular story, however, the two people, by their similarity in appearance, dress, and manner, are clearly meant to be representative of a social class, and, when we come to speak of how they respond to these stirrings, we may generalize a little more broadly. The theme might be expressed thus: "In springtime there occa-

sionally comes to those upper-middle-class people whose lives are bound by respectability and regulated by convention a peculiar impulse toward life, freedom, and beauty; but the impulse is seldom strong enough to overcome the deep-seated forces of habit and convention." Notice that we have said *seldom*, not *never*. Only occasionally will the theme of a story be expressible as a universal generalization. In "The Child by Tiger" we know from Wolfe's use of Blake's poem and from his concluding paragraphs that the author considers Dick Prosser not as a special case but as a symbol of something present in us all. The soul of every man (so the story seems to say) is mysterious in its origins and contains unfathomed possibilities for evil and violence as well as for innocence and love.

4. Theme is the *central* and *unifying* concept of a story. Therefore (a) it must account for all the major details of the story. If we cannot explain the bearing of an important incident or character on the theme, either in exemplifying it or modifying it in some way, it is probable that our interpretation is partial and incomplete, that at best we have got hold only of a subtheme. Another alternative, though it must be used with caution, is that the story itself is imperfectly constructed and lacks entire unity. (b) The theme must not be contradicted by any detail of the story. If we have to overlook or blink at or "force" the meaning of some significant detail in order to frame our statement, we may be sure that our statement is defective. (c) The theme must not rely upon supposed facts—facts not actually stated or clearly implied by the story. The theme must exist *inside*, not *outside*, the story. It must be based on the data of the story itself, not on assumptions supplied from our own experience.

5. There is no *one* way of stating the theme of a story. The story is not a guessing game or an acrostic that is supposed to yield some magic verbal formula that won't work if a syllable is changed. It merely presents a view of life, and, as long as the above conditions are fulfilled, that view may surely be stated in more than one way. Here, for instance, are three possible ways of stating the theme of "The Pot of Gold." (a) "Youthful self-confidence and dreams of success may linger into middle age despite disappointing brushes with reality, but the shattering of such dreams can lead to new values." (b) "The love of two people for each other is a more worthwhile object of desire than business success or financial prosperity." (c) "There is something primitive, delusive, and piratical in the search for money, whereas true contentment may be found in mutual love."

6. We should avoid any statement that reduces the theme to some familiar saying that we have heard all our lives, such as "You can't judge a book by its cover" or "A stitch in time saves nine." Although such a statement *may* express the theme accurately, too often it is simply the lazy

man's shortcut, which impoverishes the essential meaning of the story in order to save mental effort. When readers force every new experience into an old formula, they lose the chance for a fresh perception. Instead of letting the story expand their knowledge and awareness of the world, they fall back dully on a cliché. To come out with "Honesty is the best policy" as the theme of "I'm a Fool" is almost to lose the whole value of the story. If the impulse arises to express the meaning of a story in a ready-made phrase, it should be suppressed.

Alice Munro
AN OUNCE OF CURE

My parents didn't drink. They weren't rabid about it, and in fact I remember that when I signed the pledge in grade seven, with the rest of that superbly if impermanently indoctrinated class, my mother said, "It's just nonsense and fanaticism, children of that age." My father would drink a beer on a hot day, but my mother did not join him, and—whether accidentally or symbolically—this drink was always consumed *outside* the house. Most of the people we knew were the same, in the small town where we lived. I ought not to say that it was this which got me into difficulties, because the difficulties I got into were a faithful expression of my own incommodious nature—the same nature that caused my mother to look at me, on any occasion which traditionally calls for feelings of pride and maternal accomplishment (my departure for my first formal dance, I mean, or my hellbent preparations for a descent on college) with an expression of brooding and fascinated despair, as if she could not possibly expect, did not ask, that it should go with me as it did with other girls; the dreamed-of spoils of daughters—orchids, nice boys, diamond rings—would be borne home in due course by the daughters of her friends, but not by me; all she could do was hope for a lesser rather than a greater disaster—an elopement, say, with a boy who could never earn his living, rather than an abduction into the White Slave trade.

But ignorance, my mother said, ignorance, or innocence if you like, is not always such a fine thing as people think and I am not sure it may not be dangerous for a girl like you; then she emphasized her point, as she had a habit of doing, with some quotation which had an innocent pomposity and odor of mothballs. I didn't even wince at it, knowing full well how it must have worked wonders with Mr. Berryman.

AN OUNCE OF CURE First published in 1961. Alice Munro was born (1931) and grew up in Wingham, Ontario. She attended the University of Western Ontario for two years, was married in 1951, and has three daughters. Many of her stories are set in southwestern Ontario.

The evening I baby-sat for the Berrymans must have been in April. I had been in love all year, or at least since the first week in September, when a boy named Martin Collingwood had given me a surprised, appreciative, and rather ominously complacent smile in the school assembly. I never knew what surprised him; I was not looking like anybody but me; I had an old blouse on and my home-permanent had turned out badly. A few weeks after that he took me out for the first time, and kissed me on the dark side of the porch—also, I ought to say, on the mouth; I am sure it was the first time anybody had ever kissed me effectively, and I know that I did not wash my face that night or the next morning, in order to keep the imprint of those kisses intact. (I showed the most painful banality in the conduct of this whole affair, as you will see.) Two months, and a few amatory stages later, he dropped me. He had fallen for the girl who played opposite him in the Christmas production of *Pride and Prejudice*.

I said I was not going to have anything to do with that play, and I got another girl to work on Makeup in my place, but of course I went to it after all, and sat down in front with my girl friend Joyce, who pressed my hand when I was overcome with pain and delight at the sight of Mr. Darcy in white breeches, silk waistcoat, and sideburns. It was surely seeing Martin as Darcy that did for me; every girl is in love with Darcy anyway, and the part gave Martin an arrogance and male splendor in my eyes which made it impossible to remember that he was simply a high-school senior, passably good-looking and of medium intelligence (and with a reputation slightly tainted, at that, by such preferences as the Drama Club and the Cadet *Band*) who happened to be the first boy, the first really presentable boy, to take an interest in me. In the last act they gave him a chance to embrace Elizabeth (Mary Bishop, with a sallow complexion and no figure, but big vivacious eyes) and during this realistic encounter I dug my nails bitterly into Joyce's sympathetic palm.

That night was the beginning of months of real, if more or less self-inflicted, misery for me. Why is it a temptation to refer to this sort of thing lightly, with irony, with amazement even, at finding oneself involved with such preposterous emotions in the unaccountable past? That is what we are apt to do, speaking of love; with adolescent love, of course, it's practically obligatory; you would think we sat around, dull afternoons, amusing ourselves with these tidbit recollections of pain. But it really doesn't make me feel very gay—worse still, it doesn't really surprise me—to remember all the stupid, sad, half-ashamed things I did, that people in love always do. I hung around the places where he might be seen, and then pretended not to see him; I made absurdly roundabout approaches, in conversation, to the bitter pleasure of casually mentioning his name. I daydreamed endlessly; in fact if you want to put it mathematically, I spent perhaps ten times as many hours thinking about Martin Collingwood—yes, pining and weeping for him—as I ever spent with him; the idea of him dominated my mind relentlessly and, after a while, against my will. For if at first I had dramatized my feelings, the time came when I would have been glad to escape them; my well-worn daydreams had become depressing and not even temporarily consoling. As I worked my math problems I would torture myself, quite mechanically and helplessly, with an exact recollection of Martin kissing my throat. I had an exact recollection of *everything*. One night I had an impulse to swallow all the aspirins in the bathroom cabinet, but stopped after I had taken six.

My mother noticed that something was wrong and got me some iron pills. She said, "Are you sure everything is going all right at school?" *School!* When I told her that Martin and I had broken up all she said was, "Well so much the better for that. I never saw a boy so stuck on himself." "Martin has enough conceit to sink a battleship," I said morosely and went upstairs and cried.

The night I went to the Berrymans was a Saturday night. I baby-sat for them quite often on Saturday nights because they liked to drive over to Baileyville, a much bigger, livelier town about twenty miles away, and perhaps have supper and go to a show. They had been living in our town only two or three years—Mr. Berryman had been brought in as plant manager of the new door-factory—and they remained, I suppose by choice, on the fringes of its society; most of their friends were youngish couples like themselves, born in other places, who lived in new ranch-style houses on a hill outside town where we used to go tobogganing. This Saturday night they had two other couples in for drinks before they all drove over to Baileyville for the opening of a new supper-club; they were all rather festive. I sat in the kitchen and pretended to do Latin. Last night had been the Spring Dance at the High School. I had not gone, since the only boy who had asked me was Millerd Crompton, who asked so many girls that he was suspected of working his way through the whole class alphabetically. But the dance was held in the Armories, which was only half a block away from our house; I had been able to see the boys in dark suits, the girls in long pale formals under their coats, passing gravely under the street-lights, stepping around the last patches of snow. I could even hear the music and I have not forgotten to this day that they played "Ballerina," and—oh, song of my aching heart—"Slow Boat to China." Joyce had phoned me up this morning and told me in her hushed way (we might have been discussing an incurable disease I had) that yes, M.C. *had* been there with M.B., and she had on a formal that must have been made out of somebody's old lace tablecloth, it just *hung*.

When the Berrymans and their friends had gone I went into the living room and read a magazine. I was mortally depressed. The big softly lit room, with its green and leaf-brown colors, made an uncluttered setting for the development of the emotions, such as you would get on a stage. At home the life of the emotions went on all right, but it always seemed to get buried under the piles of mending to be done, the ironing, the children's jigsaw puzzles and rock collections. It was the sort of house where people were always colliding with one another on the stairs and listening to hockey games and Superman on the radio.

I got up and found the Berrymans' "Danse Macabre" and put it on the record player and turned out the living-room lights. The curtains were only partly drawn. A street light shone obliquely on the windowpane, making a rectangle of thin dusty gold, in which the shadows of bare branches moved, caught in the huge sweet winds of spring. It was a mild black night when the last snow was melting. A year ago all this—the music, the wind and darkness, the shadows of the branches—would have given me tremendous happiness; when they did not do so now, but only called up tediously familiar, somehow humiliatingly personal thoughts, I gave up my soul for dead and walked into the kitchen and decided to get drunk.

No, it was not like that. I walked into the kitchen to look for a coke or something in the refrigerator, and there on the front of the counter were three tall beautiful bottles, all about half full of gold. But even after I had looked at them and lifted them to feel their weight I had not decided to get drunk; I had decided to have a drink.

Now here is where my ignorance, my disastrous innocence, comes in. It is true that I had seen the Berrymans and their friends drinking their highballs as casually as I would drink a coke, but I did not apply this attitude to myself. No; I thought of hard liquor as something to be taken in extremities, and relied upon for extravagant results, one way or another. My approach could not have been less casual if I had been the Little Mermaid drinking the witch's crystal potion. Gravely, with a glance at my set face in the black window above the sink, I poured a little whisky from each of the bottles (I think now there were two brands of rye and an expensive Scotch) until I had my glass full. For I had never in my life seen anyone pour a drink and I had no idea that people frequently diluted their liquor with water, soda, et cetera, and I had seen that the glasses the Berrymans' guests were holding when I came through the living room were nearly full.

I drank it off as quickly as possible. I set the glass down and stood looking at my face in the window, half expecting to see it altered. My throat was burning, but I felt nothing else. It was very disappointing, when I had worked myself up to it. But I then filled each of the bottles with water to approximately the level I had seen when I came in. I drank the second glass only a little more slowly than the first. I put the empty glass down on the counter with care, perhaps feeling in my head a rustle of things to come, and went and sat down on a chair in the living room. I reached up and turned on a floor lamp beside the chair, and the room jumped on me.

When I say that I was expecting extravagant results I do not mean that I was expecting this. I had thought of some sweeping emotional change, an upsurge of gaiety and irresponsibility, a feeling of lawlessness and escape, accompanied by a little dizziness and perhaps a tendency to giggle out loud. I did not have in mind the ceiling spinning like a great plate somebody had thrown at me, nor the pale green blobs of the chairs swelling, converging, disintegrating, playing with me a game full of enormous senseless inanimate malice. My head sank back; I closed my eyes. And at once opened them, opened them wide, threw myself out of the chair and down the hall and reached—thank God, thank God!—the Berrymans' bathroom, where I was sick everywhere, everywhere, and dropped like a stone.

From this point on I have no continuous picture of what happened; my memories of the next hour or two are split into vivid and improbable segments, with nothing but murk and uncertainty between. I do remember lying on the bathroom floor looking sideways at the little six-sided white tiles, which lay together in such an admirable and logical pattern, seeing them with the brief broken gratitude and sanity of one who had just been torn to pieces with vomiting. Then I remember sitting on the stool in front of the hall phone, asking weakly for Joyce's number. Joyce was not home. I was told by her mother (a rather rattlebrained woman, who didn't seem to notice a thing the matter—for which I felt weakly, mechanically grateful) that she was at Kay Stringer's house. I didn't know Kay's number so I just asked the operator; I felt I couldn't risk looking down at the telephone book.

Kay Stringer was not a friend of mine but a new friend of Joyce's. She had a vague reputation for wildness and a long switch of hair, very oddly, though naturally, colored—from soap-yellow to caramel-brown. She knew a lot of boys more exciting than Martin Collingwood, boys who had quit school or been imported into town to play on the hockey team. She and Joyce rode around in these boys' cars, and sometimes went with them—having lied of course to their mothers—to the Gay-la dance hall on the highway north of town.

I got Joyce on the phone. She was very keyed-up, as she always was with boys around, and she hardly seemed to hear what I was saying.

"Oh, I can't tonight," she said. "Some kids are here. We're going to play cards. You know Bill Kline? He's here. Ross Armour—"

"I'm *sick*," I said trying to speak distinctly; it came out an inhuman croak. "I'm *drunk*. Joyce!" Then I fell off the stool and the receiver dropped out of my hand and banged for a while dismally against the wall.

I had not told Joyce where I was, so after thinking about it for a moment she phoned my mother, and using the elaborate and unnecessary subterfuge that young girls delight in, she found out. She and Kay and the boys—there were three of them—told some story about where they were going to Kay's mother, and got into the car and drove out. They found me still lying on the broadloom carpet in the hall; I had been sick again, and this time I had not made it to the bathroom.

It turned out that Kay Stringer, who arrived on this scene only by accident, was exactly the person I needed. She loved a crisis, particularly one like this, which had a shady and scandalous aspect and which must be kept secret from the adult world. She became excited, aggressive, efficient; that energy which was termed wildness was simply the overflow of a great female instinct to manage, comfort and control. I could hear her voice coming at me from all directions, telling me not to worry, telling Joyce to find the biggest coffeepot they had and make it full of coffee (*strong* coffee, she said), telling the boys to pick me up and carry me to the sofa. Later, in the fog beyond my reach, she was calling for a scrub-brush.

Then I was lying on the sofa, covered with some kind of crocheted throw they had found in the bedroom. I didn't want to lift my head. The house was full of the smell of coffee. Joyce came in, looking very pale; she said that the Berryman kids had wakened up but she had given them a cookie and told them to go back to bed, it was all right; she hadn't let them out of their room and she didn't believe they'd remember. She said that she and Kay had cleaned up the bathroom and the hall though she was afraid there was still a spot on the rug. The coffee was ready. I didn't understand anything very well. The boys had turned on the radio and were going through the Berrymans' record collection; they had it out on the floor. I felt there was something odd about this but I could not think what it was.

Kay brought me a huge breakfast mug full of coffee.

"I don't know if I can," I said. "Thanks."

"Sit up," she said briskly, as if dealing with drunks was an everyday business for her, I had no need to feel myself important. (I met, and recognized, that tone of voice years later, in the maternity ward.) "Now drink," she said. I drank, and at the same time realized that I was wearing only my slip. Joyce and Kay had taken off my blouse and skirt. They had brushed off the skirt and washed out the blouse, since it was nylon; it was hanging in the bathroom. I pulled the throw up under my arms and Kay laughed. She got everybody coffee. Joyce brought in the coffeepot and on Kay's instructions she kept filling my cup whenever I drank from it. Somebody said to me with interest. "You must have really wanted to tie one on."

"No," I said rather sulkily, obediently drinking my coffee. "I only had two drinks."

Kay laughed, "Well it certainly gets to you, I'll say that. What time do you expect *they'll* be back?" she said.

"Late. After one I think."

"You should be all right by that time. Have some more coffee."

Kay and one of the boys began dancing to the radio. Kay danced very sexily, but her face had the gently superior and indulgent, rather cold look it had when she was lifting me up to drink the coffee. The boy was whispering to her and she was smiling, shaking her head. Joyce said she was hungry, and she went out to the kitchen to see what there was—potato chips or crackers, or something like that, that you could eat without making too noticeable a dint. Bill Kline came over and sat on the sofa beside me and patted my legs through the crocheted throw. He didn't say anything to me, just patted my legs and looked at me with what seemed to me a very stupid, half-sick, absurd and alarming expression. I felt very uncomfortable; I wondered how it had ever got around that Bill Kline was so good looking, with an expression like that. I moved my legs nervously and he gave me a look of contempt, not ceasing to pat me. Then I scrambled off the sofa, pulling the throw around me, with the idea of going to the bathroom to see if my blouse was dry. I lurched a little when I started to walk, and for some reason—probably to show Bill Kline that he had not panicked me—I immediately exaggerated this, and calling out, "Watch me walk a straight line!" I lurched and stumbled, to the accompaniment of everyone's laughter, towards the hall. I was standing in the archway between the hall and the living room when the knob of the front door turned with a small matter-of-fact click and everything became silent behind me except the radio of course and the crocheted throw inspired by some delicate malice of its own slithered down around my feet and there—oh, delicious moment in a well-organized farce!—there stood the Berrymans, Mr. and Mrs., with expressions on their faces as appropriate to the occasion as any old-fashioned director of farces could wish. They must have been preparing those expressions, of course; they could not have produced them in the first moment of shock; with the noise we were making, they had no doubt heard us as soon as they got out of the car; for the same reason, we had not heard them. I don't think I ever knew what brought them home so early—a headache, an argument—and I was not really in a position to ask.

Mr. Berryman drove me home. I don't remember how I got into that car, or how I found my clothes and put them on, or what kind of a good-night, if any, I said to Mrs. Berryman. I don't remember what happened to my friends, though I imagine they gathered up their coats and fled, covering up the ignominy of their departure with a mechanical roar of defiance. I remember Joyce with a box of crackers in her hand, saying that I had become terribly sick from eating—I think she said *sauerkraut*—for supper, and that I had called them for help. (When I asked her later what they made of this she said, "It wasn't any use. You *reeked*.") I remember also her saying, "Oh, no, Mr. Berryman I beg of you, my mother is a terribly nervous person. I don't know what the shock might do to her. I will go down on my knees to you if you like but *you must not phone my mother*." I have no picture of her down on her knees—and she would have done it in a minute—so it seems this threat was not carried out.

Mr. Berryman said to me, "Well I guess you know your behavior tonight is a pretty serious thing." He made it sound as if I might be charged with criminal negligence or something worse. "It would be very wrong of me to overlook it," he said. I suppose that besides being angry and disgusted with *me*, he was worried about taking me home in this condition to my strait-laced parents, who could always say I got the liquor in his house. Plenty of Temperance people would think that enough to hold him responsible, and the town was full of Temperance people. Good relations with the town were very important to him from a business point of view.

"I have an idea it wasn't the first time," he said. "If it was the first time, would a girl be smart enough to fill three bottles up with water? No. Well in this case, she *was* smart enough, but not smart enough to know I could spot it. What do you say to that?" I opened my mouth to answer and although I was feeling quite sober the only sound that came out was a loud, desolate-sounding giggle. He stopped in front of our house. "Light's on," he said. "Now go in and tell your parents the straight truth. And if you don't, remember I will." He did not mention paying me for my baby-sitting services of the evening and the subject did not occur to me either.

I went into the house and tried to go straight upstairs but my mother called to me. She came into the front hall, where I had not turned on the light, and she must have smelled me at once for she ran forward with a cry of pure amazement, as if she had seen somebody falling, and caught me by the shoulders as I did indeed fall down against the banister, overwhelmed by my fantastic lucklessness, and I told her everything from the start, not omitting even the name of Martin Collingwood and my flirtation with the aspirin bottle, which was a mistake.

On Monday morning my mother took the bus over to Baileyville and found the liquor store and bought a bottle of Scotch whisky. Then she had to wait for a bus back, and she met some people she knew and she was not quite able to hide the bottle in her bag; she was furious with herself for not bringing a proper shopping-bag. As soon as she got back she walked out to the Berrymans'; she had not even had lunch. Mr. Berryman had not gone back to the factory. My mother went in and had a talk with both of them and made an excellent impression and then Mr. Berryman drove her home. She talked to them in the forthright and unemotional way she had, which was always agreeably surprising to people prepared to deal with a mother, and she told them that although I seemed to do well enough at school I was extremely backward—or perhaps eccentric—in my emotional development. I imagine that this analysis of my behavior was especially effective with Mrs. Berryman, a great reader of Child Guidance books. Relations between them warmed to the point where my mother brought up a specific instance of my difficulties, and disarmingly related the whole story of Martin Collingwood.

Within a few days it was all over town and the school that I had tried to commit suicide over Martin Collingwood. But it was already all over school and the town that the Berrymans had come home on Saturday night to find me drunk, staggering, wearing nothing but my slip, in a room with three boys, one of whom was Bill Kline. My mother had said that I was to pay for the bottle she had taken the Berrymans out of my baby-sitting earnings, but my clients melted away like the last April snow, and it would not be paid for yet if newcomers to town had not moved in across the street in July, and needed a baby sitter before they talked to any of their neighbors.

My mother also said that it had been a great mistake to let me go out with boys and that I would not be going out again until well after my sixteenth birthday, if then. This did not prove to be a concrete hardship at all, because it was at least that long before anybody asked me. If you think that news of the Berrymans adventure would put me in demand for whatever gambols and orgies were going on in and around that town, you could not be more mistaken. The extraordinary publicity which attended my first debauch may have made me seemed marked for a special kind of ill luck, like the girl whose illegitimate baby turns out to be triplets: nobody wants to have anything to do with her. At any rate I had at the same time one of the most silent telephones and positively the most sinful reputation in the whole High School. I had to put up with this until the next fall, when a fat blonde girl in Grade Ten ran away with a married man and was picked up two months later, living in sin—though not with the same man—in the city of Sault Ste. Marie. Then everybody forgot about me.

But there was a positive, a splendidly unexpected, result of this affair: I got completely over Martin Collingwood. It was not only that he at once said, publicly, that he had always thought I was a nut; where he was concerned I had no pride, and my tender fancy could have found a way around that, a month, a week, before. What was it that brought me back into the world again? It was the terrible and fascinating reality of my disaster; it was *the way things happened.* Not that I enjoyed it; I was a self-conscious girl and I suffered a good deal from all this exposure. But the development of events on that Saturday night—that fascinated me; I felt that I had had a glimpse of the shameless, marvelous, shattering absurdity with which the plots of life, though not of fiction, are improvised. I could not take my eyes off it.

And of course Martin Collingwood wrote his Senior Matric that June, and went away to the city to take a course at a school for Morticians, as I think it is called, and when he came back he went into his uncle's undertaking business. We lived in the same town and we would hear most things that happened to each other but I do not think we met face to face or saw one another, except at a distance, for years. I went to a shower for the girl he married, but then everybody went to everybody else's showers. No, I do not think I really saw him again until I came home after I had been married several years, to attend a relative's funeral. Then I saw him; not quite Mr. Darcy but still very nice-looking in those black clothes. And I saw him looking over at me with an expression as close to a reminiscent smile as the occasion would permit, and I knew that he had been surprised by a memory either of my devotion or my little buried catastrophe. I gave him a gentle uncomprehending look in return. I am a grown-up woman now; let him unbury his own catastrophes.

QUESTIONS

1. From what kind of family does the narrator come? Describe and evaluate her parents as they are shown by the home environment, by their attitude toward drinking and the "pledge," by the actions of the mother after the "catastrophe."

2. How old is the protagonist at the time of her "catastrophe"? What are the causes of her infatuation with Martin Collingwood? Is her behavior during her infatuation (a) highly unusual, (b) unusual, or (c) not unusual for girls of her age? How much of the "catastrophe" which follows is due to her own romantic silliness and lack of good sense, how much to simple ignorance, how much to bad luck? Are there any occasions on which she exhibits good sense?

3. Discuss the role of coincidence in the story, applying the considerations discussed in the chapter on plot to evaluating its role here. What is the narrator's attitude toward coincidence?
4. What positive result does the narrator's "catastrophe" have? Why? What does she learn from this affair? Did the "catastrophe" do her any permanent damage?
5. The story is told by a "grown-up woman" many years after the event. How early and at what points in the story is this made apparent? How does the narrator judge her adolescent self? Does she attempt to cast blame on anyone but herself? In what vein does she tell the story—humorously? self-pityingly? ruefully? angrily? Does she anywhere show a tendency to exaggerate? What do we learn of her subsequent history? What sort of woman has the girl "with the most sinful reputation in the whole High School" become?
6. To what familiar saying does the title allude, and how does it alter that saying? How does the title, though in some ways ironic, relate to the theme of the story? Formulate two statements of theme, one using and the other not using the words of the title.

William Humphrey
A JOB OF THE PLAINS

1

There was a man in the land of Oklahoma whose name was Dobbs; and this man was blameless and upright, one who feared God and turned away from evil. And there were born to him three sons and four daughters. His substance also was one lank Jersey cow, a team of spavined mules, one razorback hog, and eight or ten mongrel hound pups. So that this man was about as well off as most everybody else in eastern Pushmataha County.

Now there came a day when the sons of God came to present themselves before the Lord, and Satan also came among them. And the Lord said unto Satan, "Whence comest thou?" Then Satan answered the Lord and said, "From going to and fro in the earth and from walking up and down in it." And the Lord said unto Satan, "Hast thou considered my servant Dobbs, that there is none like him in the earth, a blameless and upright man, one that fears God and escheweth evil?" Then Satan answered the Lord and said, "Does

A JOB OF THE PLAINS   First published in 1965. As its title and the language of the opening paragraphs indicate, this story uses for its springboard the Book of Job in the Bible. Historically its background is the Great Depression of 1929-40 and the Dust Bowl storms of the early 1930s. Two of the economic recovery strategies of Franklin D. Roosevelt's New Deal involved paying farmers to withhold land from production and buying pigs from them which were then shot and buried, both designed to raise the price of farm commodities through scarcity. William Humphrey was born (1924) and grew up in Clarksville, Texas, about 25 miles across the Red River from Pushmataha County, Oklahoma.

Dobbs fear God for nought? Hast Thou not made an hedge about him, and about his house, and about all that he hath on every side? Thou hast blessed the work of his hands, and his substance is increased in the land. But put forth Thy hand now and touch all that he hath, and he will curse Thee to Thy face."

There was actually no hedge but only a single strand of barb wire about all that Chester Dobbs had. The Devil was right, though, in saying that the Lord had blessed the work of Dobbs's hands that year (1929) and his substance had increased in the land. There had been a bumper cotton crop, Dobbs had ginned five bales, and—the reverse of what you could generally count on when the crop was good—the price was staying up. In fact it was rising by the day; so that instead of selling as soon as his was ginned, Dobbs, like everybody else that fall, put his bales in storage and borrowed from the bank to live on in the meantime, and sat back to wait for the best moment. At this rate it looked as if he might at last begin paying something on the principal of the mortgage which his old daddy had left as Dobbs's legacy. And in fifteen or twenty years' time he would own a piece of paper giving him sole and undisputed right, so long as he paid the taxes, to break his back plowing those fifty acres of stiff red clay.

Then the Lord said unto Satan, "Behold, all that he hath is in your power. Only upon himself do not put forth thy hand." So Satan went forth out of the presence of the Lord.

"Well," said Dobbs, when those five fat bales he had ginned stood in the shed running up a storage bill and you couldn't give the damned stuff away that fall, "the Lord gives and the Lord takes away. I might've knowed it was too good to ever come true. I guess I ain't alone in this."

He had known bad years before—had hardly known anything else; and had instinctively protected himself against too great a disappointment by never fully believing in his own high hopes. Like the fellow in the story, he was not going to get what he thought he would for his cotton, but then he never thought he would. So he borrowed some more from the bank, and butchered the hog, and on that, and his wife's canning, they got through the winter.

But instead of things getting better the next spring they got worse. Times were so bad that a new and longer word was needed: they were in a depression. Cotton, that a man had plowed and sown and chopped and picked and ginned, was going at a price to make your codsack shrink, and the grocer in town from whom Dobbs had had credit for twenty years picked this of all times to announce that he would have to have cash from now on, and would he please settle his bill within thirty days? He hated to ask it, but they were in a depression. "Ain't I in it too?" asked Dobbs. What was the world coming to when cotton wasn't worth nothing to nobody? For when he made his annual spring trip to the loan department of the bank and was told that not only could they not advance him anything more, but that his outstanding note, due in ninety days, would not be renewed, and Dobbs offered as collateral the other two of his bales on which they did not already hold a lien, the bank manager all but laughed in his face and said, "Haven't you folks out in the country heard yet? We're in a depression."

Nevertheless, when the ground was dry enough that you could pull your foot out of it Dobbs plowed and planted more cotton. What else was a man to do? And though through the winter there had been many times when he thanked God for taking Ione's uterus after the birth of Emmagine, now he thanked Him for his big family. There was a range of just six years among them, one brace of twins being included in the number, and all were of an age to be of help around the place. The boys were broken to the plow, and the girls were learning, as plain girls did (might as well face it), to make up in the kitchen and around the house for what they lacked in looks. Level-headed, affectionate, hard-working girls, the kind to really appreciate a home and make some man a good wife. And while boys went chasing after little dollfaces that couldn't boil water, they were left at home on the shelf. But, that's how it goes. Meanwhile they were a help to their mother. And when cotton-chopping time came they knew how to wield a hoe. And when cotton-picking time came all would pick.

Still, there were nine mouths to feed. Big husky hard-working boys who devoured a pan of biscuits with their eyes alone, and where were they to find work when men with families were standing idle on the street corners in town, and in the gang working on the highway you saw former storekeepers and even young beginning lawyers swinging picks and sledge hammers for a dollar a day and glad to get it? By night around the kitchen table the whole family shelled pecans with raw fingers; the earnings, after coal-oil for the lamp, would just about keep you in shoelaces, assuming you had shoes.

On top of this a dry spell set in that seemed like it would never break. In the ground that was like ashes the seed lay unsprouting. Finally enough of a sprinkle fell to bring them up, then the sun swooped down and singed the seedlings like pinfeathers on a fowl. Stock ponds dried up into scabs, wells went dry, folks were hauling drinking water. The boll weevils came. The corn bleached and the leaves hung limp and tattered with worm holes. The next year it was the same all over again only worse.

It got so bad at last a rainmaker was called in. He pitched his tent where the medicine shows were always held, built a big smoky bonfire, set off Roman candles, firecrackers, sent up rubber balloons filled with gas and popped them with a .22 rifle, set out washtubs filled with ice water. Folks came from far and near to watch, stood around all day gawking at the sky and sunburning the roofs of their mouths, went home with a crick in their necks saying, I told you it'd never work. Church attendance picked up and the preachers prayed mightily for rain, but could not compete with the tent revivalist who came to town, pitched his tabernacle where the rainmaker had been, a real tonguelasher who told them this drought was punishment for all their sins, bunch of whiskey drinkers and fornicators and dancers and picture-show-goers and non-keepers of the Sabbath and takers of the Lord's name in vain, and if they thought they'd seen the worst of it, just to wait, the good Lord had only been warming them up so far. About this time word spread that on the second Tuesday in August the world was going to come to an end. Some folks pshawed but that Tuesday they took to their storm cellars the same as the rest. Toward milking time they began to poke their noses up, and felt pretty foolish finding the old world still there. The first ones up had a shivaree going around stomping on other folks' cellar doors and ringing cowbells and banging pots and pans. Afterwards when you threw it up to the fellow who'd told you, he said he'd got it from old So-and-so. Whoever started it nobody ever did find out.

One day the following spring an angel fell from heaven in the form of the county agricultural agent and landed at Dobbs's gate with the news that the government was ready to pay him, actually pay him, not to grow anything on twenty-five of his fifty acres.

What was the catch?

No catch. It was a new law, out of Washington. He didn't need to be told that cotton prices were down. Well, to raise them the government was taking this step to lower production. The old law of supply and demand. They would pay him as much not to grow anything on half his land as he would have made off of the cotton off of it. It sounded too good to be true. Something for nothing? From the government? And if true then there was something about it that sounded, well, a trifle shady, underhanded. Besides, what would he do?

"What would you do?"

"Yes. If I was to leave half of my land standing idle what would I do with myself half the day?"

"Hell, set on your ass half the time. Hire yourself out."

"Hire myself out? Who'll be hiring if they all go cutting back their acreage fifty percent?"

That was his problem. Now, did he have any spring shoats?

Did he! His old sow had farrowed like you never seen before. Thirteen she had throwed! Hungry as they all were, at hog-killing time this fall the Dobbses would have pigs to sell. And what pigs! Would he like to see them? Cross between Berkshire and razorback, with the lard of the one and the bacon of the other. Finest-looking litter of pigs you ever—well, see for yourself!

He had asked because the government was out to raise the price of pork, too, and would pay so and so much for every shoat not fattened for market. The government would buy them right now, pay for them as if they were grown.

"Why? What's the government going to do with all them pigs?"

"Get shut of them. Shoot them."

"What are they doing with all that meat?"

"Getting shut of it. Getting it off the market. That's the idea. So prices can—"

"Just throwing it out, you mean? With people going hungry? Just take and throw it away? Good clean hog meat?"

"Now look a-here. What difference does it make to you what they do with them, as long as you get your money? You won't have the feeding of them, and the ones you have left will be worth more."

"That ain't so good."

"How come it ain't?"

"The ones I have left I'll have to eat—the expensive ones. I won't be able to afford to eat them. Say, are you getting any takers on this offer?"

"Any takers! Why, man, you can't hardly buy a suckling pig these days, people are grabbing them up so, to sell to old Uncle Sam."

"No!"

"I'm telling you. And buying cheap land on this other deal. Land you couldn't grow a bullnettle on if you tried, then getting paid not to grow nothing on it."

"What is the world coming to! Hmm. I reckon my land and me could both use a little rest. But taking money without working for it? Naw, sir, that sound I hear is my old daddy turning over in his grave. As for them shoats there, well, when the frost is in the air, in November, and I get to thinking of sausage meat and backbone with sweet potatoes and cracklin' bread, why then I can climb into a pen and stick a hog as well as the next fellow. Then it's me or that hog. But when it comes to shooting little suckling pigs, like drownding a litter of kittens, no sir, include me out. And if this is what voting straight Democratic all your life gets you, then next time around I'll go Republican, though God should strike me dead in my tracks at the polling booth!"

The next thing was, the winds began to blow and the dust to rise. Some mornings you didn't know whether to get out of bed or not. It came in through the cracks in the wall and the floor and gritted between your teeth every bite you ate. You'd just better drop the reins and hightail it for home and the storm cellar the minute a breeze sprang up, because within five minutes more it was black as night and even if you could have stood to open your eyes you couldn't see to blow your nose. You tied a bandana over your face but still it felt like you had inhaled on a cigar. Within a month after the storms started you could no longer see out of your windowlights, they were frosted like the glass in a lawyer's office door, that was how hard the wind drove the dirt and the sand. Sometimes you holed up in the house for two or three days—nights, rather: there was no day—at a stretch. And when you had dug your way out, coughing, eyes stinging, and took a look around, you just felt like turning right around and going back in the house again. The corn lay flat, dry roots clutching the air. And the land, with the subsoil showing, looked red and raw as something skinned.

Then Faye, the oldest boy, who had been bringing in a little money finding day work in the countryside roundabout, came home one afternoon and announced he'd signed up to join the Navy. Feeling guilty, he brought it out surlily. And it was a blow. But his father couldn't blame him. Poor boy, he couldn't stand any more, he wanted to get far away from all this, out to sea where there was neither dust nor dung, and where he might be sure of three square meals a day. Trouble always comes in pairs, and one night not long afterwards Faye's little brother, Dwight, too young to volunteer, was taken over in Antlers with a pair of buddies breaking into a diner. He was let off with a suspended sentence, but only after his father had spent an arm and a leg to pay the lawyer his fee.

Then the Dobbses went on relief. Standing on line with your friends, none of you able to look another in the face, to get your handout of cornmeal and a dab of lard, pinto beans, a slab of salt-white sowbelly. And first Ione, because being the mother she scrimped herself at table on the sly, then Chester, and pretty soon all of them commenced to break out on the wrists and the hands and around the ankles and up the arms and shins and around the waist with red spots, sores, the skin cracking open. Pellagra.

A man can take just so much. And squatting on the corner of the square in town on Saturday afternoon, without a nickel for a sack of Durham, without so much as a matchstick of his own to chew on, Dobbs said to his friends, "What's it all for, will somebody please tell me? What have I done to deserve this? I worked hard all my life. I've always paid my bills. I've never diced nor gambled, never dranked, never chased after the women. I've always honored my old mama and daddy. I've done the best I could to provide for my wife and family, and tried to bring my children up decent and God-fearing. I've went to church regular. I've kept my nose out of other folkses' affairs and minded my own business. I've never knowingly done another man dirt. Whenever the hat was passed around to help out some poor woman left a widow with orphan children I've give what I could. And what have I got to show for it? Look at me. Look at them hands. If I'd kicked over the traces and misbehaved myself I'd say, all right, I've had my fling and I've got caught and now I'm going to get what's coming to me, and I'd take my punishment like a man. But I ain't never once stepped out of line, not that I know of. So what's it all for, can any of yawl tell me? I'll be much obliged to you if you will."

"Well, just hang on awhile longer, Chester. Maybe them fellows will strike oil out there on your land," said Lyman Turley.

"Like they have on yourn," said Cecil Bates. "And mine."

"Lyman, you and me been friends a long time," said Dobbs. "I never thought you would make fun of me when I was down and out."

"Hellfire, we're all in the same boat," said Lyman. "What good does it do to bellyache?"

"None. Only how can you keep from it?" asked Dobbs. "And we're not all in the same boat. I know men and so do you, right here in this county, that are driving around in big-model automobiles and sit down every night of their lives to a Kansas City T-bone steak, and wouldn't give a poor man the time of day. Are they in the same boat?"

"Their day of reckoning will come," said O.J. Carter. "And on that same day, if you've been as good as you say you have, you'll get your reward. Don't you believe that the wicked are punished and the good rewarded?"

"Search me if I know what I believe any more. When I look around me and see little children that don't know right from wrong going naked and hungry, men ready and willing to do an honest day's work being driven to steal to keep from starving to death while other men get fat off of their misery, then I don't know what I believe any more."

"Well, you can't take it with you," said Cecil.

"I don't want to take it with me," said Dobbs. "I won't need it in the sweet by-and-by. I'd just like to have a little of it in the mean old here and now."

A breeze had sprung up, hot, like somebody blowing his breath in your face, and to the south the sky was rapidly darkening over.

"Looks like rain," said Cecil.

"Looks like something," said O.J.

"Well, men, yawl can sit here and jaw if you want to, and I hope it does you lots of good," said Lyman. "Me, I'm going to the wagon. I'd like to get home while I can still see to find my way there."

"I reckon that's what we better all of us do," said Dobbs.

The sky closed down like a lid. Smells sharpened, and from off the low ceiling of clouds distant noises, such as the moan of a locomotive on the far horizon, the smoke from its stack bent down, broke startlingly close and clear. The telegraph wires along the road sagged with perching birds. They were in for something worse than just another dust storm.

To the southwest lightning began to flicker and thunder to growl. The breeze quickened and trees appeared to burst aflame as the leaves showed their undersides. Suddenly as the Dobbses came in sight of home the air was all sucked away, a vacuum fell, ears popped, lungs gasped for breath: it was as if they were drowning. Then the wind returned with a roar, and like the drops of a breaking wave, a peppering of hailstones fell, rattling in the wagonbed, bouncing off the mules' heads. A second wave followed, bigger, the size of marbles. Again silence, and the hailstones hissed and steamed on the hot dry soil. In the black cloud to the west a rent appeared, funnel-shaped, white, like smoke from a chimney by night, its point stationary, the cone gently fanning first this way then that way, as though stirred by contrary breezes. Shortly it began to blacken. Then it resembled a great gathering swarm of bees. Out of the sky fell leaves, straws, twigs, great hailstones, huge unnatural raindrops. The team balked, reared, began scrambling backwards.

"Cyclone!" Dobbs shouted. "Run for it, everybody! To the storm cellar!"

The boys helped their mother down the steps, pushed their sisters down, then tumbled in themselves while Dobbs stood holding the flapping door. He started down. As he was pulling the door shut upon his head there came an explosion. He thought at first they had been struck by lightning. Turning, he saw his house fly apart as though blown into splinters by a charge of dynamite. The chimney wobbled for a moment, then righted itself. Then the door was slammed down upon his head and Dobbs was entombed.

Hands helped him to his feet. His head hit the low ceiling. He sat down on the bench beside a shivering body, a trembling cold wet hand clutched his. God's punishment for that wild talk of his, that was what this was. Dobbs reckoned he had it coming to him. He had brought it upon himself. He had also brought it upon his innocent family. Down in the dank and moldy darkness, where he could hear his wife and children panting but could not see their faces, and where overhead through the thick roof of sod he could hear the storm stamping its mighty feet, Dobbs sat alternately wishing he was dead and shivering with dread lest his impious wish be granted and his family left without support. Someone sobbed, one of the girls, and frightened by the sound of her own voice, began to wail.

In a husky voice Dobbs said, "Well now, everybody, here we all are, all together, safe and sound. Let's be thankful for that. Now to keep our spirits up let's sing a song. All together now, loud and clear. Ready?" And with him carrying the lead in his quavering nasal tenor, they sang:

> "Jesus loves me, this I know,
> For the Bible tells me so . . ."

2

And then there is such a thing as foul-weather friends.

While people who had always been rather distant all went out of their way to be polite after oil was struck on Dobbs's land, all his old acquaintances avoided him. They had all come and bemoaned and comforted him over the evil the Lord had brought on him, every man giving him a piece of money, taking in and housing the children, chipping in with old clothes after Dobbs's house was blown down; but as soon as his luck turned they would all cross over to the other side of the street to keep from meeting him. At home Dobbs grieved aloud over this. Good riddance, his daughters all said, and wondered that he should any longer want to keep up acquaintance with the Turleys and the Maynards and the Tatums, and other poor whites like that.

"The only difference between you and them pore whites is you ain't pore no more," said Dobbs. "Which you always was and very likely will be again. Especially if you talk thataway. Now just remember that, and meanwhile thank the Lord."

The girls clamored to leave the old farmstead and move into town. They wanted to live in the biggest house in town, the old Venable mansion, which along with what was left of the family heirlooms had been on the market for years to settle the estate. You could have pastured a milch cow on the front lawn, the grass so thick you walked on tiptoe for fear of muddying it with your feet. On the lawn stood a life-size cast-iron stag, silver balls on concrete pedestals, a croquet court, a goldfish pond with a water fountain. To tally all the windows in the house would have worn a lead pencil down to a stub. Turrets and towers and cupolas, round, square, and turnip-shaped, rose here, there, and everywhere; it looked like a town. You wanted to go round to the back door with your hat in your hand. Take a while to remember that it was yours.

At the housewarming it turned out that Dobbs and his daughters had invited two separate lists of guests, he by word of mouth, on street corners on Saturday afternoon, in the barber shop, hanging over fence gaps—they by printed invitation. Nobody much from either list showed up. First to arrive were their kin from the country, in pickup trucks and mule-drawn wagons and lurching jitneys alive with kids. The men in suits smelling of mothballs, red in the face from their starched, buttoned, tieless collars, wetted-down hair drying and starting to spring up like horses' manes, all crippled by pointed shoes, licking the cigars which Dobbs passed out up and down before raking matches across the seats of their britches and setting fire to them. The women in dresses printed in jungle flowers, their hair in tight marcelled waves against their skulls. The kids sliding down banisters, tearing through the halls, and skidding across the waxed parquet floors trying to catch and goose one another.

After them came a few of the many old friends and acquaintances Dobbs had invited. Then began to arrive the others, those who knew better than to bring their children, some with colored maids at home to mind them when the folks stepped out, people whom Dobbs had always tipped his hat to, little dreaming he would one day have them to his house, the biggest house in town, some of them the owners of the land on which his kin and the people he had invited sharecropped, so that quicker than cream from milk the two groups separated, he and his finding their way out to the kitchen and the back yard, leaving the girls and theirs to the parlor and the front porch. Then through the mist of pride and pleasure of seeing all those town folks under his roof, Dobbs saw what was going on. All of them laughing up their sleeves at the things they saw, passing remarks about his girls, who would take their part against him if he tried to tell them they were being made fun of by their fine new friends. Poor things, red with pleasure, stretching their long necks like a file of ganders so as to look a little less chinless, their topmost ribs showing like rubboards above the tops of their low-cut dresses. And his wife forgetting about the Negro maid and waiting on the guests herself, passing around the teacakes and the muffins, then getting a scorching look from one of the girls which she didn't understand but blushing to the roots of her thin hair and sitting down with her big red knobby hands trembling uselessly in her lap. Jumping up to say, "Oh, yawl ain't going already? Why, you just this minute come. Let me get yawl something good to eat. Maybe you'd like to try one of these here olives. Some folks like them. You have to mind out not to bite down on the seed." And through it all his old mama upstairs in her room, dipping snuff and spitting into her coffee can, refusing to budge, saying she didn't want to put him to shame before his highfalutin new friends, only he might send that sassy nigger wench up with a bite for her, just a dry crust of bread, whatever the guests left, not now, later, she didn't want to put nobody out.

Sightseeing parties were conducted through the house, the country kin making coarse jokes over the eight flush toilets which made his daughters choke red, though it was certainly not the first time they had heard the very same jokes. Others like Mr. Henry Blankenship saying, "What! Two hundred dollars for that rug? Oh, Chester, I'm afraid they saw you coming. Why oh why"—forgetting that until the day before yesterday they had never in their lives exchanged more than good afternoon—"didn't you come to me? I could have jewed them down fifty per cent at least."

The party broke up early, leaving mounds of favors; but not before each and every one of the relatives had gotten his corns stepped on. The townspeople went home sniggering with laughter, or fuming with outrage in the name of the vanished Venables. Both groups found excuses for declining future invitations, and in the evenings the big house on the hill heaved with sighs of boredom.

Dobbs continued as before to awake at four o'clock, and could not get back to sleep. The habit of a lifetime is not easily broken. But he could and did lie there smiling to think that he did not have to get up. No cow was waiting for him to milk her, no mule to be harnessed, no field to be plowed or picked of its cotton. Except that once awake Dobbs saw no point in not getting up. In fact, it bored him to lie in bed doing nothing. What was more, it seemed sinful.

He did not want to waste a moment of his leisure. Each day, all day, was his now, to spend as he pleased, according to his whim. Mere loafing was no pleasure to Dobbs; he had to be doing. The list of pastimes known to him was somewhat short. He went hunting with his fine new gun, went fishing with his bright new tackle, went driving in his big new car. One by one he slunk back to his old singleshot with the tape around the stock, with which he was a much better shot, back to his old cane pole, relieved to be rid of his level-wind reel which was always snarling in a knot and that boxful of artificial baits of which he never seemed to be using the right one. Fishing and hunting were not nearly so much fun when the time was not stolen from work. As he sat alone on the bank of a creek enjoying the blessings of unmixed leisure and telling himself how happy he was, Dobbs's hand would steal involuntarily to the nape of his neck where a welt, a rope burn which made it look like the neck of a hanged man, was, though fading now, still visible. It corresponded to the callus rubbed by the hames on the neck of a mule, and had been bitten there by plowlines, beginning at age eight. Dobbs rubbed it with a tenderness akin to nostalgia.

Other men were not to be found on the streets of town on a weekday; they were at work, and a lifetime of doing the same had left Dobbs with the feeling that it was wicked and immoral of him to be there at that hour. Those who were on the streets were those who were there at all hours, who often slept there: the town ne'er-do-wells and drunks.

Like all farmers, Dobbs had always lived for Saturday. That had been the day when he slipped the reins and came into town. It was not the rest he enjoyed, though God knew that was sweet, so much as the company. A man can plow a field and plod along for five days at a stretch with nothing to look at but the hind end of a mule and no company but the cawing crows overhead, but then he has to see faces, hear voices. Now that every day was a Saturday Dobbs found himself looking forward to Saturday with a sense of deliverance. But though they did their best to make him welcome in his old spot, squatting among his cronies on the square and whittling away the afternoon, his company obviously embarrassed them. People he had always known began to call him Mister, and many seemed to believe that Dobbs thought they were no longer good enough for him. People still said, as they had always done on taking leave, "Well, yawl come," and Dobbs said it to them. He meant it more sincerely with each passing day. But nobody came and nobody was going to come. How could they drive up that long raked gravel drive of his in a wagon and team or a homemade pickup truck, traipse in their boots across those pastures of carpet, come calling in overalls and poke bonnets? And how could he draw up before their unhinged gates and their dirt yards in that great long-nosed Pierce-Arrow of his?

Three or four friends Dobbs lost forever by lending them money and expecting them to pay it back. He supposed they felt he would never miss it, but he thought they would despise themselves, as he would have, if they did not repay him. And he lost more by refusing them loans. Some people complained of the way he spent his money, others of the way he hoarded it.

Which last, in fact, he had begun to do. Having done nothing to deserve his sudden wealth, Dobbs feared it might just as suddenly be taken from him. Being a wagon-and-team man himself, he didn't much believe in oil, nor in money which came from it. His bank statements frightened him; he thought not how much he had, but how much it would be to lose! He developed a terror of being poor again. He knew what it was to be poor. So he told his children when they whined at him to buy them this and buy them that. Did they see him throwing money away?

True, he himself lived simply, indeed for a man in his position he lived like a beggar. But though he prided himself on his frugality, the truth was, and he knew it, that after a short while he found he simply did not like (he said he couldn't digest) filet mignon and oven-roasted beef and oysters and other unfamiliar and over-rich foods like those. After thirty years of Duke's Mixture he liked it, preferred it to ready-rolls. And cold greens and black-eyed peas and clabber: these were what he had always called food. Even they tasted less good to him now that he never worked up any appetite, now that they were never sauced with the uncertainty of whether there would be more of them for tomorrow. In fact, he just minced at his food now. Sometimes after dinner, as his girls had begun to call supper, and after everybody was in bed asleep, Dobbs would steal down to the kitchen, about half a mile from his bedroom, and make himself a glass of cornbread crumbled in sweetmilk or have some leftover cold mashed turnips, but he did not enjoy it and would leave it half finished. The Scriptures say, "Thou shalt eat thy bread in the sweat of thy face," and the sad truth is, to a man who always has, bread which does not taste of his own sweat just does not have any taste.

3

In all of Oklahoma no women were found so fair as the daughters of Dobbs; their father gave them equal inheritance among their brothers.

In his days of poverty the problem of marrying off his daughters had weighed on Dobbs's mind like a stone. He had felt beholden to them. For he had only to look in the mirror to see where they got their plainness from. But they were cheerful and uncomplaining, and when boys dressed in their best overalls and carrying bouquets went past their gate on Sunday afternoon as if past a nunnery, they had not seemed to mind. Now the problem was to keep them from marrying the first man who asked them. It was as if all four had come into heat simultaneously, and all day long and all night too, baying and snapping and snarling at one another, a pack of boys milled about the house and yard. They had given up all hope of ever catching a husband; now sweet words went to their heads like a virgin drink of spirits. "Don't you see that that rascal is just after your money?" Dobbs would say. And they would weep and pout and storm and say, "You mean you're afraid he's after your old money. That's all you ever think about. You don't know Spencer like I do. He loves me! I know he does. He would marry me if I was as poor as a churchmouse. He told me so. If you send him away you'll break my heart and I'll hate you till the day I die."

Dobbs even had to buy off one of them. One of the suitors, that is. Pay him to stay away, keep him on a regular monthly salary.

So inflamed did poor Denise get that she eloped with a fellow. Dobbs caught them in Tulsa and brought her home fainting and kicking and screaming. Even after it had been proved to her that he was wanted for passing bad checks from Atlanta to Albuquerque, she still sulked and went on pining for her Everett. The twins, who before had always gotten along together like two drops of water, now decided they each wanted the same boy, though Lord knew there were plenty to go around, and they only patched up their quarrel by turning on their father when he said that only over his dead body would either of them marry that no-good fortune-hunting drugstore cowboy.

One by one they beat him down. For Denise another Everett came along and she told her father she meant to have this one. The old refrain: he's only after your money. "I'm free, white, and twenty-one," she said, "and seeing as it's my money, I'll spend it on what I please." Dobbs shook his head and said,

"Oh, my poor girl, my poor little girl, you're buying yourself a bushel of heartache." She replied, "Nonsense. If this one don't work out to suit me I'll get shut of him and get me another one." And that in fact was how it did work out, not once but four times.

She had the biggest wedding the town had ever seen. Dobbs spared no expense. At the wedding reception in his own house he was a stranger; he knew no one there. Then the twins were married in a lavish double ceremony. People said you couldn't tell the girls apart; what Dobbs couldn't tell one from the other were their two husbands. Emmagine was not long behind them, and her wedding put theirs in the shade, for she had married a Lubbock of the Oklahoma City Lubbocks. This time there were two wedding receptions, one at Dobbs's, the other at the home of his son-in-law's people. Dobbs attended only the one, though he paid the bills for both. In fact, the day after the ceremony he began to receive unpaid bills from his son-in-law's creditors, some dated as far back as ten years.

Then Ernest, the middle boy, brought home a bride. Mickey her name was. She had hair like cotton candy, wore fishnet stockings, bathed in perfume. Thinking she might have caught cold from going around so lightly dressed, Mrs. Dobbs recommended a cure for her quinsy. But there was nothing the matter with her throat; that was her natural speaking voice. She and her sisters-in-law backed off at each other like cats. The family seldom saw Ernest after he left home. The checks his father sent him came back cashed by banks in faraway places. He wrote that he was interested in many schemes; he was always on the verge of a really big deal. To swing it he needed just this amount of cash. When he returned once every year to discuss finances with his father he came alone. His mother hinted that she would have liked to see her daughter-in-law and her grandson; as luck would have it, one or the other was always not feeling up to the trip. Once the boy was sent alone to spend a month with his grandparents. Instead of one month he was left for four. To his shame Dobbs was glad to see the boy go. When Ernest came to fetch him home he took the occasion to ask for an increase in his allowance. He and his brother quarreled; thereafter he stayed away from home for even longer stretches.

Back from his hitch in the Navy, and back from his last cruise parched with thirst and rutting like a goat, came Faye. Feeling beholden to the boy for the hard life he had had on the farm and on shipboard, Dobbs lavished money on him. When he was brought home drunk and unconscious, battered and bruised from some barroom brawl, Dobbs held his tongue. To hints that he think of his future he turned deaf. The contempt he felt for work was shown in the foul nicknames he had for men who practiced each and every trade and profession. Once to Dobbs's house came a poor young girl, obviously pregnant. She claimed the child was Faye's. He hardly bothered to deny it. When his father asked if he meant to marry the girl he snorted with laughter. He suggested that she would be happy to be bought off. Shrinking with shame, Dobbs offered her money; when she took it he felt ashamed of the whole human race. He told his son that he was breaking his mother's heart. He said there would always be money to support him but that it was time he settled down and took a wife. The one he got persuaded him that while he was away in the Navy his sisters and brothers had connived to cheat him of his share of money. He had been cheated of something, he somehow felt; maybe that was it. To have a little peace of mind, his father gave him more; whatever the amount, Faye always felt sure it was less than he had coming to him. He quarreled with his sisters. Family reunions, rare at best, grew more and more infrequent because of the bad feelings between the children.

It was Dwight, his youngest son and always his favorite child, on whom his father placed his hopes. Totally reformed after that one scrape with the law, he never drank, never even smoked, never went near a poolhall nor a honkytonk. Most important of all, girls did not interest him in the least. He was in love with the internal combustion engine. His time was spent hanging around garages, stock-car race tracks, out at the local cowpasture with the windsock and the disused haybarn which was hopefully spoken of as the hangar. He worshipped indiscriminately automobiles, motorcycles, airplanes, whatever was driven by gasoline. The smell of hot lubricating oil intoxicated him. Exhaust fumes were his native air. Silence and sitting still drove him distracted. He loved having to shout above the roar of motors. He spoke a language which his father could only marvel at, as if he had raised a child who had mastered a foreign tongue, speaking of valve compression ratio, torque, drop-head suspension, and of little else.

Dwight had known the ache, the hopeless adoration worlds removed from envy, too humble even to be called longing, of the plowboy for cars that pass the field, stopping the mule at the sound of the approaching motor and gazing trancelike long after it has disappeared in a swirl of dust, then awakening and resettling the reins about his neck and pointing the plowshare down again and saying to the mule, "Come up, mule." Now he saw no reason why he shouldn't have one of his own. He was sixteen years old and his old man had money to burn. Car or motorcycle, he would have settled for either; the mere mention of a motorcycle scared his father into buying him a car. He was not going to kill himself on one of them damned motorsickles, Dobbs said, words which just two months later came back to haunt him for the rest of his life.

It was a Ford, one of the new V-8's. No sooner was it bought than it disappeared from sight. He was working on it, said Dwight. Working on it? A brand-new car? If something was the matter with it why not take it back? All that was the matter with it was that it was a Detroit car, off the assembly line. He was improving it.

"You call that improving it!" said Dobbs on seeing it rolled out of the old Venable coach house a week later. It looked as if it had been wrecked. The body all stripped down. The entrails hanging out of the hood. Paint job spoilt, flames painted sweeping back from the nose and along the side panels in tongues of red, orange, and yellow. Dwight said he had added a supercharger, a second carburetor, advanced the timer, stripped the rear end. Well, just drive careful, that's all. Two months later the boy was brought home dead. Coming home from the funeral Dobbs's wife said, "This would never happened if we had stayed down on the farm where we belonged. Sometimes I wish we had never struck oil."

The same thought had crossed Dobbs's mind, frightening him with its ingratitude. "Ssh!" he said. "Don't talk like that."

With the death of Dwight, Dobbs and his wife were left alone in the big house with only Dobbs's old mother for company. She threatened to leave with every breath. She could see well enough where she wasn't wanted. She would not be a burden. If she wasn't good enough for her own flesh and blood just say so and she would pack her bag. The visits home of Faye and Ernest all but ceased. As for the girls, they were never mentioned. Both Dobbs and his wife knew that they were ashamed of their parents.

And so the Lord blessed the latter end of Dobbs more than his beginning. For in addition to his oil wells, he had (he never did come to trust oil, and old country boy that he was, converted much of it into livestock) fourteen thousand head of whitefaced cattle and five thousand Poland China hogs.

He also had two sons and four daughters. And he gave them equal inheritance, though there was not one who didn't believe that the rest had all been favored over him.

After this lived Dobbs not very long. Just long enough to see his sons' sons, and despair.

So Dobbs died, being old before his time, and having had his fill of days.

QUESTIONS

1. Characterize Dobbs. To what extent is he like his neighbors? Is he in any respects superior to his neighbors? How is the direct characterization of him in the opening sentence corroborated in his behavior?
2. How is Dobbs affected by adversity? by prosperity? Are the changes in his life produced by prosperity greater or less than the changes produced by adversity? Does he change in character as well as in happiness? Who wins the wager between God and Satan?
3. Compare the magnitude of the changes produced in Dobbs with that of the changes produced in his family.
4. The story is structured around a series of ironic parallels to the Book of Job in the Bible. Trace the similarities and differences, especially in regard to (a) the initial lots of Dobbs and Job (Job 1:1-12), (b) their afflictions (Job 1:13-2:10), (c) discussion with their "comforters" (Job 2:11 ff.), (d) the increased prosperity of Dobbs and Job following their adversity (Job 42:10-17). Account for the major differences. Which story has a happy ending?
5. Although the stories of Dobbs and Job are roughly parallel, the themes of the two works are quite different. What is the central question posed by the Book of Job? Where is it asked in this story? Is it answered? How does the amount of space allotted to the four matters mentioned in the preceding question signal a difference of central concern in the two works?

6. Although theme is never explicitly stated in this story, its formulation should not be difficult. State it in a brief sentence. Is a knowledge of the Book of Job necessary to its formulation?
7. The beginning and end of Humphrey's story either quote the Bible directly or echo it closely. On what is the prose style of the rest of the story based? How does the style contribute to the effectiveness of the story?

Philip Roth

DEFENDER OF THE FAITH

In May of 1945, only a few weeks after the fighting had ended in Europe, I was rotated back to the States, where I spent the remainder of the war with a training company at Camp Crowder, Missouri. Along with the rest of the Ninth Army, I had been racing across Germany so swiftly during the late winter and spring that when I boarded the plane, I couldn't believe its destination lay to the west. My mind might inform me otherwise, but there was an inertia of the spirit that told me we were flying to a new front, where we would disembark and continue our push eastward—eastward until we'd circled the globe, marching through villages along whose twisting, cobbled streets crowds of the enemy would watch us take possession of what, up till then, they'd considered their own. I had changed enough in two years not to mind the trembling of old people, the crying of the very young, the uncertainty and fear in the eyes of the once arrogant. I had been fortunate enough to develop an infantryman's heart, which, like his feet, at first aches and swells but finally grows horny enough for him to travel the weirdest paths without feeling a thing.

Captain Paul Barrett was my C.O. in Camp Crowder. The day I reported for duty, he came out of his office to shake my hand. He was short, gruff, and fiery, and—indoors or out—he wore his polished helmet liner pulled down to his little eyes. In Europe, he had received a battlefield commission and a serious chest wound, and he'd been returned to the States only a few months before. He spoke easily to me, and at the evening formation he introduced me to the troops. "Gentlemen," he said. "Sergeant Thurston, as you know, is no longer with this company. Your new first sergeant is Sergeant Nathan Marx, here. He is a veteran of the European theater, and consequently will expect to find a company of soldiers here, and not a company of *boys*."

DEFENDER OF THE FAITH   First published in 1959. World War II officially ended in Europe with the surrender of Germany on May 7, 1945; it ended in the Pacific with the surrender of Japan on September 2, 1945. The action of the story occurs within that interval. Philip Roth, of Jewish parentage, was born (1933) and grew up in Newark, New Jersey, and was educated at Rutgers, Bucknell, and the University of Chicago. He enlisted in the army in 1955 after receiving his M.A. in English but was discharged within a year due to a back injury suffered during basic training.

I sat up late in the orderly room that evening, trying half-heartedly to solve the riddle of duty rosters, personnel forms, and morning reports. The Charge of Quarters slept with his mouth open on a mattress on the floor. A trainee stood reading the next day's duty roster, which was posted on the bulletin board just inside the screen door. It was a warm evening, and I could hear radios playing dance music over in the barracks. The trainee, who had been staring at me whenever he thought I wouldn't notice, finally took a step in my direction.

"Hey, Sarge—we having a G.I. party tomorrow night?" he asked. A G.I. party is a barracks cleaning.

"You usually have them on Friday nights?" I asked him.

"Yes," he said, and then he added, mysteriously, "that's the whole thing."

"Then you'll have a G.I. party."

He turned away, and I heard him mumbling. His shoulders were moving and I wondered if he was crying.

"What's your name, soldier?" I asked.

He turned, not crying at all. Instead, his green-speckled eyes, long and narrow, flashed like fish in the sun. He walked over to me and sat on the edge of my desk. He reached out a hand. "Sheldon," he said.

"Stand on your feet, Sheldon."

Getting off the desk, he said, "Sheldon Grossbart." He smiled at the familiarity into which he'd led me.

"You against cleaning the barracks Friday night, Grossbart?" I said. "Maybe we shouldn't have G.I. parties. Maybe we should get a maid." My tone startled me. I felt I sounded like every top sergeant I had ever known.

"No, Sergeant." He grew serious, but with a seriousness that seemed to be only the stifling of a smile. "It's just—G.I. parties on Friday night, of all nights."

He slipped up onto the corner of the desk again—not quite sitting, but not quite standing, either. He looked at me with those speckled eyes flashing, and then made a gesture with his hand. It was very slight—no more than a movement back and forth of the wrist—and yet it managed to exclude from our affairs everything else in the orderly room, to make the two of us the center of the world. It seemed, in fact, to exclude everything even about the two of us except our hearts.

"Sergeant Thurston was one thing," he whispered, glancing at the sleeping C.Q., "but we thought that with you here things might be a little different."

"We?"

"The Jewish personnel."

"Why?" I asked, harshly. "What's on your mind?" Whether I was still angry at the "Sheldon" business, or now at something else, I hadn't time to tell, but clearly I was angry.

"We thought you—Marx, you know, like Karl Marx. The Marx Brothers. Those guys are all—M-a-r-x. Isn't that how *you* spell it, Sergeant?"

"M-a-r-x."

"Fishbein said—" He stopped. "What I mean to say, Sergeant—" His face and neck were red, and his mouth moved but no words came out. In a moment, he raised himself to attention, gazing down at me. It was as though he had suddenly decided he could expect no more sympathy from me than from Thurston, the reason being that I was of Thurston's faith, and not his. The young man had managed to confuse himself as to what my faith really was, but I felt no desire to straighten him out. Very simply, I didn't like him.

When I did nothing but return his gaze, he spoke, in an altered tone. "You see, Sergeant," he explained to me, "Friday nights, Jews are supposed to go to services."

"Did Sergeant Thurston tell you you couldn't go to them when there was a G.I. party?"

"No."

"Did he say you had to stay and scrub the floors?"

"No, Sergeant."

"Did the Captain say you had to stay and scrub the floors?"

"That isn't it, Sergeant. It's the other guys in the barracks." He leaned toward me. "They think we're goofing off. But we're not. That's when Jews go to services, Friday night. We have to."

"Then go."

"But the other guys make accusations. They have no right."

"That's not the Army's problem, Grossbart. It's a personal problem you'll have to work out yourself."

"But it's un*fair*."

I got up to leave. "There's nothing I can do about it," I said.

Gossbart stiffened and stood in front of me. "But this is a matter of *religion*, sir."

"Sergeant," I said.

"I mean 'Sergeant,'" he said, almost snarling.

"Look, go see the chaplain. You want to see Captain Barrett, I'll arrange an appointment."

"No, no. I don't want to make trouble, Sergeant. That's the first thing they throw up to you. I just want my rights!"

"Damn it, Grossbart, stop whining. You have your rights. You can stay and scrub floors or you can go to shul—" °

The smile swam in again. Spittle gleamed at the corners of his mouth. "You mean church, Sergeant."

"I mean shul, Grossbart!"

I walked past him and went outside. Near me, I heard the scrunching of the guard's boots on gravel. Beyond the lighted windows of the barracks, young men in T shirts and fatigue pants were sitting on their bunks, polishing their rifles. Suddenly there was a light rustling behind me. I turned and saw

shul: synagogue

Grossbart's dark frame fleeing back to the barracks, racing to tell his Jewish friends that they were right—that, like Karl and Harpo, I was one of them.

The next morning, while chatting with Captain Barrett, I recounted the incident of the previous evening. Somehow, in the telling, it must have seemed to the Captain that I was not so much explaining Grossbart's position as defending it. "Marx, I'd fight side by side with a nigger if the fella proved to me he was a man. I pride myself," he said, looking out the window, "that I've got an open mind. Consequently, Sergeant, nobody gets special treatment here, for the good *or* the bad. All a man's got to do is prove himself. A man fires well on the range, I give him a weekend pass. He scores high in P.T., he gets a weekend pass. He *earns* it." He turned from the window and pointed a finger at me. "You're a Jewish fella, am I right, Marx?"

"Yes, sir."

"And I admire you. I admire you because of the ribbons on your chest. I judge a man by what he shows me on the field of battle, Sergeant. It's what he's got *here*," he said, and then, though I expected he would point to his chest, he jerked a thumb toward the buttons straining to hold his blouse across his belly. "Guts," he said.

"O.K., sir. I only wanted to pass on to you how the men felt."

"Mr. Marx, you're going to be old before your time if you worry about how the men feel. Leave that stuff to the chaplain—that's his business, not yours. Let's us train these fellas to shoot straight. If the Jewish personnel feels the other men are accusing them of goldbricking—well, I just don't know. Seems awful funny that suddenly the Lord is calling so loud in Private Grossman's ear he's just got to run to church."

"Synagogue," I said.

"Synagogue is right, Sergeant. I'll write that down for handy reference. Thank you for stopping by."

That evening, a few minutes before the company gathered outside the orderly room for the chow formation, I called the C.Q., Corporal Robert LaHill, in to see me. LaHill was a dark, burly fellow whose hair curled out of his clothes wherever it could. He had a glaze in his eyes that made one think of caves and dinosaurs. "LaHill," I said, "when you take the formation, remind the men that they're free to attend church services *whenever* they are held, provided they report to the orderly room before they leave the area."

LaHill scratched his wrist, but gave no indication that he'd heard or understood.

"LaHill," I said, "*church*. You remember? Church, priest, Mass, confession."

He curled one lip into a kind of smile; I took it for a signal that for a second he had flickered back up into the human race.

"Jewish personnel who want to attend services this evening are to fall out in front of the orderly room at 1900," I said. Then, as an afterthought, I added, "By order of Captain Barrett."

A little while later, as the day's last light—softer than any I had seen that year—began to drop over Camp Crowder, I heard LaHill's thick, inflectionless voice outside my window: "Give me your ears, troopers. Toppie says for me to tell you that at 1900 hours all Jewish personnel is to fall out in front, here, if they want to attend the Jewish Mass."

At seven o'clock, I looked out the orderly-room window and saw three soldiers in starched khakis standing on the dusty quadrangle. They looked at their watches and fidgeted while they whispered back and forth. It was getting dimmer, and, alone on the otherwise deserted field, they looked tiny. When I opened the door, I heard the noises of the G.I. party coming from the surrounding barracks—bunks being pushed to the walls, faucets pounding water into buckets, brooms whisking at the wooden floors, cleaning the dirt away for Saturday's inspection. Big puffs of cloth moved round and round on the windowpanes. I walked outside, and the moment my foot hit the ground I thought I heard Grossbart call to the others "'Ten-*hut!*" Or maybe, when they all three jumped to attention, I imagined I heard the command.

Grossbart stepped forward, "Thank you, sir," he said.

"'Sergeant,' Grossbart," I reminded him. "You call officers 'sir.' I'm not an officer. You've been in the Army three weeks—you know that."

He turned his palms out at his sides to indicate that, in truth, he and I lived beyond convention. "Thank you anyway," he said.

"Yes," a tall boy behind him said. "Thanks a lot."

And the third boy whispered, "Thank you," but his mouth barely fluttered, so that he did not alter by more than a lip's movement his posture of attention.

"For what?" I asked.

Grossbart snorted happily. "For the announcement. The Corporal's announcement. It helped. It made it—"

"Fancier." The tall boy finished Grossbart's sentence.

Grossbart smiled. "He means formal, sir. Public," he said to me. "Now it won't seem as though we're just taking off—goldbricking because the work has begun."

"It was by order of Captain Barrett," I said.

"Aaah, but you pull a little weight," Grossbart said. "So we thank you." Then he turned to his companions. "Sergeant Marx, I want you to meet Larry Fishbein."

The tall boy stepped forward and extended his hand. I shook it. "You from New York?" he asked.

"Yes."

"Me, too." He had a cadaverous face that collapsed inward from his cheekbone to his jaw, and when he smiled—as he did at the news of our communal attachment—revealed a mouthful of bad teeth. He was blinking his eyes a good deal, as though he were fighting back tears. "What borough?" he asked.

I turned to Grossbart. "It's five after seven. What time are services?"

"Shul," he said, smiling, "is in ten minutes. I want you to meet Mickey Halpern. This is Nathan Marx, our sergeant."

The third boy hopped forward. "Private Michael Halpern." He saluted.

"Salute officers, Halpern," I said. The boy dropped his hand, and, on its way down, in his nervousness, checked to see if his shirt pockets were buttoned.

"Shall I march them over, sir?" Grossbart asked. "Or are you coming along?"

From behind Grossbart, Fishbein piped up. "Afterward, they're having refreshments. A ladies auxiliary from St. Louis, the rabbi told us last week."

"The chaplain," Halpern whispered.

"You're welcome to come along," Grossbart said.

To avoid his plea, I looked away, and saw, in the windows of the barracks, a cloud of faces staring out at the four of us. "Hurry along, Grossbart," I said.

"O.K., then," he said. He turned to the others. "Double time, *march!*"

They started off, but ten feet away Grossbart spun around and, running backward, called to me "Good *shabbus,*° sir!" And then the three of them were swallowed into the alien Missouri dusk.

Even after they had disappeared over the parade ground, whose green was now a deep blue, I could hear Grossbart singing the double-time cadence, and as it grew dimmer and dimmer, it suddenly touched a deep memory—as did the slant of the light—and I was remembering the shrill sounds of a Bronx playground where, years ago, beside the Grand Concourse, I had played on long spring evenings such as this. It was a pleasant memory for a young man so far from peace and home, and it brought so many recollections with it that I began to grow exceedingly tender about myself. In fact, I indulged myself in a reverie so strong that I felt as though a hand were reaching down inside me. It had to reach so very far to touch me! It had to reach past those days in the forests of Belgium, and past the dying I'd refused to weep over; past the nights in German farmhouses whose books we'd burned to warm us; past endless stretches when I had shut off all softness I might feel for my fellows, and had managed even to deny myself the posture of a conqueror—the swagger that I, as a Jew, might well have worn as my boots whacked against the rubble of Wesel, Münster, and Braunschweig.

But now one night noise, one rumor of home and time past, and memory plunged down through all I had anesthetized, and came to what I suddenly remembered was myself. So it was not altogether curious that, in search of more of me, I found myself following Grossbart's tracks to Chapel No. 3, where the Jewish services were being held.

I took a seat in the last row, which was empty. Two rows in front of me sat Grossbart, Fishbein, and Halpern, holding little white Dixie cups. Each row of seats was raised higher than the one in front of it, and I could see clearly what was going on. Fishbein was pouring the contents of his cup into

---

shabbus: Sabbath

Grossbart's, and Grossbart looked mirthful as the liquid made a purple arc between Fishbein's hand and his. In the glaring yellow light, I saw the chaplain standing on the platform at the front; he was chanting the first line of the responsive reading. Grossbart's prayer book remained closed on his lap; he was swishing the cup around. Only Halpern responded to the chant by praying. The fingers of his right hand were spread wide across the cover of his open book. His cap was pulled down low onto his brow, which made it round, like a yarmulke.° From time to time, Grossbart wet his lips at the cup's edge; Fishbein, his long yellow face a dying light bulb, looked from here to there, craning forward to catch sight of the faces down the row, then of those in front of him, then behind. He saw me, and his eyelids beat a tattoo. His elbow slid into Grossbart's side, his neck inclined toward his friend, he whispered something, and then, when the congregation next responded to the chant, Grossbart's voice was among the others. Fishbein looked into his book now, too; his lips, however, didn't move.

Finally, it was time to drink the wine. The chaplain smiled down at them as Grossbart swigged his in one long gulp, Halpern sipped, meditating, and Fishbein faked devotion with an empty cup. "As I look down amongst the congregation"—the chaplain grinned at the word—"this night, I see many new faces, and I want to welcome you to Friday-night services here at Camp Crowder. I am Major Leo Ben Ezra, your chaplain." Though an American, the chaplain spoke deliberately—syllable by syllable, almost—as though to communicate, above all, with the lip readers in his audience. "I have only a few words to say before we adjourn to the refreshment room, where the kind ladies of the Temple Sinai, St. Louis, Missouri, have a nice setting for you."

Applause and whistling broke out. After another momentary grin, the chaplain raised his hands, palms out, his eyes flicking upward a moment, as if to remind the troops where they were and Who Else might be in attendance. In the sudden silence that followed, I thought I heard Grossbart cackle, "Let the goyim° clean the floors!" Were those the words? I wasn't sure, but Fishbein, grinning, nudged Halpern. Halpern looked dumbly at him, then went back to his prayer book, which had been occupying him all through the rabbi's talk. One hand tugged at the black kinky hair that stuck out under his cap. His lips moved.

The rabbi continued. "It is about the food that I want to speak to you for a moment. I know, I know, I know," he intoned, wearily, "how in the mouths of most of you the *trafe*° food tastes like ashes. I know how you gag, some of you, and how your parents suffer to think of their children eating foods unclean and offensive to the palate. What can I tell you? I can only say, close your eyes and swallow as best you can. Eat what you must to live, and throw

yarmulke: skull cap
goyim: gentiles
trafe: nonkosher

away the rest. I wish I could help more. For those of you who find this impossible, may I ask that you try and try, but then come to see me in private. If your revulsion is so great, we will have to seek aid from those higher up."

A round of chatter rose and subsided. Then everyone sang "Ain Kelohainu"°; after all those years, I discovered I still knew the words. Then, suddenly, the service over, Grossbart was upon me. "Higher up? He means the General?"

"Hey, Shelly," Fishbein said, "he means God." He smacked his face and looked at Halpern. "How high can you go!"

"Sh-h-h!" Grossbart said. "What do you think, Sergeant?"

"I don't know," I said. "You better ask the chaplain."

"I'm going to. I'm making an appointment to see him in private. So is Mickey."

Halpern shook his head. "No, no, Sheldon—"

"You have rights, Mickey," Grossbart said. "They can't push us around."

"It's O.K.," said Halpern. "It bothers my mother, not me."

Grossbart looked at me. "Yesterday he threw up. From the hash. It was all ham and God knows what else."

"I have a cold—that was why," Halpern said. He pushed his yarmulke back into a cap.

"What about you, Fishbein?" I asked. "You kosher, too?"

He flushed. "A little. But I'll let it ride. I have a very strong stomach, and I don't eat a lot anyway." I continued to look at him, and he held up his wrist to reinforce what he'd just said; his watch strap was tightened to the last hole, and he pointed that out to me.

"But services are important to you?" I asked him.

He looked at Grossbart. "Sure, sir."

"'Sergeant.'"

"Not so much at home," said Grossbart, stepping between us, "but away from home it gives one a sense of his Jewishness."

"We have to stick together," Fishbein said.

I started to walk toward the door; Halpern stepped back to make way for me.

"That's what happened in Germany," Grossbart was saying, loud enough for me to hear. "They didn't stick together. They let themselves get pushed around."

I turned. "Look, Grossbart. This is the Army, not summer camp."

He smiled. "So?"

Halpern tried to sneak off, but Grossbart held his arm.

"Grossbart, how old are you?" I asked.

"Nineteen."

"And you?" I said to Fishbein.

"Ain Kelohainu": "There's no God like our God"

"The same. The same month, even."

"And what about him?" I pointed to Halpern, who had by now made it safely to the door.

"Eighteen," Grossbart whispered. "But like he can't tie his shoes or brush his teeth himself. I feel sorry for him."

"I feel sorry for all of us, Grossbart," I said, "but just act like a man. Just don't overdo it?"

"Overdo what, sir?"

"The 'sir' business, for one thing. Don't overdo that," I said.

I left him standing there. I passed by Halpern, but he did not look at me. Then I was outside, but, behind, I heard Grossbart call, "Hey, Mickey, my *leben,*° come on back. Refreshments!"

"Leben!" My grandmother's word for me!

One morning a week later, while I was working at my desk, Captain Barrett shouted for me to come into his office. When I entered, he had his helmet liner squashed down so far on his head that I couldn't even see his eyes. He was on the phone, and when he spoke to me, he cupped one hand over the mouthpiece. "Who the hell is Grossbart?"

"Third platoon, Captain," I said. "A trainee."

"What's all this stink about food? His mother called a goddam congressman about the food." He uncovered the mouthpiece and slid his helmet up until I could see his bottom eyelashes. "Yes, sir," he said into the phone. "Yes, sir. I'm still here, sir. I'm asking Marx, here, right now—"

He covered the mouthpiece again and turned his head back toward me. "Lightfoot Harry's on the phone," he said, between his teeth. "This congressman calls General Lyman, who calls Colonel Sousa, who calls the Major, who calls me. They're just dying to stick this thing on me. Whatsa matter?" He shook the phone at me. "I don't feed the troops? What is this?"

"Sir, Grossbart is strange—" Barrett greeted that with a mockingly indulgent smile. I altered my approach. "Captain, he's a very orthodox Jew, and so he's only allowed to eat certain foods."

"He throws up, the congressman said. Every time he eats something, his mother says, he throws up!"

"He's accustomed to observing the dietary laws, Captain."

"So why's his old lady have to call the White House?"

"Jewish parents, sir—they're apt to be more protective than you expect. I mean, Jews have a very close family life. A boy goes away from home, sometimes the mother is liable to get very upset. Probably the boy mentioned something in a letter, and his mother misinterpreted."

"I'd like to punch him one right in the mouth," the Captain said. "There's a war on, and he wants a silver platter!"

leben: darling

"I don't think the boy's to blame, sir. I'm sure we can straighten it out by just asking him. Jewish parents worry—"

"*All* parents worry, for Christ's sake. But they don't get on their high horse and start pulling strings—"

I interrupted, my voice higher, tighter than before. "The home life, Captain, is very important—but you're right, it may sometimes get out of hand. It's a very wonderful thing, Captain, but because it's so close, this kind of thing . . ."

He didn't listen any longer to my attempt to present both myself and Lightfoot Harry with an explanation for the letter. He turned back to the phone. "Sir?" he said. "Sir—Marx, here, tells me Jews have a tendency to be pushy. He says he thinks we can settle it right here in the company . . . Yes, sir . . . I *will* call back, sir, soon as I can." He hung up. "Where are the men, Sergeant?"

"On the range."

With a whack on the top of his helmet, he crushed it down over his eyes again, and charged out of his chair. "We're going for a ride," he said.

The Captain drove, and I sat beside him. It was a hot spring day, and under my newly starched fatigues I felt as though my armpits were melting down into my sides and chest. The roads were dry, and by the time we reached the firing range, my teeth felt gritty with dust, though my mouth had been shut the whole trip. The Captain slammed the brakes on and told me to get the hell out and find Grossbart.

I found him on his belly, firing wildly at the five-hundred-feet target. Waiting their turns behind him were Halpern and Fishbein. Fishbein, wearing a pair of steel-rimmed G.I. glasses I hadn't seen on him before, had the appearance of an old peddler who would gladly have sold you his rifle and the cartridges that were slung all over him. I stood back by the ammo boxes, waiting for Grossbart to finish spraying the distant target. Fishbein straggled back to stand near me.

"Hello, Sergeant Marx," he said.

"How are you?" I mumbled.

"Fine, thank you. Sheldon's really a good shot."

"I didn't notice."

"I'm not so good, but I think I'm getting the hang of it now. Sergeant, I don't mean to, you know, ask what I shouldn't—" The boy stopped. He was trying to speak intimately, but the noise of the shooting forced him to shout at me.

"What is it?" I asked. Down the range, I saw Captain Barrett standing up in the jeep, scanning the line for me and Grossbart.

"My parents keep asking and asking where we're going," Fishbein said. "Everybody says the Pacific. I don't care, but my parents—If I could relieve their minds, I think I could concentrate more on my shooting."

"I don't know where, Fishbein. Try to concentrate anyway."

"Sheldon says you might be able to find out."

"I don't know a thing, Fishbein. You just take it easy, and don't let Sheldon—"

"*I'm* taking it easy, Sergeant. It's at home—"

Grossbart had finished on the line, and was dusting his fatigues with one hand. I called to him. "Grossbart, the Captain wants to see you."

He came toward us. His eyes blazed and twinkled. "Hi!"

"Don't point that rifle!" I said.

"I wouldn't shoot you, Sarge." He gave me a smile as wide as a pumpkin, and turned the barrel aside.

"Damn you, Grossbart, this is no joke! Follow me."

I walked ahead of him, and had the awful suspicion that, behind me, Grossbart was *marching*, his rifle on his shoulder as though he were a one-man detachment. At the jeep, he gave the Captain a rifle salute. "Private Sheldon Grossbart, sir."

"At ease, Grossman." The Captain sat down, slid over into the empty seat, and, crooking a finger, invited Grossbart closer.

"Bart, sir. Sheldon Gross*bart*. It's a common error." Grossbart nodded at me; *I* understood, he indicated. I looked away just as the mess truck pulled up to the range, disgorging a half-dozen K.P.s with rolled-up sleeves. The mess sergeant screamed at them while they set up the chow line equipment.

"Grossbart, your mama wrote some congressman that we don't feed you right. Do your know that?" the Captain said.

"It was my father, sir. He wrote to Representative Franconi that my religion forbids me to eat certain foods."

"What religion is that, Grossbart?"

"Jewish."

"'Jewish, *sir*,'" I said to Grossbart.

"Excuse me, sir, Jewish, sir."

"What have you been living on?" the Captain asked. "You've been in the Army a month already. You don't look to me like you're falling to pieces."

"I eat because I have to, sir. But Sergeant Marx will testify to the fact that I don't eat one mouthful more than I need to in order to survive."

"Is that so, Marx?" Barrett asked.

"I've never seen Grossbart eat, sir," I said.

"But you heard the rabbi," Grossbart said. "He told us what to do, and I listened."

The Captain looked at me. "Well, Marx?"

"I still don't know what he eats and doesn't eat, sir."

Grossbart raised his arms to plead with me, and it looked for a moment as though he were going to hand me his weapon to hold. "But, Sergeant—"

"Look, Grossbart, just answer the Captain's questions," I said sharply.

Barrett smiled at me, and I resented it. "All right, Grossbart," he said. "What is it you want? The little piece of paper? You want out?"

"No, sir. Only to be allowed to live as a Jew. And for the others, too."

"What others?"

"Fishbein, sir, and Halpern."

"They don't like the way we serve, either?"

"Halpern throws up, sir. I've seen it."

"I thought *you* throw up."

"Just once, sir. I didn't know the sausage was sausage."

"We'll give menus, Grossbart. We'll show training films about the food, so you can identify when we're trying to poison you."

Grossbart did not answer. The men had been organized into two long chow lines. At the tail end of one, I spotted Fishbein—or, rather, his glasses spotted me. They winked sunlight back at me. Halpern stood next to him, patting the inside of his collar with a khaki handkerchief. They moved with the line as it began to edge up toward the food. The mess sergeant was still screaming at the K.P.s. For a moment, I was actually terrified by the thought that somehow the mess sergeant was going to become involved in Grossbart's problem.

"Marx," the Captain said, "you're a Jewish fella—am I right?"

I played straight man. "Yes, sir."

"How long you been in the Army? Tell this boy."

"Three years and two months."

"A year in combat, Grossbart. Twelve goddam months in combat all through Europe. I admire this man." The Captain snapped a wrist against my chest. "Do you hear him peeping about the food? Do you? I want an answer, Grossbart. Yes or no."

"No, sir."

"And why not? He's a Jewish fella."

"Some things are more important to some Jews than other things to other Jews."

Barrett blew up. "Look, Grossbart. Marx, here, is a good man—a goddam hero. When you were in high school, Sergeant Marx was killing Germans. Who does more for the Jews—you, by throwing up over a lousy piece of sausage, a piece of first-cut meat, or Marx, by killing those Nazi bastards? If I was a Jew, Grossbart, I'd kiss this man's feet. He's a goddam hero, and *he* eats what we give him. Why do you have to cause trouble is what I want to know! What is it you're buckin' for—a discharge?"

"No, sir."

"I'm talking to a wall! Sergeant, get him out of my way." Barrett swung himself back into the driver's seat. "I'm going to see the chaplain." The engine roared, the jeep spun around in a whirl of dust, and the Captain was headed back to camp.

For a moment, Grossbart and I stood side by side, watching the jeep. Then he looked at me and said, "I don't want to start trouble. That's the first thing they toss up to us."

When he spoke, I saw that his teeth were white and straight, and the sight of them suddenly made me understand that Grossbart actually did have parents—that once upon a time someone had taken little Sheldon to the dentist. He was their son. Despite all the talk about his parents, it was hard to believe in Grossbart as a child, an heir—as related by blood to anyone, mother, father, or, above all, to me. This realization led me to another.

"What does your father do, Grossbart?" I asked as we started to walk back toward the chow line.

"He's a tailor."

"An American?"

"Now, yes. A son in the Army," he said, jokingly.

"And your mother?" I asked.

He winked. "A *ballabusta*.° She practically sleeps with a dustcloth in her hand."

"She's also an immigrant?"

"All she talks is Yiddish, still."

"And your father, too?"

"A little English. 'Clean,' 'Press,' 'Take the pants in.' That's the extent of it. But they're good to me."

"Then, Grossbart—" I reached out and stopped him. He turned toward me, and when our eyes met, his seemed to jump back, to shiver in their sockets. "Grossbart—you were the one who wrote that letter, weren't you?"

It took only a second or two for his eyes to flash happy again. "Yes." He walked on, and I kept pace. "It's what my father *would* have written if he had known how. It was his name, though. *He* signed it. He even mailed it. I sent it home. For the New York postmark."

I was astonished, and he saw it. With complete seriousness, he thrust his right arm in front of me. "Blood is blood, Sergeant," he said, pinching the blue vein in his wrist.

"What the hell *are* you trying to do, Grossbart?" I asked. "I've seen you eat. Do you know that? I told the Captain I don't know what you eat, but I've seen you eat like a hound at chow."

"We work hard, Sergeant. We're in training. For a furnace to work, you've got to feed it coal."

"Why did you say in the letter that you threw up all the time?"

"I was really talking about Mickey there. I was talking *for* him. He would never write, Sergeant, though I pleaded with him. He'll waste away to nothing if I don't help. Sergeant, I used my name—my father's name—but it's Mickey, and Fishbein, too, I'm watching out for."

"You're a regular Messiah, aren't you?"

We were at the chow line now.

"That's a good one, Sergeant," he said, smiling. "But who knows? Who can tell? Maybe you're the Messiah—a little bit. What Mickey says is the Messiah is a collective idea. He went to Yeshiva,° Mickey, for a while. He

ballabusta: housewife
Yeshiva: seminary

says *together* we're the Messiah. Me a little bit, you a little bit. You should hear that kid talk, Sergeant, when he gets going."

"Me a little bit, you a little bit," I said. "You'd like to believe that, wouldn't you, Grossbart? That would make everything so clean for you."

"It doesn't seem too bad a thing to believe, Sergeant. It only means we should all *give* a little, is all."

I walked off to eat my rations with the other noncoms.

Two days later, a letter addressed to Captain Barrett passed over my desk. It had come through the chain of command—from the office of Congressman Franconi, where it had been received, to General Lyman, to Colonel Sousa, to Major Lamont, now to Captain Barrett. I read it over twice. It was dated May 14, the day Barrett had spoken with Grossbart on the rifle range.

Dear Congressman:

First let me thank you for your interest in behalf of my son, Private Sheldon Grossbart. Fortunately, I was able to speak with Sheldon on the phone the other night, and I think I've been able to solve our problem. He is, as I mentioned in my last letter, a very religious boy, and it was only with the greatest difficulty that I could persuade him that the religious thing to do—what God Himself would want Sheldon to do—would be to suffer the pangs of religious remorse for the good of his country and all mankind. It took some doing, Congressman, but finally he saw the light. In fact, what he said (and I wrote down the words on a scratch pad so as never to forget), what he said was "I guess you're right, Dad. So many millions of my fellow-Jews gave up their lives to the enemy, the least I can do is live for a while minus a bit of my heritage so as to help end this struggle and regain for all the children of God dignity and humanity." That, Congressman, would make any father proud.

By the way, Sheldon wanted me to know—and to pass on to you—the name of a soldier who helped him reach this decision: SERGEANT NATHAN MARX. Sergeant Marx is a combat veteran who is Sheldon's first sergeant. This man has helped Sheldon over some of the first hurdles he's had to face in the Army, and is in part responsible for Sheldon's changing his mind about the dietary laws. I know Sheldon would appreciate any recognition Marx could receive.

Thank you and good luck. I look forward to seeing your name on the next election ballot.

Respectfully,
Samuel E. Grossbart

Attached to the Grossbart communiqué was another, addressed to General Marshall Lyman, the post commander, and signed by Representative Charles E. Franconi, of the House of Representatives. The communiqué informed General Lyman that Sergeant Nathan Marx was a credit to the U.S. Army and the Jewish people.

What was Grossbart's motive in recanting? Did he feel he'd gone too far? Was the letter a strategic retreat—a crafty attempt to strengthen what he considered our alliance? Or had he actually changed his mind, via an imaginary dialogue between Grossbart *père* and Grossbart *fils?* I was puzzled, but only for a few days—that is, only until I realized that, whatever his reasons, he had actually decided to disappear from my life; he was going to allow himself to become just another trainee. I saw him at inspection, but he never winked; at chow formations, but he never flashed me a sign. On Sunday, with the other trainees, he would sit around watching the noncoms' softball team, for which I pitched, but not once did he speak an unnecessary word to me. Fishbein and Halpern retreated, too—at Grossbart's command, I was sure. Apparently he had seen that wisdom lay in turning back before he plunged over into the ugliness of privilege undeserved. Our separation allowed me to forgive him our past encounters, and finally, to admire him for his good sense.

Meanwhile, free of Grossbart, I grew used to my job and my administrative tasks. I stepped on a scale one day, and discovered I had truly become a noncombatant; I had gained seven pounds. I found patience to get past the first three pages of a book. I thought about the future more and more, and wrote letters to girls I'd known before the war. I even got a few answers. I sent away to Columbia for a Law School catalogue. I continued to follow the war in the Pacific, but it was not my war. I thought I could see the end, and sometimes, at night, I dreamed that I was walking on the streets of Manhattan—Broadway, Third Avenue, 116th Street, where I had lived the three years I attended Columbia. I curled myself around these dreams and I began to be happy.

And then, one Sunday, when everybody was away and I was alone in the orderly room reading a month-old copy of the *Sporting News,* Grossbart reappeared.

"You a baseball fan, Sergeant?"

I looked up. "How are you?"

"Fine," Grossbart said. "They're making a soldier out of me."

"How are Fishbein and Halpern?"

"Coming along," he said. "We've got no training this afternoon. They're at the movies."

"How come you're not with them?"

"I wanted to come over and say hello."

He smiled—a shy, regular-guy smile, as though he and I well knew that our friendship drew its sustenance from unexpected visits, remembered birthdays, and borrowed lawnmowers. At first it offended me, and then the feeling was swallowed by the general uneasiness I felt at the thought that everyone on the post was locked away in a dark movie theater and I was here alone with Grossbart. I folded up my paper.

"Sergeant," he said, "I'd like to ask a favor. It is a favor, and I'm making no bones about it."

He stopped, allowing me to refuse him a hearing—which, of course, forced me into a courtesy I did not intend. "Go ahead."

"Well, actually, it's two favors."

I said nothing.

"The first one's about these rumors. Everybody says we're going to the Pacific."

"As I told your friend Fishbein, I don't know," I said. "You'll just have to wait to find out. Like everybody else."

"You think there's a chance of any of us going East?"

"Germany?" I said. "Maybe."

"I meant New York."

"I don't think so, Grossbart. Offhand."

"Thanks for the information, Sergeant," he said.

"It's not information, Grossbart. Just what I surmise."

"It certainly would be good to be near home. My parents—you know." He took a step toward the door and then turned back. "Oh, the other thing. May I ask the other?"

"What is it?"

"The other thing is—I've got relatives in St. Louis, and they say they'll give me a whole Passover dinner if I can get down there. God, Sergeant, that'd mean an awful lot to me."

I stood up. "No passes during basic, Grossbart."

"But we're off from now till Monday morning, Sergeant. I could leave the post and no one would even know."

"I'd know. You'd know."

"But that's all. Just the two of us. Last night, I called my aunt, and you should have heard her. 'Come—come,' she said. 'I got gefilte fish, *chrain*°— the works!' Just a day, Sergeant. I'd take the blame if anything happened."

"The Captain isn't here to sign a pass."

"You could sign."

"Look, Grossbart—"

"Sergeant, for two months, practically, I've been eating *trafe* till I want to die."

"I thought you'd made up your mind to live with it. To be minus a little bit of heritage."

He pointed a finger at me. "You!" he said. "That wasn't for you to read."

"I read it. So what?"

"The letter was addressed to a congressman."

"Grossbart, don't feed me any baloney. You *wanted* me to read it."

"Why are you persecuting me, Sergeant?"

"Are you kidding!"

"I've run into this before," he said, "but never from my own!"

---

gefilte fish; *chrain*: seasoned chopped fish; horseradish

"Get out of here, Grossbart! Get the hell out of my sight!"

He did not move. "Ashamed, that's what you are," he said. "So you take it out on the rest of us. They say Hitler himself was half a Jew. Hearing you, I wouldn't doubt it."

"What are you trying to do with me, Grossbart?" I asked him. "What are you after? You want me to give you special privileges, to change the food, to find out about your orders, to give you weekend passes."

"You even talk like a goy!"° Grossbart shook his fist. "Is this just a weekend pass I'm asking for? Is a Seder° sacred, or not?"

Seder! It suddenly occurred to me that Passover had been celebrated weeks before. I said so.

"That's right," he replied. "Who says no? A month ago—and I was in the field eating hash! And now all I ask is a simple favor. A Jewish boy I thought would understand. My aunt's willing to go out of her way—to make a Seder a month later . . ." He turned to go, mumbling.

"Come back here!" I called. He stopped and looked at me. "Grossbart, why can't you be like the rest? Why do you have to stick out like a sore thumb?"

"Because I'm a Jew, Sergeant. I *am* different. Better, maybe not. But different."

"This is a war, Grossbart. For the time being *be* the same."

"I refuse."

"What?"

"I refuse. I can't stop being me, that's all there is to it." Tears came to his eyes. "It's a hard thing to be a Jew. But now I understand what Mickey says—it's a harder thing to stay one." He raised a hand sadly toward me. "Look at *you*."

"Stop crying!"

"Stop this, stop that, stop the other thing! *You* stop, Sergeant. Stop closing your heart to your own!" And, wiping his face with his sleeve, he ran out the door. "The least we can do for one another—the least . . ."

An hour later, looking out of the window, I saw Grossbart headed across the field. He wore a pair of starched khakis and carried a little leather ditty bag. I went out into the heat of the day. It was quiet; not a soul was in sight except, over by the mess hall, four K.P.'s sitting around a pan, sloped forward from their waists, gabbing and peeling potatoes in the sun.

"Grossbart!" I called.

He looked toward me and continued walking.

"Grossbart, get over here!"

He turned and came across the field. Finally, he stood before me.

"Where are you going?" I asked.

"St. Louis. I don't care."

goy: gentile
Seder: ceremonial dinner on first day of Passover

"You'll get caught without a pass."

"So I'll get caught without a pass."

"You'll go to the stockade."

"I'm *in* the stockade." He made an about-face and headed off.

I let him go only a step or two. "Come back here," I said, and he followed me into the office, where I typed out a pass and signed the Captain's name, and my own initials after it.

He took the pass and then, a moment later, reached out and grabbed my hand. "Sergeant, you don't know how much this means to me."

"O.K.," I said. "Don't get in any trouble."

"I wish I could show you how much this means to me."

"Don't do me any favors. Don't write any more congressmen for citations."

He smiled. "You're right. I won't. But let me do something."

"Bring me a piece of that gefilte fish. Just get out of here."

"I will!" he said. "With a slice of carrot and a little horseradish. I won't forget."

"All right. Just show your pass at the gate. And don't tell *anybody.*"

"I won't. It's a month late, but a good Yom Tov° to you."

"Good Yom Tov, Grossbart," I said.

"You're a good Jew, Sergeant. You like to think you have a hard heart, but underneath you're a fine, decent man. I mean that."

Those last three words touched me more than any words from Grossbart's mouth had the right to. "All right, Grossbart," I said. "Now call me 'sir,' and get the hell out of here."

He ran out the door and was gone. I felt very pleased with myself; it was a great relief to stop fighting Grossbart, and it had cost me nothing. Barrett would never find out, and if he did, I could manage to invent some excuse. For a while, I sat at my desk, comfortable in my decision. Then the screen door flew back and Grossbart burst in again. "Sergeant!" he said. Behind him I saw Fishbein and Halpern, both in starched khakis, both carrying ditty bags like Grossbart's.

"Sergeant, I caught Mickey and Larry coming out of the movies. I almost missed them."

"Grossbart—did I say to tell no one?" I said.

"But my aunt said I could bring friends. That I should, in fact."

"*I'm* the Sergeant, Grossbart—not your aunt!"

Grossbart looked at me in disbelief. He pulled Halpern up by his sleeve. "Mickey, tell the Sergeant what this would mean to you."

Halpern looked at me and, shrugging, said, "A lot."

Fishbein stepped forward without prompting. "This would mean a great deal to me and my parents, Sergeant Marx."

"No!" I shouted.

Yom Tov: holiday (literally, good day)

Grossbart was shaking his head. "Sergeant, I could see you denying me, but how can you deny Mickey, a Yeshiva boy—that's beyond me."

"I'm not denying Mickey anything," I said. "You just pushed a little too hard, Grossbart. *You* denied him."

"I'll give him my pass, then," Grossbart said. "I'll give him my aunt's address and a little note. At least let him go."

In a second, he had crammed the pass into Halpern's pants pocket. Halpern looked at me, and so did Fishbein. Grossbart was at the door, pushing it open. "Mickey, bring me a piece of gefilte fish, at least," he said, and then he was outside again.

The three of us looked at one another, and then I said, "Halpern, hand that pass over."

He took it from his pocket and gave it to me. Fishbein had now moved to the doorway, where he lingered. He stood there for a moment with his mouth slightly open, and then he pointed to himself. "And me?" he asked.

His utter ridiculousness exhausted me. I slumped down in my seat and felt pulses knocking at the back of my eyes. "Fishbein," I said, "you understand I'm not trying to deny you anything, don't you? If it was my Army, I'd serve gefilte fish in the mess hall. I'd sell *kugel*° in the PX, honest to God."

Halpern smiled.

"You understand, don't you, Halpern?"

"Yes, Sergeant."

"And you, Fishbein? I don't want enemies. I'm just like you—I want to serve my time and go home. I miss the same things you miss."

"Then, Sergeant," Fishbein said, "why don't you come, too?"

"Where?"

"To St. Louis. To Shelly's aunt. We'll have a regular Seder. Play hide-the-matzoh."° He gave me a broad, black-toothed smile.

I saw Grossbart again, on the other side of the screen.

"Psst!" He waved a piece of paper. "Mickey, here's the address. Tell her I couldn't get away."

Halpern did not move. He looked at me, and I saw the shrug moving up his arms into his shoulders again. I took the cover off my typewriter and made out passes for him and Fishbein. "Go," I said. "The three of you."

I thought Halpern was going to kiss my hand.

That afternoon, in a bar in Joplin, I drank beer and listened with half an ear to the Cardinal game. I tried to look squarely at what I'd become involved in, and began to wonder if perhaps the struggle with Grossbart wasn't as much my fault as his. What was I that I had to *muster* generous feelings? Who was I to have been feeling so grudging, so tight-hearted? After all, I wasn't being asked to move the world. Had I a right, then, or a reason, to clamp

kugel: noodle pudding
matzoh: unleavened bread eaten at Passover

down on Grossbart, when that meant clamping down on Halpern, too? And Fishbein—that ugly, agreeable soul? Out of the many recollections of my childhood that had tumbled over me these past few days I heard my grandmother's voice: "What are you making a *tsimmes*?"° It was what she would ask my mother when, say, I had cut myself while doing something I shouldn't have done, and her daughter was busy bawling me out. I needed a hug and a kiss, and my mother would moralize. But my grandmother knew—mercy overrides justice. I should have known it, too. Who was Nathan Marx to be such a penny pincher with kindness? Surely, I thought, the Messiah himself—if He should ever come—won't niggle over nickels and dimes. God willing, he'll hug and kiss.

The next day, while I was playing softball over on the parade ground, I decided to ask Bob Wright, who was noncom in charge of Classification and Assignment, where he thought our trainees would be sent when their cycle ended, in two weeks. I asked casually, between innings, and he said, "They're pushing them all into the Pacific. Shulman cut the orders on your boys the other day."

The news shocked me, as though I were the father of Halpern, Fishbein, and Grossbart.

That night, I was just sliding into sleep when someone tapped on my door. "Who is it?" I asked.

"Sheldon."

He opened the door and came in. For a moment, I felt his presence without being able to see him. "How was it?" I asked.

He popped into sight in the near-darkness before me. "Great, Sergeant." Then he was sitting on the edge of the bed. I sat up.

"How about you?" he asked. "Have a nice weekend?"

"Yes."

"The others went to sleep." He took a deep, paternal breath. We sat silent for a while, and a homey feeling invaded my ugly little cubicle; the door was locked, the cat was out, the children were safely in bed.

"Sergeant, can I tell you something? Personal?"

I did not answer, and he seemed to know why. "Not about me. About Mickey. Sergeant, I never felt for anybody like I feel for him. Last night I heard Mickey in the bed next to me. He was crying so, it could have broken your heart. Real sobs."

"I'm sorry to hear that."

"I had to talk to him to stop him. He held my hand, Sergeant—he wouldn't let it go. He was almost hysterical. He kept saying if he only knew where we were going. Even if he knew it *was* the Pacific, that would be better than nothing. Just to know."

Long ago, someone had taught Grossbart the sad rule that only lies can

tsimmes: a to-do

get the truth. Not that I couldn't believe in the fact of Halpern's crying; his eyes *always* seemed red-rimmed. But, fact or not, it became a lie when Grossbart uttered it. He was entirely strategic. But then—it came with the force of indictment—so was I! There are strategies of aggression, but there are strategies of retreat as well. And so, recognizing that I myself had not been without craft and guile, I told him what I knew. "It is the Pacific."

He let out a small gasp, which was not a lie. "I'll tell him. I wish it was otherwise."

"So do I."

He jumped on my words. "You mean you think you could do something? A change, maybe?"

"No, I couldn't do a thing."

"Don't you know anybody over at C. and A.?"

"Grossbart, there's nothing I can do," I said. "If your orders are for the Pacific, then it's the Pacific."

"But Mickey—"

"Mickey, you, me—everybody, Grossbart. There's nothing to be done. Maybe the war'll end before you go. Pray for a miracle."

"But—"

"Good night, Grossbart." I settled back, and was relieved to feel the springs unbend as Grossbart rose to leave. I could see him clearly now; his jaw had dropped, and he looked like a dazed prizefighter. I noticed for the first time a little paper bag in his hand.

"Grossbart." I smiled. "My gift?"

"Oh, yes, Sergeant. Here—from all of us." He handed me the bag. "It's egg roll."

"Egg roll?" I accepted the bag and felt a damp grease spot on the bottom. I opened it, sure that Grossbart was joking.

"We thought you'd probably like it. You know—Chinese egg roll. We thought you'd probably have a taste for—"

"Your aunt served egg roll?"

"She wasn't home."

"Grossbart, she invited you. You told me she invited you and your friends."

"I know," he said. "I just reread the letter. *Next* week."

I got out of bed and walked to the window. "Grossbart," I said. But I was not calling to him.

"What?"

"What are you, Grossbart? Honest to God, what are you?"

I think it was the first time I'd asked him a question for which he didn't have an immediate answer.

"How can you do this to people?" I went on.

"Sergeant, the day away did us all a world of good. Fishbein, you should see him, he *loves* Chinese food."

"But the Seder," I said.

"We took second best, Sergeant."

Rage came charging at me. I didn't sidestep. "Grossbart, you're a liar!" I said. "You're a schemer and a crook. You've got no respect for anything. Nothing at all. Not for me, the truth—not even for poor Halpern! You use us all—"

"Sergeant, Sergeant, I feel for Mickey. Honest to God, I do. I *love* Mickey. I try—"

"You try! You feel!" I lurched toward him and grabbed his shirt front. I shook him furiously. "Grossbart, get out! Get out and stay the hell away from me. Because if I see you, I'll make your life miserable. *You understand that?*"

"Yes."

I let him free, and when he walked from the room, I wanted to spit on the floor where he had stood. I couldn't stop the fury. It engulfed me, owned me, till it seemed I could only rid myself of it with tears or an act of violence. I snatched from the bed the bag Grossbart had given me and, with all my strength, threw it out the window. And the next morning, as the men policed the area around the barracks, I heard a great cry go up from one of the trainees, who had been anticipating only his morning handful of cigarette butts and candy wrappers. "Egg roll!" he shouted. "Holy Christ, Chinese goddam egg roll!"

A week later, when I read the orders that had come down from C. and A., I couldn't believe my eyes. Every single trainee was to be shipped to Camp Stoneman, California, and from there to the Pacific—every trainee but one. Private Sheldon Grossbart. He was to be sent to Fort Monmouth, New Jersey. I read the mimeographed sheet several times. Dee, Farrell, Fishbein, Fuselli, Fylypowycz, Glinicki, Gromke, Gucwa, Halpern, Hardy, Helebrandt, right down to Anton Zygadlo—all were to be headed West before the month was out. All except Grossbart. He had pulled a string, and I wasn't it.

I lifted the phone and called C. and A.

The voice on the other end said smartly, "Corporal Shulman, sir."

"Let me speak to Sergeant Wright."

"Who is this calling, sir?"

"Sergeant Marx."

And, to my surprise, the voice said, *"Oh!"* Then, "Just a minute, Sergeant."

Shulman's *"Oh!"* stayed with me while I waited for Wright to come to the phone. Why *"Oh!"*? Who was Shulman? And then, so simply, I knew I'd discovered the string that Grossbart had pulled. In fact, I could hear Grossbart the day he'd discovered Shulman in the PX, or in the bowling alley, or maybe even at services. "Glad to meet you. Where you from? Bronx? Me, too. Do you know So-and-So? And So-and-So? Me, too! You work at C. and A.? Really? Hey, how's chances of getting East? Could you do something? Change something? Swindle, cheat, lie? We gotta help each other, you know.

If the Jews in Germany . . ."

Bob Wright answered the phone. "How are you, Nate? How's the pitching arm?"

"Good. Bob, I wonder if you could do me a favor." I heard clearly my own words, and they so reminded me of Grossbart that I dropped more easily than I could have imagined into what I had planned. "This may sound crazy, Bob, but I got a kid here on orders to Monmouth who wants them changed. He had a brother killed in Europe, and he's hot to go to the Pacific. Says he'd feel like a coward if he wound up Stateside. I don't know, Bob—can anything be done? Put somebody else in the Monmouth slot?"

"Who?" he asked cagily.

"Anybody. First guy in the alphabet. I don't care. The kid just asked if something could be done."

"What's his name?"

"Grossbart, Sheldon."

Wright didn't answer.

"Yeah," I said. "He's a Jewish kid, so he thought I could help him out. You know."

"I guess I can do something," he finally said. "The Major hasn't been around for weeks. Temporary duty to the golf course. I'll try, Nate, that's all I can say."

"I'd appreciate it, Bob. See you Sunday." And I hung up, perspiring.

The following day, the corrected orders appeared: Fishbein, Fuselli, Fylypowycz, Glinicki, Gromke, Grossbart, Gucwa, Halpern, Hardy . . . Lucky Private Harley Alton was to go to Fort Monmouth, New Jersey, where, for some reason or other, they wanted an enlisted man with infantry training.

After chow that night, I stopped back at the orderly room to straighten out the guard-duty roster. Grossbart was waiting for me. He spoke first.

"You son of a bitch!"

I sat down at my desk, and while he glared at me, I began to make the necessary alterations in the duty roster.

"What do you have against me?" he cried. "Against my family? Would it kill you for me to be near my father, God knows how many months he has left to him?"

"Why so?"

"His heart," Grossbart said. "He hasn't had enough troubles in a lifetime, you've got to add to them. I curse the day I ever met you, Marx! Shulman told me what happened over there. There's no limit to your anti-Semitism, is there? The damage you've done here isn't enough. You have to make a special phone call! You really want me dead!"

I made the last notations in the duty roster and got up to leave. "Good night, Grossbart."

"You owe me an explanation!" He stood in my path.

"Sheldon, you're the one who owes explanations."

He scowled. "To *you?*"

"To me, I think so—yes. Mostly to Fishbein and Halpern."

"That's right, twist things around. I owe nobody nothing. I've done all I could for them. Now I think I've got the right to watch out for myself."

"For each other we have to learn to watch out, Sheldon. You told me yourself."

"You call this watching out for me—what you did?"

"No. For all of us."

I pushed him aside and started for the door. I heard his furious breathing behind me, and it sounded like steam rushing from an engine of terrible strength.

"You'll be all right," I said from the door. And, I thought, so would Fishbein and Halpern be all right, even in the Pacific, if only Grossbart continued to see—in the obsequiousness of the one, the soft spirituality of the other—some profit for himself.

I stood outside the orderly room, and I heard Grossbart weeping behind me. Over in the barracks, in the lighted windows, I could see the boys in their T shirts sitting on their bunks talking about their orders, as they'd been doing for the past two days. With a kind of quiet nervousness, they polished shoes, shined belt buckles, squared away underwear, trying as best they could to accept their fate. Behind me, Grossbart swallowed hard, accepting his. And then, resisting with all my will an impulse to turn and seek pardon for my vindictiveness, I accepted my own.

QUESTIONS

1. More use of dilemma is made in this story than in any other in this text. Identify some of the dilemmas the protagonist finds himself in. Are they used primarily to create suspense, to reveal character, or to illuminate theme? Might all of these dilemmas be classified as specific applications of one general dilemma? If so, how might this general dilemma be described? (One suggestion for an answer is contained in the terms used by Nathan Marx's grandmother on page 155).

2. Sergeant Marx finds himself in so many dilemmas because he is trying to reconcile three roles—top sergeant, Jew, and human being. To what extent do these roles conflict? Point out places where Marx is thinking or acting primarily as a sergeant, as a Jew, as a human being.

3. The plot has four major episodes, centering in conflicts over (a) attendance at Friday night services, (b) company food, (c) pass to St. Louis, (d) shipping orders. Insofar as these involve conflict between Sergeant Marx and Grossbart, which is the victor in each?

4. "What are you, Grossbart? Honest to God, what are you?" asks Sergeant Marx. Answer this question as precisely as possible. What is Grossbart's philosophy? Catalogue the various methods he uses to achieve his goals.

5. Even more important to Sergeant Marx is the question, Who is Sergeant Marx? What does the fact that he asks this question (pages 154-55) tell us about him? By what principles does he try to govern his conduct? On page

156, Marx speaks of "strategies of aggression" and "strategies of retreat"; on what occasions does *he* use strategies similar to Grossbart's?

6. What are Sergeant Marx's motivations in his final decision? In which of his roles—sergeant, Jew, human being—is he acting at this point? Is his decision right?

7. What is meant by Sergeant Marx's final statement that he accepted his fate? What *is* his fate?

8. Describe as precisely as possible Captain Barrett's attitude toward Jews.

9. Differentiate Grossbart, Fishbein, and Halpern. How would you rank these three, Captain Barrett, and Sergeant Marx on a scale of human worth?

10. To what character (or characters) does the title refer? Is it used straightforwardly or ironically?

11. This story—by a Jewish author about Jewish characters—has a complex theme. Does the theme at its most general level necessarily involve the idea of Jewishness? Is it more crucial to the story that Nathan Marx is a Jew or a top sergeant? Try stating the theme without mentioning the idea of Jewishness. Now expand it to include the idea of Jewishness. Can it be stated without mentioning the idea of responsibility for command and judgment?

5. Point of View

The primitive storyteller, unbothered by considerations of form, simply spun a tale. "Once upon a time," he began, and proceeded to narrate the story to his listeners, describing the characters when necessary, telling what they thought and felt as well as what they did, and interjecting comments and ideas of his own. Modern fiction writers are artistically more self-conscious. They realize that there are many ways of telling a story; they decide upon a method before they begin and may even set up rules for themselves. Instead of telling the story themselves, they may let one of the characters tell it; they may tell it by means of letters or diaries; they may confine themselves to recording the thoughts of one of the characters. With the growth of artistic consciousness, the question of POINT OF VIEW, of who tells the story, and, therefore, of how it gets told, has assumed especial importance.

To determine the point of view of a story we ask, "Who tells the story?" and "How much is this person allowed to know?" and, especially, "To what extent does the author look inside the characters and report their thoughts and feelings?"

Though many variations and combinations are possible, the basic points of view are four, as follows:

1.	Omniscient	
2.	Limited omniscient	(a) Major character
		(b) Minor character
3.	First person	(a) Major character
		(b) Minor character
4.	Objective	

1. In the OMNISCIENT POINT OF VIEW, the story is told by the author, using the third person, and his knowledge and prerogatives are unlimited. He is free to go wherever he wishes, to peer inside the minds and hearts of his characters at will and tell us what they are thinking or feeling. He can interpret their behavior, and he can comment, if he wishes, on the significance of the story he is telling. He knows all. He can tell us as much or as little as he pleases.

The following version of Aesop's fable "The Ant and the Grasshopper" is told from the omniscient point of view. Notice that in it we are told not only what both characters do and say, but also what they think and feel; also, that the author comments at the end on the significance of the story. (The phrases in which the author enters into the thoughts or feelings of the ant and the grasshopper have been italicized; the comment by the author is printed in small capitals.)

> *Weary in every limb,* the ant tugged over the snow a piece of corn he had stored up last summer. *It would taste mighty good at dinner tonight.*
>
> A grasshopper, *cold and hungry,* looked on. *Finally he could bear it no longer.* "Please, friend ant, may I have a bite of corn?"
>
> "What were you doing all last summer?" asked the ant. He looked the grasshopper up and down. *He knew its kind.*
>
> "I sang from dawn till dark," replied the grasshopper, *happily unaware of what was coming next.*
>
> "Well," said the ant, *hardly bothering to conceal his contempt,* "since you sang all summer, you can dance all winter."
>
> HE WHO IDLES WHEN HE'S YOUNG
> WILL HAVE NOTHING WHEN HE'S OLD

Stories told from the omniscient point of view may differ widely in the amount of omniscience the author allows himself. In "The Bride Comes to Yellow Sky" (page 406) we share the thoughts and perceptions, though sometimes fleetingly, of most of the characters in the story: Jack Potter, the town marshall; his new bride; Scratchy Wilson, the drunk gunman; the porter and passengers on the train; the waiter in the dining car; the drummer and others in the Weary Gentleman Saloon; even the barkeeper's dog.

In "The Destructors," though we are taken into the minds of Blackie, Mike, the gang as a group, Old Misery, and the lorry driver, we are not taken into the mind of Trevor—the most important character. In "The Most Dangerous Game," we are confined to the thoughts and feelings of Rainsford, except for the brief passage between Rainsford's leap into the sea and his waking in Zaroff's bed, during which the point of view shifts to General Zaroff. In "The Pot of Gold" we are taken freely into the minds of Ralph and Laura, both separately and together, and the author comments in his own voice on their strengths and weaknesses of character, but he scrupulously stays out of the minds of other characters, letting us know about them only what Ralph or Laura can perceive.

The omniscient is the most flexible point of view and permits the widest scope. It is also the most subject to abuse. It offers constant danger that the author may come between the readers and the story, or that the continual shifting of viewpoint from character to character may cause a breakdown in coherence or unity. Used skillfully it enables the author to achieve simultaneous breadth and depth. Unskillfully used, it can destroy the illusion of reality that the story attempts to create.

2. In the LIMITED OMNISCIENT POINT OF VIEW, the author tells the story in the third person, but he tells it from the viewpoint of one character in the story. The author places himself at the elbow of this character, so to speak, and looks at the events of the story through his eyes and through his mind. He moves both inside and outside this character but never leaves his side. He tells us what this character sees and hears and what he thinks and feels; he possibly interprets the character's thoughts and behavior. He knows everything about this character—more than the character knows about himself—but he shows no knowledge of what *other* characters are thinking or feeling or doing, except for what his chosen character knows or can infer. The chosen character may be either a major or a minor character, a participant or an observer, and this choice also will be a very important one for the story. "The Japanese Quince" and "Miss Brill" are told from the limited omniscient point of view, from the viewpoint of the main character. The use of this viewpoint with a minor character is rare and is not illustrated in this book. Here is "The Ant and the Grasshopper" told, in the third person, from the point of view of the ant. Notice that this time we are told nothing of what the grasshopper thinks or feels. We see and hear and know of him only what the ant sees and hears and knows.

Weary in every limb, the ant tugged over the snow a piece of corn he had stored up last summer. *It would taste mighty good at dinner tonight. It was then that he noticed the grasshopper, looking cold and pinched.*

"Please, friend ant, may I have a bite of your corn?" asked the grasshopper.

He looked the grasshopper up and down. "What were you doing all last summer?" he asked. *He knew its kind.*

"I sang from dawn till dark," replied the grasshopper.

"Well," said the ant, *hardly bothering to conceal his contempt,* "since you sang all summer, you can dance all winter."

The limited omniscient point of view, since it acquaints us with the world through the mind and senses of only one person, approximates more closely than the omniscient the conditions of real life; it also offers a ready-made unifying element, since all details of the story are the experience of one person. At the same time it offers a limited field of observation, for the readers can go nowhere except where the chosen character goes, and there may be difficulty in having the character naturally cognizant of all important events. Clumsy writers will constantly have the focal character listening at keyholes, accidentally overhearing important conversations, or coincidentally being present when important events occur.

3. In the FIRST-PERSON POINT OF VIEW, the author disappears into one of the characters, who tells the story in the first person. This character, again, may be either a major or minor character, protagonist or observer, and it will make considerable difference whether the protagonist tells the story or someone else tells it. In "I'm a Fool," "An Ounce of Cure," and "Defender of the Faith," the protagonist tells the story in the first person. In "The Child by Tiger," "That Evening Sun," and "Spotted Horses," the story is told by an observer. The story below is told in the first person from the point of view of the grasshopper. (The whole story is italicized, because it all comes out of the grasshopper's mind.)

Cold and hungry, I watched the ant tugging over the snow a piece of corn he had stored up last summer. My feelers twitched, and I was conscious of a tic in my left hind leg. Finally I could bear it no longer. "Please, friend ant," I asked, "may I have a bite of your corn?"

He looked me up and down. "What were you doing all last summer?" he asked, rather too smugly it seemed to me.

"I sang from dawn till dark," I said innocently, remembering the happy times.

"Well," he said, with a priggish sneer, "since you sang all summer, you can dance all winter."

The first-person point of view shares the virtues and limitations of the limited omniscient. It offers, sometimes, a gain in immediacy and reality, since we get the story directly from a participant, the author as intermediary being eliminated. It offers no opportunity, however, for *direct* interpretation by the author, and there is constant danger that the narrator may be made to transcend his sensitivity, his knowledge, or his powers of language in telling the story. A good author, however, can make tremendous literary capital out of the very limitations of the narrator. The first-person point of view offers excellent opportunities for dramatic irony and for studies in limited or blunted human perceptivity. Often, as in "I'm a Fool," the very heart of the story may lie in the difference between what the narrator perceives and what the reader perceives. In such stories the author offers an interpretation of his materials *indirectly,* through the use of irony. He may also indicate his own judgment, more straightforwardly though still indirectly, by expressing it through the lips of a discerning and sympathetic narrator. In "Defender of the Faith" the reader is disposed to accept Sergeant Marx's interpretation of characters and events as being largely the author's own. Such identifications of a narrator's attitude with the author's, however, must always be undertaken with extreme caution; they are justified only if the total material of the story supports them. In "Defender of the Faith" the moral sensitivity and intelligence of the narrator reflects the author's own; nevertheless, much of the interest of the story arises from Marx's own uncertainty about his judgments—the nagging apprehension that he may be mistaken.

4. In the OBJECTIVE POINT OF VIEW, the author disappears into a kind of roving sound camera. This camera can go anywhere but can record only what is seen and heard. It cannot comment, interpret, or enter a character's mind. With this point of view (sometimes called also the DRAMATIC POINT OF VIEW) the reader is placed in the position of a spectator at a movie or play. He sees what the characters do and hears what they say but can only infer what they think or feel and what they are like. The author is not there to explain. The purest example of a story told from the objective point of view would be one written entirely in dialogue, for as soon as the author adds words of his own, he begins to interpret through his very choice of words. Actually, few stories using this point of view are antiseptically pure, for the limitations it imposes on the author are severe. "Hills Like White Elephants" is an excellent example, however, and "The Lottery" is essentially objective in its narration. The following version of "The Ant and the Grasshopper" is also told from the objective point of view. (Since we are nowhere taken into the thoughts or feelings of the characters, none of this version is printed in italics.)

> The ant tugged over the snow a piece of corn he had stored up last summer, perspiring in spite of the cold.
> A grasshopper, its feelers twitching and with a tic in its left hind leg,

looked on for some time. Finally he asked, "Please, friend ant, may I have a bite of your corn?"

The ant looked the grasshopper up and down. "What were you doing all last summer?" he snapped.

"I sang from dawn till dark," replied the grasshopper, not changing his tone.

"Well," said the ant, and a faint smile crept into his face, "since you sang all summer, you can dance all winter."

The objective point of view has the most speed and the most action; also, it forces readers to make their own interpretations. On the other hand, it must rely heavily on external action and dialogue, and it offers no opportunities for interpretation by the author.

Each of the points of view has its advantages, its limitations, and its peculiar uses. Ideally the choice of the author will depend on his story materials and his purpose. He should choose the point of view that enables him to present his particular materials most effectively in terms of his purpose. If he is writing a murder mystery, he will ordinarily avoid using the point of view of the murderer or the brilliant detective: otherwise he would have to reveal at the beginning the secrets he wishes to conceal till the end. On the other hand, if he is interested in exploring criminal psychology, the murderer's point of view might be by far the most effective. In the Sherlock Holmes stories, A. Conan Doyle effectively uses the somewhat imperceptive Dr. Watson as his narrator, so that the reader may be kept in the dark as long as possible and then be as amazed as Watson is by Holmes's deductive powers. In Dostoevsky's *Crime and Punishment,* however, the author is interested not in mystifying and surprising but in illuminating the moral and psychological operations of the human soul in the act of taking life; he therefore tells the story from the viewpoint of a sensitive and intelligent murderer.

For readers, the examination of point of view may be important both for understanding and for evaluating the story. First, they should know whether the events of the story are being interpreted by the author or by one of the characters. If the latter, they must ask how this character's mind and personality affect his interpretation, whether the character is perceptive or imperceptive, and whether his interpretation can be accepted at face value or must be discounted because of ignorance, stupidity, or self-deception. Often, as in "I'm a Fool" and "That Evening Sun," an author achieves striking and significant effects by using a narrator not aware of the full import of the events he is reporting.

Next, readers should ask whether the writer has chosen his point of view for maximum revelation of his material or for another reason. The author may choose his point of view mainly to conceal certain information till the end of the story and thus maintain suspense and create surprise. He may even deliberately mislead readers by presenting the events through a character who puts a false interpretation on them. Such a false interpretation may be justified if it leads eventually to more effective revelation of character and theme. If it is there merely to trick readers, it is obviously less justifiable.

Finally, readers should ask whether the author has used his selected point of view fairly and consistently. Even with the escape story, we have a right to demand fair treatment. If the person to whose thoughts and feelings we are admitted has pertinent information that he does not reveal, we legitimately feel cheated. To have a chance to solve a murder mystery, we must know what the detective knows. A writer also should be consistent in his point of view; or, if he shifts it, he should do so for a just artistic reason. Serious interpretive writers choose and use point of view so as to yield ultimately the greatest possible insight, either in fullness or in intensity.

Ring Lardner

HAIRCUT

I got another barber that comes over from Carterville and helps me out Saturdays, but the rest of the time I can get along all right alone. You can see for yourself that this ain't no New York City and besides that, the most of the boys works all day and don't have no leisure to drop in here and get themselves prettied up.

You're a newcomer, ain't you? I thought I hadn't seen you round before. I hope you like it good enough to stay. As I say, we ain't no New York City or Chicago, but we have pretty good times. Not as good, though, since Jim Kendall got killed. When he was alive, him and Hod Meyers used to keep this town in an uproar. I bet they was more laughin' done here than any town its size in America.

Jim was comical, and Hod was pretty near a match for him. Since Jim's gone, Hod tries to hold his end up just the same as ever, but it's tough goin' when you ain't got nobody to kind of work with.

They used to be plenty fun in here Saturdays. This place is jam-packed Saturdays, from four o'clock on. Jim and Hod would show up right after their supper, round six o'clock. Jim would set himself down in that big chair,

---

nearest the blue spittoon. Whoever had been settin' in that chair, why they'd get up when Jim come in and give it to him.

You'd of thought it was a reserved seat like they have sometimes in a theayter. Hod would generally always stand or walk up and down, or some Saturdays, of course, he'd be settin' in this chair part of the time, gettin' a haircut.

Well, Jim would set there a w'ile without openin' his mouth only to spit, and then finally he'd say to me, "Whitey,"—my right name, that is, my right first name, is Dick, but everybody round here calls me Whitey—Jim would say, "Whitey, your nose looks like a rosebud tonight. You must of been drinkin' some of your aw de cologne."

So I'd say, "No, Jim, but you look like you'd been drinking somethin' of that kind or somethin' worse."

Jim would have to laugh at that, but then he'd speak up and say, "No, I ain't had nothin' to drink, but that ain't sayin' I wouldn't like somethin'. I wouldn't even mind if it was wood alcohol."

Then Hod Meyers would say, "Neither would your wife." That would set everybody to laughin' because Jim and his wife wasn't on very good terms. She'd of divorced him only they wasn't no chance to get alimony and she didn't have no way to take care of herself and the kids. She couldn't never understand Jim. He *was* kind of rough, but a good fella at heart.

Him and Hod had all kinds of sport with Milt Sheppard. I don't suppose you've seen Milt. Well, he's got an Adam's apple that looks more like a mushmelon. So I'd be shavin' Milt and when I'd start to shave down here on his neck, Hod would holler, "Hey, Whitey, wait a minute! Before you cut into it, let's make up a pool and see who can guess closest to the number of seeds."

And Jim would say, "If Milt hadn't of been so hoggish, he'd of ordered a half a canteloupe instead of a whole one and it might not of stuck in his throat."

All the boys would roar at this and Milt himself would force a smile, though the joke was on him. Jim certainly was a card!

There's his shavin' mug, settin' on the shelf, right next to Charley Vail's. "Charles M. Vail." That's the druggist. He comes in regular for his shave, three times a week. And Jim's is the cup next to Charley's. "James H. Kendall." Jim won't need no shavin' mug no more, but I'll leave it there just the same for old time's sake. Jim certainly was a character!

Years ago, Jim used to travel for a canned goods concern over in Carterville. They sold canned goods. Jim had the whole northern half of the State and was on the road five days out of every week. He'd drop in here Saturdays and tell his experiences for that week. It was rich.

I guess he paid more attention to playin' jokes than makin' sales. Finally the concern let him out and he come right home here and told everybody he'd been fired instead of sayin' he'd resigned like most fellas would of.

It was a Saturday and the shop was full and Jim got up out of that chair and says, "Gentlemen, I got an important announcement to make. I been fired from my job."

Well, they asked him if he was in earnest and he said he was and nobody could think of nothin' to say till Jim finally broke the ice himself. He says, "I been sellin' canned goods and now I'm canned goods myself."

You see, the concern he'd been workin' for was a factory that made canned goods. Over in Carterville. And now Jim said he was canned himself. He was certainly a card!

For instance, they'd be a sign, "Henry Smith, Dry Goods." Well, Jim would write down the name and the name of the town and when he got to wherever he was goin' he'd mail back a postal card to Henry Smith at Benton and not sign no name to it, but he'd write on the card, well, somethin' like "Ask your wife about that book agent that spent the afternoon last week," or "Ask your Missus who kept her from gettin' lonesome the last time you was in Carterville." And he'd sign the card, "A Friend."

Of course, he never knew what really come of none of these jokes, but he could picture what *probably* happened and that was enough.

Jim didn't work very steady after he lost his position with the Carterville people. What he did earn, doin' odd jobs round town, why he spent pretty near all of it on gin and his family might of starved if the stores hadn't of carried them along. Jim's wife tried her hand at dressmakin', but they ain't nobody goin' to get rich makin' dresses in this town.

As I say, she'd of divorced Jim, only she seen that she couldn't support herself and the kids and she was always hopin' that some day Jim would cut his habits and give her more than two or three dollars a week.

There was a time when she would go to whoever he was workin' for and ask them to give her his wages, but after she done this once or twice, he beat her to it by borrowin' most of his pay in advance. He told it all round town, how he had outfoxed his Missus. He certainly was a caution!

But he wasn't satisfied with just outwittin' her. He was sore the way she had acted, tryin' to grab off his pay. And he made up his mind he'd get even. Well, he waited till Evans's Circus was advertised to come to town. Then he told his wife and kiddies that he was goin' to take them to the circus. The day of the circus, he told them he would get the tickets and meet them outside the entrance to the tent.

Well, he didn't have no intentions of bein' there or buyin' tickets or nothin'. He got full of gin and laid round Wright's poolroom all day. His wife and the kids waited and waited and of course he didn't show up. His wife didn't have a dime with her, or nowhere else, I guess. So she finally had to tell the kids it was all off and they cried like they wasn't never goin' to stop.

Well, it seems, w'ile they was cryin', Doc Stair came along and he asked what was the matter, but Mrs. Kendall was stubborn and wouldn't tell him, but the kids told him and he insisted on takin' them and their mother in the show. Jim found this out afterwards and it was one reason why he had it in for Doc Stair.

Doc Stair come here about a year and a half ago. He's a mighty handsome young fella and his clothes always look like he has them made to order. He goes to Detroit two or three times a year and w'ile he's there he must have a tailor take his measure and then make him a suit to order. They cost pretty near twice as much, but they fit a whole lot better than if you just bought them in a store.

For a w'ile everybody was wonderin' why a young doctor like Doc Stair should come to a town like this where we already got old Doc Gamble and Doc Foote that's both been here for years and all the practice in town was always divided between the two of them.

Then they was a story got round that Doc Stair's gal had throwed him over, a gal up in the Northern Peninsula somewhere, and the reason he come here was to hide himself away and forget it. He said himself that he thought they wasn't nothin' like general practice in a place like ours to fit a man to be a good all round doctor. And that's why he'd came.

Anyways, it wasn't long before he was makin' enough to live on, though they tell me that he never dunned nobody for what they owed him, and the folks here certainly has got the owin' habit, even in my business. If I had all that was comin' to me for just shaves alone, I could go to Carterville and put up at the Mercer for a week and see a different picture every night. For instance, they's old George Purdy—but I guess I shouldn't ought to be gossipin'.

Well, last year, our coroner died, died of the flu. Ken Beatty, that was his name. He was the coroner. So they had to choose another man to be coroner in his place and they picked Doc Stair. He laughed at first and said he didn't want it, but they made him take it. It ain't no job anybody would fight for and what a man makes out of it in a year would just about buy seeds for their garden. Doc's the kind, though, that can't say no to nothin' if you keep at him long enough.

But I was goin' to tell you about a poor boy we got here in town—Paul Dickson. He fell out of a tree when he was about ten years old. Lit on his head and it done somethin' to him and he ain't never been right. No harm in him, but just silly. Jim Kendall used to call him cuckoo; that's a name Jim had for anybody that was off their head, only he called people's head their bean. That was another of his gags, callin' head bean and callin' crazy people cuckoo. Only poor Paul ain't crazy, but just silly.

You can imagine that Jim used to have all kinds of fun with Paul. He'd send him to the White Front Garage for a left-handed monkey wrench. Of course they ain't no such a thing as a left-handed monkey wrench.

And once we had a kind of a fair here and they was a baseball game between the fats and the leans and before the game started Jim called Paul over and sent him way down to Schrader's hardware store to get a key for the pitcher's box.

They wasn't nothin' in the way of gags that Jim couldn't think up, when he put his mind to it.

Poor Paul was always kind of suspicious of people, maybe on account of how Jim had kept foolin' him. Paul wouldn't have much to do with anybody only his own mother and Doc Stair and a girl here in town named Julie Gregg. That is, she ain't a girl no more, but pretty near thirty or over.

When Doc first come to town, Paul seemed to feel like here was a real friend and he hung around Doc's office most of the w'ile; the only time he wasn't there was when he'd go home to eat or sleep or when he seen Julie Gregg doin' her shoppin'.

When he looked out Doc's window and seen her, he'd run downstairs and join her and tag along with her to the different stores. The poor boy was crazy about Julie and she always treated him mighty nice and made him feel like he was welcome, though of course it wasn't nothin' but pity on her side.

Doc done all he could to improve Paul's mind and he told me once that he really thought the boy was gettin' better, that they was times when he was as bright and sensible as anybody else.

But I was goin' to tell you about Julie Gregg. Old Man Gregg was in the lumber business, but got to drinkin' and lost most of his money and when he died, he didn't leave nothin' but the house and just enough insurance for the girl to skimp along on.

Her mother was a kind of half invalid and didn't hardly ever leave the house. Julie wanted to sell the place and move somewheres else after the old man died, but the mother said she was born here and would die here. It was tough on Julie, as the young people round this town—well, she's too good for them.

She's been away to school and Chicago and New York and different places and they ain't no subject she can't talk on, where you take the rest of the young folks here and you mention anything to them outside of Gloria Swanson or Tommy Meighan and they think you're delirious. Did you see Gloria in *Wages of Virtue?* You missed somethin'!

Well, Doc Stair hadn't been here more than a week when he come in one day to get shaved and I recognized who he was as he had been pointed out to me, so I told him about my old lady. She's been ailin' for a couple years and either Doc Gamble or Doc Foote, neither one, seemed to be helpin' her. So he said he would come out and see her, but if she was able to get out herself, it would be better to bring her to his office where he could make a completer examination.

So I took her to his office and w'ile I was waiting for her in the reception room, in come Julie Gregg. When somebody comes in Doc Stair's office, they's a bell that rings in his inside office so he can tell they's somebody to see him.

So he left my old lady inside and come out to the front office and that's the first time him and Julie met and I guess it was what they call love at first sight. But it wasn't fifty-fifty. This young fella was the slickest lookin' fella she'd ever seen in this town and she went wild over him. To him she was just a young lady that wanted to see the doctor.

She'd came on about the same business I had. Her mother had been doctorin' for years with Doc Gamble and Doc Foote and without no results. So she'd heard they was a new doc in town and decided to give him a try. He promised to call and see her mother that same day.

I said a minute ago that it was love at first sight on her part. I'm not only judgin' by how she acted afterwards but how she looked at him that first day in his office. I ain't no mind reader, but it was wrote all over her face that she was gone.

Now Jim Kendall, besides bein' a jokesmith and a pretty good drinker, well, Jim was quite a lady-killer. I guess he run pretty wild durin' the time he was on the road for them Carterville people, and besides that, he'd had a couple little affairs of the heart right here in town. As I say, his wife could of divorced him, only she couldn't.

But Jim was like the majority of men, and women, too, I guess. He wanted what he couldn't get. He wanted Julie Gregg and worked his head off tryin' to land her. Only he'd of said bean instead of head.

Well, Jim's habits and his jokes didn't appeal to Julie and of course he was a married man, so he didn't have no more chance than, well, than a rabbit. That's an expression of Jim's himself. When somebody didn't have no chance to get elected or somethin', Jim would always say they didn't have no more chance than a rabbit.

He didn't make no bones about how he felt. Right in here, more than once, in front of the whole crowd, he said he was stuck on Julie and anybody that could get her for him was welcome to his house and his wife and kids included. But she wouldn't have nothin' to do with him; wouldn't even speak to him on the street. He finally seen he wasn't gettin' nowheres with his usual line so he decided to try the rough stuff. He went right up to her house one evenin' and when she opened the door he forced his way in and grabbed her. But she broke loose and before he could stop her, she run in the next room and locked the door and phoned to Joe Barnes. Joe's the marshal. Jim could hear who she was phonin' to and he beat it before Joe got there.

Joe was an old friend of Julie's pa. Joe went to Jim the next day and told him what would happen if he ever done it again.

I don't know how the news of this little affair leaked out. Chances is that Joe Barnes told his wife and she told somebody else's wife and they told their husband. Anyways, it did leak out and Hod Meyers had the nerve to kid Jim about it, right here in this shop. Jim didn't deny nothin' and kind of laughed it off and said for us all to wait; that lots of people had tried to make a monkey out of him, but he always got even.

Meanw'ile everybody in town was wise to Julie's bein' wild mad over the Doc. I don't suppose she had any idear how her face changed when him and her was together; of course she couldn't of, or she'd of kept away from him. And she didn't know that we was all noticin' how many times she made excuses to go up to his office or pass it on the other side of the street and look up in his window to see if he was there. I felt sorry for her and so did most other people.

Hod Meyers kept rubbin' it into Jim about how the Doc had cut him out. Jim didn't pay no attention to the kiddin' and you could see he was plannin' one of his jokes.

One trick Jim had was the knack of changin' his voice. He could make you think he was a girl talkin' and he could mimic any man's voice. To show you how good he was along this line, I'll tell you the joke he played on me once.

You know, in most towns of any size, when a man is dead and needs a shave, why the barber that shaves him soaks him five dollars for the job; that is, he don't soak *him*, but whoever ordered the shave. I just charge three dollars because personally I don't mind much shavin' a dead person. They lay a whole lot stiller than live customers. The only thing is that you don't feel like talkin' to them and you get kind of lonesome.

Well, about the coldest day we ever had here, two years ago last winter, the phone rung at the house w'ile I was home to dinner and I answered the phone and it was a woman's voice and she said she was Mrs. John Scott and her husband was dead and would I come out and shave him.

Old John had always been a good customer of mine. But they live seven miles out in the country, on the Streeter road. Still I didn't see how I could say no.

So I said I would be there, but would have to come in a jitney and it might cost three or four dollars besides the price of the shave. So she, or the voice, said that was all right, so I got Frank Abbott to drive me out to the place and when I got there, who should open the door but old John himself! He wasn't no more dead than, well, than a rabbit.

It didn't take no private detective to figure out who had played me this little joke. Nobody could of thought it up but Jim Kendall. He certainly was a card!

I tell you this incident just to show you how he could disguise his voice and make you believe it was somebody else talkin'. I'd of swore it was Mrs. Scott had called me. Anyways, some woman.

Well, Jim waited till he had Doc Stair's voice down pat; then he went after revenge.

He called Julie up on a night when he knew Doc was over in Carterville. She never questioned but what it was Doc's voice. Jim said he must see her that night; he couldn't wait no longer to tell her somethin'. She was all excited and told him to come to the house. But he said he was expectin' an important long distance call and wouldn't she please forget her manners for once and come to his office. He said they couldn't nothin' hurt her and nobody would see her and he just *must* talk to her a little w'ile. Well, poor Julie fell for it.

Doc always keeps a night light in his office, so it looked to Julie like they was somebody there.

Meanw'ile Jim Kendall had went to Wright's poolroom, where they was a whole gang amusin' themselves. The most of them had drank plenty of gin, and they was a rough bunch even when sober. They was always strong for Jim's jokes and when he told them to come with him and see some fun they give up their card games and pool games and followed along.

Doc's office is on the second floor. Right outside his door they's a flight of stairs leadin' to the floor above. Jim and his gang hid in the dark behind these stairs.

Well, Julie come up to Doc's door and rung the bell and they was nothin' doin'. She rung it again and she rung it seven or eight times. Then she tried the door and found it locked. Then Jim made some kind of a noise and she heard it and waited a minute, and then she says, "Is that you, Ralph?" Ralph is Doc's first name.

They was no answer and it must of came to her all of a sudden that she'd been bunked. She pretty near fell downstairs and the whole gang after her. They chased her all the way home, hollerin', "Is that you, Ralph?" and "Oh, Ralphie, dear, is that you?" Jim says he couldn't holler it himself, as he was laughin' too hard.

Poor Julie! She didn't show up here on Main Street for a long, long time afterward.

And of course Jim and his gang told everybody in town, everybody but Doc Stair. They was scared to tell him, and he might of never knowed only for Paul Dickson. The poor cuckoo, as Jim called him, he was here in the shop one night when Jim was still gloatin' yet over what he'd done to Julie. And Paul took in as much of it as he could understand and he run to Doc with the story.

It's a cinch Doc went up in the air and swore he'd make Jim suffer. But it was a kind of a delicate thing, because if it got out that he had beat Jim up, Julie was bound to hear of it and then she'd know that Doc knew and of course knowin' that he knew would make it worse for her than ever. He was goin' to do somethin', but it took a lot of figurin'.

Well, it was a couple days later when Jim was here in the shop again, and so was the cuckoo. Jim was goin' duck-shootin' the next day and had come in lookin' for Hod Meyers to go with him. I happened to know that Hod went over to Carterville and wouldn't be home till the end of the week. So Jim said he hated to go alone and he guessed he would call it off. Then poor Paul spoke up and said if Jim would take him he would go along. Jim thought a w'ile and then he said, well, he guessed a half-wit was better than nothin'.

I suppose he was plottin' to get Paul out in the boat and play some joke on him, like pushin' him in the water. Anyways, he said Paul could go. He asked him had he ever shot a duck and Paul said no, he'd never even had a gun in his hands. So Jim said he could set in the boat and watch him and if he behaved himself, he might lend him his gun for a couple of shots. They made a date to meet in the mornin' and that's the last I seen of Jim alive.

Next mornin', I hadn't been open more than ten minutes when Doc Stair come in. He looked kind of nervous. He asked me had I seen Paul Dickson. I said no, but I knew where he was, out duck-shootin' with Jim Kendall. So Doc says that's what he had heard, and he couldn't understand it because Paul had told him he wouldn't never have no more to do with Jim as long as he lived.

He said Paul had told him about the joke Jim played on Julie. He said Paul had asked him what he thought of the joke and the Doc had told him anybody that would do a thing like that ought not to be let live.

I said it had been a kind of a raw thing, but Jim just couldn't resist no kind of a joke, no matter how raw. I said I thought he was all right at heart, but just bubblin' over with mischief. Doc turned and walked out.

At noon he got a phone call from old John Scott. The lake where Jim and Paul had went shootin' is on John's place. Paul had came runnin' up to the house a few minutes before and said they'd been an accident. Jim had shot a few ducks and then give the gun to Paul and told him to try his luck. Paul hadn't never handled a gun and he was nervous. He was shakin' so hard that he couldn't control the gun. He let fire and Jim sunk back in the boat, dead.

Doc Stair, bein' the coroner, jumped in Frank Abbott's flivver and rushed out to Scott's farm. Paul and old John was down on the shore of the lake. Paul had rowed the boat to shore, but they'd left the body in it, waitin' for Doc to come.

Doc examined the body and said they might as well fetch it back to town. They was no use leavin' it there or callin' a jury, as it was a plain case of accidental shootin'.

Personally I wouldn't never leave a person shoot a gun in the same boat I was in unless I was sure they knew somethin' about guns. Jim was a sucker to leave a new beginner have his gun, let alone a half-wit. It probably served Jim right, what he got. But still we miss him round here. He certainly was a card!

Comb it wet or dry?

QUESTIONS

1. The barber makes much of the unique quality of his town. "We ain't no New York City or Chicago," he says, "but we have pretty good times. . . . When [Jim Kendall] was alive, . . . I bet they was more laughin' done here than any town its size in America." Evaluate the barber's opinion.
2. How good are the jokes made in Whitey's barbershop? Do they have any characteristics in common? In addition to the jokes that are "made," the story concerns jokes that are "played." What is that kind of joke called? What is its chief characteristic? Does it have anything in common with the jokes "made" in the barbershop? What are Jim Kendall's motivations for playing these jokes? Does he have just cause?
3. What kind of person is Jim Kendall? Make a thorough characterization.
4. Explain the circumstances of Jim Kendall's death. Was it "a plain case of accidental shootin'"? Does Doc Stair think so? Does the barber?
5. What kind of person is the barber? As a narrator, how reliable is he? Study him thoroughly, taking into consideration such things as (a) his evaluations of and attitude toward Jim Kendall, (b) his delight with Jim Kendall's "expressions" and his admiration of Jim's "jokes"—"They wasn't nothin' in the way of gags that Jim couldn't think up, when he put his mind to it," (c) his idea of a good time, (d) his remark, "they's old George Purdy—but I guess I shouldn't ought to be gossipin'," (e) his explanation that "Jim used to travel for a canned goods concern over in Carterville. They sold canned goods" (find other examples of the same characteristic), and (f) his evaluation of the circumstances of Jim's death.
6. Who is the most important character in the story?
7. What is the story fundamentally about?

Willa Cather
PAUL'S CASE

It was Paul's afternoon to appear before the faculty of the Pittsburgh High School to account for his various misdemeanors. He had been suspended a week ago, and his father had called at the Principal's office and confessed his perplexity about his son. Paul entered the faculty room suave and smiling. His clothes were a trifle outgrown, and the tan velvet on the collar of his open overcoat was frayed and worn; but for all that there was something of a dandy about him, and he wore an opal pin in his neatly knotted black four-in-hand, and a red carnation in his buttonhole. This latter adornment the faculty somehow felt was not properly significant of the contrite spirit befitting a boy under the ban of suspension.

Paul was tall for his age and very thin, with high, cramped shoulders and a narrow chest. His eyes were remarkable for a certain hysterical brilliancy, and he continually used them in a conscious, theatrical sort of way, peculiarly offensive in a boy. The pupils were abnormally large, as though he were addicted to belladonna, but there was a glassy glitter about them which that drug does not produce.

When questioned by the Principal as to why he was there, Paul stated, politely enough, that he wanted to come back to school. This was a lie, but Paul was quite accustomed to lying; found it, indeed, indispensable for overcoming friction. His teachers were asked to state their respective charges against him, which they did with such a rancor and aggrievedness as evinced that this was not a usual case. Disorder and impertinence were among the offences named, yet each of his instructors felt that it was scarcely possible to put into words the real cause of the trouble, which lay in a sort of hysterically defiant manner of the boy's; in the contempt which they all knew he felt for them, and which he seemingly made not the least effort to conceal. Once, when he had been making a synopsis of a paragraph at the blackboard, his English teacher had stepped to his side and attempted to guide his hand. Paul had started back with a shudder and thrust his hands violently behind him. The astonished woman could scarcely have been more hurt and embarrassed had he struck at her. The insult was so involuntary and definitely personal as to be unforgettable. In one way and another, he had made all his teachers, men and women alike, conscious of the same feeling of physical aversion. In one class he habitually sat with his hand shading his eyes; in another he always looked out of the window during the recitation; in another he made a running commentary on the lecture, with humorous intent.

PAUL'S CASE   Written in 1904, first published in 1905. Willa Cather (1873-1947), born in Virginia, grew up and was educated in Nebraska. From 1895 to 1905 she lived and worked in Pittsburgh, first as a journalist, writing dramatic and music criticism, later as a teacher of English and Latin in two Pittsburgh high schools. In 1902 she traveled in Europe.

His teachers felt this afternoon that his whole attitude was symbolized by his shrug and his flippantly red carnation flower, and they fell upon him without mercy, his English teacher leading the pack. He stood through it smiling, his pale lips parted over his white teeth. (His lips were continually twitching, and he had a habit of raising his eyebrows that was contemptuous and irritating to the last degree.) Older boys than Paul had broken down and shed tears under that ordeal, but his set smile did not once desert him, and his only sign of discomfort was the nervous trembling of the fingers that toyed with the buttons of his overcoat, and an occasional jerking of the other hand which held his hat. Paul was always smiling, always glancing about him, seeming to feel that people might be watching him and trying to detect something. This conscious expression, since it was as far as possible from boyish mirthfulness, was usually attributed to insolence or "smartness."

As the inquisition proceeded, one of his instructors repeated an impertinent remark of the boy's, and the Principal asked him whether he thought that a courteous speech to make to a woman. Paul shrugged his shoulders slightly and his eyebrows twitched.

"I don't know," he replied. "I didn't mean to be polite or impolite, either. I guess it's a sort of way I have, of saying things regardless."

The Principal asked him whether he didn't think that a way it would be well to get rid of. Paul grinned and said he guessed so. When he was told that he could go, he bowed gracefully and went out. His bow was like a repetition of the scandalous red carnation.

His teachers were in despair, and his drawing-master voiced the feeling of them all when he declared there was something about the boy which none of them understood. He added: "I don't really believe that smile of his comes altogether from insolence; there's something sort of haunted about it. The boy is not strong for one thing. There is something wrong about the fellow."

The drawing-master had come to realize that, in looking at Paul, one saw only his white teeth and the forced animation of his eyes. One warm afternoon the boy had gone to sleep at his drawing-board, and his master had noted with amazement what a white, blue-veined face it was; drawn and wrinkled like an old man's about the eyes, the lips twitching even in his sleep.

His teachers left the building dissatisfied and unhappy; humiliated to have felt so vindictive toward a mere boy, to have uttered this feeling in cutting terms, and to have set each other on, as it were, in the gruesome game of intemperate reproach. One of them remembered having seen a miserable street cat set at bay by a ring of tormentors.

As for Paul, he ran down the hill whistling the Soldiers' Chorus from *Faust,* looking behind him now and then to see whether some of his teachers were not there to witness his light-heartedness. As it was now late in the afternoon and Paul was on duty that evening as usher at Carnegie Hall, he decided that he would not go home to supper.

When he reached the concert hall, the doors were not yet open. It was chilly outside, and he decided to go up into the picture gallery—always deserted at this hour—where there were some of Raffelli's gay studies of Paris streets and an airy blue Venetian scene or two that always exhilarated him. He was delighted to find no one in the gallery but the old guard, who sat in the corner, a newspaper on his knee, a black patch over one eye and the other closed. Paul possessed himself of the place and walked confidently up and down, whistling under his breath. After a while he sat down before a blue Rico and lost himself. When he bethought him to look at his watch, it was after seven o'clock, and he rose with a start and ran downstairs, making a face at Augustus Caesar, peering out from the cast-room, and an evil gesture at the Venus of Milo as he passed her on the stairway.

When Paul reached the ushers' dressing-room, half a dozen boys were there already, and he began excitedly to tumble into his uniform. It was one of the few that at all approached fitting, and Paul thought it very becoming—though he knew the tight, straight coat accentuated his narrow chest, about which he was exceedingly sensitive. He was always excited while he dressed, twanging all over to the tuning of the strings and the preliminary flourishes of the horns in the music-room; but tonight he seemed quite beside himself, and he teased and plagued the boys until, telling him that he was crazy, they put him down on the floor and sat on him.

Somewhat calmed by his suppression, Paul dashed out to the front of the house to seat the early comers. He was a model usher. Gracious and smiling he ran up and down the aisles. Nothing was too much trouble for him; he carried messages and brought programs as though it were his greatest pleasure in life, and all the people in his section thought him a charming boy, feeling that he remembered and admired them. As the house filled, he grew more and more vivacious and animated, and the color came to his cheeks and lips. It was very much as though this were a great reception and Paul were the host. Just as the musicians came out to take their places, his English teacher arrived with checks for the seats which a prominent manufacturer had taken for the season. She betrayed some embarrassment when she handed Paul the tickets, and a *hauteur* which subsequently made her feel very foolish. Paul was startled for a moment, and had the feeling of wanting to put her out; what business had she here among all these fine people and gay colors? He looked her over and decided that she was not appropriately dressed and must be a fool to sit downstairs in such togs. The tickets had probably been sent her out of kindness, he reflected, as he put down a seat for her, and she had about as much right to sit there as he had.

When the symphony began, Paul sank into one of the rear seats with a long sigh of relief, and lost himself as he had done before the Rico. It was not that symphonies, as such, meant anything in particular to Paul, but the first sight of the instruments seemed to free some hilarious spirit within him; something that struggled there like the Genius in the bottle found by the Arab fisherman. He felt a sudden zest of life; the lights danced before his eyes and the concert hall blazed into unimaginable splendor. When the soprano soloist came on, Paul forgot even the nastiness of his teacher's being there, and gave himself up to the peculiar intoxication such personages always had for him. The soloist chanced to be a German woman, by no means in her first youth, and the mother of many children; but she wore a satin gown and a tiara, and she had that indefinable air of achievement, that world-shine upon her, which always blinded Paul to any possible defects.

After a concert was over, Paul was often irritable and wretched until he got to sleep—and tonight he was even more than usually restless. He had the feeling of not being able to let down; of its being impossible to give up his delicious excitement which was the only thing that could be called living at all. During the last number he withdrew and, after hastily changing his clothes in the dressing-room, slipped out to the side door where the singer's carriage stood. Here he began pacing rapidly up and down the walk, waiting to see her come out.

Over yonder the Schenley, in its vacant stretch, loomed big and square through the fine rain, the windows of its twelve stories glowing like those of a lighted cardboard house under a Christmas tree. All the actors and singers of any importance stayed there when they were in Pittsburgh, and a number of the big manufacturers of the place lived there in the winter. Paul had often hung about the hotel, watching the people go in and out, longing to enter and leave schoolmasters and dull care behind him forever.

At last the singer came out, accompanied by the conductor, who helped her into her carriage and closed the door with a cordial *auf wiedersehen*—which set Paul to wondering whether she were not an old sweetheart of his. Paul followed the carriage over to the hotel, walking so rapidly as not to be far from the entrance when the singer alighted and disappeared behind the swinging glass doors which were opened by a Negro in a tall hat and a long coat. In the moment that the door was ajar, it seemed to Paul that he, too, entered. He seemed to feel himself go after her up the steps, into the warm, lighted building, into an exotic, a tropical world of shiny, glistening surfaces and basking ease. He reflected upon the mysterious dishes that were brought into the dining-room, the green bottles in buckets of ice, as he had seen them in the supper-party pictures of the Sunday supplement. A quick gust of wind brought the rain down with sudden vehemence, and Paul was startled to find that he was still outside in the slush of the gravel driveway; that his boots were letting in the water and his scanty overcoat was clinging wet about him; that the lights in front of the concert hall were out, and that the rain was driving in sheets between him and the orange glow of the windows above him. There it was, what he wanted—tangibly before him, like the fairy world of a Christmas pantomime; as the rain beat in his face, Paul wondered whether he were destined always to shiver in the black night outside, looking up at it.

He turned and walked reluctantly toward the car tracks. The end had to come sometime; his father in his night-clothes at the top of the stairs, explanations that did not explain, hastily improvised fictions that were forever tripping him up, his upstairs room and its horrible yellow wallpaper, the creaking bureau with the greasy plush collar-box, and over his painted wooden bed the pictures of George Washington and John Calvin, and the framed motto, 'Feed my Lambs,' which had been worked in red worsted by his mother, whom Paul could not remember.

Half an hour later, Paul alighted from the Negley Avenue car and went slowly down one of the side streets off the main thoroughfare. It was a highly respectable street, where all the houses were exactly alike, and where business men of moderate means begot and reared large families of children, all of whom went to Sabbath School and learned the shorter catechism, and were interested in arithmetic; all of whom were as exactly alike as their homes, and of a piece with the monotony in which they lived. Paul never went up Cordelia Street without a shudder of loathing. His home was next the house of the Cumberland minister. He approached it tonight with the nerveless sense of defeat, the hopeless feeling of sinking back forever into ugliness and commonness that he had always had when he came home. The moment he turned into Cordelia Street he felt the waters close above his head. After each of these orgies of living, he experienced all the physical depression which follows a debauch; the loathing of respectable beds, of common food, of a house permeated by kitchen odors; a shuddering repulsion for the flavorless, colorless mass of every-day existence; a morbid desire for cool things and soft lights and fresh flowers.

The nearer he approached the house, the more absolutely unequal Paul felt to the sight of it all: his ugly sleeping chamber; the old bathroom with the grimy zinc tub, the cracked mirror, the dripping spigots; his father, at the top of the stairs, his hairy legs sticking out from his nightshirt, his feet thrust into carpet slippers. He was so much later than usual that there would certainly be enquiries and reproaches. Paul stopped short before the door. He felt that he could not be accosted by his father tonight; that he could not toss again on that miserable bed. He would not go in. He would tell his father that he had no carfare, and it was raining so hard he had gone home with one of the boys and stayed all night.

Meanwhile, he was wet and cold. He went around to the back of the house and tried one of the basement windows, found it open, and raised it cautiously, and scrambled down the cellar wall to the floor. There he stood, holding his breath, terrified by the noise he had made; but the floor above him was silent, and there was no creak on the stairs. He found a soap-box, and carried it over to the soft ring of light that streamed from the furnace door, and sat down. He was horribly afraid of rats, so he did not try to sleep, but sat looking distrustfully at the dark, still terrified lest he might have awakened his father.

In such reactions, after one of the experiences which made days and nights out of the dreary blanks of the calendar, when his senses were deadened, Paul's head was always singularly clear. Suppose his father had heard him getting in at the window and had come down and shot him for a burglar? Then, again, suppose his father had come down, pistol in hand, and he had cried out in time to save himself, and his father had been horrified to think how nearly he had killed him? Then again, suppose a day should come when his father would remember that night, and wish there had been no warning cry to stay his hand? With this last supposition Paul entertained himself until daybreak.

The following Sunday was fine; the sodden November chill was broken by the last flash of autumnal summer. In the morning Paul had to go to church and Sabbath School, as always. On seasonable Sunday afternoons the burghers of Cordelia Street usually sat out on their front "stoops," and talked to their neighbors on the next stoop, or called to those across the street in neighborly fashion. The men sat placidly on gay cushions placed upon the steps that led down to the sidewalk, while the women, in their Sunday "waists," sat in rockers on the cramped porches, pretending to be greatly at their ease. The children played in the streets; there were so many of them that the place resembled the recreation grounds of a kindergarten. The men on the steps, all in their shirt-sleeves, their vests unbuttoned, sat with their legs well apart, their stomachs comfortably protruding, and talked of the prices of things, or told anecdotes of the sagacity of their various chiefs and overlords. They occasionally looked over the multitude of squabbling children, listened affectionately to their high-pitched, nasal voices, smiling to see their own proclivities reproduced in their offspring, and interspersed their legends of the iron kings with remarks about their sons' progress at school, their grades in arithmetic, and the amounts they had saved in their toy banks.

On this last Sunday of November, Paul sat all afternoon on the lowest step of his "stoop," staring into the street, while his sisters, in their rockers, were talking to the minister's daughters next door about how many shirt-waists they had made in the last week, and how many waffles someone had eaten at the last church supper. When the weather was warm, and his father was in a particularly jovial frame of mind, the girls made lemonade, which was always brought out in a red-glass pitcher, ornamented with forget-me-nots in blue enamel. This the girls thought very fine, and the neighbors joked about the suspicious color of the pitcher.

Today Paul's father, on the top step, was talking to a young man who shifted a restless baby from knee to knee. He happened to be the young man who was daily held up to Paul as a model, and after whom it was his father's dearest hope that he would pattern. This young man was of a ruddy complexion, with a compressed, red mouth, and faded, nearsighted eyes, over which he wore thick spectacles, with gold bows that curved about his ears. He was clerk to one of the magnates of a great steel corporation, and was looked upon in Cordelia Street as a young man with a future. There was a story that, some five years ago—he was now barely twenty-six—he had been a trifle "dissipated," but in order to curb his appetites and save the loss of time and strength that a sowing of wild oats might have entailed, he had taken his chief's advice, oft reiterated to his employees, and at twenty-one had married the first woman whom he could persuade to share his fortunes. She happened to be an angular schoolmistress, much older than he, who also wore thick glasses, and who had now borne him four children, all nearsighted like herself.

The young man was relating how his chief, now cruising in the Mediterranean, kept in touch with all the details of the business, arranging his office hours on his yacht just as though he were at home, and "knocking off work enough to keep two stenographers busy." His father told, in turn, the plan his corporation was considering, of putting in an electric railway plant at Cairo. Paul snapped his teeth; he had an awful apprehension that they might spoil it all before he got there. Yet he rather liked to hear these legends of the iron kings, that were told and retold on Sundays and holidays; these stories of palaces in Venice, yachts on the Mediterranean, and high play at Monte Carlo appealed to his fancy, and he was interested in the triumphs of cash-boys who had become famous, though he had no mind for the cash-boy stage.

After supper was over, and he had helped to dry the dishes, Paul nervously asked his father whether he could go to George's to get some help in his geometry, and still more nervously asked for carfare. This latter request he had to repeat, as his father, on principle, did not like to hear requests for money, whether much or little. He asked Paul whether he could not go to some boy who lived nearer, and told him that he ought not to leave his school work until Sunday; but he gave him the dime. He was not a poor man, but he had a worthy ambition to come up in the world. His only reason for allowing Paul to usher was that he thought a boy ought to be earning a little.

Paul bounded upstairs, scrubbed the greasy odor of the dishwater from his hands with the ill-smelling soap he hated, and then shook over his fingers a few drops of violet water from the bottle he kept hidden in his drawer. He left the house with his geometry conspicuously under his arm, and the moment he got out of Cordelia Street and boarded a downtown car, he shook off the lethargy of two deadening days, and began to live again.

The leading juvenile of the permanent stock company which played at one of the downtown theaters was an acquaintance of Paul's, and the boy had been invited to drop in at the Sunday-night rehearsals whenever he could. For more than a year Paul had spent every available moment loitering about Charley Edwards's dressing-room. He had won a place among Edwards's following not only because the young actor, who could not afford to employ a dresser, often found him useful, but because he recognized in Paul something akin to what churchmen term "vocation."

It was at the theater and at Carnegie Hall that Paul really lived; the rest was but a sleep and a forgetting. This was Paul's fairy tale, and it had for him all the allurement of a secret love. The moment he inhaled the gassy, painty, dusty odor behind the scenes, he breathed like a prisoner set free, and felt within him the possibility of doing or saying splendid, brilliant things. The moment the cracked orchestra beat out the overture from *Martha*, or jerked at the serenade from *Rigoletto*, all stupid and ugly things slid from him, and his senses were deliciously, yet delicately fired.

Perhaps it was because, in Paul's world, the natural nearly always wore the guise of ugliness, that a certain element of artificiality seemed to him necessary in beauty. Perhaps it was because his experience of life elsewhere was so full of Sabbath-School picnics, petty economies, wholesome advice as to how to succeed in life, and the unescapable odors of cooking, that he found this existence so alluring, these smartly clad men and women so attractive, that he was so moved by these starry apple orchards that bloomed perennially under the limelight. It would be difficult to put it strongly enough how convincingly the stage entrance of the theater was for Paul the actual portal of Romance. Certainly none of the company ever suspected it, least of all Charley Edwards. It was very like the old stories that used to float about London of fabulously rich Jews, who had subterranean halls, with palms, and fountains, and soft lamps and richly appareled women who never saw the disenchanting light of London day. So, in the midst of that smoke-palled city, enamored of figures and grimy toil, Paul had his secret temple, his wishing-carpet, his bit of blue-and-white Mediterranean shore bathed in perpetual sunshine.

Several of Paul's teachers had a theory that his imagination had been perverted by garish fiction; but the truth was he scarcely ever read at all. The books at home were not such as would either tempt or corrupt a youthful mind, and as for reading the novels that some of his friends urged upon him—well, he got what he wanted much more quickly from music; any sort of music, from an orchestra to a barrel-organ. He needed only the spark, the indescribable thrill that made his imagination master of his senses, and he could make plots and pictures enough of his own. It was equally true that he was not stage-struck— not, at any rate, in the usual acceptation of the expression. He had no desire to become an actor, any more than he had to become a musician. He felt no necessity to do any of these things; what he wanted was to see, to be in the atmosphere, float on the wave of it, to be carried out, blue league after league, away from everything.

After a night behind the scenes, Paul found the schoolroom more than ever repulsive; the bare floors and naked walls; the prosy men who never wore frock coats, or violets in their buttonholes; the women with their dull gowns, shrill voices, and pitiful seriousness about prepositions that govern the dative. He could not bear to have the other pupils think, for a moment, that he took these people seriously; he must convey to them that he considered it all trivial, and was there only by way of a joke, anyway. He had autographed pictures of all the members of the stock company which he showed his classmates, telling them the most incredible stories of his familiarity with these people, of his acquaintance with the soloists who came to Carnegie Hall, his suppers with them and the flowers he sent them. When these stories lost their effect, and his audience grew listless, he would bid all the boys goodbye, announcing that he was going to travel for a while; going to Naples, to California, to Egypt. Then, next Monday, he would slip back, conscious and nervously smiling; his sister was ill, and he would have to defer his voyage until spring.

Matters went steadily worse with Paul at school. In the itch to let his instructors know how heartily he despised them, and how thoroughly he was appreciated elsewhere, he mentioned once or twice that he had no time to fool with theorems; adding—with a twitch of the eyebrows and a touch of that nervous bravado which so perplexed them—that he was helping the people down at the stock company; they were old friends of his.

The upshot of the matter was that the Principal went to Paul's father, and Paul was taken out of school and put to work. The manager at Carnegie Hall was told to get another usher in his stead; the doorkeeper at the theater was warned not to admit him to the house; and Charley Edwards remorsefully promised the boy's father not to see him again.

The members of the stock company were vastly amused when some of Paul's stories reached them—especially the women. They were hard-working women, most of them supporting indolent husbands or brothers, and they laughed rather bitterly at having stirred the boy to such fervid and florid inventions. They agreed with the faculty and with his father, that Paul's was a bad case.

The east-bound train was plowing through a January snowstorm; the dull dawn was beginning to show grey when the engine whistled a mile out of Newark. Paul started up from the seat where he had lain curled in uneasy slumber, rubbed the breath-misted window-glass with his hand, and peered out. The snow was whirling in curling eddies above the white bottom lands, and the drifts lay already deep in the fields and along the fences, while here and there the tall dead grass and dried weed stalks protruded black above it. Lights shone from the scattered houses, and a gang of laborers who stood beside the track waved their lanterns.

Paul had slept very little, and he felt grimy and uncomfortable. He had made the all-night journey in a day coach because he was afraid if he took a Pullman he might be seen by some Pittsburgh business man who had noticed him in Denny and Carson's office. When the whistle woke him, he clutched quickly at his breast pocket, glancing about him with an uncertain smile. But the little, clay-bespattered Italians were still sleeping, the slatternly women across the aisle were in open-mouthed oblivion, and even the crumby, crying babies were for the time stilled. Paul settled back to struggle with his impatience as best he could.

When he arrived at the Jersey City station, he hurried through his breakfast, manifestly ill at ease and keeping a sharp eye about him. After he reached the Twenty-Third Street station, he consulted a cabman, and had himself driven to a men's furnishing establishment which was just opening for the day. He spent upward of two hours there, buying with endless reconsidering and great care. His new street suit he put on in the fitting-room; the frock coat and dress clothes he had bundled into the cab with his new shirts. Then he drove to a hatter's and a shoe house. His next errand was at Tiffany's, where he selected silver-mounted brushes and a scarf-pin. He would not wait to have his silver marked, he said. Lastly, he stopped at a trunk shop on Broadway, and had his purchases packed into various traveling-bags.

It was a little after one o'clock when he drove up to the Waldorf, and, after settling with the cabman, went into the office. He registered from Washington; said his mother and father had been abroad, and that he had come down to await the arrival of their steamer. He told his story plausibly and had no trouble, since he offered to pay for them in advance, in engaging his rooms; a sleeping-room, sitting-room, and bath.

Not once, but a hundred times Paul had planned this entry into New York. He had gone over every detail of it with Charley Edwards, and in his scrapbook at home there were pages of description about New York hotels, cut from the Sunday papers.

When he was shown to his sitting-room on the eighth floor, he saw at a glance that everything was as it should be; there was but one detail in his mental picture that the place did not realize, so he rang for the bell-boy and sent him down for flowers. He moved about nervously until the boy returned, putting away his new linen and fingering it delightedly as he did so. When the flowers came, he put them hastily into water, and then tumbled into a hot bath. Presently he came out of his white bathroom, resplendent in his new silk underwear, and playing with the tassels of his red robe. The snow was whirling so fiercely outside his windows that he could scarcely see across the street; but within, the air was deliciously soft and fragrant. He put the violets and jonquils on the taboret beside the couch, and threw himself down with a long sigh, covering himself with a Roman blanket. He was thoroughly tired; he had been in such haste, he had stood up to such a strain, covered so much ground in the last twenty-four hours, that he wanted to think how it had all come about. Lulled by the sound of the wind, the warm air, and the cool fragrance of the flowers, he sank into deep, drowsy retrospection.

It had been wonderfully simple; when they had shut him out of the theater and concert hall, when they had taken away his bone, the whole thing was virtually determined. The rest was a mere matter of opportunity. The only thing that at all surprised him was his own courage—for he realized well enough that he had always been tormented by fear, a sort of apprehensive dread which, of late years, as the meshes of the lies he had told closed about him, had been pulling the muscles of his body tighter and tighter. Until now, he could not remember a time when he had not been dreading something. Even when he was a little boy, it was always there—behind him, or before, or on either side. There had always been the shadowed corner, the dark place into which he dared not look, but from which something seemed always to be watching him—and Paul had done things that were not pretty to watch, he knew.

But now he had a curious sense of relief, as though he had at last thrown down the gauntlet to the thing in the corner.

Yet it was but a day since he had been sulking in the traces; but yesterday afternoon that he had been sent to the bank with Denny and Carson's deposit, as usual—but this time he was instructed to leave the book to be balanced. There was above two thousand dollars in checks, and nearly a thousand in the banknotes which he had taken from the book and quietly transferred to his pocket. At the bank he had made out a new deposit slip. His nerves had been steady enough to permit of his returning to the office, where he had finished his work and asked for a full day's holiday tomorrow, Saturday, giving a perfectly reasonable pretext. The bank book, he knew, would not be returned before Monday or Tuesday, and his father would be out of town for the next week. From the time he slipped the banknotes into his pocket until he boarded the night train for New York, he had not known a moment's hesitation.

How astonishingly easy it had all been; here he was, the thing done; and this time there would be no awakening, no figure at the top of the stairs. He watched the snowflakes whirling by his window until he fell asleep.

When he awoke, it was four o'clock in the afternoon. He bounded up with a start; one of his precious days gone already! He spent nearly an hour in dressing, watching every stage of his toilet carefully in the mirror. Everything was quite perfect; he was exactly the kind of boy he had always wanted to be.

When he went downstairs, Paul took a carriage and drove up Fifth Avenue toward the Park. The snow had somewhat abated; carriages and tradesmen's wagons were hurrying soundlessly to and fro in the winter twilight; boys in woolen mufflers were shoveling off the doorsteps; the Avenue stages made fine spots of color against the white street. Here and there on the corners whole flower gardens blooming behind glass windows, against which the snowflakes stuck and melted; violets, roses, carnations, lilies-of-the-valley—somehow vastly more lovely and alluring that they blossomed thus unnaturally in the snow. The Park itself was a wonderful stage winter-piece.

When he returned, the pause of the twilight had ceased, and the tune of the streets had changed. The snow was falling faster, lights streamed from the hotels that reared their many stories fearlessly up into the storm, defying the raging Atlantic winds. A long, black stream of carriages poured down the Avenue, intersected here and there by other streams, tending horizontally. There were a score of cabs about the entrance of his hotel, and his driver had to wait. Boys in livery were running in and out of the awning stretched across the sidewalk, up and down the red velvet carpet laid from the door to the street. Above, about, within it all, was the rumble and roar, the hurry and toss of thousands of human beings as hot for pleasure as himself, and on every side of him towered the glaring affirmation of the omnipotence of wealth.

The boy set his teeth and drew his shoulders together in a spasm of realization; the plot of all dramas, the text of all romances, the nerve-stuff of all sensations was whirling about him like the snowflakes. He burnt like a fagot in a tempest.

When Paul came down to dinner, the music of the orchestra floated up the elevator shaft to greet him. As he stepped into the thronged corridor, he sank back into one of the chairs against the wall to get his breath. The lights, the chatter, the perfumes, the bewildering medley of color—he had, for a moment, the feeling of not being able to stand it. But only for a moment; these were his own people, he told himself. He went slowly about the corridors, through the writing-rooms, smoking-rooms, reception-rooms, as though he were exploring the chambers of an enchanted palace, built and peopled for him alone.

When he reached the dining-room he sat down at a table near a window. The flowers, the white linen, the many-colored wine-glasses, the gay toilettes of the women, the low popping of corks, the undulating repetitions of the "Blue Danube" from the orchestra, all flooded Paul's dream with bewildering radiance. When the roseate tinge of his champagne was added—that cold, precious, bubbling stuff that creamed and foamed in his glass—Paul wondered that there were honest men in the world at all. This was what all the world was fighting for, he reflected; this was what all the struggle was about. He doubted the reality of his past. Had he ever known a place called Cordelia Street, a place where fagged-looking business men boarded the early car? Mere rivets in a machine they seemed to Paul—sickening men, with combings of children's hair always hanging to their coats, and the smell of cooking in their clothes. Cordelia Street—Ah, that belonged to another time and country! Had he not always been thus, had he not sat here night after night, from as far back as he could remember, looking pensively over just such shimmering textures, and slowly twirling the stem of a glass like this one between his thumb and middle finger? He rather thought he had.

He was not in the least abashed or lonely. He had no especial desire to meet or to know any of these people; all he demanded was the right to look on and conjecture, to watch the pageant. The mere stage properties were all he contended for. Nor was he lonely later in the evening, in his loge at the Opera. He was entirely rid of his nervous misgivings, of his forced aggressiveness, of the imperative desire to show himself different from his surroundings. He felt now that his surroundings explained him. Nobody questioned the purple; he had only to wear it passively. He had only to glance down at his dress coat to reassure himself that here it would be impossible for anyone to humiliate him.

He found it hard to leave his beautiful sitting-room to go to bed that night, and sat long watching the raging storm from his turret window. When he went to sleep, it was with the lights turned on in his bedroom; partly because of his old timidity, and partly so that, if he should wake in the night, there would be no wretched moment of doubt, no horrible suspicion of yellow wallpaper, or of Washington and Calvin above his bed.

On Sunday morning the city was practically snowbound. Paul breakfasted late, and in the afternoon he fell in with a wild San Francisco boy, a freshman at Yale, who said he had run down for a "little flyer" over Sunday. The young man offered to show Paul the night side of the town, and the two boys went off together after dinner, not returning to the hotel until seven o'clock the next morning. They had started out in the confiding warmth of a champagne friendship, but their parting in the elevator was singularly cool.

The freshman pulled himself together to make his train, and Paul went to bed. He awoke at two o'clock in the afternoon, very thirsty and dizzy, and rang for ice-water, coffee, and the Pittsburgh papers.

On the part of the hotel management, Paul excited no suspicion. There was this to be said for him, that he wore his spoils with dignity and in no way made himself conspicuous. His chief greediness lay in his ears and eyes, and his excesses were not offensive ones. His dearest pleasures were the grey winter twilights in his sitting-room; his quiet enjoyment of his flowers, his clothes, his wide divan, his cigarette, and his sense of power. He could not remember a time when he had felt so at peace with himself. The mere release from the necessity of petty lying, lying every day and every day, restored his self-respect. He had never lied for pleasure, even at school; but to make himself noticed and admired, to assert his difference from other Cordelia Street boys; and he felt a good deal more manly, more honest, even, now that he had no need for boastful pretensions, now that he could, as his actor friends used to say, "dress the part." It was characteristic that remorse did not occur to him. His golden days went by without a shadow, and he made each as perfect as he could.

On the eighth day after his arrival in New York, he found the whole affair exploited in the Pittsburgh papers, exploited with a wealth of detail which indicated that local news of a sensational nature was at a low ebb. The firm of Denny and Carson announced that the boy's father had refunded the full amount of his theft, and that they had no intention of prosecuting. The Cumberland minister had been interviewed, and expressed his hope of yet reclaiming the motherless lad, and Paul's Sabbath-School teacher declared that she would spare no effort to that end. The rumor had reached Pittsburgh that the boy had been seen in a New York hotel, and his father had gone East to find him and bring him home.

Paul had just come in to dress for dinner; he sank into the chair, weak in the knees, and clasped his head in his hands. It was to be worse than jail, even; the tepid waters of Cordelia Street were to close over him finally and forever. The grey monotony stretched before him in hopeless, unrelieved years;— Sabbath School, Young People's Meeting, the yellow-papered room, the damp dish-towels; it all rushed back upon him with sickening vividness. He had the old feeling that the orchestra had suddenly stopped, the sinking sensation that the play was over. The sweat broke out on his face, and he sprang to his feet, looked about him with his white, conscious smile, and winked at himself in the mirror. With something of the childish belief in miracles with which he had so often gone to class, all his lessons unlearned, Paul dressed and dashed whistling down the corridor to the elevator.

He had no sooner entered the dining-room and caught the measure of the music than his remembrance was lightened by his old elastic power of claiming the moment, mounting with it, and finding it all-sufficient. The glare and glitter about him, the mere scenic accessories had again, and for the last time, their old potency. He would show himself that he was game, he would finish the thing splendidly. He doubted, more than ever, the existence of Cordelia Street, and for the first time he drank his wine recklessly. Was he not, after all, one of these fortunate beings? Was he not still himself, and in his own place? He drummed a nervous accompaniment to the music and looked about him, telling himself over and over that it had paid.

He reflected drowsily, to the swell of the violin and the chill sweetness of his wine, that he might have done it more wisely. He might have caught an outbound steamer and been well out of their clutches before now. But the other side of the world had seemed too far away and too uncertain then; he could not have waited for it; his need had been too sharp. If he had to choose over again, he would do the same thing tomorrow. He looked affectionately about the dining-room, now gilded with a soft mist. Ah, it had paid indeed!

Paul was awakened next morning by a painful throbbing in his head and feet. He had thrown himself across the bed without undressing, and had slept with his shoes on. His limbs and hands were lead-heavy, and his tongue and throat were parched. There came upon him one of those fateful attacks of clear-headedness that never occurred except when he was physically exhausted and his nerves hung loose. He lay still and closed his eyes and let the tide of realities wash over him.

His father was in New York; "stopping at some joint or other," he told himself. The memory of successive summers on the front stoop fell upon him like a weight of black water. He had not a hundred dollars left; and he knew now, more than ever, that money was everything, the wall that stood between all he loathed and all he wanted. The thing was winding itself up; he had thought of that on his first glorious day in New York, and had even provided a way to snap the thread. It lay on his dressing-table now; he had got it out last night when he came blindly up from dinner—but the shiny metal hurt his eyes, and he disliked the look of it, anyway.

He rose and moved about with a painful effort, succumbing now and again to attacks of nausea. It was the old depression exaggerated; all the world had become Cordelia Street. Yet somehow he was not afraid of anything, was absolutely calm; perhaps because he had looked into the dark corner at last, and knew. It was bad enough, what he saw there; but somehow not so bad as his long fear of it had been. He saw everything clearly now. He had a feeling that he had made the best of it, that he had lived the sort of life he was meant to live, and for half an hour he sat staring at the revolver. But he told himself that was not the way, so he went downstairs and took a cab to the ferry.

When Paul arrived at Newark, he got off the train and took another cab, directing the driver to follow the Pennsylvania tracks out of town. The snow lay heavy on the roadways and had drifted deep in the open fields. Only here and there the dead grass or dried weed stalks projected, singularly black, above it.

Once well into the country, Paul dismissed the carriage and walked, floundering along the tracks, his mind a medley of irrelevant things. He seemed to hold in his brain an actual picture of everything he had seen that morning. He remembered every feature of both his drivers, the toothless old woman from whom he had bought the red flowers in his coat, the agent from whom he had got his ticket, and all of his fellow-passengers on the ferry. His mind, unable to cope with vital matters near at hand, worked feverishly and deftly at sorting and grouping these images. They made for him a part of the ugliness of the world, of the ache in his head, and the bitter burning on his tongue. He stooped and put a handful of snow into his mouth as he walked, but that, too, seemed hot. When he reached a little hillside, where the tracks ran through a cut some twenty feet below him, he stopped and sat down.

The carnations in his coat were drooping with cold, he noticed; their red glory over. It occurred to him that all the flowers he had seen in the show windows that first night must have gone the same way, long before this. It was only one splendid breath they had, in spite of their brave mockery at the winter outside the glass. It was a losing game in the end, it seemed, this revolt against the homilies by which the world is run. Paul took one of the blossoms carefully from his coat and scooped a little hole in the snow, where he covered it up. Then he dozed awhile, from his weak condition, seeming insensible to the cold.

The sound of an approaching train woke him and he started to his feet, remembering only his resolution, and afraid lest he should be too late. He stood watching the approaching locomotive, his teeth chattering, his lips drawn away from them in a frightened smile; once or twice he glanced nervously sidewise, as though he were being watched. When the right moment came, he jumped. As he fell, the folly of his haste occurred to him with merciless clearness, the vastness of what he had left undone. There flashed through his brain, clearer than ever before, the blue of Adriatic water, the yellow of Algerian sands.

He felt something strike his chest—his body being thrown swiftly through the air, on and on, immeasurably far and fast, while his limbs gently relaxed. Then, because the picture-making mechanism was crushed, the disturbing visions flashed into black, and Paul dropped back into the immense design of things.

QUESTIONS

1. Technically we should classify the author's point of view as omniscient, for she enters into the minds of characters at will. Nevertheless early in the story the focus changes rather abruptly. Locate the point where the change occurs. Through whose eyes do we see Paul prior to this point? Through whose eyes do we see him afterward? What is the purpose of this shift? Does it offer any clue to the purpose of the story?

2. What details of Paul's appearance and behavior, as his teachers see him, indicate that he is abnormal?

3. Explain Paul's behavior. Why does he lie? What does he hate? What does he want? Contrast the world of Cordelia Street with the worlds that Paul finds at Carnegie Hall, at the Schenley, at the stock theater, and in New York.

4. Is Paul artistic? Describe his reactions to music, to painting, to literature, and to the theater. What value does he find in the arts?
5. Is Paul a static or a developing character? If the latter, at what points does he change? Why?
6. What do Paul's clandestine trips to the stock theater, his trip to New York, and his suicide have in common?
7. Compare Paul and the college boy he meets in New York. Are they two of a kind? If not, how do they differ?
8. What are the implications of the title? What does the last sentence of the story do to the reader's focus of vision?
9. Are there any clues to the causes of Paul's abnormality? How many? In what is the author chiefly interested?
10. In what two cities is the story set? Does this choice of setting have any symbolic value? Could the story have been set as validly in Cleveland and Detroit? In San Francisco and Los Angeles? In New Orleans and Birmingham?

Ernest Hemingway

HILLS LIKE WHITE ELEPHANTS

The hills across the valley of the Ebro were long and white. On this side there was no shade and no trees and the station was between two lines of rails in the sun. Close against the side of the station there was the warm shadow of the building and a curtain, made of strings of bamboo beads, hung across the open door into the bar, to keep out flies. The American and the girl with him sat at a table in the shade, outside the building. It was very hot and the express from Barcelona would come in forty minutes. It stopped at this junction for two minutes and went on to Madrid.

"What should we drink?" the girl asked. She had taken off her hat and put it on the table.

"It's pretty hot," the man said.

"Let's drink beer."

"Dos cervezas," the man said into the curtain.

"Big ones?" a woman asked from the doorway.

"Yes. Two big ones."

The woman brought two glasses of beer and two felt pads. She put the felt pads and the beer glasses on the table and looked at the man and the girl. The girl was looking off at the line of hills. They were white in the sun and the country was brown and dry.

HILLS LIKE WHITE ELEPHANTS   First published in 1927. Ernest Hemingway (1899–1961) was born and grew up in Oak Park, Illinois, with summer vacations in northern Michigan. By the time he wrote this story he had been wounded in Italy during World War I; had traveled extensively in Europe as a newspaper correspondent and writer; had married, fathered a son, been divorced, and remarried.

"They look like white elephants," she said.

"I've never seen one," the man drank his beer.

"No, you wouldn't have."

"I might have," the man said. "Just because you say I wouldn't have doesn't prove anything."

The girl looked at the bead curtain. "They've painted something on it," she said. "What does it say?"

"Anis del Toro. It's a drink."

"Could we try it?"

The man called "Listen" through the curtain. The woman came out from the bar.

"Four reales."

"We want two Anis del Toro."

"With water?"

"Do you want it with water?"

"I don't know," the girl said. "Is it good with water?"

"It's all right."

"You want them with water?" asked the woman.

"Yes, with water."

"It tastes like licorice," the girl said and put the glass down.

"That's the way with everything."

"Yes," said the girl. "Everything tastes of licorice. Especially all the things you've waited so long for, like absinthe."

"Oh, cut it out."

"You started it," the girl said. "I was being amused. I was having a fine time."

"Well, let's try to have a fine time."

"All right. I was trying. I said the mountains looked like white elephants. Wasn't that bright?"

"That was bright."

"I wanted to try this new drink. That's all we do, isn't it—look at things and try new drinks."

"I guess so."

The girl looked across at the hills.

"They're lovely hills," she said. "They don't really look like white elephants. I just meant the coloring of their skin through the trees."

"Should we have another drink?"

"All right."

The warm wind blew the bead curtain against the table.

"The beer's nice and cool," the man said.

"It's lovely," the girl said.

"It's really an awfully simple operation, Jig," the man said. "It's not really an operation at all."

The girl looked at the ground the table legs rested on.

"I know you wouldn't mind it, Jig. It's really not anything. It's just to let the air in."

The girl did not say anything.

"I'll go with you and I'll stay with you all the time. They just let the air in and then it's all perfectly natural."

"Then what will we do afterward?"

"We'll be fine afterward. Just like we were before."

"What makes you think so?"

"That's the only thing that bothers us. It's the only thing that's made us unhappy."

The girl looked at the bead curtain, put her hand out and took hold of two of the strings of beads.

"And you think then we'll be all right and be happy."

"I know we will. You don't have to be afraid. I've known lots of people that have done it."

"So have I," said the girl. "And afterward they were all so happy."

"Well," the man said, "if you don't want to you don't have to. I wouldn't have you do it if you didn't want to. But I know it's perfectly simple."

"And you really want to?"

"I think it's the best thing to do. But I don't want you to do it if you don't really want to."

"And if I do it you'll be happy and things will be like they were and you'll love me?"

"I love you now. You know I love you."

"I know. But if I do it, then it will be nice again if I say things are like white elephants, and you'll like it?"

"I'll love it. I love it now but I just can't think about it. You know how I get when I worry."

"If I do it you won't ever worry?"

"I won't worry about that because it's perfectly simple."

"Then I'll do it. Because I don't care about me."

"What do you mean?"

"I don't care about me."

"Well, I care about you."

"Oh, yes. But I don't care about me. And I'll do it and then everything will be fine."

"I don't want you to do it if you feel that way."

The girl stood up and walked to the end of the station. Across, on the other side, were fields of grain and trees along the banks of the Ebro. Far away, beyond the river, were mountains. The shadow of a cloud moved across the field of grain and she saw the river through the trees.

"And we could have all this," she said. "And we could have everything and every day we make it more impossible."

"What did you say?"

"I said we could have everything."

"We can have everything."

"No, we can't."

"We can have the whole world."

"No, we can't."

"We can go everywhere."

"No, we can't. It isn't ours any more."

"It's ours."

"No, it isn't. And once they take it away, you never get it back."

"But they haven't taken it away."

"We'll wait and see."

"Come on back in the shade," he said. "You mustn't feel that way."

"I don't feel any way," the girl said. "I just know things."

"I don't want you to do anything that you don't want to do—"

"Nor that isn't good for me," she said. "I know. Could we have another beer."

"All right. But you've got to realize—"

"I realize," the girl said. "Can't we stop talking?"

They sat down at the table and the girl looked across at the hills on the dry side of the valley and the man looked at her and at the table.

"You've got to realize," he said, "that I don't want you to do it if you don't want to. I'm perfectly willing to go through with it if it means anything to you."

"Doesn't it mean anything to you? We could get along."

"Of course it does. But I don't want anybody but you. I don't want any one else. And I know it's perfectly simple."

"Yes, you know it's perfectly simple."

"It's all right for you to say that, but I do know it."

"Would you do something for me now?"

"I'd do anything for you."

"Would you please please please please please please please stop talking?"

He did not say anything but looked at the bags against the wall of the station. There were labels on them from all the hotels where they had spent nights.

"But I don't want you to," he said. "I don't care anything about it."

"I'll scream," said the girl.

The woman came out through the curtains with two glasses of beer and put them down on the damp felt pads. "The train comes in five minutes," she said.

"What did she say?" asked the girl.

"That the train is coming in five minutes."

The girl smiled brightly at the woman, to thank her.

"I'd better take the bags over to the other side of the station," the man said. She smiled at him.

"All right. Then come back and we'll finish the beer."

He picked up the two heavy bags and carried them around the station to the other tracks. He looked up the tracks but could not see the train. Coming back, he walked through the barroom, where people waiting for the train were drinking. He drank an Anis at the bar and looked at the people. They were all waiting reasonably for the train. He went out through the bead curtain. She was sitting at the table and smiled at him.

"Do you feel better?" he asked.

"I feel fine," she said. "There's nothing wrong with me. I feel fine."

QUESTIONS

1. The main topic of discussion between the man and the girl is never named. What is the "awfully simple operation"? Why is it not named? What different attitudes are taken toward it by the man and the girl? Why?
2. What is indicated about the past life of the man and the girl? How? What has happened to the quality of their relationship? Why? How do we know? How accurate is the man's judgment about their future?
3. Though the story consists mostly of dialogue, and though it contains strong emotional conflict, it is entirely without adverbs indicating the tone of the remarks. How does Hemingway indicate tone? At what points are the characters insincere? Self-deceived? Ironic or sarcastic? To what extent do they give open expression to their feelings? Does either want an open conflict? Why or why not? Trace the various phases of emotion in the girl.
4. How sincere is the man in his insistence that he would not have the girl undergo the operation if she does not want to and that he is "perfectly willing to go through with it" (what is "it"?) if it means anything to the girl? How many times does he repeat these ideas? What significance has the man's drinking an Anis by himself before rejoining the girl at the end of the story?
5. Much of the conversation seems to be about trivial things (ordering drinks, the weather, and so on). What purposes does this conversation serve? What relevance has the girl's remarks about absinthe?
6. What is the point of the girl's comparison of the hills to white elephants? Does the remark assume any significance for the reader beyond its significance for the characters? Why does the author use it for his title?
7. What purpose does the setting serve—the hills across the valley, the treeless railroad tracks and station? What is contributed by the precise information about time at the end of the first paragraph?
8. Which of the two characters is more "reasonable"? Which "wins" the conflict between them? The point of view is objective. Does this mean that we cannot tell whether the sympathy of the author lies more with one character than with the other? Explain your answer.

6. Symbol and Irony

ost successful stories are characterized by compression. The writer's aim is to say as much as possible as briefly as possible. This does not mean that most good stories are brief. It means only that nothing is wasted and that each word and detail are chosen for maximum effectiveness. The force of an explosion is proportionate to the strength and amount of powder used and the smallness of the space it is confined in.

Good writers achieve compression by exercising a rigid selectivity. They choose the details and incidents that contribute most to the meaning they are after; they omit those whose usefulness is minimal. As far as possible they choose details that are multi-valued—that serve a variety of purposes at once. A detail that expresses character at the same time that it advances plot is more useful than a detail that does only one or the other.

This chapter will discuss two contributory resources of the writer for gaining compression: symbol and irony. Both of them may increase the explosive force of a story, but both demand awareness and maturity on the part of the reader.

A literary SYMBOL* is something that means *more* than what it is. It is an object, a person, a situation, an action, or some other item that has a literal meaning in the story but suggests or represents other meanings as

---

*Literary symbols are to be distinguished from *arbitrary* symbols, like letters of the alphabet, numbers, and algebraic signs, which have no meaning in and of themselves but which mean only something *else*, not something *more* than what they are.

well. A very simple illustration is to be found in name symbolism. Most names are simply labels. Seldom does a name tell anything about the person to whom it is attached, except possibly the individual's nationality. In a story, however, authors may choose names for their characters that serve not only to label them but also to suggest something about them. In his fictional trilogy *The Forsyte Saga*, John Galsworthy chooses Forsyte as the family name of his principal characters to indicate their practical foresightedness. Does he follow a similar practice in "The Japanese Quince"? The name of Mr. Nilson might be analyzed as "Nil's son"— son of Nil or nothing. The name of his counterpart Mr. Tandram (it sounds like both *tandem* and *humdrum*) is made up of *dram*—a very small measure—and *tan*—a substance for converting skin into leather. Whether Galsworthy consciously chose the names with these meanings in view or picked them because they "sounded right"—and whether or not the reader recognizes these suggestions—the names are *felt* to be appropriate. The name of General Zaroff in "The Most Dangerous Game" is fitting for a former "officer of the Czar" who now behaves like a czar himself. Trevor's name in Greene's "The Destructors" suggests his upper-class origins. Equally meaningful in that story is the name of the Wormsley Common Gang. First, the word "Common," here designating a small public park or green, also suggests the "common people" or the lower middle and laboring classes as opposed to the upper class. More significant, when Trevor advocates his plan for gutting the old house—"We'd do it from inside. . . . We'd be like worms, don't you see, in an apple" (page 52), we see that Greene's choice of the name Wormsley was quite deliberate, and that it is appropriate also (as well as perfectly natural) that Wormsley Common should have an Underground Station. (The word "apple," in Trevor's speech, also has symbolic resonances. Though it is often a mistake to push symbolism too hard, the reader may well ask himself whether anything would be lost if Trevor had compared the gang's activities to that of worms in a peach or a pear.)

More important than name symbolism is the symbolic use of objects and actions. In some stories these symbols will fit so naturally into the literal context that their symbolic value will not at first be apparent except to the most perceptive reader. In other stories—usually stories with a less realistic surface—they will be so central and so obvious that they will demand symbolical interpretation if the story is to yield significant meaning. In the first kind of story the symbols *reinforce* and *add* to the meaning. In the second kind of story they *carry* the meaning.

In "Hills Like White Elephants" a man and a girl sit waiting for the train to Madrid, where the girl is to have an abortion. But the girl is not fully persuaded that she wants an abortion (at the deepest levels of her being, she does not). The man is aware of this, and seeks to reassure her: "It's really an awfully simple operation. . . . It's not really an operation at all. . . . But I don't want you to do it if you don't really want to." The man *does* want her to do it even if she doesn't really want to; nevertheless, the decision is not irrevocable. They are at a railroad junction, a place where one can change directions. Symbolically it represents a juncture where they can change the direction of their lives. Their bags, with "labels on them from all the hotels where they had spent nights," indicate the kind of rootless, pleasure-seeking existence without responsibility they have hitherto lived. The man wants the girl to have the abortion so that they can go on living as they have before.

The railway station is situated in a river valley between two mountain ranges. On one side of the valley there is no shade and no trees and the country is "brown and dry." It is on this side, "the dry side," that the station sits in the heat, "between two lines of rails." It is also this side which the couple see from their table and which prompts the girl's remark that the hills look "like white elephants." On the other side of the valley, which the girl can see when she walks to the end of the station, lies the river, with "fields of grain and trees" along its banks, the "shadow of a cloud" moving across a field of grain, and another range of mountains in the distance. Looking in this direction, the girl remarks, "And we could have all this." The two landscapes, on opposite sides of the valley, have symbolic meaning in relation to the decision that the girl is being asked to reconfirm. The hot arid side of the valley represents sterility; the other side, with water in the river and the cloud, a hint of coolness in the cloud's moving shadow, and growing things along the river banks, represents fertility. The girl's remark about this other side shows a conscious recognition of its symbolism.

But what does the girl mean by her remark that the mountains on the dry side of the valley look "like white elephants"? Perhaps nothing at all. It is intended as a "bright" remark, a clever if far-fetched comparison made to amuse the man, as it would have in their earlier days together. But whether or not the girl means anything by it, almost certainly Hemingway means something. Or perhaps several things. Clearly the child begun in the girl's womb is a "white elephant" for the man, who says, "I don't want anybody but you. I don't want any one else." For the girl, on the other hand, the abortion itself, the decision to continue living as they have been living, without responsibility, may be considered a "white elephant." We already know that this life has lost its savor for her. When she remarks that the Anis del Toro "tastes like licorice," the man's response—"That's the way with everything"—is probably meant to apply only to the drinks and food in this section of the country, but the girl's confirmation of his observation seems to enlarge its meaning to the whole life they have been living together, which consists, she says, only of looking at things and trying new drinks. Thus the licorice flavor, suggesting tedium and disillusion, joins the "hills like white elephants," the opposed sides of the river valley, and the railroad junction in a network of symbols that intensify the meaning and impact of the story.*

The ability to recognize and identify symbols requires perception and tact. The great danger facing students when they first become aware of symbolical values is a tendency to run wild—to find symbols everywhere and to read into the details of a story all sorts of fanciful meanings not legitimately supported by it. Beginning readers need to remember that most stories operate almost wholly at the literal level and that, even in highly symbolical stories, the majority of the details are purely literal. A story should not be made the excuse for an exercise in ingenuity. It is better, indeed, to miss the symbolical meanings of a story than to pervert its meaning by discovering symbols that are nonexistent. Better to miss the boat than to jump wildly for it and drown.

The ability to interpret symbols is nevertheless essential for a full understanding of literature. Beginning readers should be alert for symbolical meanings but should observe the following cautions:

1. The story itself must furnish a clue that a detail is to be taken symbolically. In Hemingway's story, for instance, the comparison of the hills to white elephants is used for the title of the story and is mentioned four times within the story, while the opposed sides of the river valley are rather pointedly described in a story that otherwise has very little description in it. Both items are given emphasis, yet neither has any part in the action. Even greater emphasis is given to the flowering quince in the story by Galsworthy. Symbols nearly always signal their existence by emphasis, repetition, or position. In the absence of such signals, we should be reluctant to identify an idea as symbolical.

2. The meaning of a literary symbol must be established and supported by the entire context of the story. The symbol has its meaning *in* the story, not *outside* it. Our meaning, for instance, in "Hills Like White Elephants," for the "shadow of a cloud" moving over the field of grain, is supported by and dependent on its relation to other elements in the story,

---

*Some critics have found symbolism also in the bead curtain that separates the bar from the table where the man and girl are sitting. But there is not space here, nor need, to discuss all symbolical implications of the story.

the river, the field of grain, the stifling heat at the station, the brown, dry country on the near side of the valley, and so on. In another work of literature, in another context, a shadow or a cloud might have an almost opposite meaning, or no symbolical meaning at all. The cloud in the ancient saying "Every cloud has a silver lining," and the shadow in the Twenty-third Psalm—"though I walk through the valley of the shadow of death"—have entirely different meanings than they have here. Here, by suggesting the possibility of rain, a spot of shade from the sun, and the existence of a breeze, the moving cloud shadow extends the meaning of the fertility symbol of which it is a part.

3. To be called a symbol, an item must suggest a meaning different in *kind* from its literal meaning: a symbol is something more than the representative of a class or type. In "An Ounce of Cure," for instance, the protagonist, at the time of her "catastrophe," is an inexperienced, love-struck, adolescent girl, and, in so far as her behavior is not untypical of girls at this stage of life, she may stand for inexperienced, love-struck, adolescent girls everywhere. The story acquaints us with a truth of human nature, not with just an imaginary biographical fact. But to say this is to say no more than that the story has a theme. Every interpretive story suggests a generalization about life, is more than a recounting of the specific fortunes of specific individuals. There is no point, therefore, in calling the protagonist of "An Ounce of Cure" a *symbol* of inexperienced, love-struck, adolescent girls; she *is* an inexperienced, love-struck, adolescent girl: a member of the class of inexperienced, love-struck, adolescent girls. We ought not to use the phrase *is a symbol of* when we can as easily use *is,* or *is an example of* or *is an evidence of.* Dick Prosser, in "The Child by Tiger," through his association with the tiger in Blake's poem, and by the way he is spoken of in the story's concluding paragraphs, is clearly meant to be something more than an *example* of any class of men, or of mankind in general; he is a symbol of something *in* man, of hidden possibilities that are latent in us all.

In "Hills Like White Elephants" the railroad junction is neither an example nor an evidence of a point in time in the characters' lives when a crucial decision must be made, nor are the opposed sides of the valley examples or evidences of the two kinds of future that might result from their choice. The meanings these things suggest are different from what they are. The label-covered suitcases of the traveling couple, on the other hand, are an *evidence* or sign of their past and should not properly be called a symbol of their past.

4. A symbol may have more than one meaning. It may suggest a cluster of meanings. At its most effective a symbol is like a many-faceted

jewel: it flashes different colors when turned in the light. This is not to say that it can mean anything we want it to: the area of possible meanings is always controlled by the context. Nevertheless, this possibility of complex meaning, plus concreteness and emotional power, gives the symbol its peculiar compressive value. We have identified the far side of the valley in "Hills Like White Elephants" with fertility, but it suggests also pleasantness, growth, beauty, fulfillment—everything that the girl vaguely includes in her statement, "And we could have all this." The Japanese quince in Galsworthy's story has an equally wide range of meaning—life, growth, beauty, freedom, joy—all qualities opposed to convention and habit and "foreign" to the proper and "respectable" English upper-middle-class environment it finds itself in. The meaning cannot be confined to any one of these qualities: it is all of them, and therein lies the symbol's value.

IRONY is a term with a range of meanings, all of them involving some sort of discrepancy or incongruity. It is a contrast in which one term of the contrast in some way mocks the other term. It is not to be confused with sarcasm, however, which is simply language designed to cause pain. The story writer uses irony to suggest the complexity of experience, to furnish indirectly an evaluation of the material, and at the same time to achieve compression.

Three kinds of irony may be distinguished here. VERBAL IRONY, the simplest and, for the story writer, the least important kind, is a figure of speech in which the opposite is said from what is intended. The discrepancy is between what is said and what is meant. In "An Ounce of Cure," the protagonist uses verbal irony when, just before the return of the Berrymans, she rises from the sofa, lurches a little as she begins to walk, and immediately exaggerating the lurch into a stagger, calls out to her friends, "Watch me walk a straight line!" In "The Child by Tiger," when the narrator tells us that the man who fired the first shot into Dick Prosser was "telling the story of his own heroic accomplishments" and refers to him as "the hero," he is using the words "heroic" and "hero" ironically, for it is clear that he feels only contempt for both the man and his actions. In "Defender of the Faith," when Sergeant Marx says to Grossbart, "You're a regular Messiah, aren't you?" he is speaking ironically—and sarcastically—for he thinks Grossbart's motives are self-interested rather than Messianic. Another use of irony for sarcastic purposes is made by the girl in "Hills Like White Elephants." The man has been assuring her that, after the operation, they will be "just like" they were before, for her pregnancy has been the only thing making them unhappy:

"And you think then we'll be all right and be happy."

"I know we will. You don't have to be afraid. I've known lots of people that have done it."

"So have I," said the girl. "And afterward they were all so happy."

Abortions, the girl implies, make couples anything but "all so happy" afterward. In most of these examples what is meant is only the opposite of what is said; but, in some uses of verbal irony, the literal meaning and its opposite are both implied at once. When William Humphrey, at the end of "A Job of the Plains," tells us, "And so the Lord blessed the latter end of Dobbs more than his beginning," he is saying what is true in one sense but fundamentally false in another.

In DRAMATIC IRONY the contrast is between what a character says and what the reader knows to be true. The value of this kind of irony lies in the comment it implies on the speaker or the speaker's expectations. Thus, in "Haircut," when the barber says of Jim Kendall, near the end of the story, "I thought he was all right at heart, but just bubblin' over with mischief," the comment really reveals the barber's own crudeness and moral insensitivity, for the reader knows by this time that Jim is mean, vicious, and cruel—a selfish egotist who takes pleasure in hurting other people. When the barber concludes his narration with the words "Personally I wouldn't never leave a person shoot a gun in the same boat I was in unless I was sure they knew somethin' about guns. Jim was a sucker to leave a new beginner have his gun, let alone a half-wit," he further reveals his stupidity, for the reader knows, from the evidence provided by the barber himself, that Jim's death was anything but "a plain case of accidental shootin'." Another effective example occurs in "I'm a Fool" when the swipe blames his lie at the race track on the whisky he had drunk and the man in the Windsor tie. The reader sees, as the swipe does not, that these are simply additional symptoms of his plight, not its cause. In "The Black Madonna," dramatic irony and verbal irony are blended when Michele goes off to drink red wine with a friend and refuses to paint any more portraits while his money lasts, and the narrator tells us:

> There was a good deal of talk among the ladies about the dignity of labor, a subject in which they were well versed, and one felt they might almost go so far as to compare a white man [Michele] with a kaffir [native], who did not understand the dignity of labor either.

The reader knows that the persons who understand the dignity of labor least are the British ruling class, "whose leisure is guaranteed by a hardworking majority [the natives]," and who, whatever they lack, do not lack leisure. Later the reader learns that Captain Stocker disapproves "on principle of white men doing heavy manual labor" (it would be undignified) and therefore keeps six Africans back "to do the heavy work." If the British "military gentlemen" understand "the dignity of labor" so little, the reader surmises that their "culture-loving ladies" understand it even less.

In IRONY OF SITUATION, usually the most important kind for the story writer, the discrepancy is between appearance and reality, or between expectation and fulfillment, or between what is and what would seem appropriate. In "The Most Dangerous Game," it is ironic that Rainsford, "the celebrated hunter," should become the hunted, for this is a reversal of his expected and appropriate role. In "The Destructors," it is ironic that Old Misery's horoscope should read, "Abstain from any dealings in first half of week. Danger of serious crash," for the horoscope is valid in a sense that is quite different from that which the words seem to indicate. In "A Job of the Plains" it is ironic that prosperity is a severer affliction for Dobbs than adversity, and this irony leads us to the theme of the story. In "The Black Madonna" it is ironic at the end of the story that nothing should have hurt Captain Stocker in all his life as much as Michele's crisp parting salute and mocking *Yes, sir,* for when the Captain, a month earlier, had first met Michele, untidy, unshaven, singing, mildly drunk, a man who a year earlier had been "a mortal enemy to be shot at sight" and six months earlier "an enemy prisoner," the Captain's first desire had been that Michele should salute him. This irony emphasizes how great a change has been wrought in the Captain by his association with Michele, even though now he is trying to repudiate that change. In "The Pot of Gold" it is ironic that old Mr. Hadaam's riches only make it harder for him to meet people and that the only way he can make new friends is through "automobile accidents, fires, things like that." This irony, of course, correlates with and prepares for Ralph's discovery that his wife's love is the true "pot of gold."

As a final example, the title of "Defender of the Faith" points to a complex irony, partly verbal, partly situational. The phrase "defender of the faith" ordinarily suggests a staunch religious champion and partisan, but, insofar as Sergeant Marx fills this role, he does so against his will, even against his intention, for his motivation is to give fair and equal treatment to all his men—he does not want to be partial to Jews. Unwillingly, he is trapped into being a "defender of the faith" by Private Grossbart.

> The next morning, while chatting with Captain Barrett, I recounted the incident of the previous evening. Somehow, in the telling, it must have seemed to the Captain that I was not so much explaining Grossbart's position as defending it.

At the end of the story, however, when Marx has Grossbart's orders changed to the Pacific, the irony is that he becomes most truly a defender of his faith when he seems to be turning against it. "You call this watching out for me—what you did?" asks Grossbart. "No," answers Marx. "For all of us." The cause of the whole Jewish faith is set back when Jews like Grossbart get special favors for themselves, for other peoples will mistakenly attribute Grossbart's objectionable qualities to the Jewish people as a whole. Thus Marx is unwillingly a "defender of the faith" when he helps his coreligionist, and becomes truly defender of the faith when he turns against him. These ironies underscore the difficulties involved in being at the same time a good Jew and a good person in a world where Jews are so often the objects of prejudice and persecution.

In all these examples, irony enables the author to gain power with economy. Like symbolism, irony makes it possible to suggest meanings without stating them. Simply by juxtaposing two discordant facts in the right solution, the writer can start a current of meaning flowing between them, as between the two poles in an electric battery. We do not need to be *told* that Whitey the barber is stupid and morally insensitive; we see it. We do not need to be told that the race-track swipe is lacking in self-knowledge; we see it. We do not need to be told how difficult it is for a Jewish sergeant to balance justice and mercy in a position of command; we feel it. The ironic contrast generates meaning.

Shirley Jackson

THE LOTTERY

The morning of June 27th was clear and sunny, with the fresh warmth of a full-summer day; the flowers were blossoming profusely and the grass was richly green. The people of the village began to gather in the square, between the post office and the bank, around ten o'clock; in some towns there were so many people that the lottery took two days and had to be started on June 26th, but in this village, where there were only about three hundred people, the whole lottery took less than two hours, so it could begin at ten o'clock in the morning and still be through in time to allow the villagers to get home for noon dinner.

The children assembled first, of course. School was recently over for the summer, and the feeling of liberty sat uneasily on most of them; they tended to gather together quietly for a while before they broke into boisterous play,

THE LOTTERY First published in 1948. Shirley Jackson (1919–1965) was born in San Francisco and spent most of her early life in California. After her marriage in 1940 she lived in a quiet rural community in Vermont.

and their talk was still of the classroom and the teacher, of books and reprimands. Bobby Martin had already stuffed his pockets full of stones, and the other boys soon followed his example, selecting the smoothest and roundest stones; Bobby and Harry Jones and Dickie Delacroix—the villagers pronounced this name "Dellacroy"—eventually made a great pile of stones in one corner of the square and guarded it against the raids of the other boys. The girls stood aside, talking among themselves, looking over their shoulders at the boys, and the very small children rolled in the dust or clung to the hands of their older brothers or sisters.

Soon the men began to gather, surveying their own children, speaking of planting and rain, tractors and taxes. They stood together, away from the pile of stones in the corner, and their jokes were quiet and they smiled rather than laughed. The women, wearing faded house dresses and sweaters, came shortly after their menfolk. They greeted one another and exchanged bits of gossip as they went to join their husbands. Soon the women, standing by their husbands, began to call to their children, and the children came reluctantly, having to be called four or five times. Bobby Martin ducked under his mother's grasping hand and ran, laughing, back to the pile of stones. His father spoke up sharply, and Bobby came quickly and took his place between his father and his oldest brother.

The lottery was conducted—as were the square dances, the teen-age club, the Halloween program—by Mr. Summers, who had time and energy to devote to civic activities. He was a round-faced, jovial man and he ran the coal business, and people were sorry for him, because he had no children and his wife was a scold. When he arrived in the square, carrying the black wooden box, there was a murmur of conversation among the villagers, and he waved and called, "Little late today, folks." The postmaster, Mr. Graves, followed him, carrying a three-legged stool, and the stool was put in the center of the square and Mr. Summers set the black box down on it. The villagers kept their distance, leaving a space between themselves and the stool, and when Mr. Summers said, "Some of you fellows want to give me a hand?" there was a hesitation before two men, Mr. Martin and his oldest son, Baxter, came forward to hold the box steady on the stool while Mr. Summers stirred up the papers inside it.

The original paraphernalia for the lottery had been lost long ago, and the black box now resting on the stool had been put into use even before Old Man Warner, the oldest man in town, was born. Mr. Summers spoke frequently to the villagers about making a new box, but no one liked to upset even as much tradition as was represented by the black box. There was a story that the present box had been made with some pieces of the box that had preceded it, the one that had been constructed when the first people settled down to make a village here. Every year, after the lottery, Mr. Summers began talking again about a new box, but every year the subject was allowed to fade off without anything's being done. The black box grew shabbier each year; by now it was no longer completely black but splintered badly along one side to show the original wood color, and in some places faded or stained.

Mr. Martin and his oldest son, Baxter, held the black box securely on the stool until Mr. Summers had stirred the papers thoroughly with his hand. Because so much of the ritual had been forgotten or discarded, Mr. Summers had been successful in having slips of paper substituted for the chips of wood that had been used for generations. Chips of wood, Mr. Summers had argued, had been all very well when the village was tiny, but now that the population was more than three hundred and likely to keep on growing, it was necessary to use something that would fit more easily into the black box. The night before the lottery, Mr. Summers and Mr. Graves made up the slips of paper and put them in the box, and it was then taken to the safe of Mr. Summers' coal company and locked up until Mr. Summers was ready to take it to the square next morning. The rest of the year, the box was put away, sometimes one place, sometimes another; it had spent one year in Mr. Graves's barn and another year underfoot in the post office, and sometimes it was set on a shelf in the Martin grocery and left there.

There was a great deal of fussing to be done before Mr. Summers declared the lottery open. There were the lists to make up—of heads of families, heads of households in each family, members of each household in each family. There was the proper swearing-in of Mr. Summers by the postmaster, as the official of the lottery; at one time, some people remembered, there had been a recital of some sort, performed by the official of the lottery, a perfunctory, tuneless chant that had been rattled off duly each year; some people believed that the official of the lottery used to stand just so when he said or sang it, others believed that he was supposed to walk among the people, but years and years ago this part of the ritual had been allowed to lapse. There had been, also, a ritual salute, which the official of the lottery had had to use in addressing each person who came up to draw from the box, but this also had changed with time, until now it was felt necessary only for the official to speak to each person approaching. Mr. Summers was very good at all this; in his clean white shirt and blue jeans, with one hand resting carelessly on the black box, he seemed very proper and important as he talked interminably to Mr. Graves and the Martins.

Just as Mr. Summers finally left off talking and turned to the assembled villagers, Mrs. Hutchinson came hurriedly along the path to the square, her sweater thrown over her shoulders, and slid into place in the back of the crowd. "Clean forgot what day it was," she said to Mrs. Delacroix, who stood next to her, and they both laughed softly. "Thought my old man was out back stacking wood," Mrs. Hutchinson went on, "and then I looked out the window and the kids were gone, and then I remembered it was the twenty-seventh and came a-running." She dried her hands on her apron, and Mrs. Delacroix said, "You're in time, though. They're still talking away up there."

Mrs. Hutchinson craned her neck to see through the crowd and found her husband and children standing near the front. She tapped Mrs. Delacroix on the arm as a farewell and began to make her way through the crowd. The people separated good-humoredly to let her through; two or three people said, in voices just loud enough to be heard across the crowd, "Here comes your Missus, Hutchinson," and "Bill, she made it after all." Mrs. Hutchinson reached her husband, and Mr. Summers, who had been waiting, said cheerfully, "Thought we were going to have to get on without you, Tessie." Mrs. Hutchinson said, grinning, "Wouldn't have me leave m'dishes in the sink, now, would you, Joe?" and soft laughter ran through the crowd as the people stirred back into position after Mrs. Hutchinson's arrival.

"Well, now," Mr. Summers said soberly, "guess we better get started, get this over with, so's we can go back to work. Anybody ain't here?"

"Dunbar," several people said. "Dunbar, Dunbar."

Mr. Summers consulted his list. "Clyde Dunbar," he said. "That's right. He's broke his leg, hasn't he? Who's drawing for him?

"Me, I guess," a woman said, and Mr. Summers turned to look at her. "Wife draws for her husband," Mr. Summers said. "Don't you have a grown boy to do it for you, Janey?" Although Mr. Summers and everyone else in the village knew the answer perfectly well, it was the business of the official of the lottery to ask such questions formally. Mr. Summers waited with an expression of polite interest while Mrs. Dunbar answered.

"Horace's not but sixteen yet," Mrs. Dunbar said regretfully. "Guess I gotta fill in for the old man this year."

"Right," Mr. Summers said. He made a note on the list he was holding. Then he asked, "Watson boy drawing this year?"

A tall boy in the crowd raised his hand. "Here," he said. "I'm drawing for m'mother and me." He blinked his eyes nervously and ducked his head as several voices in the crowd said things like "Good fellow, Jack," and "Glad to see your mother's got a man to do it."

"Well," Mr. Summers said, "guess that's everyone. Old Man Warner make it?"

"Here," a voice said, and Mr. Summers nodded.

A sudden hush fell on the crowd as Mr. Summers cleared his throat and looked at the list. "All ready?" he called. "Now, I'll read the names—heads of families first—and the men come up and take a paper out of the box. Keep the paper folded in your hand without looking at it until everyone has had a turn. Everything clear?"

The people had done it so many times that they only half listened to the directions; most of them were quiet, wetting their lips, not looking around. Then Mr. Summers raised one hand high and said, "Adams." A man disengaged himself from the crowd and came forward. "Hi, Steve," Mr. Summers said, and Mr. Adams said, "Hi, Joe." They grinned at one another humorlessly and nervously. Then Mr. Adams reached into the black box and took out a folded paper. He held it firmly by one corner as he turned and went hastily back to his place in the crowd, where he stood a little apart from his family, not looking down at his hand.

"Allen," Mr. Summers said. "Anderson . . . Bentham."

"Seems like there's no time at all between lotteries any more," Mrs. Delacroix said to Mrs. Graves in the back row. "Seems like we got through with the last one only last week."

"Time sure goes fast," Mrs. Graves said.

"Clark . . . Delacroix."

"There goes my old man," Mrs. Delacroix said. She held her breath while her husband went forward.

"Dunbar," Mr. Summers said, and Mrs. Dunbar went steadily to the box while one of the women said, "Go on, Janey," and another said, "There she goes."

"We're next," Mrs. Graves said. She watched while Mr. Graves came around from the side of the box, greeted Mr. Summers gravely, and selected a slip of paper from the box. By now, all through the crowd there were men holding the small folded papers in their large hands, turning them over and over nervously. Mrs. Dunbar and her two sons stood together, Mrs. Dunbar holding the slip of paper.

"Harburt . . . Hutchinson."

"Get up there, Bill," Mrs. Hutchinson said, and the people near her laughed.

"Jones."

"They do say," Mr. Adams said to Old Man Warner, who stood next to him, "that over in the north village they're talking of giving up the lottery."

Old Man Warner snorted. "Pack of crazy fools," he said. "Listening to the young folks, nothing's good enough for *them*. Next thing you know, they'll be wanting to go back to living in caves, nobody work any more, live *that* way for a while. Used to be a saying about 'Lottery in June, corn be heavy soon.' First thing you know, we'd all be eating stewed chickweed and acorns. There's *always* been a lottery," he added petulantly. "Bad enough to see young Joe Summers up there joking with everybody."

"Some places have already quit lotteries," Mrs. Adams said.

"Nothing but trouble in *that*," Old Man Warner said stoutly. "Pack of young fools."

"Martin." And Bobby Martin watched his father go forward. "Overdyke . . . Percy."

"I wish they'd hurry," Mrs. Dunbar said to her older son. "I wish they'd hurry."

"They're almost through," her son said.

"You get ready to run tell Dad," Mrs. Dunbar said.

Mr. Summers called his own name and then stepped forward precisely and selected a slip from the box. Then he called, "Warner."

"Seventy-seventh year I been in the lottery," Old Man Warner said as he went through the crowd. "Seventy-seventh time."

"Watson." The tall boy came awkwardly through the crowd. Someone said, "Don't be nervous, Jack," and Mr. Summers said, "Take your time, son."

"Zanini."

After that, there was a long pause, a breathless pause, until Mr. Summers, holding his slip of paper in the air, said, "All right, fellows." For a minute, no one moved, and then all the slips of paper were opened. Suddenly, all the women began to speak at once, saying, "Who is it?" "Who's got it?" "Is it the Dunbars?" "Is it the Watsons?" Then the voices began to say, "It's Hutchinson. It's Bill," "Bill Hutchinson's got it."

"Go tell your father," Mrs. Dunbar said to her older son.

People began to look around to see the Hutchinsons. Bill Hutchinson was standing quiet, staring down at the paper in his hand. Suddenly, Tessie Hutchinson shouted to Mr. Summers. "You didn't give him time enough to take any paper he wanted. I saw you. It wasn't fair."

"Be a good sport, Tessie," Mrs. Delacroix called, and Mrs. Graves said, "All of us took the same chance."

"Shut up, Tessie," Bill Hutchinson said.

"Well, everyone," Mr. Summers said, "that was done pretty fast, and now we've got to be hurrying a little more to get done in time." He consulted his next list. "Bill," he said, "you draw for the Hutchinson family. You got any other households in the Hutchinsons?"

"There's Don and Eva," Mrs. Hutchinson yelled. "Make *them* take their chance!"

"Daughters draw with their husband's families, Tessie," Mr. Summers said gently. "You know that as well as anyone else."

"It wasn't *fair*," Tessie said.

"I guess not, Joe," Bill Hutchinson said regretfully. "My daughter draws with her husband's family, that's only fair. And I've got no other family except the kids."

"Then, as far as drawing for families is concerned, it's you," Mr. Summers said in explanation, "and as far as drawing for households is concerned, that's you, too. Right?"

"Right," Bill Hutchinson said.

"How many kids, Bill?" Mr. Summers asked formally.

"Three," Bill Hutchinson said. "There's Bill, Jr., and Nancy, and little Dave. And Tessie and me."

"All right, then," Mr. Summers said. "Harry, you got their tickets back?"

Mr. Graves nodded and held up the slips of paper. "Put them in the box, then," Mr. Summers directed. "Take Bill's and put it in."

"I think we ought to start over," Mrs. Hutchinson said, as quietly as she could. "I tell you it wasn't *fair*. You didn't give him time enough to choose. *Every*body saw that."

Mr. Graves had selected the five slips and put them in the box, and he dropped all the papers but those onto the ground, where the breeze caught them and lifted them off.

"Listen, everybody," Mrs. Hutchinson was saying to the people around her.

"Ready, Bill?" Mr. Summers asked, and Bill Hutchinson, with one quick glance around at his wife and children, nodded.

"Remember," Mr. Summers said, "take the slips and keep them folded until each person has taken one. Harry, you help little Dave." Mr. Graves took the hand of the little boy, who came willingly with him up to the box. "Take a paper out of the box, Davy," Mr. Summers said. Davy put his hand into the box and laughed. "Take just *one* paper," Mr. Summers said. "Harry, you hold it for him." Mr. Graves took the child's hand and removed the folded paper from the tight fist and held it while little Dave stood next to him and looked up at him wonderingly.

"Nancy next," Mr. Summers said. Nancy was twelve, and her school friends breathed heavily as she went forward, switching her skirt, and took a slip daintily from the box. "Bill, Jr.," Mr. Summers said, and Billy, his face red and his feet over-large, nearly knocked the box over as he got a paper out. "Tessie," Mr. Summers said. She hesitated for a minute, looking around defiantly, and then set her lips and went up to the box. She snatched a paper out and held it behind her.

"Bill," Mr. Summers said, and Bill Hutchinson reached into the box and felt around, bringing his hand out at last with the slip of paper in it.

The crowd was quiet. A girl whispered, "I hope it's not Nancy," and the sound of the whisper reached the edges of the crowd.

"It's not the way it used to be," Old Man Warner said clearly. "People ain't the way they used to be."

"All right," Mr. Summers said. "Open the papers. Harry, you open little Dave's."

Mr. Graves opened the slip of paper and there was a general sigh through the crowd as he held it up and everyone could see that it was blank. Nancy and Bill, Jr., opened theirs at the same time, and both beamed and laughed, turning around to the crowd and holding their slips of paper above their heads.

"Tessie," Mr. Summers said. There was a pause, and then Mr. Summers looked at Bill Hutchinson, and Bill unfolded his paper and showed it. It was blank.

"It's Tessie," Mr. Summers said, and his voice was hushed. "Show us her paper, Bill."

Bill Hutchinson went over to his wife and forced the slip of paper out of her hand. It had a black spot on it, the black spot Mr. Summers had made the night before with the heavy pencil in the coal-company office. Bill Hutchinson held it up, and there was a stir in the crowd.

"All right, folks," Mr. Summers said. "Let's finish quickly."

Although the villagers had forgotten the ritual and lost the original black box, they still remembered to use stones. The pile of stones the boys had made earlier was ready; there were stones on the ground with the blowing scraps of paper that had come out of the box. Mrs. Delacroix selected a stone so large she had to pick it up with both hands and turned to Mrs. Dunbar. "Come on," she said. "Hurry up."

Mrs. Dunbar had small stones in both hands, and she said, gasping for breath, "I can't run at all. You'll have to go ahead and I'll catch up with you."

The children had stones already, and someone gave little Davy Hutchinson a few pebbles.

Tessie Hutchinson was in the center of a cleared space by now, and she held her hands out desperately as the villagers moved in on her. "It isn't fair," she said. A stone hit her on the side of the head.

Old Man Warner was saying, "Come on, come on, everyone." Steve Adams was in the front of the crowd of villagers, with Mrs. Graves beside him.

"It isn't fair, it isn't right," Mrs. Hutchinson screamed, and then they were upon her.

QUESTIONS

1. What is a scapegoat? Who is the scapegoat in this story? Look up other examples of scapegoats (Sir James Frazer's *The Golden Bough* is an excellent source).
2. What law of probability has the author suspended in writing this story? Granting this initial implausibility, does the story proceed naturally?
3. What is the fundamental irony of the story?
4. What is the significance of the fact that the original box has been lost and many parts of the ritual have been forgotten?
5. What different attitudes toward the ritual are represented by (a) Mr. Summers, (b) Old Man Warner, (c) Mr. and Mrs. Adams, (d) Mrs. Hutchinson, (e) the villagers in general? Which would you suppose most nearly represents the attitude of the author? Why?
6. By transporting a primitivistic ritual into a modern setting, the author is enabled to say something about human nature and human society. What?
7. "The Lottery" must obviously be interpreted symbolically or allegorically (as a pattern of symbols corresponding to some pattern in the outside world). How far is the meaning of its symbols fixed? How far open to various interpretations? What specific interpretations can you suggest?

Albert Camus

THE GUEST

The schoolmaster was watching the two men climb toward him. One was on horseback, the other on foot. They had not yet tackled the abrupt rise leading to the schoolhouse built on the hillside. They were toiling onward,

THE GUEST First published in 1957. Translated into English by Justin O'Brien. Algeria, now a republic, was until mid-century a French territory with a population about 88 percent Moslem (either Arab or Berber). Daru and Balducci, in the story, are French civil servants. Algeria gained its independence as a result of the Algerian War, 1954–1962, a Moslem revolt against French rule. Albert Camus (1913–1960), though a Frenchman, was born in northeastern Algeria, was educated in Algiers, and did not see France until 1939. In 1940, with the fall of France to Germany, he returned to Algiers and taught for two years in a private school in Oran, on the seacoast. In 1942 he returned to Paris and engaged actively in the resistance movement by writing for the underground press. He continued his residence in Paris after World War II.

making slow progress in the snow, among the stones, on the vast expanse of the high, deserted plateau. From time to time the horse stumbled. He could not be heard yet but the breath issuing from his nostrils could be seen. The schoolmaster calculated that it would take them a half hour to get onto the hill. It was cold; he went back into the school to get a sweater.

He crossed the empty, frigid classroom. On the blackboard the four rivers of France, drawn with four different colored chalks, had been flowing toward their estuaries for the past three days. Snow had suddenly fallen in mid-October after eight months of drought without the transition of rain, and the twenty pupils, more or less, who lived in the villages scattered over the plateau had stopped coming. With fair weather they would return. Daru now heated only the single room that was his lodging, adjoining the classroom. One of the windows faced, like the classroom windows, the south. On that side the school was a few kilometers from the point where the plateau began to slope toward the south. In clear weather the purple mass of the mountain range where the gap opened onto the desert could be seen.

Somewhat warmed, Daru returned to the window from which he had first noticed the two men. They were no longer visible. Hence they must have tackled the rise. The sky was not so dark, for the snow had stopped falling during the night. The morning had dawned with a dirty light which had scarcely become brighter as the ceiling of clouds lifted. At two in the afternoon it seemed as if the day were merely beginning. But still this was better than those three days when the thick snow was falling amidst unbroken darkness with little gusts of wind that rattled the double door of the classroom. Then Daru had spent long hours in his room, leaving it only to go to the shed and feed the chickens or get some coal. Fortunately the delivery truck from Tadjid, the nearest village to the north, had brought his supplies two days before the blizzard. It would return in forty-eight hours.

Besides, he had enough to resist a siege, for the little room was cluttered with bags of wheat that the administration had left as a supply to distribute to those of his pupils whose families had suffered from the drought. Actually they had all been victims because they were all poor. Every day Daru would distribute a ration to the children. They had missed it, he knew, during these bad days. Possibly one of the fathers or big brothers would come this afternoon and he could supply them with grain. It was just a matter of carrying them over to the next harvest. Now shiploads of wheat were arriving from France and the worst was over. But it would be hard to forget that poverty, that army of ragged ghosts wandering in the sunlight, the plateaus burned to a cinder month after month, the earth shriveled up little by little, literally scorched, every stone bursting into dust under one's foot. The sheep had died then by thousands, and even a few men, here and there, sometimes without anyone's knowing.

In contrast with such poverty, he who lived almost like a monk, in his remote schoolhouse, had felt like a lord with his whitewashed walls, his narrow couch, his unpainted shelves, his well, and his weekly provisioning with water and food. And suddenly this snow, without warning, without the foretaste of rain. This is the way the region was, cruel to live in, even without men, who didn't help matters either. But Daru had been born here. Everywhere else, he felt exiled.

He went out and stepped forward on the terrace in front of the schoolhouse. The two men were now halfway up the slope. He recognized the horseman to be Balducci, the old gendarme he had known for a long time. Balducci was holding at the end of a rope an Arab walking behind him with hands bound and head lowered. The gendarme waved a greeting to which Daru did not reply, lost as he was in contemplation of the Arab dressed in a faded blue *jellaba*, his feet in sandals but covered with socks of heavy raw wool, his head crowned with a narrow, short *chèche*. Balducci was holding back his horse in order not to hurt the Arab, and the group was advancing slowly.

Within earshot, Balducci shouted, "One hour to do the three kilometers from El Ameur!" Daru did not answer. Short and square in his thick sweater, he watched them climb. Not once had the Arab raised his head. "Hello," said Daru when they got up onto the terrace. "Come in and warm up." Balducci painfully got down from his horse without letting go of the rope. He smiled at the schoolmaster from under his bristling mustache. His little dark eyes, deepset under a tanned forehead, and his mouth surrounded with wrinkles made him look attentive and studious. Daru took the bridle, led the horse to the shed, and came back to the two men who were now waiting for him in the school. He led them into his room. "I am going to heat up the classroom," he said. "We'll be more comfortable there."

When he entered the room again, Balducci was on the couch. He had undone the rope tying him to the Arab, who had squatted near the stove. His hands still bound, the *chèche* pushed back on his head, the Arab was looking toward the window. At first Daru noticed only his huge lips, fat, smooth, almost Negroid; yet his nose was straight, his eyes dark and full of fever. The *chèche* uncovered an obstinate forehead and, under the weathered skin now rather discolored by the cold, the whole face had a restless and rebellious look. "Go into the other room," said the schoolmaster, "and I'll make you some mint tea." "Thanks," Balducci said. "What a chore! How I long for retirement." And addressing his prisoner in Arabic, he said, "Come on, you." The Arab got up and, slowly, holding his bound wrists in front of him, went into the classroom.

With the tea, Daru brought a chair. But Balducci was already sitting in state at the nearest pupil's desk, and the Arab had squatted against the teacher's platform facing the stove, which stood between the desk and the window. When he held out the glass of tea to the prisoner, Daru hesitated at the sight of his bound hands. "He might perhaps be untied." "Sure," said Balducci. "That was for the trip." He started to get to his feet. But Daru, setting the glass on the floor, had knelt beside the Arab. Without saying anything, the Arab watched him with his feverish eyes. Once his hands were free, he rubbed his swollen wrists against each other, took the glass of tea and sucked up the burning liquid in swift little sips.

"Good," said Daru. "And where are you headed?"

Balducci withdrew his mustache from the tea. "Here, son."

"Odd pupils! And you're spending the night?"

"No. I'm going back to El Ameur. And you will deliver this fellow to Tinguit. He is expected at police headquarters."

Balducci was looking at Daru with a friendly little smile.

"What's this story?" asked the schoolmaster. "Are you pulling my leg?"

"No, son. Those are the orders."

"The orders? I'm not . . ." Daru hesitated, not wanting to hurt the old Corsican. "I mean, that's not my job."

"What! What's the meaning of that? In wartime people do all kinds of jobs."

"Then I'll wait for the declaration of war!"

Balducci nodded. "O.K. But the orders exist and they concern you too. Things are bubbling, it appears. There is talk of a forthcoming revolt. We are mobilized, in a way."

Daru still had his obstinate look.

"Listen, son," Balducci said. "I like you and you've got to understand. There's only a dozen of us at El Ameur to patrol the whole territory of a small department and I must be back in a hurry. He couldn't be kept there. His village was beginning to stir; they wanted to take him back. You must take him to Tinguit tomorrow before the day is over. Twenty kilometers shouldn't faze a husky fellow like you. After that, all will be over. You'll come back to your pupils and your comfortable life."

Behind the wall the horse could be heard snorting and pawing the earth. Daru was looking out the window. Decidedly the weather was clearing and the light was increasing over the snowy plateau. When all the snow was melted, the sun would take over again and once more would burn the fields of stone. For days still, the unchanging sky would shed its dry light on the solitary expanse where nothing had any connection with man.

"After all," he said, turning around toward Balducci, "what did he do?" And, before the gendarme had opened his mouth, he asked, "Does he speak French?"

"No, not a word. We had been looking for him for a month, but they were hiding him. He killed his cousin."

"Is he against us?"

"I don't think so. But you can never be sure."

"Why did he kill?"

"A family squabble, I think. One owed grain to the other, it seems. It's not at all clear. In short, he killed his cousin with a billhook. You know, like a sheep, *kreezk!*"

Balducci made the gesture of drawing a blade across his throat, and the

Arab, his attention attracted, watched him with a sort of anxiety. Daru felt a sudden wrath against the man, against all men with their rotten spite, their tireless hates, their blood lust.

But the kettle was singing on the stove. He served Balducci more tea, hesitated, then served the Arab again, who drank avidly a second time. His raised arms made the *jellaba* fall open, and the schoolmaster saw his thin, muscular chest.

"Thanks, son," Balducci said. "And now I'm off."

He got up and went toward the Arab, taking a small rope from his pocket.

"What are you doing?" Daru asked dryly.

Balducci, disconcerted, showed him the rope.

"Don't bother."

The old gendarme hesitated. "It's up to you. Of course, you are armed?"

"I have my shotgun."

"Where?"

"In the trunk."

"You ought to have it near your bed."

"Why? I have nothing to fear."

"You're crazy, son. If there's an uprising, no one is safe; we're all in the same boat."

"I'll defend myself. I'll have time to see them coming."

Balducci began to laugh, then suddenly the mustache covered the white teeth. "You'll have time? O.K. That's just what I was saying. You always have been a little cracked. That's why I like you; my son was like that."

At the same time he took out his revolver and put it on the desk. "Keep it; I don't need two weapons from here to El Ameur."

The revolver shone against the black paint of the table. When the gendarme turned toward him, the schoolmaster caught his smell of leather and horseflesh.

"Listen, Balducci," Daru said suddenly, "all this disgusts me, beginning with your fellow here. But I won't hand him over. Fight, yes, if I have to. But not that."

The old gendarme stood in front of him and looked at him severely.

"You're being a fool," he said slowly. "I don't like it either. You don't get used to putting a rope on a man even after years of it, and you're even ashamed—yes, ashamed. But you can't let them have their way."

"I won't hand him over," Daru said again.

"It's an order, son, and I repeat it."

"That's right. Repeat to them what I've said to you: I won't hand him over."

Balducci made a visible effort to reflect. He looked at the Arab and at Daru. At last he decided.

"No, I won't tell them anything. If you want to drop us, go ahead; I'll not denounce you. I have an order to deliver the prisoner and I'm doing so. And now you'll just sign this paper for me."

"There's no need. I'll not deny that you left him with me."

"Don't be mean with me. I know you'll tell the truth. You're from around these parts and you are a man. But you must sign; that's the rule."

Daru opened his drawer, took out a little square bottle of purple ink, the red wooden penholder with the "sergeant-major" pen he used for models of handwriting, and signed. The gendarme carefully folded the paper and put it into his wallet. Then he moved toward the door.

"I'll see you off," Daru said.

"No," said Balducci. "There's no use being polite. You insulted me."

He looked at the Arab, motionless in the same spot, sniffed peevishly, and turned away toward the door. "Good-by, son," he said. The door slammed behind him. His footsteps were muffled by the snow. The horse stirred on the other side of the wall and several chickens fluttered in fright. A moment later Balducci reappeared outside the window leading the horse by the bridle. He walked toward the little rise without turning around and disappeared from sight with the horse following him.

Daru walked back toward the prisoner, who, without stirring, never took his eyes off him. "Wait," the schoolmaster said in Arabic and went toward the bedroom. As he was going through the door, he had a second thought, went to the desk, took the revolver, and stuck it in his pocket. Then, without looking back, he went into his room.

For some time he lay on his couch watching the sky gradually close over, listening to the silence. It was this silence that had seemed painful to him during the first days here, after the war. He had requested a post in the little town at the base of the foothills separating the upper plateaus from the desert. There rocky walls, green and black to the north, pink and lavender to the south, marked the frontier of eternal summer. He had been named to a post farther north, on the plateau itself. In the beginning, the solitude and the silence had been hard for him on these wastelands peopled only by stones. Occasionally, furrows suggested cultivation, but they had been dug to uncover a certain kind of stone good for building. The only plowing here was to harvest rocks. Elsewhere a thin layer of soil accumulated in the hollows would be scraped out to enrich paltry village gardens. This is the way it was: bare rock covered three quarters of the region. Towns sprang up, flourished, then disappeared; men came by, loved one another or fought bitterly, then died. No one in this desert, neither he nor his guest, mattered. And yet, outside this desert neither of them, Daru knew, could have really lived.

When he got up, no noise came from the classroom. He was amazed at the unmixed joy he derived from the mere thought that the Arab might have fled and that he would be alone with no decision to make. But the prisoner was there. He had merely stretched out between the stove and the desk and he was staring at the ceiling. In that position, his thick lips were particularly noticeable, giving him a pouting look. "Come," said Daru. The Arab got up and followed him. In the bedroom the schoolmaster pointed to a chair near the table under the window. The Arab sat down without ceasing to watch Daru.

"Are you hungry?"

"Yes," the prisoner said.

Daru set the table for two. He took flour and oil, shaped a cake in a frying pan, and lighted the little stove that functioned on bottled gas. While the cake was cooking, he went out to the shed to get cheese, eggs, dates, and condensed milk. When the cake was done he set it on the window sill to cool, heated some condensed milk diluted with water, and beat up the eggs into an omelette. In one of his motions he bumped into the revolver stuck in his right pocket. He set the bowl down, went into the classroom, and put the revolver in his desk drawer. When he came back to the room, night was falling. He put on the light and served the Arab. "Eat," he said. The Arab took a piece of the cake, lifted it eagerly to his mouth, and stopped short.

"And you?" he asked.

"After you. I'll eat too."

The thick lips opened slightly. The Arab hesitated, then bit into the cake determinedly.

The meal over, the Arab looked at the schoolmaster. "Are you the judge?"

"No, I'm simply keeping you until tomorrow."

"Why do you eat with me?"

"I'm hungry."

The Arab fell silent. Daru got up and went out. He brought back a camp cot from the shed and set it up between the table and the stove, at right angles to his own bed. From a large suitcase which, upright in a corner, served as a shelf for papers, he took two blankets and arranged them on the cot. Then he stopped, felt useless, and sat down on his bed. There was nothing more to do or to get ready. He had to look at this man. He looked at him therefore, trying to imagine his face bursting with rage. He couldn't do so. He could see nothing but the dark yet shining eyes and the animal mouth.

"Why did you kill him?" he asked in a voice whose hostile tone surprised him.

The Arab looked away. "He ran away. I ran after him."

He raised his eyes to Daru again and they were full of a sort of woeful interrogation. "Now what will they do to me?"

"Are you afraid?"

The Arab stiffened, turning his eyes away.

"Are you sorry?"

The Arab stared at him openmouthed. Obviously he did not understand. Daru's annoyance was growing. At the same time he felt awkward and selfconscious with his big body wedged between the two beds.

"Lie down there," he said impatiently. "That's your bed."

The Arab didn't move. He cried out, "Tell me!"

The schoolmaster looked at him.

"Is the gendarme coming back tomorrow?"

"I don't know."

"Are you coming with us?"

"I don't know. Why?"

The prisoner got up and stretched out on top of the blankets, his feet toward the window. The light from the electric bulb shone straight into his eyes and he closed them at once.

"Why?" Daru repeated, standing beside the bed.

The Arab opened his eyes under the blinding light and looked at him, trying not to blink. "Come with us," he said.

In the middle of the night, Daru was still not asleep. He had gone to bed after undressing completely; he generally slept naked. But when he suddenly realized that he had nothing on, he wondered. He felt vulnerable and the temptation came to him to put his clothes back on. Then he shrugged his shoulders; after all, he wasn't a child and, if it came to that, he could break his adversary in two. From his bed, he could observe him lying on his back, still motionless, his eyes closed under the harsh light. When Daru turned out the light, the darkness seemed to congeal all of a sudden. Little by little, the night came back to life in the window where the starless sky was stirring gently. The schoolmaster soon made out the body lying at his feet. The Arab was still motionless but his eyes seemed open. A faint wind was prowling about the schoolhouse. Perhaps it would drive away the clouds and the sun would reappear.

During the night the wind increased. The hens fluttered a little and then were silent. The Arab turned over on his side with his back to Daru, who thought he heard him moan. Then he listened for his guest's breathing, which had become heavier and more regular. He listened to that breathing so close to him and mused without being able to go to sleep. In the room where he had been sleeping alone for a year, this presence bothered him. But it bothered him also because it imposed on him a sort of brotherhood he refused to accept in the present circumstances; yet he was familiar with it. Men who share the same rooms, soldiers or prisoners, develop a strange alliance as if, having cast off their armor with their clothing, they fraternized every evening, over and above their differences, in the ancient community of dream and fatigue. But Daru shook himself; he didn't like such musings, and it was essential for him to sleep.

A little later, however, when the Arab stirred slightly, the schoolmaster was still not asleep. When the prisoner made a second move, he stiffened, on the alert. The Arab was lifting himself slowly on his arms with almost the motion of a sleepwalker. Seated upright in bed, he waited motionless without turning his head toward Daru, as if he were listening attentively. Daru did not stir; it had just occurred to him that the revolver was still in the drawer of his desk. It was better to act at once. Yet he continued to observe the prisoner, who, with the same slithery motion, put his feet on the ground, waited again, then stood up slowly. Daru was about to call out to him when the Arab began to walk, in a quite natural but extraordinarily silent way. He was heading toward the door at the end of the room that opened into the shed. He lifted the latch with precaution and went out, pushing the door behind him but without shutting it.

Daru had not stirred. "He is running away," he merely thought. "Good riddance!" Yet he listened attentively. The hens were not fluttering; the guest must be on the plateau. A faint sound of water reached him, and he didn't know what it was until the Arab again stood framed in the doorway, closed the door carefully, and came back to bed without a sound. Then Daru turned his back on him and fell asleep. Still later he seemed, from the depths of his sleep, to hear furtive steps around the schoolhouse. "I'm dreaming! I'm dreaming!" he repeated to himself. And he went on sleeping.

When he awoke, the sky was clear; the loose window let in a cold, pure air. The Arab was asleep, hunched up under the blankets now, his mouth open, utterly relaxed. But when Daru shook him he started dreadfully, staring at Daru with wild eyes as if he had never seen him and with such a frightened expression that the schoolmaster stepped back. "Don't be afraid. It is I. You must eat." The Arab nodded his head and said yes. Calm had returned to his face, but his expression was vacant and listless.

The coffee was ready. They drank it seated together on the cot as they munched their pieces of the cake. Then Daru led the Arab under the shed and showed him the faucet where he washed. He went back into the room, folded the blankets on the cot, made his own bed, and put the room in order. Then he went through the classroom and out onto the terrace. The sun was already rising in the blue sky; a soft, bright light enveloped the deserted plateau. On the ridge the snow was melting in spots. The stones were about to reappear. Crouched on the edge of the plateau, the schoolmaster looked at the deserted expanse. He thought of Balducci. He had hurt him, for he had sent him off as though he didn't want to be associated with him. He could still hear the gendarme's farewell and, without knowing why, he felt strangely empty and vulnerable.

At that moment, from the other side of the schoolhouse, the prisoner coughed. Daru listened to him almost despite himself and then, furious, threw a pebble that whistled through the air before sinking into the snow. That man's stupid crime revolted him, but to hand him over was contrary to honor; just thinking of it made him boil with humiliation. He simultaneously cursed his own people who had sent him this Arab and the Arab who had dared to kill and not managed to get away. Daru got up, walked in a circle on the terrace, waited motionless, and then went back into the schoolhouse.

The Arab, leaning over the cement floor of the shed, was washing his teeth with two fingers. Daru looked at him and said, "Come." He went back into the room ahead of the prisoner. He slipped a hunting jacket on over his sweater and put on walking shoes. Standing, he waited until the Arab had put on his *chèche* and sandals. They went into the classroom, and the schoolmaster pointed to the exit saying, "Go ahead." The fellow didn't budge. "I'm coming," said Daru. The Arab went out. Daru went back into the room and made a package with pieces of rusk, dates, and sugar in it. In the classroom, before going out, he hesitated a second in front of his desk, then crossed the threshold and locked the door. "That's the way," he said. He started toward the east, followed by the prisoner. But a short distance from the schoolhouse he thought he heard a slight sound behind him. He retraced his steps and examined the surroundings of the house; there was no one there. The Arab watched him without seeming to understand. "Come on," said Daru.

They walked for an hour and rested beside a sharp needle of limestone. The snow was melting faster and faster and the sun was drinking up the puddles just as quickly, rapidly cleaning the plateau, which gradually dried and vibrated like the air itself. When they resumed walking, the ground rang under their feet. From time to time a bird rent the space in front of them with a joyful cry. Daru felt a sort of rapture before the vast familiar expanse, now almost entirely yellow under its dome of blue sky. They walked an hour more, descending toward the south. They reached a sort of flattened elevation made up of crumbly rocks. From there on, the plateau sloped down—eastward toward a low plain on which could be made out a few spindly trees, and to the south toward outcroppings of rock that gave the landscape a chaotic look.

Daru surveyed the two directions. Not a man could be seen. He turned toward the Arab, who was looking at him blankly. Daru offered the package to him. "Take it," he said. "There are dates, bread, and sugar. You can hold out for two days. Here are a thousand francs too."

The Arab took the package and the money but kept his full hands at chest level as if he didn't know what to do with what was being given him.

"Now look," the schoolmaster said as he pointed in the direction of the east, "there's the way to Tinguit. You have a two-hour walk. At Tinguit are the adminstration and the police. They are expecting you."

The Arab looked toward the east, still holding the package and the money against his chest. Daru took his elbow and turned him rather roughly toward the south. At the foot of the elevation on which they stood could be seen a faint path. "That's the trail across the plateau. In a day's walk from here you'll find pasturelands and the first nomads. They'll take you in and shelter you according to their law."

The Arab had now turned toward Daru, and a sort of panic was visible in his expression. "Listen," he said.

Daru shook his head. "No, be quiet. Now I'm leaving you." He turned his back on him, took two long steps in the direction of the school, looked hesitantly at the motionless Arab, and started off again. For a few minutes he heard nothing but his own step resounding on the cold ground, and he did not turn his head. A moment later, however, he turned around. The Arab was still there on the edge of the hill, his arms hanging now, and he was looking at the schoolmaster. Daru felt something rise in his throat. But he swore with impatience, waved vaguely, and started off again. He had already gone a distance when he again stopped and looked. There was no longer anyone on the hill.

Daru hesitated. The sun was now rather high in the sky and beginning to beat down on his head. The schoolmaster retraced his steps, at first somewhat uncertainly, then with decision. When he reached the little hill, he was bathed in sweat. He climbed it as fast as he could and stopped, out of breath, on the top. The rock fields to the south stood out sharply against the blue sky, but on the plain to the east a steamy heat was rising. And in that slight haze, Daru, with heavy heart, made out the Arab walking slowly on the road to prison.

A little later, standing before the window of the classroom, the schoolmaster was watching the clear light bathing the whole surface of the plateau. Behind him on the blackboard, among the winding French rivers, sprawled the clumsily chalked up words he had just read: "You handed over our brother. You will pay for this." Daru looked at the sky, the plateau, and beyond, the invisible lands stretching all the way to the sea. In this vast landscape he had loved so much, he was alone.

QUESTIONS

1. What is the central conflict of the story? Is it external or internal? Can it be defined in terms of a dilemma?
2. Compare and contrast the attitudes of Daru and Balducci toward the prisoner and the situation. What is their attitude toward each other? Is either a bad or a cruel man? How does the conflict between Daru and Balducci intensify the central conflict?
3. Why did Daru give the prisoner his freedom? What reasons were there for not giving him his freedom?
4. In what respect is the title ironical? Why does "The Guest" make a better title than "The Prisoner"? And why does the French title, "L'Hôte" (which can mean either "The Guest" or "The Host") make an even better title than its English translation?
5. This story contains the materials of explosive action—a revolver, a murderer, a state of undeclared war, an incipient uprising, a revenge note—but no violence occurs in the story. In what aspect of the situation is Camus principally interested?
6. This story has as its background a specific political situation—the French Algerian crisis in the years following World War II. How does Daru reflect France's plight? Is the story's meaning limited to this situation? What does the story tell us about good and evil and the nature of moral choice? How does the story differ in its treatment of these things from the typical Western story or the patriotic editorial?
7. In what respect is the ending of the story ironical? What kind of irony is this? What does it contribute to the meaning of the story?
8. Besides the ironies of the title and the ending, there are other ironies in the story. Find and explain them. Daru uses verbal irony on page 214 when he exclaims, "Odd pupils!" Is verbal irony the same thing as sarcasm?
9. Comment on the following: (a) Daru's behavior toward firearms and how it helps reveal him; (b) Camus's reason for making the Arab a murderer; (c) the Arab's reason for taking the road to prison.

Flannery O'Connor

GREENLEAF

Mrs. May's bedroom window was low and faced on the east and the bull, silvered in the moonlight, stood under it, his head raised as if he listened— like some patient god come down to woo her—for a stir inside the room. The window was dark and the sound of her breathing too light to be carried outside. Clouds crossing the moon blackened him and in the dark he began to tear at the hedge. Presently they passed and he appeared again in the same spot, chewing steadily, with a hedge-wreath that he had ripped loose for himself caught in the tips of his horns. When the moon drifted into retirement again, there was nothing to mark his place but the sound of steady chewing. Then abruptly a pink glow filled the window. Bars of light slid across him as the venetian blind was slit. He took a step backward and lowered his head as if to show the wreath across his horns.

For almost a minute there was no sound from inside, then as he raised his crowned head again, a woman's voice, guttural as if addressed to a dog, said, "Get away from here, Sir!" and in a second muttered, "Some nigger's scrub bull."

The animal pawed the ground and Mrs. May, standing bent forward behind the blind, closed it quickly lest the light make him charge into the shrubbery. For a second she waited, still bent forward, her nightgown hanging loosely from her narrow shoulders. Green rubber curlers sprouted neatly over her forehead and her face beneath them was smooth as concrete with an egg-white paste that drew the wrinkles out while she slept.

She had been conscious in her sleep of a steady rhythmic chewing as if something were eating one wall of the house. She had been aware that whatever it was had been eating as long as she had the place and had eaten everything from the beginning of her fence line up to the house and now was eating the house and calmly with the same steady rhythm would continue through the house, eating her and the boys, and then on, eating everything but the Greenleafs, on and on, eating everything until nothing was left but the Greenleafs on a little island all their own in the middle of what had been her place. When the munching reached her elbow, she jumped up and found herself, fully awake, standing in the middle of her room. She identified the sound at once: a cow was tearing at the shrubbery under her window. Mr. Greenleaf had left the lane gate open and she didn't doubt that the entire herd

GREENLEAF First published in 1956. Flannery O'Connor (1925–1964), Roman Catholic by birth and belief, was born in Savannah and lived, from 1938 till 1945, in Milledgeville, Georgia. After five years spent writing in Iowa, New York, and Connecticut, she was stricken with an incurable disease (which had already killed her father) and spent several months in an Atlanta hospital. In the summer of 1951, with the disease only partially checked, she and her mother moved to a dairy farm a few miles outside of Milledgeville, which her mother managed, while she continued to write.

was on her lawn. She turned on the dim pink table lamp and then went to the window and slit the blind. The bull, gaunt and long-legged, was standing about four feet from her, chewing calmly like an uncouth country suitor.

For fifteen years, she thought as she squinted at him fiercely, she had been having shiftless people's hogs root up her oats, their mules wallow on her lawn, their scrub bulls breed her cows. If this one was not put up now, he would be over the fence, ruining her herd before morning—and Mr. Greenleaf was soundly sleeping a half mile down the road in the tenant house. There was no way to get him unless she dressed and got in her car and rode down there and woke him up. He would come but his expression, his whole figure, his every pause, would say: "Hit looks to me like one or both of them boys would not make their maw ride out in the middle of the night thisaway. If hit was my boys, they would have got thet bull up theirself."

The bull lowered his head and shook it and the wreath slipped down to the base of his horns where it looked like a menacing prickly crown. She had closed the blind then; in a few seconds she heard him move off heavily.

Mr. Greenleaf would say, "If hit was my boys they would never have allowed their maw to go after the hired help in the middle of the night. They would have did it theirself."

Weighing it, she decided not to bother Mr. Greenleaf. She returned to bed thinking that if the Greenleaf boys had risen in the world it was because she had given their father employment when no one else would have him. She had had Mr. Greenleaf fifteen years but no one else would have had him five minutes. Just the way he approached an object was enough to tell anybody with eyes what kind of a worker he was. He walked with a high-shouldered creep and he never appeared to come directly forward. He walked on the perimeter of some invisible circle and if you wanted to look him in the face, you had to move and get in front of him. She had not fired him because she had always doubted she could do better. He was too shiftless to go out and look for another job; he didn't have the initiative to steal, and after she had told him three or four times to do a thing, he did it; but he never told her about a sick cow until it was too late to call the veterinarian and if her barn had caught fire, he would have called his wife to see the flames before he began to put them out. And of the wife, she didn't even like to think. Beside the wife, Mr. Greenleaf was an aristocrat.

"If it had been my boys," he would have said, "they would have cut off their right arm before they would have allowed their maw to . . ."

"If your boys had any pride, Mr. Greenleaf," she would like to say to him some day, "there are many things that they would not *allow* their mother to do."

The next morning as soon as Mr. Greenleaf came to the back door, she told him there was a stray bull on the place and that she wanted him penned up at once.

"Done already been here three days," he said, addressing his right foot which he held forward, turned slightly as if he were trying to look at the sole. He was standing at the bottom of the three back steps while she leaned out the kitchen door, a small woman with pale near-sighted eyes and grey hair that rose on top like the crest of some disturbed bird.

"Three days!" she said in the restrained screech that had become habitual with her.

Mr. Greenleaf, looking into the distance over the near pasture, removed a package of cigarets from his shirt pocket and let one fall into his hand. He put the package back and stood for a while looking at the cigaret. "I put him in the bull pen but he torn out of there," he said presently. "I didn't see him none after that." He bent over the cigaret and lit it and then turned his head briefly in her direction. The upper part of his face sloped gradually into the lower which was long and narrow, shaped like a rough chalice. He had deep-set fox-colored eyes shadowed under a grey felt hat that he wore slanted forward following the line of his nose. His build was insignificant.

"Mr. Greenleaf," she said, "get the bull up this morning before you do anything else. You know he'll ruin the breeding schedule. Get him up and keep him up and the next time there's a stray bull on this place, tell me at once. Do you understand?"

"Where do you want him put at?" Mr. Greenleaf asked.

"I don't care where you put him," she said. "You are supposed to have some sense. Put him where he can't get out. Whose bull is he?"

For a moment Mr. Greenleaf seemed to hesitate between silence and speech. He studied the air to the left of him. "He must be somebody's bull," he said after a while.

"Yes, he must!" she said and shut the door with a precise little slam.

She went into the dining room where the two boys were eating breakfast and sat down on the edge of her chair at the head of the table. She never ate breakfast but she sat with them to see that they had what they wanted. "Honestly!" she said, and began to tell about the bull, aping Mr. Greenleaf saying, "It must be *somebody's* bull."

Wesley continued to read the newspaper folded beside his plate but Scofield interrupted his eating from time to time to look at her and laugh. The two boys never had the same reaction to anything. They were as different, she said, as night and day. The only thing they did have in common was neither of them cared what happened on the place. Scofield was a business type and Wesley was an intellectual.

Wesley, the younger child, had had rheumatic fever when he was seven and Mrs. May thought that this was what had caused him to be an intellectual. Scofield, who had never had a day's sickness in his life, was an insurance salesman. She would not have minded his selling insurance if he had sold a nicer kind but he sold the kind that only Negroes buy. He was what Negroes call a "policy man." He said there was more money in nigger-insurance than any other kind, and before company, he was very loud about it. He would shout, "Mama don't like to hear me say it but I'm the best nigger-insurance salesman in this county!"

Scofield was thirty-six and he had a broad pleasant smiling face but he was not married. "Yes," Mrs. May would say, "and if you sold decent insurance, some *nice* girl would be willing to marry you. What nice girl wants to marry a nigger-insurance man? You'll wake up some day and it'll be too late."

And at this Scofield would yodel and say, "Why Mamma, I'm not going to marry until you're dead and gone and then I'm going to marry me some nice fat girl that can take over this place!" And once he had added, "—some nice lady like Mrs. Greenleaf." When he had said this, Mrs. May had risen from her chair, her back stiff as a rake handle, and had gone to her room. There she had sat down on the edge of her bed for some time with her small face drawn. Finally she had whispered, "I work and slave, I struggle and sweat to keep this place for them and as soon as I'm dead, they'll marry trash and bring it in here and ruin everything. They'll marry trash and ruin everything I've done," and she had made up her mind at that moment to change her will. The next day she had gone to her lawyer and had had the property entailed so that if they married, they could not leave it to their wives.

The idea that one of them might marry a woman even remotely like Mrs. Greenleaf was enough to make her ill. She had put up with Mr. Greenleaf for fifteen years, but the only way she had endured his wife had been by keeping entirely out of her sight. Mrs. Greenleaf was large and loose. The yard around her house looked like a dump and her five girls were always filthy; even the youngest one dipped snuff. Instead of making a garden or washing their clothes, her preoccupation was what she called "prayer healing."

Every day she cut all the morbid stories out of the newspaper—the accounts of women who had been raped and criminals who had escaped and children who had been burned and of train wrecks and plane crashes and the divorces of movie stars. She took these to the woods and dug a hole and buried them and then she fell on the ground over them and mumbled and groaned for an hour or so, moving her huge arms back and forth under her and out again and finally just lying down flat and, Mrs. May suspected, going to sleep in the dirt.

She had not found out about this until the Greenleafs had been with her a few months. One morning she had been out to inspect a field that she wanted planted in rye but that had come up in clover because Mr. Greenleaf had used the wrong seeds in the grain drill. She was returning through a wooded path that separated two pastures, muttering to herself and hitting the ground methodically with a long stick she carried in case she saw a snake. "Mr. Greenleaf," she was saying in a low voice, "I cannot afford to pay for your mistakes. I am a poor woman and this place is all I have. I have two boys to educate. I cannot . . ."

Out of nowhere a guttural agonized voice groaned, "Jesus! Jesus!" In a second it came again with a terrible urgency. "Jesus! Jesus!"

Mrs. May stopped still, one hand lifted to her throat. The sound was so piercing that she felt as if some violent unleashed force had broken out of the ground and was charging toward her. Her second thought was more reasonable: somebody had been hurt on the place and would sue her for everything she had. She had no insurance. She rushed forward and turning a bend in the path, she saw Mrs. Greenleaf sprawled on her hands and knees off the side of the road, her head down.

"Mrs. Greenleaf!" she shrilled, "what's happened!"

Mrs. Greenleaf raised her head. Her face was a patchwork of dirt and tears and her small eyes, the color of two field peas, were red-rimmed and swollen, but her expression was as composed as a bulldog's. She swayed back and forth on her hands and knees and groaned, "Jesus, Jesus."

Mrs. May winced. She thought the word, Jesus, should be kept inside the church building like other words inside the bedroom. She was a good Christian woman with a large respect for religion, though she did not, of course, believe any of it was true. "What is the matter with you?" she asked sharply.

"You broke my healing," Mrs. Greenleaf said, waving her aside. "I can't talk to you until I finish."

Mrs. May stood, bent forward, her mouth open and her stick raised off the ground as if she were not sure what she wanted to strike with it.

"Oh Jesus, stab me in the heart!" Mrs. Greenleaf shrieked. "Jesus, stab me in the heart!" and she fell back flat in the dirt, a huge human mound, her legs and arms spread out as if she were trying to wrap them around the earth.

Mrs. May felt as furious and helpless as if she had been insulted by a child. "Jesus," she said, drawing herself back, "would be *ashamed* of you. He would tell you to get up from there this instant and go wash your children's clothes!" and she had turned and walked off as fast as she could.

Whenever she thought of how the Greenleaf boys had advanced in the world, she had only to think of Mrs. Greenleaf sprawled obscenely on the ground, and say to herself, "Well, no matter how far they go, they *came* from that."

She would like to have been able to put in her will that when she died, Wesley and Scofield were not to continue to employ Mr. Greenleaf. She was capable of handling Mr. Greenleaf; they were not. Mr. Greenleaf had pointed out to her once that her boys didn't know hay from silage. She had pointed out to him that they had other talents, that Scofield was a successful businessman and Wesley a successful intellectual. Mr. Greenleaf did not comment, but he never lost an opportunity of letting her see, by his expression or some simple gesture, that he held the two of them in infinite contempt. As scrubhuman as the Greenleafs were, he never hesitated to let her know that in any like circumstance in which his own boys might have been involved, they—O. T. and E. T. Greenleaf—would have acted to better advantage.

The Greenleaf boys were two or three years younger than the May boys. They were twins and you never knew when you spoke to one of them whether you were speaking to O. T. or E. T., and they never had the politeness to enlighten you. They were long-legged and raw-boned and red-skinned, with bright grasping fox-colored eyes like their father's. Mr. Greenleaf's pride in them began with the fact that they were twins. He acted, Mrs. May said, as if this were something smart they had thought of themselves. They were energetic and hard-working and she would admit to anyone that they had come a long way—and that the Second World War was responsible for it.

They had both joined the service and, disguised in their uniforms, they could not be told from other people's children. You could tell, of course, when they opened their mouths but they did that seldom. The smartest thing they had done was to get sent overseas and there to marry French wives. They hadn't married French trash either. They had married nice girls who naturally couldn't tell that they murdered the king's English or that the Greenleafs were who they were.

Wesley's heart condition had not permitted him to serve his country but Scofield had been in the army for two years. He had not cared for it and at the end of his military service, he was only a Private First Class. The Greenleaf boys were both some kind of sergeants, and Mr. Greenleaf, in those days, had never lost an opportunity of referring to them by their rank. They had both managed to get wounded and now they both had pensions. Further, as soon as they were released from the army, they took advantage of all the benefits and went to the school of agriculture at the university—the taxpayers meanwhile supporting their French wives. The two of them were living now about two miles down the highway on a piece of land that the government had helped them to buy and in a brick duplex bungalow that the government had helped to build and pay for. If the war had made anyone, Mrs. May said, it had made the Greenleaf boys. They each had three little children apiece, who spoke Greenleaf English and French, and who, on account of their mothers' background, would be sent to the convent school and brought up with manners. "And in twenty years," Mrs. May asked Scofield and Wesley, "do you know what those people will be?

"*Society,*" she said blackly.

She had spent fifteen years coping with Mr. Greenleaf and, by now, handling him had become second nature with her. His disposition on any particular day was as much a factor in what she could and couldn't do as the weather was, and she had learned to read his face the way real country people read the sunrise and sunset.

She was a country woman only by persuasion. The late Mr. May, a business man, had bought the place when land was down, and when he died it was all he had to leave her. The boys had not been happy to move to the country to a broken-down farm, but there was nothing else for her to do. She had the timber on the place cut and with the proceeds had set herself up in the dairy business after Mr. Greenleaf had answered her ad. "i seen yor add and i will come have 2 boys," was all his letter said, but he arrived the next day in a pieced-together truck, his wife and five daughters sitting on the floor in the back, himself and the two boys in the cab.

Over the years they had been on her place, Mr. and Mrs. Greenleaf had aged hardly at all. They had no worries, no responsibilities. They lived like the lilies of the field, off the fat that she struggled to put into the land. When she was dead and gone from overwork and worry, the Greenleafs, healthy and thriving, would be just ready to begin draining Scofield and Wesley.

Wesley said the reason Mrs. Greenleaf had not aged was because she released all her emotions in prayer healing. "You ought to start praying, Sweetheart," he had said in the voice that, poor boy, he could not help making deliberately nasty.

Scofield only exasperated her beyond endurance but Wesley caused her real anxiety. He was thin and nervous and bald and being an intellectual was a terrible strain on his disposition. She doubted if he would marry until she died but she was certain that then the wrong woman would get him. Nice girls didn't like Scofield but Wesley didn't like nice girls. He didn't like anything. He drove twenty miles every day to the university where he taught and twenty miles back every night, but he said he hated the twenty-mile drive and he hated the second-rate university and he hated the morons who attended it. He hated the country and he hated the life he lived; he hated living with his mother and his idiot brother and he hated hearing about the damn dairy and the damn help and the damn broken machinery. But in spite of all he said, he never made any move to leave. He talked about Paris and Rome but he never went even to Atlanta.

"You'd go to those places and you'd get sick," Mrs. May would say. "Who in Paris is going to see that you get a salt-free diet? And do you think if you married one of those odd numbers you take out that *she* would cook a salt-free diet for you? No indeed, she would not!" When she took this line, Wesley would turn himself roughly around in his chair and ignore her. Once when she had kept it up too long, he had snarled, "Well, why don't you do something practical, Woman? Why don't you pray for me like Mrs. Greenleaf would?"

"I don't like to hear you boys make jokes about religion," she had said. "If you would go to church, you would meet some nice girls."

But it was impossible to tell them anything. When she looked at the two of them now, sitting on either side of the table, neither one caring the least if a stray bull ruined her herd—which was their herd, their future—when she looked at the two of them, one hunched over a paper and the other teetering back in his chair, grinning at her like an idiot, she wanted to jump up and beat her fist on the table and shout, "You'll find out one of these days, you'll find out what *Reality* is when it's too late!"

"Mamma," Scofield said, "don't you get excited now but I'll tell you whose bull that is." He was looking at her wickedly. He let his chair drop forward and he got up. Then with his shoulders bent and his hands held up to cover his head, he tiptoed to the door. He backed into the hall and pulled the door almost to so that it hid all of him but his face. "You want to know, Sugar-pie?" he asked.

Mrs. May sat looking at him coldly.

"That's O. T. and E. T.'s bull," he said. "I collected from their nigger yesterday and he told me they were missing it," and he showed her an exaggerated expanse of teeth and disappeared silently.

Wesley looked up and laughed.

Mrs. May turned her head forward again, her expression unaltered. "I am the only *adult* on this place," she said. She leaned across the table and pulled the paper from the side of his plate. "Do you see how it's going to be when I die and you boys have to handle him?" she began. "Do you see why he didn't know whose bull that was? Because it was theirs. Do you see what I have to put up with? Do you see that if I hadn't kept my foot on his neck all these years, you boys might be milking cows every morning at four o'clock?"

Wesley pulled the paper back toward his plate and staring at her full in the face, he murmured, "I wouldn't milk a cow to save your soul from hell."

"I know you wouldn't," she said in a brittle voice. She sat back and began rapidly turning her knife over at the side of her plate. "O. T. and E. T. are fine boys," she said. "They ought to have been my sons." The thought of this was so horrible that her vision of Wesley was blurred at once by a wall of tears. All she saw was his dark shape, rising quickly from the table. "And you two," she cried, "you two should have belonged to that woman!"

He was heading for the door.

"When I die," she said in a thin voice, "I don't know what's going to become of you."

"You're always yapping about when-you-die," he growled as he rushed out, "but you look pretty healthy to me."

For some time she sat where she was, looking straight ahead through the window across the room into a scene of indistinct greys and greens. She stretched her face and her neck muscles and drew in a long breath but the scene in front of her flowed together anyway into a watery grey mass. "They needn't think I'm going to die any time soon," she muttered, and some more defiant voice in her added: I'll die when I get good and ready.

She wiped her eyes with the table napkin and got up and went to the window and gazed at the scene in front of her. The cows were grazing on two pale green pastures across the road and behind them, fencing them in, was a black wall of trees with a sharp sawtooth edge that held off the indifferent sky. The pastures were enough to calm her. When she looked out any window in her house, she saw the reflection of her own character. Her city friends said she was the most remarkable woman they knew, to go, practically penniless and with no experience, out to a rundown farm and make a success of it. "Everything is against you," she would say, "the weather is against you and the dirt is against you and the help is against you. They're all in league against you. There's nothing for it but an iron hand!"

"Look at Mamma's iron hand!" Scofield would yell and grab her arm and hold it up so that her delicate blue-veined little hand would dangle from her wrist like the head of a broken lily. The company always laughed.

The sun, moving over the black and white grazing cows, was just a little brighter than the rest of the sky. Looking down, she saw a darker shape that might have been its shadow cast at an angle, moving among them. She uttered a sharp cry and turned and marched out of the house.

Mr. Greenleaf was in the trench silo, filling a wheelbarrow. She stood on the edge and looked down at him. "I told you to get up that bull. Now he's in with the milk herd."

"You can't do two thangs at oncet," Mr. Greenleaf remarked.

"I told you to do that first."

He wheeled the barrow out of the open end of the trench toward the barn and she followed close behind him. "And you needn't think, Mr. Greenleaf," she said, "that I don't know exactly whose bull that is or why you haven't been in any hurry to notify me he was here. I might as well feed O. T. and E. T.'s bull as long as I'm going to have him here ruining my herd."

Mr. Greenleaf paused with the wheelbarrow and looked behind him. "Is that them boys' bull?" he asked in an incredulous tone.

She did not say a word. She merely looked away with her mouth taut.

"They told me their bull was out but I never known that was him," he said.

"I want that bull put up now," she said, "and I'm going to drive over to O. T. and E. T.'s and tell them they'll have to come get him today. I ought to charge for the time he's been here—then it wouldn't happen again."

"They didn't pay but seventy-five dollars for him," Mr. Greenleaf offered.

"I wouldn't have had him as a gift," she said.

"They was just going to beef him," Mr. Greenleaf went on, "but he got loose and run his head into their pickup truck. He don't like cars and trucks. They had a time getting his horn out the fender and when they finally got him loose, he took off and they was too tired to run after him—but I never known that was him there."

"It wouldn't have paid you to know, Mr. Greenleaf," she said. "But you know now. Get a horse and get him."

In a half hour, from her front window she saw the bull, squirrel-colored, with jutting hips and long light horns, ambling down the dirt road that ran in front of the house. Mr. Greenleaf was behind him on the horse. "That's a Greenleaf bull if I ever saw one," she muttered. She went out on the porch and called, "Put him where he can't get out."

"He likes to bust loose," Mr. Greenleaf said, looking with approval at the bull's rump. "This gentleman is a sport."

"If those boys don't come for him, he's going to be a dead sport," she said. "I'm just warning you."

He heard her but he didn't answer.

"That's the awfullest looking bull I ever saw," she called but he was too far down the road to hear.

It was mid-morning when she turned into O. T. and E. T.'s driveway. The house, a new red-brick, low-to-the-ground building that looked like a warehouse with windows, was on top of a treeless hill. The sun was beating down directly on the white roof of it. It was the kind of house that everybody built now and nothing marked it as belonging to Greenleafs except three dogs, part hound and part spitz, that rushed out from behind it as soon as she stopped her car. She reminded herself that you could always tell the class of people by the class of dog, and honked her horn. While she sat waiting for someone to come, she continued to study the house. All the windows were down and she wondered if the government could have air-conditioned the thing. No one came and she honked again. Presently a door opened and several children appeared in it and stood looking at her, making no move to come forward. She recognized this as a true Greenleaf trait—they could hang in a door, looking at you for hours.

"Can't one of you children come here?" she called.

After a minute they all began to move forward, slowly. They had on overalls and were barefooted but they were not as dirty as she might have expected. There were two or three that looked distinctly like Greenleafs; the others not so much so. The smallest child was a girl with untidy black hair. They stopped about six feet from the automobile and stood looking at her.

"You're mighty pretty," Mrs. May said, addressing herself to the smallest girl.

There was no answer. They appeared to share one dispassionate expression between them.

"Where's your Mamma?" she asked.

There was no answer to this for some time. Then one of them said something in French. Mrs. May did not speak French.

"Where's your daddy?" she asked.

After a while, one of the boys said, "He ain't hyar neither."

"Ahhhh," Mrs. May said as if something had been proven. "Where's the colored man?"

She waited and decided no one was going to answer. "The cat has six little tongues," she said. "How would you like to come home with me and let me teach you how to talk?" She laughed and her laugh died on the silent air. She felt as if she were on trial for her life, facing a jury of Greenleafs, "I'll go down and see if I can find the colored man," she said.

"You can go if you want to," one of the boys said.

"Well, thank you," she murmured and drove off.

The barn was down the lane from the house. She had not seen it before but Mr. Greenleaf had described it in detail for it had been built according to the latest specifications. It was a milking parlor arrangement where the cows are milked from below. The milk ran in pipes from the machines to the milk house and was never carried in no bucket, Mr. Greenleaf said, by no human hand. "When you gonter get you one?" he had asked.

"Mr. Greenleaf," she had said, "I have to do for myself. I am not assisted hand and foot by the government. It would cost me $20,000 to install a milking parlor. I barely make ends meet as it is."

"My boys done it," Mr. Greenleaf had murmured and then—"but all boys ain't alike."

"No indeed!" she had said. "I thank God for that!"

"I thank Gawd for ever-thang," Mr. Greenleaf had drawled.

You might as well, she had thought in the fierce silence that followed; you've never done anything for yourself.

She stopped by the side of the barn and honked but no one appeared. For several minutes she sat in the car, observing the various machines parked around, wondering how many of them were paid for. They had a forage harvester and a rotary hay baler. She had those too. She decided that since no one was here, she would get out and have a look at the milking parlor and see if they kept it clean.

She opened the milking room door and stuck her head in and for the first second she felt as if she were going to lose her breath. The spotless white concrete room was filled with sunlight that came from a row of windows head-high along both walls. The metal stanchions gleamed ferociously and she had to squint to be able to look at all. She drew her head out the room quickly and closed the door and leaned against it, frowning. The light outside was not so bright but she was conscious that the sun was directly on top of her head, like a silver bullet ready to drop into her brain.

A Negro carrying a yellow calf-feed bucket appeared from around the corner of the machine shed and came toward her. He was a light yellow boy dressed in the cast-off army clothes of the Greenleaf twins. He stopped at a respectable distance and set the bucket on the ground.

"Where's Mr. O. T. and Mr. E. T.?" she asked.

"Mist O. T. he in town, Mist E. T. he off yonder in the field," the Negro said, pointing first to the left and then to the right as if he were naming the position of two planets.

"Can you remember a message?" she asked, looking as if she thought this doubtful.

"I'll remember it if I don't forget it," he said with a touch of sullenness.

"Well, I'll write it down then," she said. She got in her car and took a stub of pencil from her pocket book and began to write on the back of an empty envelope. The Negro came and stood at the window. "I'm Mrs. May," she said as she wrote. "Their bull is on my place and I want him off *today*. You can tell them I'm furious about it."

"That bull lef here Sareday," the Negro said, "and none of us ain't seen him since. We ain't knowed where he was."

"Well, you know now," she said, "and you can tell Mr. O. T. and Mr. E. T. that if they don't come get him today, I'm going to have their daddy shoot him the first thing in the morning. I can't have that bull ruining my herd." She handed him the note.

"If I knows Mist O. T. and Mist E. T.," he said, taking it, "they goin to say you go ahead on and shoot him. He done busted up one of our trucks already and we be glad to see the last of him."

She pulled her head back and gave him a look from slightly bleared eyes. "Do they expect me to take my time and my worker to shoot their bull?" she asked. "They don't want him so they just let him loose and expect somebody else to kill him? He's eating my oats and ruining my herd and I'm expected to shoot him too?"

"I speck you is," he said softly. "He done busted up . . ."

She gave him a very sharp look and said, "Well, I'm not surprised. That's just the way some people are," and after a second she asked, "Which is boss, Mr. O. T. or Mr. E. T.?" She had always suspected that they fought between themselves secretly.

"They never quarls," the boy said. "They like one man in two skins."

"Hmp. I expect you just never heard them quarrel."

"Nor nobody else heard them neither," he said, looking away as if this insolence were addressed to someone else.

"Well," she said, "I haven't put up with their father for fifteen years not to know a few things about Greenleafs."

The Negro looked at her suddenly with a gleam of recognition. "Is you my policy man's mother?" he asked.

"I don't know who your policy man is," she said sharply. "You give them that note and tell them if they don't come for that bull today, they'll be making their father shoot it tomorrow," and she drove off.

She stayed at home all afternoon waiting for the Greenleaf twins to come for the bull. They did not come. I might as well be working for them, she thought furiously. They are simply going to use me to the limit. At the supper table, she went over it again for the boys' benefit because she wanted them to see exactly what O. T. and E. T. would do. "They don't want that bull," she said, "—pass the butter—so they simply turn him loose and let somebody else worry about getting rid of him for them. How do you like that? I'm the victim. I've always been the victim."

"Pass the butter to the victim," Wesley said. He was in a worse humor than usual because he had had a flat tire on the way home from the university.

Scofield handed her the butter and said, "Why, Mamma, ain't you ashamed to shoot an old bull that ain't done nothing but give you a little scrub strain in your herd? I declare," he said, "with the Mamma I got it's a wonder I turned out to be such a nice boy!"

"You ain't her boy, Son," Wesley said.

She eased back in her chair, her fingertips on the edge of the table.

"All I know is," Scofield said, "I done mighty well to be as nice as I am seeing what I come from."

When they teased her they spoke Greenleaf English but Wesley made his own particular tone come through it like a knife edge. "Well lemme tell you one thang, Brother," he said, leaning over the table, "that if you had half a mind you would already know."

"What's that, Brother?" Scofield asked, his broad face grinning into the thin constricted one across from him.

"That is," Wesley said, "that neither you nor me is her boy . . . ," but he stopped abruptly as she gave a kind of hoarse wheeze like an old horse lashed unexpectedly. She reared up and ran from the room.

"Oh, for God's sake," Wesley growled, "what did you start her off for?"

"I never started her off," Scofield said. "You started her off."

"Hah."

"She's not as young as she used to be and she can't take it."

"She can only give it out," Wesley said. "I'm the one that takes it." His brother's pleasant face had changed so that an ugly family resemblance showed between them. "Nobody feels sorry for a lousy bastard like you," he said and grabbed across the table for the other's shirtfront.

From her room she heard a crash of dishes and she rushed back through the kitchen into the dining room. The hall door was open and Scofield was going out of it. Wesley was lying like a large bug on his back with the edge of the over-turned table cutting him across the middle and broken dishes scattered on top of him. She pulled the table off him and caught his arm to help him rise but he scrambled up and pushed her off with a furious charge of energy and flung himself out the door after his brother.

She would have collapsed but a knock on the back door stiffened her and she swung around. Across the kitchen and back porch, she could see Mr. Greenleaf peering eagerly through the screenwire. All her resources returned in full strength as if she had only needed to be challenged by the devil himself to regain them. "I heard a thump," he called, "and I thought the plastering might have fell on you."

If he had been wanted someone would have had to go on a horse to find him. She crossed the kitchen and the porch and stood inside the screen and said, "No, nothing happened but the table turned over. One of the legs was weak," and without pausing, "the boys didn't come for the bull so tomorrow you'll have to shoot him."

The sky was crossed with thin red and purple bars and behind them the sun was moving down slowly as if it were descending a ladder. Mr. Greenleaf squatted down on the step, his back to her, the top of his hat on a level with her feet. "Tomorrow I'll drive him home for you," he said.

"Oh no, Mr. Greenleaf," she said in a mocking voice, "you drive him home tomorrow and next week he'll be back here. I know better than that." Then in a mournful tone, she said, "I'm surprised at O. T. and E. T. to treat me this way. I thought they'd have more gratitude. Those boys spent some mighty happy days on this place, didn't they, Mr. Greenleaf?"

Mr. Greenleaf didn't say anything.

"I think they did," she said. "I think they did. But they've forgotten all the nice little things I did for them now. If I recall, they wore my boys' old clothes and played with my boys' old toys and hunted with my boys' old guns. They swam in my pond and shot my birds and fished in my stream and I never forgot their birthday and Christmas seemed to roll around very often if

I remember it right. And do they think of any of those things now?" she asked. "NOOOOO," she said.

For a few seconds she looked at the disappearing sun and Mr. Greenleaf examined the palms of his hands. Presently as if it had just occurred to her, she asked, "Do you know the real reason they didn't come for that bull?"

"Naw I don't," Mr. Greenleaf said in a surly voice.

"They didn't come because I'm a woman," she said. "You can get away with anything when you're dealing with a woman. If there were a man running this place . . . "

Quick as a snake striking Mr. Greenleaf said, "You got two boys. They know you got two men on the place."

The sun had disappeared behind the tree line. She looked down at the dark crafty face, upturned now, and at the wary eyes, bright under the shadow of the hatbrim. She waited long enough for him to see that she was hurt and then she said, "Some people learn gratitude too late, Mr. Greenleaf, and some never learn it at all," and she turned and left him sitting on the steps.

Half the night in her sleep she heard a sound as if some large stone were grinding a hole on the outside wall of her brain. She was walking on the inside, over a succession of beautiful rolling hills, planting her stick in front of each step. She became aware after a time that the noise was the sun trying to burn through the tree line and she stopped to watch, safe in the knowledge that it couldn't, that it had to sink the way it always did outside of her property. When she first stopped it was a swollen red ball, but as she stood watching it began to narrow and pale until it looked like a bullet. Then suddenly it burst through the tree line and raced down the hill toward her. She woke up with her hand over her mouth and the same noise, diminished but distinct, in her ear. It was the bull munching under her window. Mr. Greenleaf had let him out.

She got up and made her way to the window in the dark and looked out through the slit blind, but the bull had moved away from the hedge and at first she didn't see him. Then she saw a heavy form some distance away, paused as if observing her. This is the last night I am going to put up with this, she said, and watched until the iron shadow moved away in the darkness.

The next morning she waited until exactly eleven o'clock. Then she got in her car and drove to the barn. Mr. Greenleaf was cleaning milk cans. He had seven of them standing up outside the milk room to get the sun. She had been telling him to do this for two weeks. "All right, Mr. Greenleaf," she said, "go get your gun. We're going to shoot that bull."

"I thought you wanted theseyer cans . . ."

"Go get your gun, Mr. Greenleaf," she said. Her voice and face were expressionless.

"That gentleman torn out of there last night," he murmured in a tone of regret and bent again to the can he had his arm in.

"Go get your gun, Mr. Greenleaf," she said in the same triumphant toneless voice. "The bull is in the pasture with the dry cows. I saw him from my upstairs window. I'm going to drive you up to the field and you can run him into the empty pasture and shoot him there."

He detached himself from the can slowly. "Ain't nobody ever ast me to shoot my boys' own bull!" he said in a high rasping voice. He removed a rag from his back pocket and began to wipe his hands violently, then his nose.

She turned as if she had not heard this and said, "I'll wait for you in the car. Go get your gun."

She sat in the car and watched him stalk off toward the harness room where he kept a gun. After he had entered the room, there was a crash as if he had kicked something out of his way. Presently he emerged again with the gun, circled behind the car, opened the door violently and threw himself onto the seat beside her. He held the gun between his knees and looked straight ahead. He'd like to shoot me instead of the bull, she thought, and turned her face away so that he could not see her smile.

The morning was dry and clear. She drove through the woods for a quarter of a mile and then out into the open where there were fields on either side of the narrow road. The exhilaration of carrying her point had sharpened her senses. Birds were screaming everywhere, the grass was almost too bright to look at, the sky was an even piercing blue. "Spring is here!" she said gaily. Mr. Greenleaf lifted one muscle somewhere near his mouth as if he found this the most asinine remark ever made. When she stopped at the second pasture gate, he flung himself out of the car door and slammed it behind him. Then he opened the gate and she drove through. He closed it and flung himself back in, silently, and she drove around the rim of the pasture until she spotted the bull, almost in the center of it, grazing peacefully among the cows.

"The gentleman is waiting on you," she said and gave Mr. Greenleaf's furious profile a sly look. "Run him into that next pasture and when you get him in, I'll drive in behind you and shut the gate myself."

He flung himself out again, this time deliberately leaving the car door open so that she had to lean across the seat and close it. She sat smiling as she watched him make his way across the pasture toward the opposite gate. He seemed to throw himself forward at each step and then pull back as if he were calling on some power to witness that he was being forced. "Well," she said aloud as if he were still in the car, "it's your own boys who are making you do this, Mr. Greenleaf." O. T. and E. T. were probably splitting their sides laughing at him now. She could hear their identical nasal voices saying, "Made Daddy shoot our bull for us. Daddy don't know no better than to think that's a fine bull he's shooting. Gonna kill Daddy to shoot that bull!"

"If those boys cared a thing about you, Mr. Greenleaf," she said, "they would have come for that bull. I'm surprised at them."

He was circling around to open the gate first. The bull, dark among the spotted cows, had not moved. He kept his head down, eating constantly. Mr.

Greenleaf opened the gate and then began circling back to approach him from the rear. When he was about ten feet behind him, he flapped his arms at his sides. The bull lifted his head indolently and then lowered it again and continued to eat. Mr. Greenleaf stooped again and picked up something and threw it at him with a vicious swing. She decided it was a sharp rock for the bull leapt and then began to gallop until he disappeared over the rim of the hill. Mr. Greenleaf followed at his leisure.

"You needn't think you're going to lose him!" she cried and started the car straight across the pasture. She had to drive slowly over the terraces and when she reached the gate, Mr. Greenleaf and the bull were nowhere in sight. This pasture was smaller than the last, a green arena, encircled almost entirely by woods. She got out and closed the gate and stood looking for some sign of Mr. Greenleaf but he had disappeared completely. She knew at once that his plan was to lose the bull in the woods. Eventually, she would see him emerge somewhere from the circle of trees and come limping toward her and when he finally reached her, he would say, "If you can find that gentleman in them woods, you're better than me."

She was going to say, "Mr. Greenleaf, if I have to walk into those woods with you and stay all afternoon, we are going to find that bull and shoot him. You are going to shoot him if I have to pull the trigger for you." When he saw she meant business, he would return and shoot the bull quickly himself.

She got back into the car and drove to the center of the pasture where he would not have so far to walk to reach her when he came out of the woods. At this moment she could picture him sitting on a stump, marking lines in the ground with a stick. She decided she would wait exactly ten minutes by her watch. Then she would begin to honk. She got out of the car and walked around a little and then sat down on the front bumper to wait and rest. She was very tired and she lay her head back against the hood and closed her eyes. She did not understand why she should be so tired when it was only mid-morning. Through her closed eyes, she could feel the sun, red-hot overhead. She opened her eyes slightly but the white light forced her to close them again.

For some time she lay back against the hood, wondering drowsily why she was so tired. With her eyes closed, she didn't think of time as divided into days and nights but into past and future. She decided she was tired because she had been working continuously for fifteen years. She decided she had every right to be tired, and to rest for a few minutes before she began working again. Before any kind of judgment seat, she would be able to say: I've worked, I have not wallowed. At this very instant while she was recalling a lifetime of work, Mr. Greenleaf was loitering in the woods and Mrs. Greenleaf was probably flat on the ground, asleep over her holeful of clippings. The woman had got worse over the years and Mrs. May believed that now she was actually demented. "I'm afraid your wife has let religion warp her," she said once tactfully to Mr. Greenleaf. "Everything in moderation, you know."

"She cured a man oncet that half his gut was eat out with worms," Mr. Greenleaf said, and she had turned away, half-sickened. Poor souls, she thought now, so simple. For a few seconds she dozed.

When she sat up and looked at her watch, more than ten minutes had passed. She had not heard any shot. A new thought occurred to her; suppose Mr. Greenleaf had aroused the bull chunking stones at him and the animal had turned on him and run him up against a tree and gored him? The irony of it deepened: O. T. and E. T. would then get a shyster lawyer and sue her. It would be the fitting end to her fifteen years with the Greenleafs. She thought of it almost with pleasure as if she had hit on the perfect ending for a story she was telling her friends. Then she dropped it, for Mr. Greenleaf had a gun with him and she had insurance.

She decided to honk. She got up and reached inside the car window and gave three sustained honks and two or three shorter ones to let him know she was getting impatient. Then she went back and sat down on the bumper again.

In a few minutes something emerged from the tree line, a black heavy shadow that tossed its head several times and then bounded forward. After a second she saw it was the bull. He was crossing the pasture toward her at a slow gallop, a gay almost rocking gait as if he were overjoyed to find her again. She looked beyond him to see if Mr. Greenleaf was coming out of the woods too but he was not. "Here he is, Mr. Greenleaf!" she called and looked on the other side of the pasture to see if he could be coming out there but he was not in sight. She looked back and saw that the bull, his head lowered, was racing toward her. She remained perfectly still, not in fright, but in a freezing disbelief. She stared at the violent black streak bounding toward her as if she had no sense of distance, as if she could not decide at once what his intention was, and the bull had buried his head in her lap, like a wild tormented lover, before her expression changed. One of his horns sank until it pierced her heart and the other curved around her side and held her in an unbreakable grip. She continued to stare straight ahead but the entire scene in front of her had changed—the tree line was a dark wound in a world that was nothing but sky—and she had the look of a person whose sight has been suddenly restored but who finds the light unbearable.

Mr. Greenleaf was running toward her from the side with his gun raised and she saw him coming though she was not looking in his direction. She saw him approaching on the outside of some invisible circle, the tree line gaping behind him and nothing under his feet. He shot the bull four times through the eye. She did not hear the shots but she felt the quake in the huge body as it sank, pulling her forward on its head, so that she seemed, when Mr. Greenleaf reached her, to be bent over whispering some last discovery into the animal's ear.

QUESTIONS

1. The characters and events of the story are all seen as reflected through Mrs. May's mind. How objective are her evaluations? How far are they reliable testimony and how far only an index of her own mind?

2. What is Mrs. May's mental image of herself? How does it compare with the image her sons have of her? How does it compare with the reader's image?

3. What is Mrs. May's dominant emotion? What is the consuming preoccupation of her mind? Are there any occasions on which she feels joy? What are they?

4. Describe the behavior of Mrs. May and Greenleaf toward each other. Why does Mrs. May keep Greenleaf on when she despises him so?

5. The two families—the Mays and the Greenleafs—are obviously contrasted. Describe this contrast as fully as possible, considering especially the following: (a) their social and economic status, past, present, and future, (b) their religious attitudes, (c) the attitudes of Mrs. May and Greenleaf respectively toward their children, (d) Wesley and Scofield versus O. T. and E. T. What are the reasons for Mrs. May's feelings toward the Greenleafs?

6. The turning point of the story comes when Mrs. May commands Greenleaf to get his gun. What emotional reversal takes place at this point? What are Mrs. May's motivations in having the bull shot?

7. "Suppose [thinks Mrs. May on page 238] Mr. Greenleaf had aroused the bull chunking stones at him and the animal had turned on him and run him up against a tree and gored him? . . . She thought of it almost with pleasure as if she had hit on the perfect ending for the story she was telling her friends." From what points of view is the actual ending of the story a perfect ending? Is the ending of the story purely chance, or is there a sense in which Mrs. May has brought this on herself?

8. What symbolical implications, if any, have the following: (a) the name Greenleaf, (b) the bull, (c) the sun, (d) Mrs. May's two dreams (pages 222 and 235)? How important is symbolism to the final effect of the story?

9. What kinds of irony predominate in the story? Identify examples of each of the three kinds of irony. How important is irony to the final effect of the story?

7. Emotion and Humor

Interpretive fiction presents the reader with significant and therefore durable insights into life. But these insights represent something more than mere intellectual comprehension; otherwise, the story does nothing that cannot be done as well or better by psychology, history, or philosophy. Fiction derives its unique value from its power to give *felt* insights. Its truths take a deeper hold on our minds because they are conveyed through our feelings. Its effectiveness in awakening a sensuous and emotional apprehension of experience that enriches understanding is what distinguishes imaginative literature from other forms of discourse.

All successful stories arouse emotions in the reader. The adventure thriller causes fear, excitement, suspense, anxiety, exultation, surprise. Some stories make us laugh; some cause us to thrill with horror; some make us cry. We value all the arts precisely because they enrich and diversify our emotional life.

A truly significant story pursues emotion indirectly, not directly. Emotion accompanying and producing insight, not emotion for itself, is the end of the interpretive writer. He writes in order to present a sample of experience truthfully; the emotions he arouses flow naturally from the experience presented.

Over a century ago, in a review of Hawthorne's *Tales,* Edgar Allan Poe made a famous but misleading pronouncement about the short story:

A skilful literary artist has constructed a tale. If wise, he has not fashioned his thoughts to accommodate his incidents; but having conceived with deliberate care, a certain unique or single *effect* to be brought out, he then invents such incidents—he then combines such events as may best aid him in establishing this preconceived effect. If his very initial sentence tend not to the outbringing of this effect, then he has failed in his first step. In the whole composition there should be no word written, of which the tendency, direct or indirect, is not to the one preestablished design.

Poe's formulation has been enormously influential, for both good and bad. Historically it is important as being one of the first discussions of the short story as a unique form. Critically it is important because Poe so clearly here enunciates the basic critical principle of all art—the principle of artistic unity, requiring all details and elements of a piece to contribute harmoniously to the total design. Its influence has been deleterious because of the emphasis Poe put on a "unique" and "preconceived" *effect*.

The serious writer is an interpreter, not an inventor. Like a good actor, he is an intermediary between a segment of experience and an audience. The actor must pay some consideration to his audience: he must be careful, for instance, to face *toward* it, not away from it. But the great actor is the one who is wrapped up in the thoughts and feelings of a role, not the one who is continually stealing glances at the audience to determine the effect of his last gesture or bit of business. The actor who begins taking cues from the audience rather than from the script soon becomes a "ham," exaggerating and falsifying for the sake of effects. The writer, too, though he must pay some consideration to the reader, must focus primarily on the subject. If he begins to think primarily of the effect of the tale on the reader, he begins to manipulate the material, to heighten reality, to contrive and falsify for the sake of effects. The serious writer selects and arranges his material in order to convey most effectively the feeling or truth of a human situation. The less serious writer selects and arranges his material so as to stimulate a response in the reader.

The discriminating reader, then, will distinguish between contrived emotion and that which springs naturally from a human story truly told. He will mark a difference between the story that attempts to "play upon" his feelings directly, as if he were a piano, and one that draws emotion forth as naturally as a plucked string draws forth sympathetic vibrations from another instrument in a room. The difference between the two types of story is the difference between escape and interpretation. In interpretive fiction, emotion is the by-product, not the goal.

No doubt there is pleasure in having our emotions directly stimulated, and in some forms such pleasure is both delightful and innocent. We all enjoy the laugh that follows a good joke, and the story that attempts no more than to provoke laughter may be both pleasant and harmless. There is a difference, nevertheless, between the story written for humor's sake and that in which humor springs from a way of viewing experience. Humor may be as idle as the wisecrack or as vicious as the practical joke; it becomes of significant value when it flows from a comic perception of life.

Most of us enjoy the gooseflesh and the tingle along the spine produced by the successful ghost story. There is something agreeable in letting our blood be chilled by bats in the moonlight, guttering candles, creaking doors, eerie shadows, piercing screams, inexplicable bloodstains, and weird noises. But the terror aroused by tricks and external "machinery" is a far cry from the terror evoked by some terrifying treatment of the human situation. The horror we experience in watching the Werewolf or Dracula or the Frankenstein monster is far less significant than that we get from watching the bloody ambition of Macbeth or the jealousy of Othello. In the first, terror is the end-product; in the second, it is the natural accompaniment of a powerful revelation of life. In the first, we are always aware of a basic unreality; in the second, reality is terrifying.

The story designed merely to provoke laughter or to arouse terror may be an enjoyable and innocent pleasure. The story directed at stimulating tears belongs to a less innocent category. The difference is that the humor story and the terror story seldom ask to be taken for more than what they are: pleasant diversions to help us pass the time agreeably. We enjoy the custard pie in the face and the ghost in the moonlight without taking them seriously. The fiction that depends on such ingredients is pure escape. The tear-jerker, however, asks to be taken seriously. Like the street beggar who artfully disposes his rags, puts on dark glasses over perfectly good eyes, holds out a tin cup and wails about his seven starving children (there are really only two, and he doesn't know what has become of them), the tear-jerker cheats us. It is escape literature posing as its opposite; it is counterfeit interpretation. It cheats us by exaggerating and falsifying reality by asking for compassion that is not deserved.

The quality in a story that aims at drawing forth unmerited tender feeling is known as SENTIMENTALITY. Sentimentality is not the same as genuine emotion. Sentimentality is contrived or excessive or faked emotion. A story contains genuine emotion when it treats life faithfully and perceptively. The sentimentalized story oversimplifies and sweetens life to get its feeling. It exaggerates, manipulates, and prettifies. It mixes tears with sugar.

Genuine emotion, like character, must be presented *indirectly*—must be *dramatized*. It cannot be produced by words that *describe* emotions, like *angry, sad, pathetic, heart-breaking,* or *passionate*. If a writer is to draw forth genuine emotion, he must produce a character in a situation that deserves our sympathy and must tell us enough about the character and the situation to make them real and convincing.

Sentimental writers are recognizable by a number of characteristics. First, they often try to make words do what the situation faithfully presented by itself will not do. They *editorialize*—that is, comment on the story and, in a manner, instruct us how to feel. Or they overwrite and *poeticize*—use an immoderately heightened and distended language to accomplish their effects. Second, they make an excessively selective use of detail. All artists, of course, must be selective in their use of detail, but good writers use representative details while sentimentalists use details that all point one way—toward producing emotion rather than conveying truth. The little child that dies will be shown as always uncomplaining and cheerful under adversity, never as naughty, querulous, or ungrateful. It will possibly be an orphan or the only child of a mother who loves it dearly; in addition, it may be lame, hungry, ragged, and possessed of one toy, from which it cannot be parted. The villain will be all-villain, with a cruel laugh and a sharp whip, though he may reform at the end, for sentimentalists are firm believers in the heart of gold beneath the rough exterior. In short, reality will be unduly heightened and drastically over-simplified. Third, sentimentalists rely heavily on the stock response—an emotion that has its source outside the facts established by the story. In some readers certain situations and objects—babies, mothers, grand-mothers, young love, patriotism, worship—produce an almost automatic response, whether the immediate situation warrants it or not. Sentimental writers, to affect such readers, have only to draw out certain stops, as on an organ, to produce an easily anticipated effect. They depend on stock materials to produce a stock response. They thus need not go to the trouble of picturing the situation in realistic and convincing detail. Finally, sentimental writers present, nearly always, a fundamentally "sweet" picture of life. They rely not only on stock characters and situations but also on stock themes. For them every cloud has its silver lining, every bad event its good side, every storm its rainbow. If the little child dies, it goes to heaven or makes some life better by its death. Virtue is characteristically triumphant: the villain is defeated, the ne'er-do-well redeemed. True love is rewarded in some fashion; it is love—never hate—that makes the world go round. In short, sentimental writers specialize in the sad but sweet. The tears called for are warm tears, never bitter. There is always sugar at the bottom of the cup.

For mature readers, emotion is a highly valued but not easily achieved component of a story. It is a by-product, not the end-product. It is gained by honestly portrayed characters in honestly drawn situations that reflect the complexity, the ambiguity, and the endless variety of life. It is produced by a carefully exercised restraint on the part of the writer rather than by "pulling out all the stops." It is one of the chief rewards of art.

EXERCISES

The six stories that follow are paired. In the first pair each story depicts terror; in the second pair each story is humorous; in the third pair each story contains sentiment. In each of the first two pairs, one story is more purely interpretive than the other; in the third pair, one story is guilty of sentimentality. For each pair decide which story is more authentic or significant, and give reasons for your choice.

McKnight Malmar
THE STORM

She inserted her key in the lock and turned the knob. The March wind snatched the door out of her hand and slammed it against the wall. It took strength to close it against the pressure of the gale, and she had no sooner closed it than the rain came in a pounding downpour, beating noisily against the windows as if trying to follow her in. She could not hear the taxi as it started up and went back down the road.

She breathed a sigh of thankfulness at being home again and in time. In rain like this, the crossroads always were flooded. Half an hour later her cab could not have got through the rising water, and there was no alternative route.

There was no light anywhere in the house. Ben was not home, then. As she turned on the lamp by the sofa she had a sense of anticlimax. All the way home—she had been visiting her sister—she had seen herself going into a lighted house, to Ben, who would be sitting by the fire with his paper. She had taken delight in picturing his happy surprise at seeing her, home a week earlier than he had expected her. She had known just how his round face would light up, how his eyes would twinkle behind his glasses, how he would catch her by the shoulders and look down into her face to see the changes a month had made in her, and then kiss her resoundingly on both cheeks, like a French general bestowing a decoration. Then she would make coffee and find a piece of cake, and they would sit together by the fire and talk.

THE STORM   First published in 1944. McKnight Malmar was born in 1903 in Albany, New York, and grew up in suburban New York. She presently resides in Virginia.

But Ben wasn't here. She looked at the clock on the mantel and saw it was nearly ten. Perhaps he had not planned to come home tonight, as he was not expecting her; even before she had left he frequently was in the city all night because business kept him too late to catch the last train. If he did not come soon, he would not be able to make it at all.

She did not like the thought. The storm was growing worse. She could hear the wild lash of the trees, the whistle of the wind around the corners of the little house. For the first time she regretted this move to the far suburbs. There had been neighbors at first, a quarter-mile down the road; but they moved away several months ago, and now their house stood empty.

She had thought nothing of the lonesomeness. It was perfect here—for two. She had taken such pleasure in fixing up her house—her very own house—and caring for it that she had not missed company other than Ben. But now, alone and with the storm trying to batter its way in, she found it frightening to be so far away from other people. There was no one this side of the crossroads; the road that passed the house wandered past farmland into nothingness in the thick woods a mile farther on.

She hung her hat and her coat in the closet and went to stand before the hall mirror to pin up the soft strands of hair that the wind had loosened. She did not really see the pale face with its blunt little nose, the slender, almost childish figure in its grown-up black dress, or the big brown eyes that looked back at her.

She fastened the last strands into the pompadour and turned away from the mirror. Her shoulders drooped a little. There was something childlike about her, like a small girl craving protection, something immature and yet appealing, in spite of her plainness. She was thirty-one and had been married for fifteen months. The fact that she had married at all still seemed a miracle to her.

Now she began to walk through the house, turning on lights as she went. Ben had left it in fairly good order. There was very little trace of an untidy masculine presence; but then, he was a tidy man. She began to realize that the house was cold. Of course, Ben would have lowered the thermostat. He was very careful about things like that. He would not tolerate waste.

No wonder it was cold; the thermostat was set at fifty-eight. She pushed the little needle up to seventy, and the motor in the cellar started so suddenly and noisily that it frightened her for a moment.

She went into the kitchen and made some coffee. While she waited for it to drip she began to prowl around the lower floor. She was curiously restless and could not relax. Yet it was good to be back again among her own things, in her own home. She studied the living-room with fresh eyes. Yes, it was a pleasant room even though it was small. The bright, flowered chintzes on the furniture and at the windows were cheerful and pretty, and the lowboy she had bought three months ago was just right for the middle of the long wall. But her plants, set so bravely along the window sill, had died. Ben had forgotten to water them, in spite of all her admonitions, and now they drooped, shrunken and pale, in whitened, powdery soil. The sight of them added to the depression that was beginning to blot out all the pleasure of homecoming.

She returned to the kitchen and poured herself a cup of coffee, wishing that Ben would come home to share it with her. She carried her cup into the living-room and set it on the small, round table beside Ben's special big chair. The furnace was still mumbling busily, sending up heat, but she was colder than ever. She shivered and got an old jacket of Ben's from the closet and wrapped it around her before she sat down.

The wind hammered at the door and the windows, and the air was full of the sound of water, racing in the gutters, pouring from the leaders, thudding on the roof. Listening, she wished for Ben almost feverishly. She never had felt so alone. And he was such a comfort. He had been so good about her going for this long visit, made because her sister was ill. He had seen to everything and had put her on the train with her arms loaded with books and candy and fruit. She knew those farewell gifts had meant a lot to him—he didn't spend money easily. To be quite honest, he was a little close.

But he was a good husband. She sighed unconsciously, not knowing it was because of youth and romance missed. She repeated it to herself, firmly, as she sipped her coffee. He was a good husband. Suppose he was ten years older than she, and a little set in his ways; a little—perhaps—dictatorial at times, and moody. He had given her what she thought she wanted, security and a home of her own; if security were not enough, she could not blame him for it.

Her eye caught a shred of white protruding under a magazine on the table beside her. She put out a hand toward it, yet her fingers were almost reluctant to grasp it. She pulled it out nevertheless and saw that it was, as she had known instinctively, another of the white envelopes. It was empty, and it bore, as usual, the neat, typewritten address: *Benj. T. Willsom, Esq., Wildwood Road, Fairport, Conn.* The postmark was *New York City.* It never varied.

She felt the familiar constriction about the heart as she held it in her hands. What these envelopes contained she never had known. What she did know was their effect on Ben. After receiving one—one came every month or two—he was irritable, at times almost ugly. Their peaceful life together fell apart. At first she had questioned him, had striven to soothe and comfort him; but she soon had learned that this only made him angry, and of late she had avoided any mention of them. For a week after one came they shared the same room and the same table like two strangers, in a silence that was morose on his part and a little frightened on hers.

This one was postmarked three days before. If Ben got home tonight he would probably be cross, and the storm would not help his mood. Just the same she wished he would come.

She tore the envelope into tiny pieces and tossed them into the fireplace. The wind shook the house in its giant grip, and a branch crashed on the roof. As she straightened, a movement at the window caught her eye.

She froze there, not breathing, still half-bent toward the cold fireplace, her hand still extended. The glimmer of white at the window behind the sheeting blur of rain had been—she was sure of it—a human face. There had been eyes. She was certain there had been eyes staring in at her.

The wind's shout took on a personal, threatening note. She was rigid for a long time, never taking her eyes from the window. But nothing moved there now except the water on the windowpane; beyond it there was blackness, and that was all. The only sounds were the thrashing of the trees, the roar of water, and the ominous howl of the wind.

She began to breathe again, at last found courage to turn out the light and go to the window. The darkness was a wall, impenetrable and secret, and the blackness within the house made the storm close in, as if it were a pack of wolves besieging the house. She hastened to put on the light again.

She must have imagined those staring eyes. Nobody could be out on a night like this. Nobody. Yet she found herself terribly shaken.

If only Ben would come home. If only she were not so alone.

She shivered and pulled Ben's coat tighter about her and told herself she was becoming a morbid fool. Nevertheless, she found the aloneness intolerable. Her ears strained to hear prowling footsteps outside the windows. She became convinced that she did hear them, slow and heavy.

Perhaps Ben could be reached at the hotel where he sometimes stayed. She no longer cared whether her homecoming was a surprise to him. She wanted to hear his voice. She went to the telephone and lifted the receiver.

The line was quite dead.

The wires were down, of course.

She fought panic. The face at the window had been an illusion, a trick of the light reflected on the sluicing pane; and the sound of footsteps was an illusion, too. Actual ones would be inaudible in the noise made by the wild storm. Nobody would be out tonight. Nothing threatened her, really. The storm was held at bay beyond these walls, and in the morning the sun would shine again.

The thing to do was to make herself as comfortable as possible and settle down with a book. There was no use going to bed—she couldn't possibly sleep. She would only lie there wide awake and think of that face at the window, hear those footsteps.

She would get some wood for a fire in the fireplace. She hesitated at the top of the cellar stairs. The light, as she switched it on, seemed insufficient; the concrete wall at the foot of the stairs was dank with moisture and somehow gruesome. And wind was chilling her ankles. Rain was beating in through the outside door to the cellar, because that door was standing open.

The inner bolt sometimes did not hold, she knew very well. If it had not been carefully closed, the wind could have loosened it. Yet the open door increased her panic. It seemed to argue the presence of something less impersonal than the gale. It took her a long minute to nerve herself to go down the steps and reach out into the darkness for the doorknob.

In just that instant she was soaked; but her darting eyes could find nothing outdoors but the black, wavering shapes of the maples at the side of the house. The wind helped her and slammed the door resoundingly. She jammed the bolt home with all her strength and then tested it to make sure it would hold. She almost sobbed with the relief of knowing it to be firm against any intruder.

She stood with her wet clothes clinging to her while the thought came that turned her bones to water. Suppose—suppose the face at the window had been real, after all. Suppose its owner had found shelter in the only shelter to be had within a quarter-mile—this cellar.

She almost flew up the stairs again, but then she took herself firmly in hand. She must not let herself go. There had been many storms before; just because she was alone in this one, she must not let morbid fancy run away with her. But she could not throw off the reasonless fear that oppressed her, although she forced it back a little. She began to hear again the tread of the prowler outside the house. Although she knew it to be imagination, it was fearfully real—the crunch of feet on gravel, slow, persistent, heavy, like the patrol of a sentinel.

She had only to get an armful of wood. Then she could have a fire, she would have light and warmth and comfort. She would forget these terrors.

The cellar smelled of dust and old moisture. The beams were fuzzed with cobwebs. There was only one light, a dim one in the corner. A little rivulet was running darkly down the wall and already had formed a foot-square pool on the floor.

The woodpile was in the far corner away from the light. She stopped and peered around. Nobody could hide here. The cellar was too open, the supporting stanchions too slender to hide a man.

The oil burner went off with a sharp click. Its mutter, she suddenly realized, had had something human and companionable about it. Nothing was down here with her now but the snarl of the storm.

She almost ran to the woodpile. Then something made her pause and turn before she bent to gather the logs.

What was it? Not a noise. Something she had seen as she hurried across that dusty floor. Something odd.

She searched with her eyes. It was a spark of light she had seen, where no spark should be.

An inexplicable dread clutched at her heart. Her eyes widened, round and dark as a frightened deer's. Her old trunk that stood against the wall was open just a crack; from the crack came this tiny pinpoint of reflected light to prick the cellar's gloom.

She went toward it like a woman hypnotized. It was only one more insignificant thing, like the envelope on the table, the vision of the face at the window, the open door. There was no reason for her to feel smothered in terror.

Yet she was sure she had not only closed, but clamped the lid on the trunk; she was sure because she kept two or three old coats in it, wrapped in newspapers and tightly shut away from moths.

Now the lid was raised perhaps an inch. And the twinkle of light was still there.

She threw back the lid.

For a long moment she stood looking down into the trunk, while each detail of its contents imprinted itself on her brain like an image on a film. Each tiny detail was indelibly clear and never to be forgotten.

She could not have stirred a muscle in that moment. Horror was a black cloak thrown around her, stopping her breath, hobbling her limbs.

Then her face dissolved into formlessness. She slammed down the lid and ran up the stairs like a mad thing. She was breathing again, in deep, sobbing breaths that tore at her lungs. She shut the door at the top of the stairs with a crash that shook the house; then she turned the key. Gasping she clutched one of the sturdy maple chairs by the kitchen table and wedged it under the knob with hands she could barely control.

The wind took the house in its teeth and shook it as a dog shakes a rat.

Her first impulse was to get out of the house. But in the time it took to get to the front door she remembered the face at the window.

Perhaps she had not imagined it. Perhaps it was the face of a murderer—a murderer waiting for her out there in the storm; ready to spring on her out of the dark.

She fell into the big chair, her huddled body shaken by great tremors. She could not stay here—not with that thing in her trunk. Yet she dared not leave. Her whole being cried out for Ben. He would know what to do. She closed her eyes, opened them again, rubbed them hard. The picture still burned into her brain as if it had been etched with acid. Her hair, loosened, fell in soft straight wisps about her forehead, and her mouth was slack with terror.

Her old trunk had held the curled-up body of a woman.

She had not seen the face; the head had been tucked down into the hollow of the shoulder, and a shower of fair hair had fallen over it. The woman had worn a red dress. One hand had rested near the edge of the trunk, and on its third finger there had been a man's ring, a signet bearing the raised figure of a rampant lion with a small diamond between its paws. It had been the diamond that caught the light. The little bulb in the corner of the cellar had picked out this ring from the semidarkness and made it stand out like a beacon.

She never would be able to forget it. Never forget how the woman looked: the pale, luminous flesh of her arms; her doubled-up knees against the side of the trunk, with their silken covering shining softly in the gloom; the strands of hair that covered her face . . .

Shudders continued to shake her. She bit her tongue and pressed her hand against her jaw to stop the chattering of her teeth. The salty taste of blood in her mouth steadied her. She tried to force herself to be rational, to plan; yet all the time the knowledge that she was imprisoned with the body of a murdered woman kept beating at her nerves like a flail.

She drew the coat closer about her, trying to dispel the mortal cold that held her. Slowly something beyond the mere fact of murder, of death, began to penetrate her mind. Slowly she realized that beyond this fact there would be consequences. That body in the cellar was not an isolated phenomenon; some train of events had led to its being there and would follow its discovery there.

There would be policemen.

At first the thought of policemen was a comforting one; big, brawny men in blue, who would take the thing out of her cellar, take it away so she never need think of it again.

Then she realized it was *her* cellar—hers and Ben's; and policemen are suspicious and prying. Would they think *she* killed the woman? Could they be made to believe she never had seen her before?

Or would they think Ben had done it? Would they take the letters in the white envelopes, and Ben's absences on business, and her own visit to her sister, about which Ben was so helpful, and out of them build a double life for him? Would they insist that the woman had been a discarded mistress, who had hounded him with letters until out of desperation he had killed her? That was a fantastic theory, really; but the police might do that.

They might.

Now a sudden new panic invaded her. The dead woman must be taken out of the cellar, must be hidden. The police must never connect her with this house.

Yet the dead woman was bigger than she herself was; she could never move her.

Her craving for Ben became a frantic need. If only he would come home! Come home and take that body away, hide it somewhere so the police could not connect it with this house. He was strong enough to do it.

Even with the strength to move the body by herself she would not dare do it, because there was the prowler—real or imaginary—outside the house. Perhaps the cellar door had not been open by chance. Or perhaps it had been, and the murderer, seeing it so welcoming, had seized the opportunity to plant the evidence of his crime upon the Willsoms' innocent shoulders.

She crouched there, shaking. It was as if the jaws of a great trap had closed on her: on one side the storm and the silence of the telephone, on the other the presence of the prowler and of that still, cramped figure in her trunk. She was caught between them, helpless.

As if to accent her helplessness, the wind stepped up its shriek and a tree crashed thunderously out in the road. She heard glass shatter.

Her quivering body stiffened like a drawn bow. Was it the prowler attempting to get in? She forced herself to her feet and made a round of the windows on the first floor and the one above. All the glass was intact, staunchly resisting the pounding of the rain.

Nothing could have made her go into the cellar to see if anything had happened there.

The voice of the storm drowned out all other sounds, yet she could not rid herself of the fancy that she heard footsteps going round and round the house, that eyes sought an opening and spied upon her.

She pulled the shades down over the shiny black windows. It helped a little to make her feel more secure, more sheltered; but only a very little. She told herself sternly that the crash of glass had been nothing more than a branch blown through a cellar window.

The thought brought her no comfort—just the knowledge that it would not disturb that other woman. Nothing could comfort her now but Ben's plump shoulder and his arms around her and his neat, capable mind planning to remove the dead woman from this house.

A kind of numbness began to come over her, as if her capacity for fear were exhausted. She went back to the chair and curled up in it. She prayed mutely for Ben and for daylight.

The clock said half-past twelve.

She huddled there, not moving and not thinking, not even afraid, only numb, for another hour. Then the storm held its breath for a moment, and in the brief space of silence she heard footsteps on the walk—actual footsteps, firm and quick and loud. A key turned in the lock. The door opened and Ben came in.

He was dripping, dirty, and white with exhaustion. But it was Ben. Once she was sure of it she flung herself on him, babbling incoherently of what she had found.

He kissed her lightly on the cheek and took her arms down from around his neck. "Here, here, my dear. You'll get soaked. I'm drenched to the skin." He removed his glasses and handed them to her, and she began to dry them for him. His eyes squinted at the light. "I had to walk in from the crossroads. What a night!" He began to strip off rubbers and coat and shoes. "You'll never know what a difference it made, finding the place lighted. Lord, but it's good to be home."

She tried again to tell him of the past hours, but again he cut her short. "Now, wait a minute, my dear. I can see you're bothered about something. Just wait until I get into some dry things; then I'll come down and we'll straighten it out. Suppose you rustle up some coffee and toast. I'm done up—the whole trip out was a nightmare, and I didn't know if I'd ever make it from the crossing. I've been hours."

He did look tired, she thought with concern. Now that he was back, she could wait. The past hours had taken on the quality of a nightmare, horrifying but curiously unreal. With Ben here, so solid and commonplace and cheerful, she began to wonder if the hours *were* nightmare. She even began to doubt the reality of the woman in the trunk, although she could see her as vividly as ever. Perhaps only the storm was real.

She went to the kitchen and began to make fresh coffee. The chair, still wedged against the kitchen door, was a reminder of her terror. Now that Ben was home it seemed silly, and she put it back in its place by the table.

He came down very soon, before the coffee was ready. How good it was to see him in that old gray bathrobe of his, his hands thrust into its pockets. How normal and wholesome he looked with his round face rubbed pink by a rough towel and his hair standing up in damp little spikes around his bald spot. She was almost shamefaced when she told him of the face at the window, the open door, and finally of the body in the trunk. None of it, she saw quite clearly now, could possibly have happened.

Ben said so, without hesitation. But he came to put an arm around her. "You poor child. The storm scared you to death, and I don't wonder. It's given you the horrors."

She smiled dubiously. "Yes. I'm almost beginning to think so. Now that you're back, it seems so safe. But—but you will *look* in the trunk, Ben? I've got to *know*. I can see her so plainly. How could I imagine a thing like that?"

He said indulgently, "Of course I'll look, if it will make you feel better. I'll do it now. Then I can have my coffee in peace."

He went to the cellar door and opened it and snapped on the light. Her heart began to pound once more, a deafening roar in her ears. The opening of the cellar door opened, again, the whole vista of fear: the body, the police, the suspicions that would cluster about her and Ben. The need to hide this evidence of somebody's crime.

She could not have imagined it; it was incredible that she could have believed, for a minute, that her mind had played such tricks on her. In another moment Ben would know it, too.

She heard the thud as he threw back the lid of the trunk. She clutched at the back of a chair, waiting for his voice. It came in an instant.

She could not believe it. It was as cheerful and reassuring as before. He said, "There's nothing here but a couple of bundles. Come take a look."

Nothing!

Her knees were weak as she went down the stairs, down into the cellar again.

It was still musty and damp and draped with cobwebs. The rivulet was still running down the wall, but the pool was larger now. The light was still dim.

It was just as she remembered it except that the wind was whistling through a broken window and rain was splattering in on the bits of shattered glass on the floor. The branch lying across the sill had removed every scrap of glass from the frame and left not a single jagged edge.

Ben was standing by the open trunk, waiting for her. His stocky body was a bulwark. "See," he said, "there's nothing. Just some old clothes of yours, I guess."

She went to stand beside him. Was she losing her mind? Would she, now, see that crushed figure in there, see the red dress and the smooth shining knees, when Ben could not? And the ring with the diamond between the lion's paws?

Her eyes looked, almost reluctantly, into the trunk. "It *is* empty!"

There were the neat, newspaper-wrapped packages she had put away so carefully, just as she had left them deep in the bottom of the trunk. And nothing else.

She must have imagined the body. She was light with the relief the knowledge brought her, and yet confused and frightened, too. If her mind could play such tricks, if she could imagine anything so gruesome in the complete detail with which she had seen the dead woman in the trunk, the thought of the future was terrifying. When might she not have another such hallucination?

The actual, physical danger did not exist, however, and never existed. The threat of the law hanging over Ben had been based on a dream.

"I—dreamed it all. I must have," she admitted. "Yet it was so horribly clear and I wasn't asleep." Her voice broke. "I thought—oh, Ben, I thought—"

"What did you think, my dear?" His voice was odd, not like Ben's at all. It had a cold cutting edge to it.

He stood looking down at her with an immobility that chilled her more than the cold wind that swept in through the broken window. She tried to read his face, but the light from the little bulb was too weak. It left his features shadowed in broad, dark planes that made him look like a stranger, and somehow sinister.

She said, "I—" and faltered.

He still did not move, but his voice hardened. "What was it you thought?"

She backed away from him.

He moved, then. It was only to take his hands from his pockets to stretch his arms toward her; but she stood for an instant staring at the thing that left her stricken, with a voiceless scream forming in her throat.

She was never to know whether his arms had been outstretched to take her within their shelter or to clutch at her white neck. For she turned and fled, stumbling up the stairs in a mad panic of escape.

He shouted, "Janet! Janet!" His steps were heavy behind her. He tripped on the bottom step and fell on one knee and cursed.

Terror lent her strength and speed. She could not be mistaken. Although she had seen it only once, she knew that on the little finger of his left hand there had been the same, the unmistakable ring the dead woman had worn.

The blessed wind snatched the front door from her and flung it wide, and she was out in the safe, dark shelter of the storm.

QUESTIONS

1. By what means does this story create and build suspense? What uses does it make of mystery? At what points does it employ surprise?
2. Is the ending of the story determinate or indeterminate?
3. From what point of view is the story told? What advantages has this point of view for this story? Are there any places where the contents of Mrs. Willsom's consciousness are suppressed, at least temporarily? For what purpose?
4. Put together an account of Ben's activities that will explain as many as possible of the phenomena that Mrs. Willsom observes—or thinks she observes—during the course of the evening. Are any left unexplained? Is any motivation provided for the murder of the woman in the trunk? How?
5. What are the chief features of Ben's characterization? Why is he characterized as he is? Has the characterization been fashioned to serve the story or the story to serve the characterization?
6. To what extent does the story depend on coincidence?
7. What is the main purpose of the story? Does it have a theme? If so, what?
8. What do you find most effective in the story?

William Faulkner

THAT EVENING SUN

1

Monday is no different from any other weekday in Jefferson now. The streets are paved now, and the telephone and electric companies are cutting down more and more of the shade trees—the water oaks, the maples and locusts and elms— to make room for iron poles bearing clusters of bloated and ghostly and bloodless grapes, and we have a city laundry which makes the rounds on Monday morning, gathering the bundles of clothes into bright-colored, specially made motorcars: the soiled wearing of a whole week now flees apparitionlike behind alert and irritable electric horns, with a long diminishing noise of rubber and asphalt like tearing silk, and even the Negro women who still take in white people's washing after the old custom, fetch and deliver it in automobiles.

But fifteen years ago, on Monday morning the quiet, dusty shady streets

THAT EVENING SUN   First published in its present form in the collection *These Thirteen* (1931). A slightly modified version was published earlier that year in *The American Mercury*, 22 (March 1931), 257-67, under the title "That Evening Sun Go Down." For the setting of many of his novels and stories Faulkner created the mythical county of Yoknapatawpha, Mississippi, whose chief town is Jefferson. The fictional Jefferson is roughly based on Oxford, Mississippi, of which Faulkner (1897-1962) was a life-long resident. Most of Faulkner's fiction is interconnected: the characters in this story reappear in various other works, notably *The Sound and the Fury* (1929).

would be full of Negro women with, balanced on their steady, turbaned heads, bundles of clothes tied up in sheets, almost as large as cotton bales, carried so without touch of hand between the kitchen door of the white house and the blackened washpot beside a cabin door in Negro Hollow.

Nancy would set her bundle on top of her head, then upon the bundle in turn she would set the black straw sailor hat which she wore winter and summer. She was tall, with a high, sad face sunken a little where her teeth were missing. Sometimes we would go a part of the way down the lane and across the pasture with her, to watch the balanced bundle and the hat that never bobbed or wavered, even when she walked down into the ditch and up the other side and stooped through the fence. She would go down on her hands and knees and crawl through the gap, her head rigid, uptilted, the bundle steady as a rock or a balloon, and rise to her feet again and go on.

Sometimes the husbands of the washing women would fetch and deliver the clothes, but Jesus never did that for Nancy, even before Father told him to stay away from our house, even when Dilsey was sick and Nancy would come to cook for us.

And then about half the time we'd have to go down the lane to Nancy's cabin and tell her to come on and cook breakfast. We would stop at the ditch, because Father told us to not have anything to do with Jesus—he was a short black man, with a razor scar down his face—and we would throw rocks at Nancy's house until she came to the door, leaning her head around it without any clothes on.

"What yawl mean, chunking my house?" Nancy said. "What you little devils mean?"

"Father says for you to come on and get breakfast," Caddy said. "Father says it's over a half an hour now, and you've got to come this minute."

"I ain't studying no breakfast," Nancy said. "I going to get my sleep out."

"I bet you're drunk," Jason said. "Father says you're drunk. Are you drunk, Nancy?"

"Who says I is?" Nancy said. "I got to get my sleep out. I ain't studying no breakfast."

So after a while we quit chunking the cabin and went back home. When she finally came, it was too late for me to go to school. So we thought it was whiskey until that day they arrested her again and they were taking her to jail and they passed Mr. Stovall. He was the cashier in the bank and a deacon in the Baptist church, and Nancy began to say:

"When you going to pay me, white man? When you going to pay me, white man? It's been three times now since you paid me a cent—" Mr. Stovall knocked her down, but she kept on saying, "When you going to pay me, white man? It's been three times now since—" until Mr. Stovall kicked her in the mouth with his heel and the marshal caught Mr. Stovall back, and Nancy lying in the street, laughing. She turned her head and spat out some blood and teeth and said, "It's been three times now since he paid me a cent."

That was how she lost her teeth, and all that day they told about Nancy and Mr. Stovall, and all that night the ones that passed the jail could hear Nancy singing and yelling. They could see her hands holding to the window bars, and a lot of them stopped along the fence, listening to her and the jailer trying to make her stop. She didn't shut up until almost daylight, when the jailer began to hear a bumping and scraping upstairs and he went up there and found Nancy hanging from the window bar. He said that it was cocaine and not whiskey, because no nigger would try to commit suicide unless he was full of cocaine, because a nigger full of cocaine wasn't a nigger any longer.

The jailer cut her down and revived her; then he beat her, whipped her. She had hung herself with her dress. She had fixed it all right, but when they arrested her she didn't have on anything except a dress and so she didn't have anything to tie her hands with and she couldn't make her hands let go of the window ledge. So the jailer heard the noise and ran up there and found Nancy hanging from the window, stark naked, her belly already swelling out a little, like a little balloon.

When Dilsey was sick in her cabin and Nancy was cooking for us, we could see her apron swelling out; that was before Father told Jesus to stay away from the house. Jesus was in the kitchen, sitting behind the stove, with his razor scar on his black face like a piece of dirty string. He said it was a watermelon that Nancy had under her dress.

"It never come off of your vine, though," Nancy said.

"Off of what vine?" Caddy said.

"I can cut down the vine it did come off of," Jesus said.

"What makes you want to talk like that before these chillen?" Nancy said. "Whyn't you go on to work? You done et. You want Mr. Jason to catch you hanging around his kitchen, talking that way before these chillen?"

"Talking what way?" Caddy said. "What vine?"

"I can't hang around white man's kitchen," Jesus said. "But white man can hang around mine. White man can come in my house, but I can't stop him. When white man want to come in my house, I ain't got no house. I can't stop him, but he can't kick me outen it. He can't do that."

Dilsey was still sick in her cabin. Father told Jesus to stay off our place. Dilsey was still sick. It was a long time. We were in the library after supper.

"Isn't Nancy through in the kitchen yet?" Mother said. "It seems to me that she has had plenty of time to have finished the dishes."

"Let Quentin go and see," Father said. "Go and see if Nancy is through, Quentin. Tell her she can go on home."

I went to the kitchen. Nancy was through. The dishes were put away and the fire was out. Nancy was sitting in a chair, close to the cold stove. She looked at me.

"Mother wants to know if you are through," I said.

"Yes," Nancy said. She looked at me. "I done finished." She looked at me.

"What is it?" I said. "What is it?"

"I ain't nothing but a nigger," Nancy said. "It ain't none of my fault."

She looked at me, sitting in the chair before the cold stove, the sailor hat on her head. I went back to the library. It was the cold stove and all, when you think of a kitchen being warm and busy and cheerful. And with a cold stove and the dishes all put away, and nobody wanting to eat at that hour.

"Is she through?" Mother said.

"Yessum," I said.

"What is she doing?" Mother said.

"She's not doing anything. She's through."

"I'll go and see," Father said.

"Maybe she's waiting for Jesus to come and take her home," Caddy said.

"Jesus is gone," I said. Nancy told us how one morning she woke up and Jesus was gone.

"He quit me," Nancy said. "Done gone to Memphis, I reckon. Dodging them city *po*-lice for a while, I reckon."

"And a good riddance," Father said. "I hope he stays there."

"Nancy's scaired of the dark," Jason said.

"So are you," Caddy said.

"I'm not," Jason said.

"Scairy cat," Caddy said.

"I'm not," Jason said.

"You, Candace!" Mother said. Father came back.

"I am going to walk down the lane with Nancy," he said. "She says that Jesus is back."

"Has she seen him?" Mother said.

"No. Some Negro sent her word that he was back in town. I won't be long."

"You'll leave me alone, to take Nancy home?" Mother said. "Is her safety more precious to you than mine?"

"I won't be long," Father said.

"You'll leave these children unprotected, with that Negro about?"

"I'm going, too," Caddy said. "Let me go, Father."

"What would he do with them, if he were unfortunate enough to have them?" Father said.

"I want to go, too," Jason said.

"Jason!" Mother said. She was speaking to Father. You could tell that by the way she said the name. Like she believed that all day Father had been trying to think of doing the thing she wouldn't like the most, and that she knew all the time that after a while he would think of it. I stayed quiet, because Father and I both knew that Mother would want him to make me stay with her if she just thought of it in time. So Father didn't look at me. I was the oldest. I was nine and Caddy was seven and Jason was five.

"Nonsense," Father said. "We won't be long."

Nancy had her hat on. We came to the lane. "Jesus always been good to me," Nancy said. "Whenever he had two dollars, one of them was mine." We walked in the lane. "If I can just get through the lane," Nancy said, "I be all right then."

The lane was always dark. "This is where Jason got scaired on Halloween," Caddy said.

"I didn't," Jason said.

"Can't Aunt Rachel do anything with him?" Father said. Aunt Rachel was old. She lived in a cabin beyond Nancy's by herself. She had white hair and she smoked a pipe in the door, all day long; she didn't work any more. They said she was Jesus' mother. Sometimes she said she was and sometimes she said she wasn't any kin to Jesus.

"Yes you did," Caddy said. "You were scairder than Frony. You were scairder than T. P. even. Scairder than niggers."

"Can't nobody do nothing with him," Nancy said. "He say I done woke up the devil in him and ain't but one thing going to lay it down again."

"Well, he's gone now," Father said. "There's nothing for you to be afraid of now. And if you'd just let white men alone."

"Let white men alone?" Caddy said. "How let them alone?"

"He ain't gone nowhere," Nancy said. "I can feel him. I can feel him now, in this lane. He hearing us talk, every word, hid somewhere, waiting. I ain't seen him, and I ain't going to see him again but once more, with that razor in his mouth. That razor on that string down his back, inside his shirt. And then I ain't going to be even surprised."

"I wasn't scaired," Jason said.

"If you'd behave yourself, you'd have kept out of this," Father said. "But it's all right now. He's probably in Saint Louis now. Probably got another wife by now and forgot all about you."

"If he has, I better not find out about it," Nancy said. "I'd stand there right over them, and every time he wropped her, I'd cut that arm off. I'd cut his head off and I'd slit her belly and I'd shove—"

"Hush," Father said.

"Slit whose belly, Nancy?" Caddy said.

"I wasn't scaired," Jason said. "I'd walk right down this lane by myself."

"Yah," Caddy said. "You wouldn't dare to put your foot down in it if we were not here too."

2

Dilsey was still sick, so we took Nancy home every night until Mother said, "How much longer is this going on? I to be left alone in this big house while you take home a frightened Negro?"

We fixed a pallet in the kitchen for Nancy. One night we waked up, hearing the sound. It was not singing and it was not crying, coming up the dark stairs. There was a light in Mother's room and we heard Father going down the hall, down the back stairs, and Caddy and I went into the hall. The floor was cold. Our toes curled away from it while we listened to the sound. It was like singing and it wasn't like singing, like the sound that Negroes make.

Then it stopped and we heard Father going down the back stairs, and we went to the head of the stairs. Then the sound began again, in the stairway, not loud, and we could see Nancy's eyes halfway up the stairs, against the wall. They looked like cat's eyes do, like a big cat against the wall, watching us. When we came down the steps to where she was, she quit making the sound again, and we stood there until Father came back up from the kitchen, with his pistol in his hand. He went back down with Nancy and they came back with Nancy's pallet.

We spread the pallet in our room. After the light in Mother's room went off, we could see Nancy's eyes again. "Nancy," Caddy whispered, "are you asleep, Nancy?"

Nancy whispered something. It was oh or no, I don't know which. Like nobody had made it, like it came from nowhere and went nowhere, until it was like Nancy was not there at all; that I had looked so hard at her eyes on the stairs that they had got printed on my eyeballs, like the sun does when you have closed your eyes and there is no sun. "Jesus," Nancy whispered. "Jesus."

"Was it Jesus?" Caddy said. "Did he try to come into the kitchen?"

"Jesus," Nancy said. Like this: Jeeeeeeeeeeeeeeesus, until the sound went out, like a match or a candle does.

"It's the other Jesus she means," I said.

"Can you see us, Nancy?" Caddy whispered. "Can you see our eyes too?"

"I ain't nothing but a nigger," Nancy said. "God knows. God knows."

"What did you see down there in the kitchen?" Caddy whispered. "What tried to get in?"

"God knows," Nancy said. We could see her eyes. "God knows."

Dilsey got well. She cooked dinner. "You'd better stay in bed a day or two longer," Father said.

"What for?" Dilsey said. "If I had been a day later, this place would be to rack and ruin. Get on out of here now, and let me get my kitchen straight again."

Dilsey cooked supper too. And that night, just before dark, Nancy came into the kitchen.

"How do you know he's back?" Dilsey said. "You ain't seen him."

"Jesus is a nigger," Jason said.

"I can feel him," Nancy said. "I can feel him laying yonder in the ditch."

"Tonight?" Dilsey said. "Is he there tonight?"

"Dilsey's a nigger too," Jason said.

"You try to eat something," Dilsey said.

"I don't want nothing," Nancy said.

"I ain't a nigger," Jason said.

"Drink some coffee," Dilsey said. She poured a cup of coffee for Nancy. "Do you know he's out there tonight? How come you know it's tonight?"

"I know," Nancy said. "He's there, waiting. I know. I done lived with him too long. I know what he is fixing to do fore he know it himself."

"Drink some coffee," Dilsey said. Nancy held the cup to her mouth and blew into the cup. Her mouth pursed out like a spreading adder's, like a rubber mouth, like she had blown all the color out of her lips with blowing the coffee.

"I ain't a nigger," Jason said. "Are you a nigger, Nancy?"

"I hellborn, child," Nancy said. "I won't be nothing soon. I going back where I come from soon."

3

She began to drink the coffee. While she was drinking, holding the cup in both hands, she began to make the sound again. She made the sound into the cup and the coffee sploshed out onto her hands and her dress. Her eyes looked at us and she sat there, her elbows on her knees, holding the cup in both hands, looking at us across the wet cup, making the sound.

"Look at Nancy," Jason said. "Nancy can't cook for us now. Dilsey's got well now."

"You hush up," Dilsey said. Nancy held the cup in both hands, looking at us, making the sound, like there were two of them: one looking at us and the other making the sound. "Whyn't you let Mr. Jason telefoam the marshal?" Dilsey said. Nancy stopped then, holding the cup in her long brown hands. She tried to drink some coffee again, but it sploshed out of the cup, onto her hands and her dress, and she put the cup down. Jason watched her.

"I can't swallow it," Nancy said. "I swallows but it won't go down me."

"You go down to the cabin," Dilsey said. "Frony will fix you a pallet and I'll be there soon."

"Won't no nigger stop him," Nancy said.

"I ain't a nigger," Jason said. "Am I, Dilsey?"

"I reckon not," Dilsey said. She looked at Nancy. "I don't reckon so. What you going to do, then?"

Nancy looked at us. Her eyes went fast, like she was afraid there wasn't time to look, without hardly moving at all. She looked at us, at all three of us at one time. "You remember that night I stayed in yawls' room?" she said. She told about how we waked up early the next morning, and played. We had to play quiet, on her pallet, until Father woke up and it was time to get breakfast. "Go and ask your maw to let me stay here tonight," Nancy said. "I won't need no pallet. We can play some more."

Caddy asked Mother. Jason went too. "I can't have Negroes sleeping in the bedrooms," Mother said. Jason cried. He cried until Mother said he couldn't have any dessert for three days if he didn't stop. Then Jason said he would stop if Dilsey would make a chocolate cake. Father was there.

"Why don't you do something about it?" Mother said. "What do we have officers for?"

"Why is Nancy afraid of Jesus?" Caddy said. "Are you afraid of Father, Mother?"

"What could the officers do?" Father said. "If Nancy hasn't seen him, how could the officers find him?"

"Then why is she afraid?" Mother said.

"She says he is there. She says she knows he is there tonight."

"Yet we pay taxes," Mother said. "I must wait here alone in this big house while you take a Negro woman home."

"You know that I am not lying outside with a razor," Father said.

"I'll stop if Dilsey will make a chocolate cake," Jason said. Mother told us to go out and Father said he didn't know if Jason would get a chocolate cake or not, but he knew what Jason was going to get in about a minute. We went back to the kitchen and told Nancy.

"Father said for you to go home and lock the door, and you'll be all right," Caddy said. "All right from what, Nancy? Is Jesus mad at you?" Nancy was holding the coffee cup in her hands again, her elbows on her knees and her hands holding the cup between her knees. She was looking into the cup. "What have you done that made Jesus mad?" Caddy said. Nancy let the cup go. It didn't break on the floor, but the coffee spilled out, and Nancy sat there with her hands still making the shape of the cup. She began to make the sound again, not loud. Not singing and not unsinging. We watched her.

"Here," Dilsey said. "You quit that, now. You get aholt of yourself. You wait here. I going to get Versh to walk home with you." Dilsey went out.

We looked at Nancy. Her shoulders kept shaking, but she quit making the sound. We stood and watched her.

"What's Jesus going to do to you?" Caddy said. "He went away."

Nancy looked at us. "We had fun that night I stayed in yawls' room, didn't we?"

"I didn't," Jason said. "I didn't have any fun."

"You were asleep in Mother's room," Caddy said. "You were not there."

"Let's go down to my house and have some more fun," Nancy said.

"Mother won't let us," I said. "It's too late now."

"Don't bother her," Nancy said. "We can tell her in the morning. She won't mind."

"She wouldn't let us," I said.

"Don't ask her now," Nancy said. "Don't bother her now."

"She didn't say we couldn't go," Caddy said.

"We didn't ask," I said.

"If you go, I'll tell," Jason said.

"We'll have fun," Nancy said. "They won't mind, just to my house. I been working for yawl a long time. They won't mind."

"I'm not afraid to go," Caddy said. "Jason is the one that's afraid. He'll tell."

"I'm not," Jason said.

"Yes, you are," Caddy said. "You'll tell."

"I won't tell," Jason said. "I'm not afraid."

"Jason ain't afraid to go with me," Nancy said. "Is you, Jason?"

"Jason is going to tell," Caddy said. The lane was dark. We passed the pasture gate. "I bet if something was to jump out from behind that gate, Jason would holler."

"I wouldn't," Jason said. We walked down the lane. Nancy was talking loud.

"What are you talking so loud for, Nancy?" Caddy said.

"Who, me?" Nancy said. "Listen at Quentin and Caddy and Jason saying I'm talking loud."

"You talk like there was five of us here," Caddy said. "You talk like Father was here too."

"Who; me talking loud, Mr. Jason?" Nancy said.

"Nancy called Jason 'Mister,'" Caddy said.

"Listen how Caddy and Quentin and Jason talk," Nancy said.

"We're not talking loud," Caddy said. "You're the one that's talking like Father—"

"Hush," Nancy said; "hush, Mr. Jason."

"Nancy called Jason 'Mister' aguh—"

"Hush," Nancy said. She was talking loud when we crossed the ditch and stooped through the fence where she used to stoop through with the clothes on her head. Then we came to her house. We were going fast then. She opened the door. The smell of the house was like the lamp and the smell of Nancy was like the wick, like they were waiting for one another to begin to smell. She lit the lamp and closed the door and put the bar up. Then she quit talking loud, looking at us.

"What're we going to do?" Caddy said.

"What do yawl want to do?" Nancy said.

"You said we would have some fun," Caddy said.

There was something about Nancy's house; something you could smell besides Nancy and the house. Jason smelled it, even. "I don't want to stay here," he said. "I want to go home."

"Go home, then," Caddy said.

"I don't want to go by myself," Jason said.

"We're going to have some fun," Nancy said.

"How?" Caddy said.

Nancy stood by the door. She was looking at us, only it was like she had emptied her eyes, like she had quit using them. "What do you want to do?" she said.

"Tell us a story," Caddy said. "Can you tell a story?"

"Yes," Nancy said.

"Tell it," Caddy said. We looked at Nancy. "You don't know any stories."

"Yes," Nancy said. "Yes I do."

She came and sat in a chair before the hearth. There was a little fire there. Nancy built it up, when it was already hot inside. She built a good blaze. She told a story. She talked like her eyes looked, like her eyes watching us and her voice talking to us did not belong to her. Like she was living somewhere else, waiting somewhere else. She was outside the cabin. Her voice was inside and the shape of her, that Nancy that could stoop under a barbed wire fence with a bundle of clothes balanced on her head as though without weight, like a balloon, was there. But that was all. "And so this here queen come walking up to the ditch, where that bad man was hiding. She was walking up to the ditch, and she say, 'If I can just get past this here ditch,' was what she say . . ."

"What ditch?" Caddy said. "A ditch like that one out there? Why did a queen want to go into a ditch?"

"To get to her house," Nancy said. She looked at us. "She had to cross the ditch to get into her house quick and bar the door."

"Why did she want to go home and bar the door?" Caddy said.

4

Nancy looked at us. She quit talking. She looked at us. Jason's legs stuck straight out of his pants where he sat on Nancy's lap. "I don't think that's a good story," he said. "I want to go home."

"Maybe we had better," Caddy said. She got up from the floor. "I bet they are looking for us right now." She went toward the door.

"No," Nancy said. "Don't open it." She got up quick and passed Caddy. She didn't touch the door, the wooden bar.

"Why not?" Caddy said.

"Come back to the lamp," Nancy said. "We'll have fun. You don't have to go."

"We ought to go," Caddy said. "Unless we have a lot of fun." She and Nancy came back to the fire, the lamp.

"I want to go home," Jason said. "I'm going to tell."

"I know another story," Nancy said. She stood close to the lamp. She looked at Caddy, like when your eyes look up at a stick balanced on your nose. She had to look down to see Caddy, but her eyes looked like that, like when you are balancing a stick.

"I won't listen to it," Jason said. "I'll bang on the door."

"It's a good one," Nancy said. "It's better than the other one."

"What's it about?" Caddy said. Nancy was standing by the lamp. Her hand was on the lamp, against the light, long and brown.

"Your hand is on that hot globe," Caddy said. "Don't it feel hot to your hand?"

Nancy looked at her hand on the lamp chimney. She took her hand away, slow. She stood there, looking at Caddy, wringing her long hand as though it were tied to her wrist with a string.

"Let's do something else," Caddy said.

"I want to go home," Jason said.

"I got some popcorn," Nancy said. She looked at Caddy and then at Jason and then at me and then at Caddy again. "I got some popcorn."

"I don't like popcorn," Jason said. "I'd rather have candy."

Nancy looked at Jason. "You can hold the popper." She was still wringing her hand; it was long and limp and brown.

"All right," Jason said. "I'll stay a while if I can do that. Caddy can't hold it. I'll want to go home again if Caddy holds the popper."

Nancy built up the fire. "Look at Nancy putting her hands in the fire," Caddy said. "What's the matter with you, Nancy?"

"I got popcorn," Nancy said. "I got some." She took the popper from under the bed. It was broken. Jason began to cry.

"Now we can't have any popcorn," he said.

"We ought to go home anyway," Caddy said. "Come on, Quentin."

"Wait," Nancy said; "wait. I can fix it. Don't you want to help me fix it?"

"I don't think I want any," Caddy said. "It's too late now."

"You help me, Jason," Nancy said. "Don't you want to help me?"

"No," Jason said. "I want to go home."

"Hush," Nancy said; "hush. Watch. Watch me. I can fix it so Jason can hold it and pop the corn." She got a piece of wire and fixed the popper.

"It won't hold good," Caddy said.

"Yes it will," Nancy said. "Yawl watch. Yawl help me shell some corn."

The popcorn was under the bed too. We shelled it into the popper and Nancy helped Jason hold the popper over the fire.

"It's not popping," Jason said. "I want to go home."

"You wait," Nancy said. "It'll begin to pop. We'll have fun then."

She was sitting close to the fire. The lamp was turned up so high it was beginning to smoke. "Why don't you turn it down some?" I said.

"It's all right," Nancy said. "I'll clean it. Yawl wait. The popcorn will start in a minute."

"I don't believe it's going to start," Caddy said. "We ought to start home, anyway. They'll be worried."

"No," Nancy said. "It's going to pop. Dilsey will tell um yawl with me. I been working for yawl long time. They won't mind if yawl at my house. You wait, now. It'll start popping any minute now."

Then Jason got some smoke in his eyes and he began to cry. He dropped the popper into the fire. Nancy got a wet rag and wiped Jason's face, but he didn't stop crying.

"Hush," she said. "Hush." He didn't hush. Caddy took the popper out of the fire.

"It's burned up," she said. "You'll have to get some more popcorn, Nancy."

"Did you put all of it in?" Nancy said.

"Yes," Caddy said. Nancy looked at Caddy. Then she took the popper and opened it and poured the cinders into her apron and began to sort the grains, her hands long and brown, and we watched her.

"Haven't you got any more?" Caddy said.

"Yes," Nancy said; "yes. Look. This here ain't burnt. All we need to do is—"

"I want to go home," Jason said. "I'm going to tell."

"Hush," Caddy said. We all listened. Nancy's head was already turned toward the door, her eyes filled with red lamplight. "Somebody is coming," Caddy said.

Then Nancy began to make that sound again, not loud, sitting there above the fire, her long hands dangling between her knees; all of a sudden water began to come out on her face in big drops, running down her face, carrying in each one a little turning ball of firelight like a spark until it dropped off her chin. "She's not crying," I said.

"I ain't crying," Nancy said. Her eyes were closed. "I ain't crying. Who is it?"

"I don't know," Caddy said. She went to the door and looked out. "We've got to go now," she said. "Here comes Father."

"I'm going to tell," Jason said. "Yawl made me come."

The water still ran down Nancy's face. She turned in her chair. "Listen. Tell him. Tell him we going to have fun. Tell him I take good care of yawl until in the morning. Tell him to let me come home with yawl and sleep on the floor. Tell him I won't need no pallet. We'll have fun. You member last time how we had so much fun?"

"I didn't have fun," Jason said. "You hurt me. You put smoke in my eyes. I'm going to tell."

5

Father came in. He looked at us. Nancy did not get up.

"Tell him," she said.

"Caddy made us come down here," Jason said. "I didn't want to."

Father came to the fire. Nancy looked up at him. "Can't you go to Aunt Rachel's and stay?" he said. Nancy looked up at Father, her hands between her knees. "He's not here," Father said. "I would have seen him. There's not a soul in sight."

"He in the ditch," Nancy said. "He waiting in the ditch yonder."

"Nonsense," Father said. He looked at Nancy. "Do you know he's there?"

"I got the sign," Nancy said.

"What sign?"

"I got it. It was on the table when I came in. It was a hog-bone, with blood meat still on it, laying by the lamp. He's out there. When yawl walk out that door, I gone."

"Gone where, Nancy?" Caddy said.

"I'm not a tattletale," Jason said.

"Nonsense," Father said.

"He out there," Nancy said. "He looking through that window this minute, waiting for yawl to go. Then I gone."

"Nonsense," Father said. "Lock up your house and we'll take you on to Aunt Rachel's."

" 'Twon't do no good," Nancy said. She didn't look at Father now, but he looked down at her, at her long limp, moving hands. "Putting it off won't do no good."

"Then what do you want to do?" Father said.

"I don't know," Nancy said. "I can't do nothing. Just put it off. And that don't do no good. I reckon it belong to me. I reckon what I going to get ain't no more than mine."

"Get what?" Caddy said. "What's yours?"

"Nothing," Father said. "You all must get to bed."

"Caddy made me come," Jason said.

"Go on to Aunt Rachel's," Father said.

"It won't do no good." Nancy said. She sat down before the fire, her elbows on her knees, her long hands between her knees. "When even your own kitchen wouldn't do no good. When even if I was sleeping on the floor in the room with your chillen, and the next morning there I am, and blood—"

"Hush," Father said. "Lock your door and put out the lamp and go to bed."

"I scaired of the dark," Nancy said. "I scaired for it to happen in the dark."

"You mean you're going to sit right here with the lamp lighted?" Father said. Then Nancy began to make the sound again, sitting before the fire, her long hands between her knees. "Ah, damnation," Father said. "Come along, chillen. It's past bedtime."

"When yawl go home, I gone," Nancy said. She talked quieter now, and her face looked quiet, like her hands. "Anyway, I got my coffin money saved up with Mr. Lovelady." Mr. Lovelady was a short, dirty man who collected the Negro insurance, coming around to the cabins or the kitchens every Saturday morning, to collect fifteen cents. He and his wife lived at the hotel. One morning his wife committed suicide. They had a child, a little girl. He and the child went away. After a week or two he came back alone. We would see him going along the lanes and the back streets on Saturday mornings.

"Nonsense," Father said. "You'll be the first thing I'll see in the kitchen tomorrow morning."

"You'll see what you'll see, I reckon," Nancy said. "But it will take the Lord to say what that will be."

6

We left her sitting before the fire.

"Come and put the bar up," Father said. But she didn't move. She didn't look at us again, sitting quietly there between the lamp and the fire. From some distance down the lane we could look back and see her through the open door.

"What, Father?" Caddy said. "What's going to happen?"

"Nothing," Father said. Jason was on Father's back, so Jason was the tallest of all of us. We went down into the ditch. I looked at it, quiet. I couldn't see much where the moonlight and the shadows tangled.

"If Jesus *is* hid here, he can see us, can't he?" Caddy said.

"He's not there," Father said. "He went away a long time ago."

"You made me come," Jason said, high; against the sky it looked like Father had two heads, a little one and a big one. "I didn't want to."

We went up out of the ditch. We could still see Nancy's house and the open door, but we couldn't see Nancy now, sitting before the fire with the door open, because she was tired. "I just done got tired," she said. "I just a nigger. It ain't no fault of mine."

But we could hear her, because she began just after we came up out of the ditch, the sound that was not singing and not unsinging. "Who will do our washing now, Father?" I said.

"I'm not a nigger," Jason said, high and close above Father's head.

"You're worse," Caddy said, "you are a tattletale. If something was to jump out, you'd be scairder than a nigger."

"I wouldn't," Jason said.

"You'd cry," Caddy said.

"Caddy," Father said.

"I wouldn't!" Jason said.

"Scairy cat," Caddy said.

"Candace!" Father said.

QUESTIONS

1. Who is the protagonist of this story? Characterize her fully. Is she a round or flat character? How does she differ from the typical protagonist of a commercial story?

2. The central conflict in this story is man versus man and is partly physical, the favorite kind of conflict of the writers of pulp fiction. But in this story the conflict is not resolved. The story ends without our knowing whether Jesus ever killed Nancy or not. Why? What is the real subject of the story?

3. Is Faulkner primarily interested in presenting Nancy's terror or in producing terror in the reader? Is he interested in terror for its own sake, or is he interested also in exploring the human causes of the terror?

4. Why is Jesus angry with Nancy? Is Jesus the villain of the story? Is Mr. Stovall? Explore the causes of the central situation, taking into account: (a) Jesus' speech about his house and the white man's house, (b) Nancy's attitude toward her sin, (c) Father's advice to Nancy and his treatment of Jesus, (d) the jailer's treatment of Nancy, (e) Mother's attitude toward Negroes, (f) the attitudes of Caddy and Jason toward Negroes.

5. The story explores the relationships between two worlds—the black and the

white—and also the relationships within each. In reference to the latter, describe the following relationships: (a) Jesus and Nancy, (b) Father and Mother, (c) Caddy and Jason. Does each of these involve a conflict? Is fright confined to the first?

6. How is Nancy's terror *dramatized?* How rational or irrational is it?
7. Explain the title.
8. This story is given an unusual twist because an adult problem is seen through the eyes of children. How much do the three children understand of what is going on? What advantages does this point of view have?
9. Compare this story with "The Storm" as a study in human terror. What are the most significant differences?

James Thurber

THE CATBIRD SEAT

Mr. Martin bought the pack of Camels on Monday night in the most crowded cigar store on Broadway. It was theater time and seven or eight men were buying cigarettes. The clerk didn't even glance at Mr. Martin, who put the pack in his overcoat pocket and went out. If any of the staff at F & S had seen him buy the cigarettes, they would have been astonished, for it was generally known that Mr. Martin did not smoke, and never had. No one saw him.

It was just a week to the day since Mr. Martin had decided to rub out Mrs. Ulgine Barrows. The term "rub out" pleased him because it suggested nothing more than the correction of an error—in this case an error of Mr. Fitweiler. Mr. Martin had spent each night of the past week working out his plan and examining it. As he walked home now he went over it again. For the hundredth time he resented the element of imprecision, the margin of guesswork that entered into the business. The project as he had worked it out was casual and bold, the risks were considerable. Something might go wrong anywhere along the line. And therein lay the cunning of his scheme. No one would ever see in it the cautious, painstaking hand of Erwin Martin, head of the filing department at F & S of whom Mr. Fitweiler had once said, "Man is fallible but Martin isn't." No one would see his hand, that is, unless it were caught in the act.

Sitting in his apartment, drinking a glass of milk, Mr. Martin reviewed his case against Mrs. Ulgine Barrows, as he had every night for seven nights. He began at the beginning. Her quacking voice and braying laugh had first

THE CATBIRD SEAT   First published in 1942 in *The New Yorker*. At that time the "Dodgers" were located in Brooklyn, and Red Barber, originally from Mississippi, was the beloved announcer over the radio for all the Dodgers' games. James Thurber (1894–1961), cartoonist and writer, was born and grew up in Columbus, Ohio. In 1925, after a year's sojourn in France, he joined the staff of *The New Yorker*, with which he was associated until his death.

profaned the halls of F & S on March 7, 1941 (Mr. Martin had a head for dates). Old Roberts, the personnel chief, had introduced her as the newly appointed special adviser to the president of the firm, Mr. Fitweiler. The woman had appalled Mr. Martin instantly, but he hadn't shown it. He had given her his dry hand, a look of studious concentration, and a faint smile. "Well," she had said, looking at the papers on his desk, "are you lifting the oxcart out of the ditch?" As Mr. Martin recalled the moment, over his milk, he squirmed slightly. He must keep his mind on her crimes as a special adviser, not on her peccadillos as a personality. This he found difficult to do, in spite of entering an objection and sustaining it. The faults of the woman as a woman kept chattering on in his mind like an unruly witness. She had, for almost two years now, baited him. In the halls, in the elevator, even in his own office, into which she romped now and then like a circus horse, she was constantly shouting these silly questions at him. "Are you lifting the oxcart out of the ditch? Are you tearing up the pea patch? Are you hollering down the rain barrel? Are you scraping around the bottom of the pickle barrel? Are you sitting in the catbird seat?"

It was Joey Hart, one of Mr. Martin's two assistants, who had explained what the gibberish meant. "She must be a Dodger fan," he had said. "Red Barber announces the Dodger games over the radio and he uses those expressions—picked 'em up down South." Joey had gone on to explain one or two. "Tearing up the pea patch" meant going on a rampage; "sitting in the catbird seat" meant sitting pretty, like a batter with three balls and no strikes on him. Mr. Martin dismissed all this with an effort. It had been annoying, it had driven him near to distraction, but he was too solid a man to be moved to murder by anything so childish. It was fortunate, he reflected as he passed on to the important charges against Mrs. Barrows, that he had stood up under it so well. He had maintained always an outward appearance of polite tolerance. "Why, I even believe you like the woman," Miss Paird, his other assistant, had once said to him. He had simply smiled.

A gavel rapped in Mr. Martin's mind and the case was resumed. Mrs. Ulgine Barrows stood charged with willful, blatant, and persistent attempts to destroy the efficiency and system of F & S. It was competent, material, and relevant to review her advent and rise to power. Mr. Martin had got the story from Miss Paird, who seemed always able to find things out. According to her, Mrs. Barrows had met Mr. Fitweiler at a party, where she had rescued him from the embraces of a powerfully built drunken man who had mistaken the president of F & S for a famous retired Middle Western football coach. She had led him to a sofa and somehow worked upon him a monstrous magic. The aging gentleman had jumped to the conclusion there and then that this was a woman of singular attainments, equipped to bring out the best in him and the firm. A week later he had introduced her into F & S as his special adviser. On that day confusion got its foot in the door. After Miss Tyson, Mr. Brundage and Mr. Bartlett had been fired and Mr. Munson had taken his hat and stalked out, mailing in his resignation later, old Roberts had been emboldened to speak to Mr. Fitweiler. He mentioned that Mr. Munson's depart-ment had been "a little disrupted" and hadn't they perhaps better resume the old system there? Mr. Fitweiler had said certainly not. He had the greatest faith in Mrs. Barrows' ideas. "They require a little seasoning, a little season-ing, is all," he had added. Mr. Roberts had given it up. Mr. Martin reviewed in detail all the changes wrought by Mrs. Barrows. She had begun chipping at the cornices of the firm's edifice and now she was swinging at the foundation with a pickaxe.

Mr. Martin came now, in his summing up, to the afternoon of Monday, November 2, 1942—just one week ago. On that day, at 3 P.M., Mrs. Barrows had bounced into his office. "Boo!" she had yelled. "Are you scraping around the bottom of the pickle barrel?" Mr. Martin had looked at her from under his green eyeshade, saying nothing. She had begun to wander about the office, taking it in with her great, popping eyes. "Do you really need *all* these filing cabinets?" she had demanded suddenly. Mr. Martin's heart had jumped. "Each of these files," he had said, keeping his voice even, "plays an indispen-sable part in the system of F & S." She had brayed at him, "Well, don't tear up the pea patch!" and gone to the door. From there she had bawled, "But you sure have got a lot of fine scrap in here!" Mr. Martin could no longer doubt that the finger was on his beloved department. Her pickaxe was on the upswing, poised for the first blow. It had not come yet; he had received no blue memo from the enchanted Mr. Fitweiler bearing nonsensical instruc-tions deriving from the obscene woman. But there was no doubt in Mr. Martin's mind that one would be forthcoming. He must act quickly. Already a precious week had gone by. Mr. Martin stood up in his living room, still holding his milk glass. "Gentlemen of the jury," he said to himself, "I de-mand the death penalty for this horrible person."

The next day Mr. Martin followed his routine, as usual. He polished his glasses more often and once sharpened an already sharp pencil, but not even Miss Paird noticed. Only once did he catch sight of his victim; she swept past him in the hall with a patronizing "Hi!" At five-thirty he walked home, as usual, and had a glass of milk, as usual. He had never drunk anything stronger in his life—unless you could count ginger ale. The late Sam Schlosser, the S of F & S, had praised Mr. Martin at a staff meeting several years before for his temperate habits. "Our most efficient worker neither drinks nor smokes," he had said. "The results speak for themselves." Mr. Fitweiler had sat by, nodding approval.

Mr. Martin was still thinking about that red-letter day as he walked over to the Schrafft's on Fifth Avenue near Forty-sixth Street. He got there, as he always did, at eight o'clock. He finished his dinner and the financial page of the *Sun* at a quarter to nine, as he always did. It was his custom after dinner to take a walk. This time he walked down Fifth Avenue at a casual pace. His gloved hands felt moist and warm, his forehead cold. He transferred the Camels from his overcoat to a jacket pocket. He wondered, as he did so, if they did not represent an unnecessary note of strain. Mrs. Barrows smoked only Luckies. It was his idea to puff a few puffs on a Camel (after the rubbing-out), stub it out in the ashtray holding her lipstick-stained Luckies, and thus drag a small red herring across the trail. Perhaps it was not a good idea. It would take time. He might even choke, too loudly.

Mr. Martin had never seen the house on West Twelfth Street where Mrs. Barrows lived, but he had a clear enough picture of it. Fortunately, she had bragged to everybody about her ducky first-floor apartment in the perfectly darling three-story red-brick. There would be no doorman or other attendants; just the tenants of the second and third floors. As he walked along, Mr. Martin realized that he would get there before nine-thirty. He had considered walking north on Fifth Avenue from Schrafft's to a point from which it would take him until ten o'clock to reach the house. At that hour people were less likely to be coming in or going out. But the procedure would have made an awkward loop in the straight thread of his casualness, and he had abandoned it. It was impossible to figure when people would be entering or leaving the house, anyway. There was a great risk at any hour. If he ran into anybody, he would simply have to place the rubbing-out of Ulgine Barrows in the inactive file forever. The same thing would hold true if there were someone in her apartment. In that case he would just say that he had been passing by, recognized her charming house, and thought to drop in.

It was eighteen minutes after nine when Mr. Martin turned into Twelfth Street. A man passed him, and a man and a woman, talking. There was no one within fifty paces when he came to the house, halfway down the block. He was up the steps and in the small vestibule in no time, pressing the bell under the card that said "Mrs. Ulgine Barrows." When the clicking in the lock started he jumped forward against the door. He got inside fast, closing the door behind him. A bulb in a lantern hung from the hall ceiling on a chain seemed to give a monstrously bright light. There was nobody on the stair, which went up ahead of him along the left wall. A door opened down the hall in the wall on the right. He went toward it swiftly, on tiptoe.

"Well, for God's sake, look who's here!" bawled Mrs. Barrows, and her braying laugh rang out like the report of a shotgun. He rushed past her like a football tackle, bumping her. "Hey, quit shoving!" she said, closing the door behind them. They were in her living room, which seemed to Mr. Martin to be lighted by a hundred lamps. "What's after you?" she said. "You're as jumpy as a goat." He found he was unable to speak. His heart was wheezing in his throat. "I—yes," he finally brought out. She was jabbering and laughing as she started to help him off with his coat. "No, no," he said. "I'll put it here." He took it off and put it on a chair near the door. "Your hat and gloves, too," she said. "You're in a lady's house." He put his hat on top of the coat. Mrs. Barrows seemed larger than he had thought. He kept his gloves on. "I was passing by," he said. "I recognized—is there anyone here?" She laughed louder than ever. "No," she said, "we're all alone. You're as white as a sheet, you funny man. Whatever *has* come over you? I'll mix you a toddy." She started toward a door across the room. "Scotch-and-soda be all right? But say, you don't drink, do you?" She turned and gave him her amused look. Mr. Martin pulled himself together. "Scotch-and-soda will be all right," he heard himself say. He could hear her laughing in the kitchen.

Mr. Martin looked quickly around the living room for the weapon. He had counted on finding one there. There were andirons and a poker and something in a corner that looked like an Indian club. None of them would do. It couldn't be that way. He began to pace around. He came to a desk. On it lay a metal paper knife with an ornate handle. Would it be sharp enough? He reached for it and knocked over a small brass jar. Stamps spilled out of it and it fell to the floor with a clatter. "Hey," Mrs. Barrows yelled from the kitchen, "are you tearing up the pea patch?" Mr. Martin gave a strange laugh. Picking up the knife, he tried its point against his left wrist. It was blunt. It wouldn't do.

When Mrs. Barrows reappeared, carrying two highballs, Mr. Martin, standing there with his gloves on, became acutely conscious of the fantasy he had wrought. Cigarettes in his pocket, a drink prepared for him—it was all too grossly improbable. It was more than that; it was impossible. Somewhere in the back of his mind a vague idea stirred, sprouted. "For heaven's sake, take off those gloves," said Mrs. Barrows. "I always wear them in the house," said Mr. Martin. The idea began to bloom, strange and wonderful. She put the glasses on a coffee table in front of a sofa and sat on the sofa. "Come over here, you odd little man," she said. Mr. Martin went over and sat beside her. It was difficult getting a cigarette out of the pack of Camels, but he managed it. She held a match for him, laughing. "Well," she said, handing him his drink, "this is perfectly marvelous. You with a drink and a cigarette."

Mr. Martin puffed, not too awkwardly, and took a gulp of the highball. "I drink and smoke all the time," he said. He clinked his glass against hers. "Here's nuts to that old windbag, Fitweiler," he said, and gulped again. The stuff tasted awful, but he made no grimace. "Really, Mr. Martin," she said, her voice and posture changing, "you are insulting our employer." Mrs. Barrows was now all special adviser to the president. "I am preparing a bomb," said Mr. Martin, "which will blow the old goat higher than hell." He had only had a little of the drink, which was not strong. It couldn't be that. "Do you take dope or something?" Mrs. Barrows asked coldly. "Heroin," said Mr. Martin. "I'll be coked to the gills when I bump the old buzzard off." "Mr. Martin!" she shouted, getting to her feet. "That will be all of that. You must go at once." Mr. Martin took another swallow of his drink. He tapped his cigarette out in the ashtray and put the pack of Camels on the coffee table. Then he got up. She stood glaring at him. He walked over and put on his hat and coat. "Not a word about this," he said, and laid an index finger against his lips. All Mrs. Barrows could bring out was "Really!" Mr. Martin put his hand on the doorknob. "I'm sitting in the catbird seat," he said. He stuck his tongue out at her and left. Nobody saw him go.

Mr. Martin got to his apartment, walking, well before eleven. No one saw him go in. He had two glasses of milk after brushing his teeth, and he felt elated. It wasn't tipsiness, because he hadn't been tipsy. Anyway, the walk had worn off all effects of the whiskey. He got in bed and read a magazine for a while. He was asleep before midnight.

Mr. Martin got to the office at eight-thirty the next morning, as usual. At a quarter to nine, Ulgine Barrows, who had never before arrived at work before ten, swept into his office. "I'm reporting to Mr. Fitweiler now!" she shouted. "If he turns you over to the police, it's no more than you deserve!" Mr. Martin gave her a look of shocked surprise. "I beg your pardon?" he said. Mrs. Barrows snorted and bounced out of the room, leaving Miss Paird and Joey Hart staring after her. "What's the matter with that old devil now?" asked Miss Paird. "I have no idea," said Mr. Martin, resuming his work. The other two looked at him and then at each other. Miss Paird got up and went out. She walked slowly past the closed door of Mr. Fitweiler's office. Mrs. Barrows was yelling inside, but she was not braying. Miss Paird could not hear what the woman was saying. She went back to her desk.

Forty-five minutes later, Mrs. Barrows left the president's office and went into her own, shutting the door. It wasn't until half an hour later that Mr. Fitweiler sent for Mr. Martin. The head of the filing department, neat, quiet, attentive, stood in front of the old man's desk. Mr. Fitweiler was pale and nervous. He took his glasses off and twiddled them. He made a small, bruffing sound in his throat. "Martin," he said, "you have been with us more than twenty years." "Twenty-two, sir," said Mr. Martin. "In that time," pursued the president, "your work and your—uh—manner have been exemplary." "I trust so, sir," said Mr. Martin. "I have understood, Martin," said Mr. Fitweiler, "that you have never taken a drink or smoked." "That is correct, sir," said Mr. Martin. "Ah, yes." Mr. Fitweiler polished his glasses. "You may describe what you did after leaving the office yesterday, Martin," he said. Mr. Martin allowed less than a second for his bewildered pause. "Certainly, sir," he said. "I walked home. Then I went to Schrafft's for dinner. Afterward I walked home again. I went to bed early, sir, and read a magazine for a while. I was asleep before eleven." "Ah, yes," said Mr. Fitweiler again. He was silent for a moment, searching for the proper words to say to the head of the filing department. "Mrs. Barrows," he said finally, "Mrs. Barrows has worked hard, Martin, very hard. It grieves me to report that she has suffered a severe breakdown. It has taken the form of a persecution complex accompanied by distressing hallucinations." "I am very sorry, sir," said Mr. Martin. "Mrs. Barrows is under the delusion," continued Mr. Fitweiler, "that you visited her last evening and behaved yourself in an—uh—unseemly manner." He raised his hand to silence Mr. Martin's little pained outcry. "It is the nature of these psychological diseases," Mr. Fitweiler said, "to fix upon the least likely and most innocent party as the—uh—source of persecution. These matters are not for the lay mind to grasp, Martin. I've just had my psychiatrist, Dr. Fitch, on the phone. He would not, of course, commit himself, but he made enough generalizations to substantiate my suspicions. I suggested to Mrs. Barrows, when she had completed her—uh—story to me this morning, that she visit Dr. Fitch, for I suspected a condition at once. She flew, I regret to say, into a rage, and demanded—uh—requested that I call you on the carpet. You may not know, Martin, but Mrs. Barrows had planned a reorganization of your department—subject to my approval, of course, subject to my approval. This brought you, rather than anyone else, to her mind—but again that is a phenomenon for Dr. Fitch and not for us. So, Martin, I am afraid Mrs. Barrows' usefulness here is at an end." "I am dreadfully sorry, sir," said Mr. Martin.

It was at this point that the door to the office blew open with the suddenness of a gas-main explosion and Mrs. Barrows catapulted through it. "Is the little rat denying it?" she screamed. "He can't get away with that!" Mr. Martin got up and moved discreetly to a point beside Mr. Fitweiler's chair. "You drank and smoked at my apartment," she bawled at Mr. Martin, "and you know it! You called Mr. Fitweiler an old windbag and said you were going to blow him up when you got coked to the gills on your heroin!" She stopped yelling to catch her breath and a new glint came into her popping eyes. "If you weren't such a drab, ordinary little man," she said, "I'd think you'd planned it all. Sticking your tongue out, saying you were sitting in the catbird seat, because you thought no one would believe me when I told it! My God, it's really too perfect!" She brayed loudly and hysterically, and the fury was on her again. She glared at Mr. Fitweiler. "Can't you see how he has tricked us, you old fool? Can't you see his little game?" But Mr. Fitweiler had been surreptitiously pressing all the buttons under the top of his desk and employees of F & S began pouring into the room. "Stockton," said Mr. Fitweiler, "you and Fishbein will take Mrs. Barrows to her home. Mrs. Powell, you will go with them." Stockton, who had played a little football in high school, blocked Mrs. Barrows as she made for Mr. Martin. It took him and Fishbein together to force her out of the door into the hall, crowded with stenographers and office boys. She was still screaming imprecations at Mr. Martin, tangled and contradictory imprecations. The hubbub finally died out down the corridor.

"I regret that this has happened," said Mr. Fitweiler. "I shall ask you to dismiss it from your mind, Martin." "Yes sir," said Mr. Martin, anticipating his chief's "That will be all" by moving to the door. "I will dismiss it." He went out and shut the door, and his step was light and quick in the hall. When he entered his department he had slowed down to his customary gait, and he walked quietly across the room to the W20 file, wearing a look of studious concentration.

QUESTIONS

1. How is suspense aroused and maintained in the story? What is the story's principal surprise?
2. Through whose consciousness are the events of the story chiefly seen? Are

there any departures from this strictly limited point of view? Where in the
story are we taken most fully into Mr. Martin's mind? For what purpose?
3. At what point in the story do Mr. Martin's plans change? What happens to
the point of view at this point? What does Thurber's handling of the point of
view here tell us about the seriousness of the story's purpose?
4. Characterize Mr. Martin and Mrs. Barrows respectively. In what ways are
they character foils?
5. Analyze the story in terms of its conflicts. What kinds of conflict are involved?
Is there any internal conflict? What kind of conflict that *might* be expected in
a murder story is missing?
6. Evaluate the surprise ending of the story by the criteria suggested on page 45.
7. What insights into the life of a business office does the story provide? What
kind of insight does the story not provide? What is the story's greatest improbability?
8. What are the main sources of the story's humor?
9. Why does Thurber choose this particular expression of Mrs. Barrows' for his
title rather than one of her others?

Frank O'Connor

THE DRUNKARD

It was a terrible blow to Father when Mr. Dooley on the terrace died. Mr.
Dooley was a commercial traveler with two sons in the Dominicans and a car
of his own, so socially he was miles ahead of us, but he had no false pride. Mr.
Dooley was an intellectual, and, like all intellectuals, the thing he loved best
was conversation, and in his own limited way Father was a well-read man and
could appreciate an intelligent talker. Mr. Dooley was remarkably intelligent.
Between business acquaintances and clerical contacts, there was very little he
didn't know about what went on in town, and evening after evening he
crossed the road to our gate to explain to Father the news behind the news.
He had a low, palavering voice and a knowing smile, and Father would listen
in astonishment, giving him a conversational lead now and again, and then
stump triumphantly in to Mother with his face aglow and ask: "Do you know
what Mr. Dooley is after telling me?" Ever since, when somebody has given
me some bit of information off the record I have found myself on the point of
asking: "Was it Mr. Dooley told you that?"

Till I actually saw him laid out in his brown shroud with the rosary beads
entwined between his waxy fingers I did not take the report of his death
seriously. Even then I felt there must be a catch and that some summer

THE DRUNKARD   First published in 1948. Frank O'Connor (1903–1966) was born Michael
O'Donovan, the only child of very poor, Roman Catholic parents in Cork, Ireland. He used
his mother's maiden name as a pseudonym when he began to publish. "The Drunkard" is
based on an incident from his boyhood in Cork, as revealed in the first two chapters of his
autobiographical volume, *An Only Son* (1961).

evening Mr. Dooley must reappear at our gate to give us the lowdown on the next world. But Father was very upset, partly because Mr. Dooley was about one age with himself, a thing that always gives a distinctly personal turn to another man's demise; partly because now he would have no one to tell him what dirty work was behind the latest scene at the Corporation.° You could count on your fingers the number of men in Blarney Lane who read the papers as Mr. Dooley did, and none of these would have overlooked the fact that Father was only a laboring man. Even Sullivan, the carpenter, a mere nobody, thought he was a cut above Father. It was certainly a solemn event.

"Half past two to the Curragh," Father said meditatively, putting down the paper.

"But you're not thinking of going to the funeral?" Mother asked in alarm.

" 'Twould be expected," Father said, scenting opposition. "I wouldn't give it to say to them."

"I think," said Mother with suppressed emotion, "it will be as much as anyone will expect if you go to the chapel with him."

("Going to the chapel," of course, was one thing, because the body was removed after work, but going to a funeral meant the loss of a half-day's pay.)

"The people hardly know us," she added.

"God between us and all harm," Father replied with dignity, "we'd be glad if it was our own turn."

To give Father his due, he was always ready to lose a half day for the sake of an old neighbor. It wasn't so much that he liked funerals as that he was a conscientious man who did as he would be done by, and nothing could have consoled him so much for the prospect of his own death as the assurance of a worthy funeral. And, to give Mother her due, it wasn't the half-day's pay she begrudged, badly as we could afford it.

Drink, you see, was Father's great weakness. He could keep steady for months, even for years, at a stretch, and while he did he was as good as gold. He was first up in the morning and brought the mother a cup of tea in bed, stayed home in the evenings and read the paper; saved money and bought himself a new blue serge suit and bowler hat. He laughed at the folly of men who, week in, week out, left their hard-earned money with the publicans; and sometimes, to pass an idle hour, he took pencil and paper and calculated precisely how much he saved each week through being a teetotaller. Being a natural optimist he sometimes continued this calculation through the whole span of his prospective existence and the total was breathtaking. He would die worth hundreds.

If I had only known it, this was a bad sign; a sign he was becoming stuffed up with spiritual pride and imagining himself better than his neighbors. Sooner or later, the spiritual pride grew till it called for some form of celebration. Then he took a drink—not whisky, of course; nothing like that—just a glass of some harmless drink like lager beer. That was the end of Father. By the time he had taken the first he already realized that he had made a fool of

Corporation: the officials of the city (mayor, aldermen, councillors)

himself, took a second to forget it and a third to forget that he couldn't forget, and at last came home reeling drunk. From this on it was "The Drunkard's Progress," as in the moral prints. Next day he stayed in from work with a sick head while Mother went off to make his excuses at the works, and inside a fortnight he was poor and savage and despondent again. Once he began he drank steadily through everything down to the kitchen clock. Mother and I knew all the phases and dreaded all the dangers. Funerals were one.

"I have to go to Dunphy's to do a half-day's work," said Mother in distress. "Who's to look after Larry?"

"I'll look after Larry," Father said graciously. "The little walk will do him good."

There was no more to be said, though we all knew I didn't need anyone to look after me, and that I could quite well have stayed home and looked after Sonny, but I was being attached to the party to act as a brake on Father. As a brake I had never achieved anything, but Mother still had great faith in me.

Next day, when I got home from school, Father was there before me and made a cup of tea for both of us. He was very good at tea, but too heavy in the hand for anything else; the way he cut bread was shocking. Afterwards, we went down the hill to the church, Father wearing his best blue serge and a bowler cocked to one side of his head with the least suggestion of the masher. To his great joy he discovered Peter Crowley among the mourners. Peter was another danger signal, as I knew well from certain experiences after Mass on Sunday morning: a mean man, as Mother said, who only went to funerals for the free drinks he could get at them. It turned out that he hadn't even known Mr. Dooley! But Father had a sort of contemptuous regard for him as one of the foolish people who wasted their good money in public-houses when they could be saving it. Very little of his own money Peter Crowley wasted!

It was an excellent funeral from Father's point of view. He had it all well studied before we set off after the hearse in the afternoon sunlight.

"Five carriages!" he exclaimed. "Five carriages and sixteen covered cars! There's one alderman, two councillors and 'tis unknown how many priests. I didn't see a funeral like this from the road since Willie Mack, the publican, died."

"Ah, he was well liked," said Crowley in his husky voice.

"My goodness, don't I know that?" snapped Father. "Wasn't the man my best friend? Two nights before he died—only two nights—he was over telling me the goings-on about the housing contract. Them fellows in the Corporation are night and day robbers. But even I never imagined he was as well connected as that."

Father was stepping out like a boy, pleased with everything: the other mourners, and the fine houses along Sunday's Well. I knew the danger signals were there in full force: a sunny day, a fine funeral, and a distinguished company of clerics and public men were bringing out all the natural vanity and flightiness of Father's character. It was with something like genuine pleasure that he saw his old friend lowered into the grave; with the sense of having performed a duty and the pleasant awareness that however much he would miss poor Mr. Dooley in the long summer evenings, it was he and not poor Mr. Dooley who would do the missing.

"We'll be making tracks before they break up," he whispered to Crowley as the gravediggers tossed in the first shovelfuls of clay, and away he went, hopping like a goat from grassy hump to hump. The drivers, who were probably in the same state as himself, though without months of abstinence to put an edge on it, looked up hopefully.

"Are they nearly finished, Mick?" bawled one.

"All over now bar the last prayers," trumpeted Father in the tone of one who brings news of great rejoicing.

The carriages passed us in a lather of dust several hundred yards from the public-house, and Father, whose feet gave him trouble in hot weather, quickened his pace, looking nervously over his shoulder for any sign of the main body of mourners crossing the hill. In a crowd like that a man might be kept waiting.

When we did reach the pub the carriages were drawn up outside, and solemn men in black ties were cautiously bringing out consolation to mysterious females whose hands reached out modestly from behind the drawn blinds of the coaches. Inside the pub there were only the drivers and a couple of shawly women. I felt if I was to act as a brake at all, this was the time, so I pulled Father by the coattails.

"Dadda, can't we go home now?" I asked.

"Two minutes now," he said, beaming affectionately. "Just a bottle of lemonade and we'll go home."

This was a bribe, and I knew it, but I was always a child of weak character. Father ordered lemonade and two pints. I was thirsty and swallowed my drink at once. But that wasn't Father's way. He had long months of abstinence behind him and an eternity of pleasure before. He took out his pipe, blew through it, filled it, and then lit it with loud pops, his eyes bulging above it. After that he deliberately turned his back on the pint, leaned one elbow on the counter in the attitude of a man who did not know there was a pint behind him, and deliberately brushed the tobacco from his palms. He had settled down for the evening. He was steadily working through all the important funerals he had ever attended. The carriages departed and the minor mourners drifted in till the pub was half full.

"Dadda," I said, pulling his coat again, "can't we go home now?"

"Ah, your mother won't be in for a long time yet," he said benevolently enough. "Run out in the road and play, can't you."

It struck me very cool, the way grown-ups assumed that you could play all by yourself on a strange road. I began to get bored as I had so often been bored before. I knew Father was quite capable of lingering there till nightfall. I knew I might have to bring him home, blind drunk, down Blarney Lane, with all the old women at their doors, saying: "Mick Delaney is on it again." I knew that my mother would be half crazy with anxiety; that next day Father wouldn't go out to work; and before the end of the week she would be running down to the pawn with the clock under her shawl. I could never get over the lonesomeness of the kitchen without a clock.

I was still thirsty. I found if I stood on tiptoe I could just reach Father's glass, and the idea occurred to me that it would be interesting to know what the contents were like. He had his back to it and wouldn't notice. I took down the glass and sipped cautiously. It was a terrible disappointment. I was astonished that he could even drink such stuff. It looked as if he had never tried lemonade.

I should have advised him about lemonade but he was holding forth himself in great style. I heard him say that bands were a great addition to a funeral. He put his arms in the position of someone holding a rifle in reverse and hummed a few bars of Chopin's Funeral March. Crowley nodded reverently. I took a longer drink and began to see that porter might have its advantages. I felt pleasantly elevated and philosophic. Father hummed a few bars of the Dead March in *Saul*. It was a nice pub and a very fine funeral, and I felt sure that poor Mr. Dooley in Heaven must be highly gratified. At the same time I thought they might have given him a band. As Father said, bands were a great addition.

But the wonderful thing about porter was the way it made you stand aside, or rather float aloft like a cherub rolling on a cloud, and watch yourself with your legs crossed, leaning against a bar counter, not worrying about trifles but thinking deep, serious, grown-up thoughts about life and death. Looking at yourself like that, you couldn't help thinking after a while how funny you looked, and suddenly you got embarrassed and wanted to giggle. But by the time I had finished the pint, that phase too had passed; I found it hard to put back the glass, the counter seemed to have grown so high. Melancholia was supervening again.

"Well," Father said reverently, reaching behind him for his drink, "God rest the poor man's soul, wherever he is!" He stopped, looked first at the glass, and then at the people around him. "Hello," he said in a fairly good-humored tone, as if he were just prepared to consider it a joke, even if it was in bad taste, "who was at this?"

There was silence for a moment while the publican and the old women looked first at Father and then at his glass.

"There was no one at it, my good man," one of the women said with an offended air. "Is it robbers you think we are?"

"Ah, there's no one here would do a thing like that, Mick," said the publican in a shocked tone.

"Well, someone did it," said Father, his smile beginning to wear off.

"If they did, they were them that were nearer it," said the woman darkly, giving me a dirty look; and at the same moment the truth began to dawn on Father. I suppose I must have looked a bit starry-eyed. He bent and shook me.

"Are you all right, Larry?" he asked in alarm.

Peter Crowley looked down at me and grinned.

"Could you beat that?" he exclaimed in a husky voice.

I could and without difficulty. I started to get sick. Father jumped back in holy terror that I might spoil his good suit, and hastily opened the back door.

"Run! run! run!" he shouted.

I saw the sunlit wall outside with the ivy overhanging it, and ran. The intention was good but the performance was exaggerated, because I lurched right into the wall, hurting it badly, as it seemed to me. Being always very polite, I said "Pardon" before the second bout came on me. Father, still concerned for his suit, came up behind and cautiously held me while I got sick.

"That's a good boy!" he said encouragingly. "You'll be grand when you get that up."

Begor, I was not grand! Grand was the last thing I was. I gave one unmerciful wail out of me as he steered me back to the pub and put me sitting on the bench near the shawlies. They drew themselves up with an offended air, still sore at the suggestion that they had drunk his pint.

"God help us!" moaned one, looking pityingly at me. "Isn't it the likes of them would be fathers?"

"Mick," said the publican in alarm, spraying sawdust on my tracks, "that child isn't supposed to be in here at all. You'd better take him home quick in case a bobby would see him."

"Merciful God!" whimpered Father, raising his eyes to heaven and clapping his hands silently as he only did when distraught. "What misfortune was on me? Or what will his mother say? . . . If women might stop at home and look after their children themselves!" he added in a snarl for the benefit of the shawlies. "Are them carriages all gone, Bill?"

"The carriages are finished long ago, Mick," replied the publican.

"I'll take him home," Father said despairingly . . . "I'll never bring you out again," he threatened me. "Here," he added, giving me the clean handkerchief from his breast pocket, "put that over your eye."

The blood on the handkerchief was the first indication I got that I was cut, and instantly my temple began to throb and I set up another howl. "Whisht, whisht, whisht!" Father said testily, steering me out the door. "One'd think you were killed. That's nothing. We'll wash it when we get home."

"Steady now, old scout!" Crowley said, taking the other side of me. "You'll be all right in a minute."

I never met two men who knew less about the effects of drink. The first breath of fresh air and the warmth of the sun made me groggier than ever and I pitched and rolled between wind and tide till Father started to whimper again.

"God Almighty, and the whole road out! What misfortune was on me didn't stop at my work! Can't you walk straight?"

I couldn't. I saw plain enough that, coaxed by the sunlight, every woman old and young in Blarney Lane was leaning over her half-door or sitting on her doorstep. They all stopped gabbling to gape at the strange spectacle of two sober, middle-aged men bringing home a drunken small boy with a cut over his eye. Father, torn between the shamefast desire to get me home as quick as he could, and the neighborly need to explain that it wasn't his fault, finally halted outside Mrs. Roche's. There was a gang of old women outside a door at the opposite side of the road. I didn't like the look of them from the first. They seemed altogether too interested in me. I leaned against the wall of Mrs. Roche's cottage with my hands in my trousers pockets, thinking mournfully of poor Mr. Dooley in his cold grave on the Curragh, who would never walk down the road again, and, with great feeling, I began to sing a favorite song of Father's.

> Though lost to Mononia and cold in the grave
> He returns to Kincora no more.

"Wisha, the poor child!" Mrs. Roche said, "Haven't he a lovely voice, God bless him!"

That was what I thought myself, so I was the more surprised when Father said "Whisht!" and raised a threatening finger at me. He didn't seem to realize the appropriateness of the song, so I sang louder than ever.

"Whisht, I tell you!" he snapped, and then tried to work up a smile for Mrs. Roche's benefit. "We're nearly home now. I'll carry you the rest of the way."

But, drunk and all as I was, I knew better than to be carried home ignominiously like that.

"Now," I said severely, "can't you leave me alone? I can walk all right. 'Tis only my head. All I want is a rest."

"But you can rest at home in bed," he said viciously, trying to pick me up, and I knew by the flush on his face that he was very vexed.

"Ah, Jasus," I said crossly, "what do I want to go home for? Why the hell can't you leave me alone?"

For some reason the gang of old women at the other side of the road thought this very funny. They nearly split their sides over it. A gassy fury began to expand in me at the thought that a fellow couldn't have a drop taken without the whole neighborhood coming out to make game of him.

"Who are ye laughing at?" I shouted, clenching my fists at them. "I'll make ye laugh at the other side of yeer faces if ye don't let me pass."

They seemed to think this funnier still; I had never seen such ill-mannered people.

"Go away, ye bloody bitches!" I said.

"Whisht, whisht, whisht, I tell you!" snarled Father, abandoning all pretence of amusement and dragging me along behind him by the hand. I was maddened by the women's shrieks of laughter. I was maddened by Father's bullying. I tried to dig in my heels but he was too powerful for me, and I could only see the women by looking back over my shoulder.

"Take care or I'll come back and show ye!" I shouted. "I'll teach ye to let decent people pass. Fitter for ye to stop at home an wash yeer dirty faces."

" 'Twill be all over the road," whimpered Father. "Never again, never again, not if I live to be a thousand!"

To this day I don't know whether he was forswearing me or the drink. By way of a song suitable to my heroic mood I bawled "The Boys of Wexford," as he dragged me in home. Crowley, knowing he was not safe, made off and Father undressed me and put me to bed. I couldn't sleep because of the whirling in my head. It was very unpleasant, and I got sick again. Father came in with a wet cloth and mopped up after me. I lay in a fever, listening to him chopping sticks to start a fire. After that I heard him lay the table.

Suddenly the front door banged open and Mother stormed in with Sonny in her arms, not her usual gentle, timid self, but a wild, raging woman. It was clear that she had heard it all from the neighbors.

"Mick Delaney," she cried hysterically, "what did you do to my son?"

"Whisht, woman, whisht, whisht!" he hissed, dancing from one foot to the other. "Do you want the whole road to hear?"

"Ah," she said with a horrifying laugh, "the road knows all about it by this time. The road knows the way you filled your unfortunate innocent child with drink to make sport for you and that other rotten, filthy brute."

"But I gave him no drink," he shouted, aghast at the horrifying interpretation the neighbors had chosen to give his misfortune. "He took it while my back was turned. What the hell do you think I am?"

"Ah," she replied bitterly, "everyone knows what you are now. God forgive you, wasting our hard-earned few ha'pence on drink, and bringing up your child to be a drunken corner-boy like yourself."

Then she swept into the bedroom and threw herself on her knees by the bed. She moaned when she saw the gash over my eye. In the kitchen Sonny set up a loud bawl on his own, and a moment later Father appeared in the bedroom door with his cap over his eyes, wearing an expression of the most intense self-pity.

"That's a nice way to talk to me after all I went through," he whined. "That's a nice accusation, that I was drinking. Not one drop of drink crossed my lips the whole day. How could it when he drank it all? I'm the one that ought to be pitied, with my day ruined on me, and I after being made a show for the whole road."

But the next morning, when he got up and went out quietly to work with his dinner-basket, Mother threw herself on me in the bed and kissed me. It seemed it was all my doing, and I was being given a holiday till my eye got better.

"My brave little man!" she said with her eyes shining. "It was God did it you were there. You were his guardian angel."

1. What are the sources of humor in this story? Does the humor rise from observation of life or from distortion of life? What elements of the story seem to you funniest?
2. Is this a purely humorous story, or are there undertones of pathos in it? If the latter, from what does the pathos arise?
3. List what seem to you the chief insights into life and character presented by the story.
4. Is the title seriously meant? To whom does it refer?
5. The boy's drunkenness is seen from four points of view. What are they, and how do they differ?
6. What is the principal irony in the story?
7. The story is told in retrospect by a man recalling an incident from his boyhood. What does this removal in time do to the treatment of the material?
8. Which story—this one or "The Catbird Seat"—is more purely an interpretive story? Discuss.
9. *Did* Larry's father forswear liquor? Support your answer with evidence from the story.

Truman Capote

A CHRISTMAS MEMORY

Imagine a morning in late November. A coming of winter morning more than twenty years ago. Consider the kitchen of a spreading old house in a country town. A great black stove is its main feature; but there is also a big round table and a fireplace with two rocking chairs placed in front of it. Just today the fireplace commenced its seasonal roar.

A woman with shorn white hair is standing at the kitchen window. She is wearing tennis shoes and a shapeless gray sweater over a summery calico dress. She is small and sprightly, like a bantam hen; but, due to a long youthful illness, her shoulders are pitifully hunched. Her face is remarkable—not unlike Lincoln's, craggy like that, and tinted by sun and wind; but it is delicate too, finely boned, and her eyes are sherry-colored and timid. "Oh my," she exclaims, her breath smoking the windowpane, "it's fruitcake weather!"

The person to whom she is speaking is myself. I am seven; she is sixty-something. We are cousins, very distant ones, and we have lived together—

A CHRISTMAS MEMORY   First published in 1956. Truman Capote was born in 1924 in New Orleans. His parents divorced when he was four, and Capote lived until he was nine or ten with a family of distant and elderly cousins in the small town of Monroeville, Alabama. Miss Sook Faulk, the real-life distant cousin on whom this story is based, died in 1938 while Capote was a student in a military academy in New York State.

well, as long as I can remember. Other people inhabit the house, relatives; and though they have power over us, and frequently make us cry, we are not, on the whole, too much aware of them. We are each other's best friend. She calls me Buddy, in memory of a boy who was formerly her best friend. The other Buddy died in the 1880's, when she was still a child. She is still a child.

"I knew it before I got out of bed," she says, turning away from the window with a purposeful excitement in her eyes. "The courthouse bell sounded so cold and clear. And there were no birds singing; they've gone to warmer country, yes indeed. Oh, Buddy, stop stuffing biscuit and fetch our buggy. Help me find my hat. We've thirty cakes to bake."

It's always the same: a morning arrives in November, and my friend, as though officially inaugurating the Christmas time of year that exhilarates her imagination and fuels the blaze of her heart, announces: "It's fruitcake weather! Fetch our buggy. Help me find my hat."

The hat is found, a straw cartwheel corsaged with velvet roses out-of-doors has faded: it once belonged to a more fashionable relative. Together, we guide our buggy, a dilapidated baby carriage, out to the garden and into a grove of pecan trees. The buggy is mine; that is, it was bought for me when I was born. It is made of wicker, rather unraveled, and the wheels wobble like a drunkard's legs. But it is a faithful object; springtimes, we take it to the woods and fill it with flowers, herbs, wild fern for our porch pots; in the summer, we pile it with picnic paraphernalia and sugar-cane fishing poles and roll it down to the edge of a creek; it has its winter uses, too: as a truck for hauling firewood from the yard to the kitchen, as a warm bed for Queenie, our tough little orange and white rat terrier who has survived distemper and two rattle-snake bites. Queenie is trotting beside it now.

Three hours later we are back in the kitchen hulling a heaping buggyload of windfall pecans. Our backs hurt from gathering them: how hard they were to find (the main crop having been shaken off the trees and sold by the orchard's owners, who are not us) among the concealing leaves, the frosted, deceiving grass. Caarackle! A cheery crunch, scraps of miniature thunder sound as the shells collapse and the golden mound of sweet oily ivory meat mounts in the milk-glass bowl. Queenie begs to taste, and now and again my friend sneaks her a mite, though insisting we deprive ourselves. "We mustn't, Buddy. If we start, we won't stop. And there's scarcely enough as there is. For thirty cakes." The kitchen is growing dark. Dusk turns the window into a mirror: our reflections mingle with the rising moon as we work by the fireside in the firelight. At last, when the moon is quite high, we toss the final hull into the fire and, with joined sighs, watch it catch flame. The buggy is empty, the bowl is brimful.

We eat our supper (cold biscuits, bacon, blackberry jam) and discuss tomorrow. Tomorrow the kind of work I like best begins: buying. Cherries and citron, ginger and vanilla and canned Hawaiian pineapple, rinds and raisins and walnuts and whiskey and oh, so much flour, butter, so many eggs, spices, flavoring: why we'll need a pony to pull the buggy home.

But before these purchases can be made, there is the question of money. Neither of us has any. Except for skinflint sums persons in the house occasionally provide (a dime is considered very big money); or what we earn ourselves from various activities: holding rummage sales, selling buckets of hand-picked blackberries, jars of homemade jam and apple jelly and peach preserves, rounding up flowers for funerals and weddings. Once we won seventy-ninth prize, five dollars, in a national football contest. Not that we know a fool thing about football. It's just that we enter any contest we hear about: at the moment our hopes are centered on the fifty-thousand-dollar Grand Prize being offered to name a new brand of coffee (we suggest "A.M."; and, after some hesitation, for my friend thought it perhaps sacrilegious, the slogan "A.M.! Amen!"). To tell the truth, our only *really* profitable enterprise was the Fun and Freak Museum we conducted in a back-yard woodshed two summers ago. The Fun was a stereopticon with slide views of Washington and New York lent us by a relative who had been to those places (she was furious when she discovered why we'd borrowed it); the Freak was a three-legged biddy chicken hatched by one of our hens. Everybody hereabouts wanted to see that biddy: we charged grownups a nickel, kids two cents. And took in a good twenty dollars before the museum shut down due to the decease of the main attraction.

But one way and another we do each year accumulate Christmas savings, a Fruitcake Fund. These moneys we keep hidden in an ancient bead purse under a loose board under the floor under a chamber pot under my friend's bed. The purse is seldom removed from this safe location except to make a deposit, or, as happens every Saturday, a withdrawal; for on Saturdays I am allowed ten cents to go to the picture show. My friend has never been to a picture show, nor does she intend to: "I'd rather hear you tell the story, Buddy. That way I can imagine it more. Besides, a person my age shouldn't squander their eyes. When the Lord comes, let me see him clear." In addition to never having seen a movie, she has never: eaten in a restaurant, traveled more than five miles from home, received or sent a telegram, read anything except funny papers and the Bible, worn cosmetics, cursed, wished someone harm, told a lie on purpose, let a hungry dog go hungry. Here are a few things she has done, does do: killed with a hoe the biggest rattlesnake ever seen in this county (sixteen rattles), dip snuff (secretly), tame hummingbirds (just try it) till they balance on her finger, tell ghost stories (we both believe in ghosts) so tingling they chill you in July, talk to herself, take walks in the rain, grow the prettiest japonicas in town, know the recipe for every sort of old-time Indian cure, including a magical wart remover.

Now, with supper finished, we retire to the room in a faraway part of the house where my friend sleeps in a scrap-quilt-covered iron bed painted rose pink, her favorite color. Silently, wallowing in the pleasures of conspiracy, we take the bead purse from its secret place and spill its contents on the scrap quilt. Dollar bills, tightly rolled and green as May buds. Somber fifty-cent pieces, heavy enough to weight a dead man's eyes. Lovely dimes, the liveliest coin, the one that really jingles. Nickels and quarters, worn smooth as creek pebbles. But mostly a hateful heap of bitter-odored pennies. Last summer others in the house contracted to pay us a penny for every twenty-five flies we killed. Oh, the carnage of August: the flies that flew to heaven! Yet it was not work in which we took pride. And, as we sit counting pennies, it is as though we were back tabulating dead flies. Neither of us has a head for figures; we count slowly, lose track, start again. According to her calculation, we have $12.73. According to mine, exactly $13. "I do hope you're wrong, Buddy. We can't mess around with thirteen. The cakes will fall. Or put somebody in the cemetery. Why, I wouldn't dream of getting out of bed on the thirteenth." This is true: she always spends thirteenths in bed. So, to be on the safe side, we subtract a penny and toss it out the window.

Of the ingredients that go into our fruitcakes, whiskey is the most expensive, as well as the hardest to obtain: State laws forbid its sale. But everybody knows you can buy a bottle from Mr. Haha Jones. And the next day, having completed our more prosaic shopping, we set out for Mr. Haha's business address, a "sinful" (to quote public opinion) fish-fry and dancing café down by the river.We've been there before, and on the same errand; but in previous years our dealings have been with Haha's wife, an iodine-dark Indian woman with brazzy peroxided hair and a dead-tired disposition. Actually, we've never laid eyes on her husband, though we've heard that he's an Indian too. A giant with razor scars across his cheeks. They call him Haha because he's so gloomy, a man who never laughs. As we approach his café (a large log cabin festooned inside and out with chains of garish-gay naked lightbulbs and standing by the river's muddy edge under the shade of river trees where moss drifts through the branches like gray mist) our steps slow down. Even Queenie stops prancing and sticks close by. People have been murdered in Haha's café. Cut to pieces. Hit on the head. There's a case coming up in court next month. Naturally these goings-on happen at night when the colored lights cast crazy patterns and the victrola wails. In the daytime Haha's is shabby and deserted. I knock at the door, Queenie barks, my friend calls: "Mrs. Haha, ma'am? Anyone to home?"

Footsteps. The door opens. Our hearts overturn. It's Mr. Haha Jones himself! And he *is* a giant; he *does* have scars; he *doesn't* smile. No, he glowers at us through Satan-tilted eyes and demands to know: "What you want with Haha?"

For a moment we are too paralyzed to tell. Presently my friend half-finds her voice, a whispery voice at best: "If you please, Mr. Haha, we'd like a quart of your finest whiskey."

His eyes tilt more. Would you believe it? Haha is smiling! Laughing, too. "Which one of you is a drinkin' man?"

"It's for making fruitcakes, Mr. Haha. Cooking."

This sobers him. He frowns. "That's no way to waste good whiskey." Nevertheless, he retreats into the shadowed café and seconds later appears carrying a bottle of daisy yellow unlabeled liquor. He demonstrates its sparkle in the sunlight and says: "Two dollars."

We pay him with nickels and dimes and pennies. Suddenly, jangling the coins in his hands like a fistful of dice, his face softens. "Tell you what," he proposes, pouring the money back into our bead purse, "just send me one of them fruitcakes instead."

"Well," my friend remarks on our way home, "there's a lovely man. We'll put an extra cup of raisins in *his* cake."

The black stove, stoked with coal and firewood, glows like a lighted pumpkin. Eggbeaters whirl, spoons spin round in bowls of butter and sugar, vanilla sweetens the air, ginger spices it; melting, nose-tingling odors saturate the kitchen, suffuse the house, drift out to the world on puffs of chimney smoke. In four days our work is done. Thirty-one cakes, dampened with whiskey, bask on window sills and shelves.

Who are they for?

Friends. Not necessarily neighbor friends: indeed, the larger share are intended for persons we've met maybe once, perhaps not at all. People who've struck our fancy. Like President Roosevelt. Like the Reverend and Mrs. J. C. Lucey, Baptist missionaries to Borneo who lectured here last winter. Or the little knife grinder who comes through town twice a year. Or Abner Packer, the driver of the six o'clock bus from Mobile, who exchanges waves with us every day as he passes in a dust-cloud whoosh. Or the young Wistons, a California couple whose car one afternoon broke down outside the house and who spent a pleasant hour chatting with us on the porch (young Mr. Wiston snapped our picture, the only one we've ever had taken). Is it because my friend is shy with everyone *except* strangers that these strangers, and merest acquaintances, seem to us our truest friends? I think yes. Also, the scrapbooks we keep of thank-you's on White House stationery, time-to-time communications from California and Borneo, the knife grinder's penny post cards, make us feel connected to eventful worlds beyond the kitchen with its view of a sky that stops.

Now a nude December fig branch grates against the window. The kitchen is empty, the cakes are gone; yesterday we carted the last of them to the post office, where the cost of stamps turned our purse inside out. We're broke. That rather depresses me, but my friend insists on celebrating—with two inches of whiskey left in Haha's bottle. Queenie has a spoonful in a bowl of coffee (she likes her coffee chicory-flavored and strong). The rest we divide between a pair of jelly glasses. We're both quite awed at the prospect of drinking straight whiskey; the taste of it brings screwed-up expressions and sour shudders. But by and by we begin to sing, the two of us singing different songs simultaneously. I don't know the words to mine, just: *Come on along, come on along, to the dark-town strutters' ball.* But I can dance: that's what I mean to be, a tap dancer in the movies. My dancing shadow rollicks on the walls; our voices rock the chinaware; we giggle: as if unseen hands were tickling us. Queenie rolls on her back, her paws plow the air, something like a grin stretches her black lips. Inside myself, I feel warm and sparky as those crumbling logs, carefree as the wind in the chimney. My friend waltzes round the stove, the hem of her poor calico skirt pinched between her fingers as though it were a party dress: *Show me the way to go home*, she sings, her tennis shoes squeaking on the floor. *Show me the way to go home.*

Enter: two relatives. Very angry. Potent with eyes that scold, tongues that scald. Listen to what they have to say, the words tumbling together into a wrathful tune: "A child of seven! whiskey on his breath! are you out of your mind? feeding a child of seven! must be loony! road to ruination! remember Cousin Kate? Uncle Charlie? Uncle Charlie's brother-in-law? shame! scandal! humiliation! kneel, pray, beg the Lord!"

Queenie sneaks under the stove. My friend gazes at her shoes, her chin quivers, she lifts her skirt and blows her nose and runs to her room. Long after the town has gone to sleep and the house is silent except for the chimings of clocks and the sputter of fading fires, she is weeping into a pillow already as wet as a widow's handkerchief.

"Don't cry," I say, sitting at the bottom of her bed and shivering despite my flannel nightgown that smells of last winter's cough syrup, "Don't cry," I beg, teasing her toes, tickling her feet, "you're too old for that."

"It's because," she hiccups, "I *am* too old. Old and funny."

"Not funny. Fun. More fun than anybody. Listen. If you don't stop crying you'll be so tired tomorrow we can't go cut a tree."

She straightens up. Queenie jumps on the bed (where Queenie is not allowed) to lick her cheeks. "I know where we'll find pretty trees, Buddy. And holly, too. With berries big as your eyes. It's way off in the woods. Farther than we've ever been. Papa used to bring us Christmas trees from there: carry them on his shoulder. That's fifty years ago. Well now: I can't wait for morning."

Morning. Frozen rime lusters the grass; the sun, round as an orange and orange as hot-weather moons, balances on the horizon, burnishes the silvered winter woods. A wild turkey calls. A renegade hog grunts in the undergrowth. Soon, by the edge of knee-deep, rapid-running water, we have to abandon the buggy. Queenie wades the stream first, paddles across barking complaints at the swiftness of the current, the pneumonia-making coldness of it. We follow, holding our shoes and equipment (a hatchet, a burlap sack) above our heads. A mile more: of chastising thorns, burs and briers that catch at our clothes; of rusty pine needles brilliant with gaudy fungus and molted feathers. Here, there, a flash, a flutter, an ecstasy of shrillings remind us that not all the birds have flown south. Always, the path unwinds through lemony sun pools and pitch vine tunnels. Another creek to cross: a disturbed armada of speckled trout froths the water round us, and frogs the size of plates practice belly flops; beaver workmen are building a dam. On the farther shore, Queenie shakes herself and trembles. My friend shivers, too: not with cold but enthusiasm. One of her hat's ragged roses sheds a petal as she lifts her head and inhales the pine-heavy air. "We're almost there; can you smell it, Buddy?" she says, as though we were approaching an ocean.

And, indeed, it is a kind of ocean. Scented acres of holiday trees, prickly-leafed holly. Red berries shiny as Chinese bells: black crows swoop upon them screaming. Having stuffed our burlap sacks with enough greenery and crimson to garland a dozen windows, we set about choosing a tree. "It should be," muses my friend, "twice as tall as a boy. So a boy can't steal the star." The one we pick is twice as tall as me. A brave handsome brute that survives thirty hatchet strokes before it keels with a creaking rending cry. Lugging it like a kill, we commence the long trek out. Every few yards we abandon the struggle, sit down and pant. But we have the strength of triumphant hunts-men; that and the tree's virile, icy perfume revive us, goad us on. Many compliments accompany our sunset return along the red clay road to town; but my friend is sly and noncommital when passers-by praise the treasure perched on our buggy: what a fine tree and where did it come from? "Yonderways," she murmurs vaguely. Once a car stops and the rich mill owner's lazy wife leans out and whines: "Giveya two-bits cash for that ol tree." Ordinarily my friend is afraid of saying no; but on this occasion she promptly shakes her head: "We wouldn't take a dollar." The mill owner's wife persists. "A dollar, my foot! Fifty cents. That's my last offer. Goodness, woman, you can get another one." In answer, my friend gently reflects: "I doubt it. There's never two of anything."

Home: Queenie slumps by the fire and sleeps till tomorrow, snoring loud as a human.

A trunk in the attic contains: a shoebox of ermine tails (off the opera cape of a curious lady who once rented a room in the house), coils of frazzled tinsel gone gold with age, one silver star, a brief rope of dilapidated, undoubtedly dangerous candy-like light bulbs. Excellent decorations, as far as they go, which isn't far enough: my friend wants our tree to blaze "like a Baptist window," droop with weighty snows of ornament. But we can't afford the made-in-Japan splendors at the five-and-dime. So we do what we've always done: sit for days at the kitchen table with scissors and crayons and stacks of colored paper. I make sketches and my friend cuts them out: lots of cats, fish too (because they're easy to draw), some apples, some watermelons, a few winged angels devised from saved-up sheets of Hershey-bar tin foil. We use safety pins to attach these creations to the tree; as a final touch, we sprinkle the branches with shredded cotton (picked in August for this purpose). My friend, surveying the effects, clasps her hands together. "Now honest, Buddy. Doesn't it look good enough to eat?" Queenie tries to eat an angel.

After weaving and ribboning holly wreaths for all the front windows, our next project is the fashioning of family gifts. Tie-dye scarves for the ladies, for the men a home-brewed lemon and licorice and aspirin syrup to be taken "at the first Symptoms of a Cold and after Hunting." But when it comes time for making each other's gift, my friend and I separate to work secretly. I

would like to buy her a pearl-handled knife, a radio, a whole pound of choco-
late-covered cherries (we tasted some once, and she always swears: "I could
live on them, Buddy, Lord yes I could—and that's not taking His name in
vain"). Instead, I am building her a kite. She would like to give me a bicycle
(she's said so on several million occasions: "If only I could, Buddy. It's bad
enough in life to do without something *you* want; but confound it, what gets
my goat is not being able to give somebody something you want *them* to have.
Only one of these days I will, Buddy. Locate you a bike. Don't ask how. Steal
it, maybe"). Instead, I'm fairly certain that she is building me a kite—the
same as last year, and the year before: the year before that we exchanged
slingshots. All of which is fine by me. For we are champion kite-fliers who
study the wind like sailors; my friend, more accomplished than I, can get a
kite aloft when there isn't enough breeze to carry clouds.

Christmas Eve afternoon we scrape together a nickel and go to the butcher's to buy Queenie's traditional gift, a good gnawable beef bone. The bone,
wrapped in funny paper, is placed high in the tree near the silver star.
Queenie knows it's there. She squats at the foot of the tree staring up in a
trance of greed: when bedtime arrives she refuses to budge. Her excitement is
equaled by my own. I kick the covers and turn my pillow as though it were a
scorching summer's night. Somewhere a rooster crows: falsely, for the sun is
still on the other side of the world.

"Buddy, are you awake?" It is my friend, calling from her room, which is
next to mine; and an instant later she is sitting on my bed holding a candle.
"Well, I can't sleep a hoot," she declares. "My mind's jumping like a jack
rabbit. Buddy, do you think Mrs. Roosevelt will serve our cake at dinner?"
We huddle in the bed, and she squeezes my hand I-love-you. "Seems like
your hand used to be so much smaller. I guess I hate to see you grow up.
When you're grown up, will we still be friends?" I say always. "But I feel so
bad, Buddy. I wanted so bad to give you a bike. I tried to sell my cameo Papa
gave me. Buddy"—she hesitates, as though embarrassed—"I made you another kite." Then I confess that I made her one, too; and we laugh. The
candle burns too short to hold. Out it goes, exposing the starlight, the stars
spinning at the window like a visible caroling that slowly, slowly daybreak
silences. Possibly we doze; but the beginnings of dawn splash us like cold
water: we're up, wide-eyed and wandering while we wait for others to waken.
Quite deliberately my friend drops a kettle on the kitchen floor. I tap-dance in
front of closed doors. One by one the household emerges, looking as though
they'd like to kill us both: but it's Christmas, so they can't. First, a gorgeous
breakfast: just everything you can imagine—from flapjacks and fried squirrel
to hominy grits and honey-in-the-comb. Which puts everyone in a good
humor except my friend and I. Frankly, we're so impatient to get at the
presents we can't eat a mouthful.

Well, I'm disappointed. Who wouldn't be? With socks, a Sunday school
shirt, some handkerchiefs, a hand-me-down sweater and a year's subscription

to a religious magazine for children. *The Little Shepherd.* It makes me boil. It really does.

My friend has a better haul. A sack of Satsumas, that's her best present. She is proudest, however, of a white wool shawl knitted by her married sister. But she *says* her favorite gift is the kite I built her. And it *is* very beautiful; though not as beautiful as the one she made me, which is blue and scattered with gold and green Good Conduct stars; moreover, my name is painted on it, "Buddy."

"Buddy, the wind is blowing."

The wind is blowing, and nothing will do till we've run to a pasture below the house where Queenie has scooted to bury her bone (and where, a winter hence, Queenie will be buried, too). There, plunging through the healthy waist-high grass, we unreel our kites, feel them twitching at the string like sky fish as they swim into the wind. Satisfied, sun-warmed, we sprawl in the grass and peel Satsumas and watch our kites cavort. Soon I forget the socks and hand-me-down sweater. I'm as happy as if we'd already won the fifty-thousand-dollar Grand Prize in that coffee-naming contest.

"My, how foolish I am!" my friend cries, suddenly alert, like a woman remembering too late she has biscuits in the oven. "You know what I've always thought?" she asks in a tone of discovery, and not smiling at me but a point beyond. "I've always thought a body would have to be sick and dying before they saw the Lord. And I imagined that when He came it would be like looking at the Baptist window: pretty as colored glass with the sun pouring through, such a shine you don't know it's getting dark. And it's been a comfort: to think of that shine taking away all the spooky feeling. But I'll wager it never happens. I'll wager at the very end a body realizes the Lord has already shown Himself. That things as they are"—her hand circles in a gesture that gathers clouds and kites and grass and Queenie pawing earth over her bone—"just what they've always seen, was seeing Him. As for me, I could leave the world with today in my eyes."

This is our last Christmas together.

Life separates us. Those who Know Best decide that I belong in a military school. And so follows a miserable succession of bugle-blowing prisons, grim reveille-ridden summer camps. I have a new home too. But it doesn't count. Home is where my friend is, and there I never go.

And there she remains, puttering around the kitchen. Alone with Queenie. Then alone. ("Buddy dear," she writes in her wild hard-to-read script, "yesterday Jim Macy's horse kicked Queenie bad. Be thankful she didn't feel much. I wrapped her in a Fine Linen sheet and rode her in the buggy down to Simpson's pasture where she can be with all her Bones . . ."). For a few Novembers she continues to bake her fruitcakes single-handed; not as many, but some: and, of course, she always sends me "the best of the batch." Also, in every letter she encloses a dime wadded in toilet paper: "See a picture show and write me the story." But gradually in her letters she tends to confuse me with her other friend, the Buddy who died in the 1880's; more and more thirteenths are not the only days she stays in bed: a morning arrives in November, a leafless birdless coming of winter morning, when she cannot rouse herself to exclaim: "Oh my, it's fruitcake weather!"

And when that happens, I know it. A message saying so merely confirms a piece of news some secret vein had already received, severing from me an irreplaceable part of myself, letting it loose like a kite on a broken string. That is why, walking across a school campus on this particular December morning, I keep searching the sky. As if I expected to see, rather like hearts, a lost pair of kites hurrying toward heaven.

QUESTIONS

1. Although the Christmas memory of the title is more than twenty years old, it is recollected in the present tense. How is this managed? What advantages has it for the story?
2. What does the narrator mean by saying that his more than sixty-year-old friend "is still a child"? Is she like a child in more than one sense? Cite instances of behavior to support different meanings. What does she herself mean when she says that she is "old and funny" (page 288)? What are her chief sources of pleasure? Why does she make a perfect companion for the narrator? Are there places where she exhibits a superior wisdom to that of the adults in the story? Is she in any sense a developing character?
3. If the narrator and his friend—and Queenie—be taken as the protagonists of the story, who are the antagonists? At what points do they enter the story, and with what results? What are the sources of conflict? Who ultimately have the upper hand?
4. Where does the primary interest of the story lie? What are the principal sources of its appeal? Does it illuminate human character?
5. Can you formulate a theme for the story?

Bill Adams

GOD REST YOU MERRY, GENTLEMEN

1

The carrier's cart was drawn by two very slow old white horses. Only now and again, where the road was not too slippery with ice, did the carrier urge them to a heavy trot. There was a stout canvas cover over the cart, in which, besides myself, were five old village women. Young women walked to and from town on market day, saving tuppence each way. The carrier, who'd been

GOD REST YOU MERRY, GENTLEMEN   First published in 1938. Bill Adams is the pseudonym of Bertram Martin Adams (1879-1958), who lived his early years in England and his later years in California.

paid tuppence to bring me from the little market town three miles away, whither I'd come by train, set me down where Bowers lane leaves the highroad at the edge of Peterstow village. I'd my clothes in a brown paper parcel. I'd been traveling since nine in the morning, and had come about a hundred miles.

It was very cold. There was snow on the ground. I had mittens on my hands, and a thick muffler round my neck. The tip of my nose felt frozen, and so did my feet. The old women each side of me helped keep me warm while I was in the carrier's cart; but when I was put down I set my parcel on the snow, stamped my feet, and beat my hands on my sides before starting down Bowers lane.

It was maybe three-quarters of a mile from the highroad to Bowers. The lane was steep, narrow, and full of curves. It had high banks on the top of which were tall leafless hawthorn hedges. The oaks and elms that stood here and there in the hedgerows were leafless too. Everything was bleak and bare and cold, except for the holly trees, which were covered with bright red berries.

Because I stopped to make snowballs, and to slide where there was smooth ice in the wheel ruts, it took a long time to reach Bowers farm. My paper parcel burst open, and I had to stop to tie it up. I didn't tie it very well, and it kept bursting open. By the time I came to Bowers a pair of my stockings, my toothbrush, and some handkerchiefs were missing. Garge Gwilliam found them, and brought them to Bowers next day. But this has little to do with what I'm writing about. I'm grown-up now, and have a good deal of gray in my hair and a great many wrinkles. My socks, toothbrush and handkerchiefs are in their right places. Yet it was on this same pair of feet that I first went to Bowers, and with this same heart pulsing. I'm still me.

It's Christmas night, and Bowers farm is very far away in that quiet valley through which the little silvery river flows westward to the wide Atlantic. Very long ago it is; yet also it is very near, and only yesterday. Things do not change unless you let them—not the things that count, the lovely things. The stars are bright tonight, and all is still, save for the echo of an echo on the silent air.

My wife and our two daughters—Apple Dumpling, aged thirteen, and Honey Bee, aged six—are in bed and asleep. Ellison, our grown son, and Helen, his wife, are gone home an hour or more ago. It is late. The floor is strewn with toys. I have just turned out the lights upon the Christmas tree—electric lights of many colors which one turns on and off by one switch. Artificial icicles that are quite safe hang from the tree, which is covered with artificial snow that is quite safe. When the lights are turned on, ice and snow glimmer and gleam. The sole gleam now is from a big red candle that stands in the window, its light shining out into the darkness of the night. By the gleam of the big red candle I am writing this.

I had not thought of Bowers farm for many years till yesterday, when we were all trimming the Christmas tree and hanging our stockings in a row along the wide mantel above the sunken open fireplace.

2

It was getting dark when at last I came to the door of Bowers farmhouse. As I approached it, I heard shouting and laughter. When it opened at my rap, a wave of warm air streamed out, as though to cheer all the cold world outside. It was the night before Christmas Eve, and what happened that night from the time the door opened I have no memory of. But the two following nights I can see very plainly, and can hear very plainly their sounds.

Bowers farm was owned and managed by a widow with four young daughters and a son of my own age. An old Welsh servant named Mary Llewelyn lived in the house, and two nephews and a niece of the widow were visiting. On Christmas Eve, John Thomas the wagoner, who lived in a cottage across the lane from the farmhouse, came with his wife and their fourteen children. Bill Weevin the shepherd, and the girl he was going to marry in the spring, came too, and Jack Evans the cowman, who was going with Thomas' eldest girl Annie. Last came old Garge Gwilliam, the gardener, with his old deaf wife and their grown half-witted daughter Jane. Everyone gathered in the stone-floored kitchen, from the whitewashed ceiling of which hung sides of bacon, and hams, and great bunches of herbs. There was a huge plum cake on the table, and there were loaves of fresh bread, with cheese, and ale and cider. For Mrs. Thomas, because she was nursing a baby, there was stout. For the children there were pitchers of milk. Mistletoe hung from the oaken beams of the ceiling. There were red-berried holly wreaths on the white-washed walls, and in the windows.

We played "Here we go gathering nuts in May," and "London bridge is falling down," and "Oranges and lemons said the bells of St. Clemens." Everyone but Garge Gwilliam's old deaf wife, and their grown half-witted daughter Jane, danced the quadrille, the lancers and the Sir Roger de Coverley, to the tune of old Garge's fiddle. The kitchen was lighted by one big bright oil lamp and several cow-horn lanterns. In the large window was a big thick candle burning to show the Christ child the way to Bowers farm.

While we were dancing the Sir Roger de Coverley there was a rap on the door. Mary Llewelyn opened to the bell ringers. They came in, sat just within the door, and rang their bells. Then they ate bread and cheese and drank ale, and went on to the next farm: Weir End, a mile away through the snow.

The bell ringers were but a little while gone when we heard voices without. Mary opened the door and there, in the snow, one of them carrying a cow-horn lantern, were six village children, necks muffled up, woolly caps drawn down on their foreheads, snow thick upon their ragged clothes. They sang "O come, all ye faithful," and "Hark! the herald angels," and about "peace on earth and mercy mild." And when they had sung:

The roads are very dirty,
My shoes are very thin,
I've got a little pocket
To put a penny in . . .

they were brought into the warm kitchen, and ate plum cake and drank milk and were given pennies by the widow. Then they went on their way to Weir End farm, and were gone but a little while when more carol singers came. Lads and lasses of round eighteen and twenty, they too sang, "O come, all ye faithful" and "Hark! the herald angels," and about "peace on earth and mercy mild," singing with strong voices in which was lightheartedness, and a note as of challenge. With flushed faces and sparkling eyes, they came jesting into the warm kitchen and ate bread and cheese and plum cake. Lifting mugs of ale and of cider, they drank to the health and the happiness of the widow and all our company, and went merrily off into the snow on their way to Weir End.

And not long had they been gone when again we heard voices and, opening the great oaken door, looked out upon a company of men and women of and beyond middle age. First they sang "O come, all ye faithful," and then one carol after another, singing as though for the joy and delight of it, all unconscious of the snow and the cold. Not till they had been bidden several times did they enter the snug kitchen, and eat and drink. In their wrinkled faces and steady eyes was a strong and a merry contentment. Yet also they resembled in a manner children, because of the frankness of their countenances. When, lifting their mugs, they wished us happiness—why, then it seemed that happiness must of a certainty be, so honest, so stolidly determined, were the tones of their friendly voices.

These, when they went, left behind them a great sense of peace in Bowers kitchen; yet also a something of regret, a sort of rue, because they had not stayed longer. But that sense of regret swiftly ceased; for of a sudden we heard their upraised voices again, and opened the great oak door and looked out after them. They had stopped at the end of the driveway, and stood in a ring in the snow singing "God rest you merry, gentlemen, Let nothing you dismay," singing for their own joy, with the light of the cow-horn lantern shining in their smiling faces.

A little after the last carol singers were gone the widow took down a lantern from its hook, wrapped a shawl about her head and shoulders, and went forth from the snug kitchen into the thickly falling snow. John Thomas, Bill Weevin, Jack Evans, and old Garge Gwilliam each took a horn lantern and followed. Her son and her daughters, her niece and her nephew; John Thomas' wife, carrying at her breast her last infant; the girl Bill Weevin was going to marry in the spring; old Garge Gwilliam's old deaf wife and their grown half-witted daughter Jane, and all the children, went out from the snug kitchen into the thickly falling snow, with Bill Weevin's two sheep dogs following after them. Last from the kitchen, old Mary Llewelyn shut the great oak door, then, holding tight to my hand, followed after Bill Weevin's dogs.

Down the long drive we walked, the light of the lanterns shining on the snow laurels, lilacs and red-berried holly trees that bordered it. Through the old iron gate we went, and across the lane, and through the high five-barred gate opposite, into the great fold upon which opened the stables and cow houses and sheep pens.

There was a jingle of halter chains, and a shifting of hoofs, as we entered the stable. Boxer and Dobbin, Prince and old Tom, Taffy and Merlin, looked round at us from questioning eyes.

"There be good 'ay in h'every manger, missis," said John Thomas.

"That's right, John," replied the widow, and, having handed to him her lantern, went to one after another of her horses and laid her hand upon it gently, speaking a few soft words.

From the stable we passed to the cow house, where Molly and Creamcup, Hilda and Bess, lying soft in deep straw, looked up at us with big round eyes. Beyond the milch cows the long row of great red oxen with white faces gazed at us from warm straw-strewn stalls.

"Good dry beddin' an' a manger full for each on 'em, missis," said Jack Evans.

"That's as it should be, Jack," replied the widow, and, having spoken a few low words to her milch cows, passed slowly down the long narrow passage in front of the white faces of the great red oxen that gazed at her placidly.

We looked into the pen folds where lay the quiet sheep, and into the small pen where by himself the horned ram dwelt. Silent, they gazed at us, expectant-eyed. The night was far advanced when we went from the fold through the big five-barred gate back to the lane. Sleepily holding to old Mary's hand, I heard Jack Evans say, "Midnight be a-comin', John!"

"Aye, Jack, lad! Soon they'uns'll be a-talkin' same as you an' me," replied John Thomas.

"Mary, who'll be talking?" I asked.

"The be-asts," replied old Mary Llewelyn.

"But, Mary, animals can't talk!" I argued.

"It be Christmas Eve, little lad," she answered me.

And then John Thomas and Jack Evans and Bill Weevin, old Garge and the women and sleepy children, were calling "Good night" and "Merry Christmas," and disappearing toward their cottages through the thickly falling snow.

We came back to the warm kitchen. The widow put out her lantern. Mary lighted tallow candles and handed them round for us to go to bed by. With the bright oil lamp extinguished, and our candles in our hands, we went from the kitchen into the hallway. Only the tortoise-shell cat was left in the kitchen, curled in her box by the stove. On the window sill the big candle still burned clear and steady, gleaming out into the snow, to show the Christ child the way to Bowers farm.

On our way to bed we were allowed to peep into the drawing room, in which, all along the wide mantel, hung a row of empty stockings high above the bright fire.

"Mary, how can Santa Claus come with a fire burning?" I fearfully asked.

"Doant'ee be a-frettin', little lad! Just'ee wait!" replied old Mary.

3

All I know of the rest of that night is that Santa came. I didn't see him, but my stocking was full next morning—as were those of all the other children. There was no question about his having been, for in those days there was no cynical child. In those days when you heard the carol singers' "O come, all ye faithful," that "ye" meant yourself. Without question you accepted the invitation. If ever a child wondered why the Christ child did not see the candle in the window and come to Bowers farm, the explanation was simple. We didn't fret about His coming. We waited. There were so many other farms for Him to go to. In time He'd come!

We opened our stockings in the drawing room, where was also the Christmas tree. The Christmas tree was covered with tiny wax candles of many colors, and every candle had to be lighted with a match. On the branches of the tree, to represent snow, was cotton wool. In those days a Christmas tree was not alone a thing of beauty and of joy. It was a thing of danger, too—a thing for small children not to come too close to.

Though we scattered paper and string everywhere, the widow didn't mind at all. The drawing room was a very special room, used only on very special occasions, such as weddings and funerals, and when the rector came to call, and at Christmas. On one wall was a photograph of the widow as a bride, and her husband. They had been married in the drawing room, and he had been buried from it. On the opposite wall hung the widow's "marriage lines" in a gilt frame. On another wall was a picture of Queen Victoria and the Prince Consort; and opposite them, on the remaining wall, one of a champion cow and bull together. The chairs and sofas were covered with antimacassars.

The widow always swept and dusted the drawing room herself, and no one else was permitted to enter it on ordinary days. But today we were allowed to play in it as though it were just like any other room. The widow, busy helping old Mary in the kitchen, came to look in on us now and then. Once when I chanced to look up I saw old Mary in the door watching us. There were tears in her eyes. I jumped up, ran to her, pulled her under the mistletoe that hung from the chandelier in the center of the ceiling, drew her head down, and kissed her withered cheek. "Oh, God bless'ee, little lad!" she cried.

Old Mary was alone in the world. She had been engaged for twenty-two years before she married David Llewelyn, who was killed by a white-faced bull one evening eight months later while he was taking a short cut through a meadow, being in a hurry to get home because Mary wasn't very well. Her son, who was born a month later, grew up to take the Queen's shilling on market day, and was killed a little while afterward at Tell el-Kebir, in the Sudan.

I don't recall anything else very definitely of that day till evening. I see wrapping paper and string, toys and books and sweets, all over the house. I see turkey and goose, turnips and carrots, parsnips and baked potatoes, onions and cabbage and pickles; shiny apples, red, yellow, and green; big juicy deep-green winter pears; walnuts, hazelnuts, cobnuts, and filberts; and, from lands beyond the sea, oranges, figs, dates, raisins, prunes, coconuts, tangerines wrapped in tinfoil, and almonds and Brazil nuts. There was a sprig of red-berried holly stuck in the top of the Christmas pudding. The widow poured brandy over the pudding, set fire to it, cut it up, and passed it round while it was blazing. There was a dish of blazing snapdragon, too. I see it all in a sort of happy haze, and hear a continuous murmur of talk, with laughter rising and falling, young feet running to and fro, and young and old faces shining.

And I see old Mary come to the drawing room from the kitchen, where she has just finished washing the dishes. She says something in a low voice to the widow, who replies, "You stay here now, Mary. I'll go see to him."

The widow went to the kitchen. I followed, curious.

He stood with his back to the great oak door, his battered hat in his thin fingers. Bare knees showed through holes in his ragged trousers. A jacket with frayed sleeves and holes at the elbows, its collar missing, hung loosely from his sharp shoulders. His face was pale. He was shivering, at his feet a little pool of water from the snow that had melted and run from him.

The widow set a plate heaped with food on the table, and bade him sit down to it. About it she set other plates, with fruits and pudding and nuts, and a tankard of ale. Then, without having noticed me, she went back to the drawing room.

He didn't seem able to eat. He nibbled a bite of this and of that. The tortoise-shell cat leaped to a chair beside him and regarded him solemnly. He reached out a hand and stroked her soft warm fur. Having eaten scarce anything, he leaned wearily back in his chair. The oil lamp went out. Mary must have forgotten to fill it that morning. The only light in the kitchen was that of the big candle burning in the window to show the Christ child the way to Bowers farm. He gazed at it, his eyes full of longing. There wasn't a sound. By the light of the candle I could see beyond the windowpane the big flakes falling. He rose, picked his hat up from the floor, and looked uncertainly about the dimly lighted kitchen. Something told me that he wanted to say "Thank you" before he went away.

I was just starting to the drawing room to call the widow when he became aware of my presence. Without a word, reading my mind, he shook his head. Had he said aloud, "Don't disturb anyone any more on my account," his meaning could have been no plainer. Next moment he was gone through the great oak door out to the cold snowy night. Left alone in the dim kitchen, I was suddenly very frightened. Of just what I was afraid I could not have said. Old Mary Llewelyn appeared, closing the kitchen door behind her, shutting away the sounds of merriment in the drawing room. Unaware of me, she sat down in the just-vacated chair, longing eyes fixed upon the big red candle that burned on the window sill, her aspect one of utter loneliness. I ran to her and buried my face upon her flat breast.

"Doant 'ee be a-frettin', little lad! Yonder's the candle burnin'. Just 'ee wait!" said old Mary, stroking my head.

4

Now, as I say, Bowers farm had been forgotten till yesterday, when my wife, Apple Dumpling, Honey Bee, Helen and Ellison, and I were trimming the Christmas tree and hanging our stockings along the wide mantel above the sunken fireplace, in which a bright fire burned.

I paused and looked from a window out to the starry dark. Faintly I could hear the murmur of the creek that, a short distance away, flows westward to the wide Pacific. Dim in the starshine I could see the trees that border our drive, the branches of the great oak that spread over our roof. On a hill a little to the north of the drive's end an air-mail beacon flashed alternate red and white rays across the sky. From high above our roof came the drone of a passenger plane. Round a curve in the paved highway that passes between the drive's end and the beacon hill came the lights of a transcontinental auto stage. It was at that instant that Honey Bee spoke.

"Daddy, how can Santa Claus come down the chimney with a fire burning?" asked Honey Bee. And spark touched spark. Memory's embers were fanned to flame, and I heard old Mary Llewelyn answering that same question asked by me so long ago when I was Honey Bee's age. And I wondered if in stage or plane was some small boy on his way to spend Christmas many hundreds of miles, perhaps a thousand miles, away. "How different it all is to when I was a child," I thought.

On our little farm, so little that it scarce can be called a farm, is neither wagoner, cowman, shepherd, gardener nor serving woman. It is but a few months since we moved here from the city, twenty miles away, where live many friends. Distance precludes neighborliness. Now, on Christmas Eve, no one would be dropping in upon us to wish us good cheer and to share for a space the warmth of our hearth. A sort of sadness came over me, a longing. There was too much haste, too much noise, in this modern world where all was so changed.

The trimming of our tree was finished. The stockings were hung in a row on the mantel. The many-colored lights on the the tree twinkled and gleamed, the fire blazed bright, and in a window, on the window sill, a big red candle burned, as long ago a big red candle had burned at Bowers farm.

I took a powerful flashlight, opened the French door, and stepped out to the starry dark, my wife at my side, the children old and young following, and the two little terriers that keep the rats from our outbuildings and the gophers from our two acres following them. Under the branches of the great oak we went, past the pomegranate, oleander, deodar and redwood trees; beneath the sky in which, now far away, the lights of the passenger plane still winked, along which the beacon sent its constant ray, under which, along the paved highway, countless hurrying cars sped.

There was the jingle of a halter chain, and a shifting of hoofs, as we looked into the little barn where Moby the saddle horse, and Molly the cow, and Honey Bee's pet lamb, lay bedded in deep dry straw. They looked at us expectant-eyed. Honey Bee wanted to stay, to hear them talk. "They'd not talk with people about," I assured her. We looked in at my wife's turkeys, geese, chickens, ducks and pigeons. There was a rustle of feathers, and a low cooing from the gloom. When we went back to the porch Dumpling suggested that, since the night was not cold, we might leave the door open, and so overhear the beasts talking. When I negatived that, she said that she didn't believe animals talked on Christmas Eve, and asked if I had ever heard them.

"If I'd been near enough to overhear, they'd not have talked," I told her.

When the others went in, she lingered on the porch. I stayed with her. The ridges of the near hills were distinct in the starshine. The canyons were black gashes. In them, when spring came, the buckeye would flower, the madroña, and the wild mountain lilac. On hill and in canyon, in place of the red-berried holly of Bowers lane, were the no less bright red berries of the toyon. To match the memories of my boyhood, there was beauty for beauty. Home was very sweet. And yet upon me there was still that longing.

"Ah, if only the carol singers would come! If I could just hear carol singers again!" thought I, and thought also, "There was neighborliness in the lanes in the old days."

Dumpling went in. I followed. We all sat on the step of the sunken fireplace, with the firelight in our faces; behind us the lights of the tree, on each wall wreaths of red-berried toyon and of evergreen, and in the window, burning with a clear unwavering flame, the big red candle to show the Christ child the way to Oakcroft farm.

We had but sat down when there was a step on our porch. Our little lane is a blind lane. Sometimes someone from the paved highway near by mistakenly takes it and comes to ask directions. This would be someone from the hurrying mob. I rose and opened the door.

" 'Appee Kreesmas!" cried Tony Giammona. " 'Appy Kreemas!" cried Mrs. Giammona. "Happy Christmas!" came a chorus from the eight Giammona children.

Tony and his wife are from Sicily; the children were born in America. Mrs. Giammona has done our washing a few times. Dumpling takes it, the eldest Giammona child brings it back. My wife and I had scarce set eyes on Mr. or Mrs. Giammona.

Tony was dressed in his best suit, from a mail-order house. He can't write English, but his eldest girl goes to high school and writes his orders for him. Mrs. Giammona was dressed in an old silk dress worn long ago in Palermo and used on only the most special occasions. The girls were all in brightly colored new silk dresses from the mail-order house. Very lovely they were, with their black shoe-button eyes and olive faces. The boys were in gay, green, new sweaters, and new trousers.

"Dees not hurt you, my vren! You dreenk whole bottle, eet not hurt you!"

cried Tony Giammona, handing me a bottle of his homemade wine. "I breeng eet you for 'appee Kreesmas!"

"I make two doz' loafs today. Dey not last long, I tell you! I vants you try my bread, for 'appee Kreesmas!" cried Mrs. Giammona, handing my wife two big loaves fresh from her oven.

While the little Giammonas laughed and talked with Dumpling and Honey Bee, Tony and his wife sat down and gazed round the big room. "Dees verra nice 'ome," said Tony. Mrs. Giammona said, "You sure got nice 'ome, you folks!" Their dwelling has some windows missing, and is devoid of carpets; in places wallpaper hangs in shreds. Tony prunes fruit trees for a living, but for a long time has not been well enough to work. Mrs. Giammona takes in washing. They "make out."

"We'ave to go. We got forty peoples come tomorrow," said Tony presently. He had five brothers, each married and with a family. "We wants you folks to come. We goin' to dance old countree dances!" he added.

"Sure, we wants you folks to come! We goin' to barbecue a goat. Maybe two, t'ree goats!" cried Mrs. Giammona. We might have been her own kin.

Having allowed Dumpling to accept the invitation, being unable to do so ourselves because of other plans, we promised to come next time the Giammonas had a party. We loaded the children with oranges and candy and saw them away. As they disappeared in the darkness, Tony's voice came back to us. "Dose ees nice peoples. I 'opes zey 'ave 'appee Kreesmas!"

So here again was beauty for beauty. In place of John Thomas' honest friendship, that of Tony Giammona.

5

"Ah, if only the carol singers would come!" thought I. But that would not be. A memory of the tramp came to me. There was something very pleasant in the memory. The tramp had, in a sort of way, helped to make Christmas. There had been no need for him to go off as he did. He could have stayed the night, and have gone forth in the morning warm and dry. I remembered how the widow had made up for him a big bundle of her dead husband's clothes. But he had gone away out of pride, and an unwillingness to intrude his poverty. I wondered if, perhaps, some poor wanderer would come to our door tonight. But no one would come, of course. No longer were there any tramps. A thing called "relief," coming in many forms and under many subtitles, had destroyed pride and made willing beggars out of people. The tramp had not been a beggar. Had there been work for him, he'd have worked eagerly. Today no one who can avoid it works; save for such Old World people as the Giammonas, who, despite poverty, manage to "make out" and would utterly scorn "relief."

I sat down on the step of the sunken fireplace, where all the others save Dumpling were seated. Dumpling sat on the couch in the far corner. Close by her burned the big red candle. From above our roof came the noise of another plane. Flying low, it passed with a roar of motors. From the paved highway came the insistent honk of another transcontinental auto stage demanding the right of way.

I glanced toward Dumpling, and I shuddered. A thoroughgoing radio fan, she knows all the programs, and the special time for each. Her finger was on the button. In a moment she would turn it, and flood the room with something about "gang busters," or "phantom pilots," or with jazz or buffoonery.

"Dumpling, it's time for bed!" I called.

"Let me stay a little while. There's something I like coming on," pleaded Dumpling. And what could I say? Could a man with gray hair have his child think him an old crab, upon Christmas Eve? What could my child know or understand of the longing that was in me? If all was changed since I was a child, that was none of her doing.

There was silence now, no sound from sky or highway. In silence I sat thinking, waiting with dread the noise that Dumpling all too soon would turn loose.

"The lights of a plane, seen amongst stars, are beautiful," I thought. And I thought too, "So is a plane beautiful when the sun shines on it." And the beacon on the hill, its constant ray was beautiful, I admitted. Even the modern carrier's cart, speeding along concrete roads and honking for the right of way, had its own peculiar beauty. I was willing to admit all that. It was admitted not without some effort, true; and not without a distinct feeling of magnanimity. And besides, one could always forget these things by going into one's house. In one's home, in the sanctity of one's rooftree, one could shut modernity away and be at rest. But as for this thing upon which Dumpling had her finger, this thing I loathed. There was no escape from it. It was the very essence of all that was banal in modernity. And now, beneath the roof of home, on Christmas Eve, with my heart hungry for rest and for beauty, I must submit to its blatant banality.

I bowed my head. With my eyes on those same feet on which, so long ago, I walked down Bowers lane, I thought of Bowers farm. I said to myself, "I'll just keep thinking of when I was a child at Bowers, and of the carol singers. If I just keep thinking, it will drown out the horror of modernity."

There was a faint click as Dumpling turned the button.

And then, in a moment, my wife and our grown son and his wife, and our two small daughters, were singing, their voices joining with the air-borne chorus of many singers far away—singing, all of them, as though for the joy and the delight of it.

"O come, all ye faithful," they sang, and "Hark! the herald angels," and of peace on earth. And last they sang:

> *God rest you merry, gentlemen,*
> *Let nothing you dismay . . .*
> *For Jesus Christ, our Savior,*
> *Was born on Christmas Day!*

While they were singing that last carol there came again from above our rooftree the drone of a plane, and a transcontinental auto stage upon the paved highway honked for the right of way. With my eyes uplifted, I saw the beacon's ray across the sky. Upon our window sill the big red candle burned, with faithful flame unwavering. And of a sudden it was as though nothing were changed—as though all were as it had been so long ago at Bowers farm. Bowers farm and Oakcroft were become one. And I said to myself, "Things do not change unless you let them change—not the things that count, the lovely things."

QUESTIONS

1. Although this story, like Truman Capote's, utilizes a first person narrator and is largely taken up with a Christmas memory, it differs in being concerned with two Christmases, widely separated in space and time, and in focusing on differences and similarities between them. Where are the settings of the two Christmases?

2. Draw up a list of parallels between the Christmas at Bowers farm and the Christmas at Oakcroft. How many of them seem natural? Are any coincidental, forced, or unlikely?

3. Unlike most stories in this book, this story explicitly states its theme—states it twice in fact. What is the theme? Where is it expressed?

4. Does the theme grow naturally out of the materials of the story, or is the story written to illustrate the theme? Does the story convince you of the truth of the theme? Why or why not? Do any elements in the story run counter to the theme?

5. Which story—this, or Capote's—relies primarily for its effect on unique, precisely imagined details? Which relies heavily on traditional Christmas motifs (evoking a stock response)?

6. Without rereading, can you remember or guess which story each of the following phrases is taken from—"friendly voices," "smiling faces," "the frankness of their countenances," "young feet running to and fro," "a strong and merry contentment," "a great sense of peace," "It makes me boil," "looking as though they'd like to kill us"? Of what significance is this question?

7. Compare the final paragraphs of the two stories. How do they fundamentally differ? Which is designed to leave us with a happy glow? Which takes us into a deeper understanding of life?

8. Which is the more authentic story? Which is a confection manufactured for the Christmas season? Explain your answer fully.

8. Fantasy

Truth in fiction is not the same as fidelity to fact. Fiction, after all, is the opposite of fact. It is a game of make-believe—though, at its best, a serious game—in which the author conceives characters and situations in his mind and sets them down on paper. And yet these characters and situations, if deeply imagined, may embody truths of human life and behavior more fully and significantly than any number of the miscellaneous facts reported on the front pages of our morning papers. The purpose of the interpretive artist is to communicate truths by means of imagined facts.

The story writer begins, then, by saying "Let's suppose. . . ." "Let's suppose," for instance, "that a fair-minded, conscientious, but not cold-hearted Jewish top sergeant, during World War II, is placed in charge of a training company in which a Jewish recruit tries to play on their common Jewishness to obtain special favors for himself and his friends." From this initial assumption the author goes on to develop a story ("Defender of the Faith") which, though entirely imaginary in the sense that it never happened, nevertheless reveals convincingly to us some truths of human behavior.

But now, what if the author goes a step further and supposes not just something that might very well have happened though it didn't but something highly improbable—something that could happen, say, only as the result of a very surprising coincidence? What if he begins, "Let's suppose that a woman hater and a charming female siren find themselves alone on a desert island"? This initial supposition causes us to stretch our imaginations a bit further, but is not this situation just as capable of revealing human truths as the former? The psychologist puts a rat in a maze (certainly an improbable situation for a rat), observes its reactions to the maze, and discovers some truth of rat nature. The author may put his imagined characters on an imagined desert island, imaginatively study their reactions, and reveal some truth of human nature. The improbable initial situation may yield as much truth as the probable one.

From the improbable it is but one step further to the impossible (as we know it in this life). Why should not our author begin "Let's suppose that a miser and his termagant wife find themselves in hell" or "Let's suppose that a timid but ambitious man discovers how to make himself invisible" or "Let's suppose that a primitive scapegoat ritual still survives in contemporary America." Could not these situations also be used to exhibit human truth?

The nonrealistic story, or FANTASY, is one that transcends the bounds of known reality. Commonly, it conjures up a strange and marvelous world, which one enters by falling down a rabbit hole or climbing up a beanstalk or getting shipwrecked in an unfamiliar ocean or dreaming a dream; or else it introduces strange powers and occult forces into the world of ordinary reality, allowing one to foretell the future or communicate with the dead or separate his mind from his body or turn himself into a monster. It introduces human beings into a world where the ordinary laws of nature are suspended or superseded and where the landscape and its creatures are unfamiliar, or it introduces ghosts or fairies or dragons or werewolves or talking animals or invaders from Mars or miraculous occurrences into the normal world of human beings. Fables, ghost stories, science fiction—all are types of fantasy.

Fantasy may be escapist or interpretive, true or false. The space ship on its way to a distant planet may be filled with stock characters or with human beings. The author may be interested chiefly in exhibiting its mechanical marvels or providing thrills and adventures, or he may use it as a means of creating exacting circumstances in which human behavior may be sharply observed and studied. Fantasy, like other elements of fiction, may be employed sheerly for its own sake or as a means of communicating an important insight. The appeal may be to our taste for the strange or to our need for the true. The important point to remember is that truth in fiction is not to be identified with realism in method. Stories that never depart from the three dimensions of actuality may distort and falsify life. Stories that fly on the wings of fantasy may be vehicles for truth. Fantasy may convey truth through symbolism or allegory or simply by providing an unusual setting for the observation of human beings.

Some of the world's greatest works of literature have been partly or wholly fantasy: *The Odyssey, The Book of Job, The Divine Comedy, The Tempest, Pilgrim's Progress, Gulliver's Travels, Faust, Alice in Wonderland.* All these have had important things to say about the human condition.

We must not judge a story, then, by whether or not it stays within the limits of the possible. Rather, we begin by granting every story a "Let's suppose"—an initial assumption. The initial assumption may be plausible or implausible. The writer may begin with an ordinary, everyday situation or with a far-fetched, improbable coincidence. Or he may be allowed to suspend a law of nature or to create a marvelous being or machine or place. But once we have granted him his impossibility, we have a right to demand probability in his treatment of it. The realm of fantasy is not a realm in which *all* laws of logic are suspended. We need to ask, too, for what reason the story employs the element of fantasy. Is it used simply for its own strangeness or for thrills or surprises or laughs? Or is it used to illumine the more normal world of our experience? What is the purpose of the author's invention? Is it, like a roller coaster, simply a machine for producing thrills? Or does it, like an observation balloon, provide a vantage point from which we may view the world?

D. H. Lawrence

THE ROCKING-HORSE WINNER

There was a woman who was beautiful, who started with all the advantages, yet she had no luck. She married for love, and the love turned to dust. She had bonny children, yet she felt they had been thrust upon her, and she could not love them. They looked at her coldly, as if they were finding fault with her. And hurriedly she felt she must cover up some fault in herself. Yet what it was that she must cover up she never knew. Nevertheless, when her children were present, she always felt the center of her heart go hard. This troubled her, and in her manner she was all the more gentle and anxious for her children, as if she loved them very much. Only she herself knew that at the center of her heart was a hard little place that could not feel love, no, not for anybody. Everybody else said of her: "She is such a good mother. She adores her children." Only she herself, and her children themselves, knew it was not so. They read it in each other's eyes.

THE ROCKING-HORSE WINNER   First published in 1933. D. H. Lawrence (1885-1930), son of a coal miner and a school teacher, was born and grew up in Nottinghamshire, England, was rejected for military service in World War I because of lung trouble, and lived most of his adult life abroad.

There were a boy and two little girls. They lived in a pleasant house, with a garden, and they had discreet servants, and felt themselves superior to anyone in the neighborhood.

Although they lived in style, they felt always an anxiety in the house. There was never enough money. The mother had a small income, and the father had a small income, but not nearly enough for the social position which they had to keep up. The father went into town to some office. But though he had good prospects, these prospects never materialized. There was always the grinding sense of the shortage of money, though the style was always kept up.

At last the mother said: "I will see if I can't make something." But she did not know where to begin. She racked her brains, and tried this thing and the other, but could not find anything successful. The failure made deep lines come into her face. Her children were growing up, they would have to go to school. There must be more money, there must be more money. The father, who was always very handsome and expensive in his tastes, seemed as if he never would be able to do anything worth doing. And the mother, who had a great belief in herself, did not succeed any better, and her tastes were just as expensive.

And so the house came to be haunted by the unspoken phrase: There must be more money! There must be more money! The children could hear it all the time, though nobody said it aloud. They heard it at Christmas, when the expensive and splendid toys filled the nursery. Behind the shining modern rocking horse, behind the smart doll's-house, a voice would start whispering: "There must be more money! There must be more money!" And the children would stop playing, to listen for a moment. They would look into each other's eyes, to see if they had all heard. And each one saw in the eyes of the other two that they too had heard. "There must be more money! There must be more money!"

It came whispering from the springs of the still-swaying rocking horse, and even the horse, bending his wooden, champing head, heard it. The big doll, sitting so pink and smirking in her new pram, could hear it quite plainly, and seemed to be smirking all the more self-consciously because of it. The foolish puppy, too, that took the place of the Teddy bear, he was looking so extraordinarily foolish for no other reason but that he heard the secret whisper all over the house: "There must be more money!"

Yet nobody ever said it aloud. The whisper was everywhere, and therefore no one spoke it. Just as no one ever says: "We are breathing!" in spite of the fact that breath is coming and going all the time.

"Mother," said the boy Paul one day, "why don't we keep a car of our own? Why do we always use uncle's, or else a taxi?"

"Because we're the poor members of the family," said the mother.

"But why are we, mother?"

"Well—I suppose," she said slowly and bitterly, "it's because your father has no luck."

The boy was silent for some time.

"Is luck money, mother?" he asked, rather timidly.

"No, Paul. Not quite. It's what causes you to have money."

"Oh!" said Paul vaguely. "I thought when Uncle Oscar said filthy lucker, it meant money."

"Filthy lucre° does mean money," said the mother, "But it's lucre, not luck."

"Oh!" said the boy. "Then what is luck, mother?"

"It's what causes you to have money. If you're lucky you have money. That's why it's better to be born lucky than rich. If you're rich, you may lose your money. But if you're lucky, you will always get more money."

"Oh! Will you? And is father not lucky?"

"Very unlucky, I should say," she said bitterly.

The boy watched her with unsure eyes.

"Why?" he asked.

"I don't know. Nobody ever knows why one person is lucky and another unlucky."

"Don't they? Nobody at all? Does nobody know?"

"Perhaps God. But He never tells."

"He ought to, then. And aren't you lucky either, mother?"

"I can't be, if I married an unlucky husband."

"But by yourself, aren't you?"

"I used to think I was, before I married. Now I think I am very unlucky indeed."

"Why?"

"Well—never mind! Perhaps I'm not really," she said.

The child looked at her, to see if she meant it. But he saw, by the lines of her mouth, that she was only trying to hide something from him.

"Well, anyhow," he said stoutly, "I'm a lucky person."

"Why?" said his mother, with a sudden laugh.

He stared at her. He didn't even know why he had said it.

"God told me," he asserted, brazening it out.

"I hope He did, dear!" she said, again with a laugh, but rather bitter.

"He did, mother!"

"Excellent!" said the mother, using one of her husband's exclamations.

The boy saw she did not believe him; or, rather, that she paid no attention to his assertion. This angered him somewhat, and made him want to compel her attention.

He went off by himself, vaguely, in a childish way, seeking for the clue to "luck." Absorbed, taking no heed of other people, he went about with a sort of stealth, seeking inwardly for luck. He wanted luck, he wanted it, he wanted it. When the two girls were playing dolls in the nursery, he would sit on his big rocking horse, charging madly into space, with a frenzy that made the little girls peer at him uneasily. Wildly the horse careered, the waving dark

filthy lucre: see New Testament, I Timothy 3:3

hair of the boy tossed, his eyes had a strange glare in them. The little girls dared not speak to him.

When he had ridden to the end of his mad little journey, he climbed down and stood in front of his rocking horse, staring fixedly into its lowered face. Its red mouth was slightly open, its big eye was wide and glassy-bright.

"Now!" he would silently command the snorting steed. "Now, take me to where there is luck! Now take me!"

And he would slash the horse on the neck with the little whip he had asked Uncle Oscar for. He knew the horse could take him to where there was luck, if only he forced it. So he would mount again, and start on his furious ride, hoping at last to get there. He knew he could get there.

"You'll break your horse, Paul!" said the nurse.

"He's always riding like that! I wish he'd leave off!" said his elder sister Joan.

But he only glared down on them in silence. Nurse gave him up. She could make nothing of him. Anyhow he was growing beyond her.

One day his mother and his Uncle Oscar came in when he was on one of his furious rides. He did not speak to them.

"Hallo, you young jockey! Riding a winner?" said his uncle.

"Aren't you growing too big for a rocking horse? You're not a very little boy any longer, you know," said his mother.

But Paul only gave a blue glare from his big, rather close-set eyes. He would speak to nobody when he was in full tilt. His mother watched him with an anxious expression on her face.

At last he suddenly stopped forcing his horse into the mechanical gallop, and slid down.

"Well, I got there!" he announced fiercely, his blue eyes still flaring, and his sturdy long legs straddling apart.

"Where did you get to?" asked his mother.

"Where I wanted to go," he flared back at her.

"That's right, son!" said Uncle Oscar. "Don't you stop till you get there. What's the horse's name?"

"He doesn't have a name," said the boy.

"Gets on without all right?" asked the uncle.

"Well, he has different names. He was called Sansovino last week."

"Sansovino, eh? Won the Ascot. How did you know his name?"

"He always talks about horse races with Bassett," said Joan.

The uncle was delighted to find that his small nephew was posted with all the racing news. Bassett, the young gardener, who had been wounded in the left foot in the war and got his present job through Oscar Cresswell, whose batman he had been, was a perfect blade of the "turf." He lived in the racing events, and the small boy lived with him.

Oscar Cresswell got it all from Bassett.

"Master Paul comes and asks me, so I can't do more than tell him, sir," said Bassett, his face terribly serious, as if he were speaking of religious matters.

"And does he ever put anything on a horse he fancies?"

"Well—I don't want to give him away—he's a young sport, a fine sport, sir. Would you mind asking him yourself? He sort of takes a pleasure in it, and perhaps he'd feel I was giving him away, sir, if you don't mind."

Bassett was serious as a church.

The uncle went back to his nephew, and took him off for a ride in the car.

"Say, Paul, old man, do you ever put anything on a horse?" the uncle asked.

The boy watched the handsome man closely.

"Why, do you think I oughtn't to?" he parried.

"Not a bit of it! I thought perhaps you might give me a tip for the Lincoln."

The car sped on into the country, going down to Uncle Oscar's place in Hampshire.

"Honor bright?" said the nephew.

"Honor bright, son!" said the uncle.

"Well, then, Daffodil."

"Daffodil! I doubt it, sonny. What about Mirza?"

"I only know the winner," said the boy. "That's Daffodil."

"Daffodil, eh?"

There was a pause. Daffodil was an obscure horse comparatively.

"Uncle!"

"Yes, son?"

"You won't let it go any further, will you? I promised Bassett."

"Bassett be damned, old man! What's he got to do with it?"

"We're partners. We've been partners from the first. Uncle, he lent me my first five shillings, which I lost. I promised him, honor bright, it was only between me and him; only you gave me that ten-shilling note I started winning with, so I thought you were lucky. You won't let it go any further, will you?"

The boy gazed at his uncle from those big, hot, blue eyes, set rather close together. The uncle stirred and laughed uneasily.

"Right you are, son! I'll keep your tip private. Daffodil, eh? How much are you putting on him?"

"All except twenty pounds," said the boy. "I keep that in reserve."

The uncle thought it a good joke.

"You keep twenty pound in reserve, do you, you young romancer? What are you betting, then?"

"I'm betting three hundred," said the boy gravely. "But it's between you and me, Uncle Oscar! Honor bright?"

The uncle burst into a roar of laughter.

"It's between you and me all right, you young Nat Gould,"° he said, laughing. "But where's your three hundred?"

Nat Gould: a journalist and novelist (1857-1919) who wrote about horse racing

"Bassett keeps it for me. We're partners."

"You are, are you! And what is Bassett putting on Daffodil?"

"He won't go quite as high as I do, I expect. Perhaps he'll go a hundred and fifty."

"What, pennies?" laughed the uncle.

"Pounds," said the child, with a surprised look at his uncle. "Bassett keeps a bigger reserve than I do."

Between wonder and amusement Uncle Oscar was silent. He pursued the matter no further, but he determined to take his nephew with him to the Lincoln races.

"Now, son," he said, "I'm putting twenty on Mirza, and I'll put five for you on any horse you fancy. What's your pick?"

"Daffodil, uncle."

"No, not the fiver on Daffodil!"

"I should if it was my own fiver," said the child.

"Good! Good! Right you are! A fiver for me and a fiver for you on Daffodil."

The child had never been to a race meeting before, and his eyes were blue fire. He pursed his mouth tight, and watched. A Frenchman just in front had put his money on Lancelot. Wild with excitement, he flayed his arms up and down, yelling "Lancelot! Lancelot!" in his French accent.

Daffodil came in first, Lancelot second, Mirza third. The child, flushed and with eyes blazing, was curiously serene. His uncle brought him four five-pound notes, four to one.

"What am I to do with these?" he cried, waving them before the boy's eyes.

"I suppose we'll talk to Bassett," said the boy. "I expect I have fifteen hundred now; and twenty in reserve; and this twenty."

His uncle studied him for some moments.

"Look here, son!" he said, "You're not serious about Bassett and that fifteen hundred, are you?"

"Yes, I am. But it's between you and me, uncle. Honor bright!"

"Honor bright all right, son! But I must talk to Bassett."

"If you'd like to be a partner, uncle, with Bassett and me, we could all be partners. Only, you'd have to promise, honor bright, uncle, not to let it go beyond us three. Bassett and I are lucky, and you must be lucky, because it was your ten shillings I started winning with . . ."

Uncle Oscar took both Bassett and Paul into Richmond Park for an afternoon, and there they talked.

"It's like this, you see, sir," Bassett said. "Master Paul would get me talking about racing events, spinning yarns, you know, sir. And he was always keen on knowing if I'd made or if I'd lost. It's about a year since, now, that I put five shillings on Blush of Dawn for him—and we lost. Then the luck turned, with that ten shillings he had from you, that we put on Singhalese. And since that time, it's been pretty steady, all things considering. What do you say, Master Paul?"

"We're all right when we're sure," said Paul. "It's when we're not quite sure that we go down."

"Oh, but we're careful then," said Bassett.

"But when are you sure?" smiled Uncle Oscar.

"It's Master Paul, sir," said Bassett, in a secret, religious voice. "It's as if he had it from heaven. Like Daffodil, now, for the Lincoln. That was as sure as eggs."

"Did you put anything on Daffodil?" asked Oscar Cresswell.

"Yes, sir, I made my bit."

"And my nephew?"

Bassett was obstinately silent, looking at Paul.

"I made twelve hundred, didn't I, Bassett? I told uncle I was putting three hundred on Daffodil."

"That's right," said Bassett, nodding.

"But where's the money?" asked the uncle.

"I keep it safe locked up, sir. Master Paul he can have it any minute he likes to ask for it."

"What, fifteen hundred pounds?"

"And twenty! and forty, that is, with the twenty he made on the course."

"It's amazing!" said the uncle.

"If Master Paul offers you to be partners, sir, I would, if I were you; if you'll excuse me," said Bassett.

Oscar Cresswell thought about it.

"I'll see the money," he said.

They drove home again, and sure enough, Bassett came round to the garden-house with fifteen hundred pounds in notes. The twenty pounds reserve was left with Joe Glee, in the Turf Commission deposit.

"You see, it's all right, uncle, when I'm sure! Then we go strong, for all we're worth. Don't we, Bassett?"

"We do that, Master Paul."

"And when are you sure?" said the uncle, laughing.

"Oh, well, sometimes I'm absolutely sure, like about Daffodil," said the boy; "and sometimes I have an idea; and sometimes I haven't even an idea, have I, Bassett? Then we're careful, because we mostly go down."

"You do, do you! And when you're sure, like about Daffodil, what makes you sure, sonny?"

"Oh, well, I don't know," said the boy uneasily. "I'm sure, you know, uncle; that's all."

"It's as if he had it from heaven, sir," Bassett reiterated.

"I should say so!" said the uncle.

But he became a partner. And when the Leger was coming on, Paul was "sure" about Lively Spark, which was a quite inconsiderable horse. The boy insisted on putting a thousand on the horse, Bassett went for five hundred, and Oscar Cresswell two hundred. Lively Spark came in first, and the betting had been ten to one against him. Paul had made ten thousand.

"You see," he said, "I was absolutely sure of him."

Even Oscar Cresswell had cleared two thousand.

"Look here son," he said, "this sort of thing makes me nervous."

"It needn't, uncle! Perhaps I shan't be sure again for a long time."

"But what are you going to do with your money?" asked the uncle.

"Of course," said the boy, "I started it for mother. She said she had no luck, because father is unlucky, so I thought if I was lucky, it might stop whispering."

"What might stop whispering?"

"Our house. I hate our house for whispering."

"What does it whisper?"

"Why—why"—the boy fidgeted—"why, I don't know. But it's always short of money, you know, uncle."

"I know it, son, I know it."

"You know people send mother writs, don't you, uncle?"

"I'm afraid I do," said the uncle.

"And then the house whispers, like people laughing at you behind your back. It's awful, that is! I thought if I was lucky . . ."

"You might stop it," added the uncle.

The boy watched him with big blue eyes that had an uncanny cold fire in them, and he said never a word.

"Well, then!" said the uncle. "What are we doing?"

"I shouldn't like mother to know I was lucky," said the boy.

"Why not, son?"

"She'd stop me."

"I don't think she would."

"Oh!"—and the boy writhed in an odd way—"I don't want her to know, uncle."

"All right, son! We'll manage it without her knowing."

They managed it very easily. Paul, at the other's suggestion, handed over five thousand pounds to his uncle, who deposited it with the family lawyer, who was then to inform Paul's mother that a relative had put five thousand pounds into his hands, which sum was to be paid out a thousand pounds at a time, on the mother's birthday, for the next five years.

"So she'll have a birthday present of a thousand pounds for five successive years," said Uncle Oscar. "I hope it won't make it all the harder for her later."

Paul's mother had her birthday in November. The house had been "whispering" worse than ever lately, and, even in spite of his luck, Paul could not bear up against it. He was very anxious to see the effect of the birthday letter, telling his mother about the thousand pounds.

When there were no visitors, Paul now took his meals with his parents, as he was beyond the nursery control. His mother went into town nearly every day. She had discovered that she had an odd knack of sketching furs and dress materials, so she worked secretly in the studio of a friend who was the chief "artist" for the leading drapers. She drew the figures of ladies in furs and ladies in silk and sequins for the newspaper advertisements. This young woman artist earned several thousand pounds a year, but Paul's mother only made several hundreds, and she was again dissatisfied. She so wanted to be first in something, and she did not succeed, even in making sketches for drapery advertisements.

She was down to breakfast on the morning of her birthday. Paul watched her face as she read her letters. He knew the lawyer's letter. As his mother read it, her face hardened and became more expressionless. Then a cold, determined look came on her mouth. She hid the letter under the pile of others, and said not a word about it.

"Didn't you have anything nice in the post for your birthday, mother?" said Paul.

"Quite moderately nice," she said, her voice cold and absent.

She went away to town without saying more.

But in the afternoon Uncle Oscar appeared. He said Paul's mother had had a long interview with the lawyer, asking if the whole five thousand could be advanced at once, as she was in debt.

"What do you think, uncle?" said the boy.

"I leave it to you, son."

"Oh, let her have it, then! We can get some more with the other," said the boy.

"A bird in the hand is worth two in the bush, laddie!" said Uncle Oscar.

"But I'm sure to know for the Grand National; or the Lincolnshire; or else the Derby. I'm sure to know for one of them," said Paul.

So Uncle Oscar signed the agreement, and Paul's mother touched the whole five thousand. Then something very curious happened. The voices in the house suddenly went mad, like a chorus of frogs on a spring evening. There were certain new furnishings, and Paul had a tutor. He was really going to Eton,° his father's school, in the following autumn. There were flowers in the winter, and a blossoming of the luxury Paul's mother had been used to. And yet the voices in the house, behind the sprays of mimosa and almond blossom, and from under the piles of iridescent cushions, simply trilled and screamed in a sort of ectasy: "There must be more money! Oh-h-h, there must be more money. Oh, now, now-w! Now-w-w—there must be more money—more than ever! More than ever!"

It frightened Paul terribly. He studied away at his Latin and Greek with his tutors. But his intense hours were spent with Bassett. The Grand National had gone by: he had not "known," and had lost a hundred pounds. Summer was at hand. He was in agony for the Lincoln. But even for the Lincoln he didn't "know" and he lost fifty pounds. He became wild-eyed and strange, as if something were going to explode in him.

Eton: England's most prestigious privately supported secondary school

"Let it alone, son! Don't you bother about it!" urged Uncle Oscar. But it was as if the boy couldn't really hear what his uncle was saying.

"I've got to know for the Derby! I've got to know for the Derby!" the child reiterated, his big blue eyes blazing with a sort of madness.

His mother noticed how overwrought he was.

"You'd better go to the seaside. Wouldn't you like to go now to the seaside, instead of waiting? I think you'd better," she said, looking down at him anxiously, her heart curiously heavy because of him.

But the child lifted his uncanny blue eyes.

"I couldn't possibly go before the Derby, mother!" he said. "I couldn't possibly!"

"Why not?" she said, her voice becoming heavy when she was opposed. "Why not? You can still go from the seaside to see the Derby with your Uncle Oscar, if that's what you wish. No need for you to wait here. Besides, I think you care too much about these races. It's a bad sign. My family has been a gambling family, and you won't know till you grow up how much damage it has done. But it has done damage. I shall have to send Bassett away, and ask Uncle Oscar not to talk racing to you, unless you promise to be reasonable about it; go away to the seaside and forget it. You're all nerves!"

"I'll do what you like, mother, so long as you don't send me away till after the Derby," the boy said.

"Send you away from where? Just from this house?"

"Yes," he said, gazing at her.

"Why, you curious child, what makes you care about this house so much, suddenly? I never knew you loved it."

He gazed at her without speaking. He had a secret within a secret, something he had not divulged, even to Bassett or to his Uncle Oscar.

But his mother, after standing undecided and a little bit sullen for some moments, said:

"Very well, then! Don't go to the seaside till after the Derby, if you don't wish it. But promise me you won't let your nerves go to pieces. Promise you won't think so much about horse racing and events, as you call them!"

"Oh, no," said the boy casually. "I won't think much about them, mother. You needn't worry. I wouldn't worry, mother, if I were you."

"If you were me and I were you," said his mother, "I wonder what we should do!"

"But you know you needn't worry, mother, don't you?" the boy repeated.

"I should be awfully glad to know it," she said wearily.

"Oh, well, you can, you know. I mean, you ought to know you needn't worry," he insisted.

"Ought I? Then I'll see about it," she said.

Paul's secret of secrets was his wooden horse, that which had no name. Since he was emancipated from a nurse and a nursery-governess, he had had his rocking horse removed to his own bedroom at the top of the house.

"Surely, you're too big for a rocking horse!" his mother had remonstrated.

"Well, you see mother, till I can have a real horse, I like to have some sort of animal about," had been his quaint answer.

"Do you feel he keeps you company?" she laughed.

"Oh, yes! He's very good, he always keeps me company, when I'm there," said Paul.

So the horse, rather shabby, stood in an arrested prance in the boy's bedroom.

The Derby was drawing near, and the boy grew more and more tense. He hardly heard what was spoken to him, he was very frail, and his eyes were really uncanny. His mother had sudden seizures of uneasiness about him. Sometimes, for half-an-hour, she would feel a sudden anxiety about him that was almost anguish. She wanted to rush to him at once, and know he was safe.

Two nights before the Derby, she was at a big party in town, when one of her rushes of anxiety about her boy, her first-born, gripped her heart till she could hardly speak. She fought with the feeling, might and main, for she believed in common sense. But it was too strong. The children's nursery-governess was terribly surprised and startled at being rung up in the night.

"Are the children all right, Miss Wilmot?"

"Oh, yes, they are quite all right."

"Master Paul? Is he all right?"

"He went to bed as right as a trivet. Shall I run up and look at him?"

"No," said Paul's mother reluctantly. "No! Don't trouble. It's all right. Don't sit up. We shall be home fairly soon." She did not want her son's privacy intruded upon.

"Very good," said the governess.

It was about one o'clock when Paul's mother and father drove up to their house. All was still. Paul's mother went to her room and slipped off her white fur coat. She had told her maid not to wait up for her. She heard her husband downstairs, mixing a whisky-and-soda.

And then, because of the strange anxiety at her heart, she stole upstairs to her son's room. Noiselessly she went along the upper corridor. Was there a faint noise? What was it?

She stood, with arrested muscles, outside his door, listening. There was a strange, heavy, and yet not loud noise. Her heart stood still. It was a soundless noise, yet rushing and powerful. Something huge, in violent, hushed motion. What was it? What in God's name was it? She ought to know. She felt that she knew the noise. She knew what it was.

Yet she could not place it. She couldn't say what it was. And on and on it went, like madness.

Softly, frozen with anxiety and fear, she turned the door handle.

The room was dark. Yet in the space near the window, she heard and saw something plunging to and fro. She gazed in fear and amazement.

Then suddenly she switched on the light, and saw her son, in his green pyjamas, madly surging on the rocking horse. The blaze of light suddenly lit him up, as he urged the wooden horse, and lit her up, as she stood, blonde, in her dress of pale green and crystal, in the doorway.

"Paul!" she cried. "Whatever are you doing?"

"It's Malabar!" he screamed, in a powerful, strange voice. "It's Malabar."

His eyes blazed at her for one strange and senseless second, as he ceased urging his wooden horse. Then he fell with a crash to the ground, and she, all her tormented motherhood flooding upon her, rushed to gather him up.

But he was unconscious, and unconscious he remained, with some brain-fever. He talked and tossed, and his mother sat stonily by his side.

"Malabar! It's Malabar! Bassett, Bassett, I know it! It's Malabar!"

So the child cried, trying to get up and urge the rocking horse that gave him his inspiration.

"What does he mean by Malabar?" asked the heart-frozen mother.

"I don't know," said his father stonily.

"What does he mean by Malabar?" she asked her brother Oscar.

"It's one of the horses running for the Derby," was the answer.

And, in spite of himself, Oscar Cresswell spoke to Bassett, and himself put a thousand on Malabar: at fourteen to one.

The third day of the illness was critical: they were waiting for a change. The boy, with his rather long, curly hair, was tossing ceaselessly on the pillow. He neither slept nor regained consciousness, and his eyes were like blue stones. His mother sat, feeling her heart had gone, turned actually into a stone.

In the evening, Oscar Cresswell did not come, but Bassett sent a message, saying could he come up for one moment, just one moment? Paul's mother was very angry at the intrusion, but on second thought she agreed. The boy was the same. Perhaps Bassett might bring him to consciousness.

The gardener, a shortish fellow with a little brown mustache, and sharp little brown eyes, tiptoed into the room, touched his imaginary cap to Paul's mother, and stole to the bedside, staring with glittering, smallish eyes, at the tossing, dying child.

"Master Paul!" he whispered. "Master Paul! Malabar came in first all right, a clean win. I did as you told me. You've made over seventy thousand pounds, you have; you've got over eighty thousand. Malabar came in all right, Master Paul."

"Malabar! Malabar! Did I say Malabar, mother? Did I say Malabar? Do you think I'm lucky, mother? I knew Malabar, didn't I? Over eighty thousand pounds! I call that lucky, don't you, mother? Over eighty thousand pounds! I knew, didn't I know I knew? Malabar came in all right. If I ride my horse till I'm sure, then I tell you, Bassett, you can go as high as you like. Did you go for all you were worth, Bassett?"

"I went a thousand on it, Master Paul."

"I never told you, mother, that if I can ride my horse, and get there, then I'm absolutely sure—oh, absolutely! Mother, did I ever tell you? I'm lucky."

"No, you never did," said the mother.

But the boy died in the night.

And even as he lay dead, his mother heard her brother's voice saying to her: "My God, Hester, you're eighty-odd thousand to the good and a poor devil of a son to the bad. But, poor devil, poor devil, he's best gone out of a life where he rides his rocking horse to find a winner."

QUESTIONS

1. In the phraseology of its beginning ("There was a woman . . ."), its simple style, its direct characterization, and its use of the wish motif—especially that of the wish that is granted only on conditions that nullify its desirability (compare the story of King Midas)—this story has the qualities of a fairy tale. Its differences, however—in characterization, setting, and ending—are especially significant. What do they tell us about the purpose of the story?
2. Characterize the mother fully. How does she differ from the stepmothers in fairy tales like "Cinderella" and "Hansel and Gretel"? How does the boy's mistake about *filthy lucker* clarify her thinking and her motivations? Why had her love for her husband turned to dust? Why is she "unlucky"?
3. What kind of a child is Paul? What are his motivations?
4. The initial assumptions of the story are that (a) a boy might get divinatory powers by riding a rocking horse, (b) a house can whisper. Could the second of these be accepted as little more than a metaphor? Once we have granted these initial assumptions, does the story develop plausibly?
5. It is ironical that the boy's attempt to stop the whispers should only increase them. Is this a plausible irony? Why? What does it tell us about the theme of the story? Why is it ironical that the whispers should be especially audible at Christmas time? What irony is contained in the boy's last speech?
6. In what way is the boy's furious riding on the rocking horse an appropriate symbol for materialistic pursuits?
7. How might a sentimental writer have ended the story?
8. How many persons in the story are affected (or infected) by materialism?
9. What is the theme of the story?

James Agee

A MOTHER'S TALE

The calf ran up the hill as fast as he could and stopped sharp. "Mama!" he cried, all out of breath. "What *is* it! What are they *doing?* Where are they *going!*"

Other spring calves came galloping too.

They all were looking up at her and awaiting her explanation, but she looked out over their excited eyes. As she watched the mysterious and majes-

A MOTHER'S TALE First published in 1952. James Agee (1909–1955) was born and grew up in Knoxville, Tennessee, was graduated from Harvard, and became a staff writer for *Fortune* and, later, *Time* magazines in New York City. During his Harvard years he worked one summer as a harvest hand in Oklahoma, Kansas, and Nebraska. He wrote this story while hospitalized in Santa Barbara, California.

tic thing they had never seen before, her own eyes became even more than ordinarily still, and during the considerable moment before she answered, she scarcely heard their urgent questioning.

Far out along the autumn plain, beneath the sloping light, an immense drove of cattle moved eastward. They went at a walk, not very fast, but faster than they could imaginably enjoy. Those in front were compelled by those behind; those at the rear, with few exceptions, did their best to keep up; those who were locked within the herd could no more help moving than the particles inside a falling rock. Men on horses rode ahead, and alongside, and behind, or spurred their horses intensely back and forth, keeping the pace steady, and the herd in shape; and from man to man a dog sped back and forth incessantly as a shuttle, barking, incessantly, in a hysterical voice. Now and then one of the men shouted fiercely, and this like the shrieking of the dog was tinily audible above a low and awesome sound which seemed to come not from the multitude of hooves but from the center of the world, and above the sporadic bawlings and bellowings of the herd.

From the hillside this tumult was so distant that it only made more delicate the prodigious silence in which the earth and sky were held; and, from the hill, the sight was as modest as its sound. The herd was virtually hidden in the dust it raised, and could be known, in general, only by the horns which pricked this flat sunlit dust like little briars. In one place a twist of the air revealed the trembling fabric of many backs; but it was only along the near edge of the mass that individual animals were discernible, small in a driven frieze, walking fast, stumbling and recovering, tossing their armed heads, or opening their skulls heavenward in one of those cries which reached the hillside long after the jaws were shut.

From where she watched, the mother could not be sure whether there were any she recognized. She knew that among them there must be a son of hers; she had not seen him since some previous spring, and she would not be seeing him again. Then the cries of the young ones impinged on her bemusement: "Where are they going?"

She looked in their ignorant eyes.

"Away," she said.

"Where?" they cried. "Where? Where?" her own son cried again.

She wondered what to say.

"On a long journey."

"But where *to?*" they shouted. "Yes, where *to?*" her son exclaimed; and she could see that he was losing his patience with her, as he always did when he felt she was evasive.

"I'm not sure," she said.

Their silence was so cold that she was unable to avoid their eyes for long.

"Well, not *really* sure. Because, you see," she said in her most reasonable tone, "I've never seen it with my own eyes, and that's the only way to *be* sure; *isn't* it."

They just kept looking at her. She could see no way out.

"But I've *heard* about it," she said with shallow cheerfulness, "from those who *have* seen it, and I don't suppose there's any good reason to doubt them."

She looked away over them again, and for all their interest in what she was about to tell them, her eyes so changed that they turned and looked, too.

The herd, which had been moving broadside to them, was being turned away, so slowly that like the turning of stars it could not quite be seen from one moment to the next; yet soon it was moving directly away from them, and even during the little while she spoke and they all watched after it, it steadily and very noticeably diminished, and the sounds of it as well.

"It happens always about this time of year," she said quietly while they watched. "Nearly all the men and horses leave, and go into the North and the West."

"Out on the range," her son said, and by his voice she knew what enchantment the idea already held for him.

"Yes," she said, "out on the range." And trying, impossibly, to imagine the range, they were touched by the breath of grandeur.

"And then before long," she continued, "everyone has been found, and brought into one place; and then . . . what you see, happens. All of them.

"Sometimes when the wind is right," she said more quietly, "you can hear them coming long before you can see them. It isn't even like a sound, at first. It's more as if something were moving far under the ground. It makes you uneasy. You wonder, why, what in the world can *that* be! Then you remember what it is and then you can really hear it. And then, finally, there they all are."

She could see this did not interest them at all.

"But where are they *going?*" one asked, a little impatiently.

"I'm coming to that," she said; and she let them wait. Then she spoke slowly but casually.

"They are on their way to a railroad."

There, she thought; that's for that look you all gave me when I said I wasn't sure. She waited for them to ask; they waited for her to explain.

"A railroad," she told them, "is great hard bars of metal lying side by side, or so they tell me, and they go on and on over the ground as far as the eye can see. And great wagons run on the metal bars on wheels, like wagon wheels but smaller, and these wheels are made of solid metal too. The wagons are much bigger than any wagon you've ever seen, as big as, big as sheds, they say, and they are pulled along on the iron bars by a terrible huge dark machine, with a loud scream."

"Big as *sheds?*" one of the calves said skeptically.

"Big *enough*, anyway," the mother said. "I told you I've never seen it myself. But those wagons are so big that several of us can get inside at once. And that's exactly what happens."

Suddenly she became very quiet, for she felt that somehow, she could not imagine just how, she had said altogether too much.

"Well, *what* happens?" her son wanted to know. "What do you mean, *happens?*"

She always tried hard to be a reasonably modern mother. It was probably better, she felt, to go on, than to leave them all full of imaginings and mystification. Besides, there was really nothing at all awful about what happened . . . if only one could know *why*.

"Well," she said, "it's nothing much, really. They just—why, when they all finally *get* there, why there are all the great cars waiting in a long line, and the big dark machine is up ahead . . . smoke comes out of it, they say . . . and . . . well, then, they just put us into the wagons, just as many as will fit in each wagon, and when everybody is in, why . . ." She hesitated, for again, though she couldn't be sure why, she was uneasy.

"Why then," her son said, "the train takes them away."

Hearing that word, she felt a flinching of the heart. Where had he picked it up, she wondered, and she gave him a shy and curious glance. Oh dear, she thought. I should never have even *begun* to explain. "Yes," she said, "when everybody is safely in, they slide the doors shut."

They were all silent for a little while. Then one of them asked thoughtfully, "Are they taking them somewhere they don't want to go?"

"Oh, I don't think so," the mother said. "I imagine it's very nice."

"I want to go," she heard her son say with ardor. "I want to go right now," he cried. "Can I, Mama? *Can* I? *Please?*" And looking into his eyes, she was overwhelmed by sadness.

"Silly thing," she said, "there'll be time enough for that when you're grown up. But what I very much hope," she went on, "is that instead of being chosen to go out on the range and to make the long journey, you will grow up to be very strong and bright so they will decide that you may stay here at home with Mother. And you, too," she added, speaking to the other little males; but she could not honestly wish this for any but her own, least of all for the eldest, strongest and most proud, for she knew how few are chosen.

She could see that what she said was not received with enthusiasm.

"But I want to go," her son said.

"Why?" she asked. "I don't think any of you realize that it's a great *honor* to be chosen to stay. A great privilege. Why, it's just the most ordinary ones are taken out onto the range. But only the very pick are chosen to stay here at home. If you want to go out on the range," she said in hurried and happy inspiration, "all you have to do is be ordinary and careless and silly. If you want to have even a chance to be chosen to stay, you have to try to be stronger and bigger and braver and brighter than anyone else, and that takes *hard work. Every day.* Do you see?" and she looked happily and hopefully from one to another. "Besides," she added, aware that they were not won over. "I'm told it's a very rough life out there, and the men are unkind."

"Don't you see," she said again; and she pretended to speak to all of them, but it was only to her son.

But he only looked at her. "Why do you want me to stay home?" he asked flatly; in their silence she knew the others were asking the same question.

"Because it's safe here," she said before she knew better; and realized she had put it in the most unfortunate way possible. "Not safe, not just that," she fumbled. "I mean . . . because here we *know* what happens, and what's going to happen, and there's never any doubt about it, never any reason to wonder, to worry. Don't you see? It's just *Home,*" and she put a smile on the word, "where we all know each other and are happy and well."

They were so merely quiet, looking back at her, that she felt they were neither won over nor alienated. Then she knew of her son that he, anyhow, was most certainly not persuaded, for he asked the question most dreaded: "Where do they go on the train?" And hearing him, she knew that she would stop at nothing to bring that curiosity and eagerness, and that tendency toward skepticism, within safe bounds.

"Nobody knows," she said, and she added, in just the tone she knew would most sharply engage them, "Not for sure, anyway."

"What do you mean, *not for sure,*" her son cried. And the oldest, biggest calf repeated the question, his voice cracking.

The mother deliberately kept silence as she gazed out over the plain, and while she was silent they all heard the last they would ever hear of all those who were going away: one last great cry, as faint almost as a breath; the infinitesimal jabbing vituperation of the dog; the solemn muttering of the earth.

"Well," she said, after even this sound was entirely lost, "there was one who came back." Their instant, trustful eyes were too much for her. She added, "Or so they say."

They gathered a little more closely around her, for now she spoke very quietly.

"It was my great-grandmother who told me," she said. "She was told it by *her* great-grandmother, who claimed she saw it with her own eyes, though of course I can't vouch for that. Because of course I wasn't even dreamed of then; and Great-grandmother was so very, very old, you see, that you couldn't always be sure she knew quite *what* she was saying."

Now that she began to remember it more clearly, she was sorry she had committed herself to telling it.

"Yes," she said, "the story is, there was one, *just* one, who ever came back, and he told what happened on the train, and where the train went and what happened after. He told it all in a rush, they say, the last things first and every which way, but as it was finally sorted out and gotten in order by those who heard it and those who they told it to, this is more or less what happened:

"He said that after the men had gotten just as many of us as they could into the car he was in, so that their sides pressed tightly together and nobody could lie down, they slid the door shut with a startling rattle and a bang, and then there was a sudden jerk, so strong they might have fallen except that they were packed so closely together, and the car began to move. But after it had moved only a little way, it stopped as suddenly as it had started, so that they all nearly fell down again. You see, they were just moving up the next car that was joined on behind, to put more of us into it. He could see it all between the boards of the car, because the boards were built a little apart from each other, to let in air."

Car, her son said again to himself. Now he would never forget the word.

"He said that then, for the first time in his life, he became very badly frightened, he didn't know why. But he was sure, at that moment, that there was something dreadfully to be afraid of. The others felt this same great fear. They called out loudly to those who were being put into the car behind, and the others called back, but it was no use; those who were getting aboard were between narrow white fences and then were walking up a narrow slope and the men kept jabbing them as they do when they are in an unkind humor, and there was no way to go but on into the car. There was no way to get out of the car, either: he tried, with all his might, and he was the one nearest the door.

"After the next car behind was full, and the door was shut, the train jerked forward again, and stopped again, and they put more of us into still another car, and so on, and on, until all the starting and stopping no longer frightened anybody; it was just something uncomfortable that was never going to stop, and they began instead to realize how hungry and thirsty they were. But there was no food and no water, so they just had to put up with this; and about the time they became resigned to going without their suppers (for now it was almost dark), they heard a sudden and terrible scream which frightened them even more deeply than anything had frightened them before, and the train began to move again, and they braced their legs once more for the jolt when it would stop, but this time, instead of stopping, it began to go fast, and then even faster, so fast that the ground nearby slid past like a flooded creek and the whole country, he claimed, began to move too, turning slowly around a far mountain as if it were all one great wheel. And then there was a strange kind of disturbance inside the car, he said, or even inside his very bones. He felt as if everything in him was *falling,* as if he had been filled full of a heavy liquid that all wanted to flow one way, and all the others were leaning as he was leaning, away from this queer heaviness that was trying to pull them over, and then just as suddenly this leaning heaviness was gone and they nearly fell again before they could stop leaning against it. He could never understand what this was, but it too happened so many times that they got used to it, just as they got used to seeing the country turn like a slow wheel, and just as they got used to the long cruel screams of the engine, and the steady iron noise beneath them which made the cold darkness so fearsome, and the hunger and the thirst and the continual standing up, and the moving on and on and on as if they would never stop."

"Didn't they ever stop?" one asked.

"Once in a great while," she replied. "Each time they did," she said, "he thought, Oh, now *at last! At last* we can get out and stretch our tired legs and lie down! *At last* we'll be given food and water! But they never let them out. And they never gave them food or water. They never even cleaned up under them. They had to stand in their manure and in the water they made."

"Why did the train stop?" her son asked; and with somber gratification she saw that he was taking all this very much to heart.

"He could never understand why," she said. "Sometimes men would walk up and down alongside the cars, and the more nervous and the more trustful of us would call out; but they were only looking around, they never seemed to do anything. Sometimes he could see many houses and bigger buildings together where people lived. Sometimes it was far out in the country and after they had stood still for a long time they would hear a little noise which quickly became louder, and then became suddenly a noise so loud it stopped their breathing, and during this noise something black would go by, very close, and so fast it couldn't be seen. And then it was gone as suddenly as it had appeared, and the noise became small, and then in the silence their train would start up again.

"Once, he tells us, something very strange happened. They were standing still, and cars of a very different kind began to move slowly past. These cars were not red, but black, with many glass windows like those in a house; and he says they were as full of human beings as the car he was in was full of our kind. And one of these people looked into his eyes and smiled, as if he liked him, or as if he knew only too well how hard the journey was.

"So by this account it happens to them, too," she said with a certain pleased vindictiveness. "Only they were sitting down at their ease, not standing. And the one who smiled was eating."

She was still, trying to think of something; she couldn't quite grasp the thought.

"But didn't they *ever* let them out?" her son asked.

The oldest calf jeered. "Of *course* they did. He came back, didn't he? How would he ever come back if he didn't get out?"

"They didn't let them out," she said, "for a long, long time."

"How long?"

"So long, and he was so tired, he could never quite be sure. But he said that it turned from night to day and from day to night and back again several times over, with the train moving nearly all of this time, and that when it finally stopped, early one morning, they were all so tired and so discouraged that they hardly even noticed any longer, let alone felt any hope that anything would change for them, ever again; and then all of a sudden men came up and put up a wide walk and unbarred the door and slid it open, and it was the most wonderful and happy moment of his life when he saw the door open, and walked into the open air with all his joints trembling, and drank the water and ate the delicious food they had ready for him; it was worth the whole terrible journey."

Now that these scenes came clear before her, there was a faraway shining in her eyes, and her voice, too, had something in it of the faraway.

"When they had eaten and drunk all they could hold they lifted up their heads and looked around, and everything they saw made them happy. Even the trains made them cheerful now, for now they were no longer afraid of them. And though these trains were forever breaking to pieces and joining again with other broken pieces, with shufflings and clashings and rude cries, they hardly paid them attention any more, they were so pleased to be in their new home, and so surprised and delighted to find they were among thousands upon thousands of strangers of their own kind, all lifting up their voices in peacefulness and thanksgiving, and they were so wonderstruck by all they could see, it was so beautiful and so grand.

"For he has told us that now they lived among fences as white as bone, so many, and so spiderishly complicated, and shining so pure, that there's no use trying even to hint at the beauty and the splendor of it to anyone who knows only the pitiful little outfittings of a ranch. Beyond these mazy fences, through the dark and bright smoke which continually turned along the sunlight, dark buildings stood shoulder to shoulder in a wall as huge and proud as mountains. All through the air, all the time, there was an iron humming like the humming of the iron bar after it has been struck to tell the men it is time to eat, and in all the air, all the time, there was that same strange kind of iron strength which makes the silence before lightning so different from all other silence.

"Once for a little while the wind shifted and blew over them straight from the great buildings, and it brought a strange and very powerful smell which confused and disturbed them. He could never quite describe this smell, but he has told us it was unlike anything he had ever known before. It smelled like old fire, he said, and old blood and fear and darkness and sorrow and most terrible and brutal force and something else, something in it that made him want to run away. This sudden uneasiness and this wish to run away swept through every one of them, he tells us, so that they were all moved at once as restlessly as so many leaves in a wind, and there was great worry in their voices. But soon the leaders among them concluded that it was simply the way men must smell when there are a great many of them living together. Those dark buildings must be crowded very full of men, they decided, probably as many thousands of them, indoors, as there were of us, outdoors; so it was no wonder their smell was so strong and, to our kind, so unpleasant. Besides, it was so clear now in every other way that men were not as we had always supposed, but were doing everything they knew how to make us comfortable and happy, that we ought to just put up with their smell, which after all they couldn't help, any more than we could help our own. Very likely men didn't like the way we smelled, any more than we liked theirs. They passed along these ideas to the others, and soon everyone felt more calm, and then the wind changed again, and the fierce smell no longer came to them, and the smell of their own kind was back again, very strong of course, in such a crowd, but ever so homey and comforting, and everyone felt easy again.

"They were fed and watered so generously, and treated so well, and the majesty and the loveliness of this place where they had all come to rest was so far beyond anything they had ever known or dreamed of, that many of the simple and ignorant, whose memories were short, began to wonder whether that whole difficult journey, or even their whole lives up to now, had ever really been. Hadn't it all been just shadows, they murmured, just a bad dream?

"Even the sharp ones, who knew very well it had all really happened, began to figure that everything up to now had been made so full of pain only so that all they had come to now might seem all the sweeter and the more glorious. Some of the oldest and deepest were even of a mind that all the puzzle and tribulation of the journey had been sent us as a kind of harsh trying or proving of our worthiness; and that it was entirely fitting and proper that we could earn our way through to such rewards as these, only through suffering, and through being patient under pain which was beyond our understanding; and that now at the last, to those who had borne all things well, all things were made known: for the mystery of suffering stood revealed in joy. And now as they looked back over all that was past, all their sorrows and bewilderments seemed so little and so fleeting that, from the simplest among them even to the most wise, they could feel only the kind of amused pity we feel toward the very young when, with the first thing that hurts them or they are forbidden, they are sure there is nothing kind or fair in all creation, and carry on accordingly, raving and grieving as if their hearts would break."

She glanced among them with an indulgent smile, hoping the little lesson would sink home. They seemed interested but somewhat dazed. I'm talking way over their heads, she realized. But by now she herself was too deeply absorbed in her story to modify it much. *Let* it be, she thought, a little impatient; it's over *my* head, for that matter.

"They had hardly before this even wondered that they were alive," she went on, "and now all of a sudden they felt they understood *why* they were. This made them very happy, but they were still only beginning to enjoy this new wisdom when quite a new and different kind of restiveness ran among them. Before they quite knew it they were all moving once again, and now they realized that they were being moved, once more, by men, toward still some other place and purpose they could not know. But during these last hours they had been so well that now they felt no uneasiness, but all moved forward calm and sure toward better things still to come; he had told us that he no longer felt as if he were being driven, even as it became clear that they were going toward the shade of those great buildings; but guided.

"He was guided between fences which stood ever more and more narrowly near each other, among companions who were pressed ever more and more closely against one another; and now as he felt their warmth against him it was not uncomfortable, and his pleasure in it was not through any need to be close among others through anxiousness, but was a new kind of strong and gentle delight, at being so very close, so deeply of his own kind, that it seemed as if the very breath and heartbeat of each one were being exchanged through all that multitude, and each was another, and others were each, and each was a multitude, and the multitude was one. And quieted and made mild within this melting, they now entered the cold shadow cast by the buildings, and now with every step the smell of the buildings grew stronger, and in the darkening air the glittering of the fences was ever more queer.

"And now as they pressed ever more intimately together he could see ahead of him a narrow gate, and he was strongly pressed upon from either side and from behind, and went in eagerly, and now he was between two fences so narrowly set that he brushed either fence with either flank, and walked alone, seeing just one other ahead of him, and knowing of just one other behind him, and for a moment the strange thought came to him, that the one ahead was his father, and that the one behind was the son he had never begotten.

"And now the light was so changed that he knew he must have come inside one of the gloomy and enormous buildings, and the smell was so much stronger that it seemed almost to burn his nostrils, and the smell and the somber new light blended together and became some other thing again, beyond his describing to us except to say that the whole air beat with it like one immense heart and it was as if the beating of this heart were pure violence infinitely manifolded upon violence: so that the uneasy feeling stirred in him again that it would be wise to turn around and run out of this place just as fast and as far as ever he could go. This he heard, as if he were telling it to himself at the top of his voice, but it came from somewhere so deep and so dark inside him that he could only hear the shouting of it as less than a whisper, as just a hot and chilling breath, and he scarcely heeded it, there was so much else to attend to.

"For as he walked along in this sudden and complete loneliness, he tells us, this wonderful knowledge of being one with all his race meant less and less to him, and in its place came something still more wonderful: he knew what it was to be himself alone, a creature separate and different from any other, who had never been before, and would never be again. He could feel this in his whole weight as he walked, and in each foot as he put it down and gave his weight to it and moved above it, and in every muscle as he moved, and it was a pride which lifted him up and made him feel large, and a pleasure which pierced him through. And as he began with such wondering delight to be aware of his own exact singleness in this world, he also began to understand (or so he thought) just why these fences were set so very narrow, and just why he was walking all by himself. It stole over him, he tells us, like the feeling of a slow cool wind, that he was being guided toward some still more wonderful reward or revealing, up ahead, which he could not of course imagine, but he was sure it was being held in store for him alone.

"Just then the one ahead of him fell down with a great sigh, and was so quickly taken out of the way that he did not even have to shift the order of his hooves as he walked on. The sudden fall and the sound of that sigh dismayed him, though, and something within him told him that it would be wise to look up: and there he saw Him.

"A little bridge ran crosswise above the fences. He stood on this bridge with His feet as wide apart as He could set them. He wore spattered trousers but from the belt up He was naked and as wet as rain. Both arms were raised high above His head and in both hands He held an enormous Hammer. With a grunt which was hardly like the voice of a human being, and with all His strength, He brought this Hammer down into the forehead of our friend: who, in a blinding blazing, heard from his own mouth the beginning of a gasping sigh; then there was only darkness."

Oh, this is *enough!* it's *enough!* she cried out within herself, seeing their terrible young eyes. How *could* she have been so foolish as to tell so much!

"What happened then?" she heard, in the voice of the oldest calf, and she was horrified. This shining in their eyes: was it only excitement? no pity? no fear?

"What happened?" two others asked.

Very well, she said to herself. I've gone so far; now I'll go the rest of the way. She decided not to soften it, either. She'd teach them a lesson they wouldn't forget in a hurry.

"Very well," she was surprised to hear herself say aloud.

"How long he lay in this darkness he couldn't know, but when he began to come out of it, all he knew was the most unspeakably dreadful pain. He was upside down and very slowly swinging and turning, for he was hanging by the tendons of his heels from great frightful hooks, and he has told us that the feeling was as if his hide were being torn from him inch by inch, in one piece. And then as he became more clearly aware he found that this was exactly what was happening. Knives would sliver and slice along both flanks, between the hide and the living flesh; then there was a moment of most precious relief; then red hands seized his hide and there was a jerking of the hide and a tearing of tissue which it was almost as terrible to hear as to feel, turning his whole body and the poor head at the bottom of it; and then the knives again.

"It was so far beyond anything he had ever known unnatural and amazing that he hung there through several more such slicings and jerkings and tearings before he was fully able to take it all in: then, with a scream, and a supreme straining of all his strength, he tore himself from the hooks and collapsed sprawling to the floor and, scrambling right to his feet, charged the men with the knives. For just a moment they were so astonished and so terrified they could not move. Then they moved faster than he had ever known men could—and so did all the other men who chanced to be in his way. He ran down a glowing floor of blood and down endless corridors which were hung with the bleeding carcasses of our kind and with bleeding fragments of carcasses, among blood-clothed men who carried bleeding weapons, and out of that vast room into the open, and over and through one fence after another, shoving aside many an astounded stranger and shouting out warnings as he ran, and away up the railroad toward the West.

"How he ever managed to get away, and how he ever found his way home, we can only try to guess. It's told that he scarcely knew, himself, by the time he came to this part of his story. He was impatient with those who interrupted him to ask about that, he had so much more important things to tell them, and by then he was so exhausted and so far gone that he could say nothing very clear about the little he did know. But we can realize that he must have had really tremendous strength, otherwise he couldn't have outlived the Hammer; and that strength such as his—which we simply don't see these days, it's of the olden time—is capable of things our own strongest and bravest would sicken to dream of. But there was something even stronger than his strength. There was his righteous fury, which nothing could stand up against, which brought him out of that fearful place. And there was his high and burning and heroic purpose, to keep him safe along the way, and to guide him home, and to keep the breath of life in him until he could warn us. He did manage to tell us that he just followed the railroad, but how he chose one among the many which branched out from that place, he couldn't say. He told us, too, that from time to time he recognized shapes of mountains and other landmarks, from his journey by train, all reappearing backward and with a changed look and hard to see, too (for he was shrewd enough to travel mostly at night), but still recognizable. But that isn't enough to account for it. For he has told us, too, that he simply *knew* the way; that he didn't hesitate one moment in choosing the right line of railroad, or even think of it as choosing; and that the landmarks didn't really guide him, but just made him the more sure of what he was already sure of; and that whenever he *did* encounter human beings—and during the later stages of his journey, when he began to doubt he would live to tell us, he traveled day and night—they never so much as moved to make him trouble, but stopped dead in their tracks, and their jaws fell open.

"And surely we can't wonder that their jaws fell open. I'm sure yours would, if you had seen him as he arrived, and I'm very glad I wasn't there to see it, either, even though it is said to be the greatest and most momentous day of all the days that ever were or shall be. For we have the testimony of eyewitnesses, how he looked, and it is only too vivid, even to hear of. He came up out of the East as much staggering as galloping (for by now he was so worn out by pain and exertion and loss of blood that he could hardly stay upright), and his heels were so piteously torn by the hooks that his hooves doubled under more often than not, and in his broken forehead the mark of the Hammer was like the socket for a third eye.

"He came to the meadow where the great trees made shade over the water. 'Bring them all together!' he cried out, as soon as he could find breath. 'All!' Then he drank; and then he began to speak to those who were already there: for as soon as he saw himself in the water it was as clear to him as it was to those who watched him that there was no time left to send for the others. His hide was all gone from his head and his neck and his forelegs and his chest and most of one side and a part of the other side. It was flung backward from his naked muscles by the wind of his running and now it lay around him in the dust like a ragged garment. They say there is no imagining how terrible and in some way how grand the eyeball is when the skin has been taken entirely from around it: his eyes, which were bare in this way, also burned with pain, and with the final energies of his life, and with his desperate concern to warn us while he could; and he rolled his eyes wildly while he talked, or looked piercingly from one to another of the listeners, interrupting himself to cry out, *'Believe* me! Oh, *believe* me!' For it had evidently never occurred to him that he might not be believed, and must make this last great effort, in addition to all he had gone through for us, to *make* himself believed; so that he groaned with sorrow and with rage and railed at them without tact or mercy for their slowness to believe. He had scarcely what you could call a voice left, but with this relic of a voice he shouted and bellowed and bullied us and insulted us, in the agony of his concern. While he talked he bled from the mouth, and the mingled blood and saliva hung from his chin like the beard of a goat.

"Some say that with his naked face, and his savage eyes, and that beard and the hide lying off his bare shoulders like shabby clothing, he looked almost human. But others feel this is an irreverence even to think; and others, that it is a poor compliment to pay the one who told us, at such cost to himself, the true ultimate purpose of Man. Some did not believe he had ever come from our ranch in the first place, and of course he was so different from us in appearance and even in his voice, and so changed from what he might ever have looked or sounded like before, that nobody could recognize him for sure, though some were sure they did. Others suspected that he had been sent among us with his story for some mischievous and cruel purpose, and the fact that they could not imagine what this purpose might be, made them, naturally, all the more suspicious. Some believed he was actually a man, trying—and none too successfully, they said—to disguise himself as one of us; and again the fact that they could not imagine why a man would do this, made them all the more uneasy. There were quite a few who doubted that anyone who could get into such bad condition as he was in, was fit even to give reliable information, let alone advice, to those in good health. And some whispered, even while he spoke, that he had turned lunatic; and many came to believe this. It wasn't only that his story was so fantastic; there was good reason to wonder, many felt, whether anybody in his right mind would go to such trouble for others. But even those who did not believe him listened intently, out of curiosity to hear so wild a tale, and out of the respect it is only proper to show any creature who is in the last agony.

"What he told, was what I have just told you. But his purpose was away beyond just the telling. When they asked questions, no matter how curious or suspicious or idle or foolish, he learned, toward the last, to answer them with all the patience he could and in all the detail he could remember. He even invited them to examine his wounded heels and the pulsing wound in his head as closely as they pleased. He even begged them to, for he knew that before everything else, he must be believed. For unless we could believe him, wherever could we find any reason, or enough courage, to do the hard and dreadful things he told us we must do!

"It was only these things, he cared about. Only for these, he came back."

Now clearly remembering what these things were, she felt her whole being quail. She looked at the young ones quickly and as quickly looked away.

"While he talked," she went on, "and our ancestors listened, men came quietly among us; one of them shot him. Whether he was shot in kindness or to silence him is an endlessly disputed question which will probably never be settled. Whether, even, he died of the shot, or through his own great pain and weariness (for his eyes, they say, were glazing for some time before the men came), we will never be sure. Some suppose even that he may have died of his sorrow and his concern for us. Others feel that he had quite enough to die of, without that. All these things are tangled and lost in the disputes of those who love to theorize and to argue. There is no arguing about his dying words, though; they were very clearly remembered:

" *'Tell them! Believe!'* "

After a while her son asked, "What did he tell them to do?"

She avoided his eyes. "There's a great deal of disagreement about that, too," she said after a moment. "You see, he was so very tired."

They were silent.

"So tired," she said, "some think that toward the end, he really *must* have been out of his mind."

"Why?" asked her son.

"Because he was so tired out and so badly hurt."

They looked at her mistrustfully.

"And because of what he told us to do."

"What did he tell us to do?" her son asked again.

Her throat felt dry. "Just . . . things you can hardly bear even to think of. That's all."

They waited. "Well, *what?*" her son asked in a cold, accusing voice.

" *'Each one is himself,'* " she said shyly. " *'Not of the herd. Himself alone.'* That's one."

"What else?"

" *'Obey nobody. Depend on none.'* "

"What else?"

She found that she was moved. " *'Break down the fences,'* " she said less shyly. " *'Tell everybody, everywhere.'* "

"Where?"

"Everywhere. You see, he thought there must be ever so many more of us than we had ever known."

They were silent. "What else?" her son asked.

" *'For if even a few do not hear me, or disbelieve me, we are all betrayed.'* "

"Betrayed?"

"He meant, doing as men want us to. Not for ourselves, or the good of each other."

They were puzzled.

"Because, you see, he felt there was no other way." Again her voice altered: " *'All who are put on the range are put onto trains. All who are put onto trains meet the Man With The Hammer. All who stay home are kept there to breed others to go onto the range, and so betray themselves and their kind and their children forever.*

" *'We are brought into this life only to be victims; and there is no other way for us unless we save ourselves.' "*

"Do you understand?"

Still they were puzzled, she saw; and no wonder, poor things. But now the ancient lines rang in her memory, terrible and brave. They made her somehow proud. She began actually to want to say them.

" *'Never be taken,' "* she said. " *'Never be driven. Let those who can, kill Man. Let those who cannot, avoid him.' "*

She looked around at them.

"What else?" her son asked, and in his voice there was a rising valor.

She looked straight into his eyes. " *'Kill the yearlings,' "* she said very gently. " *'Kill the calves.' "*

She saw the valor leave his eyes.

"Kill us?"

She nodded, " *'So long as Man holds dominion over us,' "* she said. And in dread and amazement she heard herself add, " *'Bear no young.'"*

With this they all looked at her at once in such a way that she loved her child, and all these others, as never before; and there dilated within her such a sorrowful and marveling grandeur that for a moment she was nothing except her own inward whisper, "Why, *I* am one alone. And of the herd, too. Both at once. All one."

Her son's voice brought her back: "Did they do what he told them to?"

The oldest one scoffed, "Would we be here, if they had?"

"They say some did," the mother replied. "Some tried. Not all."

"What did the men do to them?" another asked.

"I don't know," she said. "It was such a very long time ago."

"Do you believe it?" asked the oldest calf.

"There are some who believe it," she said.

"Do *you?*"

"I'm told that far back in the wildest corners of the range there are some of us, mostly very, very old ones, who have never been taken. It's said that they meet, every so often, to talk and just to think together about the heroism and the terror of two sublime Beings, The One Who Came Back, and The Man With The Hammer. Even here at home, some of the old ones, and some of us who are just old-fashioned, believe it, or parts of it anyway. I know there are some who say that a hollow at the center of the forehead—a sort of shadow of the Hammer's blow—is a sign of very special ability. And I remember how Great-grandmother used to sing an old, pious song, let's see now, yes, 'Be not like dumb-driven cattle, be a hero in the strife.' But there aren't many. Not any more."

"Do *you* believe it?" the oldest calf insisted; and now she was touched to realize that every one of them, from the oldest to the youngest, needed very badly to be sure about that.

"Of course not, silly," she said; and all at once she was overcome by a most curious shyness, for it occurred to her that in the course of time, this young thing might be bred to her. "It's just an old, old legend." With a tender little laugh she added, lightly, "We use it to frighten children with."

By now the light was long on the plain and the herd was only a fume of gold near the horizon. Behind it, dung steamed, and dust sank gently to the shattered ground. She looked far away for the moment, wondering. Something—it was like a forgotten word on the tip of the tongue. She felt the sudden chill of the late afternoon and she wondered what she had been wondering about. "Come, children," she said briskly, "it's high time for supper." And she turned away; they followed.

The trouble was, her son was thinking, you could never trust her. If she said a thing was so, she was probably just trying to get her way with you. If she said a thing wasn't so, it probably was so. But you never could be sure. Not without seeing for yourself. I'm going to go, he told himself; I don't care *what* she wants. And if it isn't so, why then I'll live on the range and make the great journey and find out what *is* so. And if what she told was true, why then I'll know ahead of time and the one *I* will charge is The Man With The Hammer. I'll put Him and His Hammer out of the way forever, and that will make me an even better hero than The One Who Came Back.

So, when his mother glanced at him in concern, not quite daring to ask her question, he gave her his most docile smile, and snuggled his head against her, and she was comforted.

The littlest and youngest of them was doing double skips in his efforts to keep up with her. Now that he wouldn't be interrupting her, and none of the big ones would hear and make fun of him, he shyly whispered his question, so warmly moistly ticklish that she felt as if he were licking her ear.

"What is it, darling?" she asked, bending down.

"What's a train?"

QUESTIONS

1. This is a *story* containing a *tale*. The characters in the *story* are a cow and some spring calves, one of whom is her son. The principal characters in the *tale* are The One Who Came Back and The Man With The Hammer. To what extent are the characters in the *story* animals? To what extent are they human? How do they illuminate human motherhood, childhood, problems of education?
2. Can the cattle in the *tale* also be taken as both animal and human? Discuss the events of the tale from the trainride to the return of The One Who Came Back as they illuminate the experience of cattle.
3. At the allegorical level of interpretation, discuss the possible human applications or meanings of (a) the cowherds, (b) the trainride, (c) the train with glass windows full of human beings (page 324), (d) the stockyards (pages 324–26), (e) The Man With The Hammer, (f) the slaughterhouse (pages 327–28).
4. Explain the strange thought of the protagonist (page 327) "that the one ahead was his father, and that the one behind was the son he had never begotten."

5. Discuss The One Who Came Back as a religious prophet who, on his return, attempts to found a new religion and preach a new social gospel. Does his experience parallel that of any prophet you can think of? In what ways? How is his preaching received? What comes of his attempt?
6. What is the essence of this prophet's message? How does it differ from traditional religious messages? What meanings does the tale suggest about the possible ultimate government, destiny, and meaning of human life?
7. Does the *story* provide any alleviation of the grim message of the *tale*?
8. Does the mother believe the tale? Why does she tell it? How much validity or truth-value does the tale have? Should *we* believe it?

9. The Scale of Value

Our purpose in the preceding chapters has been to develop not literary critics but proficient readers—readers who choose wisely and read well. Yet good reading involves criticism, for choice necessitates judgment. Though we need not, to read well, be able to settle the relative claims of Welty and Mansfield or of Hemingway and Faulkner, we do need to discriminate between the genuine and the spurious, the consequential and the trivial, the significant and the merely entertaining. Our first object, naturally, is enjoyment; but full development as human beings requires that we enjoy most what is most worth enjoying.

There are no easy rules for literary judgment. Such judgment depends ultimately on our perceptivity, intelligence, and experience; it is a product of how much and how alertly we have lived and how much and how well we have read. Yet at least two basic principles may be set up. *First, every story is to be initially judged by how fully it achieves its central purpose.* Each element in the story is to be judged by the effectiveness of its contribution to the central purpose. In a good story every element works with every other element for the accomplishment of this central purpose. It follows that no element in the story may be judged in isolation.

Perhaps the most frequent mistake made by inexperienced readers when called upon for a judgment is to judge the elements of the story in isolation, independently of each other. For example, a student once wrote of "I'm a Fool" that it is not a very good story "because it is not written in good English." And certainly the style of the story, if judged by itself, is very poor indeed: the language is slangy and ungrammatical; the sentences are often disjointed and broken-backed; the narrator constantly digresses and is at times so incapable of expressing himself that he can only say "etc., etc., you know." But no high level of discrimination is needed to see that just such a style is essential to the purpose of the story. The uneducated race-track swipe, whose failure in school life has made him feel both scornful and envious of boys who "go to high schools and college," can hardly speak otherwise than as he does here; the digressions, moreover, are not truly digressions, for each of them supplies additional insight into the character of the swipe, which is the true subject of the story. The same kind of claim can be made for the style of "Haircut."

The principle of judgment just applied to style may be applied to every other element in a story. We cannot say that "The Japanese Quince" is a poor story because it does not have an exciting, fast-moving plot: plot can be judged only in relation to the other elements in the story and to its central purpose, and in this relationship the plot of "The Japanese Quince" is a good one. We cannot say that "The Lottery" is a poor story because it contains no such complex characterization as is to be found in "I'm a Fool." The purpose of "The Lottery" is to make a generalization about the persistence of dark communal impulses in human life, and for this purpose its characterization is adequate: a more complete characterization might obscure this central purpose.

Every first-rate story is an organic whole. All its parts are related, and all are necessary to the central purpose. Near the beginning of "The Most Dangerous Game" there is a suggestion of theme. When Whitney declares that hunting is a great sport—for the hunter, not for the jaguar—Rainsford replies, "Who cares how a jaguar feels? . . . They've no understanding." To this, Whitney replies: "I rather think they understand one thing—fear. The fear of pain and the fear of death." Evidently Rainsford has something to learn about how it feels to be hunted, and presumably during the hunt Rainsford learns it, for when General Zaroff turns back the first time—playing cat and mouse—we are told, "Then it was that Rainsford knew the full meaning of terror." Later, on the morning of the third day, Rainsford is awakened by the baying of hounds—"a sound that made him know that he had new things to learn about fear." But, really, little is made of Rainsford's terror during the hunt. The main interest focuses on Malay man-catchers, Burmese tiger pits, Uganda knife-throwers—in short, on what Zaroff refers to as "Your brain against mine. Your woodcraft against mine. Your strength and stamina against mine. Outdoor chess!" The story ends with the physical triumph of Rainsford over Zaroff. Has Rainsford been altered by the experience? Has he learned anything significant? Has he changed his attitudes toward hunting? We cannot answer, for the author's interest has been elsewhere. What connection has the final sentence—"He had never slept in a better bed, Rainsford decided"—to the question "Who cares how a jaguar feels?"

In "The Storm" we are presented with an experience of mounting terror in a woman who (1) returns to an empty, lonely house during the outbreak of a storm and who (2) discovers that her husband is a murderer. There is, of course, no logical connection between the storm and the fact that her husband is a murderer or her discovery of that fact: the coincidence of the storm and the discovery is simply that—a coincidence. The presence of this coincidence and the author's manipulation of point of view (her temporary suppression of Mrs. Willsom's consciousness, in order to prolong suspense, when she sees the body in the trunk and when she recognizes the ring on her husband's finger) are partial clues that the author's purpose is not really to provide insight into human terror so much as to produce terror in the reader. In the light of this purpose, the storm and the discovery of the murder are both justified in the story, for both help to produce terror in the reader. At the same time, their co-presence largely prevents the story from being more meaningful, for what might have been either (1) a study of irrational terror in a woman left alone in an isolated house during a storm or (2) a study of rational terror in a woman who discovers that her husband is a murderer is prevented from being either. Thus "The Storm" is a skillfully written suspense story rather than a story of human insight.

Once a story has been judged successful in achieving its central purpose, we may apply a second principle of judgment. *A story, if successful, may be judged by the significance of its purpose.* If every story is to be judged by how successfully it integrates its materials into an organic unity, it is also to be judged by the extent, the range, and the value of the materials integrated. This principle returns us to our distinction between escape and interpretation. If a story's only aim is to entertain, whether by mystifying, surprising, thrilling, provoking to laughter or tears, or furnishing a substitute dream life, we may judge it of less value than a story whose aim is to *reveal.* "That Evening Sun," "The Storm," "The Drunkard," and "The Catbird Seat" are all successful stories if we judge them by the degree to which they fulfill their central purpose. But "That Evening Sun" has a more significant purpose than "The Storm" and "The Drunkard" a more significant purpose than "The Catbird Seat." When a story does provide some revelation—does make some serious statement about life—we may measure it by the breadth and depth of that revelation. "The Drunkard" and "That Evening Sun" are both fine stories, but

"That Evening Sun" attempts a deeper probing than does "The Drunkard." The situation with which is it is concerned is more crucial, cuts deeper. The story reveals a more significant range and depth of life.

Some stories, then, like "The Storm" and "The Catbird Seat" provide good fun and innocent merriment, and even may convey some measure of interpretation along the way. Others, like "The Drunkard" and "That Evening Sun" afford the reader a deeper enjoyment through the profounder and more consistent insights they give into life. A third type, like many of the soap operas of television and radio, offers a cheaper and less innocent pleasure by providing escape under the guise of interpretation. Such stories, while professing to present real-life situations and everyday people and happenings, actually, by their shallowness of characterization, their falsifications of plot, their use of stock themes and stock emotions, present us with dangerous oversimplifications and distortions. They seriously misrepresent life and are harmful to the extent that they keep us from a more sensitive, more discriminating response to experience.

The above types of stories do not fall into sharp, distinct categories. There are no fortified barriers running between them to inform us when we are passing from one realm into another. There are no appointed officials to whom we can apply for certain information. Our only passports are our own good judgments, based on our accumulated experience with both literature and life. Nevertheless, certain questions, if asked wisely and with consideration for the two principles developed in this chapter, may help us both to understand the stories we read and to place them with rough accuracy on a scale of value that rises through many gradations from "poor" to "good" to "great." These questions, most of them explored in the previous chapters of this book, are, for convenience, summarized here.

GENERAL QUESTIONS FOR ANALYSIS AND EVALUATION

Plot
1. Who is the protagonist of the story? What are the conflicts? Are they physical, intellectual, moral, or emotional? Is the main conflict between sharply differentiated good and evil, or is it more subtle and complex?
2. Does the plot have unity? Are all the episodes relevant to the total meaning or effect of the story? Does each incident grow logically out of the preceding incident and lead naturally to the next? Is the ending happy, unhappy, or indeterminate? Is it fairly achieved?
3. What use does the story make of chance and coincidence? Are these occurrences used to initiate, to complicate, or to resolve the story? How improbable are they?

4. How is suspense created in the story? Is the interest confined to "What happens next?" or are larger concerns involved? Can you find examples of mystery? of dilemma?
5. What use does the story make of surprise? Are the surprises achieved fairly? Do they serve a significant purpose? Do they divert the reader's attention from weaknesses in the story?
6. To what extent is this a "formula" story?

Characters

7. What means does the author use to reveal character? Are the characters sufficiently dramatized? What use is made of character contrasts?
8. Are the characters consistent in their actions? adequately motivated? plausible? Does the author successfully avoid stock characters?
9. Is each character fully enough developed to justify its role in the story? Are the main characters round or flat?
10. Is any of the characters a developing character? If so, is the change a large or a small one? Is it a plausible change for such a person? Is it sufficiently motivated? Is it given sufficient time?

Theme

11. Does the story have a theme? What is it? Is it implicit or explicit?
12. Does the theme reinforce or oppose popular notions of life? Does it furnish a new insight or refresh or deepen an old one?

Point of View

13. What point of view does the story use? Is it consistent in its use of this point of view? If shifts are made, are they justified?
14. What advantages has the chosen point of view? Does it furnish any clues as to the purpose of the story?
15. If the point of view is that of one of the characters, does this character have any limitations that affect his interpretation of events or persons?
16. Does the author use point of view primarily to reveal or conceal? Does he ever unfairly withhold important information known to the focal character?

Symbol and Irony

17. Does the story make use of symbols? If so, do the symbols carry or merely reinforce the meaning of the story?
18. Does the story anywhere utilize irony of situation? dramatic irony? verbal irony? What functions do the ironies serve?

Emotion and Humor

19. Does the story aim directly at an emotional *effect*, or is emotion merely its natural by-product?
20. Is the emotion sufficiently dramatized? Is the author anywhere guilty of sentimentality?

Fantasy

21. Does the story employ fantasy? If so, what is the initial assumption? Does the story operate logically from this assumption?

22. Is the fantasy employed for its own sake or to express some human truth? If the latter, what truth?

General

23. Is the primary interest of the story in plot, character, theme, or some other element?
24. What contribution to the story is made by its setting? Is the particular setting essential, or could the story have happened anywhere?
25. What are the characteristics of the author's style? Are they appropriate to the nature of his story?
26. What light is thrown on the story by its title?
27. Do all the elements of the story work together to support a central purpose? Is any part irrelevant or inappropriate?
28. What do you conceive to be the story's central purpose? How fully has it achieved that purpose?
29. Does the story offer chiefly escape or interpretation? How significant is the story's purpose?
30. Does the story gain or lose on a second reading?

EXERCISE

The two stories that follow have a number of plot features in common; in purpose, however, they are quite different. One attempts to reveal certain truths about aspects of human life and succeeds in doing so. The other attempts to do little more than entertain the reader, and, in achieving this end, it falsifies human life. Which story is which? Support your decision by making a thorough analysis of both.

O. Henry
A MUNICIPAL REPORT

> The cities are full of pride,
>   Challenging each to each—
> This from her mountainside,
>   That from her burthened beach.

> —R. KIPLING

Fancy a novel about Chicago or Buffalo, let us say, or Nashville, Tennessee! There are just three big cities in the United States that are "story cities"—New York, of course, New Orleans, and, best of the lot, San Francisco.—FRANK NORRIS.

East is east°, and west is San Francisco, according to Californians. Californians are a race of people; they are not merely inhabitants of a State. They

East is east . . . : cf. Rudyard Kipling's poem "The Ballad of East and West"

are the Southerners of the West. Now, Chicagoans are no less loyal to their city; but when you ask them why, they stammer and speak of lake fish and the new Odd Fellows Building. But Californians go into detail.

Of course they have, in the climate, an argument that is good for half an hour while you are thinking of your coal bills and heavy underwear. But as soon as they come to mistake your silence for conviction, madness comes upon them, and they picture the city of the Golden Gate as the Bagdad of the New World. So far, as a matter of opinion, no refutation is necessary. But dear cousins all (from Adam and Eve descended), it is a rash one who will lay his finger on the map and say "In this town there can be no romance—what could happen here?" Yes, it is a bold and a rash deed to challenge in one sentence history, romance, and Rand and McNally.

Nashville.—A city, port of delivery, and the capital of the State of Tennessee, is on the Cumberland River and on the N.C. & St.L. and the L. & N. railroads. This city is regarded as the most important educational center in the South.

I stepped off the train at 8 P.M. Having searched the thesaurus in vain for adjectives, I must, as a substitution, hie me to comparison in the form of a recipe.

Take of London fog 30 parts; malaria 10 parts; gas leaks 20 parts; dewdrops gathered in a brick yard at sunrise, 25 parts; odor of honeysuckle 15 parts. Mix.

The mixture will give you an approximate conception of a Nashville drizzle. It is not so fragrant as a moth-ball nor as thick as peasoup; but 'tis enough—'twill serve.°

I went to a hotel in a tumbril. It required strong self-suppression for me to keep from climbing to the top of it and giving an imitation of Sidney Carton.° The vehicle was drawn by beasts of a bygone era and driven by something dark and emancipated.

I was sleepy and tired, so when I got to the hotel I hurriedly paid it the fifty cents it demanded (with approximate lagniappe, I assure you). I knew its

A MUNICIPAL REPORT   First published in 1909. Rand McNally and Co. (see end of second paragraph), founded in 1856, are well-known publishers of atlases and gazeteers. The statistical and historical notes about Nashville in the story are such as might be excerpted from one of their books. Generals Hood, Thomas, Sherman, and Longstreet, Fort Sumter and Appomattox, are all names connected with the Civil War, during which, in 1863, the slaves were emancipated. William Sydney Porter (1862-1919), who wrote under the pseudonym O. Henry, was born in North Carolina, but his immensely varied life took him to Texas, Central and South America, Mexico, Ohio, and Pittsburgh, before he arrived in New York City in 1901 to become a writer very much in demand for his short stories.

not so fragrant . . . 'twill serve: cf. Mercutio's dying speech, *Romeo and Juliet,* III, i, 99–100
   Sidney Carton: in Dickens' novel *A Tale of Two Cities* a dissipated character who dies nobly on the guillotine

habits; and I did not want to hear it prate about its old "marster" or anything that happened "befo' de wah."

The hotel was one of the kind described as "renovated." That means $20,000 worth of new marble pillars, tiling, electric lights and brass cuspidors in the lobby, and a new L. & N. time table and a lithograph of Lookout Mountain in each one of the great rooms above. The management was without reproach, the attention full of exquisite Southern courtesy, the service as slow as the progress of a snail and as good-humored as Rip Van Winkle. The food was worth traveling a thousand miles for. There is no other hotel in the world where you can get such chicken livers *en brochette.*

At dinner I asked a Negro waiter if there was anything doing in town. He pondered gravely for a minute, and then replied: "Well, boss, I don't really reckon there's anything at all doin' after sundown."

Sundown had been accomplished: it had been drowned in drizzle long before. So that spectacle was denied me. But I went forth upon the streets in the drizzle to see what might be there.

It is built on undulating grounds; and the streets are lighted by electricity at a cost of $32,470 per annum.

As I left the hotel there was a race riot. Down upon me charged a company of freedmen, or Arabs, or Zulus, armed with—no, I saw with relief that they were not rifles, but whips. And I saw dimly a caravan of black, clumsy vehicles; and at the reassuring shouts, "Kyar you anywhere in the town, boss, fuh fifty cents," I reasoned that I was merely a "fare" instead of a victim.

I walked through long streets, all leading uphill. I wondered how those streets ever came down again. Perhaps they didn't until they were "graded." On a few of the "main streets" I saw lights in stores here and there; saw street cars go by conveying worthy burghers hither and yon; saw people pass engaged in the art of conversation, and heard a burst of semi-lively laughter issuing from a soda-water and ice-cream parlor. The streets other than "main" seemed to have enticed upon their borders houses consecrated to peace and domesticity. In many of them lights shone behind discreetly drawn window shades, in a few pianos tinkled orderly and irreproachable music. There was indeed, little "doing." I wished I had come before sundown. So I returned to my hotel.

In November, 1864, the Confederate General Hood advanced against Nashville, where he shut up a National force under General Thomas. The latter then sallied forth and defeated the Confederates in a terrible conflict.

All my life I have heard of, admired, and witnessed the fine marksmanship of the South in its peaceful conflicts in the tobacco-chewing regions. But in my hotel a surprise awaited me. There were twelve bright, new, imposing, capacious brass cuspidors in the great lobby, tall enough to be called urns and so wide-mouthed that the crack pitcher of a lady baseball team should have been able to throw a ball into one of them at five paces distant. But, although a terrible battle had raged and was still raging, the enemy had not suffered. Bright, new, imposing, capacious, untouched, they stood. But, shades of Jefferson Brick!° the tile floor—the beautiful tile floor! I could not avoid thinking of the battle of Nashville, and trying to draw, as is my foolish habit, some deductions about hereditary marksmanship.

Here I first saw Major (by misplaced courtesy) Wentworth Caswell. I knew him for a type the moment my eyes suffered from the sight of him. A rat has no geographical habitat. My old friend, A. Tennyson,° said, as he so well said almost everything:

> Prophet, curse me the blabbing lip,
> And curse me the British vermin, the rat.

Let us regard the word "British" as interchangeable *ad lib.* A rat is a rat.

This man was hunting about the hotel lobby like a starved dog that had forgotten where he had buried a bone. He had a face of great acreage, red, pulpy, and with a kind of sleepy massiveness like that of Buddha. He possessed one single virtue—he was very smoothly shaven. The mark of the beast is not indelible upon a man until he goes about with a stubble. I think that if he had not used his razor that day I would have repulsed his advances, and the criminal calendar of the world would have been spared the addition of one murder.

I happened to be standing within five feet of a cuspidor when Major Caswell opened fire upon it. I had been observant enough to perceive that the attacking force was using Gatlings instead of squirrel rifles, so I sidestepped so promptly that the major seized the opportunity to apologize to a noncombatant. He had the blabbing lip. In four minutes he had become my friend and had dragged me to the bar.

I desire to interpolate here that I am a Southerner. But I am not one by profession or trade. I eschew the string tie, the slouch hat, the Prince Albert, the number of bales of cotton destroyed by Sherman, and plug chewing. When the orchestra plays "Dixie" I do not cheer. I slide a little lower on the leather-cornered seat and, well, order another Würzburger and wish that Longstreet had—but what's the use?

Major Caswell banged the bar with his fist, and the first gun at Fort Sumter re-echoed. When he fired the last one at Appomattox I began to hope. But then he began on family trees, and demonstrated that Adam was only a third cousin of a collateral branch of the Caswell family. Genealogy disposed of, he took up, to my distaste, his private family matters. He spoke of his wife,

---

Jefferson Brick: in Dickens' novel *Martin Chuzzlewit* an American journalist "unwholesomely pale" from "excessive use of [chewing] tobacco"

A. Tennyson: The quoted lines are from Tennyson's *Maud,* Part II, V, vi.

traced her descent back to Eve, and profanely denied any possible rumor that she may have had relations in the land of Nod.°

By this time I began to suspect that he was trying to obscure by noise the fact that he had ordered the drinks, on the chance that I would be bewildered into paying for them. But when they were down he crashed a silver dollar loudly upon the bar. Then, of course, another serving was obligatory. And when I had paid for that I took leave of him brusquely; for I wanted no more of him. But before I had obtained my release he had prated loudly of an income that his wife received, and showed a handful of silver money.

When I got my key at the desk the clerk said to me courteously: "If that man Caswell has annoyed you, and if you would like to make a complaint, we will have him ejected. He is a nuisance, a loafer, and without any known means of support, although he seems to have some money most of the time. But we don't seem to be able to hit upon any means of throwing him out legally."

"Why, no," said I, after some reflection; "I don't see my way clear to making a complaint. But I would like to place myself on record as asserting that I do not care for his company. Your town," I continued, "seems to be a quiet one. What manner of entertainment, adventure, or excitement, have you to offer to the stranger within your gates?"°

"Well, sir," said the clerk, "there will be a show here next Thursday. It is—I'll look it up and have the announcement sent up to your room with the ice water. Good-night."

After I went up to my room I looked out the window. It was only about ten o'clock, but I looked upon a silent town. The drizzle continued, spangled with dim lights, as far apart as currants in a cake sold at the Ladies' Exchange.

"A quiet place," I said to myself, as my first shoe struck the ceiling of the occupant of the room beneath mine. "Nothing of the life here that gives color and good variety to the cities in the East and West. Just a good, ordinary, humdrum, business town."

Nashville occupies a foremost place among the manufacturing centers of the country. It is the fifth boot and shoe market in the United States, the largest candy and cracker manufacturing city in the South, and does an enormous wholesale drygoods, grocery, and drug business.

I must tell you how I came to be in Nashville, and I assure you the digression brings as much tedium to me as it does to you. I was traveling elsewhere on my own business, but I had a commission from a Northern literary magazine to stop over there and establish a personal connection between the publication and one of its contributors, Azalea Adair.

land of Nod: where Cain, the exiled son of Adam and Eve, found a wife (Genesis 4:16ff.)
stranger within your gates: cf. Exodus 20:10

Adair (there was no clue to the personality except the handwriting) had sent in some essays (lost art!) and poems that had made the editors swear approvingly over their one o'clock luncheon. So they had commissioned me to round up said Adair and corner by contract his or her output at two cents a word before some other publisher offered her ten or twenty.

At nine o'clock the next morning, after my chicken livers *en brochette* (try them if you can find that hotel), I strayed out into the drizzle, which was still on for an unlimited run. At the first corner I came upon Uncle Caesar. He was a stalwart Negro, older than the pyramids, with gray wool and a face that reminded me of Brutus,° and a second afterwards of the late King Cettiwayo.° He wore the most remarkable coat that I ever had seen or expect to see. It reached to his ankles and had once been a Confederate gray in color. But rain and sun and age had so variegated it that Joseph's coat,° beside it, would have faded to a pale monochrome. I must linger with that coat, for it has to do with the story—the story that is so long in coming, because you can hardly expect anything to happen in Nashville.

Once it must have been the military coat of an officer. The cape of it had vanished, but all adown its front it had been frogged and tasseled magnificently. But now the frogs and tassels were gone. In their stead had been patiently stitched (I surmised by some surviving "black mammy") new frogs made of cunningly twisted common hempen twine. This twine was frayed and disheveled. It must have been added to the coat as a substitute for vanished splendors, with tasteless but painstaking devotion, for it followed faithfully the curves of the long-missing frogs. And, to complete the comedy and pathos of the garment, all its buttons were gone save one. The second button from the top alone remained. The coat was fastened by other twine strings tied through the buttonholes and other holes rudely pierced in the opposite side. There was never such a weird garment so fantastically bedecked and of so many mottled hues. The lone button was the size of a half-dollar, made of yellow horn and sewed on with coarse twine.

This Negro stood by a carriage so old that Ham° himself might have started a hack line with it after he left the ark with the two animals hitched to it. As I approached he threw open the door, drew out a feather duster, waved it without using it, and said in deep, rumbling tones:

"Step right in, suh; ain't a speck of dust in it—jus' got back from a funeral, suh."

I inferred that on such gala occasions carriages were given an extra cleaning. I looked up and down the street and perceived that there was little choice among the vehicles for hire that lined the curb. I looked in my memorandum book for the address of Azalea Adair.

Brutus: tragic hero of Shakespeare's *Julius Caesar*
King Cettiwayo: king of the Zulus (1872–1884)
Joseph's coat: cf. Genesis 37
Ham: son of Noah who, according to tradition, settled in Africa and was the ancestor of the black races

"I want to go to 861 Jessamine Street," I said, and was about to step into the hack. But for an instant the thick, long, gorilla-like arm of the Negro barred me. On his massive and saturnine face a look of sudden suspicion and enmity flashed for a moment. Then, with quickly returning conviction, he asked, blandishingly: "What are you gwine there for, boss?"

"What is that to you?" I asked, a little sharply.

"Nothin', suh, jus' nothin'. Only it's a lonesome kind of part of town and few folks ever has business out there. Step right in. The seats is clean—jes' got back from a funeral, suh."

A mile and a half it must have been to our journey's end. I could hear nothing but the fearful rattle of the ancient hack over the uneven brick paving; I could smell nothing but the drizzle, now further flavored with coal smoke and something like a mixture of tar and oleander blossoms. All I could see through the streaming windows were two rows of dim houses.

The city has an area of 10 square miles; 181 miles of streets, of which 137 miles are paved; a system of waterworks that cost $2,000,000, with 77 miles of mains.

Eight-sixty-one Jessamine Street was a decayed mansion. Thirty yards back from the street it stood, outmerged in a splendid grove of trees and untrimmed shrubbery. A row of box bushes overflowed and almost hid the paling fence from sight; the gate was kept closed by a rope noose that encircled the gate post and the first paling of the gate. But when you got inside you saw that 861 was a shell, a shadow, a ghost of former grandeur and excellence. But in the story, I have not yet got inside.

When the hack had ceased from rattling and the weary quadrupeds came to a rest I handed my jehu° his fifty cents with an additional quarter, feeling a glow of conscious generosity as I did so. He refused it.

"It's two dollars, suh," he said.

"How's that?" I asked. "I plainly heard you call at the hotel. 'Fifty cents to any part of town.'"

"It's two dollars, suh," he repeated obstinately. "It's a long ways from the hotel."

"It is within the city limits and well within them," I argued. "Don't think that you have picked up a greenhorn Yankee. Do you see those hills over there?" I went on, pointing toward the east (I could not see them, myself, for the drizzle); "well, I was born and raised on their other side. You old fool nigger, can't you tell people from other people when you see 'em?"

The grim face of King Cettiwayo softened. "Is you from the South, suh? I reckon it was them shoes of yourn' fooled me. They is somethin' sharp in the toes for a Southern gen'l'man to wear."

"Then the charge is fifty cents, I suppose?" said I, inexorably.

jehu: a fast driver (cf. II Kings 9:20)

His former expression, a mingling of cupidity and hostility, returned, remained ten seconds, and vanished.

"Boss," he said, "fifty cents is right; but I *needs* two dollars, suh; I'm *obleeged* to have two dollars. I ain't *demandin'* it now, suh; after I knows whar you's from; I'm jus sayin' that I *has* to have two dollars to-night and business is mighty po'."

Peace and confidence settled upon his heavy features. He had been luckier than he had hoped. Instead of having picked up a greenhorn, ignorant of rates, he had come upon an inheritance.

"You confounded old rascal," I said, reaching down to my pocket, "you ought to be turned over to the police."

For the first time I saw him smile. He knew; *he knew;* HE KNEW.

I gave him two one-dollar bills. As I handed them over I noticed that one of them had seen parlous times. Its upper right-hand corner was missing, and it had been torn through in the middle, but joined again. A strip of blue tissue paper, pasted over the split, preserved its negotiablility.

Enough of the African bandit for the present: I left him happy, lifted the rope, and opened the creaky gate.

The house, as I said, was a shell. A paint brush had not touched it in twenty years. I could not see why a strong wind should not have bowled it over like a house of cards until I looked again at the trees that hugged it close—the trees that saw the battle of Nashville and still drew their protecting branches around it against storm and enemy and cold.

Azalea Adair, fifty years old, white-haired, a descendant of the cavaliers, as thin and frail as the house she lived in, robed in the cheapest and cleanest dress I ever saw, with an air as simple as a queen's, received me.

The reception room seemed a mile square, because there was nothing in it except some rows of books, on unpainted white-pine bookshelves, a cracked marble-topped table, a rag rug, a hairless horsehair sofa, and two or three chairs. Yes, there was a picture on the wall, a colored crayon drawing of a cluster of pansies. I looked around for the portrait of Andrew Jackson and the pine-cone hanging basket but they were not there.

Azalea Adair and I had conversation, a little of which will be repeated to you. She was a product of the old South, gently nurtured in the sheltered life. Her learning was not broad, but was deep and of splendid originality in its somewhat narrow scope. She had been educated at home, and her knowledge of the world was derived from inference and by inspiration. Of such is the precious, small group of essayists made. While she talked to me I kept brushing my fingers, trying, unconsciously, to rid them guiltily of the absent dust from the half-calf backs of Lamb, Chaucer, Hazlitt, Marcus Aurelius, Montaigne, and Hood. She was exquisite, she was a valuable discovery. Nearly everybody nowadays knows too much—oh, so much too much—of real life.

I could perceive clearly that Azalea Adair was very poor. A house and a dress she had, not much else, I fancied. So, divided between my duty to the magazine and my loyalty to the poets and essayists who fought Thomas in the valley of the Cumberland, I listened to her voice which was like a harpsichord's and found that I could not speak of contracts. In the presence of the nine Muses and the three Graces one hesitated to lower the topic to two cents. There would have to be another colloquy after I had regained my commercialism. But I spoke of my mission, and three o'clock of the next afternoon was set for the discussion of the business proposition.

"Your town," I said, as I began to make ready to depart (which is the time for smooth generalities), "seems to be a quiet, sedate place. A home town, I should say, where few things out of the ordinary ever happen."

It carries on an extensive trade in stoves and hollow ware with the West and South, and its flouring mills have a daily capacity of more than 2,000 barrels.

Azalea Adair seemed to reflect.

"I have never thought of it that way," she said, with a kind of sincere intensity that seemed to belong to her. "Isn't it in the still, quiet places that things do happen? I fancy that when God began to create the earth on the first Monday morning one could have leaned out one's window and heard the drops of mud splashing from His trowel as He built up the everlasting hills. What did the noisiest project in the world—I mean the building of the tower of Babel—result in finally? A page and a half of Esperanto in the *North American Review*."

"Of course," said I, platitudinously, "human nature is the same everywhere; but there is more color—er—more drama and movement and—er—romance in some cities than in others."

"On the surface," said Azalea Adair. "I have traveled many times around the world in a golden airship wafted on two wings—print and dreams. I have seen (on one of my imaginary tours) the Sultan of Turkey bowstring° with his own hands one of his wives who had uncovered her face in public. I have seen a man in Nashville tear up his theater tickets because his wife was going out with her face covered—with rice powder. In San Francisco's Chinatown I saw the slave girl Sing Yee dipped slowly, inch by inch, in boiling almond oil to make her swear she would never see her American lover again. She gave in when the boiling oil had reached three inches above her knees. At a euchre party in East Nashville the other night I saw Kitty Morgan cut dead by seven of her schoolmates and lifelong friends because she had married a house painter. The boiling oil was sizzling as high as her heart; but I wish you could have seen the fine little smile that she carried from table to table. Oh, yes, it is a humdrum town. Just a few miles of red brick houses and mud and stores and lumber yards."

Some one had knocked hollowly at the back of the house. Azalea Adair

bowstring: strangle with a bowstring

breathed a soft apology and went to investigate the sound. She came back in three minutes with brightened eyes, a faint flush on her cheeks, and ten years lifted from her shoulders.

"You must have a cup of tea before you go," she said, "and a sugar cake."

She reached and shook a little iron bell. In shuffled a small Negro girl about twelve, barefoot, not very tidy, glowering at me with thumb in mouth and bulging eyes.

Azalea Adair opened a tiny, worn purse and drew out a dollar bill, a dollar bill with the upper right-hand corner missing, torn in two pieces and pasted together again with a strip of blue tissue paper. It was one of those bills I had given the piratical Negro—there was no doubt of it.

"Go up to Mr. Baker's store on the corner, Impy," she said, handing the girl the dollar bill, "and get a quarter of a pound of tea—the kind he always sends me—and ten cents' worth of sugar cakes. Now, hurry. The supply of tea in the house happens to be exhausted," she explained to me.

Impy left by the back way. Before the scrape of her hard, bare feet had died away on the back porch, a wild shriek—I was sure it was hers—filled the hollow house. Then the deep, gruff tones of an angry man's voice mingled with the girl's further squeals and unintelligible words.

Azalea Adair rose without surprise or emotion and disappeared. For two minutes I heard the hoarse rumble of the man's voice; then something like an oath and a slight scuffle, and she returned calmly to her chair.

"This is a roomy house," she said, "and I have a tenant for part of it. I am sorry to have to rescind my invitation to tea. It is impossible to get the kind I always use at the store. Perhaps tomorrow Mr. Baker will be able to supply me."

I was sure that Impy had not had time to leave the house. I inquired concerning street-car lines and took my leave. After I was well on my way I remembered that I had not learned Azalea Adair's name. But tomorrow would do.

The same day I started in on the course of iniquity that this uneventful city forced upon me. I was in the town only two days, but in that time I managed to lie shamelessly by telegraph, and to be an accomplice—after the fact, if that is the correct legal term—to a murder.

As I rounded the corner nearest my hotel the Afrite coachman of the polychromatic, nonpareil coat seized me, swung open the dungeony door of his peripatetic sarcophagus, flirted his feather duster and began his ritual: "Step right in, boss. Carriage is clean—jus' got back from a funeral. Fifty cents to any—"

And then he knew me and grinned broadly. " 'Scuse me, boss; you is de gen'l'man what rid out with me dis mawnin.' Thank you kindly, suh."

"I am going out to 861 again to-morrow afternoon at three," said I, "and if you will be here, I'll let you drive me. So you know Miss Adair?" I concluded, thinking of my dollar bill.

"I belonged to her father, Judge Adair, suh," he replied.

"I judge that she is pretty poor," I said. "She hasn't much money to speak of, has she?"

For an instant I looked again at the fierce countenance of King Cettiwayo, and then he changed back to an extortionate old Negro hack driver.

"She ain't gwine to starve, suh," he said. "She has reso'ces, suh; she has reso'ces."

"I shall pay you fifty cents for the trip," said I.

"Dat is puffeckly correct, suh," he answered, humbly. "I just *had* to have dat two dollars dis mawnin', boss."

I went to the hotel and lied by electricity. I wired the magazine: "A. Adair holds out for eight cents a word."

The answer that came back was: "Give it to her quick, you duffer."

Just before dinner "Major" Wentworth Caswell bore down upon me with the greetings of a long-lost friend. I have seen few men whom I have so instantaneously hated, and of whom it was so difficult to be rid. I was standing at the bar when he invaded me; therefore I could not wave the white ribbon in his face. I would have paid gladly for the drinks, hoping thereby to escape another; but he was one of those despicable, roaring, advertising bibbers who must have brass bands and fireworks attend upon every cent that they waste in their follies.

With an air of producing millions he drew two one-dollar bills from a pocket and dashed one of them upon the bar. I looked once more at the dollar bill with the upper right-hand corner missing, torn through the middle, and patched with a strip of blue tissue paper. It was my dollar again. It could have been no other.

I went up to my room. The drizzle and the monotony of a dreary, eventless Southern town had made me tired and listless. I remember that just before I went to bed I mentally disposed of the mysterious dollar bill (which might have formed the clue to a tremendously fine detective story of San Francisco) by saying to myself sleepily: "Seems as if a lot of people here own stock in the Hack-Drivers' Trust. Pays dividends promptly, too. Wonder if—" Then I fell asleep.

King Cettiwayo was at his post the next day, and rattled my bones over the stones out to 861. He was to wait and rattle me back again when I was ready.

Azalea Adair looked paler and cleaner and frailer than she had looked on the day before. After she had signed the contract at eight cents per word she grew still paler and began to slip out of her chair. Without much trouble I managed to get her up on the antediluvian horsehair sofa and then I ran out to the sidewalk and yelled to the coffee-colored Pirate to bring a doctor. With a wisdom that I had not suspected in him, he abandoned his team and struck off up the street afoot, realizing the value of speed. In ten minutes he returned with a grave, gray-haired, and capable man of medicine. In a few words (worth much less than eight cents each) I explained to him my presence in the hollow house of mystery. He bowed with stately understanding, and turned to the old Negro.

"Uncle Caesar," he said, calmly, "run up to my house and ask Miss Lucy to give you a cream pitcher full of fresh milk and half a tumbler of port wine. And hurry back. Don't drive—run. I want you to get back sometime this week."

It occurred to me that Dr. Merriman also felt a distrust as to the speeding powers of the land-pirate's steeds. After Uncle Caesar was gone, lumberingly, but swiftly, up the street, the doctor looked me over with great politeness and as much careful calculation until he had decided that I might do.

"It is only a case of insufficient nutrition," he said. "In other words, the result of poverty, pride, and starvation. Mrs. Caswell has many devoted friends who would be glad to aid her, but she will accept nothing except from that old Negro, Uncle Caesar, who was once owned by her family."

"Mrs. Caswell!" said I, in surprise. And then I looked at the contract and saw that she had signed it "Azalea Adair Caswell."

"I thought she was Miss Adair," I said.

"Married to a drunken, worthless loafer, sir," said the doctor. "It is said that he robs her even of the small sums that her old servant contributes toward her support."

When the milk and wine had been brought the doctor soon revived Azalea Adair. She sat up and talked of the beauty of the autumn leaves that were then in season and their height of color. She referred lightly to her fainting seizure as the outcome of an old palpitation of her heart. Impy fanned her as she lay on the sofa. The doctor was due elsewhere, and I followed him to the door. I told him that it was within my power and intentions to make a reasonable advance of money to Azalea Adair on future contributions to the magazine, and he seemed pleased.

"By the way," he said, "perhaps you would like to know that you have had royalty for a coachman. Old Caesar's grandfather was a king in Congo. Caesar himself has royal ways, as you may have observed."

As the doctor was moving off I heard Uncle Caesar's voice inside: "Did he git bofe of dem two dollars from you, Mis' Zalea?"

"Yes, Caesar," I heard Azalea Adair answer, weakly. And then I went in and concluded business negotiations with our contributor. I assumed the responsibility of advancing fifty dollars, putting it as a necessary formality in binding our bargain. And then Uncle Caesar drove me back to the hotel.

Here ends all of the story as far as I can witness. The rest must be only bare statements of facts.

At about six o'clock I went out for a stroll. Uncle Caesar was at his corner. He threw open the door of his carriage, flourished his duster, and began his depressing formula: "Step right in, suh. Fifty cents to anywhere in the city— hack's puffickly clean, suh—jus' got back from a funeral—"

And then he recognized me. I think his eyesight was getting bad. His coat had taken on a few more faded shades of color, the twine strings were more frayed and ragged, the last remaining button—the button of yellow horn—was gone. A motley descendant of kings was Uncle Caesar!

About two hours later I saw an excited crowd besieging the front of the drug store. In a desert where nothing happens this was manna; so I wedged my way inside. On an extemporized couch of empty boxes and chairs was stretched the mortal corporeality of Major Wentworth Caswell. A doctor was testing him for the mortal ingredient. His decision was that it was conspicuous by its absence.

The erstwhile Major had been found dead on a dark street and brought by curious and ennuied citizens to the drug store. The late human being had been engaged in terrific battle—the details showed that. Loafer and reprobate though he had been, he had been also a warrior. But he had lost. His hands were yet clinched so tightly that his fingers could not be opened. The gentle citizens who had known him stood about and searched their vocabularies to find some good words, if it were possible, to speak of him. One kind-looking man said, after much thought: "When 'Cas' was about fo'teen he was one of the best spellers in the school."

While I stood there the fingers of the right hand of "the man that was," which hung down the side of a white pine box, relaxed, and dropped something at my feet. I covered it with one foot quietly, and a little later on I picked it up and pocketed it. I reasoned that in his last struggle his hand must have seized that object unwittingly and held it in a death grip.

At the hotel that night the main topic of conversation, with the possible exceptions of politics and prohibition, was the demise of Major Caswell. I heard one man say to a group of listeners:

"In my opinion, gentlemen, Caswell was murdered by some of these no-account niggers for his money. He had fifty dollars this afternoon which he showed to several gentlemen in the hotel. When he was found the money was not on his person."

I left the city the next morning at nine, and as the train was crossing the bridge over the Cumberland River I took out of my pocket a yellow horn overcoat button the size of a fifty-cent piece, with frayed ends of coarse twine hanging from it, and cast it out of the window into the slow, muddy waters below.

I wonder what's doing in Buffalo!

Susan Glaspell

A JURY OF HER PEERS

When Martha Hale opened the storm-door and got a cut of the north wind, she ran back for her big woolen scarf. As she hurriedly wound that round her head her eye made a scandalized sweep of her kitchen. It was no ordinary thing that called her away—it was probably farther from ordinary than anything that had ever happened in Dickson County. But what her eye took in was that her kitchen was in no shape for leaving: her bread all ready for mixing, half the flour sifted and half unsifted.

She hated to see things half done; but she had been at that when the team from town stopped to get Mr. Hale, and then the sheriff came running in to say his wife wished Mrs. Hale would come too—adding, with a grin, that he guessed she was getting scarey and wanted another woman along. So she had dropped everything right where it was.

"Martha!" now came her husband's impatient voice. "Don't keep folks waiting out here in the cold."

She again opened the storm-door, and this time joined the three men and the one woman waiting for her in the big two-seated buggy.

After she had the robes tucked around her she took another look at the woman who sat beside her on the back seat. She had met Mrs. Peters the year before at the county fair, and the thing she remembered about her was that she didn't seem like a sheriff's wife. She was small and thin and didn't have a strong voice. Mrs. Gorman, sheriff's wife before Gorman went out and Peters came in, had a voice that somehow seemed to be backing up the law with every word. But if Mrs. Peters didn't look like a sheriff's wife, Peters made it up in looking like a sheriff. He was to a dot the kind of man who could get himself elected sheriff—a heavy man with a big voice, who was particularly genial with the law-abiding, as if to make it plain that he knew the difference between criminals and non-criminals. And right there it came into Mrs. Hale's mind, with a stab, that this man who was so pleasant and lively with all of them was going to the Wrights' now as a sheriff.

"The country's not very pleasant this time of year," Mrs. Peters at last ventured, as if she felt they ought to be talking as well as the men.

Mrs. Hale scarcely finished her reply, for they had gone up a little hill and could see the Wright place now, and seeing it did not make her feel like talking. It looked very lonesome this cold March morning. It had always been a lonesome-looking place. It was down in a hollow, and the poplar trees around it were lonesome-looking trees. The men were looking at it and talking about what had happened. The county attorney was bending to one side of the buggy, and kept looking steadily at the place as they drew up to it.

"I'm glad you came with me," Mrs. Peters said nervously, as the two women were about to follow the men in through the kitchen door.

Even after she had her foot on the door-step, her hand on the knob, Martha Hale had a moment of feeling she could not cross that threshold. And the reason it seemed she couldn't cross it now was simply because she hadn't crossed it before. Time and time again it had been in her mind, "I ought to

A JURY OF HER PEERS First published in 1917, the story is based on the author's one-act play *Trifles*, written in 1916 for the Provincetown Players. Susan Glaspell (1882–1948) lived for the first thirty-two years of her life in Iowa. She has said that *Trifles* (and hence this short story) was suggested to her by an experience she had while working for a Des Moines newspaper.

go over and see Minnie Foster"—she still thought of her as Minnie Foster, though for twenty years she had been Mrs. Wright. And then there was always something to do and Minnie Foster would go from her mind. But *now* she could come.

The men went over to the stove. The women stood close together by the door. Young Henderson, the county attorney, turned around and said, "Come up to the fire, ladies."

Mrs. Peters took a step forward, then stopped. "I'm not—cold," she said.

And so the two women stood by the door, at first not even so much as looking around the kitchen.

The men talked for a minute about what a good thing it was the sheriff had sent his deputy out that morning to make a fire for them, and then Sheriff Peters stepped back from the stove, unbuttoned his outer coat, and leaned his hands on the kitchen table in a way that seemed to mark the beginning of official business. "Now, Mr. Hale," he said in a sort of semi-official voice, "before we move things about, you tell Mr. Henderson just what it was you saw when you came here yesterday morning."

The county attorney was looking around the kitchen.

"By the way," he said, "has anything been moved?" He turned to the sheriff. "Are things just as you left them yesterday?"

Peters looked from cupboard to sink; from that to a small worn rocker a little to one side of the kitchen table.

"It's just the same."

"Somebody should have been left here yesterday," said the county attorney.

"Oh—yesterday," returned the sheriff, with a little gesture as of yesterday having been more than he could bear to think of. "When I had to send Frank to Morris Center for that man who went crazy—let me tell you, I had my hands full *yesterday*. I knew you could get back from Omaha by to-day, George, and as long as I went over everything here myself—"

"Well, Mr. Hale," said the county attorney, in a way of letting what was past and gone go, "tell just what happened when you came here yesterday morning."

Mrs. Hale, still leaning against the door, had that sinking feeling of the mother whose child is about to speak a piece. Lewis often wandered along and got things mixed up in a story. She hoped he would tell this straight and plain, and not say unnecessary things that would just make things harder for Minnie Foster. He didn't begin at once, and she noticed that he looked queer—as if standing in that kitchen and having to tell what he had seen there yesterday morning made him almost sick.

"Yes, Mr. Hale?" the county attorney reminded.

"Harry and I had started to town with a load of potatoes," Mrs. Hale's husband began.

Harry was Mrs. Hale's oldest boy. He wasn't with them now, for the very good reason that those potatoes never got to town yesterday and he was taking them this morning, so he hadn't been home when the sheriff stopped to say he wanted Mr. Hale to come over to the Wright place and tell the county attorney his story there, where he could point it all out. With all Mrs. Hale's other emotions came the fear that maybe Harry wasn't dressed warm enough—they hadn't any of them realized how that north wind did bite.

"We come along this road," Hale was going on, with a motion of his hand to the road over which they had just come, "and as we got in sight of the house I says to Harry, 'I'm goin' to see if I can't get John Wright to take a telephone.' You see," he explained to Henderson, "unless I can get somebody to go in with me they won't come out this branch road except for a price *I* can't pay. I'd spoke to Wright about it once before; but he put me off, saying folks talked too much anyway, and all he asked was peace and quiet—guess you know about how much he talked himself. But I thought maybe if I went to the house and talked about it before his wife, and said all the women-folks liked the telephones, and that in this lonesome stretch of road it would be a good thing—well, I said to Harry that that was what I was going to say— though I said at the same time that I didn't know as what his wife wanted made much difference to John—"

Now, there he was!—saying things he didn't need to say. Mrs. Hale tried to catch her husband's eye, but fortunately the county attorney interrupted with:

"Let's talk about that a little later, Mr. Hale. I do want to talk about that, but I'm anxious now to get along to just what happened when you got here."

When he began this time, it was very deliberately and carefully:

"I didn't see or hear anything. I knocked at the door. And still it was all quiet inside. I knew they must be up—it was past eight o'clock. So I knocked again, louder, and I thought I heard somebody say 'Come in.' I wasn't sure—I'm not sure yet. But I opened the door—this door," jerking a hand toward the door by which the two women stood, "and there, in that rocker"—pointing to it—"sat Mrs. Wright."

Every one in the kitchen looked at the rocker. It came into Mrs. Hale's mind that that rocker didn't look in the least like Minnie Foster—the Minnie Foster of twenty years before. It was a dingy red, with wooden rungs up the back, and the middle rung was gone, and the chair sagged to one side.

"How did she—look?" the county attorney was inquiring.

"Well," said Hale, "she looked—queer."

"How do you mean—queer?"

As he asked it he took out a note-book and pencil. Mrs. Hale did not like the sight of that pencil. She kept her eye fixed on her husband, as if to keep him from saying unnecessary things that would go into that note-book and make trouble.

Hale did speak guardedly, as if the pencil had affected him too.

"Well, as if she didn't know what she was going to do next. And kind of—done up."

"How did she seem to feel about your coming?"

"Why, I don't think she minded—one way or other. She didn't pay much attention. I said, 'Ho' do, Mrs. Wright? It's cold, ain't it?' And she said, 'Is it?'—and went on pleatin' at her apron.

"Well, I was surprised. She didn't ask me to come up to the stove, or to sit down, but just set there, not even lookin' at me. And so I said: 'I want to see John.'

"And then she—laughed. I guess you would call it a laugh.

"I thought of Harry and the team outside, so I said, a little sharp, 'Can I see John?' 'No,' says she—kind of dull like. 'Ain't he home?' says I. Then she looked at me. 'Yes,' says she, 'he's home.' 'Then why can't I see him?' I asked her, out of patience with her now. ''Cause he's dead,' says she, just as quiet and dull—and fell to pleatin' her apron. 'Dead?' says I, like you do when you can't take in what you've heard.

"She just nodded her head, not getting a bit excited, but rockin' back and forth.

" 'Why—where is he?' says I, not knowing *what* to say.

"She just pointed upstairs—like this"—pointing to the room above.

"I got up, with the idea of going up there myself. By this time I—didn't know what to do. I walked from there to here; then I says: 'Why, what did he die of?'

" 'He died of a rope around his neck,' says she; and just went on pleatin' at her apron."

Hale stopped speaking, and stood staring at the rocker, as if he were still seeing the woman who had sat there the morning before. Nobody spoke; it was as if every one were seeing the woman who had sat there the morning before.

"And what did you do then?" the county attorney at last broke the silence.

"I went out and called Harry. I thought I might—need help. I got Harry in, and we went upstairs." His voice fell almost to a whisper. "There he was—lying over the—"

"I think I'd rather have you go into that upstairs," the county attorney interrupted, "where you can point it all out. Just go on now with the rest of the story."

"Well, my first thought was to get that rope off. It looked—"

He stopped, his face twitching.

"But Harry, he went up to him, and he said, 'No, he's dead all right, and we'd better not touch anything.' So we went downstairs.

"She was still sitting that same way. 'Has anybody been notified?' I asked. 'No,' says she, unconcerned.

" 'Who did this, Mrs. Wright?' said Harry. He said it business-like, and she stopped pleatin' at her apron. 'I don't know,' she says. 'You don't *know?*' says Harry. 'Weren't you sleepin' in the bed with him?' 'Yes,' says she, 'but I was on the inside.' 'Somebody slipped a rope round his neck and strangled him, and you didn't wake up?' says Harry. 'I didn't wake up,' she said after him.

"We may have looked as if we didn't see how that could be, for after a minute she said, 'I sleep sound.'

"Harry was going to ask her more questions, but I said maybe that weren't our business; maybe we ought to let her tell her story first to the coroner or the sheriff. So Harry went fast as he could over to High Road—the Rivers' place, where there's a telephone."

"And what did she do when she knew you had gone for the coroner?" The attorney got his pencil in his hand all ready for writing.

"She moved from that chair to this one over here"—Hale pointed to a small chair in the corner—"and just sat there with her hands held together and looking down. I got a feeling that I ought to make some conversation, so I said I had come in to see if John wanted to put in a telephone; and at that she started to laugh, and then she stopped and looked at me—scared."

At the sound of a moving pencil the man who was telling the story looked up.

"I dunno—maybe it wasn't scared," he hastened; "I wouldn't like to say it was. Soon Harry got back, and then Dr. Lloyd came, and you, Mr. Peters, and so I guess that's all I know that you don't."

He said that last with relief, and moved a little, as if relaxing. Every one moved a little. The county attorney walked toward the stair door.

"I guess we'll go upstairs first—then out to the barn and around there."

He paused and looked around the kitchen.

"You're convinced there was nothing important here?" he asked the sheriff. "Nothing that would—point to any motive?"

The sheriff too looked all around, as if to re-convince himself.

"Nothing here but kitchen things," he said, with a little laugh for the insignificance of kitchen things.

The county attorney was looking at the cupboard—a peculiar, ungainly structure, half closet and half cupboard, the upper part of it being built in the wall, and the lower part just the old-fashioned kitchen cupboard. As if its queerness attracted him, he got a chair and opened the upper part and looked in. After a moment he drew his hand away sticky.

"Here's a nice mess," he said resentfully.

The two women had drawn nearer, and now the sheriff's wife spoke.

"Oh—her fruit," she said, looking to Mrs. Hale for sympathetic understanding. She turned back to the county attorney and explained: "She worried about that when it turned so cold last night. She said the fire would go out and her jars might burst."

Mrs. Peters' husband broke into a laugh.

"Well, can you beat the women! Held for murder, and worrying about her preserves!"

The young attorney set his lips.

"I guess before we're through with her she may have something more serious than preserves to worry about."

"Oh, well," said Mrs. Hale's husband, with good-natured superiority, "women are used to worrying over trifles."

The two women moved a little closer together. Neither of them spoke. The county attorney seemed suddenly to remember his manners—and think of his future.

"And yet," said he, with the gallantry of a young politician, "for all their worries, what would we do without the ladies?"

The women did not speak, did not unbend. He went to the sink and began washing his hands. He turned to wipe them on the roller towel—whirled it for a cleaner place.

"Dirty towels! Not much of a housekeeper, would you say, ladies?"

He kicked his foot against some dirty pans under the sink.

"There's a great deal of work to be done on a farm," said Mrs. Hale stiffly.

"To be sure. And yet"—with a little bow to her—"I know there are some Dickson County farm-houses that do not have such roller towels." He gave it a pull to expose its full length again.

"Those towels get dirty awful quick. Men's hands aren't always as clean as they might be."

"Ah, loyal to your sex, I see," he laughed. He stopped and gave her a keen look. "But you and Mrs. Wright were neighbors. I suppose you were friends, too."

Martha Hale shook her head.

"I've seen little enough of her of late years. I've not been in this house— it's more than a year."

"And why was that? You didn't like her?"

"I liked her well enough," she replied with spirit. "Farmers' wives have their hands full, Mr. Henderson. And then"—She looked around the kitchen.

"Yes?" he encouraged.

"It never seemed a very cheerful place," said she, more to herself than to him.

"No," he agreed; "I don't think any one would call it cheerful. I shouldn't say she had the home-making instinct."

"Well, I don't know as Wright had, either," she muttered.

"You mean they didn't get on very well?" he was quick to ask.

"No; I don't mean anything," she answered, with decision. As she turned a little away from him, she added: "But I don't think a place would be any the cheerfuler for John Wright's bein' in it."

"I'd like to talk to you about that a little later, Mrs. Hale," he said. "I'm anxious to get the lay of things upstairs now."

He moved toward the stair door, followed by the two men.

"I suppose anything Mrs. Peters does'll be all right?" the sheriff inquired. "She was to take in some clothes for her, you know—and a few little things. We left in such a hurry yesterday."

The county attorney looked at the two women whom they were leaving alone there among the kitchen things.

"Yes—Mrs. Peters," he said, his glance resting on the woman who was not Mrs. Peters, the big farmer woman who stood behind the sheriff's wife. "Of course Mrs. Peters is one of us," he said, in a manner of entrusting responsibility. "And keep your eye out, Mrs. Peters, for anything that might be of use. No telling; you women might come upon a clue to the motive—and that's the thing we need."

Mr. Hale rubbed his face after the fashion of a show man getting ready for a pleasantry.

"But would the women know a clue if they did come upon it?" he said; and, having delivered himself of this, he followed the others through the stair door.

The women stood motionless and silent, listening to the footsteps, first upon the stairs, then in the room above them.

Then, as if releasing herself from something strange, Mrs. Hale began to arrange the dirty pans under the sink, which the county attorney's disdainful push of the foot had deranged.

"I'd hate to have men comin' into my kitchen," she said testily—"snoopin' round and criticizin'."

"Of course it's no more than their duty," said the sheriff's wife, in her manner of timid acquiescence.

"Duty's all right," replied Mrs. Hale bluffly; "but I guess that deputy sheriff that come out to make the fire might have got a little of this on." She gave the roller towel a pull. "Wish I'd thought of that sooner! Seems mean to talk about her for not having things slicked up, when she had to come away in such a hurry."

She looked around the kitchen. Certainly it was not "slicked up." Her eye was held by a bucket of sugar on a low shelf. The cover was off the wooden bucket, and beside it was a paper bag—half full.

Mrs. Hale moved toward it.

"She was putting this in there," she said to herself—slowly.

She thought of the flour in her kitchen at home—half sifted, half not sifted. She had been interrupted, and had left things half done. What had interrupted Minnie Foster? Why had that work been left half done? She made a move as if to finish it,—unfinished things always bothered her,—and then she glanced around and saw that Mrs. Peters was watching her—and she didn't want Mrs. Peters to get that feeling she had got of work begun and then—for some reason—not finished.

"It's a shame about her fruit," she said, and walked toward the cupboard that the county attorney had opened, and got on the chair, murmuring: "I wonder if it's all gone."

It was a sorry enough looking sight, but "Here's one that's all right," she said at last. She held it toward the light. "This is cherries, too." She looked again. "I declare I believe that's the only one."

With a sigh, she got down from the chair, went to the sink, and wiped off the bottle.

"She'll feel awful bad, after all her hard work in the hot weather. I remember the afternoon I put up my cherries last summer."

She set the bottle on the table, and, with another sigh, started to sit down in the rocker. But she did not sit down. Something kept her from sitting down in that chair. She straightened—stepped back, and, half turned away, stood looking at it, seeing the woman who sat there "pleatin' at her apron."

The thin voice of the sheriff's wife broke in upon her: "I must be getting those things from the front room closet." She opened the door into the other room, started in, stepped back. "You coming with me, Mrs. Hale?" she asked nervously. "You—you could help me get them."

They were soon back—the stark coldness of that shut-up room was not a thing to linger in.

"My!" said Mrs. Peters, dropping the things on the table and hurrying to the stove.

Mrs. Hale stood examining the clothes the woman who was being detained in town had said she wanted.

"Wright was close!" she exclaimed, holding up a shabby black skirt that bore the marks of much making over. "I think maybe that's why she kept so much to herself. I s'pose she felt she couldn't do her part; and then, you don't enjoy things when you feel shabby. She used to wear pretty clothes and be lively—when she was Minnie Foster, one of the town girls, singing in the choir. But that—oh, that was twenty years ago."

With a carefulness in which there was something tender, she folded the shabby clothes and piled them at one corner of the table. She looked at Mrs. Peters, and there was something in the other woman's look that irritated her.

"She don't care," she said to herself. "Much difference it makes to her whether Minnie Foster had pretty clothes when she was a girl."

Then she looked again, and she wasn't so sure; in fact, she hadn't at any time been perfectly sure about Mrs. Peters. She had that shrinking manner, and yet her eyes looked as if they could see a long way into things.

"This all you was to take in?" asked Mrs. Hale.

"No," said the sheriff's wife; "she said she wanted an apron. Funny thing to want," she ventured in her nervous little way, "for there's not much to get you dirty in jail, goodness knows. But I suppose just to make her feel more natural. If you're used to wearing an apron—. She said they were in the bottom drawer of this cupboard. Yes—here they are. And then her little shawl that always hung on the stair door."

She took the small gray shawl from behind the door leading upstairs, and stood a minute looking at it.

Suddenly Mrs. Hale took a quick step toward the other woman.

"Mrs. Peters!"

"Yes, Mrs. Hale?"

"Do you think she—did it?"

A frightened look blurred the other things in Mrs. Peters' eyes.

"Oh, I don't know," she said, in a voice that seemed to shrink away from the subject.

"Well, I don't think she did," affirmed Mrs. Hale stoutly. "Asking for an apron, and her little shawl. Worryin' about her fruit."

"Mr. Peters says—." Footsteps were heard in the room above; she stopped, looked up, then went on in a lowered voice: "Mr. Peters says—it looks bad for her. Mr. Henderson is awful sarcastic in a speech, and he's going to make fun of her saying she didn't—wake up."

For a moment Mrs. Hale had no answer. Then, "Well, I guess John Wright didn't wake up—when they was slippin' that rope under his neck," she muttered.

"No, it's *strange*," breathed Mrs. Peters. "They think it was such a— funny way to kill a man."

She began to laugh; at sound of the laugh, abruptly stopped.

"That's just what Mr. Hale said," said Mrs. Hale, in a resolutely natural voice. "There was a gun in the house. He says that's what he can't under- stand."

"Mr. Henderson said, coming out, that what was needed for the case was a motive. Something to show anger—or sudden feeling."

"Well, I don't see any signs of anger around here," said Mrs. Hale. "I don't—"

She stopped. It was as if her mind tripped on something. Her eye was caught by a dish-towel in the middle of the kitchen table. Slowly she moved toward the table. One half of it was wiped clean, the other half messy. Her eyes made a slow, almost unwilling turn to the bucket of sugar and the half empty bag beside it. Things begun—and not finished.

After a moment she stepped back, and said, in that manner of releasing herself:

"Wonder how they're finding things upstairs? I hope she had it a little more red up up there. You know,"—she paused, and feeling gathered,—"it seems kind of *sneaking;* locking her up in town and coming out here to get her own house to turn against her!"

"But, Mrs. Hale," said the sheriff's wife, "the law is the law."

"I s'pose 'tis," answered Mrs. Hale shortly.

She turned to the stove, saying something about that fire not being much to brag of. She worked with it a minute, and when she straightened up she said aggressively:

"The law is the law—and a bad stove is a bad stove. How'd you like to cook on this?"—pointing with the poker to the broken lining. She opened the oven door and started to express her opinion of the oven; but she was swept into her own thoughts, thinking of what it would mean, year after year, to have that stove to wrestle with. The thought of Minnie Foster trying to bake in that oven—and the thought of her never going over to see Minnie Foster—.

She was startled by hearing Mrs. Peters say: "A person gets discour- aged—and loses heart."

The sheriff's wife had looked from the stove to the sink—to the pail of water which had been carried in from outside. The two women stood there silent, above them the footsteps of the men who were looking for evidence against the woman who had worked in that kitchen. That look of seeing into things, of seeing through a thing to something else, was in the eyes of the sheriff's wife now. When Mrs. Hale next spoke to her, it was gently:

"Better loosen up your things, Mrs. Peters. We'll not feel them when we go out."

Mrs. Peters went to the back of the room to hang up the fur tippet she was wearing. A moment later she exclaimed, "Why, she was piecing a quilt," and held up a large sewing basket piled high with quilt pieces.

Mrs. Hale spread some of the blocks on the table.

"It's log-cabin pattern," she said, putting several of them together. "Pretty, isn't it?"

They were so engaged with the quilt that they did not hear the footsteps on the stairs. Just as the stair door opened Mrs. Hale was saying:

"Do you suppose she was going to quilt it or just knot it?"

The sheriff threw up his hands.

"They wonder whether she was going to quilt it or just knot it!"

There was a laugh for the ways of women, a warming of hands over the stove, and then the county attorney said briskly:

"Well, let's go right out to the barn and get that cleared up."

"I don't see as there's anything so strange," Mrs. Hale said resentfully, after the outside door had closed on the three men—"our taking up our time with little things while we're waiting for them to get the evidence. I don't see as it's anything to laugh about."

"Of course they've got awful important things on their minds," said the sheriff's wife apologetically.

They returned to an inspection of the blocks for the quilt. Mrs. Hale was looking at the fine, even sewing, and preoccupied with thoughts of the woman who had done that sewing, when she heard the sheriff's wife say, in a queer tone:

"Why, look at this one."

She turned to take the block held out to her.

"The sewing," said Mrs. Peters, in a troubled way. "All the rest of them have been so nice and even—but—this one. Why, it looks as if she didn't know what she was about!"

Their eyes met—something flashed to life, passed between them; then, as if with an effort, they seemed to pull away from each other. A moment Mrs. Hale sat there, her hands folded over that sewing which was so unlike all the rest of the sewing. Then she had pulled a knot and drawn the threads.

"Oh, what are you doing, Mrs. Hale?" asked the sheriff's wife, startled.

"Just pulling out a stitch or two that's not sewed very good," said Mrs. Hale mildly.

"I don't thing we ought to touch things," Mrs. Peters said, a little help-lessly.

"I'll just finish up this end," answered Mrs. Hale, still in that mild, matter-of-fact fashion.

She threaded a needle and started to replace bad sewing with good. For a little while she sewed in silence. Then, in that thin, timid voice, she heard:

"Mrs. Hale!"

"Yes, Mrs. Peters?"

"What do you suppose she was so—nervous about?"

"Oh, *I* don't know," said Mrs. Hale, as if dismissing a thing not important enough to spend much time on. "I don't know as she was—nervous. I sew awful queer sometimes when I'm just tired."

She cut a thread, and out of the corner of her eye looked up at Mrs. Peters. The small, lean face of the sheriff's wife seemed to have tightened up. Her eyes had that look of peering into something. But the next moment she moved, and said in her thin, indecisive way:

"Well, I must get those clothes wrapped. They may be through sooner than we think. I wonder where I could find a piece of paper—and string."

"In that cupboard, maybe," suggested Mrs. Hale, after a glance around.

One piece of the crazy sewing remained unripped. Mrs. Peters' back turned, Martha Hale now scrutinized that piece, compared it with the dainty, accurate sewing of the other blocks. The difference was startling. Holding this block made her feel queer, as if the distracted thoughts of the woman who had perhaps turned to it to try and quiet herself were communicating themselves to her.

Mrs. Peters' voice roused her.

"Here's a bird-cage," she said. "Did she have a bird, Mrs. Hale?"

"Why, I don't know whether she did or not." She turned to look at the cage Mrs. Peters was holding up. "I've not been here in so long." She sighed. "There was a man round last year selling canaries cheap—but I don't know as she took one. Maybe she did. She used to sing real pretty herself."

Mrs. Peters looked around the kitchen.

"Seems kind of funny to think of a bird here." She half laughed—an attempt to put up a barrier. "But she must have had one—or why would she have a cage? I wonder what happened to it."

"I suppose maybe the cat got it," suggested Mrs. Hale, resuming her sewing.

"No; she didn't have a cat. She's got that feeling some people have about cats—being afraid of them. When they brought her to our house yesterday, my cat got in the room, and she was real upset and asked me to take it out."

"My sister Bessie was like that," laughed Mrs. Hale.

The sheriff's wife did not reply. The silence made Mrs. Hale turn around. Mrs. Peters was examining the bird-cage.

"Look at this door," she said slowly. "It's broke. One hinge has been pulled apart."

Mrs. Hale came nearer.

"Looks as if some one must have been—rough with it."

Again their eyes met—startled, questioning, apprehensive. For a moment neither spoke nor stirred. Then Mrs. Hale, turning away, said brusquely: "If they're going to find any evidence, I wish they'd be about it. I don't like this place."

"But I'm awful glad you came with me, Mrs. Hale." Mrs. Peters put the bird-cage on the table and sat down. "It would be lonesome for me—sitting here alone."

"Yes, it would, wouldn't it?" agreed Mrs. Hale, a certain determined naturalness in her voice. She picked up the sewing, but now it dropped in her lap, and she murmured in a different voice: "But I tell you what I *do* wish, Mrs. Peters. I wish I had come over sometimes when she was here. I wish—I had."

"But of course you were awful busy, Mrs. Hale. Your house—and your children."

"I could've come," retorted Mrs. Hale shortly. "I stayed away because it weren't cheerful—and that's why I ought to have come. I"—she looked around—"I've never liked this place. Maybe because it's down in a hollow and you don't see the road. I don't know what it is, but it's a lonesome place, and always was. I wish I had come over to see Minnie Foster sometimes. I can see now—" She did not put it into words.

"Well, you mustn't reproach yourself," counseled Mrs. Peters. "Somehow, we just don't see how it is with other folks till—something comes up."

"Not having children makes less work," mused Mrs. Hale, after a silence, "but it makes a quiet house—and Wright out to work all day—and no company when he did come in. Did you know John Wright, Mrs. Peters?"

"Not to know him. I've seen him in town. They say he was a good man."

"Yes—good," conceded John Wright's neighbor grimly. "He didn't drink, and kept his word as well as most, I guess, and paid his debts. But he was a hard man, Mrs. Peters. Just to pass the time of day with him—." She stopped, shivered a little. "Like a raw wind that gets to the bone." Her eye fell upon the cage on the table before her, and she added, almost bitterly: "I should think she would've wanted a bird!"

Suddenly she leaned forward, looking intently at the cage. "But what do you s'pose went wrong with it?"

"I don't know," returned Mrs. Peters; "unless it got sick and died."

But after she said it she reached over and swung the broken door. Both women watched it as if somehow held by it.

"You didn't know—her?" Mrs. Hale asked, a gentler note in her voice.

"Not till they brought her yesterday," said the sheriff's wife.

"She—come to think of it, she was kind of like a bird herself. Real sweet and pretty, but kind of timid and—fluttery. How—she—did—change."

That held her for a long time. Finally, as if struck with a happy thought and relieved to get back to everyday things, she exclaimed:

"Tell you what, Mrs. Peters, why don't you take the quilt in with you? It might take up her mind."

"Why, I think that's a real nice idea, Mrs. Hale," agreed the sheriff's wife, as if she too were glad to come into the atmosphere of a simple kindness. "There couldn't possibly be any objection to that, could there? Now, just what will I take? I wonder if her patches are in here—and her things."

They turned to the sewing basket.

"Here's some red," said Mrs. Hale, bringing out a roll of cloth. Underneath that was a box. "Here, maybe her scissors are in here—and her things." She held it up. "What a pretty box! I'll warrant that was something she had a long time ago—when she was a girl."

She held it in her hand a moment; then, with a little sigh, opened it. Instantly her hand went to her nose.

"Why—!"

Mrs. Peters drew nearer—then turned away.

"There's something wrapped up in this piece of silk," faltered Mrs. Hale.

"This isn't her scissors," said Mrs. Peters in a shrinking voice.

Her hand not steady, Mrs. Hale raised the piece of silk. "Oh, Mrs. Peters!" she cried. "It's—"

Mrs. Peters bent closer.

"It's the bird," she whispered.

"But, Mrs. Peters!" cried Mrs. Hale. "*Look* at it! Its neck—look at its neck! It's all—other side *to*."

She held the box away from her.

The sheriff's wife again bent closer.

"Somebody wrung its neck," said she, in a voice that was slow and deep.

And then again the eyes of the two women met—this time clung together in a look of dawning comprehension, of growing horror. Mrs. Peters looked from the dead bird to the broken door of the cage. Again their eyes met. And just then there was a sound at the outside door.

Mrs. Hale slipped the box under the quilt pieces in the basket, and sank into the chair before it. Mrs. Peter stood holding to the table. The county attorney and the sheriff came in from outside.

"Well, ladies," said the county attorney, as one turning from serious things to little pleasantries, "have you decided whether she was going to quilt it or knot it?"

"We think," began the sheriff's wife in a flurried voice, "that she was going to—knot it."

He was too preoccupied to notice the change that came in her voice on that last.

"Well, that's very interesting, I'm sure," he said tolerantly. He caught sight of the bird-cage. "Has the bird flown?"

"We think the cat got it," said Mrs. Hale in a voice curiously even.

He was walking up and down, as if thinking something out.

"Is there a cat?" he asked absently.

Mrs. Hale shot a look up at the sheriff's wife.

"Well, not *now*," said Mrs. Peters. "They're superstitious, you know; they leave."

She sank into her chair.

The county attorney did not heed her. "No sign at all of any one having come in from the outside," he said to Peters, in the manner of continuing an interrupted conversation. "Their own rope. Now let's go upstairs again and go over it, piece by piece. It would have to have been some one who knew just the—"

The stair door closed behind them and their voices were lost.

The two women sat motionless, not looking at each other, but as if peering into something and at the same time holding back. When they spoke now it was as if they were afraid of what they were saying, but as if they could not help saying it.

"She liked the bird," said Martha Hale, low and slowly. "She was going to bury it in that pretty box."

"When I was a girl," said Mrs. Peters, under her breath, "my kitten—there was a boy took a hatchet, and before my eyes—before I could get there—" She covered her face an instant. "If they hadn't held me back I would have"—she caught herself, looked upstairs where footsteps were heard, and finished weakly—"hurt him."

Then they sat without speaking or moving.

"I wonder how it would seem," Mrs. Hale at last began, as if feeling her way over strange ground—"never to have had any children around?" Her eyes made a slow sweep of the kitchen, as if seeing what that kitchen had meant through all the years. "No, Wright wouldn't like the bird," she said after that—"a thing that sang. She used to sing. He killed that too." Her voice tightened.

Mrs. Peters moved uneasily.

"Of course we don't know who killed the bird."

"I knew John Wright," was Mrs. Hale's answer.

"It was an awful thing was done in this house that night, Mrs. Hale," said the sheriff's wife. "Killing a man while he slept—slipping a thing round his neck that choked the life out of him."

Mrs. Hale's hand went out to the bird-cage.

"His neck. Choked the life out of him."

"We don't *know* who killed him," whispered Mrs. Peters wildly. "We don't *know*."

Mrs. Hale had not moved. "If there had been years and years of—nothing, then a bird to sing to you, it would be awful—still—after the bird was still."

It was as if something within her not herself had spoken, and it found in Mrs. Peters something she did not know as herself.

"I know what stillness is," she said, in a queer, monotonous voice. "When we homesteaded in Dakota, and my first baby died—after he was two years old—and me with no other then—"

Mrs. Hale stirred.

"How soon do you suppose they'll be through looking for evidence?"

"I know what stillness is," repeated Mrs. Peters, in just that same way. Then she too pulled back. "The law has got to punish crime, Mrs. Hale," she said in her tight little way.

"I wish you'd seen Minnie Foster," was the answer, "when she wore a white dress with blue ribbons, and stood up there in the choir and sang."

The picture of that girl, the fact that she had lived neighbor to that girl for twenty years, and had let her die for lack of life, was suddenly more than she could bear.

"Oh, I *wish* I'd come over here once in a while!" she cried. "That was a crime! That was a crime! Who's going to punish that?"

"We mustn't take on," said Mrs. Peters, with a frightened look toward the stairs.

"I might 'a' *known* she needed help! I tell you, it's *queer*, Mrs. Peters. We live close together, and we live far apart. We all go through the same things—it's all just a different kind of the same thing! If it weren't—why do you and I *understand?* Why do we *know*—what we know this minute?"

She dashed her hand across her eyes. Then, seeing the jar of fruit on the table, she reached for it and choked out:

"If I was you I wouldn't *tell* her her fruit was gone! Tell her it *ain't.* Tell her it's all right—all of it. Here—take this in to prove it to her! She—she may never know whether it was broke or not."

She turned away.

Mrs. Peters reached out for the bottle of fruit as if she were glad to take it—as if touching a familiar thing, having something to do, could keep her from something else. She got up, looked about for something to wrap the fruit in, took a petticoat from the pile of clothes she had brought from the front room, and nervously started winding that round the bottle.

"My!" she began, in a high, false voice, "it's a good thing the men couldn't hear us! Getting all stirred up over a little thing like a—dead canary." She hurried over that. "As if that could have anything to do with—with—My, wouldn't they *laugh?*"

Footsteps were heard on the stairs.

"Maybe they would," muttered Mrs. Hale—"maybe they wouldn't."

"No, Peters," said the county attorney incisively; "it's all perfectly clear, except the reason for doing it. But you know juries when it comes to women. If there was some definite thing—something to show. Something to make a story about. A thing that would connect up with this clumsy way of doing it."

In a covert way Mrs. Hale looked at Mrs. Peters. Mrs. Peters was looking at her. Quickly they looked away from each other. The outer door opened and Mr. Hale came in.

"I've got the team round now," he said. "Pretty cold out there."

"I'm going to stay here awhile by myself," the county attorney suddenly announced. "You can send Frank out for me, can't you?" he asked the sheriff. "I want to go over everything. I'm not satisfied we can't do better."

Again, for one brief moment, the two women's eyes found one another.

The sheriff came up to the table.

"Did you want to see what Mrs. Peters was going to take in?"

The county attorney picked up the apron. He laughed.

"Oh, I guess they're not very dangerous things the ladies have picked out."

Mrs. Hale's hand was on the sewing basket in which the box was concealed. She felt that she ought to take her hand off the basket. She did not seem able to. He picked up one of the quilt blocks which she had piled on to cover the box. Her eyes felt like fire. She had a feeling that if he took up the basket she would snatch it from him.

But he did not take it up. With another little laugh, he turned away, saying:

"No; Mrs. Peters doesn't need supervising. For that matter, a sheriff's wife is married to the law. Ever think of it that way, Mrs. Peters?"

Mrs. Peters was standing beside the table. Mrs. Hale shot a look up at her; but she could not see her face. Mrs. Peters had turned away. When she spoke, her voice was muffled.

"Not—just that way," she said.

"Married to the law!" chuckled Mrs. Peters' husband. He moved toward the door into the front room, and said to the county attorney:

"I just want you to come in here a minute, George. We ought to take a look at these windows."

"Oh—windows," said the county attorney scoffingly.

"We'll be right out, Mr. Hale," said the sheriff to the farmer, who was still waiting by the door.

Hale went to look after the horses. The sheriff followed the county attorney into the other room. Again—for one moment—the two women were alone in that kitchen.

Martha Hale sprang up, her hands tight together, looking at that other woman, with whom it rested. At first she could not see her eyes, for the sheriff's wife had not turned back since she turned away at that suggestion of being married to the law. But now Mrs. Hale made her turn back. Her eyes made her turn back. Slowly, unwillingly, Mrs. Peters turned her head until her eyes met the eyes of the other woman. There was a moment when they held each other in a steady, burning look in which there was no evasion nor flinching. Then Martha Hale's eyes pointed the way to the basket in which was hidden the thing that would make certain the conviction of the other woman—that woman who was not there and yet who had been there with them all through the hour.

For a moment Mrs. Peters did not move. And then she did it. With a rush forward, she threw back the quilt pieces, got the box, tried to put it in her handbag. It was too big. Desperately she opened it, started to take the bird out. But there she broke—she could not touch the bird. She stood helpless, foolish.

There was the sound of a knob turning in the inner door. Martha Hale snatched the box from the sheriff's wife, and got it in the pocket of her big coat just as the sheriff and the county attorney came back into the kitchen.

"Well, Henry," said the county attorney facetiously, "at least we found out that she was not going to quilt it. She was going to—what is it you call it, ladies?"

Mrs. Hale's hand was against the pocket of her coat.

"We call it—knot it, Mr. Henderson."

EXERCISE

The two stories by William Faulkner that follow, both revolving around an animal chase and financial transactions related thereto, are both comic interpretive stories of indisputable merit. The majority of qualified judges, however, would rank one story higher on the scale of literary value than the other. Which story, in your estimation, deserves the higher ranking? Support your decision with a reasoned and thorough analysis, using the study questions for what help they may provide.

William Faulkner

SPOTTED HORSES

1

Yes, sir. Flem Snopes has filled that whole country full of spotted horses. You can hear folks running them all day and all night, whooping and hollering, and the horses running back and forth across them little wooden bridges ever now and then kind of like thunder. Here I was this morning pretty near half way to town, with the team ambling along and me setting in the buckboard about half asleep, when all of a sudden something come swurging up outen the bushes and jumped the road clean, without touching hoof to it. It flew right over my team, big as a billboard and flying through the air like a hawk. It taken me thirty minutes to stop my team and untangle the harness and the buckboard and hitch them up again.

That Flem Snopes. I be dog if he ain't a case, now. One morning about ten years ago, the boys was just getting settled down on Varner's porch for a little talk and tobacco, when here come Flem from behind the counter, with his coat off and his hair all parted, like he might have been clerking for Varner

---

SPOTTED HORSES First published in 1931. An expanded, considerably altered version of the story constitutes book IV, chapter 1, of *The Hamlet* (1940). Like "That Evening Sun" (page 254) the story is set in Yoknapatawpha county. Faulkner's trilogy—*The Hamlet*, *The Town*, and *The Mansion*—charts the spread of the Snopes tribe and the rise of Flem Snopes, son of a tenant farmer, to the foremost position of power and wealth in the county.

for ten years already. Folks all knowed him; it was a big family of them about five miles down the bottom. That year, at least. Share-cropping. They never stayed on any place over a year. Then they would move on to another place, with the chap or maybe the twins of that year's litter. It was a regular nest of them. But Flem. The rest of them stayed tenant farmers, moving ever year, but here come Flem one day, walking out from behind Jody Varner's counter like he owned it. And he wasn't there but a year or two before folks knowed that, if him and Jody was both still in that store in ten years more, it would be Jody clerking for Flem Snopes. Why, that fellow could make a nickel where it wasn't but four cents to begin with. He skun me in two trades, myself, and the fellow that can do that, I just hope he'll get rich before I do; that's all.

All right. So here Flem was, clerking at Varner's, making a nickel here and there and not telling nobody about it. No, sir. Folks never knowed when Flem got the better of somebody lessen the fellow he beat told it. He'd just set there in the store-chair, chewing his tobacco and keeping his own business to hisself, until about a week later we'd find out it was somebody else's business he was keeping to hisself—provided the fellow he trimmed was mad enough to tell it. That's Flem.

We give him ten years to own ever thing Jody Varner had. But he never waited no ten years. I reckon you-all know that gal of Uncle Billy Varner's, the youngest one; Eula. Jody's sister. Ever Sunday ever yellow-wheeled buggy and curried riding horse in that country would be hitched to Bill Varner's fence, and the young bucks setting on the porch, swarming around Eula like bees around a honey pot. One of these here kind of big, soft-looking gals that could giggle richer than plowed new-ground. Wouldn't none of them leave before the others, and so they would set there on the porch until time to go home, with some of them with nine or ten miles to ride and then get up tomorrow and go back to the field. So they would all leave together and they would ride in a clump down to the creek ford and hitch them curried horses and yellow-wheeled buggies and get out and fight one another. Then they would get in the buggies again and go on home

Well, one day about a year ago, one of them yellow-wheeled buggies and one of them curried saddle-horses quit this country. We heard they was heading for Texas. The next day Uncle Billy and Eula and Flem come in to town in Uncle Bill's surrey, and when they come back, Flem and Eula was married. And on the next day we heard that two more of them yellow-wheeled buggies had left the country. They mought have gone to Texas, too. It's a big place.

Anyway, about a month after the wedding, Flem and Eula went to Texas, too. They was gone pretty near a year. Then one day last month, Eula come back, with a baby. We figgured up, and we decided that it was as well-growed a three-months-old baby as we ever see. It can already pull up on a chair. I reckon Texas makes big men quick, being a big place. Anyway, if it keeps on like it started, it'll be chewing tobacco and voting time it's eight years old.

And so last Friday here come Flem himself. He was on a wagon with another fellow. The other fellow had one of these two-gallon hats and a ivory-handled pistol and a box of gingersnaps sticking out of his hind pocket, and tied to the tail-gate of the wagon was about two dozen of them Texas ponies, hitched to one another with barbed wire. They was colored like parrots and they was quiet as doves, and ere a one of them would kill you quick as a rattlesnake. Nere a one of them had two eyes the same color, and nere a one of them had ever see a bridle, I reckon; and when that Texas man got down offen the wagon and walked up to them to show how gentle they was, one of them cut his vest clean offen him, same as with a razor.

Flem had done already disappeared; he had went on to see his wife, I reckon, and to see if that ere baby had done gone on to the field to help Uncle Billy plow maybe. It was the Texas man that taken the horses on to Mrs. Littlejohn's lot. He had a little trouble at first, when they come to the gate, because they hadn't never see a fence before, and when he finally got them in and taken a pair of wire cutters and unhitched them and got them into the barn and poured some shell corn into the trough, they durn nigh tore down the barn. I reckon they thought that shell corn was bugs, maybe. So he left them in the lot and he announced that the auction would begin at sunup to-morrow.

That night we was setting on Mrs. Littlejohn's porch. You-all mind the moon was nigh full that night, and we could watch them spotted varmints swirling along the fence and back and forth across the lot same as minnows in a pond. And then now and then they would all kind of huddle up against the barn and rest themselves by biting and kicking one another. We would hear a squeal, and then a set of hoofs would go Bam! against the barn, like a pistol. It sounded just like a fellow with a pistol, in a nest of cattymounts, taking his time.

2

It wasn't ere a man knowed yet if Flem owned them things or not. They just knowed one thing: that they wasn't never going to know for sho if Flem did or not, or if maybe he didn't just get on that wagon at the edge of town, for the ride or not. Even Eck Snopes didn't know, Flem's own cousin. But wasn't nobody surprised at that. We knowed that Flem would skin Eck quick as he would ere a one of us.

They was there by sunup next morning, some of them come twelve and sixteen miles, with seed-money tied up in tobacco sacks in their overalls, standing along the fence, when the Texas man come out of Mrs. Littlejohn's after breakfast and clumb onto the gate post with that ere white pistol butt sticking outen his hind pocket. He taken a new box of gingersnaps outen his pocket and bit the end offen it like a cigar and spit out the paper, and said the auction was open. And still they was coming up in wagons and a horse- and mule-back and hitching the teams across the road and coming to the fence. Flem wasn't nowhere in sight.

But he couldn't get them started. He begun to work on Eck, because Eck holp him last night to get them into the barn and feed them that shell corn. Eck got out just in time. He come outen that barn like a chip on the crest of a busted dam of water, and clumb into the wagon just in time.

He was working on Eck when Henry Armstid come up in his wagon. Eck was saying he was skeered to bid on one of them, because he might get it, and the Texas man says, "Them ponies? Them little horses?" He clumb down offen the gate post and went toward the horses. They broke and run, and him following them, kind of chirping to them, with his hand out like he was fixing to catch a fly, until he got three or four of them cornered. Then he jumped into them, and then we couldn't see nothing for a while because of the dust. It was a big cloud of it, and them blare-eyed, spotted things swoaring outen it twenty foot to a jump, in forty directions without counting up. Then the dust settled and there they was, the Texas man and the horse. He had its head twisted clean around like a owl's head. Its legs was braced and it was trembling like a new bride and groaning like a saw mill, and him holding its head wrung clean around on its neck so it was snuffing sky. "Look it over," he says, with his heels dug too and that white pistol sticking outen his pocket and his neck swole up like a spreading adder's until you could just tell what he was saying, cussing the horse and talking to us all at once: "Look him over, the fiddle-headed son of fourteen fathers. Try him, buy him; you will get the best—" Then it was all dust again, and we couldn't see nothing but spotted hide and mane, and that ere Texas man's boot-heels like a couple of walnuts on two strings, and after a while that two-gallon hat come sailing out like a fat old hen crossing a fence.

When the dust settled again, he was just getting outen the far fence corner, brushing himself off. He come and got his hat and brushed it off and come and clumb onto the gate post again. He was breathing hard. He taken the gingersnap box outen his pocket and et one, breathing hard. The hammer-head horse was still running round and round the lot like a merry-go-round at a fair. That was when Henry Armstid come shoving up to the gate in them patched overalls and one of them dangle-armed shirts of hisn. Hadn't nobody noticed him until then. We was all watching the Texas man and the horses. Even Mrs. Littlejohn; she had done come out and built a fire under the wash-pot in her back yard, and she would stand at the fence a while and then go back into the house and come out again with a arm full of wash and stand at the fence again. Well, here come Henry shoving up, and then we see Mrs. Armstid right behind him, in that ere faded wrapper and sunbonnet and them tennis shoes. "Git on back to that wagon," Henry says.

"Henry," she says.

"Here, boys," the Texas man says; "make room for missus to git up and see. Come on, Henry," he says; "here's your chance to buy that saddle-horse missus has been wanting. What about ten dollars, Henry?"

"Henry," Mrs. Armstid says. She put her hand on Henry's arm. Henry knocked her hand down.

"Git on back to that wagon, like I told you," he says.

Mrs. Armstid never moved. She stood behind Henry, with her hands rolled into her dress, not looking at nothing. "He hain't no more despair than to buy one of them things," she says. "And us not five dollars ahead of the pore house, he hain't no more despair." It was the truth, too. They ain't never made more than a bare living offen that place of theirs, and them with four chaps and the very clothes they wears she earns by weaving by the firelight at night while Henry's asleep.

"Shut your mouth and git on back to that wagon," Henry says. "Do you want I taken a wagon stake to you here in the big road?"

Well, that Texas man taken one look at her. Then he begun on Eck again, like Henry wasn't even there. But Eck was skeered. "I can git me a snapping turtle or a water moccasin for nothing. I ain't going to buy none."

So the Texas man said he would give Eck a horse. "To start the auction, and because you holp me last night. If you'll start the bidding on the next horse," he says, "I'll give you that fiddle-head horse."

I wish you could have seen them, standing there with their seed-money in their pockets, watching that Texas man give Eck Snopes a live horse, all fixed to call him a fool if he taken it or not. Finally Eck says he'll take it. "Only I just starts the bidding," he says. "I don't have to buy the next one lessen I ain't overtopped." The Texas man said all right, and Eck bid a dollar on the next one, with Henry Armstid standing there with his mouth already open, watching Eck and the Texas man like a mad-dog or something. "A dollar," Eck says.

The Texas man looked at Eck. His mouth was already open too, like he had started to say something and what he was going to say had up and died on him. "A dollar?" he says. "One dollar? You mean, *one* dollar, Eck?"

"Durn it," Eck says; "two dollars, then."

Well, sir, I wish you could a seen that Texas man. He taken out that gingersnap box and held it up and looked into it, careful, like it might have been a diamond ring in it, or a spider. Then he throwed it away and wiped his face with a bandanna. "Well," he says. "Well. Two dollars. Two dollars. Is your pulse all right, Eck?" he says. "Do you have ager-sweats at night, maybe?" he says. "Well," he says, "I got to take it. But are you boys going to stand there and see Eck get two horses at a dollar a head?"

That done it. I be dog if he wasn't nigh as smart as Flem Snopes. He hadn't no more than got the words outen his mouth before here was Henry Armstid, waving his hand. "Three dollars," Henry says. Mrs. Armstid tried to hold him again. He knocked her hand off, shoving up to the gate post.

"Mister," Mrs. Armstid says, "we got chaps in the house and not corn to feed the stock. We got five dollars I earned my chaps a-weaving after dark, and him snoring in the bed. And he hain't no more despair."

"Henry bids three dollars," the Texas man says. "Raise him a dollar, Eck, and the horse is yours."

"Henry," Mrs. Armstid says.

"Raise him, Eck," the Texas man says.

"Four dollars," Eck says.

"Five dollars," Henry says, shaking his fist. He shoved up right under the gate post. Mrs. Armstid was looking at the Texas man too.

"Mister," she says, "if you take that five dollars I earned my chaps a-weaving for one of them things, it'll be a curse onto you and yourn during all the time of man."

But it wasn't no stopping Henry. He had shoved up, waving his fist at the Texas man. He opened it; the money was in nickels and quarters, and one dollar bill that looked like a cow's cud. "Five dollars," he says. "And the man that raises it'll have to beat my head off, or I'll beat hisn."

"All right," the Texas man says. "Five dollars is bid. But don't you shake your hand at me."

3

It taken till nigh sundown before the last one was sold. He got them hotted up once and the bidding got up to seven dollars and a quarter, but most of them went around three or four dollars, him setting on the gate post and picking the horses out one at a time by mouth-word, and Mrs. Littlejohn pumping up and down at the tub and stopping and coming to the fence for a while and going back to the tub again. She had done got done too, and the wash was hung on the line in the back yard, and we could smell supper cooking. Finally they was all sold; he swapped the last two and the wagon for a buckboard.

We was all kind of tired, but Henry Armstid looked more like a mad-dog than ever. When he bought, Mrs. Armstid had went back to the wagon, setting in it behind them two rabbit-sized bone-pore mules, and the wagon itself looking like it would fall all to pieces soon as the mules moved. Henry hadn't even waited to pull it outen the road; it was still in the middle of the road and her setting in it, not looking at nothing, ever since this morning.

Henry was right up against the gate. He went up to the Texas man. "I bought a horse and I paid cash," Henry says. "And yet you expect me to stand around here until they are all sold before I can get my horse. I'm going to take my horse outen that lot."

The Texas man looked at Henry. He talked like he might have been asking for a cup of coffee at the table. "Take your horse," he says.

Then Henry quit looking at the Texas man. He begun to swallow, holding onto the gate. "Ain't you going to help me?" he says.

"It ain't my horse," the Texas man says.

Henry never looked at the Texas man again, he never looked at nobody. "Who'll help me catch my horse?" he says. Never nobody said nothing. "Bring the plowline," Henry says. Mrs. Armstid got outen the wagon and brought the plowline. The Texas man got down off the post. The woman made to pass him, carrying the rope.

"Don't you go in there, missus," the Texas man says. Henry opened the gate. He didn't look back. "Come on here," he says. "Don't you go in there, missus," the Texas man says.

Mrs. Armstid wasn't looking at nobody, neither, with her hands across her middle, holding the rope. "I reckon I better," she says. Her and Henry went into the lot. The horses broke and run. Henry and Mrs. Armstid followed.

"Get him into the corner," Henry says. They got Henry's horse cornered finally, and Henry taken the rope, but Mrs. Armstid let the horse get out. They hemmed it up again, but Mrs. Armstid let it get out again, and Henry turned and hit her with the rope. "Why didn't you head him back?" Henry says. He hit her again. "Why didn't you?" It was about that time I looked around and see Flem Snopes standing there.

It was the Texas man that done something. He moved fast for a big man. He caught the rope before Henry could hit the third time, and Henry whirled and made like he would jump at the Texas man. But he never jumped. The Texas man went and taken Henry's arm and led him outen the lot. Mrs. Armstid come behind them and the Texas man taken some money outen his pocket and he give it into Mrs. Armstid's hand. "Get him into the wagon and take him on home," the Texas man says, like he might have been telling them he enjoyed his supper.

Then here come Flem. "What's that for, Buck?" Flem says.

"Thinks he bought one of them ponies," the Texas man says. "Get him on away, missus."

But Henry wouldn't go. "Give him back that money," he says. "I bought that horse and I aim to have him if I have to shoot him."

And there was Flem, standing there with his hands in his pockets, chewing, like he had just happened to be passing.

"You take your money and I take my horse," Henry says. "Give it back to him," he says to Mrs. Armstid.

"You don't own no horse of mine," the Texas man says. "Get him on home, missus."

Then Henry seen Flem. "You got something to do with these horses," he says. "I bought one. Here's the money for it." He taken the bill outen Mrs. Armstid's hand. He offered it to Flem. "I bought one. Ask him. Here. Here's the money," he says, giving the bill to Flem.

When Flem taken the money, the Texas man dropped the rope he had snatched outen Henry's hand. He had done sent Eck Snopes's boy up to the store for another box of gingersnaps, and he taken the box outen his pocket and looked into it. It was empty and he dropped it on the ground. "Mr. Snopes will have your money for you to-morrow," he says to Mrs. Armstid. "You can get it from him to-morrow. He don't own no horse. You get him into the wagon and get him on home." Mrs. Armstid went back to the wagon and got in. "Where's that ere buckboard I bought?" the Texas man says. It was after sundown then. And then Mrs. Littlejohn come out on the porch and rung the supper bell.

4

I come on in and et supper. Mrs. Littlejohn would bring in a pan of bread or something, then she would go out to the porch a minute and come back and tell us. The Texas man had hitched his team to the buckboard he had swapped them last two horses for, and him and Flem had gone, and then she told that the rest of them that never had ropes had went back to the store with I. O. Snopes to get some ropes, and wasn't nobody at the gate but Henry Armstid, and Mrs. Armstid setting in the wagon in the road, and Eck Snopes and that boy of hisn. "I don't care how many of them fool men gets killed by them things," Mrs. Littlejohn says, "but I ain't going to let Eck Snopes take that boy into that lot again." So she went down to the gate, but she come back without the boy or Eck neither.

"It ain't no need to worry about that boy," I says. "He's charmed." He was right behind Eck last night when Eck went to help feed them. The whole drove of them jumped clean over that boy's head and never touched him. It was Eck that touched him. Eck snatched him into the wagon and taken a rope and frailed the tar out of him.

So I had done et and went to my room and was undressing, long as I had a long trip to make the next day; I was trying to sell a machine to Mrs. Bundren up past Whiteleaf; when Henry Armstid opened that gate and went in by hisself. They couldn't make him wait for the balance of them to get back with their ropes. Eck Snopes said he tried to make Henry wait, but Henry wouldn't do it. Eck said Henry walked right up to them and that when they broke, they run clean over Henry like a hay-mow breaking down. Eck said he snatched that boy of hisn out of the way just in time and that them things went through the gate like a creek flood and into the wagons and teams hitched side the road, busting wagon tongues and snapping harness like it was fishing-line, with Mrs. Armstid still setting in their wagon in the middle of it like something carved outen wood. Then they scattered, wild horses and tame mules with pieces of harness and single trees dangling offen them, both ways up and down the road.

"There goes ourn, paw!" Eck says his boy said. "There it goes, into Mrs. Littlejohn's house." Eck says it run right up the steps and into the house like a boarder late for supper. I reckon so. Anyway, I was in my room, in my underclothes, with one sock on and one sock in my hand, leaning out the window when the commotion busted out, when I heard something run into the melodeon in the hall; it sounded like a railroad engine. Then the door to my room come sailing in like when you throw a tin bucket top into the wind and I looked over my shoulder and see something that looked like a fourteen-foot pinwheel a-blaring its eyes at me. It had to blare them fast, because I was already done jumped out the window.

I reckon it was anxious, too. I reckon it hadn't never seen barbed wire or shell corn before, but I know it hadn't never seen underclothes before, or maybe it was a sewing-machine agent it hadn't never seen. Anyway, it swirled and turned to run back up the hall and outen the house, when it met Eck Snopes and that boy just coming in, carrying a rope. It swirled again and run down the hall and out the back door just in time to meet Mrs. Littlejohn. She had just gathered up the clothes she had washed, and she was coming onto the back porch with a armful of washing in one hand and a scrubbing-board in the other, when the horse skidded up to her, trying to stop and swirl again. It never taken Mrs. Littlejohn no time a-tall.

"Git outen here, you son," she says. She hit it across the face with the scrubbing board; that ere scrubbing-board split as neat as ere a axe could have done it, and when the horse swirled to run back up the hall, she hit it again with what was left of the scrubbing-board, not on the head this time. "And stay out," she says.

Eck and that boy was half-way down the hall by this time. I reckon that horse looked like a pinwheel to Eck too. "Git to hell outen here, Ad!" Eck says. Only there wasn't time. Eck dropped flat on his face, but the boy never moved. The boy was about a yard tall maybe, in overhalls just like Eck's; that horse swoared over his head without touching a hair. I saw that, because I was just coming back up the front steps, still carrying that ere sock and still in my underclothes, when the horse come onto the porch again. It taken one look at me and swirled again and run to the end of the porch and jumped the banisters and the lot fence like a hen-hawk and lit in the lot running and went out the gate again and jumped eight or ten upside-down wagons and went on down the road. It was a full moon then. Mrs. Armstid was still setting in the wagon like she had done been carved outen wood and left there and forgot.

That horse. It ain't never missed a lick. It was going about forty miles a hour when it come to the bridge over the creek. It would have had a clear road, but it so happened that Vernon Tull was already using the bridge when it got there. He was coming back from town; he hadn't heard about the auction; him and his wife and three daughters and Mrs. Tull's aunt, all setting in chairs in the wagon bed, and all asleep, including the mules. They waked up when the horse hit the bridge one time, but Tull said the first he knew was when the mules tried to turn the wagon around in the middle of the bridge and he seen that spotted varmint run right twixt the mules and run up the wagon tongue like a squirrel. He said he just had time to hit it across the face with his whip-stock, because about that time the mules turned the wagon around on that ere one-way bridge and that horse clumb across one of the mules and jumped down onto the bridge again and went on, with Vernon standing up in the wagon and kicking at it.

Tull said the mules turned in the harness and clumb back into the wagon too, with Tull trying to beat them out again, with the reins wrapped around his wrist. After that he says all he seen was overturned chairs and womenfolks' legs and white drawers shining in the moonlight, and his mules and that spotted horse going on up the road like a ghost.

The mules jerked Tull outen the wagon and drug him a spell on the bridge before the reins broke. They thought at first that he was dead, and while they was kneeling around him, picking the bridge splinters outen him, here come Eck and that boy, still carrying the rope. They was running and breathing a little hard. "Where'd he go?" Eck says.

5

I went back and got my pants and shirt and shoes on just in time to go and help get Henry Armstid outen the trash in the lot. I be dog if he didn't look like he was dead, with his head hanging back and his teeth showing in the moonlight, and a little rim of white under his eyelids. We could still hear them horses, here and there; hadn't none of them got more than four-five miles away yet, not knowing the country, I reckon. So we could hear them and folks yelling now and then: "Whooey. Head him!"

We toted Henry into Mrs. Littlejohn's. She was in the hall; she hadn't put down the armful of clothes. She taken one look at us, and she laid down the busted scrubbing-board and taken up the lamp and opened a empty door. "Bring him in here," she says.

We toted him in and laid him on the bed. Mrs. Littlejohn set the lamp on the dresser, still carrying the clothes. "I'll declare, you men," she says. Our shadows was way up the wall, tiptoeing too; we could hear ourselves breathing. "Better get his wife," Mrs. Littlejohn says. She went out, carrying the clothes.

"I reckon we had," Quick says. "Go get her, somebody."

"Whyn't you go?" Winterbottom says.

"Let Ernest git her," Durley says. "He lives neighbors with them."

Ernest went to fetch her. I be dog if Henry didn't look like he was dead. Mrs. Littlejohn come back, with a kettle and some towels. She went to work on Henry, and then Mrs. Armstid and Ernest come in. Mrs. Armstid come to the foot of the bed and stood there, with her hands rolled into her apron, watching what Mrs. Littlejohn was doing, I reckon.

"You men git outen the way," Mrs. Littlejohn says. "Git outside," she says. "See if you can't find something else to play with that will kill some more of you."

"Is he dead?" Winterbottom says.

"It ain't your fault if he ain't," Mrs. Littlejohn says. "Go tell Will Varner to come up here. I reckon a man ain't so different from a mule, come long come short. Except maybe a mule's got more sense."

We went to get Uncle Billy. It was a full moon. We could hear them, now and then, four mile away: "Whooey. Head him." The country was full of them, one on ever wooden bridge in the land, running across it like thunder: "Whooey. There he goes. Head him."

We hadn't got far before Henry begun to scream. I reckon Mrs. Littlejohn's water had brung him to; anyway, he wasn't dead. We went on to Uncle Billy's. The house was dark. We called to him, and after a while the window opened and Uncle Billy put his head out, peart as a peckerwood, listening. "Are they still trying to catch them durn rabbits?" he says.

He come down, with his britches on over his night-shirt and his suspenders dangling, carrying his horse-doctoring grip. "Yes, sir," he says, cocking his head like a woodpecker; "they're still a-trying."

We could hear Henry before we reached Mrs. Littlejohn's. He was going Ah-Ah-Ah. We stopped in the yard. Uncle Billy went on in. We could hear Henry. We stood in the yard, hearing them on the bridges, this-a-way and that: "Whooey. Whooey."

"Eck Snopes ought to caught hisn," Ernest says.

"Looks like he ought," Winterbottom said.

Henry was going Ah-Ah-Ah steady in the house; then he begun to scream. "Uncle Billy's started," Quick says. We looked into the hall. We could see the light where the door was. Then Mrs. Littlejohn come out.

"Will needs some help," she says. "You, Ernest. You'll do." Ernest went into the house.

"Hear them?" Quick said. "That one was on Four Mile bridge." We could hear them; it sounded like thunder a long way off; it didn't last long. "Whooey."

We could hear Henry: "Ah-Ah-Ah-Ah-Ah."

"They are both started now," Winterbottom says. "Ernest too."

That was early in the night. Which was a good thing, because it taken a long night for folks to chase them things right and for Henry to lay there and holler, being as Uncle Billy never had none of this here chloryfoam to set Henry's leg with. So it was considerate in Flem to get them started early. And what do you reckon Flem's com-ment was?

That's right. Nothing. Because he wasn't there. Hadn't nobody see him since that Texas man left.

6

That was Saturday night. I reckon Mrs. Armstid got home about daylight, to see about the chaps. I don't know where they thought her and Henry was. But lucky the oldest one was a gal, about twelve, big enough to take care of the little ones. Which she did for the next two days. Mrs. Armstid would nurse Henry all night and work in the kitchen for hern and Henry's keep, and in the afternoon she would drive home (it was about four miles) to see to the chaps. She would cook up a pot of victuals and leave it on the stove, and the gal would bar the house and keep the little ones quiet. I would hear Mrs. Littlejohn and Mrs. Armstid talking in the kitchen. "How are the chaps making out?" Mrs. Littlejohn says.

"All right," Mrs. Armstid says.

"Don't they git skeered at night?" Mrs. Littlejohn says.

"Ina May bars the door when I leave," Mrs. Armstid says. "She's got the axe in bed with her. I reckon she can make out."

I reckon they did. And I reckon Mrs. Armstid was waiting for Flem to come back to town; hadn't nobody seen him until this morning; to get her money the Texas man said Flem was keeping for her. Sho. I reckon she was.

Anyway, I heard Mrs. Armstid and Mrs. Littlejohn talking in the kitchen this morning while I was eating breakfast. Mrs. Littlejohn had just told Mrs. Armstid that Flem was in town. "You can ask him for that five dollars," Mrs. Littlejohn says.

"You reckon he'll give it to me?" Mrs. Armstid says.

Mrs. Littlejohn was washing dishes, washing them like a man, like they was made out of iron. "No," she says. "But asking him won't do no hurt. It might shame him. I don't reckon it will, but it might."

"If he wouldn't give it back, it ain't no use to ask," Mrs. Armstid says.

"Suit yourself," Mrs. Littlejohn says. "It's your money."

I could hear the dishes.

"Do you reckon he might give it back to me?" Mrs. Armstid says. "That Texas man said he would. He said I could get it from Mr. Snopes later."

"Then go and ask him for it," Mrs. Littlejohn says.

I could hear the dishes.

"He won't give it back to me," Mrs. Armstid says.

"All right," Mrs. Littlejohn says. "Don't ask him for it, then."

I could hear the dishes; Mrs. Armstid was helping. "You don't reckon he would, do you?" she says. Mrs. Littlejohn never said nothing. It sounded like she was throwing the dishes at one another. "Maybe I better go and talk to Henry about it," Mrs. Armstid says.

"I would," Mrs. Littlejohn says. I be dog if it didn't sound like she had two plates in her hands, beating them together. "Then Henry can buy another five-dollar horse with it. Maybe he'll buy one next time that will out and out kill him. If I thought that, I'd give you back the money, myself."

"I reckon I better talk to him first," Mrs. Armstid said. Then it sounded like Mrs. Littlejohn taken up all the dishes and throwed them at the cookstove, and I come away.

That was this morning. I had been up to Bundren's and back, and I thought that things would have kind of settled down. So after breakfast, I went up to the store. And there was Flem, setting in the store-chair and whittling, like he might not have ever moved since he come to clerk for Jody Varner. I. O. was leaning in the door, in his shirt sleeves and with his hair parted too, same as Flem was before he turned the clerking job over to I. O. It's a funny thing about them Snopes: they all looks alike, yet there ain't ere a two of them that claims brothers. They're always just cousins, like Flem and Eck and Flem and I. O. Eck was there too, squatting against the wall, him and that boy, eating cheese and crackers outen a sack; they told me that Eck hadn't been home a-tall. And that Lon Quick hadn't got back to town, even. He followed his horse clean down to Samson's Bridge, with a wagon and a camp outfit. Eck finally caught one of hisn. It run into a blind lane at Freeman's and Eck and the boy taken and tied their rope across the end of the lane, about three foot high. The horse come to the end of the lane and whirled and run back without ever stopping. Eck says it never seen the rope a-tall. He says it looked just like one of these here Christmas pinwheels. "Didn't it try to run again?" I says.

"No," Eck says, eating a bite of cheese offen his knife blade. "Just kicked some."

"Kicked some?" I says.

"It broke its neck," Eck says.

Well, they was squatting there, about six of them, talking, talking at Flem; never nobody knowed yet if Flem had ere a interest in them horses or not. So finally I come right out and asked him. "Flem's done skun all of us so much," I says, "that we're proud of him. Come on, Flem," I says, "how much did you and that Texas man make offen them horses? You can tell us. Ain't nobody here but Eck that bought one of them; the others ain't got back to town yet, and Eck's your own cousin; he'll be proud to hear, too. How much did you-all make?"

They was all whittling, not looking at Flem, making like they was studying. But you could a heard a pin drop. And I. O. He had been rubbing his back up and down on the door, but he stopped now, watching Flem like a pointing dog. Flem finished cutting the sliver offen his stick. He spit across the porch, into the road. "'Twarn't none of my horses," he says.

I. O. cackled, like a hen, slapping his legs with both hands. "You boys might just as well quit trying to get ahead of Flem," he said.

Well, about that time I see Mrs. Armstid come outen Mrs. Littlejohn's gate, coming up the road. I never said nothing. I says, "Well, if a man can't take care of himself in a trade, he can't blame the man that trims him."

Flem never said nothing, trimming at the stick. He hadn't seen Mrs. Armstid. "Yes, sir," I says. "A fellow like Henry Armstid ain't got nobody but hisself to blame."

"Course he ain't," I. O. says. He ain't seen her, neither. "Henry Armstid's a born fool. Always is been. If Flem hadn't a got his money, somebody else would."

We looked at Flem. He never moved. Mrs. Armstid come on up the road.

"That's right," I says. "But, come to think of it, Henry never bought no horse." We looked at Flem; you could a heard a match drop. "That Texas man told her to get that five dollars back from Flem next day. I reckon Flem's done already taken that money to Mrs. Littlejohn's and give it to Mrs. Armstid."

We watched Flem. I. O. quit rubbing his back against the door again. After a while Flem raised his head and spit across the porch, into the dust. I. O. cackled, just like a hen. "Ain't he a beating fellow, now?" I. O. says.

Mrs. Armstid was getting closer, so I kept on talking, watching to see if Flem would look up and see her. But he never looked up. I went on talking about Tull, about how he was going to sue Flem, and Flem setting there, whittling his stick, not saying nothing else after he said they wasn't none of his horses.

Then I. O. happened to look around. He seen Mrs. Armstid. "Pssssst!" he says. Flem looked up. "Here she comes!" I. O. says. "Go out the back. I'll tell her you done went in to town to-day."

But Flem never moved. He just set there, whittling, and we watched Mrs.

Armstid come up onto the porch, in that ere faded sunbonnet and wrapper and them tennis shoes that made a kind of hissing noise on the porch. She come onto the porch and stopped, her hands rolled into her dress in front, not looking at nothing.

"He said Saturday," she says, "that he wouldn't sell Henry no horse. He said I could get the money from you."

Flem looked up. The knife never stopped. It went on trimming off a sliver same as if he was watching it. "He taken that money off with him when he left," Flem says.

Mrs. Armstid never looked at nothing. We never looked at her, neither, except that boy of Eck's. He had a half-et cracker in his hand, watching her, chewing.

"He said Henry hadn't bought no horse," Mrs. Armstid says. "He said for me to get the money from you to-day."

"I reckon he forgot about it," Flem said. "He taken that money off with him Saturday." He whittled again. I. O. kept on rubbing his back, slow. He licked his lips. After a while the woman looked up the road, where it went on up the hill, toward the graveyard. She looked up that way for a while, with that boy of Eck's watching her and I. O. rubbing his back slow against the door. Then she turned back toward the steps.

"I reckon it's time to get dinner started," she says.

"How's Henry this morning, Mrs. Armstid?" Winterbottom says.

She looked at Winterbottom; she almost stopped. "He's resting, I thank you kindly," she says.

Flem got up, outen the chair, putting his knife away. He spit across the porch. "Wait a minute, Mrs. Armstid," he says. She stopped again. She didn't look at him. Flem went on into the store, with I. O. done quit rubbing his back now, with his head craned after Flem, and Mrs. Armstid standing there with her hands rolled into her dress, not looking at nothing. A wagon come up the road and passed; it was Freeman, on the way to town. Then Flem come out again, with I. O. still watching him. Flem had one of these little striped sacks of Jody Varner's candy; I bet he still owes Jody that nickel, too. He put the sack into Mrs. Armstid's hand, like he would have put it into a hollow stump. He spit again across the porch. "A little sweetening for the chaps," he says.

"You're right kind," Mrs. Armstid says. She held the sack of candy in her hand, not looking at nothing. Eck's boy was watching the sack, the half-et cracker in his hand; he wasn't chewing now. He watched Mrs. Armstid roll the sack into her apron. "I reckon I better get on back and help with dinner," she says. She turned and went back across the porch. Flem set down in the chair again and opened his knife. He spit across the the porch again, past Mrs. Armstid where she hadn't went down the steps yet. Then she went on, in that ere sunbonnet and wrapper all the same color, back down the road toward Mrs. Littlejohn's. You couldn't see her dress move, like a natural woman walking. She looked like a old snag still standing up and moving along on a high water. We watched her turn in at Mrs. Littlejohn's and go outen sight. Flem was whittling. I. O. begun to rub his back on the door. Then he begun to cackle, just like a durn hen.

"You boys might just as well quit trying," I. O. says. "You can't git ahead of Flem. You can't touch him. Ain't he a sight, now?"

I be dog if he ain't. If I had brung a herd of wild cattymounts into town and sold them to my neighbors and kinfolks, they would have lynched me. Yes, sir.

QUESTIONS

1. Characterize Flem Snopes and trace his history in the story. What is his principal motivation? What inferences may be drawn about his marriage? about his involvement in the auction? Is there any point in the story where Flem can be proved to be lying? Is any of his actions motivated by generosity? How is he regarded by his cousins? Why?
2. Who is the narrator of the story? Characterize him as a person, and comment on his abilities as a story-teller, illustrating particularly by an analysis of some single paragraph (e.g., the opening one). What kind of story, as he tells it, is this—comic? tragic? pathetic? horrifying? What kind would it be if told by Mrs. Armstid? by Mr. Armstid? How does the narrator regard his characters? What is his attitude toward Flem? What are the chief sources of his humor?
3. Characterize the Texan. How is he different from Flem? What details of his characterization make him memorable?
4. Characterize Mrs. Armstid. What characteristics individuate her and make her more than just a "victim" of social and marital injustice? Is she a sympathetic character? What are her values and loyalties? How is she regarded by (a) her husband, (b) the Texan, (c) Flem, (d) Mrs. Littlejohn, (e) the narrator?
5. For a story of its length, this story has an unusual number of characters. How many are more than mere names? Identify each of the following, characterize each briefly, and comment on characteristics that make them memorable in any way: (a) Henry Armstid, (b) Mrs. Littlejohn, (c) Eck Snopes, (d) Eck's son, Ad, (e) I. O. Snopes, (f) Eula Varner, (g) "Uncle" Billy Varner, (h) the spotted horses. What is the irony of Vernon Tull's role in the story?
6. Who is the protagonist? Who are the antagonists? Who is victorious in their conflict? Does the story have a happy ending?

William Faulkner

MULE IN THE YARD

It was a gray day in late January, though not cold because of the fog. Old Het, just walked in from the poorhouse, ran down the hall toward the kitchen,

MULE IN THE YARD First published in 1934. A considerably altered version of the story is incorporated in chapter 16 of *The Town* (1957). The action of the story occurs many years after that of "Spotted Horses." The town is Jefferson.

shouting in a strong, bright, happy voice. She was about seventy probably, though by her own counting, calculated from the ages of various housewives in the town from brides to grandmothers whom she claimed to have nursed in infancy, she would have to be around a hundred and at least triplets. Tall, lean, fog-beaded, in tennis shoes and a long rat-colored cloak trimmed with what forty or fifty years ago had been fur, a modish though not new purple toque set upon her headrag and carrying (time was when she made her weekly rounds from kitchen to kitchen carrying a brocaded carpetbag though since the advent of the ten-cent stores the carpetbag became an endless succession of the convenient paper receptacles with which they supply their customers for a few cents) the shopping-bag, she ran into the kitchen and shouted with strong and childlike pleasure: "Miss Mannie! Mule in de yard!"

Mrs. Hait, stooping to the stove, in the act of drawing from it a scuttle of live ashes, jerked upright; clutching the scuttle, she glared at old Het, then she too spoke at once, strong too, immediate. "Them sons of bitches," she said. She left the kitchen, not running exactly, yet with a kind of outraged celerity, carrying the scuttle—a compact woman of forty-odd, with an air of indomitable yet relieved bereavement, as though that which had relicted her had been a woman and a not particularly valuable one at that. She wore a calico wrapper and a sweater coat, and a man's felt hat which they in the town knew had belonged to her ten years' dead husband. But the man's shoes had not belonged to him. They were high shoes which buttoned, with toes like small tulip bulbs, and in the town they knew that she had bought them new for herself. She and old Het ran down the kitchen steps and into the fog. That's why it was not cold: as though there lay supine and prisoned between earth and mist the long winter night's suspiration of the sleeping town in dark, close rooms—the slumber and the rousing; the stale waking thermostatic, by reheating heat-engendered: it lay like a scum of cold grease upon the steps and the wooden entrance to the basement and upon the narrow plank walk which led to a shed building in the corner of the yard: upon these planks, running and still carrying the scuttle of live ashes, Mrs. Hait skated viciously.

"Watch out!" old Het, footed securely by her rubber soles, cried happily. "Dey in de front!" Mrs. Hait did not fall. She did not even pause. She took in the immediate scene with one cold glare and was running again when there appeared at the corner of the house and apparently having been born before their eyes of the fog itself, a mule. It looked taller than a giraffe. Longheaded, with a flying halter about its scissorlike ears, it rushed down upon them with violent and apparitionlike suddenness.

"Dar hit!" old Het cried, waving the shopping-bag. "Hoo!" Mrs. Hait whirled. Again she skidded savagely on the greasy planks as she and the mule rushed parallel with one another toward the shed building, from whose open doorway there now projected the static and astonished face of a cow. To the cow the fog-born mule doubtless looked taller and more incredibly sudden than a giraffe even, and apparently bent upon charging right through the shed as though it were made of straw or were purely and simply mirage. The cow's head likewise had a quality transient and abrupt and unmundane. It vanished, sucked into invisibility like a match flame, though the mind knew and the reason insisted that she had withdrawn into the shed, from which, as proof's burden, there came an indescribable sound of shock and alarm by shed and beast engendered, analogous to a single note from a profoundly struck lyre or harp. Toward this sound Mrs. Hait sprang, immediately, as if by pure reflex, as though in invulnerable compact of female with female against a world of mule and man. She and the mule converged upon the shed at top speed, the heavy scuttle poised lightly in her hand to hurl. Of course it did not take this long, and likewise it was the mule which refused the gambit. Old Het was still shouting "Dar hit! Dar hit!" when it swerved and rushed at her where she stood tall as a stove pipe, holding the shopping-bag which she swung at the beast as it rushed past her and vanished beyond the other corner of the house as though sucked back into the fog which had produced it, profound and instantaneous and without any sound.

With that unhasteful celerity Mrs. Hait turned and set the scuttle down on the brick coping of the cellar entrance and she and old Het turned the corner of the house in time to see the now wraithlike mule at the moment when its course converged with that of a choleric-looking rooster and eight Rhode Island Red hens emerging from beneath the house. Then for an instant its progress assumed the appearance and trappings of an apotheosis: hell-born and hell-returning, in the act of dissolving completely into the fog, it seemed to rise vanishing into a sunless and dimensionless medium borne upon and enclosed by small winged goblins.

"Dey's mo in de front!" old Het cried.

"Them sons of bitches," Mrs. Hait said, again in that grim, prescient voice without rancor or heat. It was not the mules to which she referred; it was not even the owner of them. It was her whole town-dwelling history as dated from that April dawn ten years ago when what was left of Hait had been gathered from the mangled remains of five mules and several feet of new Manila rope on a blind curve of the railroad just out of town; the geographical hap of her very home; the very components of her bereavement—the mules, the defunct husband, and the owner of them. His name was Snopes; in the town they knew about him too—how he bought his stock at the Memphis market and brought it to Jefferson and sold it to farmers and widows and orphans black and white, for whatever he could contrive—down to a certain figure; and about how (usually in the dead season of winter) teams and even small droves of his stock would escape from the fenced pasture where he kept them and, tied one to another with sometimes quite new hemp rope (and which item Snopes included in the subsequent claim), would be annihilated by freight trains on the same blind curve which was to be the scene of Hait's exit from this world; once a town wag sent him through the mail a printed train schedule for the division. A squat, pasty man perennially tieless and with a strained, harried expression, at stated intervals he passed athwart the peaceful and somnolent life of the town in dust and uproar, his advent heralded by shouts and cries, his passing marked by a yellow cloud filled with tossing jug-shaped heads and clattering hooves and the same forlorn and earnest cries of the drovers; and last of all and well back out of the dust, Snopes himself moving at a harried and panting trot, since it was said in the town that he was deathly afraid of the very beasts in which he cleverly dealt.

The path which he must follow from the railroad station to his pasture crossed the edge of town near Hait's home; Hait and Mrs. Hait had not been in the house a week before they waked one morning to find it surrounded by galloping mules and the air filled with the shouts and cries of the drovers. But it was not until that April dawn some years later, when those who reached the scene first found what might be termed foreign matter among the mangled mules and the savage fragments of new rope, that the town suspected that Hait stood in any closer relationship to Snopes and the mules than that of helping at periodical intervals to drive them out of his front yard. After that they believed that they knew; in a three days' recess of interest, surprise, and curiosity they watched to see if Snopes would try to collect on Hait also.

But they learned only that the adjuster appeared and called upon Mrs. Hait and that a few days later she cashed a check for eight thousand five hundred dollars, since this was back in the old halcyon days when even the companies considered their southern branches and divisions the legitimate prey of all who dwelt beside them. She took the cash: she stood in her sweater coat and the hat which Hait had been wearing on the fatal morning a week ago and listened in cold, grim silence while the teller counted the money and the president and the cashier tried to explain to her the virtues of a bond, then of a savings account, then of a checking account, and departed with the money in a salt sack under her apron; after a time she painted her house: that serviceable and time-defying color which the railroad station was painted, as though out of sentiment or (as some said) gratitude.

The adjuster also summoned Snopes into conference, from which he emerged not only more harried-looking than ever, but with his face stamped with a bewildered dismay which it was to wear from then on, and that was the last time his pasture fence was ever to give inexplicably away at dead of night upon mules coupled in threes and fours by adequate rope even though not always new. And then it seemed as though the mules themselves knew this, as if, even while haltered at the Memphis block at his bid, they sensed it somehow as they sensed that he was afraid of them. Now, three or four times a year and as though by fiendish concord and as soon as they were freed of the box car, the entire uproar—the dust cloud filled with shouts earnest, harried, and dismayed, with plunging demoniac shapes—would become translated in a single burst of perverse and uncontrollable violence, without any intervening contact with time, space, or earth, across the peaceful and astonished town and into Mrs. Hait's yard, where, in a certain hapless despair which abrogated for the moment even physical fear, Snopes ducked and dodged among the thundering shapes about the house (for whose very impervious paint the town believed that he felt he had paid and whose inmate lived within it a life of idle and queenlike ease on money which he considered at least partly his own) while gradually that section and neighborhood gathered to look on from behind adjacent window curtains and porches screened and not, and from the sidewalks and even from halted wagons and cars in the street—housewives in the wrappers and boudoir caps of morning, children on the way to school, casual Negroes and casual whites in static and entertained repose.

They were all there when, followed by old Het and carrying the stub of a worn-out broom, Mrs. Hait ran around the next corner and onto the handkerchief-sized plot of earth which she called her front yard. It was small; any creature with a running stride of three feet could have spanned it in two paces, yet at the moment, due perhaps to the myopic and distortive quality of the fog, it seemed to be as incredibly full of mad life as a drop of water beneath the microscope. Yet again she did not falter. With the broom clutched in her hand and apparently with a kind of sublime faith in her own invulnerability, she rushed on after the haltered mule which was still in that arrested and wraithlike process of vanishing furiously into the fog, its wake indicated by the tossing and dispersing shapes of the nine chickens like so many jagged scraps of paper in the dying air blast of an automobile, and the madly dodging figure of a man. The man was Snopes; beaded too with moisture, his wild face gaped with hoarse shouting and the two heavy lines of shaven beard descending from the corners of it as though in alluvial retrospect of years of tobacco, he screamed at her: "Fore God, Miz Hait! I done everything I could!" She didn't even look at him.

"Ketch that big un with the bridle on," she said in her cold, panting voice. "Git that big un outen here."

"Sho!" Snopes shrieked. "Jest let um take their time. Jest don't git um excited now."

"Watch out!" old Het shouted. "He headin fer de back again!"

"Git the rope," Mrs. Hait said, running again. Snopes glared back at old Het.

"Fore God, where is ere rope?" he shouted.

"In de cellar fo God!" old Het shouted, also without pausing. "Go roun de udder way en head um." Again she and Mrs. Hait turned the corner in time to see again the still-vanishing mule with the halter once more in the act of floating lightly onward in its cloud of chickens with which, they being able to pass under the house and so on the chord of a circle while it had to go around on the arc, it had once more coincided. When they turned the next corner they were in the back yard again.

"Fo God!" old Het cried. "He fixin' to misuse de cow!" For they had gained on the mule now, since it had stopped. In fact, they came around the corner on a tableau. The cow now stood in the center of the yard. She and the mule faced one another a few feet apart. Motionless, with lowered heads and braced forelegs, they looked like two book ends from two distinct pairs of a general pattern which some one of amateurly bucolic leanings might have purchased, and which some child had salvaged, brought into idle juxtaposition and then forgotten; and, his head and shoulders projecting above the back-flung slant of the cellar entrance where the scuttle still sat, Snopes standing as though buried to the armpits for a Spanish-Indian-American suttee. Only again it did not take this long. It was less than tableau; it was one of those things which later even memory cannot quite affirm. Now and in turn, man and cow and mule vanished beyond the next corner, Snopes now in the lead, carrying the rope, the cow next with her tail rigid and raked slightly like the stern staff of a boat. Mrs. Hait and old Het ran on, passing the open cellar gaping upon its accumulation of human necessities and widowed womanyears—boxes for kindling wood, old papers and magazines, the broken and outworn furniture and utensils which no woman ever throws away; a pile of coal and another of pitch pine for priming fires—and ran on and turned the next corner to see man and cow and mule all vanishing now in the wild cloud of ubiquitous chickens which had once more crossed beneath the house and emerged. They ran on, Mrs. Hait in grim and unflagging silence, old Het with the eager and happy amazement of a child. But when they gained the front again they saw only Snopes. He lay flat on his stomach, his head and shoulders upreared by his outstretched arms, his coat tail swept forward by its own arrested momentum about his head so that from beneath it his slack-jawed face mused in wild repose like that of a burlesqued nun.

"Whar'd dey go?" old Het shouted at him. He didn't answer.

"Dey tightenin' on de curves!" she cried. "Dey already in de back again!" That's where they were. The cow made a feint at running into her shed, but deciding perhaps that her speed was too great, she whirled in a final desperation of despair-like valor. But they did not see this, nor see the mule, swerving to pass her, crash and blunder for an instant at the open cellar door before going on. When they arrived, the mule was gone. The scuttle was gone too, but they did not notice it; they saw only the cow standing in the center of the yard as before, panting, rigid, with braced forelegs and lowered head facing nothing, as if the child had returned and removed one of the book ends for some newer purpose or game. They ran on. Mrs. Hait ran heavily now, her mouth too open, her face putty-colored and one hand pressed to her side. So slow was their progress that the mule in its third circuit of the house overtook them from behind and soared past with undiminished speed, with brief demon thunder and a keen ammonia-sweet reek of sweat sudden and sharp as a jeering cry, and was gone. Yet they ran doggedly on around the next corner in time to see it succeed at last in vanishing into the fog; they heard its hoofs, brief, staccato, and derisive, on the paved street, dying away.

"Well!" old Het said, stopping. She panted, happily. "Gentlemen, hush! Ain't we had—" Then she became stone still; slowly her head turned, high-nosed, her nostrils pulsing; perhaps for the instant she saw the open cellar door as they had last passed it, with no scuttle beside it. "Fo God I smells smoke!" she said. "Chile, run, git yo money."

That was still early, not yet ten o'clock. By noon the house had burned to the ground. There was a farmers' supply store where Snopes could be usually found; more than one had made a point of finding him there by that time. They told him about how when the fire engine and the crowd reached the scene, Mrs. Hait, followed by old Het carrying her shopping-bag in one hand and a framed portrait of Mr. Hait in the other, emerged with an umbrella and wearing a new, dun-colored, mail-order coat, in one pocket of which lay a fruit jar filled with smoothly rolled banknotes and in the other a heavy, nickel-plated pistol, and crossed the street to the house opposite, where with old Het beside her in another rocker, she had been sitting ever since on the veranda, grim, inscrutable, the two of them rocking steadily, while hoarse and tireless men hurled her dishes and furniture and bedding up and down the street.

"What are you telling me for?" Snopes said. "Hit warn't me that set that ere scuttle of live fire where the first thing that passed would knock hit into the cellar."

"It was you that opened the cellar door, though."

"Sho. And for what? To git that rope, her own rope, where she told me to get it."

"To catch your mule with, that was trespassing on her property. You can't get out of it this time, I. O. There ain't a jury in the county that won't find for her."

"Yes. I reckon not. And just because she is a woman. That's why. Because she is a durn woman. All right. Let her go to her durn jury with hit. I can talk too; I reckon hit's a few things I could tell a jury myself about—" He ceased. They were watching him.

"What? Tell a jury about what?"

"Nothing. Because hit ain't going to no jury. A jury between her and me? Me and Mannie Hait? You boys don't know her if you think she's going to make trouble over a pure acci-dent couldn't nobody help. Why, there ain't a fairer, finer woman in the county than Miz Mannie Hait. I just wisht I had a opportunity to tell her so." The opportunity came at once. Old Het was behind her, carrying the shopping-bag. Mrs. Hait looked once, quietly, about at the faces, making no response to the murmur of curious salutation, then not again. She didn't look at Snopes long either, nor talk to him long.

"I come to buy that mule," she said.

"What mule?" They looked at one another. "You'd like to own that mule?" She looked at him. "Hit'll cost you a hundred and fifty, Miz Mannie."

"You mean dollars?"

"I don't mean dimes nor nickels neither, Miz Mannie."

"Dollars," she said. "That's more than mules was in Hait's time."

"Lots of things is different since Hait's time. Including you and me."

"I reckon so," she said. Then she went away. She turned without a word, old Het following.

"Maybe one of them others you looked at this morning would suit you," Snopes said. She didn't answer. Then they were gone.

"I don't know as I would have said that last to her," one said.

"What for?" Snopes said. "If she was aiming to law something outen me about that fire, you reckon she would have come and offered to pay me money for hit?" That was about one o'clock. About four o'clock he was shouldering his way through a throng of Negroes before a cheap grocery store when one called his name. It was old Het, the now bulging shopping-bag on her arm, eating bananas from a paper sack.

"Fo God I wuz jest dis minute huntin fer you," she said. She handed the banana to a woman beside her and delved and fumbled in the shopping-bag and extended a greenback. "Miz Mannie gimme dis to give you; I wuz just on de way to de sto whar you stay at. Here." He took the bill.

"What's this? From Miz Hait?"

"Fer de mule." The bill was for ten dollars. "You don't need to gimme no receipt. I kin be de witness I give hit to you."

"Ten dollars? For that mule? I told her a hundred and fifty dollars."

"You'll have to fix dat up wid her yo'self. She jest gimme dis to give ter you when she sot out to fetch de mule."

"Set out to fetch—She went out there herself and taken my mule outen my pasture?"

"Lawd, chile," old Het said, "Miz Mannie ain't skeered of no mule. Ain't you done foun dat out?"

And then it became late, what with the yet short winter days; when she came in sight of the two gaunt chimneys against the sunset, evening was already finding itself. But she could smell the ham cooking before she came in sight of the cow shed even, though she could not see it until she came around in front where the fire burned beneath an iron skillet set on bricks and where nearby Mrs. Hait was milking the cow. "Well," old Het said, "you is settled down, ain't you?" She looked into the shed, neated and raked and swept even, and floored now with fresh hay. A clean new lantern burned on a box, beside it a pallet bed was spread neatly on the straw and turned neatly back for the night. "Why, you is fixed up," she said with pleased astonishment. Within the door was a kitchen chair. She drew it out and sat down beside the skillet and laid the bulging shopping-bag beside her.

"I'll tend dis meat whilst you milks. I'd offer to strip dat cow fer you ef I wuzn't so wo out wid all dis excitement we been had." She looked around her. "I don't believe I sees yo new mule, dough." Mrs. Hait grunted, her head against the cow's flank. After a moment she said,

"Did you give him that money?"

"I give um ter him. He ack surprise at first, lak maybe he think you didn't aim to trade dat quick. I tole him to settle de details wid you later. He taken de money, dough. So I reckin dat's offen his mine en yo'n bofe." Again Mrs. Hait grunted. Old Het turned the ham in the skillet. Beside it the coffee pot bubbled and steamed. "Cawfee smell good too," she said. "I ain't had no appetite in years now. A bird couldn't live on de vittles I eats. But jest lemme git a whiff er cawfee en seem lak hit always whets me a little. Now, ef you jest had nudder little piece o dis ham, now—Fo God, you got company aready."

But Mrs. Hait did not even look up until she had finished. Then she turned without rising from the box on which she sat.

"I reckon you and me better have a little talk," Snopes said. "I reckon I got something that belongs to you and I hear you got something that belongs to me." He looked about, quickly, ceaselessly, while old Het watched him. He turned to her. "You go away, aunty. I don't reckon you want to set here and listen to us."

"Lawd, honey," old Het said. "Don't you mind me. I done already had so much troubles myself dat I kin set en listen to udder folks' widout hit worryin me a-tall. You gawn talk whut you came ter talk; I jest set here en tend de ham." Snopes looked at Mrs. Hait.

"Ain't you going to make her go away?" he said.

"What for?" Mrs. Hait said. "I reckon she ain't the first critter that ever come on this yard when hit wanted and went or stayed when hit liked." Snopes made a gesture, brief, fretted, restrained.

"Well," he said. "All right. So you taken the mule."

"I paid you for it. She give you the money."

"Ten dollars. For a hundred-and-fifty-dollar mule. Ten dollars."

"I don't know anything about hundred-and-fifty-dollar mules. All I know is what the railroad paid." Now Snopes looked at her for a full moment. "What do you mean?"

"Them sixty dollars a head the railroad used to pay you for mules back when you and Hait——"

"Hush," Snopes said; he looked about again, quick, ceaseless. "All right. Even call it sixty dollars. But you just sent me ten."

"Yes. I sent you the difference." He looked at her, perfectly still. "Between that mule and what you owed Hait."

"What I owed——"

"For getting them five mules onto the tr——"

"Hush!" he cried. "Hush!" Her voice went on, cold, grim, level.

"For helping you. You paid him fifty dollars each time, and the railroad paid you sixty dollars a head for the mules. Ain't that right?" He watched her. "The last time you never paid him. So I taken that mule instead. And I sent you the ten dollars difference."

"Yes," he said in a tone of quiet, swift, profound bemusement; then he cried: "But look! Here's where I got you. Hit was our agreement that I wouldn't never owe him nothing until after the mules was——"

"I reckon you better hush yourself," Mrs. Hait said.

"—until hit was over. And this time, when over had come, I never owed nobody no money because the man hit would have been owed to wasn't nobody," he cried triumphantly. "You see?" Sitting on the box, motionless, downlooking, Mrs. Hait seemed to muse. "So you just take your ten dollars back and tell me where my mule is and we'll just go back good friends to where we started at. Fore God, I'm as sorry as ere a living man about that fire——"

"Fo God!" old Het said, "hit was a blaze, wuzn't it?"

"—but likely with all that ere railroad money you still got, you just been wanting a chance to build new, all along. So here. Take hit." He put the money into her hand. "Where's my mule?" But Mrs. Hait didn't move at once.

"You want to give it back to me?" she said.

"Sho. We been friends all the time; now we'll just go back to where we left off being. I don't hold no hard feelings and don't you hold none. Where you got the mule hid?"

"Up at the end of that ravine ditch behind Spilmer's," she said.

"Sho. I know. A good, sheltered place, since you ain't got nere barn. Only if you'd a just left hit in the pasture, hit would a saved us both trouble. But hit ain't no hard feelings though. And so I'll bid you goodnight. You're all fixed up, I see. I reckon you could save some more money by not building no house a-tall."

"I reckon I could," Mrs. Hait said. But he was gone.

"Whut did you leave de mule dar fer?" old Het said.

"I reckon that's far enough," Mrs. Hait said.

"Fer enough?" But Mrs. Hait came and looked into the skillet, and old Het said, "Wuz hit me er you dat mentioned something erbout er nudder piece o dis ham?" So they were both eating when in the not-quite-yet accomplished twilight Snopes returned. He came up quietly and stood, holding his hands to the blaze as if he were quite cold. He did not look at any one now.

"I reckon I'll take that ere ten dollars," he said.

"What ten dollars?" Mrs. Hait said. He seemed to muse upon the fire. Mrs. Hait and old Het chewed quietly, old Het alone watching him.

"You ain't going to give hit back to me?" he said.

"You was the one that said to let's go back to where we started," Mrs. Hait said.

"Fo God you wuz, en dat's de fack," old Het said. Snopes mused upon the fire; he spoke in a tone of musing and amazed despair:

"I go to the worry and the risk and the agoment for years and years and I get sixty dollars. And you, one time, without no trouble and no risk, without even knowing you are going to git it, git eighty-five hundred dollars. I never begrudged hit to you; can't nere a man say I did, even if hit did seem a little strange that you should git it all when he wasn't working for you and you never even knowed where he was at and what doing; that all you done to git it was to be married to him. And now, after all these ten years of not begrudging you hit, you taken the best mule I had and you ain't even going to pay me ten dollars for hit. Hit ain't right. Hit ain't justice."

"You got de mule back, en you ain't satisfried yit," old Het said. "Whut does you want?" Now Snopes looked at Mrs. Hait.

"For the last time I ask hit," he said. "Will you or won't you give hit back?"

"Give what back?" Mrs. Hait said. Snopes turned. He stumbled over something—it was old Het's shopping-bag—and recovered and went on. They could see him in silhouette, as though framed by the two blackened chimneys against the dying west; they saw him fling up both clenched hands in a gesture almost Gallic, of resignation and impotent despair. Then he was gone. Old Het was watching Mrs. Hait.

"Honey," she said. "Whut did you do wid de mule?" Mrs. Hait leaned forward to the fire. On her plate lay a stale biscuit. She lifted the skillet and poured over the biscuit the grease in which the ham had cooked.

"I shot it," she said.

"You which?" old Het said. Mrs. Hait began to eat the biscuit. "Well," old Het said, happily, "de mule burnt de house en you shot de mule. Dat's whut I calls justice." It was getting dark fast now, and before her was still the three-mile walk to the poorhouse. But the dark would last a long time in January, and the poorhouse too would not move at once. She sighed with weary and happy relaxation. "Gentlemen, hush! Ain't we had a day!"

QUESTIONS

1. This story has one character in common with "Spotted Horses." Is he a logical projection of the character as seen in that story? How is he like and unlike his cousin Flem? How does he make his living?
2. Characterize Mrs. Hait. Explain in detail her final transactions with I. O.
3. Characterize Old Het. What color is she?
4. From what narrative point of view is this story told? Compare and contrast its narrative style with that of "Spotted Horses." Give specific examples.
5. What are the chief sources of comedy in this story? Is there any difference in the flavor of its humor?
6. Who is the protagonist? Who is the antagonist? Which is successful in their conflict?
7. Like "Spotted Horses," this is a comic story involving an animal chase. Which story is more powerful, broader in scope, deeper in insight and effect? Justify your answer.

Stories for
Further Reading

Nathaniel Hawthorne

YOUNG GOODMAN BROWN

Young Goodman Brown came forth at sunset, into the street of Salem village, but put his head back, after crossing the threshold, to exchange a parting kiss with his young wife. And Faith, as the wife was aptly named, thrust her own pretty head into the street, letting the wind play with the pink ribbons of her cap, while she called to Goodman Brown.

"Dearest heart," whispered she, softly and rather sadly, when her lips were close to his ear, "prithee, put off your journey until sunrise, and sleep in your own bed to-night. A lone woman is troubled with such dreams and such thoughts, that she's afeard of herself, sometimes. Pray, tarry with me this night, dear husband, of all nights in the year!"

"My love and my Faith," replied young Goodman Brown, "of all nights in the year, this one must I tarry away from thee. My journey, as thou callest it, forth and back again must needs be done 'twixt now and sunrise. What, my sweet, pretty wife, dost thou doubt me already, and we but three months married!"

"Then God bless you!" said Faith with the pink ribbons, "and may you find all well, when you come back."

"Amen!" cried Goodman Brown. "Say thy prayers, dear Faith, and go to bed at dusk, and no harm will come to thee."

So they parted; and the young man pursued his way, until, being about to turn the corner by the meeting-house, he looked back and saw the head of Faith still peeping after him, with a melancholy air, in spite of her pink ribbons.

"Poor little Faith!" thought he, for his heart smote him. "What a wretch am I, to leave her on such an errand! She talks of dreams, too. Methought, as she spoke, there was trouble in her face, as if a dream had warned her what work is to be done to-night. But no, no! 't would kill her to think it. Well; she's a blessed angel on earth and after this one night, I'll cling to her skirts and follow her to Heaven."

With this excellent resolve for the future, Goodman Brown felt himself justified in making more haste on his present evil purpose. He had taken a

---

YOUNG GOODMAN BROWN First published in 1835. "Goodman" was a title of respect, but at a social rank lower than "gentleman." "Goody" (or "Goodwife") was the feminine equivalent. Deacon Gookin in the story is a historical personage (1612–1687), as are also Goody Cloyse, Goody Cory, and Martha Carrier, all three executed at the Salem witchcraft trials in 1692. Nathaniel Hawthorne (1804–1864) was born and grew up in Salem, Massachusetts, where Hawthornes had lived since the seventeenth century. One ancestor had been a judge at the Salem witch trials; another had been a leader in the persecution of Quakers. "Young Goodman Brown" is one of several stories in which Hawthorne explored the Puritan past of New England.

dreary road, darkened by all the gloomiest trees of the forest, which barely stood aside to let the narrow path creep through, and closed immediately behind. It was all as lonely as could be; and there is this peculiarity in such a solitude, that the traveler knows not who may be concealed by the innumerable trunks and the thick boughs overhead; so that, with lonely footsteps, he may be passing through an unseen multitude.

"There may be a devilish Indian behind every tree," said Goodman Brown to himself; and he glanced fearfully behind him, as he added, "What if the devil himself should be at my very elbow!"

His head being turned back, he passed a crook of the road, and looking forward again, beheld the figure of a man, in grave and decent attire, seated at the foot of an old tree. He rose at Goodman Brown's approach, and walked onward, side by side with him.

"You are late, Goodman Brown," said he. "The clock of the Old South was striking, as I came through Boston; and that is full fifteen minutes agone."°

"Faith kept me back awhile," replied the young man, with a tremor in his voice, caused by the sudden appearance of his companion, though not wholly unexpected.

It was now deep dusk in the forest, and deepest in that part of it where these two were journeying. As nearly as could be discerned, the second traveler was about fifty years old, apparently in the same rank of life as Goodman Brown, and bearing a considerable resemblance to him, though perhaps more in expression than features. Still, they might have been taken for father and son. And yet, though the elder person was as simply clad as the younger, and as simple in manner too, he had an indescribable air of one who knew the world, and would not have felt abashed at the governor's dinner-table, or in King William's court,° were it possible that his affairs should call him thither. But the only thing about him that could be fixed upon as remarkable, was his staff, which bore the likeness of a great black snake, so curiously wrought that it might almost be seen to twist and wriggle itself like a living serpent. This, of course, must have been an ocular deception, assisted by the uncertain light.

"Come, Goodman Brown!" cried his fellow-traveler, "this is a dull pace for the beginning of a journey. Take my staff, if you are so soon weary."

"Friend," said the other, exchanging his slow pace for a full stop, "having kept covenant by meeting thee here, it is my purpose now to return whence I came. I have scruples, touching the matter thou wot'st of."

"Sayest thou so?" replied he of the serpent, smiling apart. "Let us walk on nevertheless, reasoning as we go, and if I convince thee not, thou shalt turn back. We are but a little way in the forest yet."

full fifteen minutes agone: The distance from the center of Boston to the forest was over 20 miles.
King William's court: William III, King of England, 1689–1702

"Too far, too far!" exclaimed the goodman, unconsciously resuming his walk. "My father never went into the woods on such an errand, nor his father before him. We have been a race of honest men and good Christians since the days of the martyrs. And shall I be the first of the name of Brown that ever took this path and kept—"

"Such company, thou wouldst say," observed the elder person, interrupting his pause. "Well said, Goodman Brown! I have been as well acquainted with your family as with ever a one among the Puritans; and that's no trifle to say. I helped your grandfather, the constable, when he lashed the Quaker woman so smartly through the streets of Salem. And it was I that brought your father a pitch-pine knot, kindled at my own hearth, to set fire to an Indian village, in King Philip's war.° They were my good friends, both; and many a pleasant walk have we had along this path, and returned merrily after midnight. I would fain be friends with you, for their sake."

"If it be as thou sayest," replied Goodman Brown, "I marvel they never spoke of these matters. Or, verily, I marvel not, seeing that the least rumor of the sort would have driven them from New England. We are a people of prayer, and good works to boot, and abide no such wickedness."

"Wickedness or not," said the traveler with twisted staff, "I have a general acquaintance here in New England. The deacons of many a church have drunk the communion wine with me; the selectmen of divers towns make me their chairman; and a majority of the Great and General Court° are firm supporters of my interest. The governor and I, too—but these are state secrets."

"Can this be so!" cried Goodman Brown, with a stare of amazement at his undisturbed companion. "Howbeit, I have nothing to do with the governor and council; they have their own ways, and are no rule for a simple husbandman like me. But, were I to go on with thee, how should I meet the eye of that good old man, our minister, at Salem village? Oh, his voice would make me tremble, both Sabbath-day and lecture-day!"

Thus far, the elder traveler had listened with due gravity, but now burst into a fit of irrepressible mirth, shaking himself so violently, that his snakelike staff actually seemed to wriggle in sympathy.

"Ha! ha! ha!" shouted he, again and again; then composing himself, "Well, go on, Goodman Brown, go on; but, prithee, don't kill me with laughing!"

"Well, then, to end the matter at once," said Goodman Brown, considerably nettled, "there is my wife, Faith. It would break her dear little heart; and I'd rather break my own!"

"Nay, if that be the case," answered the other, "e'en go thy ways, Goodman Brown. I would not, for twenty old women like the one hobbling before us, that Faith should come to any harm."

King Philip's War: a war between the colonists and Indians, 1675-76
Great and General Court: the legislature of the Massachusetts Bay Colony

As he spoke, he pointed his staff at a female figure on the path, in whom Goodman Brown recognized a very pious and exemplary dame, who had taught him his catechism in youth, and was still his moral and spiritual adviser, jointly with the minister and Deacon Gookin.

"A marvel, truly, that Goody Cloyse should be so far in the wilderness, at nightfall!" said he. "But, with your leave, friend, I shall take a cut through the woods, until we have left this Christian woman behind. Being a stranger to you, she might ask whom I was consorting with, and whither I was going."

"Be it so," said his fellow-traveler. "Betake you to the woods, and let me keep the path."

Accordingly, the young man turned aside, but took care to watch his companion, who advanced softly along the road, until he had come within a staff's length of the old dame. She, meanwhile, was making the best of her way, with singular speed for so aged a woman, and mumbling some indistinct words, a prayer, doubtless, as she went. The traveler put forth his staff, and touched her withered neck with what seemed the serpent's tail.

"The devil!" screamed the pious old lady.

"Then Goody Cloyse knows her old friend?" observed the traveler, confronting her, and leaning on his writhing stick.

"Ah, forsooth, and is it your worship, indeed?" cried the good dame. "Yea, truly is it, and in the very image of my old gossip, Goodman Brown, the grandfather of the silly fellow that now is. But, would your worship believe it? my broomstick hath strangely disappeared, stolen, as I suspect, by that unhanged witch, Goody Cory, and that, too, when I was all anointed with the juice of smallage and cinque-foil and wolf's-bane—"

"Mingled with fine wheat and the fat of a new-born babe," said the shape of old Goodman Brown.

"Ah, your worship knows the recipe," cried the old lady, cackling aloud. "So, as I was saying, being all ready for the meeting, and no horse to ride on, I made up my mind to foot it; for they tell me there is a nice young man to be taken into communion to-night. But now your good worship will lend me your arm, and we shall be there in a twinkling."

"That can hardly be," answered her friend. "I may not spare you my arm, Goody Cloyse, but here is my staff, if you will."

So saying, he threw it down at her feet, where, perhaps, it assumed life, being one of the rods which its owner had formerly lent to the Egyptian Magi. Of this fact, however, Goodman Brown could not take cognizance. He had cast up his eyes in astonishment, and looking down again, beheld neither Goody Cloyse nor the serpentine staff, but his fellow-traveler alone, who waited for him as calmly as if nothing had happened.

"That old woman taught me my catechism!" said the young man; and there was a world of meaning in this simple comment.

They continued to walk onward, while the elder traveler exhorted his companion to make good speed and persevere in the path, discoursing so aptly that his arguments seemed rather to spring up in the bosom of his auditor, than to be suggested by himself. As they went he plucked a branch of maple, to serve for a walking-stick, and began to strip it of the twigs and little boughs, which were wet with evening dew. The moment his fingers touched them, they became strangely withered and dried up, as with a week's sunshine. Thus the pair proceeded, at a good free pace, until suddenly, in a gloomy hollow of the road, Goodman Brown sat himself down on the stump of a tree and refused to go any farther.

"Friend," said he, stubbornly, "my mind is made up. Not another step will I budge on this errand. What if a wretched old woman do choose to go to the devil when I thought she was going to Heaven! Is that any reason why I should quit my dear Faith and go after her?"

"You will think better of this by and by," said his acquaintance, composedly. "Sit here and rest yourself awhile; and when you feel like moving again, there is my staff to help you along."

Without more words, he threw his companion the maple stick, and was as speedily out of sight as if he had vanished into the deepening gloom. The young man sat a few moments by the roadside, applauding himself greatly, and thinking with how clear a conscience he should meet the minister, in his morning walk, nor shrink from the eye of good old Deacon Gookin. And what calm sleep would be his, that very night, which was to have been spent so wickedly, but purely and sweetly now, in the arms of Faith! Amidst these pleasant and praiseworthy meditations, Goodman Brown heard the tramp of horses along the road, and deemed it advisable to conceal himself within the verge of the forest, conscious of the guilty purpose that had brought him thither, though now so happily turned from it.

On came the hoof-tramps and the voices of the riders, two grave old voices, conversing soberly as they drew near. These mingled sounds appeared to pass along the road, within a few yards of the young man's hiding-place; but owing, doubtless, to the depth of the gloom at that particular spot, neither the travelers nor their steeds were visible. Though their figures brushed the small boughs by the wayside, it could not be seen that they intercepted, even for a moment, the faint gleam from the strip of bright sky, athwart which they must have passed. Goodman Brown alternately crouched and stood on tiptoe, pulling aside the branches and thrusting forth his head as far as he durst, without discerning so much as a shadow. It vexed him the more, because he could have sworn, were such a thing possible, that he recognized the voices of the minister and Deacon Gookin, jogging along quietly, as they were wont to do, when bound to some ordination or ecclesiastical council. While yet within hearing, one of the riders stopped to pluck a switch.

"Of the two, reverend Sir," said the voice like the deacon's, "I had rather miss an ordination dinner than tonight's meeting. They tell me that some of our community are to be here from Falmouth and beyond, and others from Connecticut and Rhode Island, besides several of the Indian powwows, who, after their fashion, know almost as much deviltry as the best of us. Moreover, there is a goodly young woman to be taken into communion."

"Mighty well, Deacon Gookin!" replied the solemn old tones of the minister. "Spur up, or we shall be late. Nothing can be done, you know, until I get on the ground."

The hoofs clattered again, and the voices, talking so strangely in the empty air, passed on through the forest, where no church had ever been gathered nor solitary Christian prayed. Whither, then, could these holy men be journeying, so deep into the heathen wilderness? Young Goodman Brown caught hold of a tree for support, being ready to sink down on the ground, faint and over-burthened with the heavy sickness of his heart. He looked up to the sky, doubting whether there really was a Heaven above him. Yet there was the blue arch, and the stars brightening in it.

"With Heaven above, and Faith below, I will yet stand firm against the devil!" cried Goodman Brown.

While he still gazed upward into the deep arch of the firmament and had lifted his hands to pray, a cloud, though no wind was stirring, hurried across the zenith and hid the brightening stars. The blue sky was still visible, except directly overhead, where this black mass of cloud was sweeping swiftly northward. Aloft in the air, as if from the depths of the cloud, came a confused and doubtful sound of voices. Once the listener fancied that he could distinguish the accents of town's-people of his own, men and women, both pious and ungodly, many of whom he had met at the communion-table, and had seen others rioting at the tavern. The next moment, so indistinct were the sounds, he doubted whether he had heard aught but the murmur of the old forest, whispering without a wind. Then came a stronger swell of those familiar tones, heard daily in the sunshine, at Salem village, but never, until now, from a cloud at night. There was one voice, of a young woman, uttering lamentations, yet with an uncertain sorrow, and entreating for some favor, which, perhaps, it would grieve her to obtain. And all the unseen multitude, both saints and sinners, seemed to encourage her onward.

"Faith!" shouted Goodman Brown, in a voice of agony and desperation; and the echoes of the forest mocked him, crying—"Faith! Faith!" as if bewildered wretches were seeking her all through the wilderness.

The cry of grief, rage, and terror was yet piercing the night, when the unhappy husband held his breath for a response. There was a scream, drowned immediately in a louder murmur of voices fading into far-off laughter, as the dark cloud swept away, leaving the clear and silent sky above Goodman Brown. But something fluttered lightly down through the air and caught on the branch of a tree. The young man seized it and beheld a pink ribbon.

"My Faith is gone!" cried he, after one stupefied moment. "There is no good on earth, and sin is but a name. Come, devil! for to thee is this world given."

And maddened with despair, so that he laughed loud and long, did Goodman Brown grasp his staff and set forth again, at such a rate that he seemed to fly along the forest path rather than to walk or run. The road grew wilder and drearier and more faintly traced, and vanished at length, leaving him in the heart of the dark wilderness, still rushing onward with the instinct that guides mortal man to evil. The whole forest was peopled with frightful sounds—the creaking of the trees, the howling of wild beasts, and the yell of Indians; while sometimes the wind tolled like a distant church bell, and sometimes gave a broad roar around the traveler, as if all Nature were laughing him to scorn. But he was himself the chief horror of the scene, and shrank not from its other horrors.

"Ha! ha! ha!" roared Goodman Brown when the wind laughed at him. "Let us hear which will laugh loudest! Think not to frighten me with your deviltry! come witch, come wizard, come Indian powwow, come devil himself! and here comes Goodman Brown. You may as well fear him as he fear you!"

In truth, all through the haunted forest there could be nothing more frightful than the figure of Goodman Brown. On he flew among the black pines, brandishing his staff with frenzied gestures, now giving vent to an inspiration of horrid blasphemy, and now shouting forth such laughter as set all the echoes of the forest laughing like demons around him. The fiend in his own shape is less hideous than when he rages in the breast of man. Thus sped the demoniac on his course, until, quivering among the trees, he saw a red light before him, as when the felled trunks and branches of a clearing have been set on fire, and throw up their lurid blaze against the sky, at the hour of midnight. He paused, in a lull of the tempest that had driven him onward, and heard the swell of what seemed a hymn, rolling solemnly from a distance with the weight of many voices. He knew the tune. It was a familiar one in the choir of the village meeting-house. The verse died heavily away, and was lengthened by a chorus, not of human voices, but of all the sounds of the benighted wilderness pealing in awful harmony together. Goodman Brown cried out, and his cry was lost to his own ear by its unison with the cry of the desert.

In the interval of silence he stole forward until the light glared full upon his eyes. At one extremity of an open space, hemmed in by the dark wall of the forest, arose a rock, bearing some rude, natural resemblance either to an altar or a pulpit, and surrounded by four blazing pines, their tops aflame, their stems untouched, like candles at an evening meeting. The mass of foliage that had overgrown the summit of the rock was all on fire, blazing high into the night and fitfully illuminating the whole field. Each pendent twig and leafy festoon was in a blaze. As the red light arose and fell, a numerous congregation alternately shone forth, then disappeared in shadow, and again grew, as it were, out of the darkness, peopling the heart of the solitary woods at once.

"A grave and dark-clad company!" quoth Goodman Brown.

In truth, they were such. Among them, quivering to and fro, between gloom and splendor, appeared faces that would be seen next day at the council-board of the province, and others which, Sabbath after Sabbath, looked devoutly heavenward, and benignantly over the crowded pews, from the holiest pulpits in the land. Some affirm that the lady of the governor was there. At least, there were high dames well known to her, and wives of honored husbands, and widows a great multitude, and ancient maidens, all of excellent repute, and fair young girls who trembled lest their mothers should espy them. Either the sudden gleams of light flashing over the obscure field bedazzled Goodman Brown, or he recognized a score of the church members of Salem village famous for their especial sanctity. Good old Deacon Gookin had arrived, and waited at the skirts of that venerable saint, his reverend pastor. But, irreverently consorting with these grave, reputable, and pious people, these elders of the church, these chaste dames and dewy virgins, there were men of dissolute lives and women of spotted fame, wretches given over to all mean and filthy vice, and suspected even of horrid crimes. It was strange to see that the good shrank not from the wicked, nor were the sinners abashed by the saints. Scattered also among their pale-faced enemies were the Indian priests, or powwows, who had often scared their native forest with more hideous incantations than any known to English witchcraft.

"But where is Faith?" thought Goodman Brown; and, as hope came into his heart, he trembled.

Another verse of the hymn arose, a slow and mournful strain, such as the pious love, but joined to words which expressed all that our nature can conceive of sin, and darkly hinted at far more. Unfathomable to mere mortals is the lore of fiends. Verse after verse was sung, and still the chorus of the desert swelled between, like the deepest tone of a mighty organ. And, with the final peal of that dreadful anthem, there came a sound, as if the roaring wind, the rushing streams, the howling beasts, and every other voice of the unconverted wilderness were mingling and according with the voice of guilty man in homage to the prince of all. The four blazing pines threw up a loftier flame, and obscurely discovered shapes and visages of horror on the smoke-wreaths, above the impious assembly. At the same moment the fire on the rock shot redly forth and formed a glowing arch above its base, where now appeared a figure. With reverence be it spoken, the apparition bore no slight similitude, both in garb and manner, to some grave divine of the New England churches.

"Bring forth the converts!" cried a voice, that echoed through the field and rolled into the forest.

At the word, Goodman Brown stepped forth from the shadow of the trees and approached the congregation, with whom he felt a loathful brotherhood by the sympathy of all that was wicked in his heart. He could have well-nigh sworn that the shape of his own dead father beckoned him to advance, looking downward from a smoke-wreath, while a woman, with dim features of despair, threw out her hand to warn him back. Was it his mother? But he had no power to retreat one step, nor to resist, even in thought, when the minister and good old Deacon Gookin seized his arms and led him to the blazing rock. Thither came also the slender form of a veiled female, led between Goody Cloyse, that pious teacher of the catechism, and Martha Carrier, who had received the devil's promise to be queen of hell. A rampant hag was she! And there stood the proselytes beneath the canopy of fire.

"Welcome, my children," said the dark figure, "to the communion of your race! Ye have found, thus young, your nature and your destiny. My children, look behind you!"

They turned; and flashing forth, as it were, in a sheet of flame, the fiend-worshippers were seen; the smile of welcome gleamed darkly on every visage.

"There," resumed the sable form, "are all whom ye have reverenced from youth. Ye deemed them holier than yourselves, and shrank from your own sin, contrasting it with their lives of righteousness and prayerful aspirations heavenward. Yet here are they all in my worshipping assembly! This night it shall be granted you to know their secret deeds: how hoary-bearded elders of the church have whispered wanton words to the young maids of their households; how many a woman, eager for widow's weeds, has given her husband a drink at bedtime, and let him sleep his last sleep in her bosom; how beardless youths have made haste to inherit their father's wealth; and how fair damsels—blush not, sweet ones!—have dug little graves in the garden, and bidden me, the sole guest, to an infant's funeral. By the sympathy of your human hearts for sin, ye shall scent out all the places—whether in church, bedchamber, street, field, or forest—where crime has been committed, and shall exult to behold the whole earth one stain of guilt, one mighty blood-spot. Far more than this! It shall be yours to penetrate, in every bosom, the deep mystery of sin, the fountain of all wicked arts, and which inexhaustibly supplies more evil impulses than human power—than my power, at its utmost!—can make manifest in deeds. And now, my children, look upon each other."

They did so; and, by the blaze of the hell-kindled torches, the wretched man beheld his Faith, and the wife her husband, trembling before that unhallowed altar.

"Lo! there ye stand, my children," said the figure, in a deep and solemn tone, almost sad with its despairing awfulness, as if his once angelic nature could yet mourn for our miserable race. "Depending upon one another's hearts, ye had still hoped that virtue were not all a dream! Now are ye undeceived!—Evil is the nature of mankind. Evil must be your only happiness. Welcome, again, my children, to the communion of your race!"

"Welcome!" repeated the fiend-worshippers, in one cry of despair and triumph.

And there they stood, the only pair, as it seemed, who were yet hesitating on the verge of wickedness in this dark world. A basin was hollowed, naturally, in the rock. Did it contain water, reddened by the lurid light? or was it blood? or, perchance, a liquid flame? Herein did the Shape of Evil dip his hand and prepare to lay the mark of baptism upon their foreheads, that they might be partakers of the mystery of sin, more conscious of the secret guilt of others, both in deed and thought, than they could now be of their own. The husband cast one look at his pale wife, and Faith at him. What polluted wretches would the next glance show them to each other, shuddering alike at what they disclosed and what they saw!

"Faith! Faith!" cried the husband. "Look up to Heaven, and resist the Wicked One!"

Whether Faith obeyed he knew not. Hardly had he spoken when he found himself amid calm night and solitude, listening to a roar of the wind which died heavily away through the forest. He staggered against the rock, and felt it chill and damp, while a hanging twig, that had been all on fire, besprinkled his cheek with the coldest dew.

The next morning, young Goodman Brown came slowly into the street of Salem village staring around him like a bewildered man. The good old minister was taking a walk along the graveyard to get an appetite for breakfast and meditate his sermon, and bestowed a blessing, as he passed, on Goodman Brown. He shrank from the venerable saint as if to avoid an anathema. Old Deacon Gookin was at domestic worship, and the holy words of his prayer were heard through the open window. "What God doth the wizard pray to?" quoth Goodman Brown. Goody Cloyse, that excellent old Christian, stood in the early sunshine at her own lattice, catechizing a little girl who had brought her a pint of morning's milk. Goodman Brown snatched away the child, as from the grasp of the fiend himself. Turning the corner by the meeting-house, he spied the head of Faith, with the pink ribbons, gazing anxiously forth, and bursting into such joy at sight of him that she skipt along the street and almost kissed her husband before the whole village. But Goodman Brown looked sternly and sadly into her face, and passed on without a greeting.

Had Goodman Brown fallen asleep in the forest and only dreamed a wild dream of a witch-meeting?

Be it so, if you will. But, alas! it was a dream of evil omen for young Goodman Brown. A stern, a sad, a darkly meditative, a distrustful, if not a desperate man did he become from the night of that fearful dream. On the Sabbath-day, when the congregation were singing a holy psalm, he could not listen, because an anthem of sin rushed loudly upon his ear and drowned all the blessed strain. When the minister spoke from the pulpit with power and fervid eloquence, and with his hand on the open Bible, of the sacred truths of our religion, and of saint-like lives and triumphant deaths, and of future bliss or misery unutterable, then did Goodman Brown turn pale, dreading lest the roof should thunder down upon the gray blasphemer and his hearers. Often, awaking suddenly at midnight, he shrank from the bosom of Faith, and at morning or eventide, when the family knelt down at prayer, he scowled and muttered to himself, and gazed sternly at his wife, and turned away. And when he had lived long, and was borne to his grave a hoary corpse, followed by Faith, an aged woman, and children and grand-children, a goodly procession, besides neighbors not a few, they carved no hopeful verse upon his tombstone; for his dying hour was gloom.

Stephen Crane

THE BRIDE COMES TO YELLOW SKY

1

The great Pullman was whirling onward with such dignity of motion that a glance from the window seemed simply to prove that the plains of Texas were pouring eastward. Vast flats of green grass, dull-hued spaces of mesquite and cactus, little groups of frame houses, woods of light and tender trees, all were sweeping into the east, sweeping over the horizon, a precipice.

A newly married pair had boarded this coach at San Antonio. The man's face was reddened from many days in the wind and sun, and a direct result of his new black clothes was that his brick-colored hands were constantly performing in a most conscious fashion. From time to time he looked down respectfully at his attire. He sat with a hand on each knee, like a man waiting in a barber's shop. The glances he devoted to other passengers were furtive and shy.

The bride was not pretty, nor was she very young. She wore a dress of blue cashmere, with small reservations of velvet here and there, and with steel buttons abounding. She continually twisted her head to regard her puff sleeves, very stiff, straight, and high. They embarrassed her. It was quite apparent that she had cooked, and that she expected to cook, dutifully. The blushes caused by the careless scrutiny of some passengers as she had entered the car were strange to see upon this plain, underclass countenance, which was drawn in placid, almost emotionless lines.

They were evidently very happy. "Ever been in a parlor car before?" he asked, smiling with delight.

"No," she answered, "I never was. It's fine, ain't it?"

"Great! And then after a while we'll go forward to the diner, and get a big lay-out. Finest meal in the world. Charge a dollar."

"Oh, do they?" cried the bride. "Charge a dollar? Why, that's too much—for us—ain't it, Jack?"

"Not this trip, anyhow," he answered bravely. "We're going to go the whole thing."

Later he explained to her about the trains. "You see, it's a thousand miles from one end of Texas to the other; and this train runs right across it, and never stops but four times." He had the pride of an owner. He pointed out to her the dazzling fittings of the coach; and in truth her eyes opened wider as

THE BRIDE COMES TO YELLOW SKY First published in 1898. Stephen Crane (1871–1900), son of a Methodist minister, grew up in New Jersey and New York States and did his early writing in New York City. A newspaper assignment in the West (including Texas, Arizona, Nevada, and Mexico), in the early months of 1895, provided background for this story.

she contemplated the sea-green figured velvet, the shining brass, silver, and glass, the wood that gleamed as darkly brilliant as the surface of a pool of oil. At one end a bronze figure sturdily held a support for a separated chamber, and at convenient places on the ceiling were frescos in olive and silver.

To the minds of the pair, their surroundings reflected the glory of their marriage that morning in San Antonio; this was the environment of their new estate; and the man's face in particular beamed with an elation that made him appear ridiculous to the Negro porter. This individual at times surveyed them from afar with an amused and superior grin. On other occasions he bullied them with skill in ways that did not make it exactly plain to them that they were being bullied. He subtly used all the manners of the most unconquerable kind of snobbery. He oppressed them; but of this oppression they had small knowledge, and they speedily forgot that infrequently a number of travelers covered them with stares of derisive enjoyment. Historically there was supposed to be something infinitely humorous in their situation.

"We are due in Yellow Sky at 3:42," he said, looking tenderly into her eyes.

"Oh, are we?" she said, as if she had not been aware of it. To evince surprise at her husband's statement was part of her wifely amiability. She took from a pocket a little silver watch; and as she held it before her, and stared at it with a frown of attention, the new husband's face shone.

"I bought it in San Anton' from a friend of mine," he told her gleefully.

"It's seventeen minutes past twelve," she said, looking up at him with a kind of shy and clumsy coquetry. A passenger, noting this play, grew excessively sardonic, and winked at himself in one of the numerous mirrors.

At last they went to the dining car. Two rows of Negro waiters, in glowing white suits, surveyed their entrance with the interest, and also the equanimity, of men who had been forewarned. The pair fell to the lot of a waiter who happened to feel pleasure in steering them through their meal. He viewed them with the manner of a fatherly pilot, his countenance radiant with benevolence. The patronage, entwined with the ordinary deference, was not plain to them. And yet, as they returned to their coach, they showed in their faces a sense of escape.

To the left, miles down a long purple slope, was a little ribbon of mist where moved the keening Rio Grande. The train was approaching it at an angle, and the apex was Yellow Sky. Presently it was apparent that, as the distance from Yellow Sky grew shorter, the husband became commensurately restless. His brick-red hands were more insistent in their prominence. Occasionally he was even rather absent-minded and faraway when the bride leaned forward and addressed him.

As a matter of truth, Jack Potter was beginning to find the shadow of a deed weigh upon him like a leaden slab. He, the town marshal of Yellow Sky, a man known, liked, and feared in his corner, a prominent person, had gone to San Antonio to meet a girl he believed he loved, and there, after the usual prayers, had actually induced her to marry him, without consulting Yellow

Sky for any part of the transaction. He was now bringing his bride before an innocent and unsuspecting community.

Of course people in Yellow Sky married as it pleased them, in accordance with a general custom; but such was Potter's thought of his duty to his friends, or of their idea of his duty, or of an unspoken form which does not control men in these matters, that he felt he was heinous. He had committed an extraordinary crime. Face to face with this girl in San Antonio, and spurred by his sharp impulse, he had gone headlong over all the social hedges. At San Antonio he was like a man hidden in the dark. A knife to sever any friendly duty, any form, was easy to his hand in that remote city. But the hour of Yellow Sky—the hour of daylight—was approaching.

He knew full well that his marriage was an important thing to his town. It could only be exceeded by the burning of the new hotel. His friends could not forgive him. Frequently he had reflected on the advisability of telling them by telegraph, but a new cowardice had been upon him. He feared to do it. And now the train was hurrying him toward a scene of amazement, glee, and reproach. He glanced out of the window at the line of haze swinging slowly in toward the train.

Yellow Sky had a kind of brass band, which played painfully, to the delight of the populace. He laughed without heart as he thought of it. If the citizens could dream of his prospective arrival with his bride, they would parade the band at the station and escort them, amid cheers and laughing congratulations, to his adobe home.

He resolved that he would use all the devices of speed and plains-craft in making the journey from the station to his house. Once within that safe citadel, he could issue some sort of vocal bulletin, and then not go among the citizens until they had time to wear off a little of their enthusiasm.

The bride looked anxiously at him. "What's worrying you, Jack?"

He laughed again. "I'm not worrying, girl; I'm only thinking of Yellow Sky."

She flushed in comprehension.

A sense of mutual guilt invaded their minds and developed a finer tenderness. They looked at each other with eyes softly aglow. But Potter often laughed the same nervous laugh; the flush upon the bride's face seemed quite permanent.

The traitor to the feelings of Yellow Sky narrowly watched the speeding landscape. "We're nearly there," he said.

Presently the porter came and announced the proximity of Potter's home. He held a brush in his hand, and, with all his airy superiority gone, he brushed Potter's new clothes as the latter slowly turned this way and that way. Potter fumbled out a coin and gave it to the porter, as he had seen others do. It was a heavy and muscle-bound business, as that of a man shoeing his first horse.

The porter took their bag, and as the train began to slow they moved forward to the hooded platform of the car. Presently the two engines and their long string of coaches rushed into the station of Yellow Sky.

"They have to take water here," said Potter, from a constricted throat and in mournful cadence, as one announcing death. Before the train stopped, his eye had swept the length of the platform, and he was glad and astonished to see there was none upon it but the station agent, who, with a slightly hurried and anxious air, was walking toward the water tanks. When the train had halted, the porter alighted first, and placed in position a little temporary step. "Come on, girl," said Potter, hoarsely. As he helped her down they each laughed on a false note. He took the bag from the Negro, and bade his wife cling to his arm. As they slunk rapidly away, his hangdog glance perceived that they were unloading the two trunks, and also that the station agent, far ahead near the baggage car, had turned and was running toward him, making gestures. He laughed, and groaned as he laughed, when he noted the first effect of his marital bliss upon Yellow Sky. He gripped his wife's arm firmly to his side, and they fled. Behind them the porter stood, chuckling fatuously.

2

The California express on the Southern Railway was due at Yellow Sky in twenty-one minutes. There were six men at the bar of the Weary Gentleman saloon. One was a drummer° who talked a great deal and rapidly; three were Texans who did not care to talk at that time; and two were Mexican sheep-herders, who did not talk as a general practice in the Weary Gentleman saloon. The barkeeper's dog lay on the boardwalk that crossed in front of the door. His head was on his paws, and he glanced drowsily here and there with the constant vigilance of a dog that is kicked on occasion. Across the sandy street were some vivid green grass-plots, so wonderful in appearance, amid the sands that burned near them in a blazing sun, that they caused a doubt in the mind. They exactly resembled the grass mats used to represent lawns on the stage. At the cooler end of the railway station, a man without a coat sat in a tilted chair and smoked his pipe. The fresh-cut bank of the Rio Grande circled near the town, and there could be seen beyond it a great plum-colored plain of mesquite.

Save for the busy drummer and his companions in the saloon, Yellow Sky was dozing. The newcomer leaned gracefully upon the bar, and recited many tales with the confidence of a bard who has come upon a new field.

"—and at the moment that the old man fell downstairs with the bureau in his arms, the old woman was coming up with two scuttles of coal, and of course—"

The drummer's tale was interrupted by a young man who suddenly appeared in the open door. He cried: "Scratchy Wilson's drunk, and has turned loose with both hands." The two Mexicans at once set down their glasses and faded out of the rear entrance of the saloon.

The drummer, innocent and jocular, answered: "All right, old man. S'pose he has? Come in and have a drink, anyhow."

drummer: traveling salesman

But the information had made such an obvious cleft in every skull in the room that the drummer was obliged to see its importance. All had become instantly solemn. "Say," said he, mystified, "what is this?" His three companions made the introductory gesture of eloquent speech; but the young man at the door forestalled them.

"It means, my friend," he answered, as he came into the saloon, "that for the next two hours this town won't be a health resort."

The barkeeper went to the door, and locked and barred it; reaching out of the window, he pulled in heavy wooden shutters, and barred them. Immediately a solemn, chapel-like gloom was upon the place. The drummer was looking from one to another.

"But say," he cried, "what is this, anyhow? You don't mean there is going to be a gun fight?"

"Don't know whether there'll be a fight or not," answered one man, grimly, "but there'll be some shootin'—some good shootin'."

The young man who had warned them waved his hand. "Oh, there'll be a fight fast enough, if any one wants it. Anybody can get a fight out there in the street. There's a fight just waiting."

The drummer seemed to be swayed between the interest of a foreigner and a perception of personal danger.

"What did you say his name was?" he asked.

"Scratchy Wilson," they answered in chorus.

"And will he kill anybody? What are you going to do? Does this happen often? Does he rampage around like this once a week or so? Can he break in that door?"

"No, he can't break down that door," replied the barkeeper. "He's tried it three times. But when he comes you'd better lay down on the floor, stranger. He's dead sure to shoot at it, and a bullet may come through."

Thereafter the drummer kept a strict eye upon the door. The time had not yet been called for him to hug the floor, but, as a minor precaution, he sidled near to the wall. "Will he kill anybody?" he said again.

The men laughed low and scornfully at the question.

"He's out to shoot, and he's out for trouble. Don't see any good in experimentin' with him."

"But what do you do in a case like this? What do you do?"

A man responded: "Why, he and Jack Potter—"

"But," in chorus the other men interrupted, "Jack Potter's in San Anton'."

"Well, who is he? What's he got to do with it?"

"Oh, he's the town marshal. He goes out and fights Scratchy when he gets on one of these tears."

"Wow!" said the drummer, mopping his brow. "Nice job he's got."

The voices had toned away to mere whisperings. The drummer wished to ask further questions, which were born of an increasing anxiety and bewilderment; but when he attempted them, the men merely looked at him in irritation and motioned him to remain silent. A tense waiting hush was upon them. In the deep shadows of the room their eyes shone as they listened for sounds from the street. One man made three gestures at the barkeeper; and the latter, moving like a ghost, handed him a glass and a bottle. The man poured a full glass of whisky, and set down the bottle noiselessly. He gulped the whisky in a swallow, and turned again toward the door in immovable silence. The drummer saw that the barkeeper, without a sound, had taken a Winchester from beneath the bar. Later he saw this individual beckoning to him, so he tip-toed across the room.

"You better come with me back of the bar."

"No, thanks," said the drummer, perspiring; "I'd rather be where I can make a break for the back door."

Whereupon the man of bottles made a kindly but peremptory gesture. The drummer obeyed it, and, finding himself seated on a box with his head below the level of the bar, balm was laid upon his soul at a sight of various zinc and copper fittings that bore a resemblance to armor plate. The barkeeper took a seat comfortably upon an adjacent box.

"You see," he whispered, "this here Scratchy Wilson is a wonder with a gun—a perfect wonder; and when he goes on the war-trail, we hunt our holes—naturally. He's about the last one of the old gang that used to hang out along the river here. He's a terror when he's drunk. When he's sober he's all right—kind of simple—wouldn't hurt a fly—nicest fellow in town. But when he's drunk—whoo!"

There were periods of stillness. "I wish Jack Potter was back from San Anton'," said the barkeeper. "He shot Wilson up once—in the leg—and he would sail in and pull out the kinks in this thing."

Presently they heard from a distance the sound of a shot, followed by three wild yowls. It instantly removed a bond from the men in the darkened saloon. There was a shuffling of feet. They looked at each other. "Here he comes," they said.

3

A man in a maroon-colored flannel shirt, which had been purchased for purposes of decoration, and made principally by some Jewish women on the East Side of New York, rounded a corner and walked into the middle of the main street of Yellow Sky. In either hand the man held a long, heavy, blue-black revolver. Often he yelled, and these cries rang through a semblance of a deserted village, shrilly flying over the roofs in a volume that seemed to have no relation to the ordinary vocal strength of a man. It was as if the surrounding stillness formed the arch of a tomb over him. These cries of ferocious challenge rang against walls of silence. And his boots had red tops with gilded imprints, of the kind beloved in winter by little sledding boys on the hillsides of New England.

The man's face flamed in a rage begot of whisky. His eyes, rolling, and yet keen for ambush, hunted the still doorways and windows. He walked with the creeping movement of the midnight cat. As it occurred to him, he roared menacing information. The long revolvers in his hands were as easy as straws; they were moved with an electric swiftness. The little fingers of each hand played sometimes in a musician's way. Plain from the low collar of the shirt, the cords of his neck straightened and sank, straightened and sank, as passion moved him. The only sounds were his terrible invitations. The calm adobes preserved their demeanor at the passing of this small thing in the middle of the street.

There was no offer of fight—no offer of fight. The man called to the sky. There were no attractions. He bellowed and fumed and swayed his revolvers here and everywhere.

The dog of the barkeeper of the Weary Gentleman saloon had not appreciated the advance of events. He yet lay dozing in front of his master's door. At sight of the dog, the man paused and raised his revolver humorously. At sight of the man, the dog sprang up and walked diagonally away, with a sullen head, and growling. The man yelled, and the dog broke into a gallop. As it was about to enter an alley, there was a loud noise, a whistling, and something spat the ground directly before it. The dog screamed, and, wheeling in terror, galloped headlong in a new direction. Again there was a noise, a whistling, and sand was kicked viciously before it. Fear-stricken, the dog turned and flurried like an animal in a pen. The man stood laughing, his weapons at his hips.

Ultimately the man was attracted by the closed door of the Weary Gentleman saloon. He went to it and, hammering with a revolver, demanded drink.

The door remaining imperturbable, he picked a bit of paper from the walk, and nailed it to the framework with a knife. He then turned his back contemptuously upon this popular resort and, walking to the opposite side of the street and spinning there on his heel quickly and lithely, fired at the bit of paper. He missed it by a half-inch. He swore at himself, and went away. Later he comfortably fusilladed the windows of his most intimate friend. The man was playing with this town; it was a toy for him.

But still there was no offer of fight. The name of Jack Potter, his ancient antagonist, entered his mind, and he concluded that it would be a glad thing if he should go to Potter's house, and by bombardment induce him to come out and fight. He moved in the direction of his desire, chanting Apache scalp-music.

When he arrived at it, Potter's house presented the same still front as had the other adobes. Taking up a strategic position, the man howled a challenge. But this house regarded him as might a great stone god. It gave no sign. After a decent wait, the man howled further challenges, mingling with them wonderful epithets.

Presently there came the spectacle of a man churning himself into deepest rage over the immobility of a house. He fumed at it as the winter wind attacks a prairie cabin in the North. To the distance there should have gone the sound of a tumult like the fighting of two hundred Mexicans. As necessity bade him, he paused for breath or to reload his revolvers.

4

Potter and his bride walked sheepishly and with speed. Sometimes they laughed together shamefacedly and low.

"Next corner, dear," he said finally.

They put forth the efforts of a pair walking bowed against a strong wind. Potter was about to raise a finger to point the first appearance of the new home when, as they circled the corner, they came face to face with a man in a maroon-colored shirt, who was feverishly pushing cartridges into a large revolver. Upon the instant the man dropped his revolver to the ground and, like lightning, whipped another from its holster. The second weapon was aimed at the bridegroom's chest.

There was a silence. Potter's mouth seemed to be merely a grave for his tongue. He exhibited an instinct to at once loosen his arm from the woman's grip, and he dropped the bag to the sand. As for the bride, her face had gone as yellow as old cloth. She was a slave to hideous rites, gazing at the apparitional snake.

The two men faced each other at a distance of three paces. He of the revolver smiled with a new and quiet ferocity.

"Tried to sneak up on me," he said. "Tried to sneak up on me!" His eyes grew more baleful. As Potter made a slight movement, the man thrust his revolver venomously forward, "No, don't you do it, Jack Potter. Don't you move a finger toward a gun just yet. Don't you move an eyelash. The time has come for me to settle with you, and I'm goin' to do it my own way, and loaf along with no interferin'. So if you don't want a gun bent on you, just mind what I tell you."

Potter looked at his enemy. "I ain't got a gun on me, Scratchy," he said. "Honest, I ain't." He was stiffening and steadying, but yet somewhere at the back of his mind a vision of the Pullman floated; the sea-green figured velvet, the shining brass, silver, and glass, the wood that gleamed as darkly brilliant as the surface of a pool of oil—all the glory of the marriage, the environment of the new estate. "You know I fight when it comes to fighting, Scratchy Wilson; but I ain't got a gun on me. You'll have to do all the shootin' yourself."

His enemy's face went livid. He stepped forward and lashed his weapon to and fro before Potter's chest. "Don't you tell me you ain't got no gun on you, you whelp. Don't tell me no lie like that. There ain't a man in Texas ever seen you without no gun. Don't take me for no kid." His eyes blazed with light, and his throat worked like a pump.

"I ain't takin' you for no kid," answered Potter. His heels had not moved an inch backward. "I'm takin' you for a damn fool. I tell you I ain't got a gun, and I ain't. If you're goin' to shoot me up, you better begin now; you'll never get a chance like this again."

So much enforced reasoning had told on Wilson's rage; he was calmer. "If you ain't got a gun, why ain't you got a gun?" he sneered. "Been to Sunday school?"

"I ain't got a gun because I've just come from San Anton' with my wife. I'm married," said Potter. "And if I'd thought there was going to be any galoots like you prowling around when I brought my wife home, I'd had a gun, and don't you forget it."

"Married!" said Scratchy, not at all comprehending.

"Yes, married. I'm married," said Potter, distinctly.

"Married?" said Scratchy. Seemingly for the first time, he saw the drooping, drowning woman at the other man's side. "No!" he said. He was like a creature allowed a glimpse of another world. He moved a pace backward, and his arm, with the revolver, dropped to his side. "Is this the lady?" he asked.

"Yes, this is the lady," answered Potter.

There was another period of silence.

"Well," said Wilson at last, slowly, "I s'pose it's all off now."

"It's all off if you say so, Scratchy. You know I didn't make the trouble." Potter lifted his valise.

"Well, I 'low it's off, Jack," said Wilson. He was looking at the ground. "Married!" He was not a student of chivalry; it was merely that in the presence of this foreign condition he was a simple child of the earlier plains. He picked up his starboard revolver, and, placing both weapons in their holsters, he went away. His feet made funnel-shaped tracks in the heavy sand.

Katherine Anne Porter

ROPE

On the third day after they moved to the country he came walking back from the village carrying a basket of groceries and a twenty-four-yard coil of rope. She came out to meet him, wiping her hands on her green smock. Her hair was tumbled, her nose was scarlet with sunburn; he told her that already she looked like a born country woman. His gray flannel shirt stuck to him, his heavy shoes were dusty. She assured him he looked like a rural character in a play.

Had he brought the coffee? She had been waiting all day long for coffee. They had forgot it when they ordered at the store the first day.

Gosh, no, he hadn't. Lord, now he'd have to go back. Yes, he would if it

ROPE   First published in 1928. Katherine Anne Porter (1890–1980) was born and grew up in Texas, was educated at convent schools in New Orleans, and had lived in Chicago, Fort Worth, Denver, Mexico, and New York City before writing this story.

killed him. He thought, though, he had everything else. She reminded him it was only because he didn't drink coffee himself. If he did he would remember it quick enough. Suppose they ran out of cigarettes? Then she saw the rope. What was that for? Well, he thought it might do to hang clothes on, or something. Naturally she asked him if he thought they were going to run a laundry? They already had a fifty-foot line hanging right before his eyes? Why, hadn't he noticed it, really? It was a blot on the landscape to her.

He thought there were a lot of things a rope might come in handy for. She wanted to know what, for instance. He thought a few seconds, but nothing occurred. They could wait and see, couldn't they? You need all sorts of strange odds and ends around a place in the country. She said, yes, that was so; but she thought just at that time when every penny counted, it seemed funny to buy more rope. That was all. She hadn't meant anything else. She hadn't just seen, not at first, why he felt it was necessary.

Well, thunder, he had bought it because he wanted to, and that was all there was to it. She thought that was reason enough, and couldn't understand why he hadn't said so, at first. Undoubtedly it would be useful, twenty-four yards of rope, there were hundreds of things, she couldn't think of any at the moment, but it would come in. Of course. As he had said, things always did in the country.

But she was a little disappointed about the coffee, and oh, look, look, look at the eggs! Oh, my, they're all running! What had he put on top of them? Hadn't he known eggs mustn't be squeezed? Squeezed, who squeezed them, he wanted to know. What a silly thing to say. He had simply brought them along in the basket with the other things. If they got broke it was the grocer's fault. He should know better than to put heavy things on top of eggs.

She believed it was the rope. That was the heaviest thing in the pack, she saw him plainly when he came in from the road, the rope was a big package on top of everything. He desired the whole wide world to witness that this was not a fact. He had carried the rope in one hand and the basket in the other, and what was the use of her having eyes if that was the best they could do for her?

Well, anyhow, she could see one thing plain: no eggs for breakfast. They'd have to scramble them now, for supper. It was too damned bad. She had planned to have steak for supper. No ice, meat wouldn't keep. He wanted to know why she couldn't finish breaking the eggs in a bowl and set them in a cool place.

Cool place! if he could find one for her, she'd be glad to set them there. Well, then, it seemed to him they might very well cook the meat at the same time they cooked the eggs and then warm up the meat for tomorrow. The idea simply choked her. Warmed-over meat, when they might as well have had it fresh. Second best and scraps and makeshifts, even to the meat! He rubbed her shoulder a little. It doesn't really matter so much, does it, darling? Sometimes when they were playful, he would rub her shoulder and she would arch and purr. This time she hissed and clawed. He was getting ready to say that they could surely manage somehow when she turned to him and said, if he told her they could manage somehow she would certainly slap his face.

He swallowed the words red hot, his face burned. He picked up the rope and started to put it on the top shelf. She would not have it on the top shelf, the jars and tins belonged there; positively she would not have the top shelf cluttered up with a lot of rope. She had borne all the clutter she meant to bear in the flat in town, there was space here at least and she meant to keep things in order.

Well, in that case, he wanted to know what the hammer and nails were doing up there? And why had she put them there when she knew very well he needed that hammer and those nails upstairs to fix the window sashes? She simply slowed down everything and made double work on the place with her insane habit of changing things around and hiding them.

She was sure she begged his pardon, and if she had any reason to believe he was going to fix the sashes this summer she would have left the hammer and nails right where he put them; in the middle of the bedroom floor where they could step on them in the dark. And now if he didn't clear the whole mess out of there she would throw them down the well.

Oh, all right, all right—could he put them in the closet? Naturally not, there were brooms and mops and dustpans in the closet, and why couldn't he find a place for his rope outside her kitchen? Had he stopped to consider there were seven God-forsaken rooms in the house, and only one kitchen?

He wanted to know what of it? And did she realize that she was making a complete fool of herself? And what did she take him for, a three-year-old idiot? The whole trouble with her was she needed something weaker than she was to heckle and tyrannize over. He wished to God now they had a couple of children she could take it out on. Maybe he'd get some rest.

Her face changed at this, she reminded him he had forgot the coffee and had bought a worthless piece of rope. And when she thought of all the things they actually needed to make the place even decently fit to live in, well, she could cry, that was all. She looked so forlorn, so lost and despairing he couldn't believe it was only a piece of rope that was causing all the racket. What *was* the matter, for God's sake?

Oh, would he please hush and go away, and *stay* away, if he could, for five minutes? By all means, yes, he would. He'd stay away indefinitely if she wished. Lord, yes, there was nothing he'd like better than to clear out and never come back. She couldn't for the life of her see what was holding him, then. It was a swell time. Here she was, stuck, miles from a railroad, with a half-empty house on her hands, and not a penny in her pocket, and everything on earth to do; it seemed the God-sent moment for him to get out from under. She was surprised he hadn't stayed in town as it was until she had come out and done the work and got things straightened out. It was his usual trick.

It appeared to him that this was going a little far. Just a touch out of bounds, if she didn't mind his saying so. Why the hell had he stayed in town the summer before? To do a half-dozen extra jobs to get the money he had sent her. That was it. She knew perfectly well they couldn't have done it otherwise. She had agreed with him at the time. And that was the only time so help him he had ever left her to do anything by herself.

Oh, he could tell that to his great-grandmother. She had her notion of what had kept him in town. Considerably more than a notion, if he wanted to know. So, she was going to bring all that up again, was she? Well, she could just think what she pleased. He was tired of explaining. It may have looked funny but he had simply got hooked in, and what could he do? It was impossible to believe that she was going to take it seriously. Yes, yes, she knew how it was with a man: if he was left by himself a minute, some woman was certain to kidnap him. And naturally he couldn't hurt her feelings by refusing!

Well, what was she raving about? Did she forget she had told him those two weeks alone in the country were the happiest she had known for four years? And how long had they been married when she said that? All right, shut up! If she thought that hadn't stuck in his craw.

She hadn't meant she was happy because she was away from him. She meant she was happy getting the devilish house nice and ready for him. That was what she had meant, and now look! Bringing up something she said a year ago simply to justify himself for forgetting her coffee and breaking the eggs and buying a wretched piece of rope they couldn't afford. She really thought it was time to drop the subject, and now she wanted only two things in the world. She wanted him to get that rope from underfoot, and go back to the village and get her coffee, and if he could remember it, he might bring a metal mitt for the skillets, and two more curtain rods, and if there were any rubber gloves in the village, her hands were simply raw, and a bottle of milk of magnesia from the drugstore.

He looked out at the dark blue afternoon, sweltering on the slopes, and mopped his forehead and sighed heavily and said, if only she could wait a minute for *anything*, he was going back. He had said so, hadn't he, the very instant they found he had overlooked it?

Oh, yes, well . . . run along. She was going to wash the windows. The country was so beautiful! She doubted they'd have a moment to enjoy it. He meant to go, but he could not until he had said that if she wasn't such a hopeless melancholiac she might see that this was only for a few days. Couldn't she remember anything pleasant about the other summers? Hadn't they ever had any fun? She hadn't time to talk about it, and now would he please not leave that rope lying around for her to trip on? He picked it up, somehow it had toppled off the table, and walked out with it under his arm.

Was he going this minute? He certainly was. She thought so. Sometimes it seemed to her he had second sight about the precisely perfect moment to leave her ditched. She had meant to put the mattresses out to sun, if they put them out this minute they would get at least three hours, he must have heard her say that morning she meant to put them out. So of course he would walk off and leave her to it. She supposed he thought the exercise would do her good.

Well, he was merely going to get her coffee. A four-mile walk for two pounds of coffee was ridiculous, but he was perfectly willing to do it. The habit was making a wreck of her, but if she wanted to wreck herself there was nothing he could do about it. If he thought it was coffee that was making a wreck of her, she congratulated him: he must have a damned easy conscience.

Conscience or no conscience, he didn't see why the mattresses couldn't very well wait until tomorrow. And anyhow, for God's sake, were they living *in* the house, or were they going to let the house ride them to death? She paled at this, her face grew livid about the mouth, she looked quite dangerous, and reminded him that housekeeping was no more her work than it was his: she had other work to do as well, and when did he think she was going to find time to do it at this rate?

Was she going to start on that again? She knew as well as he did that his work brought in the regular money, hers was only occasional, if they depended on what *she* made—and she might as well get straight on this question once for all!

That was positively not the point. The question was, when both of them were working on their own time, was there going to be a division of housework, or wasn't there? She merely wanted to know, she had to make her plans. Why, he thought that was all arranged. It was understood that he was to help. Hadn't he always, in the summers?

Hadn't he, though? Oh, just hadn't he? And when, and where, and doing what? Lord, what an uproarious joke!

It was such a very uproarious joke that her face turned slightly purple, and she screamed with laughter. She laughed so hard she had to sit down, and finally a rush of tears spurted from her eyes and poured down into the lifted corners of her mouth. He dashed towards her and dragged her up to her feet and tried to pour water on her head. The dipper hung by a string on a nail and he broke it loose. Then he tried to pump water with one hand while she struggled in the other. So he gave it up and shook her instead.

She wrenched away, crying out for him to take his rope and go to hell, she had simply given him up: and ran. He heard her high-heeled bedroom slippers clattering and stumbling on the stairs.

He went out around the house and into the lane; he suddenly realized he had a blister on his heel and his shirt felt as if it were on fire. Things broke so suddenly you didn't know where you were. She could work herself into a fury about simply nothing. She was terrible, damn it: not an ounce of reason. You might as well talk to a sieve as that woman when she got going. Damned if he'd spend his life humoring her! Well, what to do now? He would take back the rope and exchange it for something else. Things accumulated, things were mountainous, you couldn't move them or sort them out or get rid of them. They just lay and rotted around. He'd take it back. Hell, why should he? He wanted it. What was it anyhow? A piece of rope. Imagine anybody caring more about a piece of rope than about a man's feelings. What earthly right had she to say a word about it? He remembered all the useless, meaningless things she bought for herself: Why? because I wanted it, that's why! He stopped and selected a large stone by the road. He would put the rope behind it. He would put it in the tool-box when he got back. He'd heard enough about it to last him a life-time.

When he came back she was leaning against the post box beside the road waiting. It was pretty late, the smell of broiled steak floated nose high in the cooling air. Her face was young and smooth and fresh-looking. Her unmanageable funny black hair was all on end. She waved to him from a distance, and he speeded up. She called out that supper was ready and waiting, was he starved?

You bet he was starved. Here was the coffee. He waved it at her. She looked at his other hand. What was that he had there?

Well, it was the rope again. He stopped short. He had meant to exchange it but forgot. She wanted to know why he should exchange it, if it was something he really wanted. Wasn't the air sweet now, and wasn't it fine to be here?

She walked beside him with one hand hooked into his leather belt. She pulled and jostled him a little as he walked, and leaned against him. He put his arm clear around her and patted her stomach. They exchanged wary smiles. Coffee, coffee for the Ootsum-Wootsoms! He felt as if he were bringing her a beautiful present.

He was a love, she firmly believed, and if she had had her coffee in the morning, she wouldn't have behaved so funny . . . There was a whippoorwill still coming back, imagine, clear out of season, sitting in the crab-apple tree calling all by himself. Maybe his girl stood him up. Maybe she did. She hoped to hear him once more, she loved whippoorwills . . . He knew how she was, didn't he?

Sure, he knew how she was.

Eudora Welty

DEATH OF A TRAVELING SALESMAN

R. J. Bowman, who for fourteen years had traveled for a shoe company through Mississippi, drove his Ford along a rutted dirt path. It was a long day! The time did not seem to clear the noon hurdle and settle into soft afternoon. The sun, keeping its strength here even in winter, stayed at the top of the sky, and every time Bowman stuck his head out of the dusty car to stare up the road, it seemed to reach a long arm down and push against the top of his head, right through his hat—like the practical joke of an old drummer, long on the road. It made him feel all the more angry and helpless. He was feverish, and he was not quite sure of the way.

This was his first day back on the road after a long siege of influenza. He

DEATH OF A TRAVELING SALESMAN   First published in 1936. A traveling salesman was also called a drummer. Eudora Welty was born in 1909 in Jackson, Mississippi, of which she has been a lifelong resident.

had had very high fever, and dreams, and had become weakened and pale, enough to tell the difference in the mirror, and he could not think clearly . . . All afternoon, in the midst of his anger, and for no reason, he had thoughts of his dead grandmother. She had been a comfortable soul. Once more Bowman wished he could fall into the big feather bed that had been in her room . . . Then he forgot her again.

This desolate hill country! And he seemed to be going the wrong way—it was as if he were going back, far back. There was not a house in sight. . . . There was no use wishing he were back in bed, though. By paying the hotel doctor his bill he had proved his recovery. He had not even been sorry when the pretty trained nurse said good-bye. He did not like illness, he distrusted it, as he distrusted the road without signposts. It angered him. He had given the nurse a really expensive bracelet, just because she was packing up her bag and leaving.

But now—what if in fourteen years on the road he had never been ill before and never had an accident? His record was broken, and he had even begun almost to question it . . . He had gradually put up at better hotels, in the bigger towns, but weren't they all, eternally, stuffy in summer and draughty in winter? Women? He could only remember little rooms within little rooms, like a nest of Chinese paper boxes, and if he thought of one woman he saw the worn loneliness that the furniture of that room seemed built of. And he himself—he was a man who always wore rather wide-brimmed black hats, and in the wavy hotel mirrors had looked something like a bullfighter, as he paused for that inevitable instant on the landing, walking downstairs to supper . . . He leaned out of the car again, and once more the sun pushed at his head.

Bowman had wanted to reach Beulah by dark, to go to bed and sleep off his fatigue. As he remembered, Beulah was fifty miles away from the last town, on a graveled road. This was only a cow trail. How had he ever come to such a place? One hand wiped the sweat from his face, and he drove on.

He had made the Beulah trip before. But he had never seen this hill or this petering-out path before—or that cloud, he thought shyly, looking up and then down quickly—any more than he had seen this day before. Why did he not admit he was simply lost and had been for miles? . . . He was not in the habit of asking the way of strangers, and these people never knew where the very roads they lived on went to; but then he had not even been close enough to anyone to call out. People standing in the fields now and then, or on top of the haystacks, had been too far away, looking like leaning sticks or weeds, turning a little at the solitary rattle of his car along their countryside, watching the pale sobered winter dust where it chunked out behind like big squashes down the road. The stares of these distant people had followed him solidly like a wall, impenetrable, behind which they turned back after he had passed.

The cloud floated there to one side like the bolster on his grandmother's bed. It went over a cabin on the edge of a hill, where two bare chinaberry trees clutched at the sky. He drove through a heap of dead oak leaves, his wheels stirring their weightless sides to make a silvery melancholy whistle as the car passed through their bed. No car had been along this way ahead of him. Then he saw that he was on the edge of a ravine that fell away, a red erosion, and that this was indeed the road's end.

He pulled the brake. But it did not hold, though he put all his strength into it. The car, tipped toward the edge, rolled a little. Without a doubt, it was going over the bank.

He got out quietly, as though some mischief had been done him and he had his dignity to remember. He lifted his bag and sample case out, set them down and stood back and watched the car roll over the edge. He heard something—not the crash he was listening for, but a slow un-uproarious crackle. Rather distastefully he went to look over, and he saw that his car had fallen into a tangle of immense grape vines as thick as his arm, which caught it and held it, rocked it like a grotesque child in a dark cradle, and then, as he watched, concerned somehow that he was not still inside it, released it gently to the ground.

He sighed.

Where am I? he wondered with a shock. Why didn't I do something? All his anger seemed to have drifted away from him. There was the house, back on the hill. He took a bag in each hand and with almost childlike willingness went toward it. But his breathing came with difficulty, and he had to stop and rest.

It was a shotgun house, two rooms and an open passage between, perched on the hill. The whole cabin slanted a little under the heavy heaped-up vine that covered the roof, light and green, as though forgotten from summer. A woman stood in the passage.

He stopped still. Then all of a sudden his heart began to behave strangely. Like a rocket set off, it began to leap and expand into uneven patterns of beats which showered into his brain, and he could not think. But in scattering and falling it made no noise. It shot up with great power, almost elation, and fell gently, like acrobats into nets. It began to pound profoundly, then waited irresponsibly, hitting in some sort of inward mockery first at his ribs, then against his eyes, then under his shoulder blades, and against the roof of his mouth when he tried to say, "Good afternoon, madam." But he could not hear his heart—it was as quiet as ashes falling. This was rather comforting; still, it was shocking to Bowman to feel his heart beating at all.

Stockstill in his confusion, he dropped his bags, which seemed to drift in slow bulks gracefully through the air and to cushion themselves on the gray prostrate grass near the doorstep.

As for the woman standing there, he saw at once that she was old. Since she could not possibly hear his heart, he ignored the pounding and now looked at her carefully, and yet in his distraction dreamily, with his mouth open.

She had been cleaning the lamp, and held it, half blackened, half clear, in front of her. He saw her with the dark passage behind her. She was a big woman with a weather-beaten but unwrinkled face; her lips were held tightly together, and her eyes looked with a curious dulled brightness into his. He looked at her shoes, which were like bundles. If it were summer she would be barefoot . . . Bowman, who automatically judged a woman's age on sight, set her age at fifty. She wore a formless garment of some gray coarse material, rough-dried from a washing, from which her arms appeared pink and unexpectedly round. When she never said a word, and sustained her quiet pose holding the lamp, he was convinced of the strength in her body.

"Good afternoon, madam," he said.

She stared on, whether at him or at the air around he could not tell, but after a moment she lowered her eyes to show that she would listen to whatever he had to say.

"I wonder if you would be interested—" He tried once more. "An accident—my car . . . "

Her voice emerged low and remote, like a sound across the lake. "Sonny he ain't here."

"Sonny?"

"Sonny ain't here now."

Her son—a fellow able to bring my car up, he decided in blurred relief. He pointed down the hill. "My car's in the bottom of the ditch. I'll need help."

"Sonny ain't here, but he'll be here."

She was becoming clearer to him and her voice stronger, and Bowman saw that she was stupid.

He was hardly surprised at the deepening postponement and tedium of his journey. He took a breath, and heard his voice speaking over the silent blows of his heart. "I was sick. I am not strong yet . . . May I come in?"

He stooped and laid his big black hat over the handle of his bag. It was a humble motion, almost a bow, that instantly struck him as absurd and betraying of all his weakness. He looked up at the woman, the wind blowing his hair. He might have continued for a long time in this unfamiliar attitude; he had never been a patient man, but when he was sick he had learned to sink submissively into the pillows, or to wait for his medicine. He waited on the woman.

Then she, looking at him with blue eyes, turned and held open the door; and after a moment Bowman, as if convinced in his action, stood erect and followed her in.

Inside, the darkness of the house touched him like a professional hand, the doctor's. The woman set the half-cleaned lamp on a table in the center of the room and pointed, also like a professional person, a guide, to a chair with a yellow cowhide seat. She herself crouched on the hearth, drawing her knees up under the shapeless dress.

At first he felt hopefully secure. His heart was quieter. The room was enclosed in the gloom of yellow pine boards. He could see the other room, with the foot of an iron bed showing, across the passage. The bed had been made up with a red-and-yellow pieced quilt that looked like a map or a picture, a little like his grandmother's girlhood painting of Rome burning.

He had ached for coolness, but in this room it was cold. He stared at the hearth with the dead coals lying on it and iron pots in the corners. The hearth and smoked chimney were of the stone he had seen ribbing the hills, mostly slate. Why is there no fire? he wondered.

And it was so still. The silence of the fields seemed to enter and move familiarly through the house. The wind used the open hall. He felt that he was in a mysterious, quiet, cool danger. It was necessary to do what? . . . To talk.

"I have a nice line of women's low-priced shoes . . . " he said.

But the woman answered, "Sonny'll be here. He's strong. Sonny'll move your car."

"Where is he now?"

"Farms for Mr. Redmond."

Mr. Redmond. Mr. Redmond. That was someone he would never have to encounter, and he was glad. Somehow the name did not appeal to him . . . In a flare of touchiness and anxiety, Bowman wished to avoid even mention of unknown men and their unknown farms.

"Do you two live here alone?" He was surprised to hear his old voice, chatty, confidential, inflected for selling shoes, asking a question like that—a thing he did not even want to know.

"Yes. We are alone."

He was surprised at the way she answered. She had taken a long time to say that. She had nodded her head in a deep way too. Had she wished to affect him with some sort of premonition? he wondered unhappily. Or was it only that she would not help him, after all, by talking with him? For he was not strong enough to receive the impact of unfamiliar things without a little talk to break their fall. He had lived a month in which nothing had happened except in his head and his body—an almost inaudible life of heartbeats and dreams that came back, a life of fever and privacy, a delicate life which had left him weak to the point of—what? Of begging. The pulse in his palm leapt like a trout in a brook.

He wondered over and over why the woman did not go ahead with cleaning the lamp. What prompted her to stay there across the room, silently bestowing her presence upon him? He saw that with her it was not a time for doing little tasks. Her face was grave; she was feeling how right she was. Perhaps it was only politeness. In docility he held his eyes stiffly wide; they fixed themselves on the woman's clasped hands as though she held the cord they were strung on.

Then, "Sonny's coming," she said.

He himself had not heard anything, but there came a man passing the window and then plunging in at the door, with two hounds beside him. Sonny was a big enough man, with his belt slung low about his hips. He looked at least thirty. He had a hot, red face that was yet full of silence. He wore muddy blue pants and an old military coat stained and patched. World War? Bowman wondered. Great God, it was a Confederate coat. On the back of his light hair he had a wide filthy black hat which seemed to insult Bowman's own. He pushed down the dogs from his chest. He was strong with dignity and heaviness in his way of moving . . . There was the resemblance to his mother.

They stood side by side . . . He must account again for his presence here.

"Sonny, this man, he had his car to run off over the prec'pice an' wants to know if you will git it out for him," the woman said after a few minutes.

Bowman could not even state his case.

Sonny's eyes lay upon him.

He knew he should offer explanations and show money—at least appear either penitent or authoritative. But all he could do was to shrug slightly.

Sonny brushed by him going to the window, followed by the eager dogs, and looked out. There was effort even in the way he was looking, as if he could throw his sight out like a rope. Without turning Bowman felt that his own eyes could have seen nothing: it was too far.

"Got me a mule out there an' got me a block an' tackle," said Sonny meaningfully. "I *could* catch me my mule an' git me my ropes, an' before long I'd git your car out the ravine."

He looked completely round the room, as if in meditation, his eyes roving in their own distance. Then he pressed his lips firmly and yet shyly together, and with the dogs ahead of him this time, he lowered his head and strode out. The hard earth sounded, cupping to his powerful way of walking—almost a stagger.

Mischievously, at the suggestion of those sounds, Bowman's heart leapt again. It seemed to walk about inside him.

"Sonny's goin' to do it," the woman said. She said it again, singing it almost, like a song. She was sitting in her place by the hearth.

Without looking out, he heard some shouts and the dogs barking and the pounding of hoofs in short runs on the hill. In a few minutes Sonny passed under the window with a rope, and there was a brown mule with quivering, shining, purple-looking ears. The mule actually looked in the window. Under its eyelashes it turned target-like eyes into his. Bowman averted his head and saw the woman looking serenely back at the mule, with only satisfaction on her face.

She sang a little more, under her breath. It occurred to him, and it seemed quite marvelous, that she was not really talking to him, but rather following the thing that came about with words that were unconscious and part of her looking.

So he said nothing, and this time when he did not reply he felt a curious and strong emotion, not fear, rise up in him.

This time, when his heart leapt, something—his soul—seemed to leap too, like a little colt invited out of a pen. He stared at the woman while the frantic nimbleness of his feeling made his head sway. He could not move; there was nothing he could do, unless perhaps he might embrace this woman who sat there growing old and shapeless before him.

But he wanted to leap up, to say to her, I have been sick and I found out then, only then, how lonely I am. Is it too late? My heart puts up a struggle inside me, and you may have heard it, protesting against emptiness . . . It should be full, he would rush on to tell her, thinking of his heart now as a deep lake, it should be holding love like other hearts. It should be flooded with love. There would be a warm spring day . . . Come and stand in my heart, whoever you are, and a whole river would cover your feet and rise higher and take your knees in whirlpools, and draw you down to itself, your whole body, your heart too.

But he moved a trembling hand across his eyes, and looked at the placid crouching woman across the room. She was as still as a statue. He felt ashamed and exhausted by the thought that he might, in one more moment, have tried by simple words and embraces to communicate some strange thing—something which seemed always to have just escaped him . . .

Sunlight touched the farthest pot on the hearth. It was late afternoon. This time tomorrow he would be somewhere on a good graveled road, driving his car past things that happened to people, quicker than their happening. Seeing ahead to the next day, he was glad, and knew that this was no time to embrace an old woman. He could feel in his pounding temples the readying of his blood for motion and for hurrying away.

"Sonny's hitched up your car by now," said the woman. "He'll git it out of the ravine right shortly."

"Fine!" he cried with his customary enthusiasm.

Yet it seemed a long time that they waited. It began to get dark. Bowman was cramped in his chair. Any man should know enough to get up and walk around while he waited. There was something like guilt in such stillness and silence.

But instead of getting up, he listened . . . His breathing restrained, his eyes powerless in the growing dark, he listened uneasily for a warning sound, forgetting in wariness what it would be. Before long he heard something— soft, continuous, insinuating.

"What's the noise?" he asked, his voice jumping into the dark. Then wildly he was afraid it would be his heart beating so plainly in the quiet room, and she would tell him so.

"You might hear the stream," she said grudgingly.

Her voice was closer. She was standing by the table. He wondered why she did not light the lamp. She stood there in the dark and did not light it.

Bowman would never speak to her now, for the time was past. I'll sleep in the dark, he thought, in his bewilderment pitying himself.

Heavily she moved on to the window. Her arm, vaguely white, rose straight from her full side and she pointed out into the darkness.

"That white speck's Sonny," she said, talking to herself.

He turned unwillingly and peered over her shoulder; he hesitated to rise and stand beside her. His eyes searched the dusky air. The white speck floated smoothly toward her finger, like a leaf on a river, growing whiter in the dark. It was as if she had shown him something secret, part of her life, but had offered no explanation. He looked away. He was moved almost to tears, feeling for no reason that she had made a silent declaration equivalent to his own. His hand waited upon his chest.

Then a step shook the house, and Sonny was in the room. Bowman felt how the woman left him there and went to the other man's side.

"I done got your car out, mister," said Sonny's voice in the dark. "She's settin' a-waitin' in the road, turned to go back where she come from."

"Fine!" said Bowman, projecting his own voice to loudness. "I'm surely much obliged—I could never have done it myself—I was sick . . ."

"I could do it easy," said Sonny.

Bowman could feel them both waiting in the dark, and he could hear the dogs panting out in the yard, waiting to bark when he should go. He felt strangely helpless and resentful. Now that he could go, he longed to stay. From what was he being deprived? His chest was rudely shaken by the violence of his heart. These people cherished something here that he could not see, they withheld some ancient promise of food and warmth and light. Between them they had a conspiracy. He thought of the way she had moved away from him and gone to Sonny, she had flowed toward him. He was shaking with cold, he was tired, and it was not fair. Humbly and yet angrily he stuck his hand into his pocket.

"Of course I'm going to pay you for everything—"

"We don't take money for such," said Sonny's voice belligerently.

"I want to pay. But do something more . . . Let me stay—tonight . . ." He took another step toward them. If only they could see him, they would know his sincerity, his real need! His voice went on, "I'm not very strong yet, I'm not able to walk far, even back to my car, maybe, I don't know—I don't know exactly where I am—"

He stopped. He felt as if he might burst into tears. What would they think of him!

Sonny came over and put his hands on him. Bowman felt them pass (they were professional too) across his chest, over his hips. He could feel Sonny's eyes upon him in the dark.

"You ain't no revenuer° come sneakin' here, mister, ain't got no gun?"

To this end of nowhere! And yet *he* had come. He made a grave answer. "No."

"You can stay."

"Sonny," said the woman, "you'll have to borry some fire."

"I'll go git it from Redmond's," said Sonny.

revenuer: a government agent searching for sources of illegal revenue, such as whiskey stills

"What?" Bowman strained to hear their words to each other.

"Our fire, it's out, and Sonny's got to borry some, because it's dark an' cold," she said.

"But matches—I have matches—"

"We don't have no need for 'em," she said proudly. "Sonny's goin' after his own fire."

"I'm goin' to Redmond's," said Sonny with an air of importance, and he went out.

After they had waited a while, Bowman looked out the window and saw a light moving over the hill. It spread itself out like a little fan. It zigzagged along the field, darting and swift, not like Sonny at all . . . Soon enough, Sonny staggered in, holding a burning stick behind him in tongs, fire flowing in his wake, blazing light into the corners of the room.

"We'll make a fire now," the woman said, taking the brand.

When that was done she lit the lamp. It showed its dark and light. The whole room turned golden-yellow like some sort of flower, and the walls smelled of it and seemed to tremble with the quiet rushing of the fire and the waving of the burning lampwick in its funnel of light.

The woman moved among the iron pots. With the tongs she dropped hot coals on top of the iron lids. They made a set of soft vibrations, like the sound of a bell far away.

She looked up and over at Bowman, but he could not answer. He was trembling . . .

"Have a drink, mister?" Sonny asked. He had brought in a chair from the other room and sat astride it with his folded arms across the back. Now we are all visible, to one another, Bowman thought, and cried, "Yes sir, you bet, thanks!"

"Come after me and do just what I do," said Sonny.

It was another excursion into the dark. They went through the hall, out to the back of the house, past a shed and a hooded well. They came to a wilderness of thicket.

"Down on your knees," said Sonny.

"What?" Sweat broke out on his forehead.

He understood when Sonny began to crawl through a sort of tunnel that the bushes made over the ground. He followed, startled in spite of himself when a twig or a thorn touched him gently without making a sound, clinging to him and finally letting go.

Sonny stopped crawling and, crouched on his knees, began to dig with both his hands into the dirt. Bowman shyly struck matches and made a light. In a few minutes Sonny pulled up a jug. He poured out some of the whisky into a bottle from his coat pocket, and buried the jug again. "You never know who's liable to knock at your door," he said, and laughed. "Start back," he said, almost formally. "Ain't no need for us to drink outdoors, like hogs."

At the table by the fire, sitting opposite each other in their chairs, Sonny and Bowman took drinks out of the bottle, passing it across. The dogs slept; one of them was having a dream.

"This is good," said Bowman. "This is what I needed." It was just as though he were drinking the fire off the hearth.

"He makes it," said the woman with quiet pride.

She was pushing the coals off the pots, and the smells of corn bread and coffee circled the room. She set everything on the table before the men, with a bone-handled knife stuck into one of the potatoes, splitting out its golden fiber. Then she stood for a minute looking at them, tall and full above them where they sat. She leaned a little toward them.

"You-all can eat now," she said, and suddenly smiled.

Bowman had just happened to be looking at her. He set his cup back on the table in unbelieving protest. A pain pressed at his eyes. He saw that she was not an old woman. She was young, still young. He could think of no number of years for her. She was the same age as Sonny, and she belonged to him. She stood with the deep dark corner of the room behind her, the shifting yellow light scattering over her head and her gray formless dress, trembling over her tall body when it bent over them in its sudden communication. She was young. Her teeth were shining and her eyes glowed. She turned and walked slowly and heavily out of the room, and he heard her sit down on the cot and then lie down. The pattern on the quilt moved.

"She's goin' to have a baby," said Sonny, popping a bite into his mouth.

Bowman could not speak. He was shocked with knowing what was really in this house. A marriage, a fruitful marriage. That simple thing. Anyone could have had that.

Somehow he felt unable to be indignant or protest, although some sort of joke had certainly been played upon him. There was nothing remote or mysterious here—only something private. The only secret was the ancient communication between two people. But the memory of the woman's waiting silently by the cold hearth, of the man's stubborn journey a mile away to get fire, and how they finally brought out their food and drink and filled the room proudly with all they had to show, was suddenly too clear and too enormous within him for response . . .

"You ain't as hungry as you look," said Sonny.

The woman came out of the bedroom as soon as the men had finished, and ate her supper while her husband stared peacefully into the fire.

Then they put the dogs out, with the food that was left.

"I think I'd better sleep here by the fire, on the floor," said Bowman.

He felt that he had been cheated, and that he could afford now to be generous. Ill though he was, he was not going to ask them for their bed. He was through with asking favors in this house, now that he understood what was there.

"Sure, mister."

But he had not known yet how slowly he understood. They had not meant to give him their bed. After a little interval they both rose and looking at him gravely went into the other room.

He lay stretched by the fire until it grew low and dying. He watched every tongue of blaze lick out and vanish. "There will be special reduced prices on all footwear during the month of January," he found himself repeating quietly, and then he lay with his lips tight shut.

How many noises the night had! He heard the stream running, the fire dying, and he was sure now that he heard his heart beating, too, the sound it made under his ribs. He heard breathing, round and deep, of the man and his wife in the room across the passage. And that was all. But emotion swelled patiently within him, and he wished that the child were his.

He must get back to where he had been before. He stood weakly before the red coals, and put on his overcoat. It felt too heavy on his shoulders. As he started out he looked and saw that the woman had never got through with cleaning the lamp. On some impulse he put all the money from his bill-fold under its fluted base, almost ostentatiously.

Ashamed, shrugging a little, and then shivering, he took his bags and went out. The cold of the air seemed to lift him bodily. The moon was in the sky.

On the slope he began to run, he could not help it. Just as he reached the road, where his car seemed to sit in the moonlight like a boat, his heart began to give off tremendous explosions like a rifle, bang bang bang.

He sank in fright onto the road, his bags falling about him. He felt as if all this had happened before. He covered his heart with both hands to keep anyone from hearing the noise it made.

But nobody heard it.

Ralph Ellison

BATTLE ROYAL

It goes a long way back, some twenty years. All my life I had been looking for something, and everywhere I turned someone tried to tell me what it was. I accepted their answers too, though they were often in contradiction and even self-contradictory. I was naïve. I was looking for myself and asking everyone except myself questions which I, and only I, could answer. It took me a long time and much painful boomeranging of my expectations to achieve a realization everyone else appears to have been born with: That I am nobody but myself. But first I had to discover that I am an invisible man!

BATTLE ROYAL   First published in 1947; five years later, with the addition of a brief transitional paragraph at the end, it appeared as chapter 1 of Ellison's novel *The Invisible Man* (1952). Ralph Ellison was born in Oklahoma City in 1914 and attended high school there. He then studied for three years as a scholarship student at Tuskegee Institute, in Alabama, founded in 1881 by the Negro leader and educator Booker T. Washington (1856-1915), whose famous speech at the opening of an exposition at Atlanta in 1895 is quoted from by the protagonist on page 438. After leaving Tuskegee, Ellison went to New York City, where he has mostly lived since.

And yet I am no freak of nature, nor of history. I was in the cards, other things having been equal (or unequal) eighty-five years ago. I am not ashamed of my grandparents for having been slaves. I am only ashamed of myself for having at one time been ashamed. About eighty-five years ago° they were told they were free, united with others of our country in everything pertaining to the common good, and, in everything social, separate like the fingers of the hand. And they believed it. They exulted in it. They stayed in their place, worked hard, and brought up my father to do the same. But my grandfather is the one. He was an odd old guy, my grandfather, and I am told I take after him. It was he who caused the trouble. On his deathbed he called my father to him and said, "Son, after I'm gone I want you to keep up the good fight. I never told you, but our life is a war and I have been a traitor all my born days, a spy in the enemy's country ever since I give up my gun back in the Reconstruction. Live with your head in the lion's mouth. I want you to overcome 'em with yeses, undermine 'em with grins, agree 'em to death and destruction, let 'em swoller you till they vomit or bust wide open." They thought the old man had gone out of his mind. He had been the meekest of men. The younger children were rushed from the room, the shades drawn and the flame of the lamp turned so low that it sputtered on the wick like the old man's breathing. "Learn it to the younguns," he whispered fiercely; then he died.

But my folks were more alarmed over his last words than over his dying. It was as though he had not died at all, his words caused so much anxiety. I was warned emphatically to forget what he had said and, indeed, this is the first time it has been mentioned outside the family circle. It had a tremendous effect upon me, however. I could never be sure of what he meant. Grandfather had been a quiet old man who never made any trouble, yet on his deathbed he had called himself a traitor and a spy, and he had spoken of his meekness as a dangerous activity. It became a constant puzzle which lay unanswered in the back of my mind. And whenever things went well for me I remembered my grandfather and felt guilty and uncomfortable. It was as though I was carrying out his advice in spite of myself. And to make it worse, everyone loved me for it. I was praised by the most lily-white men in town. I was considered an example of desirable conduct—just as my grandfather had been. And what puzzled me was that the old man had defined it as *treachery*. When I was praised for my conduct I felt a guilt that in some way I was doing something that was really against the wishes of the white folks, that if they had understood they would have desired me to act just the opposite, that I should have been sulky and mean, and that that really would have been what they wanted, even though they were fooled and thought they wanted me to act as I did. It made me afraid that some day they would look upon me as a traitor and I would be lost. Still I was more afraid to act any other way because they didn't like that at all. The old man's words were like a curse. On my graduation day I delivered an oration in which I showed that humility was

About eighty-five years ago: The Emancipation Proclamation was issued in 1863.

the secret, indeed, the very essence of progress. (Not that I believed this—how could I, remembering my grandfather?—I only believed that it worked.) It was a great success. Everyone praised me and I was invited to give the speech at a gathering of the town's leading white citizens. It was a triumph for the whole community.

It was in the main ballroom of the leading hotel. When I got there I discovered that it was on the occasion of a smoker, and I was told that since I was to be there anyway I might as well take part in the battle royal to be fought by some of my schoolmates as part of the entertainment. The battle royal came first.

All of the town's big shots were there in their tuxedoes, wolfing down the buffet foods, drinking beer and whiskey and smoking black cigars. It was a large room with a high ceiling. Chairs were arranged in neat rows around three sides of a portable boxing ring. The fourth side was clear, revealing a gleaming space of polished floor. I had some misgivings over the battle royal, by the way. Not from a distaste for fighting but because I didn't care too much for the other fellows who were to take part. They were tough guys who seemed to have no grandfather's curse worrying their minds. No one could mistake their toughness. And besides, I suspected that fighting a battle royal might detract from the dignity of my speech. In those pre-invisible days I visualized myself as a potential Booker T. Washington. But the other fellows didn't care too much for me either, and there were nine of them. I felt superior to them in my way, and I didn't like the manner in which we were all crowded together in the servants' elevator. Nor did they like my being there. In fact, as the warmly lighted floors flashed past the elevator we had words over the fact that I, by taking part in the fight, had knocked one of their friends out of a night's work.

We were led out of the elevator through a rococo hall into an anteroom and told to get into our fighting togs. Each of us was issued a pair of boxing gloves and ushered out into the big mirrored hall, which we entered looking cautiously about us and whispering, lest we might accidentally be heard above the noise of the room. It was foggy with cigar smoke. And already the whiskey was taking effect. I was shocked to see some of the most important men of the town quite tipsy. They were all there—bankers, lawyers, judges, doctors, fire chiefs, teachers, merchants. Even one of the more fashionable pastors. Something we could not see was going on up front. A clarinet was vibrating sensuously and the men were standing up and moving eagerly forward. We were a small tight group, clustered together, our bare upper bodies touching and shining with anticipatory sweat; while up front the big shots were becoming increasingly excited over something we still could not see. Suddenly I heard the school superintendent, who had told me to come, yell, "Bring up the shines, gentlemen! Bring up the little shines!"

We were rushed up to the front of the ballroom, where it smelled even more strongly of tobacco and whiskey. Then we were pushed into place. I almost wet my pants. A sea of faces, some hostile, some amused, ringed around us, and in the center, facing us, stood a magnificent blonde—stark naked. There was dead silence. I felt a blast of cold air chill me. I tried to back away, but they were behind me and around me. Some of the boys stood with lowered heads, trembling. I felt a wave of irrational guilt and fear. My teeth chattered, my skin turned to goose flesh, my knees knocked. Yet I was strongly attracted and looked in spite of myself. Had the price of looking been blindness, I would have looked. The hair was yellow like that of a circus kewpie doll, the face heavily powdered and rouged, as though to form an abstract mask, the eyes hollow and smeared a cool blue, the color of a baboon's butt. I felt a desire to spit upon her as my eyes brushed slowly over her body. Her breasts were firm and round as the domes of East Indian temples, and I stood so close as to see the fine skin texture and beads of pearly perspiration glistening like dew around the pink and erected buds of her nipples. I wanted at one and the same time to run from the room, to sink through the floor, or go to her and cover her from my eyes and the eyes of the others with my body; to feel the soft thighs, to caress her and destroy her, to love her and to murder her, to hide from her, and yet to stroke where below the small American flag tattooed upon her belly her thighs formed a capital V. I had a notion that of all in the room she saw only me with her impersonal eyes.

And then she began to dance, a slow sensuous movement; the smoke of a hundred cigars clinging to her like the thinnest of veils. She seemed like a fair bird-girl girdled in veils calling to me from the angry surface of some gray and threatening sea. I was transported. Then I became aware of the clarinet playing and the big shots yelling at us. Some threatened us if we looked and others if we did not. On my right I saw one boy faint. And now a man grabbed a silver pitcher from a table and stepped close as he dashed ice water upon him and stood him up and forced two of us to support him as his head hung and moans issued from his thick bluish lips. Another boy began to plead to go home. He was the largest of the group, wearing dark red fighting trunks much too small to conceal the erection which projected from him as though in answer to the insinuating low-registered moaning of the clarinet. He tried to hide himself with his boxing gloves.

And all the while the blonde continued dancing, smiling faintly at the big shots who watched her with fascination, and faintly smiling at our fear. I noticed a certain merchant who followed her hungrily, his lips loose and drooling. He was a large man who wore diamond studs in a shirtfront which swelled with the ample paunch underneath, and each time the blonde swayed her undulating hips he ran his hand through the thin hair of his bald head and, with his arms upheld, his posture clumsy like that of an intoxicated panda, wound his belly in a slow and obscene grind. This creature was completely hypnotized. The music had quickened. As the dancer flung herself about with a detached expression on her face, the men began reaching out to touch her. I could see their beefy fingers sink into her soft flesh. Some of the others tried to stop them and she began to move around the floor in graceful circles, as they gave chase, slipping and sliding over the polished floor. It was mad. Chairs went crashing, drinks were spilt, as they ran laughing and howling after her. They caught her just as she reached a door, raised her from the floor, and tossed her as college boys are tossed at a hazing, and above her red, fixed-smiling lips I saw the terror and disgust in her eyes, almost like my own terror and that which I saw in some of the other boys. As I watched, they tossed her twice and her soft breasts seemed to flatten against the air and her legs flung wildly as she spun. Some of the more sober ones helped her to escape. And I started off the floor, heading for the anteroom with the rest of the boys.

Some were still crying and in hysteria. But as we tried to leave we were stopped and ordered to get into the ring. There was nothing to do but what we were told. All ten of us climbed under the ropes and allowed ourselves to be blindfolded with broad bands of white cloth. One of the men seemed to feel a bit sympathetic and tried to cheer us up as we stood with our backs against the ropes. Some of us tried to grin. "See that boy over there?" one of the men said. "I want you to run across at the bell and give it to him right in the belly. If you don't get him, I'm going to get you. I don't like his looks." Each of us was told the same. The blindfolds were put on. Yet even then I had been going over my speech. In my mind each word was as bright as a flame. I felt the cloth pressed into place, and frowned so that it would be loosened when I relaxed.

But now I felt a sudden fit of blind terror. I was unused to darkness. It was as though I had suddenly found myself in a dark room filled with poisonous cottonmouths. I could hear the bleary voices yelling insistently for the battle royal to begin.

"Get going in there!"

"Let me at that big nigger!"

I strained to pick up the school superintendent's voice, as though to squeeze some security out of that slightly more familiar sound.

"Let me at those black sonsabitches!" someone yelled.

"No, Jackson, no!" another voice yelled. "Here, somebody, help me hold Jack."

"I want to get at that ginger-colored nigger. Tear him limb from limb," the first voice yelled.

I stood against the ropes trembling. For in those days I was what they called ginger-colored, and he sounded as though he might crunch me between his teeth like a crisp ginger cookie.

Quite a struggle was going on. Chairs were being kicked about and I could hear voices grunting as with terrific effort. I wanted to see, to see more desperately than ever before. But the blindfold was as tight as a thick skin-puckering scab and when I raised my gloved hands to push the layers of white aside a voice yelled, "Oh, no you don't, black bastard! Leave that alone!"

"Ring the bell before Jackson kills him a coon!" someone boomed in the sudden silence. And I heard the bell clang and the sound of the feet scuffling forward.

A glove smacked against my head. I pivoted, striking out stiffly as some-one went past, and felt the jar ripple along the length of my arm to my shoulder. Then it seemed as though all nine of the boys had turned upon me at once. Blows pounded me from all sides while I struck out as best I could. So many blows landed upon me that I wondered if I were not the only blindfolded fighter in the ring, or if the man called Jackson hadn't succeeded in getting me after all.

Blindfolded, I could no longer control my motions. I had no dignity. I stumbled about like a baby or a drunken man. The smoke had become thicker and with each new blow it seemed to sear and further restrict my lungs. My saliva became like hot bitter glue. A glove connected with my head, filling my mouth with warm blood. It was everywhere. I could not tell if the moisture I felt upon my body was sweat or blood. A blow landed hard against the nape of my neck. I felt myself going over, my head hitting the floor. Streaks of blue light filled the black world behind the blindfold. I lay prone, pretending that I was knocked out, but felt myself seized by hands and yanked to my feet. "Get going, black boy! Mix it up!" My arms were like lead, my head smarting from blows. I managed to feel my way to the ropes and held on, trying to catch my breath. A glove landed in my midsection and I went over again, feeling as though the smoke had become a knife jabbed into my guts. Pushed this way and that by the legs milling around me, I finally pulled erect and discovered that I could see the black, sweatwashed forms weaving in the smoky-blue atmosphere like drunken dancers weaving to the rapid drum-like thuds of blows.

Everyone fought hysterically. It was complete anarchy. Everybody fought everybody else. No group fought together for long. Two, three, four, fought one, then turned to fight each other, were themselves attacked. Blows landed below the belt and in the kidney, with the gloves open as well as closed, and with my eye partly opened now there was not so much terror. I moved carefully, avoiding blows, although not too many to attract attention, fighting group to group. The boys groped about like blind, cautious crabs crouching to protect their midsections, their heads pulled in short against their shoulders, their arms stretched nervously before them, with their fists testing the smoke-filled air like the knobbed feelers of hypersensitive snails. In one cor-ner I glimpsed a boy violently punching the air and heard him scream in pain as he smashed his hand against a ring post. For a second I saw him bent over holding his hand, then going down as a blow caught his unprotected head. I played one group against the other, slipping in and throwing a punch then stepping out of range while pushing the others into the melee to take the blows blindly aimed at me. The smoke was agonizing and there were no rounds, no bells at three minute intervals to relieve our exhaustion. The room spun round me, a swirl of lights, smoke, sweating bodies surrounded by tense white faces. I bled from both nose and mouth, the blood spattering upon my chest.

The men kept yelling, "Slug him, black boy! Knock his guts out!"

"Uppercut him! Kill him! Kill that big boy!"

Taking a fake fall, I saw a boy going down heavily beside me as though we were felled by a single blow, saw a sneaker-clad foot shoot into his groin as the two who had knocked him down stumbled upon him. I rolled out of range, feeling a twinge of nausea.

The harder we fought the more threatening the men became. And yet, I had begun to worry about my speech again. How would it go? Would they recognize my ability? What would they give me?

I was fighting automatically when suddenly I noticed that one after another of the boys was leaving the ring. I was surprised, filled with panic, as though I had been left alone with an unknown danger. Then I understood. The boys had arranged it among themselves. It was the custom for the two men left in the ring to slug it out for the winner's prize. I discovered this too late. When the bell sounded two men in tuxedoes leaped into the ring and removed the blindfold. I found myself facing Tatlock, the biggest of the gang. I felt sick at my stomach. Hardly had the bell stopped ringing in my ears than it clanged again and I saw him moving swiftly toward me. Thinking of nothing else to do I hit him smash on the nose. He kept coming, bringing the rank sharp violence of stale sweat. His face was a black blank of a face, only his eyes alive—with hate of me and aglow with a feverish terror from what had happened to us all. I became anxious. I wanted to deliver my speech and he came at me as though he meant to beat it out of me. I smashed him again and again, taking his blows as they came. Then on a sudden impulse I struck him lightly and we clinched. I whispered, "Fake like I knocked you out, you can have the prize."

"I'll break your behind," he whispered hoarsely.

"For *them?*"

"For *me,* sonofabitch!"

They were yelling for us to break it up and Tatlock spun me half around with a blow, and as a joggled camera sweeps in a reeling scene, I saw the howling red faces crouching tense beneath the cloud of blue-gray smoke. For a moment the world wavered, unraveled, flowed, then my head cleared and Tatlock bounced before me. That fluttering shadow before my eyes was his jabbing left hand. Then falling forward, my head against his damp shoulder, I whispered,

"I'll make it five dollars more."

"Go to hell!"

But his muscles relaxed a trifle beneath my pressure and I breathed, "Seven?"

"Give it to your ma," he said, ripping me beneath the heart.

And while I still held him I butted him and moved away. I felt myself bombarded with punches. I fought back with hopeless desperation. I wanted to deliver my speech more than anything else in the world, because I felt that only these men could judge truly my ability, and now this stupid clown was ruining my chances. I began fighting carefully now, moving in to punch him and out again with my greater speed. A lucky blow to his chin and I had him going too—until I heard a loud voice yell, "I got my money on the big boy."

Hearing this, I almost dropped my guard. I was confused: Should I try to win against the voice out there? Would not this go against my speech, and was not this a moment for humility, for nonresistance? A blow to my head as I danced about sent my right eye popping like a jack-in-the-box and settled my dilemma. The room went red as I fell. It was a dream fall, my body languid and fastidious as to where to land, until the floor became impatient and smashed up to meet me. A moment later I came to. An hypnotic voice said FIVE emphatically. And I lay there, hazily watching a dark red spot of my own blood shaping itself into a butterfly, glistening and soaking into the soiled gray world of the canvas.

When the voice drawled TEN I was lifted up and dragged to a chair. I sat dazed. My eye pained and swelled with each throb of my pounding heart and I wondered if now I would be allowed to speak. I was wringing wet, my mouth still bleeding. We were grouped along the wall now. The other boys ignored me as they congratulated Tatlock and speculated as to how much they would be paid. One boy whimpered over his smashed hand. Looking up front, I saw attendants in white jackets rolling the portable ring away and placing a small square rug in the vacant space surrounded by chairs. Perhaps, I thought, I will stand on the rug to deliver my speech.

Then the M.C. called to us, "Come on up here boys and get your money."

We ran forward to where the men laughed and talked in their chairs, waiting. Everyone seemed friendly now.

"There it is on the rug," the man said. I saw the rug covered with coins of all dimensions and a few crumpled bills. But what excited me, scattered here and there, were the gold pieces.

"Boys, it's all yours," the man said. "You get all you grab."

"That's right, Sambo," a blond man said, winking at me confidentially.

I trembled with excitement, forgetting my pain. I would get the gold and the bills, I thought. I would use both hands. I would throw my body against the boys nearest me to block them from the gold.

"Get down around the rug now," the man commanded, "and don't anyone touch it until I give the signal."

"This ought to be good," I heard.

As told, we got around the square rug on our knees. Slowly the man raised his freckled hand as we followed it upward with our eyes.

I heard, "These niggers look like they're about to pray!"

Then, "Ready," the man said. "Go!"

I lunged for a yellow coin lying on the blue design of the carpet, touching it and sending a surprised shriek to join those around me. I tried frantically to remove my hand but could not let go. A hot, violent force tore through my body, shaking me like a wet rat. The rug was electrified. The hair bristled up on my head as I shook myself free. My muscles jumped, my nerves jangled, writhed. But I saw that this was not stopping the other boys. Laughing in fear and embarrassment, some were holding back and scooping up the coins knocked off by the painful contortions of others. The men roared above us as we struggled.

"Pick it up, goddamnit, pick it up!" someone called like a bass-voiced parrot. "Go on, get it!"

I crawled rapidly around the floor, picking up the coins, trying to avoid the coppers and to get greenbacks and the gold. Ignoring the shock by laughing, as I brushed the coins off quickly, I discovered that I could contain the electricity—a contradiction but it works. Then the men began to push us onto the rug. Laughing embarrassedly, we struggled out of their hands and kept after the coins. We were all wet and slippery and hard to hold. Suddenly I saw a boy lifted into the air, glistening with sweat like a circus seal, and dropped, his wet back landing flush upon the charged rug, heard him yell and saw him literally dance upon his back, his elbows beating a frenzied tattoo upon the floor, his muscles twitching like the flesh of a horse stung by many flies. When he finally rolled off, his face was gray and no one stopped him when he ran from the floor amid booming laughter.

"Get the money," the M.C. called. "That's good hard American cash!"

And we snatched and grabbed, snatched and grabbed. I was careful not to come too close to the rug now, and when I felt the hot whiskey breath descend upon me like a cloud of foul air I reached out and grabbed the leg of a chair. It was occupied and I held on desperately.

"Leggo, nigger! Leggo!"

The huge face wavered down to mine as he tried to push me free. But my body was slippery and he was too drunk. It was Mr. Colcord, who owned a chain of movie houses and "entertainment palaces." Each time he grabbed me I slipped out of his hands. It became a real struggle. I feared the rug more than I did the drunk, so I held on, surprising myself for a moment by trying to topple *him* upon the rug. It was such an enormous idea that I found myself actually carrying it out. I tried not to be obvious, yet when I grabbed his leg, trying to tumble him out of the chair, he raised up roaring with laughter, and, looking at me with soberness dead in the eye, kicked me viciously in the chest. The chair leg flew out of my hand and I felt myself going and rolled. It was as though I had rolled through a bed of hot coals. It seemed a whole century would pass before I would roll free, a century in which I was seared through the deepest levels of my body to the fearful breath within me and the breath seared and heated to the point of explosion. It'll all be over in a flash, I thought as I rolled clear. It'll all be over in a flash.

But not yet, the men on the other side were waiting, red faces swollen as though from apoplexy as they bent forward in their chairs. Seeing their fingers coming toward me I rolled away as a fumbled football rolls off the receiver's fingertips, back into the coals. That time I luckily sent the rug sliding out of place and heard the coins ringing against the floor and the boys scuffling to pick them up and the M.C. calling, "All right, boys, that's all. Go get dressed and get your money."

I was limp as a dish rag. My back felt as though it had been beaten with wires.

When we had dressed the M.C. came in and gave us each five dollars, except Tatlock, who got ten for being the last in the ring. Then he told us to leave. I was not to get a chance to deliver my speech, I thought. I was going out into the dim alley in despair when I was stopped and told to go back. I returned to the ballroom, where the men were pushing back their chairs and gathering in small groups to talk.

The M.C. knocked on a table for quiet. "Gentlemen," he said, "we almost forgot an important part of the program. A most serious part, gentlemen. This boy was brought here to deliver a speech which he made at his graduation yesterday . . ."

"Bravo!"

"I'm told that he is the smartest boy we've got out there in Greenwood. I'm told that he knows more big words than a pocket-sized dictionary."

Much applause and laughter.

"So now, gentlemen, I want you to give him your attention."

There was still laughter as I faced them, my mouth dry, my eyes throbbing. I began slowly, but evidently my throat was tense, because they began shouting, "Louder! Louder!"

"We of the younger generation extol the wisdom of that great leader and educator," I shouted, "who first spoke these flaming words of wisdom: 'A ship lost at sea for many days suddenly sighted a friendly vessel. From the mast of the unfortunate vessel was seen a signal: "Water, water; we die of thirst!" The answer from the friendly vessel came back: "Cast down your bucket where you are." The captain of the distressed vessel, at last heeding the injunction, cast down his bucket, and it came up full of fresh sparkling water from the mouth of the Amazon River.' And like him I say, and in his words, 'To those of my race who depend upon bettering their condition in a foreign land, or who underestimate the importance of cultivating friendly relations with the Southern white man, who is his next-door neighbor, I would say: "Cast down your bucket where you are"—cast it down in making friends in every manly way of the people of all races by whom we are surrounded . . .'"

I spoke automatically and with such fervor that I did not realize that the men were still talking and laughing until my dry mouth, filling up with blood from the cut, almost strangled me. I coughed, wanting to stop and go to one of the tall brass, sand-filled spittoons to relieve myself, but a few of the men, especially the superintendent, were listening and I was afraid. So I gulped it down, blood, saliva and all, and continued. (What powers of endurance I had during those days! What enthusiasm! What a belief in the rightness of things!) I spoke even louder in spite of the pain. But still they talked and still they laughed, as though deaf with cotton in dirty ears. So I spoke with greater emotional emphasis. I closed my ears and swallowed blood until I was nauseated. The speech seemed a hundred times as long as before, but I could not leave out a single word. All had to be said, each memorized nuance considered, rendered. Nor was that all. Whenever I uttered a word of three or more syllables a group of voices would yell for me to repeat it. I used the phrase "social responsibility" and they yelled:

"What's that word you say, boy?"

"Social responsibility," I said.

"What?"

"Social . . ."

"Louder."

". . . responsibility."

"More!"

"Respon—"

"Repeat!"

"—sibility."

The room filled with the uproar of laughter until, no doubt, distracted by having to gulp down my blood, I made a mistake and yelled a phrase I had often seen denounced in newspaper editorials, heard debated in private.

"Social . . ."

"What?" they yelled.

" . . . equality—"

The laughter hung smokelike in the sudden stillness. I opened my eyes, puzzled. Sounds of displeasure filled the room. The M.C. rushed forward. They shouted hostile phrases at me. But I did not understand.

A small dry mustached man in the front row blared out, "Say that slowly, son!"

"What, sir?"

"What you just said!"

"Social responsibility, sir," I said.

"You weren't being smart, were you, boy?" he said, not unkindly.

"No, sir!"

"You sure that about 'equality' was a mistake?"

"Oh, yes, sir," I said. "I was swallowing blood."

"Well, you had better speak more slowly so we can understand. We mean to do right by you, but you've got to know your place at all times. All right, now, go on with your speech."

I was afraid. I wanted to leave but I wanted also to speak and I was afraid they'd snatch me down.

"Thank you, sir," I said, beginning where I had left off, and having them ignore me as before.

Yet when I finished there was a thunderous applause. I was surprised to see the superintendent come forth with a package wrapped in white tissue paper, and, gesturing for quiet, address the men.

"Gentlemen, you see that I did not overpraise the boy. He makes a good speech and some day he'll lead his people in the proper paths. And I don't have to tell you that this is important in these days and times. This is a good, smart boy, and so to encourage him in the right direction, in the name of the Board of Education I wish to present him a prize in the form of this . . . "

He paused, removing the tissue paper and revealing a gleaming calfskin briefcase.

" . . . in the form of this first-class article from Shad Whitmore's shop."

"Boy," he said, addressing me, "take this prize and keep it well. Consider it a badge of office. Prize it. Keep developing as you are and some day it will be filled with important papers that will help shape the destiny of your people."

I was so moved that I could hardly express my thanks. A rope of bloody saliva forming a shape like an undiscovered continent drooled upon the leather and I wiped it quickly away. I felt an importance that I had never dreamed.

"Open it and see what's inside," I was told.

My fingers a-tremble, I complied, smelling fresh leather and finding an official-looking document inside. It was a scholarship to the state college for Negroes. My eyes filled with tears and I ran awkwardly off the floor.

I was overjoyed; I did not even mind when I discovered the gold pieces I had scrambled for were brass pocket tokens advertising a certain make of automobile.

When I reached home everyone was excited. Next day the neighbors came to congratulate me. I even felt safe from grandfather, whose deathbed curse usually spoiled my triumphs. I stood beneath his photograph with my briefcase in hand and smiled triumphantly into his stolid black peasant's face. It was a face that fascinated me. The eyes seemed to follow everywhere I went.

That night I dreamed I was at a circus with him and that he refused to laugh at the clowns no matter what they did. Then later he told me to open my briefcase and read what was inside and I did, finding an official envelope stamped with the state seal; and inside the envelope I found another and another, endlessly, and I thought I would fall of weariness. "Them's years," he said. "Now open that one." And I did and in it I found an engraved stamp containing a short message in letters of gold. "Read it," my grandfather said. "Out loud."

"To Whom It May Concern," I intoned. "Keep This Nigger-Boy Running."

I awoke with the old man's laughter ringing in my ears.

Alice Walker

TO HELL WITH DYING

"To hell with dying," my father would say. "These children want Mr. Sweet!"

Mr. Sweet was a diabetic and an alcoholic and a guitar player and lived down the road from us on a neglected cotton farm. My older brothers and sisters got the most benefit from Mr. Sweet, for when they were growing up he had quite a few years ahead of him and so was capable of being called back from the brink of death any number of times—whenever the voice of my father reached him as he lay expiring. "To hell with dying, man," my father would say, pushing the wife away from the bedside (in tears although she knew the death was not necessarily the last one unless Mr. Sweet really wanted it to be). "These children want Mr. Sweet!" And they did want him, for at a signal from Father they would come crowding around the bed and throw themselves on the covers, and whoever was the smallest at the time would kiss him all over his wrinkled brown face and begin to tickle him so that he would laugh all down in his stomach, and his mustache, which was long and sort of straggly, would shake like Spanish moss and was also that color.

Mr. Sweet had been ambitious as a boy, wanted to be a doctor or lawyer or sailor, only to find that black men fare better if they are not. Since he could become none of these things he turned to fishing as his only earnest career and playing the guitar as his only claim to doing anything extraordinarily well. His son, the only one that he and his wife, Miss Mary, had, was shiftless as the day is long and spent money as if he were trying to see the bottom of the mint, which Mr. Sweet would tell him was the clean brown palm of his hand. Miss Mary loved her "baby," however, and worked hard to get him the "li'l necessaries" of life, which turned out mostly to be women.

Mr. Sweet was a tall, thinnish man with thick kinky hair going dead white. He was dark brown, his eyes were very squinty and sort of bluish, and he chewed Brown Mule tobacco. He was constantly on the verge of being blind drunk, for he brewed his own liquor and was not in the least a stingy sort of man, and was always very melancholy and sad, though frequently when he was "feelin' good" he'd dance around the yard with us, usually keeling over just as my mother came to see what the commotion was.

Toward all of us children he was very kind, and had the grace to be shy with us, which is unusual in grown-ups. He had great respect for my mother

TO HELL WITH DYING First published in 1967 in *The Best Stories by Negro Writers*, ed. Langston Hughes. Alice Walker was born in Georgia in 1944, attended Spelman College for two years, got her B.A. from Sarah Lawrence, and has taught at Jackson State, Tougaloo, Wellesley, and the University of Massachusetts in Boston.

for she never held his drunkenness against him and would let us play with him even when he was about to fall in the fireplace from drink. Although Mr. Sweet would sometimes lose complete or nearly complete control of his head and neck so that he would loll in his chair, his mind remained strangely acute and his speech not too affected. His ability to be drunk and sober at the same time made him an ideal playmate, for he was as weak as we were and we could usually best him in wrestling, all the while keeping a fairly coherent conversation going.

We never felt anything of Mr. Sweet's age when we played with him. We loved his wrinkles and would draw some on our brows to be like him, and his white hair was my special treasure and he knew it and would never come to visit us just after he had had his hair cut off at the barbershop. Once he came to our house for something, probably to see my father about fertilizer for his crops because, although he never paid the slightest attention to his crops, he liked to know what things would be best to use on them if he ever did. Anyhow, he had not come with his hair since he had just had it shaved off at the barbershop. He wore a huge straw hat to keep off the sun and also to keep his head away from me. But as soon as I saw him I ran up and demanded that he take me up and kiss me with his funny beard which smelled so strongly of tobacco. Looking forward to burying my small fingers into his woolly hair I threw away his hat only to find he had done something to his hair, that it was no longer there! I let out a squall which made my mother think that Mr. Sweet had finally dropped me in the well or something and from that day I've been wary of men in hats. However, not long after, Mr. Sweet showed up with his hair grown out and just as white and kinky and impenetrable as it ever was.

Mr. Sweet used to call me his princess, and I believed it. He made me feel pretty at five and six, and simply outrageously devastating at the blazing age of eight and a half. When he came to our house with his guitar the whole family would stop whatever they were doing to sit around him and listen to him play. He liked to play "Sweet Georgia Brown," that was what he called me sometimes, and also he liked to play "Caldonia" and all sorts of sweet, sad, wonderful songs which he sometimes made up. It was from one of these songs that I learned that he had had to marry Miss Mary when he had in fact loved somebody else (now living in Chi-ca-go, or De-stroy, Michigan). He was not sure that Joe Lee, her "baby," was also his baby. Sometimes he would cry and that was an indication that he was about to die again. And so we would all get prepared, for we were sure to be called upon.

I was seven the first time I remember actually participating in one of Mr. Sweet's "revivals"—my parents told me I had participated before, I had been the one chosen to kiss him and tickle him long before I knew the rite of Mr. Sweet's rehabilitation. He had come to our house, it was a few years after his wife's death, and was very sad, and also, typically, very drunk. He sat on the floor next to me and my older brother, the rest of the children were grown up and lived elsewhere, and began to play his guitar and cry. I held his woolly head in my arms and wished I could have been old enough to have been the woman he loved so much and that I had not been lost years and years ago.

When he was leaving, my mother said to us that we'd better sleep light that night for we'd probably have to go over to Mr. Sweet's before daylight. And we did. For soon after we had gone to bed one of the neighbors knocked on our door and called my father and said that Mr. Sweet was sinking fast and if he wanted to get in a word before the crossover he'd better shake a leg and get over to Mr. Sweet's house. All the neighbors knew to come to our house if something was wrong with Mr. Sweet, but they did not know how we always managed to make him well, or at least stop him from dying, when he was so often near death. As soon as we heard the cry we got up, my brother and I and my mother and father, and put on our clothes. We hurried out of the house and down the road for we were always afraid that we might someday be too late and Mr. Sweet would get tired of dallying.

When we got to the house, a very poor shack really, we found the front room full of neighbors and relatives and someone met us at the door and said it was all very sad that old Mr. Sweet Little (for Little was his family name, although we mostly ignored it) was about to kick the bucket. My parents were advised not to take my brother and me into the "death room," seeing we were so young and all, but we were so much more accustomed to the death room than he that we ignored him and dashed in without giving his warning a second thought. I was almost in tears, for these deaths upset me fearfully, and the thought of how much depended on me and my brother (who was such a ham most of the time) made me very nervous.

The doctor was bending over the bed and turned back to tell us for at least the tenth time in the history of my family that, alas, old Mr. Sweet Little was dying and that the children had best not see the face of implacable death (I didn't know what "implacable" was, but whatever it was, Mr. Sweet was not!). My father pushed him rather abruptly out of the way saying, as he always did and very loudly for he was saying it to Mr. Sweet, "To hell with dying, man, these children want Mr. Sweet"—which was my cue to throw myself upon the bed and kiss Mr. Sweet all around the whiskers and under the eyes and around the collar of his nightshirt where he smelled so strongly of all sorts of things, mostly liniment.

I was very good at bringing him around, for as soon as I saw that he was struggling to open his eyes I knew he was going to be all right, and so could finish my revival sure of success. As soon as his eyes were open he would begin to smile and that way I knew that I had surely won. Once, though, I got a tremendous scare, for he could not open his eyes and later I learned that he had had a stroke and that one side of his face was stiff and hard to get into motion. When he began to smile I could tickle him in earnest because I was sure that nothing would get in the way of his laughter, although once he began to cough so hard that he almost threw me off his stomach, but that was when I was very small, little more than a baby, and my bushy hair had gotten in his nose.

When we were sure he would listen to us we would ask him why he was in bed and when he was coming to see us again and could we play with his guitar, which more than likely would be leaning against the bed. His eyes would get all misty and he would sometimes cry out loud, but we never let it embarrass us, for he knew that we loved him and that we sometimes cried too for no reason. My parents would leave the room to just the three of us; Mr. Sweet, by that time, would be propped up in bed with a number of pillows behind his head and with me sitting and lying on his shoulder and along his chest. Even when he had trouble breathing he would not ask me to get down. Looking into my eyes he would shake his white head and run a scratchy old finger all around my hairline, which was rather low down, nearly to my eyebrows, and made some people say I looked like a baby monkey.

My brother was very generous in all this, he let me do all the revivaling—he had done it for years before I was born and so was glad to be able to pass it on to someone new. What he would do while I talked to Mr. Sweet was pretend to play the guitar, in fact pretend that he was a young version of Mr. Sweet, and it always made Mr. Sweet glad to think that someone wanted to be like him—of course, we did not know this then, we played the thing by ear, and whatever he seemed to like, we did. We were desperately afraid that he was just going to take off one day and leave us.

It did not occur to us that we were doing anything special; we had not learned that death was final when it did come. We thought nothing of triumphing over it so many times, and in fact became a trifle contemptuous of people who let themselves be carried away. It did not occur to us that if our father had been dying we could not have stopped it, that Mr. Sweet was the only person over whom we had power.

When Mr. Sweet was in his eighties I was studying in the university many miles from home. I saw him whenever I went home, but he was never on the verge of dying that I could tell and I began to feel that my anxiety for his health and psychological well-being was unnecessary. By this time he not only had a mustache but a long flowing snow-white beard, which I loved and combed and braided for hours. He was very peaceful, fragile, gentle, and the only jarring note about him was his old steel guitar, which he still played in the old sad, sweet, down-home blues way.

On Mr. Sweet's ninetieth birthday I was finishing my doctorate in Massachusetts and had been making arrangements to go home for several weeks' rest. That morning I got a telegram telling me that Mr. Sweet was dying again and could I please drop everything and come home. Of course I could. My dissertation could wait and my teachers would understand when I explained to them when I got back. I ran to the phone, called the airport, and within four hours I was speeding along the dusty road to Mr. Sweet's.

The house was more dilapidated than when I was last there, barely a shack, but it was overgrown with yellow roses which my family had planted many years ago. The air was heavy and sweet and very peaceful. I felt strange walking through the gate and up the old rickety steps. But the strangeness left me as I caught sight of the long white beard I loved so well flowing down the thin body over the familiar quilt coverlet. Mr. Sweet!

His eyes were closed tight and his hands, crossed over his stomach, were thin and delicate, no longer scratchy. I remembered how always before I had run and jumped up on him just anywhere; now I knew he would not be able to support my weight. I looked around at my parents, and was surprised to see that my father and mother also looked old and frail. My father, his own hair very gray, leaned over the quietly sleeping old man, who, incidentally, smelled still of wine and tobacco, and said, as he'd done so many times, "To hell with dying, man! My daughter is home to see Mr. Sweet!" My brother had not been able to come as he was in the war in Asia. I bent down and gently stroked the closed eyes and gradually they began to open. The closed, wine-stained lips twitched a little, then parted in a warm, slightly embarrassed smile. Mr. Sweet could see me and he recognized me and his eyes looked very spry and twinkly for a moment. I put my head down on the pillow next to his and we just looked at each other for a long time. Then he began to trace my peculiar hairline with a thin, smooth finger. I closed my eyes when his finger halted above my ear (he used to rejoice at the dirt in my ears when I was little), his hand stayed cupped around my cheek. When I opened my eyes, sure that I had reached him in time, his were closed.

Even at twenty-four how could I believe that I had failed? that Mr. Sweet was really gone? He had never gone before. But when I looked at my parents I saw that they were holding back tears. They had loved him dearly. He was like a piece of rare and delicate china which was always being saved from breaking and which finally fell. I looked long at the old face, the wrinkled forehead, the red lips, the hands that still reached out to me. Soon I felt my father pushing something cool into my hands. It was Mr. Sweet's guitar. He had asked them months before to give it to me; he had known that even if I came next time he would not be able to respond in the old way. He did not want me to feel that my trip had been for nothing.

The old guitar! I plucked the strings, hummed "Sweet Georgia Brown." The magic of Mr. Sweet lingered still in the cool steel box. Through the window I could catch the fragrant delicate scent of tender yellow roses. The man on the high old-fashioned bed with the quilt coverlet and the flowing white beard had been my first love.

Donald Barthelme

SOME OF US HAD BEEN THREATENING OUR FRIEND COLBY

Some of us had been threatening our friend Colby for a long time, because of the way he had been behaving. And now he'd gone too far, so we decided to hang him. Colby argued that just because he had gone too far (he did not deny that he had gone too far) did not mean that he should be subjected to hanging. Going too far, he said, was something everybody did sometimes. We didn't pay much attention to this argument. We asked him what sort of music he would like played at the hanging. He said he'd think about it but it would take him a while to decide. I pointed out that we'd have to know soon, because Howard, who is a conductor, would have to hire and rehearse the musicians and he couldn't begin until he knew what the music was going to be. Colby said he'd always been fond of Ives' Fourth Symphony. Howard said that this was a "delaying tactic" and that everybody knew that Ives was almost impossible to perform and would involve weeks of rehearsal, and that the size of the orchestra and chorus would put us way over the music budget. "Be reasonable," he said to Colby. Colby said he'd try to think of something a little less exacting.

Hugh was worried about the wording of the invitations. What if one of them fell into the hands of the authorities? Hanging Colby was doubtless against the law, and if the authorities learned in advance what the plan was they would very likely come in and try to mess everything up. I said that although hanging Colby was almost certainly against the law, we had a perfect *moral* right to do so because he was *our* friend, *belonged* to us in various important senses, and he had after all gone too far. We agreed that the invitations would be worded in such a way that the person invited could not know for sure what he was being invited to. We decided to refer to the event as "An Event Involving Mr. Colby Williams." A handsome script was selected from a catalogue and we picked a cream-colored paper. Magnus said he'd see to having the invitations printed, and wondered whether we should serve drinks. Colby said he thought drinks would be nice but was worried about the expense. We told him kindly that the expense didn't matter, that we were after all his dear friends and if a group of his dear friends couldn't get together and do the thing with a little bit of *éclat*, why, what was the world coming to? Colby asked if he would be able to have drinks, too, before the event. We said, "Certainly."

The next item of business was the gibbet. None of us knew too much about gibbet design, but Tomás, who is an architect, said he'd look it up in old books and draw the plans. The important thing, as far as he recollected, was that the trapdoor function perfectly. He said that just roughly, counting labor and materials, it shouldn't run us more than four hundred dollars. "Good God!" Howard said. He said what was Tomás figuring on, rosewood? No, just a good grade of pine, Tomás said. Victor asked if unpainted pine wouldn't look kind of "raw," and Tomás replied that he thought it could be stained a dark walnut without too much trouble.

I said that although I thought the whole thing ought to be done really

SOME OF US HAD BEEN THREATENING OUR FRIEND COLBY   First published in 1973. Donald Barthelme was born in Philadelphia, Pennsylvania, in 1931, but grew up in Houston, Texas, and presently lives in New York City.

446   SOME OF US HAD BEEN THREATENING OUR FRIEND COLBY

well, and all, I also thought four hundred dollars for a gibbet, on top of the expense for the drinks, invitations, musicians and everything, was a bit steep, and why didn't we just use a tree—a nice-looking oak, or something? I pointed out that since it was going to be a June hanging the trees would be in glorious leaf and that not only would a tree add a kind of "natural" feeling but it was also strictly traditional, especially in the West. Tomás, who had been sketching gibbets on the backs of envelopes, reminded us that an outdoor hanging always had to contend with the threat of rain. Victor said he liked the idea of doing it outdoors, possibly on the bank of a river, but noted that we would have to hold it some distance from the city, which presented the problem of getting the guests, musicians, etc., to the site and then back to town.

At this point everybody looked at Harry, who runs a car-and-truck-rental business. Harry said he thought he could round up enough limousines to take care of that end but that the drivers would have to be paid. The drivers, he pointed out, wouldn't be friends of Colby's and couldn't be expected to donate their services, any more than the bartender or the musicians. He said that he had about ten limousines, which he used mostly for funerals, and that he could probably obtain another dozen by calling around to friends of his in the trade. He said also that if we did it outside, in the open air, we'd better figure on a tent or awning of some kind to cover at least the principals and the orchestra, because if the hanging was being rained on he thought it would look kind of dismal. As between gibbet and tree, he said, he had no particular preferences, and he really thought that the choice ought to be left up to Colby, since it was his hanging. Colby said that everybody went too far, sometimes, and weren't we being a little Draconian. Howard said rather sharply that all that had already been discussed, and which did he want, gibbet or tree? Colby asked if he could have a firing squad. No, Howard said, he could not. Howard said a firing squad would just be an ego trip for Colby, the blindfold and last-cigarette bit, and that Colby was in enough hot water already without trying to "upstage" everyone with unnecessary theatrics. Colby said he was sorry, he hadn't meant it that way, he'd take the tree. Tomás crumpled up the gibbet sketches he'd been making, in disgust.

Then the question of the hangman came up. Paul said did we really need a hangman? Because if we used a tree, the noose could be adjusted to the appropriate level and Colby could just jump off something—a chair or stool or something. Besides, Paul said, he very much doubted if there were any free-lance hangmen wandering around the country, now that capital punishment has been done away with absolutely, temporarily, and that we'd probably have to fly one in from England or Spain or one of the South American countries, and even if we did that how could we know in advance that the man was a professional, a real hangman, and not just some moneyhungry amateur who might bungle the job and shame us all, in front of everybody? We all agreed that Colby should just jump off something and that a chair was not what he should jump off of, because that would look, we felt, extremely tacky—some old kitchen chair sitting out there under our beautiful tree. Tomás, who is quite modern in outlook and not afraid of innovation, proposed that Colby be standing on a large round rubber ball ten feet in diameter. This, he said, would afford a sufficient "drop" and would also roll out of the way if Colby suddenly changed his mind after jumping off. He reminded us that by not using a regular hangman we were placing an awful lot of the responsibility for the success of the affair on Colby himself, and that although he was sure Colby would perform creditably and not disgrace his friends at the last minute, still, men have been known to get a little irresolute at times like that, and the ten-foot-round rubber ball, which could probably be fabricated rather cheaply, would insure a "bang-up" production right down to the wire.

At the mention of "wire," Hank, who had been silent all this time, suddenly spoke up and said he wondered if it wouldn't be better if we used wire instead of rope—more efficient and in the end kinder to Colby, he suggested. Colby began looking a little green, and I didn't blame him, because there is something extremely distasteful in thinking about being hanged with wire instead of rope—it gives you sort of a revulsion, when you think about it. I thought it was really quite unpleasant of Hank to be sitting there talking about wire, just when we had solved the problem of what Colby was going to jump off of so neatly, with Tomás's idea about the rubber ball, so I hastily said that wire was out of the question, because it would injure the tree—cut into the branch it was tied to when Colby's full weight hit it—and that in these days of increased respect for environment, we didn't want that, did we? Colby gave me a grateful look, and the meeting broke up.

Everything went off very smoothly on the day of the event (the music Colby finally picked was standard stuff, Elgar, and it was played very well by Howard and his boys). It didn't rain, the event was well attended, and we didn't run out of Scotch, or anything. The ten-foot rubber ball had been painted a deep green and blended in well with the bucolic setting. The two things I remember best about the whole episode are the grateful look Colby gave me when I said what I said about the wire, and the fact that nobody has ever gone too far again.

James Joyce

CLAY

The matron had given her leave to go out as soon as the women's tea was over and Maria looked forward to her evening out. The kitchen was spick and span: the cook said you could see yourself in the big copper boilers. The fire was nice and bright and on one of the side-tables were four very big barmbracks. These barmbracks seemed uncut; but if you went closer you would see that they had been cut into long thick even slices and were ready to be handed round at tea. Maria had cut them herself.

Maria was a very, very small person indeed but she had a very long nose and a very long chin. She talked a little through her nose, always soothingly: *Yes, my dear,* and *No, my dear.* She was always sent for when the women quarreled over their tubs and always succeeded in making peace. One day the matron had said to her:

—Maria, you are a veritable peacemaker!

And the sub-matron and two of the Board ladies had heard the compliment. And Ginger Mooney was always saying what she wouldn't do to the dummy who had charge of the irons if it wasn't for Maria. Everyone was so fond of Maria.

The women would have their tea at six o'clock and she would be able to get away before seven. From Ballsbridge to the Pillar, twenty minutes; from the Pillar to Drumcondra, twenty minutes; and twenty minutes to buy the things. She would be there before eight. She took out her purse with the silver clasps and read again the words *A Present from Belfast.* She was very fond of that purse because Joe had brought it to her five years before when he and Alphy had gone to Belfast on a Whit-Monday trip. In the purse were two half-crowns and some coppers. She would have five shillings clear after paying tram fare. What a nice evening they would have, all the children singing! Only she hoped that Joe wouldn't come in drunk. He was so different when he took any drink.

Often he had wanted her to go and live with them; but she would have felt herself in the way (though Joe's wife was ever so nice with her) and she had become accustomed to the life of the laundry. Joe was a good fellow. She had nursed him and Alphy too; and Joe used often say:

—Mamma is mamma but Maria is my proper mother.

After the break-up at home the boys had got her that position in the *Dublin by Lamplight* laundry, and she liked it. She used to have such a bad opinion of Protestants but now she thought they were very nice people, a little quiet and serious, but still very nice people to live with. Then she had her plants in the conservatory and she liked looking after them. She had lovely ferns and wax-plants and, whenever anyone came to visit her, she always gave the visitor one or two slips from her conservatory. There was one thing she didn't like and that was the tracts on the walls; but the matron was such a nice person to deal with, so genteel.

CLAY Written in 1905. First published in 1916 in the collection *Dubliners*. The *Dublin by Lamplight* laundry, where Maria is employed, was a Protestant-run Home for Fallen Women. Barmbracks are currant buns. The game played at the Donnellys' party is a fortune-telling game. The participants, blindfolded, choose one of various symbolic objects arranged on a table: the ring signifies marriage; water, a long journey; the prayer-book, life in a convent; clay, death. The song mis-sung by Maria is from Balfe's romantic opera *The Bohemian Girl*. James Joyce (1882-1941), born a Catholic and educated at Catholic schools, lived in Dublin until 1904 and for the rest of his life lived abroad and wrote about Dublin.

When the cook told her everything was ready she went into the women's room and began to pull the big bell. In a few minutes the women began to come in by twos and threes, wiping their steaming hands in their petticoats and pulling down the sleeves of their blouses over their red steaming arms. They settled down before their huge mugs which the cook and the dummy filled up with hot tea, already mixed with milk and sugar in huge tin cans. Maria superintended the distribution of the barmbrack and saw that every woman got her four slices. There was a great deal of laughing and joking during the meal. Lizzie Fleming said Maria was sure to get the ring and, though Fleming had said that for so many Hallow Eves, Maria had to laugh and say she didn't want any ring or man either; and when she laughed her grey-green eyes sparkled with disappointed shyness and the tip of her nose nearly met the tip of her chin. Then Ginger Mooney lifted up her mug of tea and proposed Maria's health while all the other women clattered with their mugs on the table, and said she was sorry she hadn't a sup of porter to drink it in. And Maria laughed again till the tip of her nose nearly met the tip of her chin and till her minute body nearly shook itself asunder because she knew that Mooney meant well though, of course, she had the notions of a common woman.

But wasn't Maria glad when the women had finished their tea and the cook and the dummy had begun to clear away the tea-things! She went into her little bedroom and, remembering that the next morning was a mass morning, changed the hand of the alarm from seven to six. Then she took off her working skirt and her house-boots and laid her best skirt out on the bed and her tiny dress-boots beside the foot of the bed. She changed her blouse too and, as she stood before the mirror, she thought of how she used to dress for mass on Sunday morning when she was a young girl; and she looked with quaint affection at the diminutive body which she had so often adorned. In spite of its years she found it a nice tidy little body.

When she got outside the streets were shining with rain and she was glad of her old brown raincloak. The tram was full and she had to sit on the little stool at the end of the car, facing all the people, with her toes barely touching the floor. She arranged in her mind all she was going to do and thought how much better it was to be independent and to have your own money in your pocket. She hoped they would have a nice evening. She was sure they would but she could not help thinking what a pity it was Alphy and Joe were not speaking. They were always falling out now but when they were boys together they used to be the best of friends: but such was life.

She got out of her tram at the Pillar and ferreted her way quickly among the crowds. She went into Downes's cakeshop but the shop was so full of people that it was a long time before she could get herself attended to. She bought a dozen of mixed penny cakes, and at last came out of the shop laden with a big bag. Then she thought what else would she buy: she wanted to buy something really nice. They would be sure to have plenty of apples and nuts. It was hard to know what to buy and all she could think of was cake. She decided to buy some plumcake but Downes's plumcake had not enough almond icing on top of it so she went over to a shop in Henry Street. Here she was a long time in suiting herself and the stylish young lady behind the counter, who was evidently a little annoyed by her, asked her was it wedding-cake she wanted to buy. That made Maria blush and smile at the young lady; but the young lady took it all very seriously and finally cut a thick slice of plumcake, parceled it up and said:

—Two-and-four, please.

She thought she would have to stand in the Drumcondra tram because none of the young men seemed to notice her but an elderly gentleman made room for her. He was a stout gentleman and he wore a brown hard hat; he had a square red face and a greyish mustache. Maria thought he was a colonel-looking gentleman and she reflected how much more polite he was than the young men who simply stared straight before them. The gentleman began to chat with her about Hallow Eve and the rainy weather. He supposed the bag was full of good things for the little ones and said it was only right that the youngsters should enjoy themselves while they were young. Maria agreed with him and favored him with demure nods and hems. He was very nice with her, and when she was getting out at the Canal Bridge she thanked him and bowed, and he bowed to her and raised his hat and smiled agreeably; and while she was going up along the terrace, bending her tiny head under the rain, she thought how easy it was to know a gentleman even when he has a drop taken.

Everybody said: *O, here's Maria!* when she came to Joe's house. Joe was there, having come home from business, and all the children had their Sunday dresses on. There were two big girls in from next door and games were going on. Maria gave the bag of cakes to the eldest boy, Alphy, to divide and Mrs. Donnelly said it was too good of her to bring such a big bag of cakes and made all the children say:

—Thanks, Maria.

But Maria said she had brought something special for papa and mamma, something they would be sure to like, and she began to look for her plumcake. She tried in Downes's bag and then in the pockets of her raincloak and then the hall-stand but nowhere could she find it. Then she asked all the children had any of them eaten it—by mistake, of course—but the children all said no and looked as if they did not like to eat cakes if they were to be accused of stealing. Everybody had a solution for the mystery and Mrs. Donnelly said it was plain that Maria had left it behind her in the tram. Maria, remembering how confused the gentleman with the greyish mustache had made her, colored with shame and vexation and disappointment. At the thought of the failure of her little surprise and of the two and fourpence she had thrown away for nothing she nearly cried outright.

But Joe said it didn't matter and made her sit down by the fire. He was very nice with her. He told her all that went on in his office, repeating for her a smart answer which he had made to the manager. Maria did not understand why Joe laughed so much over the answer he had made but she said that the manager must have been a very overbearing person to deal with. Joe said he wasn't so bad when you knew how to take him, that he was a decent sort so long as you didn't rub him the wrong way. Mrs. Donnelly played the piano for the children and they danced and sang. Then the two next-door girls handed round the nuts. Nobody could find the nutcrackers and Joe was nearly getting cross over it and asked how did they expect Maria to crack nuts without a nutcracker. But Maria said she didn't like nuts and that they weren't to bother about her. Then Joe asked would she take a bottle of stout and Mrs. Donnelly said there was port wine too in the house if she would prefer that. Maria said she would rather they didn't ask her to take anything: but Joe insisted.

So Maria let him have his way and they sat by the fire talking over old times and Maria thought she would put in a good word for Alphy. But Joe cried that God might strike him stone dead if ever he spoke a word to his brother again and Maria said she was sorry she had mentioned the matter. Mrs. Donnelly told her husband it was a great shame for him to speak that way of his own flesh and blood but Joe said that Alphy was no brother of his and there was nearly being a row on the head of it. But Joe said he would not lose his temper on account of the night it was and asked his wife to open some more stout. The two next-door girls had arranged some Hallow Eve games and soon everything was merry again. Maria was delighted to see the children so merry and Joe and his wife in such good spririts. The next-door girls put some saucers on the table and then led the children up to the table, blindfold. One got the prayer-book and the other three got the water; and when one of the next-door girls got the ring Mrs. Donnelly shook her finger at the blushing girl as much as to say: *O, I know all about it!* They insisted then on blindfolding Maria and leading her up to the table to see what she would get; and, while they were putting on the bandage, Maria laughed and laughed again till the tip of her nose nearly met the tip of her chin.

They led her up to the table amid laughing and poking and she put her hand out in the air as she was told to do. She moved her hand about here and there in the air and descended on one of the saucers. She felt a soft wet substance with her fingers and was surprised nobody spoke or took off her bandage. There was a pause for a few seconds; and then a great deal of scuffling and whispering. Somebody said something about the garden, and at last Mrs. Donnelly said something very cross to one of the next-door girls and told her to throw it out at once: that was no play. Maria understood that it was wrong that time and so she had to do it over again: and this time she got the prayer-book.

After that Mrs. Donnelly played Miss McCloud's Reel for the children and Joe made Maria take a glass of wine. Soon they were all quite merry again and Mrs. Donnelly said Maria would enter a convent before the year was out because she had got the prayer-book. Maria had never seen Joe so nice to her as he was that night, so full of pleasant talk and reminiscences. She said they were all very good to her.

At last the children grew tired and sleepy and Joe asked Maria would she not sing some little song before she went, one of the old songs. Mrs. Donnelly said *Do, please, Maria!* and so Maria had to get up and stand beside the piano. Mrs. Donnelly bade the children be quiet and listen to Maria's song. Then she played the prelude and said *Now, Maria!* and Maria, blushing very much, began to sing in a tiny quavering voice. She sang *I Dreamt that I Dwelt*, and when she came to the second verse she sang again:

> I dreamt that I dwelt in marble halls
> With vassals and serfs at my side
> And of all who assembled within those walls
> That I was the hope and the pride.
> I had riches too great to count, could boast
> Of a high ancestral name,
> But I also dreamt, which pleased me most,
> That you loved me still the same.

But no one tried to show her her mistake;° and when she had ended her song Joe was very much moved. He said that there was no time like the long ago and no music for him like poor old Balfe, whatever other people might say; and his eyes filled up so much with tears that he could not find what he was looking for and in the end he had to ask his wife to tell him where the corkscrew was.

Katherine Mansfield

MISS BRILL

Although it was so brilliantly fine—the blue sky powdered with gold and great spots of light like white wine splashed over the Jardins Publiques—Miss Brill was glad that she had decided on her fur. The air was motionless, but when you opened your mouth there was just a faint chill, like a chill from a glass of iced water before you sip, and now and again a leaf came drifting—from nowhere, from the sky. Miss Brill put up her hand and touched her fur. Dear little thing! It was nice to feel it again. She had taken it out of its box that afternoon, shaken out the moth powder, given it a good brush, and rubbed the life back into the dim little eyes. "What has been happening to me?" said the sad little eyes. Oh, how sweet it was to see them snap at her again from the

MISS BRILL   Written in 1921; first published in 1922. "Jardins Publiques" is French for Public Gardens. Katherine Mansfield (1888-1923) was born and grew up in New Zealand, but lived her adult life in London with various sojourns on the Continent.

mistake: The "second verse," omitted by Maria, is as follows: *I dreamt that suitors sought my hand, / That knights on bended knee, / And with vows no maiden heart could withstand / They pledged their faith to me. / And I dreamt that one of that noble band / Came forth my hand to claim, / But I also dreamt, which charmed me most, / That you loved me still the same.*

red eiderdown! . . . But the nose, which was of some black composition, wasn't at all firm. It must have had a knock, somehow. Never mind—a little dab of black sealing-wax when the time came—when it was absolutely necessary . . . Little rogue! Yes, she really felt like that about it. Little rogue biting its tail just by her left ear. She could have taken it off and laid it on her lap and stroked it. She felt a tingling in her hands and arms, but that came from walking, she supposed. And when she breathed, something light and sad—no, not sad, exactly—something gentle seemed to move in her bosom.

There were a number of people out this afternoon, far more than last Sunday. And the band sounded louder and gayer. That was because the Season had begun. For although the band played all the year round on Sundays, out of season it was never the same. It was like some one playing with only the family to listen; it didn't care how it played if there weren't any strangers present. Wasn't the conductor wearing a new coat, too? She was sure it was new. He scraped with his foot and flapped his arms like a rooster about to crow, and the bandsmen sitting in the green rotunda blew out their cheeks and glared at the music. Now there came a little "flutey" bit—very pretty!—a little chain of bright drops. She was sure it would be repeated. It was; she lifted her head and smiled.

Only two people shared her "special" seat: a fine old man in a velvet coat, his hands clasped over a huge carved walking-stick, and a big old woman, sitting upright, with a roll of knitting on her embroidered apron. They did not speak. This was disappointing, for Miss Brill always looked forward to the conversation. She had become really quite expert, she thought, at listening as though she didn't listen, at sitting in other people's lives just for a minute while they talked round her.

She glanced, sideways, at the old couple. Perhaps they would go soon. Last Sunday, too, hadn't been as interesting as usual. An Englishman and his wife, he wearing a dreadful Panama hat and she button boots. And she'd gone on the whole time about how she ought to wear spectacles; she knew she needed them; but that it was no good getting any; they'd be sure to break and they'd never keep on. And he'd been so patient. He'd suggested everything—gold rims, the kind that curve round your ears, little pads inside the bridge. No, nothing would please her. "They'll always be sliding down my nose!" Miss Brill had wanted to shake her.

The old people sat on the bench, still as statues. Never mind, there was always the crowd to watch. To and fro, in front of the flower beds and the band rotunda, the couples and groups paraded, stopped to talk, to greet, to buy a handful of flowers from the old beggar who had his tray fixed to the railings. Little children ran among them, swooping and laughing; little boys with big white silk bows under their chins, little girls, little French dolls, dressed up in velvet and lace. And sometimes a tiny staggerer came suddenly rocking into the open from under the trees, stopped, stared, as suddenly sat down "flop," until its small high-stepping mother, like a young hen, rushed scolding to its rescue. Other people sat on the benches and green chairs, but they were nearly always the same, Sunday after Sunday, and—Miss Brill had often noticed—there was something funny about nearly all of them. They were odd, silent, nearly all old, and from the way they stared they looked as though they'd just come from dark little rooms or even—even cupboards!

Behind the rotunda the slender trees with yellow leaves down drooping, and through them just a line of sea, and beyond the blue sky with gold-veined clouds.

Tum-tum-tum tiddle-um! tiddle-um! tum tiddley-um tum ta! blew the band.

Two young girls in red came by and two young soldiers in blue met them, and they laughed and paired and went off arm-in-arm. Two peasant women with funny straw hats passed, gravely, leading beautiful smoke-colored donkeys. A cold, pale nun hurried by. A beautiful woman came along and dropped her bunch of violets, and a little boy ran after to hand them to her, and she took them and threw them away as if they'd been poisoned. Dear me! Miss Brill didn't know whether to admire that or not! And now an ermine toque and a gentleman in gray met just in front of her. He was tall, stiff, dignified, and she was wearing the ermine toque she'd bought when her hair was yellow. Now everything, her hair, her face, even her eyes, was the same color as the shabby ermine, and her hand, in its cleaned glove, lifted to dab her lips, was a tiny yellowish paw. Oh, she was so pleased to see him— delighted! She rather thought they were going to meet that afternoon. She described where she'd been—everywhere, here, there, along by the sea. The day was so charming—didn't he agree? And wouldn't he, perhaps? . . . But he shook his head, lighted a cigarette, slowly breathed a great deep puff into her face, and, even while she was still talking and laughing, flicked the match away and walked on. The ermine toque was alone; she smiled more brightly than ever. But even the band seemed to know what she was feeling and played more softly, played tenderly, and the drum beat, "The Brute! The Brute!" over and over. What would she do? What was going to happen now? But as Miss Brill wondered, the ermine toque turned, raised her hand as though she'd seen some one else, much nicer, just over there, and pattered away. And the band changed again and played more quickly, more gayly than ever, and the old couple on Miss Brill's seat got up and marched away, and such a funny old man with long whiskers hobbled along in time to the music and was nearly knocked over by four girls walking abreast.

Oh, how fascinating it was! How she enjoyed it! How she loved sitting here, watching it all! It was like a play. It was exactly like a play. Who could believe the sky at the back wasn't painted? But it wasn't till a little brown dog trotted on solemn and then slowly trotted off, like a little "theater" dog, a little dog that had been drugged, that Miss Brill discovered what it was that made it so exciting. They were all on stage. They weren't only the audience, not only looking on; they were acting. Even she had a part and came every Sunday. No doubt somebody would have noticed if she hadn't been there; she was part of the performance after all. How strange she'd never thought of it like that before! And yet it explained why she made such a point of starting from home at just the same time each week—so as not to be late for the performance—and it also explained why she had quite a queer, shy feeling at telling her English pupils how she spent her Sunday afternoons. No wonder! Miss Brill nearly laughed out loud. She was on the stage. She thought of the old invalid gentleman to whom she read the newspaper four afternoons a week while he slept in the garden. She had got quite used to the frail head on the cotton pillow, the hollowed eyes, the open mouth and the high pinched nose. If he'd been dead she mightn't have noticed for weeks; she wouldn't have minded. But suddenly he knew he was having the paper read to him by an actress! "An actress!" The old head lifted; two points of light quivered in the old eyes. "An actress—are ye?" And Miss Brill smoothed the newspaper as though it were the manuscript of her part and said gently: "Yes, I have been an actress for a long time."

The band had been having a rest. Now they started again. And what they played was warm, sunny, yet there was just a faint chill—a something, what was it?—not sadness—no, not sadness—a something that made you want to sing. The tune lifted, lifted, the light shone; and it seemed to Miss Brill that in another moment all of them, all the whole company, would begin singing. The young ones, the laughing ones who were moving together, they would begin, and the men's voices, very resolute and brave, would join them. And then she too, she too, and the others on the benches—they would come in with a kind of accompaniment—something low, that scarcely rose or fell, something so beautiful—moving . . . And Miss Brill's eyes filled with tears and she looked smiling at all the other members of the company. Yes, we understand, we understand, she thought—though what they understood she didn't know.

Just at that moment a boy and girl came and sat down where the old couple had been. They were beautifully dressed; they were in love. The hero and heroine, of course, just arrived from his father's yacht. And still soundlessly singing, still with that trembling smile, Miss Brill prepared to listen.

"No, not now," said the girl. "Not here, I can't."

"But why? Because of that stupid old thing at the end there?" asked the boy. "Why does she come here at all—who wants her? Why doesn't she keep her silly old mug at home?"

"It's her fu-fur which is so funny," giggled the girl. "It's exactly like a fried whiting."

"Ah, be off with you!" said the boy in an angry whisper. Then: "Tell me, ma petite chère—"

"No, not here," said the girl. "Not *yet.*"

On her way home she usually bought a slice of honeycake at the baker's. It was her Sunday treat. Sometimes there was an almond in her slice, sometimes not. It made a great difference. If there was an almond it was like carrying home a tiny present—a surprise—something that might very well not have been there. She hurried on the almond Sundays and struck the match for the kettle in quite a dashing way.

But today she passed the baker's by, climbed the stairs, went into the little dark room—her room like a cupboard—and sat down on the red eiderdown. She sat there for a long time. The box that the fur came out of was on the bed. She unclasped the necklet quickly; quickly, without looking, laid it inside. But when she put the lid on she thought she heard something crying.

Margaret Atwood

RAPE FANTASIES

The way they're going on about it in the magazines you'd think it was just invented, and not only that but it's something terrific, like a vaccine for cancer. They put it in capital letters on the front cover, and inside they have these questionnaires like the ones they used to have about whether you were a good enough wife or an endomorph or an ectomorph, remember that? with the scoring upside down on page 73, and then these numbered do-it-yourself dealies, you know? RAPE, TEN THINGS TO DO ABOUT IT, like it was ten new hairdos or something. I mean, what's so new about it?

So at work they all have to talk about it because no matter what magazine you open, there it is, staring you right between the eyes, and they're beginning to have it on the television, too. Personally I'd prefer a June Allyson movie anytime but they don't make them any more and they don't even have them that much on the Late Show. For instance, day before yesterday, that would be Wednesday, thank god it's Friday as they say, we were sitting around in the women's lunch room—the *lunch* room, I mean you'd think you could get some peace and quiet in there—and Chrissy closes up the magazine she's been reading and says, "How about it, girls, do you have rape fantasies?"

The four of us were having our game of bridge the way we always do, and I had a bare twelve points counting the singleton with not that much of a bid in anything. So I said one club, hoping Sondra would remember about the one club convention, because the time before when I used that she thought I really meant clubs and she bid us up to three, and all I had was four little ones with nothing higher than a six, and we went down two and on top of that we were vulnerable. She is not the world's best bridge player. I mean, neither am I but there's a limit.

Darlene passed but the damage was done, Sondra's head went round like it was on ball bearings and she said, *"What* fantasies?"

RAPE FANTASIES First published in 1977. Margaret Atwood was born in 1939 in Ottawa, and grew up there, in Sault Ste. Marie, and in Toronto, all in Ontario. She has published several volumes of poetry.

"Rape fantasies," Chrissy said. She's a receptionist and she looks like one; she's pretty but cool as a cucumber, like she's been painted all over with nail polish, if you know what I mean. Varnished. "It says here all women have rape fantasies."

"For Chrissake, I'm eating an egg sandwich," I said, "and I bid one club and Darlene passed."

"You mean, like some guy jumping you in an alley or something," Sondra said. She was eating her lunch, we all eat our lunches during the game, and she bit into a piece of that celery she always brings and started to chew away on it with this thoughtful expression in her eyes and I knew we might as well pack it in as far as the game was concerned.

"Yeah, sort of like that," Chrissy said. She was blushing a little, you could see it even under her makeup.

"I don't think you should go out alone at night," Darlene said, "you put yourself in a position," and I may have been mistaken but she was looking at me. She's the oldest, she's forty-one though you wouldn't know it and neither does she, but I looked it up in the employees' file. I like to guess a person's age and then look it up to see if I'm right. I let myself have an extra pack of cigarettes if I am, though I'm trying to cut down. I figure it's harmless as long as you don't tell. I mean, not everyone has access to that file, it's more or less confidential. But it's all right if I tell you, I don't expect you'll ever meet her, though you never know, it's a small world. Anyway.

"For *heaven's* sake, it's only *Toronto*," Greta said. She worked in Detroit for three years and she never lets you forget it, it's like she thinks she's a war hero or something, we should all admire her just for the fact that she's still walking this earth, though she was really living in Windsor the whole time, she just worked in Detroit. Which for me doesn't really count. It's where you sleep, right?

"Well, do you?" Chrissy said. She was obviously trying to tell us about hers but she wasn't about to go first, she's cautious, that one.

"I certainly don't," Darlene said, and she wrinkled up her nose, like this, and I had to laugh. "I think it's disgusting." She's divorced, I read that in the file too, she never talks about it. It must've been years ago anyway. She got up and went over to the coffee machine and turned her back on us as though she wasn't going to have anything more to do with it.

"Well," Greta said. I could see it was going to be between her and Chrissy. They're both blondes, I don't mean that in a bitchy way but they do try to outdress each other. Greta would like to get out of Filing, she'd like to be a receptionist too so she could meet more people. You don't meet much of anyone in Filing except other people in Filing. Me, I don't mind it so much, I have outside interests.

"Well," Greta said, "I sometimes think about, you know my apartment? It's got this little balcony, I like to sit out there in the summer and I have a few plants out there. I never bother that much about locking the door to the balcony, it's one of those sliding glass ones, I'm on the eighteenth floor for heaven's sake, I've got a good view of the lake and the CN Tower and all. But I'm sitting around one night in my housecoat, watching TV with my shoes off, you know how you do, and I see this guy's feet, coming down past the window, and the next thing you know he's standing on the balcony, he's let himself down by a rope with a hook on the end of it from the floor above, that's the nineteenth, and before I can even get up off the chesterfield he's inside the apartment. He's all dressed in black with black gloves on"—I knew right away what show she got the black gloves off because I saw the same one—"and then he, well, you know."

"You know what?" Chrissy said, but Greta said, "And afterwards he tells me that he goes all over the outside of the apartment building like that, from one floor to another, with his rope and his hook . . . and then he goes out to the balcony and tosses his rope, and he climbs up it and disappears."

"Just like Tarzan," I said, but nobody laughed.

"Is that all?" Chrissy said. "Don't you ever think about, well, I think about being in the bathtub, with no clothes on . . ."

"So who takes a bath in their clothes?" I said, you have to admit it's stupid when you come to think of it, but she just went on, " . . . with lots of bubbles, what I use is Vitabath, it's more expensive but it's so relaxing, and my hair pinned up, and the door opens and this fellow's standing there. . . . "

"How'd he get in?" Greta said.

"Oh, I don't know, through a window or something. Well, I can't very well get out of the bathtub, the bathroom's too small and besides he's blocking the doorway, so I just *lie* there, and he starts to very slowly take his own clothes off, and then he gets into the bathtub with me."

"Don't you scream or anything?" said Darlene. She'd come back with her cup of coffee, she was getting really interested. "I'd scream like bloody murder."

"Who'd hear me?" Chrissy said. "Besides, all the articles say it's better not to resist, that way you don't get hurt."

"Anyway you might get bubbles up your nose," I said, "from the deep breathing," and I swear all four of them looked at me like I was in bad taste, like I'd insulted the Virgin Mary or something. I mean, I don't see what's wrong with a little joke now and then. Life's too short, right?

"Listen," I said, "those aren't *rape* fantasies. I mean, you aren't getting *raped*, it's just some guy you haven't met formally who happens to be more attractive than Derek Cummins"—he's the Assistant Manager, he wears elevator shoes or at any rate they have these thick soles and he has this funny way of talking, we call him Derek Duck—"and you have a good time. Rape is when they've got a knife or something and you don't want to."

"So what about you, Estelle," Chrissy said, she was miffed because I laughed at her fantasy, she thought I was putting her down. Sondra was miffed too, by this time she'd finished her celery and she wanted to tell about hers, but she hadn't got in fast enough.

"All right, let me tell you one," I said. "I'm walking down this dark street at night and this fellow comes up and grabs my arm. Now it so happens that I have a plastic lemon in my purse, you know how it always says you should carry a plastic lemon in your purse? I don't really do it, I tried it once but the darn thing leaked all over my checkbook, but in this fantasy I have one, and I say to him, 'You're intending to rape me, right?' and he nods, so I open my purse to get the plastic lemon, and I can't find it! My purse is full of all this junk, Kleenex and cigarettes and my change purse and my lipstick and my driver's license, you know the kind of stuff; so I ask him to hold out his hands, like this, and I pile all this junk into them and down at the bottom there's the plastic lemon, and I can't get the top off. So I hand it to him and he's very obliging, he twists the top off and hands it back to me, and I squirt him in the eye."

I hope you don't think that's too vicious. Come to think of it, it is a bit mean, especially when he was so polite and all.

"*That's* your rape fantasy?" Chrissy says. "I don't believe it."

"She's a card," Darlene says, she and I are the ones that've been here the longest and she never will forget the time I got drunk at the office party and insisted I was going to dance under the table instead of on top of it, I did a sort of Cossack number but then I hit my head on the bottom of the table— actually it was a desk—when I went to get up, and I knocked myself out cold. She's decided that's the mark of an original mind and she tells everyone new about it and I'm not sure that's fair. Though I did do it.

"I'm being totally honest," I say. I always am and they know it. There's no point in being anything else, is the way I look at it, and sooner or later the truth will out so you might as well not waste the time, right? "You should hear the one about the Easy-Off Oven Cleaner."

But that was the end of the lunch hour, with one bridge game shot to hell, and the next day we spent most of the time arguing over whether to start a new game or play out the hands we had left over from the day before, so Sondra never did get a chance to tell about her rape fantasy.

It started me thinking though, about my own rape fantasies. Maybe I'm abnormal or something, I mean I have fantasies about handsome strangers coming in through the window too, like Mr. Clean, I wish one would, please god somebody without flat feet and big sweat marks on his shirt, and over five feet five, believe me being tall is a handicap though it's getting better, tall guys are starting to like someone whose nose reaches higher than their belly button. But if you're being totally honest you can't count those as rape fantasies. In a real rape fantasy, what you should feel is this anxiety, like when you think about your apartment building catching on fire and whether you should use the elevator or the stairs or maybe just stick your head under a wet towel, and you try to remember everything you've read about what to do but you can't decide.

For instance, I'm walking along this dark street at night and this short, ugly fellow comes up and grabs my arm, and not only is he ugly, you know, with a sort of puffy nothing face, like those fellows you have to talk to in the bank when your account's overdrawn— of course I don't mean they're all like that—but he's absolutely covered in pimples. So he gets me pinned against the wall, he's short but he's heavy, and he starts to undo himself and the zipper gets stuck. I mean, one of the most significant moments in a girl's life, it's almost like getting married or having a baby or something, and he sticks the zipper.

So I say, kind of disgusted, "Oh for Chrissake," and he starts to cry. He tells me he's never been able to get anything right in his entire life, and this is the last straw, he's going to go jump off a bridge.

"Look," I say, I feel so sorry for him, in my rape fantasies I always end up feeling sorry for the guy, I mean there has to be something *wrong* with them, if it was Clint Eastwood it'd be different but worse luck it never is. I was the kind of little girl who buried dead robins, know what I mean? It used to drive my mother nuts, she didn't like me touching them, because of the germs I guess. So I say, "Listen, I know how you feel. You really should do something about those pimples, if you got rid of them you'd be quite good looking, honest; then you wouldn't have to go around doing stuff like this. I had them myself once," I say, to comfort him, but in fact I did, and it ends up I give him the name of my old dermatologist, the one I had in high school, that was back in Leamington, except I used to go to St. Catharines for the dermatologist. I'm telling you, I was really lonely when I first came here; I thought it was going to be such a big adventure and all, but it's a lot harder to meet people in a city. But I guess it's different for a guy.

Or I'm lying in bed with this terrible cold, my face is all swollen up, my eyes are red and my nose is dripping like a leaky tap, and this fellow comes in through the window and *he* has a terrible cold too, it's a new kind of flu that's been going around. So he says, "I'b goig do rabe you"—I hope you don't mind me holding my nose like this but that's the way I imagine it—and he lets out this terrific sneeze, which slows him down a bit, also I'm no object of beauty myself, you'd have to be some kind of pervert to want to rape someone with a cold like mine, it'd be like raping a bottle of LePages mucilage the way my nose is running. He's looking wildly around the room, and I realize it's because he doesn't have a piece of Kleenex! "Id's ride here," I say, and I pass him the Kleenex, god knows why he even bothered to get out of bed, you'd think if you were going to go around climbing in windows you'd wait till you were healthier, right? I mean, that takes a certain amount of energy. So I ask him why doesn't he let me fix him a Neo-Citran and scotch, that's what I always take, you still have the cold but you don't feel it, so I do and we end up watching the Late Show together. I mean, they aren't all sex maniacs, the rest of the time they must lead a normal life. I figure they enjoy watching the Late Show just like anybody else.

I do have a scarier one though . . . where the fellow says he's hearing angel voices that're telling him he's got to kill me, you know, you read about things like that all the time in the papers. In this one I'm not in the apartment where I live now, I'm back in my mother's house in Leamington and the fellow's been hiding in the cellar, he grabs my arm when I go downstairs to get a jar of jam and he's got hold of the axe too, out of the garage, that one is really scary. I mean, what do you say to a nut like that?

So I start to shake but after a minute I get control of myself and I say, is he sure the angel voices have got the right person, because I hear the same angel voices and they've been telling me for some time that I'm going to give birth to the reincarnation of St. Anne who in turn has the Virgin Mary and right after that comes Jesus Christ and the end of the world, and he wouldn't want to interfere with that, would he? So he gets confused and listens some more, and then he asks for a sign and I show him my vaccination mark, you can see it's sort of an odd-shaped one, it got infected because I scratched the top off, and that does it, he apologizes and climbs out the coal chute again, which is how he got in in the first place, and I say to myself there's some advantage in having been brought up a Catholic even though I haven't been to church since they changed the service into English, it just isn't the same, you might as well be a Protestant. I must write to Mother and tell her to nail up that coal chute, it always has bothered me. Funny, I couldn't tell you at all what this man looks like but I know exactly what kind of shoes he's wearing, because that's the last I see of him, his shoes going up the coal chute, and they're the old-fashioned kind that lace up the ankles, even though he's a young fellow. That's strange, isn't it?

Let me tell you though I really sweat until I see him safely out of there and I go upstairs right away and make myself a cup of tea. I don't think about that one much. My mother always said you shouldn't dwell on unpleasant things and I generally agree with that, I mean, dwelling on them doesn't make them go away. Though not dwelling on them doesn't make them go away either, when you come to think of it.

Sometimes I have these short ones where the fellow grabs my arm but I'm really a Kung-Fu expert, can you believe it, in real life I'm sure it would just be a conk on the head and that's that, like getting your tonsils out, you'd wake up and it would be all over except for the sore places, and you'd be lucky if your neck wasn't broken or something, I could never even hit the volleyball in gym and a volleyball is fairly large, you know?—and I just go *zap* with my fingers into his eyes and that's it, he falls over, or I flip him against a wall or something. But I could never really stick my fingers in anyone's eyes, could you? It would feel like hot jello and I don't even like cold jello, just thinking about it gives me the creeps. I feel a bit guilty about that one, I mean how would you like walking around knowing someone's been blinded for life because of you?

But maybe it's different for a guy.

The most touching one I have is when the fellow grabs my arm and I say, sad and kind of dignified, "You'd be raping a corpse." That pulls him up short and I explain that I've just found out I have leukemia and the doctors have only given me a few months to live. That's why I'm out pacing the streets alone at night, I need to think, you know, come to terms with myself. I don't really have leukemia but in the fantasy I do, I guess I chose that particular disease because a girl in my grade four class died of it, the whole class sent her flowers when she was in the hospital. I didn't understand then that she was going to die and I wanted to have leukemia too so I could get flowers. Kids are funny, aren't they? Well, it turns out that he has leukemia himself, and *he* only has a few months to live, that's why he's going around raping people, he's very bitter because he's so young and his life is being taken from him before he's really lived it. So we walk along gently under the street lights, it's spring and sort of misty, and we end up going for coffee, we're happy we've found the only other person in the world who can understand what we're going through, it's almost like fate, and after a while we just sort of look at each other and our hands touch, and he comes back with me and moves into my apartment and we spend our last months together before we die, we just sort of don't wake up in the morning, though I've never decided which one of us gets to die first. If it's him I have to go on and fantasize about the funeral, if it's me I don't have to worry about that, so it just about depends on how tired I am at the time. You may not believe this but sometimes I even start crying. I cry at the ends of movies, even the ones that aren't all that sad, so I guess it's the same thing. My mother's like that too.

The funny thing about these fantasies is that the man is always someone I don't know, and the statistics in the magazines, well, most of them anyway, they say it's often someone you do know, at least a little bit, like your boss or something—I mean, it wouldn't be *my* boss, he's over sixty and I'm sure he couldn't rape his way out of a paper bag, poor old thing, but it might be someone like Derek Duck, in his elevator shoes, perish the thought—or someone you just met, who invites you up for a drink, it's getting so you can hardly be sociable any more, and how are you supposed to meet people if you can't trust them even that basic amount? You can't spend your whole life in the Filing Department or cooped up in your own apartment with all the doors and windows locked and the shades down. I'm not what you would call a drinker but I like to go out now and then for a drink or two in a nice place, even if I am by myself, I'm with Women's Lib on that even though I can't agree with a lot of other things they say. Like here for instance, the waiters all know me and if anyone, you know, bothers me. . . . I don't know why I'm telling you all this, except I think it helps you get to know a person, especially at first, hearing some of the things they think about. At work they call me the office worry wart, but it isn't so much like worrying, it's more like figuring out what you should do in an emergency, like I said before.

Anyway, another thing about it is that there's a lot of conversation, in fact I spend most of my time, in the fantasy that is, wondering what I'm going to say and what he's going to say, I think it would be better if you could get a conversation going. Like, how could a fellow do that to a person he's just had a long conversation with, once you let them know you're human, you have a life too, I don't see how they could go ahead with it, right? I mean, I know it happens but I just don't understand it, that's the part I really don't understand.

Anton Chekhov

IN EXILE

Old Semyon, whose nickname was Preacher, and a young Tartar, whose name no one knew, were sitting by a campfire on the bank of the river; the other three ferrymen were inside the hut. Semyon, a gaunt, toothless old man of sixty, broad-shouldered and still healthy-looking, was drunk; he would have gone to bed long ago, but he had a bottle in his pocket and was afraid his comrades in the hut would ask him for a drink of vodka. The Tartar was worn out and ill, and, wrapping himself in his rags, he talked about how good it was in the province of Simbirsk, and what a beautiful and clever wife he had left at home. He was not more than twenty-five, and in the firelight his pale, sickly face and woebegone expression made him seem like a boy.

"Well, this is no paradise, of course," said Preacher. "You can see for yourself: water, bare banks, nothing but clay wherever you look. . . . It's long past Easter and there's still ice on the river . . . and this morning there was snow."

"Bad! Bad!" said the Tartar, surveying the landscape with dismay.

A few yards away the dark, cold river flowed, growling and sluicing against the pitted clay banks as it sped on to the distant sea. At the edge of the bank loomed a capacious barge, which ferrymen call a *karbas*. Far away on the opposite bank crawling snakes of fire were dying down then reappearing—last year's grass being burned. Beyond the snakes there was darkness again. Little blocks of ice could be heard knocking against the barge. It was cold and damp. . . .

The Tartar glanced at the sky. There were as many stars as there were at home, the same blackness, but something was lacking. At home, in the province of Simbirsk, the stars and the sky seemed altogether different.

"Bad! Bad!" he repeated.

"You'll get used to it!" said Preacher with a laugh. "You're still young and foolish—the milk's hardly dry on your lips—and in your foolishness you think there's no one more unfortunate than you, but the time will come when you'll say to yourself: may God give everyone such a life. Just look at me. In a week's time the floods will be over and we'll launch the ferry; you'll all go

IN EXILE First published in 1892. Translated from the Russian by Ann Dunnigan. Although old Semyon in the story comes from Kursk, about three hundred miles south of Moscow, and the young Tartar from Simbirsk (now named Ulyanovsk), only about five hundred miles to the east, the Tartar, whose native tongue is Turkish-related, can talk to Semyon only in broken Russian. Siberia, under the czars (as under the Soviets), was a place for sending exiles and criminals. Anton Chekhov (1860-1904), though he earned a medical degree from the University of Moscow, pursued writing as his main career. In 1890 he made a hazardous ten-thousand mile trip by river boat and carriage across Siberia to the Pacific, writing about his experiences for a newspaper. Near Omsk he was forced to spend one night at a ferry shelter when the boatmen would not take him across the flooded river because of dangerous winds. For information on Russian names, see the note on page 471.

gadding about Siberia, while I stay here, going back and forth, from one bank to the other. For twenty-two years now that's what I've been doing. Day and night. The pike and the salmon under the water and me on it. That's all I want. God give everyone such a life."

The Tartar threw some brushwood onto the fire, lay down closer to it, and said, "My father is sick man. When he dies, my mother, my wife, will come here. Have promised."

"And what do you want a mother and a wife for?" asked Preacher. "Just foolishness, brother. It's the devil stirring you up, blast his soul! Don't listen to him, the Evil One! Don't give in to him. When he goes on about women, spite him: I don't want them! When he talks to you about freedom, you stand up to him: I don't want it! I want nothing! No father, no mother, no wife, no freedom, no house nor home! I want nothing, damn their souls!"

Preacher took a swig at the bottle and went on, "I'm no simple peasant, brother; I don't come from the servile class; I'm a deacon's son, and when I was free I lived in Kursk, and used to go around in a frock coat; but now I've brought myself to such a point that I can sleep naked on the ground and eat grass. And God give everyone such a life. I don't want anything. I'm not afraid of anyone, and the way I see it, there's no man richer or freer than I am. When they sent me here from Russia, from the very first day I jibbed: I want nothing! The devil was at me about my wife, about my kin, about freedom, but I told him: I want nothing! And I stuck to it; and here, you see, I live well, I don't complain. But if anyone humors the devil and listens to him even once, he's lost, no salvation for him. He'll be stuck fast in the bog, up to his ears, and he'll never get out.

"It's not only the likes of you, foolish peasants, that are lost, but even the well-born and educated. Fifteen years ago they sent a gentleman here from Russia. He forged a will or something—wouldn't share with his brothers. It was said he was a prince or a baron, but maybe he was only an official, who knows? Well, the gentleman came here, and the first thing, he bought himself a house and land in Mukhortinskoe. 'I want to live by my own labor,' says he, 'in the sweat of my brow, because I'm no longer a gentleman, but an exile.'. . . 'Well,' says I, 'may God help you, that's the right thing.' He was a young man then, a hustler, always on the move; he used to do the mowing himself, catch fish, ride sixty versts on horseback. But here was the trouble: from the very first year he began riding to Gyrino to the post office. He used to stand on my ferry and sigh, 'Ah, Semyon, for a long time now they haven't sent me any money from home.' . . . 'You don't need money, Vasily Sergeich. What good is it? Throw off the past, forget it as if it had never happened, as if it was only a dream, and start life afresh. Don't listen to the devil,' I tell him, 'he'll bring you to no good; he'll tighten the noose. Now you want money,' says I, 'and in a little while, before you know it, you'll want something else, and then more and more. But,' says I, 'if you want to be happy, the very first thing is not to want anything.' Yes. . . .'And if fate has cruelly wronged you and me,' says I, 'it's no good going down on your knees to her and asking her favor; you have to spurn her and laugh at her, otherwise she'll laugh at you.' That's what I said to him. . . .

"Two years later I ferried him over to this side, and he was rubbing his hands together and laughing. 'I'm going to Gyrino,' says he, 'to meet my wife. She has taken pity on me and come here. She's so kind and good!' He was panting with joy. Next day he comes with his wife. A young, beautiful lady in a hat, carrying a baby girl in her arms. And plenty of baggage of all sorts. My Vasily Sergeich was spinning around her; couldn't take his eyes off her; couldn't praise her enough. 'Yes, brother Semyon, even in Siberia people can live!' . . . 'Well,' thinks I, 'just you wait; better not rejoice too soon.' . . . And from that time on, almost every week he went to Gyrino to find out if money had been sent from Russia. As for money—it took plenty! 'It's for my sake that her youth and beauty are going to ruin here in Siberia,' he says, 'sharing with me my bitter fate, and for this,' he says, 'I ought to provide her with every diversion.' To make it more cheerful for his lady he took up with the officials and with all sorts of riff-raff. And there had to be food and drink for this crowd, of course, and they must have a piano, and a fuzzy little lap dog on the sofa—may it croak! . . . Luxury, in short, indulgence. The lady did not stay with him long. How could she? Clay, water, cold, no vegetables for you, no fruit; uneducated and drunken people all around, no manners at all, and she a pampered lady from the capital. . . . Naturally, she grew tired of it. Besides, her husband, say what you like, was no longer a gentleman, but an exile—not exactly an honor.

"Three years later, I remember, on the eve of the Assumption, someone shouted from the other side. I went over in the ferry, and what do I see but the lady—all muffled up, and with her a young gentleman, an official. There was a troika. . . . And after I ferried them across, they got in it and vanished into thin air! That was the last that was seen of them. Toward morning Vasily Sergeich galloped up to the ferry. 'Didn't my wife pass this way, Semyon, with a gentleman in spectacles?' . . . 'She did,' says I. 'Seek the wind in the fields!' He galloped off in pursuit of them, and didn't stop for five days and five nights. Afterwards, when I took him over to the other side, he threw himself down on the ferry, beat his head against the planks, and howled. 'So that's how it is,' says I. . . . I laughed and recalled to him: 'Even in Siberia people can live!' And he beat his head all the more.

"After that he began to long for freedom. His wife had slipped away to Russia, so, naturally, he was drawn there, both to see her and to rescue her from her lover. And, my friend, he took to galloping off every day, either to the post office or the authorities; he kept sending in petitions, and presenting them personally, asking to be pardoned so he could go back home; and he used to tell how he had spent some two hundred rubles on telegrams alone. He sold his land, and mortgaged his house to the Jews. He grew gray, stooped, and yellow in the face, as if he was consumptive. He'd talk to you and go: khe-khe-khe . . . and there would be tears in his eyes. He struggled with those petitions for eight years, but now he has recovered his spirits and is more cheerful: he's thought up a new indulgence. His daughter, you see, has grown up. He keeps an eye on her, dotes on her. And, to tell the truth, she's all right, a pretty little thing, black-browed, and with a lively disposition. Every Sunday he goes to church with her in Gyrino. Side by side they stand on the ferry, she laughing and he not taking his eyes off her. 'Yes, Semyon,' says he, 'even in Siberia people can live. Even in Siberia there is happiness. Look,' says he, 'see what a daughter I've got! I suppose you wouldn't find another like her if you went a thousand versts.'. . . 'Your daughter,' says I, 'is a fine young lady, that's true, certainly. . . .' But I think to myself: Wait a while. . . . The girl is young, her blood is dancing, she wants to live, and what life is there here? And, my friend, she did begin to fret. . . . She withered and withered, wasted away, fell ill; and now she's completely worn out. Consumption.

"That's your Siberian happiness for you, the pestilence take it! That's how people can live in Siberia! . . . He's taken to running after doctors and taking them home with him. As soon as he hears that there's a doctor or quack two or three hundred versts away, he goes to fetch him. A terrible lot of money has been spent on doctors; to my way of thinking, it would have been better to spend it on drink. . . . She'll die anyway. She's certain to die, and then he'll be completely lost. He'll hang himself from grief, or run away to Russia—that's sure. He'll run away, they'll catch him, there'll be a trial, and then hard labor; they'll give him a taste of the lash. . . ."

"Good, good," muttered the Tartar, shivering with cold.

"What's good?" asked Preacher.

"Wife and daughter. . . . Let hard labor, let suffer; he saw his wife and daughter. . . . You say: want nothing. But nothing is bad! Wife was with him three years—God gave him that. Nothing is bad; three years is good. How you not understand?"

Shivering and stuttering, straining to pick out the Russian words, of which he knew so few, the Tartar said God forbid one should fall sick and die in a strange land, and be buried in the cold, sodden earth; that if his wife came to him even for one day, even for one hour, he would be willing to accept any torture whatsoever, and thank God for it. Better one day of happiness than nothing.

After that he again described the beautiful and clever wife he had left at home; then, clutching his head with both hands, he began crying and assuring Semyon that he was innnocent and had been falsely accused. His two brothers and his uncle stole some horses from a peasant, and beat the old man till he was half dead, and the commune had not judged fairly, but had contrived a sentence by which all three brothers were sent to Siberia, while the uncle, a rich man, remained at home.

"You'll get u-u-used to it!" said Semyon.

The Tartar relapsed into silence and fixed his tearful eyes on the fire; his face expressed bewilderment and fright, as though he still did not understand why he was here in the dark, in the damp, among strangers, instead of in the province of Simbirsk. Preacher lay down near the fire, chuckled at something, and began singing in an undertone.

"What joy has she with her father?" he said a little later. "He loves her, she's a consolation to him, it's true; but you have to mind your p's and q's with him, brother: he's a strict old man, a severe old man. And strictness is not what young girls want. . . . They want petting and ha-ha-ha and ho-ho-ho, scents and pomades! Yes. . . . Ekh, life, life!" sighed Semyon, getting up with difficulty. "The vodka's all gone, so it's time to sleep. Eh? I'm going, my boy."

Left alone, the Tartar put more brushwood onto the fire, lay down, and, looking into the blaze, began thinking of his native village, and of his wife: if she would come only for a month, even for a day, then, if she liked, she might go back again. Better a month or even a day than nothing. But if she kept her promise and came, how could he provide for her? Where could she live?

"If not something to eat, how you live?" the Tartar asked aloud.

He was paid only ten kopecks for working at the oars a day and a night; the passengers gave him tips, it was true, but the ferrymen shared everything among themselves, giving nothing to the Tartar, but only making fun of him. And he was hungry, cold, and frightened from want. . . . Now, when his whole body was shivering and aching, he ought to go into the hut and lie down to sleep, but he had nothing there to cover himself with, and it was colder there than on the river bank; here, too, he had nothing to put over him, but at least he could make a fire. . . .

In another week, when the floods had subsided and the ferry could sail, none of the ferrymen except Semyon would be needed, and the Tartar would begin going from village to village, looking for work and begging alms. His wife was only seventeen years old; beautiful, pampered, shy—could she possibly go from village to village, her face unveiled, begging? No, even to think of it was dreadful. . . .

It was already growing light; the barge, the bushes of rose-willow, and the ripples on the water were clearly distinguishable, and looking back there was the steep clay precipice, below it the little hut thatched with brown straw, and above clung the huts of the villagers. The cocks were already crowing in the village.

The red clay precipice, the barge, the river, the strange, unkind people, hunger, cold, illness—perhaps all this did not exist in reality. Probably it was all a dream, thought the Tartar. He felt that he was asleep, and hearing his own snoring. . . . Of course, he was at home in the province of Simbirsk, and he had only to call his wife by name for her to answer, and in the next room his mother. . . . However, what awful dreams there are! Why? The Tartar smiled and opened his eyes. What river was this? The Volga?

"Bo-o-at!" someone shouted from the other side. "Kar-ba-a-s!"

The Tartar woke up and went to wake his comrades, to row over to the other side. Putting on their torn sheepskins as they came, the ferrymen appeared on the bank, swearing in hoarse, sleepy voices, and shivering from the cold. After their sleep, the river, from which there came a piercing gust of cold air, evidently struck them as revolting and sinister. They were not quick to jump into the barge. The Tartar and the three ferrymen took up the long, broad-bladed oars, which looked like crabs' claws in the darkness. Semyon leaned his belly against the long tiller. The shouting from the other side continued, and two shots were fired from a revolver; the man probably thought that the ferrymen were asleep or had gone off to the village tavern.

"All right, plenty of time!" said Preacher in the tone of a man who is convinced that there is no need to hurry in this world—that it makes no difference, really, and nothing will come of it.

The heavy, clumsy barge drew away from the bank and floated between the rose-willows; and only because the willows slowly receded was it possible to see that the barge was not standing still but moving. The ferrymen plied the oars evenly, in unison; Preacher hung over the tiller on his belly, and, describing an arc in the air, flew from one side of the boat to the other. In the darkness it looked as if the men were sitting on some antideluvian animal with long paws, and sailing to a cold, bleak land, the very one of which we sometimes dream in nightmares.

They passed beyond the willows and floated out into the open. The rhythmic thump and splash of the oars were now audible on the further shore, and someone shouted, "Hurry! Hurry!" Another ten minutes passed and the barge bumped heavily against the landing stage.

"And it keeps coming down, and coming down!" muttered Semyon, wiping the snow from his face. "Where it comes from, God only knows!"

On the other side stood a thin old man of medium height wearing a jacket lined with fox fur and a white lambskin cap. He was standing at a little distance from his horses and not moving; he had a concentrated, morose expression, as if, trying to remember something, he had grown angry with his unyielding memory. When Semyon went up to him with a smile and took off his cap, he said, "I'm hastening to Anastasyevka. My daughter is worse again, and they say there's a new doctor at Anastasyevka."

They dragged the tarantass° onto the barge and rowed back. The man, whom Semyon called Vasily Sergeich, stood motionless all the way back, his thick lips tightly compressed, his eyes fixed on one spot; when the coachman asked permission to smoke in his presence, he made no reply, as if he had not heard. And Semyon, hanging over the tiller on his belly, glanced mockingly at him and said, "Even in Siberia people can live. Li-i-ve!"

There was a triumphant expression on Preacher's face, as if he had proved something and was rejoicing that it had turned out exactly as he had surmised. The helpless, unhappy look of the man in the fox-lined jacket evidently afforded him great satisfaction.

"It's muddy driving now, Vasily Sergeich," he said when the horses were harnessed on the bank. "You'd better have waited a week or two till it gets

---

tarantass: a heavy four-wheeled carriage

drier. . . . Or else not have gone at all. . . . If there were any sense in going, but, as you yourself know, people have been driving about for ever and ever, by day and by night, and there's never any sense in it. That's the truth!"

Vasily Sergeich tipped him without a word, got into the tarantass, and drove off.

"See there, he's gone galloping off for a doctor!" said Semyon, shrinking with cold. "Yes, looking for a real doctor is like chasing the wind in the fields, or catching the devil by the tail, damn your soul! What freaks! Lord forgive me, a sinner!"

The Tartar went up to Preacher and, looking at him with hatred and abhorrence, trembling, mixing Tartar words with his broken Russian, said, "He is good—good. You bad! You bad! Gentleman is good soul, excellent, and you beast, you bad! Gentleman alive and you dead. . . . God created man to be live, be joyful, be sad and sorrow, but you want nothing. . . .You not live, you stone, clay! Stone want nothing and you want nothing. . . . You stone—and God not love you, love gentleman!"

Everyone laughed; the Tartar frowned scornfully and, with a gesture of despair, wrapped himself in his rags and went to the fire. Semyon and the ferrymen trailed off to the hut.

"It's cold," said one of the ferrymen hoarsely as he stretched out on the straw that covered the damp floor.

"Well, it's not warm!" one of the others agreed. "It's a hard life!"

They all lay down. The door was blown open by the wind, and snow drifted into the hut. No one felt like getting up and closing the door; it was cold and they were lazy.

"I'm all right!" said Semyon, falling asleep. "God give everyone such a life."

"You're a hard case, we know that. Even the devils won't take you!"

From outside there came sounds like the howling of a dog.

"What's that? Who's there?"

"It's the Tartar crying."

"He'll get u-u-used to it!" said Semyon, and instantly fell asleep.

Soon the others fell asleep too. And the door remained unclosed.

Leo Tolstoy

THE DEATH OF IVAN ILYCH

1

During an interval in the Melvinski trial in the large building of the Law Courts, the members and public prosecutor met in Ivan Egorovich Shebek's private room, where the conversation turned on the celebrated Krasovski case. Fëdor Vasilievich warmly maintained that it was not subject to their jurisdiction, Ivan Egorovich maintained the contrary, while Peter Ivanovich, not having entered into the discussion at the start, took no part in it but looked through the *Gazette* which had just been handed in.

"Gentlemen," he said, "Ivan Ilych has died!"

"You don't say so!"

"Here, read it yourself," replied Peter Ivanovich, handing Fëdor Vasilievich the paper still damp from the press. Surrounded by a black border were the words: "Praskovya Fëdorovna Golovina, with profound sorrow, informs relatives and friends of the demise of her beloved husband Ivan Ilych Golovin, Member of the Court of Justice, which occurred on February the 4th of this year 1882. The funeral will take place on Friday at one o'clock in the afternoon."

Ivan Ilych had been a colleague of the gentlemen present and was liked by them all. He had been ill for some weeks with an illness said to be incurable. His post had been kept open for him, but there had been conjectures that in the case of his death Alexeev might receive his appointment, and that either Vinnikov or Shtabel would succeed Alexeev. So on receiving the news of Ivan Ilych's death the first thought of each of the gentlemen in that private room was of the changes and promotions it might occasion among themselves or their acquaintances.

"I shall be sure to get Shtabel's place or Vinnikov's," thought Fëdor

---

THE DEATH OF IVAN ILYCH   First published in 1886. Translated from the Russian by Louise and Aylmer Maude. Leo Tolstoy (1828-1910), a Russian nobleman, after writing his two great novels *War and Peace* (1869) and *Anna Karenina* (1877), underwent a period of spiritual turmoil in which he was obsessed with answering the question, What is the meaning of life? The crisis, which reached a head in 1879, resulted in a radical acceptance and interpretation of the teaching of Christ: one must do good for others and not live for oneself. In 1890, no longer willing to own property, he divided his large estate among his wife and nine children, gave up his royalties, and tried to live like a peasant. His new principles brought him into conflict with his family, the government, and the Church, which in 1901 excommunicated him.

A note on Russian names: In Russia, persons are identified by three names—a given name (such as Ivan), a patronymic middle name (Ilych), and a family or surname (Golovin). The patronymic indicates one's father's given name, and for men is formed by adding the suffix -ch, or -ich, or -ovich; for women, the suffixes are -evna or -ovna. "Ivan Ilych" is thus Ivan, son of Ilya Golovin. Ivan Ilych's wife has the feminine surname Golovina, and is the daughter of a man named Fëdor. It was customary, even in informal address, to call a person by both the given name and the patronymic, as a sign of politeness. Children were usually called by nicknames derived from the given name, of which (as in English) there are many. Ivan Ilych as a child was called Vanya; and his schoolboy son, Vladimir Ivanich Golovin, is called Volodya by his mother and Vasya by his father. Among intimates, also, given names or nicknames are used. Thus Ivan Ilych is called Jean by his wife. (Jean is the French equivalent of Ivan—as John is the English—and the wife's use of the French form reflects the nineteenth-century Russian upper-class belief that to be civilized was to know French and French culture.) Peasants and lower servants were generally called by their given names—Peter, the footman; Gerasim, the butler's assistant.

Vasilievich. "I was promised that long ago, and the promotion means an extra eight hundred rubles a year for me beside the allowance."

"Now I must apply for my brother-in-law's transfer from Kaluga," thought Peter Ivanovich. "My wife will be very glad, and then she won't be able to say that I never do anything for her relations."

"I thought he would never leave his bed again," said Peter Ivanovich aloud. "It's very sad."

"But what really was the matter with him?"

"The doctors couldn't say—at least they could, but each of them said something different. When last I saw him I thought he was getting better."

"And I haven't been to see him since the holidays. I always meant to go."

"Had he any property?"

"I think his wife had a little—but something quite trifling."

"We shall have to go to see her, but they live so terribly far away."

"Far away from you, you mean. Everything's far away from your place."

"You see, he never can forgive my living on the other side of the river," said Peter Ivanovich, smiling at Shebek. Then, still talking of the distances between different parts of the city, they returned to the Court.

Besides considerations as to the possible transfers and promotions likely to result from Ivan Ilych's death, the mere fact of the death of a near acquaintance aroused, as usual, in all who heard of it the complacent feeling that, "it is he who is dead and not I."

Each one thought or felt, "Well, he's dead but I'm alive!" But the more intimate of Ivan Ilych's acquaintances, his so-called friends, could not help thinking also that they would now have to fulfill the very tiresome demands of propriety by attending the funeral service and paying a visit of condolence to the widow.

Fëdor Vasilievich and Peter Ivanovich had been his nearest acquaintances. Peter Ivanovich had studied law with Ivan Ilych and had considered himself to be under obligations to him.

Having told his wife at dinner-time of Ivan Ilych's death and of his conjecture that it might be possible to get her brother transferred to their circuit, Peter Ivanovich sacrificed his usual nap, put on his evening clothes, and drove to Ivan Ilych's house.

At the entrance stood a carriage and two cabs. Leaning against the wall in the hall downstairs near the cloak-stand was a coffin-lid covered with cloth of gold, ornamented with gold cord and tassels, that had been polished up with metal powder. Two ladies in black were taking off their fur cloaks. Peter Ivanovich recognized one of them as Ivan Ilych's sister, but the other was a stranger to him. His colleague Schwartz was just coming downstairs, but on seeing Peter Ivanovich enter he stopped and winked at him, as if to say: "Ivan Ilych has made a mess of things—not like you and me."

Schwartz's face with his Piccadilly whiskers and his slim figure in evening dress, had as usual an air of elegant solemnity which contrasted with the playfulness of his character and had a special piquancy here, or so it seemed to Peter Ivanovich.

Peter Ivanovich allowed the ladies to precede him and slowly followed them upstairs. Schwartz did not come down but remained where he was, and Peter Ivanovich understood that he wanted to arrange where they should play bridge that evening. The ladies went upstairs to the widow's room, and Schwartz with seriously compressed lips but a playful look in his eyes, indicated by a twist of his eyebrows the room to the right where the body lay.

Peter Ivanovich, like everyone else on such occasions, entered feeling uncertain what he would have to do. All he knew was that at such times it is always safe to cross oneself. But he was not quite sure whether one should make obeisances while doing so. He therefore adopted a middle course. On entering the room he began crossing himself and made a slight movement resembling a bow. At the same time, as far as the motion of his head and arm allowed, he surveyed the room. Two young men—apparently nephews, one of whom was a high-school pupil—were leaving the room, crossing themselves as they did so. An old woman was standing motionless, and a lady with strangely arched eyebrows was saying something to her in a whisper. A vigorous, resolute Church Reader, in a frock-coat, was reading something in a loud voice with an expression that precluded any contradiction. The butler's assistant, Gerasim, stepping lightly in front of Peter Ivanovich, was strewing something on the floor. Noticing this, Peter Ivanovich was immediately aware of a faint odor of a decomposing body.

The last time he had called on Ivan Ilych, Peter Ivanovich had seen Gerasim in the study. Ivan Ilych had been particularly fond of him and he was performing the duty of a sick nurse.

Peter Ivanovich continued to make the sign of the cross slightly inclining his head in an intermediate direction between the coffin, the Reader, and the icons on the table in a corner of the room. Afterwards, when it seemed to him that this movement of his arm in crossing himself had gone on too long, he stopped and began to look at the corpse.

The dead man lay, as dead men always lie, in a specially heavy way, his rigid limbs sunk in the soft cushions of the coffin, with the head forever bowed on the pillow. His yellow waxen brow with bald patches over his sunken temples was thrust up in the way peculiar to the dead, the protruding nose seeming to press on the upper lip. He was much changed and had grown even thinner since Peter Ivanovich had last seen him, but, as is always the case with the dead, his face was handsomer and above all more dignified than when he was alive. The expression on the face said that what was necessary had been accomplished, and accomplished rightly. Besides this there was in that expression a reproach and a warning to the living. This warning seemed to Peter Ivanovich out of place, or at least not applicable to him. He felt a certain discomfort and so he hurriedly crossed himself once more and turned and went out of the door—too hurriedly and too regardless of propriety, as he himself was aware.

Schwartz was waiting for him in the adjoining room with legs spread wide apart and both hands toying with his top-hat behind his back. The mere sight of that playful, well-groomed, and elegant figure refreshed Peter Ivanovich.

He felt that Schwartz was above all these happenings and would not surrender to any depressing influences. His very look said that this incident of a church service for Ivan Ilych could not be sufficient reason for infringing the order of the session—in other words, that it would certainly not prevent his unwrapping a new pack of cards and shuffling them that evening while a footman placed four fresh candles on the table: in fact, that there was no reason for supposing that this incident would hinder their spending the evening agreeably. Indeed he said this in a whisper as Peter Ivanovich passed him, proposing that they should meet for a game at Fëdor Vasilievich's. But apparently Peter Ivanovich was not destined to play bridge that evening. Praskovya Fëdorovna (a short, fat woman who despite all efforts to the contrary had continued to broaden steadily from her shoulders downwards and who had the same extraordinary arched eyebrows as the lady who had been standing by the coffin), dressed all in black, her head covered with lace, came out of her own room with some other ladies, conducted them to the room where the dead body lay, and said: "The service will begin immediately. Please go in."

Schwartz, making an indefinite bow, stood still, evidently neither accepting nor declining this invitation. Praskovya Fëdorovna, recognizing Peter Ivanovich, sighed, went close to him, took his hand, and said: "I know you were a true friend to Ivan Ilych . . . " and looked at him awaiting some suitable response. And Peter Ivanovich knew that, just as it had been the right thing to cross himself in that room, so what he had to do here was to press her hand, sigh, and say, "Believe me. . . . " So he did all this and as he did it felt that the desired result had been achieved: that both he and she were touched.

"Come with me. I want to speak to you before it begins," said the widow. "Give me your arm."

Peter Ivanovich gave her his arm and they went to the inner rooms, passing Schwartz, who winked at Peter Ivanovich compassionately.

"That does for our bridge! Don't object if we find another player. Perhaps you can cut in when you do escape," said his playful look.

Peter Ivanovich sighed still more deeply and despondently, and Praskovya Fëdorovna pressed his arm gratefully. When they reached the drawing-room, upholstered in pink cretonne and lighted by a dim lamp, they sat down at the table—she on a sofa and Peter Ivanovich on a low pouffe, the springs of which yielded spasmodically under his weight. Praskovya Fëdorovna had been on the point of warning him to take another seat, but felt that such a warning was out of keeping with her present condition and so changed her mind. As he sat down on the pouffe Peter Ivanovich recalled how Ivan Ilych had arranged this room and had consulted him regarding this pink cretonne with green leaves. The whole room was full of furniture and knick-knacks, and on her way to the sofa the lace of the widow's black shawl caught on the carved edge of the table. Peter Ivanovich rose to detach it, and the springs of the pouffe, relieved of his weight, rose also and gave him a push. The widow began detaching her shawl herself, and Peter Ivanovich again sat down, suppressing the rebellious springs of the pouffe under him. But the widow had not quite freed herself and Peter Ivanovich got up again, and again the pouffe rebelled and even creaked. When this was all over she took out a clean cambric handkerchief and began to weep. The episode with the shawl and the struggle with the pouffe had cooled Peter Ivanovich's emotions and he sat there with a sullen look on his face. This awkward situation was interrupted by Sokolov, Ivan Ilych's butler, who came to report that the plot in the cemetery that Praskovya Fëdorovna had chosen would cost two hundred rubles. She stopped weeping and, looking at Peter Ivanovich with the air of a victim, remarked in French that it was very hard for her. Peter Ivanovich made a silent gesture signifying his full conviction that it must indeed be so.

"Please smoke," she said in a magnanimous yet crushed voice, and turned to discuss with Sokolov the price of the plot for the grave.

Peter Ivanovich while lighting his cigarette heard her inquiring very circumstantially into the prices of different plots in the cemetery and finally decide which she would take. When that was done she gave instructions about engaging the choir. Sokolov then left the room.

"I look after everything myself," she told Peter Ivanovich, shifting the albums that lay on the table; and noticing that the table was endangered by his cigarette-ash, she immediately passed him an ash-tray, saying as she did so: "I consider it an affectation to say that my grief prevents my attending to practical affairs. On the contrary, if anything can—I won't say console me, but—distract me, it is seeing to everything concerning him." She again took out her handkerchief as if preparing to cry, but suddenly, as if mastering her feeling, she shook herself and began to speak calmly. "But there is something I want to talk to you about."

Peter Ivanovich bowed, keeping control of the springs of the pouffe, which immediately began quivering under him.

"He suffered terribly the last few days."

"Did he?" said Peter Ivanovich.

"Oh, terribly! He screamed unceasingly, not for minutes but for hours. For the last three days he screamed incessantly. It was unendurable. I cannot understand how I bore it; you could hear him three rooms off. Oh, what I have suffered!"

"Is it possible that he was conscious all that time?" asked Peter Ivanovich.

"Yes," she whispered. "To the last moment. He took leave of us a quarter of an hour before he died, and asked us to take Volodya away."

The thought of the sufferings of this man he had known so intimately, first as a merry little boy, then as a school-mate, and later as a grown-up colleague, suddenly struck Peter Ivanovich with horror, despite an unpleasant consciousness of his own and this woman's dissimulation. He again saw that brow, and that nose pressing down on the lip, and felt afraid for himself.

"Three days of frightful suffering and then death! Why, that might suddenly, at any time, happen to me," he thought, and for a moment felt terrified. But—he did not himself know how—the customary reflection at once occurred to him that this had happened to Ivan Ilych and not to him, and that it should not and could not happen to him, and to think that it could would be yielding to depression which he ought not to do, as Schwartz's expression plainly showed. After which reflection Peter Ivanovich felt reassured, and began to ask with interest about the details of Ivan Ilych's death, as though death was an accident natural to Ivan Ilych but certainly not to himself.

After many details of the really dreadful physical suffering Ivan Ilych had endured (which details he learnt only from the effect those sufferings had produced on Praskovya Fëdorovna's nerves) the widow apparently found it necessary to get to business.

"Oh, Peter Ivanovich, how hard it is! How terribly, terribly hard!" and she again began to weep.

Peter Ivanovich sighed and waited for her to finish blowing her nose. When she had done so he said, "Believe me . . . " and she again began talking and brought out what was evidently her chief concern with him—namely, to question him as to how she could obtain a grant of money from the government on the occasion of her husband's death. She made it appear that she was asking Peter Ivanovich's advice about her pension, but he soon saw that she already knew about that to the minutest detail, more even than he did himself. She knew how much could be got out of the government in consequence of her husband's death, but wanted to find out whether she could not possibly extract something more. Peter Ivanovich tried to think of some means of doing so, but after reflecting for a while and, out of propriety, condemning the government for its niggardliness, he said he thought that nothing more could be got. Then she sighed and evidently began to devise means of getting rid of her visitor. Noticing this, he put out his cigarette, rose, pressed her hand, and went out into the anteroom.

In the dining-room where the clock stood that Ivan Ilych had liked so much and had bought at an antique shop, Peter Ivanovich met a priest and a few acquaintances who had come to attend the service, and he recognized Ivan Ilych's daughter, a handsome young woman. She was in black and her slim figure appeared slimmer than ever. She had a gloomy, determined, almost angry expression, and bowed to Peter Ivanovich as though he were in some way to blame. Behind her, with the same offended look, stood a wealthy young man, an examining magistrate, whom Peter Ivanovich also knew and who was her fiancé, as he had heard. He bowed mournfully to them and was about to pass into the death-chamber, when from under the stairs appeared the figure of Ivan Ilych's schoolboy son, who was extremely like his father. He seemed a little like Ivan Ilych, such as Peter Ivanovich remembered when they studied law together. His tear-stained eyes had in them the look that is seen in the eyes of boys thirteen or fourteen who are not pure-minded. When he saw Peter Ivanovich he scowled morosely and shamefacedly. Peter Ivanovich nodded to him and entered the death-chamber. The service began:

candles, groans, incense, tears, and sobs. Peter Ivanovich stood looking gloomily down at his feet. He did not look once at the dead man, did not yield to any depressing influence, and was one of the first to leave the room. There was no one in the anteroom, but Gerasim darted out of the dead man's room, rummaged with his strong hands among the fur coats to find Peter Ivanovich's and helped him on with it.

"Well, friend Gerasim," said Peter Ivanovich, so as to say something. "It's a sad affair, isn't it?"

"It's God's will. We shall all come to it some day," said Gerasim, displaying his teeth—the even, white teeth of a healthy peasant—and, like a man in the thick of urgent work, he briskly opened the front door, called the coachman, helped Peter Ivanovich into the sledge, and sprang back to the porch as if in readiness for what he had to do next.

Peter Ivanovich found the fresh air particularly pleasant after the smell of incense, the dead body, and carbolic acid.

"Where to, sir?" asked the coachman.

"It's not too late even now. . . . I'll call round on Fëdor Vasilievich."

He accordingly drove there and found them just finishing the first rubber, so that it was quite convenient for him to cut in.

2

Ivan Ilych's life had been most simple and most ordinary and therefore most terrible.

He had been a member of the Court of Justice, and died at the age of forty-five. His father had been an official who after serving in various ministries and departments in Petersburg had made the sort of career which brings men to positions from which by reason of their long service they cannot be dismissed, though they are obviously unfit to hold any responsible position, and for whom therefore posts are especially created, which though fictitious carry salaries of from six to ten thousand rubles that are not fictitious, and in receipt of which they live on to a great age.

Such was the Privy Councillor and superfluous member of various superfluous institutions, Ilya Epimovich Golovin.

He had three sons, of whom Ivan Ilych was second. The eldest son was following in his father's footsteps only in another department, and was already approaching that stage in the service at which a similar sinecure would be reached. The third son was a failure. He had ruined his prospects in a number of positions and was now serving in the railway department. His father and brothers, and still more their wives, not merely disliked meeting him, but avoided remembering his existence unless compelled to do so. His sister had married Baron Greff, a Petersburg official of her father's type. Ivan Ilych was *le phénix de la famille*° as people said. He was neither as cold and

le phénix de la famille: the marvel of the family

formal as his elder brother nor as wild as the younger, but was a happy mean between them—an intelligent, polished, lively and agreeable man. He had studied with his younger brother at the School of Law, but the latter had failed to complete the course and was expelled when he was in the fifth class. Ivan Ilych finished the course well. Even when he was at the School of Law he was just what he remained for the rest of his life: a capable, cheerful, good-natured, and sociable man, though strict in the fulfillment of what he considered to be his duty: and he considered his duty to be what was so considered by those in authority. Neither as a boy nor as a man was he a toady, but from early youth was by nature attracted to people of high station as a fly is drawn to the light, assimilating their ways and views of life and establishing friendly relations with them. All the enthusiasms of childhood and youth passed without leaving much trace on him; he succumbed to sensuality, to vanity, and latterly among the highest classes to liberalism, but always within limits which his instinct unfailingly indicated to him as correct.

At school he had done things which had formerly seemed to him very horrid and made him feel disgusted with himself when he did them; but when later on he saw that such actions were done by people of good position and that they did not regard them as wrong, he was able not exactly to regard them as right, but to forget about them entirely or not be at all troubled at remembering them.

Having graduated from the School of Law and qualified for the tenth rank of the civil service, and having received money from his father for his equipment, Ivan Ilych ordered himself clothes at Scharmer's, the fashionable tailor, hung a medallion inscribed *respice finem*° on his watch-chain, took leave of his professor and the prince who was patron of the school, had a farewell dinner with his comrades at Donon's first-class restaurant, and with his new and fashionable portmanteau, linen, clothes, shaving and other toilet appliances, and a traveling rug, all purchased at the best shops, he set off for one of the provinces where, through his father's influence, he had been attached to the Governor as an official for special service.

In the province Ivan Ilych soon arranged as easy and agreeable a position for himself as he had had at the School of Law. He performed his official tasks, made his career, and at the same time amused himself pleasantly and decorously. Occasionally he paid official visits to country districts, where he behaved with dignity both to his superiors and inferiors, and performed the duties entrusted to him, which related chiefly to the sectarians,° with an exactness and incorruptible honesty of which he could not but feel proud.

In official matters, despite his youth and taste for frivolous gaiety, he was exceedingly reserved, punctilious, and even severe; but in society he was often amusing and witty, and always good-natured, correct in his manner, and *bon*

---

respice finem: look to the end
sectarians: Old Believers, dissenters from the modern church

enfant,° as the governor and his wife—with whom he was like one of the family—used to say of him.

In the province he had an affair with a lady who made advances to the elegant young lawyer, and there was also a milliner; and there were carousals with aides-de-camp who visited the district, and after-supper visits to a certain outlying street of doubtful reputation; and there was too some obsequiousness to his chief and even to his chief's wife, but all this was done with such a tone of good breeding that no hard names could be applied to it. It all came under the heading of the French saying: *"Il faut que jeunesse se passe."*° It was all done with clean hands, in clean linen, with French phrases, and above all among people of the best society and consequently with the approval of people of rank.

So Ivan Ilych served for five years and then came a change in his official life. The new and reformed judicial institutions were introduced, and new men were needed. Ivan Ilych became such a new man. He was offered the post of examining magistrate, and he accepted it though the post was in another province and obliged him to give up the connections he had formed and to make new ones. His friends met to give him a send-off; they had a group-photograph taken and presented him with a silver cigarette-case, and he set off to his new post.

As examining magistrate Ivan Ilych was just as *comme il faut*° and decorous a man, inspiring general respect and capable of separating his official duties from his private life, as he had been when acting as an official on special service. His duties now as examining magistrate were far more interesting and attractive than before. In his former position it had been pleasant to wear an undress uniform made by Scharmer, and to pass through the crowd of petitioners and officials who were timorously awaiting an audience with the governor, and who envied him as with free and easy gait he went straight into his chief's private room to have a cup of tea and a cigarette with him. But not many people had then been directly dependent on him—only police officials and the sectarians when he went on special missions—and he liked to treat them politely, almost as comrades, as if he were letting them feel that he who had the power to crush them was treating them in this simple, friendly way. There were then but few such people. But now, as an examining magistrate, Ivan Ilych felt that everyone without exception, even the most important and self-satisfied, was in his power, and that he need only write a few words on a sheet of paper with a certain heading, and this or that important, self-satisfied person would be brought before him in the role of an accused person or a witness, and if he did not choose to allow him to sit down, would have to stand before him and answer his questions. Ivan Ilych never abused

bon enfant: a good child
Il faut que jeunesse se passe: You're only young once.
comme il faut: proper

his power; he tried on the contrary to soften its expression, but the consciousness of it and of the possibility of softening its effect, supplied the chief interest and attraction of his office. In his work itself, especially in his examinations, he very soon acquired a method of eliminating all considerations irrelevant to the legal aspect of the case, and reducing even the most complicated case to a form in which it would be presented on paper only in its externals, completely excluding his personal opinion of the matter, while above all observing every prescribed formality. The work was new and Ivan Ilych was one of the first men to apply the new Code of 1864.°

On taking up the post of examining magistrate in a new town, he made new acquaintances and connections, placed himself on a new footing, and assumed a somewhat different tone. He took up an attitude of rather dignified aloofness towards the provincial authorities, but picked out the best circle of legal gentlemen and wealthy gentry living in the town and assumed a tone of slight dissatisfaction with the government, of moderate liberalism, and of enlightened citizenship. At the same time, without at all altering the elegance of his toilet, he ceased shaving his chin and allowed his beard to grow as it pleased.

Ivan Ilych settled down very pleasantly in this new town. The society there, which inclined towards opposition to the Governor, was friendly, his salary was larger, and he began to play *vint*,° which he found added not a little to the pleasure of life, for he had a capacity for cards, played good-humoredly, and calculated rapidly and astutely, so that he usually won.

After living there for two years he met his future wife, Praskovya Fëdorovna Mikhel, who was the most attractive, clever, and brilliant girl of the set in which he moved, and among other amusements and relaxations from his labors as examining magistrate, Ivan Ilych established light and playful relations with her.

While he had been an offical on special service he had been accustomed to dance, but now as an examining magistrate it was exceptional for him to do so. If he danced now, he did it as if to show that though he served under the reformed order of things, and had reached the fifth official rank, yet when it came to dancing he could do it better than most people. So at the end of an evening he sometimes danced with Praskovya Fëdorovna, and it was chiefly during these dances that he captivated her. She fell in love with him. Ivan Ilych had at first no definite intention of marrying, but when the girl fell in love with him he said to himself: "Really, why shouldn't I marry?"

Praskovya Fëdorovna came of a good family, was not bad looking, and had some little property. Ivan Ilych might have aspired to a more brilliant match, but even this was good. He had his salary, and she, he hoped, would have an equal income. She was well connected, and was a sweet, pretty, and thoroughly correct young woman. To say that Ivan Ilych married because he

---

Code of 1864: reformed judicial procedures following the 1861 emancipation of the serfs
vint: a card game resembling bridge

fell in love with Praskovya Fëdorovna and found that she sympathized with his views of life would be as incorrect as to say that he married because his social circle approved of the match. He was swayed by both these considerations: the marriage gave him personal satisfaction, and at the same time it was considered the right thing by the most highly placed of his associates.

So Ivan Ilych got married.

The preparations for marriage and the beginning of married life, with its conjugal caresses, the new furniture, new crockery, and new linen, were very pleasant until his wife became pregnant—so that Ivan Ilych had begun to think that marriage would not impair the easy, agreeable, gay and always decorous character of his life, approved of by society and regarded by himself as natural, but would even improve it. But from the first months of his wife's pregnancy, something new, unpleasant, depressing, and unseemly, and from which there was no way of escape, unexpectedly showed itself.

His wife, without any reason—*de gaieté de coeur*° as Ivan Ilych expressed it to himself—began to disturb the pleasure and propriety of their life. She began to be jealous without any cause, expected him to devote his whole attention to her, found fault with everything, and made coarse and ill-mannered scenes.

At first Ivan Ilych hoped to escape from the unpleasantness of this state of affairs by the same easy and decorous relation to life that had served him heretofore: he tried to ignore his wife's disagreeable moods, continued to live in his usual easy and pleasant way, invited friends to his house for a game of cards, and also tried going out to his club or spending his evenings with friends. But one day his wife began upbraiding him so vigorously, using such coarse words, and continued to abuse him every time he did not fulfill her demands, so resolutely and with such evident determination not to give way till he submitted—that is, till he stayed at home and was bored just as she was—that he became alarmed. He now realized that matrimony—at any rate with Praskovya Fëdorovna—was not always conducive to the pleasures and amenities of life, but on the contrary often infringed both comfort and propriety, and that he must therefore entrench himself against such infringement. And Ivan Ilych began to seek for means of doing so. His official duties were the one thing that imposed upon Praskovya Fëdorovna, and by means of his official work and the duties attached to it he began struggling with his wife to secure his own independence.

With the birth of their child, the attempts to feed it and the various failures in doing so, and with the real and imaginary illnesses of mother and child, in which Ivan Ilych's sympathy was demanded but about which he understood nothing, the need for securing for himself an existence outside his family life became still more imperative.

As his wife grew more irritable and exacting and Ivan Ilych transferred the center of gravity of his life more and more to his official work, so did he grow to like his work better and became more ambitious than before.

de gaieté de coeur: out of sheer wantonness

Very soon, within a year of his wedding, Ivan Ilych had realized that marriage, though it may add some comforts to life, is in fact a very intricate and difficult affair towards which in order to perform one's duty, that is, to lead a decorous life approved of by society, one must adopt a definite attitude just as towards one's official duties.

And Ivan Ilych evolved such an attitude towards married life. He only required of it those conveniences—dinner at home, housewife, and bed—which it could give him, and above all that propriety of external forms required by public opinion. For the rest he looked for light-hearted pleasure and propriety, and was very thankful when he found them, but if he met with antagonism and querulousness he at once retired into his separate fenced-off world of official duties, where he found satisfaction.

Ivan Ilych was esteemed a good official, and after three years was made Assistant Public Prosecutor. His new duties, their importance, the possibility of indicting and imprisoning anyone he chose, the publicity his speeches received, and the success he had in all these things, made his work still more attractive.

More children came. His wife became more and more querulous and ill-tempered, but the attitude Ivan Ilych had adopted towards his home life rendered him almost impervious to her grumbling.

After seven years' service in that town he was transferred to another province as Public Prosecutor. They moved, but were short of money and his wife did not like the place they moved to. Though the salary was higher the cost of living was greater, besides which two of their children died and family life became still more unpleasant for him.

Praskovya Fëdorovna blamed her husband for every inconvenience they encountered in their new home. Most of the conversations between husband and wife, especially as to the children's education, led to topics which recalled former disputes, and those disputes were apt to flare up again at any moment. There remained only those rare periods of amorousness which still came to them at times but did not last long. These were islets at which they anchored for a while and then again set out upon that ocean of veiled hostility which showed itself in their aloofness from one another. This aloofness might have grieved Ivan Ilych had he considered that it ought not to exist, but he now regarded the position as normal, and even made it the goal at which he aimed in family life. His aim was to free himself more and more from those unpleasantnesses and to give them a semblance of harmlessness and propriety. He attained this by spending less and less time with his family, and when obliged to be at home he tried to safeguard his position by the presence of outsiders. The chief thing however was that he had his official duties. The whole interest of his life now centered in the official world and that interest absorbed him. The consciousness of his power, being able to ruin anybody he wished to ruin, the importance, even the external dignity of his entry into court, or meetings with his subordinates, his success with superiors and inferiors, and above all his masterly handling of cases, of which he was conscious—all this gave him pleasure and filled his life, together with chats with his colleagues, dinners, and bridge. So that on the whole Ivan Ilych's life continued to flow as he considered it should do—pleasantly and properly.

So things continued for another seven years. His eldest daughter was already sixteen, another child had died, and only one son was left, a schoolboy and a subject of dissension. Ivan Ilych wanted to put him in the School of Law, but to spite him Praskovya Fëdorovna entered him at the High School. The daughter had been educated at home and had turned out well: the boy did not learn badly either.

3

So Ivan Ilych lived for seventeen years after his marriage. He was already a Public Prosecutor of long standing, and had declined several proposed transfers while awaiting a more desirable post, when an unanticipated and unpleasant occurrence quite upset the peaceful course of his life. He was expecting to be offered the post of presiding judge in a University town, but Happe somehow came to the front and obtained the appointment instead. Ivan Ilych became irritable, reproached Happe, and quarreled both with him and with his immediate superiors—who became colder to him and again passed him over when other appointments were made.

This was in 1880, the hardest year of Ivan Ilych's life. It was then that it became evident on the one hand that his salary was insufficient for them to live on, and on the other that he had been forgotten, and not only this, but that what was for him the greatest and most cruel injustice appeared to others a quite ordinary occurrence. Even his father did not consider it his duty to help him. Ivan Ilych felt himself abandoned by everyone, and that they regarded his position with a salary of 3,500 rubles as quite normal and even fortunate. He alone knew that with the consciousness of the injustices done him, with his wife's incessant nagging, and with the debts he had contracted by living beyond his means, his position was far from normal.

In order to save money that summer he obtained leave of absence and went with his wife to live in the country at her brother's place.

In the country, without his work, he experienced *ennui* for the first time in his life, and not only *ennui* but intolerable depression, and he decided that it was impossible to go on living like that, and that it was necessary to take energetic measures.

Having passed a sleepless night pacing up and down the veranda, he decided to go to Petersburg and bestir himself, in order to punish those who had failed to appreciate him and to get transferred to another ministry.

Next day, despite many protests from his wife and brother, he started for Petersburg with the sole object of obtaining a post with a salary of five thousand rubles a year. He was no longer bent on any particular department, or tendency, or kind of activity. All he now wanted was an appointment to another post with a salary of five thousand rubles, either in administration, in the banks, with the railways, in one of the Empress Marya's Institutions,° or even in customs—but it had to carry with it a salary of five thousand rubles and be in a ministry other than that in which they had failed to appreciate him.

And this quest of Ivan Ilych's was crowned with remarkable and unexpected success. At Kursk an acquaintance of his, F. I. Ilyin, got into the first-class carriage, sat down beside Ivan Ilych, and told him of a telegram just received by the Governor of Kursk announcing that a change was about to take place in the ministry: Peter Ivanovich was to be superseded by Ivan Semënovich.

The proposed change, apart from its significance for Russia, had a special significance for Ivan Ilych, because by bringing forward a new man, Peter Petrovich, and consequently his friend Zachar Ivanovich, it was highly favorable for Ivan Ilych, since Zachar Ivanovich was a friend and colleague of his.

In Moscow this news was confirmed, and on reaching Petersburg Ivan Ilych found Zachar Ivanovich and received a definite promise of an appointment in his former department of Justice.

A week later he telegraphed to his wife: "Zachar in Miller's place. I shall receive appointment on presentation of report."

Thanks to this change of personnel, Ivan Ilych had unexpectedly obtained an appointment in his former ministry which placed him two stages above his former colleagues besides giving him five thousand rubles salary and three thousand five hundred rubles for expenses connected with his removal. All his ill humor towards his former enemies and the whole department vanished, and Ivan Ilych was completely happy.

He returned to the country more cheerful and contented than he had been for a long time. Praskovya Fëdorovna also cheered up and a truce was arranged between them. Ivan Ilych told of how he had been fêted by everybody in Petersburg, how all those who had been his enemies were put to shame and now fawned on him, how envious they were of his appointment, and how much everybody in Petersburg had liked him.

Praskovya Fëdorovna listened to all this and appeared to believe it. She did not contradict anything, but only made plans for their life in the town to which they were going. Ivan Ilych saw with delight that these plans were his plans, that he and his wife agreed, and that, after a stumble, his life was regaining its due and natural character of pleasant lightheartedness and decorum.

Ivan Ilych had come back for a short time only, for he had to take up his new duties on the 10th of September. Moreover, he needed time to settle into the new place, to move all his belongings from the province, and to buy and order many additional things: in a word, to make such arrangements as he had resolved on, which were almost exactly what Praskovya Fëdorovna too had decided on.

the Empress Marya's Institutions: orphanage-schools for girls

Now that everything had happened so fortunately, and that he and his wife were at one in their aims and moreover saw so little of one another, they got on together better than they had done since the first years of marriage. Ivan Ilych had thought of taking his family away with him at once, but the insistence of his wife's brother and her sister-in-law, who had suddenly become particularly amiable and friendly to him and his family, induced him to depart alone.

So he departed, and the cheerful state of mind induced by his success and by the harmony between his wife and himself, the one intensifying the other, did not leave him. He found a delightful house, just the thing both he and his wife had dreamt of. Spacious, lofty reception rooms in the old style, a convenient and dignified study, rooms for his wife and daughter, a study for his son—it might have been specially built for them. Ivan Ilych himself superintended the arrangements, chose the wallpapers, supplemented the furniture (preferably with antiques which he considered particularly *comme il faut*), and supervised the upholstering. Everything progressed and progressed and approached the ideal he had set himself: even when things were only half completed they exceeded his expectations. He saw what a refined and elegant character, free from vulgarity, it would all have when it was ready. On falling asleep he pictured to himself how the reception-room would look. Looking at the yet unfinished drawing-room he could see the fireplace, the screen, the what-nots, the little chairs dotted here and there, the dishes and plates on the walls, and the bronzes, as they would be when everything was in place. He was pleased by the thought of how his wife and daughter, who shared his taste in this matter, would be impressed by it. They were certainly not expecting as much. He had been particularly successful in finding, and buying cheaply, antiques which gave a particularly aristocratic character to the whole place. But in his letters he intentionally understated everything in order to be able to surprise them. All this so absorbed him that his new duties—though he liked his official work—interested him less than he had expected. Sometimes he even had moments of absent-mindedness during the Court Sessions, and would consider whether he should have straight or curved cornices for his curtains. He was so interested in it all that he often did things himself, rearranging the furniture, or rehanging the curtains. Once when mounting a step-ladder to show the upholsterer, who did not understand, how he wanted the hangings draped, he made a false step and slipped, but being a strong and agile man he clung on and only knocked his side against the knob of the window frame. The bruised place was painful but the pain soon passed, and he felt particularly bright and well just then. He wrote: "I feel fifteen years younger." He thought he would have everything ready by September, but it dragged on till mid-October. But the result was charming not only in his eyes but to everyone who saw it.

In reality it was just what is usually seen in houses of people of moderate means who want to appear rich, and therefore succeed only in resembling others like themselves: there were damasks, dark wood, plants, rugs, and dull and polished bronzes—all the things people of a certain class have in order to resemble other people of that class. His house was so like the others that it would never have been noticed, but to him it all seemed to be quite exceptional. He was very happy when he met his family at the station and brought them to the newly furnished house all lit up, where a footman in a white tie opened the door into the hall decorated with plants, and when they went on into the drawing-room and the study uttering exclamations of delight. He conducted them everywhere, drank in their praises eagerly, and beamed with pleasure. At tea that evening, when Praskovya Fëdorovna among other things asked him about his fall, he laughed and showed them how he had gone flying and frightened the upholsterer.

"It's a good thing I'm a bit of an athlete. Another man might have been killed, but I merely knocked myself, just here; it hurts when touched, but it's passing off already—it's only a bruise."

So they began living in their new home—in which, as always happens, when they got thoroughly settled in they found they were just one room short—and with the increased income, which as always was just a little (some five hundred rubles) too little, but it was all very nice.

Things went particularly well at first, before everything was finally arranged and while something had still to be done: this thing bought, that thing ordered, another thing moved, and something else adjusted. Though there were some disputes between husband and wife, they were both so well satisfied and had so much to do that it all passed off without any serious quarrels. When nothing was left to arrange it became rather dull and something seemed to be lacking, but they were then making acquaintances, forming habits, and life was growing fuller.

Ivan Ilych spent his mornings at the law court and came home to dinner, and at first he was generally in a good humor, though he occasionally became irritable just on account of his house. (Every spot on the tablecloth or the upholstery, and every broken window-blind string, irritated him. He had devoted so much trouble to arranging it all that every disturbance of it distressed him.) But on the whole his life ran its course as he believed life should do: easily, pleasantly, and decorously.

He got up at nine, drank his coffee, read the paper, and then put on his undress uniform and went to the law courts. There the harness in which he worked had already been stretched to fit him and he donned it without a hitch: petitioners, inquiries at the chancery, the chancery itself, and the sittings public and administrative. In all this the thing was to exclude everything fresh and vital, which always disturbs the regular course of official business, and to admit only official relations with people, and then only on official grounds. A man would come, for instance, wanting some information. Ivan Ilych, as one in whose sphere the matter did not lie, would have nothing to do with him: but if the man had some business with him in his official capacity, something that could be expressed on officially stamped paper, he would do everything, positively everything he could within the limits of such relations, and in doing so would maintain the semblance of friendly human relations, that is, would observe the courtesies of life. As soon as the official relations ended, so did everything else. Ivan Ilych possessed this capacity to separate his real life from the official side of affairs and not mix the two, in the highest degree, and by long practice and natural aptitude had brought it to such a pitch that sometimes, in the manner of a virtuoso, he would even allow himself to let the human and official relations mingle. He let himself do this just because he felt that he could at any time he chose resume the strictly official attitude again and drop the human relation. And he did it all easily, pleasantly, correctly, and even artistically. In the intervals between the sessions he smoked, drank tea, chatted a little about politics, a little about general topics, a little about cards, but most of all about official appointments. Tired, but with the feelings of a virtuoso—one of the first violins who has played his part in an orchestra with precision—he would return home to find that his wife and daughter had been out paying calls, or had a visitor, and that his son had been to school, had done his homework with his tutor, and was duly learning what is taught at High Schools. Everything was as it should be. After dinner, if they had no visitors, Ivan Ilych sometimes read a book that was being much discussed at the time, and in the evening settled down to work, that is, read official papers, compared the depositions of witnesses, noted paragraphs of the Code applying to them. This was neither dull nor amusing. It was dull when he might have been playing bridge, but if no bridge was available it was at any rate better than doing nothing or sitting with his wife. Ivan Ilych's chief pleasure was giving little dinners to which he invited men and women of good social position, and just as his drawing-room resembled all other drawing-rooms so did his enjoyable little parties resemble all other such parties.

Once they even gave a dance. Ivan Ilych enjoyed it and everything went off well, except that it led to a violent quarrel with his wife about the cakes and sweets. Praskovya Fëdorovna had made her own plans, but Ivan Ilych insisted on getting everything from an expensive confectioner and ordered too many cakes, and the quarrel occurred because some of those cakes were left over and the confectioner's bill came to forty-five rubles. It was a great and disageeable quarrel. Praskovya Fëdorovna called him "a fool and an imbecile," and he clutched at his head and made angry allusions to divorce.

But the dance itself had been enjoyable. The best people were there, and Ivan Ilych had danced with Princess Trufonova, a sister of the distinguished founder of the Society "Bear my Burden."

The pleasures connected with his work were pleasures of ambition; his social pleasures were those of vanity; but Ivan Ilych's greatest pleasure was playing bridge. He acknowledged that whatever disagreeable incident happened in his life, the pleasure that beamed like a ray of light above everything else was to sit down to bridge with good players, not noisy partners, and of course to four-handed bridge (with five players it was annoying to have to stand out, though one pretended not to mind), to play a clever and serious game (when the cards allowed it) and then to have supper and a glass of wine. After a game of bridge, especially if he had won a little (to win a large sum was unpleasant), Ivan Ilych went to bed in specially good humor.

So they lived. They formed a circle of acquaintances among the best people and were visited by people of importance and by young folk. In their views as to their acquaintances, husband, wife and daughter were entirely agreed, and tacitly and unanimously kept at arm's length and shook off the shabby friends and relations who, with much show of affection, gushed into the drawing-room with its Japanese plates on the walls. Soon these shabby friends ceased to obtrude themselves and only the best people remained in the Golovins' set.

Young men made up to Lisa, and Petrishchev, an examining magistrate and Dmitri Ivanovich Petrishchev's son and sole heir, began to be so attentive to her that Ivan Ilych had already spoken to Praskovya Fëdorovna about it, and considered whether they should not arrange a party for them, or get up some private theatricals.

So they lived, and all went well, without change, and life flowed pleasantly.

4

They were all in good health. It could not be called ill health if Ivan Ilych sometimes said that he had a queer taste in his mouth and felt some discomfort in his left side.

But this discomfort increased and, though not exactly painful, grew into a sense of pressure in his side accompanied by ill humor. And his irritability became worse and worse and began to mar the agreeable, easy, and correct life that had established itself in the Golovin family. Quarrels between husband and wife became more and more frequent, and soon the ease and amenity disappeared and even the decorum was barely maintained. Scenes again became frequent, and very few of those islets remained on which husband and wife could meet without an explosion. Praskovya Fëdorovna now had good reason to say that her husband's temper was trying. With characteristic exaggeration she said he had always had a dreadful temper, and that it had needed all her good nature to put up with it for twenty years. It was true that now the quarrels were started by him. His bursts of temper always came just before dinner, often just as he began to eat his soup. Sometimes he noticed that a plate or dish was chipped, or the food was not right, or his son put his elbow on the table, or his daughter's hair was not done as he liked it, and for all this he blamed Praskovya Fëdorovna. At first she retorted and said disagreeable things to him, but once or twice he fell into such a rage at the beginning of dinner that she realized it was due to some physical derangement brought on by taking food, and so she restrained herself and did not answer but only hurried to get the dinner over. She regarded this self-restraint as highly praiseworthy. Having come to the conclusion that her husband had a dreadful temper and made her life miserable, she began to feel sorry for herself, and the more she pitied herself the more she hated her husband. She began to wish he would die; yet she did not want him to die because then his salary would cease. And this irritated her against him still more. She considered herself dreadfully unhappy just because not even his death could save her, and though she concealed her exasperation, that hidden exasperation of hers increased his irritation also.

After one scene in which Ivan Ilych had been particularly unfair and after which he had said in explanation that he certainly was irritable but that it was due to his not being well, she said that if he was ill it should be attended to, and insisted on his going to see a celebrated doctor.

He went. Everything took place as he had expected and as it always does. There was the usual waiting and the important air assumed by the doctor, with which he was so familiar (resembling that which he himself assumed in court), and the sounding and listening, and the questions which called for answers that were foregone conclusions and were evidently unnecessary, and the look of importance which implied that "if only you put yourself in our hands we will arrange everything—we know indubitably how it has to be done, always in the same way for everybody alike." It was all just as it was in the law courts. The doctor put on just the same air towards him as he himself put on towards an accused person.

The doctor said that so-and-so indicated that there was so-and-so inside the patient, but if the investigation of so-and-so did not confirm this, then he must assume that and that. If he assumed that and that, then . . . and so on. To Ivan Ilych only one question was important: was his case serious or not? But the doctor ignored that inappropriate question. From his point of view it was not the one under consideration, the real question was to decide between a floating kidney, chronic catarrh, or appendicitis. It was not a question of Ivan Ilych's life or death, but one between a floating kidney and appendicitis. And that question the doctor solved brilliantly, as it seemed to Ivan Ilych, in favor of appendix, with the reservation that should an examination of the urine give fresh indications the matter would be reconsidered. All this was just what Ivan Ilych had himself brilliantly accomplished a thousand times in dealing with men on trial. The doctor summed up just as brilliantly, looking over his spectacles triumphantly and even gaily at the accused. From the doctor's summing up Ivan Ilych concluded that things were bad, but that for the doctor, and perhaps for everybody else, it was a matter of indifference, though for him it was bad. And this conclusion struck him painfully, arousing in him a great feeling of pity for himself and of bitterness towards the doctor's indifference to a matter of such importance.

He said nothing of this, but rose, placed the doctor's fee on the table, and remarked with a sigh: "We sick people probably often put inappropriate questions. But tell me, in general, is this complaint dangerous, or not? . . ."

The doctor looked at him sternly over his spectacles with one eye, as if to say: "Prisoner, if you will not keep to the questions put to you, I shall be obliged to have you removed from court."

"I have already told you what I consider necessary and proper. The analysis may show something more." And the doctor bowed.

Ivan Ilych went out slowly, seated himself disconsolately in his sledge, and drove home. All the way home he was going over what the doctor had said, trying to translate those complicated, obscure, scientific phrases into plain language and find in them an answer to the question: "Is my condition bad? Is it very bad? Or is there as yet nothing much wrong?" And it seemed to him that the meaning of what the doctor had said was that it was very bad. Everything in the streets seemed depressing. The cabmen, the houses, the passers-by, and the shops, were dismal. His ache, this dull gnawing ache that never ceased for a moment, seemed to have acquired a new and more serious significance from the doctor's dubious remarks. Ivan Ilych now watched it with a new and oppressive feeling.

He reached home and began to tell his wife about it. She listened, but in the middle of his account his daughter came in with her hat on, ready to go out with her mother. She sat down reluctantly to listen to this tedious story, but could not stand it long, and her mother too did not hear him to the end.

"Well, I am very glad," she said. "Mind now to take your medicine regularly. Give me the prescription and I'll send Gerasim to the chemist's." And she went to get ready to go out.

While she was in the room Ivan Ilych had hardly taken time to breathe, but he sighed deeply when she left it.

"Well," he thought, "perhaps it isn't so bad after all."

He began taking his medicine and following the doctor's directions, which had been altered after the examination of the urine. But then it happened that there was a contradiction between the indications drawn from the examination of the urine and the symptoms that showed themselves. It turned out that what was happening differed from what the doctor had told him, and that he had either forgotten, or blundered or hidden something from him. He could not, however, be blamed for that, and Ivan Ilych still obeyed his orders implicitly and at first derived some comfort from doing so.

From the time of his visit to the doctor, Ivan Ilych's chief occupation was the exact fulfillment of the doctor's instructions regarding hygiene and the taking of medicine, and the observation of his pain and his excretions. His chief interests came to be people's ailments and people's health. When sickness, deaths, or recoveries were mentioned in his presence, especially when the illness resembled his own, he listened with agitation which he tried to hide, asked questions, and applied what he heard to his own case.

The pain did not grow less, but Ivan Ilych made efforts to force himself to think that he was better. And he could do this so long as nothing agitated him. But as soon as he had any unpleasantness with his wife, or a lack of success in his official work, or held bad cards at bridge, he was at once acutely sensible of his disease. He had formerly borne such mischances, hoping soon to adjust what was wrong, to master it and attain success, or make a grand slam. But now every mischance upset him and plunged him into despair. He would say to himself: "There now, just as I was beginning to get better and the medicine had begun to take effect, comes this accursed misfortune, or unpleasantness . . . " And he was furious with the mishap, or with the people who were causing the unpleasantness and killing him, for he felt that this fury was killing him but could not restrain it. One would have thought that it should have been clear to him that this exasperation with circumstances and people aggravated his illness, and that he ought therefore to ignore unpleasant occurrences. But he drew the very opposite conclusion: he said that he needed peace, and he watched for everything that might disturb it and became irritable at the slightest infringement of it. His condition was rendered worse by the fact that he read medical books and consulted doctors. The progress of his disease was so gradual that he could deceive himself when comparing one day with another—the difference was so slight. But when he consulted the doctors it seemed to him that he was getting worse, and even very rapidly. Yet despite this he was continually consulting them.

That month he went to see another celebrity, who told him almost the same as the first had done but put his questions rather differently, and the interview with this celebrity only increased Ivan Ilych's doubts and fears. A friend of a friend of his, a very good doctor, diagnosed his illness again quite differently from the others, and though he predicted recovery, his questions and suppositions bewildered Ivan Ilych still more and increased his doubts. A homoeopathist diagnosed the disease in yet another way, and prescribed medicine which Ivan Ilych took secretly for a week. But after a week, not feeling any improvement and having lost confidence both in the former doctor's treatment and in this one's, he became more despondent. One day a lady acquaintance mentioned a cure effected by a wonder-working icon. Ivan Ilych caught himself listening attentively and beginning to believe that it had occurred. This incident alarmed him. "Has my mind really weakened to such an extent?" he asked himself. "Nonsense! It's all rubbish. I mustn't give way to nervous fears but having chosen a doctor must keep strictly to his treatment. That is what I will do. Now it's all settled. I won't think about it, but will follow the treatment seriously till summer, and then we shall see. From now there must be no more of this wavering!" This was easy to say but impossible to carry out. The pain in his side oppressed him and seemed to grow worse and more incessant, while the taste in his mouth grew stranger and stranger. It seemed to him that his breath had a disgusting smell, and he was conscious of a loss of appetite and strength. There was no deceiving himself: something terrible, new, and more important than anything before in his life, was taking place within him of which he alone was aware. Those about him did not understand or would not understand it, but thought everything in the world was going on as usual. That tormented Ivan Ilych more than anything. He saw that his household, especially his wife and daughter who were in a perfect whirl of visiting, did not understand anything of it and were annoyed that he was so depressed and so exacting, as if he were to blame for it. Though they tried to disguise it he saw that he was an obstacle in their path, and that his wife had adopted a definite line in regard to his illness and kept to it regardless of anything he said or did. Her attitude was this: "You know," she would say to her friends, "Ivan Ilych can't do as other people do, and keep to the treatment prescribed for him. One day he'll take his drops and keep strictly to his diet and go to bed in good time, but the next day unless I watch him he'll suddenly forget his medicine, eat sturgeon—which is forbidden—and sit up playing cards till one o'clock in the morning."

"Oh, come, when was that?" Ivan Ilych would ask in vexation. "Only once at Peter Ivanovich's."

"And yesterday with Shebek."

"Well, even if I hadn't stayed up, this pain would have kept me awake."

"Be that as it may you'll never get well like that, but will always make us wretched."

Praskovya Fëdorovna's attitude to Ivan Ilych's illness, as she expressed it both to others and to him, was that it was his own fault and was another of the annoyances he caused her. Ivan Ilych felt that this opinion escaped her involuntarily—but that did not make it easier for him.

At the law courts too, Ivan Ilych noticed, or thought he noticed, a strange attitude toward himself. It sometimes seemed to him that people were watching him inquisitively as a man whose place might soon be vacant. Then again, his friends would suddenly begin to chaff him in a friendly way about his low spirits, as if the awful, horrible, and unheard-of thing that was going on within him, incessantly gnawing at him and irresistibily drawing him away, was a very agreeable subject for jests. Schwartz in particular irritated him by his jocularity, vivacity, and *savoir-faire*, which reminded him of what he himself had been ten years ago.

Friends came to make up a set and they sat down to cards. They dealt, bending the new cards to soften them, and he sorted the diamonds in his hands and found he had seven. His partner said "No trumps" and supported him with two diamonds. What more could be wished for? It ought to be jolly and lively. They would make a grand slam. But suddenly Ivan Ilych was conscious of that gnawing pain, that taste in his mouth, and it seemed ridiculous that in such circumstances he should be pleased to make a grand slam.

He looked at his partner, Mikhail Mikhaylovich, who rapped the table with his strong hand and instead of snatching up the tricks pushed the cards courteously and indulgently towards Ivan Ilych that he might have the pleasure of gathering them up without the trouble of stretching out his hand for them. "Does he think I am too weak to stretch my arm?" thought Ivan Ilych, and forgetting what he was doing he over-trumped his partner, missing the grand slam by three tricks. And what was most awful of all was that he saw how upset Mikhail Mikhaylovich was about it but did not himself care. And it was dreadful to realize why he did not care.

They all saw that he was suffering, and said: "We can stop if you are tired. Take a rest." Lie down? No, he was not at all tired, and finished the rubber. All were gloomy and silent. Ivan Ilych felt that he had diffused the gloom over them and could not dispel it. They had supper and went away, and Ivan Ilych was left alone with the consciousness that his life was poisoned and was poisoning the lives of others, and that this poison did not weaken but penetrated more and more deeply into his whole being.

With this consciousness, and with physical pain besides that terror, he must go to bed, often to lie awake the greater part of the night. Next morning he had to get up again, dress, go to the law courts, speak, and write; or if he did not go out, spend at home those twenty-four hours a day each of which was a torture. And he had to live thus all alone on the brink of an abyss, with no one who understood or pitied him.

5

So one month passed and then another. Just before the New Year his brother-in-law came to town and stayed at their house. Ivan Ilych was at the law courts and Praskovya Fëdorovna had gone shopping. When Ivan Ilych came home and entered his study he found his brother-in-law there—a healthy, florid man— unpacking his portmanteau himself. He raised his head on hearing Ivan Ilych's footsteps and looked up at him for a moment without a word. That stare told Ivan Ilych everything. His brother-in-law opened his mouth to utter an exclamation of surprise but checked himself, and that action confirmed it all.

"I have changed, eh?"

"Yes, there is a change."

And after that, try as he would to get his brother-in-law to return to the subject of his looks, the latter would say nothing about it. Praskovya Fëdorovna came home and her brother went out to her. Ivan Ilych locked the door and began to examine himself in the glass, first full face, then in profile. He took up a portrait of himself taken with his wife, and compared it with what he saw in the glass. The change in him was immense. Then he bared his arms to the elbow, looked at them, drew the sleeves down again, sat down on an ottoman, and grew blacker than night.

"No, no, this won't do!" he said to himself, and jumped up, went to the table, took up some law papers and began to read them, but could not continue. He unlocked the door and went into the reception-room. The door leading to the drawing-room was shut. He approached it on tiptoe and listened.

"No, you are exaggerating!" Praskovya Fëdorovna was saying.

"Exaggerating! Don't you see it? Why, he's a dead man! Look at his eyes—there's no light in them. But what is wrong with him?"

"No one knows. Nikolaevich (that was another doctor) said something, but I don't know what. And Leshchetitsky (this was the celebrated specialist) said quite the contrary . . . "

Ivan Ilych walked away, went to his own room, lay down, and began musing: "The kidney, a floating kidney." He recalled all the doctors had told him of how it detached itself and swayed about. And by an effort of imagination he tried to catch that kidney and arrest it and support it. So little was needed for this, it seemed to him. "No, I'll go to see Peter Ivanovich again." (That was the friend whose friend was a doctor.) He rang, ordered the carriage, and got ready to go.

"Where are you going, Jean?" asked his wife, with a specially sad and exceptionally kind look.

The exceptionally kind look irritated him. He looked morosely at her. "I must go to see Peter Ivanovich."

He went to see Peter Ivanovich, and together they went to see his friend, the doctor. He was in, and Ivan Ilych had a long talk with him.

Reviewing the anatomical and physiological details of what in the doctor's opinion was going on inside him, he understood it all.

There was something, a small thing, in the vermiform appendix. It might all come right. Only stimulate the energy of one organ and check the activity of another, then absorption would take place and everything would come right. He got home rather late for dinner, ate his dinner, conversed cheerfully, but could not for a long time bring himself to go back to work in his room. At last, however, he went to his study and did what was necessary, but the consciousness that he had put something aside—an important, intimate matter which he would revert to when his work was done—never left him. When he had finished his work he remembered that this intimate matter was the thought of the vermiform appendix. But he did not give himself up to it, and went to the drawing-room for tea. There were callers there, including the examining magistrate who was a desirable match for his daughter, and they were conversing, playing the piano, and singing. Ivan Ilych, as Praskovya Fëdorovna remarked, spent the evening more cheerfully than usual, but he never for a moment forgot that he had postponed the important matter of the appendix. At eleven o'clock he said good-night and went to his bedroom. Since his illness he had slept alone in a small room next to his study. He undressed and took up a novel by Zola, but instead of reading it fell into thought, and in his imagination that desired improvement in the vermiform appendix occurred. There was the absorption and evacuation and the re-establishment of normal activity. "Yes, that's it!" he said to himself. "One need only assist nature, that's all." He remembered his medicine, rose, took it, and lay down on his back watching for the beneficent action of the medicine and for it to lessen the pain. "I need only take it regularly and avoid all injurious influences. I am already feeling better, much better." He began touching his side: it was not painful to the touch. "There, I really don't feel it. It's much better already." He put out the light and turned on his side . . . "The appendix is getting better, absorption is occurring." Suddenly he felt the old familiar, dull, gnawing pain, stubborn and serious. There was the same loathsome taste in his mouth. His heart sank and he felt dazed. "My God! My God!" he muttered. "Again, again! and it will never cease." And suddenly the matter presented itself in a quite different aspect. "Vermiform appendix! Kidney!" he said to himself. "It's not a question of appendix or kidney, but of life and . . . death. Yes, life was there and now it is going, going and I cannot stop it. Yes. Why deceive myself? Isn't it obvious to everyone but me that I'm dying, and that it's only a question of weeks, days . . . it may happen this moment. There was light and now there is darkness. I was here and now I'm going there! Where?" A chill came over him, his breathing ceased, and he felt only the throbbing of his heart.

"When I am not, what will there be? There will be nothing. Then where shall I be when I am no more? Can this be dying? No, I don't want to!" He jumped up and tried to light the candle, felt for it with trembling hands, dropped the candle and candlestick on the floor, and fell back to his pillow.

"What's the use? It makes no difference," he said to himself, staring with wide-open eyes into the darkness. "Death. Yes, death. And none of them know or wish to know it, and they have no pity for me. Now they are playing." (He heard through the door the distant sound of a song and its accompaniment.) "It's all the same to them, but they will die too! Fools! I first, and they later, but it will be the same for them. And now they are merry . . . the beasts!"

Anger choked him and he was agonizingly, unbearably, miserable. "It is impossible that all men have been doomed to suffer this awful horror!" He raised himself.

"Something must be wrong. I must calm myself—must think it over from the beginning." And he again began thinking. "Yes, the beginning of my illness: I knocked my side, but I was quite well that day and the next. It hurt a little, then rather more. I saw the doctor, then followed despondency and anguish, more doctors, and I drew nearer to the abyss. My strength grew less and I kept coming nearer and nearer, and now I have wasted away and there is no light in my eyes. I think of the appendix—but this is death! I think of mending the appendix, and all the while here is death! Can it really be death?" Again terror seized him and he gasped for breath. He leant down and began feeling for the matches, pressing with his elbow on the stand beside the bed. It was in the way and hurt him, he grew furious with it, pressed on it still harder, and upset it. Breathless and in despair he fell on his back, expecting death to come immediately.

Meanwhile the visitors were leaving. Praskovya Fëdorovna was seeing them off. She heard something fall and came in.

"What has happened?"

"Nothing. I knocked it over accidentally."

She went out and returned with a candle. He lay there panting heavily, like a man who has run a thousand yards, and stared upwards at her with a fixed look.

"What is it, Jean?"

"No . . . o . . . thing. I upset it." ("Why speak of it? She won't understand," he thought.)

And in truth she did not understand. She picked up the stand, lit his candle, and hurried away to see another visitor off. When she came back he still lay on his back, looking upwards.

"What is it? Do you feel worse?"

"Yes."

She shook her head and sat down.

"Do you know, Jean, I think we must ask Leshchetitsky to come and see you here."

This meant calling in the famous specialist, regardless of expense. He smiled malignantly and said "No." She remained a little longer and then went up to him and kissed his forehead.

While she was kissing him he hated her from the bottom of his soul and with difficulty refrained from pushing her away.

"Good-night. Please God you'll sleep."

"Yes."

6

Ivan Ilych saw that he was dying, and he was in continual despair.

In the depth of his heart he knew he was dying, but not only was he not accustomed to the thought, he simply did not and could not grasp it.

The syllogism he had learnt from Kiezewetter's Logic:° "Caius is a man, men are mortal, therefore Caius is mortal," had always seemed to him correct as applied to Caius, but certainly not as applied to himself. That Caius—man in the abstract—was mortal, was perfectly correct, but he was not Caius, not an abstract man, but a creature quite, quite separate from all others. He had been little Vanya, with a mamma and a papa, with Mitya and Volodya, with the toys, a coachman and a nurse, afterwards with Katenka and with all the joys, griefs, and delights of childhood, boyhood, and youth. What did Caius know of the smell of that striped leather ball Vanya had been so fond of? Had Caius kissed his mother's hand like that, and did the silk of her dress rustle so for Caius? Had he rioted like that at school when the pastry was bad? Had Caius been in love like that? Could Caius preside at a session as he did? "Caius really was mortal, and it was right for him to die; but for me, little Vanya, Ivan Ilych, with all my thoughts and emotions, it's altogether a different matter. It cannot be that I ought to die. That would be too terrible."

Such was his feeling.

"If I had to die like Caius, I should have known it was so. An inner voice would have told me so, but there was nothing of the sort in me and I and all my friends felt that our case was quite different from that of Caius. And now here it is!" he said to himself. "It can't be. It's impossible! But here it is. How is this? How is one to understand it?"

Kiezewetter's Logic: a widely used textbook

He could not understand it, and tried to drive this false, incorrect, morbid thought away and to replace it by other proper and healthy thoughts. But that thought, and not the thought only but the reality itself, seemed to come and confront him.

And to replace that thought he called up a succession of others, hoping to find in them some support. He tried to get back into the former current of thoughts that had once screened the thought of death from him. But strange to say, all that had formerly shut off, hidden, and destroyed, his consciousness of death, no longer had that effect. Ivan Ilych now spent most of his time in attempting to re-establish that old current. He would say to himself: "I will take up my duties again—after all I used to live by them." And banishing all doubts he would go to the law courts, enter into conversation with his colleagues, and sit carelessly as was his wont, scanning the crowd with a thoughtful look and leaning both his emaciated arms on the arms of his oak chair; bending over as usual to a colleague and drawing his papers nearer he would interchange whispers with him, and then suddenly raising his eyes and sitting erect would pronounce certain words and open the proceedings. But suddenly in the midst of those proceedings the pain in his side, regardless of the stage the proceedings had reached, would begin its own gnawing work. Ivan Ilych would turn his attention to it and try to drive the thoughts of it away, but without success. *It* would come and stand before him and look at him, and he would be petrified and the light would die out of his eyes, and he would again begin asking himself whether *It* alone was true. And his colleagues and subordinates would see with surprise and distress that he, the brilliant and subtle judge, was becoming confused and making mistakes. He would shake himself, try to pull himself together, manage somehow to bring the sitting to a close, and return home with the sorrowful consciousness that his judicial labors could not as formerly hide from him what he wanted them to hide, and could not deliver him from *It*. And what was worst of all was that *It* drew his attention to itself not in order to take some action but only that he should look at *It*, look it straight in the face: look at it without doing anything, suffer inexpressibly.

And to save himself from this condition Ivan Ilych looked for consolations—new screens—and new screens were found and for a while seemed to save him, but then they immediately fell to pieces or rather became transparent, as if *It* penetrated them and nothing could veil *It*.

In these latter days he would go into the drawing-room he had arranged—that drawing-room where he had fallen and for the sake of which (how bitterly ridiculous it seemed) he had sacrificed his life—for he knew that his illness originated with that knock. He would enter and see that something had scratched the polished table. He would look for the cause of this and find that it was the bronze ornamentation of an album, that had got bent. He would take up the expensive album which he had lovingly arranged, and feel vexed with his daughter and her friends for their untidiness—for the album was torn here and there and some of the photographs turned upside down. He would put it carefully in order and bend the ornamentation back into position. Then it would occur to him to place all those things in another corner of the room, near the plants. He would call the footman, but his daughter or wife would come to help him. They would not agree, and his wife would contradict him, and he would dispute and grow angry. But that was all right, for then he did not think about *It*. *It* was invisible.

But then, when he was moving something himself, his wife would say: "Let the servants do it. You will hurt yourself again." And suddenly *It* would flash through the screen and he would see it. It was just a flash, and he hoped it would disappear, but he would involuntarily pay attention to his side. "It sits there as before, gnawing just the same!" And he could no longer forget *It*, but could distinctly see it looking at him from behind the flowers. "What is it all for?"

"It really is so! I lost my life over the curtain as I might have done when storming a fort. Is that possible? How terrible and how stupid. It can't be true! It can't, but it is."

He would go to his study, lie down, and again be alone with *It*: face to face with *It*. And nothing could be done with *It* except to look at it and shudder.

7

How it happened it is impossible to say because it came about step by step, unnoticed, but in the third month of Ivan Ilych's illness, his wife, his daughter, his son, his acquaintances, the doctors, the servants, and above all he himself, were aware that the whole interest he had for other people was whether he would soon vacate his place, and at last release the living from the discomfort caused by his presence and be himself released from his sufferings.

He slept less and less. He was given opium and hypodermic injections of morphine, but this did not relieve him. The dull depression he experienced in a somnolent condition at first gave him a little relief, but only as something new, afterwards it became as distressing as the pain itself or even more so.

Special foods were prepared for him by the doctors' orders, but all those foods became increasingly distasteful and disgusting to him.

For his excretions also special arrangements had to be made, and this was a torment to him every time—a torment from the uncleanliness, the unseemliness, and the smell, and from knowing that another person had to take part in it.

But just through this most unpleasant matter, Ivan Ilych obtained comfort. Gerasim, the butler's young assistant, always came in to carry the things out. Gerasim was a clean, fresh peasant lad, grown stout on town food and always cheerful and bright. At first the sight of him, in his clean Russian peasant costume, engaged in that disgusting task embarrassed Ivan Ilych.

Once when he got up from the commode too weak to draw up his trousers, he dropped into a soft armchair and looked with horror at his bare, enfeebled thighs with the muscles so sharply marked on them.

Gerasim with a firm light tread, his heavy boots emitting a pleasant smell of tar and fresh winter air, came in wearing a clean Hessian apron, the sleeves of his print shirt tucked up over his strong bare young arms; and refraining from looking at his sick master out of consideration for his feelings, and restraining the joy of life that beamed from his face, he went up to the commode.

"Gerasim!" said Ivan Ilych in a weak voice.

Gerasim started, evidently afraid he might have committed some blunder, and with a rapid movement turned his fresh, kind, simple young face which just showed the first downy signs of a beard.

"Yes, sir?"

"That must be very unpleasant for you. You must forgive me. I am helpless."

"Oh, why, sir," and Gerasim's eyes beamed and he showed his glistening white teeth, "what's a little trouble? It's a case of illness with you, sir."

And his deft strong hands did their accustomed task, and he went out of the room stepping lightly. Five minutes later he as lightly returned.

Ivan Ilych was still sitting in the same position in the armchair.

"Gerasim," he said when the latter had replaced the freshly-washed utensil. "Please come here and help me." Gerasim went up to him. "Lift me up. It is hard for me to get up, and I have sent Dmitri away."

Gerasim went up to him, grasped his master with his strong arms deftly but gently, in the same way that he stepped—lifted him, supported him with one hand, and with the other drew up his trousers and would have set him down again, but Ivan Ilych asked to be led to the sofa. Gerasim, without an effort and without apparent pressure, led him, almost lifting him, to the sofa and placed him on it.

"Thank you. How easily and well you do it all!"

Gerasim smiled again and turned to leave the room. But Ivan Ilych felt his presence such a comfort that he did not want to let him go.

"One thing more, please move up that chair. No, the other one—under my feet. It is easier for me when my feet are raised."

Gerasim brought the chair, set it down gently in place, and raised Ivan Ilych's legs on to it. It seemed to Ivan Ilych that he felt better while Gerasim was holding up his legs.

"It's better when my legs are higher," he said. "Place that cushion under them."

Gerasim did so. He again lifted the legs and placed them, and again Ivan Ilych felt better while Gerasim held his legs. When he set them down Ivan Ilych fancied he felt worse.

"Gerasim," he said. "Are you busy now?"

"Not at all, sir," said Gerasim, who had learnt from the townfolk how to speak to gentlefolk.

"What have you still to do?"

"What have I to do? I've done everything except chopping the logs for tomorrow."

"Then hold my legs up a bit higher, can you?"

"Of course I can. Why not?" And Gerasim raised his master's legs higher and Ivan Ilych thought that in that position he did not feel any pain at all.

"And how about the logs?"

"Don't trouble about that, sir. There's plenty of time."

Ivan Ilych told Gerasim to sit down and hold his legs, and began to talk to him. And strange to say it seemed to him that he felt better while Gerasim held his legs up.

After that Ivan Ilych would sometimes call Gerasim and get him to hold his legs on his shoulders, and he liked talking to him. Gerasim did it all easily, willingly, simply, and with a good nature that touched Ivan Ilych. Health, strength, and vitality in other people were offensive to him, but Gerasim's strength and vitality did not mortify but soothed him.

What tormented Ivan Ilych most was the deception, the lie, which for some reason they all accepted, that he was not dying but was simply ill, and that he only need keep quiet and undergo a treatment and then something very good would result. He however knew that do what they would nothing would come of it, only still more agonizing suffering and death. This deception tortured him—their not wishing to admit what they all knew and what he knew, but wanting to lie to him concerning his terrible condition, and wishing and forcing him to participate in that lie. Those lies—lies enacted over him on the eve of his death and destined to degrade this awful, solemn act to the level of their visitings, their curtains, their sturgeon for dinner—were a terrible agony for Ivan Ilych. And strangely enough, many times when they were going through their antics over him he had been within a hairbreadth of calling out to them: "Stop lying! You know and I know that I am dying. Then at least stop lying about it!" But he had never had the spirit to do it. The awful, terrible act of his dying was, he could see, reduced by those about him to the level of a casual, unpleasant, and almost indecorous incident (as if someone entered a drawing-room diffusing an unpleasant odor) and this was done by that very decorum which he had served all his life long. He saw that no one felt for him, because no one even wished to grasp his position. Only Gerasim recognized it and pitied him. And so Ivan Ilych felt at ease only with him. He felt comforted when Gerasim supported his legs (sometimes all night long) and refused to go to bed, saying: "Don't you worry, Ivan Ilych. I'll get sleep enough later on," or when he suddenly became familiar and exclaimed: "If you weren't sick it would be another matter, but as it is, why should I grudge a little trouble?" Gerasim alone did not lie; everything showed that he alone understood the facts of the case and did not consider it necessary to disguise them, but simply felt sorry for his emaciated and enfeebled master. Once when Ivan Ilych was sending him away he even said straight out: "We shall all of us die, so why should I grudge a little trouble?"—expressing the fact that he did not think his work burdensome, because he was doing it for a dying man and hoped someone would do the same for him when his time came.

Apart from this lying, or because of it, what most tormented Ivan Ilych was that no one pitied him as he wished to be pitied. At certain moments after prolonged suffering he wished most of all (though he would have been ashamed to confess it) for someone to pity him as a sick child is pitied. He longed to be petted and comforted. He knew he was an important functionary, that he had a beard turning grey, and that therefore what he longed for was impossible, but still he longed for it. And in Gerasim's attitude towards him there was something akin to what he wished for, and so that attitude comforted him. Ivan Ilych wanted to weep, wanted to be petted and cried over, and then his colleague Shebek would come, and instead of weeping and being petted, Ivan Ilych would assume a serious, severe, and profound air, and by force of habit would express his opinion on a decision of the Court of Cassation° and would stubbornly insist on that view. This falsity around him and within him did more than anything else to poison his last days.

8

It was morning. He knew it was morning because Gerasim had gone, and Peter the footman had come and put out the candles, drawn back one of the curtains, and begun quietly to tidy up. Whether it was morning or evening, Friday or Sunday, made no difference, it was all just the same: the gnawing, unmitigated, agonizing pain, never ceasing for an instant, the consciousness of life inexorably waning but not yet extinguished, the approach of that ever dreaded and hateful Death which was the only reality, and always the same falsity. What were days, weeks, hours, in such a case?

"Will you have some tea, sir?"

"He wants things to be regular, and wishes the gentlefolk to drink tea in the morning," thought Ivan Ilych, and only said "No."

"Wouldn't you like to move onto the sofa, sir?"

"He wants to tidy up the room, and I'm in the way. I am uncleanliness and disorder," he thought, and said only:

"No, leave me alone."

The man went on bustling about. Ivan Ilych stretched out his hand. Peter came up, ready to help.

"What is it, sir?"

"My watch."

Peter took the watch which was close at hand and gave it to his master.

"Half-past eight. Are they up?"

"No, sir, except Vladimir Ivanich" (the son) "who has gone to school. Praskovya Fëdorovna ordered me to wake her if you asked for her. Shall I do so?"

Court of Cassation: the highest court of appeals

"No, there's no need to." "Perhaps I'd better have some tea," he thought, and added aloud: "Yes, bring me some tea."

Peter went to the door, but Ivan Ilych dreaded being left alone. "How can I keep him here? Oh yes, my medicine." "Peter, give me my medicine." "Why not? Perhaps it may do me some good." He took a spoonful and swallowed it. "No, it won't help. It's all tomfoolery, all deception," he decided as soon as he became aware of the familiar, sickly, hopeless taste. "No, I can't believe in it any longer. But the pain, why this pain? If it would only cease just for a moment!" And he moaned. Peter turned towards him. "It's all right. Go and fetch me some tea."

Peter went out. Left alone Ivan Ilych groaned not so much with pain, terrible though that was, as from mental anguish. Always and for ever the same, always these endless days and nights. If only it would come quicker! If only *what* would come quicker? Death, darkness? . . . No, no! Anything rather than death!

When Peter returned with the tea on a tray, Ivan Ilych stared at him for a time in perplexity, not realizing who and what he was. Peter was disconcerted by that look and his embarrassment brought Ivan Ilych to himself.

"Oh, tea! All right, put it down. Only help me to wash and put on a clean shirt."

And Ivan Ilych began to wash. With pauses for rest, he washed his hands and then his face, cleaned his teeth, brushed his hair, and looked in the glass. He was terrified by what he saw, especially by the limp way in which his hair clung to his pallid forehead.

While his shirt was being changed he knew that he would be still more frightened at the sight of his body, so he avoided looking at it. Finally he was ready. He drew on a dressing-gown, wrapped himself in a plaid, and sat down in the armchair to take his tea. For a moment he felt refreshed, but as soon as he began to drink the tea he was again aware of the same taste, and the pain also returned. He finished it with an effort, and then lay down stretching out his legs, and dismissed Peter.

Always the same. Now a spark of hope flashes up, then a sea of despair rages, and always pain; always pain, always despair, and always the same. When alone he had a dreadful and distressing desire to call someone, but he knew beforehand that with others present it would be still worse. "Another dose of morphine—to lose consciousness. I will tell him, the doctor, that he must think of something else. It's impossible, impossible, to go on like this."

An hour and another pass like that. But now there is a ring at the door bell. Perhaps it's the doctor? It is. He comes in fresh, hearty, plump, and cheerful, with that look on his face that seems to say: "There now, you're in a panic about something, but we'll arrange it all for you directly!" The doctor knows this expression is out of place here, but he has put it on once for all and can't take it off—like a man who has put on a frock-coat in the morning to pay a round of calls.

The doctor rubs his hands vigorously and reassuringly.

"Brr! How cold it is! There's such a sharp frost; just let me warm myself!"

he says, as if it were only a matter of waiting till he was warm, and then he would put everything right.

"Well now, how are you?"

Ivan Ilych feels that the doctor would like to say: "Well, how are your affairs?" but that even he feels that this would not do, and says instead: "What sort of a night have you had?"

Ivan Ilych looks at him as much as to say: "Are you really never ashamed of lying?" But the doctor does not wish to understand this question, and Ivan Ilych says: "Just as terrible as ever. The pain never leaves me and never subsides. If only something . . ."

"Yes, you sick people are always like that . . . There, now I think I am warm enough. Even Praskovya Fëdorovna, who is so particular, could find no fault with my temperature. Well, now I can say good-morning," and the doctor presses his patient's hand.

Then, dropping his former playfulness, he begins with a most serious face to examine the patient, feeling his pulse and taking his temperature, and then begins the sounding and auscultation.

Ivan Ilych knows quite well and definitely that all this is nonsense and pure deception, but when the doctor, getting down on his knee, leans over him, putting the ear first higher then lower, and performs various gymnastic movements over him with a significant expression on his face, Ivan Ilych submits to it all as he used to submit to the speeches of the lawyers, though he knew very well they were all lying and why they were lying.

The doctor, kneeling on the sofa, is still sounding him when Praskovya Fëdorovna's silk dress rustles at the door and she is heard scolding Peter for not having let her know of the doctor's arrival.

She comes in, kisses her husband, and at once proceeds to prove that she has been up a long time already, and only owing to a misunderstanding failed to be there when the doctor arrived.

Ivan Ilych looks at her, scans her all over, sets against her the whiteness and plumpness and cleanness of her hands and neck, the gloss of her hair, and the sparkle of her vivacious eyes. He hates her with his whole soul. And the thrill of hatred he feels for her makes him suffer from her touch.

Her attitude towards him and his disease is still the same. Just as the doctor had adopted a certain relation to his patient which he could not abandon, so had she formed one towards him—that he was not doing something he ought to do and was himself to blame, and that she reproached him lovingly for this—and she could not now change that attitude.

"You see he doesn't listen to me and doesn't take his medicine at the proper time. And above all he lies in a position that is no doubt bad for him—with his legs up."

She described how he made Gerasim hold his legs up.

The doctor smiled with a contemptuous affability that said: "What's to be done? These sick people do have foolish fancies of that kind, but we must forgive them."

When the examination was over the doctor looked at his watch, and then

Praskovya Fëdorovna announced to Ivan Ilych that it was of course as he pleased, but she had sent today for a celebrated specialist who would examine him and have a consultation with Michael Danilovich (their regular doctor).

"Please don't raise any objections. I am doing this for my own sake," she said ironically, letting it be felt that she was doing this all for his sake and only said this to leave him no right to refuse. He remained silent, knitting his brows. He felt that he was so surrounded and involved in a mesh of falsity that it was hard to unravel anything.

Everything she did for him was entirely for her own sake, and she told him she was doing for herself what she actually was doing for herself, as if that was so incredible that he must understand the opposite.

At half-past eleven the celebrated specialist arrived. Again the sounding began and the significant conversations in his presence and in another room about the kidneys and the appendix, and the questions and answers, with such an air of importance that again, instead of the real question of life and death which now alone confronted him, the question arose of the kidney and appendix which were not behaving as they ought to and would now be attacked by Michael Danilovich and the specialist and forced to mend their ways.

The celebrated specialist took leave of him with a serious though not hopeless look, and in reply to the timid question Ivan Ilych, with eyes glistening with fear and hope, put to him as to whether there was a chance of recovery, said that he could not vouch for it but there was a possibility. The look of hope with which Ivan Ilych watched the doctor out was so pathetic that Praskovya Fëdorovna, seeing it, even wept as she left the room to hand the doctor his fee.

The gleam of hope kindled by the doctor's encouragement did not last long. The same room, the same pictures, curtains, wall-paper, medicine bottles, were all there, and the same aching suffering body, and Ivan Ilych began to moan. They gave him a subcutaneous injection and he sank into oblivion.

It was twilight when he came to. They brought him his dinner and he swallowed some beef tea with difficulty, and then everything was the same again and night was coming on.

After dinner, at seven o'clock, Praskovya Fëdorovna came into the room in evening dress, her full bosom pushed up by her corset, and with traces of powder on her face. She had reminded him in the morning that they were going to the theater. Sarah Bernhardt was visiting the town and they had a box, which he had insisted on their taking. Now he had forgotten about it and her toilet offended him, but he concealed his vexation when he remembered that he had himself insisted on their securing a box and going because it would be an instructive and aesthetic pleasure for the children.

Praskovya Fëdorovna came in, self-satisfied but yet with a rather guilty air. She sat down and asked how he was, but as he saw, only for the sake of asking and not in order to learn about it, knowing that there was nothing to learn—and then went on to what she really wanted to say: that she would not on any account have gone but that the box had been taken and Helen and their daughter were going, as well as Petrishchev (the examining magistrate, their daughter's fiancé) and that it was out of the question to let them go alone; but that she would have much preferred to sit with him for a while; and he must be sure to follow the doctor's orders while she was away.

"Oh, and Fëdor Petrovich" (the fiancé) "would like to come in. May he? And Lisa?"

"All right."

Their daughter came in in full evening dress, her fresh young flesh exposed (making a show of that very flesh which in his own case caused so much suffering), strong, healthy, evidently in love, and impatient with illness, suffering, and death, because they interfered with her happiness.

Fëdor Petrovich came in too, in evening dress, his hair curled à la Capoul, a tight stiff collar round his long sinewy neck, an enormous white shirt-front and narrow black trousers tightly stretched over his strong thighs. He had one white glove tightly drawn on, and was holding his opera hat in his hand.

Following him the schoolboy crept in unnoticed, in a new uniform, poor little fellow, and wearing gloves. Terribly dark shadows showed under his eyes, the meaning of which Ivan Ilych knew well.

His son had always seemed pathetic to him, and now it was dreadful to see the boy's frightened look of pity. It seemed to Ivan Ilych that Vasya was the only one besides Gerasim who understood and pitied him.

They all sat down and again asked how he was. A silence followed. Lisa asked her mother about the opera-glasses, and there was an altercation between mother and daughter as to who had taken them and where they had been put. This occasioned some unpleasantness.

Fëdor Petrovich inquired of Ivan Ilych whether he had ever seen Sarah Bernhardt. Ivan Ilych did not at first catch the question, but then replied: "No, have you seen her before?"

"Yes, in *Adrienne Lecouvreur*."

Praskovya Fëdorovna mentioned some rôles in which Sarah Bernhardt was particularly good. Her daughter disagreed. Conversation sprang up as to the elegance and realism of her acting—the sort of conversation that is always repeated and is always the same.

In the midst of the conversation Fëdor Petrovich glanced at Ivan Ilych and became silent. Ivan Ilych was staring with glittering eyes straight before him, evidently indignant with them. This had to be rectified, but it was impossible to do so. The silence had to be broken, but for a time no one dared to break it and they all became afraid that the conventional deception would suddenly become obvious and the truth become plain to all. Lisa was the first to pluck up courage and break the silence, but by trying to hide what everybody was feeling, she betrayed it.

"Well, if we are going it's time to start," she said, looked at her watch, a present from her father, and with a faint and significant smile at Fëdor Petrovich relating to something known only to them. She got up with a rustle of her dress.

They all rose, said good-night, and went away.

When they had gone it seemed to Ivan Ilych that he felt better; the falsity had gone with them. But the pain remained—that same pain and that same fear that made everything monotonously alike, nothing harder and nothing easier. Everything was worse.

Again minute followed minute and hour followed hour. Everything remained the same and there was no cessation. And the inevitable end of it all became more and more terrible.

"Yes, send Gerasim here," he replied to a question Peter asked.

9

His wife returned late at night. She came in on tiptoe, but he heard her, opened his eyes, and made haste to close them again. She wished to send Gerasim away and to sit with him herself, but he opened his eyes and said: "No, go away."

"Are you in great pain?"

"Always the same."

"Take some opium."

He agreed and took some. She went away.

Till about three in the morning he was in a state of stupefied misery. It seemed to him that he and his pain were being thrust into a narrow, deep black sack, but though they were pushed further and further in they could not be pushed to the bottom. And this, terrible enough in itself, was accompanied by suffering. He struggled but yet cooperated. And suddenly he broke through, fell, and regained consciousness. Gerasim was sitting at the foot of the bed dozing quietly, while he himself lay with his emaciated stockinged legs resting on Gerasim's shoulders; the same shaded candle was there and the same unceasing pain.

"Go away, Gerasim," he whispered.

"It's all right, sir. I'll stay a while."

"No. Go away."

He removed his legs from Gerasim's shoulders, turned sideways onto his arm, and felt sorry for himself. He only waited till Gerasim had gone into the next room and then restrained himself no longer but wept like a child. He wept on account of his helplessness, his terrible loneliness, the cruelty of man, the cruelty of God, and the absence of God.

"Why hast Thou done all this? Why hast Thou brought me here? Why, why dost Thou torment me so terribly?"

He did not expect an answer and yet wept because there was no answer and could be none. The pain grew more acute, but he did not stir and did not call. He said to himself: "Go on! Strike me! But what is it for? What have I done to Thee? What is it for?"

Then he grew quiet and not only ceased weeping but even held his breath and became all attention. It was as though he were listening not to an audible voice but to the voice of his soul, to the current of thoughts arising within him.

"What is it you want?" was the first clear conception of expression in words, that he heard.

"What do you want? What do you want?" he repeated to himself.

"What do I want? To live and not to suffer," he answered.

And again he listened with such concentrated attention that even his pain did not distract him.

"To live? How?" asked his inner voice.

"Why, to live as I used to—well and pleasantly."

"As you lived before, well and pleasantly?" the voice repeated.

And in imagination he began to recall the best moments of his pleasant life. But strange to say none of those best moments of his pleasant life now seemed at all what they had then seemed—none of them except the first recollections of childhood. There, in childhood, there had been something really pleasant with which it would be possible to live if it could return. But the child who had experienced that happiness existed no longer, it was like a reminiscence of somebody else.

As soon as the period began which had produced the present Ivan Ilych, all that had then seemed joys now melted before his sight and turned into something trivial and often nasty.

And the further he departed from childhood and the nearer he came to the present the more worthless and doubtful were the joys. This began with the School of Law. A little that was really good was still found there—there was light-heartedness, friendship, and hope. But in the upper classes there had already been fewer of such good moments. Then during the first years of his official career, when he was in the service of the Governor, some pleasant moments again occurred: they were memories of love for a woman. Then all became confused and there was still less of what was good; later on again there was still less that was good, and the further he went the less there was. His marriage, a mere accident, then the disenchantment that followed it, his wife's bad breath and the sensuality and hypocrisy: then that deadly official life and those preoccupations about money, a year of it, and two, and ten, and twenty, and always the same thing. And the longer it lasted the more deadly it became. "It is as if I had been going downhill while I imagined I was going up. And that is really what it was. I was going up in public opinion, but to the same extent life was ebbing away from me. And now it is all done and there is only death."

"Then what does it mean? Why? It can't be that life is so senseless and horrible. But if it really has been so horrible and senseless, why must I die and die in agony? There is something wrong!"

"Maybe I did not live as I ought to have done," it suddenly occurred to him. "But how could that be, when I did everything properly?" he replied, and immediately dismissed from his mind this, the sole solution of all the riddles of life and death, as something quite impossible.

"Then what do you want now? To live? Live how? Live as you lived in the law courts when the usher proclaimed 'The judge is coming!' The judge is coming, the judge!" he repeated to himself. "Here he is, the judge. But I am not guilty!" he exclaimed angrily. "What is it for?" And he ceased crying, but turning his face to the wall continued to ponder on the same question: Why, and for what purpose, is there all this horror? But however much he pondered he found no answer. And whenever the thought occurred to him, as it often did, that it all resulted from his not having lived as he ought to have done, he at once recalled the correctness of his whole life and dismissed so strange an idea.

10

Another fortnight passed. Ivan Ilych now no longer left his sofa. He would not lie in bed but lay on the sofa, facing the wall nearly all the time. He suffered ever the same unceasing agonies and in his loneliness pondered always on the same insoluble question: "What is this? Can it be that it is Death?" And the inner voice answered: "Yes, it is Death."

"Why these sufferings?" And the voice answered, "For no reason—they just are so." Beyond and besides this there was nothing.

From the very beginning of his illness, ever since he had first been to see the doctor, Ivan Ilych's life had been divided between two contrary and alternating moods: now it was despair and the expectation of this uncomprehended and terrible death, and now hope and an intently interested observation of the functioning of his organs. Now before his eyes there was only a kidney or an intestine that temporarily evaded its duty, and now only that incomprehensible and dreadful death from which it was impossible to escape.

These two states of mind had alternated from the very beginning of his illness, but the further it progressed the more doubtful and fantastic became the conception of the kidney, and the more real the sense of impending death.

He had but to call to mind what he had been three months before and what he was now, to call to mind with what regularity he had been going downhill, for every possibility of hope to be shattered.

Latterly during that loneliness in which he found himself as he lay facing the back of the sofa, a loneliness in the midst of a populous town and surrounded by numerous acquaintances and relations but that yet could not have been more complete anywhere—either at the bottom of the sea or under the earth—during that terrible loneliness Ivan Ilych had lived only in memories of the past. Pictures of his past rose before him one after another. They always began with what was nearest in time and then went back to what was the most remote—to his childhood—and rested there. If he thought of the stewed prunes that had been offered him that day, his mind went back to the raw shriveled French plums of his childhood, their peculiar flavor and the flow of saliva when he sucked their stones, and along with the memory of that taste came a whole series of memories of those days: his nurse, his brother, and their toys. "No, I mustn't think of that . . . It is too painful," Ivan Ilych said to himself, and brought himself back to the present—to the button on the back of the sofa and the creases in its morocco. "Morocco is expensive, but it does not wear well: there had been a quarrel about it. It was a different kind of quarrel and a different kind of morocco that time when we tore father's portfolio and were punished, and Mamma brought us some tarts . . ." And again his thoughts dwelt on his childhood, and again it was painful and he tried to banish them and fix his mind on something else.

Then again together with that chain of memories another series passed through his mind—of how his illness had progressed and grown worse. There also the further back he looked the more life there had been. There had been more of what was good in life and more of life itself. The two merged together. "Just as the pain went on getting worse and worse, so my life grew worse and worse," he thought. "There is one bright spot there at the back, at the beginning of life, and afterwards all becomes blacker and blacker and proceeds more and more rapidly—in inverse ratio to the square of the distance from death," thought Ivan Ilych. And the example of a stone falling downwards with increasing velocity entered his mind. Life, a series of increasing sufferings, flies further and further towards its end—the most terrible suffering. "I am flying . . ." He shuddered, shifted himself, and tried to resist, but was already aware that resistance was impossible, and again with eyes weary of gazing but unable to cease seeing what was before them, he stared at the back of the sofa and waited—awaiting that dreadful fall and shock and destruction.

"Resistance is impossible!" he said to himself. "If I could only understand what it is all for! But that too is impossible. An explanation would be possible if it could be said that I have not lived as I ought to. But it is impossible to say that," and he remembered all the legality, correctitude, and propriety of his life. "That at any rate can certainly not be admitted," he thought, and his lips smiled ironically as if someone could see that smile and be taken in by it. "There is no explanation! Agony, death . . . What for?"

11

Another two weeks went by in this way and during that fortnight an event occurred that Ivan Ilych and his wife had desired. Petrishchev formally proposed. It happened in the evening. The next day Praskovya Fëdorovna came into her husband's room considering how best to inform him of it, but that very night there had been a fresh change for the worse in his condition. She found him lying on the sofa but in a different position. He lay on his back, groaning and staring fixedly in front of him.

She began to remind him of his medicines, but he turned his eyes toward her with such a look that she did not finish what she was saying; so great an animosity, to her in particular, did that look express.

"For Christ's sake let me die in peace!" he said.

She would have gone away, but just then their daughter came in and went up to say good morning. He looked at her as he had done at his wife, and in reply to her inquiry about his health said dryly that he would soon free them all of himself. They were both silent and after sitting with him for a while went away.

"Is it our fault?" Lisa said to her mother. "It's as if we were to blame! I am sorry for papa, but why should we be tortured?"

The doctor came at his usual time. Ivan Ilych answered "Yes" and "No," never taking his angry eyes from him, and at last said: "You know you can do nothing for me, so leave me alone."

"We can ease your sufferings."

"You can't even do that. Let me be."

The doctor went into the drawing-room and told Praskovya Fëdorovna that the case was very serious and that the only resource left was opium to allay her husband's sufferings, which must be terrible.

It was true, as the doctor said, that Ivan Ilych's physical sufferings were terrible, but worse than the physical sufferings were his mental sufferings, which were his chief torture.

His mental sufferings were due to the fact that that night, as he looked at Gerasim's sleepy, good-natured face with its prominent cheek-bones, the question suddenly occurred to him: "What if my whole life has really been wrong?"

It occurred to him that what had appeared perfectly impossible before, namely that he had not spent his life as he should have done, might after all be true. It occurred to him that his scarcely perceptible attempts to struggle against what was considered good by the most highly placed people, those scarcely noticeable impulses which he had immediately suppressed, might have been the real thing, and all the rest false. And his professional duties and the whole arrangement of his life and of his family, and all his social and official interests, might all have been false. He tried to defend all those things to himself and suddenly felt the weakness of what he was defending. There was nothing to defend.

"But if that is so," he said to himself, "and I am leaving this life with the consciousness that I have lost all that was given me and it is impossible to rectify it—what then?"

He lay on his back and began to pass his life in review in quite a new way. In the morning when he saw first his footman, then his wife, then his daughter, and then the doctor, their every word and movement confirmed to him the awful truth that had been revealed to him during the night. In them he saw himself—all that for which he had lived—and saw clearly that it was not real at all, but a terrible and huge deception which had hidden both life and death. This consciousness intensified his physical suffering tenfold. He groaned and tossed about, and pulled at his clothing which choked and stifled him. And he hated them on that account.

He was given a large dose of opium and became unconscious, but at noon his sufferings began again. He drove everybody away and tossed from side to side.

His wife came to him and said:

"Jean, my dear, do this for me. It can't do any harm and often helps. Healthy people often do it."

He opened his eyes wide.

"What? Take communion? Why? It's unnecessary! However . . ."

She began to cry.

"Yes, do, my dear. I'll send for our priest. He is such a nice man."

"All right. Very well," he muttered.

When the priest came and heard his confession, Ivan Ilych was softened and seemed to feel a relief from his doubts and consequently from his sufferings, and for a moment there came a ray of hope. He again began to think of the vermiform appendix and the possibility of correcting it. He received the sacrament with tears in his eyes.

When they laid him down again afterwards he felt a moment's ease, and the hope that he might live awoke in him again. He began to think of the operation that had been suggested to him. "To live! I want to live!" he said to himself.

His wife came to congratulate him after his communion, and when uttering the usual conventional words she added:

"You feel better, don't you?"

Without looking at her he said "Yes."

Her dress, her figure, the expression of her face, the tone of her voice, all revealed the same thing. "This is wrong, it is not as it should be. All you have lived for and still live for is falsehood and deception, hiding life and death from you." And as soon as he admitted that thought, his hatred and his agonizing physical suffering again sprang up, and with that suffering a consciousness of the unavoidable, approaching end. And to this was added a new sensation of grinding shooting pain and a feeling of suffocation.

The expression of his face when he uttered that "yes" was dreadful. Having uttered it, he looked her straight in the eyes, turned on his face with a rapidity extraordinary in his weak state and shouted:

"Go away! Go away and leave me alone!"

12

From that moment the screaming began that continued for three days, and was so terrible that one could not hear it through two closed doors without horror. At the moment he answered his wife he realized that he was lost, that there was no return, that the end had come, the very end, and his doubts were still unsolved and remained doubts.

"Oh! Oh! Oh!" he cried in various intonations. He had begun by screaming "I won't!" and continued screaming on the letter O.

For three whole days, during which time did not exist for him, he struggled in that black sack into which he was being thrust by an invisible, resistless force. He struggled as a man condemned to death struggles in the hands of the executioner, knowing that he cannot save himself. And every moment he felt that despite all his efforts he was drawing nearer and nearer to what terrified him. He felt that his agony was due to his being thrust into that black hole and still more to his not being able to get right into it. He was hindered from getting into it by his conviction that his life had been a good one. That very justification of his life held him fast and prevented his moving forward, and it caused him most torment of all.

Suddenly some force struck him in the chest and side, making it still harder to breathe, and he fell through the hole and there at the bottom was a light. What had happened to him was like the sensation one sometimes experiences in a railway carriage when one thinks one is going backwards while one is really going forwards and suddenly becomes aware of the real direction.

"Yes, it was all not the right thing," he said to himself, "but that's no matter. It can be done. But what *is* the right thing?" he asked himself, and suddenly grew quiet.

This occurred at the end of the third day, two hours before his death. Just then his schoolboy son had crept softly in and gone up to the bedside. The dying man was still screaming and waving his arms. His hand fell on the boy's head, and the boy caught it, pressed it to his lips, and began to cry.

At that very moment Ivan Ilych fell through and caught sight of the light, and it was revealed to him that though his life had not been what it should have been, this could still be rectified. He asked himself, "What *is* the right thing?" and grew still, listening. Then he felt that someone was kissing his hand. He opened his eyes, looked at his son, and felt sorry for him. His wife came up to him and he glanced at her. She was gazing at him openmouthed with undried tears on her nose and cheek and a despairing look on her face. He felt sorry for her too.

"Yes, I am making them wretched," he thought. "They are sorry, but it will be better for them when I die." He wished to say this but had not the strength to utter it. "Besides, why speak? I must act," he thought. With a look at his wife he indicated his son and said: "Take him away . . . sorry for him . . . sorry for you too . . ." He tried to add, "forgive me," but said "forgo" and waved his hand, knowing that He whose understanding mattered would understand.

And suddenly it grew clear to him that what had been oppressing him and would not leave him was dropping away at once from two sides, from ten sides, and from all sides. He was sorry for them, he must act so as not to hurt them and free himself from these sufferings. "How good and how simple!" he thought. "And the pain?" he asked himself. "What has become of it? Where are you, pain?"

He turned his attention to it.

"Yes, here it is. Well, what of it? Let the pain be."

"And death . . . where is it?"

He sought his former accustomed fear of death and did not find it. "Where is it? What death?" There was no fear because there was no death.

In place of death there was light.

"So that's what it is!" he suddenly exclaimed aloud. "What joy!"

To him all this happened in a single instant, and the meaning of that instant did not change. For those present his agony continued for another two hours. Something rattled in his throat, his emaciated body twitched, then the gasping and rattle became less and less frequent.

"It is finished!" said someone near him.

He heard these words and repeated them in his soul.

"Death is finished," he said to himself. "It is no more!"

He drew in a breath, stopped in the midst of a sigh, stretched out, and died.

Poetry

The Elements
of Poetry

1. What Is Poetry?

Poetry is as universal as language and almost as ancient. The most primitive peoples have used it, and the most civilized have cultivated it. In all ages, and in all countries, poetry has been written—and eagerly read or listened to—by all kinds and conditions of people, by soldiers, statesmen, lawyers, farmers, doctors, scientists, clergymen, philosophers, kings, and queens. In all ages it has been especially the concern of the educated, the intelligent, and the sensitive, and it has appealed, in its simpler forms, to the uneducated and to children. Why? First, because it has given pleasure. People have read it or listened to it or recited it because they liked it, because it gave them enjoyment. But this is not the whole answer. Poetry in all ages has been regarded as important, not simply as one of several alternative forms of amusement, as one person might choose bowling, another chess, and another poetry. Rather, it has been regarded as something central to existence, something having unique value to the fully realized life, something that we are better off for having and spiritually impoverished without. To understand the reasons for this, we need to have at least a provisional understanding of what poetry is—provisional, because people have always been more successful at appreciating poetry than at defining it.

Initially, poetry might be defined as a kind of language that says *more* and says it *more intensely* than does ordinary language. In order to understand this fully, we need to understand what it is that poetry "says." For language is employed on different occasions to say quite different kinds of things; in other words, language has different uses.

Perhaps the commonest use of language is to communicate *information*. We say that it is nine o'clock, that there is a good movie downtown, that George Washington was the first president of the United States, that bromine and iodine are members of the halogen group of chemical elements. This we might call the *practical* use of language; it helps us with the ordinary business of living.

But it is not primarily to communicate information that novels and short stories and plays and poems are written. These exist to bring us a sense and a perception of life, to widen and sharpen our contacts with existence. Their concern is with *experience*. We all have an inner need to live more deeply and fully and with greater awareness, to know the experience of others and to know better our own experience. Poets, from their own store of felt, observed, or imagined experiences, select, combine, and reorganize. They create significant new experiences for their readers—significant because focused and formed—in which readers can participate and which they may use to give themselves a greater awareness and understanding of their world. Literature, in other words, can be used as a gear for stepping up the intensity and increasing the range of our experience and as a glass for clarifying it. This is the *literary* use of language, for literature is not only an aid to living but a means of living.*

Suppose, for instance, that we are interested in eagles. If we want simply to acquire information about eagles, we may turn to an encyclopedia or a book of natural history. There we find that the family Falconidae, to which eagles belong, is characterized by imperforate nostrils, legs of medium length, a hooked bill, the hind toe inserted on a level with the three front ones, and the claws roundly curved and sharp; that land eagles are feathered to the toes and sea-fishing eagles halfway to the toes; that their length is about three feet, the extent of wing seven feet; that the nest is usually placed on some inaccessible cliff; that the eggs are spotted and do not exceed three; and perhaps that the eagle's "great power of vision, the vast height to which it soars in the sky, the wild grandeur of its abode, have . . . commended it to the poets of all nations."†

But unless we are interested in this information only for practical purposes, we are likely to feel a little disappointed, as though we had

---

*A third use of language is as an instrument of persuasion. This is the use we find in advertisements, propaganda bulletins, sermons, and political speeches. These three uses of language—the practical, the literary, and the hortatory—are not sharply divided. They may be thought of as three points of a triangle; most actual specimens of written language fall somewhere within the triangle. Most poetry conveys some information, and some poetry has a design on the reader. But language becomes *literature* when the desire to communicate experience predominates.

†*Encyclopedia Americana,* IX, 473–74.

grasped the feathers of the eagle but not its soul. True, we have learned many facts about the eagle, but we have missed somehow its lonely majesty, its power, and the "wild grandeur" of its surroundings that would make the eagle a living creature rather than a mere museum specimen. For the living eagle we must turn to literature.

THE EAGLE

He clasps the crag with crooked hands;
Close to the sun in lonely lands,
Ringed with the azure world, he stands.

The wrinkled sea beneath him crawls;
He watches from his mountain walls,
And like a thunderbolt he falls.

Alfred, Lord Tennyson (1809–1892)

QUESTIONS

1. What is peculiarly effective about the expressions "crooked hands," "close to the sun," "ringed with the azure world," "wrinkled," "crawls," and "like a thunderbolt"?
2. Notice the formal pattern of the poem, particularly the contrast of "he stands" in the first stanza and "he falls" in the second. Is there any other contrast between the two stanzas?

When the preceding poem has been read well, readers will feel that they have enjoyed a significant experience and understand eagles better, though in a different way, than they did from the encyclopedia article alone. For if the article *analyzes* man's experience with eagles, the poem in some sense *synthesizes* such an experience. Indeed, the two approaches to experience—the scientific and the literary—may be said to complement each other. And it may be contended that the kind of understanding we get from the second is at least as valuable as the kind we get from the first.

Literature, then, exists to communicate significant experience—significant because concentrated and organized. Its function is not to tell us *about* experience but to allow us imaginatively to *participate* in it. It is a means of allowing us, through the imagination, to live more fully, more deeply, more richly, and with greater awareness. It can do this in two ways: by *broadening* our experience—that is, by making us acquainted with a range of experience with which, in the ordinary course of events, we might have no contact—or by *deepening* our experience—that is, by making us feel more poignantly and more understandingly the everyday experiences all of us have.

Two false approaches often taken to poetry can be avoided if we keep this conception of literature firmly in mind. The first approach always looks for a lesson or a bit of moral instruction. The second expects to find poetry always beautiful. Let us consider a song from Shakespeare:

WINTER

When icicles hang by the wall,
    And Dick the shepherd blows his nail,
And Tom bears logs into the hall,
    And milk comes frozen home in pail,
When blood is nipped and ways be foul,   5
Then nightly sings the staring owl,
    "Tu-whit, tu-who!"

A merry note,
While greasy Joan doth keel° the pot.   skim

When all aloud the wind doth blow,   10
    And coughing drowns the parson's saw,
And birds sit brooding in the snow,
    And Marian's nose looks red and raw,
When roasted crabs° hiss in the bowl,   crab apples
Then nightly sings the staring owl,   15
    "Tu-whit, tu-who!"

A merry note,
While greasy Joan doth keel the pot.

William Shakespeare (1564–1616)

QUESTIONS

1. What are the meanings of "nail" (2) and "saw" (11)?
2. Is the owl's cry really a "merry" note? How are this adjective and the verb "sings" employed?
3. In what way does the owl's cry contrast with the other details of the poem?

In the poem "Winter" Shakespeare is attempting to communicate the quality of winter life around a sixteenth-century English country house. But instead of telling us flatly that winter in such surroundings is cold and in many respects unpleasant, though with some pleasant features too (the adjectives *cold, unpleasant,* and *pleasant* are not even used in the poem), he gives us a series of concrete homely details that suggest these qualities and enable us, imaginatively, to experience this winter life ourselves. The shepherd lad blows on his fingernails to warm his hands; the milk freezes in the pail between the cowshed and the kitchen; the roads are muddy; the folk listening to the parson have colds; the birds "sit brooding in the snow"; and the servant girl's nose is raw from cold. But pleasant things are in prospect. Logs are being brought in for a fire, hot cider or ale is being prepared, and the kitchen maid is making a hot soup or stew. In contrast to all these homely, familiar details of country life comes in the mournful, haunting, and eerie note of the owl.

Obviously the poem contains no moral. Readers who always look in poetry for some lesson, message, or noble truth about life are bound to be disappointed. Moral-hunters see poetry as a kind of sugar-coated pill—a wholesome truth or lesson made palatable by being put into pretty words. What they are really after is a sermon—not a poem, but something inspirational. Yet "Winter," which has appealed to readers now for nearly four centuries, is not inspirational and contains no moral preachment.

Neither is the poem "Winter" beautiful. Though it is appealing in its way and contains elements of beauty, there is little that is really beautiful in red raw noses, coughing in chapel, nipped blood, foul roads, and greasy kitchen maids. Yet some readers think that poetry deals exclusively with beauty—with sunsets, flowers, butterflies, love, God—and that the one appropriate response to any poem is, after a moment of awed silence, "Isn't that beautiful!" For such readers poetry is a precious affair, the enjoyment only of delicate souls, removed from the heat and sweat of ordinary life. But theirs is too narrow an approach to poetry. The function of poetry is sometimes to be ugly rather than beautiful. And poetry may deal with common colds and greasy kitchen maids as legitimately as with sunsets and flowers. Consider another example:

DULCE ET DECORUM EST

Bent double, like old beggars under sacks,
Knock-kneed, coughing like hags, we cursed through sludge,
Till on the haunting flares we turned our backs,
And towards our distant rest began to trudge.
Men marched asleep. Many had lost their boots,   5
But limped on, blood-shod. All went lame, all blind;
Drunk with fatigue; deaf even to the hoots
Of gas-shells dropping softly behind.

Gas! GAS! Quick, boys!—An ecstasy of fumbling,
Fitting the clumsy helmets just in time,   10
But someone still was yelling out and stumbling
And flound'ring like a man in fire or lime.—
Dim through the misty panes and thick green light,
As under a green sea, I saw him drowning.

In all my dreams before my helpless sight   15
He plunges at me, guttering, choking, drowning.

If in some smothering dreams, you too could pace
Behind the wagon that we flung him in,
And watch the white eyes writhing in his face,
His hanging face, like a devil's sick of sin,   20
If you could hear, at every jolt, the blood
Come gargling from the froth-corrupted lungs
Bitter as the cud
Of vile, incurable sores on innocent tongues,—
My friend, you would not tell with such high zest   25
To children ardent for some desperate glory,
The old lie: *Dulce et decorum est
Pro patria mori.*

Wilfred Owen (1893–1918)

QUESTIONS

1. The Latin quotation, from the Roman poet Horace, means "It is sweet and
   becoming to die for one's country." (Wilfred Owen died fighting for England
   in World War I, a week before the armistice.) What is the poem's comment on
   this statement?
2. List the elements of the poem that to you seem not beautiful and therefore
   unpoetic. Are there any elements of beauty in the poem?
3. How do the comparisons in lines 1, 14, 20, and 23–24 contribute to the
   effectiveness of the poem?

Poetry takes all life as its province. Its primary concern is not with
beauty, not with philosophical truth, not with persuasion, but with experience. Beauty and philosophical truth are aspects of experience, and the
poet is often engaged with them. But poetry as a whole is concerned with
all kinds of experience—beautiful or ugly, strange or common, noble or
ignoble, actual or imaginary. One of the paradoxes of human existence is
that all experience—even painful experience—when transmitted through
the medium of art is, for the good reader, enjoyable. In real life, death and
pain and suffering are not pleasurable, but in poetry they may be. In real

life, getting soaked in a rainstorm is not pleasurable, but in poetry it can be. In actual life, if we cry, usually we are unhappy; but if we cry in a movie, we are manifestly enjoying it. We do not ordinarily like to be terrified in real life, but we sometimes seek movies or books that will terrify us. We find some value in all intense living. To be intensely alive is the opposite of being dead. To be dull, to be bored, to be imperceptive is in one sense to be dead. Poetry comes to us bringing life and therefore pleasure. Moreover, art focuses and so organizes experience as to give us a better understanding of it. And to understand life is partly to be master of it.

Between poetry and other forms of imaginative literature there is no sharp distinction. You may have been taught to believe that poetry can be recognized by the arrangement of its lines on the page or by its use of rime and meter. Such superficial tests are almost worthless. The Book of Job in the Bible and Melville's *Moby Dick* are highly poetical, but the familiar verse that begins: "Thirty days hath September, / April, June, and November . . ." is not. The difference between poetry and other literature is one only of degree. Poetry is the most condensed and concentrated form of literature, saying most in the fewest number of words. It is language whose individual lines, either because of their own brilliance or because they focus so powerfully what has gone before, have a higher voltage than most language has. It is language that grows frequently incandescent, giving off both light and heat.

Ultimately, therefore, poetry can be recognized only by the response made to it by a good reader, someone who has acquired some sensitivity to poetry. But there is a catch here. We are not all good readers. To a poor reader, poetry will often seem dull and boring, a fancy way of writing something that could be said more simply. So might a colorblind man deny that there is such a thing as color.

The act of communication involved in reading poetry is like the act of communication involved in receiving a message by radio. Two factors are involved: a transmitting station and a receiving set. The completeness of the communication depends on both the power and clarity of the transmitter and the sensitivity and tuning of the receiver. When a person reads a poem and no experience is transmitted, either the poem is not a good poem or the reader is a poor reader or not properly tuned. With new poetry, we cannot always be sure which is at fault. With older poetry, if it has acquired critical acceptance—has been enjoyed by generations of good readers—we may assume that the receiving set is at fault. Fortunately, the fault is not irremediable. Though we cannot all become expert readers, we can become good enough to find both pleasure and value in much good poetry, or we can increase the amount of pleasure we already find in poetry and the number of kinds of poetry we find it in. To help you increase your sensitivity and range as a receiving set is the purpose of this book.

Poetry, finally, is a kind of multidimensional language. Ordinary language—the kind that we use to communicate information—is one-dimensional. It is directed at only part of the listener, his understanding. Its one dimension is intellectual. Poetry, which is language used to communicate experience, has at least four dimensions. If it is to communicate experience, it must be directed at the *whole* person, not just at his understanding. It must involve not only his intelligence but also his senses, emotions, and imagination. Poetry, to the intellectual dimension, adds a sensuous dimension, an emotional dimension, and an imaginative dimension.

Poetry achieves its extra dimensions—its greater pressure per word and its greater tension per poem—by drawing more fully and more consistently than does ordinary language on a number of language resources, none of which is peculiar to poetry. These various resources form the subjects of a number of the following chapters. Among them are connotation, imagery, metaphor, symbol, paradox, irony, allusion, sound repetition, rhythm, and pattern. Using these resources and the materials of life, the poet shapes and makes his poem. Successful poetry is never effusive language. If it is to come alive it must be as cunningly put together and as efficiently organized as a tree. It must be an organism whose every part serves a useful purpose and cooperates with every other part to preserve and express the life that is within it.

*   *   *

SPRING

When daisies pied and violets blue,
    And lady-smocks all silver-white,
And cuckoo-buds of yellow hue
    Do paint the meadows with delight,
The cuckoo then, on every tree,   5
Mocks married men; for thus sings he,
                "Cuckoo!
Cuckoo, cuckoo!" O word of fear,
Unpleasing to a married ear!

When shepherds pipe on oaten straws,   10
    And merry larks are ploughmen's clocks,

When turtles tread, and rooks, and daws,
    And maidens bleach their summer smocks,
The cuckoo then, on every tree,
Mocks married men; for thus sings he,   15
            "Cuckoo!
Cuckoo, cuckoo!" O word of fear,
Unpleasing to a married ear!

                                                William Shakespeare (1564–1616)

QUESTIONS

1. Vocabulary: *pied* (1), *lady-smocks* (2), *oaten straws* (10), *turtles* (12), *tread* (12), *daws* (12).
2. This song is a companion piece to "Winter." In what respects are the two poems similar? How do they contrast? What details show that this poem, like "Winter," was written by a realist, not simply by a man carried away with the beauty of spring?
3. The word "cuckoo" is "unpleasing to a married ear" because it sounds like *cuckold.* Cuckolds were a frequent butt of humor in earlier English literature. If you do not know the meaning of the word, look it up.
4. Is the tone of this poem solemn or light and semihumorous?

A BIRD CAME DOWN THE WALK*

A bird came down the walk.
He did not know I saw.
He bit an angle-worm in halves
And ate the fellow, raw.

And then he drank a dew   5
From a convenient grass,
And then hopped sideways to the wall
To let a beetle pass.

He glanced with rapid eyes
That hurried all around;   10
They looked like frightened beads, I thought.
He stirred his velvet head

Like one in danger; cautious,
I offered him a crumb,

---

*Whenever a title duplicates the first line of the poem or a substantial portion thereof, it is probable that the poet left the poem untitled and that the anthologist has substituted the first line or part of it as an editorial convenience. This is standard practice, and is true for this poem and for two of the three poems that follow in this chapter.

And he unrolled his feathers 15
And rowed him softer home

Than oars divide the ocean,
Too silver for a seam,
Or butterflies, off banks of noon,
Leap, plashless, as they swim. 20

Emily Dickinson (1830–1886)

QUESTIONS

1. The poem is based on a pair of contrasts: that between the observer (the human world) and the bird (the natural world); and that between the bird on the ground (1–14) and the bird in flight (15–20). Discuss the first contrast. What is the relationship between observer and bird? How do their "worlds" contrast?
2. How does the bird in the air differ from the bird on the ground? How do the sounds of the words in lines 15–20 reflect that difference?
3. Discuss the appropriateness of the word "rowed" (16). What is referred to in line 18? What image is suggested in lines 19–20, and how is *it* lightly reflected in the sounds of the words used?

CONSTANTLY RISKING ABSURDITY

Constantly risking absurdity
                            and death
            whenever he performs
                        above the heads
                                    of his audience 5
        the poet like an acrobat
                    climbs on rime
                        to a high wire of his own making
and balancing on eyebeams
                        above a sea of faces 10
            paces his way
                        to the other side of day
        performing entrechats
                        and sleight-of-foot tricks
and other high theatrics 15
                        and all without mistaking
            any thing
                        for what it may not be

        For he's the super realist
                        who must perforce perceive 20
            taut truth
                        before the taking of each stance or step

in his supposed advance
                    toward that still higher perch
where Beauty stands and waits   25
                    with gravity
                    to start her death-defying leap

            And he
                a little charleychaplin man
                            who may or may not catch   30
                    her fair eternal form
                            spreadeagled in the empty air
                of existence

                                        Lawrence Ferlinghetti (b. 1919)

QUESTIONS

1. Vocabulary: *entrechats* (13). What meanings have "above the heads" (4), "sleight-of-foot tricks" (14), "high theatrics" (15), "with gravity" (26)?
2. The poet, it is said, "climbs on rime" (7). To what extent does this poem utilize rime and other sound correspondences? Point out examples.
3. What statement does the poem make about poetry, truth, and beauty?
4. What additional comments about poetry are implied by the figures of speech employed?
5. Does Ferlinghetti take poets and poetry seriously? Solemnly?

THE PASTURE

I'm going out to clean the pasture spring;
I'll only stop to rake the leaves away
(And wait to watch the water clear, I may):
I shan't be gone long.—You come too.

I'm going out to fetch the little calf
That's standing by the mother. It's so young
It totters when she licks it with her tongue.
I shan't be gone long.—You come too.

                                        Robert Frost (1874–1963)

QUESTIONS

1. Who and what kind of person is the speaker? Who is addressed?
2. Frost, as a poet, characteristically strove to capture the speech rhythms and language of the actual human voice in poems retaining a metrical form. In what lines is he particularly successful at this?

3. Originally the initial poem in Frost's second volume of verse, "The Pasture" was retained by Frost as the initial poem in collections of his verse. What additional meaning does the poem acquire from this position? Are poets usually concerned, would you guess, with the *arrangement* of poems in their books? Why or why not?

TERENCE, THIS IS STUPID STUFF

"Terence, this is stupid stuff:
You eat your victuals fast enough;
There can't be much amiss, 'tis clear,
To see the rate you drink your beer.
But oh, good Lord, the verse you make,   5
It gives a chap the belly-ache.
The cow, the old cow, she is dead;
It sleeps well, the horned head:
We poor lads, 'tis our turn now
To hear such tunes as killed the cow.   10
Pretty friendship 'tis to rhyme
Your friends to death before their time
Moping melancholy mad:
Come, pipe a tune to dance to, lad."

Why, if 'tis dancing you would be,   15
There's brisker pipes than poetry.
Say, for what were hop-yards meant,
Or why was Burton built on Trent?
Oh many a peer of England brews
Livelier liquor than the Muse,   20
And malt does more than Milton can
To justify God's ways to man.
Ale, man, ale's the stuff to drink
For fellows whom it hurts to think:
Look into the pewter pot   25
To see the world as the world's not.
And faith, 'tis pleasant till 'tis past:
The mischief is that 'twill not last.
Oh I have been to Ludlow fair
And left my necktie god knows where,   30
And carried half-way home, or near,
Pints and quarts of Ludlow beer:
Then the world seemed none so bad,
And I myself a sterling lad;
And down in lovely muck I've lain,   35

Happy till I woke again.
Then I saw the morning sky:
Heigho, the tale was all a lie;
The world, it was the old world yet,
I was I, my things were wet,   40
And nothing now remained to do
But begin the game anew.

   Therefore, since the world has still
Much good, but much less good than ill,
And while the sun and moon endure   45
Luck's a chance, but trouble's sure,
I'd face it as a wise man would,
And train for ill and not for good.
'Tis true, the stuff I bring for sale
Is not so brisk a brew as ale: 50
Out of a stem that scored the hand
I wrung it in a weary land.
But take it: if the smack is sour,
The better for the embittered hour;
It should do good to heart and head   55
When your soul is in my soul's stead;
And I will friend you, if I may,
In the dark and cloudy day.

   There was a king reigned in the East:
There, when kings will sit to feast,   60
They get their fill before they think
With poisoned meat and poisoned drink.
He gathered all that springs to birth
From the many-venomed earth;
First a little, thence to more,   65
He sampled all her killing store;
And easy, smiling, seasoned sound,
Sate the king when healths went round.
They put arsenic in his meat
And stared aghast to watch him eat;   70
They poured strychnine in his cup
And shook to see him drink it up:
They shook, they stared as white's their shirt:
Them it was their poison hurt.
—I tell the tale that I heard told.   75
Mithridates, he died old.

                                    A. E. Housman (1859–1936)

QUESTIONS

1. "Terence" (1) is Housman's poetic name for himself. Housman's poetry is
   largely pessimistic or sad; and this poem, placed near the end of his volume *A
   Shropshire Lad*, is his defense of the kind of poetry he wrote. Who is the
   speaker in the first fourteen lines? Who is the speaker in the rest of the poem?
   What is "the stuff I bring for sale" (49)?
2. "Hops" (17) and "malt" (21) are principal ingredients of beer and ale. Bur-
   ton-upon-Trent (18) is an English city famous for its breweries. Milton
   (21), in the invocation of his epic poem *Paradise Lost*, declares that his purpose is to "justify the ways of God to men." What, in Housman's eyes, is the
   efficacy of liquor in helping one live a difficult life?
3. What six lines of the poem most explicitly sum up the poet's philosophy?
   Most people like reading material that is cheerful and optimistic (on the
   argument that "there's enough suffering and unhappiness in the world already"). What for Housman is the value of pessimistic and tragic literature?
4. "Mithridates" (76) was a king of Pontus and contemporary of Julius Caesar;
   his "tale" is told in Pliny's *Natural History*. What is the connection of this last
   verse paragraph with the rest of the poem?

HAST THOU GIVEN THE HORSE STRENGTH

Hast thou given the horse strength?
Hast thou clothed his neck with thunder?
Canst thou make him afraid as a grasshopper?
The glory of his nostrils is terrible.
He paweth in the valley, and rejoiceth in his strength: 5
He goeth on to meet the armed men.
He mocketh at fear, and is not affrighted;
Neither turneth he back from the sword.
The quiver rattleth against him,
The glittering spear and the shield.   10
He swalloweth the ground with fierceness and rage;
Neither believeth he that it is the sound of the trumpet.
He saith among the trumpets, Ha, ha;
And he smelleth the battle afar off,
The thunder of the captains, and the shouting.   15

From the Book of Job 39:19–25

QUESTION

These words are spoken to Job by the Lord, out of a whirlwind. In the Bible
they are generally printed as prose. What justifies their being regarded as poetry?

2. Reading the Poem

The primary purpose of this book is to develop your ability to understand and appreciate poetry. Here are some preliminary suggestions:

1. Read a poem more than once. A good poem will no more yield its full meaning on a single reading than will a Beethoven symphony on a single hearing. Two readings may be necessary simply to let you get your bearings. And if the poem is a work of art, it will repay repeated and prolonged examination. One does not listen to a good piece of music once and forget it; one does not look at a good painting once and throw it away. A poem is not like a newspaper, to be hastily read and cast into the wastebasket. It is to be hung on the wall of one's mind.

2. Keep a dictionary by you and use it. It is futile to try to understand poetry without troubling to learn the meanings of the words of which it is composed. One might as well attempt to play tennis without a ball. One of your primary purposes while in college should be to build a good vocabulary, and the study of poetry gives you an excellent opportunity. A few other reference books will also be invaluable. Particularly desirable are a good book on mythology (your instructor can recommend one) and a Bible.

3. Read so as to hear the sounds of the words in your mind. Poetry is written to be heard: its meanings are conveyed through sound as well as through print. Every word is therefore important. The best way to read a poem is just the opposite of the best way to read a newspaper. One reads a newspaper as rapidly as possible; one should read a poem as slowly as possible. When you cannot read a poem aloud, lip-read it: form the words with your tongue and mouth though you do not utter them. With ordi-

nary reading material, lip reading is a bad habit; with poetry it is a good habit.

4. Always pay careful attention to what the poem is saying. Though you should be conscious of the sounds of the poem, you should never be so exclusively conscious of them that you pay no attention to what the poem means. For some readers, reading a poem is like getting on board a rhythmical roller coaster. The car starts, and off they go, up and down, paying no attention to the landscape flashing past them, arriving at the end of the poem breathless, with no idea of what it has been about.* This is the wrong way to read a poem. One should make the utmost effort to follow the thought continuously and to grasp the full implications and suggestions. Because a poem says so much, several readings may be necessary, but on the very first reading you should determine the subjects of the verbs and the antecedents of the pronouns.

5. Practice reading poems aloud. When you find one you especially like, make friends listen to it. Try to read it to them in such a way that they will like it too. (a) Read it affectionately, but not affectedly. The two extremes oral readers often fall into are equally deadly. One is to read as if one were reading a tax report or a railroad timetable, unexpressively, in a monotone. The other is to elocute, with artificial flourishes and vocal histrionics. It is not necessary to put emotion into reading a poem. The emotion is already there. It only wants a fair chance to get out. It will express *itself* if the poem is read naturally and sensitively. (b) Of the two extremes, reading too fast offers greater danger than reading too slow. Read slowly enough that each word is clear and distinct and that the meaning has time to sink in. Remember that your friends do not have the advantage, as you do, of having the text before them. Your ordinary rate of reading will probably be too fast. (c) Read the poem so that the rhythmical pattern is felt but not exaggerated. Remember that poetry is written in sentences, just as prose is, and that punctuation is a signal as to how it should be read. Give all grammatical pauses their full due. Do not distort the natural pronunciation of words or a normal accentuation of the sentence to fit into what you have decided is its metrical pattern. One of the worst ways to read a poem is to read it ta-*dum* ta-*dum* ta-*dum* with an exaggerated emphasis on every other syllable. On the other hand, it should not be read as if it were prose. An important test of your reading will be how you handle the end of a line when there is no punctuation there. A frequent mistake of the beginning reader is to treat each line as if it were a complete thought, whether grammatically complete or not,

---

*Some poems encourage this type of reading. When this is so, usually the poet has not made the best use of rhythm to support sense.

and to drop his voice at the end of it. A frequent mistake of the sophisticated reader is to take a running start upon approaching the end of a line and fly over it as if it were not there. The line is a rhythmical unit, and its end should be observed whether there is punctuation or not. If there is no punctuation, one observes it ordinarily by the slightest of pauses or by holding onto the last word in the line just a little longer than usual, without dropping one's voice. In line 12 of the following poem, you should hold onto the word "although" longer than if it occurred elsewhere in the line. But do not lower your voice on it: it is part of the clause that follows in the next stanza.

THE MAN HE KILLED

    Had he and I but met
    By some old ancient inn,
We should have sat us down to wet
    Right many a nipperkin!°   half-pint cup

    But ranged as infantry,   5
    And staring face to face,
I shot at him as he at me,
    And killed him in his place.

    I shot him dead because—
    Because he was my foe,   10
Just so: my foe of course he was;
    That's clear enough; although

    He thought he'd 'list, perhaps,
    Off-hand-like—just as I—
Was out of work—had sold his traps—   15
    No other reason why.

    Yes; quaint and curious war is!
    You shoot a fellow down
You'd treat, if met where any bar is,
    Or help to half-a-crown.   20

                              Thomas Hardy (*1840–1928*)

QUESTIONS

1. Vocabulary: *traps* (15).
2. In informational prose the repetition of a word like "because" (9–10) would be an error. What purpose does the repetition serve here? Why does the

speaker repeat to himself his "clear" reason for killing a man (10–11)? The word "although" (12) gets more emphasis than it ordinarily would because it comes not only at the end of a line but at the end of a stanza. What purpose does this emphasis serve? Can the redundancy of "old ancient" (2) be poetically justified?

3. Someone has defined poetry as "the expression of elevated thought in elevated language." Comment on the adequacy of this definition in the light of Hardy's poem.

To aid us in the understanding of a poem, we may ask ourselves a number of questions about it. One of the most important is *Who is the speaker and what is the occasion?* A cardinal error of some readers is to assume always that the speaker is the poet himself. A far safer course is to assume always that the speaker is someone other than the poet himself. For even when the poet does speak directly and express his own thoughts and emotions, he does so ordinarily as a representative human being rather than as an individual who lives at a particular address, dislikes dill pickles, and favors blue neckties. We must always be cautious about identifying anything in a poem with the biography of the poet. Like the novelist and the playwright, he is fully justified in changing actual details of his own experience to make the experience of the poem more universal. We may well think of every poem, therefore, as being to some degree *dramatic*, that is, the utterance of a fictional character rather than of the poet himself. Many poems are expressly dramatic.

In "The Man He Killed" the speaker is a soldier; the occasion is his having been in battle and killed a man—obviously for the first time in his life. We can tell a good deal about him. He is not a career soldier: he enlisted only because he was out of work. He is a workingman: he speaks a simple and colloquial language ("nipperkin," "'list," "off-hand-like," "traps"), and he has sold the tools of his trade—he may have been a tinker or plumber. He is a friendly, kindly sort who enjoys a neighborly drink of ale in a bar and will gladly lend a friend a half crown when he has it. He has known what it is to be poor. In any other circumstances he would have been horrified at taking a human life. He has been given pause as it is. He is trying to figure it out. But he is not a deep thinker and thinks he has supplied a reason when he has only supplied a name: "I killed the man . . . because he was my foe." The critical question, of course, is *Why was the man his "foe"?* Even the speaker is left unsatisfied by his answer, though he is not analytical enough to know what is wrong with it. Obviously this poem is expressly dramatic. We need know nothing about Thomas Hardy's life (he was never a soldier and never killed a man) to realize that the poem is dramatic. The internal evidence of the poem tells us so.

A second important question that we should ask ourselves upon reading any poem is *What is the central purpose of the poem?** The purpose may be to tell a story, to reveal human character, to impart a vivid impression of a scene, to express a mood or an emotion, or to convey to us vividly some idea or attitude. Whatever the purpose is, we must determine it for ourselves and define it mentally as precisely as possible. Only then can we fully understand the function and meaning of the various details in the poem, by relating them to this central purpose. Only then can we begin to assess the value of the poem and determine whether it is a good one or a poor one. In "The Man He Killed" the central purpose is quite clear: it is to make us realize more keenly the irrationality of war. The puzzlement of the speaker may be our puzzlement. But even if we are able to give a more sophisticated answer than his as to why men kill each other, we ought still to have a greater awareness, after reading the poem, of the fundamental irrationality in war that makes men kill who have no grudge against each other and who might under different circumstances show each other considerable kindness.

IS MY TEAM PLOUGHING

"Is my team ploughing,
    That I was used to drive
And hear the harness jingle
    When I was man alive?"

Aye, the horses trample,   5
    The harness jingles now;
No change though you lie under
    The land you used to plough.

"Is football playing
    Along the river shore,   10
With lads to chase the leather,
    Now I stand up no more?"

Aye, the ball is flying,
    The lads play heart and soul;

---

*Our only reliable evidence of the poem's purpose, of course, is the poem itself. External evidence, when it exists, though often helpful, may also be misleading. Some critics have objected to the use of such terms as "purpose" and "intention" altogether; we cannot know, they maintain, what was *attempted* in the poem; we can know only what was *done*. Philosophically this position is impeccable. Yet it is possible to make inferences about what was attempted, and such inferences furnish a convenient and helpful way of talking about poetry.

The goal stands up, the keeper   15
    Stands up to keep the goal.

"Is my girl happy,
    That I thought hard to leave,
And has she tired of weeping
    As she lies down at eve?"   20

Aye, she lies down lightly,
    She lies not down to weep:
Your girl is well contented.
    Be still, my lad, and sleep.

"Is my friend hearty,   25
    Now I am thin and pine;
And has he found to sleep in
    A better bed than mine?"

Yes, lad, I lie easy,
    I lie as lads would choose;   30
I cheer a dead man's sweetheart,
    Never ask me whose.

                        A. E. Housman (1859–1936)

QUESTIONS

1. What is meant by "whose" in line 32?
2. Is Housman cynical in his observation of human nature and human life?
3. The word "sleep" in the concluding stanzas suggests three different meanings. What are they? How many meanings are suggested by the word "bed"?

   Once we have answered the question *What is the central purpose of the
poem?* we can consider another question, equally important to full understanding: *By what means is that purpose achieved?* It is important to distinguish means from ends. A student on an examination once used the
poem "Is my team ploughing" as evidence that A. E. Housman believed
in immortality, because in it a man speaks from the grave. This is as much
a misconstruction as to say that Thomas Hardy in "The Man He Killed"
joined the army because he was out of work. The purpose of Housman's
poem is to communicate poignantly a certain truth about human life: life
goes on after our deaths pretty much as it did before—our dying does not
disturb the universe. This purpose is achieved by means of a fanciful
dramatic framework in which a dead man converses with his still-living

friend. The framework tells us nothing about whether Housman believed in immortality (as a matter of fact, he did not). It is simply an effective means by which we *can* learn how Housman felt a man's death affected the life he left behind. The question *By what means is the purpose of the poem achieved?* is partially answered by describing the poem's dramatic framework, if it has any. The complete answer requires an accounting of various resources of communication that we will discuss in the rest of this book.

The most important preliminary advice we can give for reading poetry is to maintain always, while reading it, the utmost mental alertness. The most harmful idea one can get about poetry is that its purpose is to soothe and relax and that the best place to read it is lying in a hammock with a cool drink beside one and low music in the background. One *can* read poetry lying in a hammock but only if he refuses to put his mind in the same attitude as his body. Its purpose is not to soothe and relax but to arouse and awake, to shock one into life, to make one more alive. Poetry is not a substitute for a sedative.

An analogy can be drawn between reading poetry and playing tennis. Both offer great enjoyment if the game is played hard. A good tennis player must be constantly on the tip of his toes, concentrating on his opponent's every move. He must be ready for a drive to the right or a drive to the left, a lob overhead or a drop shot barely over the net. He must be ready for top spin or underspin, a ball that bounces crazily to the left or crazily to the right. He must jump for the high ones and run for the far ones. He will enjoy the game almost exactly in proportion to the effort he puts into it. The same is true of poetry. Great enjoyment is there, but this enjoyment demands a mental effort equivalent to the physical effort one puts into tennis.

The reader of poetry has one advantage over the tennis player. The poet is not trying to win a match. He may expect the reader to stretch for his shots, but he *wants* the reader to return them.

EXERCISE

Most of the poems in this book are accompanied by study questions that are by no means exhaustive. Following is a list of questions that you may apply to any poem. You will not be able to answer many of them until you have read further into the book.

1. Who is the speaker? What kind of person is he?
2. To whom is he speaking? What kind of person is he?
3. What is the occasion?
4. What is the setting in time (hour, season, century, etc.)?

5. What is the setting in place (indoors or out, city or country, land or sea, region, country, hemisphere, etc.)?
6. What is the central purpose of the poem?
7. State the central idea or theme of the poem in a sentence.
8. Discuss the tone of the poem. How is it achieved?
9. a. Outline the poem so as to show its structure and development, or
   b. Summarize the events of the poem.
10. Paraphrase the poem.
11. Discuss the diction of the poem. Point out words that are particularly well chosen and explain why.
12. Discuss the imagery of the poem. What kinds of imagery are used?
13. Point out examples of metaphor, simile, personification, and metonymy and explain their appropriateness.
14. Point out and explain any symbols. If the poem is allegorical, explain the allegory.
15. Point out and explain examples of paradox, overstatement, understatement, and irony. What is their function?
16. Point out and explain any allusions. What is their function?
17. Point out significant examples of sound repetition and explain their function.
18. a. What is the meter of the poem?
    b. Copy the poem and mark its scansion.
19. Discuss the adaptation of sound to sense.
20. Describe the form or pattern of the poem.
21. Criticize and evaluate the poem.

*   *   *

HYLA BROOK

By June our brook's run out of song and speed.
Sought for much after that, it will be found
Either to have gone groping underground
(And taken with it all the Hyla breed
That shouted in the mist a month ago,   5
Like ghost of sleigh bells in a ghost of snow)—
Or flourished and come up in jewelweed,
Weak foliage that is blown upon and bent
Even against the way its waters went.
Its bed is left a faded paper sheet   10
Of dead leaves stuck together by the heat—
A brook to none but who remember long.
This as it will be seen is other far
Than with brooks taken otherwise in song.
We love the things we love for what they are.   15

Robert Frost (1874–1963)

QUESTIONS

1. Your instructor may occasionally ask you, as a test of your understanding of a poem at its lowest level, or as a means of clearing up misunderstanding, to paraphrase its content. To PARAPHRASE a poem means to restate it in different language, so as to make its prose sense as plain as possible. A paraphrase may be longer or shorter than the poem, but it should contain as far as possible all the ideas in the poem in such a way as to make them clear to a puzzled reader. Figurative language should be reduced when possible to literal language; metaphors should be turned into similes. Though it is neither necessary nor possible to avoid using some words occurring in the original, you should in general use your own language.

   The central idea, or THEME, of the above poem is stated in its last line; but this line, despite its simplicity of language, is given full meaning only in the context of the fourteen lines preceding. The poem may be paraphrased as follows:

   > By June our brook is almost dry. The water no longer flows swiftly or makes a pleasant rippling sound. Soon after that, the water will have disappeared altogether (and with it all the tree toads that made such a racket along the banks a month ago, sounding like ghostly sleighbells in the April mist, which itself looked like the ghost of snow). Either the water will be creeping underground or will have spent itself nourishing the abundant jewelweed, a feeble plant easily bent down by the wind in a direction opposed to the brook's former flow ("against the current" of the now vanished brook). The bed of the brook by this time will be covered with dead leaves matted by the summer heat into the appearance of a faded paper sheet. The brook will be no longer a brook except to people who recall what it was like in mid-spring and earlier. This (the brook as it will then appear) is quite different from the brooks that other poets have celebrated.* But when we truly love things, we cherish them in all their aspects.

   A paraphrase is useful only if you understand that it is the barest, most inadequate expression of what the poem really says and is no more equivalent to the poem than a corpse is to a man. Once you have made the paraphrase, you should endeavor to see how far short of the poem it falls and why. If the above paraphrase clarifies the poem for you in any respect, does it also falsify the poem in any way? What features make the poem more appealing, more forceful, and more memorable than the paraphrase?

2. The above paraphrase is more consistent than the poem in its use of verb tenses. Does it gain or lose thereby? Why? What does the paraphrase lose by ignoring most of line 2? Can you think of a different meaning for the phrase "as it will be seen" (13)? Does the paraphrase adequately express the meaning of the final line? How might the paraphrase at this point be further expanded?

---

*The poet is thinking especially of Tennyson's well-known poem "The Brook," with its refrain, "For men may come and men may go, / But I go on forever."

THINK'ST THOU TO SEDUCE ME THEN

Think'st thou to seduce me then with words that have no meaning?
Parrots so can learn to prate, our speech by pieces gleaning;
Nurses teach their children so about the time of weaning.

Learn to speak first, then to woo; to wooing much pertaineth;
He that courts us, wanting art, soon falters when he feigneth,   5
Looks asquint on his discourse, and smiles when he complaineth.

Skillful anglers hide their hooks, fit baits for every season;
But with crooked pins fish thou, as babes do that want reason:
Gudgeons only can be caught with such poor tricks of treason.

Ruth forgive me, if I erred from human heart's compassion,   10
When I laughed sometimes too much to see thy foolish fashion;
But, alas, who less could do that found so good occasion?

Thomas Campion (1567–1620)

QUESTIONS

1. Vocabulary: *feigneth* (5), *gudgeons* (9). Is "fit" (7) an adjective or a verb? Is "Ruth" (10) a common or proper noun? What does "erred" (10) mean in this context?
2. Who is speaking to whom? What is the occasion?
3. What kind of person is the speaker? By what is the speaker offended in the person addressed? Why does the speaker change from "me" (1) to "us" (5)? Does the speaker's attitude undergo any change in stanza 4?

THERE'S BEEN A DEATH
IN THE OPPOSITE HOUSE

There's been a death in the opposite house
As lately as today.
I know it by the numb look
Such houses have alway.

The neighbors rustle in and out,   5
The doctor drives away.
A window opens like a pod,
Abrupt, mechanically;

Somebody flings a mattress out,—
The children hurry by;   10
They wonder if it died on that,—
I used to when a boy.

The minister goes stiffly in
As if the house were his,
And he owned all the mourners now,   15
And little boys besides;

And then the milliner, and the man
Of the appalling trade,
To take the measure of the house.
There'll be that dark parade   20

Of tassels and of coaches soon;
It's easy as a sign,—
The intuition of the news
In just a country town.

Emily Dickinson (1830–1886)

QUESTIONS

1. What can we know about the speaker in the poem?
2. By what signs does the speaker recognize that a death has occurred? Explain
   them stanza by stanza.
3. Comment on the words "appalling" (18) and "dark" (20).
4. What is the speaker's attitude toward death?

WHEN IN ROME

Marrie dear
the box is full . . .
take
whatever you like
to eat . . .   5

        (an egg
        or soup
        . . . there ain't no meat.)

there's endive there
and   10
cottage cheese . . .

        (whew! if I had some
        black-eyed peas . . .)

there's sardines
on the shelves   15
and such . . .

but
don't
get my anchovies . . .
they cost   20
too much!

(me get the
anchovies indeed!
what she think, she got—
a bird to feed?)   25

there's plenty in there
to fill you up . . .

(yes'm. just the
sight's
enough!   30

Hope I lives till I get
home
I'm tired of eatin'
what they eats in Rome . . .)

Mari Evans

QUESTIONS

1. Who are the two speakers? What is the situation? Why are the second speaker's words enclosed in parentheses?
2. What are the attitudes of the two speakers toward one another?
3. What implications have the title and the last two lines?

O WHAT IS THAT SOUND

O what is that sound which so thrills the ear
    Down in the valley drumming, drumming?
Only the scarlet soldiers, dear,
    The soldiers coming.

O what is that light I see flashing so clear   5
    Over the distance brightly, brightly?
Only the sun on their weapons, dear,
    As they step lightly.

O what are they doing with all that gear,
    What are they doing this morning, this morning?   10

Only their usual manoeuvres, dear,
    Or perhaps a warning.

O why have they left the road down there,
    Why are they suddenly wheeling, wheeling?
Perhaps a change in their orders, dear.   15
    Why are you kneeling?

O haven't they stopped for the doctor's care,
    Haven't they reined their horses, their horses?
Why, they are none of them wounded, dear,
    None of these forces.   20

O is it the parson they want, with white hair,
    Is it the parson, is it, is it?
No, they are passing his gateway, dear,
    Without a visit.

O it must be the farmer who lives so near.   25
    It must be the farmer so cunning, so cunning?
They have passed the farmyard already, dear,
    And now they are running.

O where are you going? Stay with me here!
    Were the vows you swore deceiving, deceiving?   30
No, I promised to love you, dear,
    But I must be leaving.

O it's broken the lock and splintered the door,
    O it's the gate where they're turning, turning;
Their boots are heavy on the floor   35
    And their eyes are burning.

W. H. Auden (1907–1973)

QUESTIONS

1. Even before it is understood, this *ballad* (see Glossary) manifests considerable power. What are the sources of that power? What aspects of human life are brought into conflict?
2. The first eight stanzas are pretty clearly divided between a male and a female speaker. Which is which? Try to form a consistent hypothesis that takes into account (a) the mounting anxiety of the first speaker, (b) the calm reassurance and final departure of the second speaker, (c) the action of the first speaker indicated in line 16 (how do this speaker's questions after line 16 differ from those before?), and (d) the behavior of the soldiers. (Note: At one point in its publishing history this poem was titled "The Quarry.")
3. Who speaks the final stanza?

MIRROR

I am silver and exact. I have no preconceptions.
Whatever I see I swallow immediately
Just as it is, unmisted by love or dislike.
I am not cruel, only truthful—
The eye of a little god, four-cornered.   5
Most of the time I meditate on the opposite wall.
It is pink, with speckles. I have looked at it so long
I think it is a part of my heart. But it flickers.
Faces and darkness separate us over and over.

Now I am a lake. A woman bends over me,   10
Searching my reaches for what she really is.
Then she turns to those liars, the candles or the moon.
I see her back, and reflect it faithfully.
She rewards me with tears and an agitation of hands.
I am important to her. She comes and goes.   15
Each morning it is her face that replaces the darkness.
In me she has drowned a young girl, and in me an old woman
Rises toward her day after day, like a terrible fish.

Sylvia Plath (1932-1963)

QUESTIONS

1. Who is the speaker? Distinguish means from ends.
2. In what ways is the mirror like and unlike a person (stanza 1)? In what ways is
   it like a lake (stanza 2)?
3. What is the meaning of the last two lines?

A STUDY OF READING HABITS

When getting my nose in a book
Cured most things short of school,
It was worth ruining my eyes
To know I could still keep cool,
And deal out the old right hook   5
To dirty dogs twice my size.

Later, with inch-thick specs,
Evil was just my lark:
Me and my cloak and fangs
Had ripping times in the dark.   10
The women I clubbed with sex!
I broke them up like meringues.

Don't read much now: the dude
Who lets the girl down before
The hero arrives, the chap   15
Who's yellow and keeps the store,
Seem far too familiar. Get stewed:
Books are a load of crap.

Philip Larkin (b. 1922)

QUESTIONS

1. The three stanzas delineate three stages in the speaker's life. Describe each.
2. What kind of person is the speaker? What kind of books does he read? May he
   be identified with the poet?
3. Contrast the advice given by the speaker in stanza 3 with the advice given by
   Terence in "Terence, this is stupid stuff" (page 528). Are A. E. Housman and
   Philip Larkin at odds in their attitudes toward drinking and reading? Discuss.

HOW ROSES CAME RED

Roses at first were white,
    Till they could not agree
Whether my Sappho's breast
    Or they more white should be.

But being vanquished quite,
    A blush their cheeks bespread;
Since which (believe the rest)
    The roses first came red.

Robert Herrick (1591–1674)

QUESTION

Distinguish means from end in this poem. Was it written by a naturalist or a
lover?

3. Denotation and Connotation

A primary distinction between the practical use of language and the literary use is that in literature, especially in poetry, a *fuller* use is made of individual words. To understand this, we need to examine the composition of a word.

The average word has three component parts: sound, denotation, and connotation. It begins as a combination of tones and noises, uttered by the lips, tongue, and throat, for which the written word is a notation. But it differs from a musical tone or a noise in that it has a meaning attached to it. The basic part of this meaning is its DENOTATION or denotations: that is, the dictionary meaning or meanings of the word. Beyond its denotations, a word may also have connotations. The CONNOTATIONS are what it suggests beyond what it expresses: its overtones of meaning. It acquires these connotations by its past history and associations, by the way and the circumstances in which it has been used. The word *home*, for instance, by denotation means only a place where one lives, but by connotation it suggests security, love, comfort, and family. The words *childlike* and *childish* both mean "characteristic of a child," but *childlike* suggests meekness, innocence, and wide-eyed wonder, while *childish* suggests pettiness, willfulness, and temper tantrums. If we name over a series of coins: *nickel, peso, lira, shilling, sen, doubloon,* the word *doubloon,* to four out of five readers, will immediately suggest pirates, though one will find nothing about pirates in looking up its meaning in the dictionary. Pirates are part of its connotation.

Connotation is very important in poetry, for it is one of the means by which the poet can concentrate or enrich meaning—say more in fewer words. Consider, for instance, the following short poem:

THERE IS NO FRIGATE LIKE A BOOK

> There is no frigate like a book
> To take us lands away,
> Nor any coursers like a page
> Of prancing poetry:
> This traverse may the poorest take
> Without oppress of toll;
> How frugal is the chariot
> That bears the human soul!

Emily Dickinson (1830–1886)

In this poem Emily Dickinson is considering the power of a book or of poetry to carry us away, to let us escape from our immediate surroundings into a world of the imagination. To do this she has compared literature to various means of transportation: a boat, a team of horses, a wheeled land vehicle. But she has been careful to choose kinds of transportation and names for them that have romantic connotations. "Frigate" suggests exploration and adventure; "coursers," beauty, spirit, and speed; "chariot," speed and the ability to go through the air as well as on land. (Compare "Swing Low, Sweet Chariot" and the myth of Phaëthon, who tried to drive the chariot of Apollo, and the famous painting of Aurora with her horses, once hung in almost every school.) How much of the meaning of the poem comes from this selection of vehicles and words is apparent if we try to substitute for them, say, *steamship, horses,* and *streetcar.*

QUESTIONS

1. What is lost if *miles* is substituted for "lands" (2) or *cheap* for "frugal" (7)?
2. How is "prancing" (4) peculiarly appropriate to poetry as well as to coursers? Could the poet have without loss compared a book to coursers and poetry to a frigate?
3. Is this account appropriate to all kinds of poetry or just to certain kinds? That is, was the poet thinking of poems like Wilfred Owen's "Dulce et Decorum Est" (page 521) or of poems like Coleridge's "Kubla Khan" (page 781) and Walter de la Mare's "The Listeners" (page 783)?

Just as a word has a variety of connotations, so may it have more than one denotation. If we look up the word *spring* in the dictionary, for instance, we will find that it has between twenty-five and thirty distinguishable meanings: It may mean (1) a pounce or leap, (2) a season of the year, (3) a natural source of water, (4) a coiled elastic wire, and so forth. This variety of denotation, complicated by additional tones of connotation, makes language confusing and difficult to use. Any person using words must be careful to define precisely by context the meanings that he wishes. But the difference between the writer using language to communicate information and the poet is this: the practical writer will always attempt to confine his words to one meaning at a time; the poet will often take advantage of the fact that the word has more than one meaning by using it to mean more than one thing at the same time. Thus when Edith Sitwell in one of her poems writes, "This is the time of the wild spring and the mating of tigers," she uses the word *spring* to denote both a season of the year and a sudden leap (and she uses *tigers* rather than *lambs* or *birds* because it has a connotation of fierceness and wildness that the other two lack).

WHEN MY LOVE SWEARS
THAT SHE IS MADE OF TRUTH

When my love swears that she is made of truth,
I do believe her, though I know she lies,
That she might think me some untutored youth,
Unlearnèd in the world's false subtleties.
Thus vainly thinking that she thinks me young,   5
Although she knows my days are past the best,
Simply I credit her false-speaking tongue;
On both sides thus is simple truth supprest.
But wherefore says she not she is unjust?°   unfaithful
And wherefore say not I that I am old?   10
Oh, love's best habit is in seeming trust,
And age in love loves not to have years told:
Therefore I lie with her and she with me,
And in our faults by lies we flattered be.

William Shakespeare (1564–1616)

QUESTIONS

1. How old is the speaker in the poem? How old is his beloved? What is the nature of their relationship?
2. How is the contradiction in line 2 to be resolved? How is the one in lines 5–6 to be resolved? Who is lying to whom?

3. How do "simply" (7) and "simple" (8) differ in meaning? The words "vainly" (5), "habit" (11), "told" (12), and "lie" (13) all have double meanings. What are they?
4. What is the tone of the poem—that is, the attitude of the speaker toward his situation? Should line 11 be taken as an expression of (a) wisdom, (b) conscious rationalization, or (c) self-deception? In answering these questions, consider both the situation and the connotations of all the important words beginning with "swears" (1) and ending with "flattered" (14).

A frequent misconception of poetic language is that the poet seeks always the most beautiful or noble-sounding words. What he really seeks are the most *meaningful* words, and these vary from one context to another. Language has many levels and varieties, and the poet may choose from them all. His words may be grandiose or humble, fanciful or matter of fact, romantic or realistic, archaic or modern, technical or everyday, monosyllabic or polysyllabic. Usually his poem will be pitched pretty much in one key. The words in Emily Dickinson's "There is no frigate like a book" and those in Thomas Hardy's "The Man He Killed" (page 533) are chosen from quite different areas of language, but both poets have chosen the words most meaningful for their own poetic context. Sometimes a poet may import a word from one level or area of language into a poem composed mostly of words from a different level or area. If he does this clumsily, the result will be incongruous and sloppy. If he does it skillfully, the result will be a shock of surprise and an increment of meaning for the reader. In fact, the many varieties of language open to the poet provide his richest resource. The poet's task is one of constant exploration and discovery. He searches always for the secret affinities of words that allow them to be brought together with soft explosions of meaning.

THE NAKED AND THE NUDE

For me, the naked and the nude
(By lexicographers construed
As synonyms that should express
The same deficiency of dress
Or shelter) stand as wide apart   5
As love from lies, or truth from art.

Lovers without reproach will gaze
On bodies naked and ablaze;
The Hippocratic eye will see

In nakedness, anatomy;   10
And naked shines the Goddess when
She mounts her lion among men.

The nude are bold, the nude are sly
To hold each treasonable eye.
While draping by a showman's trick   15
Their dishabille in rhetoric,
They grin a mock-religious grin
Of scorn at those of naked skin.

The naked, therefore, who compete
Against the nude may know defeat;   20
Yet when they both together tread
The briary pastures of the dead,
By Gorgons with long whips pursued,
How naked go the sometime nude!

Robert Graves (b. 1895)

QUESTIONS

1. Vocabulary: *lexicographers* (2), *construed* (2), *Hippocratic* (9), *dishabille* (16), *Gorgons* (23), *sometime* (24).
2. What kind of language is used in lines 2-5? Why? (For example, why is "deficiency" used in preference to *lack?* Purely because of meter?)
3. What is meant by "rhetoric" (16)? Why is the word "dishabille" used in this line instead of some less fancy word?
4. Explain why the poet chose his wording instead of the following alternatives: *brave* for "bold" (13), *clever* for "sly" (13), *clothing* for "draping" (15), *smile* for "grin" (17).
5. What, for the poet, is the difference in connotation between "naked" and "nude"? Try to explain reasons for the difference. If your own sense of the two words differs from that of Graves, state the difference and give reasons to support your sense of them.
6. Explain the reversal in the last line.

   The person using language to convey information is largely indifferent to the sound of his words and is hampered by their connotations and multiple denotations. He tries to confine each word to a single exact meaning. He uses, one might say, a fraction of the word and throws the rest away. The poet, on the other hand, tries to use as much of the word as he can. He is interested in sound and uses it to reinforce meaning (see chapter 13). He is interested in connotation and uses it to enrich and convey meaning. And he may use more than one denotation.

The purest form of practical language is scientific language. Scientists need a precise language for conveying information precisely. The fact that words have multiple denotations and various overtones of meaning is a hindrance to them in accomplishing their purpose. Their ideal language would be a language with a one-to-one correspondence between word and meaning; that is, every word would have one meaning only, and for every meaning there would be only one word. Since ordinary language does not fulfill these conditions, they have invented some that do. A statement in one of these languages may look like this:

$$SO_2 + H_2O = H_2SO_3$$

In such a statement the symbols are entirely unambiguous; they have been stripped of all connotation and of all denotations but one. The word *sulfurous*, if it occurred in poetry, might have all kinds of connotations: fire, smoke, brimstone, hell, damnation. But H_2SO_3 means one thing and one thing only: sulfurous acid.

The ambiguity and multiplicity of meanings possessed by words are an obstacle to the scientist but a resource to the poet. Where the scientist wants singleness of meaning, the poet wants richness of meaning. Where the scientist requires and has invented a strictly one-dimensional language, in which every word is confined to one denotation, the poet needs a multidimensional language, and he creates it partly by using a multidimensional vocabulary, in which to the dimension of denotation he adds the dimensions of connotation and sound.

The poet, we may say, plays on a many-stringed instrument. And he sounds more than one note at a time.

The first problem in reading poetry, therefore, or in reading any kind of literature, is to develop a sense of language, a feeling for words. One needs to become acquainted with their shape, their color, and their flavor. There are two ways of doing this: extensive use of the dictionary and extensive reading.

EXERCISES

1. Robert Frost has said that "Poetry is what evaporates from all translations." On the basis of this chapter, can you explain why this statement is true? How much of a word can be translated?
2. Which word in each group has the most "romantic" connotations? (a) horse, nag, steed; (b) king, ruler, tyrant, autocrat; (c) China, Cathay; (d) crow, sparrow, nightingale, catbird; (e) kiss, osculate, buss; (f) Pittsburgh, Birmingham, Samarkand, Podunk; (g) spy, secret agent.

3. Which word in each group has the most favorable connotation? (a) skinny, thin, slender; (b) old-fashioned, out-of-date, obsolete; (c) dwarfish, elfin, pigmy; (d) small, little, petite; (e) doting, loving, amorous; (f) prosperous, rich, moneyed, opulent; (g) revelation, exposure; (h) cur, bitch, dog; (i) scribble, write, indite; (j) brainy, intelligent, smart; (k) famous, notorious.
4. Which word in each group is most emotionally connotative? (a) offspring, children, progeny; (b) brother, sibling.
5. Which of the following is most likely to suggest an off-color remark? (a) pun, (b) play on words, (c) double meaning, (d) *double entendre*.
6. Which of the following should you be least offended at being accused of? (a) having acted foolishly, (b) having acted like a fool.
7. Fill each blank with the word richest in meaning in the given context. Explain.

a. I still had hopes, my latest hours to crown,
   Amidst these humble bowers to lay me down;
   To husband out life's _____ at the close,   *candle, taper*
   And keep the flame from wasting by repose.
                                        Goldsmith

b. She was a _____ of delight   *ghost, phantom,*
   When first she gleamed upon my sight.   *spectre, spook*
                                        Wordsworth

c. His sumptuous watch-case, though concealed it lies,
   Like a good conscience, _____ joy supplies. *perfect, solid,*
                                        Edward Young *thorough*

d. Charmed magic _____ opening on the foam   *casements, windows*
   Of _____ seas, in faery lands forlorn.   *dangerous, perilous*
                                        Keats

e. Thou _____ unravished bride of quietness.   *still, yet*
                                        Keats

f. I'll _____ the guts into the neighbor room. *bear, carry,*
                                        Shakespeare *convey, lug*

g. The iron tongue of midnight hath _____   *said, struck,*
   twelve.   *told*
                                        Shakespeare

h. In poetry each word reverberates like the note of a
         well-tuned _____ and always leaves   *banjo, guitar,*
   behind it a multitude of vibrations.   *lyre*
                                        Joubert

i. Sweet are the uses of adversity,
   Which like the toad, ugly and venomous,
   Wears yet a _____ jewel in his head.   *costly, high-priced,*
                                        Shakespeare *precious*

j. Care on thy maiden brow shall put
   A wreath of wrinkles, and thy foot
   Be shod with pain: not silken dress
   But toil shall _____ thy loveliness.

   C. Day Lewis   *clothe, tire,*
                            weary

8. Ezra Pound has defined great literature as being "simply language charged
   with meaning to the utmost possible degree." Would this be a good definition
   of poetry? The word "charged" is roughly equivalent to *filled*. Why is
   "charged" a better word in Pound's definition? What do its associations with
   storage batteries, guns, and dynamite suggest about poetry?

                    *   *   *

RICHARD CORY

Whenever Richard Cory went down town,
We people on the pavement looked at him:
He was a gentleman from sole to crown,
Clean favored, and imperially slim.

And he was always quietly arrayed,   5
And he was always human when he talked;
But still he fluttered pulses when he said,
"Good-morning," and he glittered when he walked.

And he was rich—yes, richer than a king—
And admirably schooled in every grace: 10
In fine, we thought that he was everything
To make us wish that we were in his place.

So on we worked, and waited for the light,
And went without the meat, and cursed the bread;
And Richard Cory, one calm summer night,   15
Went home and put a bullet through his head.

               Edwin Arlington Robinson (1869–1935)

QUESTIONS

1. In how many senses is Richard Cory a gentleman?
2. The word "crown" (3), meaning the top of the head, is familiar to you from
   "Jack and Jill," but why does Robinson use the unusual phrase "from sole to
   crown" instead of the common *from head to foot* or *from top to toe?*
3. List the words that express or suggest the idea of aristocracy or royalty.
4. Try to explain why the poet chose his wording rather than the following

alternatives: *sidewalk* for "pavement" (2), *good-looking* for "Clean favored" (4), *thin* for "slim" (4), *dressed* for "arrayed" (5), *courteous* for "human" (6), *wonderfully* for "admirably" (10), *trained* for "schooled" (10), *manners* for "every grace" (10), *in short* for "in fine" (11). What other examples of effective diction do you find in the poem?

5. Why is "Richard Cory" a good name for the character in this poem?
6. This poem is a good example of how ironic contrast (see chapter 7) generates meaning. The poem makes no direct statement about life; it simply relates an incident. What larger meanings about life does it suggest?
7. A leading American critic has said of this poem: "In 'Richard Cory' . . . we have a superficially neat portrait of the elegant man of mystery; the poem builds up deliberately to a very cheap surprise ending; but all surprise endings are cheap in poetry, if not, indeed, elsewhere, for poetry is written to be read not once but many times."* Do you agree with this evaluation? Discuss.

NAMING OF PARTS

To-day we have naming of parts. Yesterday,
We had daily cleaning. And to-morrow morning,
We shall have what to do after firing. But to-day,
To-day we have naming of parts. Japonica
Glistens like coral in all of the neighboring gardens,   5
     And to-day we have naming of parts.

This is the lower sling swivel. And this
Is the upper sling swivel, whose use you will see,
When you are given your slings. And this is the piling swivel,
Which in your case you have not got. The branches   10
Hold in the gardens their silent, eloquent gestures,
     Which in our case we have not got.

This is the safety-catch, which is always released
With an easy flick of the thumb. And please do not let me
See anyone using his finger. You can do it quite easy   15
If you have any strength in your thumb. The blossoms
Are fragile and motionless, never letting anyone see
     Any of them using their finger.

And this you can see is the bolt. The purpose of this
Is to open the breech, as you see. We can slide it   20
Rapidly backwards and forwards: we call this
Easing the spring. And rapidly backwards and forwards
The early bees are assaulting and fumbling the flowers:
     They call it easing the Spring.

---

*Yvor Winters, *Edwin Arlington Robinson* (Norfolk, Conn.: New Directions, 1946), p. 52.

They call it easing the Spring: it is perfectly easy   25
If you have any strength in your thumb: like the bolt,
And the breech, and the cocking-piece, and the point of balance,
Which in our case we have not got; and the almond-blossom
Silent in all of the gardens and the bees going backwards and forwards,
      For to-day we have naming of parts.   30

Henry Reed (b. 1914)

QUESTIONS

1. Who is the speaker (or who are the speakers) in the poem, and what is the situation?
2. What basic contrasts are represented by the trainees and by the gardens?
3. What is it that the trainees "have not got" (28)? How many meanings have the phrases "easing the Spring" (22) and "point of balance" (27)?
4. What differences in language and rhythm do you find between the lines concerning "naming of parts" and those describing the gardens?
5. Does the repetition of certain phrases throughout the poem have any special function or is it done only to create a kind of refrain?
6. What statement does the poem make about war as it affects men and their lives?

JUDGING DISTANCES

Not only how far away, but the way that you say it
Is very important. Perhaps you may never get
The knack of judging a distance, but at least you know
How to report on a landscape: the central sector,
The right of arc and that, which we had last Tuesday,   5
      And at least you know

That maps are of time, not place, so far as the army
Happens to be concerned—the reason being,
Is one which need not delay us. Again, you know
There are three kinds of tree, three only, the fir and the poplar,   10
And those which have bushy tops to; and lastly
      That things only seem to be things.

A barn is not called a barn, to put it more plainly,
Or a field in the distance, where sheep may be safely grazing.
You must never be over-sure. You must say, when reporting: 15
At five o'clock in the central sector is a dozen
Of what appear to be animals; whatever you do,
      Don't call the bleeders *sheep*.

I am sure that's quite clear; and suppose, for the sake of example,
The one at the end, asleep, endeavors to tell us   20
What he sees over there to the west, and how far away,
After first having come to attention. There to the west,
On the fields of summer the sun and the shadows bestow
      Vestments of purple and gold.

The still white dwellings are like a mirage in the heat,   25
And under the swaying elms a man and a woman
Lie gently together. Which is, perhaps, only to say
That there is a row of houses to the left of arc,
And that under some poplars a pair of what appear to be humans
      Appear to be loving.   30

Well that, for an answer, is what we might rightly call
Moderately satisfactory only, the reason being,
Is that two things have been omitted, and those are important.
The human beings, now: in what direction are they,
And how far away, would you say? And do not forget   35
      There may be dead ground in between.

There may be dead ground in between; and I may not have got
The knack of judging a distance; I will only venture
A guess that perhaps between me and the apparent lovers,
(Who, incidentally, appear by now to have finished,)   40
At seven o'clock from the houses, is roughly a distance
      Of about one year and a half.

Henry Reed (b. 1914)

QUESTIONS

1. In what respect are maps "of time, not place" (7) in the army?
2. Though they may be construed as belonging to the same speaker, there are two speaking voices in this poem. Identify each and put quotation marks around the lines spoken by the second voice.
3. Two kinds of language are used in this poem—army "officialese" and the language of human experience. What are the characteristics of each? What is the purpose of each? Which is more precise?
4. The word "bleeders" (18)—that is, "bloody creatures"—is British profanity. To which of the two kinds of language does it belong? Or is it perhaps a third kind of language?
5. As in "Naming of Parts" (these two poems are part of a series of four with the general title "Lessons of War") the two kinds of language used might possibly be called "unpoetic" and "poetic." Is the "unpoetic" language *really* unpoetic? In other words, is its use inappropriate in these two poems? Explain.
6. The phrase "dead ground" (36) takes on symbolic meaning in the last stanza.

What is its literal meaning? What is its symbolic meaning? What does the second speaker mean by saying that the distance between himself and the lovers is "about one year and a half" (42)? In what respect is the contrast between the recruits and the lovers similar to that between the recruits and the gardens in "Naming of Parts"? What meanings are generated by the former contrast?

BEING HERDED PAST THE PRISON'S HONOR FARM

The closer I come to their huge black-and-white sides, the less
Room there is in the world for anything but Holsteins.
I thought I could squeeze past them, but I'm stuck now
Among them, dwarfed in my car, while they plod gigantically
To pasture ahead of me, beside me, behind me, cow eyes   5
As big as eightballs staring down at another prisoner.

They seem enormously pregnant, bulging with mash and alfalfa,
But their low-slung sacks and rawboned high-rise rumps look insur-
Mountable for any bull. One side-swipes my fender
And gives it a cud-slow look. What fingers would dare   10
Milk those veiny bags? Not mine. I'm cowed. My hands
On the steering wheel are squeezing much too tight to be trusted.

They all wear numbers clipped to their ears. They're going to feed
Behind barbed wire like a work-gang or, later, like solitaries
Stalled in concrete, for the milk of inhuman kindness.   15
They clomp muddily forward. Now splatting his boots down
Like cowflops, the tall black numbered trusty cowpoke tells me
Exactly where I can go, steering me, cutting me out of the herd.

David Wagoner (b. 1926)

QUESTIONS

1. Why did the poet choose to write about Holsteins rather than Jerseys or Guernseys? Why did he make the "cowpoke" (17) black rather than tanned, brown, or white?
2. Explain why the poet chose his wording rather than the following possible alternatives: *guided* for "Herded" (title), *nearer* for "closer" (1), *walk* for "plod" (4), *cueballs* instead of "eightballs" (6), *swollen* for "pregnant" (7), *snail-slow* for "cud-slow" (10), *scared* for "cowed" (11), *hermits* for "solitaries" (14), *stopped* for "stalled" (15), *trod* for "clomp" (16), *putting* for "splatting" (16), *snowshoes* instead of "cowflops" (17), *reliable* for "trusty" (17), *gives me*

good directions for "tells me / Exactly where I can go" (17–18), *getting* for "cutting" (18). Comment on the phrase "the milk of inhuman kindness" (15).

3. How many kinds of "prisoners" are referred to in the poem? Is there any suggestion of the speaker's attitude toward each?

CROSS

My old man's a white old man
And my old mother's black.
If ever I cursed my white old man
I take my curses back.

If ever I cursed my black old mother   5
And wished she were in hell,
I'm sorry for that evil wish
And now I wish her well.

My old man died in a fine big house.
My ma died in a shack.   10
I wonder where I'm gonna die,
Being neither white nor black?

Langston Hughes (1902–1967)

QUESTIONS

1. What different denotations does the title have? Explain.
2. The language in this poem, such as "old man" (1, 3, 9), "ma" (10), and "gonna" (11), is plain, and even colloquial. Is it appropriate to the subject? Why?

BASE DETAILS

If I were fierce, and bald, and short of breath,
    I'd live with scarlet Majors at the Base,
And speed glum heroes up the line to death.
    You'd see me with my puffy petulant face,
Guzzling and gulping in the best hotel,   5
    Reading the Roll of Honor. "Poor young chap,"
I'd say—"I used to know his father well;
    Yes, we've lost heavily in this last scrap."
And when the war is done and youth stone dead,
I'd toddle safely home and die—in bed.   10

Siegfried Sassoon (1886–1967)

1. Vocabulary: *petulant* (4).
2. In what two ways may the title be interpreted? (Both words have two pertinent meanings.) What applications has "scarlet" (2)? What is the force of "fierce" (1)? Try to explain why the poet chose his wording rather than the following alternatives: *fleshy* for "puffy" (4), *eating and drinking* for "guzzling and gulping" (5), *battle* for "scrap" (8), *totter* for "toddle" (10).
3. Who evidently is the speaker? (The poet, a British captain in World War I, was decorated for bravery on the battlefield.) Does he mean what he says? What is the purpose of the poem?

THE CAREFUL ANGLER

The careful angler chose his nook
At morning by the lilied brook,
And all the noon his rod he plied
By that romantic riverside.
Soon as the evening hours decline
Tranquilly he'll return to dine,
And, breathing forth a pious wish,
Will cram his belly full of fish.

Robert Louis Stevenson (1850–1894)

QUESTION

At what point in the poem does the kind of connotative language used by the poet abruptly change? Explain the change. What does it do to the tone of the poem?

4. Imagery

Experience comes to us largely through the senses. My experience of a spring day, for instance, may consist partly of certain emotions I feel and partly of certain thoughts I think, but most of it will be a cluster of sense impressions. It will consist of *seeing* blue sky and white clouds, budding leaves and daffodils; of *hearing* robins and bluebirds singing in the early morning; of *smelling* damp earth and blossoming hyacinths; and of *feeling* a fresh wind against my cheek. The poet seeking to express his experience of a spring day must therefore provide a selection of the sense impressions he has. Like Shakespeare (page 524), he must give the reader "daisies pied" and "lady-smocks all silver-white" and "merry larks" and the song of the cuckoo and maidens bleaching their summer smocks. Without doing so he will probably fail to evoke the emotions that accompanied his sensations. The poet's language, therefore, must be more *sensuous* than ordinary language. It must be more full of imagery.

IMAGERY may be defined as the representation through language of sense experience. Poetry appeals directly to our senses, of course, through its music and rhythms, which we actually hear when it is read aloud. But indirectly it appeals to our senses through imagery, the representation to the imagination of sense experience. The word *image* perhaps most often suggests a mental picture, something seen in the mind's eye—and *visual* imagery is the kind of imagery that occurs most frequently in poetry. But an image may also represent a sound; a smell; a taste; a tactile experience, such as hardness, wetness, or cold; an internal sensation, such as hunger, thirst, or nausea; or movement or tension in the muscles or joints. If we wished to be scientific, we could extend this list further, for psychologists no longer confine themselves to five or even six senses, but for purposes of discussing poetry the above classification should ordinarily be sufficient.

MEETING AT NIGHT

The gray sea and the long black land;
And the yellow half-moon large and low;
And the startled little waves that leap
In fiery ringlets from their sleep,
As I gain the cove with pushing prow,   5
And quench its speed i' the slushy sand.

Then a mile of warm sea-scented beach;
Three fields to cross till a farm appears;
A tap at the pane, the quick sharp scratch
And blue spurt of a lighted match,   10
And a voice less loud, through its joys and fears,
Than the two hearts beating each to each!

Robert Browning (1812-1889)

"Meeting at Night" is a poem about love. It makes, one might say, a number of statements about love: being in love is a sweet and exciting experience; when one is in love everything seems beautiful, and the most trivial things become significant; when one is in love one's sweetheart seems the most important object in the world. But the poet actually *tells* us none of these things directly. He does not even use the word *love* in his poem. His business is to communicate experience, not information. He does this largely in two ways. First, he presents us with a specific situation, in which a lover goes to meet his sweetheart. Second, he describes the lover's journey so vividly in terms of sense impressions that the reader not only sees and hears what the lover saw and heard but also shares his anticipation and excitement.

Every line in the poem contains some image, some appeal to the senses: the gray sea, the long black land, the yellow half-moon, the startled little waves with their fiery ringlets, the blue spurt of the lighted match—all appeal to our sense of sight and convey not only shape but also color and motion. The warm sea-scented beach appeals to the senses of both smell and touch. The pushing prow of the boat on the slushy sand, the tap at the pane, the quick scratch of the match, the low speech of the lovers, and the sound of their hearts beating—all appeal to the sense of hearing.

PARTING AT MORNING

> Round the cape of a sudden came the sea,
> And the sun looked over the mountain's rim:
> And straight was a path of gold for him,
> And the need of a world of men for me.

Robert Browning (1812–1889)

QUESTIONS

1. This poem is a sequel to "Meeting at Night." "Him" (3) refers to the sun. Does the last line mean that the lover needs the world of men or that the world of men needs the lover? Or both?
2. Does the sea *actually* come suddenly around the cape or *appear* to? Why does Browning mention the *effect* before its *cause* (the sun looking over the mountain's rim)?
3. Do these two poems, taken together, suggest any larger truths about love? Browning, in answer to a question, said that the second part is the man's confession of "how fleeting is the belief (implied in the first part) that such raptures are self-sufficient and enduring—as for the time they appear."

The sharpness and vividness of any image will ordinarily depend on how specific it is and on the poet's use of effective detail. The word *hummingbird*, for instance, conveys a more definite image than does *bird*, and *ruby-throated hummingbird* is sharper and more specific still. For a vivid representation, however, it is not necessary that something be completely described. One or two especially sharp and representative details will ordinarily serve, allowing the reader's imagination to fill in the rest. Tennyson in "The Eagle" (page 519) gives only one detail about the eagle itself—that he clasps the crag with "crooked hands"—but this detail is an effective and memorable one. Robinson tells us that Richard Cory (page 553) was "clean favored," "slim," and "quietly arrayed," but the detail that really brings Cory before us is that he "glittered when he walked." Browning, in "Meeting at Night," calls up a whole scene with "A tap at the pane, the quick sharp scratch / And blue spurt of a lighted match."

Since imagery is a peculiarly effective way of evoking vivid experience, and since it may be used to convey emotion and suggest ideas as well as to cause a mental reproduction of sensations, it is an invaluable resource of the poet. In general, the poet will seek concrete or image-bearing words in preference to abstract or non-image-bearing words. We cannot evaluate a poem, however, by the amount or quality of its imagery alone. Sense impression is only one of the elements of experience. A poet may attain his ends by other means. We should never judge any single element of a poem except in reference to the total intention of that poem.

*　　　*　　　*

A LATE AUBADE

You could be sitting now in a carrel
Turning some liver-spotted page,
Or rising in an elevator-cage
Toward Ladies' Apparel.

You could be planting a raucous bed   5
Of salvia, in rubber gloves,
Or lunching through a screed of someone's loves
With pitying head,

Or making some unhappy setter
Heel, or listening to a bleak   10
Lecture on Schoenberg's serial technique.
Isn't this better?

Think of all the time you are not
Wasting, and would not care to waste,
Such things, thank God, not being to your taste. 15
Think what a lot

Of time, by woman's reckoning,
You've saved, and so may spend on this,
You who had rather lie in bed and kiss
Than anything.   20

It's almost noon, you say? If so,
Time flies, and I need not rehearse
The rosebuds-theme of centuries of verse.
If you *must* go,

Wait for a while, then slip downstairs   25
And bring us up some chilled white wine,
And some blue cheese, and crackers, and some fine
Ruddy-skinned pears.

Richard Wilbur (b. 1921)

QUESTIONS

1. Vocabulary: *Aubade* (see Glossary), *carrel* (1), *screed* (7), *Schoenberg* (11).
2. Who is the speaker? What is the situation? What plea is the speaker making?
3. As lines 22–23 suggest, this poem treats an age-old theme of poetry. What is it? In what respects is this an original treatment of it? Though line 23 is general in reference, it alludes specifically to a famous poem by Robert Herrick (see page 596). In what respects are these two poems similar? In what respects are they different?
4. What clues are there in the poem as to the characters and personalities of the two people involved?
5. How does the last stanza provide a fitting conclusion to the poem?

ON MOONLIT HEATH AND LONESOME BANK

On moonlit heath and lonesome bank
    The sheep beside me graze;
And yon the gallows used to clank
    Fast by the four cross ways.

A careless shepherd once would keep   5
    The flocks by moonlight there,
And high amongst the glimmering sheep
    The dead man stood on air.

They hang us now in Shrewsbury jail:
    The whistles blow forlorn,   10
And trains all night groan on the rail
    To men that die at morn.

There sleeps in Shrewsbury jail to-night,
    Or wakes, as may betide,
A better lad, if things went right,   15
    Than most that sleep outside.

And naked to the hangman's noose
    The morning clocks will ring
A neck God made for other use
    Than strangling in a string.   20

And sharp the link of life will snap,
    And dead on air will stand
Heels that held up as straight a chap
    As treads upon the land.

So here I'll watch the night and wait   25
    To see the morning shine,
When he will hear the stroke of eight
    And not the stroke of nine;

And wish my friend as sound a sleep
    As lads' I did not know,   30
That shepherded the moonlit sheep
    A hundred years ago.

A. E. Housman (1859–1936)

QUESTIONS

1. Vocabulary: *heath* (1).
2. Housman explains in a note to lines 5–6 that "Hanging in chains was called keeping sheep by moonlight." Where is this idea repeated?
3. What is the speaker's attitude toward his friend? Toward other young men who have died by hanging? What is the purpose of the reference to the young men hanged "A hundred years ago"?
4. Discuss the kinds of imagery present in the poem and their role in the development of the dramatic situation.
5. Discuss the use of language in stanza 5.

A NARROW FELLOW IN THE GRASS

A narrow fellow in the grass
Occasionally rides;
You may have met him. Did you not,
His notice sudden is:

The grass divides as with a comb,   5
A spotted shaft is seen,
And then it closes at your feet
And opens further on.

He likes a boggy acre,
A floor too cool for corn,   10
Yet when a boy, and barefoot,
I more than once at noon

Have passed, I thought, a whip-lash
Unbraiding in the sun,
When, stooping to secure it,   15
It wrinkled, and was gone.

Several of nature's people
I know, and they know me;
I feel for them a transport
Of cordiality;   20

But never met this fellow,
Attended or alone,
Without a tighter breathing
And zero at the bone.

                                    Emily Dickinson (1830–1886)

QUESTIONS

1. The subject of this poem is never named. What is it? How does the imagery identify it?
2. The last two lines might be paraphrased as "without being frightened." Why is Dickinson's wording more effective?
3. Who is the speaker?

LIVING IN SIN

She had thought the studio would keep itself;
no dust upon the furniture of love.
Half heresy, to wish the taps less vocal,
the panes relieved of grime. A plate of pears,
a piano with a Persian shawl, a cat   5
stalking the picturesque amusing mouse
had risen at his urging.
Not that at five each separate stair would writhe
under the milkman's tramp; that morning light
so coldly would delineate the scraps   10
of last night's cheese and three sepulchral bottles;
that on the kitchen shelf among the saucers
a pair of beetle-eyes would fix her own—
envoy from some village in the moldings . . .
Meanwhile, he, with a yawn,   15
sounded a dozen notes upon the keyboard,
declared it out of tune, shrugged at the mirror,
rubbed at his beard, went out for cigarettes;
while she, jeered by the minor demons,

pulled back the sheets and made the bed and found   20
a towel to dust the table-top,
and let the coffee-pot boil over on the stove.
By evening she was back in love again,
though not so wholly but throughout the night
she woke sometimes to feel the daylight coming   25
like a relentless milkman up the stairs.

Adrienne Rich (b. 1929)

QUESTIONS

1. Explain the grammatical structure and meaning of the sentence in lines 4–7.
   What are its subject and verb? To whom or what does "his" (7) refer? What
   kind of life do its images conjure up?
2. On what central contrast is the poem based? What is its central mood or
   emotion?
3. Discuss the various kinds of imagery used and their function in conveying the
   experience of the poem.

THOSE WINTER SUNDAYS

Sundays too my father got up early
and put his clothes on in the blueblack cold,
then with cracked hands that ached
from labor in the weekday weather made
banked fires blaze. No one ever thanked him.   5

I'd wake and hear the cold splintering, breaking.
When the rooms were warm, he'd call,
and slowly I would rise and dress,
fearing the chronic angers of that house,

Speaking indifferently to him,   10
who had driven out the cold
and polished my good shoes as well.
What did I know, what did I know
of love's austere and lonely offices?

Robert Hayden (1913–1980)

QUESTIONS

1. Vocabulary: *offices* (14).
2. What kind of imagery is central to the poem? How is this imagery related to
   the emotional concerns of the poem?
3. How do the subsidiary images relate to the central images?

4. From what point in time does the speaker view the subject matter of the poem? What has happened to him in the interval?

SPRING

Nothing is so beautiful as spring—
    When weeds, in wheels, shoot long and lovely and lush;
    Thrush's eggs look little low heavens, and thrush
Through the echoing timber does so rinse and wring
The ear, it strikes like lightnings to hear him sing;   5
    The glassy peartree leaves and blooms, they brush
    The descending blue; that blue is all in a rush
With richness; the racing lambs too have fair their fling.

What is all this juice and all this joy?
    A strain of the earth's sweet being in the beginning   10
In Eden garden.—Have, get, before it cloy,

    Before it cloud, Christ, lord, and sour with sinning,
Innocent mind and Mayday in girl and boy,
    Most, O maid's child, thy choice and worthy the winning.

Gerard Manley Hopkins (1844–1889)

QUESTIONS

1. The first line makes an abstract statement. How is this statement brought to carry conviction?
2. The sky is described as being "all in a rush / With richness" (7–8). In what other respects is the poem "rich"?
3. The author was a Catholic priest as well as a poet. To what two things does he compare the spring in lines 9–14? In what ways are the comparisons appropriate?

TO AUTUMN

Season of mists and mellow fruitfulness,
    Close bosom-friend of the maturing sun;
Conspiring with him how to load and bless
    With fruit the vines that round the thatch-eves run;
To bend with apples the mossed cottage-trees,   5
    And fill all fruit with ripeness to the core;
        To swell the gourd, and plump the hazel shells
With a sweet kernel; to set budding more,
    And still more, later flowers for the bees,
    Until they think warm days will never cease,   10
        For summer has o'er-brimmed their clammy cells.

Who hath not seen thee oft amid thy store?
    Sometimes whoever seeks abroad may find
Thee sitting careless on a granary floor,
    Thy hair soft-lifted by the winnowing wind;   15
Or on a half-reaped furrow sound asleep,
    Drowsed with the fume of poppies, while thy hook
      Spares the next swath and all its twinèd flowers:
And sometimes like a gleaner thou dost keep
    Steady thy laden head across a brook;   20
Or by a cider-press, with patient look,
    Thou watchest the last oozings hours by hours.

Where are the songs of Spring? Ay, where are they?
    Think not of them, thou hast thy music too,—
While barred clouds bloom the soft-dying day,   25
    And touch the stubble-plains with rosy hue;
Then in a wailful choir the small gnats mourn
    Among the river sallows, borne aloft
      Or sinking as the light wind lives or dies;
And full-grown lambs loud bleat from hilly bourn;   30
    Hedge-crickets sing; and now with treble soft
    The red-breast whistles from a garden-croft;
      And gathering swallows twitter in the skies.

John Keats (1795–1821)

QUESTIONS

1. Vocabulary: *hook* (17), *barred* (25), *sallows* (28), *bourn* (30), *croft* (32).
2. How many kinds of imagery do you find in the poem? Give examples of each.
3. Are the images arranged haphazardly or are they carefully organized? In answering this question, consider: (a) With what aspect of autumn is each stanza particularly concerned? (b) What kind of imagery is dominant in each stanza? (c) What time of the season is presented in each stanza? (d) Is there any progression in time of day?
4. What is Autumn personified as in stanza 2? Is there any suggestion of personification in the other two stanzas?
5. Although the poem is primarily descriptive, what attitude toward transience and passing beauty is implicit in it?

5. Figurative Language 1
METAPHOR, PERSONIFICATION, METONYMY

> *Poetry provides the one permissible way of saying one thing and meaning another.*
>
> ROBERT FROST

Let us assume that your brother has just come in out of a rainstorm and you say to him, "Well, you're a pretty sight! Got slightly wet, didn't you?" And he replies, "Wet? I'm drowned! It's raining cats and dogs, and my raincoat's like a sieve!"

It is likely that you and your brother understand each other well enough, and yet if you examine this conversation literally, that is to say unimaginatively, you will find that you have been speaking nonsense. Actually you have been speaking figuratively. You have been saying less than what you mean, or more than what you mean, or the opposite of what you mean, or something other than what you mean. You did not mean that your brother was a pretty sight but that he was a wretched sight. You did not mean that he got slightly wet but that he got very wet. Your brother did not mean that he got drowned but that he got drenched. It was not raining cats and dogs; it was raining water. And your brother's raincoat is so unlike a sieve that not even a baby would confuse them.

If you are familiar with Molière's play *Le Bourgeois Gentilhomme,* you will remember how delighted M. Jourdain was to discover that he had been speaking prose all his life. Many people might be equally surprised to learn that they have been speaking a kind of subpoetry all their lives. The difference between their figures of speech and the poet's is that theirs are probably worn and trite, the poet's fresh and original.

On first examination, it might seem absurd to say one thing and mean another. But we all do it and with good reason. We do it because we can say what we want to say more vividly and forcefully by figures than we can by saying it directly. And we can say more by figurative statement than we can by literal statement. Figures of speech are another way of adding extra dimensions to language. We shall examine their usefulness more particularly later in this chapter.

Broadly defined, a FIGURE OF SPEECH is any way of saying something other than the ordinary way, and some rhetoricians have classified as many as 250 separate figures. For our purposes, however, a figure of speech is more narrowly definable as a way of saying one thing and meaning another, and we need be concerned with no more than a dozen. FIGURATIVE LANGUAGE—language using figures of speech—is language that cannot be taken literally (or should not be taken literally only).

METAPHOR and SIMILE are both used as a means of comparing things that are essentially unlike. The only distinction between them is that in simile the comparison is *expressed* by the use of some word or phrase, such as *like, as, than, similar to, resembles,* or *seems;* in metaphor the comparison is *implied*—that is, the figurative term is *substituted for* or *identified with* the literal term.

THE GUITARIST TUNES UP

With what attentive courtesy he bent
Over his instrument;
Not as a lordly conquerer who could
Command both wire and wood,
But as a man with a loved woman might,
Inquiring with delight
What slight essential things she had to say
Before they started, he and she, to play.

Frances Cornford (1886-1960)

QUESTION

Explore the comparison. Does it principally illuminate the guitarist or the lovers or both? What one word brings its two terms together?

THE HOUND

Life the hound
Equivocal
Comes at a bound
Either to rend me
Or to befriend me.   5
I cannot tell

The hound's intent
Till he has sprung
At my bare hand
With teeth or tongue.   10
Meanwhile I stand
And wait the event.

Robert Francis (b. 1901)

QUESTION

What does "equivocal" (2) mean? Show how this is the key word in the poem.
What is the effect of placing it on a line by itself?

Metaphors may take one of four forms, depending on whether the
literal and figurative terms are respectively *named* or *implied.* In the first
form of metaphor, as in simile, both the literal and figurative terms are
named. In Francis's poem, for example, the literal term is "life" and the
figurative term is "hound." In the second form, the literal term is *named*
and the figurative term is *implied.*

BEREFT

Where had I heard this wind before
Change like this to a deeper roar?
What would it take my standing there for,
Holding open a restive door,
Looking downhill to a frothy shore?   5
Summer was past and day was past.
Somber clouds in the west were massed.
Out in the porch's sagging floor
Leaves got up in a coil and hissed,
Blindly struck at my knee and missed.   10
Something sinister in the tone
Told me my secret must be known:
Word I was in the house alone
Somehow must have gotten abroad,
Word I was in my life alone,   15
Word I had no one left but God.

Robert Frost (1874–1963)

QUESTIONS

1. Describe the situation precisely. What time of day and year is it? Where is the speaker? What is happening to the weather?
2. To what are the leaves in lines 9–10 compared?
3. The word "hissed" (9) is onomatopoetic (see page 701). How is its effect reinforced in the lines following?
4. Though lines 9–10 present the clearest example of the second form of metaphor, there are others. To what is the wind ("it") compared in line 3? Why is the door (4) "restive" and what does this do (figuratively) to the door? To what is the speaker's "life" compared (15)?
5. What is the tone of the poem? How reassuring is the last line?

In the third form of metaphor, the literal term is *implied* and the figurative term is *named*. In the fourth form, both the literal *and* figurative terms are *implied*. The following poem exemplifies both types:

IT SIFTS FROM LEADEN SIEVES

It sifts from leaden sieves,
It powders all the wood.
It fills with alabaster wool
The wrinkles of the road.

It makes an even face   5
Of mountain and of plain—
Unbroken forehead from the east
Unto the east again.

It reaches to the fence,
It wraps it rail by rail   10
Till it is lost in fleeces;
It deals celestial veil

To stump and stack and stem—
A summer's empty room—
Acres of joints where harvests were,   15
Recordless,° but for them.   unrecorded

It ruffles wrists of posts
As ankles of a queen,
Then stills its artisans like ghosts,
Denying they have been.   20

Emily Dickinson (1830–1886)

QUESTIONS

1. This poem consists essentially of a series of metaphors having the same literal term, identified only as "It." What is "It"?
2. In several of these metaphors the figurative term is named—"alabaster wool" (3), "fleeces" (11), "celestial veil" (12). In two of them, however, the figurative term as well as the literal term is left unnamed. To what is "It" compared in lines 1–2? In lines 17–18?
3. Comment on the additional metaphorical expressions or complications contained in "leaden sieves" (1), "alabaster wool" (3), "even face" (5), "unbroken forehead" (7), "a summer's empty room" (14), "artisans" (19).

Metaphors of the fourth form, as one might guess, are comparatively rare. An extended example, however, is provided by Dickinson's "I like to see it lap the miles" (page 710).

PERSONIFICATION consists in giving the attributes of a human being to an animal, an object, or a concept. It is really a subtype of metaphor, an implied comparison in which the figurative term of the comparison is always a human being. When Sylvia Plath makes a mirror speak and think (page 544), she is personifying an object. When Keats describes autumn as a harvester "sitting careless on a granary floor" or "on a half-reaped furrow sound asleep" (page 569), he is personifying a concept. Personifications differ in the degree to which they ask the reader actually to visualize the literal term in human form. In Keats's comparison we are asked to make a complete identification of autumn with a human being. In Sylvia Plath's, though the mirror speaks and thinks, we continue to visualize it as a mirror; similarly, in Frost's "Bereft" (page 572), the "restive" door remains in appearance a door tugged by the wind. In Browning's reference to "the startled little waves" (page 561), a personification is barely suggested; we would make a mistake if we tried to visualize the waves in human form or even, really, to think of them as having human emotions.*

Closely related to personification is APOSTROPHE, which consists in addressing someone absent or dead or something nonhuman as if that person or thing were present and alive and could reply to what is being

---

*The various figures of speech blend into each other, and it is sometimes difficult to classify a specific example as definitely metaphor or symbol, symbolism or allegory, understatement or irony, irony or paradox. Often a given example may exemplify two or more figures at once. In "The Guitarist Tunes Up" (page 571), "wire and wood" are metonymies (see page 576) for a guitar and are personified as subjects, slaves, or soldiers who could be commanded by a lordly conquerer. In "A bird came down the walk" (page 525), when the bird glances around with eyes that look "like frightened beads," the beads function as part of a simile and are personified as something that can be "frightened." The important consideration in reading poetry is not that we classify figures definitely but that we construe them correctly.

said. The speaker in A. E. Housman's "To an Athlete Dying Young" (page 798) apostrophizes a dead runner. William Blake apostrophizes a tiger throughout his famous poem (page 778) but does not otherwise personify it. Keats apostrophizes as well as personifies autumn (page 568). Personification and apostrophe are both ways of giving life and immediacy to one's language, but since neither requires great imaginative power on the part of the poet—apostrophe especially does not—they may degenerate into mere mannerisms and are to be found as often in bad and mediocre poetry as in good. We need to distinguish between their effective use and their merely conventional use.

DR. SIGMUND FREUD DISCOVERS
THE SEA SHELL

Science, that simple saint, cannot be bothered
Figuring what anything is for:
Enough for her devotions that things are
And can be contemplated soon as gathered.

She knows how every living thing was fathered,   5
She calculates the climate of each star,
She counts the fish at sea, but cannot care
Why any one of them exists, fish, fire or feathered.

Why should she? Her religion is to tell
By rote her rosary of perfect answers.   10
Metaphysics she can leave to man:
She never wakes at night in heaven or hell

Staring at darkness. In her holy cell
There is no darkness ever: the pure candle
Burns, the beads drop briskly from her hand.   15

Who dares to offer Her the curled sea shell!
She will not touch it!—knows the world she sees
Is all the world there is! Her faith is perfect!

And still he offers the sea shell . . .

                What surf
Of what far sea upon what unknown ground   20
Troubles forever with that asking sound?
What surge is this whose question never ceases?

Archibald MacLeish (1892-1982)

QUESTIONS

1. Vocabulary: *metaphysics* (11).
2. This poem employs an extended personification. List the ways in which science is appropriately compared to a saint. In what way is its faith "perfect" (18)?
3. Who is "he" in line 19?
4. Who was Sigmund Freud, and what discoveries did he make about human nature?
5. What does the sea shell represent?

PACK, CLOUDS, AWAY

> Pack, clouds, away; and welcome, day!
> With night we banish sorrow.
> Sweet air, blow soft; mount, lark, aloft
> To give my love good morrow.
> Wings from the wind to please her mind,   5
> Notes from the lark I'll borrow;
> Bird, prune thy wing, nightingale, sing,
> To give my love good morrow.
>> To give my love good morrow,
>> Notes from them all I'll borrow.   10
>
> Wake from thy nest, robin redbreast!
> Sing, birds, in every furrow;
> And from each bill let music shrill
> Give my fair love good morrow.
> Black-bird and thrush in every bush,   15
> Stare, linnet, and cock-sparrow,
> You pretty elves, amongst yourselves
> Sing my fair love good morrow.
>> To give my love good morrow,
>> Sing, birds, in every furrow.   20

Thomas Heywood (c. 1575–1641)

QUESTIONS

1. Vocabulary: *prune* (7), *stare* (16). Could this poem be called an *aubade?*
2. Count the apostrophes in the poem. Why are they effective? Would the poem be damaged if lines 10 and 20 were interchanged? Why?
3. Describe the rime-patterns of the poem. Does the frequency of the rimes serve a poetic function, or are they merely decorative?

SYNECDOCHE (the use of the part for the whole) and METONYMY (the use of something closely related for the thing actually meant) are alike in that both substitute some significant detail or aspect of an experience for the experience itself. Thus, Shakespeare uses synecdoche when he says that the cuckoo's song is unpleasing to a "married ear" (page 524), for he means a married *man*. Robert Graves uses synecdoche in "The Naked and the Nude" (page 549) when he refers to a doctor as a "Hippocratic eye," and T. S. Eliot uses it in "The Love Song of J. Alfred Prufrock" when he refers to a crab or lobster as "a pair of ragged claws" (page 761). Shakespeare uses metonymy when he says that the yellow cuckoo-buds "paint the meadows with delight" (page 524), for he means with bright color, which produces delight. Robert Frost uses metonymy in "Out, Out—" (page 630) when he describes an injured boy holding up his cut hand "as if to keep / The life from spilling," for literally he means to keep the blood from spilling. In each case, however, there is a gain in vividness and meaning. Eliot, by substituting for the crab that part which seizes its prey, tells us something important about the crab and makes us see it more vividly. Shakespeare, by referring to bright color as "delight," evokes not only the visual effect but the emotional response it arouses. Frost tells us both that the boy's hand is bleeding and that his life is in danger.

Many synecdoches and metonymies, of course, like many metaphors, have become so much a part of the language that they no longer strike us as figurative; such is the case with *redhead* for a red-haired person, *wheel* for a bicycle, and *salt* and *tar* for sailor. Such figures are referred to as dead metaphors or dead figures. Synecdoche and metonymy are so much alike that it is hardly worth while to distinguish between them, and the latter term is increasingly coming to be used for both. In this book metonymy will be used for both figures—that is, for any figure in which a part or something closely related is substituted for the thing literally meant.

A HUMMINGBIRD

> A route of evanescence
> With a revolving wheel;
> A resonance of emerald,
> A rush of cochineal;
> And every blossom on the bush
> Adjusts its tumbled head,—
> The mail from Tunis, probably,
> An easy morning's ride.

> *Emily Dickinson (1830–1886)*

QUESTIONS

1. Vocabulary: *evanescence* (1), *cochineal* (4). "Tunis" (7), on the north coast of Africa, is literally quite distant from Amherst, Massachusetts, where the poet lived, but as a symbol for remoteness it gets its main force from Shakespeare's *Tempest* (II, i, 246-48), where the next heir to the throne of Naples is described as "She that is Queen of Tunis; she that dwells / Ten leagues beyond man's life; she that from Naples / Can have no note, unless the sun were post— / The man i' th' moon's too slow."
2. Identify and explain three metonymies and a metaphor in lines 1-4.
3. Account fully for the vividness of the poem.

We said at the beginning of this chapter that figurative language often provides a more effective means of saying what we mean than does direct statement. What are some of the reasons for that effectiveness?

First, figurative language affords us imaginative pleasure. Imagination might be described in one sense as that faculty or ability of the mind that proceeds by sudden leaps from one point to another, that goes up a stair by leaping in one jump from the bottom to the top rather than by climbing up one step at a time.* The mind takes delight in these sudden leaps, in seeing likenesses between unlike things. We have probably all taken pleasure in staring into a fire and seeing castles and cities and armies in it, or in looking into the clouds and shaping them into animals or faces, or in seeing a man in the moon. We name our plants and flowers after fancied resemblances: jack-in-the-pulpit, babies'-breath, Queen Anne's lace. Figures of speech are therefore satisfying in themselves, providing us with a source of pleasure in the exercise of the imagination.

Second, figures of speech are a way of bringing additional imagery into verse, of making the abstract concrete, of making poetry more sensuous. When MacLeish personifies science (page 575), he gives body and form to what had previously been only a concept. When Emily Dickinson compares poetry to prancing coursers (page 547), she objectifies imaginative and rhythmical qualities by presenting them in visual terms. When Robert Browning compares the crisping waves to "fiery ringlets" (page 561), he starts with one image and transforms it into three. Figurative language is a way of multiplying the sense appeal of poetry.

Third, figures of speech are a way of adding emotional intensity to otherwise merely informative statements and of conveying attitudes along with information. If we say, "So-and-so is a rat" or "My feet are

---

*It is also the faculty of mind that is able to "picture" or "image" absent objects as if they were present. It was with imagination in this sense that we were concerned in the chapter on imagery.

killing me," our meaning is as much emotional as informative. When Thomas Hardy compares "tangled bine-stems" to "strings of broken lyres" (page 795), he not only draws an exact visual comparison but also conjures up a feeling of despondency through the suggestion of discarded instruments no longer capable of making music. When Wilfred Owen compares a soldier caught in a gas attack to a man drowning under a green sea (page 522), he conveys a feeling of despair and suffocation as well as a visual image.

Fourth, figures of speech are a means of concentration, a way of saying much in brief compass. Like words, they may be multidimensional. Consider, for instance, the merits of comparing life to a candle, as Shakespeare does in a passage from *Macbeth* (page 632). Life is like a candle in that it begins and ends in darkness; in that while it burns, it gives off light and energy, is active and colorful; in that it gradually consumes itself, gets shorter and shorter; in that it can be snuffed out at any moment; in that it is brief at best, burning only for a short duration. Possibly your imagination can suggest other similarities. But at any rate, Macbeth's compact metaphorical description of life as a "brief candle" suggests certain truths about life that would require dozens of words to state in literal language. At the same time it makes the abstract concrete, provides imaginative pleasure, and adds a degree of emotional intensity.

Obviously one of the necessary abilities for reading poetry is the ability to interpret figurative language. Every use of figurative language involves a risk of misinterpretation, though the risk is well worth taking. For the person who can translate the figure, the dividends are immense. Fortunately all people have imagination to some degree, and imagination can be cultivated. By practice one's ability to interpret figures of speech can be increased.

EXERCISE

Identify each of the following quotations as literal or figurative. If figurative, explain what is being compared to what and explain the appropriateness of the comparison. EXAMPLE: "Talent is a cistern; genius is a fountain." ANSWER: A metaphor. Talent = cistern; genius = fountain. Talent exists in finite supply; it can be used up. Genius is inexhaustible, ever renewing.

1. O tenderly the haughty day
   Fills his blue urn with fire.   *Emerson*

2. It is with words as with sunbeams—the more they are condensed, the
   deeper they burn.   *Robert Southey*

3. Joy and Temperance and Repose
   Slam the door on the doctor's nose.
                                                              Anonymous

4. The pen is mightier than the sword.   *Edward Bulwer-Lytton*

5. The strongest oaths are straw
   To the fire i' the blood.   *Shakespeare*

6. The Cambridge ladies . . . live in furnished souls.   *e. e. cummings*

7. The green lizard and the golden snake,
   Like unimprisoned flames, out of their trance awake.   *Shelley*

8. Dorothy's eyes, with their long brown lashes, looked very much like her
   mother's.   *Laetitia Johnson*

9. Was this the face that launched a thousand ships?   *Marlowe*

10. What should such fellows as I do crawling between earth and heaven?
                                                               Shakespeare

11. Love's feeling is more soft and sensible
    Than are the tender horns of cockled snails.   *Shakespeare*

12. The tawny-hided desert crouches watching her.   *Francis Thompson*

13. . . . Let us sit upon the ground
    And tell sad stories of the death of kings.   *Shakespeare*

14. See, from his [Christ's, on the cross] head, his hands, his side
    Sorrow and love flow mingled down.   *Isaac Watts*

15. Now half [of the departing guests] to the setting moon are gone,
    And half to the rising day.   *Tennyson*

16. I do not know whether my present poems are better than the earlier ones.
    But this is certain: they are much sadder and sweeter, like pain dipped in
    honey.   *Heinrich Heine*

17. . . . clouds. . . . Shepherded by the slow, unwilling wind.   *Shelley*

18. Let us eat and drink, for tomorrow we shall die.   *Isaiah 22:13*

19. Let us eat and drink, for tomorrow we may die.
                                            Common misquotation of the above

*   *   *

THE SILKEN TENT

>   She is as in a field a silken tent
>   At midday when a sunny summer breeze
>   Has dried the dew and all its ropes relent,
>   So that in guys it gently sways at ease,
>   And its supporting central cedar pole,   5
>   That is its pinnacle to heavenward

And signifies the sureness of the soul,
Seems to owe naught to any single cord,
But strictly held by none, is loosely bound
By countless silken ties of love and thought   10
To everything on earth the compass round,
And only by one's going slightly taut
In the capriciousness of summer air
Is of the slightest bondage made aware.

Robert Frost (1874–1963)

QUESTIONS

1. A poet may use a variety of metaphors and similes in developing his subject or may, as Frost does here, develop a single figure at length (this poem is an excellent example of EXTENDED or SUSTAINED SIMILE). What are the advantages of each type of development?
2. Explore the similarities between the two things compared.

METAPHORS

I'm a riddle in nine syllables,
An elephant, a ponderous house,
A melon strolling on two tendrils.
O red fruit, ivory, fine timbers!
This loaf's big with its yeasty rising.
Money's new-minted in this fat purse.
I'm a means, a stage, a cow in calf.
I've eaten a bag of green apples,
Boarded the train there's no getting off.

Sylvia Plath (1932–1963)

QUESTIONS

1. Like its first metaphor, this poem is a riddle to be solved by identifying the literal terms of its metaphors. After you have identified the speaker ("riddle," "elephant," "house," "melon," "stage," "cow"), identify the literal meanings of the related metaphors ("syllables," "tendrils," "fruit," "ivory," "timbers," "loaf," "yeasty rising," "money," "purse," "train"). How is line 8 to be interpreted?
2. How does the form of the poem relate to its content?

TOADS

Why should I let the toad *work*
    Squat on my life?
Can't I use my wit as a pitchfork
    And drive the brute off?

Six days of the week it soils   5
    With its sickening poison—
Just for paying a few bills!
    That's out of proportion.

Lots of folk live on their wits:
    Lecturers, lispers,   10
Losels,° loblolly-men,° louts—   scoundrels; bumpkins
    They don't end as paupers;

Lots of folk live up lanes
    With fires in a bucket,
Eat windfalls and tinned sardines—   15
    They seem to like it.

Their nippers° have got bare feet,   children
    Their unspeakable wives
Are skinny as whippets—and yet
    No one actually *starves*.   20

Ah, were I courageous enough
    To shout *Stuff your pension!*
But I know, all too well, that's the stuff
    That dreams are made on;

For something sufficiently toad-like   25
    Squats in me, too;
Its hunkers° are heavy as hard luck,   haunches
    And cold as snow,

And will never allow me to blarney
    My way to getting   30
The fame and the girl and the money
    All at one sitting.

I don't say, one bodies the other
    One's spiritual truth;
But I do say it's hard to lose either,   35
    When you have both.

Philip Larkin (*b. 1922*)

1. How many "toads" are described in the poem? Where is each located? How are they described? What are the antecedents of the pronouns "one" and "the other / one" (33-34) respectively?
2. What characteristics have the people mentioned in stanza 3 in common? Those mentioned in stanzas 4-5?
3. Explain the pun in stanza 6 and the literary allusion it leads into. (If you don't recognize it, check Shakespeare's *Tempest*, Act IV, Scene 1, lines 156-58.)
4. The first "toad" is explicitly identified as "work" (1). The literal term for the second "toad" is not named. Why not? What do you take it to be?
5. What kind of person is the speaker? What are his attitudes toward work?

A VALEDICTION: FORBIDDING MOURNING

As virtuous men pass mildly away,
    And whisper to their souls to go,
While some of their sad friends do say,
    The breath goes now, and some say, no:

So let us melt, and make no noise,   5
    No tear-floods, nor sigh-tempests move;
'Twere profanation of our joys
    To tell the laity our love.

Moving of th' earth brings harms and fears,
    Men reckon what it did and meant,   10
But trepidation of the spheres,
    Though greater far, is innocent.

Dull sublunary lovers' love
    (Whose soul is sense) cannot admit
Absence, because it doth remove   15
    Those things which elemented it.

But we by a love so much refined,
    That ourselves know not what it is,
Inter-assurèd of the mind,
    Care less, eyes, lips, and hands to miss.   20

Our two souls therefore, which are one,
    Though I must go, endure not yet
A breach, but an expansion,
    Like gold to airy thinness beat.

If they be two, they are two so   25
    As stiff twin compasses are two;

Thy soul the fixed foot, makes no show
To move, but doth, if th' other do.

And though it in the center sit,
    Yet when the other far doth roam,   30
It leans, and hearkens after it,
    And grows erect, as that comes home.

Such wilt thou be to me, who must
    Like th' other foot, obliquely run;
Thy firmness makes my circle just,   35
    And makes me end, where I begun.

John Donne (1572–1631)

QUESTIONS

1. Vocabulary: *valediction* (title), *mourn* (title), *profanation* (7), *laity* (8), *trepidation* (11), *innocent* (12), *sublunary* (13), *elemented* (16). Line 11 is a reference to the spheres of the Ptolemaic cosmology, whose movements caused no such disturbance as does a movement of the earth—that is, an earthquake.
2. Is the speaker in the poem about to die? Or about to leave on a journey? (The answer may be found in a careful analysis of the simile in the last three stanzas.)
3. The poem is organized around a contrast of two kinds of lovers: the "laity" (8) and, as their implied opposite, the "priesthood." Are these terms literal or metaphorical? What is the essential difference between their two kinds of love? How, according to the speaker, does their behavior differ when they must separate from each other? What is the motivation of the speaker in this "valediction"?
4. Find and explain three similes and one metaphor used to describe the parting of true lovers. The figure in the last three stanzas is one of the most famous in English literature. Demonstrate its appropriateness by obtaining a drawing compass or by using two pencils to imitate the two legs.
5. What kind of language is used in the poem? Is the language consonant with the figures of speech?

TO HIS COY MISTRESS

        Had we but world enough, and time,
    This coyness, lady, were no crime.
    We would sit down, and think which way
    To walk, and pass our long love's day.
    Thou by the Indian Ganges' side   5
    Shouldst rubies find; I by the tide
    Of Humber would complain. I would
    Love you ten years before the Flood,

And you should, if you please, refuse
Till the conversion of the Jews.
My vegetable love should grow   10
Vaster than empires, and more slow;
An hundred years should go to praise
Thine eyes, and on thy forehead gaze;
Two hundred to adore each breast,   15
But thirty thousand to the rest;
An age at least to every part,
And the last age should show your heart.
For, lady, you deserve this state,
Nor would I love at lower rate.   20
    But at my back I always hear
Time's wingèd chariot hurrying near;
And yonder all before us lie
Deserts of vast eternity.
Thy beauty shall no more be found,   25
Nor, in thy marble vault, shall sound
My echoing song; then worms shall try
That long-preserved virginity,
And your quaint honor turn to dust,
And into ashes all my lust: 30
The grave's a fine and private place,
But none, I think, do there embrace.
    Now therefore, while the youthful hue
Sits on thy skin like morning dew,
And while thy willing soul transpires   35
At every pore with instant fires,
Now let us sport us while we may,
And now, like amorous birds of prey,
Rather at once our time devour
Than languish in his slow-chapped power.   40
Let us roll all our strength and all
Our sweetness up into one ball,
And tear our pleasures with rough strife
Thorough° the iron gates of life.   through
Thus, though we cannot make our sun   45
Stand still, yet we will make him run.

Andrew Marvell (1621–1678)

QUESTIONS

1. Vocabulary: *coy* (title), *Humber* (7), *transpires* (35). "Mistress" (title) has the
now archaic meaning of *sweetheart;* "slow-chapped" (40) derives from *chap,*
meaning *jaw.*

2. What is the speaker urging his sweetheart to do? Why is she being "coy"?
3. Outline the speaker's argument in three sentences that begin with the words *If, But,* and *Therefore.* Is the argument valid?
4. Explain the appropriateness of "vegetable love" (11). What simile in the third section contrasts with it and how? What image in the third section contrasts with the distance between the Ganges and the Humber? Of what would the speaker be "complaining" by the Humber (7)?
5. Explain the figures in lines 22, 24, and 40 and their implications.
6. Explain the last two lines. For what is "sun" a metonymy?
7. Is this poem principally about love or about time? If the latter, what might making love represent? What philosophy is the poet advancing here?

WEEP YOU NO MORE, SAD FOUNTAINS

> Weep you no more, sad fountains;
>   What need you flow so fast?
> Look how the snowy mountains
>   Heaven's sun doth gently waste.
> But my sun's heavenly eyes   5
>   View not your weeping,
>   That now lies sleeping
>   Softly, now softly lies
>   Sleeping.
>
> Sleep is a reconciling,   10
>   A rest that peace begets.
> Doth not the sun rise smiling
>   When fair at even he sets?
> Rest you then, rest, sad eyes,
>   Melt not in weeping   15
>   While she lies sleeping
>   Softly, now softly lies
>   Sleeping.

Anonymous (c. 1603)

QUESTIONS

1. Are *fountains* (1), *sun* (4), *sun* (5), and *sleeping* (7, 9) respectively literal or metaphorical? Explain.
2. What figures of speech are used in lines 12, 14, and 15?
3. To what do the pronouns *your* (6) and *that* (7) respectively refer? Is *peace* (11) the subject or object of *begets?*
4. Explain the situation and the argument of the poem.

LOVELIEST OF TREES

Loveliest of trees, the cherry now
Is hung with bloom along the bough,
And stands about the woodland ride
Wearing white for Eastertide.

Now, of my threescore years and ten,   5
Twenty will not come again,
And take from seventy springs a score,
It only leaves me fifty more.

And since to look at things in bloom
Fifty springs are little room,   10
About the woodlands I will go
To see the cherry hung with snow.

A. E. Housman (1859–1936)

QUESTIONS

1. Very briefly, this poem presents a philosophy of life. In a sentence, what is it?
2. How old is the speaker? Why does he assume that his life will be seventy years in length? What is surprising about the words "only" (8) and "little" (10)?
3. A good deal of ink has been spilt over whether "snow" (12) is literal or figurative. What do you say? Justify your answer.

DREAM DEFERRED

What happens to a dream deferred?

Does it dry up
like a raisin in the sun?
Or fester like a sore—
And then run?   5
Does it stink like rotten meat?
Or crust and sugar over—
like a syrupy sweet?

Maybe it just sags
like a heavy load.   10

Or does it explode?

Langston Hughes (1902–1967)

QUESTIONS

1. Of the six images, five are similes. Which is a metaphor? Comment on its position and its effectiveness.
2. Since the dream could be any dream, the poem is general in its implication. What happens to your understanding of it on learning that its author was a black American?

DEATH STANDS ABOVE ME

> Death stands above me, whispering low
> I know not what into my ear;
> Of his strange language all I know
> Is, there is not a word of fear.

Walter Savage Landor (1775–1864)

QUESTIONS

1. To what degree is Death personified, and what is the effect of this personification? What is implied by the poet's not knowing what is said in Death's "strange language"?
2. Define as precisely as possible the poet's attitude toward the possibility of some kind of future life.

6. Figurative Language 2

SYMBOL, ALLEGORY

THE ROAD NOT TAKEN

Two roads diverged in a yellow wood,
And sorry I could not travel both
And be one traveler, long I stood
And looked down one as far as I could
To where it bent in the undergrowth;   5

Then took the other, as just as fair,
And having perhaps the better claim,
Because it was grassy and wanted wear;
Though as for that the passing there
Had worn them really about the same,   10

And both that morning equally lay
In leaves no step had trodden black.
Oh, I kept the first for another day!
Yet knowing how way leads on to way,
I doubted if I should ever come back.   15

I shall be telling this with a sigh
Somewhere ages and ages hence:
Two roads diverged in a wood, and I—
I took the one less traveled by,
And that has made all the difference.   20

Robert Frost (1874–1963)

QUESTIONS

1. Does the speaker feel that he made the wrong choice in taking the road "less traveled by"? If not, why will he sigh? What does he regret?
2. Why will the choice between two roads that seem very much alike make such a big difference many years later?

A SYMBOL may be roughly defined as something that means *more* than what it is. "The Road Not Taken," for instance, concerns a choice made between two roads by a person out walking in the woods. He would like to explore both roads. He tells himself that he will explore one and then come back and explore the other, but he knows that he shall probably be unable to do so. By the last stanza, however, we realize that the poet is talking about something more than the choice of paths in a wood, for such a choice would be relatively unimportant, while this choice is one that will make a great difference in the speaker's life and that he will remember with a sigh "ages and ages hence." We must interpret his choice of a road as a symbol for any choice in life between alternatives that appear almost equally attractive but will result through the years in a large difference in the kind of experience one knows.

Image, metaphor, and symbol shade into each other and are sometimes difficult to distinguish. In general, however, an image means only what it is; the figurative term of a metaphor means something other than what it is; and a symbol means what it is and something more too.* If I say that a shaggy brown dog was rubbing its back against a white picket fence, I am talking about nothing but a dog (and a picket fence) and am therefore presenting an image. If I say, "Some dirty dog stole my wallet at the party," I am not talking about a dog at all and am therefore using a metaphor. But if I say, "You can't teach an old dog new tricks," I am talking not only about dogs but about living creatures of any species and am therefore speaking symbolically. Images, of course, do not cease to be images when they become incorporated in metaphors or symbols. If we are discussing the sensuous qualities of "The Road Not Taken" we should refer to the two leaf-strewn roads in the yellow wood as an image; if we are discussing the significance of the poem, we talk about them as symbols.

Symbols vary in the degree of identification and definition given them

---

* This account does not hold for nonliterary symbols such as the letters of the alphabet and algebraic signs (the symbol ∞ for infinity or = for equals). Here, the symbol is meaningless except as it stands for something else, and the connection between the sign and what it stands for is purely arbitrary.

by their authors. Frost in this poem forces us to interpret the choice of roads symbolically by the degree of importance he gives it in the last stanza. Sometimes poets are much more specific in identifying their symbols. Sometimes they do not identify them at all. Consider, for instance, the following poems.

A WHITE ROSE

The red rose whispers of passion,
    And the white rose breathes of love;
Oh, the red rose is a falcon,
    And the white rose is a dove.

But I send you a cream-white rosebud,
    With a flush on its petal tips;
For the love that is purest and sweetest
    Has a kiss of desire on the lips.

John Boyle O'Reilly (1844–1890)

QUESTIONS

1. Could the poet have made the white rose a symbol of passion and the red rose a symbol of love? Why not?
2. In the second stanza, why does the speaker send a rosebud rather than a rose?

MY STAR

All that I know
    Of a certain star
Is, it can throw
    (Like the angled spar)
Now a dart of red,   5
    Now a dart of blue;
Till my friends have said
    They would fain° see, too,   gladly
My star that dartles the red and the blue!
Then it stops like a bird; like a flower, hangs furled: 10
    They must solace themselves with the Saturn above it.
What matter to me if their star is a world?
    Mine has opened its soul to me; therefore I love it.

Robert Browning (1812–1889)

In his first two lines O'Reilly indicates so clearly that his red rose is a symbol of physical desire and his white rose a symbol of spiritual attachment that when we get to the metaphor in the third line, we unconsciously substitute passion for the red rose in our minds, knowing without thinking that what O'Reilly is really likening is falcons and passion, not falcons and roses. Similarly in the second stanza, the symbolism of the white rosebud with pink tips is specifically indicated in the last two lines, although, as a matter of fact, it would have been clear from the first stanza. In Browning's poem, on the other hand, there is nothing specific to tell us that Browning is talking about anything other than just a star, and it is only the star's importance to him that makes us suspect that he is talking about something more.

The symbol is the richest and at the same time the most difficult of the poetical figures. Both its richness and its difficulty result from its imprecision. Although the poet may pin down the meaning of his symbol to something fairly definite and precise, as O'Reilly does in "A White Rose," more often the symbol is so general in its meaning that it is able to suggest a great variety of more specific meanings. It is like an opal that flashes out different colors when slowly turned in the light. The choice in "The Road Not Taken," for instance, concerns some choice in life, but what choice? Was it a choice of profession? (Frost took the road "less traveled by" in deciding to become a poet.) A choice of hobby? A choice of mate? It might be any or all or none of these. We cannot determine what particular choice the poet had in mind, if any, and it is not important that we do so. The general meaning of the poem is clear enough. It is an expression of regret that the possibilities of life-experience are so sharply limited. One must live with one mate, have one native country, follow one profession. The speaker in the poem would have liked to explore both roads, but he could explore only one. The person with a craving for life, however satisfied with his own choice, will always long for the realms of experience that had to be passed by. Because the symbol is a rich one, the poem suggests other meanings too. It affirms a belief in the possibility of choice and says something of the nature of choice—how each choice limits the range of possible future choices, so that we make our lives as we go, both freely choosing and being determined by past choices. Though not primarily a philosophical poem, it obliquely comments on the issue of free will versus determinism and indicates the poet's own position. It is able to do all these things, concretely and compactly, by its use of an effective symbol.

"My Star," if we interpret it symbolically, likewise suggests a variety of meanings. It has been most often interpreted as a tribute to Browning's wife, Elizabeth Barrett Browning. As one critic writes, "She shone upon his life like a star of various colors; but the moment the world attempted to pry into the secret of her genius, she shut off the light altogether."* The poem has also been taken to refer to Browning's own peculiar genius, "his gift for seeing in events and things a significance hidden from other men."† A third suggestion is that Browning was thinking of his own peculiar poetic style. He loved harsh, jagged sounds and rhythms and grotesque images; most people of his time found beauty only in the smoother-flowing, melodic rhythms and more conventionally poetic images of his contemporary Tennyson's style, which could be symbolized by Saturn in the poem. The point is not that any one of these interpretations is right or necessarily wrong. We cannot say what the poet had specifically in mind. Literally, the poem is an expression of affection for a particular star in the sky that has a unique beauty and fascination for the poet but in which no one else can see the qualities that the poet sees. If we interpret the poem symbolically, the star is a symbol for anything in life that has unique meanings and value for an individual, which other people cannot see. Beyond this, the meaning is "open." And because the meaning is open, the reader is justified in bringing his own experience to its interpretation. Browning's cherished star might remind him of, for instance, an old rag doll he particularly loved as a child, though its button eyes were off and its stuffing coming out and it had none of the crisp bright beauty of waxen dolls with real hair admired by other children.

Between the extremes represented by "The White Rose" and "My Star" a poem may exercise all degrees of control over the range and meaning of its symbolism. Consider another example.

YOU, ANDREW MARVELL

> And here face down beneath the sun
> And here upon earth's noonward height
> To feel the always coming on
> The always rising of the night:
>
> To feel creep up the curving east   5
> The earthly chill of dusk and slow
> Upon those under lands the vast
> And ever-climbing shadow grow

*William Lyon Phelps, *Robert Browning: How to Know Him* (Indianapolis: Bobbs-Merrill, 1932), p. 165.

†Quoted from William Clyde DeVane, *A Browning Handbook* (New York: Crofts, 1935), p. 202.

And strange at Ecbatan the trees
Take leaf by leaf the evening strange   10
The flooding dark about their knees
The mountains over Persia change

And now at Kermanshah the gate
Dark empty and the withered grass
And through the twilight now the late   15
Few travelers in the westward pass

And Baghdad darken and the bridge
Across the silent river gone
And through Arabia the edge
Of evening widen and steal on   20

And deepen on Palmyra's street
The wheel rut in the ruined stone
And Lebanon fade out and Crete
High through the clouds and overblown

And over Sicily the air   25
Still flashing with the landward gulls
And loom and slowly disappear
The sails above the shadowy hulls

And Spain go under and the shore
Of Africa the gilded sand   30
And evening vanish and no more
The low pale light across that land

Nor now the long light on the sea:
And here face downward in the sun
To feel how swift how secretly   35
The shadow of the night comes on . . .

Archibald MacLeish (1892–1982)

QUESTIONS

1. We ordinarily speak of *nightfall*. Why does MacLeish speak of the "rising" of the night? What implicit metaphorical comparison is suggested by phrases like "rising of the night" (4), "the flooding dark" (11), "the bridge / Across the silent river gone" (17–18), "deepen on Palmyra's street" (21), "Spain go under" (29), and so on?
2. Does the comparative lack of punctuation serve any function? What is the effect of the repetition of "and" throughout the poem?

3. Ecbatan was founded in 700 B.C. and is associated in history with Cyrus the Great, founder of the Persian Empire, and with Alexander the Great. Kermanshah was another ancient city of Persia. Where are Baghdad, Palmyra, Lebanon, Crete?

On the literal level, "You, Andrew Marvell" is about the coming on of night. The poet, lying at noon full length in the sun somewhere in the United States,* pictures in his mind the earth's shadow, halfway around the world, moving silently westward over Persia, Syria, Crete, Sicily, Spain, Africa, and finally the Atlantic—approaching swiftly, in fact, the place where he himself lies. But the title of the poem tells us that, though particularly concerned with the passage of a day, it is more generally concerned with the swift passage of time; for the title is an allusion to a famous poem on this subject by Andrew Marvell ("To His Coy Mistress," page 584) and especially to two lines of that poem:

> But at my back I always hear
> Time's wingèd chariot hurrying near.

Once we are aware of this larger concern of the poem, two symbolical levels of interpretation open to us. Marvell's poem is primarily concerned with the swift passing of man's life; and the word *night*, we know, from our experience with other literature, is a natural and traditional metaphor or symbol for death. The poet, then, is thinking not only about the passing of a day but about the passing of his life. He is at present "upon earth's noonward height"—in the full flush of manhood—but he is acutely conscious of the declining years ahead and of "how swift how secretly" his death comes on.

If we are to account fully for all the data of the poem, however, a third level of interpretation is necessary. What has dictated the poet's choice of geographical references? The places named, of course, progress from east to west; but they have a further linking characteristic. Ecbatan, Kermanshah, Baghdad, and Palmyra are all ancient or ruined cities, the relics of past empires and crumbled civilizations. Lebanon, Crete, Sicily, Spain, and North Africa are places where civilization once flourished more vigorously than it does at present. On a third level, then, the poet is concerned, not with the passage of a day nor with the passage of a lifetime, but with the passage of historical epochs. The poet's own coun-

---

* MacLeish has identified the fixed location of the poem as Illinois on the shore of Lake Michigan.

try—the United States—now shines "upon earth's noonward height" as a favored nation in the sun of history, but its civilization, too, will pass.

Meanings ray out from a symbol, like the corona around the sun or like connotations around a richly suggestive word. But the very fact that a symbol may be so rich in its meanings makes it necessary that we use the greatest tact in its interpretation. Though Browning's "My Star" might, because of personal associations, make us think of a rag doll, still we should not go around telling people that in this poem Browning uses the star to symbolize a rag doll, for this interpretation is private, idiosyncratic, and narrow. The poem allows it but does not itself suggest it. Moreover, we should never assume that because the meaning of a symbol is more or less open, we may make it mean anything we choose. We would be wrong, for instance, in interpreting the choice in "The Road Not Taken" as some choice between good and evil, for the poem tells us that the two roads are much alike and that both lie "in leaves no step had trodden black." Whatever the choice is, it is a choice between two goods. Whatever our interpretation of a symbolical poem, it must be tied firmly to the facts of the poem. We must not let loose of the string and let our imaginations go ballooning up among the clouds. Because the symbol is capable of adding so many dimensions to a poem, it is a peculiarly effective resource of the poet, but it is also peculiarly susceptible of misinterpretation by the incautious reader.

Accurate interpretation of the symbol requires delicacy, tact, and good sense. The reader must keep his balance while walking a tightrope between too little and too much—between underinterpretation and overinterpretation. If he falls off, however, it is much more desirable that he fall off on the side of too little. The reader who reads "The Road Not Taken" as being only about a choice between two roads in a wood has at least gotten part of the experience that the poem communicates, but the reader who reads into it anything he chooses might as well discard the poem and simply daydream.

Above all, we should avoid the disease of seeing symbols everywhere, like a man with hallucinations, whether there are symbols there or not. It is better to miss a symbol now and then than to walk constantly among shadows and mirages.

TO THE VIRGINS, TO MAKE MUCH OF TIME

> Gather ye rosebuds while ye may,
> Old Time is still a-flying;
> And this same flower that smiles today
> Tomorrow will be dying.

The glorious lamp of heaven, the Sun,   5
    The higher he's a-getting,
The sooner will his race be run,
    And nearer he's to setting.

That age is best which is the first,
    When youth and blood are warmer;   10
But being spent, the worse, and worst
    Times still succeed the former.

Then be not coy, but use your time;
    And while ye may, go marry;
For having lost but once your prime,   15
    You may forever tarry.

Robert Herrick (1591–1674)

QUESTIONS

1. The first two stanzas might be interpreted literally if the third and fourth stanzas did not force us to interpret them symbolically. What do the rosebuds symbolize (stanza 1)? What does the course of a day symbolize (stanza 2)? Does the poet fix the meaning of the rosebud symbol in the last stanza or merely name *one* of its specific meanings?
2. How does the title help us interpret the meaning of the symbol? Why did Herrick use "virgins" instead of *maidens?*
3. Why is such haste necessary in gathering the rosebuds? True, the blossoms die quickly, but they are replaced by others. Who *really* is dying?
4. What are the "worse, and worst" times (11)? Why?
5. Why did the poet use his wording rather than the following alternatives: *blooms* for "smiles" (3), *course* for "race" (7), *used* for "spent" (11), *spend* for "use" (13)?

ALLEGORY is a narrative or description that has a second meaning beneath the surface one. Although the surface story or description may have its own interest, the author's major interest is in the ulterior meaning. When Pharaoh in the Bible, for instance, has a dream in which seven fat kine are devoured by seven lean kine, the story does not really become significant until Joseph interprets its allegorical meaning: that Egypt is to enjoy seven years of fruitfulness and prosperity followed by seven years of famine. Allegory has been defined sometimes as an extended metaphor and sometimes as a series of related symbols. But it is usually distinguishable from both of these. It is unlike extended metaphor in that it involves a *system* of related comparisons rather than one comparison drawn out. It differs from symbolism in that it puts less emphasis on the images for their own sake and more on their ulterior meanings. Also, these meanings are more fixed. In allegory usually there is a one-to-one correspondence between the details and a single set of ulterior meanings. In complex allegories the details may have more than one meaning, but these meanings tend to be definite. Meanings do not ray out from allegory as they do from a symbol.

Allegory is less popular in modern literature than it was in medieval and Renaissance writing, and it is much less often found in short poems than in long works such as *The Faerie Queene, Everyman,* and *Pilgrim's Progress.* It has sometimes, especially with political allegory, been used to disguise meaning rather than reveal it (or, rather, to disguise it from some people while revealing it to others). Though less rich than the symbol, allegory is an effective way of making the abstract concrete and has occasionally been used effectively even in fairly short poems.

REDEMPTION

Having been tenant long to a rich Lord,
   Not thriving, I resolvèd to be bold,
   And make a suit unto him, to afford
A new small-rented lease and cancel the old.
In heaven at his manor I him sought: 5
   They told me there that he was lately gone
   About some land which he had dearly bought
Long since on earth, to take possession.
I straight returned, and knowing his great birth,
   Sought him accordingly in great resorts;   10
   In cities, theaters, gardens, parks, and courts:
At length I heard a ragged noise and mirth
   Of thieves and murderers; there I him espied,
   Who straight, "Your suit is granted," said, and died.

George Herbert (*1593–1633*)

QUESTIONS

1. Vocabulary: *suit* (3, 14), *afford* (3), *dearly* (7).
2. On the surface this poem tells about a business negotiation between a tenant landholder and his landlord. What clues indicate that the poem really concerns something deeper?
3. Who is the "rich Lord"? Who is the tenant? What is the old lease? What is the new one? Where does the tenant find his Lord? What is the significance of his suit being granted just as the landlord dies?
4. What are the implications of the landlord's having gone to take possession of

some land which he "had dearly bought / Long since on earth"? In what senses (on both levels of meaning) is the landlord of "great birth"? What is "a ragged noise and mirth / Of thieves and murderers"?

EXERCISE

Determine whether "sleep," in the following poems, is literal, metaphorical, symbolical, or other. In each case explain and justify your answer.

1. "On moonlit heath and lonesome bank," page 564, line 13.
2. "On moonlit heath and lonesome bank," line 29.
3. "Dulce et Decorum Est," page 521, line 5.
4. "Terence, this is stupid stuff," page 528, line 8.
5. "Is my team ploughing," page 535, lines 24, 27.
6. "Meeting at Night," page 561, line 4.
7. "Weep ye no more, sad fountains," page 586, lines 7, 9, 16, 18.
8. "Reveille," page 599, line 24.
9. "Ulysses," page 601, line 5.
10. "Stopping by Woods on a Snowy Evening," page 642, line 16.

*   *   *

REVEILLE

Wake: the silver dusk returning
   Up the beach of darkness brims,
And the ship of sunrise burning
   Strands upon the eastern rims.

Wake: the vaulted shadow shatters,   5
   Trampled to the floor it spanned,
And the tent of night in tatters
   Straws the sky-pavilioned land.

Up, lad, up, 'tis late for lying:
   Hear the drums of morning play;   10
Hark, the empty highways crying
   "Who'll beyond the hills away?"

Towns and countries woo together,
   Forelands beacon, belfries call;
Never lad that trod on leather   15
   Lived to feast his heart with all.

Up, lad: thews that lie and cumber
   Sunlit pallets never thrive;

Morns abed and daylight slumber
Were not meant for man alive. 20

Clay lies still, but blood's a rover;
Breath's a ware that will not keep.
Up, lad: when the journey's over
There'll be time enough to sleep.

A. E. Housman (1859–1936)

QUESTIONS

1. Are *Reveille* (title) and *drums* (10) literal or metaphorical? Explain.
2. Explain the metaphors in lines 1–4, 5–8, and 22. What figure of speech predominates in lines 11–14?
3. Identify and explain the metonymies in lines 15, 17, 21, and 22.
4. What symbolical meanings have *journey* (23) and *sleep* (24)?
5. What philosophy does the poem express?

FIRE AND ICE

Some say the world will end in fire,
Some say in ice.
From what I've tasted of desire
I hold with those who favor fire.
But if it had to perish twice,
I think I know enough of hate
To say that for destruction ice
Is also great
And would suffice.

Robert Frost (1874–1963)

QUESTIONS

1. Who are "Some"? To what two theories do lines 1–2 refer?
2. What do "fire" and "ice" respectively symbolize? What two meanings has "the world"?
3. The poem ends with an *understatement* (see chapter 7). How does it affect the tone of the poem?

THE SICK ROSE

O Rose, thou art sick!
The invisible worm
That flies in the night,
In the howling storm,

Has found out thy bed
Of crimson joy,
And his dark secret love
Does thy life destroy.

William Blake (1757–1827)

QUESTIONS

1. As in Browning's "My Star," the meaning of the symbolism in this poem is
   left fairly open. The poem might be interpreted as being only about a rose
   which has been attacked on a stormy night by a cankerworm. But the connotations of certain words and details are so powerful as to suggest that more is
   meant: "sick" (applied to a flower), "invisible," "night," "howling storm,"
   "bed of crimson joy," "dark secret love." Can you suggest specific meanings
   for the rose and the worm? What broad boundaries of meaning must any
   specific interpretations observe? Can the poem be read as about the overcoming of something evil by something good?
2. Besides being a symbol, the rose is to some degree personified. What words or
   details of the poem contribute to this personification?

ULYSSES

It little profits that an idle king,
By this still hearth, among these barren crags,
Matched with an aged wife, I mete and dole
Unequal laws unto a savage race,
That hoard, and sleep, and feed, and know not me.   5
I cannot rest from travel; I will drink
Life to the lees. All times I have enjoyed
Greatly, have suffered greatly, both with those
That loved me, and alone; on shore, and when
Through scudding drifts the rainy Hyades   10
Vext the dim sea. I am become a name;
For always roaming with a hungry heart
Much have I seen and known,—cities of men
And manners, climates, councils, governments,
Myself not least, but honored of them all;   15
And drunk delight of battle with my peers,
Far on the ringing plains of windy Troy.
I am a part of all that I have met;
Yet all experience is an arch wherethrough
Gleams that untraveled world, whose margin fades   20
For ever and for ever when I move.
How dull it is to pause, to make an end,
To rust unburnished, not to shine in use!

As though to breathe were life! Life piled on life
Were all too little, and of one to me   25
Little remains; but every hour is saved
From that eternal silence, something more,
A bringer of new things; and vile it were
For some three suns to store and hoard myself,
And this grey spirit yearning in desire   30
To follow knowledge like a sinking star,
Beyond the utmost bound of human thought.

This is my son, mine own Telemachus,
To whom I leave the scepter and the isle—
Well-loved of me, discerning to fulfil   35
This labor, by slow prudence to make mild
A rugged people, and through soft degrees
Subdue them to the useful and the good.
Most blameless is he, centered in the sphere
Of common duties, decent not to fail   40
In offices of tenderness, and pay
Meet adoration to my household gods,
When I am gone. He works his work, I mine.

There lies the port; the vessel puffs her sail:
There gloom the dark, broad seas. My mariners,   45
Souls that have toiled, and wrought, and thought with me—
That ever with a frolic welcome took
The thunder and the sunshine, and opposed
Free hearts, free foreheads—you and I are old;
Old age hath yet his honor and his toil.   50
Death closes all; but something ere the end,
Some work of noble note, may yet be done,
Not unbecoming men that strove with Gods.
The lights begin to twinkle from the rocks;
The long day wanes; the slow moon climbs; the deep   55
Moans round with many voices. Come, my friends,
'Tis not too late to seek a newer world.
Push off, and sitting well in order smite
The sounding furrows; for my purpose holds
To sail beyond the sunset, and the baths   60
Of all the western stars, until I die.
It may be that the gulfs will wash us down;
It may be we shall touch the Happy Isles,
And see the great Achilles, whom we knew.
Though much is taken, much abides; and though   65
We are not now that strength which in old days
Moved earth and heaven, that which we are, we are:

One equal temper of heroic hearts,
Made weak by time and fate, but strong in will
To strive, to seek, to find, and not to yield.   70

Alfred, Lord Tennyson (1809–1892)

QUESTIONS

1. Vocabulary: *lees* (7), *Hyades* (10), *meet* (42).
2. Ulysses, king of Ithaca, is a legendary Greek hero, a major figure in Homer's *Iliad*, the hero of Homer's *Odyssey*, and a minor figure in Dante's *Divine Comedy*. After ten years at the siege of Troy, Ulysses set sail for home but, having incurred the wrath of the god of the sea, he was subjected to storms and vicissitudes and was forced to wander for another ten years, having many adventures and seeing most of the Mediterranean world before again reaching Ithaca, his wife, and his son. Once back home, according to Dante, he still wished to travel and "to follow virtue and knowledge." In Tennyson's poem, Ulysses is represented as about to set sail on a final voyage from which he will not return. Locate Ithaca on a map. Where exactly, in geographical terms, does Ulysses intend to sail (59–64)? (The Happy Isles were the Elysian fields, or Greek paradise; Achilles was another Greek prince, the hero of the *Iliad*, who was killed at the siege of Troy.)
3. Ulysses' speech is divided into three sections. What is the topic or purpose of each section? To whom, specifically, is the third section addressed? To whom, would you infer, are sections 1 and 2 addressed? Where do you visualize Ulysses as standing during his speech?
4. Characterize Ulysses. What kind of person is he as Tennyson represents him?
5. What does Ulysses symbolize? What way of life is being recommended? Find as many evidences as you can that Ulysses' desire for travel represents something more than mere wanderlust and wish for adventure.
6. Give two symbolical implications of the westward direction of Ulysses' journey.
7. Interpret lines 18–21 and 26–29. What is symbolized by "the thunder and the sunshine" (48)? What do the two metonymies in line 49 stand for? What metaphor is implied in line 23?

CURIOSITY

may have killed the cat; more likely
the cat was just unlucky, or else curious
to see what death was like, having no cause
to go on licking paws, or fathering
litter on litter of kittens, predictably.   5

Nevertheless, to be curious
is dangerous enough. To distrust
what is always said, what seems,
to ask odd questions, interfere in dreams,

leave home, smell rats, have hunches
do not endear cats to those doggy circles
where well-smelt baskets, suitable wives, good lunches
are the order of things, and where prevails
much wagging of incurious heads and tails. 10

Face it. Curiosity 15
will not cause us to die—
only lack of it will.
Never to want to see
the other side of the hill
or that improbable country 20
where living is an idyll
(although a probable hell)
would kill us all.
Only the curious
have, if they live, a tale 25
worth telling at all.

Dogs say cats love too much, are irresponsible,
are changeable, marry too many wives,
desert their children, chill all dinner tables
with tales of their nine lives. 30
Well, they are lucky. Let them be
nine-lived and contradictory,
curious enough to change, prepared to pay
the cat price, which is to die
and die again and again, 35
each time with no less pain.
A cat minority of one
is all that can be counted on
to tell the truth. And what cats have to tell
on each return from hell 40
is this: that dying is what the living do,
that dying is what the loving do,
and that dead dogs are those who do not know
that dying is what, to live, each has to do.

Alastair Reid (b. 1926)

QUESTIONS

1. On the surface this poem is a dissertation on cats. What deeper comments
   does it make? Of what are cats and dogs, in this poem, symbols?
2. In what different senses are the words "death," "die," and "dying" here used?
3. Compare and contrast this poem in meaning and manner with "Ulysses."

LOVE SONG: I AND THOU

Nothing is plumb, level or square:
    the studs are bowed, the joists
are shaky by nature, no piece fits
    any other piece without a gap
or pinch, and bent nails   5
    dance all over the surfacing
like maggots. By Christ
    I am no carpenter, I built
the roof for myself, the walls
    for myself, the floors   10
for myself, and got
    hung up in it myself. I
danced with a purple thumb
    at this house-warming, drunk
with my prime whiskey: rage.   15
    Oh I spat rage's nails
into the frame-up of my work:
    it held. It settled plumb,
level, solid, square and true
    for that one moment. Then   20
it screamed and went on through
    skewing as wrong the other way.
God damned it. This is hell,
    but I planned it, I sawed it,
I nailed it, and I   25
    will live in it until it kills me.
I can nail my left palm
    to the left-hand cross-piece but
I can't do everything myself.
    I need a hand to nail the right,   30
a help, a love, a you, a wife.

Alan Dugan (b. 1923)

QUESTIONS

1. What clues are there that this house is not literal? What does it stand for?
2. Why does the speaker swear "By Christ" rather than *By God* (7)? Where else in the poem is Christ alluded to? What parallels and differences does the speaker see between himself and Christ?
3. "God damned it" (23) at first sounds like another curse, but the past tense makes its meaning more precise. What are the implications of lines 24–26? What implications are added in the phrase "by nature" (3)? What meanings has "prime" (15)?

4. What is the meaning of the last three lines? (Note: *I and Thou* is the title of a very influential book by the Jewish theologian Martin Buber. Briefly, it argues that, though suffering is inescapable, human life becomes meaningful as man forms "I–Thou" relationships, as opposed to "I–It" relationships— that is, as one becomes deeply involved with and committed to other human beings in relationships of love and concern.)

A HOLE IN THE FLOOR

The carpenter's made a hole
In the parlor floor, and I'm standing
Staring down into it now
At four o'clock in the evening,
As Schliemann stood when his shovel   5
Knocked on the crowns of Troy.

A clean-cut sawdust sparkles
On the grey, shaggy laths,
And here is a cluster of shavings
From the time when the floor was laid.   10
They are silvery-gold, the color
Of Hesperian apple-parings.

Kneeling, I look in under
Where the joists go into hiding.
A pure street, faintly littered   15
With bits and strokes of light,
Enters the long darkness
Where its parallels will meet.

The radiator-pipe
Rises in middle distance   20
Like a shuttered kiosk, standing
Where the only news is night.
Here it's not painted green
As it is in the visible world.

For God's sake, what am I after?   25
Some treasure, or tiny garden?
Or that untrodden place,
The house's very soul,
Where time has stored our footbeats
And the long skein of our voices?   30

Not these, but the buried strangeness
Which nourishes the known:
That spring from which the floor-lamp

Drinks now a wilder bloom,
Inflaming the damask love-seat   35
And the whole dangerous room.

Richard Wilbur (b. 1921)

QUESTIONS

1. Vocabulary: *laths* (8), *Hesperian* (12), *joists* (14), *kiosk* (21), *skein* (30).
2. Heinrich Schliemann (5), an archaeologist, discovered and excavated the ruins of ancient Troy. In Greek mythology a tree bearing golden apples, a wedding gift to Hera, was guarded by three nymphs called the Hesperides. What meanings are combined in the adjective "Hesperian" (12)? What do these two allusions add to the poem?
3. The first four stanzas are mainly descriptive, the fifth transitional. What associations prompt the questions in this stanza?
4. Of what does the house become a symbol in the sixth stanza? What does the region beneath the house symbolize? What do the words "nourishes," "spring," "wilder bloom," "inflaming," "love-seat," and "dangerous" suggest about its qualities? Comment on each.

SUN AND MOON

A strong man, a fair woman,
Bound fast in love,
Parted by ordered heaven,
Punishment prove.°   undergo

He suffers gnawing fires: 5
She in her frost
Beams in his sight, but dies
When he seems lost.

Not till the poles are joined
Shall the retreat   10
Of fierce brother from lost sister
End, and they meet.

Jay Macpherson (b. 1931)

QUESTIONS

1. In what ways are the personifications of sun and moon as man and woman, and brother and sister, appropriate?
2. In what senses have they been parted "by ordered heaven"? Explain their punishment.
3. When will they "meet" (12)?

FAME

See, as the prettiest graves will do in time,
Our poet's wants the freshness of its prime:
Spite of the sexton's browsing horse, the sods
Have struggled through its binding osier-rods;
Headstone and half-sunk footstone lean awry,
Wanting the brick-work promised by-and-by;
How the grey lichens, plate o'er plate,
Have softened down the crisp-cut name and date!

Robert Browning (1812–1889)

EXERCISE

In what respects are the following poems alike? In what respects are they essentially different?

DUST OF SNOW

The way a crow
Shook down on me
The dust of snow
From a hemlock tree

Has given my heart
A change of mood
And saved some part
Of a day I had rued.

Robert Frost (1874–1963)

SOFT SNOW

I walked abroad in a snowy day;
I asked the soft snow with me to play;
She played and she melted in all her prime,
And the winter called it a dreadful crime.

William Blake (1757–1827)

7. Figurative Language 3

PARADOX, OVERSTATEMENT, UNDERSTATEMENT, IRONY

Aesop tells the tale of a traveler who sought refuge with a Satyr on a bitter winter night. On entering the Satyr's lodging, he blew on his fingers, and was asked by the Satyr what he did it for. "To warm them up," he explained. Later, on being served with a piping hot bowl of porridge, he blew also on it, and again was asked what he did it for. "To cool it off," he explained. The Satyr thereupon thrust him out of doors, for he would have nothing to do with a man who could blow hot and cold with the same breath.

A PARADOX is an apparent contradiction that is nevertheless somehow true. It may be either a situation or a statement. Aesop's tale of the traveler illustrates a paradoxical situation. As a figure of speech, paradox is a statement. When Alexander Pope wrote that a literary critic of his time would "damn with faint praise," he was using a verbal paradox, for how can a man damn by praising?

When we understand all the conditions and circumstances involved in a paradox, we find that what at first seemed impossible is actually entirely plausible and not strange at all. The paradox of the cold hands and hot porridge is not strange to a man who knows that a stream of air directed upon an object of different temperature will tend to bring that object closer to its own temperature. And Pope's paradox is not strange when we realize that *damn* is being used figuratively, and that Pope means only that a too reserved praise may damage an author with the public almost as much as adverse criticism. In a paradoxical statement the contradiction usually stems from one of the words being used figuratively or in more than one sense.

The value of paradox is its shock value. Its seeming impossibility startles the reader into attention and, thus, by the fact of its apparent absurdity, it underscores the truth of what is being said.

MY LIFE CLOSED TWICE

My life closed twice before its close;
It yet remains to see
If Immortality unveil
A third event to me,

So huge, so hopeless to conceive,
As these that twice befell.
Parting is all we know of heaven,
And all we need of hell.

Emily Dickinson (1830–1886)

QUESTIONS

1. Do lines 2–6 mean: (a) I do not know yet whether there is a life after death—a continued existence in heaven and hell or (b) I do not know yet whether my entry into heaven or hell—whichever place I go—will be as "huge" an event as two events that have already happened to me during my life? Or both?
2. The poem sets forth two or possibly three paradoxes: (a) that the speaker's life closed twice before its close; (b) (if we accept the second alternative above) that death and entry into immortality may possibly be "lesser" events than two not extraordinary occurrences that happened during the speaker's lifetime; (c) that parting from a loved one is *both* heaven and hell. Resolve (that is, explain) each of these paradoxes.

Overstatement, understatement, and verbal irony form a continuous series, for they consist, respectively, of saying more, saying less, and saying the opposite of what one really means.

OVERSTATEMENT, or *hyperbole,* is simply exaggeration, but exaggeration in the service of truth. It is not the same as a fish story. If you say, "I'm starved!" or "You could have knocked me over with a feather!" or "I'll die if I don't pass this course!" you do not expect to be believed; you are merely adding emphasis to what you really mean. (And if you say, "There were literally millions of people at the dance!" you are merely piling one overstatement on top of another, for you really mean that

"There were figuratively millions of people at the dance," or, literally, "The dance hall was very crowded.") Like all figures of speech, overstatement may be used with a variety of effects. It may be humorous or grave, fanciful or restrained, convincing or unconvincing. When Tennyson says of his eagle (page 519) that it is "*Close* to the sun in lonely lands," he says what appears to be literally true, though we know from our study of astronomy that it is not. When Wordsworth reports of his daffodils in "I wandered lonely as a cloud" that they "stretched *in never-ending line*" along the margin of a bay, he too reports faithfully a visual appearance. When Frost says, at the conclusion of "The Road Not Taken" (page 589),

> I shall be telling this with a sigh
> Somewhere *ages and ages hence,*

we are scarcely aware of the overstatement, so quietly is the assertion made. Unskillfully used, however, overstatement may seem strained and ridiculous, leading us to react as Gertrude does to the player-queen's speeches in *Hamlet:* "The lady doth protest too much."

It is paradoxical that one can emphasize a truth either by overstating it or by understating it. UNDERSTATEMENT, or saying less than one means, may exist in what one says or merely in how one says it. If, for instance, upon sitting down to a loaded dinner plate, you say, "This looks like a good bite," you are actually stating less than the truth; but if you say, with Artemus Ward, that a man who holds his hand for half an hour in a lighted fire will experience "a sensation of excessive and disagreeable warmth," you are stating what is literally true but with a good deal less force than the situation might seem to warrant.

A RED, RED ROSE

> O my Luve's like a red, red rose,
>   That's newly sprung in June;
> O my Luve's like the melodie
>   That's sweetly play'd in tune.
>
> As fair art thou, my bonnie lass,   5
>   So deep in luve am I;
> And I will love thee still, my Dear,
>   Till a'° the seas gang° dry.   all; go
>
> Till a' the seas gang dry, my Dear,
>   And the rocks melt wi' the sun: 10
> I will love thee still, my Dear,
>   While the sands o' life shall run.

And fare thee weel, my only Luve!
And fare thee weel, a while!
And I will come again, my Luve,   15
Tho' it were ten thousand mile!

Attributed to *Robert Burns* (*1759-1796*)

THE ROSE FAMILY

The rose is a rose,
And was always a rose.
But the theory now goes
That the apple's a rose,
And the pear is, and so's   5
The plum, I suppose.
The dear only knows
What will next prove a rose.
You, of course, are a rose—
But were always a rose.   10

Robert Frost (*1874-1963*)

QUESTION

Burns and Frost use the same metaphor in paying tribute to their loved ones;
otherwise their methods are opposed. Burns begins with a couple of conventionally poetic similes and proceeds to a series of overstatements. Frost begins with
literal and scientific fact (the apple, pear, plum, and rose all belong to the same
botanical family, the Rosaceae), and then slips in his metaphor so casually and
quietly that the assertion has the effect of understatement. What is the function
of "of course" and "but" in the last two lines?

Like paradox, *irony* has meanings that extend beyond its use merely
as a figure of speech.

VERBAL IRONY, saying the opposite of what one means, is often confused with sarcasm and with satire, and for that reason it may be well to
look at the meanings of all three terms. SARCASM and SATIRE both imply
ridicule, one on the colloquial level, the other on the literary level. Sarcasm is simply bitter or cutting speech, intended to wound the feelings (it
comes from a Greek word meaning to tear flesh). Satire is a more formal
term, usually applied to written literature rather than to speech and ordinarily implying a higher motive: it is ridicule (either bitter or gentle) of
human folly or vice, with the purpose of bringing about reform or at least
of keeping other people from falling into similar folly or vice. Irony, on

the other hand, is a literary device or figure that may be used in the service of sarcasm or ridicule or may not. It is popularly confused with sarcasm and satire because it is so often used as their tool; but irony may be used without either sarcastic or satirical intent, and sarcasm and satire may exist (though they do not usually) without irony. If, for instance, one of the members of your class raises his hand on the discussion of this point and says, "I don't understand," and your instructor replies, with a tone of heavy disgust in his voice, "Well, I wouldn't expect *you* to," he is being sarcastic but not ironical; he means exactly what he says. But if, after you have done particularly well on an examination, your instructor brings your test papers into the classroom saying, "Here's some *bad* news for you: you all got A's and B's!" he is being ironical but not sarcastic. Sarcasm, we may say, is cruel, as a bully is cruel: it intends to give hurt. Satire is both cruel and kind, as a surgeon is cruel and kind: it gives hurt in the interest of the patient or of society. Irony is neither cruel nor kind: it is simply a device, like a surgeon's scalpel, for performing any operation more skillfully.

Though verbal irony always implies the opposite of what is said, it has many gradations, and only in its simplest forms does it mean *only* the opposite of what is said. In more complex forms it means both what is said and the opposite of what is said, at once, though in different ways and with different degrees of emphasis. When Terence's critic, in "Terence, this is stupid stuff" (page 528) says, "*Pretty* friendship 'tis to rhyme / Your friends to death before their time" (11–12), we may substitute the literal *sorry* for "pretty" with little or no loss of meaning. When Terence speaks in reply, however, of the pleasure of drunkenness—"And down in *lovely* muck I've lain, / Happy till I woke again" (35–36)—we cannot substitute *loathsome* for "lovely" without considerable loss of meaning, for, while muck is actually extremely unpleasant to lie in, it may *seem* lovely to an intoxicated person. Thus two meanings—one the opposite of the other—operate at once.

Like all figures of speech, verbal irony runs the danger of being misunderstood. With irony the risks are perhaps greater than with other figures, for if metaphor is misunderstood, the result may be simply bewilderment; but if irony is misunderstood, the reader goes away with exactly the opposite idea from what the user meant to convey. The results of misunderstanding if, for instance, you ironically called someone a villain, might be calamitous. For this reason the user of irony must be very skillful in its use, conveying by an altered tone or by a wink of the eye or pen, that he is speaking ironically; and the reader of literature must be always alert to recognize the subtle signs that irony is intended.

No matter how broad or obvious the irony, there will always be in any large audience, a number who will misunderstand. The humorist Artemus Ward used to protect himself against these people by writing at the bottom of his newspaper column, "This is writ ironical." But irony is most delightful and most effective when it is subtlest. It sets up a special understanding between writer and reader that may add either grace or force. If irony is too obvious, it sometimes seems merely crude. But if effectively used, it, like all figurative language, is capable of adding extra dimensions to meaning.

WHAT SOFT, CHERUBIC CREATURES

What soft, cherubic creatures
These gentlewomen are.
One would as soon assault a plush
Or violate a star.

Such dimity convictions,   5
A horror so refined
Of freckled human nature,
Of deity ashamed—

It's such a common glory,
A fisherman's degree.   10
Redemption, brittle lady,
Be so ashamed of thee.

Emily Dickinson (1830–1886)

QUESTIONS

1. In what sense (or senses) is the word "gentlewomen" used? What qualities are attributed to them in the first seven lines? What are "dimity convictions" (*dimity* was a thin, crisp cotton cloth fashionable for women's dresses)?
2. For whom is "Redemption" (11) a metonymy? What is the meaning of "common" (9) and of "degree" (10)? What "common glory" is referred to, and why is it a "fisherman's degree"? What is "freckled human nature" (7)? How are the gentlewomen "ashamed" of deity?
3. How is the judgment implied on the "gentlewomen" in the first half of the poem reversed in the second half? Which half is ironical?
4. Does Luke 9:26 help you with any of these questions?

The term *irony* always implies some sort of discrepancy or incongruity. In verbal irony the discrepancy is between what is said and what is meant. In other forms the discrepancy may be between appearance and reality or between expectation and fulfillment. These other forms of irony are, on the whole, more important resources for the poet than is verbal irony. Two types are especially important.

In DRAMATIC IRONY* the discrepancy is not between what the speaker says and what he means but between what the speaker says and what the author means. The speaker's words may be perfectly straightforward, but the author, by putting these words in a particular speaker's mouth, may be indicating to the reader ideas or attitudes quite opposed to those the speaker is voicing. This form of irony is more complex than verbal irony and demands a more complex response from the reader. It may be used not only to convey attitudes but also to illuminate character, for the author who uses it is indirectly commenting not only upon the value of the ideas uttered but also upon the nature of the person who utters them. Such comment may be harsh, gently mocking, or sympathetic.

THE CHIMNEY SWEEPER

When my mother died I was very young,
And my father sold me while yet my tongue
Could scarcely cry "'weep! 'weep! 'weep! 'weep!"
So your chimneys I sweep, and in soot I sleep.

There's little Tom Dacre, who cried when his head,   5
That curled like a lamb's back, was shaved; so I said,
"Hush, Tom! never mind it, for, when your head's bare,
You know that the soot cannot spoil your white hair."

And so he was quiet, and that very night,
As Tom was asleeping, he had such a sight!   10
That thousands of sweepers, Dick, Joe, Ned, and Jack,
Were all of them locked up in coffins of black.

And by came an Angel who had a bright key,
And he opened the coffins and set them all free;

---

*The term *dramatic irony*, which stems from Greek tragedy, often connotes something more specific and perhaps a little different from what I am developing here. It is used of a speech or an action in a story which has much greater significance to the audience than to the character who speaks or performs it, because of possession by the audience of knowledge the character does not have, as when the enemies of Ulysses, in the *Odyssey*, wish good luck and success to a man who the reader knows is Ulysses himself in disguise, or as when Oedipus, in the play by Sophocles, bends every effort to discover the murderer of Laius so that he may avenge the death, not knowing, as the audience does, that Laius is the man whom he himself once slew. I have appropriated the term for a perhaps slightly different situation, because no other suitable term exists. Both uses have the common characteristic—that the author conveys to the reader something different, or at least something more, than the character himself intends.

Then down a green plain leaping, laughing, they run,   15
And wash in a river, and shine in the sun.

Then naked and white, all their bags left behind,
They rise upon clouds and sport in the wind;
And the Angel told Tom, if he'd be a good boy,
He'd have God for his father, and never want joy.   20

And so Tom awoke, and we rose in the dark,
And got with our bags and our brushes to work.
Though the morning was cold, Tom was happy and warm;
So if all do their duty they need not fear harm.

William Blake (*1757–1827*)

QUESTIONS

1. In the eighteenth century small boys, sometimes no more than four or five years old, were employed to climb up the narrow chimney flues and clean them, collecting the soot in bags. Such boys, sometimes sold to the master sweepers by their parents, were miserably treated by their masters and often suffered disease and physical deformity. Characterize the boy who speaks in this poem. How do his and the poet's attitudes toward his lot in life differ? How, especially, are the meanings of the poet and the speaker different in lines 3, 7–8, and 24?
2. The dream in lines 11–20, besides being a happy dream, is capable of allegorical interpretations. Point out possible significances of the sweepers' being "locked up in coffins of black" and the Angel's releasing them with a bright key to play upon green plains.

A third type of irony is IRONY OF SITUATION. This occurs when there is a discrepancy between the actual circumstances and those that would seem appropriate or between what one anticipates and what actually comes to pass. If a man and his second wife, on the first night of their honeymoon, are accidentally seated at the theater next to the man's first wife, we should call the situation ironical. When, in O. Henry's famous short story "The Gift of the Magi" a poor young husband pawns his most prized possession, a gold watch, in order to buy his wife a set of combs for her hair for Christmas, and his wife sells her most prized possession, her long brown hair, in order to buy a fob for her husband's watch, we call the situation ironical. When King Midas, in the famous fable, is granted his fondest wish, that anything he touch turn to gold, and then finds that he cannot eat because even his food turns to gold, we call the situation ironical. When Coleridge's Ancient Mariner finds himself in the middle of the ocean with "Water, water, everywhere" but not a "drop to drink," we call the situation ironical. In each case the circumstances are not what would seem appropriate or what we would expect.

Dramatic irony and irony of situation are powerful devices for the poet, for, like symbol, they enable him to suggest meanings without stating them—to communicate a great deal more than he says. We have seen one effective use of irony of situation in "Richard Cory" (page 553). Another is in "Ozymandias," which follows.

Irony and paradox may be trivial or powerful devices, depending on their use. At their worst they may degenerate into mere mannerism and mental habit. At their best they may greatly extend the dimensions of meaning in a work of literature. Because irony and paradox are devices that demand an exercise of critical intelligence, they are particularly valuable as safeguards against sentimentality.

OZYMANDIAS

I met a traveler from an antique land
Who said: Two vast and trunkless legs of stone
Stand in the desert . . . Near them, on the sand,
Half sunk, a shattered visage lies, whose frown,
And wrinkled lip, and sneer of cold command,   5
Tell that its sculptor well those passions read
Which yet survive, stamped on these lifeless things,
The hand that mocked them, and the heart that fed;
And on the pedestal these words appear:
"My name is Ozymandias, king of kings;   10
Look on my works, ye Mighty, and despair!"
Nothing beside remains. Round the decay
Of that colossal wreck, boundless and bare
The lone and level sands stretch far away.

Percy Bysshe Shelley (1792–1822)

QUESTIONS

1. "Survive" (7) is a transitive verb with "hand" and "heart" as direct objects. Whose hand? Whose heart? What figure of speech is exemplified in "hand" and "heart"?
2. Characterize Ozymandias.
3. Ozymandias was an ancient Egyptian tyrant. This poem was first published in 1817. Of what is Ozymandias a *symbol?* What contemporary reference might the poem have had in Shelley's time?
4. What is the theme of the poem and how is it "stated"?

Identify each of the following quotations as literal or figurative. If figurative, identify the figure as paradox, overstatement, understatement, or irony and explain the use to which it is put (emotional emphasis, humor, satire, etc.).

1. Poetry is a language that tells us, through a more or less emotional reaction, something that cannot be said. *Edwin Arlington Robinson*

2. Have not the Indians been kindly and justly treated? Have not the temporal things, the vain baubles and filthy lucre of this world, which were too apt to engage their worldly and selfish thoughts, been benevolently taken from them? And have they not instead thereof, been taught to set their affections on things above? *Washington Irving*

3. A man who could make so vile a pun would not scruple to pick a pocket. *John Dennis*

4. Last week I saw a woman flayed, and you will hardly believe how much it altered her person for the worse. *Swift*

5. . . . Where ignorance is bliss,
'Tis folly to be wise. *Thomas Gray*

6. All night I made my bed to swim; with my tears I dissolved my couch. *Psalms 6:6*

7. Believe him, he has known the world too long,
And seen the death of much immortal song. *Pope*

8. Give me my Romeo: and, when he shall die,
Take him and cut him out in little stars,
And he will make the face of heaven so fine
That all the world will be in love with night,
And pay no worship to the garish sun. *Juliet, in Shakespeare*

9. Immortality will come to such as are fit for it; and he who would be a great soul in the future must be a great soul now. *Emerson*

10. Whoe'er their crimes for interest only quit,
Sin on in virtue, and good deeds *commit*. *Edward Young*

*   *   *

TO ALTHEA, FROM PRISON

When love with unconfinèd wings
Hovers within my gates,
And my divine Althea brings
To whisper at the grates;

When I lie tangled in her hair   5
    And fettered to her eye,
The birds that wanton in the air
    Know no such liberty.

When flowing cups run swiftly round
    With no allaying Thames,   10
Our careless heads with roses bound,
    Our hearts with loyal flames;
When thirsty grief in wine we steep,
    When healths and draughts go free,
Fishes that tipple in the deep   15
    Know no such liberty.

When, like committed linnets, I
    With shriller throat shall sing
The sweetness, mercy, majesty,
    And glories of my King;   20
When I shall voice aloud how good
    He is, how great should be,
Enlargèd winds that curl the flood
    Know no such liberty.

Stone walls do not a prison make,   25
    Nor iron bars a cage;
Minds innocent and quiet take
    That for an hermitage;
If I have freedom in my love
    And in my soul am free,   30
Angels alone, that soar above,
    Enjoy such liberty.

Richard Lovelace (1618–1658)

QUESTIONS

1. Vocabulary: *wanton* (7), *allaying* (10), *committed* (17), *enlargèd* (23).
2. Richard Lovelace was a Cavalier poet, a loyal follower of Charles I who because of his royalist sympathies was imprisoned by Parliament in the Gatehouse at Westminster in 1642, a few months before the outbreak of the English Civil War. What is the central paradox of the poem? To whom are healths being drunk in stanza 2 and songs or poems being "sung" in stanza 3?
3. Each of the first three stanzas names a different pleasure which the poet may enjoy even though in prison. What are they? Each stanza also develops and intensifies the central paradox by suggesting some further kind of "confinement" (besides physical) which is not inconsistent with "liberty." What? Each

of the four stanzas ends, in its last two lines, with a comparison. Show how each of these is especially appropriate to its stanza.
4. Explain the image in lines 1–2. What is the subject of "brings" (3)? "Thames" (10) is a metonymy; what does it mean?

BATTER MY HEART, THREE-PERSONED GOD

Batter my heart, three-personed God, for you
As yet but knock, breathe, shine, and seek to mend;
That I may rise and stand, o'erthrow me; and bend
Your force to break, blow, burn, and make me new.
I, like an usurped town, to another due,   5
Labor to admit you, but oh, to no end;
Reason, your viceroy in me, me should defend,
But is captived, and proves weak or untrue.
Yet dearly I love you and would be loved fain,°   gladly
But am betrothed unto your enemy;   10
Divorce me, untie or break that knot again,
Take me to you, imprison me, for I
Except° you enthrall me, never shall be free,   unless
Nor ever chaste, except you ravish me.

John Donne (1572–1631)

QUESTIONS

1. In this sonnet (No. 14 in a group called "Holy Sonnets") Donne addresses God in a series of metaphors and paradoxes. What is the paradox in the first quatrain? To what is the "three-personed God" metaphorically compared? To what is Donne compared? Can the first three verbs of the parallel lines 2 and 4 be taken as addressed to specific "persons" of the Trinity (Father, Son, Holy Spirit)? If so, to which are "knock" and "break" addressed? "breathe" and "blow"? "shine" and "burn"? (What concealed pun helps in the attribution of the last pair? What etymological pun in the attribution of the second?)
2. To what does Donne compare himself in the second quatrain? To what is God compared? Who is the usurper? What role does Reason play in this political metaphor, and why is it a weak one?
3. To what does Donne compare himself in the sestet (lines 9–14)? To what does he compare God? Who is the "enemy" (10)? Resolve the paradox in lines 12–13 by explaining the double meaning of "enthrall." Resolve the paradox in line 14 by explaining the double meaning of "ravish."
4. Sum up the meaning of the poem in a sentence.

LOVE POEM

My clumsiest dear, whose hands shipwreck vases,
At whose quick touch all glasses chip and ring,

Whose palms are bulls in china, burs in linen,
And have no cunning with any soft thing

Except all ill-at-ease fidgeting people: 5
The refugee uncertain at the door
You make at home; deftly you steady
The drunk clambering on his undulant floor.

Unpredictable dear, the taxi drivers' terror,
Shrinking from far headlights pale as a dime   10
Yet leaping before red apoplectic streetcars—
Misfit in any space. And never on time.

A wrench in clocks and the solar system. Only
With words and people and love you move at ease.
In traffic of wit expertly manoeuvre   15
And keep us, all devotion, at your knees.

Forgetting your coffee spreading on our flannel,
Your lipstick grinning on our coat,
So gayly in love's unbreakable heaven
Our souls on glory of spilt bourbon float.   20

Be with me, darling, early and late. Smash glasses—
I will study wry music for your sake.
For should your hands drop white and empty
All the toys of the world would break.

John Frederick Nims (b. 1914)

QUESTIONS

1. Overstatement is the traditional language of love poetry. Point out examples
   here. How does this poem differ from traditional love poems?
2. What is the meaning of the last two lines?

INCIDENT

Once riding in old Baltimore
    Heart-filled, head-filled with glee,
I saw a Baltimorean
    Keep looking straight at me.

Now I was eight and very small,   5
    And he was no whit bigger,
And so I smiled, but he poked out
    His tongue, and called me, "Nigger."

I saw the whole of Baltimore
    From May until December;   10
Of all the things that happened there
    That's all that I remember.

                Countee Cullen (1903–1946)

QUESTION

What accounts for the effectiveness of the last stanza? Comment on the title. Is
it in key with the meaning of the poem?

FORMAL APPLICATION

"The poets apparently want to rejoin the human race." TIME

I shall begin by learning to throw
the knife, first at trees, until it sticks
in the trunk and quivers every time;

next from a chair, using only wrist
and fingers, at a thing on the ground,   5
a fresh ant hill or a fallen leaf;

then at a moving object, perhaps
a pieplate swinging on twine, until
I pot it at least twice in three tries.

Meanwhile, I shall be teaching the birds   10
that the skinny fellow in sneakers
is a source of suet and bread crumbs,

first putting them on a shingle nailed
to a pine tree, next scattering them
on the needles, closer and closer   15

to my seat, until the proper bird,
a towhee, I think, in black and rust
and gray, takes tossed crumbs six feet away.

Finally, I shall coordinate
conditioned reflex and functional   20
form and qualify as Modern Man.

You see the splash of blood and feathers
and the blade pinning it to the tree?
It's called an "Audubon Crucifix."

The phrase has pleasing (even pious)   25
connotations, like *Arbeit Macht Frei,*
"Molotov Cocktail," and *Enola Gay.*

Donald W. Baker (b. 1923)

QUESTIONS

1. This poem has an epigraph: a quotation following the title which relates to
   the theme of the poem or provides the stimulus which gave rise to its writing.
   How is this poem related to its epigraph? Who is the speaker?
2. What meanings has the title?
3. *Arbeit Macht Frei* (26) ("Labor liberates") was the slogan of the German Nazi
   Party. "Molotov Cocktail" (27), a homemade hand grenade named after Sta-
   lin's foreign minister, was widely used during the Spanish Civil War and
   World War II. *Enola Gay* (27) was the American plane that dropped the first
   atom bomb on Hiroshima. In what ways are the connotations of these
   phrases—and of "Audubon Crucifix" (24)—"pleasing" (25)?
4. What different kinds of irony operate in this poem? Discuss.

THE UNKNOWN CITIZEN

(To JS/07/M/378 This Marble Monument Is Erected by the State)

He was found by the Bureau of Statistics to be
One against whom there was no official complaint,
And all the reports on his conduct agree
That, in the modern sense of an old-fashioned word, he was a saint,
For in everything he did he served the Greater Community.   5
Except for the War till the day he retired
He worked in a factory and never got fired,
But satisfied his employers, Fudge Motors Inc.
Yet he wasn't a scab or odd in his views,
For his Union reports that he paid his dues,   10
(Our report on his Union shows it was sound)
And our Social Psychology workers found
That he was popular with his mates and liked a drink.
The Press are convinced that he bought a paper every day
And that his reactions to advertisements were normal in every way.   15
Policies taken out in his name prove that he was fully insured,
And his Health-card shows he was once in hospital but left it cured.
Both Producers Research and High-Grade Living declare
He was fully sensible to the advantages of the Installment Plan
And had everything necessary to the Modern Man,   20
A phonograph, a radio, a car and a frigidaire.

Our researchers into Public Opinion are content
That he held the proper opinions for the time of year;
When there was peace, he was for peace; when there was war, he went.
He was married and added five children to the population,   25
Which our Eugenist says was the right number for a parent of
   his generation,
And our teachers report that he never interfered with their education.
Was he free? Was he happy? The question is absurd:
Had anything been wrong, we should certainly have heard.

W. H. Auden (*1907–1973*)

QUESTIONS

1. Vocabulary: *scab* (9), *Eugenist* (26).
2. Explain the allusion and the irony in the title. Why was the citizen "un-known"?
3. This obituary of an unknown state "hero" was apparently prepared by a functionary of the state. Give an account of the citizen's life and character from Auden's own point of view.
4. What trends in modern life and social organization does the poem satirize?

DEPARTMENTAL

An ant on the tablecloth
Ran into a dormant moth
Of many times his size.
He showed not the least surprise.
His business wasn't with such.   5
He gave it scarcely a touch,
And was off on his duty run.
Yet if he encountered one
Of the hive's enquiry squad
Whose work is to find out God   10
And the nature of time and space,
He would put him onto the case.
Ants are a curious race;
One crossing with hurried tread
The body of one of their dead   15
Isn't given a moment's arrest—
Seems not even impressed.
But he no doubt reports to any
With whom he crosses antennae,
And they no doubt report   20
To the higher up at court.

Then word goes forth in Formic:
"Death's come to Jerry McCormic,
Our selfless forager Jerry.
Will the special Janizary   25
Whose office it is to bury
The dead of the commissary
Go bring him home to his people.
Lay him in state on a sepal.
Wrap him for shroud in a petal.   30
Embalm him with ichor of nettle.
This is the word of your Queen."
And presently on the scene
Appears a solemn mortician;
And taking formal position   35
With feelers calmly atwiddle,
Seizes the dead by the middle,
And heaving him high in air,
Carries him out of there.
No one stands round to stare.   40
It is nobody else's affair.

It couldn't be called ungentle.
But how thoroughly departmental.

Robert Frost (1874–1963)

QUESTIONS

1. Vocabulary: *dormant* (2), *Formic* (22), *Janizary* (25), *commissary* (27), *sepal* (29), *ichor* (31).
2. The poem is ostensibly about ants. Is it ultimately about ants? Give reasons to support your view that it is or is not.
3. What is the author's attitude toward the "departmental" organization of ant society? How is it indicated? Could this poem be described as "gently satiric"? If so, in what sense?
4. Compare and contrast this poem with "The Unknown Citizen" in content and manner.

MR. Z

Taught early that his mother's skin was the sign of error,
He dressed and spoke the perfect part of honor;
Won scholarships, attended the best schools,
Disclaimed kinship with jazz and spirituals;
Chose prudent, raceless views for each situation,   5

Or when he could not cleanly skirt dissension,
Faced up to the dilemma, firmly seized
Whatever ground was Anglo-Saxonized.

In diet, too, his practice was exemplary:
Of pork in its profane forms he was wary;   10
Expert in vintage wines, sauces and salads,
His palate shrank from cornbread, yams and collards.

He was as careful whom he chose to kiss:
His bride had somewhere lost her Jewishness,
But kept her blue eyes; an Episcopalian   15
Prelate proclaimed them matched chameleon.
Choosing the right addresses, here, abroad,
They shunned those places where they might be barred;
Even less anxious to be asked to dine
Where hosts catered to kosher accent or exotic skin.   20

And so he climbed, unclogged by ethnic weights,
An airborne plant, flourishing without roots.
Not one false note was struck—until he died:
His subtly grieving widow could have flayed
The obit writers, ringing crude changes on a clumsy phrase: 25
"One of the most distinguished members of his race."

M. Carl Holman (b. 1919)

QUESTIONS

1. Vocabulary: *profane* (10), *kosher* (20), *exotic* (20), *ethnic* (21), *obit* (25).
2. Explain Mr. Z's motivation and the strategies he used to achieve his goal.
3. What is the author's attitude toward Mr. Z? Is he satirizing him or the society that produced him? Why does he not give Mr. Z a name?
4. What judgments on Mr. Z are implied by the metaphors in lines 16 and 22? Explain them.
5. What kind of irony is operating in the last line? As you reread the poem, where else do you detect ironic overtones?
6. What is Mr. Z's color?

MY LAST DUCHESS

FERRARA

That's my last duchess painted on the wall,
Looking as if she were alive. I call
That piece a wonder, now; Fra Pandolf's hands
Worked busily a day, and there she stands.

Will't please you sit and look at her? I said   5
"Fra Pandolf" by design, for never read
Strangers like you that pictured countenance,
The depth and passion of its earnest glance,
But to myself they turned (since none puts by
The curtain I have drawn for you, but I)   10
And seemed as they would ask me, if they durst,
How such a glance came there; so, not the first
Are you to turn and ask thus. Sir, 'twas not
Her husband's presence only, called that spot
Of joy into the Duchess' cheek; perhaps   15
Fra Pandolf chanced to say, "Her mantle laps
Over my lady's wrist too much," or, "Paint
Must never hope to reproduce the faint
Half-flush that dies along her throat." Such stuff
Was courtesy, she thought, and cause enough   20
For calling up that spot of joy. She had
A heart—how shall I say?—too soon made glad,
Too easily impressed; she liked whate'er
She looked on, and her looks went everywhere.
Sir, 'twas all one! My favor at her breast,   25
The dropping of the daylight in the West,
The bough of cherries some officious fool
Broke in the orchard for her, the white mule
She rode with round the terrace—all and each
Would draw from her alike the approving speech,   30
Or blush, at least. She thanked men—good! but thanked
Somehow—I know not how—as if she ranked
My gift of a nine-hundred-years-old name
With anybody's gift. Who'd stoop to blame
This sort of trifling? Even had you skill   35
In speech—which I have not—to make your will
Quite clear to such an one, and say, "Just this
Or that in you disgusts me; here you miss,
Or there exceed the mark"—and if she let
Herself be lessoned so, nor plainly set   40
Her wits to yours, forsooth, and made excuse—
E'en then would be some stooping; and I choose
Never to stoop. Oh, sir, she smiled, no doubt,
Whene'er I passed her; but who passed without
Much the same smile? This grew; I gave commands;   45
Then all smiles stopped together. There she stands
As if alive. Will 't please you rise? We'll meet
The company below, then. I repeat,
The Count your master's known munificence

Is ample warrant that no just pretense 50
Of mine for dowry will be disallowed;
Though his fair daughter's self, as I avowed
At starting, is my object. Nay, we'll go
Together down, sir. Notice Neptune, though,
Taming a sea-horse, thought a rarity, 55
Which Claus of Innsbruck cast in bronze for me!

Robert Browning (1812–1889)

QUESTIONS

1. Vocabulary: *officious* (27), *munificence* (49).
2. Ferrara is in Italy. The time is during the Renaissance, probably the sixteenth century. To whom is the Duke speaking? What is the occasion? Are the Duke's remarks about his last Duchess a digression, or do they have some relation to the business at hand?
3. Characterize the Duke as fully as you can. How does your characterization differ from the Duke's opinion of himself? What kind of irony is this?
4. Why was the Duke dissatisfied with his last Duchess? Was it sexual jealousy? What opinion do you get of the Duchess's personality, and how does it differ from the Duke's opinion?
5. What characteristics of the Italian Renaissance appear in the poem (marriage customs, social classes, art)? What is the Duke's attitude toward art? Is it insincere?
6. What happened to the Duchess? Should we have been told?

EARTH

"A planet doesn't explode of itself," said drily
The Martian astronomer, gazing off into the air—
"That they were able to do it is proof that highly
Intelligent beings must have been living there."

John Hall Wheelock (1886–1978)

8. Allusion

The famous English diplomat and letter writer Lord Chesterfield was once invited to a great dinner given by the Spanish ambassador. At the conclusion of the meal the host rose and proposed a toast to his master, the king of Spain, whom he compared to the sun. The French ambassador followed with a health to the king of France, whom he likened to the moon. It was then Lord Chesterfield's turn. "Your excellencies have taken from me," he said, "all the greatest luminaries of heaven, and the stars are too small for me to make a comparison of my royal master; I therefore beg leave to give your excellencies—Joshua!"*

For a reader familiar with the Bible—that is, for one who recognizes the Biblical allusion—Lord Chesterfield's story will come as a stunning revelation of his wit. For an ALLUSION—a reference to something in history or previous literature—is, like a richly connotative word or a symbol, a means of suggesting far more than it says. The one word "Joshua," in the context of Chesterfield's toast, calls up in the reader's mind the whole Biblical story of how the Israelite captain stopped the sun and the moon in order that the Israelites might finish a battle and conquer their enemies before nightfall.† The force of the toast lies in its extreme economy; it says so much in so little, and it exercises the mind of the reader to make the connection for himself.

---

*Samuel Shellabarger, *Lord Chesterfield and His World* (Boston: Little, Brown, 1951), p. 132.

† Joshua 10:12–14.

The effect of Chesterfield's allusion is chiefly humorous or witty, but allusions may also have a powerful emotional effect. The essayist William Hazlitt writes of addressing a fashionable audience about the lexicographer Samuel Johnson. Speaking of Johnson's great heart and of his charity to the unfortunate, Hazlitt recounted how, finding a drunken prostitute lying in Fleet Street late at night, Johnson carried her on his broad back to the address she managed to give him. The audience, unable to face the picture of the famous dictionary-maker doing such a thing, broke out in titters and expostulations. Whereupon Hazlitt simply said: "I remind you, ladies and gentlemen, of the parable of the Good Samaritan." The audience was promptly silenced.*

Allusions are a means of reinforcing the emotion or the ideas of one's own work with the emotion or ideas of another work or occasion. Because they are capable of saying so much in so little, they are extremely useful to the poet.

"OUT, OUT—"

The buzz-saw snarled and rattled in the yard
And made dust and dropped stove-length sticks of wood,
Sweet-scented stuff when the breeze drew across it.
And from there those that lifted eyes could count
Five mountain ranges one behind the other   5
Under the sunset far into Vermont.
And the saw snarled and rattled, snarled and rattled,
As it ran light, or had to bear a load.
And nothing happened: day was all but done.
Call it a day, I wish they might have said   10
To please the boy by giving him the half hour
That a boy counts so much when saved from work.
His sister stood beside them in her apron
To tell them "Supper." At the word, the saw,
As if to prove saws knew what supper meant,   15
Leaped out at the boy's hand, or seemed to leap—
He must have given the hand. However it was,
Neither refused the meeting. But the hand!
The boy's first outcry was a rueful laugh,
As he swung toward them holding up the hand   20
Half in appeal, but half as if to keep
The life from spilling. Then the boy saw all—

---

*Jacques Barzun, *Teacher in America* (Boston: Little, Brown, 1945), p. 160.

Since he was old enough to know, big boy
Doing a man's work, though a child at heart—
He saw all spoiled. "Don't let him cut my hand off—   25
The doctor, when he comes. Don't let him, sister!"
So. But the hand was gone already.
The doctor put him in the dark of ether.
He lay and puffed his lips out with his breath.
And then—the watcher at his pulse took fright.   30
No one believed. They listened at his heart.
Little—less—nothing!—and that ended it.
No more to build on there. And they, since they
Were not the one dead, turned to their affairs.

Robert Frost (1874–1963)

QUESTIONS

1. How does this poem differ from a newspaper account that might have dealt with the same incident?
2. To whom does "they" (33) refer? The boy's family? The doctor and hospital attendants? Casual onlookers? Need we assume that all these people—whoever they are—turned immediately "to their affairs"? Does the ending of this poem seem to you callous or merely realistic? Would a more tearful and sentimental ending have made the poem better or worse?
3. What figure of speech is used in lines 21–22?

Allusions vary widely in the burden put on them by the poet to convey his meaning. Lord Chesterfield risked his whole meaning on his hearers' recognizing his allusion. Robert Frost in "Out, Out—" makes his meaning entirely clear even for the reader who does not recognize the allusion contained in his title. His theme is the uncertainty and unpredictability of life, which may be accidentally ended at any moment, and the tragic waste of human potentiality which takes place when such premature deaths occur. A boy who is already "doing a man's work" and gives every promise of having a useful life ahead of him is suddenly wiped out. There seems no rational explanation for either the accident or the death. The only comment to be made is, "No more to build on there."

Frost's title, however, is an allusion to one of the most famous passages in all English literature, and it offers a good illustration of how a poet may use allusion not only to reinforce emotion but also to help define his theme. The passage is that in *Macbeth* in which Macbeth has just been informed of his wife's death. A good many readers will recall the key phrase, "Out, out, brief candle!" with its underscoring of the tragic brevity and uncertainty of life that can be snuffed out at any moment. For some readers, however, the allusion will summon up the whole passage in act V, scene 5, in which this phrase occurs. Macbeth's words are:

> She should have died hereafter;
> There would have been a time for such a word.
> To-morrow, and to-morrow, and to-morrow
> Creeps in this petty pace from day to day
> To the last syllable of recorded time; 5
> And all our yesterdays have lighted fools
> The way to dusty death. Out, out, brief candle!
> Life's but a walking shadow, a poor player,
> That struts and frets his hour upon the stage
> And then is heard no more. It is a tale 10
> Told by an idiot, full of sound and fury,
> Signifying nothing.

Macbeth's first words underscore the theme of premature death. The boy also "should have died hereafter." The rest of the passage, with its marvelous evocation of the vanity and meaninglessness of life, expresses neither Shakespeare's philosophy nor, ultimately, Frost's, but it is Macbeth's philosophy at the time of his bereavement, and it is likely to express the feelings of us all when such tragic accidents occur. Life does indeed seem cruel and meaningless, a tale told by an idiot, signifying nothing, when human life and potentiality are thus without explanation so suddenly ended.

Allusions vary widely in the number of readers to whom they will be familiar. The poet, in using an allusion as in using a figure of speech, is always in danger of not being understood. In appealing powerfully to one reader, he may lose another reader altogether. But the poet must assume a certain fund of common experience with his readers. He could not even write about the ocean unless he could assume that his readers had seen the ocean or pictures of it. In the same way he will assume a certain common fund of literary experience. He is often justified in expecting a rather wide range of literary experience in his readers, for the people who read poetry for pleasure are generally people of good minds and good education who have read widely. But, obviously, beginning readers will not have this range, just as they will not know the meanings of as many words as will maturer readers. Students ought therefore to be prepared to look up certain allusions, just as they should be eager to look up in their dictionaries the meanings of unfamiliar words. They will find that every increase in knowledge broadens their base for understanding both literature and life.

IN JUST-

                in Just-
                spring   when the world is mud-
                luscious the little
                lame balloonman

                whistles   far   and wee   5

                and eddieandbill come
                running from marbles and
                piracies and it's
                spring

                when the world is puddle-wonderful   10

                the queer
                old balloonman whistles
                far   and   wee
                and bettyandisbel come dancing

                from hop-scotch and jump-rope and   15

                it's
                spring
                and
                    the

                         goat-footed   20

                balloonMan   whistles
                far
                and
                wee

                                    e. e. cummings (1894–1962)

QUESTION

Why is the balloonman called "goat-footed"? How does the identification made
by this mythological allusion enrich the meaning of the poem?

ON HIS BLINDNESS

            When I consider how my light is spent
                Ere half my days in this dark world and wide,
                And that one talent which is death to hide
                Lodged with me useless, though my soul more bent

To serve therewith my Maker, and present   5
        My true account, lest he returning chide,
        "Doth God exact day-labor, light denied?"
    I fondly ask. But Patience, to prevent
That murmur, soon replies, "God doth not need
        Either man's work or his own gifts. Who best   10
        Bear his mild yoke, they serve him best. His state
    Is kingly: thousands at his bidding speed,
        And post o'er land and ocean without rest;
    They also serve who only stand and wait."

John Milton (1608-1674)

QUESTIONS

1. Vocabulary: *spent* (1), *fondly* (8), *prevent* (8), *post* (13).
2. What two meanings has "talent" (3)? What is Milton's "one talent"?
3. The poem is unified and expanded in its dimensions by a Biblical allusion that Milton's original readers would have recognized immediately. What is it? If you do not know, look up Matthew 25:14-30. In what ways is the situation in the poem similar to that in the parable? In what ways is it different?
4. What is the point of the poem?

GOD IS A DISTANT, STATELY LOVER

God is a distant, stately lover—
Woos, as he states us, by his son:
Verily, a vicarious courtship—
Miles and Priscilla were such an one,

But lest the soul, like fair Priscilla,
Choose the envoy and spurn the groom,
Vouches, with hyperbolic archness,
Miles and John Alden were synonym.

Emily Dickinson (1830-1886)

QUESTIONS

1. Vocabulary: *vicarious* (3), *hyperbolic* (7), *archness* (7).
2. In Longfellow's long narrative poem *The Courtship of Miles Standish*—once familiar to every American school child—the widower Miles Standish, Captain of the Plymouth Colony, determines to marry the virtuous Puritan maiden Priscilla. A blunt old soldier with no gift for words, he requests his literate young friend John Alden to make the proposal for him, not knowing John loves her too. Faithful to friendship, but torn by his own love, John makes the proposal and is answered by Priscilla, "Why don't you speak for

yourself, John?" Eventually the two young persons marry. How, in Dickinson's poem, is God like Miles Standish? Who is His "John Alden"? Who is the "Priscilla" whom He woos? How does He insure himself against the kind of defeat Miles Standish suffered?

3. What is Dickinson satirizing in this poem?

AUNT JANE

Aunt Jane, of whom I dreamed the nights it thundered,
was dead at ninety, buried at a hundred.
We kept her corpse a decade, hid upstairs,
where it ate porridge, slept and said its prayers.

And every night before I went to bed
they took me in to worship with the dead.
Christ Lord, if I should die before I wake,
I pray thee Lord my body take.

Alden Nowlan (b. 1933)

QUESTION

Resolve the paradox and explain the allusion.

ON THE IDLE HILL OF SUMMER

On the idle hill of summer,
    Sleepy with the flow of streams,
Far I hear the steady drummer
    Drumming like a noise in dreams.

Far and near and low and louder   5
    On the roads of earth go by,
Dear to friends and food for powder,
    Soldiers marching, all to die.

East and west on fields forgotten
    Bleach the bones of comrades slain,   10
Lovely lads and dead and rotten;
    None that go return again.

Far the calling bugles hollo,
    High the screaming fife replies,
Gay the files of scarlet follow: 15
    Woman bore me, I will rise.

A. E. Housman (1859–1936)

1. What effect does the sound of the drums, bugles, fifes, and marching soldiers have on the speaker? Is it a single or a mixed effect? Describe it as precisely as possible.
2. What syntactical qualities of the poem combine to put heavy emphasis on the two clauses in the last line? What relevance has the first to the second? (For help, see Job 14:1 and ff.) What does the speaker resolve to do in the last line? In what spirit?
3. "Scarlet" (14) refers to the bright red coats of British army dress uniforms. What figures of speech are involved in this and in "food for powder" (7)?

LEDA AND THE SWAN

A sudden blow: the great wings beating still
Above the staggering girl, her thighs caressed
By the dark webs, her nape caught in his bill,
He holds her helpless breast upon his breast.

How can those terrified vague fingers push   5
The feathered glory from her loosening thighs?
And how can body, laid in that white rush,
But feel the strange heart beating where it lies?

A shudder in the loins engenders there
The broken wall, the burning roof and tower   10
And Agamemnon dead.
                     Being so caught up,
So mastered by the brute blood of the air,
Did she put on his knowledge with his power
Before the indifferent beak could let her drop?

William Butler Yeats (*1865–1939*)

QUESTIONS

1. What is the connection between Leda and "the broken wall, the burning roof and tower / And Agamemnon dead"? If you do not know, look up the myth of Leda, and, if necessary, the story of Agamemnon.
2. What is the significance of the question asked in the last two lines?

VETERAN SIRENS

The ghost of Ninon would be sorry now
To laugh at them, were she to see them here,

So brave and so alert for learning how
To fence with reason for another year.

Age offers a far comelier diadem   5
Than theirs; but anguish has no eye for grace,
When time's malicious mercy cautions them
To think a while of number and of space.

The burning hope, the worn expectancy,
The martyred humor, and the maimed allure,   10
Cry out for time to end his levity,
And age to soften its investiture;

But they, though others fade and are still fair,
Defy their fairness and are unsubdued;
Although they suffer, they may not forswear   15
The patient ardor of the unpursued.

Poor flesh, to fight the calendar so long;
Poor vanity, so quaint and yet so brave;
Poor folly, so deceived and yet so strong,
So far from Ninon and so near the grave.   20

Edwin Arlington Robinson (1869–1935)

QUESTIONS

1. The poem is based on two allusions, one historical and one mythological. Ninon de Lenclos (1620–1705), mistress of a *salon* in Paris which attracted the most celebrated political and literary figures of her time, is famous for having retained her beauty and charm to an advanced age, and is said to have had lovers until she was seventy. If you do not recognize the allusion in the title, look up "siren" in your dictionary. In what respect is the title ironical?
2. Who are the "veteran sirens" in the poem? How old do you imagine them to be? What do they hope for? How do they "fence with reason" (4)? What is the "far comelier diadem / Than theirs" (5–6) offered them by age? What is the central irony of the poem?
3. Explain the metonymies involved in the words "anguish" (6), "number and space" (8), "flesh" (17), "calendar" (17), "vanity" (18), "folly" (19), "Ninon" (20), "grave" (20). Explain the effectiveness of the phrases "malicious mercy" (7), "worn expectancy" (9), "martyred humor" (10), "maimed allure" (10), "patient ardor of the unpursued" (16).
4. What is the poet's attitude toward the "veteran sirens"?

JOURNEY OF THE MAGI

"A cold coming we had of it,
Just the worst time of the year

For a journey, and such a long journey:
The ways deep and the weather sharp,
The very dead of winter."   5
And the camels galled, sore-footed, refractory,
Lying down in the melting snow.
There were times we regretted
The summer palaces on slopes, the terraces,
And the silken girls bringing sherbet.   10
Then the camel men cursing and grumbling
And running away, and wanting their liquor and women,
And the night-fires going out, and the lack of shelters,
And the cities hostile and the towns unfriendly
And the villages dirty and charging high prices: 15
A hard time we had of it.
At the end we preferred to travel all night,
Sleeping in snatches,
With the voices singing in our ears, saying
That this was all folly.   20

   Then at dawn we came down to a temperate valley,
Wet, below the snow line, smelling of vegetation;
With a running stream and a water-mill beating the darkness,
And three trees on the low sky,
And an old white horse galloped away in the meadow.   25
Then we came to a tavern with vine-leaves over the lintel,
Six hands at an open door dicing for pieces of silver,
And feet kicking the empty wine-skins.
But there was no information, and so we continued
And arrived at evening, not a moment too soon   30
Finding the place; it was (you may say) satisfactory.

   All this was a long time ago, I remember,
And I would do it again, but set down
This set down
This: were we led all that way for   35
Birth or Death? There was a Birth, certainly,
We had evidence and no doubt. I had seen birth and death,
But had thought they were different; this Birth was
Hard and bitter agony for us, like Death, our death.
We returned to our places, these Kingdoms,   40
But no longer at ease here, in the old dispensation,
With an alien people clutching their gods.
I should be glad of another death.

T. S. Eliot (1888–1965)

QUESTIONS

1. The Biblical account of the journey of the Magi, or wise men, to Bethlehem is given in Matthew 2:1–12 and has since been elaborated by numerous legendary accretions. It has been made familiar through countless pageants and Christmas cards. How does this account differ from the familiar one? Compare it with the Biblical account. What has been added? What has been left out? What is the poet doing? (Lines 1–5 are in quotation marks because they are taken, with very slight modification, from a Christmas sermon [1622] by the Anglican bishop Lancelot Andrewes.)
2. Who is the speaker? Where and when is he speaking? What is the "old dispensation" (41) to which he refers, and why are the people "alien" (42)? Why does he speak of the "Birth" as being "like Death" (39)? Of whose "Birth" and "Death" is he speaking? How does his life differ from the life he lived before his journey? What does he mean by saying that he would be "glad of another death" (43)?
3. This poem was written while the poet was undergoing religious conversion. (Eliot published it in 1927, the year he was confirmed in the Anglican Church.) Could the poem be considered a parable of the conversion experience? If so, how does this account differ from popular conceptions of this experience?
4. How do the images in the second section differ from those of the first? Do any of them suggest connections with the life of Christ?

IN THE GARDEN

> In the garden there strayed
> A beautiful maid
> As fair as the flowers of the morn;
> The first hour of her life
> She was made a man's wife,
> And was buried before she was born.

Anonymous

QUESTION

Resolve the paradox by identifying the allusion.

9. Meaning and Idea

Little Jack Horner
Sat in a corner
Eating a Christmas pie.
He stuck in his thumb
And pulled out a plum
And said, "What a good boy am I!"

Anonymous

The meaning of a poem is the experience it expresses—nothing less. But the reader who, baffled by a particular poem, asks perplexedly, "What does it *mean?*" is usually after something more specific than this. He wants something that he can grasp entirely with his mind. We may therefore find it useful to make a distinction between the TOTAL MEANING of a poem—the experience it communicates (and which can be communicated in no other way)—and its PROSE MEANING—the ingredient that can be separated out in the form of a prose paraphrase. If we make this distinction, however, we must be careful not to confuse the two kinds of meaning. The prose meaning is no more the poem than a plum is a pie or than a prune is a plum.

The prose meaning will not necessarily or perhaps even usually be an idea. It may be a story, it may be a description, it may be a statement of emotion, it may be a presentation of human character, or it may be some combination of these. "O what is that sound" (page 542) tells a story; "The Eagle" (page 519) is primarily descriptive; "A Red, Red Rose" (page 611) is an expression of emotion; "My Last Duchess" (page 626) is an account of human character. None of these poems is directly concerned with ideas. The message-hunter will be baffled and disappointed by poetry of this kind, for he will not find what he is looking for, and he may attempt to read some idea into the poem that is really not there. Yet ideas are also part of human experience, and therefore many poems are concerned, at least partially, with presenting ideas. But with these poems message-hunting is an even more dangerous activity. For the message-hunter is likely to think that the whole object of reading the poem is to find the message—that the idea is really the only important thing in it. Like Little Jack Horner, he will reach in and pluck it out and say, "What a good boy am I!" as if the pie existed for the plum.

The idea in a poem is only part of the total experience it communicates. The value and worth of the poem are determined by the value of the total experience, not by the truth or the nobility of the idea itself. This is not to say that the truth of the idea is unimportant, or that its validity should not be examined and appraised. But a good idea will not make a good poem, nor need an idea with which the reader does not agree ruin one. The good reader of poetry will be a reader receptive to all kinds of experience. He will be able to make that "willing suspension of disbelief" that Coleridge characterized as constituting poetic faith. When one attends a performance of *Hamlet,* one is willing to forget for the time being that such a person as Hamlet never existed and that the events on the stage are fictions. The reader of poetry should also be willing to enter imaginatively, for the time being, into ideas he objectively regards as untrue. It is one way of understanding these ideas better and of enlarging the reader's own experience. The believer in God should be able to enjoy a good poem expressing atheistic ideas, and the atheist a good poem in praise of God. The optimist by temperament should be able to find pleasure in pessimistic poetry, and the pessimist in optimistic poetry. The teetotaler should be able to enjoy "The Rubáiyát of Omar Khayyám," and the winebibber a good poem in praise of austerity. The primary value of a poem depends not so much on the truth of the idea presented as on the power with which it is communicated and on its being made a convincing part of a meaningful total experience. We must feel that the idea has been truly and deeply *felt* by the poet and that he is doing something more than merely moralizing. The plum must be made part of a pie. If the plum is properly combined with other ingredients and if the pie is well baked, it should be enjoyable even for persons who do not care for the brand of plums it is made of. Let us consider, for instance, the following two poems.

BARTER

Life has loveliness to sell,
All beautiful and splendid things,
Blue waves whitened on a cliff,
Soaring fire that sways and sings,

And children's faces looking up,   5
Holding wonder like a cup.

Life has loveliness to sell,
    Music like a curve of gold,
Scent of pine trees in the rain,
    Eyes that love you, arms that hold,   10
And for your spirit's still delight,
Holy thoughts that star the night.

Spend all you have for loveliness,
    Buy it and never count the cost;
For one white singing hour of peace   15
    Count many a year of strife well lost,
And for a breath of ecstasy
Give all you have been, or could be.

Sara Teasdale (*1884–1933*)

STOPPING BY WOODS ON A SNOWY EVENING

Whose woods these are I think I know.
His house is in the village though;
He will not see me stopping here
To watch his woods fill up with snow.

My little horse must think it queer   5
To stop without a farmhouse near
Between the woods and frozen lake
The darkest evening of the year.

He gives his harness bells a shake
To ask if there is some mistake.   10
The only other sound's the sweep
Of easy wind and downy flake.

The woods are lovely, dark and deep,
But I have promises to keep,
And miles to go before I sleep,   15
And miles to go before I sleep.

Robert Frost (*1874–1963*)

QUESTIONS

1. How do these two poems differ in idea?
2. What contrasts are suggested between the speaker in the second poem and
   (a) his horse and (b) the owner of the woods?

Both of these poems present ideas, the first more or less explicitly, the second symbolically. Perhaps the best way to get at the idea of the second poem is to ask two questions. First, why does the speaker stop? Second, why does he go on? He stops, we answer, to watch the woods fill up with snow—to observe a scene of natural beauty. He goes on, we answer, because he has "promises" to keep, that is, he has obligations to fulfill. He is momentarily torn between his love of beauty and these other various and complex claims that life has upon him. The small conflict in the poem is symbolical of a larger conflict in life. One part of the sensitive thinking person would like to give up his life to the enjoyment of beauty and art. But another part is aware of larger duties and responsibilities—responsibilities owed, at least in part, to other human beings. The speaker in the poem would like to satisfy both impulses. But when the two come into conflict, he seems to suggest, the "promises" must be given precedence.

The first poem also presents a philosophy but an opposed one. For this poet, beauty is of such supreme value that any conflicting demand should be sacrificed to it. "Spend all you have for loveliness, / Buy it and never count the cost . . . And for a breath of ecstasy / Give all you have been, or could be." The reader, if he is a thinking person, will have to choose between these two philosophies—to commit himself to one or the other—but this commitment should not destroy for him his enjoyment of either poem. If it does, he is reading for plums and not for pies.

Nothing so far said in this chapter should be construed as meaning that the truth or falsity of the idea in a poem is a matter of no importance. *Other things being equal,* the good reader naturally will, and properly should, value more highly the poem whose idea he feels to be maturer and nearer to the heart of human experience. There may be some ideas, moreover, that he feels to be so vicious or so foolish or so beyond the pale of normal human decency as to discredit *by themselves* the poems in which he finds them. A rotten plum may spoil a pie. But a good reader will strive for intellectual flexibility and tolerance, and be able to entertain sympathetically ideas other than his own. He will often like a poem whose idea he disagrees with better than one with an idea he accepts. And, above all, he will not confuse the prose meaning of any poem with its total meaning. He will not mistake plums for pies.

*   *   *

SONG

The year's at the spring,
And day's at the morn;
Morning's at seven;

The hillside's dew-pearled;
The lark's on the wing;
The snail's on the thorn;
God's in his heaven—
All's right with the world!

Robert Browning (1812-1889)

DIRGE

Rough wind, that moanest loud
    Grief too sad for song;
Wild wind, when sullen cloud
    Knells all the night long;
Sad storm, whose tears are vain,
Bare woods, whose branches strain,
Deep caves and dreary main,—
    Wail, for the world's wrong!

Percy Bysshe Shelley (1792-1822)

QUESTIONS

1. In what ways are these two poems alike? In what ways are they different?
2. How would you evaluate the two comments made on the world? Is it possible to justify both? Should you be surprised to learn that the first poet was a tremendous admirer of the second poet?

TO A WATERFOWL

Whither, midst falling dew,
While glow the heavens with the last steps of day,
Far, through their rosy depths, dost thou pursue
    Thy solitary way?

Vainly the fowler's eye   5
Might mark thy distant flight to do thee wrong,
As, darkly seen against the crimson sky,
    Thy figure floats along.

Seek'st thou the plashy brink
Of weedy lake, or marge of river wide,   10
Or where the rocking billows rise and sink
    On the chafed ocean side?

There is a Power whose care
Teaches thy way along that pathless coast—

The desert and illimitable air—   15
    Lone wandering, but not lost.

    All day thy wings have fanned,
At that far height, the cold, thin atmosphere,
Yet stoop not, weary, to the welcome land,
    Though the dark night is near.   20

    And soon that toil shall end;
Soon shalt thou find a summer home, and rest,
And scream among thy fellows; reeds shall bend,
    Soon, o'er thy sheltered nest.

    Thou'rt gone, the abyss of heaven   25
Hath swallowed up thy form; yet, on my heart
Deeply has sunk the lesson thou hast given,
    And shall not soon depart.

    He who, from zone to zone,
Guides through the boundless sky thy certain flight,   30
In the long way that I must tread alone,
    Will lead my steps aright.

William Cullen Bryant (1794-1878)

QUESTIONS

1. Vocabulary: *fowler* (5), *desert* (15), *stoop* (19).
2. What figure of speech unifies the poem?
3. Where is the waterfowl flying? Why? What is "that pathless coast" (14)?
4. What "Power" (13) "guides" (30) the waterfowl to its destination? How does it do so?
5. What lesson does the poet derive from his observations?

DESIGN

I found a dimpled spider, fat and white,
On a white heal-all, holding up a moth
Like a white piece of rigid satin cloth—
Assorted characters of death and blight
Mixed ready to begin the morning right,   5
Like the ingredients of a witches' broth—
A snow-drop spider, a flower like a froth,
And dead wings carried like a paper kite.

What had that flower to do with being white,
The wayside blue and innocent heal-all?   10

What brought the kindred spider to that height,
Then steered the white moth thither in the night?
What but design of darkness to appall?—
If design govern in a thing so small.

Robert Frost (1874–1963)

QUESTIONS

1. Vocabulary: *characters* (4).
2. The heal-all is a wildflower, usually blue or violet but occasionally white, found blooming along roadsides in the summer. It was once supposed to have healing qualities, hence its name. Of what significance, scientific and poetic, is the fact that the spider, the heal-all, and the moth are all white? Of what poetic significance is the fact that the spider is "dimpled" and "fat" and like a "snow-drop," and that the flower is "innocent" and named "heal-all"?
3. The "argument from design," as it was called, was a favorite eighteenth-century argument for the existence of God. What twist does Frost give the argument? What answer does he suggest to the question in lines 11–13? How comforting is the apparent concession in line 14?
4. Contrast Frost's poem in content and emotional effect with "To a Water-fowl." Is it possible to like both?

WHAT IF A MUCH OF A WHICH OF A WIND

what if a much of a which of a wind
gives the truth to summer's lie;
bloodies with dizzying leaves the sun
and yanks immortal stars awry?
Blow king to beggar and queen to seem   5
(blow friend to fiend:blow space to time)
—when skies are hanged and oceans drowned,
the single secret will still be man

what if a keen of a lean wind flays
screaming hills with sleet and snow: 10
strangles valleys by ropes of thing
and stifles forests in white ago?
Blow hope to terror;blow seeing to blind
(blow pity to envy and soul to mind)
—whose hearts are mountains,roots are trees,   15
it's they shall cry hello to the spring

what if a dawn of a doom of a dream
bites this universe in two,
peels forever out of his grave

and sprinkles nowhere with me and you?   20
Blow soon to never and never to twice
(blow life to isn't:blow death to was)
—all nothing's only our hugest home;
the most who die,the more we live

e. e. cummings (1894–1962)

QUESTIONS

1. What unconventional uses does cummings make of grammar and diction? Can you justify them?
2. All stanzas follow a common syntactical and structural pattern. Describe it.
3. What assertions does the poet make about man in each of the three stanzas?

WHEN SERPENTS BARGAIN FOR THE RIGHT TO SQUIRM

when serpents bargain for the right to squirm
and the sun strikes to gain a living wage—
when thorns regard their roses with alarm
and rainbows are insured against old age

when every thrush may sing no new moon in   5
if all screech-owls have not okayed his voice
—and any wave signs on the dotted line
or else an ocean is compelled to close

when the oak begs permission of the birch
to make an acorn—valleys accuse their   10
mountains of having altitude—and march
denounces april as a saboteur

then we'll believe in that incredible
unanimal mankind(and not until)

e. e. cummings (1894–1962)

QUESTIONS

1. What characteristics do the various activities not engaged in by nature have in common? What qualities of thought and feeling or kinds of behavior ought to replace these activities, in the poet's view?
2. What does the poet imply by calling man an "unanimal" (14)? What is the precise force here of "incredible" (13)?
3. How does the view of man implied in this poem differ from that implied in the preceding poem? Which of the two poems is *satirical* (see page 612)?

THE CAGED SKYLARK

As a dare-gale skylark scanted in a dull cage
    Man's mounting spirit in his bone-house, mean house, dwells—
    That bird beyond the remembering his free fells;
This in drudgery, day-laboring-out life's age.

Though aloft on turf or perch or poor low stage,   5
    Both sing sometimes the sweetest, sweetest spells,
    Yet both droop deadly sometimes in their cells
Or wring their barriers in bursts of fear or rage.

Not that the sweet-fowl, song-fowl, needs no rest—
    Why, hear him, hear him babble and drop down to his nest,   10
    But his own nest, wild nest, no prison.

Man's spirit will be flesh-bound when found at best,
But uncumbered: meadow-down is not distressed
    For a rainbow footing it nor he for his bones risen.

Gerard Manley Hopkins (*1844–1889*)

QUESTIONS

1. Vocabulary: *scanted* (1), *fells* (3). What meanings of "mean" (2) are appropriate here? "Turf" (5) is a piece of sod placed in a cage.
2. This poem, written by a poet-priest, expresses his belief in the orthodox Roman Catholic doctrine of the resurrection of the body. According to this belief, man's immortal soul, after death, will be ultimately reunited with his body; this body, however, will be a weightless, perfected, glorified body, not the gross imperfect body of mortal life. Express the analogy in the poem as a pair of mathematical statements of proportion (in the form $a:b=c:d$, and $e:f=g:h=i:j$), using the following terms: caged skylark, mortal body, meadow-down, cage, rainbow, spirit-in-life, nest, immortal spirit, wild skylark, resurrected body.
3. Discuss the image of the last two lines as a figure for weightlessness. Why would not a shadow have been equally apt as a rainbow for this comparison?

AUBADE

I work all day, and get half drunk at night.
Waking at four to soundless dark, I stare.
In time the curtain-edges will grow light.
Till then I see what's really always there:
Unresting death, a whole day nearer now,   5
Making all thought impossible but how
And where and when I shall myself die.
Arid interrogation: yet the dread

Of dying, and being dead,
Flashes afresh to hold and horrify.   10

The mind blanks at the glare. Not in remorse
—The good not done, the love not given, time
Torn off unused—nor wretchedly because
An only life can take so long to climb
Clear of its wrong beginnings, and may never;   15
But at the total emptiness for ever,
The sure extinction that we travel to
And shall be lost in always. Not to be here,
Not to be anywhere,
And soon; nothing more terrible, nothing more true.   20

This is a special way of being afraid
No trick dispels. Religion used to try,
That vast moth-eaten musical brocade
Created to pretend we never die,
And specious stuff that says *No rational being*   25
Can fear a thing it will not feel, not seeing
That this is what we fear—no sight, no sound,
No touch or taste or smell, nothing to think with,
Nothing to love or link with,
The anaesthetic from which none come round.   30

And so it stays just on the edge of vision,
A small unfocused blur, a standing chill
That slows each impulse down to indecision.
Most things may never happen: this one will,
And realization of it rages out   35
In furnace-fear when we are caught without
People or drink. Courage is no good:
It means not scaring others. Being brave
Lets no one off the grave.
Death is no different whined at than withstood.   40

Slowly light strengthens, and the room takes shape.
It stands plain as a wardrobe, what we know,
Have always known, know that we can't escape,
Yet can't accept. One side will have to go.
Meanwhile telephones crouch, getting ready to ring   45
In locked-up offices, and all the uncaring
Intricate rented world begins to rouse.
The sky is white as clay, with no sun.
Work has to be done.
Postmen like doctors go from house to house.   50

Philip Larkin (b. 1922)

1. Vocabulary: *remorse* (11), *specious* (25), *stuff* (25), *anaesthetic* (30).
2. The title of this poem, like that of Richard Wilbur's (page 563), is partially ironical, but the irony arises from a quite different source. What is the irony here?
3. How does the speaker characterize death? Why is 4 A.M. the time when he feels it most intensely?
4. Comment on Larkin's metaphor for religion (23). What are its implications?
5. What is the "specious stuff" characterized by the italicized sentence in lines 25-26?
6. The speaker dismisses courage as a useless remedy for his fear of death (37-40). Is he, then, an utter coward? Does he display *any* kind of courage?
7. Contrast this poem with "The Caged Skylark" in idea and tone. Discuss its merits as a poem.

ARS POETICA

A poem should be palpable and mute
As a globed fruit,

Dumb
As old medallions to the thumb,

Silent as the sleeve-worn stone   5
Of casement ledges where the moss has grown—

A poem should be wordless
As the flight of birds.

                              *

A poem should be motionless in time
As the moon climbs,   10

Leaving, as the moon releases
Twig by twig the night-entangled trees,

Leaving, as the moon behind the winter leaves,
Memory by memory the mind—

A poem should be motionless in time   15
As the moon climbs.

                              *

A poem should be equal to:
Not true.

For all the history of grief
An empty doorway and a maple leaf.   20

For love
The leaning grasses and two lights above the sea—

A poem should not mean
But be.

Archibald MacLeish (1892–1982)

QUESTIONS

1. How can a poem be "wordless" (7)? How can it be "motionless in time" (15)?
2. The Latin title, literally translatable as "The Art of Poetry," is a traditional title for works on the philosophy of poetry. What is *this* poet's philosophy of poetry? What does he mean by saying that a poem should not "mean" and should not be "true"?

10. Tone

Tone, in literature, may be defined as the writer's or speaker's attitude toward his subject, his audience, or himself. It is the emotional coloring, or the emotional meaning, of the work and is an extremely important part of the full meaning. In spoken language it is indicated by the inflections of the speaker's voice. If, for instance, a friend tells you, "I'm going to get married today," the facts of the statement are entirely clear. But the emotional meaning of the statement may vary widely according to the tone of voice with which it is uttered. The tone may be ecstatic ("Hooray! I'm going to get married today!"); it may be incredulous ("I can't believe it! I'm going to get married today"); it may be despairing ("Horrors! I'm going to get married today"); it may be resigned ("Might as well face it. I'm going to get married today"). Obviously, a correct interpretation of the tone will be an important part of understanding the full meaning. It may even have rather important consequences. If someone calls you a fool, your interpretation of the tone may determine whether you roll up your sleeves for a fight or walk off with your arm around his shoulder. If a woman says "No" to a proposal of marriage, the man's interpretation of her tone may determine whether he asks her again and wins her or starts going with someone else.

In poetry tone is likewise important. We have not really understood a poem unless we have accurately sensed whether the attitude it manifests is playful or solemn, mocking or reverent, calm or excited. But the correct determination of tone in literature is a much more delicate matter than it is with spoken language, for we do not have the speaker's voice to guide us. We must learn to recognize tone by other means. Almost all the elements of poetry go into indicating its tone: connotation, imagery, and metaphor; irony and understatement; rhythm, sentence construction, and formal pattern. There is therefore no simple formula for recognizing tone. It is an end product of all the elements in a poem. The best we can do is illustrate.

Robert Frost's "Stopping by Woods on a Snowy Evening" (page 642) seems a simple poem, but it has always afforded trouble to beginning readers. A very good student, asked to interpret it, once wrote this: "The poem means that we are forever passing up pleasures to go onward to what we wrongly consider our obligations. We would like to watch the snow fall on the peaceful countryside, but we always have to rush home to supper and other engagements. Frost feels that the average person considers life too short to stop and take time to appreciate true pleasures." This student did a good job in recognizing the central conflict of the poem. He went astray in recognizing its tone. Let's examine why.

In the first place, the fact that the speaker in the poem *does* stop to watch the snow fall in the woods immediately establishes him as a human being with more sensitivity and feeling for beauty than most. He is not one of the people of Wordsworth's sonnet (page 830) who, "getting and spending," have laid waste their powers and lost the capacity to be stirred by nature. Frost's speaker is contrasted with his horse, who, as a creature of habit and an animal without esthetic perception, cannot understand the speaker's reason for stopping. There is also a suggestion of contrast with the "owner" of the woods, who, if he saw the speaker stopping, might be as puzzled as the horse. (Who most truly "profits" from the woods—its absentee owner or the person who can enjoy its beauty?) The speaker goes on because he has "promises to keep." But the word "promises," though it may here have a wry ironic undertone of regret, has a favorable connotation: people almost universally agree that promises ought to be kept. If the poet had used a different term, say, "things to do," or "business to attend to," or "financial affairs to take care of," or "money to make," the connotations would have been quite different. As it is, the tone of the poem tells us that the poet is sympathetic to the speaker, is endorsing rather than censuring his action. Perhaps we may go even further. In the concluding two lines, because of their climactic position, because they are repeated, and because "sleep" in poetry is often used figuratively to refer to death, there is a suggestion of symbolic interpretation: "and many years to live before I die." If we accept this interpretation, it poses a parallel between giving oneself up to contemplation of the woods and dying. The poet's total implication would seem to be that beauty is a distinctively human value that deserves its place in a full life but that to devote one's life to its pursuit, at the expense of other obligations and duties, is tantamount to one's death as a responsible being. The poet therefore accepts the choice the speaker makes, though not without a touch of regret.

Differences in tone, and their importance, can perhaps be studied best in poems with similar content. Consider, for instance, the following pair.

THE VILLAIN

While joy gave clouds the light of stars,
    That beamed where'er they looked;
And calves and lambs had tottering knees,
    Excited, while they sucked;
While every bird enjoyed his song,   5
Without one thought of harm or wrong—
I turned my head and saw the wind,
    Not far from where I stood,
Dragging the corn by her golden hair,
    Into a dark and lonely wood.   10

W. H. Davies (1871–1940)

QUESTIONS

1. Vocabulary: *corn* (9).
2. From what realm of experience is the image in the title and the last two lines taken? What implications does your answer have for the way this image should be taken—that is, for its relation to reality?

APPARENTLY WITH NO SURPRISE

Apparently with no surprise
To any happy flower,
The frost beheads it at its play
In accidental power.

The blond assassin passes on,
The sun proceeds unmoved
To measure off another day
For an approving God.

Emily Dickinson (1830–1886)

QUESTIONS

1. What is the "blond assassin"?
2. What ironies are involved in this poem?

Both of these poems are concerned with nature; both use contrast as their basic organizing principle—a contrast between innocence and evil, joy and tragedy. But in tone the two poems are sharply different. The first is light and fanciful; its tone is one of delight or delighted surprise. The second, though superficially fanciful, is basically grim, almost savage; its tone is one of horror. Let's examine the difference.

In "The Villain" the images of the first six lines all suggest joy and innocence. The last four introduce the sinister. The poet, on turning his head, sees a villain dragging a beautiful maiden toward a dark wood to commit there some unmentionable deed, or so his metaphor tells us. But our response is one not of horror but of delight, for we realize that the poet does not mean us to take his metaphor seriously. He has actually seen only the wind blowing through the wheat and bending its golden tops gracefully toward a shady wood. The beauty of the scene has delighted him, and he has been further delighted by the fanciful metaphor which he has found to express it. The reader shares his delight both in the scene and in the metaphor.

The second poem makes the same contrast of joyful innocence (the "happy flower . . . at its play") with the sinister ("the blond assassin"). The chief difference would seem to be that the villain is this time the frost rather than the wind. But this time the poet, though her metaphor is no less fanciful, is earnest in what she is saying. For the frost actually *does* kill the flower. What makes the horror of the killing even worse is that nothing else in nature is disturbed over it or seems even to notice it. The sun "proceeds unmoved / To measure off another day." Nothing in nature stops or pauses. The flower itself is not surprised. And even God— the God who we have all been told is benevolent and concerned over the least sparrow's fall—seems to approve of what has happened, for He shows no displeasure, and it was He who created the frost as well as the flower. Further irony lies in the fact that the "assassin" (the word's connotations are of terror and violence) is not dark but "blond," or white (the connotations here are of innocence and beauty). The destructive agent, in other words, is among the most exquisite creations of God's handiwork. The poet, then, is shocked at what has happened, and is even more shocked that nothing else in nature is shocked. What has happened seems inconsistent with a rule of benevolence in the universe. In her ironic reference to an "approving God," therefore, the poet is raising a dreadful question: are the forces that created and govern the universe actually benevolent? And if we think that the poet is unduly disturbed over the death of a flower, we may consider that what is true for the flower is true throughout nature. Death—even early or accidental death, in terrible juxtaposition with beauty—is its constant condition; the fate that befalls the flower befalls us all.

These two poems, then, though superficially similar, are basically as different as night and day. And the difference is primarily one of tone.

Accurate determination of tone, therefore, is extremely important, whether in the reading of poetry or the interpretation of a woman's "No." For the experienced reader it will be instinctive and automatic. For the beginning reader it will require study. But beyond the general suggestions for reading that already have been made, no specific instructions can be given. Recognition of tone requires an increasing familiarity with the meanings and connotations of words, alertness to the presence of irony and other figures, and, above all, careful reading. Poetry cannot be read as one would skim a newspaper or a mystery novel looking merely for facts.

EXERCISES

1. Marvell's "To His Coy Mistress" (page 584), Housman's "Loveliest of trees" (page 587), and Herrick's "To the Virgins, to Make Much of Time" (page 596) all treat a traditional poetic theme known as the *carpe diem* ("seize the day") theme. They differ, however, in tone. Characterize in tone of each, and point out the differences in poetic management that account for the difference in tone.

2. Describe and account for the differences in tone between the poems in each of the following pairs:
   a. "A bird came down the walk" (page 525) and "A narrow fellow in the grass" (page 565).
   b. "The Lamb" and "The Tiger" (pages 777–78).
   c. "Spring" (Shakespeare, page 524) and "Spring" (Hopkins, page 568).
   d. "God is a distant, stately lover" (page 634) and "Batter my heart, three-personed God" (page 620).
   e. "Elegy for Alfred Hubbard" (page 659) and "The Mill" (Wilbur, page 828).
   f. "Bredon Hill" and "To an Athlete Dying Young" (pages 797–98).
   g. "When my love swears that she is made of truth" (page 548) and "The Silken Tent" (page 580).
   h. "Virtue" (page 682) and "Mr. Edwards and the Spider" (page 804).
   i. "Song" (Praed, page 677) and "Sestina: Altaforte" (page 810).
   j. "Design" (page 645) and "Some keep the Sabbath going to church" (page 747).
   k. "Pike" (page 799) and "The Truro Bear" (page 809).
   l. "I taste a liquor never brewed" (page 786) and "All day I hear" (page 715).
   m. "Landcrab" (page 773) and "Lion" (page 821).

*   *   *

THE COMING OF WISDOM WITH TIME

> Though leaves are many, the root is one;
> Through all the lying days of my youth
> I swayed my leaves and flowers in the sun;
> Now I may wither into the truth.

William Butler Yeats (1865–1939)

QUESTION

Is the poet exulting over a gain or lamenting over a loss?

SINCE THERE'S NO HELP

> Since there's no help, come let us kiss and part;
> Nay, I have done, you get no more of me,
> And I am glad, yea, glad with all my heart
> That thus so cleanly I myself can free;
> Shake hands forever, cancel all our vows,   5
> And when we meet at any time again,
> Be it not seen in either of our brows
> That we one jot of former love retain.
> Now at the last gasp of Love's latest breath,
> When, his pulse failing, Passion speechless lies,   10
> When Faith is kneeling by his bed of death,
> And Innocence is closing up his eyes,
> Now, if thou wouldst, when all have given him over,
> From death to life thou mightst him yet recover.

Michael Drayton (1563–1631)

QUESTIONS

1. What difference in tone do you find between the first eight lines and the last six? In which is the speaker more sincere? What differences in rhythm and language help to establish the difference in tone?

2. How many figures are there in the allegorical scene in lines 9–12? What do the pronouns "his" and "him" in lines 10–14 refer to? What is dying? Why? How might the person addressed still restore it from death to life?
3. Define the dramatic situation as precisely as possible, taking into consideration both the man's attitude and the woman's.

FAREWELL TO BARN AND STACK AND TREE

"Farewell to barn and stack and tree,
    Farewell to Severn shore.
Terence, look your last at me,
    For I come home no more.

"The sun burns on the half-mown hill,   5
    By now the blood is dried;
And Maurice amongst the hay lies still
    And my knife is in his side.

"My mother thinks us long away;
    'Tis time the field were mown.   10
She had two sons at rising day,
    To-night she'll be alone.

"And here's a bloody hand to shake,
    And oh, man, here's good-bye;
We'll sweat no more on scythe and rake,   15
    My bloody hands and I.

"I wish you strength to bring you pride,
    And a love to keep you clean,
And I wish you luck, come Lammastide,
    At racing on the green.   20

"Long for me the rick will wait,
    And long will wait the fold,
And long will stand the empty plate,
    And dinner will be cold."

A. E. Housman (1859–1936)

QUESTIONS

1. Vocabulary: *stack* (1), *rick* (21), *fold* (22). The *Severn* (2) is the principal river in the county of Shropshire in the west of England. *Lammastide* (19) was an annual harvest festival held on August 1.
2. Who is speaking to whom? What is the situation?
3. What kind of things does the speaker wish his friend in stanza 5?

4. Explain the effectiveness of the last stanza. What figure of speech does it use throughout?
5. What is the attitude of the poet toward the speaker? How is it conveyed?
6. Though there is no explicit allusion, the poem should remind most readers of a famous Biblical story. How does this association deepen the effect of the poem?

ELEGY FOR ALFRED HUBBARD

Hubbard is dead, the old plumber;
who will mend our burst pipes now,
the tap that has dripped all the summer,
testing the sink's overflow?

No other like him. Young men with knowledge   5
of new techniques, theories from books,
may better his work straight from college,
but who will challenge his squint-eyed looks

in kitchen, bathroom, under floorboards,
rules of thumb which were often wrong;   10
seek as erringly stopcocks in cupboards,
or make a job last half as long?

He was a man who knew the ginnels,
alleyways, streets—the whole district,
family secrets, minor annals,   15
time-honored fictions fused to fact.

Seventy years of gossip muttered
under his cap, his tufty thatch,
so that his talk was slow and clotted,
hard to follow, and too much.   20

As though nothing fell, none vanished,
and time were the maze of Cheetham Hill,
in which the dead—with jobs unfinished—
waited to hear him ring the bell.

For much he never got round to doing,   25
but meant to, when weather bucked up,
or worsened, or when his pipe was drawing,
or when he'd finished this cup.

I thought time, he forgot so often,
had forgotten him but here's Death's pomp   30
over his house, and by the coffin
the son who will inherit his blowlamp,

tools, workshop, cart, and cornet
(pride of Cheetham Prize Brass Band),
and there's his mourning widow, Janet,   35
stood at the gate he'd promised to mend.

Soon he will make his final journey;
shaved and silent, strangely trim,
with never a pause to talk to any-
body: how arrow-like, for him!   40

In St. Mark's church, whose dismal tower
he pointed and painted when a lad,
they will sing his praises amidst flowers
while, somewhere, a cellar starts to flood,

and the housewife banging his front-door knocker   45
is not surprised to find him gone,
and runs for Thwaite, who's a better worker,
and sticks at a job until it's done.

Tony Connor (b. 1930)

QUESTIONS

1. Vocabulary: *annals* (15), *pomp* (30). "Ginnels" (13) are tunnels that punctuate
   rows of houses, giving access to the "backs." "Pointed" (42) means refinishing
   the mortar between bricks.
2. Characterize Hubbard. How does this "elegy" (see Glossary) differ from the
   eulogy that will be said for him in St. Mark's church (41–43)? Compose his
   eulogy.
3. What is the poet's attitude toward his subject?

THE TELEPHONE

"When I was just as far as I could walk
From here today,
There was an hour
All still
When leaning with my head against a flower   5
I heard you talk.
Don't say I didn't, for I heard you say—
You spoke from that flower on the window sill—
Do you remember what it was you said?"

"First tell me what it was you thought you heard."   10

"Having found the flower and driven a bee away,
I leaned my head,

And holding by the stalk,
I listened and I thought I caught the word—
What was it? Did you call me by my name?   15
Or did you say—
Someone said 'Come'—I heard it as I bowed."

"I may have thought as much, but not aloud."

"Well, so I came."

Robert Frost (1874–1963)

QUESTIONS

1. When and where does the above dialogue take place? What is the relationship between the two speakers?
2. How does the title relate to the poem?
3. Characterize the first speaker. Why does he interrupt his narrative to say, "Don't say I didn't" (7)? Why does he not tell her what he heard her say (7–9, 14–16)? Why does he shift to what *"Someone"* said (17)?
4. Characterize the second speaker.
5. What is the poem about? What is its tone?

LOVE IN BROOKLYN

"I love you, Horowitz," he said, and blew his nose.
She splashed her drink. "The hell you say," she said.
Then, thinking hard, she lit a cigarette:
"Not *love*. You don't *love* me. You like my legs,
and how I make your letters nice and all.   5
You drunk your drink too fast. You don't love *me*."

"You wanna bet?" he asked. "You wanna bet?
I loved you from the day they moved you up
from Payroll, last July. I watched you, right?
You sat there on that typing chair you have   10
and swung round like a kid. It made me shake.
Like once, in World War II, I saw a tank
slide through some trees at dawn like it was god.
That's how you make me feel. I don't know why."

She turned towards him, then sat back and grinned,   15
and on the bar stool swung full circle round.
"You think I'm like a tank, you mean?" she asked.
"Some fellers tell me nicer things than that."
But then she saw his face and touched his arm
and softly said "I'm only kidding you."   20

He ordered drinks, the same again, and paid.
A fat man, wordless, staring at the floor.
She took his hand in hers and pressed it hard.
And his plump fingers trembled in her lap.

John Wakeman (b. 1928)

QUESTIONS

1. When and where does the above dialogue take place? What is the relationship between the two speakers?
2. Characterize the first speaker. How does he feel toward the other?
3. Characterize the second speaker. How does she feel toward him? Do her feelings change? If so, how?
4. Contrast this poem in tone with "The Telephone."

ONE DIGNITY DELAYS FOR ALL

One dignity delays for all,
One mitred afternoon.
None can avoid this purple,
None avoid this crown.

Coach it insures, and footmen,   5
Chamber and state and throng;
Bells, also, in the village,
As we ride grand along.

What dignified attendants,
What service when we pause!   10
How loyally at parting
Their hundred hats they raise!

How pomp surpassing ermine
When simple you and I
Present our meek escutcheon   15
And claim the rank to die!

Emily Dickinson (1830–1886)

QUESTIONS

1. Vocabulary: *mitred* (2), *state* (6), *escutcheon* (15).
2. What is the "dignity" that delays for all? What is its nature? What is being described in stanzas 2 and 3?

3. What figures of speech are combined in "our meek escutcheon" (15)? What metaphorically does it represent?

'TWAS WARM AT FIRST LIKE US

'Twas warm at first like us,
Until there crept upon
A chill, like frost upon a glass,
Till all the scene be gone.

The forehead copied stone,   5
The fingers grew too cold
To ache, and like a skater's brook
The busy eyes congealed.

It straightened—that was all,
It crowded cold to cold,   10
It multiplied indifference
As Pride were all it could.

And even when with cords
'Twas lowered like a weight,
It made no signal, nor demurred,   15
But dropped like adamant.

Emily Dickinson (1830–1886)

QUESTIONS

1. Vocabulary: *adamant* (16).
2. What is "It" in the opening line? What is being described in the poem, and between what points in time?
3. How would you describe the tone of this poem? How does it contrast with that of the preceding?

CROSSING THE BAR

Sunset and evening star,
    And one clear call for me!
And may there be no moaning of the bar
    When I put out to sea,

But such a tide as moving seems asleep,   5
    Too full for sound and foam,
When that which drew from out the boundless deep
    Turns again home.

Twilight and evening bell,
    And after that the dark!   10
And may there be no sadness of farewell
    When I embark;

For though from out our bourne of Time and Place
    The flood may bear me far,
I hope to see my Pilot face to face   15
    When I have crossed the bar.

Alfred, Lord Tennyson (1809–1892)

QUESTIONS

1. Vocabulary: *bourne* (13).
2. What two sets of figures does Tennyson use for approaching death? What is the precise moment of death in each set?
3. In troubled weather the wind and waves above the sandbar across a harbor's mouth make a moaning sound. What metaphorical meaning has the "moaning of the bar" here (3)? For what kind of death is the poet wishing? Why does he want "no sadness of farewell" (11)?
4. What is "that which drew from out the boundless deep" (7)? What is "the boundless deep"? To what is it opposed in the poem? Why is "Pilot" (15) capitalized?

THE OXEN

Christmas Eve, and twelve of the clock.
    "Now they are all on their knees,"
An elder said as we sat in a flock
    By the embers in hearthside ease.

We pictured the meek mild creatures where   5
    They dwelt in their strawy pen,
Nor did it occur to one of us there
    To doubt they were kneeling then.

So fair a fancy few would weave
    In these years! Yet, I feel,   10
If someone said on Christmas Eve,
    "Come; see the oxen kneel

"In the lonely barton° by yonder coomb°   farm; valley
    Our childhood used to know,"
I should go with him in the gloom,   15
    Hoping it might be so.

Thomas Hardy (1840–1928)

QUESTIONS

1. Is the simple superstition referred to in the poem here opposed to, or identified with, religious faith? With what implications for the meaning of the poem?
2. What are "these years" (10) and how do they contrast with the years of the poet's boyhood? What event in intellectual history between 1840 and 1915 (the date of composition of this poem) was most responsible for the change?
3. Both "Crossing the Bar" and "The Oxen" in their last lines use a form of the verb *hope*. By full discussion of tone, establish the precise meaning of hope in each poem. What degree of expectation does it imply? How should the word be handled in reading Tennyson's poem aloud?

LOVE

There's the wonderful love of a beautiful maid,
    And the love of a staunch true man,
And the love of a baby that's unafraid—
    All have existed since time began.
But the most wonderful love, the Love of all loves,
    Even greater than the love for Mother,
Is the infinite, tenderest, passionate love
    Of one dead drunk for another.

Anonymous

QUESTION

The radical shift in tone makes "Love" come off. If such a shift were unintentional in a poem, what would our view be?

ENGRAVED ON THE COLLAR OF A DOG WHICH I GAVE TO HIS ROYAL HIGHNESS

I am his Highness' dog at Kew;
Pray tell me, sir, whose dog are you?

Alexander Pope (1688–1744)

11. Musical Devices

I t is obvious that poetry makes a greater use of the "music" of language than does language that is not poetry. The poet, unlike the person who uses language to convey only information, chooses words for sound as well as for meaning, and uses the sound as a means of reinforcing meaning. So prominent is this musical quality of poetry that some writers have made it the distinguishing term in their definitions of poetry. Edgar Allan Poe, for instance, describes poetry as "music . . . combined with a pleasurable idea." Whether or not it deserves this much importance, verbal music, like connotation, imagery, and figurative language, is one of the important resources that enable the poet to do something more than communicate mere information. The poet may indeed sometimes pursue verbal music for its own sake; more often, at least in first-rate poetry, it is an adjunct to the total meaning or communication of the poem.

There are two broad ways by which the poet achieves musical quality: by the choice and arrangement of sounds and by the arrangement of accents. In this chapter we will consider one aspect of the first of these.

An essential element in all music is repetition. In fact, we might say that all art consists of giving structure to two elements: repetition and variation. All things we enjoy greatly and lastingly have these two elements. We enjoy the sea endlessly because it is always the same yet always different. We enjoy a baseball game because it contains the same complex combination of pattern and variation. Our love of art, then, is rooted in human psychology. We like the familiar, we like variety, but we like them combined. If we get too much sameness, the result is monotony and tedium; if we get too much variety, the result is bewilderment and confusion. The composer of music, therefore, repeats certain musical tones; repeats them in certain combinations, or chords; and repeats them in certain patterns, or melodies. The poet likewise repeats certain sounds in certain combinations and arrangements, and thus gives organization and structure to his verse. Consider the following short example.

THE TURTLE

> The turtle lives 'twixt plated decks
> Which practically conceal its sex.
> I think it clever of the turtle
> In such a fix to be so fertile.

Ogden Nash (1902-1971)

Here is a little joke, a paradox of animal life to which the author has cleverly drawn our attention. An experiment will show us, however, that much of its appeal lies not so much in what it says as in the manner in which it says it. If, for instance, we recast the verse as prose: "The turtle lives in a shell which almost conceals its sex. It is ingenious of the turtle, in such a situation, to be so prolific," the joke falls flat. Some of its appeal must lie in its metrical form. So now we cast it in unrimed verse:

> Because he lives between two decks,
> It's hard to tell a turtle's gender.
> The turtle is a clever beast
> In such a plight to be so fertile.

Here, perhaps, is *some* improvement, but still the piquancy of the original is missing. Much of that appeal must have consisted in the use of rime— the repetition of sound in "decks" and "sex," "turtle" and "fertile." So we try once more:

> The turtle lives 'twixt plated decks
> Which practically conceal its sex.
> I think it clever of the turtle
> In such a plight to be so fertile.

But for perceptive readers there is still something missing—they may not at first see what—but some little touch that makes the difference between a good piece of verse and a little masterpiece in its kind. And then they see it: "plight" has been substituted for "fix."

But why should "fix" make such a difference? Its meaning is little different from that of "plight"; its only important difference is in sound. But there we are. The final *x* in "fix" catches up the concluding consonant sound in "sex," and its initial *f* is repeated in the initial consonant sound of "fertile." Not only do these sound recurrences provide a subtle gratification to the ear, but they also give the verse structure; they emphasize and draw together the key words of the piece: "sex," "fix," and "fertile."

The poet may repeat any unit of sound from the smallest to the largest. He may repeat individual vowel and consonant sounds, whole syllables, words, phrases, lines, or groups of lines. In each instance, in a good poem, the repetition will serve several purposes: it will please the ear, it will emphasize the words in which the repetition occurs, and it will give structure to the poem. The popularity and initial impressiveness of such repetitions is evidenced by their becoming in many instances embedded in the language as clichés like "wild and woolly," "first and foremost," "footloose and fancy-free," "penny-wise, pound-foolish," "dead as a doornail," "might and main," "sink or swim," "do or die," "pell-mell," "helter-skelter," "harum-scarum," "hocus-pocus." Some of these kinds of repetition have names, as we will see.

A syllable consists of a vowel sound that may be preceded or followed by consonant sounds. Any of these sounds may be repeated. The repetition of initial consonant sounds, as in "tried and true," "safe and sound," "fish or fowl," "rime or reason," is ALLITERATION. The repetition of vowel sounds, as in "mad as a hatter," "time out of mind," "free and easy," "slapdash," is ASSONANCE. The repetition of final consonant sounds, as in "first and last," "odds and ends," "short and sweet," "a stroke of luck," or Shakespeare's "struts and frets" (page 632) is CONSONANCE.*

Repetitions may be used alone or in combination. Alliteration and assonance are combined in such phrases as "time and tide," "thick and thin," "kith and kin," "alas and alack," "fit as a fiddle," and Edgar Allan Poe's famous line, "The viol, the violet, and the vine." Alliteration and consonance are combined in such phrases as "crisscross," "last but not least," "lone and lorn," "good as gold," Housman's "Malt does more than Milton can" (page 528), "strangling in a string" (page 564) and "fleet foot" (page 798), and e. e. cummings's "blow friend to fiend" and "a doom of a

---

*There is no established terminology for these various repetitions. *Alliteration* is used by some writers to mean any repetition of consonant sounds. *Assonance* has been used to mean the similarity as well as the identity of vowel sounds, or even the similarity of any sounds whatever. *Consonance* has often been reserved for words in which both the initial *and* final consonant sounds correspond, as in *green* and *groan, moon* and *mine*. *Rime* (or rhyme) has been used to mean any sound repetition, including alliteration, assonance, and consonance. In the absence of clear agreement on the meanings of these terms, the terminology chosen here has appeared most useful, with support in usage. Labels are useful in analysis. The student should, however, learn to recognize the devices and, more important, to see their function, without worrying too much over nomenclature.

dream" (page 646). The combination of assonance and consonance is rime.

Rɪᴍᴇ is the repetition of the accented vowel sound and all succeeding sounds. It is called ᴍᴀsᴄᴜʟɪɴᴇ when the rime sounds involve only one syllable, as in *decks* and *sex* or *support* and *retort*. It is ꜰᴇᴍɪɴɪɴᴇ when the rime sounds involve two or more syllables, as in *turtle* and *fertile* or *spitefully* and *delightfully*. It is referred to as ɪɴᴛᴇʀɴᴀʟ ʀɪᴍᴇ when one or more riming words are within the line and as ᴇɴᴅ ʀɪᴍᴇ when the riming words are at the *ends* of lines. End rime is probably the most frequently used and most consciously sought sound repetition in English poetry. Because it comes at the end of the line, it receives emphasis as a musical effect and perhaps contributes more than any other musical resource except rhythm and meter to give poetry its musical effect as well as its structure. There exists, however, a large body of poetry that does not employ rime and for which rime would not be appropriate. Also, there has always been a tendency, especially noticeable in modern poetry, to substitute approximate rimes for perfect rimes at the ends of lines. Aᴘ-ᴘʀᴏxɪᴍᴀᴛᴇ ʀɪᴍᴇs include words with any kind of sound similarity, from close to fairly remote. Under approximate rime we include alliteration, assonance, and consonance or their combinations when used at the end of the line; half-rime (feminine rimes in which only half of the word rimes—the accented half, as in *lightly* and *frightful,* or the unaccented half, as in *yellow* and *willow*); and other similarities too elusive to name. "A bird came down the walk" (page 525) and "A narrow fellow in the grass" (page 565), "Dr. Sigmund Freud Discovers the Sea Shell" (page 575), "Toads" (page 582), and "Mr. Z" (page 625), to different degrees, all employ various kinds of approximate end rime.

THAT NIGHT WHEN JOY BEGAN

That night when joy began
Our narrowest veins to flush,
We waited for the flash
Of morning's leveled gun.

But morning let us pass,   5
And day by day relief
Outgrows his nervous laugh,
Grown credulous of peace,

As mile by mile is seen
No trespasser's reproach,   10

And love's best glasses reach
No fields but are his own.

W. H. Auden (*1907–1973*)

QUESTIONS

1. What has been the past experience with love of the two people in the poem? What is their present experience? What precisely is the tone of the poem?
2. What basic metaphor underlies the poem? Work it out stanza by stanza. What is "the flash of morning's leveled gun"? Does line 10 mean that no trespasser reproaches the lovers or that no one reproaches the lovers for being trespassers? Does "glasses" (11) refer to spectacles, tumblers, mirrors, or field glasses? Point out three personifications.
3. The rime pattern in this poem is intricate and exact. Work it out, considering alliteration, assonance, and consonance.

In addition to the repetition of individual sounds and syllables, the poet may repeat whole words, phrases, lines, or groups of lines. When such repetition is done according to some fixed pattern, it is called a REFRAIN. The refrain is especially common in songlike poetry. Examples are to be found in Shakespeare's "Winter" (page 520) and "Spring" (page 524).

It is not to be thought that we have exhausted the possibilities of sound repetition by giving names to a few of the more prominent kinds. The complete study of possible kinds of sound repetition in poetry would be so complex that it would break down under its own machinery. Some of the subtlest and loveliest effects escape our net of names. In as short a phrase as this from the prose of John Ruskin—"ivy as light and lovely as the vine"—we notice alliteration in *light* and *lovely*, assonance in *ivy*, *light*, and *vine*, and consonance in *ivy* and *lovely*, but we have no name to connect the *v* in *vine* with the *v*'s in *ivy* and *lovely*, or the second *l* in *lovely* with the first *l*, or the final syllables of *ivy* and *lovely* with each other; but these are all an effective part of the music of the line. Also contributing to the music of poetry is the use of related rather than identical sounds, such as *m* and *n* or *p* and *b* or the vowel sounds in *boat*, *boot*, and *book*.

These various musical repetitions, for trained readers, will ordinarily make an almost subconscious contribution to their reading of the poem: readers will feel their effect without necessarily being aware of what has caused it. There is value, however, in occasionally analyzing a poem for these devices in order to increase awareness of them. A few words of caution are necessary. First, the repetitions are entirely a matter of sound; spelling is irrelevant. *Bear* and *pair* are rimes, but *through* and *rough* are

eye - rime

not. *Cell* and *sin, folly* and *philosophy* alliterate, but *sin* and *sugar, gun* and *gem* do not. Second, alliteration, assonance, consonance, and masculine rime are matters that ordinarily involve only stressed or accented syllables; for only such syllables ordinarily make enough impression on the ear to be significant in the sound pattern of the poem. We should hardly consider *which* and *its* in the second line of "The Turtle," for instance, as an example of assonance, for neither word is stressed enough in the reading to make it significant as a sound. Third, the words involved in these repetitions must be close enough together that the ear retains the sound, consciously or subconsciously, from its first occurrence to its second. This distance varies according to circumstances, but for alliteration, assonance, and consonance the words ordinarily have to be in the same line or adjacent lines. End rime bridges a longer gap.

GOD'S GRANDEUR

The world is charged with the grandeur of God.
  It will flame out, like shining from shook foil;
  It gathers to a greatness, like the ooze of oil
Crushed. Why do men then now not reck his rod?
Generations have trod, have trod, have trod;   5
  And all is seared with trade; bleared, smeared with toil;
  And wears man's smudge and shares man's smell: the soil
Is bare now, nor can foot feel, being shod.

And for all this, nature is never spent;
  There lives the dearest freshness deep down things;   10
And though the last lights off the black West went
  Oh, morning, at the brown brink eastward, springs—
Because the Holy Ghost over the bent
  World broods with warm breast and with ah! bright wings.

Gerard Manley Hopkins (1844–1889)

QUESTIONS

1. What is the theme of this sonnet?
2. The image in lines 3–4 possibly refers to olive oil being collected in great vats from crushed olives, but the image is much disputed. Explain the simile in line 2 and the symbols in lines 7–8 and 11–12.
3. Explain "reck his rod" (4), "spent" (9), "bent" (13).
4. Using different-colored pencils, encircle and connect examples of alliteration, assonance, consonance, and internal rime. Do these help to carry the meaning?

We should not leave the impression that the use of these musical devices is necessarily or always valuable. Like the other resources of poetry, they can be judged only in the light of the poem's total intention. Many of the greatest works of English poetry—for instance, *Hamlet* and *King Lear* and *Paradise Lost*—do not employ end rime. Both alliteration and rime, especially feminine rime, if used excessively or unskillfully, become humorous or silly. If the intention is humorous, the result is delightful; if not, fatal. Shakespeare, who knew how to use all these devices to the utmost advantage, parodied their unskillful use in lines like "The preyful princess pierced and pricked a pretty pleasing prickett" in *Love's Labor's Lost* and

> Whereat with blade, with bloody, blameful blade,
> He bravely broached his boiling bloody breast

in *A Midsummer Night's Dream*. Swinburne parodied his own highly alliterative style in "Nephelidia" with lines like "Life is the lust of a lamp for the light that is dark till the dawn of the day when we die." Used skillfully and judiciously, however, musical devices provide a palpable and delicate pleasure to the ear and, even more important, add dimension to meaning.

EXERCISE

Discuss the various ways in which the following poems make use of refrain:

1. "Winter," page 520.
2. "The Pasture," page 527.
3. "Pack, clouds, away," page 576.
4. "Weep you no more, sad fountains," page 586.
5. "To Althea, from Prison," page 618.
6. "in Just—," page 633.
7. "When I was one-and-twenty," page 728.
8. "Edward," page 731.
9. "Southern Cop," page 779.
10. "Do not go gentle into that good night," page 822.

*   *   *

WITH RUE MY HEART IS LADEN

> With rue my heart is laden
>   For golden friends I had.
> For many a rose-lipt maiden
>   And many a lightfoot lad.

By brooks too broad for leaping
The lightfoot boys are laid;
The rose-lipt girls are sleeping
In fields where roses fade.

A. E. Housman (1859-1936)

QUESTIONS

1. Vocabulary: *rue* (1).
2. What, where, or why are the "brooks too broad for leaping" and the "fields where roses fade"?
3. What are the connotations here of "golden"? Does the use of "golden" (2), "lad" (4), and "girls" (7) remind you of any earlier poem? (If not, see page 818.) How does this submerged allusion enrich the poem?
4. Point out and discuss the contribution to the poem of alliteration, end rime (masculine and feminine), and other repetitions.

WE REAL COOL

The Pool Players.
Seven At The Golden Shovel.

We real cool. We
Left school. We

Lurk late. We
Strike straight. We

Sing sin. We
Thin gin. We

Jazz June. We
Die soon.

Gwendolyn Brooks (b. 1917)

QUESTIONS

1. In addition to end rime, what other musical devices does this poem employ?
2. Try reading this poem with the pronouns at the beginning of the lines instead of at the end. What is lost?
3. English teachers in a certain urban school were criticized recently for having their students read this poem: it was said to be immoral. Was the criticism justified? Why or why not?

SHOE SHOP

I shut the door on the racket
Of rush hour traffic,
Inhale the earthy, thick
Perfume of leather and pipe tobacco.

The place might be a barbershop   5
Where the air gets lathered with gossip.
You can almost hear the whippersnap
Of the straightedge on the razor strop.

It might be a front for agitators,
But there's no back room. A rabble   10
Of boots and shoes lies tumbled
In heaps like a hoard of potatoes.

The cobbler, broad as a blacksmith,
Turns a shoe over his pommel,
Pummels the sole, takes the nail   15
He's bit between his teeth,

And drives it into the heel. Hunched
At his workbench, he pays the old shoe
More attention than me. "Help you?"
He grunts, as if the man held a grudge   20

Against business. He gives my run-over
Loafer a look. "Plastic," he spits.
"And foreign-made. Doubt I can fix it."
I could be holding a dead gopher.

"The Europeans might make good shoes,   25
But I never see them. Cut the price.
Advertise! Never mind the merchandise.
You buy yourself a pair, brand new,

"The welt will be cardboard
Where it ought to be leather.   30
There's nothing to hold the shoe together."
He stows my pair in a cupboard.

"And all of them tan with acid.
The Mexicans make fancy boots, but they cure
Their leather in cow manure. Wear   35
Them out in the rain once. Rancid?

"I had a guy bring me a pair.
Wanted me to get rid of the stink.

Honest to God. I hate to think
My customers are crazy, but I swear."   40

He curses factories, inflation,
And I welcome the glow of conspiracy.
Together we plot, half seriously,
A counter industrial revolution.

His pride's been steeped in bitterness,   45
His politics tanned with elbow-grease.
To hear him fume and bitch, you'd guess
His guerrilla warfare's hopeless.

But talk about job satisfaction!
To take a tack from a tight-lipped smile,   50
Stick it like a thorn in an unworn sole,
To heft the hammer, and whack it!

When I step back out in the street
The city looks flimsy as a movie set.

Barton Sutter (b.1949)

QUESTIONS

1. Identify the rime scheme of the poem. What kinds of rimes does it use? What lines contain perfect rimes?
2. Contrast the language (diction and syntax) of this poem with that of "To Autumn" (p. 568) or "Ulysses" (p. 601). Is it less poetic?
3. What kinds of imagery does the poem employ? Is it less rich in imagery than the poems just named?
4. Identify and discuss the appropriateness of the metaphors and similes in lines 6, 10–12, 22, 24, 45, 46, 48. What links stanzas 3, 11, 12? What is a "counter industrial revolution"?
5. Explain the apparent contradiction between the cobbler's "bitterness" (45) and his "job satisfaction" (49). Why does the city look "flimsy as a movie set" to the narrator when he leaves the shop?

WINTER OCEAN

Many-maned scud-thumper, tub
of male whales, maker of worn wood, shrub-
ruster, sky-mocker, rave!
portly pusher of waves, wind-slave.

John Updike (b. 1932)

QUESTIONS

1. The fun of this poem lies chiefly in two features: in its invention of elaborate
   epithets (descriptive names) for something familiar (in Old English poetry,
   partially imitated here, these descriptive names were called *kennings*), and in
   its equally elaborate sound correspondences. How apt are the names? List or
   chart the sound correspondences. Are they also appropriate?
2. What figure of speech is most central to the poem?

PARTING, WITHOUT A SEQUEL

She has finished and sealed the letter
At last, which he so richly has deserved,
With characters venomous and hatefully curved,
And nothing could be better.

But even as she gave it   5
Saying to the blue-capped functioner of doom,
"Into his hands," she hoped the leering groom
Might somewhere lose and leave it.

Then all the blood
Forsook the face. She was too pale for tears,   10
Observing the ruin of her younger years.
She went and stood

Under her father's vaunting oak
Who kept his peace in wind and sun, and glistened
Stoical in the rain; to whom she listened   15
If he spoke.

And now the agitation of the rain
Rasped his sere leaves, and he talked low and gentle
Reproaching the wan daughter by the lintel;
Ceasing and beginning again.   20

Away went the messenger's bicycle,
His serpent's track went up the hill forever,
And all the time she stood there hot as fever
And cold as any icicle.

John Crowe Ransom (1888–1974)

QUESTIONS

1. Identify the figures of speech in lines 3 and 22 and discuss their effectiveness.
   Are there traces of dramatic irony in the poem? Where?

2. Is the oak literal or figurative? Neither? Both? Discuss the meanings of "vaunting" (13), "stoical" (15), "sere" (18), and "lintel" (19).
3. Do you find any trite language in the poem? Where? What does it tell us about the girl's action?
4. W. H. Auden has defined poetry as "the clear expression of mixed feelings." Discuss the applicability of the definition to this poem. Try it out on other poems.
5. A feminine rime that involves two syllables is known also as a DOUBLE RIME. Find examples in the poem of both perfect and approximate double rimes. A feminine rime that involves three syllables is a TRIPLE RIME. Find one example of a triple rime. Which lines employ masculine or SINGLE RIMES, either perfect or approximate?

SONG

The pints and the pistols, the pike-staves and pottles,
  The trooper's fierce shout and the toper's bold song;
O! theirs is such friendship that battles and bottles
  When going together can never go wrong.

The wine of the vintner, the blood of the Roundhead,   5
  The Cavalier taps them with equal delight;
And we are the boys for whom always abounded
  Good casks for the table, good casques for the fight.

Then thus do we drink to the flag and the flagon,
  The two stoutest allies the world ever saw;   10
For war without wine would so wearily drag on
  That none but a blockhead the bilbo would draw.

The can and the cannon sure never can bicker,
  Full quarts and free quarters shall still be our cry;
One hand draws the blade and the other the liquor,   15
  And grape is the best of all shot—when we're dry.

Drink sack and sack cities—whet swords and wet gullets,
  Nor blush, jolly boys, when we make it our boast
That friends as we are both to bowls and to bullets,
  We're not always fond of the charge of the host.   20

Who like not both swilling and killing are asses,
  For Bacchus was surely the brother of Mars;
So shrink not to charge to the muzzles your glasses
  And fire off a salvo for wine-cups and wars.

Attributed to *Winthrop Mackworth Praed (1802-1839)*

1. Vocabulary: *pottles* (1), *toper* (2), *casques* (8), *bilbo* (12).
2. In a drinking song we expect high spirits and jollity rather than profundity. How do the high spirits express themselves here in the very language itself? How many of the devices discussed in this chapter can you identify? How many puns do you count?

TRAVELING THROUGH THE DARK

Traveling through the dark I found a deer
dead on the edge of the Wilson River road.
It is usually best to roll them into the canyon:
that road is narrow; to swerve might make more dead.

By glow of the tail-light I stumbled back of the car   5
and stood by the heap, a doe, a recent killing;
she had stiffened already, almost cold.
I dragged her off; she was large in the belly.

My fingers touching her side brought me the reason—
her side was warm; her fawn lay there waiting,   10
alive, still, never to be born.
Beside that mountain road I hesitated.

The car aimed ahead its lowered parking lights;
under the hood purred the steady engine.
I stood in the glare of the warm exhaust turning red;   15
around our group I could hear the wilderness listen.

I thought hard for us all—my only swerving—,
then pushed her over the edge into the river.

William Stafford (b. 1914)

QUESTIONS

1. State precisely the speaker's dilemma. What kind of person is he? Does he make the right decision? Why does he call his hesitation "my only swerving" (17), and how does this connect with the word "swerve" in line 4?
2. What different kinds of imagery and of image contrasts give life to the poem? Do any of the images have symbolic overtones?
3. At first glance this poem may appear to be without end rime. Looking closer, do you find any correspondences between lines 2 and 4 in each stanza? between the final words of the concluding couplet? Can you find any line-end in the poem without some connection in sound to another line-end in its stanza?

NOTHING GOLD CAN STAY

Nature's first green is gold,
Her hardest hue to hold.
Her early leaf's a flower;
But only so an hour.
Then leaf subsides to leaf.
So Eden sank to grief,
So dawn goes down to day.
Nothing gold can stay.

Robert Frost (1874–1963)

QUESTIONS

1. Explain the paradoxes in lines 1 and 3.
2. Discuss the poem as a series of symbols. What are the symbolical meanings of "gold" in the final line of the poem?
3. Discuss the contributions of alliteration, assonance, consonance, rime, and other repetitions to the effectiveness of the poem.

AUTUMNUS

When the leaves in autumn wither,
   With a tawny tannèd face,
Warped and wrinkled-up together,
   The year's late beauty to disgrace:

There thy life's glass may'st thou find thee,
   Green now, gray now, gone anon;
   Leaving (worldling) of thine own,
Neither fruit, nor leaf behind thee.

Joshua Sylvester (1563–1618)

QUESTIONS

1. To whom is the poem addressed? What is the "glass" (5)?
2. Discuss the contribution of musical devices to the structure and meaning of the poem.

12. Rhythm and Meter

Our love of rhythm and meter is rooted even deeper in us than our love for musical repetition. It is related to the beat of our hearts, the pulse of our blood, the intake and outflow of air from our lungs. Everything that we do naturally and gracefully we do rhythmically. There is rhythm in the way we walk, the way we swim, the way we ride a horse, the way we swing a golf club or a baseball bat. So native is rhythm to us that we read it, when we can, into the mechanical world around us. Our clocks go tick-tick-tick-tick, but we hear them go tick-tock, tick-tock in an endless trochaic. The click of the railway wheels beneath us patterns itself into a tune in our heads. There is a strong appeal for us in language that is rhythmical.

The term RHYTHM refers to any wavelike recurrence of motion or sound. In speech it is the natural rise and fall of language. All language is to some degree rhythmical, for all language involves some kind of alternation between accented and unaccented syllables. Language varies considerably, however, in the degree to which it exhibits rhythm. In some forms of speech the rhythm is so unobtrusive or so unpatterned that we are scarcely, if at all, aware of it. In other forms of speech the rhythm is so pronounced that we may be tempted to tap our foot to it.

METER is the kind of rhythm we can tap our foot to. In language that is metrical the accents are so arranged as to occur at apparently equal intervals of time, and it is this interval we mark off with the tap of our foot. Metrical language is called VERSE. Nonmetrical language is PROSE.

Not all poetry is metrical, nor is all metrical language poetry. *Verse* and *poetry* are not synonymous terms, nor is a *versifier* necessarily a *poet.*

The study of meter is a fascinating but highly complex subject. It is by no means an absolute prerequisite to an enjoyment, even a rich enjoyment, of poetry. But a knowledge of its fundamentals does have certain values. It can make the beginning reader more aware of the rhythmical effects of poetry and of how poetry should be read. It can enable the more advanced reader to analyze how certain effects are achieved, to see how rhythm is adapted to thought, and to explain what makes one poem (in this respect) better than another. The beginning student ought to have at least an elementary knowledge of the subject. It is not so difficult as its terminology might suggest.

In every word of more than one syllable, one syllable is *accented* or *stressed,* that is, given more prominence in pronunciation than the rest.*
We say to*day,* to*morrow,* *yesterday,* *daily,* inter*vene.* If words of even one syllable are arranged into a sentence, we give certain words, or syllables, more prominence in pronunciation than the rest. We say: "He *went* to the *store,*" or "*Jack* is *driving* his *car.*" There is nothing mysterious about this; it is the normal process of language. The only difference between prose and verse is that in prose these accents occur more or less haphazardly; in verse the poet has arranged them to occur at regular intervals.

The word *meter* comes from a word meaning "measure." To measure something we must have a unit of measurement. For measuring length we use the inch, the foot, and the yard; for measuring time we use the second, the minute, and the hour. For measuring verse we use the foot, the line, and (sometimes) the stanza.

The basic metrical unit, the FOOT, consists normally of one accented syllable plus one or two unaccented syllables, though occasionally there may be no unaccented syllables, and very rarely there may be three. For diagramming verse, various systems of visual symbols have been invented. In this book we shall use a short curved line to indicate an unaccented syllable, a short horizontal line to indicate an accented syllable, and a vertical bar to indicate the division between feet. The basic kinds of feet are thus as follows:

---

*Though the words *accent* and *stress* are generally used interchangeably, as here, a distinction is sometimes made between them in technical discussions. ACCENT, the relative prominence given a syllable in relation to its neighbors, is then said to result from one or more of four causes: *stress,* or force of utterance, producing loudness; *duration; pitch;* and *juncture,* the manner of transition between successive sounds. Of these, *stress,* in English verse, is most important.

Example	Name of foot	Name of meter*	
to-*day* (˘ ¯)	Iamb	Iambic	⎫
dai-ly (¯ ˘)	Trochee	Trochaic	⎬ Duple meters
in-ter-*vene* (˘ ˘ ¯)	Anapest	Anapestic	⎫
yes-ter-day (¯ ˘ ˘)	Dactyl	Dactylic	⎬ Triple meters
true-blue (¯ ¯)	Spondee	(Spondaic)	
day (¯)	Monosyllabic foot		

The secondary unit of measurement, the LINE, is measured by naming the number of feet in it. The following names are used:

Monometer	one foot	Pentameter	five feet
Dimeter	two feet	Hexameter	six feet
Trimeter	three feet	Heptameter	seven feet
Tetrameter	four feet	Octameter	eight feet

The third unit, the STANZA, consists of a group of lines whose metrical pattern is repeated throughout the poem. Since not all verse is written in stanzas, we shall save our discussion of this unit till a later chapter.

The process of measuring verse is referred to as SCANSION. To *scan* any specimen of verse, we do three things: (1) we identify the prevailing foot, (2) we name the number of feet in a line—if this length follows any regular pattern, and (3) we describe the stanza pattern—if there is one. We may try out our skill on the following poem.

VIRTUE

Sweet day, so cool, so calm, so bright,
    The bridal of the earth and sky;
The dew shall weep thy fall to night,
    For thou must die.

Sweet rose, whose hue, angry and brave,   5
    Bids the rash gazer wipe his eye;

---

* In the spondee the accent is thought of as being distributed equally or almost equally over the two syllables and is sometimes referred to as a hovering accent. No whole poems are written in spondees or monosyllabic feet; hence there are only four basic meters: iambic, trochaic, anapestic, and dactylic. Iambic and trochaic are DUPLE METERS because they employ two-syllable feet; anapestic and dactylic are TRIPLE METERS because they employ three-syllable feet.

Thy root is ever in its grave,
  And thou must die.

Sweet spring, full of sweet days and roses,
  A box where sweets compacted lie;   10
My music shows ye have your closes,
  And all must die.

Only a sweet and virtuous soul,
  Like seasoned timber, never gives;
But though the whole world turn to coal,   15
  Then chiefly lives.

George Herbert (1593–1633)

QUESTIONS

1. Vocabulary: *bridal* (2), *brave* (5), *closes* (11).
2. How are the four stanzas interconnected? How do they build to a climax? How does the fourth contrast with the first three?

The first step in scanning a poem is to read it normally, listening to where the accents fall, and perhaps beating time with the hand. If we have any doubt about how a line should be marked, we should skip it temporarily and go on to lines where we feel greater confidence, that is, to those lines which seem most regular, with accents that fall unmistakably at regular intervals. In "Virtue" lines 3, 10, and 14 clearly fall into this category, as do also the short lines 4, 8, and 12. Lines 3, 10, and 14 may be marked as follows:

The dew | shall weep | thy fall | to night,| 3

A box | where sweets | com- pact- | ed lie;| 10

Like sea- | soned tim- | ber, nev- | er gives.| 14

Lines 4, 8, and 12 are so nearly identical that we may let line 4 represent all three:

For thou | must die.| 4

Surveying what we have done so far, we may with some confidence say that the prevailing metrical foot of the poem is iambic; and we may reasonably hypothesize that the second and third lines of each stanza are tetrameter (four-foot) lines and the fourth line dimeter. What about the

first line? Line 1 contains eight syllables, and the last six are clearly
iambic:

Sweet day, | so cool, | so calm, | so bright. | 1

This too, then, is a tetrameter line, and the only question is whether to
mark the first foot as another iamb or as a spondee. Many metrists, emphasizing the priority of pattern, would mark it as an iamb. Clearly,
however, the word "Sweet" is more important and receives more emphasis in a sensitive reading than the three "so's" in the line. Other metrists,
therefore, would give it equal emphasis with "day" and mark the first foot
as a spondee. Neither marking can be called incorrect. It is a matter of the
reader's personal judgment or of his metrical philosophy. Following my
own preference, I mark it as a spondee, and mark the first foot in lines 5
and 9 correspondingly. Similar choices occur at several points in the
poem (lines 11, 15, and 16). Many readers will quite legitimately perceive
line 16 as parallel to lines 4, 8, and 12. Others, however, may argue that
the word "Then"—emphasizing what happens to the virtuous soul when
everything else has perished—has an importance that should be reflected
in both the reading and the scansion and will therefore mark the first foot
of this line as a spondee:

Then chief- | ly lives. | 16

These readers will also see the third foot in line 15 as a spondee:

But though | the whole | world turn | to coal. | 15

Lines 2 and 7 introduce a different problem. Most readers, encounter-
ing these lines in a paragraph of prose, would read them thus:

The bri- dal of the earth and sky, 2

Thy root is ev- er in its grave. 7

But this reading leaves us with an anomalous situation. First, we have
only three accents where our hypothetical pattern calls for four. Second,
we have three unaccented syllables occurring together, a situation almost
never encountered in verse of duple meter. From this situation we learn
an important principle. Though normal reading of the sentences in a
poem establishes its metrical pattern, the metrical pattern so established
in turn influences the reading. A circular process is at work. In this poem
the pressure of the pattern will cause most sensitive readers to stress the
second of the three unaccented syllables slightly more than those on
either side of it. In scansion we recognize this slight increase of stress by

promoting the syllable to the status of an accented syllable. Thus we mark
lines 2 and 7 respectively thus:

The brí- | dál of | the earth | and sky, | 2

Thy root | is ev- | er in | its grave. | 7

Line 5 presents a situation about which there can be no dispute. The
word "angry," though it occurs in a position where we would expect an
iamb, *must* be accented on the first syllable, and thus must be marked as
a trochee:

Sweet rose, | whose hue, | an- gry | and brave. | 5

There is little question also that the following line begins with a trochee
in the first foot, followed by a spondee:

Bids the | rash gaz- | er wipe | his eye. | 6

Similarly, the word "Only," beginning line 13, is accented on the first
syllable, thus introducing a trochaic substitution in the first foot of that
line. Line 13 presents also another problem. A modern reader perceives
the word "virtuous" as a three-syllable word, but the poet (writing in the
seventeenth century, when metrical requirements were stricter than they
are today) would probably have meant the word to be pronounced as two
syllables (*ver-tyus*). Following the tastes of my century, I mark it as three,
thus introducing an anapest instead of the expected iamb in the last foot:

On- ly | a sweet | and vir- | tu- ous soul. | 13

In doing this, however, I am consciously "modernizing"—altering the
intention of the poet for the sake of a contemporary audience.

One problem remains. In the third stanza, lines 9 and 11 differ from
the other lines of the poem in two respects: (a) they contain nine rather
than eight syllables; (b) they end on unaccented syllables.

Sweet spring, | full of | sweet days | and ros- | es,   9

My mu- | sic shows | ye have | your clos- | es.   11

Such left-over unaccented syllables are not counted in identifying and
naming the meter. These lines are both tetrameter, and if we tap our foot
while reading them, we shall tap it four times. Metrical verse will often
have one and sometimes two left-over unaccented syllables. In iambic and
anapestic verse they will come at the end of lines; in trochaic and dactylic
at the beginning.

Our metrical analysis of "Virtue" is completed. Though (mainly for ease of discussion) we have skipped about eccentrically, we have indicated a scansion for all its lines. "Virtue" is written in iambic meter (meaning that most of its feet are iambs), and is composed of four-line stanzas, the first three lines tetrameter, and the final line dimeter. We are now ready to make a few generalizations about scansion.

1. Good readers will not ordinarily stop to scan a poem they are reading, and they certainly will not read a poem with the exaggerated emphasis on accented syllables that we sometimes give them in order to make the scansion more apparent. However, occasional scansion of a poem has value, as will become more apparent in the next chapter, which discusses the relation of sound and meter to sense. Just one example here. The structure of meaning in "Virtue" is unmistakable. It consists of three parallel stanzas concerning things that die, followed by a contrasting fourth stanza concerning the one thing that does not die. The first three stanzas all begin with the word "Sweet" preceding a noun, and the first metrical foot in these stanzas—whether we consider it iamb or spondee—is the same. The contrasting fourth stanza, however, begins with a trochee, thus departing both from the previous pattern and from the basic meter of the poem. This departure is significant, for the word "Only" is the hinge upon which the structure of the poem turns, and the metrical reversal gives it emphasis. Thus meter serves meaning.

2. Scansion is at best a gross way of describing the rhythmical quality of a poem. It depends on classifying all syllables into either accented or unaccented categories and on ignoring the sometimes considerable difference between degrees of accent. Whether we call a syllable accented or unaccented depends, moreover, on its degree of accent relative to the syllables on either side of it. In lines 2 and 7 of "Virtue," the accents on "of" and "in" are obviously much lighter than on the other accented syllables in the line. Unaccented syllables also vary in weight. In line 5 "whose" is clearly heavier than "-gry" and "and," and is arguably heavier even than the accented "of" and "in" of lines 2 and 7. The most ardent champion of spondees, moreover, would concede that the accentual weight is not really equivalent in "Sweet rose": the noun shoulders more of the burden. Scansion is thus incapable of dealing with the subtlest rhythmical effects in poetry. It is nevertheless a useful and serviceable tool. Any measurement device more refined or sensitive would be too complicated to be widely serviceable.

3. Scansion is not an altogether exact science. Within certain limits we may say that a certain scansion is right or wrong, but beyond these limits there is legitimate room for disagreement between qualified read-

ers. Line 11 of "Virtue" provides the best example. Some metrists—those wanting scansion to reflect as closely as possible the underlying pattern—would mark it as perfectly regular: a succession of four iambs. Others—those wishing the scansion to reveal more nearly the nuances of a sensitive reading—would find that three sensitive readers might read this line in three different ways. One might stress "ye"; a second, "your"; and a third, both. The result is four possible scansions for this line:

My mu- | sic shows | ye have | your close- | es, 11

My mu- | sic shows | ye have | your close- | es, 11

My mu- | sic shows | ye have | your close- | es, 11

My mu- | sic shows | ye have | your close- | es. 11

Notice that the divisions between feet have no meaning except to help us identify the meter. They do not correspond to real divisions in the line; indeed, they fall often in the middle of a word. We place them where we do only to yield the most possible of a single kind of foot; in other words, to reveal regularity. If line 14 is marked

Like sea- | soned tim- | ber, nev- | er gives, 14

it yields four regular iambs. If it were marked

Like | sea- soned | tim- ber, | nev- er | gives, 14

there would be an unaccented "left-over" syllable, three trochees, and a monosyllabic foot. The basic pattern of the poem would be obscured.

4. Finally—and this is the most important generalization of all—perfect regularity of meter is no criterion of merit. Beginning students sometimes get the notion that it is. If the meter is smooth and perfectly regular, they feel that the poet has handled his meter successfully and deserves all credit for it. Actually there is nothing easier than for any moderately talented versifier to make language go ta-*dum* ta-*dum* ta-*dum*. But there are two reasons why this is not generally desirable. The first is that, as we have said, all art consists essentially of repetition and variation. If a meter alternates too regularly between light and heavy beats, the result is to banish variation; the meter becomes mechanical and, for any sensitive reader, monotonous. The second is that, once a basic meter has been established, any deviations from it become highly significant and are the means by which the poet can use meter to reinforce meaning. If a

meter is too perfectly regular, the probability is that the poet, instead of adapting rhythm to meaning, has simply forced his meaning into a metrical straitjacket.

Actually what gives the skillful use of meter its greatest effectiveness is that it consists, not of one rhythm, but of two. One of these is the *expected* rhythm. The other is the *heard* rhythm. Once we have determined the basic meter of a poem, say, iambic tetrameter, we have an expectation that this rhythm will continue. Thus a silent drumbeat is set up in our minds, and this drumbeat constitutes the expected rhythm. But the actual rhythm of the words—the heard rhythm—will sometimes confirm this expected rhythm and sometimes not. Thus the two rhythms are counterpointed, and the appeal of the verse is magnified just as when two melodies are counterpointed in music or as when we see two swallows flying together and around each other, following the same general course but with individual variations and making a much more eye-catching pattern than one swallow flying alone. If the heard rhythm conforms too closely to the expected rhythm, the meter becomes dull and uninteresting. If it departs too far from the expected rhythm, there ceases to be an expected rhythm. If the irregularity is too great, meter disappears and the result is prose rhythm or free verse.

There are several ways by which variation can be introduced into the poet's use of meter. The most obvious way is by the substitution of other kinds of feet for regular feet. In our scansion of line 9 of "Virtue," for instance, we found a spondee, a trochee, and another spondee substituted for the expected iambs in the first three feet (plus an unexpected unaccented syllable left over at the end of the line). A less obvious but equally important means of variation is through simple phrasing and variation of degrees of accent. Though we began our scansion of "Virtue" by marking lines 3, 10, and 14 as perfectly regular, there is actually a considerable difference among them. Line 3 is quite regular, for the phrasing corresponds with the metrical pattern, and the line can be read ta-*dum* ta-*dum* ta-*dum* ta-*dum*. Line 10 is less regular, for the three-syllable word "compacted" cuts across the division between two feet. We should read it ta-*dum* ta-*dum* ta-*dump*-ty *dum*. Line 14 is the least regular of the three, for here there is no correspondence between phrasing and metrical division. We should read this line ta-*dump*-ty *dump*-ty, *dump*-ty *dum*. Finally, variation can be introduced by grammatical and rhetorical pauses. The comma in line 14, by introducing a grammatical pause, provides an additional variation from its perfect regularity. Probably the most violently irregular line in the poem is line 5,

Sweet rose, | whose hue, | an- gry | and brave, | 5 for here the spondaic substitution in the first foot, and the unusual trochaic substitution in the middle of a line in the third foot, are set off and emphasized by grammatical pauses, and also (as we have noted) the unaccented "whose" is considerably heavier than the other two unaccented syllables in the line. It is worth noting that the violent irregularity of this line (only slightly diminished in the next) corresponds with, and reinforces, the most violent image in the poem. Again, meter serves meaning.

The uses of rhythm and meter are several. Like the musical repetitions of sound, the musical repetitions of accent can be pleasing for their own sake. In addition, rhythm works as an emotional stimulus and serves, when used skillfully, to heighten our attention and awareness to what is going on in a poem. Finally, by his choice of meter, and by his skillful use of variation within the metrical framework, the poet can adapt the sound of his verse to its content and thus make meter a powerful reinforcement of meaning. We should avoid, however, the notion that there is any mystical correspondence between certain meters and certain emotions. There are no "happy" meters and no "melancholy" ones. The poet's choice of meter is probably less important than how he handles it after he has chosen it. However, some meters are swifter than others, some slower; some are more lilting than others, some more dignified. The poet can choose a meter that is appropriate or one that is inappropriate to his content, and by his handling of it can increase the appropriateness or inappropriateness. If he chooses a swift, lilting meter for a serious and grave subject, the meter will probably act to keep the reader from feeling any really deep emotion. But if he chooses a more dignified meter, it will intensify the emotion. In all great poetry, meter works intimately with the other elements of the poem to produce the appropriate total effect.

We must not forget, of course, that poetry need not be metrical at all. Like alliteration and rime, like metaphor and irony, like even imagery, meter is simply one resource the poet may or may not use. His job is to employ his resources to the best advantage for the object he has in mind—the kind of experience he wishes to express. And on no other basis can we judge him.

SUPPLEMENTAL NOTE

Of the four standard meters, iambic is by far the commonest. Perhaps 80 percent of metered poetry in English is iambic. Anapestic meter (example: Praed's "Song," page 677, in anapestic tetrameter) is next most common. Trochaic meter (example: "Think'st thou to seduce me then," page 540, in trochaic heptameter) is relatively infrequent. Dactylic meter is so rare as to be almost a museum specimen ("Bedtime Story," page 806, in stanzas consisting of three tetrameter lines followed by a dimeter line, is the sole example in this book).

Because of the predominance of iambic and anapestic meters in English verse, and because most anapestic poems have a high percentage of iambic substitutions, Robert Frost has written that in our language there are virtually but two meters: "strict iambic and loose iambic."* This is, of course, an overstatement; but, like many overstatements, it contains a good deal of truth. "Strict iambic" is strictly duple meter: it admits no trisyllabic substitutions. Trochees, spondees, and, occasionally, monosyllabic feet may be substituted for the expected iambs, but not anapests or dactyls. The presence of a triple foot has such a conspicuous effect in speeding or loosening up a line that the introduction of a few of them quite alters the nature of the meter. Herbert's "Virtue" is written in "strict iambic" (most of its feet are iambic; and, with the dubious exception of "virtuous," it contains no trisyllabic feet). Praed's "Song" is anapestic (most of its feet are anapests). e. e. cummings's "what if a much of a which of a wind" (page 646) contains more iambic than anapestic feet, but *in effect* it sounds more anapestic than iambic, more like Praed's "Song" than like Herbert's "Virtue." It would be impossible to define what percentage of anapestic feet a poem must have before it ceases seeming iambic and begins seeming anapestic, but it would be considerably less than 50 percent and might be more like 25 percent. At any rate, a large number of poems fall into an area between "strict iambic" and "prevailingly anapestic," and they might be fittingly described as iambic-anapestic (what Frost called "loose iambic").

Finally, the importance of the final paragraph preceding this note must be underscored: *poetry need not be metrical at all.* Following the prodigious example of Walt Whitman in the nineteenth century, more and more twentieth-century poets have turned to the writing of *free verse.* FREE VERSE, by our definition, is not verse at all; that is, it is not metrical. It may be rimed or unrimed (most often unrimed). The only difference between free verse and rhythmical prose is that free verse introduces one additional rhythmical unit, the line. The arrangement into lines divides the material into rhythmical units, or cadences. Beyond its line arrangement there are no necessary differences between it and rhythmical prose. Possibly 50 percent of published contemporary poetry is written in free verse.

*"The Figure a Poem Makes," *Selected Prose of Robert Frost* (New York: Holt, 1966), pp. 17–18.

To add one further variation, a number of contemporary poets have begun writing "prose poems," or poems in prose (example: Russell Edson's "The Mouse Dinners," page 791). It is too early to determine whether this is a passing fashion or will be a lasting development.

EXERCISES

1. An important term which every student of poetry should know (and should be careful not to confuse with *free verse*) is *blank verse*. BLANK VERSE has a very specific meter: it is *iambic pentameter, unrimed*. It has a special name because it is the principal English meter, that is, the meter that has been used for a large proportion of the greatest English poetry, including the tragedies of Shakespeare and the epics of Milton. Iambic pentameter in English seems especially suitable for the serious treatment of serious themes. The natural movement of the English language tends to be iambic. Lines shorter than pentameter tend to be songlike, not suited to sustained treatment of serious material. Lines longer than pentameter tend to break up into shorter units, the hexameter line being read as two three-foot units, the heptameter line as a four-foot and a three-foot unit, and so on. Rime, while highly appropriate to most short poems, often proves a handicap for a long and lofty work. (The word *blank* implies that the end of the line is "blank," that is, bare of rime.) The above generalizations, of course, represent tendencies, not laws.

   Of the following poems, four are in blank verse, four are in free verse, and two are in other meters. Determine in which category each belongs.
   a. "Hyla Brook," page 538.
   b. "Mirror," page 544.
   c. "Being Herded Past the Prison's Honor Farm," page 557.
   d. "Ulysses," page 601.
   e. Excerpt from *Macbeth*, page 632.
   f. "in Just—," page 633.
   g. "Journey of the Magi," page 637.
   h. "The Telephone," page 660.
   i. "Grace to Be Said at the Supermarket," page 808.
   j. "Mending Wall," page 792.
2. Another useful distinction is that between end-stopped lines and run-on lines. An END-STOPPED LINE is one in which the end of the line corresponds with a natural speech pause; a RUN-ON LINE is one in which the sense of the line hurries on into the next line. (There are, of course, all degrees of end-stop and run-on. A line ending with a period or semicolon is heavily end-stopped. A line without punctuation at the end is normally considered a run-on line, but it is less forcibly run-on if it ends at a natural speech pause—as between subject and predicate—than if it ends, say, between an article and its noun, between an auxiliary and its verb, or between a preposition and its object.) The use of run-on lines is one way the poet can make use of grammatical or rhetorical pauses to vary his basic meter.
   a. Examine "Sound and Sense" (page 709) and "My Last Duchess" (page 626). Both are written in the same meter: iambic pentameter, rimed in couplets. Is their general rhythmical effect quite similar or markedly dif-

ferent? What accounts for the difference? Does the contrast support our statement that the poet's choice of meter is probably less important than the way he handles it?

b. Examine "The Hound" (page 571) and "The Dance" (page 716). Which is the more forcibly run-on in the majority of its lines? Describe the difference in effect.

*   *   *

SEAL LULLABY

Oh! hush thee, my baby, the night is behind us,
    And black are the waters that sparkled so green.
The moon, o'er the combers, looks downward to find us
    At rest in the hollows that rustle between.
Where billow meets billow, there soft be thy pillow;
    Ah, weary wee flipperling, curl at thy ease!
The storm shall not wake thee, nor shark overtake thee,
    Asleep in the arms of the slow-swinging seas.

Rudyard Kipling (1865–1936)

QUESTIONS

1. Identify speaker, audience, and situation.
2. What is a "flipperling" (6)? Answer without consulting a dictionary, and explain how you know.
3. Scan the poem and name its meter. Which lines have unaccented syllables left over at the end? Is this an incidental variation from the basic pattern of the poem (as in Herbert's "Virtue," lines 9 and 11), or is it part of the pattern? How does this feature strengthen one's sense of the basic meter?
4. In scanning "Virtue" we noted a circular process in which, while normal reading established the metrical pattern, the metrical pattern in turn influenced the reading, causing us in scansion to promote to accented status certain syllables which would have been unaccented in prose. With poems in triple meter this circular pattern operates in the opposite direction, causing us to demote some syllables that would be accented in prose. It happens twice in this poem. In line 7 the first syllable of "overtake" would normally receive a slight stress, but in the poem this stress is suppressed by the metrical pattern. What syllable in the last line is even more dramatically reduced in the scansion? Does the weight of this unstressed syllable nevertheless affect the sense and movement of the line? How?

"INTRODUCTION" TO *SONGS OF INNOCENCE*

Piping down the valleys wild,
Piping songs of pleasant glee,

On a cloud I saw a child,
And he laughing said to me:

"Pipe a song about a Lamb."   5
So I piped with merry cheer.
"Piper, pipe that song again."
So I piped; he wept to hear.

"Drop thy pipe, thy happy pipe;
Sing thy songs of happy cheer."   10
So I sung the same again
While he wept with joy to hear.

"Piper, sit thee down and write
In a book that all may read."
So he vanished from my sight,   15
And I plucked a hollow reed,

And I made a rural pen,
And I stained the water clear,
And I wrote my happy songs
Every child may joy to hear.   20

William Blake (1757-1827)

QUESTIONS

1. Poets have traditionally been thought of as inspired by one of the Muses (Greek female divinities whose duties were to nurture the arts). Blake's *Songs of Innocence,* a book of poems about childhood and the state of innocence, includes "The Chimney Sweeper" (page 615) and "The Lamb" (page 777). In this introductory poem to the book, what function is played by the child upon a cloud?
2. What is symbolized by "a Lamb" (5)?
3. What three stages of poetic composition are suggested in stanzas 1-2, 3, and 4-5 respectively?
4. What features of the poems in his book does Blake indicate in this "Introduction"? Name at least four.
5. Mark the stressed and unstressed syllables in lines 1-2 and 9-10. Do they establish the basic meter of the poem? If so, is that meter iambic or trochaic? Or could it be either? Some metrists have discarded the distinction between iambic and trochaic, and between anapestic and dactylic, as being artificial. The important distinction, they feel, is between duple and triple meters. Does this poem support their claim?

THE "JE NE SAIS QUOI"

Yes, I'm in love, I feel it now,
And Celia has undone me;

And yet I'll swear I can't tell how
    The pleasing plague stole on me.

'Tis not her face that love creates,   5
    For there no Graces revel;
'Tis not her shape, for there the Fates
    Have rather been uncivil.

'Tis not her air, for sure in that,
    There's nothing more than common;   10
And all her sense is only chat,
    Like any other woman.

Her voice, her touch, might give the alarm—
    'Tis both perhaps, or neither;
In short, 'tis that provoking charm   15
    Of Celia altogether.

William Whitehead (1715-1785)

QUESTIONS

1. *Je ne sais quoi* is a French expression meaning "I do not know what"—an indefinable something. Does the use of approximate rimes rather than perfect rimes in the even lines of this poem help to establish the quality of uncertainty which is the subject of the poem?
2. Find examples of OXYMORON (a compact paradox in which two successive words seemingly contradict each other) in the first and last stanzas. What broad paradox underlies the whole poem?
3. What is the reason for the capitalization and pluralization of "grace" and "fate" in the second stanza? What is the image here conveyed? Is "love" (5) the subject or object of the verb?
4. Describe the metrical pattern of the poem. What effect does the extra unaccented syllable in lines 2 and 4 of each stanza have on the tone of the poem? (The rimes in these lines are feminine, and the lines are said to have feminine endings.)

IF EVERYTHING HAPPENS
THAT CAN'T BE DONE

    if everything happens that can't be done
    (and anything's righter
    than books
    could plan)
    the stupidest teacher will almost guess   5

(with a run
skip
around we go yes)
there's nothing as something as one

one hasn't a why or because or although   10
(and buds know better
than books
don't grow)
one's anything old being everything new
(with a what   15
which
around we come who)
one's everyanything so

so world is a leaf so tree is a bough
(and birds sing sweeter   20
than books
tell how)
so here is away and so your is a my
(with a down
up   25
around again fly)
forever was never till now

now i love you and you love me
(and books are shuter
than books   30
can be)
and deep in the high that does nothing but fall
(with a shout
each
around we go all)   35
there's somebody calling who's we

we're anything brighter than even the sun
(we're everything greater
than books
might mean)   40
we're everyanything more than believe
(with a spin
leap
alive we're alive)
we're wonderful one times one   45

e. e. cummings (*1894–1962*)

1. Explain the last line. Of what very familiar idea is this poem a fresh treatment?
2. The poem is based on a contrast between heart and mind, or love and learning. Which does the poet prefer? What symbols does he use for each?
3. What is the tone of the poem?
4. Which lines of each stanza regularly rime with each other (either perfect or approximate rime)? How does the poet link the stanzas?
5. What is the basic metrical scheme of the poem? What does the meter contribute to the tone? What line (in the fourth stanza) most clearly states the subject and occasion of the poem? How does meter underline its significance?
6. Can you suggest any reason why the poet did not write lines 2–4 and 6–8 of each stanza as one line each? What metrical variations does the poet use in lines 6–8 of each stanza and with what effect?

OH WHO IS THAT YOUNG SINNER

Oh who is that young sinner with the handcuffs on his wrists?
And what has he been after that they groan and shake their fists?
And wherefore is he wearing such a conscience-stricken air?
Oh they're taking him to prison for the color of his hair.

'Tis a shame to human nature, such a head of hair as his;⁣   5
In the good old time 'twas hanging for the color that it is;
Though hanging isn't bad enough and flaying would be fair
For the nameless and abominable color of his hair.

Oh a deal of pains he's taken and a pretty price he's paid
To hide his poll or dye it of a mentionable shade;   10
But they've pulled the beggar's hat off for the world to see and stare,
And they're taking him to justice for the color of his hair.

Now 'tis oakum for his fingers and the treadmill for his feet,
And the quarry-gang on Portland in the cold and in the heat,
And between his spells of labor in the time he has to spare   15
He can curse the God that made him for the color of his hair.

A. E. Housman (1859–1936)

1. Vocabulary: *poll* (10), *oakum* (13). Portland (14), an English peninsula, is the site of a famous criminal prison.
2. What kind of irony does the poem exhibit? Explain.
3. What symbolical meanings are suggested by "the color of his hair"?
4. This poem represents a kind of meter that we have not yet discussed. It *may* be scanned as iambic heptameter:

Oh who | is that | young sin-ner with | the hand-cuffs on | his wrists?|

But you will probably find yourself reading it as a four-beat line:

Oh who | is that young sin-ner with the hand-cuffs on his wrists?|

Although the meter is duple insofar as there is an alternation between unaccented and accented syllables, there is also an alternation in the degree of stress on the accented syllables: the first, third, fifth, and seventh stresses being heavier than the second, fourth, and sixth; the result is that the two-syllable feet tend to group themselves into larger units. We may scan it as follows, using a short line for a light accent, a longer one for a heavy accent:

Oh who | is that young sin-ner with the hand-cuffs on his wrists?|

And what | has he been af-ter that they groan | and shake their fists?|

And where-fore is he wear-ing such a con-science strick-en air?|

Oh they're tak-ing him to pris-on for the col-or of his hair.|

This kind of meter, in which there is an alternation between heavy and light stresses, is known as DIPODIC (two-footed) VERSE. The alternation may not be perfect throughout, but it will be frequent enough to establish a pattern in the reader's mind. Now scan the last three stanzas. For another example of dipodic verse, see "America for Me" (page 749).

DOWN BY THE SALLEY GARDENS

> Down by the salley gardens my love and I did meet;
> She passed the salley gardens with little snow-white feet.
> She bid me take love easy, as the leaves grow on the tree;
> But I, being young and foolish, with her would not agree.
> In a field by the river my love and I did stand,
> And on my leaning shoulder she laid her snow-white hand.
> She bid me take life easy, as the grass grows on the weirs;
> But I was young and foolish, and now am full of tears.

William Butler Yeats (1865–1939)

QUESTIONS

1. Vocabulary: *salley* (1), *weirs* (7).
2. This poem introduces an additional kind of metrical variation—the metrical pause or rest. Unlike grammatical and rhetorical pauses, the metrical pause affects scansion. If you beat out the rhythm of this poem with your hand, you will find that the fourth beat of each line (possibly excepting lines 3 and 7)

regularly falls *between* syllables. A METRICAL PAUSE, then, is a pause that replaces an accented syllable. It is usually found in verse that has a pronounced lilt or swing. The first line of Yeats's poem may be scanned as follows (the metrical pause is represented with an *x*):

$$\overline{\text{Down}} \ \breve{\text{by}} \ | \ \breve{\text{the}} \ \overline{\text{sal-}} \ | \ \breve{\text{ley}} \ \overline{\text{gar-}}\breve{\text{dens,}} \ ^{x} \ | \ \breve{\text{my}} \ \overline{\text{love}} \ | \ \breve{\text{and}} \ \overline{\text{I}} \ | \ \breve{\text{did}} \ \overline{\text{meet.}} \ |$$

The third line might be scanned in several ways, as the following alternatives suggest:

$$\breve{\text{She}} \ \overline{\text{bid}} \ | \ \breve{\text{me}} \ \overline{\text{take}} \ | \ \overline{\text{love}} \ \overline{\text{eas-}} \ | \ \breve{\text{y,}} \ \overline{\text{as}} \ | \ \breve{\text{the}} \ \overline{\text{leaves}} \ | \ \overline{\text{grow}} \ \breve{\text{on}} \ | \ \breve{\text{the}} \ \overline{\text{tree,}} \ |$$

$$\breve{\text{She}} \ \overline{\text{bid}} \ | \ \breve{\text{me}} \ \overline{\text{take}} \ | \ \overline{\text{love}} \ \overline{\text{eas-}} \ | \ \breve{\text{y,}} \ \breve{\text{as}} \ \breve{\text{the}} \ \overline{\text{leaves}} \ | \ \overline{\text{grow}} \ \breve{\text{on}} \ | \ \breve{\text{the}} \ \overline{\text{tree.}} \ |$$

Scan the rest of the poem.

HAD I THE CHOICE

Had I the choice to tally greatest bards,
To limn their portraits, stately, beautiful, and emulate at will,
Homer with all his wars and warriors—Hector, Achilles, Ajax,
Or Shakespeare's woe-entangled Hamlet, Lear, Othello—Tennyson's
    fair ladies,
Meter or wit the best, or choice conceit to wield in perfect rhyme,
    delight of singers;
These, these, O sea, all these I'd gladly barter,
Would you the undulation of one wave, its trick to me transfer,
Or breathe one breath of yours upon my verse,
And leave its odor there.

Walt Whitman (1819–1892)

QUESTIONS

1. Vocabulary: *tally* (1), *limn* (2), *conceit* (5).
2. What poetic qualities does Whitman propose to barter in exchange for what? What qualities do the sea and its waves symbolize?
3. What kind of "verse" is this? Why does Whitman prefer it to "meter" and "perfect rhyme"?

THE AIM WAS SONG

    Before man came to blow it right
        The wind once blew itself untaught,
    And did its loudest day and night
        In any rough place where it caught.

Man came to tell it what was wrong: 5
   It hadn't found the place to blow;
It blew too hard—the aim was song.
   And listen—how it ought to go!

He took a little in his mouth,
   And held it long enough for north   10
To be converted into south,
   And then by measure blew it forth.

By measure. It was word and note,
   The wind the wind had meant to be—
A little through the lips and throat.   15
   The aim was song—the wind could see.

Robert Frost (1874–1963)

QUESTIONS

1. Frost invents a myth about the origin of poetry. What implications does it suggest about the relation of man to nature and of poetry to nature?
2. Contrast the thought and form of this poem with Whitman's.
3. Scan the poem and identify its meter. How does the poet give variety to a regular metrical pattern?

METRICAL FEET

Trochee | trips from | long to | short.

From long to long in solemn sort

Slow Spondee stalks; | strong foot! | yet ill able

Ever to | come up with | Dactyl trisyllable.

Iambics march | from short | to long;—

With a leap | and a bound | the swift Anapests throng.

Samuel Taylor Coleridge (1772–1834)

QUESTION

If you have trouble remembering the metrical feet, memorize this.

13. Sound and Meaning

R hythm and sound cooperate to produce what we call the music of poetry. This music, as we have pointed out, may serve two general functions: it may be enjoyable in itself; it may be used to reinforce meaning and intensify the communication.

Pure pleasure in sound and rhythm exists from a very early age in the human being—probably from the age the baby first starts cooing in its cradle, certainly from the age that children begin chanting nursery rimes and skipping rope. The appeal of the following verse, for instance, depends almost entirely on its "music":

Pease | por-ridge | hot, |
Pease | por-ridge | cold, |
Pease | por-ridge | in the | pot |
Nine | days | old. |

There is very little sense here; the attraction comes from the emphatic rhythm, the emphatic rimes (with a strong contrast between the short vowel and short final consonant of *hot-pot* and the long vowel and long final consonant combination of *cold-old*), and the heavy alliteration (exactly half the words begin with *p*). From nonsense rimes such as this, many of us graduate into a love of more meaningful poems whose appeal resides largely in the sound they make. Much of the pleasure that we find in poems like Vachel Lindsay's "The Congo" and Edgar Allan Poe's "The Bells" lies in their musical qualities.

The peculiar function of poetry as distinguished from music, however, is to convey not sounds but meaning or experience *through* sounds. In third- and fourth-rate poetry, sound and rhythm sometimes distract attention from sense. In first-rate poetry the sound exists, not for its own sake, not for mere decoration, but as a medium of meaning. Its function is to support the leading player, not to steal the scene.

There are numerous ways in which the poet may reinforce meaning through sound. Without claiming to exhaust them, perhaps we can include most of the chief means under four general headings.

First, the poet can choose words whose sound in some degree suggests their meaning. In its narrowest sense this is called onomatopoeia. ONOMATOPOEIA, strictly defined, means the use of words which, at least supposedly, sound like what they mean, such as *hiss, snap,* and *bang.*

SONG: HARK, HARK!

Hark, hark!
  Bow-wow.
The watch-dogs bark!
  Bow-wow.
Hark, hark! I hear
The strain of strutting chanticleer
Cry, "Cock-a-doodle-doo!"

William Shakespeare (1564–1616)

In this lyric, "bark," "bow-wow," and "cock-a-doodle-doo" are onomatopoetic words. In addition, Shakespeare has reinforced the onomatopoetic effect with the repeated use of "hark," which sounds like "bark." The usefulness of onomatopoeia, of course, is strictly limited, because it can be used only where the poet is describing sound, and most poems do not describe sound. And the use of pure onomatopoeia, as in the above example, is likely to be fairly trivial except as it forms an incidental part of a more complex poem. But by combining onomatopoeia with other devices that help convey meaning, the poet can achieve subtle and beautiful effects whose recognition is one of the keenest pleasures in reading poetry.

In addition to onomatopoetic words there is another group of words, sometimes called PHONETIC INTENSIVES, whose sound, by a process as yet obscure, to some degree suggests their meaning. An initial *fl-* sound, for instance, is often associated with the idea of moving light, as in *flame, flare, flash, flicker, flimmer.* An initial *gl-* also frequently accompanies the idea of light, usually unmoving, as in *glare, gleam, glint, glow, glisten.* An initial *sl-* often introduces words meaning "smoothly wet," as in *slippery, slick, slide, slime, slop, slosh, slobber, slushy.* An initial *st-* often suggests strength, as in *staunch, stalwart, stout, sturdy, stable, steady, stocky, stern, strong, stubborn, steel.* Short *-i-* often goes with the idea of smallness, as in *inch, imp, thin, slim, little, bit, chip, sliver, chink, slit, sip, whit, tittle, snip, wink, glint, glimmer, flicker, pigmy, midge, chick, kid, kitten, minikin, miniature.* Long *-o-* or *-oo-* may suggest melancholy or sorrow, as in *moan, groan, woe, mourn, forlorn, toll, doom, gloom, moody.* Medial and final *-are* sometimes goes with the idea of a big light or noise, as *flare, glare, stare, blare.* Medial *-att-* suggests some kind of particled movement, as in *spatter, scatter, shatter, chatter, rattle, prattle, clatter, batter.* Final *-er* and *-le* indicate repetition, as in *glitter, flutter, shimmer, whisper, jabber, chatter, clatter, sputter, flicker, twitter, mutter,* and *ripple, bubble, twinkle, sparkle, rattle, rumble, jingle.* None of these various sounds is invariably associated with the idea that it seems to suggest, and, in fact, a short *-i-* is found in *thick* as well as *thin,* in *big* as well as *little.* Language is a complex phenomenon. But there is enough association between these sounds and ideas to suggest some sort of intrinsic if obscure relationship, and a word like *flicker,* though not onomatopoetic, for it does not refer to sound, would seem somehow to suggest its sense, the *fl-* suggesting moving light, the *-i-* suggesting smallness, the *-ck* suggesting sudden cessation of movement (as in *crack, peck, pick, hack,* and *flick*), and the *-er* suggesting repetition. The above list of sound-idea correspondences is only a very partial one. A complete list, though it would involve only a small proportion of words in the language, would probably be a longer list than that of the more strictly onomatopoetic words, to which they are related.

SPLINTER

> The voice of the last cricket
> across the first frost
> is one kind of good-by.
> It is so thin a splinter of singing.

> *Carl Sandburg (1878–1967)*

QUESTIONS

1. Why is "so thin a splinter" a better choice of metaphor than *so small an atom* or *so meager a morsel?*
2. How does the poet intensify the effect of the two phonetic intensives in line 4?

A second way that the poet can reinforce meaning through sound is to choose sounds and group them so that the effect is smooth and pleasant sounding (*euphonious*) or rough and harsh sounding (*cacophonous*). The vowels are in general more pleasing than the consonants, for the vowels are musical tones, whereas the consonants are merely noises. A line with a high percentage of vowel sounds in proportion to consonant sounds will therefore tend to be more melodious than one in which the proportion is low. The vowels and consonants themselves differ considerably in quality. The "long" vowels, such as those in *fate, reed, rime, coat, food,* and *dune* are fuller and more resonant than the "short" vowels, as in *fat, red, rim, cot, foot,* and *dun.* Of the consonants, some are fairly mellifluous, such as the "liquids," *l, m, n,* and *r;* the soft *v* and *f* sounds; the semi-vowels *w* and *y;* and such combinations as *th* and *wh.* Others, such as the "plosives," *b, d, g, k, p,* and *t,* are harsher and sharper in their effect. These differences in sound are the poet's materials. However, he will not necessarily seek out the sounds that are pleasing and attempt to combine them in melodious combinations. Rather, he will use euphonious and cacophonous combinations as they are appropriate to his content. Consider, for instance, the following poem.

UPON JULIA'S VOICE

> So smooth, so sweet, so silvery is thy voice,
> As, could they hear, the Damned would make no noise,
> But listen to thee (walking in thy chamber)
> Melting melodious words to Lutes of Amber.

Robert Herrick (1591-1674)

QUESTION

Literally, an amber lute is as nonsensical as a silver voice. What connotations do "Amber" and "silvery" have that contribute to the meaning of this poem?

There are no strictly onomatopoetic words in this poem, and yet the sound seems marvelously adapted to the sense. Especially remarkable are the first and last lines, those most directly concerned with Julia's voice. In the first line the sounds that most strike the ear are the unvoiced *s*'s and the soft *v*'s, supported by *th:* "*So* smoo*th, so* *sweet, so silvery* is *thy* *v*oice." In the fourth line the predominating sounds are the liquid consonants *m, l,* and *r,* supported by a *w:* "*Melting melodious words* to *Lutes* of *Amber.*" The least euphonious line in the poem, on the other hand, is the second, where the subject is the tormented in hell, not Julia's voice. Here the prominent sounds are the *d*'s, supported by a voiced *s* (a voiced *s* buzzes, unlike the unvoiced *s*'s in line 1), and two *k* sounds: "A*s,* could they hear, the *D*amne*d* would ma*k*e no noi*s*e." Throughout the poem there is a remarkable correspondence between the pleasant-sounding and the pleasant in idea, the unpleasant-sounding and the unpleasant in idea.

A third way in which a poet can reinforce meaning through sound is by controlling the speed and movement of the lines by the choice and use of meter, by the choice and arrangement of vowel and consonant sounds, and by the disposition of pauses. In meter the unaccented syllables go faster than the accented syllables; hence the triple meters are swifter than the duple. But the poet can vary the tempo of any meter by the use of substitute feet. Whenever two or more unaccented syllables come together, the effect will be to speed up the pace of the line; when two or more accented syllables come together, the effect will be to slow it down. This pace will also be affected by the vowel lengths and by whether the sounds are easily run together. The long vowels take longer to pronounce than the short ones. Some words are easily run together, while others demand that the position of the mouth be re-formed before the next word is uttered. It takes much longer, for instance, to say, "Watch dogs catch much meat" than to say, "My aunt is away," though the number of syllables is the same. And finally the poet can slow down the speed of a line through the introduction of grammatical and rhetorical pauses. Consider lines 54–56 from Tennyson's "Ulysses" (page 601):

> The lights | be-gin | to twin-kle from | the rocks; |
> The long | day wanes; | the slow | moon climbs; | the deep | 55
> Moans round | with man-ly voi-ces . . .

In these lines Tennyson wished the movement to be slow, in accordance with the slow waning of the long day and the slow climbing of the moon. His meter is iambic pentameter. This is not a swift meter, but in lines 55–56 he slows it down, (1) by introducing three spondaic feet, thus bringing three accented syllables together in three separate places; (2) by choosing for his accented syllables words that have long vowel sounds or dipthongs that the voice hangs on to: "long," "day," "wanes," "slow," "moon," "climbs," "deep," "moans," "round"; (3) by choosing words that are not easily run together (except for "day" and "slow," each of these words begins and ends with consonant sounds that demand varying degrees of readjustment of the mouth before pronunciation is continued); (4) by introducing two grammatical pauses, after "wanes" and "climbs," and a rhetorical pause after "deep." The result is an extremely effective use of the movement of the verse to accord with the movement suggested by the words.*

A fourth way for a poet to fit sound to sense is to control both sound and meter in such a way as to put emphasis on words that are important in meaning. He can do this by marking out such words by alliteration, assonance, consonance, or rime; by placing them before a pause; or by skillfully placing or displacing them in the metrical pattern. Look again at Shakespeare's "Spring" (page 524):

> When dai-sies pied | and vio-lets blue |
> And la-dy-smocks | all sil-ver-white |
> And cuck-oo-buds | of yel-low hue |
> Do paint | the mea-dows with | de-light, |
> The cuck-oo then, | on ev-ery tree, |
> Mocks mar-ried men; | for thus | sings he, |
>
> "Cuckoo!
>
> Cuckoo, cuckoo!" O, word of fear,
>
> Unpleasing to a married ear!

5

The scansion is regular until the beginning of the sixth line: there we find a spondaic substitution in the first foot. In addition, the first three words in this line are heavily alliterated, all beginning with *m*. And further, each of these words ends in a consonant, thus preventing their being run together. The result is to throw heavy emphasis on these three words: to give them, one might almost say, a tone of solemnity, or mock-solemnity. Whether or not the solemnity is in the sound, the emphasis on these three words is appropriate, for it serves to signal the shift in tone that takes place at this point. The first five lines have contained nothing but delightful images; the concluding four introduce the note of irony.

Just as Shakespeare uses metrical irregularity, plus alliteration, to give emphasis to important words, Tennyson, in the concluding line of "Ulysses," uses marked regularity, plus skillful use of grammatical pause, to achieve the same effect:

> Though much | is ta-ken, | much | a-bides; | and though |

*In addition, Tennyson uses one onomatopoetic word ("moans") and one phonetic intensive ("twinkle").

We are | not now | that strength | which in | old | days|
Moved earth | and heav-en, that | which we are, | we are:|
One e-qual tem-per of he-ro-ic hearts,|
Made weak | by time | and fate, | but strong | in will|
To strive, | to seek, | to find, | and not | to yield.|

The blank verse rhythm throughout "Ulysses" is remarkably subtle and varied, but the last line is not only regular in its scansion but heavily regular, for a number of reasons. First, all the words are monosyllables: no words cross over the divisions between feet. Second, the unaccented syllables are all very small and unimportant words—four "to's" and one "and," whereas the accented syllables consist of four important verbs and a very important "not." Third, each of the verbs is followed by a grammatical pause pointed off by a mark of punctuation. The result is to cause a pronounced alternation between light and heavy syllables that brings the accent down on the four verbs and the "not" with sledgehammer blows. The line rings out like a challenge, which it is.

THE SPAN OF LIFE

The old dog barks backward without getting up.
I can remember when he was a pup.

Robert Frost (1874–1963)

QUESTIONS

1. Is the dog a dog only or also a symbol?
2. The first line presents a visual and auditory image; the second line makes a comment. But does the second line *call up images?* Does it suggest more than it says? Would the poem have been more or less effective if the second line had been, "He was frisky and lively when he was a pup"?

We may well conclude our discussion of the adaptation of sound to sense by analyzing this very brief poem. It consists of one riming anapestic tetrameter couplet. Its content is a contrast between the decrepitude of an old dog and his friskiness as a pup. The scansion is as follows:

The old | dog barks back-ward with-out | get-ting up.|
I | can re-mem-ber when he | was a pup.|

How is sound fitted to sense? In the first place, the triple meter chosen by the poet is a swift meter, but in the first line he has jammed it up in a remarkable way by substituting a kind of foot so rare that we do not even have a name for it. It might be called a triple spondee: at any rate it is a foot in which the accent is distributed over three syllables. This foot, following the accented syllable in the first foot, creates a situation where four accented syllables are pushed up together. In addition, each of these accented syllables begins and ends with a strong consonant sound or cluster of consonant sounds, so that they cannot be run together in pronunciation: the mouth must be re-formed between each syllable: "The *old dog barks backward.*" The result is to slow down the line drastically, to almost destroy its rhythmical quality, and to make it difficult to utter. Indeed, the line is as decrepit as the old dog who turns his head to greet his master but does not get up. When we get to the second line, however, the contrast is startling. The rhythm is swift and regular, the syllables end in vowels or liquid consonants and are easily run together, the whole line ripples fluently off the tongue. In addition, where the first line has a high proportion of explosive and cacophonous consonants—"The ol*d dog barks backward* without *getting up*"—the second line contains predominantly consonants which are smoother and more graceful—"I ca*n remember when he was* a pup." Thus the motion and the sound of the lines are remarkably in accord with the visual images they suggest. In addition, in the first line the poet has supported the onomatopoetic word *barks* with a near echo *back*, so that the sound reinforces the auditory image. If the poem does a great deal in just two lines, this skillful adaptation of sound to sense is one very important reason.

In analyzing verse for correspondence between sound and sense, we need to be very cautious not to make exaggerated claims. A great deal of nonsense has been written about the moods of certain meters and the effects of certain sounds, and it is easy to suggest correspondences that exist really only in our imaginations. Nevertheless, the first-rate poet has nearly always an instinctive tact about handling his sound so that it in some degree supports his meaning; the inferior poet is usually obtuse to these correspondences. One of the few absolute rules that can be applied to the judgment of poetry is that the form should be adequate to the content. This rule does not mean that there must always be a close and easily demonstrable correspondence. It does mean that there will be no glaring discrepancies. Poor poets, and even good poets in their third-rate work, sometimes go horribly wrong.

The two selections that introduce this chapter illustrate, first, the use of sound in verse almost purely for its own sake ("Pease porridge hot"), and, second, the use of sound in verse almost purely to *imitate* meaning ("Hark, hark! Bow-wow"), and they are, as significant poetry, perhaps the most trivial pieces in the whole book. But in between these extremes there is an abundant range of poetic possibilities where sound is pleasurable for itself without violating meaning and where sound to varying degrees corresponds with and corroborates meaning; and in this rich middle range, for the reader who can learn to perceive them, lie many of the greatest pleasures of reading poetry.

EXERCISE

In which of the following pairs of quotations is sound more successfully adapted to sense? As precisely as possible, explain why. (The poet named is in each case the author of the superior version.)

1. a. Go forth—and Virtue, ever in your sight
      Shall be your guide by day, your guard by night.
   b. Go forth—and Virtue, ever in your sight,
      Shall point your way by day, and keep you safe at night.

Charles Churchill

2. a. How charming is divine philosophy!
      Not harsh and rough as foolish men suppose
      But musical as is the lute of Phoebus.
   b. How charming is divine philosophy!
      Not harsh and crabbed as dull fools suppose
      But musical as is Apollo's lute.

Milton

3. a. All day the fleeing crows croak hoarsely over the snow.
   b. All day the out-cast crows croak hoarsely across the whiteness.

Elizabeth Coatsworth

4. a. Your talk attests how bells of singing gold
      Would sound at evening over silent water.
   b. Your low voice tells how bells of singing gold
      Would sound at twilight over silent water.

Edwin Arlington Robinson

5. a. A thousand streamlets flowing through the lawn,
      The moan of doves in gnarled ancient oaks,
      And quiet murmuring of countless bees.
   b. Myriads of rivulets hurrying through the lawn,
      The moan of doves in immemorial elms,
      And murmuring of innumerable bees.

Tennyson

6. a. It is the lark that sings so out of tune,
      Straining harsh discords and unpleasing sharps.

b. It is the lark that warbles out of tune
   In harsh discordant tones with doleful flats.

Shakespeare

7. a. "Artillery" and "armaments" and "implements of war"
      Are phrases too severe to please the gentle Muse.
   b. Bombs, drums, guns, bastions, batteries, bayonets, bullets,—
      Hard words, which stick in the soft Muses' gullets.

Byron

8. a. The hands of the sisters Death and Night incessantly softly wash
         again, and ever again, this soiled world.
   b. The hands of the soft twins Death and Night repeatedly wash
         again, and ever again, this dirty world.

Whitman

9. a. The curfew sounds the knell of parting day,
      The lowing cattle slowly cross the lea,
      The plowman goes wearily plodding his homeward way,
      Leaving the world to the darkening night and me.
   b. The curfew tolls the knell of parting day,
      The lowing herd wind slowly o'er the lea,
      The plowman homeward plods his weary way,
      And leaves the world to darkness and to me.

Thomas Gray

10. a. Let me chastise this odious, gilded bug,
       This painted son of dirt, that smells and bites.
    b. Yet let me flap this bug with gilded wings,
       This painted child of dirt, that stinks and stings.

Pope

*   *   *

SOUND AND SENSE

True ease in writing comes from art, not chance,
As those move easiest who have learned to dance.
'Tis not enough no harshness gives offense,
The sound must seem an echo to the sense:
Soft is the strain when Zephyr gently blows,   5
And the smooth stream in smoother numbers flows;
But when loud surges lash the sounding shore,
The hoarse, rough verse should like the torrent roar;
When Ajax strives some rock's vast weight to throw,
The line too labors, and the words move slow;   10
Not so, when swift Camilla scours the plain,

Flies o'er the unbending corn, and skims along the main.
Hear how Timotheus' varied lays surprise,
And bid alternate passions fall and rise!

Alexander Pope (*1688–1744*)

QUESTIONS

1. Vocabulary: *numbers* (6), *lays* (13).
2. This excerpt is from a long poem (called *An Essay on Criticism*) on the arts of writing and judging poetry. Which line is the topic sentence of the passage?
3. There are four classical allusions: Zephyr (5) was god of the west wind; Ajax (9), a Greek warrior noted for his strength; Camilla (11), a legendary queen reputedly so fleet of foot that she could run over a field of grain without bending the blades or over the sea without wetting her feet; Timotheus (13), a famous Greek rhapsodic poet. Does the use of these allusions enable Pope to achieve greater economy?
4. Copy the passage and scan it. Then, considering both meter and sounds, show how Pope practices what he preaches. (Incidentally, on which syllable should "alternate" in line 14 be accented?)

I LIKE TO SEE IT LAP THE MILES

I like to see it lap the miles,
And lick the valleys up,
And stop to feed itself at tanks;
And then, prodigious, step

Around a pile of mountains,   5
And, supercilious, peer
In shanties by the sides of roads;
And then a quarry pare

To fit its ribs,
And crawl between,   10
Complaining all the while
In horrid, hooting stanza;
Then chase itself down hill

And neigh like Boanerges;
Then, punctual as a star,   15
Stop—docile and omnipotent—
At its own stable door.

Emily Dickinson (*1830–1886*)

1. Vocabulary: *prodigious* (4), *supercilious* (6), *Boanerges* (14).
2. What basic metaphor underlies the poem? Identify the literal and the metaphorical terms and explain how you were able to make both identifications.
3. What additional figures of speech do you find in lines 8, 12, 15, 16, and 17? Explain their appropriateness.
4. Point out examples of alliteration, assonance, and consonance. Does this poem have a rime scheme?
5. Considering such things as sounds and sound repetitions, grammatical pauses, run-on lines, monosyllabic and polysyllabic words, onomatopoeia, and meter, explain in detail how sound is fitted to sense in this poem.

WIND

This house has been far out at sea all night,
The woods crashing through darkness, the booming hills,
Winds stampeding the fields under the window
Floundering black astride and blinding wet

Till day rose; then under an orange sky   5
The hills had new places, and wind wielded
Blade-like, luminous black and emerald,
Flexing like the lens of a mad eye.

At noon I scaled along the house-side as far as
The coal-house door. I dared once to look up—   10
Through the brunt wind that dented the balls of my eyes
The tent of the hills drummed and strained its guyrope,

The fields quivering, the skyline a grimace,
At any second to bang and vanish with a flap:
The wind flung a magpie away and a black-   15
Back gull bent like an iron bar slowly. The house

Rang like some fine green goblet in the note
That any second would shatter it. Now deep
In chairs, in front of the great fire, we grip
Our hearts and cannot entertain book, thought,   20

Or each other. We watch the fire blazing,
And feel the roots of the house move, but sit on,
Seeing the window tremble to come in,
Hearing the stones cry out under the horizons.

Ted Hughes (b. 1930)

1. Explain the images, or metaphors, in lines 1, 3, 6, 7–8, 12–14, 15–16, 22. What kind of weather is the poem describing?
2. Discuss the adaptation of sound to sense.

HEAVEN-HAVEN

A Nun Takes the Veil

I have desired to go
    Where springs not fail,
To fields where flies no sharp and sided hail
    And a few lilies blow.

And I have asked to be
    Where no storms come,
Where the green swell is in the havens dumb,
    And out of the swing of the sea.

Gerard Manley Hopkins (1844–1889)

QUESTIONS

1. Vocabulary: *blow* (4).
2. Who is the speaker and what is the situation? Explain the metaphors that form the substance of the poem. What things are being compared?
3. Comment on the meaning of "springs" (2) and on the effectiveness of the poet's choice of "lilies" (4).
4. How do the sound repetitions of the title reinforce the meaning? Are there other instances in the poem where sound reinforces meaning?
5. Scan the poem. (The meter is basically iambic, but there is a great deal of variation.) How does the meter reinforce meaning, especially in the last line? What purpose is served by the displacement of "not" (2) from its normal order?

ANTHEM FOR DOOMED YOUTH

What passing-bells for these who die as cattle?
Only the monstrous anger of the guns.
Only the stuttering rifles' rapid rattle
Can patter out their hasty orisons.
No mockeries now for them; no prayers nor bells,   5
Nor any voice of mourning save the choirs,—
The shrill, demented choirs of wailing shells;
And bugles calling for them from sad shires.

What candles may be held to speed them all?
Not in the hands of boys, but in their eyes   10
Shall shine the holy glimmers of good-byes.
The pallor of girls' brows shall be their pall;
Their flowers the tenderness of patient minds,
And each slow dusk a drawing-down of blinds.

Wilfred Owen (1893–1918)

QUESTIONS

1. Vocabulary: *passing-bells* (1), *orisons* (4), *shires* (8), *pall* (12).
2. How do the octave and the sestet of this sonnet differ in (a) geographical setting, (b) subject matter, (c) kind of imagery used, and (d) tone? Who are the "boys" (10) and "girls" (12) referred to in the sestet? It was the custom during World War I to draw down the blinds in homes where a son had been lost (14).
3. What central metaphorical image runs throughout the poem? What secondary metaphors build up the central one?
4. Why are the "doomed youth" said to die "as cattle"? Why would prayers, bells, and so on, be "mockeries" for them (5)?
5. Show how sound is adapted to sense throughout the poem.

BOOT AND SADDLE

Boot, saddle, to horse, and away!
Rescue my castle before the hot day
Brightens to blue from its silvery gray.
    Chorus: *Boot, saddle, to horse, and away!*

Ride past the suburbs, asleep as you'd say;   5
Many's the friend there, will listen and pray,
"God's luck to gallants that strike up the lay—
    Chorus: *Boot, saddle, to horse, and away!"*

Forty miles off, like a roebuck at bay,
Flouts Castle Brancepeth the Roundheads' array;   10
Who laughs, "Good fellows ere this, by my fay,°   faith
    Chorus: *Boot, saddle, to horse, and away?"*

Who? My wife Gertrude; that, honest and gay,
Laughs when you talk of surrendering, "Nay!
I've better counselors; what counsel they?   15
    Chorus: *Boot, saddle, to horse, and away!"*

Robert Browning (1812–1889)

1. Vocabulary: *lay* (7).
2. The historical setting for this song is the English Civil War (1642-1649) between the Royalists (Cavaliers) and the Puritans (Roundheads). Who is the speaker? What is the situation? Who is imagined to be speaking in the three passages between quotation marks?
3. Comment on the choice of meter in relation to the subject, especially on the handling of the meter in the refrain.

NIGHT OF SPRING

> Slow, horses, slow,
> As through the wood we go—
> We would count the stars in heaven,
> Hear the grasses grow:
>
> Watch the cloudlets few   5
> Dappling the deep blue,
> In our open palms outspread
> Catch the blessèd dew.
>
> Slow, horses, slow,
> As through the wood we go—   10
> We would see fair Dian rise
> With her huntress bow:
>
> We would hear the breeze
> Ruffling the dim trees,
> Hear its sweet love-ditty set   15
> To endless harmonies.
>
> Slow, horses, slow,
> As through the wood we go—
> All the beauty of the night
> We would learn and know!   20

Thomas Westwood (1814-1888)

QUESTIONS

1. Vocabulary: *Dian* (11).
2. Compare and contrast this poem with the preceding poem in subject and situation, and in adaptation of sound and meter to sense, especially in the refrain.
3. Find phonetic intensives in stanzas 2 and 4. How do the rimes function in stanza 4?

EIGHT O'CLOCK

He stood, and heard the steeple
    Sprinkle the quarters on the morning town.
One, two, three, four, to market-place and people
    It tossed them down.

Strapped, noosed, nighing his hour,
    He stood and counted them and cursed his luck;
And then the clock collected in the tower
    Its strength, and struck.

A. E. Housman (1859–1936)

QUESTIONS

1. Vocabulary: *quarters* (2).
2. Eight A.M. is the traditional hour in England for putting condemned men to death. Discuss the force of "morning" (2) and "struck" (8). Discuss the appropriateness of the image of the clock collecting its strength. Can you suggest any reason for the use of "nighing" (5) rather than *nearing?*
3. Scan the poem and note its musical devices. Comment on the adaptation of sound to sense.

ALL DAY I HEAR

All day I hear the noise of waters
    Making moan,
Sad as the sea-bird is, when going
    Forth alone,
He hears the winds cry to the waters'   5
    Monotone.

The grey winds, the cold winds are blowing
    Where I go.
I hear the noise of many waters
    Far below.   10
All day, all night, I hear them flowing
    To and fro.

James Joyce (1882–1941)

QUESTIONS

1. What is the central purpose of the poem? Is it primarily descriptive?
2. What kinds of imagery does the poem contain?

3. Discuss the adaptation of sound to meaning, commenting on the use of onomatopoeia, phonetic intensives, alliteration, consonance, rime, vowel quality, stanzaic structure, the counterpointing of the rhythmically varied long lines with the rhythmically regular short lines.

THE DANCE

In Breughel's great picture, The Kermess,
the dancers go round, they go round and
around, the squeal and the blare and the
tweedle of bagpipes, a bugle and fiddles
tipping their bellies (round as the thick-   5
sided glasses whose wash they impound)
their hips and their bellies off balance
to turn them. Kicking and rolling about
the Fair Grounds, swinging their butts, those
shanks must be sound to bear up under such   10
rollicking measures, prance as they dance
in Breughel's great picture, The Kermess.

William Carlos Williams (1883–1963)

QUESTION

Peter Breughel, the Elder, was a sixteenth-century Flemish painter of peasant life. A *kermess* is an annual outdoor festival or fair. How do the form, the meter, and the sounds of this poem reinforce its content?

TO FOOL, OR KNAVE

Thy praise or dispraise is to me alike:
One doth not stroke me, nor the other strike.

Ben Jonson (1573?–1637)

14. Pattern

A rt, ultimately, is organization. It is a searching after order, after form. The primal artistic act was God's creation of the universe out of chaos, shaping the formless into form; and every artist since, on a lesser scale, has sought to imitate Him—by selection and arrangement to reduce the chaotic in experience to a meaningful and pleasing order. For this reason we evaluate a poem partially by the same criteria that an English instructor uses to evaluate a theme—by its unity, its coherence, and its proper placing of emphasis. In a well-constructed poem there is neither too little nor too much; every part of the poem belongs where it is and could be placed nowhere else; any interchanging of two stanzas, two lines, or even two words, would to some extent damage the poem and make it less effective. We come to feel, with a truly first-rate poem, that the choice and placement of every word is inevitable, that it could not be otherwise.

In addition to the internal ordering of materials—the arrangement of ideas, images, and thoughts, which we may refer to as the poem's STRUCTURE—the poet may impose some external pattern on his poem, may give it not only an inside logical order but an outside symmetry, or FORM. In doing so, he appeals to the human instinct for design, the instinct that has prompted men, at various times, to tattoo and paint their bodies, to decorate their swords and armor with beautiful and complex tracery, and to choose patterned fabrics for their clothing, carpets, curtains, and wallpapers. The poet appeals to our love of the shapely.

In general, there are three broad kinds of form into which the poet may cast his work: continuous form, stanzaic form, and fixed form.

In CONTINUOUS FORM, as illustrated by "Had I the Choice" (page

698), "Dover Beach" (page 772), "Ulysses" (page 601), and "My Last Duchess" (page 626), the element of formal design is slight. The lines follow each other without formal grouping, the only breaks being dictated by units of meaning, as paragraph breaks are in prose. Even here there are degrees of formal pattern. The free verse "Had I the Choice" has neither regular meter nor rime. "Dover Beach," on the other hand, is metrical; it has no regularity in length of line, but the meter is prevailingly iambic. "Ulysses" is regular in both meter and length of line; it is unrimed iambic pentameter, or blank verse. And to these regularities "My Last Duchess" adds regularity of rime, for it is written in riming iambic pentameter couplets. Thus, in increasing degrees, the authors of "Dover Beach," "Ulysses," and "My Last Duchess" have chosen a predetermined pattern in which to cast their work.

In STANZAIC FORM the poet writes in a series of STANZAS, that is, repeated units having the same number of lines, usually the same metrical pattern, and often an identical rime scheme. The poet may choose some traditional stanza pattern (for poetry, like colleges, is rich in tradition) or invent his own. The traditional stanza patterns (for example, terza rima, ballad meter, rime royal, Spenserian stanza) are many, and the student specializing in literature will wish to familiarize himself with some of them; the general student should know that they exist. Often the use of one of these traditional stanza forms constitutes a kind of literary allusion. The reader who is conscious of its traditional use or of its use by a previous great poet will be aware of subtleties in the communication that a less well-read reader may miss.

As with continuous form, there are degrees of formal pattern in stanzaic form. In "Being Herded Past the Prison's Honor Farm" (page 557) the stanzas are alike only in each having the same number of lines. In "Poem in October" (page 725) the stanzas are alike in length of line but are without a regular pattern of rime. In "Virtue" (page 682) a rime pattern is added to a metrical pattern. In Shakespeare's "Winter" (page 520) and "Spring" (page 524), a refrain is employed in addition to the patterns of meter and rime. The following poem illustrates additional elements of design:

THE GREEDY THE PEOPLE

the greedy the people
(as if as can yes)
they sell and they buy
and they die for because

though the bell in the steeple   5
says Why

the chary the wary
(as all as can each)
they don't and they do
and they turn to a which   10
though the moon in her glory
says Who

the busy the millions
(as you're as can i'm)
they flock and they flee   15
through a thunder of seem
though the stars in their silence
say Be

the cunning the craven
(as think as can feel)   20
they when and they how
and they live for until
though the sun in his heaven
says Now

the timid the tender   25
(as doubt as can trust)
they work and they pray
and they bow to a must
though the earth in her splendor
says May   30

e. e. cummings (1894–1962)

QUESTIONS

1. This poem is a constellation of interlocking patterns. To appreciate them
fully, read it first in the normal fashion, one line after another; then read all
the first lines of the stanzas, followed by the second lines, the third lines, and
so on. Having done this, describe (a) the rime scheme; (b) the metrical design;
(c) the sound pattern (How are the two main words in each of the first lines
related?); (d) the syntactical pattern. Prepare a model of the poem in which
the recurring words are written out, blanks are left for varying words, and
recurring parts of speech are indicated in parentheses. The model for the
third lines would be: *they* [*verb*] *and they* [*verb*]. Describe the pattern of
meaning. How do the last two lines of each stanza relate to the first four?
What blanks in your model are to be filled in by words related in meaning?
2. A trademark of e. e. cummings as a poet is his imaginative freedom with parts

of speech. For instance, in line 21 he uses conjunctions as verbs. What different parts of speech does he use as nouns in the fourth line of each stanza? Can you see meanings for these unusual nouns? Explain the contrast between the last words in the fourth and sixth lines of each stanza. What two meanings has the final word of the poem?

3. Sum up briefly the meaning of the poem.

A stanza form may be described by designating four things: the rime scheme (if there is one), the position of the refrain (if there is one), the prevailing metrical foot, and the number of feet in each line. Rime scheme is traditionally designated by using letters of the alphabet to indicate the riming lines, and x for unrimed lines. Refrain lines may be indicated by a capital letter, and the number of feet in the line by a numerical exponent after the letter. Thus the stanza pattern of Browning's "Meeting at Night" (page 561) is iambic tetrameter $abccba$ (or iambic $abccba^4$); that of cummings's "if everything happens that can't be done" (page 694) is anapestic $a^4x^2x^1a^1b^4x^1x^1b^2a^3$; that of Shakespeare's "Spring" (page 524) is iambic $ababCC^4X^1DD^4$.

A FIXED FORM is a traditional pattern that applies to a whole poem. In French poetry many fixed forms have been widely used: rondeaus, roundels, villanelles, triolets, sestinas, ballades, double ballades, and others. In English poetry, though most of the fixed forms have been experimented with, perhaps only two—the limerick and the sonnet—have really taken hold.

The LIMERICK, though really a subliterary form, will serve to illustrate the fixed form in general. Its pattern is anapestic $aa^3bb^2a^3$:

> There was | a young la-dy of Ni-ger
> Who smiled | as she rode | on a ti-ger;
> They re-turned | from the ride
> With the la-dy in-side,
> And the smile | on the face | of the ti-ger.
>
> *Anonymous*

The limerick form is used exclusively for humorous and nonsense verse, for which, with its swift catchy meter, short lines, and emphatic rimes, it is particularly suitable. By trying to recast these little jokes and bits of nonsense in a different meter and pattern or into prose, we may discover how much of their effect they owe particularly to the limerick form.

There is, of course, no magical or mysterious identity between certain forms and certain types of content, but there may be more or less correspondence. A form may be appropriate or inappropriate. The limerick form is inappropriate for the serious treatment of serious material.

The SONNET is less rigidly prescribed than the limerick. It must be fourteen lines in length, and it almost always is iambic pentameter, but in structure and rime scheme there may be considerable leeway. Most sonnets, however, conform more or less closely to one of two general models or types, the Italian and the English.

The ITALIAN or *Petrarchan* SONNET (so called because the Italian poet Petrarch practiced it so extensively) is divided usually between eight lines called the octave, using two rimes arranged *abbaabba,* and six lines called the sestet, using any arrangement of either two or three rimes: *cdcdcd* and *cdecde* are common patterns. Usually in the Italian sonnet, corresponding to the division between octave and sestet indicated by the rime scheme (and sometimes marked off in printing by a space), there is a division of thought. The octave presents a situation and the sestet a comment, or the octave an idea and the sestet an example, or the octave a question and the sestet an answer. Thus the form reflects the structure.

ON FIRST LOOKING INTO CHAPMAN'S HOMER

Much have I traveled in the realms of gold,
    And many goodly states and kingdoms seen;
    Round many western islands have I been
Which bards in fealty to Apollo hold.
Oft of one wide expanse had I been told   5
    That deep-browed Homer ruled as his demesne;
    Yet did I never breathe its pure serene
Till I heard Chapman speak out loud and bold:
Then felt I like some watcher of the skies
    When a new planet swims into his ken;   10
Or like stout Cortez when with eagle eyes
    He stared at the Pacific—and all his men
Looked at each other with a wild surmise—
    Silent, upon a peak in Darien.

John Keats (1795–1821)

QUESTIONS

1. Vocabulary: *fealty* (4), *Apollo* (4), *demesne* (6), *ken* (10). *Darien* (14) is an ancient name for the isthmus of Panama.

2. John Keats, at twenty-one, could not read Greek and was probably acquainted with Homer's *Iliad* and *Odyssey* only through the translations of Alexander Pope, which to him would have seemed prosy and stilted. Then one day he and a friend found a vigorous poetic translation by the Elizabethan poet George Chapman. Keats and his friend, enthralled, sat up late at night excitedly reading aloud to each other from Chapman's book. Toward morning Keats walked home and, before going to bed, wrote the above sonnet and sent it to his friend. What common ideas underlie the three major figures of speech in the poem?
3. What is the rime scheme? What division of thought corresponds to the division between octave and sestet?
4. Balboa, not Cortez, discovered the Pacific. How seriously does this mistake detract from the value of the poem?

The ENGLISH or *Shakespearean* SONNET (invented by the English poet Surrey and made famous by Shakespeare) is composed of three quatrains and a concluding couplet, riming *abab cdcd efef gg*. Again, there is often a correspondence between the units marked off by the rimes and the development of the thought. The three quatrains, for instance, may present three examples and the couplet a conclusion or (as in the following example) three metaphorical statements of one idea plus an application.

THAT TIME OF YEAR

That time of year thou mayst in me behold
When yellow leaves, or none, or few, do hang
Upon those boughs which shake against the cold,
Bare ruined choirs where late the sweet birds sang.
In me thou see'st the twilight of such day   5
As after sunset fadeth in the west,
Which by and by black night doth take away,
Death's second self, that seals up all in rest.
In me thou see'st the glowing of such fire,
That on the ashes of his youth doth lie   10
As the deathbed whereon it must expire,
Consumed with that which it was nourished by.
　　This thou perceivest, which makes thy love more strong,
　　To love that well which thou must leave ere long.

William Shakespeare (1564–1616)

QUESTIONS

1. What are the three major images introduced by the three quatrains? What do they have in common? Can you see any reason for presenting them in this particular order, or might they be rearranged without loss?

2. Each of the images is to some degree complicated rather than simple. For instance, what additional image is introduced by "bare ruined choirs" (4)? Explain its appropriateness.
3. What additional comparisons are introduced in the second and third quatrains? Explain line 12.
4. Whom does the speaker address? What assertion does he make in the concluding couplet, and with what degree of confidence? Paraphrase these lines so as to state their meaning as clearly as possible.

At first glance it may seem absurd that a poet should choose to confine himself in an arbitrary fourteen-line mold with prescribed meter and rime scheme. He does so partly from the desire to carry on a tradition, as all of us carry out certain traditions for their own sake, else why should we bring a tree indoors at Christmas time? But, in addition, the tradition of the sonnet has proved a useful one for, like the limerick, it seems effective for certain types of subject matter and treatment. Though this area cannot be as narrowly limited or as rigidly described as for the limerick, the sonnet is usually most effective when used for the serious treatment of love but has also been used for the discussion of death, religion, political situations, and related subjects. Again, there is no magical affinity between form and subject, or treatment, and excellent sonnets have been written outside these traditional areas. The sonnet tradition has also proved useful because it has provided a challenge to the poet. The inferior poet, of course, is often defeated by that challenge: he will use unnecessary words to fill out his meter or inappropriate words for the sake of his rime. The good poet is inspired by the challenge: it will call forth ideas and images that might not otherwise have come. He will subdue his form rather than be subdued by it; he will make it do his will. There is no doubt that the presence of a net makes good tennis players more precise in their shots than they otherwise would be. And finally, there is in all form the pleasure of form itself.

EXERCISES

1. "One Art" (page 776), "The Waking" (page 815), and "Do not go gentle into that good night" (page 822) are all examples of the French fixed form known as the *villanelle*. After reading the poems and studying their form, define the *villanelle*.
2. "Acquainted with the Night" (page 792) is written in the stanzaic form known as *terza rima* (most famous for its use by Dante in *The Divine Comedy*). Study its rime scheme and give a description of *terza rima*.
3. Reread the following sonnets; classify each (when possible) as primarily Italian or primarily English; then specify how closely each sticks to or how far it

departs from (in form and structure) the polarities represented by "On First Looking into Chapman's Homer" and "That time of year":

a. "When my love swears that she is made of truth," page 548.
b. "Spring," page 568.
c. "The Silken Tent," page 580.
d. "Redemption," page 598.
e. "Ozymandias," page 617.
f. "Batter my heart, three-personed God," page 620.
g. "On His Blindness," page 633.
h. "Leda and the Swan," page 636.
i. "Design," page 645.
j. "when serpents bargain for the right to squirm," page 647.
k. "The Caged Skylark," page 648.
l. "Since there's no help," page 657.
m. "God's Grandeur," page 671.
n. "Anthem for Doomed Youth," page 712.

*   *   *

A HANDFUL OF LIMERICKS *

I sat next the Duchess at tea.
It was just as I feared it would be:
    Her rumblings abdominal
    Were simply abominable,
And everyone thought it was me.

There was a young lady of Lynn
Who was so uncommonly thin
    That when she essayed
    To drink lemonade
She slipped through the straw and fell in.

A tutor who tooted the flute
Tried to tutor two tooters to toot.
    Said the two to the tutor,
    "Is it harder to toot or
To tutor two tooters to toot?"

There was a young maid who said, "Why
Can't I look in my ear with my eye?
    If I put my mind to it,

---

* Most limericks are anonymous. If not written anonymously, they soon become so, unfortunately for the glory of their authors, because of repeated oral transmission and reprinting without accreditation.

I'm sure I can do it.
You never can tell till you try."

There was an old man of Peru
Who dreamt he was eating his shoe.
  He awoke in the night
  In a terrible fright,
And found it was perfectly true!

A decrepit old gas man named Peter,
While hunting around for the meter,
  Touched a leak with his light.
  He arose out of sight,
And, as anyone can see by reading this, he
   also destroyed the meter.

Well, it's partly the shape of the thing
That gives the old limerick wing;
  These accordion pleats
  Full of airy conceits
Take it up like a kite on a string.

POEM IN OCTOBER

It was my thirtieth year to heaven
Woke to my hearing from harbor and neighbor wood
  And the mussel pooled and the heron
    Priested shore
   The morning beckon   5
With water praying and call of seagull and rook
And the knock of sailing boats on the net webbed wall
    Myself to set foot
    That second
In the still sleeping town and set forth.   10

My birthday began with the water-
Birds and the birds of the winged trees flying my name
  Above the farms and the white horses
    And I rose
   In rainy autumn   15
And walked abroad in a shower of all my days.
High tide and the heron dived when I took the road
    Over the border
    And the gates
Of the town closed as the town awoke.   20

A springful of larks in a rolling
Cloud and the roadside bushes brimming with whistling
   Blackbirds and the sun of October
      Summery
      On the hill's shoulder,   25
Here were fond climates and sweet singers suddenly
Come in the morning where I wandered and listened
     To the rain wringing
      Wind blow cold
In the woods faraway under me.   30

   Pale rain over the dwindling harbor
And over the sea wet church the size of a snail
    With its horns through mist and the castle
       Brown as owls
       But all the gardens   35
Of spring and summer were blooming in the tall tales
Beyond the border and under the lark full cloud.
     There could I marvel
       My birthday
Away but the weather turned around.   40

   It turned away from the blithe country
And down the other air and the blue altered sky
    Streamed again a wonder of summer
       With apples
       Pears and red currants   45
And I saw in the turning so clearly a child's
Forgotten mornings when he walked with his mother
     Through the parables
       Of sun light
And the legends of the green chapels   50

   And the twice told fields of infancy
That his tears burned my cheeks and his heart moved in mine.
    These were the woods the river and sea
       Where a boy
       In the listening   55
Summertime of the dead whispered the truth of his joy
To the trees and the stones and the fish in the tide.
     And the mystery
       Sang alive
Still in the water and singingbirds.   60

   And there could I marvel my birthday
Away but the weather turned around. And the true
    Joy of the long dead child sang burning

                    In the sun.
          It was my thirtieth   65
Year to heaven stood there then in the summer noon
Though the town below lay leaved with October blood.
          O may my heart's truth
                    Still be sung
On this high hill in a year's turning.   70

                                    Dylan Thomas (1914–1953)

QUESTIONS

1. The setting is a small fishing village on the coast of Wales. The poet's first name in Welsh means "water" (12). Trace the poet's walk in relation to the village, the weather, and the time of day.
2. "The weather turned around" is an expression indicating a change in the weather or the direction of the wind. In what psychological sense does the weather turn around during the poet's walk? Who is "the long dead child" (63), and what kind of child was he? With what wish does the poem close?
3. Explain "thirtieth year to heaven" (1), "horns" (33), "tall tales" (36), "green chapels" (50), "October blood" (67).
4. The elaborate stanza pattern in this poem is based not on the meter (which is very free) but on a syllable count. How many syllables are there in each line of the stanza? (In line 1 "thirtieth" may be counted as only two syllables.) Notice that the stanzas 1 and 3 consist of exactly one sentence each.
5. The poem makes a considerable use of approximate rime, though not according to a regular pattern. Point out examples.

TWO JAPANESE HAIKU

The lightning flashes!   A lightning gleam:
And slashing through the darkness,   into darkness travels
    A night-heron's screech.   a night heron's scream.

                              Matsuo Bashō (1644–1694)

    The falling flower   Fallen flowers rise
I saw drift back to the branch   back to the branch—I watch:
    Was a butterfly.   oh . . . butterflies!

                                 Moritake (1452–1540)

QUESTION

The *haiku,* a Japanese form, consists of three lines with five, seven, and five syllables respectively. The translators of the left-hand versions above (Earl Miner and Babette Deutsch respectively) preserve this syllable count; the translator of the right-hand versions (Harold G. Henderson) seeks to preserve the sense of formal structure by making the first and last lines rime. Moritake's haiku, as Miss Deutsch points out, "refers to the Buddhist proverb that the fallen flower never returns to the branch; the broken mirror never again reflects." From these two examples, what would you say are the characteristics of effective haiku?

WHEN I WAS ONE-AND-TWENTY

When I was one-and-twenty
    I heard a wise man say,
"Give crowns and pounds and guineas
    But not your heart away;
Give pearls away and rubies   5
    But keep your fancy free."
But I was one-and-twenty,
    No use to talk to me.

When I was one-and-twenty
    I heard him say again,   10
"The heart out of the bosom
    Was never given in vain;
'Tis paid with sighs a-plenty
    And sold for endless rue."
And I am two-and-twenty,   15
    And oh, 'tis true, 'tis true.

A. E. Housman (1859–1936)

QUESTIONS

1. Vocabulary: *fancy* (6), *rue* (14). Crowns, pounds, and guineas (3) are valuable English coins. The phrase "in vain" (12) here means "for nothing."
2. Describe (a) the metrical and rime pattern and (b) the thought structure of the two stanzas, as compared with each other. How do parallelism and contrast contribute to the poem's effectiveness? What central event is implied rather than stated?
3. Is the poem valuable primarily as an expression of wisdom or of truth of feeling?

PIAZZA PIECE

    —I am a gentleman in a dustcoat trying
To make you hear. Your ears are soft and small
And listen to an old man not at all,

They want the young men's whispering and sighing.
But see the roses on your trellis dying   5
And hear the spectral singing of the moon;
For I must have my lovely lady soon,
I am a gentleman in a dustcoat trying.

—I am a lady young in beauty waiting
Until my truelove comes, and then we kiss.   10
But what grey man among the vines is this
Whose words are dry and faint as in a dream?
Back from my trellis, Sir, before I scream!
I am a lady young in beauty waiting.

John Crowe Ransom (1888-1974)

QUESTIONS

1. What is the setting? Who is the "gentleman in a dustcoat" (a dustcoat was a light linen overcoat worn to protect the clothing of a traveler from dust)? What images and connotations suggest his identity? Do you think of any traditional subject of art and music of which this is a literary analogue?
2. What variations does this poem play on the traditional form and structure of the Italian sonnet? What is the effect in lines 8 and 14 of cutting off after the participle the thoughts expressed in lines 1-2 and 9-10 respectively?

FROM ROMEO AND JULIET

ROMEO   If I profane with my unworthiest hand
        This holy shrine, the gentle sin is this;
        My lips, two blushing pilgrims, ready stand
        To smooth that rough touch with a tender kiss.
JULIET Good pilgrim, you do wrong your hand too much,   5
        Which mannerly devotion shows in this;
        For saints have hands that pilgrims' hands do touch,
        And palm to palm is holy palmers' kiss.
ROMEO   Have not saints lips, and holy palmers too?
JULIET Ay, pilgrim, lips that they must use in prayer.   10
ROMEO   O! then, dear saint, let lips do what hands do;
        They pray, Grant thou, lest faith turn to despair.
JULIET Saints do not move,° though grant for prayers'   propose,
             sake.   instigate
ROMEO   Then move not, while my prayers' effect I take.

William Shakespeare (1564-1616)

QUESTIONS

1. These fourteen lines have been lifted out of Act I, scene 5, of Shakespeare's play. They are the first words exchanged between Romeo and Juliet, who are meeting, for the first time, at a masquerade ball given by her father. Romeo is dressed as a pilgrim. Struck by Juliet's beauty, he has come up to greet her. What stage action accompanies this passage?
2. What is the basic metaphor employed? How does it affect the tone of the relationship between Romeo and Juliet?
3. What play on words do you find in lines 8 and 13–14? What two meanings has line 11?
4. By meter and rime scheme, these lines form a sonnet. Do you think this was coincidental or intentional on Shakespeare's part? Discuss.

THE MAGICIAN SUSPENDS THE CHILDREN

With this charm I keep the boy at six
and the girl fast at five
almost safe behind the four
walls of family. We three
are a feathery totem I tattoo   5
against time: I'll be one

again. Joy here is hard-won
but possible. Protector of six
found toads, son, you feel too
much, my Halloween mouse. Your five   10
finger exercises predict no three
quarter time gliding for

you. Symphonic storms are the fore-
cast, nothing unruffled for my wun-
derkind. Have two children: make three   15
journeys upstream. Son, at six
you run into angles where five
let you curve, let me hold onto

your fingers in drugstores. Too
intent on *them,* you're before   20
or behind me five
paces at least. Let no one
tie the sturdy boat of your six
years to me the grotesque, the three

headed mother. More than three   25
times you'll deny me. And my cockatoo,
my crested girl, how you cry to be six.

Age gathers on your fore-
head with that striving. Everyone
draws your lines and five   30

breaks out like a rash, five
crouches, pariah of the three
o'clock male rendezvous. Oh wonderful girl, my impromptu
rainbow, believe it: you'll be four-   35
teen before you're six.

This is the one abracadabra I know to
keep us three, keep you five and six.
Grow now. Sing. Fly. Do what you're here for.

Carole Oles (b. 1939)

QUESTIONS

1. Vocabulary: *totem* (5), *tattoo* (5), *pariah* (32), *abracadabra* (37). "Wunderkind"
   (14-15) is a familiar German word meaning "child prodigy" (literally, "wonder child").
2. Who is the speaker in the poem? How old are her children? What would she
   like to do? How does this conflict with the wishes of her children? Does it
   conflict even with her own wish? Explain.
3. In what lines of the poem does the speaker address (a) herself, (b) her son,
   (c) her daughter, (d) both children? Does she do so in speech or in thought?
4. Who is the "Magician" of the title? What are "this charm" (1) and "the one
   abracadabra I know" (37)?
5. Explain the allusion in lines 25-26, and the paradox in lines 35-36.
6. In form this poem is a *sestina*, a fixed form consisting of six six-line stanzas, in
   which end-rime is replaced by a pattern of six recurrent end-words following
   a shifting but prescribed sequence in each stanza, plus a three-line *envoy*. The
   envoy must use the last three end-words of stanza six and must also include
   the remaining three end-words somewhere *within* its lines. The challenge to
   the poet is not only to fulfill a very demanding form gracefully, but also,
   while using the same end-words seven times, to avoid monotony. How does
   this poet meet the latter challenge? (For another example of a sestina, see page
   810.)

EDWARD

"Why dois° your brand° sae drap wi bluid,   does; sword
        Edward, Edward,
Why dois your brand sae drap wi bluid,
        And why sae sad gang° yee O?"   go
"O I hae killed my hauke sae guid,   5

Mither, mither,
O I hae killed my hauke sae guid,
And I had nae mair bot hee O."

"Your haukis bluid was nevir sae reid,
Edward, Edward,   10
Your haukis bluid was nevir sae reid,
My deir son I tell thee O."
"O I hae killed my reid-roan steid,
Mither, mither,
O I hae killed my reid-roan steid,   15
That erst° was sae fair and frie° O."   formerly; spirited

"Your steid was auld, and ye hae got mair,
Edward, Edward,
Your steid was auld, and ye hae got mair,
Sum other dule° ye drie° O."   grief; suffer 20
"O I hae killed my fadir deir,
Mither, mither,
O I hae killed my fadir deir,
Alas, and wae is mee O!"

"And whatten penance wul ye drie for that,   25
Edward, Edward,
And whatten penance wul ye drie for that?
My deir son, now tell me O."
"Ile set my feit in yonder boat,
Mither, mither,   30
Ile set my feit in yonder boat,
And Ile fare ovir the sea O."

"And what wul ye doe wi your towirs and your ha,°   hall
Edward, Edward,
And what wul ye doe wi your towirs and your ha,   35
That were sae fair to see O?"
"Ile let thame stand tul they doun fa,°   fall
Mither, mither,
Ile let thame stand tul they doun fa,
For here nevir mair maun° I bee O."   must 40

"And what wul ye leive to your bairns° and your wife,   children
Edward, Edward,
And what wul ye leive to your bairns and your wife,
Whan ye gang ovir the sea O?"   44

"The warldis° room, late them beg thrae° life,   world's; through
    Mither, mither,
The warldis room, late them beg thrae life,
    For thame nevir mair wul I see O."

"And what wul ye leive to your ain mither deir,
    Edward, Edward?   50
And what wul ye leive to your ain mither deir?
    My deir son, now tell me O."
"The curse of hell frae me sall ye beir,
    Mither, mither,
The curse of hell frae me sall ye beir,   55
    Sic° counseils ye gave to me O."   Such

Anonymous

QUESTIONS

1. What has Edward done and why? Where do the two climaxes of the poem come?
2. Tell as much as you can about Edward and his feelings toward what he has done. From what class of society is he? Why does he at first give false answers to his mother's questions? What reversal of feelings and loyalties has he undergone? Do his answers about his hawk and steed perhaps indicate his present feelings toward his father? How do you explain his behavior to his wife and children? What are his present feelings toward his mother?
3. Tell as much as you can about Edward's mother. Why does she ask what Edward has done—doesn't she already know? Is there any clue as to the motivation of her deed? How skillful is she in her questioning? What do we learn about her from her dismissal of Edward's steed as "auld" and only one of many (17)? From her asking Edward what penance *he* will do for his act (25)? From her reference to herself as Edward's "ain mither deir" (49)?
4. Structure and form are both important in this poem. Could any of the stanzas be interchanged without loss, or do they build up steadily to the two climaxes? What effect has the constant repetition of the two short refrains, "Edward, Edward" and "Mither, mither"? What is the effect of the final "O" at the end of each speech? Does the repetition of each question and answer simply waste words or does it add to the suspense and emotional intensity? (Try reading the poem omitting the third and seventh lines of each stanza. Is it improved or weakened?)
5. Much of what happened is implied, much is omitted. Does the poem gain anything in power from what is *not* told?

400-METER FREESTYLE

THE GUN full swing the swimmer catapults and cracks

                                                    s

                                                    i

                                                    x

feet   away   onto   that   perfect   glass   he   catches   at   5
a

n

d

throws behind him scoop after scoop cunningly moving

                                                    t   10

                                                    h

                                                    e

water back to move him forward. Thrift is his wonderful
s

e   15

c

ret; he has schooled out all extravagance. No muscle

                                                    r

                                                    i

                                                    p   20

ples without compensation wrist cock to heel snap to
h

i

s

mobile mouth that siphons in the air that nurtures   25

                                                    h

                                                    i

                                                    m

at half an inch above sea level so to speak.

T   30

h

e

astonishing whites of the soles of his feet rise

                                                    a

                                                    n   35

                                                    d

salute us on the turns. He flips, converts, and is gone
a

l

l   40

in one. We watch him for signs. His arms are steady at

                                                    t

                                                    h

                                                    e

catch, his cadent feet tick in the stretch, they know   45
t
h
e
lesson well. Lungs know, too; he does not list for
                                                    a   50
                                                    i

                                                    r
he drives along on little sips carefully expended
b
u   55
t
that plum red heart pumps hard cries hurt how soon
                                                    i

                                                    t

                                                    s   60
near one more and makes its final surge TIME: 4:25:9

Maxine Kumin (*b. 1925*)

QUESTIONS

1. To what quality or qualities does this poem essentially pay tribute? What sentence in the poem most nearly expresses its theme?
2. Does the poem itself exhibit the qualities which it praises? Discuss.
3. How does the visual form of the poem reflect its content?

A CHRISTMAS TREE

Star
If you are
A love compassionate,
You will walk with us this year.
We face a glacial distance, who are here
Huddld
At your feet.

William Burford (*b. 1927*)

QUESTION

Why do you think the author misspelled "huddled" in line 6?

15. Bad Poetry and Good

The attempt to evaluate a poem should never be made before the poem is understood; and, unless one has developed the capacity to feel some poetry deeply, any judgments he makes will be worthless. A person who likes no wines can hardly be a judge of them. But the ability to make judgments, to discriminate between good and bad, great and good, good and half-good, is surely a primary object of all liberal education, and one's appreciation of poetry is incomplete unless it includes discrimination. Of the mass of verse that appears each year in print, as of all literature, most is "flat, stale, and unprofitable"; a very, very little is of any enduring value.

In judging a poem, as in judging any work of art, we need to ask three basic questions: (1) *What is its central purpose?* (2) *How fully has this purpose been accomplished?* (3) *How important is this purpose?* The first question we need to answer in order to understand the poem. The last two questions are those by which we evaluate it. The first of these measures the poem on a scale of perfection. The second measures it on a scale of significance. And, just as the area of a rectangle is determined by multiplying its measurements on two scales, breadth and height, so the greatness of a poem is determined by multiplying its measurements on two scales, perfection and significance. If the poem measures well on the first of these scales, we call it a good poem, at least of its kind. If it measures well on both scales, we call it a great poem.*

---

*As indicated in the footnote on page 535, some objection has been made to the use of the term "purpose" in literary criticism. For the two criteria suggested above may be substituted these two: (1) How thoroughly are the materials of the poem integrated or unified? (2) How many and how diverse are the materials that it integrates? Thus a poem becomes successful in proportion to the tightness of its organization—that is, according to the degree to which all its elements work together and require each other to produce the total effect—and it becomes great in proportion to its scope—that is, according to the amount and diversity of the material it amalgamates into unity.

The measurement of a poem is a much more complex process, of course, than is the measurement of a rectangle. It cannot be done as exactly. Agreement on the measurements will never be complete. Yet over a period of time the judgments of qualified readers* tend to coalesce: there comes to be more agreement than disagreement. There is almost universal agreement, for instance, that Shakespeare is the greatest of English poets. Although there might be sharp disagreements among qualified readers as to whether Donne or Keats is the superior poet, or Wordsworth or Chaucer, or Shelley or Pope, there is almost universal agreement among them that each of these is superior to Kipling or Longfellow. And there is almost universal agreement that Kipling and Longfellow are superior to James Whitcomb Riley and Edgar Guest.

But your problem is to be able to discriminate, not between already established reputations, but between poems—poems you have not seen before and of which, perhaps, you do not even know the author. Here, of course, you will not always be right—even the most qualified readers occasionally go badly astray—but you should, we hope, be able to make broad distinctions with a higher average of success than you could when you began this book. And, unless you allow yourself to petrify, your ability to do this should improve throughout your college years and beyond.

For answering the first of our evaluative questions, *How fully has the poem's purpose been accomplished?* there are no easy yardsticks that we can apply. We cannot ask, Is the poem melodious? Does it have smooth meter? Does it use good grammar? Does it contain figures of speech? Are the rimes perfect? Excellent poems exist without any of these attributes. We can judge any element in a poem only as it contributes or fails to contribute to the achievement of the central purpose; and we can judge the total poem only as these elements work together to form an integrated whole. But we can at least attempt a few generalizations. In a perfect poem there are no excess words, no words that do not bear their full weight in contributing to the total meaning, and no words just to fill out the meter. Each word is the best word for expressing the total meaning: there are no inexact words forced by the rime scheme or the metrical pattern. The word order is the best order for expressing the author's total meaning; distortions or departures from normal order are for emphasis or some other meaningful purpose. The diction, the images, and the figures of speech are fresh, not trite (except, of course, when the poet uses trite language deliberately for purposes of irony). There are no clashes be-

---

*Throughout this discussion the term "qualified reader" is of utmost importance. By a qualified reader we mean briefly a person with considerable experience of literature and considerable experience of life: a person of intelligence, sensitivity, and knowledge.

tween the sound of the poem and its sense, or its form and its content; and in general the poet uses both sound and pattern in such a way as to support his meaning. The organization of the poem is the best possible organization: images and ideas are so effectively arranged that any rearrangement would be harmful to the poem. We will always remember, however, that a good poem may have flaws. We should never damn a poem for its flaws if these flaws are amply compensated for by positive excellence.

If a poem is to have true excellence, it must be in some sense a "new" poem; it must exact a fresh response from the qualified reader—make him respond in a new way. It will not be merely imitative of previous literature nor appeal to stock, preestablished ways of thinking and feeling that in some readers are automatically stimulated by words like *mother, baby, home, country, faith,* or *God,* as a coin put into a slot always gets an expected reaction.

And here, perhaps, may be discussed the kinds of poems that most frequently "fool" poor readers (and occasionally a few good ones) and achieve sometimes a tremendous popularity without winning the respect of most good readers. These poems are found pasted in great numbers in the scrapbooks of sweet old ladies and appear in anthologies entitled *Poems of Inspiration, Poems of Courage,* or *Heart-Throbs.* The people who write such poems and the people who like them are often the best of people, but they are not poets or lovers of poetry in any genuine sense. They are lovers of conventional ideas or sentiments or feelings, which they like to see expressed with the adornment of rime and meter, and which, when so expressed, they respond to in predictable ways.

Of the several varieties of inferior poetry, we shall concern ourselves with three: the sentimental, the rhetorical, and the purely didactic. All three are perhaps unduly dignified by the name of poetry. They might more aptly be described as verse.

SENTIMENTALITY is indulgence in emotion for its own sake, or expression of more emotion than an occasion warrants. A sentimental *person* is gushy, stirred to tears by trivial or inappropriate causes; he weeps at all weddings and all funerals; he is made ecstatic by manifestations of young love; he clips locks of hair, gilds baby shoes, and talks baby talk; he grows compassionate over hardened criminals when he hears of their being punished. His opposite is the callous or unfeeling person. The ideal is the person who responds sensitively on appropriate occasions and feels deeply on occasions that deserve deep feeling, but who has nevertheless a certain amount of emotional reserve, a certain command over his feelings. Sentimental *literature* is *"tear-jerking"* literature. It aims primarily at stimulating the emotions directly rather than at communicating experience truly and freshly; it depends on trite and well-tried formulas for exciting emotion; it revels in old oaken buckets, rocking chairs, mother love, and the pitter-patter of little feet; it oversimplifies; it is unfaithful to the full complexity of human experience. In our book the best example of sentimental verse is the first seven lines of the anonymous "Love" (page 665). If this verse had ended as it began, it would have been pure sentimentalism. The eighth line redeems it by making us realize that the writer is not serious and thus transfers the piece from the classification of sentimental verse to that of humorous verse. In fact, the writer is poking fun at sentimentality by showing that in its most maudlin form it is characteristic of drunks.

RHETORICAL poetry uses a language more glittering and high flown than its substance warrants. It offers a spurious vehemence of language—language without a corresponding reality of emotion or thought underneath. It is oratorical, overelegant, artificially eloquent. It is superficial and, again, often basically trite. It loves rolling phrases like "from the rocky coast of Maine to the sun-washed shores of California" and "our heroic dead" and "Old Glory." It deals in generalities. At its worst it is bombast. In this book an example is offered by the two lines quoted from the play-within-a-play in Shakespeare's *A Midsummer Night's Dream:*

> Whereat with blade, with bloody, blameful blade,
> He bravely broached his boiling bloody breast.

Another example may be found in the player's recitation in *Hamlet* (in Act II, scene 2):

> Out, out, thou strumpet Fortune! All you gods,
> In general synod take away her power,
> Break all the spokes and fellies from her wheel,
> And bowl the round nave down the hill of heaven
> As low as to the fiends!

DIDACTIC poetry has as a primary purpose to teach or preach. It is probable that all the very greatest poetry teaches in subtle ways, without being expressly didactic; and much expressly didactic poetry ranks high in poetic excellence: that is, it accomplishes its teaching without ceasing to be poetry. But when the didactic purpose supersedes the poetic purpose, when the poem communicates information or moral instruction only, then it ceases to be didactic poetry and becomes didactic verse. Such verse appeals to people who go to poetry primarily for noble thoughts or inspiring lessons and like them prettily expressed. It is recognizable often by its lack of any specific situation, the flatness of its diction, the poverty of its imagery and figurative language, its emphasis on moral platitudes, its lack of poetic freshness. It is either very trite or has little to distinguish it from informational prose except rime or meter. Bryant's "To a Waterfowl" (page 644) is an example of didactic *poetry*. The familiar couplet

> Early to bed and early to rise,
> Makes a man healthy, wealthy, and wise

is more aptly characterized as didactic *verse*.

Undoubtedly, so far in this chapter, we have spoken too categorically, have made our distinctions too sharp and definite. All poetic excellence is a matter of degree. There are no absolute lines between sentimentality and true emotion, artificial and genuine eloquence, didactic verse and didactic poetry. Though the difference between extreme examples is easy to recognize, subtler discriminations are harder to make. But a primary distinction between the educated person and the ignorant one is the ability to make informed judgments.

A final caution to students. In making judgments on literature, always be honest. Do not pretend to like what you really do not like. Do not be afraid to admit a liking for what you do like. A genuine enthusiasm for the second-rate is much better than false enthusiasm or no enthusiasm at all. Be neither hasty nor timorous in making your judgments. When you have attentively read a poem and thoroughly considered it, decide what you think. Do not hedge, equivocate, or try to find out others' opinions before forming your own. Having formed an opinion and expressed it, do not allow it to petrify. Compare your opinion *then* with the opinions of others; allow yourself to change it when convinced of its error: in this way you learn. Honesty, courage, and humility are the necessary moral foundations for all genuine literary judgment.

In the poems for comparison in this chapter, the distinction to be made is not always between black and white; it may be between varying degrees of poetic merit.

EXERCISE

Poetry is not so much a thing as a quality; it exists in varying degrees in different specimens of language. Though we cannot always say definitely, "This is poetry; that is not," we can often say, "This is more poetical than that." Rank the following passages from most poetical to least poetical or not poetical at all.

1. Why should we be in such desperate haste to succeed and in such desperate enterprises? If a man does not keep pace with his companions, perhaps it is

because he hears a different drummer. Let him step to the music which he hears, however measured or far away.

2. $(x - 12)(x - 2) = x^2 - 14x + 24.$

3. Thirty days hath September,
April, June, and November.
All the rest have thirty-one,
Except February alone,
To which we twenty-eight assign,
Till leap year makes it twenty-nine.

4. "Meeting at Night" (page 561).

5. Thus, through the serene tranquilities of the tropical sea, among waves whose handclappings were suspended by exceeding rapture, Moby Dick moved on, still withholding from sight the full terrors of his submerged trunk, entirely hiding the wrenched hideousness of his jaw. But soon the fore part of him slowly rose from the water; for an instant his whole marbleized body formed a high arch, like Virginia's Natural Bridge, and warningly waving his bannered flukes in the air, the grand god revealed himself, sounded, and went out of sight. Hoveringly halting, and dipping on the wing, the white sea fowls longingly lingered over the agitated pool that he left.

6. Nature in the abstract is the aggregate of the powers and properties of all things. Nature means the sum of all phenomena, together with the causes which produce them; including not only all that happens, but all that is capable of happening; the unused capabilities of causes being as much a part of the idea of Nature, as those which take effect.

*   *   *

SAY NOT THE STRUGGLE NOUGHT AVAILETH

Say not the struggle nought availeth,
　　The labor and the wounds are vain,
The enemy faints not, nor faileth,
　　And as things have been they remain.

If hopes were dupes, fears may be liars;　　　　5
　　It may be, in yon smoke concealed,
Your comrades chase e'en now the fliers,
　　And, but for you, possess the field.

For while the tired waves, vainly breaking,
　　Seem here no painful inch to gain,　　　　10
Far back, through creeks and inlets making,
　　Comes silent, flooding in, the main.

And not by eastern windows only,
　　When daylight comes, comes in the light,

In front, the sun climbs slow, how slowly,   15
  But westward, look, the land is bright.

THE MAN WHO THINKS HE CAN

If you think you are beaten, you are;
  If you think you dare not, you don't.
If you'd like to win, but think you can't,
  It's almost a cinch you won't.
If you think you'll lose, you're lost,   5
  For out in the world we find
Success begins with a fellow's will;
  It's all in the state of mind.

If you think you're outclassed, you are;
  You've got to think high to rise.   10
You've got to be sure of yourself before
  You can ever win a prize.
Life's battles don't always go
  To the stronger or faster man;
But soon or late the man who wins   15
  Is the one who thinks he can.

QUESTION

Which of the above poems has more poetic merit? Discuss.

GOD'S WILL FOR YOU AND ME

Just to be tender, just to be true,
Just to be glad the whole day through,
Just to be merciful, just to be mild,
Just to be trustful as a child,
Just to be gentle and kind and sweet,   5
Just to be helpful with willing feet,
Just to be cheery when things go wrong,
Just to drive sadness away with a song,
Whether the hour is dark or bright,
Just to be loyal to God and right,   10
Just to believe that God knows best,
Just in his promises ever to rest—
Just to let love be our daily key,
That is God's will for you and me.

PIED BEAUTY

Glory be to God for dappled things—
  For skies of couple-color as a brinded cow;
    For rose-moles all in stipple upon trout that swim;
Fresh-firecoal chestnut-falls; finches' wings;
  Landscape plotted and pieced—fold, fallow and plow;   5
    And all trades, their gear and tackle and trim.

All things counter, original, spare, strange;
  Whatever is fickle, freckled (who knows how?)
    With swift, slow; sweet, sour; adazzle, dim;
He fathers-forth whose beauty is past change: 10
    Praise him.

QUESTION

Which is the superior poem? Explain in full.

PITCHER

His art is eccentricity, his aim
How not to hit the mark he seems to aim at,

His passion how to avoid the obvious,
His technique how to vary the avoidance.

The others throw to be comprehended. He   5
Throws to be a moment misunderstood.

Yet not too much. Not errant, arrant, wild,
But every seeming aberration willed.

Not to, yet still, still to communicate
Making the batter understand too late.   10

THE OLD-FASHIONED PITCHER

How dear to my heart was the old-fashioned hurler
  Who labored all day on the old village green.
He did not resemble the up-to-date twirler
  Who pitches four innings and ducks from the scene.
The up-to-date twirler I'm not very strong for;   5
  He has a queer habit of pulling up lame.
And that is the reason I hanker and long for
  The pitcher who started and finished the game.

                    The old-fashioned pitcher,
                         The iron-armed pitcher,   10
                    The stout-hearted pitcher
                         Who finished the game.

QUESTION

Which poem is the more interesting and more meaningful? Why?

TO MY SON

        Do you know that your soul is of my soul such part
        That you seem to be fibre and cord of my heart?
        None other can pain me as you, dear, can do;
        None other can please me or praise me as you.

        Remember the world will be quick with its blame   5
        If shadow or stain ever darken your name;
        "Like mother like son" is a saying so true,
        The world will judge largely of "Mother" by you.

        Be yours then the task, if task it shall be,
        To force the proud world to do homage to me;   10
        Be sure it will say when its verdict you've won,
        "She reaped as she sowed, Lo! this is her son."

ON THE BEACH AT FONTANA

        Wind whines and whines the shingle,
        The crazy pierstakes groan;
        A senile sea numbers each single
        Slimesilvered stone.

        From whining wind and colder   5
        Gray sea I wrap him warm
        And touch his trembling fineboned shoulder
        And boyish arm.

        Around us fear, descending
        Darkness of fear above   10
        And in my heart how deep unending
        Ache of love!

QUESTIONS

1. Vocabulary: *shingle* (1).
2. Identify the speaker in each poem (the first was written by a woman, the
   second by a man). Which is the better poem, and why?

744 BAD POETRY AND GOOD

A POISON TREE

I was angry with my friend:
I told my wrath, my wrath did end.
I was angry with my foe:
I told it not, my wrath did grow.

And I watered it in fears,   5
Night and morning with my tears;
And I sunnèd it with smiles,
And with soft deceitful wiles.

And it grew both day and night
Till it bore an apple bright;   10
And my foe beheld it shine,
And he knew that it was mine,

And into my garden stole
When the night had veiled the pole:°   sky
In the morning glad I see   15
My foe outstretched beneath the tree.

THE MOST VITAL THING IN LIFE

When you feel like saying something
   That you know you will regret,
Or keenly feel an insult
   Not quite easy to forget,
That's the time to curb resentment   5
   And maintain a mental peace,
For when your mind is tranquil
   All your ill-thoughts simply cease.

It is easy to be angry
   When defrauded or defied,   10
To be peeved and disappointed
   If your wishes are denied;
But to win a worthwhile battle
   Over selfishness and spite,
You must learn to keep strict silence   15
   Though you know you're in the right.

So keep your mental balance
   When confronted by a foe,
Be it enemy in ambush
   Or some danger that you know.   20
If you are poised and tranquil

When all around is strife,
Be assured that you have mastered
The most vital thing in life.

QUESTION

Which poem has more poetic merit? Explain.

ON A DEAD CHILD

Man proposes, God in His time disposes,
　　And so I wandered up to where you lay,
A little rose among the little roses,
　　And no more dead than they.

It seemed your childish feet were tired of straying,　　5
　　You did not greet me from your flower-strewn bed,
Yet still I knew that you were only playing—
　　Playing at being dead.

I might have thought that you were really sleeping,
　　So quiet lay your eyelids to the sky,　　10
So still your hair, but surely you were peeping;
　　And so I did not cry.

God knows, and in His proper time disposes,
　　And so I smiled and gently called your name,
Added my rose to your sweet heap of roses,　　15
　　And left you to your game.

BELLS FOR JOHN WHITESIDE'S DAUGHTER

There was such speed in her little body,
And such lightness in her footfall,
It is no wonder her brown study
Astonishes us all.

Her wars were bruited in our high window.　　5
We looked among orchard trees and beyond
Where she took arms against her shadow,
Or harried unto the pond

The lazy geese, like a snow cloud
Dripping their snow on the green grass,　　10

Tricking and stopping, sleepy and proud,
Who cried in goose, Alas,

For the tireless heart within the little
Lady with rod that made them rise
From their noon apple-dreams and scuttle   15
Goose-fashion under the skies!

But now go the bells, and we are ready,
In one house we are sternly stopped
To say we are vexed at her brown study,
Lying so primly propped.   20

QUESTIONS

1. Vocabulary: *brown study* (3, 19), *bruited* (5).
2. Which is the sentimental poem? Which is the honest one? Explain.

SOME KEEP THE SABBATH GOING TO CHURCH

Some keep the Sabbath going to church;
I keep it staying at home,
With a bobolink for a chorister,
And an orchard for a dome.

Some keep the Sabbath in surplice;   5
I just wear my wings,
And instead of tolling the bell for church,
Our little sexton sings.

God preaches,—a noted clergyman,—
And the sermon is never long;   10
So instead of getting to heaven at last,
I'm going all along!

MY CHURCH

My church has but one temple,
    Wide as the world is wide,
Set with a million stars,
    Where a million hearts abide.

My church has no creed to bar   5
    A single brother man

But says, "Come thou and worship"
To every one who can.

My church has no roof nor walls,
    Nor floors save the beautiful sod—   10
For fear, I would seem to limit
    The love of the illimitable God.

QUESTION

Which is the better poem, and why?

BOY-MAN

England's lads are miniature men
To start with, grammar in their shiny hats,
And serious: in America who knows when
Manhood begins? Presidents dance and hug
And while the kind King waves and gravely chats   5
America wets on England's old green rug.

The boy-man roars. Worry alone will give
This one the verisimilitude of age.
Those white teeth are his own, for he must live
Longer, grow taller than the Texas race.   10
Fresh are his eyes, his darkening skin the gauge
Of bloods that freely mix beneath his face.

He knows the application of the book
But not who wrote it; shuts it like a shot.
Rather than read he thinks that he will look,   15
Rather than look he thinks that he will talk,
Rather than talk he thinks that he will not
Bother at all; would rather ride than walk.

His means of conversation is the joke,
Humor his language underneath which lies   20
The undecoded dialect of the folk.
Abroad he scorns the foreigner: what's old
Is worn, what's different bad, what's odd unwise.
He gives off heat and is enraged by cold.

Charming, becoming to the suits he wears,   25
The boy-man, younger than his eldest son,
Inherits the state; upon his silver hairs

Time like a panama hat sits at a tilt
And smiles. To him the world has just begun
And every city waiting to be built.   30

Mister, remove your shoulder from the wheel
And say this prayer, "Increase my vitamins,
Make my decisions of the finest steel,
Pour motor oil upon my troubled spawn,
Forgive the Europeans for their sins,   35
Establish them, that values may go on."

QUESTIONS

1. Vocabulary: *verisimilitude* (8), *spawn* (34).
2. What is the subject of the poem?
3. What is the tone—admiration? mockery? or both?
4. Explain fully the figures of speech in lines 2, 6, 26, 28-29, and their appropriateness. What kind of irony appears in the last stanza?

AMERICA FOR ME

'Tis fine to see the Old World, and travel up and down
Among the famous palaces and cities of renown,
To admire the crumbly castles and the statues of the kings—
But now I think I've had enough of antiquated things.

So it's home again, and home again, America for me!   5
My heart is turning home again, and there I long to be,
In the land of youth and freedom beyond the ocean bars,
Where the air is full of sunlight and the flag is full of stars.

Oh, London is a man's town, there's power in the air;
And Paris is a woman's town, with flowers in her hair;   10
And it's sweet to dream in Venice, and it's great to study Rome;
But when it comes to living there is no place like home.

I like the German fir-woods, in green battalions drilled;
I like the gardens of Versailles with flashing fountains filled;
But, oh, to take your hand, my dear, and ramble for a day   15
In the friendly western woodlands where Nature has her way!

I know that Europe's wonderful, yet something seems to lack:
The Past is too much with her, and the people looking back.
But the glory of the Present is to make the Future free—
We love our land for what she is and what she is to be.   20

Oh, it's home again, and home again, America for me!
I want a ship that's westward bound to plow the rolling sea,
To the blessèd Land of Room Enough beyond the ocean bars,
Where the air is full of sunlight and the flag is full of stars.

QUESTIONS

1. In what respects do the attitudes expressed in this poem fit the characterization made in "Boy-Man"?
2. "America for Me" and "Boy-Man" were both written by Americans. Which is more worthy of prolonged consideration? Why?

LITTLE BOY BLUE

The little toy dog is covered with dust,
    But sturdy and staunch he stands;
And the little toy soldier is red with rust,
    And his musket moulds in his hands.
Time was when the little toy dog was new,   5
    And the soldier was passing fair;
And that was the time when our Little Boy Blue
    Kissed them and put them there.

"Now, don't you go till I come," he said,
    "And don't you make any noise!"   10
So, toddling off to his trundle-bed,
    He dreamt of the pretty toys;
And, as he was dreaming, an angel song
    Awakened our Little Boy Blue—
Oh! the years are many, the years are long,   15
    But the little toy friends are True!

Ay, faithful to Little Boy Blue they stand
    Each in the same old place—
Awaiting the touch of a little hand,
    The smile of a little face;   20
And they wonder, as waiting the long years through
    In the dust of that little chair,
What has become of our Little Boy Blue,
    Since he kissed them and put them there.

THE TOYS

My little Son, who looked from thoughtful eyes
And moved and spoke in quiet grown-up wise,
Having my law the seventh time disobeyed,

I struck him, and dismissed
With hard words and unkissed,   5
His Mother, who was patient, being dead.
Then, fearing lest his grief should hinder sleep,
I visited his bed,
But found him slumbering deep,
With darkened eyelids, and their lashes yet   10
From his late sobbing wet.
And I, with moan,
Kissing away his tears, left others of my own;
For, on a table drawn beside his head,
He had put, within his reach,   15
A box of counters and a red-veined stone,
A piece of glass abraded by the beach,
And six or seven shells,
A bottle with bluebells,
And two French copper coins, ranged there with careful art,   20
To comfort his sad heart.
So when that night I prayed
To God, I wept, and said:
Ah, when at last we lie with trancèd breath,
Not vexing Thee in death,   25
And thou rememberest of what toys
We made our joys,
How weakly understood
Thy great commanded good,
Then, fatherly not less   30
Than I whom Thou hast moulded from the clay,
Thou'lt leave Thy wrath, and say,
"I will be sorry for their childishness."

QUESTION

One of these poems has an obvious appeal for the beginning reader. The other is
likely to have more meaning for the mature reader. Try to explain in terms of
sentimentality and honesty.

16. Good Poetry and Great

I f a poem has successfully met the test in the question, *How fully has it accomplished its purpose?* we are ready to subject it to our second question, *How important is its purpose?*

Great poetry must, of course, be good poetry. Noble intent alone cannot redeem a work that does not measure high on the scale of accomplishment; otherwise the sentimental and purely didactic verse of much of the last chapter would stand with the world's masterpieces. But once a work has been judged as successful on the scale of execution, its final standing will depend on its significance of purpose.

Suppose, for instance, we consider three poems in our text: the limerick "There was a young lady of Niger" (page 720), Emily Dickinson's poem "It sifts from leaden sieves" (page 573), and Shakespeare's sonnet "That time of year" (page 722). Each of these would probably be judged by competent critics as highly successful in accomplishing what it sets out to do. The limerick tells its little story without an unnecessary word, with no "wrong" word, with no distortion of normal sentence order forced by exigencies of meter or rime; the limerick form is ideally suited to the author's humorous purpose; and the manner in which the story is told, with its understatement, its neat shift in position of the lady and her smile, is economical and delicious. Yet we should hardly call this poetry at all: it does not really communicate experience, nor does it attempt to. It attempts merely to relate a brief anecdote humorously and effectively. On the other hand, Emily Dickinson's poem *is* poetry, and very good poetry. It appeals richly to our senses and to our imaginations, and it succeeds excellently in its purpose: to convey the appearance and the quality of falling and newly fallen snow as well as a sense of the magic and the mystery of nature. Yet, when we compare this excellent poem with Shakespeare's, we again see important differences. Although the first poem engages the senses and the imagination and may affect us with wonder and cause us to meditate on nature, it does not deeply engage the emotions or the intellect. It does not come as close to the core of human living and suffering as does Shakespeare's sonnet. In fact, it is concerned primarily with that staple of small talk, the weather. On the other hand, Shakespeare's sonnet is concerned with the universal human tragedy of growing old, with approaching death, and with love. Of these three selections, then, Shakespeare's is the greatest. It "says" more than Emily Dickinson's poem or the limerick; it communicates a richer experience; it successfully accomplishes a more significant purpose. The discriminating reader will get from it a deeper enjoyment, because he has been nourished as well as delighted.

Great poetry engages the whole person—senses, imagination, emotion, intellect; it does not touch him merely on one or two sides of his nature. Great poetry seeks not merely to entertain the reader, but to bring him—along with pure pleasure—fresh insights, or renewed insights, and important insights, into the nature of human experience. Great poetry, we might say, gives its reader a broader and deeper understanding of life, of his fellow men, and of himself, always with the qualification, of course, that the kind of insight literature gives is not necessarily the kind that can be summed up in a simple "lesson" or "moral." It is *knowledge—felt* knowledge, *new* knowledge—of the complexities of human nature and of the tragedies and sufferings, the excitements and joys, that characterize human experience.

Is Shakespeare's sonnet a *great* poem? It is, at least, a great *sonnet*. Greatness, like goodness, is relative. If we compare any of Shakespeare's sonnets with his greatest plays—*Macbeth, Othello, Hamlet, King Lear*— another big difference appears. What is undertaken and accomplished in these tragedies is enormously greater, more difficult, and more complex than could ever be undertaken or accomplished in a single sonnet. Greatness in literature, in fact, cannot be entirely dissociated from size. In literature, as in basketball and football, a good big man is better than a good little man. The greatness of a poem is in proportion to the range and depth and intensity of experience that it brings to us: its amount of life. Shakespeare's plays offer us a multiplicity of life and a depth of living that could never be compressed into the fourteen lines of a sonnet. They organize a greater complexity of life and experience into unity.

Yet, after all, we have provided no easy yardsticks or rule-of-thumb measures for literary judgment. There are no mechanical tests. The final measuring rod can be only the responsiveness, the maturity, the taste and discernment of the cultivated reader. Such taste and discernment are partly a native endowment, partly the product of maturity and experience, partly the achievement of conscious study, training, and intellectual effort. They cannot be achieved suddenly or quickly; they can never be achieved in perfection. The pull is a long and a hard one. But success, even relative success, brings enormous rewards in enrichment and command of life.

*   *   *

ODE TO A NIGHTINGALE

My heart aches, and a drowsy numbness pains
  My sense, as though of hemlock° I had drunk,   *a poisonous*
Or emptied some dull opiate to the drains   *drink*
  One minute past, and Lethe-wards had sunk:
'Tis not through envy of thy happy lot,   5
  But being too happy in thine happiness,—
    That thou, light-wingèd Dryad° of the trees, *wood nymph*
      In some melodious plot
Of beechen green, and shadows numberless,
  Singest of summer in full-throated ease.   10

O, for a draught of vintage! that hath been
  Cooled a long age in the deep-delvèd earth,
Tasting of Flora° and the country green,.   *goddess of flowers*
  Dance, and Provençal song, and sunburnt mirth!
O for a beaker full of the warm South,   15
  Full of the true, the blushful Hippocrene,
    With beaded bubbles winking at the brim,
      And purple-stainèd mouth;
That I might drink, and leave the world unseen,
  And with thee fade away into the forest dim: 20

Fade far away, dissolve, and quite forget
  What thou among the leaves hast never known,
The weariness, the fever, and the fret
  Here, where men sit and hear each other groan;
Where palsy shakes a few, sad, last gray hairs,   25
  Where youth grows pale, and specter-thin, and dies;
    Where but to think is to be full of sorrow
      And leaden-eyed despairs,

Where Beauty cannot keep her lustrous eyes,
    Or new Love pine at them beyond to-morrow.   30

Away! away! for I will fly to thee,
    Not charioted by Bacchus and his pards,
But on the viewless° wings of Poesy,   invisible
    Though the dull brain perplexes and retards:
Already with thee! tender is the night,   35
    And haply the Queen-Moon is on her throne,
        Clustered around by all her starry Fays;
           But here there is no light,
    Save what from heaven is with the breezes blown
        Through verdurous glooms and winding mossy ways.   40

I cannot see what flowers are at my feet,
    Nor what soft incense hangs upon the boughs,
But, in embalmèd° darkness, guess each sweet   perfumed
    Wherewith the seasonable month endows
The grass, the thicket, and the fruit-tree wild;   45
    White hawthorn, and the pastoral eglantine;
        Fast fading violets covered up in leaves;
           And mid-May's eldest child,
    The coming musk-rose, full of dewy wine,
        The murmurous haunt of flies on summer eves.   50

Darkling° I listen; and, for many a time   in darkness
    I have been half in love with easeful Death,
Called him soft names in many a musèd rhyme,
    To take into the air my quiet breath;
Now more than ever seems it rich to die,   55
    To cease upon the midnight with no pain,
        While thou art pouring forth thy soul abroad
           In such an ecstasy!
    Still wouldst thou sing, and I have ears in vain—
    To thy high requiem become a sod.   60

Thou wast not born for death, immortal Bird!
    No hungry generations tread thee down;
The voice I hear this passing night was heard
    In ancient days by emperor and clown:
Perhaps the self-same song that found a path   65
    Through the sad heart of Ruth, when, sick for home,
        She stood in tears amid the alien corn;
           The same that oft-times hath
    Charmed magic casements, opening on the foam
    Of perilous seas, in faery lands forlorn.   70

Forlorn! the very word is like a bell
    To toll me back from thee to my sole self!
Adieu! the fancy cannot cheat so well
    As she is famed to do, deceiving elf.
Adieu! adieu! thy plaintive anthem fades   75
    Past the near meadows, over the still stream,
        Up the hill-side; and now 'tis buried deep
    In the next valley-glades:
Was it a vision, or a waking dream?
    Fled is that music:—Do I wake or sleep?   80

John Keats (1795–1821)

QUESTIONS

1. Vocabulary: *vintage* (11), *haply* (36), *Fays* (37), *verdurous* (40), *musèd* (53), *requiem* (60), *clown* (64). *Lethe* (4) was the river of forgetfulness in the Greek underworld. *Provençal* (14) refers to Provence, a wine-growing region in southern France, famous in the Middle Ages for its troubadours. *Hippocrene* (16) in Greek mythology was the fountain of the Muses on Mt. Helicon. *Bacchus* (32), the god of wine, went about in a chariot drawn by leopards.
2. Why does the poet experience the sensations described in lines 1–4?
3. The poet expresses a desire to escape from his world into the world of the nightingale. What is unsatisfactory about *his* world? In what two ways especially do his world and the world of the nightingale contrast (stanzas 3, 6, 7)? How is the fancied process of leaving the actual world described (lines 19–21)?
4. What means of escape does the poet first consider? How is it described? Why does he reject it? What means does he choose instead (what constitutes the "viewless wings" of poesy)?
5. Discuss the imagery in stanzas 4 and 5. From what to what (in terms of place and time) has the poet been transported? Why cannot the poet see what flowers are at his feet? How does he identify them? Why does this beautiful scene make him think of death?
6. Dying under the conditions described in stanza 6 is made to seem very attractive. How do the last two lines of the stanza affect this attractiveness? Why has the poet often been "half in love" with death? Why has he been *only* "half in love" with it?
7. In what sense (or senses) is the nightingale "immortal"? How is this immortality illustrated in stanza 7? Of what has the nightingale (or its song) become a symbol? (There may be more than one answer.)
8. Why does the word "forlorn" break the poet's reverie? Are its meanings the same in stanza 8 as in stanza 7? How are the poet's return to the actual world and the distancing of the nightingale's song described? In what two ways is the imagination a "deceiving elf"? What is the difference between a "vision" and a "waking dream"? Are we meant to be able to answer the questions in the last two lines?

9. What final conclusions, if any, does the poem reach about the possibilities of escaping from the actual world to that of the nightingale? about the desirability of doing so?

THE DEATH OF THE HIRED MAN

Mary sat musing on the lamp-flame at the table
Waiting for Warren. When she heard his step,
She ran on tip-toe down the darkened passage
To meet him in the doorway with the news
And put him on his guard. "Silas is back."   5
She pushed him outward with her through the door
And shut it after her. "Be kind" she said.
She took the market things from Warren's arms
And set them on the porch, then drew him down
To sit beside her on the wooden steps.   10

"When was I ever anything but kind to him?
But I'll not have the fellow back," he said.
"I told him so last haying, didn't I?
If he left then, I said, that ended it.
What good is he? Who else will harbor him   15
At his age for the little he can do?
What help he is there's no depending on.
Off he goes always when I need him most.
He thinks he ought to earn a little pay,
Enough at least to buy tobacco with,   20
So he won't have to beg and be beholden.
'All right,' I say, 'I can't afford to pay
Any fixed wages, though I wish I could.'
'Someone else can.' 'Then someone else will have to.'
I shouldn't mind his bettering himself   25
If that was what it was. You can be certain,
When he begins like that, there's someone at him
Trying to coax him off with pocket-money—
In haying time, when any help is scarce.
In winter he comes back to us. I'm done."   30

"Sh! not so loud: he'll hear you," Mary said.

"I want him to: he'll have to soon or late."

"He's worn out. He's asleep beside the stove.
When I came up from Rowe's I found him here,
Huddled against the barn-door fast asleep,   35
A miserable sight, and frightening, too—

You needn't smile—I didn't recognize him—
I wasn't looking for him—and he's changed.
Wait till you see."

                "Where did you say he'd been?"

"He didn't say, I dragged him to the house,   40
And gave him tea and tried to make him smoke.
I tried to make him talk about his travels.
Nothing would do: he just kept nodding off."

"What did he say? Did he say anything?"

"But little."

        "Anything? Mary, confess   45
He said he'd come to ditch the meadow for me."

"Warren!"

        "But did he? I just want to know."

"Of course he did. What would you have him say?
Surely you wouldn't grudge the poor old man
Some humble way to save his self-respect.   50
He added, if you really care to know,
He meant to clear the upper pasture, too.
That sounds like something you have heard before?
Warren, I wish you could have heard the way
He jumbled everything. I stopped to look   55
Two or three times—he made me feel so queer—
To see if he was talking in his sleep.
He ran on Harold Wilson—you remember—
The boy you had in haying four years since.
He's finished school, and teaching in his college.   60
Silas declares you'll have to get him back.
He says they two will make a team for work:
Between them they will lay this farm as smooth!
The way he mixed that in with other things.
He thinks young Wilson a likely lad, though daft   65
On education—you know how they fought
All through July under the blazing sun,
Silas up on the cart to build the load,
Harold along beside to pitch it on."

"Yes, I took care to keep well out of earshot."   70

"Well, those days trouble Silas like a dream.
You wouldn't think they would. How some things linger!

Harold's young college boy's assurance piqued him.
After so many years he still keeps finding
Good arguments he sees he might have used.   75
I sympathize. I know just how it feels
To think of the right thing to say too late.
Harold's associated in his mind with Latin.
He asked me what I thought of Harold's saying
He studied Latin like the violin   80
Because he liked it—that an argument!
He said he couldn't make the boy believe
He could find water with a hazel prong—
Which showed how much good school had ever done him.
He wanted to go over that. But most of all   85
He thinks if he could have another chance
To teach him how to build a load of hay—"

"I know, that's Silas' one accomplishment.
He bundles every forkful in its place,
And tags and numbers it for future reference,   90
So he can find and easily dislodge it
In the unloading. Silas does that well.
He takes it out in bunches like big birds' nests.
You never see him standing on the hay
He's trying to lift, straining to lift himself."   95

"He thinks if he could teach him that, he'd be
Some good perhaps to someone in the world.
He hates to see a boy the fool of books.
Poor Silas, so concerned for other folk,
And nothing to look backward to with pride,   100
And nothing to look forward to with hope,
So now and never any different."

Part of a moon was falling down the west,
Dragging the whole sky with it to the hills.
Its light poured softly in her lap. She saw it   105
And spread her apron to it. She put out her hand
Among the harp-like morning-glory strings,
Taut with the dew from garden bed to eaves,
As if she played unheard some tenderness
That wrought on him beside her in the night.   110
"Warren," she said, "he has come home to die:
You needn't be afraid he'll leave you this time."

"Home," he mocked gently.

                    "Yes, what else but home?

It all depends on what you mean by home.
Of course he's nothing to us, any more   115
Than was the hound that came a stranger to us
Out of the woods, worn out upon the trail."

"Home is the place where, when you have to go there,
They have to take you in."

                     "I should have called it
Something you somehow haven't to deserve."   120

Warren leaned out and took a step or two,
Picked up a little stick, and brought it back
And broke it in his hand and tossed it by.
"Silas has better claim on us you think
Than on his brother? Thirteen little miles   125
As the road winds would bring him to his door.
Silas has walked that far no doubt today.
Why doesn't he go there? His brother's rich,
A somebody—director in the bank."

"He never told us that."

                "We know it though."   130

"I think his brother ought to help, of course.
I'll see to that if there is need. He ought of right
To take him in, and might be willing to—
He may be better than appearances.
But have some pity on Silas. Do you think   135
If he had any pride in claiming kin
Or anything he looked for from his brother,
He'd keep so still about him all this time?"

"I wonder what's between them."

                       "I can tell you.
Silas is what he is—we wouldn't mind him—   140
But just the kind that kinsfolk can't abide.
He never did a thing so very bad.
He don't know why he isn't quite as good
As anybody. Worthless though he is,
He won't be made ashamed to please his brother."   145

"*I* can't think Si ever hurt anyone."

"No, but he hurt my heart the way he lay
And rolled his old head on that sharp-edged chair-back.
He wouldn't let me put him on the lounge.

You must go in and see what you can do.   150
I made the bed up for him there tonight.
You'll be surprised at him—how much he's broken.
His working days are done; I'm sure of it."

"I'd not be in a hurry to say that."

"I haven't been. Go, look, see for yourself.   155
But, Warren, please remember how it is:
He's come to help you ditch the meadow.
He has a plan. You mustn't laugh at him.
He may not speak of it, and then he may.
I'll sit and see if that small sailing cloud   160
Will hit or miss the moon."

                    It hit the moon.
Then there were three there, making a dim row,
The moon, the little silver cloud, and she.

Warren returned—too soon, it seemed to her,
Slipped to her side, caught up her hand and waited.   165

"Warren?" she questioned.

                    "Dead," was all he answered.

                              Robert Frost (1874–1963)

QUESTIONS

1. Vocabulary: *beholden* (21), *piqued* (73).
2. What kind of person is Silas? Characterize him as fully as possible, showing, especially, what is revealed about his character by his relationships with Harold Wilson, with his brother, and with Warren and Mary.
3. Characterize Warren and Mary. Are they basically unlike in their natures and attitudes, or not really too far apart? Can you suggest reasons why Warren should at first be less solicitous than Mary?
4. Define as precisely as possible the moral problem faced by Warren and Mary. How would Warren finally have answered it (if an answer had not been made unnecessary)? Give reasons for your answer.
5. Is the poem written in free verse or blank verse? How would you describe its rhythm and language?

THE LOVE SONG OF J. ALFRED PRUFROCK

> *S'io credesse che mia risposta fosse*
> *A persona che mai tornasse al mondo,*
> *Questa fiamma staria senza piu scosse.*

Ma perciocche giammai di questo fondo
Non torno vivo alcun, s'i'odo il vero,
Senza tema d'infamia ti rispondo.

Let us go then, you and I,
When the evening is spread out against the sky
Like a patient etherized upon a table;
Let us go, through certain half-deserted streets,
The muttering retreats   5
Of restless nights in one-night cheap hotels
And sawdust restaurants with oyster-shells:
Streets that follow like a tedious argument
Of insidious intent
To lead you to an overwhelming question . . .   10
Oh, do not ask, "What is it?"
Let us go and make our visit.

In the room the women come and go
Talking of Michelangelo.

The yellow fog that rubs its back upon the window-panes,   15
The yellow smoke that rubs its muzzle on the window-panes
Licked its tongue into the corners of the evening,
Lingered upon the pools that stand in drains,
Let fall upon its back the soot that falls from chimneys,
Slipped by the terrace, made a sudden leap,   20
And seeing that it was a soft October night,
Curled once about the house, and fell asleep.

And indeed there will be time
For the yellow smoke that slides along the street,
Rubbing its back upon the window-panes;   25
There will be time, there will be time
To prepare a face to meet the faces that you meet;
There will be time to murder and create,
And time for all the works and days of hands
That lift and drop a question on your plate;   30
Time for you and time for me,
And time yet for a hundred indecisions,
And for a hundred visions and revisions,
Before the taking of a toast and tea.

In the room the women come and go   35
Talking of Michelangelo.

And indeed there will be time
To wonder, "Do I dare?" and "Do I dare?"

Time to turn back and descend the stair,
With a bald spot in the middle of my hair—   40
(They will say: "How his hair is growing thin!")
My morning coat, my collar mounting firmly to the chin,
My necktie rich and modest, but asserted by a simple pin—
(They will say: "But how his arms and legs are thin!")
Do I dare   45
Disturb the universe?
In a minute there is time
For decisions and revisions which a minute will reverse.

    For I have known them all already, known them all:—
Have known the evenings, mornings, afternoons,   50
I have measured out my life with coffee spoons;
I know the voices dying with a dying fall
Beneath the music from a farther room.
    So how should I presume?

    And I have known the eyes already, known them all—   55
The eyes that fix you in a formulated phrase,
And when I am formulated, sprawling on a pin,
When I am pinned and wriggling on the wall,
Then how should I begin
To spit out all the butt-ends of my days and ways   60
    And how should I presume?

    And I have known the arms already, known them all—
Arms that are braceleted and white and bare
(But in the lamplight, downed with light brown hair!)
Is it perfume from a dress   65
That makes me so digress?
Arms that lie along a table, or wrap about a shawl.
    And should I then presume?
    And how should I begin?

      *   *   *

Shall I say, I have gone at dusk through narrow streets   70
And watched the smoke that rises from the pipes
Of lonely men in shirt-sleeves, leaning out of windows? . . .

    I should have been a pair of ragged claws
Scuttling across the floors of silent seas.

      *   *   *

And the afternoon, the evening, sleeps so peacefully!   75
Smoothed by long fingers,
Asleep . . . tired . . . or it malingers,
Stretched on the floor, here beside you and me.
Should I, after tea and cakes and ices,
Have the strength to force the moment to its crisis?   80
But though I have wept and fasted, wept and prayed,
Though I have seen my head (grown slightly bald) brought in
      upon a platter,
I am no prophet—and here's no great matter;
I have seen the moment of my greatness flicker,
And I have seen the eternal Footman hold my coat, and snicker,   85
And in short, I was afraid.

      And would it have been worth it, after all,
After the cups, the marmalade, the tea,
Among the porcelain, among some talk of you and me,
Would it have been worth while,   90
To have bitten off the matter with a smile,
To have squeezed the universe into a ball
To roll it toward some overwhelming question,
To say: "I am Lazarus, come from the dead,
Come back to tell you all, I shall tell you all"—   95
If one, settling a pillow by her head,
      Should say: "That is not what I meant at all.
      That is not it, at all."

      And would it have been worth it, after all,
Would it have been worth while,   100
After the sunsets and the dooryards and the sprinkled streets,
After the novels, after the teacups, after the skirts that trail
      along the floor—
And this, and so much more?—
It is impossible to say just what I mean!
But as if a magic lantern threw the nerves in patterns on a screen: 105
Would it have been worth while
If one, settling a pillow or throwing off a shawl,
And turning toward the window, should say:
      "That is not it at all,
      That is not what I meant, at all."   110

                  *   *   *

No! I am not Prince Hamlet, nor was meant to be;
Am an attendant lord, one that will do

To swell a progress, start a scene or two,
Advise the prince; no doubt, an easy tool,
Deferential, glad to be of use,   115
Politic, cautious, and meticulous:
Full of high sentence, but a bit obtuse;
At times, indeed, almost ridiculous—
Almost, at times, the Fool.

    I grow old . . . I grow old . . .   120
I shall wear the bottoms of my trousers rolled.°   cuffed

    Shall I part my hair behind? Do I dare to eat a peach?
I shall wear white flannel trousers, and walk upon the beach.
I have heard the mermaids singing, each to each.

    I do not think that they will sing to me.   125

    I have seen them riding seaward on the waves
Combing the white hair of the waves blown back
When the wind blows the water white and black.

    We have lingered in the chambers of the sea
By sea-girls wreathed with seaweed red and brown   130
Till human voices wake us, and we drown.

T. S. Eliot (1888–1965)

QUESTIONS

1. Vocabulary: *insidious* (9), *Michelangelo* (14), *muzzle* (16), *malingers* (77), *progress* (113), *deferential* (115), *politic* (116), *meticulous* (116), *sentence* (117).
2. This poem may be for you the most difficult in the book, because it uses a "stream of consciousness" technique (that is, presents the apparently random thoughts going through a person's head within a certain time interval), in which the transitional links are psychological rather than logical, and also because it uses allusions you may be unfamiliar with. Even if you do not at first understand the poem in detail, you should be able to get from it a quite accurate picture of Prufrock's character and personality. What kind of person is he? (Answer this as fully as possible.) From what class of society is he? What one line especially well sums up the nature of his past life? A brief initial orientation may be helpful: Prufrock is apparently on his way, at the beginning of the poem, to a late afternoon tea, at which he wishes (or does he?) to make a declaration of love to some lady who will be present. The "you and I" of the first line are divided parts of Prufrock's own nature, for he is undergoing internal conflict. Does he or does he not make the declaration? Where does the climax of the poem come? If the first half of the poem (up to the climax) is devoted to Prufrock's effort to prepare himself psychologically to make the declaration (or to postpone such effort), what is the latter half (after the climax) devoted to?

3. There are a number of striking or unusual figures of speech in the poem. Most of them in some way reflect Prufrock's own nature or his desires or fears. From this point of view discuss lines 2-3; 15-22 and 75-78; 57-58; 73-74; and 124-31. What figure of speech is lines 73-74? In what respect is the title ironical?

4. The poem makes an extensive use of literary allusion. The Italian epigraph is a passage from Dante's *Inferno* in which a man in Hell tells a visitor that he would never tell his story if there were a chance that it would get back to living ears. In line 29 the phrase "works and days" is the title of a long poem—a description of agricultural life and a call to toil—by the early Greek poet Hesiod. Line 52 echoes the opening speech of Shakespeare's *Twelfth Night*. The prophet of lines 81-83 is John the Baptist, whose head was delivered to Salome by Herod as a reward for her dancing (Matthew 14:1-11, and Oscar Wilde's play *Salome*). Line 92 echoes the closing six lines of Marvell's "To His Coy Mistress" (page 584). Lazarus (94-95) may be either the beggar Lazarus (of Luke 16) who was not permitted to return from the dead to warn the brothers of a rich man about Hell or the Lazarus (of John 11) whom Christ raised from death or both. Lines 111-19 allude to a number of characters from Shakespeare's *Hamlet:* Hamlet himself, the chamberlain Polonius, and various minor characters including probably Rosencrantz, Guildenstern, and Osric. "Full of high sentence" (117) echoes Chaucer's description of the Clerk of Oxford in the Prologue to *The Canterbury Tales*. Relate as many of these allusions as you can to the character of Prufrock. How is Prufrock particularly like Hamlet, and how is he unlike him? Contrast Prufrock with the speaker in "To His Coy Mistress."

5. This poem and "The Death of the Hired Man" are dramatic in structure. Frost's poem (though it has a slight narrative element) is largely a dialogue between two characters who speak in their own voices; Eliot's is a highly allusive soliloquy, or interior monologue. In what ways do their dramatic structures facilitate what they have to say?

EXERCISES

In the following exercises, use both scales of poetic measurement—perfection and significance of accomplishment.

1. Considering such matters as economy and richness of poetic communication, inevitability of organization, and the complexity and maturity of the attitude or philosophy expressed, decide whether "Barter" (page 641) or "Stopping by Woods on a Snowy Evening" (page 642) is the superior poem.

2. Rank the following short poems and explain the reasons for your ranking:
   a. "In the Garden" (page 639), "The Death of the Ball Turret Gunner" (page 800), "Fog" (page 816).
   b. "The Coming of Wisdom with Time" (page 657), "The Turtle" (page 667), "Splinter" (page 702).
   c. "Little Jack Horner" (page 640), "Seal Lullaby" (page 692), "Heaven-Haven" (page 712).
   d. "There is no frigate like a book" (page 547), "Apparently with no surprise" (page 654), "Love" (page 665).

3. The following poems are all on seasons of the year. Rank them on a scale of poetic accomplishment: "Winter" (page 520), "Spring" (Shakespeare, page 524), "Spring" (Hopkins, page 568), "To Autumn" (page 568).
4. "The Man He Killed" (page 533) and "Naming of Parts" (page 554) both treat the subject of war. Which is the superior poem?
5. "A Valediction: Forbidding Mourning" (page 583), "The 'Je Ne Sais Quoi'" (page 693), and "if everything happens that can't be done" (page 694) all treat the subject of love. Evaluate and rank them.
6. Rank the following poems by Robert Browning in order of their excellence and defend your ranking: "Meeting at Night" and "Parting at Morning" (considered as one poem) (pages 561–62), "My Star" (page 591), "My Last Duchess" (page 626).
7. Bryant's "To a Waterfowl" and Frost's "Design" (pages 644–45) have a similar subject. Which is the greater poem? Why?
8. Herrick's "To the Virgins, to Make Much of Time" (page 596) and Marvell's "To His Coy Mistress" (page 584) are both *carpe diem* poems of acknowledged excellence. Which achieves the more complex unity?
9. The following poems are all in praise of a beloved. Evaluate and rank them: "A Silken Tent" (page 580), "A Red, Red Rose" (page 611), "My mistress' eyes are nothing like the sun" (page 819).
10. The following poems all explore discord or disenchantment in love. Evaluate and rank them: "When my love swears that she is made of truth" (page 548), "Living in Sin" (page 566), "The Mouse Dinners" (page 791).
11. Each of the following pairs is written by a single author. Pick the poem of each pair that you think represents the higher poetic accomplishment and explain why.
    a. "Bredon Hill" and "To an Athlete Dying Young" (pages 797–98).
    b. "There's been a death in the opposite house" (page 540) and "Because I could not stop for death" (page 785).
    c. "Departmental" (page 624) and "Mending Wall" (page 792).
    d. "The Coming of Wisdom with Time" (page 657) and "Down by the Salley Gardens" (page 697).
    e. "The Lamb" and "The Tiger" (pages 777–78).
    f. "All day I hear" (page 715) and "On the Beach at Fontana" (page 744).
    g. "Song" (page 786) and "The Sun Rising" (page 789).
    h. "Naming of Parts" and "Judging Distances" (pages 554–55).
    i. "Bereft" (page 572) and "Design" (page 645).
    j. "A Hummingbird" (page 577) and "Apparently with no surprise" (page 654).
    k. "Loveliest of trees" (page 587) and "When I was one-and-twenty" (page 728).
    l. "Heaven-Haven" (page 712) and "Pied Beauty" (page 743).
    m. "The Sick Rose" (page 600) and "Soft Snow" (page 608).
    n. "Richard Cory" (page 553) and "Mr. Flood's Party" (page 813).
    o. "Winter" (page 520) and "Spring" (page 524).
    p. "A Silken Tent" (page 580) and "The Aim Was Song" (page 698).
    q. "There is no frigate like a book" (page 547) and "My life closed twice before its close" (page 610).
    r. "Reveille" (page 599) and "Farewell to barn and stack and tree" (page 658).

Poems for
Further Reading

BLACK AND WHITE

"Rhodesia, sweaty
flank of the world . . ."
i read as quietly
as they lay: "guerillas,"
it went on,   5
"put here as a lesson . . ."

they lay like a catch
in the plaza sun,
still damp, the eyes
not yet clouded,   10
the African heat
raising the bellies . . .

"it is the way
of our generals
to count what is theirs,   15
what is done
in their name,"
the secretary announced . . .

from their circle
photographers stare   20
and snap at the dead men,
at the keyboard of rifles
above their heads,
at the small town
that leads to   25
the jungle's edge—
they snap and freeze
it all, store it
in the silent world
of black and white . . .   30

Leonard Adame (b. 1947)

TO SATCH

Sometimes I feel like I will *never* stop
Just go on forever
Till one fine mornin'

BLACK AND WHITE.   This poem was first published in 1977 before Rhodesia, then ruled by
a white minority comprising about 3 percent of its population, became the present African
state of Zimbabwe, in which Blacks have a majority voice.

I'm gonna reach up and grab me a handfulla stars
Throw out my long lean leg
And whip three hot strikes burnin' down the heavens
And look over at God and say
How about that!

Samuel Allen (b. 1917)

THE LAST WAR

The first country to die was normal in the evening,
Ate a good but plain dinner, chatted with some friends
Over a glass, and went to bed soon after ten;
And in the morning was found disfigured and dead.
      That was a lucky one.   5

At breakfast the others heard about it, and kept
Their eyes on their plates. Who was guilty? No one knew,
But by lunch-time three more would never eat again.
The rest appealed for frankness, quietly cocked their guns,
      Declared "This can't go on."   10

They were right. Only the strongest turned up for tea:
The old ones with the big estates hadn't survived
The slobbering blindfold violence of the afternoon.
One killer or many? Was it a gang, or all-against-all?
      Somebody must have known.   15

But each of them sat there watching the others, until
Night came and found them anxious to get it over.
Then the lights went out. A few might have lived, even then;
Innocent, they thought (at first) it still mattered what
      You had or hadn't done.   20

They were wrong. One had been lenient with his servants;
Another ran an island brothel, but rarely left it;
The third owned a museum, the fourth a remarkable gun;
The name of the fifth was quite unknown, but in the end
      What was the difference? None.   25

Homicide, pacifist, crusader, cynic, gentile, jew
Staggered about moaning, shooting into the dark.

TO SATCH. "Satch" or "Satchelfoot" Paige, one of the great baseball pitchers of all time,
had an extraordinarily prolonged career. After more than two brilliant decades of pitching
in organized Negro baseball, he played in the major leagues after their integration. As late
as 1953, when he was over forty-seven years old, he participated in over fifty-seven games
as a relief pitcher.

Next day, to tidy up as usual, the sun came in
When they and their ammunition were all used up,
        And found himself alone.   30

Upset, he looked them over, to separate, if he could,
The assassins from the victims, but every face
Had taken on the flat anonymity of pain;
And soon they'll all smell alike, he thought, and felt sick,
        And went to bed at noon.   35

                                    Kingsley Amis (b. 1922)

DOVER BEACH

                The sea is calm tonight,
                The tide is full, the moon lies fair
                Upon the straits;—on the French coast the light
                Gleams and is gone; the cliffs of England stand,
                Glimmering and vast, out in the tranquil bay.   5
                Come to the window, sweet is the night-air!
                Only, from the long line of spray
                Where the sea meets the moon-blanched land,
                Listen! you hear the grating roar
                Of pebbles which the waves draw back, and fling,   10
                At their return, up the high strand,
                Begin, and cease, and then again begin,
                With tremulous cadence slow, and bring
                The eternal note of sadness in.

                Sophocles long ago   15
                Heard it on the Aegean, and it brought
                Into his mind the turbid ebb and flow
                Of human misery; we
                Find also in the sound a thought,
                Hearing it by this distant northern sea.   20

                The Sea of Faith
                Was once, too, at the full, and round earth's shore
                Lay like the folds of a bright girdle furled.
                But now I only hear
                Its melancholy, long, withdrawing roar,   25
                Retreating, to the breath
                Of the night-wind, down the vast edges drear
                And naked shingles° of the world.   pebbled beaches

                Ah, love, let us be true
                To one another! for the world, which seems   30

To lie before us like a land of dreams,
So various, so beautiful, so new,
Hath really neither joy, nor love, nor light,
Nor certitude, nor peace, nor help for pain;
And we are here as on a darkling plain   35
Swept with confused alarms of struggle and flight,
Where ignorant armies clash by night.

Matthew Arnold (1822–1888)

LANDCRAB

A lie, that we come from water.
The truth is we were born
from stones, dragons, the sea's
teeth, as you testify,
with your crust and jagged scissors.   5

Hermit, hard socket
for a timid eye,
you're a soft gut scuttling
sideways, a blue skull,
round bone on the prowl.   10
Wolf of treeroots and gravelly holes,
a mouth on stilts,
the husk of a small demon.

Attack, voracious
eating, and flight: 15
it's a sound routine
for staying alive on edges.
Then there's the tide, and that dance
you do for the moon
on wet sand, claws raised   20
to fend off your mate,
your coupling a quick
dry clatter of rocks.
For mammals
with their lobes and bulbs,   25
scruples and warm milk,
you've nothing but contempt.

Here you are, a frozen scowl
targeted in flashlight,
then gone: a piece of what   30
we are, not all,

my stunted child, my momentary
face in the mirror,
my tiny nightmare.

Margaret Atwood (*b. 1939*)

MUSÉE DES BEAUX ARTS

About suffering they were never wrong,
The Old Masters: how well they understood
Its human position; how it takes place
While someone else is eating or opening a window or just
    walking dully along;
How, when the aged are reverently, passionately waiting   5
For the miraculous birth, there always must be
Children who did not specially want it to happen, skating
On a pond at the edge of the wood:
They never forgot
That even the dreadful martyrdom must run its course   10
Anyhow in a corner, some untidy spot
Where the dogs go on with their doggy life and the
    torturer's horse
Scratches its innocent behind on a tree.

In Brueghel's *Icarus,* for instance: how everything turns away
Quite leisurely from the disaster; the ploughman may   15
Have heard the splash, the forsaken cry,
But for him it was not an important failure; the sun shone
As it had to on the white legs disappearing into the green
Water; and the expensive delicate ship that must have seen
Something amazing, a boy falling out of the sky,   20
Had somewhere to get to and sailed calmly on.

W. H. Auden (*1907–1973*)

"O WHERE ARE YOU GOING?"

"O where are you going?" said reader to rider,
"That valley is fatal when furnaces burn,
Yonder's the midden whose odors will madden,
That gap is the grave where the tall return."

"O do you imagine," said fearer to farer,   5
"That dusk will delay on your path to the pass,
Your diligent looking discover the lacking
Your footsteps feel from granite to grass?"

"O what was that bird," said horror to hearer,
"Did you see that shape in the twisted trees?   10
Behind you swiftly the figure comes softly,
The spot on your skin is a shocking disease?"

"Out of this house"—said rider to reader,
"Yours never will"—said farer to fearer,
"They're looking for you"—said hearer to horror,   15
As he left them there, as he left them there.

W. H. Auden (1907–1973)

ON READING POEMS TO A
SENIOR CLASS AT SOUTH HIGH

Before
I opened my mouth
I noticed them sitting there
as orderly as frozen fish
in a package.   5

Slowly water began to fill the room
though I did not notice it
till it reached
my ears

and then I heard the sounds   10
of fish in an aquarium

and I knew that though I had
tried to drown them
with my words
that they had only opened up   15
like gills for them
and let me in.

Together we swam around the room
like thirty tails whacking words
till the bell rang   20
puncturing
a hole in the door

where we all leaked out

They went to another class
I suppose and I home   25

where Queen Elizabeth
my cat met me
and licked my fins
till they were hands again.

D. C. Berry (b. 1947)

TWENTY-THIRD FLIGHT

Lo as I pause in the alien vale of the airport
fearing ahead the official ambush
a voice languorous and strange as these winds of Oahu
calleth my name and I turn to be quoited in orchids
and amazed with a kiss perfumed and soft as the *lei*   5
Straight from a travel poster thou steppest
thy arms like mangoes for smoothness
o implausible shepherdess for this one aging sheep
and leadest me through the righteous paths of the Customs
in a mist of my own wild hopes   10
Yea though I walk through the valley of Immigration
I fear no evil   for thou art a vision beside me
and my name is correctly spelled
and I shall dwell in the Hawaiian Village Hotel
where thy kindred prepareth a table before me   15
Thou restorest my baggage   and by limousine leadest me
to where I may lie on coral sands by a stream-lined pool

Nay but thou stayest not?
Thou anointest not my naked head with oil?
O shepherdess of Flight Number Twenty-three only   20
thou hastenest away on thy long brown legs to enchant
thy fellow-members in Local Five of the Greeters' Union
or that favored professor of Commerce mayhap
who leadeth thee into higher courses in Hotel Management
O nubile goddess of the Kaiser Training Programme   25
is it possible that tonight my cup runneth not over
and that I shall sit in the still pastures of the lobby
whilst thou leadest another old ram in garlands past me,
and   bland as papaya   appearest not to remember me?
And that I shall lie by the waters of Waikiki   and want?   30

Honolulu 1958   *Earle Birney (b. 1904)*

ONE ART

The art of losing isn't hard to master;
so many things seem filled with the intent
to be lost that their loss is no disaster.

Lose something every day. Accept the fluster
of lost door keys, the hour badly spent.   5
The art of losing isn't hard to master.

Then practice losing farther, losing faster:
places, and names, and where it was you meant
to travel. None of these will bring disaster.

I lost my mother's watch. And look! my last, or   10
next-to-last, of three loved houses went.
The art of losing isn't hard to master.

I lost two cities, lovely ones. And, vaster,
some realms I owned, two rivers, a continent.
I miss them, but it wasn't a disaster.   15

—Even losing you (the joking voice, a gesture
I love) I shan't have lied. It's evident
the art of losing's not too hard to master
though it may look like (*Write* it!) like disaster.

                                        Elizabeth Bishop (1911–1979)

THE LAMB

    Little Lamb, who made thee?
    Dost thou know who made thee?
Gave thee life and bid thee feed
By the stream and o'er the mead;
Gave thee clothing of delight,   5
Softest clothing wooly bright;
Gave thee such a tender voice,
Making all the vales rejoice!
    Little Lamb, who made thee?
    Dost thou know who made thee?   10

    Little Lamb, I'll tell thee,
    Little Lamb, I'll tell thee!
He is callèd by thy name,
For he calls himself a Lamb;
He is meek and he is mild,   15
He became a little child;
I a child and thou a lamb,
We are callèd by his name.
    Little Lamb, God bless thee.
    Little Lamb, God bless thee.   20

                                        William Blake (1757–1827)

THE TIGER

Tiger! Tiger! burning bright
In the forests of the night,
What immortal hand or eye
Could frame thy fearful symmetry?

In what distant deeps or skies   5
Burnt the fire of thine eyes?
On what wings dare he aspire?
What the hand dare seize the fire?

And what shoulder, and what art,
Could twist the sinews of thy heart?   10
And when thy heart began to beat,
What dread hand forged thy dread feet?

What the hammer? what the chain?
In what furnace was thy brain?
What the anvil? what dread grasp   15
Dare its deadly terrors clasp?

When the stars threw down their spears,
And watered heaven with their tears,
Did he smile his work to see?
Did he who made the Lamb make thee?   20

Tiger! Tiger! burning bright
In the forests of the night,
What immortal hand or eye
Dare frame thy fearful symmetry?

William Blake (1757–1827)

THE GARDEN OF LOVE

I went to the Garden of Love,
And saw what I never had seen:
A Chapel was built in the midst,
Where I used to play on the green.

And the gates of this Chapel were shut,   5
And "Thou shalt not" writ over the door;
So I turned to the Garden of Love
That so many sweet flowers bore;

And I saw it was filled with graves,
And tomb-stones where flowers should be;   10

And Priests in black gowns were walking their rounds,
And binding with briars my joys and desires.

William Blake (1757–1827)

SOUTHERN COP

Let us forgive Ty Kendricks.
The place was Darktown. He was young.
His nerves were jittery. The day was hot.
The Negro ran out of the alley.
And so Ty shot.   5

Let us understand Ty Kendricks.
The Negro must have been dangerous,
Because he ran;
And here was a rookie with a chance
To prove himself a man.   10

Let us condone Ty Kendricks
If we cannot decorate.
When he found what the Negro was running for,
It was too late;
And all we can say for the Negro is   15
It was unfortunate.

Let us pity Ty Kendricks.
He has been through enough,
Standing there, his big gun smoking,
Rabbit-scared, alone,   20
Having to hear the wenches wail
And the dying Negro moan.

Sterling Brown (b. 1901)

THE SCIENTIST

"There's nothing mysterious about the skull."
He may have been suspicious of my request,
That being mainly a poet, I mainly guessed
There might be an esoteric chance to cull

Some succulent, unfamiliar word; that being   5
Mainly a woman, I now for his sake embraced
An object I held in fact in some distaste.
But he complied, his slender fingers freeing

(There must be a surgeon somewhere with stubby hands)
The latch that held a coil across "The suture   10
Between the parietals and occipital feature."
And gently, his flesh on the bone disturbed the bands

Which illustrated the way that "The mandible
Articulates with the temple next to the ear.
The nasal bone gives onto the maxilla here."   15
He laughed, "It's a bore, but it's not expendable;

"The features depend, if not for their shape, on the narrow
Cranium, formed of the commonest elements;
Weighing nine ounces, worth about fourteen cents;
Not even room for what you would call a marrow."   20

In words resembling these, he judged them dull;
The specimen, his detail, and my suggestion.
"The skin and the brain, of course, are another question,"
He said again, "but there's nothing to the skull."

And that must be so. The quick mind most demands a   25
Miracle in the covering or the core.
What lies between is shallow and functional fare:
My hand between this thought and the posturing stanza.

But his face belied us both. As he spoke his own
Eyes rhymed depth from the sockets of that example;   30
His jawline articulated with the temple
Over the words, and his fingers along the bone

Revealed his god in the praying of their plying.
So that, wonderfully, I justify his doubt:
Am moved, as woman to love, as poet to write,   35
By the mystery and the function of his denying.

                                              Janet Burroway (b. *1936*)

LISA

Under the great down-curving lilac branches,
a dome of coolness and a cave of bloom,
Lisa, vague-eyed, chin-propped, cross-legged, is sitting
within a leaf-walled room.

Beyond the curtaining green, her brothers wrangle,   5
cars pass, a huckster shouts, a bicycle bell
is brisk, is brief, dogs bark. She does not hear them.
She is netted in silence, she is lost in a spell.

She has chosen to come here, but she is not hiding,
nor in disgrace, nor sulky. She is alone   10
of her free will—alone and yet not lonely:
this quarter hour her own.

She could not tell you herself what she is thinking,
or what she makes of this kingdom she has found.
Presently she will go and join the others: 15
her voice will sound

with theirs. But now the candid light, come sifting
thro leaves, illuminates another view.
O leaf and light, that can divide thus cleanly
the world in two   20

and give the halves to a child, so to acquaint her
with the mind's need of quietude for growth,
yet interpose no barrier between them,
that she may move in both.

Constance Carrier (b. 1908)

GIFT

You tell me that silence
is nearer to peace than poems
but if for my gift
I brought you silence
(for I know silence)
you would say
    This is not silence
    this is another poem
and you would hand it back to me.

Leonard Cohen (b. 1934)

KUBLA KHAN

In Xanadu did Kubla Khan
A stately pleasure-dome decree:
Where Alph, the sacred river, ran
Through caverns measureless to man
    Down to a sunless sea.   5
So twice five miles of fertile ground
With walls and towers were girdled round:
And here were gardens bright with sinuous rills,

Where blossomed many an incense-bearing tree;
And here were forests ancient as the hills,   10
Enfolding sunny spots of greenery.

But oh! that deep romantic chasm which slanted
Down the green hill athwart a cedarn cover!
A savage place! as holy and enchanted
As e'er beneath a waning moon was haunted   15
By woman wailing for her demon-lover!
And from this chasm, with ceaseless turmoil seething,
As if this earth in fast thick pants were breathing,
A mighty fountain momently was forced:
Amid whose swift half-intermitted burst   20
Huge fragments vaulted like rebounding hail,
Or chaffy grain beneath the thresher's flail:
And 'mid these dancing rocks at once and ever
It flung up momently the sacred river.
Five miles meandering with a mazy motion   25
Through wood and dale the sacred river ran,
Then reached the caverns measureless to man,
And sank in tumult to a lifeless ocean:
And 'mid this tumult Kubla heard from far
Ancestral voices prophesying war!   30

        The shadow of the dome of pleasure
        Floated midway on the waves;
        Where was heard the mingled measure
        From the fountain and the caves.
It was a miracle of rare device,   35
A sunny pleasure-dome with caves of ice!

        A damsel with a dulcimer
        In a vision once I saw:
        It was an Abyssinian maid,
        And on her dulcimer she played,   40
        Singing of Mount Abora.
        Could I revive within me
        Her symphony and song,
To such a deep delight, 'twould win me,
That with music loud and long,   45
I would build that dome in air,
That sunny dome! those caves of ice!
And all who heard should see them there,
And all should cry, Beware! Beware!
His flashing eyes, his floating hair!   50
Weave a circle round him thrice,

And close your eyes with holy dread,
For he on honey-dew hath fed,
And drunk the milk of Paradise.

Samuel Taylor Coleridge (1772–1834)

THE LISTENERS

"Is there anybody there?" said the Traveler,
    Knocking on the moonlit door;
And his horse in the silence champed the grasses
    Of the forest's ferny floor:
And a bird flew up out of the turret,   5
    Above the Traveler's head:
And he smote upon the door again a second time;
    "Is there anybody there?" he said.
But no one descended to the Traveler;
    No head from the leaf-fringed sill   10
Leaned over and looked into his grey eyes,
    Where he stood perplexed and still.
But only a host of phantom listeners
    That dwelt in the lone house then
Stood listening in the quiet of the moonlight   15
    To that voice from the world of men:
Stood thronging the faint moonbeams on the dark stair,
    That goes down to the empty hall,
Hearkening in an air stirred and shaken
    By the lonely Traveler's call.   20
And he felt in his heart their strangeness,
    Their stillness answering his cry,
While his horse moved, cropping the dark turf,
    'Neath the starred and leafy sky;
For he suddenly smote on the door, even   25
    Louder, and lifted his head:—
"Tell them I came, and no one answered,
    That I kept my word," he said.
Never the least stir made the listeners,
    Though every word he spake   30
Fell echoing through the shadowiness of the still house
    From the one man left awake:
Ay, they heard his foot upon the stirrup,
    And the sound of iron on stone,
And how the silence surged softly backward,   35
    When the plunging hoofs were gone.

Walter de la Mare (1873–1956)

THE BEE

To the football coaches of Clemson College, 1942

One dot
Grainily shifting   we at roadside and
The smallest wings coming   along the rail fence out
Of the woods   one dot   of all that green. It now
Becomes flesh-crawling   then the quite still   5
Of stinging. I must live faster for my terrified
Small son   it is on him. Has come. Clings.

Old wingback, come
To life. If your knee action is high
Enough, the fat may fall in time   God damn   10
You, Dickey, *dig*   this is your last time to cut
And run   but you must give it everything you have
Left, for screaming near your screaming child is the sheer
Murder of California traffic: some bee hangs driving

Your child   15
Blindly onto the highway. Get there however
Is still possible. Long live what I badly did
At Clemson   and all of my clumsiest drives
For the ball   all of my trying to turn
The corner downfield   and my spindling explosions   20
Through the five-hole over tackle. O backfield

Coach Shag Norton,
Tell me as you never yet have told me
To get the lead out   scream whatever will get
The slow-motion of middle age off me   I cannot   25
Make it this way   I will have to leave
My feet   they are gone   I have him where
He lives   and down we go singing with screams into

The dirt,
Son-screams of fathers   screams of dead coaches turning   30
To approval   and from between us the bee rises screaming
With flight   grainily shifting   riding the rail fence
Back into the woods   traffic blasting past us
Unchanged, nothing heard through the air-
conditioning glass   we lying at roadside full   35

Of the forearm prints
Of roadrocks   strawberries on our elbows as from
Scrimmage with the varsity   now we can get

Up   stand   turn away from the highway   look straight
Into trees. See, there is nothing coming out   no   40
Smallest wing   no shift of a flight-grain   nothing
Nothing. Let us go in, son, and listen

For some tobacco-
mumbling voice in the branches   to say "That's
a little better,"   to our lives still hanging   45
By a hair. There is nothing to stop us   we can go
Deep   deeper   into elms, and listen to traffic die
Roaring, like a football crowd from which we have
Vanished. Dead coaches live in the air, son   live

In the ear   50
Like fathers, and *urge*   and *urge*. They want you better
Than you are. When needed, they rise and curse you   they scream
When something must be saved. Here, under this tree,
We can sit down. You can sleep, and I can try
To give back what I have earned by keeping us   55
Alive, and safe from bees: the smile of some kind

Of savior—
Of touchdowns, of fumbles, battles,
Lives. Let me sit here with you, son
As on the bench, while the first string takes back   60
Over, far away   and say with my silentest tongue, with the man-
creating bruises of my arms   with a live leaf a quick
Dead hand on my shoulder, "Coach Norton, I am your boy."

James Dickey (b. 1923)

BECAUSE I COULD NOT STOP FOR DEATH

Because I could not stop for Death,
He kindly stopped for me;
The carriage held but just ourselves
And Immortality.

We slowly drove; he knew no haste,   5
And I had put away
My labor and my leisure too,
For his civility.

We passed the school, where children strove,
At recess, in the ring,   10
We passed the fields of gazing grain,
We passed the setting sun,

Or rather, he passed us;
The dews drew quivering and chill;
For only gossamer, my gown;   15
My tippet, only tulle.

We paused before a house that seemed
A swelling of the ground;
The roof was scarcely visible.
The cornice, in the ground.   20

Since then, 'tis centuries, and yet
Feels shorter than the day
I first surmised the horses' heads
Were toward eternity.

Emily Dickinson (1830–1886)

I TASTE A LIQUOR NEVER BREWED

I taste a liquor never brewed,
From tankards scooped in pearl;
Not all the vats upon the Rhine
Yield such an alcohol!

Inebriate of air am I,   5
And debauchee of dew,
Reeling, through endless summer days,
From inns of molten blue.

When landlords turn the drunken bee
Out of the foxglove's door,   10
When butterflies renounce their drams,
I shall but drink the more!

Till seraphs swing their snowy hats,
And saints to windows run,
To see the little tippler   15
Leaning against the sun!

Emily Dickinson (1830–1886)

SONG: GO AND CATCH A FALLING STAR

Go and catch a falling star,
    Get with child a mandrake root,
Tell me where all past years are,

SONG. 2. *mandrake:* supposed to resemble a human being because of its forked root.

Or who cleft the devil's foot,
Teach me to hear mermaids singing, 5
    Or to keep off envy's stinging,
            And find
            What wind
Serves to advance an honest mind.

If thou be'st born to strange sights, 10
    Things invisible to see,
Ride ten thousand days and nights,
    Till age snow white hairs on thee,
Thou, when thou return'st, wilt tell me
    All strange wonders that befell thee, 15
            And swear
            No where
Lives a woman true and fair.

If thou find'st one, let me know;
    Such a pilgrimage were sweet. 20
Yet do not; I would not go,
    Though at next door we might meet.
Though she were true when you met her,
    And last till you write your letter,
            Yet she 25
            Will be
False, ere I come, to two or three.

John Donne (1572–1631)

THE FLEA

Mark but this flea, and mark in this
How little that which thou deny'st me is;
It sucked me first, and now sucks thee,
And in this flea our two bloods mingled be;
Thou know'st that this cannot be said 5
A sin, nor shame, nor loss of maidenhead;
    Yet this enjoys before it woo,
    And pampered swells with one blood made of two,
    And this, alas, is more than we would do.

Oh stay, three lives in one flea spare, 10
Where we almost, yea more than married are.
This flea is you and I, and this
Our marriage bed, and marriage temple is;
Though parents grudge, and you, we are met

And cloistered in these living walls of jet. 15

    Though use° make you apt to kill me, habit

    Let not to that, self-murder added be,

    And sacrilege, three sins in killing three.

Cruel and sudden, hast thou since

Purpled thy nail in blood of innocence? 20

Wherein could this flea guilty be,

Except in that drop which it sucked from thee?

Yet thou triumph'st and say'st that thou

Find'st not thyself, nor me the weaker now.

    'Tis true. Then learn how false fears be: 25

    Just so much honor, when thou yield'st to me,

    Will waste, as this flea's death took life from thee.

John Donne (1572–1631)

THE GOOD-MORROW

I wonder, by my troth, what thou and I

Did till we loved? were we not weaned till then,

But sucked on country pleasures childishly?

Or snorted we in the seven sleepers' den?

'Twas so; but this, all pleasures fancies be. 5

If ever any beauty I did see,

Which I desired, and got, 'twas but a dream of thee.

And now good-morrow to our waking souls,

Which watch not one another out of fear;

For love all love of other sights controls, 10

And makes one little room an everywhere.

Let sea-discoverers to new worlds have gone;

Let maps to other,° worlds on worlds have shown; others

Let us possess one world; each hath one, and is one.

My face in thine eye, thine in mine appears, 15

And true plain hearts do in the faces rest;

Where can we find two better hemispheres

Without sharp north, without declining west?

Whatever dies was not mixed equally;

If our two loves be one, or thou and I 20

Love so alike that none can slacken, none can die.

John Donne (1572–1631)

THE GOOD-MORROW. 4. *seven sleepers' den:* a cave where, according to Christian legend, seven youths escaped persecution and slept for two centuries.

THE SUN RISING

        Busy old fool, unruly Sun,
        Why dost thou thus
Through windows and through curtains call on us?
Must to thy motions lovers' seasons run?
        Saucy pedantic wretch, go chide   5
        Late schoolboys and sour prentices,
  Go tell court-huntsmen that the king will ride,
  Call country ants to harvest offices;
Love, all alike, no season knows, nor clime,
Nor hours, days, months, which are the rags of time.   10

        Thy beams so reverend and strong
        Why shouldst thou think?
I could eclipse and cloud them with a wink,
But that I would not lose her sight so long;
        If her eyes have not blinded thine,   15
        Look, and tomorrow late tell me,
  Whether both th' Indias of spice and mine
  Be where thou left'st them, or lie here with me.
Ask for those kings whom thou saw'st yesterday,
And thou shalt hear, "All here in one bed lay."   20

        She's all states, and all princes I;
        Nothing else is.
Princes do but play us; compared to this,
All honor's mimic, all wealth alchemy.
        Thou, Sun, art half as happy as we,   25
        In that the world's contracted thus;
  Thine age asks ease, and since thy duties be
  To warm the world, that's done in warming us.
Shine here to us, and thou art everywhere;
This bed thy center is, these walls thy sphere.   30

John Donne (1572–1631)

VERGISSMEINNICHT

        Three weeks gone and the combatants gone,
        returning over the nightmare ground
        we found the place again, and found
        the soldier sprawling in the sun.

VERGISSMEINNICHT. The German title means "Forget me not." The author, an English poet, fought with a tank battalion in World War II and was killed in the invasion of Normandy.

The frowning barrel of his gun   5
overshadowing. As we came on
that day, he hit my tank with one
like the entry of a demon.

Look. Here in the gunpit spoil
the dishonored picture of his girl   10
who has put: *Steffi.° Vergissmeinnicht*   a girl's name
in a copybook gothic script.

We see him almost with content
abased, and seeming to have paid
and mocked at by his own equipment   15
that's hard and good when he's decayed.

But she would weep to see to-day
how on his skin the swart flies move;
the dust upon the paper eye
and the burst stomach like a cave.   20

For here the lover and killer are mingled
who had one body and one heart.
And death who had the soldier singled
has done the lover mortal hurt.

Keith Douglas (1920-1944)

THE DEBT

This is the debt I pay
Just for one riotous day,
Years of regret and grief,
Sorrow without relief.

Pay it I will to the end—   5
Until the grave, my friend,
Gives me a true release—
Gives me the clasp of peace.

Slight was the thing I bought,
Small was the debt I thought,   10
Poor was the loan at best—
God but the interest!

Paul Laurence Dunbar (1872-1906)

AWARD

A Gold Watch to the FBI
Man who has followed
me for 25 years.

Well, old spy
looks like I
led you down some pretty blind alleys,
took you on several trips to Mexico,
fishing in the high Sierras,   5
jazz at the Philharmonic.
You've watched me all your life,
I've clothed your wife,
put your two sons through college.
what good has it done?   10
the sun keeps rising every morning.
ever see me buy an Assistant President?
or close a school?
or lend money to Trujillo?
ever catch me rigging airplane prices?   15
I bought some after-hours whiskey in L. A.
but the Chief got his pay.
I ain't killed no Koreans
or fourteen-year-old boys in Mississippi.
neither did I bomb Guatemala,   20
or lend guns to shoot Algerians.
I admit I took a Negro child
to a white rest room in Texas,
but she was my daughter, only three,
who had to pee.   25

Ray Durem (1915–1963)

THE MOUSE DINNERS

A woman was cooking a mouse for her husband's dinner, roasting it with a blueberry in its mouth.

He'll use a dentist's pick and a surgeon's scalpel to get the meat off, bending over the tiny roastling with a jeweler's loupe in his eye . . . Twenty years of this . . .

AWARD. 14. *Trujillo:* Dictator of the Dominican Republic, 1930–1961.

After dinner he'll make a long gassy belch as he pats his stomach, saying, it's the best mouse he's ever had, and (as he always reminds her) one less vermin in this world.

Then she'll say, you say that every night, like last night, the curried mouse, the night before, the garlic and butter mouse, sauteed in its own fur. Oh, and then there was the mouse pie. Or was it my mouse-in-the-trap, the mouse I baked in its own trap for variety? My mouse tartare? Or was it mouse poached in menstrual blood at the full of the moon, the best you'd ever had?—Hypocrite!

Hypocrite? No no, I never liked mouse. I thought you liked mouse, so I liked mouse so you'd like me, cried the husband.

You mouse! cried his wife.

Ah yes, he is a mouse; but it came so slowly he hadn't noticed . . . Perhaps it was the twenty years of mouse, eaten to please a wife, who he thought liked mice, has worked the metamorphosis. But now he sees she never liked mouse, and sees this only now that he has himself become a mouse . . .

Russell Edson (b. 1935)

ACQUAINTED WITH THE NIGHT

I have been one acquainted with the night.
I have walked out in rain—and back in rain.
I have outwalked the furthest city light.

I have looked down the saddest city lane.
I have passed by the watchman on his beat   5
And dropped my eyes, unwilling to explain.

I have stood still and stopped the sound of feet
When far away an interrupted cry
Came over houses from another street,

But not to call me back or say good-by;   10
And further still at an unearthly height
One luminary clock against the sky

Proclaimed the time was neither wrong nor right.
I have been one acquainted with the night.

Robert Frost (1874–1963)

MENDING WALL

Something there is that doesn't love a wall,
That sends the frozen-ground-swell under it

And spills the upper boulders in the sun,
And makes gaps even two can pass abreast.
The work of hunters is another thing: 5
I have come after them and made repair
Where they have left not one stone on a stone,
But they would have the rabbit out of hiding,
To please the yelping dogs. The gaps I mean,
No one has seen them made or heard them made, 10
But at spring mending-time we find them there.
I let my neighbor know beyond the hill;
And on a day we meet to walk the line
And set the wall between us once again.
We keep the wall between us as we go. 15
To each the boulders that have fallen to each.
And some are loaves and some so nearly balls
We have to use a spell to make them balance:
"Stay where you are until our backs are turned!"
We wear our fingers rough with handling them. 20
Oh, just another kind of outdoor game,
One on a side. It comes to little more:
There where it is we do not need the wall:
He is all pine and I am apple orchard.
My apple trees will never get across 25
And eat the cones under his pines, I tell him.
He only says, "Good fences make good neighbors."
Spring is the mischief in me, and I wonder
If I could put a notion in his head:
"*Why* do they make good neighbors? Isn't it 30
Where there are cows? But here there are no cows.
Before I built a wall I'd ask to know
What I was walling in or walling out,
And to whom I was like to give offense.
Something there is that doesn't love a wall, 35
That wants it down." I could say "Elves" to him,
But it's not elves exactly, and I'd rather
He said it for himself. I see him there,
Bringing a stone grasped firmly by the top
In each hand, like an old-stone savage armed. 40
He moves in darkness as it seems to me,
Not of woods only and the shade of trees.
He will not go behind his father's saying,
And he likes having thought of it so well
He says again, "Good fences make good neighbors." 45

Robert Frost (*1874–1963*)

CHANNEL FIRING

That night your great guns, unawares,
Shook all our coffins as we lay,
And broke the chancel window-squares,
We thought it was the Judgment-day

And sat upright. While drearisome   5
Arose the howl of wakened hounds:
The mouse let fall the altar-crumb,
The worms drew back into the mounds,

The glebe cow drooled. Till God called, "No;
It's gunnery practice out at sea   10
Just as before you went below;
The world is as it used to be:

"All nations striving strong to make
Red war yet redder. Mad as hatters
They do no more for Christès sake   15
Than you who are helpless in such matters.

"That this is not the judgment-hour
For some of them's a blessed thing,
For if it were they'd have to scour
Hell's floor for so much threatening. . . .   20

"Ha, ha. It will be warmer when
I blow the trumpet (if indeed
I ever do; for you are men,
and rest eternal sorely need)."

So down we lay again. "I wonder,   25
Will the world ever saner be,"
Said one, "than when He sent us under
In our indifferent century!"

And many a skeleton shook his head.
"Instead of preaching forty year,"   30
My neighbor Parson Thirdly said,
"I wish I had stuck to pipes and beer."

CHANNEL FIRING.   35–36. *Stourton Tower:* memorial at the spot where Alfred the Great
resisted the invading Danes in 879; *Camelot:* legendary capital of Arthur's kingdom; *Stonehenge:* mysterious circle of huge stones erected in Wiltshire by very early inhabitants of
Britain. The three references move backward in time through the historic, the legendary,
and the prehistoric.

Again the guns disturbed the hour,
Roaring their readiness to avenge,
As far inland as Stourton Tower,   35
And Camelot, and starlit Stonehenge.

April 1914.

Thomas Hardy (1840–1928)

THE DARKLING THRUSH

I leant upon a coppice gate
    When Frost was specter-gray,
And Winter's dregs made desolate
    The weakening eye of day.
The tangled bine-stems scored the sky   5
    Like strings of broken lyres,
And all mankind that haunted nigh
    Had sought their household fires.

The land's sharp features seemed to be
    The Century's corpse outleant,   10
His crypt the cloudy canopy,
    The wind his death-lament.
The ancient pulse of germ and birth
    Was shrunken hard and dry,
And every spirit upon earth   15
    Seemed fervorless as I.

At once a voice arose among
    The bleak twigs overhead
In a full-hearted evensong
    Of joy illimited;   20
An aged thrush, frail, gaunt, and small,
    In blast-beruffled plume,
Had chosen thus to fling his soul
    Upon the growing gloom.

So little cause for carolings   25
    Of such ecstatic sound
Was written on terrestrial things
    Afar or nigh around,
That I could think there trembled through
    His happy good-night air   30

Some blessed Hope, whereof he knew
And I was unaware.

December 1900.

Thomas Hardy (1840–1928)

"MORE LIGHT! MORE LIGHT!"

Composed in the Tower before his execution
These moving verses, and being brought at that time
Painfully to the stake, submitted, declaring thus:
"I implore my God to witness that I have made no crime."

Nor was he forsaken of courage, but the death was horrible,   5
The sack of gunpowder failing to ignite.
His legs were blistered sticks on which the black sap
Bubbled and burst as he howled for the Kindly Light.

And that was but one, and by no means one of the worst;
Permitted at least his pitiful dignity;   10
And such as were by made prayers in the name of Christ,
That shall judge all men, for his soul's tranquility.

We move now to outside a German wood.
Three men are there commanded to dig a hole
In which the two Jews are ordered to lie down   15
And be buried alive by the third, who is a Pole.

Not light from the shrine at Weimar beyond the hill
Nor light from heaven appeared. But he did refuse.
A Lüger settled back deeply in its glove.
He was ordered to change places with the Jews.   20

Much casual death had drained away their souls.
The thick dirt mounted toward the quivering chin.

"MORE LIGHT! MORE LIGHT!" Title: These words are sometimes said to have been the last
uttered by Goethe (1749–1832), the great German poet and scientist, before his death.
1. *Tower:* the Tower of London, for centuries a place of imprisonment for high-ranking
offenders against the English Crown. The account in stanzas 1–3 is composite, but based
largely on the death of Bishop Nicholas Ridley, burned at Oxford in 1553.   6. *gunpowder:*
used to ignite the faggots and thus make the death occur more quickly.   8. *Kindly Light:*
"Lead, Kindly Light" are the opening words of a famous hymn ("The Pillar of Cloud") by
Cardinal Newman (1801–1890).   13. *German wood:* Stanzas 4–8 give an accurate account
of an incident that occurred at Buchenwald in 1944.   17. *Weimar:* the intellectual center of
Germany during the late eighteenth and early nineteenth centuries; Goethe died there. It is
near Buchenwald.

When only the head was exposed the order came
To dig him out again and to get back in.

No light, no light in the blue Polish eye. 25
When he finished a riding boot packed down the earth.
The Lüger hovered lightly in its glove.
He was shot in the belly and in three hours bled to death.

No prayers or incense rose up in those hours
Which grew to be years, and every day came mute 30
Ghosts from the ovens, sifting through crisp air,
And settled upon his eyes in a black soot.

Anthony Hecht (b. 1923)

BREDON HILL

In summertime on Bredon
    The bells they sound so clear;
Round both the shires they ring them
    In steeples far and near,
    A happy noise to hear. 5

Here of a Sunday morning
    My love and I would lie,
And see the colored counties,
    And hear the larks so high
    About us in the sky. 10

The bells would ring to call her
    In valleys miles away:
"Come all to church, good people;
    Good people, come and pray."
    But here my love would stay. 15

And I would turn and answer
    Among the springing thyme,
"Oh, peal upon our wedding,
    And we will hear the chime,
    And come to church in time." 20

But when the snows at Christmas
    On Bredon top were strown,
My love rose up so early
    And stole out unbeknown
    And went to church alone. 25

They tolled the one bell only,
    Groom there was none to see,
The mourners followed after,
    And so to church went she,
    And would not wait for me.   30

The bells they sound on Bredon,
    And still the steeples hum.
"Come all to church, good people,"—
    Oh, noisy bells, be dumb;
    I hear you, I will come.   35

A. E. Housman (*1859–1936*)

TO AN ATHLETE DYING YOUNG

The time you won your town the race
We chaired you through the market-place;
Man and boy stood cheering by,
And home we brought you shoulder-high.

To-day, the road all runners come,   5
Shoulder-high, we bring you home,
And set you at your threshold down,
Townsman of a stiller town.

Smart lad, to slip betimes away
From fields where glory does not stay   10
And early though the laurel grows
It withers quicker than the rose.

Eyes the shady night has shut
Cannot see the record cut,
And silence sounds no worse than cheers   15
After earth has stopped the ears:

Now you will not swell the rout
Of lads that wore their honors out,
Runners whom renown outran
And the name died before the man.   20

So set, before its echoes fade,
The fleet foot on the sill of shade,
And hold to the low lintel up
The still-defended challenge-cup.

And round that early-laureled head   25
Will flock to gaze the strengthless dead,
And find unwithered on its curls
The garland briefer than a girl's.

A. E. Housman (1859–1936)

PIKE

Pike, three inches long, perfect
Pike in all parts, green tigering the gold.
Killers from the egg: the malevolent aged grin.
They dance on the surface among the flies.

Or move, stunned by their own grandeur   5
Over a bed of emerald, silhouette
Of submarine delicacy and horror.
A hundred feet long in their world.

In ponds, under the heat-struck lily pads—
Gloom of their stillness: 10
Logged on last year's black leaves, watching upwards.
Or hung in an amber cavern of weeds

The jaws' hooked clamp and fangs
Not to be changed at this date;
A life subdued to its instrument;   15
The gills kneading quietly, and the pectorals.

Three we kept behind glass,
Jungled in weed: three inches, four,
And four and a half: fed fry to them—
Suddenly there were two. Finally one.   20

With a sag belly and the grin it was born with.
And indeed they spare nobody.
Two, six pounds each, over two feet long,
High and dry and dead in the willow-herb—

One jammed past its gills down the other's gullet: 25
The outside eye stared: as a vice locks—
The same iron in this eye
Though its film shrank in death.

A pond I fished, fifty yards across,
Whose lilies and muscular tench   30

Had outlasted every visible stone
Of the monastery that planted them—

Stilled legendary depth:
It was as deep as England. It held
Pike too immense to stir, so immense and old   35
That past nightfall I dared not cast

But silently cast and fished
With the hair frozen on my head
For what might move, for what eye might move.
The still splashes on the dark pond,   40

Owls hushing the floating woods
Frail on my ear against the dream
Darkness beneath night's darkness had freed,
That rose slowly towards me, watching.

Ted Hughes (b. 1930)

THE DEATH OF THE BALL TURRET GUNNER

From my mother's sleep I fell into the State,
And I hunched in its belly till my wet fur froze.
Six miles from earth, loosed from its dream of life,
I woke to black flak and the nightmare fighters.
When I died they washed me out of the turret with a hose.

Randall Jarrell (1914–1965)

PATHEDY OF MANNERS

At twenty she was brilliant and adored,
Phi Beta Kappa, sought for every dance;
Captured symbolic logic and the glance
Of men whose interest was their sole reward.

She learned the cultured jargon of those bred   5
To antique crystal and authentic pearls,
Scorned Wagner, praised the Degas dancing girls,
And when she might have thought, conversed instead.

PATHEDY OF MANNERS. *Pathedy:* a coined word formed from the Greek root *path-* (as in *pathetic, pathology*) plus the suffix *-edy* (as in *tragedy, comedy*).

She hung up her diploma, went abroad,
Saw catalogues of domes and tapestry,   10
Rejected an impoverished marquis,
And learned to tell real Wedgwood from a fraud.

Back home her breeding led her to espouse
A bright young man whose pearl cufflinks were real.
They had an ideal marriage, and ideal   15
But lonely children in an ideal house.

I saw her yesterday at forty-three
Her children gone, her husband one year dead,
Toying with plots to kill time and re-wed
Illusions of lost opportunity.   20

But afraid to wonder what she might have known
With all that wealth and mind had offered her,
She shuns conviction, choosing to infer
Tenets of every mind except her own.

A hundred people call, though not one friend,   25
To parry a hundred doubts with nimble talk.
Her meanings lost in manners, she will walk
Alone in brilliant circles to the end.

Ellen Kay (b. 1931)

LA BELLE DAME SANS MERCI
A BALLAD

O, what can ail thee, knight-at-arms,
    Alone and palely loitering?
The sedge has withered from the lake,
    And no birds sing.

O, what can ail thee, knight-at-arms,   5
    So haggard and so woe-begone?
The squirrel's granary is full,
    And the harvest's done.

I see a lily on thy brow,
    With anguish moist and fever dew;   10

LA BELLE DAME SANS MERCI. The title means "The beautiful woman without mercy."

And on thy cheeks a fading rose
    Fast withereth too.

I met a lady in the meads,
    Full beautiful—a faery's child
Her hair was long, her foot was light,   15
    And her eyes were wild.

I made a garland for her head,
    And bracelets too, and fragrant zone;
She looked at me as she did love,
    And made sweet moan.   20

I set her on my pacing steed,
    And nothing else saw all day long;
For sidelong would she bend, and sing
    A faery's song.

She found me roots of relish sweet,   25
    And honey wild, and manna dew,
And sure in language strange she said—
    "I love thee true."

She took me to her elfin grot,
    And there she wept and sighed full sore,   30
And there I shut her wild wild eyes
    With kisses four.

And there she lullèd me asleep
    And there I dreamed—Ah! woe betide!
The latest dream I ever dreamed   35
    On the cold hill side.

I saw pale kings and princes too,
    Pale warriors, death-pale were they all;
They cried—"La Belle Dame sans Merci
    Hath thee in thrall!"   40

I saw their starved lips in the gloam
    With horrid warning gapèd wide,
And I awoke and found me here
    On the cold hill's side.

And this is why I sojourn here   45
    Alone and palely loitering,
Though the sedge has withered from the lake,
    And no birds sing.

John Keats (1795-1821)

ODE ON A GRECIAN URN

Thou still unravished bride of quietness,
  Thou foster-child of silence and slow time,
Sylvan historian, who canst thus express
  A flowery tale more sweetly than our rhyme:
What leaf-fringed legend haunts about thy shape   5
  Of deities or mortals, or of both,
    In Tempe or the dales of Arcady?
What men or gods are these? What maidens loth?
What mad pursuit? What struggle to escape?
    What pipes and timbrels? What wild ecstasy?   10

Heard melodies are sweet, but those unheard
  Are sweeter; therefore, ye soft pipes, play on;
Not to the sensual ear, but, more endeared,
  Pipe to the spirit ditties of no tone:
Fair youth, beneath the trees, thou canst not leave   15
  Thy song, nor ever can those trees be bare;
    Bold Lover, never, never canst thou kiss,
Though winning near the goal—yet, do not grieve;
    She cannot fade, though thou hast not thy bliss,
For ever wilt thou love, and she be fair!   20

Ah, happy, happy boughs! that cannot shed
  Your leaves, nor ever bid the Spring adieu;
And, happy melodist, unwearièd,
  For ever piping songs for ever new;
More happy love! more happy, happy love!   25
  For ever warm and still to be enjoyed,
    For ever panting and for ever young;
All breathing human passion far above,
    That leaves a heart high-sorrowful and cloyed,
    A burning forehead, and a parching tongue.   30

Who are these coming to the sacrifice?
  To what green altar, O mysterious priest,
Lead'st thou that heifer lowing at the skies,
  And all her silken flanks with garlands drest?
What little town by river or sea shore,   35

ODE ON A GRECIAN URN.   49–50. In the 1820 edition of Keats's poems the words "Beauty is truth, truth beauty" were enclosed in quotation marks, and the poem is often reprinted that way. It is now generally agreed, however, on the basis of examination of contemporary transcripts of Keats's poem, that Keats intended the entire last two lines of the poem to be spoken by the Urn.

Or mountain-built with peaceful citadel,
        Is emptied of its folk, this pious morn?
And, little town, thy streets for evermore
        Will silent be; and not a soul to tell
                Why thou art desolate, can e'er return.   40

O Attic shape! Fair attitude! with brede
        Of marble men and maidens overwrought,
With forest branches and the trodden weed;
        Thou, silent form, dost tease us out of thought
As doth eternity: Cold Pastoral!   45
        When old age shall this generation waste,
                Thou shalt remain, in midst of other woe
        Than ours, a friend to man, to whom thou say'st,
Beauty is truth, truth beauty,—that is all
        Ye know on earth, and all ye need to know.   50

John Keats (1795-1821)

FOR THE SISTERS OF THE HOTEL DIEU

In pairs,
as if to illustrate their sisterhood,
the sisters pace the hospital garden walks.
In their robes black and white immaculate hoods
they are like birds,   5
the safe domestic fowl of the House of God.

O biblic birds,
who fluttered to me in my childhood illnesses
—me little, afraid, ill, not of your race,—
the cool wing for my fever, the hovering solace,   10
the sense of angels—
be thanked, O plumage of paradise, be praised.

A. M. Klein (1909-1972)

MR. EDWARDS AND THE SPIDER

I saw the spiders marching through the air,
Swimming from tree to tree that mildewed day
        In latter August when the hay
        Came creaking to the barn. But where

FOR THE SISTERS OF THE HOTEL DIEU.   9. *not of your race:* The poet was born in Montreal to immigrant Jewish parents.

The wind is westerly,   5
Where gnarled November makes the spiders fly
Into the apparitions of the sky,
They purpose nothing but their ease and die
Urgently beating east to sunrise and the sea;

What are we in the hands of the great God?   10
It was in vain you set up thorn and briar
    In battle array against the fire
    And treason crackling in your blood;
        For the wild thorns grow tame
And will do nothing to oppose the flame;   15
Your lacerations tell the losing game
You play against a sickness past your cure.
How will the hands be strong? How will the heart endure?

A very little thing, a little worm,
Or hourglass-blazoned spider, it is said,   20
    Can kill a tiger. Will the dead
    Hold up his mirror and affirm
        To the four winds the smell
And flash of his authority? It's well
If God who holds you to the pit of hell,   25
Much as one holds a spider, will destroy,
Baffle and dissipate your soul. As a small boy

On Windsor Marsh, I saw the spider die
When thrown into the bowels of fierce fire:
    There's no long struggle, no desire   30
    To get up on its feet and fly—
        It stretches out its feet
And dies. This is the sinner's last retreat;
Yes, and no strength exerted on the heat
Then sinews the abolished will, when sick   35
And full of burning, it will whistle on a brick.

But who can plumb the sinking of that soul?
Josiah Hawley, picture yourself cast
    Into a brick-kiln where the blast
    Fans your quick vitals to a coal—   40

MR. EDWARDS AND THE SPIDER. Title: Jonathan Edwards, Puritan preacher and theologian
(1703–1758), as a boy of eleven wrote an essay describing how spiders are borne on the
wind, at the end of a strand of web, toward the sea, where they die. The images in the poem
are taken from this essay and from his famous sermons "Sinners in the Hands of an Angry
God" and "The Future Punishment of the Wicked." 38. *Joseph (or Josiah) Hawley:* leader
of the faction that got Edwards dismissed from his pastorate in Northhampton, Mass.

If measured by a glass
How long would it seem burning! Let there pass
A minute, ten, ten trillion; but the blaze
Is infinite, eternal: this is death,
To die and know it. This is the Black Widow, death.   45

Robert Lowell (1917–1977)

BEDTIME STORY

Long long ago when the world was a wild place
Planted with bushes and peopled by apes, our
Mission Brigade was at work in the jungle.
    Hard by the Congo

Once, when a foraging detail was active   5
Scouting for green-fly, it came on a grey man, the
Last living man, in the branch of a baobab
    Stalking a monkey.

Earlier men had disposed of, for pleasure,
Creatures whose names we scarcely remember—   10
Zebra, rhinoceros, elephants, wart-hog,
    Lion, rats, deer. But

After the wars had extinguished the cities
Only the wild ones were left, half-naked
Near the Equator: and here was the last one,   15
    Starved for a monkey.

By then the Mission Brigade had encountered
Hundreds of such men: and their procedure,
History tells us, was only to feed them:
    Find them and feed them;   20

Those were the orders. And this was the last one.
Nobody knew that he was, but he was. Mud
Caked on his flat grey flanks. He was crouched, half-
    Armed with a shaved spear

Glinting beneath broad leaves. When their jaws cut   25
Swathes through the bark and he saw fine teeth shine,
Round eyes roll round and forked arms waver
    Huge as the rough trunks

Over his head, he was frightened. Our workers
Marched through the Congo before he was born, but   30

This was the first time perhaps that he'd seen one.
　　Staring in hot still

Silence, he crouched there: then jumped. With a long swing
Down from his branch, he had angled his spear too
Quickly, before they could hold him, and hurled it　　　　　35
　　Hard at the soldier

Leading the detail. How could he know Queen's
Orders were only to help him? The soldier
Winced when the tipped spear pricked him. Unsheathing his
　　Sting was a reflex.　　　　　40

Later the Queen was informed. There were no more
Men. An impetuous soldier had killed off,
Purely by chance, the penultimate primate.
　　When she was certain,

Squadrons of workers were fanned through the Congo　　　　　45
Detailed to bring back the man's picked bones to be
Sealed in the archives in amber. I'm quite sure
　　Nobody found them

After the most industrious search, though.
Where had the bones gone? Over the earth, dear,　　　　　50
Ground by the teeth of the termites, blown by the
　　Wind, like the dodo's.

George MacBeth (b. 1932)

NEVERTHELESS

　　　　you've seen a strawberry
　　　　　　that's had a struggle; yet
　　　　　　was, where the fragments met,

　　　　a hedgehog or a star-
　　　　　　fish for the multitude　　　　　5
　　　　　　of seeds. What better food

　　　　than apple seeds—the fruit
　　　　　　within the fruit—locked in
　　　　　　like counter-curved twin

NEVERTHELESS.　12. *kok-saghyz:* a perennial dandelion native to south central U.S.S.R.,
cultivated for its fleshy roots, which contain a high rubber content.　15. *prickly-pear:* a
flat-jointed cactus with edible fruit.　19. *mandrakes:* The root of the carrot sometimes is
forked, resembling the root of the mandrake plant, the subject of superstition because it
may look like a human being.

hazelnuts? Frost that kills   10
    the little rubber-plant-
    leaves of *kok-saghyz*-stalks, can't

harm the roots; they still grow
    in frozen ground. Once where
    there was a prickly-pear-   15

leaf clinging to barbed wire,
    a root shot down to grow
    in earth two feet below;

as carrots form mandrakes
    or a ram's-horn root some-   20
    times. Victory won't come

to me unless I go
    to it; a grape tendril
    ties a knot in knots till

knotted thirty times—so   25
    the bound twig that's under-
    gone and over-gone, can't stir.

The weak overcomes its
    menace, the strong over-
    comes itself. What is there   30

like fortitude! What sap
    went through that little thread
    to make the cherry red!

Marianne Moore (*1887–1972*)

GRACE TO BE SAID AT THE SUPERMARKET

That God of ours, the Great Geometer,
Does something for us here, where He hath put
(if you want to put it that way) things in shape,
Compressing the little lambs in orderly cubes,
Making the roast a decent cylinder,   5
Fairing the tin ellipsoid of a ham,
Getting the luncheon meat anonymous
In squares and oblongs with the edges bevelled
Or rounded (streamlined, maybe, for greater speed).

Praise Him, He hath conferred aesthetic distance   10
Upon our appetites, and on the bloody

Mess of our birthright, our unseemly need,
Imposed significant form. Through Him the brutes
Enter the pure Euclidean kingdom of number,
Free of their bulging and blood-swollen lives   15
They come to us holy, in cellophane
Transparencies, in the mystical body,

That we may look unflinchingly on death
As the greatest good, like a philosopher should.

Howard Nemerov (b. 1920)

THE TRURO BEAR

There's a bear in the Truro woods.
People have seen it—three or four,
or two, or one. I think
of the thickness of the serious woods
around the dark bowls of the Truro ponds;   5
I think of the blueberry fields, the blackberry tangles,
the cranberry bogs. And the sky
with its new moon, its familiar star-trails,
burns down like a brand-new heaven,
while everywhere I look on the scratchy hillsides   10
shadows seem to grow shoulders. Surely
a beast might be clever, be lucky, move quietly
through the woods for years, learning to stay away
from roads and houses. Common sense mutters:
it can't be true, it must be somebody's   15
runaway dog. But the seed
has been planted, and when has happiness ever
required much evidence to begin
its leaf-green breathing?

Mary Oliver (b. 1935)

THE LANDLADY

Through sepia air the boarders come and go,
impersonal as trains. Pass silently
the craving silence swallowing her speech;
click doors like shutters on her camera eye.

Because of her their lives become exact: 5
their entrances and exits are designed;

phone calls are cryptic. Oh, her ticklish ears
advance and fall back stunned.

Nothing is unprepared. They hold the walls
about them as they weep or laugh. Each face   10
is dialed to zero publicly. She peers
stippled with curious flesh;

pads on the patient landing like a pulse,
unlocks their keyholes with the wire of sight,
searches their rooms for clues when they are out,   15
pricks when they come home late.

Wonders when they are quiet, jumps when they move,
dreams that they dope or drink, trembles to know
the traffic of their brains, jaywalks their street
in clumsy shoes.   20

Yet knows them better than their closest friends:
their cupboards and the secrets of their drawers,
their books, their private mail, their photographs
are theirs and hers.

Knows when they wash, how frequently their clothes   25
go to the cleaners, what they like to eat,
their curvature of health, but even so
is not content.

And like a lover must know all, all, all.
Prays she may catch them unprepared at last   30
and palm the dreadful riddle of their skulls—
hoping the worst.

                                        P. K. Page (b. *1917*)

SESTINA: ALTAFORTE

LOQUITUR: *En* Bertrans de Born. Dante Alighieri put this man in hell for that
he was a stirrer up of strife. Eccovi! Judge ye! Have I dug him up again? The
scene is at his castle, Altaforte. "Papiols" is his jongleur. "The Leopard," the
device of Richard Coeur de Lion.

SESTINA: ALTAFORTE.   The speaker (*Loquitur*) is Sir (*En*) Bertran de Born, a twelfth-century
French nobleman and troubadour, whom the great Italian poet Dante pictures in hell in the
Inferno, first part of his *Divine Comedy*. *Eccovi!:* Here you are! *jongleur:* singer. *Richard
Coeur de Lion:* Duke of Aquitaine, later Richard I, king of England; Bertran's enemy.

Damn it all! all this our South stinks peace.
You whoreson dog, Papiols, come! Let's to music!
I have no life save when the swords clash.
But ah! when I see the standards gold, vair, purple, opposing
And the broad fields beneath them turn crimson,   5
Then howl I my heart nigh mad with rejoicing.

In hot summer have I great rejoicing
When the tempests kill the earth's foul peace,
And the lightnings from black heav'n flash crimson,
And the fierce thunders roar me their music   10
And the winds shriek through the clouds mad, opposing,
And through all the riven skies God's swords clash.

Hell grant soon we hear again the swords clash!
And the shrill neighs of destriers° in battle rejoicing,   war horses
Spiked breast to spiked breast opposing!   15
Better one hour's stour° than a year's peace   battle
With fat boards, bawds, wine and frail music!
Bah! there's no wine like the blood's crimson!

And I love to see the sun rise blood-crimson.
And I watch his spears through the dark clash   20
And it fills all my heart with rejoicing
And pries wide my mouth with fast music
When I see him so scorn and defy peace,
His lone might 'gainst all darkness opposing.

The man who fears war and squats opposing   25
My words for stour, hath no blood of crimson
But is fit only to rot in womanish peace
Far from where worth's won and the swords clash
For the death of such sluts I go rejoicing;
Yea, I fill all the air with my music.   30

Papiols, Papiols, to the music!
There's no sound like to swords swords opposing,
No cry like the battle's rejoicing
When our elbows and swords drip the crimson
And our charges 'gainst "The Leopard's" rush clash.   35
May God damn for ever all who cry "Peace!"

And let the music of the swords make them crimson!
Hell grant soon we hear again the swords clash!
Hell blot black for alway the thought "Peace!"

                                          Ezra Pound (1885–1972)

AFTER THE KILLING

"We will kill,"
said the blood-thirster,
"and after the killing
there will be peace."

But after the killing   5
their sons
killed his sons,
and his sons
killed their sons,
and their sons   10
killed his sons

until

at last

a blood-thirster said,
"We will kill.   15
And after the killing
there will be   peace."

Dudley Randall (b. 1914)

THE MILL

The miller's wife had waited long,
    The tea was cold, the fire was dead;
And there might yet be nothing wrong
    In how he went and what he said:
"There are no millers any more,"   5
    Was all that she had heard him say;
And he had lingered at the door
    So long that it seemed yesterday.

Sick with a fear that had no form
    She knew that she was there at last;   10
And in the mill there was a warm
    And mealy fragrance of the past.
What else there was would only seem
    To say again what he had meant;
And what was hanging from a beam   15
    Would not have heeded where she went.

And if she thought it followed her,
    She may have reasoned in the dark

That one way of the few there were
    Would hide her and would leave no mark: 20
Black water, smooth above the weir
    Like starry velvet in the night,
Though ruffled once, would soon appear
    The same as ever to the sight.

Edwin Arlington Robinson (1869-1935)

MR. FLOOD'S PARTY

Old Eben Flood, climbing alone one night
Over the hill between the town below
And the forsaken upland hermitage
That held as much as he should ever know
On earth again of home, paused warily.   5
The road was his with not a native near;
And Eben, having leisure, said aloud,
For no man else in Tilbury Town to hear:

"Well, Mr. Flood, we have the harvest moon
Again, and we may not have many more;   10
The bird is on the wing, the poet says,
And you and I have said it here before.
Drink to the bird." He raised up to the light
The jug that he had gone so far to fill,
And answered huskily: "Well, Mr. Flood,   15
Since you propose it, I believe I will."

Alone, as if enduring to the end
A valiant armor of scarred hopes outworn,
He stood there in the middle of the road
Like Roland's ghost winding a silent horn.   20
Below him, in the town among the trees,
Where friends of other days had honored him,
A phantom salutation of the dead
Rang thinly till old Eben's eyes were dim.

Then, as a mother lays her sleeping child   25
Down tenderly, fearing it may awake,
He set the jug down slowly at his feet

MR. FLOOD'S PARTY.   11. *bird:* Mr. Flood is quoting from *The Rubáiyát of Omar Khayyám,*
"The bird of Time . . . is on the wing."   20. *Roland:* hero of the French epic poem *The
Song of Roland.* He died fighting a rearguard action for Charlemagne against the Moors in
Spain; before his death he sounded a call for help on his famous horn, but the king's army
arrived too late.

With trembling care, knowing that most things break;
And only when assured that on firm earth
It stood, as the uncertain lives of men   30
Assuredly did not, he paced away,
And with his hand extended paused again:

"Well, Mr. Flood, we have not met like this
In a long time; and many a change has come
To both of us, I fear, since last it was   35
We had a drop together. Welcome home!"
Convivially returning with himself,
Again he raised the jug up to the light;
And with an acquiescent quaver said:
"Well, Mr. Flood, if you insist, I might.   40

"Only a very little, Mr. Flood—
For auld lang syne. No more, sir; that will do."
So, for the time, apparently it did,
And Eben evidently thought so too;
For soon amid the silver loneliness   45
Of night he lifted up his voice and sang,
Secure, with only two moons listening,
Until the whole harmonious landscape rang—

"For auld lang syne." The weary throat gave out,
The last word wavered, and the song was done.   50
He raised again the jug regretfully
And shook his head, and was again alone.
There was not much that was ahead of him,
And there was nothing in the town below—
Where strangers would have shut the many doors   55
That many friends had opened long ago.

Edwin Arlington Robinson (1869–1935)

I KNEW A WOMAN

I knew a woman, lovely in her bones,
When small birds sighed, she would sigh back at them;
Ah, when she moved, she moved more ways than one:
The shapes a bright container can contain!
Of her choice virtues only gods should speak,   5
Or English poets who grew up on Greek
(I'd have them sing in chorus, cheek to cheek).

How well her wishes went! She stroked my chin,
She taught me Turn, and Counter-turn, and Stand;

She taught me Touch, that undulant white skin;   10
I nibbled meekly from her proffered hand;
She was the sickle; I, poor I, the rake,
Coming behind her for her pretty sake
(But what prodigious mowing we did make).

Love likes a gander, and adores a goose: 15
Her full lips pursed, the errant note to seize;
She played it quick, she played it light and loose;
My eyes, they dazzled at her flowing knees;
Her several parts could keep a pure repose,
Or one hip quiver with a mobile nose   20
(She moved in circles, and those circles moved).

Let seed be grass, and grass turn into hay:
I'm martyr to a motion not my own;
What's freedom for? To know eternity.
I swear she cast a shadow white as stone.   25
But who would count eternity in days?
These old bones live to learn her wanton ways:
(I measure time by how a body sways).

Theodore Roethke (1908–1963)

THE WAKING

I wake to sleep, and take my waking slow.
I feel my fate in what I cannot fear.
I learn by going where I have to go.

We think by feeling. What is there to know?
I hear my being dance from ear to ear.   5
I wake to sleep, and take my waking slow.

Of those so close beside me, which are you?
God bless the Ground! I shall walk softly there,
And learn by going where I have to go.

Light takes the Tree; but who can tell us how?   10
The lowly worm climbs up a winding stair;
I wake to sleep, and take my waking slow.

Great Nature has another thing to do
To you and me; so take the lively air,
And, lovely, learn by going where to go.   15

This shaking keeps me steady. I should know.
What falls away is always. And is near.

I wake to sleep, and take my waking slow.
I learn by going where I have to go.

Theodore Roethke (1908–1963)

SONG

When I am dead, my dearest,
    Sing no sad songs for me;
Plant thou no roses at my head,
    Nor shady cypress tree;
Be the green grass above me   5
    With showers and dewdrops wet;
And if thou wilt, remember,
    And if thou wilt, forget.

I shall not see the shadows,
    I shall not feel the rain;   10
I shall not hear the nightingale
    Sing on, as if in pain;
And dreaming through the twilight
    That doth not rise nor set,
Haply I may remember,   15
    And haply may forget.

Christina Rossetti (1830–1894)

FOG

The fog comes
on little cat feet.

It sits looking
over harbor and city
on silent haunches
and then moves on.

Carl Sandburg (1878–1967)

PAIN FOR A DAUGHTER

Blind with love, my daughter
has cried nightly for horses,
those long-necked marchers and churners
that she has mastered, any and all,
reigning them in like a circus hand—   5

the excitable muscles and the ripe neck—
tending, this summer, a pony and a foal.
She who is too squeamish to pull
a thorn from the dog's paw
watched her pony blossom with distemper,   10
the underside of the jaw swelling
like an enormous grape.
Gritting her teeth with love,
she drained the boil and scoured it
with hydrogen peroxide until pus   15
ran like milk on the barn floor.

Blind with loss all winter,
in dungarees, a ski jacket, and a hard hat,
she visits the neighbors' stable,
our acreage not zoned for barns,   20
they who own the flaming horses
and the swan-whipped thoroughbred
that she tugs at and cajoles,
thinking it will burn like a furnace
under her small-hipped English seat.   25

Blind with pain, she limps home.
The thoroughbred has stood on her foot.
He rested there like a building.
He grew into her foot until they were one.
The marks of the horseshoe printed   30
into her flesh, the tips of her toes
ripped off like pieces of leather,
three toenails swirled like shells
and left to float in blood in her riding boot.

Blind with fear, she sits on the toilet,   35
her foot balanced over the washbasin,
her father, hydrogen peroxide in hand,
performing the rites of the cleansing.
She bites on a towel, sucked in breath,
sucked in and arched against the pain,   40
her eyes glancing off me where
I stand at the door, eyes locked
on the ceiling, eyes of a stranger,
and then she cries . . .
Oh, my God, help me!   45
Where a child would have cried *Mama!*
Where a child would have believed *Mama!*
She bit the towel and called on God,

and I saw her life stretch out . . .
I saw her torn in childbirth,   50
and I saw her, at that moment,
in her own death, and I knew that she
knew.

Anne Sexton (1928-1974)

FEAR NO MORE

Fear no more the heat o' the sun,
    Nor the furious winter's rages;
Thou thy worldly task hast done,
    Home art gone, and ta'en thy wages.
Golden lads and girls all must,   5
As chimney-sweepers, come to dust.

Fear no more the frown o' the great;
    Thou art past the tyrant's stroke;
Care no more to clothe and eat;
    To thee the reed is as the oak.   10
The scepter, learning, physic,° must   art of healing
All follow this, and come to dust.

Fear no more the lightning-flash,
    Nor the all-dreaded thunder-stone;°   thunderbolt
Fear not slander, censure rash;   15
    Thou hast finished joy and moan.
All lovers young, all lovers must
Consign to thee,° and come to dust. yield to your condition

William Shakespeare (1564-1616)

LET ME NOT TO THE MARRIAGE
OF TRUE MINDS

Let me not to the marriage of true minds
Admit impediments. Love is not love
Which alters when it alteration finds,
Or bends with the remover to remove.
O no! it is an ever-fixèd mark   5
That looks on tempests and is never shaken;
It is the star to every wandering bark,
Whose worth's unknown, although his height be taken.
Love's not Time's fool, though rosy lips and cheeks
Within his bending sickle's compass come;   10

Love alters not with his brief hours and weeks,
But bears it out even to the edge of doom.
    If this be error and upon me proved,
    I never writ, nor no man ever loved.

William Shakespeare (1564–1616)

MY MISTRESS' EYES ARE NOTHING LIKE THE SUN

My mistress' eyes are nothing like the sun;
Coral is far more red than her lips' red:
If snow be white, why then her breasts are dun;
If hairs be wires, black wires grow on her head.   4
I have seen roses damasked,° red and white,   of different colors
But no such roses see I in her cheeks;
And in some perfumes is there more delight
Than in the breath that from my mistress reeks.°   exhales
I love to hear her speak, yet well I know
That music hath a far more pleasing sound: 10
I grant I never saw a goddess go,—
My mistress, when she walks, treads on the ground.
    And yet, by heaven, I think my love as rare
    As any she belied with false compare.

William Shakespeare (1564–1616)

TELEPHONE CONVERSATION

The price seemed reasonable, location
Indifferent. The landlady swore she lived
Off premises. Nothing remained
But self-confession. "Madam," I warned,
"I hate a wasted journey—I am African."   5
Silence. Silenced transmission of
Pressurized good-breeding. Voice, when it came,
Lipstick-coated, long gold-rolled
Cigarette-holder tipped. Caught I was, foully.
"HOW DARK?" . . . I had not misheard . . . "ARE YOU LIGHT   10

TELEPHONE CONVERSATION. 11–14. Public telephones in England once required the pushing of buttons to make connections and deposit coins. Telephone booths, mailboxes (called pillar boxes), and buses are painted red. 19. *plain chocolate:* dark chocolate.

OR VERY DARK?" Button B. Button A. Stench
Of rancid breath of public hide-and-speak.
Red booth. Red pillar box. Red double-tiered
Omnibus squelching tar. It *was* real! Shamed
By ill-mannered silence, surrender   15
Pushed dumbfounded to beg simplification.
Considerate she was, varying the emphasis—
"ARE YOU DARK? OR VERY LIGHT?" Revelation came.
"You mean—like plain or milk chocolate?"
Her assent was clinical, crushing in its light   20
Impersonality. Rapidly, wave-length adjusted,
I chose. "West African sepia"—and as afterthought,
"Down in my passport." Silence for spectroscopic
Flight of fancy, till truthfulness clanged her accent
Hard on the mouthpiece. "WHAT'S THAT?" conceding   25
"DON'T KNOW WHAT THAT IS." "Like brunette."
"THAT'S DARK, ISN'T IT?" "Not altogether.
Facially, I am brunette, but madam, you should see
The rest of me. Palm of my hand, soles of my feet
Are a peroxide blonde. Friction, caused—   30
Foolishly madam—by sitting down, has turned
My bottom raven black—One moment, madam!—sensing
Her receiver rearing on the thunderclap
About my ears—"Madam," I pleaded, "wouldn't you rather
See for yourself?"   35

Wole Soyinka (b. *1935*)

THE SNOW MAN

One must have a mind of winter
To regard the frost and the boughs
Of the pine-trees crusted with snow;

And have been cold a long time
To behold the junipers shagged with ice,   5
The spruces rough in the distant glitter

Of the January sun; and not to think
Of any misery in the sound of the wind,
In the sound of a few leaves,

Which is the sound of the land   10
Full of the same wind
That is blowing in the same bare place

For the listener, who listens in the snow,
And, nothing himself, beholds
Nothing that is not there and the nothing that is.   15

Wallace Stevens (1879–1955)

LION

In the bend of your mouth soft murder
   in the flints of your eyes
   the sun-stained openings of caves
Your nostrils breathe the ordained air
   of chosen loneliness   5

Magnificently maned as the lustrous pampas
   your head heavy with heraldic curls
   wears a regal frown between the brows

The wide bundle of your chest
   your loose-skinned belly frilled with fur   10
   you carry easily sinuously pacing on suede paws

Between tight thighs
   under the thick root of your tufted tail
   situated like a full-stoned fruit beneath a bough
   the quiver of your never-used malehood is slung   15

You pace in dung on cement
   the bars flick past your eyeballs
   fixed beyond the awestruck stares of children
Watching you they remember their fathers
   the frightening hairs in their fathers' ears   20

Young girls remember lovers too timid and white
   and I remember how I played lion with my brothers
   under the round yellow-grained table
   the shadow our cave in the lamplight

Your beauty burns the brain   25
   though your paws slue on foul cement
   the fetor of captivity you do right to ignore
   the bars too an illusion

Your heroic paranoia plants you in the Indian jungle
   pacing by the cool water-hole as dawn streaks the sky   30
   and the foretaste of the all-day hunt

is sweet as yearling's blood
in the corners of your lips

May Swenson (b. 1919)

A DESCRIPTION OF THE MORNING

Now hardly here and there a hackney-coach
Appearing, showed the ruddy morn's approach.
Now Betty from her master's bed had flown,
And softly stole to discompose her own.
The slip-shod 'prentice from his master's door   5
Had pared the dirt, and sprinkled round the floor.
Now Moll had whirled her mop with dextrous airs,
Prepared to scrub the entry and the stairs.
The youth with broomy stumps began to trace
The kennel's edge, where wheels had worn the place.   10
The small-coal man was heard with cadence deep,
Till drowned in shriller notes of chimney-sweep.
Duns at his lordship's gate began to meet;
And Brickdust Moll had screamed through half the street.
The turnkey now his flock returning sees,   15
Duly let out a-nights to steal for fees.
The watchful bailiffs take their silent stands;
And schoolboys lag with satchels in their hands.

Jonathan Swift (1667–1745)

DO NOT GO GENTLE INTO THAT GOOD NIGHT

Do not go gentle into that good night,
Old age should burn and rave at close of day;
Rage, rage against the dying of the light.

Though wise men at their end know dark is right,
Because their words had forked no lightning they   5
Do not go gentle into that good night.

Good men, the last wave by, crying how bright
Their frail deeds might have danced in a green bay,
Rage, rage against the dying of the light.

A DESCRIPTION OF THE MORNING.   9. *youth:* he is apparently searching for salvage.
10. *kennel:* gutter.   14. *Brickdust:* red-complexioned.

Wild men who caught and sang the sun in flight,   10
And learn, too late, they grieved it on its way
Do not go gentle into that good night.

Grave men, near death, who see with blinding sight
Blind eyes could blaze like meteors and be gay,
Rage, rage against the dying of the light.   15

And you, my father, there on the sad height,
Curse, bless, me now with your fierce tears, I pray.
Do not go gentle into that good night.
Rage, rage against the dying of the light.

Dylan Thomas (1914–1953)

FERN HILL

Now as I was young and easy under the apple boughs
About the lilting house and happy as the grass was green,
   The night above the dingle starry,
     Time let me hail and climb
   Golden in the heydays of his eyes,   5
And honored among wagons I was prince of the apple towns
And once below a time I lordly had the trees and leaves
     Trail with daisies and barley
   Down the rivers of the windfall light.

And as I was green and carefree, famous among the barns   10
About the happy yard and singing as the farm was home,
   In the sun that is young once only,
     Time let me play and be
   Golden in the mercy of his means,
And green and golden I was huntsman and herdsman, the calves   15
Sang to my horn, the foxes on the hills barked clear and cold,
     And the sabbath rang slowly
   In the pebbles of the holy streams.

All the sun long it was running, it was lovely, the hay
Fields high as the house, the tunes from the chimneys, it was air 20
   And playing, lovely and watery
     And fire green as grass.
   And nightly under the simple stars
As I rode to sleep the owls were bearing the farm away,
All the moon long I heard, blessed among stables, the nightjars   25
   Flying with the ricks, and the horses
     Flashing into the dark.

And then to awake, and the farm, like a wanderer white
With the dew, come back, the cock on his shoulder: it was all
    Shining, it was Adam and maiden,   30
        The sky gathered again
    And the sun grew round that very day.
So it must have been after the birth of the simple light
In the first, spinning place, the spellbound horses walking warm
    Out of the whinnying green stable   35
        On to the fields of praise.

And honored among foxes and pheasants by the gay house
Under the new made clouds and happy as the heart was long,
    In the sun born over and over,
        I ran my heedless ways,   40
    My wishes raced through the house high hay
And nothing I cared, at my sky blue trades, that time allows
In all his tuneful turning so few and such morning songs
    Before the children green and golden
        Follow him out of grace,   45

Nothing I cared, in the lamb white days, that time would take me
Up to the swallow thronged loft by the shadow of my hand,
    In the moon that is always rising,
        Nor that riding to sleep
I should hear him fly with the high fields   50
And wake to the farm forever fled from the childless land.
Oh as I was young and easy in the mercy of his means,
        Time held me green and dying
    Though I sang in my chains like the sea.

Dylan Thomas (1914–1953)

THE OWL

    Downhill I came, hungry, and yet not starved;
    Cold, yet had heat within me that was proof
    Against the North wind; tired, yet so that rest
    Had seemed the sweetest thing under a roof.

    Then at the inn I had food, fire, and rest,   5
    Knowing how hungry, cold, and tired was I.
    All of the night was quite barred out except
    An owl's cry, a most melancholy cry

    Shaken out long and clear upon the hill,
    No merry note, nor cause of merriment,   10

But one telling me plain what I escaped
And others could not, that night, as in I went.

And salted was my food, and my repose,
Salted and sobered, too, by the bird's voice
Speaking for all who lay under the stars,   15
Soldiers and poor, unable to rejoice.

Edward Thomas (1878–1917)

THE VIRGINS

Down the dead streets of sun-stoned Frederiksted,
the first free port to die for tourism,
strolling at funeral pace, I am reminded
of life not lost to the American dream;
but my small-islander's simplicities   5
can't better our new empire's civilized
exchange of cameras, watches, perfumes, brandies
for the good life, so cheaply underpriced
that only the crime rate is on the rise
in streets blighted with sun, stone arches   10
and plazas blown dry by the hysteria
of rumor. A condominium drowns
in vacancy; its bargains are dusted,
but only a jeweled housefly drones
over the bargains. The roulettes spin   15
rustily to the wind—the vigorous trade
that every morning would begin afresh
by revving up green water round the pierhead
heading for where the banks of silver thresh.

Derek Walcott (b. 1930)

BOY WANDERING IN SIMMS' VALLEY

Through brush and love-vine, well blooded by blackberry thorn
Long dry past prime, all under the molten light
Of late summer, and past the last rock-slide at ridge-top and stubborn,
Raw cedar, I clambered, breath short and spit white

THE VIRGINS. 1. *Frederiksted:* chief port of St. Croix, largest of the American Virgin Islands, is a free port where goods can be bought without payment of customs duties and therefore at bargain prices. The economy of St. Croix, once based on sugar cane, is now chiefly dependent on tourism. Like the other American Virgin Islands, it has suffered from uncontrolled growth, building booms, unevenly distributed prosperity, destruction of natural beauty, and pollution. 5. *my . . . simplicities:* The poet is a native of St. Lucia in the West Indies. 16. *trade:* cf. trade wind.

From lung-depth. Then down the lone valley, called Simms' Valley still,   5
Where Simms, for long years, had nursed a sick wife till she died.
Then turned out his spindly stock to forage at will,
And took down his .12 gauge, and simply lay down by her side.

No kin they had, and nobody came just to jaw.
It was two years before some straggling hunter sat down   10
On the porch-edge to rest, then started to prowl. He saw
What he saw, saw no reason to linger, but high-tailed to town.

A dirt-farmer needs a good wife to keep a place trim,
So the place must have gone to wrack with his old lady sick.
And when I came there, years later, old furrows were dim,   15
And dimmer in fields where grew maples and such, two-span thick.

So for years the farm had contracted: now barn down, and all
The yard gone part of the wilderness, and only
The house to mark human hope, and that ready to fall.
No buyer at tax-sale. It waited, forgotten and lonely.   20

I stood in the bedroom upstairs, in lowering sun,
And saw sheets hang spiderweb-rotten, and blankets a mass
Of what weather and leaves from the broken window had done,
Not to mention the rats, and thought what had there come to pass.

But lower was sinking the sun. I shook myself,   25
And flung a last glance around, then suddenly
Saw the old enameled bedpan, high on a shelf.
I stood still again, as the last sun fell on me,

And stood wondering what life is, and love, and what they may be.

Robert Penn Warren (*b. 1905*)

A NOISELESS PATIENT SPIDER

A noiseless patient spider,
I marked where on a little promontory it stood isolated,
Marked how to explore the vacant vast surrounding,
It launched forth filament, filament, filament, out of itself,
Ever unreeling them, ever tirelessly speeding them.   5

And you O my soul where you stand,
Surrounded, detached, in measureless oceans of space,
Ceaselessly musing, venturing, throwing, seeking the spheres to connect them,
Till the bridge you will need be formed, till the ductile anchor hold,
Till the gossamer thread you fling catch somewhere, O my soul.   10

Walt Whitman (*1819–1892*)

THERE WAS A CHILD WENT FORTH

There was a child went forth every day,
And the first object he looked upon, that object he became,
And that object became part of him for the day or a
   certain part of the day,
Or for many years or stretching cycles of years.

The early lilacs became part of this child,   5
And grass and white and red morning-glories, and white and red
   clover, and the song of the phoebe-bird,
And the Third-month lambs and the sow's pink-faint litter, and the
   mare's foal and the cow's calf,
And the noisy brood of the barnyard or by the mire of the
   pond-side,
And the fish suspending themselves so curiously below there,
   and the beautiful curious liquid,
And the water-plants with their graceful flat heads, all became
   part of him.   10

The field-sprouts of Fourth-month and Fifth-month became
   part of him,
Winter-grain sprouts and those of the light-yellow corn, and the
   esculent roots of the garden,
And the apple-trees covered with blossoms and the fruit afterward,
   and wood-berries, and the commonest weeds by the road,
And the old drunkard staggering home from the outhouse of the
   tavern whence he had lately risen,
And the schoolmistress that passed on her way to the school,   15
And the friendly boys that passed, and the quarrelsome boys,
And the tidy and fresh-cheeked girls, and the barefoot negro boy
   and girl,
And all the changes of city and country wherever he went.

His own parents, he that had fathered him and she that had conceived
   him in her womb and birthed him,
They gave this child more of themselves than that,   20
They gave him afterward every day, they became part of him.

The mother at home quietly placing the dishes on the supper-table,
The mother with mild words, clean her cap and gown, a wholesome
   odor falling off her person and clothes as she walks by,
The father, strong, self-sufficient, manly, mean, angered, unjust,
The blow, the quick loud word, the tight bargain, the crafty lure,   25
The family usages, the language, the company, the furniture,
   the yearning and swelling heart,
Affection that will not be gainsayed, the sense of what is real,
   the thought if after all it should prove unreal,

The doubts of day-time and the doubts of night-time, the curious
 whether and how,
Whether that which appears so is so, or is it all flashes and specks?
Men and women crowding fast in the streets, if they are not
 flashes and specks what are they?   30
The streets themselves and the façades of houses, and goods
 in the windows,
Vehicles, teams, the heavy-planked wharves, the huge crossing
 at the ferries,
The village on the highland seen from afar at sunset, the river between,
Shadows, aureola and mist, the light falling on roofs and gables
 of white or brown two miles off,
The schooner near by sleepily dropping down the tide, the little boat
 slack-towed astern,   35
The hurrying tumbling waves, quick-broken crests, slapping,
The strata of colored clouds, the long bar of maroon-tint away
 solitary by itself, the spread of purity it lies motionless in,
The horizon's edge, the flying sea-crow, the fragrance of salt marsh
 and shore mud,
These became part of that child who went forth every day, and who
 now goes, and will always go forth every day.

Walt Whitman (1819–1892)

WHEN I HEARD THE LEARN'D ASTRONOMER

When I heard the learn'd astronomer,
When the proofs, the figures, were ranged in columns before me,
When I was shown the charts and diagrams, to add, divide,
 and measure them,
When I sitting heard the astronomer where he lectured with much
 applause in the lecture-room,
How soon unaccountable I became tired and sick,
Till rising and gliding out I wandered off by myself,
In the mystical moist night-air, and from time to time,
Looked up in perfect silence at the stars.

Walt Whitman (1819–1892)

THE MILL

The spoiling daylight inched along the bar-top,
Orange and cloudy, slowly igniting lint,
And then that glow was gone, and still your voice,
Serene with failure and with the ease of dying,
Rose from the shades that more and more became you.   5

Turning among its images, your mind
Produced the names of streets, the exact look
Of lilacs, 1903, in Cincinnati,
—Random, as if your testament were made,
The round sums all bestowed, and now you spent   10
Your pocket change, so as to be rid of it.
Or was it that you half-hoped to surprise
Your dead life's sound and sovereign anecdote?
What I remember best is the wrecked mill
You stumbled on in Tennessee; or was it   15
Somewhere down in Brazil? It slips my mind
Already. But there it was in a still valley
Far from the towns. No road or path came near it.
If there had been a clearing now it was gone,
And all you found amidst the choke of green   20
Was three walls standing, hurdled by great vines
And thatched by height on height of hushing leaves.
But still the mill-wheel turned! its crazy buckets
Creaking and lumbering out of the clogged race
And sounding, as you said, as if you'd found   25
Time all alone and talking to himself
In his eternal rattle.
                    How should I guess
Where they are gone to, now that you are gone,
Those fading streets and those most fragile lilacs,
Those fragmentary views, those times of day?   30
All that I can be sure of is the mill-wheel.
It turns and turns in my mind, over and over.

Richard Wilbur (b. 1921)

THE RED WHEELBARROW

so much depends
upon

a red wheel
barrow

glazed with rain
water

beside the white
chickens.

William Carlos Williams (1883-1963)

THE SOLITARY REAPER

Behold her, single in the field,
Yon solitary Highland lass!
Reaping and singing by herself;
Stop here, or gently pass!
Alone she cuts and binds the grain,   5
And sings a melancholy strain;
O listen! for the vale profound
Is overflowing with the sound.

No nightingale did ever chaunt
More welcome notes to weary bands   10
Of travelers in some shady haunt
Among Arabian sands.
A voice so thrilling ne'er was heard
In springtime from the cuckoo-bird,
Breaking the silence of the seas   15
Among the farthest Hebrides.

Will no one tell me what she sings?—
Perhaps the plaintive numbers° flow   measures
For old, unhappy, far-off things,
And battles long ago.   20
Or is it some more humble lay,°   song
Familiar matter of today?
Some natural sorrow, loss, or pain,
That has been, and may be again?

Whate'er the theme, the maiden sang   25
As if her song could have no ending;
I saw her singing at her work,
And o'er the sickle bending—
I listened, motionless and still;
And, as I mounted up the hill,   30
The music in my heart I bore
Long after it was heard no more.

William Wordsworth (*1770–1850*)

THE WORLD IS TOO MUCH WITH US

The world is too much with us; late and soon,
Getting and spending, we lay waste our powers:
Little we see in Nature that is ours;

THE SOLITARY REAPER. 2. *Highland:* Scottish upland. The girl is singing in the Highland language, a form of Gaelic, quite different from English. 16. *Hebrides:* islands off the northwest tip of Scotland.

We have given our hearts away, a sordid boon!
This Sea that bares her bosom to the moon;   5
The winds that will be howling at all hours,
And are up-gathered now like sleeping flowers;
For this, for everything, we are out of tune;
It moves us not.—Great God! I'd rather be
A Pagan suckled in a creed outworn;   10
So might I, standing on this pleasant lea,
Have glimpses that would make me less forlorn;
Have sight of Proteus rising from the sea;
Or hear old Triton blow his wreathèd horn.

William Wordsworth (1770–1850)

SAILING TO BYZANTIUM

That is no country for old men. The young
In one another's arms, birds in the trees
—Those dying generations—at their song,
The salmon-falls, the mackerel-crowded seas,
Fish, flesh, or fowl, commend all summer long   5
Whatever is begotten, born, and dies.
Caught in that sensual music all neglect
Monuments of unaging intellect.

An aged man is but a paltry thing,
A tattered coat upon a stick, unless   10
Soul clap its hands and sing, and louder sing
For every tatter in its mortal dress,
Nor is there singing school but studying
Monuments of its own magnificence;
And therefore I have sailed the seas and come   15
To the holy city of Byzantium.

O sages standing in God's holy fire
As in the gold mosaic of a wall,
Come from the holy fire, perne in a gyre,°   spin in spiraling or
And be the singing-masters of my soul.   cone-shaped flight
Consume my heart away; sick with desire   21
And fastened to a dying animal
It knows not what it is; and gather me
Into the artifice of eternity.

SAILING TO BYZANTIUM. *Byzantium:* Ancient eastern capital of the Roman Empire; here
symbolically a holy city of the imagination. 1. *That:* Ireland, or the ordinary sensual
world. 27–31. *such . . . Byzantium:* The Byzantine Emperor Theophilus had made for
himself mechanical golden birds which sang upon the branches of a golden tree.

Once out of nature I shall never take   25
My bodily form from any natural thing,
But such a form as Grecian goldsmiths make
Of hammered gold and gold enameling
To keep a drowsy Emperor awake;
Or set upon a golden bough to sing   30
To lords and ladies of Byzantium
Of what is past, or passing, or to come.

William Butler Yeats (1865–1939)

THE SECOND COMING

Turning and turning in the widening gyre°   spiral
The falcon cannot hear the falconer;
Things fall apart; the center cannot hold;
Mere anarchy is loosed upon the world,
The blood-dimmed tide is loosed, and everywhere   5
The ceremony of innocence is drowned;
The best lack all conviction, while the worst
Are full of passionate intensity.

Surely some revelation is at hand;
Surely the Second Coming is at hand.   10
The Second Coming! Hardly are those words out
When a vast image out of *Spiritus Mundi*
Troubles my sight: somewhere in sands of the desert
A shape with lion body and the head of a man,
A gaze blank and pitiless as the sun,   15
Is moving its slow thighs, while all about it
Reel shadows of the indignant desert birds.
The darkness drops again; but now I know
That twenty centuries of stony sleep
Were vexed to nightmare by a rocking cradle,   20
And what rough beast, its hour come round at last,
Slouches towards Bethlehem to be born?

William Butler Yeats (1865–1939)

THE SECOND COMING.   In Christian legend the prophesied "Second Coming" may refer either to Christ or to Antichrist. Yeats believed in a cyclical theory of history in which one historical era would be replaced by an opposite kind of era every two thousand years. Here, the anarchy in the world following World War I (the poem was written in 1919) heralds the end of the Christian era.   12. *Spiritus Mundi:* the racial memory or collective unconscious mind of mankind (literally, world spirit).

THE WILD SWANS AT COOLE

The trees are in their autumn beauty,
The woodland paths are dry,
Under the October twilight the water
Mirrors a still sky;
Upon the brimming water among the stones   5
Are nine-and-fifty swans.

The nineteenth autumn has come upon me
Since I first made my count;
I saw, before I had well finished,
All suddenly mount   10
And scatter wheeling in great broken rings
Upon their clamorous wings.

I have looked upon those brilliant creatures,
And now my heart is sore,
All's changed since I, hearing at twilight,   15
The first time on this shore,
The bell-beat of their wings above my head,
Trod with a lighter tread.

Unwearied still, lover by lover,
They paddle in the cold   20
Companionable streams or climb the air;
Their hearts have not grown old;
Passion or conquest, wander where they will,
Attend upon them still.

But now they drift on the still water,   25
Mysterious, beautiful;
Among what rushes will they build,
By what lake's edge or pool
Delight men's eyes when I awake some day
To find they have flown away?   30

William Butler Yeats (1865-1939)

THE WILD SWANS AT COOLE. Coole Park, in County Galway, Ireland, was the estate of Lady Augusta Gregory, Yeats's patroness and friend. Beginning in 1897, Yeats regularly summered there for many years.

Drama

The Elements
of Drama

1. The Nature of Drama

Drama, like prose fiction, utilizes plot and characters, develops a theme, arouses emotion or appeals to humor, and may be either escapist or interpretive in its dealings with life.* Like poetry, it may draw upon all the resources of language, including verse. Much drama *is* poetry. But drama has one characteristic peculiar to itself. It is written primarily to be *performed*, not read. It normally presents its action (1) *through* actors, (2) *on* a stage, and (3) *before* an audience. Each of these circumstances has important consequences for the nature of drama. Each presents the playwright with a potentially enormous source of power, and each imposes limitations on the directions his work may take.

Because a play presents its action *through* actors, its impact is direct, immediate, and heightened by the actor's skills. Instead of responding to words on a printed page, the spectator sees what is done and hears what is said. The experience of the play is registered directly upon his senses. It may therefore be fuller and more compact. Where the work of prose fiction may tell us what a character looks like in one paragraph, how he moves or speaks in a second, what he says in a third, and how his auditors respond in a fourth, the acted play presents this material all at once. Simultaneous impressions are not temporally separated. Moreover, this experience is interpreted by actors who may be highly skilled in rendering nuances of meaning and strong emotion. Through facial expression, gesture, speech rhythm, and intonation, they may be able to make a

---

*Plot, character, theme, symbol, irony, and other elements of literature have been discussed in the fiction section and the poetry section.

speaker's words more expressive than can the reader's unaided imagination. Thus, the performance of a play by skilled actors expertly directed gives the playwright* a tremendous source of power.

But the playwright pays a price for this increased power. Of the four major points of view open to the fiction writer, the dramatist is practically limited to one—the *objective,* or *dramatic.* He cannot directly comment on the action or the characters. He cannot enter the minds of his characters and tell us what is going on there. Although there are ways around these limitations, each has its own limitations. Authorial commentary may be placed in the mouth of a character, but only at the risk of distorting characterization and of leaving the character's reliability uncertain. (Does the character speak for the author or only for himself?) Entry can be made into a character's mind through the conventions of the soliloquy and the aside. In the SOLILOQUY, a character is presented as speaking to himself—that is, he is made to think out loud. In the ASIDE, a character turns from the person with whom he is conversing to speak directly to, or for the benefit of, the audience, thus letting the audience know what he is really thinking or feeling as opposed to what he pretends to be thinking or feeling. Characters speaking in soliloquy or in asides are always presumed to be telling the truth, to the extent that they know the truth. Both devices can be used very effectively in the theater, but they interrupt the action and are therefore used sparingly. Also, they are inappropriate if the playwright is working in a strictly realistic mode.

Because a play presents its action *on* a stage, it is able powerfully to focus the spectator's attention. The stage is lighted; the theater is dark; extraneous noises are shut out; the spectator is almost literally pinned to his seat; there is nowhere he can go; there is nothing else to look at; there is nothing to distract. The playwright has extraordinary means by which to command the undivided attention of the audience. Unlike the fiction writer or the poet, the playwright is not dependent on the power of words alone.

But the necessity to confine his action to a stage, rather than to the imagination's vast arena, limits the kind of materials the playwright can easily and effectively present. For the most part, he must present human beings in spoken interaction with each other. He cannot easily use materials in which the main interest is in unspoken thoughts and reflections. He cannot present complex actions that involve nonhuman creatures such as

*The word *wright*—as in *playwright, shipwright, wheelwright, cartwright,* and the common surname *Wright*—comes from an Anglo-Saxon word meaning a workman or craftsman. It is related to the verb *wrought* (a past-tense form of *work*) and has nothing whatever to do with the verb *write.*

wild horses or charging bulls. He finds it more difficult to shift scenes rapidly than the writer of prose fiction does. The latter may whisk his reader from heaven to earth and back again in the twinkling of an eye, but the playwright must usually stick to one setting for an extended period of time, and may feel constrained to do so for the whole play.* Moreover, the events he depicts must be of a magnitude appropriate to the stage. He cannot present the movements of armies and warfare on the vast scale that Tolstoy uses in *War and Peace*. He cannot easily present adventures at sea or action on a ski slope. Conversely, he cannot depict a fly crawling around the rim of a saucer or falling into a cup of milk. At best he can present a general on a hilltop reporting the movements of a battle or two persons bending over a cup of milk reacting to a fly that the members of the audience cannot see.

Because a play presents its action *before* an audience, the experience it creates is a communal experience, and its impact is intensified. Reading a short story or a novel is a private transaction between the reader and a book, but the performance of a play is public. The spectator's response is affected by the presence of other spectators. A comedy becomes funnier when one hears others laughing, a tragedy more moving when others are present to carry the current of feeling. A dramatic experience, in fact, becomes more intense almost exactly to the extent that it is shared and the individual spectator becomes aware that others are having the same experience. This intensification is partly dependent on the size of the audience, but more on their sense of community with each other. A play will be more successful performed before a small audience in a packed auditorium than before a large audience in a half-filled hall.

But, again, the advantage given the playwright by the fact of theatrical

---

* The ease, and therefore the rapidity, with which a playwright can change from one scene to another depends, first, on the elaborateness of the stage setting and, second, on the means by which one scene is separated from another. In ancient plays and in many modern ones, stage settings have been extremely simple, depending only on a few easily moved properties or even entirely on the actors' words and the spectators' imaginations. In such cases, change of scenes is made fairly easily, especially if the actors themselves are allowed to carry on and off any properties that may be needed. Various means have been used to separate scenes from each other. In Greek plays, dancing and chanting by a chorus served as a scene divider. More recently, the closing and opening or dropping and raising of a curtain has been the means used. In contemporary theater, with its command of electrical technology, increased reliance has been placed on darkening and illuminating the stage or on darkening one part of it while lighting up another. But even where there is no stage scenery and where the shift of scene is made only by a change in lighting, the playwright can seldom change his setting as rapidly as the writer of prose fiction. On the stage, too frequent shifts of scene make a play seem jerky. A reader's imagination, on the other hand, can change from one setting to another without even shifting gears.

performance is paid for by limitations on the material he can present. His play must be able to hold the attention of a group audience. A higher premium than in prose fiction is placed on a well-defined plot, swift exposition, strong conflict, dramatic confrontations. Unless the play is very brief, it is usually divided into parts separated by an intermission or intermissions, and each part works up to its own climax or point of suspense. It is written so that its central meanings may be grasped in a single hearing. The spectator at a play cannot back up and rerun a passage whose import he has missed; he cannot, in one night, sit through the whole performance a second time. In addition, the playwright usually avoids extensive use of materials that are purely narrative or lyrical. Long narrative passages are usually interrupted, descriptive passages short or eliminated altogether. Primarily, human beings are presented in spoken interaction with each other. Clearly, many of the world's literary masterpieces—stories and poems that enthrall the reader of a book—would not hold the attention of a group audience in a theater.

Drama, then, imposes sharp limitations on its writer but holds out the opportunity for extraordinary power. The successful playwright combines the power of words, the power of fiction, and the power of dramatic technique to make possible the achievement of that extraordinary power.

EXERCISES AND TOPICS FOR DISCUSSION

1. Works written as short stories, novels, or poems have sometimes been dramatized for stage production. In light of the advantages and limitations discussed in this chapter, however, some are clearly more easily adapted for the stage than others. Of the following works, which could be most easily and effectively dramatized? Which would be possible but more difficult? Which would be impossible? Why? "Miss Brill" (page 453), "Mule in the Yard" (page 383), "The Lottery" (page 204), "The Guest" (page 211), "Hills Like White Elephants" (page 191), "The Death of the Hired Man" (page 757), "The Love Song of J. Alfred Prufrock" (page 761).

2. Write a stage adaptation of "The Ant and the Grasshopper" (page 162). What are the difficulties involved? How effective would such a presentation be?

3. Movie and TV production are in many ways more flexible than stage production and are more easily brought to a mass audience. What limitations of stage performance discussed in this chapter can be minimized or circumvented in a movie or TV production? In view of the greater flexibility of movies and TV as media, why is there still an eager audience for plays? What advantages do stage performances have over moving pictures and TV?

4. If plays are written to be *performed*, what justification is there for reading them?

August Strindberg
THE STRONGER

CHARACTERS

MRS. X., *an actress, married*
MISS Y., *an actress, unmarried*
A WAITRESS

SCENE. *The corner of a ladies' cafe. Two little iron tables, a red velvet sofa, several chairs. Enter* MRS. X., *dressed in winter clothes, carrying a Japanese basket on her arm.*

MISS Y. *sits with a half-empty beer bottle before her, reading an illustrated paper, which she changes later for another.*

MRS. X.   Good afternoon, Amelia. You're sitting here alone on Christmas eve like a poor bachelor!

MISS Y.   (*Looks up, nods, and resumes her reading.*)

MRS. X.   Do you know it really hurts me to see you like this, alone, in a café, and on Christmas eve, too. It makes me feel as I did one time when I saw a bridal party in a Paris restaurant, and the bride sat reading a comic paper, while the groom played billiards with the witnesses. Huh, thought I, with such a beginning, what will follow, and what will be the end? He played billiards on his wedding eve! (MISS Y. *starts to speak*) And she read a comic paper, you mean? Well, they are not altogether the same thing.

(A WAITRESS *enters, places a cup of chocolate before* MRS. X. *and goes out.*)

MRS. X.   You know what, Amelia! I believe you would have done better to have kept him! Do you remember, I was the first to say "Forgive him?" Do you remember that? You would be married now and have a home. Remember that Christmas when you went out to visit your fiancé's parents in the country? How you gloried in the happiness of home life and really longed to quit the theater forever? Yes, Amelia dear, home is the best of all—next to the theater—and as for children—well, you don't understand that.

MISS Y. (*Looks up scornfully.*)

THE STRONGER   Written and first performed in 1889. English translation by Edith and Warner Oland. August Strindberg (1849–1912) was born in Stockholm, Sweden, published his first play in 1870, and in 1875–76 began an intense love affair with an aspiring actress, Siri von Essen, then the Baroness Wrangel, whom he married in 1877 after her divorce. Though the marriage produced four children, it was a troubled one, largely because of Strindberg's irrational jealousies. *The Stronger,* though written while husband and wife were living apart, was done for a joint theatrical project, and Siri played Mrs. X in the opening production.

(MRS. X. *sips a few spoonfuls out of the cup, then opens her basket and shows Christmas presents.*)

MRS. X.   Now you shall see what I bought for my piggywigs. (*Takes up a doll.*) Look at this! This is for Lisa, ha! Do you see how she can roll her eyes and turn her head, eh? And here is Maja's popgun.

(*Loads it and shoots at* MISS Y.)

MISS Y. (*Makes a startled gesture.*)

MRS. X.   Did I frighten you? Do you think I would like to shoot you, eh? On my soul, if I don't think you did! If you wanted to shoot *me* it wouldn't be so surprising, because I stood in your way—and I know you can never forget that—although I was absolutely innocent. You still believe I intrigued and got you out of the Stora theater, but I didn't. I didn't do that, although you think so. Well, it doesn't make any difference what I say to you. You still believe I did it. (*Takes up a pair of embroidered slippers.*) And these are for my better half. I embroidered them myself—I can't bear tulips, but he wants tulips on everything.

MISS Y. (*Looks up ironically and curiously.*)

Mrs. X. (*putting a hand in each slipper*).   See what little feet Bob has! What? And you should see what a splendid stride he has! You've never seen him in slippers! (MISS Y. *laughs aloud.*) Look! (*She makes the slippers walk on the table.* MISS Y. *laughs loudly.*) And when he is grumpy he stamps like this with his foot. "What! damn those servants who can never learn to make coffee. Oh, now those creatures haven't trimmed the lamp wick properly!" And then there are drafts on the floor and his feet are cold. "Ugh, how cold it is; the stupid idiots can never keep the fire going." (*She rubs the slippers together, one sole over the other.*)

MISS Y. (*Shrieks with laughter.*)

MRS. X.   And then he comes home and has to hunt for his slippers which Marie has stuck under the chiffonier—oh, but it's sinful to sit here and make fun of one's husband this way when he is kind and a good little man. You ought to have had such a husband, Amelia. What are you laughing at? What? What? And you see he's true to me. Yes, I'm sure of that, because he told me himself—what are you laughing at?—that when I was touring in Norway that brazen Frederika came and wanted to seduce him! Can you fancy anything so infamous? (*pause*) I'd have torn her eyes out if she had come to see him when I was at home. (*pause*) It was lucky that Bob told me about it himself and that it didn't reach me through gossip. (*pause*) But would you believe it, Frederika wasn't the only one! I don't know why, but the women are crazy about my husband. They must think he has influence about getting them theatrical engagements, because he is connected with the government. Perhaps you were after him yourself. I didn't use to trust you any too much. But now I know he never bothered his head about you, and you always seemed to have a grudge against him someway.

(Pause. They look at each other in a puzzled way.)

MRS. X.   Come and see us this evening, Amelia, and show us that you're not put out with us—not put out with me at any rate. I don't know, but I think it would be uncomfortable to have you for an enemy. Perhaps it's because I stood in your way (*more slowly*) or—I really—don't know why—in particular.

(Pause. MISS Y. stares at MRS. X. curiously.)

MRS. X. (*thoughtfully*).   Our acquaintance has been so queer. When I saw you for the first time I was afraid of you, so afraid that I didn't dare let you out of my sight; no matter when or where, I always found myself near you—I didn't dare have you for an enemy, so I became your friend. But there was always discord when you came to our house, because I saw that my husband couldn't endure you, and the whole thing seemed as awry to me as an ill-fitting gown—and I did all I could to make him friendly toward you, but with no success until you became engaged. Then came a violent friendship between you, so that it looked all at once as though you both dared show your real feelings only when you were secure—and then—how was it later? I didn't get jealous—strange to say! And I remember at the christening, when you acted as godmother, I made him kiss you—he did so, and you became so confused—as it were; I didn't notice it then—didn't think about it later, either—have never thought about it until—now! (*Rises suddenly.*) Why are you silent? You haven't said a word this whole time, but you have let me go on talking! You have sat there, and your eyes have reeled out of me all these thoughts which lay like raw silk in its cocoon—thoughts—suspicious thoughts, perhaps. Let me see—why did you break your engagement? Why do you never come to our house any more? Why won't you come to see us tonight?

(MISS Y. appears as if about to speak.)

MRS. X.   Hush, you needn't speak—I understand it all! It was because—and because—and because! Yes, yes! Now all the accounts balance. That's it. Fie, I won't sit at the same table with you. (*Moves her things to another table.*) That's the reason I had to embroider tulips—which I hate—on his slippers, because you are fond of tulips; that's why (*throws slippers on the floor*) we go to Lake Mälarn in the summer, because you don't like salt water; that's why my boy is named Eskil—because it's your father's name; that's why I wear your colors, read your authors, eat your favorite dishes, drink your drinks—chocolate, for instance; that's why—oh—my God—it's terrible, when I think about it; it's terrible. Everything, everything came from you to me, even your passions. Your soul crept into mine, like a worm into an apple, ate and ate, bored and bored, until nothing was left but the rind and a little black dust within. I wanted to get away from you, but I couldn't; you lay like a snake and charmed me with your black eyes; I felt that when I lifted my wings they only dragged me down; I lay in the water with bound feet, and the stronger I strove to keep up the deeper I worked myself down, down, until I sank to the bottom, where you lay like a giant crab to clutch me in your claws—and there I am lying now.

I hate you, hate you, hate you! And you only sit there silent—silent and indifferent; indifferent whether it's new moon or waning moon, Christmas or New Year's, whether others are happy or unhappy; without power to hate or to love; as quiet as a stork by a rat hole—you couldn't scent your prey and capture it, but you could lie in wait for it! You sit here in your corner of the café—did you know it's called "The Rat Trap" for you?—and read the papers to see if misfortune hasn't befallen someone, to see if someone hasn't been given notice at the theater, perhaps; you sit here and calculate about your next victim and reckon on your chances of recompense like a pilot in a shipwreck. Poor Amelia, I pity you, nevertheless, because I know you are unhappy, unhappy like one who has been wounded, and angry because you are wounded. I can't be angry with you, no matter how much I want to be—because you come out the weaker one. Yes, all that with Bob doesn't trouble me. What is that to me, after all? And what difference does it make whether I learned to drink chocolate from you or some one else. (*Sips a spoonful from her cup*) Besides, chocolate is very healthful. And if you taught me how to dress—*tant mieux!*°—that has only made me more attractive to my husband; so you lost and I won there. Well, judging by certain signs, I believe you have already lost him; and you certainly intended that I should leave him—do as you did with your fiancé and regret as you now regret; but, you see, I don't do that—we mustn't be too exacting. And why should I take only what no one else wants?

Perhaps, take it all in all, I am at this moment the stronger one. You received nothing from me, but you gave me much. And now I seem like a thief since you have awakened and find I possess what is your loss. How could it be otherwise when everything is worthless and sterile in your hands? You can never keep a man's love with your tulips and your passions—but I can keep it. You can't learn how to live from your authors, as I have learned. You have no little Eskil to cherish, even if your father's name was Eskil. And why are you always silent, silent, silent? I thought that was strength, but perhaps it is because you have nothing to say! Because you never think about anything! (*Rises and picks up slippers.*) Now I'm going home—and take the tulips with me—*your* tulips! You are unable to learn from another; you can't bend—therefore, you broke like a dry stalk. But I won't break! Thank you, Amelia, for all your good lessons. Thanks for teaching my husband how to love. Now I'm going home to love him. (*Goes.*)

tant mieux!: so much the better

QUESTIONS

1. Much of the action of this play lies in the past, but to reconstruct that action we must separate what is true from what is untrue and from what may or may not be true in Mrs. X's account of it. Point out places where Mrs. X (a) is probably lying, (b) is clearly rationalizing, (c) has very likely or has certainly been deceived, (d) is clearly giving an accurate account. In each case, explain your reason for your opinion. To what extent can we be certain of what has happened in the past?

2. Now put together as reliable an account as possible of the past relationships of Mrs. X, her husband, and Miss Y. How did the friendship between the two women start? How did it proceed? How and why did it terminate? In what two ways have the two women consciously or unconsciously been rivals? In what ways and by what means has Miss Y influenced Mrs. X's behavior and her life?

3. In a sense the play has two plots, one in the past and one in the present, though the plot in the present is really only the culminating phase of that in the past. At what point does Mrs. X discover something about the past that she had not known before? What is it she discovers? How does she react to the discovery? Why can this discovery be called the turning point of the play?

4. Trace the successive attitudes expressed by Mrs. X toward Miss Y, together with the real attitudes underlying the expressed attitudes. At what points do the expressed attitudes and the real attitudes coincide? At what points do they clearly differ?

5. What kind of person is Mrs. X? Characterize her.

6. Although Miss Y says nothing during the course of the play, we can infer a good deal about her from her reactions to Mrs. X, from her past actions, and from what Mrs. X says about her (cautiously interpreted). What kind of person is she? How, especially, does she differ from Mrs. X? What is the nature of her present life? Would this role be easy or difficult to act?

7. Although Mr. X never appears, he also is an important character in the play. What kind of man is he?

8. To which character does the title refer? Consider carefully before answering, and support your answer with a reasoned argument, including a definition of what is meant by "stronger."

Anonymous

EVERYMAN

CHARACTERS

MESSENGER	GOOD DEEDS
GOD	KNOWLEDGE
DEATH	CONFESSION
EVERYMAN	BEAUTY
FELLOWSHIP	STRENGTH
COUSIN	DISCRETION
KINDRED	FIVE WITS
GOODS	ANGEL

DOCTOR

Here beginneth a treatise how the High Father of Heaven sendeth Death to summon every creature to come and give account of their lives in this world, and is in manner of a moral play.

Enter MESSENGER *as Prologue.*

MESSENGER. I pray you all give your audience,
 And hear this matter with reverence,
 By figure a moral play—
 The *Summoning of Everyman* called it is,
 That of our lives and ending shows   5
 How transitory we be all day.
 This matter is wondrous precious,
 But the intent of it is more gracious,
 And sweet to bear away.
 The story saith: Man, in the beginning,   10
 Look well, and take good heed to the ending,
 Be you never so gay!
 Ye think sin in the beginning full sweet,
 Which in the end causeth the soul to weep,
 When the body lieth in clay.   15
 Here shall you see how Fellowship and Jollity,
 Both Strength, Pleasure, and Beauty,
 Will fade from thee as flower in May.
 For ye shall hear how our Heaven King
 Calleth Everyman to a general reckoning.   20

EVERYMAN The author and date of this play are unknown. The earliest existing printed versions date from the early 1500s.

Give audience, and hear what he doth say. (*Exit.*)

(GOD *speaks from above.*)

GOD. I perceive, here in my majesty,
    How that all creatures be to me unkind,
    Living without dread in worldly prosperity.
    Of ghostly° sight the people be so blind,   25
    Drowned in sin, they know me not for their God.
    In worldly riches is all their mind,
    They fear not my rightwiseness, the sharp rod;
    My love that I showed when I for them died
    They forget clean, and shedding of my blood red;   30
    I hanged between two, it cannot be denied;
    To get them life I suffered to be dead;
    I healed their feet, with thorns hurt was my head.
    I could do no more than I did, truly;
    And now I see the people do clean forsake me.   35
    They use the seven deadly sins damnable,
    As pride, covetise,° wrath, and lechery,
    Now in the world be made commendable;
    And thus they leave of angels the heavenly company.
    Every man liveth so after his own pleasure,   40
    And yet of their life they be nothing sure.
    I see the more that I them forbear
    The worse they be from year to year;
    All that liveth appaireth° fast.
    Therefore I will, in all the haste,   45
    Have a reckoning of every man's person;
    For, and° I leave the people thus alone
    In their life and wicked tempests,
    Verily they will become much worse than beasts;
    For now one would by envy another up eat;   50
    Charity they all do clean forget.
    I hoped well that every man
    In my glory should make his mansion,
    And thereto I had them all elect,°
    But now I see, like traitors deject,°   55
    They thank me not for the pleasure that I to them meant,
    Nor yet for their being that I them have lent.
    I proffered the people great multitude of mercy,

---

25. ghostly: spiritual. **37. covetise:** covetousness. **44. appaireth:** becomes worse. **47. and:** if; so used frequently throughout the play. **54. elect:** numbered among the redeemed. **55. deject:** abject.

And few there be that asketh it heartily;
They be so cumbered with worldly riches,   60
That needs on them I must do justice,
On every man living without fear.
Where art thou, Death, thou mighty messenger?

(*Enter* DEATH.)

DEATH. Almighty God, I am here at your will,
    Your commandment to fulfil.   65
GOD. Go thou to Everyman,
    And show him, in my name,
    A pilgrimage he must on him take,
    Which he in no wise may escape;
    And that he bring with him a sure reckoning   70
    Without delay or any tarrying. (*Exit* GOD.)
DEATH. Lord, I will in the world go run over all,
    And cruelly out search both great and small.
    Every man will I beset that liveth beastly
    Out of God's laws, and dreadeth not folly.   75
    He that loveth riches I will strike with my dart,
    His sight to blind, and from heaven to depart,
    Except that alms be his good friend,
    In hell for to dwell, world without end.

(EVERYMAN *enters, at a distance.*)

    Lo, yonder I see Everyman walking;   80
    Full little he thinketh on my coming.
    His mind is on fleshly lusts and his treasure,
    And great pain it shall cause him to endure
    Before the Lord, Heaven King.
    Everyman, stand still! Whither art thou going   85
    Thus gaily? Hast thou thy Maker forgot?
EVERYMAN. Why askest thou?
    Wouldst thou wete?°
DEATH. Yea, sir, I will show you:
    In great haste I am sent to thee   90
    From God out of his Majesty.
EVERYMAN. What, sent to me?
DEATH. Yea, certainly.
    Though thou have forgot him here,
    He thinketh on thee in the heavenly sphere,   95
    As, ere we depart, thou shalt know.
EVERYMAN. What desireth God of me?

88. **wete:** know.

DEATH. That shall I show thee:
  A reckoning he will needs have
  Without any longer respite.   100
EVERYMAN. To give a reckoning, longer leisure I crave.
  This blind matter troubleth my wit.
DEATH. On thee thou must take a long journey;
  Therefore thy book of count° with thee thou bring;
  For turn again thou can not by no way.   105
  And look thou be sure of thy reckoning,
  For before God thou shalt answer and show
  Thy many bad deeds, and good but a few,
  How thou hast spent thy life, and in what wise,
  Before the Chief Lord of paradise.   110
  Have ado that we were in that way,°
  For, wete thou well, thou shalt make none attourney.°
EVERYMAN. Full unready I am such reckoning to give.
  I know thee not. What messenger art thou?
DEATH. I am Death, that no man dreadeth.°   115
  For every man I 'rest,° and no man spareth;
  For it is God's commandment
  That all to me should be obedient.
EVERYMAN. O Death! thou comest when I had thee least in mind!
  In thy power it lieth me to save.   120
  Yet of my goods will I give thee, if thou will be kind;
  Yea, a thousand pound shalt thou have,
  If thou defer this matter till another day.
DEATH. Everyman, it may not be, by no way!
  I set not by° gold, silver, nor riches,   125
  Nor by pope, emperor, king, duke, nor princes.
  For, and I would receive gifts great,
  All the world I might get;
  But my custom is clean contrary.
  I give thee no respite. Come hence, and not tarry.   130
EVERYMAN. Alas! shall I have no longer respite?
  I may say Death giveth no warning.
  To think on thee, it maketh my heart sick,
  For all unready is my book of reckoning.
  But twelve year and I might have abiding,   135
  My counting-book I would make so clear,
  That my reckoning I should not need to fear.
  Wherefore, Death, I pray thee, for God's mercy,

---

104. count: accounts.   **111. Have ado . . . way:** get busy so that we may be on the way.
112. thou shalt . . . attourney: you shall have no attorney to plead for you.   **115. no man dreadeth:** fears no man.   **116. 'rest:** arrest.   **125. set not by:** care nothing for.

Spare me till I be provided of remedy.

DEATH. Thee availeth not to cry, weep, and pray; 140
But haste thee lightly that thou were gone that journey,
And prove thy friends if thou can.
For wete thou well the tide abideth no man;
And in the world each living creature
For Adam's sin must die of nature. 145

EVERYMAN. Death, if I should this pilgrimage take,
And my reckoning surely make,
Show me, for saint charity,
Should I not come again shortly?

DEATH. No, Everyman; and thou be once there, 150
Thou mayest never more come here,
Trust me verily.

EVERYMAN. O gracious God, in the high seat celestial,
Have mercy on me in this most need!
Shall I have no company from this vale terrestrial 155
Of mine acquaintance that way me to lead?

DEATH. Yea, if any be so hardy,
That would go with thee and bear thee company.
Hie thee that thou were gone to God's magnificence,
Thy reckoning to give before his presence. 160
What! weenest° thou thy life is given thee,
And thy worldly goods also?

EVERYMAN. I had weened so, verily.

DEATH. Nay, nay; it was but lent thee;
For, as soon as thou art gone, 165
Another a while shall have it, and then go therefrom
Even as thou hast done.
Everyman, thou art mad! Thou hast thy wits five,
And here on earth will not amend thy life;
For suddenly I do come. 170

EVERYMAN. O wretched caitiff! whither shall I flee,
That I might 'scape endless sorrow?
Now, gentle Death, spare me till tomorrow,
That I may amend me
With good advisement.° 175

DEATH. Nay, thereto I will not consent,
Nor no man will I respite,
But to the heart suddenly I shall smite
Without any advisement.
And now out of thy sight I will me hie; 180
See thou make thee ready shortly,

---

161. weenest: think. **175. advisement:** warning.

For thou mayst say this is the day
That no man living may 'scape away. (*Exit* DEATH.)
EVERYMAN. Alas! I may well weep with sighs deep.
Now have I no manner of company   185
To help me in my journey and me to keep;
And also my writing is full unready.
How shall I do now for to excuse me?
I would to God I had never been get!
To my soul a full great profit it had be,   190
For now I fear pains huge and great.
The time passeth; Lord, help, that all wrought.
For though I mourn it availeth naught.
The day passeth, and is almost a-go;
I wot° not well what for to do.   195
To whom were I best my complaint to make?
What if I to Fellowship thereof spake,
And showed him of this sudden chance?
For in him is all mine affiance,°
We have in the world so many a day   200
Been good friends in sport and play.
I see him yonder, certainly;
I trust that he will bear me company;
Therefore to him will I speak to ease my sorrow.

(*Enter* FELLOWSHIP.)

Well met, good Fellowship, and good morrow!   205
FELLOWSHIP. Everyman, good morrow, by this day!
Sir, why lookest thou so piteously?
If any thing be amiss, I pray thee me say,
That I may help to remedy.
EVERYMAN. Yea, good Fellowship, yea,   210
I am in great jeopardy.
FELLOWSHIP. My true friend, show to me your mind.
I will not forsake thee to my life's end
In the way of good company.
EVERYMAN. That was well spoken, and lovingly.   215
FELLOWSHIP. Sir, I must needs know your heaviness;
I have pity to see you in any distress;
If any have you wronged, ye shall revenged be,
Though I on the ground be slain for thee,
Though that I know before that I should die.   220
EVERYMAN. Verily, Fellowship, gramercy.°
FELLOWSHIP. Tush! by thy thanks I set not a straw!

195. wot: know. **199. affiance:** trust. **221. gramercy:** thanks.

Show me your grief, and say no more.

EVERYMAN. If I my heart should to you break,°
    And then you to turn your mind from me,   225
    And would not me comfort when you hear me speak,
    Then should I ten times sorrier be.

FELLOWSHIP. Sir, I say as I will do, indeed.

EVERYMAN. Then be you a good friend at need;
    I have found you true here before.   230

FELLOWSHIP. And so ye shall evermore;
    For, in faith, and thou go to hell,
    I will not forsake thee by the way!

EVERYMAN. Ye speak like a good friend. I believe you well;
    I shall deserve it, and I may.   235

FELLOWSHIP. I speak of no deserving, by this day!
    For he that will say and nothing do
    Is not worthy with good company to go;
    Therefore show me the grief of your mind,
    As to your friend most loving and kind.   240

EVERYMAN. I shall show you how it is:
    Commanded I am to go a journey,
    A long way, hard and dangerous,
    And give a strait° count without delay
    Before the high judge, Adonai.°   245
    Wherefore, I pray you, bear me company,
    As ye have promised, in this journey.

FELLOWSHIP. That is matter indeed! Promise is duty;
    But, and I should take such a voyage on me,
    I know it well, it should be to my pain.   250
    Also it maketh me afeared, certain.
    But let us take counsel here as well as we can,
    For your words would fear° a strong man.

EVERYMAN. Why, ye said if I had need,
    Ye would me never forsake, quick° nor dead,   255
    Though it were to hell, truly.

FELLOWSHIP. So I said, certainly,
    But such pleasures be set aside, the sooth to say.
    And also, if we took such a journey,
    When should we come again?   260

EVERYMAN. Nay, never again till the day of doom.

FELLOWSHIP. In faith, then will not I come there!
    Who hath you these tidings brought?

EVERYMAN. Indeed, Death was with me here.

---

224. **break:** reveal. 244. **strait:** strict. 245. **Adonai:** an Old Testament name for God.
253. **fear:** frighten. 255. **quick:** living.

FELLOWSHIP. Now, by God that all hath bought,   265
    If Death were the messenger,
    For no man that is living today
    I will not go that loath° journey—
    Not for the father that begat me!
EVERYMAN. Ye promised otherwise, pardie.°   270
FELLOWSHIP. I wot well I said so, truly;
    And yet if thou wilt eat, and drink, and make good cheer,
    Or haunt to women the lusty company,
    I would not forsake you while the day is clear,
    Trust me verily!   275
EVERYMAN. Yea, thereto you would be ready.
    To go to mirth, solace, and play,
    Your mind will sooner apply
    Than to bear me company in my long journey.
FELLOWSHIP. Now, in good faith, I will not that way.   280
    But and thou wilt murder, or any man kill,
    In that I will help thee with a good will!
EVERYMAN. O, that is a simple advice indeed!
    Gentle fellow, help me in my necessity;
    We have loved long, and now I need,   285
    And now, gentle Fellowship, remember me!
FELLOWSHIP. Whether ye have loved me or no,
    By Saint John, I will not with thee go.
EVERYMAN. Yet, I pray thee, take the labor, and do so much for me
    To bring me forward, for saint charity,   290
    And comfort me till I come without the town.
FELLOWSHIP. Nay, and thou would give me a new gown,
    I will not a foot with thee go;
    But, and thou had tarried, I would not have left thee so.
    And as now God speed thee in thy journey,   295
    For from thee I will depart as fast as I may.
EVERYMAN. Whither away, Fellowship? Will you forsake me?
FELLOWSHIP. Yea, by my fay,° to God I betake° thee.
EVERYMAN. Farewell, good Fellowship! For thee my heart is sore;
    Adieu for ever! I shall see thee no more.   300
FELLOWSHIP. In faith, Everyman, farewell now at the end!
    For you I will remember that parting is mourning.

                                              (*Exit* FELLOWSHIP.)

EVERYMAN. Alack! shall we thus depart indeed
    (Ah, Lady, help), without any more comfort?
    Lo, Fellowship foresaketh me in my most need.   305

268. **loath:** loathsome. 270. **pardie:** by God. 298. **fay:** faith. **betake:** commend.

For help in this world whither shall I resort?
Fellowship here before with me would merry make,
And now little sorrow for me doth he take.
It is said, "In prosperity men friends may find,
Which in adversity be full unkind."   310
Now whither for succor shall I flee,
Sith° that Fellowship hath forsaken me?
To my kinsmen I will, truly,
Praying them to help me in my necessity;
I believe that they will do so,   315
For "kind° will creep where it may not go.°"
I will go say,° for yonder I see them go.
Where be ye now, my friends and kinsmen?

(*Enter* KINDRED *and* COUSIN.)

KINDRED. Here be we now, at your commandment.
    Cousin, I pray you show us your intent   320
    In any wise, and do not spare.
COUSIN. Yea, Everyman, and to us declare
    If ye be disposed to go any whither,
    For, wete you well, we will live and die together.
KINDRED. In wealth° and woe we will with you hold,   325
    For over his kin a man may be bold.
EVERYMAN. Gramercy, my friends and kinsmen kind.
    Now shall I show you the grief of my mind.
    I was commanded by a messenger
    That is a high king's chief officer;   330
    He bade me go a pilgrimage, to my pain,
    And I know well I shall never come again;
    Also I must give a reckoning straight,
    For I have a great enemy that hath me in wait,°
    Which intended me for to hinder.   335
KINDRED. What account is that which ye must render?
    That would I know.
EVERYMAN. Of all my works I must show
    How I have lived, and my days spent;
    Also of ill deeds that I have used   340
    In my time, sith life was me lent;
    And of all virtues that I have refused.
    Therefore I pray you go thither with me,
    To help to make mine account, for saint charity.
COUSIN. What, to go thither? Is that the matter?   345

---

312. Sith: since. **316. kind:** kinship. **go:** walk. **317. say:** assay, try. **325. wealth:** weal, happiness. **334. hath me in wait:** lies in wait for me.

Nay, Everyman, I had liefer fast bread and water
All this five year and more.
EVERYMAN. Alas, that ever I was bore!
For now shall I never be merry
If that you forsake me.   350
KINDRED. Ah, sir, what! Ye be a merry man!
Take good heart to you, and make no moan.
But one thing I warn you, by Saint Anne,
As for me, ye shall go alone.
EVERYMAN. My Cousin, will you not with me go?   355
COUSIN. No, by our Lady! I have the cramp in my toe.
Trust not to me, for, so God me speed,°
I will deceive you in your most need.
KINDRED. It availeth not us to tice.°
Ye shall have my maid with all my heart;   360
She loveth to go to feasts, there to be nice,°
And to dance, and abroad to start;
I will give her leave to help you in that journey,
If that you and she may agree.
EVERYMAN. Now show me the very effect of your mind.   365
Will you go with me, or abide behind?
KINDRED. Abide behind? Yea, that will I, and I may!
Therefore, farewell till another day. (*Exit* KINDRED.)
EVERYMAN. How should I be merry or glad?
For fair promises men to me make,   370
But when I have most need, they me forsake.
I am deceived; that maketh me sad.
COUSIN. Cousin Everyman, farewell now,
For verily I will not go with you;
Also of mine own life an unready reckoning   375
I have to account; therefore I make tarrying.
Now, God keep thee, for now I go. (*Exit* COUSIN.)
EVERYMAN. Ah, Jesus! is all come hereto?
Lo, fair words maketh fools fain;°
They promise and nothing will do, certain.   380
My kinsmen promised me faithfully
For to abide with me steadfastly,
And now fast away do they flee.
Even so Fellowship promised me.
What friend were best me of to provide?   385
I lose my time here longer to abide.
Yet in my mind a thing there is:
All my life I have loved riches;

---

357. speed: prosper. **359. tice:** entice. **361. nice:** wanton, gay. **379. fain:** joyful.

If that my good now help me might,
He would make my heart full light.
I will speak to him in this distress.   390
Where art thou, my Goods and riches?

(GOODS *speaks from within.*)

GOODS. Who calleth me? Everyman? What, hast thou haste?
  I lie here in corners, trussed and piled so high,
  And in chests I am locked so fast,   395
  Also sacked in bags—thou mayest see with thine eye—
  I cannot stir; in packs low I lie.
  What would ye have? Lightly me say.°
EVERYMAN. Come hither, Goods, in all the haste thou may.
  For of counsel I must desire thee.   400

(*Enter* GOODS.)

GOODS. Sir, and ye in the world have sorrow or adversity,
  That can I help you to remedy shortly.
EVERYMAN. It is another disease that grieveth me;
  In this world it is not, I tell thee so.
  I am sent for another way to go,   405
  To give a strict count general
  Before the highest Jupiter of all;
  And all my life I have had joy and pleasure in thee,
  Therefore I pray thee go with me,
  For, peradventure, thou mayst before God Almighty   410
  My reckoning help to clean and purify;
  For it is said ever among,
  That "money maketh all right that is wrong."
GOODS. Nay, Everyman; I sing another song,
  I follow no man in such voyages;   415
  For, and I went with thee,
  Thou shouldst fare much the worse for me;
  For because on me thou did set thy mind,
  Thy reckoning I have made blotted and blind,
  That thine account thou cannot make truly;   420
  And that hast thou for the love of me.
EVERYMAN. That would grieve me full sore,
  When I should come to that fearful answer.
  Up, let us go thither together.
GOODS. Nay, not so! I am too brittle, I may not endure;   425
  I will follow no man one foot, be ye sure.
EVERYMAN. Alas! I have thee loved, and had great pleasure

398. **Lightly me say:** tell me quickly.

All my life-days on goods and treasure.

GOODS. That is to thy damnation, without lesing!°
For my love is contrary to the love everlasting.   430
But if thou had me loved moderately during,°
As to the poor to give part of me,
Then shouldst thou not in this dolor be,
Nor in this great sorrow and care.

EVERYMAN. Lo, now was I deceived ere I was ware,   435
And all I may wyte° my spending of time.

GOODS. What, weenest thou that I am thine?

EVERYMAN. I had weened so.

GOODS. Nay, Everyman, I say no;
As for a while I was lent thee,   440
A season thou hast had me in prosperity.
My condition is man's soul to kill;
If I save one, a thousand I do spill;°
Weenest thou that I will follow thee
From this world? Nay, verily.   445

EVERYMAN. I had weened otherwise.

GOODS. Therefore to thy soul Goods is a thief;
For when thou art dead, this is my guise,°
Another to deceive in the same wise
As I have done thee, and all to his soul's reprief.°   450

EVERYMAN. O false Goods, curséd may thou be!
Thou traitor to God, that hast deceived me
And caught me in thy snare.

GOODS. Marry!° thou brought thyself in care,°
Whereof I am right glad.   455
I must needs laugh, I cannot be sad.

EVERYMAN. Ah, Goods, thou hast had long my heartly love;
I gave thee that which should be the Lord's above.
But wilt thou not go with me indeed?
I pray thee truth to say.   460

GOODS. No, so God me speed!
Therefore farewell, and have good day. (*Exit* GOODS.)

EVERYMAN. O, to whom shall I make my moan
For to go with me in that heavy journey?
First Fellowship said he would with me gone;   465
His words were very pleasant and gay,
But afterward he left me alone.
Then spake I to my kinsmen, all in despair,

---

429. lesing: lying. **431. during:** while living. **436. wyte:** blame on. **443. spill:** destroy.
448. guise: custom. **450. reprief:** reproach. **454. Marry:** "by Mary," a mild oath.
care: trouble.

And also they gave me words fair,
They lacked no fair speaking, 470
But all forsook me in the ending.
Then went I to my Goods, that I loved best,
In hope to have comfort, but there had I least;
For my Goods sharply did me tell
That he bringeth many into hell. 475
Then of myself I was ashamed,
And so I am worthy to be blamed;
Thus may I well myself hate.
Of whom shall I now counsel take?
I think that I shall never speed 480
Till that I go to my Good Deeds.
But alas! she is so weak
That she can neither go nor speak.
Yet will I venture on her now.
My Good Deeds, where be you? 485

(GOOD DEEDS *speaks from the ground.*)

GOOD DEEDS. Here I lie, cold in the ground.
    Thy sins hath me sore bound,
    That I cannot stir.
EVERYMAN. O Good Deeds, I stand in fear!
    I must you pray of counsel, 490
    For help now should come right well.
GOOD DEEDS. Everyman, I have understanding
    That ye be summoned account to make
    Before Messias, of Jerusalem King;
    And you do by me,° that journey with you will I take. 495
EVERYMAN. Therefore I come to you my moan to make;
    I pray you that ye will go with me.
GOOD DEEDS. I would full fain, but I cannot stand, verily.
EVERYMAN. Why, is there anything on you fall?
GOOD DEEDS. Yea, sir, I may thank you of all;° 500
    If ye had perfectly cheered° me,
    Your book of count full ready had be.
    Look, the books of your works and deeds eke,°
    Behold how they lie under the feet,
    To your soul's heaviness. 505
EVERYMAN. Our Lord Jesus help me!
    For one letter here I can not see.°
GOOD DEEDS. There is a blind reckoning in time of distress!°

---

495. do by me: follow my advice. **500. of all:** for everything. **501. cheered:** cherished.
503. eke: also. **507. one . . . see:** I cannot make out a single letter. **508. There . . .**
distress: the account is hard to read in time of trouble.

EVERYMAN. Good Deeds, I pray you, help me in this need,
Or else I am for ever damned indeed.   510
Therefore help me to make my reckoning
Before the Redeemer of all thing,
That King is, and was, and ever shall.
GOOD DEEDS. Everyman, I am sorry of your fall,
And fain would I help you, and I were able.   515
EVERYMAN. Good Deeds, your counsel I pray you give me.
GOOD DEEDS. That shall I do verily;
Though that on my feet I may not go,
I have a sister that shall with you also,
Called Knowledge,° which shall with you abide,   520
To help you to make that dreadful reckoning.

(*Enter* KNOWLEDGE.)

KNOWLEDGE. Everyman, I will go with thee, and be thy guide,
In thy most need to go by thy side.
EVERYMAN. In good condition I am now in every thing,
And am wholly content with this good thing;   525
Thanked be God my Creator.
GOOD DEEDS. And when he hath brought thee there,
Where thou shalt heal thee of thy smart,
Then go you with your reckoning and your Good Deeds together
For to make you joyful at heart   530
Before the blessed Trinity.
EVERYMAN. My Good Deeds, gramercy!
I am well content, certainly,
With your words sweet.
KNOWLEDGE. Now go we together lovingly   535
To Confession, that cleansing river.
EVERYMAN. For Joy I weep; I would we were there!
But, I pray you, give me cognition°
Where dwelleth that holy man, Confession.
KNOWLEDGE. In the house of salvation,   540
We shall find him in that place,
That shall us comfort, by God's grace.

(*Enter* CONFESSION.)

Lo, this is Confession. Kneel down and ask mercy,
For he is in good conceit° with God almighty.
EVERYMAN. O glorious fountain, that all uncleanness doth clarify,   545
Wash from me the spots of vice unclean,
That on me no sin may be seen.

---

520. Knowledge: i.e., knowledge of sin. **538. cognition:** understanding. **544. conceit:**
favor.

I come with Knowledge, for my redemption,
Redempt with hearty and full contrition;
For I am commanded a pilgrimage to take,   550
And great accounts before God to make.
Now, I pray you, Shrift,° mother of salvation,
Help my Good Deeds for my piteous exclamation.
CONFESSION. I know your sorrow well, Everyman.
Because with Knowledge ye come to me,   555
I will you comfort as well as I can,
And a precious jewel I will give thee,
Called penance, voider of adversity.
Therewith shall your body chastised be
With abstinence and perseverance in God's service.   560
Here shall you receive that scourge of me

(*Gives* EVERYMAN *a scourge.*)

Which is penance strong that ye must endure
To remember thy Savior was scourged for thee
With sharp scourges and suffered it patiently.
So must thou ere thou 'scape° that painful pilgrimage.   565
Knowledge, keep him in this voyage,
And by that time Good Deeds will be with thee.
But in any wise be sure of mercy,
For your time draweth fast, and ye will saved be;
Ask God mercy, and He will grant truly;   570
When with the scourge of penance man doth him bind,
The oil of forgiveness then shall he find. (*Exit* CONFESSION.)
EVERYMAN. Thanked be God for his gracious work!
For now I will my penance begin;
This hath rejoiced and lighted my heart,   575
Though the knots be painful and hard within.
KNOWLEDGE. Everyman, look your penance that ye fulfil,
What pain that ever it to you be,
And Knowledge shall give you counsel at will
How your account ye shall make clearly.   580

(EVERYMAN *kneels.*)

EVERYMAN. O eternal God! O heavenly figure!
O way of rightwiseness! O goodly vision!
Which descended down in a virgin pure
Because he would Everyman redeem,
Which Adam forfeited by his disobedience.   585
O blesséd Godhead! elect and high divine,

552. **Shrift:** absolution. 565. **'scape:** finish.

Forgive me my grievous offence;
Here I cry thee mercy in this presence.
O ghostly treasure! O ransomer and redeemer!
Of all the world hope and conductor, 590
Mirror of joy, and founder of mercy,
Which illumineth heaven and earth thereby,
Hear my clamorous complaint, though it late be.
Receive my prayers; unworthy in this heavy life.
Though I be a sinner most abominable, 595
Yet let my name be written in Moses' table.°
O Mary! pray to the Maker of all thing,
Me for to help at my ending,
And save me from the power of my enemy,
For Death assaileth me strongly. 600
And, Lady, that I may by means of thy prayer
Of your Son's glory to be partner,
By the means of his passion I it crave.
I beseech you, help my soul to save. (*He rises.*)
Knowledge, give me the scourge of penance. 605
My flesh therewith shall give you a quittance.°
I will now begin, if God give me grace.
KNOWLEDGE. Everyman, God give you time and space.
Thus I bequeath you in the hands of our Savior,
Now may you make your reckoning sure. 610
EVERYMAN. In the name of the Holy Trinity,
My body sore punished shall be. (*Scourges himself.*)
Take this, body, for the sin of the flesh.
Also thou delightest to go gay and fresh,
And in the way of damnation thou did me bring; 615
Therefore suffer now strokes of punishing.
Now of penance I will wade the water clear,
To save me from purgatory, that sharp fire.

(GOOD DEEDS *rises.*)

GOOD DEEDS. I thank God, now I can walk and go,
And am delivered of my sickness and woe. 620
Therefore with Everyman I will go, and not spare;
His good works I will help him to declare.
KNOWLEDGE. Now, Everyman, be merry and glad!
Your Good Deeds cometh now, ye may not be sad.
Now is your Good Deeds whole and sound, 625
Going upright upon the ground.
EVERYMAN. My heart is light, and shall be evermore.

596. table: tablets, i.e., among the saved.   **606. a quittance:** full payment.

Now will I smite faster than I did before.

GOOD DEEDS. Everyman, pilgrim, my special friend,
  Blesséd be thou without end.   630
  For thee is prepared the eternal glory.
  Ye have me made whole and sound,
  Therefore I will bide by thee in every stound.°

EVERYMAN. Welcome, my Good Deeds; now I hear thy voice,
  I weep for very sweetness of love.   635

KNOWLEDGE. Be no more sad, but ever rejoice;
  God seeth thy living in his throne above.
  Put on this garment to thy behoof,°
  Which is wet with your tears,
  Or else before God you may it miss,   640
  When you to your journey's end come shall.

EVERYMAN. Gentle Knowledge, what do ye it call?

KNOWLEDGE. It is the garment of sorrow;
  From pain it will you borrow,°
  Contrition it is   645
  That getteth forgiveness;
  It pleaseth God passing well.

GOOD DEEDS. Everyman, will you wear it for your heal?

(EVERYMAN *puts on garment of contrition.*)

EVERYMAN. Now blesséd be Jesu, Mary's Son,
  For now have I on true contrition.   650
  And let us go now without tarrying;
  Good Deeds, have we clear our reckoning?

GOOD DEEDS. Yea, indeed I have it here.

EVERYMAN. Then I trust we need not fear.
  Now, friends, let us not part in twain.   655

KNOWLEDGE. Nay, Everyman, that will we not, certain.

GOOD DEEDS. Yet must thou lead with thee
  Three persons of great might.

EVERYMAN. Who should they be?

GOOD DEEDS. Discretion and Strength they hight,°   660
  And thy Beauty may not abide behind.

KNOWLEDGE. Also ye must call to mind
  Your Five Wits° as for your counselors.

GOOD DEEDS. You must have them ready at all hours.

EVERYMAN. How shall I get them hither?   665

KNOWLEDGE. You must call them all together,
  And they will hear you incontinent.°

---

633. stound: trial. **638. behoof:** benefit. **644. borrow:** redeem. **660. hight:** are called.
663. Five Wits: five senses. **667. incontinent:** at once.

EVERYMAN. My friends, come hither and be present,
Discretion, Strength, my Five Wits, and Beauty.

(*Enter* DISCRETION, STRENGTH, FIVE WITS, *and* BEAUTY.)

BEAUTY. Here at your will we be all ready.   670
What will ye that we should do?
GOOD DEEDS. That ye would with Everyman go,
And help him in his pilgrimage.
Advise you, will ye with him or not in that voyage?
STRENGTH. We will bring him all thither,   675
To his help and comfort, ye may believe me.
DISCRETION. So will we go with him all together.
EVERYMAN. Almighty God, lovéd may thou be!
I give thee laud° that I have hither brought
Strength, Discretion, Beauty, and Five Wits. Lack I naught.   680
And my Good Deeds, with Knowledge clear,
All be in company at my will here.
I desire no more to my business.
STRENGTH. And I, Strength, will by you stand in distress,
Though thou would in battle fight on the ground.   685
FIVE WITS. And though it were through the world round,
We will not depart for sweet nor sour.
BEAUTY. No more will I, unto death's hour,
Whatsoever thereof befall.
DISCRETION. Everyman, advise you first of all,   690
Go with a good advisement and deliberation.
We all give you virtuous monition
That all shall be well.
EVERYMAN. My friends, hearken what I will tell:
I pray God reward you in his heavenly sphere.   695
Now hearken, all that be here,
For I will make my testament
Here before you all present:
In alms half my goods I will give my hands twain
In the way of charity, with good intent,   700
And the other half still shall remain,
I it bequeath to be returned there it ought to be.
This I do in despite of the fiend of hell,
To go quite out of his peril
Ever after and this day.   705
KNOWLEDGE. Everyman, hearken what I say;
Go to Priesthood, I you advise,
And receive of him in any wise

679. laud: praise.

The holy sacrament and ointment together,°
Then shortly see ye turn again hither;   710
We will all abide you here.
FIVE WITS. Yea, Everyman, hie you that ye ready were.
There is no emperor, king, duke, nor baron,
That of God hath commission
As hath the least priest in the world being;   715
For of the blessèd sacraments pure and benign
He beareth the keys, and thereof hath the cure
For man's redemption—it is ever sure—
Which God for our soul's medicine
Gave us out of his heart with great pain,   720
Here in this transitory life, for thee and me.
The blessèd sacraments seven there be:
Baptism, confirmation, with priesthood good,
And the sacrament of God's precious flesh and blood,
Marriage, the holy extreme unction, and penance.   725
These seven be good to have in remembrance,
Gracious sacraments of high divinity.
EVERYMAN. Fain would I receive that holy body
And meekly to my ghostly father I will go.
FIVE WITS. Everyman, that is the best that ye can do.   730
God will you to salvation bring,
For priesthood exceedeth all other thing;
To us Holy Scripture they do teach,
And converteth man from sin, heaven to reach;
God hath to them more power given,   735
Than to any angel that is in heaven.
With five words he may consecrate
God's body in flesh and blood to make,
And handleth his Maker between his hands.
The priest bindeth and unbindeth all bands,   740
Both in earth and in heaven.
Thou minister all the sacraments seven,
Though we kissed thy feet, thou wert worthy;
Thou art the surgeon that cureth sin deadly:
No remedy we find under God   745
But all only priesthood.
Everyman, God gave priests that dignity,
And setteth them in his stead among us to be;
Thus be they above angels, in degree.

(EVERYMAN *goes out to receive the last rites of the church.*)

709. **The . . . together:** Communion and extreme unction.

KNOWLEDGE. If priests be good, it is so, surely.   750
   But when Jesus hanged on the cross with great smart,
   There he gave out of his blesséd heart
   The same sacrament in great torment.
   He sold them not to us, that Lord omnipotent.
   Therefore Saint Peter the Apostle doth say   755
   That Jesus' curse hath all they
   Which God their Savior do buy or sell,
   Or they for any money do take or tell.°
   Sinful priests giveth the sinners example bad;
   Their children sitteth by other men's fires, I have heard;   760
   And some haunteth women's company
   With unclean life, as lusts of lechery.
   These be with sin made blind.
FIVE WITS. I trust to God no such way we find.
   Therefore let us priesthood honor,   765
   And follow their doctrine for our souls' succor.
   We be their sheep, and they shepherds be
   By whom we all be kept in surety.
   Peace! for yonder I see Everyman come,
   Which hath made true satisfaction.   770
GOOD DEEDS. Methinketh it is he indeed.

   (*Re-enter* EVERYMAN.)

EVERYMAN. Now Jesu be your alder speed.°
   I have received the sacrament for my redemption,
   And then mine extreme unction.
   Blesséd be all they that counseled me to take it!   775
   And now, friends, let us go without longer respite.
   I thank God that ye have tarried so long.
   Now set each of you on this rood° your hand,
   And shortly follow me.
   I go before, there I would be. God be our guide.   780
STRENGTH. Everyman, we will not from you go,
   Till ye have done this voyage long.
DISCRETION. I, Discretion, will bide by you also.
KNOWLEDGE. And though this pilgrimage be never so strong,°
   I will never part you fro.°   785
   Everyman, I will be as sure by thee
   As ever I did by Judas Maccabee.

   (*They go to a grave.*)

---

758. tell: count. **772. your alder speed:** the help of you all. **778. rood:** cross. **784. strong:** hard. **785. fro:** from.

EVERYMAN. Alas! I am so faint I may not stand,
My limbs under me do fold.
Friends, let us not turn again to this land,   790
Not for all the world's gold;
For into this cave must I creep
And turn to earth, and there to sleep.
BEAUTY. What, into this grave? Alas!
EVERYMAN. Yea, there shall you consume, more and less.   795
BEAUTY. And what, should I smother here?
EVERYMAN. Yea, by my faith, and never more appear.
In this world live no more we shall,
But in heaven before the highest Lord of all.
BEAUTY. I cross out all this; adieu; by Saint John!   800
I take my cap in my lap and am gone.
EVERYMAN. What, Beauty, whither will ye?
BEAUTY. Peace! I am deaf. I look not behind me,
Not and thou would give me all the gold in thy chest.

(*Exit* BEAUTY.)

EVERYMAN. Alas, whereto may I trust?   805
Beauty goeth fast away from me;
She promised with me to live and die.
STRENGTH. Everyman, I will thee also forsake and deny.
Thy game liketh me not at all.
EVERYMAN. Why, then ye will forsake me all?   810
Sweet Strength, tarry a little space.
STRENGTH. Nay, sir, by the rood of grace,
I will hie me from thee fast,
Though thou weep till thy heart to-brast.°
EVERYMAN. Ye would ever bide by me, ye said.   815
STRENGTH. Yea, I have you far enough conveyed.
Ye be old enough, I understand,
Your pilgrimage to take on hand.
I repent me that I hither came.
EVERYMAN. Strength, you to displease I am to blame;   820
Yet promise is debt, this ye well wot.
STRENGTH. In faith, I care not!
Thou art but a fool to complain.
You spend your speech and waste your brain.
Go, thrust thee into the ground. (*Exit* STRENGTH.)   825
EVERYMAN. I had weened surer I should you have found.
He that trusteth in his Strength
She him deceiveth at the length.

814. to-brast: burst.

Both Strength and Beauty forsaketh me,
Yet they promised me fair and lovingly.   830
DISCRETION. Everyman, I will after Strength be gone;
As for me I will leave you alone.
EVERYMAN. Why, Discretion, will ye forsake me?
DISCRETION. Yea, in faith, I will go from thee;
For when Strength goeth before   835
I follow after evermore.
EVERYMAN. Yet, I pray thee, for the love of the Trinity,
Look in my grave once piteously.
DISCRETION. Nay, so nigh will I not come.
Farewell, every one! (*Exit* DISCRETION.)   840
EVERYMAN. O all thing faileth, save God alone,
Beauty, Strength, and Discretion;
For when Death bloweth his blast,
They all run from me full fast.
FIVE WITS. Everyman, my leave now of thee I take;   845
I will follow the other, for here I thee forsake.
EVERYMAN. Alas! then may I wail and weep,
For I took you for my best friend.
FIVE WITS. I will no longer thee keep;
Now farewell, and there an end. (*Exit* FIVE WITS.)   850
EVERYMAN. O Jesu, help! All hath forsaken me!
GOOD DEEDS. Nay, Everyman; I will bide with thee,
I will not forsake thee indeed;
Thou shalt find me a good friend at need.
EVERYMAN. Gramercy, Good Deeds! Now may I true friends see.   855
They have forsaken me, every one;
I loved them better than my Good Deeds alone.
Knowledge, will ye forsake me also?
KNOWLEDGE. Yea, Everyman, when ye to death shall go;
But not yet, for no manner of danger.   860
EVERYMAN. Gramercy, Knowledge, with all my heart.
KNOWLEDGE. Nay, yet I will not from hence depart
Till I see where ye shall be come.
EVERYMAN. Methink, alas, that I must be gone
To make my reckoning and my debts pay,   865
For I see my time is nigh spent away.
Take example, all ye that this do hear or see,
How they that I loved best do forsake me,
Except my Good Deeds that bideth truly.
GOOD DEEDS. All earthly things is but vanity.   870
Beauty, Strength, and Discretion do man forsake,
Foolish friends and kinsmen, that fair spake,
All fleeth save Good Deeds, and that am I.

EVERYMAN. Have mercy on me, God most mighty;
   And stand by me, thou Mother and Maid, holy Mary!   875
GOOD DEEDS. Fear not, I will speak for thee.
EVERYMAN. Here I cry God mercy!
GOOD DEEDS. Short° our end, and 'minish° our pain.
   Let us go and never come again.
EVERYMAN. Into thy hands, Lord, my soul I commend.   880
   Receive it, Lord, that it be not lost.
   As thou me boughtest, so me defend.
   And save me from the fiend's boast,
   That I may appear with that blessèd host.
   That shall be saved at the day of doom.   885
   In manus tuas—of might's most
   For ever—*commendo spiritum meum.*°

(EVERYMAN *and* GOOD DEEDS *go into the grave.*)

KNOWLEDGE. Now hath he suffered that we all shall endure;
   The Good Deeds shall make all sure.
   Now hath he made ending.   890
   Methinketh that I hear angels sing
   And make great joy and melody
   Where Everyman's soul received shall be.
ANGEL. Come, excellent elect spouse to Jesu!
   Here above thou shalt go   895
   Because of thy singular virtue.
   Now the soul is taken the body fro,
   Thy reckoning is crystal clear.
   Now shalt thou into the heavenly sphere,
   Unto the which all ye shall come   900
   That liveth well before the day of doom. (*Exit* KNOWLEDGE.)

(*Enter* DOCTOR *as Epilogue.*)

DOCTOR.° This moral men may have in mind;
   Ye hearers, take it of worth, old and young,
   And forsake Pride, for he deceiveth you in the end,
   And remember Beauty, Five Wits, Strength, and Discretion,   905
   They all at the last do Everyman forsake,
   Save his Good Deeds there doth he take.
   But beware, and they be small
   Before God he hath no help at all.
   None excuse may be there for Everyman.   910
   Alas, how shall he do then?

878. Short: shorten. **'minish:** diminish. **886–87. In manus . . . meum:** "Into thy hands
I commend my spirit." **902. Doctor:** teacher.

For, after death, amends may no man make,
For then mercy and pity doth him forsake.
If his reckoning be not clear when he doth come,
God will say, *"Ite, maledicti, in ignem aeternum."*°
And he that hath his account whole and sound,
High in heaven he shall be crowned.
Unto which place God bring us all thither,
That we may live body and soul together.
Thereto help the Trinity!   920
Amen, say ye, for saint charity.

Thus endeth this moral play of EVERYMAN.

QUESTIONS

1. Composed by an unknown author probably before 1500, *Everyman* is a
   characteristically medieval play, yet it has been produced in recent years on
   radio and stage with notable success. What qualities continue to make it
   effective and moving?
2. *Everyman* belongs to a class of medieval plays known as moralities. Briefly, a
   morality is a moral allegory in dramatic form. What characteristics of this
   play make it an allegory? On what central metaphor is the allegory based?
3. Unlike most plays, this play is frankly didactic (intended to teach). List its
   didactic devices. Does this didacticism weaken the force or appeal of the
   play? Why or why not? What are the central lessons of the play? Draw up a
   brief account of the religious doctrines it embodies.
4. Of what relative importance are plot, character, and theme in the play?
   Discuss the importance of each.
5. At what points in the play does Everyman undergo a change of mood or
   attitude? Chart the rising and falling of his morale. What causes each
   change?
6. Everyman has four soliloquies during the first half of the play, none during
   the second half. Can you relate this fact to the action and meaning of the
   play? What effect do the soliloquies have?
7. Discuss the characterization of (a) God, (b) Death, (c) Everyman. How is
   each conceived? How might they have been conceived differently?
8. What sort of stage setting would you design for this play? Would it be
   effective if performed on the steps of a cathedral? How would you present
   God? How old an actor would you choose for Everyman? What parts would
   you assign to female actors? How would you costume the various characters?
9. Contrast this play with *The Stronger*. What qualities does *The Stronger* have
   that *Everyman* lacks? What qualities does *Everyman* have that *The Stronger*
   lacks?

---

915. Ite, maledicti, in ignem aeternum: "Go, ye accursed, into everlasting fire."

Edward Albee

THE SANDBOX

A Brief Play, in Memory of My Grandmother (1876–1959)

PLAYERS

THE YOUNG MAN, *25, a good-looking, well-built boy in a bathing suit*
MOMMY, *55, a well-dressed, imposing woman*
DADDY, *60, a small man; gray, thin*
GRANDMA, *86, a tiny, wizened woman with bright eyes*
THE MUSICIAN, *no particular age, but young would be nice*

NOTE. *When, in the course of the play,* MOMMY *and* DADDY *call each other by these names, there should be no suggestion of regionalism. These names are of empty affection and point up the pre-senility and vacuity of their characters.*

THE SCENE. *A bare stage, with only the following: Near the footlights, far stage-right, two simple chairs set side by side, facing the audience; near the footlights, far stage-left, a chair facing stage-right with a music stand before it; farther back, and stage-center, slightly elevated and raked, a large child's sandbox with a toy pail and shovel; the background is the sky, which alters from brightest day to deepest night.*

At the beginning, it is brightest day; the YOUNG MAN *is alone on stage to the rear of the sandbox, and to one side. He is doing calisthenics; he does calisthenics until quite at the very end of the play. These calisthenics, employing the arms only, should suggest the beating and fluttering of wings. The* YOUNG MAN *is, after all, the Angel of Death.*

MOMMY *and* DADDY *enter from stage-left,* MOMMY *first.*

MOMMY (*motioning to* DADDY). Well, here we are; this is the beach.
DADDY (*whining*). I'm cold.

THE SANDBOX Written in 1959. Edward Albee, abandoned by his natural parents, was adopted two weeks after birth in 1928 by a wealthy couple in Westchester County, New York, and named after his adoptive grandfather, part owner of the Keith-Albee string of movie-and-vaudeville theaters. His early schooling frequently interrupted by family vacations, Albee attended a variety of private schools. Dismissed from Trinity College (Connecticut) after three semesters, he went to Greenwich Village, against his foster parents' wishes, determined to write. For about ten years he tried poetry and fiction while working at various odd jobs to supplement a weekly allowance from a trust fund established by his grandmother. After the success of his first play, *Zoo Story* (1959), and the completion of a second, Albee interrupted work on *The American Dream* when commissioned to do a short play for an international theatrical festival. For this play (*The Sandbox*) he used characters from the work in progress placed in a different situation and setting. Despite its overlap of characters and themes with *The American Dream* (1961), it is a separate play, and Albee in 1966 declared it his favorite among his plays (which then numbered about ten including *Who's Afraid of Virginia Woolf?*).

MOMMY (*dismissing him with a little laugh*). Don't be silly; it's as warm as toast. Look at that nice young man over there: *he* doesn't think it's cold. (*Waves to the* YOUNG MAN) Hello.

YOUNG MAN (*with an endearing smile*). Hi!

MOMMY (*looking about*). This will do perfectly . . . don't you think so, Daddy? There's sand there . . . and the water beyond. What do you think, Daddy?

DADDY (*vaguely*). Whatever you say, Mommy.

MOMMY (*with the same little laugh*). Well, of course . . . whatever I say. Then, it's settled, is it?

DADDY (*shrugs*). She's *your* mother, not mine.

MOMMY. *I* know she's my mother. What do you take me for? (*A pause*) All right, now; let's get on with it. (*She shouts into the wings, stage-left*) You! Out there! You can come in now.

(*The* MUSICIAN *enters, seats himself in the chair, stage-left, places music on the music stand, is ready to play.* MOMMY *nods approvingly.*)

MOMMY. Very nice; very nice. Are you ready, Daddy? Let's go get Grandma.

DADDY. Whatever you say, Mommy.

MOMMY (*leading the way out, stage-left*). Of course, whatever I say. (*To the* MUSICIAN) You can begin now.

(*The* MUSICIAN *begins playing;* MOMMY *and* DADDY *exit; the* MUSICIAN, *all the while playing, nods to the* YOUNG MAN.)

YOUNG MAN (*with the same endearing smile*). Hi!

(*After a moment,* MOMMY *and* DADDY *re-enter, carrying* GRANDMA. *She is borne in by their hands under her armpits; she is quite rigid; her legs are drawn up; her feet do not touch the ground; the expression on her ancient face is that of puzzlement and fear.*)

DADDY. Where do we put her?

MOMMY (*the same little laugh*). Wherever I say, of course. Let me see . . . well . . . all right, over there . . . in the sandbox. (*Pause*) Well, what are you waiting for, Daddy? . . . The sandbox!

(*Together they carry* GRANDMA *over to the sandbox and more or less dump her in.*)

GRANDMA (*righting herself to a sitting position; her voice a cross between a baby's laugh and cry*). Ahhhhhh! Graaaaa!

DADDY (*dusting himself*). What do we do now?

MOMMY (*to the* MUSICIAN). You can stop now. (*The* MUSICIAN *stops.*) (*Back to* DADDY) What do you mean, what do we do now? We go over there and sit down, of course. (*To the* YOUNG MAN) Hello there.

YOUNG MAN (*again smiling*) Hi!

(MOMMY *and* DADDY *move to the chairs, stage-right, and sit down. A pause.*)

GRANDMA (*same as before*). Ahhhhhh! Ah-haaaaaa! Graaaaaa!

DADDY. Do you think . . . do you think she's . . . comfortable?

MOMMY (*impatiently*). How would I know?

DADDY (*pause*). What do we do now?

MOMMY (*as if remembering*). We . . . wait. We . . . sit here . . . and we wait . . . that's what we do.

DADDY (*after a pause*). Shall we talk to each other?

MOMMY (*with that little laugh; picking something off her dress*). Well, *you* can talk, if you want to . . . if you can think of anything to say . . . if you can think of anything *new*.

DADDY (*thinks*). No . . . I suppose not.

MOMMY (*with a triumphant laugh*). Of course not!

GRANDMA (*banging the toy shovel against the pail*). Haaaaaa! Ah-haaaaaa!

MOMMY (*out over the audience*). Be quiet, Grandma . . . just be quiet, and wait.

(GRANDMA *throws a shovelful of sand at* MOMMY.)

MOMMY (*still out over the audience*). She's throwing sand at me! You stop that, Grandma; you stop throwing sand at Mommy! (*To* DADDY) She's throwing sand at me.

(DADDY *looks around at* GRANDMA, *who screams at him.*)

GRANDMA. GRAAAAAA!

MOMMY. Don't look at her. Just . . . sit here . . . be very still . . . and wait. (*To the* MUSICIAN) You . . . uh . . . you go ahead and do whatever it is you do.

(*The* MUSICIAN *plays.* MOMMY *and* DADDY *are fixed, staring out beyond the audience.* GRANDMA *looks at them, looks at the* MUSICIAN, *looks at the sandbox, throws down the shovel.*)

GRANDMA. Ah-haaaaaa! Graaaaaa! (*Looks for reaction; gets none. Now . . . directly to the audience*) Honestly! What a way to treat an old woman! Drag her out of the house . . . stick her in a car . . . bring her out here from the city . . . dump her in a pile of sand . . . and leave her here to set. I'm eighty-six years old! I was married when I was seventeen. To a farmer. He died when I was thirty. (*To the* MUSICIAN) Will you stop that, please? (*The* MUSICIAN *stops playing.*) I'm a feeble old woman . . . how do you expect anybody to hear me over that peep! peep! peep! (*To herself*) There's no respect around here. (*To the* YOUNG MAN) There's no respect around here!

YOUNG MAN (*same smile*). Hi!

GRANDMA (*after a pause, a mild double-take, continues, to the audience*). My husband died when I was thirty (*indicates* MOMMY), and I had to raise that big cow over there all by my lonesome. You can imagine what *that was like*. Lordy! (*To the* YOUNG MAN) Where'd they get *you?*

YOUNG MAN. Oh . . . I've been around for a while.

GRANDMA. I'll bet you have! Heh, heh, heh. Will you look at you!

YOUNG MAN (*flexing his muscles*). Isn't that something? (*Continues his calisthenics.*)

GRANDMA. Boy, oh boy; I'll say. Pretty good.

YOUNG MAN (*sweetly*). I'll say.

GRANDMA. Where ya from?

YOUNG MAN. Southern California.

GRANDMA (*nodding*). Figgers; figgers. What's your name, honey?

YOUNG MAN. I don't know . . .

GRANDMA (*to the audience*). Bright, too!

YOUNG MAN. I mean . . . I mean, they haven't given me one yet . . . the studio . . .

GRANDMA (*giving him the once-over*). You don't say . . . you don't say. Well . . . uh, I've got to talk some more . . . don't you go 'way.

YOUNG MAN. Oh, no.

GRANDMA (*turning her attention back to the audience*). Fine; fine. (*Then, once more, back to the* YOUNG MAN) You're . . . you're an actor, hunh?

YOUNG MAN (*beaming*). Yes. I am.

GRANDMA (*to the audience again; shrugs*). I'm smart that way. *Anyhow*, I had to raise . . . *that* over there all by my lonesome; and what's next to her there . . . that's what she married. Rich? I tell you . . . money, money, money. They took me off the *farm* . . . which was real decent of them . . . and they moved me into the big town house with *them* . . . fixed a nice place for me under the stove . . . gave me an army blanket . . . and my own dish . . . my very own dish! So, what have I got to complain about? Nothing, of course. I'm not complaining. (*She looks up at the sky, shouts to someone off stage*) Shouldn't it be getting dark now, dear?

(*The lights dim; night comes on. The* MUSICIAN *begins to play; it becomes deepest night. There are spots on all the players, including the* YOUNG MAN, *who is, of course, continuing his calisthenics.*)

DADDY (*stirring*). It's nighttime.

MOMMY. Shhhh. Be still . . . wait.

DADDY (*whining*). It's so hot.

MOMMY. Shhhhhh. Be still . . . wait.

GRANDMA (*to herself*). That's better. Night. (*To the* MUSICIAN) Honey, do you play all through this part? (*The* MUSICIAN *nods.*) Well, keep it nice and soft; that's a good boy. (*The* MUSICIAN *nods again; plays softly.*) That's nice.

(*There is an off-stage rumble.*)

DADDY (*starting*). What was that?

MOMMY (*beginning to weep*). It was nothing.

DADDY. It was . . . it was . . . thunder . . . or a wave breaking . . . or something.

MOMMY (*whispering, through her tears*). It was an off-stage rumble . . . and you know what *that* means . . .

DADDY. I forget . . .

MOMMY (*barely able to talk*). It means the time has come for poor Grandma . . . and I can't bear it!

DADDY (*vacantly*). I . . . I suppose you've got to be brave.

GRANDMA (*mocking*). That's right, kid; be brave. You'll bear up; you'll get over it.

(*Another off-stage rumble . . . louder.*)

MOMMY. Ohhhhhhhhhh . . . poor Grandma . . . poor Grandma . . .

GRANDMA (*to* MOMMY). I'm fine! I'm all right! It hasn't happened yet!

(*A violent off-stage rumble. All the lights go out, save the spot on the* YOUNG MAN; *the* MUSICIAN *stops playing.*)

MOMMY. Ohhhhhhhhh . . . Ohhhhhhhhhh . . .

(*Silence.*)

GRANDMA. Don't put the lights up yet . . . I'm not ready; I'm not quite ready. (*Silence*) All right, dear . . . I'm about done.

(*The lights come up again, to brightest day; the* MUSICIAN *begins to play.* GRANDMA *is discovered, still in the sandbox, lying on her side, propped up on an elbow, half covered, busily shoveling sand over herself.*)

GRANDMA (*muttering*). I don't know how I'm supposed to do anything with this goddam toy shovel . . .

DADDY. Mommy! It's daylight!

MOMMY (*brightly*). So it is! Well! Our long night is over. We must put away our tears, take off our mourning . . . and face the future. It's our duty.

GRANDMA (*still shoveling; mimicking*). . . . take off our mourning . . . face the future . . . Lordy!

(MOMMY *and* DADDY *rise, stretch.* MOMMY *waves to the* YOUNG MAN.)

YOUNG MAN (*with that smile*). Hi!

(GRANDMA *plays dead.* (!) MOMMY *and* DADDY *go over to look at her; she is a little more than half buried in the sand; the toy shovel is in her hands, which are crossed on her breast.*)

MOMMY (*before the sandbox; shaking her head*). Lovely! It's . . . it's hard to be sad . . . she looks . . . so happy. (*With pride and conviction*) It pays to do things well. (*To the* MUSICIAN) All right, you can stop now, if you want to. I mean, stay around for a swim, or something; it's all right with us. (*She sighs heavily*) Well, Daddy . . . off we go.

DADDY. Brave Mommy!
MOMMY. Brave Daddy!

(*They exit, stage left.*)

GRANDMA (*after they leave; lying quite still*). It pays to do things well . . .
Boy, oh boy! (*She tries to sit up*) . . . well, kids . . . (*but she finds she can't*) . . .
I . . . I can't get up. I . . . I can't move . . .

(*The* YOUNG MAN *stops his calisthenics, nods to the* MUSICIAN, *walks over to*
GRANDMA, *kneels down by the sandbox.*)

GRANDMA. I . . . can't move . . .
YOUNG MAN. Shhhhh . . . be very still . . .
GRANDMA. I . . . I can't move . . .
YOUNG MAN. Uh . . . ma'am; I . . . I have a line here.
GRANDMA. Oh, I'm sorry, sweetie; you go right ahead.
YOUNG MAN. I am . . . uh . . .
GRANDMA Take your time, dear.
YOUNG MAN (*prepares; delivers the line like a real amateur*). I am the
Angel of Death. I am . . . uh . . . I am come for you.
GRANDMA. What . . . wha . . . (*then, with resignation*) . . . ohhhh . . .
ohhhh, I see.

(*The* YOUNG MAN *bends over, kisses* GRANDMA *gently on the forehead.*)

GRANDMA (*her eyes closed, her hands folded on her breast again, the shovel
between her hands, a sweet smile on her face*). Well . . . that was very nice
dear . . .
YOUNG MAN (*still kneeling*). Shhhhh . . . be still . . .
GRANDMA. What I meant was . . . you did that very well, dear . . .
YOUNG MAN (*blushing*). . . . oh . . .
GRANDMA. No; I mean it. You've got that . . . you've got a quality.
YOUNG MAN (*with his endearing smile*). Oh . . . thank you; thank you
very much . . . ma'am.
GRANDMA (*slowly; softly—as the* YOUNG MAN *puts his hands on top of*
GRANDMA'*s*). You're . . . you're welcome . . . dear.

(*Tableau. The* MUSICIAN *continues to play as the curtain slowly comes
down.*)

QUESTIONS

1. On the face of it, this little play is absurd—absurd both in the way it is
   presented and in what happens in it. Is it therefore simply horseplay, or does
   it have a serious subject? What is its subject?
2. The word *absurd*, used above, itself demands attention, since it has been
   much used with reference to contemporary theater. The word suggests two

different meanings: (a) funny, (b) meaningless. Do both meanings function here? Does either meaning predominate over the other?

3. Characterize Mommy and Daddy. In what ways are they alike? In what ways are they foils? Two of Daddy's speeches are repeated. What do they tell us about his relationship to Mommy?

4. Discuss the treatment by Mommy and Daddy, especially Mommy, of Grandma and her death and burial. What discrepancy exists between appearance and reality? Is their treatment of her in death similar to or different from their treatment of her in life? What metaphor is submerged in Granny's account of their fixing her a place under the stove with an army blanket and her own dish? What is the function of the musician?

5. How does the treatment accorded the young man by most of the characters (Mommy, the musician, Grandma) contrast with their treatment of Grandma? What accounts for the difference? What kind of person is the young man?

6. What aspects of contemporary American life are presented in the play? In answering this question, consider your answers to questions 3, 4, and 5. What judgment does the play make on contemporary American life?

7. Contrast Grandma with the young man and with Mommy and Daddy. What admirable qualities does she have? What disagreeable qualities does she have? Why? On the whole, is she presented as more, or less, worthy of respect than the other characters in the play? Why?

8. Both in the notes and in the dialogue, the young man is identified as the Angel of Death. How is he a very unusual Angel of Death? Is he a simple or a multiple symbol? What other meanings does he suggest?

9. What symbolical meanings are suggested by the following? Which of them, like the young man, are multiple symbols? (a) the bareness of the stage, (b) the sandbox, (c) the toy pail and shovel, (d) the dimming and extinguishing of the lights, (e) Grandma's burying herself with sand, (f) the fact that Grandma is buried before she is dead, (g) the young man's kissing Grandma.

2. Realistic and Nonrealistic Drama

As in fiction and poetry, so in drama, literary truth is not the same as fidelity to fact. Fantasy is as much the property of the theater as of poetry or the prose tale. Shakespeare in *A Midsummer Night's Dream* and *The Tempest* uses fairies and goblins and monsters as characters, and in *Hamlet* and *Macbeth* he introduces ghosts and witches. These supernatural characters, nevertheless, serve as a vehicle for truth. When Bottom, in *A Midsummer Night's Dream,* is given an ass's head, the enchantment is a visual metaphor. The witches in *Macbeth* truthfully prefigure a tragic destiny.

Because it is written to be performed, however, drama adds still another dimension of possible unreality. It may be realistic or unrealistic in mode of production as well as in content. Staging, make-up, costuming, and acting may all be handled in such a way as to emphasize the realistic or the fanciful.

It must be recognized, however, that all stage production, no matter how realistic, involves a certain necessary artificiality. If an indoor scene is presented on a picture-frame stage, the spectator is asked to imagine that a room with only three walls is actually a room with four walls. In an arena-type theater, where the audience is seated on all sides of the acting area, the spectator must imagine all four walls. Both types of presentation, moreover, require adjustments in the acting. In a traditional theater, the actors must be facing the missing fourth wall most of the time. In an arena-type theater, they must not turn their backs too long on any "wall." Both types of staging, in the interests of effective presentation, require the actors to depart from an absolute realism.

From this point on, the departure from the appearance of reality may be little or great. In many late nineteenth- and early twentieth-century productions, an effort was made to make stage sets as realistic as possible. If the play called for a setting in a study, there had to be real bookshelves on the wall and real books on the shelves. If the room contained a wash basin, real water had to flow from the taps. More recently, however, plays have been performed on a stage furnished only with drapes and platforms. In between these two extremes, all degrees of realism are possible. The scenery may consist of painted flats, with painted bookshelves and painted books and painted pictures on the wall. Or, instead of scenery, a play may use only a few movable properties to suggest the required setting. Thornton Wilder's famous play *Our Town* (1938) utilized a bare stage, without curtain, with exposed ropes and backstage equipment, and with a few chairs, two ladders, and a couple of trellises as the only properties. For a scene at a soda fountain, a plank was laid across the backs of two chairs. In fact, provision of elaborately realistic stage sets has been the exception rather than the rule in the long history of the theater. Neither in Greek nor in Shakespearean theater was setting much more than suggested.

But the choice of realistic or unrealistic stage sets, costuming, and make-up may lie with the producer rather than the playwright. When we move to the realm of language and the management of dialogue, the choice is entirely the playwright's. Here again all degrees of realism and nonrealism are possible. In the realistic theater of the early twentieth century, playwrights often made an elaborate effort to reproduce the flat quality of ordinary speech, with all its stumblings and inarticulateness. In real life, of course, few lovers speak with the eloquence of Romeo and Juliet, and many people, in daily conversation, have difficulty getting through a grammatically correct sentence of any length or complexity. They break off, they begin again, they end lamely like the swipe in "I'm a Fool" with "etc., etc., you know." Such broken-backed and inadequate speech, skillfully used by the playwright, may faithfully render the quality of human life at some levels, yet its limitations for expressing the heights and depths of human experience are obvious. Most dramatic dialogue, even when most realistic, is more coherent and expressive than speech in actual life. Art is always a heightening or an intensification of reality; else it would have no value. The heightening may be little or great. It is greatest in poetic drama. The love exchanges of Romeo and Juliet, spoken in rhymed iambic pentameter and at one point taking the form of a perfect sonnet (see page 729), are absurdly unrealistic if judged as an imitation of actual speech, but they vividly express the emotional truth of passionate, idealistic young love. It is no criticism of Shakespearean tragedy, therefore, to say that in real life people do not speak in blank verse. The deepest purpose of the playwright is not to imitate actual human speech but to give accurate and powerful expression to human thought and emotion.

All drama asks us to accept certain departures from reality—certain DRAMATIC CONVENTIONS. That a room with three walls or fewer may represent one with four walls, that the actors speak in the language of the audience whatever the nationality of the persons they play, that the actors stand or sit so as to face the audience most of the time—these are all necessary conventions. Other conventions are optional—for example, that the characters may reveal their inner thoughts through soliloquies and asides or may speak in the heightened language of poetry. The playwright working in a strictly realistic mode will avoid the optional conventions, for they conflict with the realistic method that he has chosen to achieve his purpose. The playwright working in a freer mode will feel free to use any or all of them, for they make possible the revelation of dimensions of reality unreachable by a strictly realistic method. Hamlet's famous soliloquy that begins "To be or not to be," in which he debates in blank verse the merits of onerous life and untimely death, is unrealistic on two counts, but it enables Shakespeare to present Hamlet's introspective mind more powerfully than he otherwise could have done. The characteristic device of Greek drama, a chorus—a group of actors speaking in unison, often in a chant, while going through the steps of an elaborate formalized dance—is another unrealistic device but a useful one for conveying communal or group emotion. It has been revived, in different forms, in many modern plays. The use of a narrator, as in *Our Town*, is a related unrealistic device that has served playwrights as a vehicle for dramatic truth.

The history of the drama might be told in a history of conventions that have arisen, flourished, and been replaced; and those readers and audiences who experience plays most fully are those who have learned to understand the main conventions of its various periods and major dramatists. The inexperienced reader or spectator often judges a play defective because it makes use of conventions other than those in common current acceptance (whether or not consciously recognized as such). Most contemporary audiences, for example, have been trained by their experience with movies and television, two media based on the realistic conventions of photography. Few people pause to consider that looking at a photograph, whether filmed by a still camera or a movie camera, requires the acceptance of the simple convention that three-dimensional reality is being represented two-dimensionally, or that the full spectrum of color may be represented by shades of white, gray, or black. We accept these conventions without question, as we also accept the emotional reinforcement that comes with a musical background even though there is no justification for the presence of an orchestra in a living room or on a beach. The study of drama requires the purposeful learning of its conventions, both realistic and nonrealistic.

In most plays, however unreal the world into which we are taken, this world is treated as self-contained, and we are asked to regard it temporarily as a real world. Thus Shakespeare's world of fairies in *A Midsummer Night's Dream* is real to us while we watch the play. Because of Shakespeare's magic, we quite willingly make that "temporary suspension of disbelief" that, according to Coleridge, "constitutes poetic faith." And the step from crediting Bottom as real, though we know in fact he is only a dressed-up actor, to regarding Bottom with an ass's head as real is relatively a small one. But some playwrights abandon even this much attempt to give their work an illusion of reality. They deliberately violate the self-containment of the fictional world and keep reminding us that we are only seeing a play. Thus Edward Albee, in *The Sandbox*, not only presents as his main character a Grandma who buries herself alive and speaks after she is presumably dead; he systematically breaks down the barriers between his fictional world and the real one. The musician, instead of being concealed in an orchestra pit, is summoned onstage and told by Mommy and Grandma when to play and when not to play. Grandma addresses herself much of the time directly to the audience and at one time shouts to the electricians offstage, instructing them to dim the lights. The young man reminds us that he is an actor by telling Grandma that he has "a line here" and by delivering the line "like a real amateur." When Mommy and Daddy hear a noise offstage, Daddy thinks it may be thunder or a breaking wave, but Mommy says, with literal accuracy, "It was an off-stage rumble." In short, Albee keeps reminding us that this is a play, not reality, and not even an imitation of reality but a symbolic representation of it. The effects he gains thereby are various: partly comic, partly antisentimental, partly intellectual; and the play that results is both theatrically effective and dramatically significant.

The adjective *realistic*, then, as applied to literature, must be regarded as a descriptive, not an evaluative, term. When we call a play realistic, we are saying something about its mode of presentation, not praising nor dispraising it. Realism indicates fidelity to the outer appearances of life. The serious dramatist is interested in life's inner meanings, which he may approach through either realistic or nonrealistic presentation. Great plays have been written in both the realistic and the nonrealistic modes. It is not without significance, however, that the three greatest plays in this book are probably *Oedipus Rex, Othello,* and *The Misanthrope*—one originally written in quantitative Greek verse, one in English blank verse, and one in French rimed couplets. Human truth, rather than fidelity to fact, is the highest achievement of literary art.

EXERCISE

In any classification of plays, Strindberg's *The Stronger* would undoubtedly be called realistic, Albee's *The Sandbox* nonrealistic. Are there any respects, however, in which Albee's play is more "realistic" than Strindberg's? Examine particularly the quality of the language. Pick out samples for contrast, and try to account for the difference.

Henrik Ibsen
AN ENEMY OF THE PEOPLE

CHARACTERS

DR. THOMAS STOCKMANN, *Medical Officer of the Municipal Baths*
MRS. STOCKMANN, *his wife*
PETRA, *their daughter, a teacher*
EJLIF } *their sons, aged 13 and 10 respectively*
MORTEN
PETER STOCKMANN, *the Doctor's elder brother; Mayor of the Town and Chief Constable, Chairman of the Baths' Committee, etc., etc.*
MORTEN KIIL, *a tanner* (MRS. STOCKMANN'S *adoptive father*)
HOVSTAD, *editor of the* People's Messenger
BILLING, *subeditor*
CAPTAIN HORSTER
ASLAKSEN, *a printer*
MEN, *of various conditions and occupations, some few women, and a troop of schoolboys—the audience at a public meeting.*

The action takes place in a coast town in southern Norway.

ACT I

SCENE.   DR. STOCKMANN'S *sitting-room. It is evening. The room is plainly but neatly appointed and furnished. In the right-hand wall are two doors; the farther leads out to the hall, the nearer to the doctor's study. In the left-hand wall, opposite the door leading to the hall, is a door leading to the other rooms occupied by the family. In the middle of the same wall stands the stove, and, further forward, a couch with a looking-glass hanging over it and an oval table in front of it. On the table, a lighted lamp, with a lampshade. At the back of the room, an open door leads to the dining-room.* BILLING *is seen sitting at the dining table, on which a lamp is burning. He has a napkin tucked under his chin, and* MRS. STOCKMANN *is standing by the table handing him a large plateful of roast beef. The other places at the table are empty, and the table somewhat in disorder, a meal having evidently recently been finished.*

AN ENEMY OF THE PEOPLE First performed in 1882. English translation by R. Farquharson Sharp. Henrik Ibsen (1828–1906), widely regarded as the father of modern drama, was born in Norway. Between 1851–1864, while associated with theaters in Bergen and Christiana, he gained experience by helping produce some 145 different plays. A small state grant enabled him after 1863 to live abroad with his wife and child (mainly in Rome and Germany) and devote full time to writing. The plot of *An Enemy of the People* is partially based on two actual incidents: the first, about an outbreak of disease at a health spa in the 1830s, was related to Ibsen by a friend; the second, about an interrupted public meeting, was reported in Norwegian newspapers in 1881 (see Michael Meyer, *Ibsen* [Garden City, N.Y.: Doubleday, 1971], pp. 500–01).

MRS. STOCKMANN. You see, if you come an hour late, Mr. Billing, you have to put up with cold meat.

BILLING (*as he eats*). It is uncommonly good, thank you—remarkably good.

MRS. STOCKMANN. My husband makes such a point of having his meals punctually, you know—

BILLING. That doesn't affect me a bit. Indeed, I almost think I enjoy a meal all the better when I can sit down and eat all by myself and undisturbed.

MRS. STOCKMANN. Oh well, as long as you are enjoying it—. (*Turns to the hall door, listening.*) I expect that is Mr. Hovstad coming too.

BILLING. Very likely.

(PETER STOCKMANN *comes in. He wears an overcoat and his official hat, and carries a stick.*)

PETER STOCKMANN. Good evening, Katherine.

MRS. STOCKMANN (*coming forward into the sitting-room*). Ah, good evening—is it you? How good of you to come up and see us!

PETER STOCKMANN. I happened to be passing, and so— (*Looks into the dining-room.*) But you have company with you, I see.

MRS. STOCKMANN (*a little embarrassed*). Oh, no—it was quite by chance he came in. (*Hurriedly.*) Won't you come in and have something, too?

PETER STOCKMANN. I! No, thank you. Good gracious—hot meat at night! Not with my digestion.

MRS. STOCKMANN. Oh, but just once in a way—

PETER STOCKMANN. No, no, my dear lady; I stick to my tea and bread and butter. It is much more wholesome in the long run—and a little more economical, too.

MRS. STOCKMANN (*smiling*). Now you mustn't think that Thomas and I are spendthrifts.

PETER STOCKMANN. Not you, my dear; I would never think that of you. (*Points to the Doctor's study.*) Is he not at home?

MRS. STOCKMANN. No, he went out for a little turn after supper—he and the boys.

PETER STOCKMANN. I doubt if that is a wise thing to do. (*Listens.*) I fancy I hear him coming now.

MRS. STOCKMANN. No, I don't think it is he. (*A knock is heard at the door.*) Come in! (HOVSTAD *comes in from the hall.*) Oh, it is you, Mr. Hovstad!

HOVSTAD. Yes, I hope you will forgive me, but I was delayed at the printer's. Good evening, Mr. Mayor.

PETER STOCKMANN (*bowing a little distantly*). Good evening. You have come on business, no doubt.

HOVSTAD. Partly. It's about an article for the paper.

PETER STOCKMANN. So I imagined. I hear my brother has become a prolific contributor to the *People's Messenger*.

HOVSTAD. Yes, he is good enough to write in the *People's Messenger* when he has any home truths to tell.

MRS. STOCKMANN (*to* HOVSTAD). But won't you—? (*Points to the dining-room.*)

PETER STOCKMANN. Quite so, quite so. I don't blame him in the least, as a writer, for addressing himself to the quarters where he will find the readiest sympathy. And, besides that, I personally have no reason to bear any ill will to your paper, Mr. Hovstad.

HOVSTAD. I quite agree with you.

PETER STOCKMANN. Taking one thing with another, there is an excellent spirit of toleration in the town—an admirable municipal spirit. And it all springs from the fact of our having a great common interest to unite us—an interest that is in an equally high degree the concern of every right-minded citizen—

HOVSTAD. The Baths, yes.

PETER STOCKMANN. Exactly—our fine, new, handsome Baths. Mark my words, Mr. Hovstad—the Baths will become the focus of our municipal life! Not a doubt of it!

MRS. STOCKMANN. That is just what Thomas says.

PETER STOCKMANN. Think how extraordinarily the place has developed within the last year or two! Money has been flowing in, and there is some life and some business doing in the town. Houses and landed property are rising in value every day.

HOVSTAD. And unemployment is diminishing.

PETER STOCKMANN. Yes, that is another thing. The burden of the poor rates has been lightened, to the great relief of the propertied classes; and that relief will be even greater if only we get a really good summer this year, and lots of visitors—plenty of invalids, who will make the Baths talked about.

HOVSTAD. And there is a good prospect of that, I hear.

PETER STOCKMANN. It looks very promising. Enquiries about apartments and that sort of thing are reaching us every day.

HOVSTAD. Well, the doctor's article will come in very suitably.

PETER STOCKMANN. Has he been writing something just lately?

HOVSTAD. This is something he wrote in the winter; a recommendation of the Baths—an account of the excellent sanitary conditions here. But I held the article over, temporarily.

PETER STOCKMANN. Ah,—some little difficulty about it, I suppose?

HOVSTAD. No, not at all; I thought it would be better to wait till the spring, because it is just at this time that people begin to think seriously about their summer quarters.

PETER STOCKMANN. Quite right; you were perfectly right, Mr. Hovstad.

HOVSTAD. Yes, Thomas is really indefatigable when it is a question of the Baths.

PETER STOCKMANN. Well—remember, he is the Medical Officer to the Baths.

HOVSTAD. Yes, and what is more, they owe their existence to him.

PETER STOCKMANN. To him? Indeed! It is true I have heard from time to time that some people are of that opinion. At the same time I must say I imagined that I took a modest part in the enterprise.

MRS. STOCKMANN. Yes, that is what Thomas is always saying.

HOVSTAD. But who denies it, Mr. Stockmann? You set the thing going and made a practical concern of it; we all know that. I only meant that the idea of it came first from the doctor.

PETER STOCKMANN. Oh, ideas—yes! My brother has had plenty of them in his time—unfortunately. But when it is a question of putting an idea into practical shape, you have to apply to a man of different mettle, Mr. Hovstad. And I certainly should have thought that in this house at least—

MRS. STOCKMANN. My dear Peter—

HOVSTAD. How can you think that—?

MRS. STOCKMANN. Won't you go in and have something, Mr. Hovstad? My husband is sure to be back directly.

HOVSTAD. Thank you, perhaps just a morsel. (*Goes into the dining-room.*)

PETER STOCKMANN (*lowering his voice a little*). It is a curious thing that these farmers' sons never seem to lose their want of tact.

MRS. STOCKMANN. Surely it is not worth bothering about! Cannot you and Thomas share the credit as brothers?

PETER STOCKMANN. I should have thought so; but apparently some people are not satisfied with a share.

MRS. STOCKMANN. What nonsense! You and Thomas get on so capitally together. (*Listens.*) There he is at last, I think. (*Goes out and opens the door leading to the hall.*)

DR. STOCKMANN (*laughing and talking outside*). Look here—here is another guest for you, Katherine. Isn't that jolly! Come in, Captain Horster; hang your coat up on this peg. Ah, you don't wear an overcoat. Just think, Katherine; I met him in the street and could hardly persuade him to come up! (*CAPTAIN HORSTER comes into the room and greets MRS. STOCKMANN. He is followed by DR. STOCKMANN.*) Come along in, boys. They are ravenously hungry again, you know. Come along, Captain Horster; you must have a slice of beef. (*Pushes HORSTER into the dining-room. EJLIF and MORTEN go in after them.*)

MRS. STOCKMANN. But, Thomas, don't you see—?

DR. STOCKMANN (*turning in the doorway*). Oh, is it you, Peter? (*Shakes hands with him.*) Now that is very delightful.

PETER STOCKMANN. Unfortunately I must go in a moment—

DR. STOCKMANN. Rubbish! There is some toddy just coming in. You haven't forgotten the toddy, Katherine?

MRS. STOCKMANN. Of course not; the water is boiling now. (*Goes into the dining-room.*)

PETER STOCKMANN. Toddy too!

DR. STOCKMANN. Yes, sit down and we will have it comfortably.

PETER STOCKMANN. Thanks, I never care about an evening's drinking.

DR. STOCKMANN. But this isn't an evening's drinking.

PETER STOCKMANN. It seems to me—. (*Looks towards the dining-room.*) It is extraordinary how they can put away all that food.

DR. STOCKMANN (*rubbing his hands*). Yes, isn't it splendid to see young people eat? They have always got an appetite, you know! That's as it should be. Lots of food—to build up their strength! They are the people who are going to stir up the fermenting forces of the future, Peter.

PETER STOCKMANN. May I ask what they will find here to "stir up," as you put it?

DR. STOCKMANN. Ah, you must ask the young people that—when the time comes. We shan't be able to see it, of course. That stands to reason—two old fogies, like us—

PETER STOCKMANN. Really, really! I must say that is an extremely odd expression to—

DR. STOCKMANN. Oh, you mustn't take me too literally, Peter. I am so heartily happy and contented, you know. I think it is such an extraordinary piece of good fortune to be in the middle of all this growing, germinating life. It is a splendid time to live in! It is as if a whole new world were being created around one.

PETER STOCKMANN. Do you really think so?

DR. STOCKMANN. Ah, naturally you can't appreciate it as keenly as I. You have lived all your life in these surroundings, and your impressions have got blunted. But I, who have been buried all these years in my little corner up north, almost without ever seeing a stranger who might bring new ideas with him—well, in my case it has just the same effect as if I had been transported into the middle of a crowded city.

PETER STOCKMANN. Oh, a city—!

DR. STOCKMANN. I know, I know; it is all cramped enough here, compared with many other places. But there is life here—there is promise—there are innumerable things to work for and fight for; and that is the main thing. (*Calls.*) Katherine, hasn't the postman been here?

MRS. STOCKMANN (*from the dining-room*). No.

DR. STOCKMANN. And then to be comfortably off, Peter! That is something one learns to value, when one has been on the brink of starvation, as we have.

PETER STOCKMANN. Oh, surely—

DR. STOCKMANN. Indeed I can assure you we have often been very hard put to it, up there. And now to be able to live like a lord! Today, for instance, we had roast beef for dinner—and, what is more, for supper too. Won't you come and have a little bit? Or let me show it you, at any rate? Come here—

PETER STOCKMANN. No, no—not for worlds!

DR. STOCKMANN. Well, but just come here then. Do you see, we have got a table-cover?

PETER STOCKMANN. Yes, I noticed it.

DR. STOCKMANN. And we have got a lamp-shade too. Do you see? All out of Katherine's savings! It makes the room so cosy. Don't you think so? Just stand here for a moment—no, no, not there—just here, that's it! Look now, when you get the light on it altogether—I really think it looks very nice, doesn't it?

PETER STOCKMANN. Oh, if you can afford luxuries of this kind—

DR. STOCKMANN. Yes, I can afford it now. Katherine tells me I earn almost as much as we spend.

PETER STOCKMANN. Almost—yes!

DR. STOCKMANN. But a scientific man must live in a little bit of style. I am quite sure an ordinary civil servant spends more in a year than I do.

PETER STOCKMANN. I daresay. A civil servant—a man in a well-paid position—

DR. STOCKMANN. Well, any ordinary merchant, then! A man in that position spends two or three times as much as—

PETER STOCKMANN. It just depends on circumstances.

DR. STOCKMANN. At all events I assure you I don't waste money unprofitably. But I can't find it in my heart to deny myself the pleasure of entertaining my friends. I need that sort of thing, you know. I have lived for so long shut out of it all, that it is a necessity of life to me to mix with young, eager, ambitious men, men of liberal and active minds; and that describes every one of those fellows who are enjoying their supper in there. I wish you knew more of Hovstad—

PETER STOCKMANN. By the way, Hovstad was telling me he was going to print another article of yours.

DR. STOCKMANN. An article of mine?

PETER STOCKMANN. Yes, about the Baths. An article you wrote in the winter.

DR. STOCKMANN. Oh, that one! No, I don't intend that to appear just for the present.

PETER STOCKMANN. Why not? It seems to me that this would be the most opportune moment.

DR. STOCKMANN. Yes, very likely—under normal conditions. (*Crosses the room.*)

PETER STOCKMANN (*following him with his eyes*). Is there anything abnormal about the present conditions?

DR. STOCKMANN (*standing still*). To tell you the truth, Peter, I can't say just at this moment—at all events not tonight. There may be much that is very abnormal about the present conditions—and it is possible there may be nothing abnormal about them at all. It is quite possible it may be merely my imagination.

PETER STOCKMANN. I must say it all sounds most mysterious. Is there something going on that I am to be kept in ignorance of? I should have imagined that I, as Chairman of the governing body of the Baths—

DR. STOCKMANN. And I should have imagined that I—. Oh, come, don't let us fly out at one another, Peter.

PETER STOCKMANN. Heaven forbid! I am not in the habit of flying out at people, as you call it. But I am entitled to request most emphatically that all arrangements shall be made in a business-like manner, through the proper channels, and shall be dealt with by the legally constituted authorities. I can allow no going behind our backs by any roundabout means.

DR. STOCKMANN. Have I ever at any time tried to go behind your backs!

PETER STOCKMANN. You have an ingrained tendency to take your own way, at all events; and that is almost equally inadmissible in a well-ordered community. The individual ought undoubtedly to acquiesce in subordinating himself to the community—or, to speak more accurately, to the authorities who have the care of the community's welfare.

DR. STOCKMANN. Very likely. But what the deuce has all this got to do with me?

PETER STOCKMANN. That is exactly what you never appear to be willing to learn, my dear Thomas. But, mark my words, some day you will have to suffer for it—sooner or later. Now I have told you. Good-bye.

DR. STOCKMANN. Have you taken leave of your senses? You are on the wrong scent altogether.

PETER STOCKMANN. I am not usually that. You must excuse me now if I—(*calls into the dining-room.*) Good night, Katherine. Good night, gentlemen. (*Goes out.*)

MRS. STOCKMANN (*coming from the dining-room*). Has he gone?

DR. STOCKMANN. Yes, and in such a bad temper.

MRS. STOCKMANN. But, dear Thomas, what have you been doing to him again?

DR. STOCKMANN. Nothing at all. And, anyhow, he can't oblige me to make my report before the proper time.

MRS. STOCKMANN. What have you got to make a report to him about?

DR. STOCKMANN. Hm! Leave that to me, Katherine.—It is an extraordinary thing that the postman doesn't come.

(HOVSTAD, BILLING *and* HORSTER *have got up from the table and come into the sitting-room.* EJLIF *and* MORTEN *come in after them.*)

BILLING (*stretching himself*). Ah—one feels a new man after a meal like that.

HOVSTAD. The mayor wasn't in a very sweet temper tonight, then.

DR. STOCKMANN. It is his stomach; he has a wretched digestion.

HOVSTAD. I rather think it was us two of the *People's Messenger* that he couldn't digest.

MRS. STOCKMANN. I thought you came out of it pretty well with him.

HOVSTAD. Oh yes; but it isn't anything more than a sort of truce.

BILLING. That is just what it is! That word sums up the situation.

DR. STOCKMANN. We must remember that Peter is a lonely man, poor chap. He has no home comforts of any kind; nothing but everlasting business. And all that infernal weak tea wash that he pours into himself! Now then, my boys, bring chairs up to the table. Aren't we going to have that toddy, Katherine?

MRS. STOCKMANN (*going into the dining-room*). I am just getting it.

DR. STOCKMANN. Sit down here on the couch beside me, Captain Horster. We so seldom see you—. Please sit down, my friends.

(*They sit down at the table.* MRS. STOCKMANN *brings a tray, with a spirit-lamp, glasses, bottles, etc., upon it.*)

MRS. STOCKMANN. There you are! This is arrack, and this is rum, and this one is the brandy. Now every one must help himself.

DR. STOCKMANN (*taking a glass*). We will. (*They all mix themselves some toddy.*) And let us have the cigars. Ejlif, you know where the box is. And you, Morten, can fetch my pipe. (*The two boys go into the room on the right.*) I have a suspicion that Ejlif pockets a cigar now and then!—but I take no notice of it. (*Calls out.*) And my smoking-cap too, Morten. Katherine, you can tell him where I left it. Ah, he has got it. (*The boys bring the various things.*) Now, my friends. I stick to my pipe, you know. This one has seen plenty of bad weather with me up north. (*Touches glasses with them.*) Your good health! Ah! it is good to be sitting snug and warm here.

MRS. STOCKMANN (*who sits knitting*). Do you sail soon, Captain Horster?

HORSTER. I expect to be ready to sail next week.

MRS. STOCKMANN. I suppose you are going to America?

HORSTER. Yes, that is the plan.

MRS. STOCKMANN. Then you won't be able to take part in the coming election.

HORSTER. Is there going to be an election?

BILLING. Didn't you know?

HORSTER. No, I don't mix myself up with those things.

BILLING. But do you not take an interest in public affairs?

HORSTER. No, I don't know anything about politics.

BILLING. All the same, one ought to vote, at any rate.

HORSTER. Even if one doesn't know anything about what is going on?

BILLING. Doesn't know! What do you mean by that? A community is like a ship; every one ought to be prepared to take the helm.

HORSTER. Maybe that is all very well on shore; but on board ship it wouldn't work.

HOVSTAD. It is astonishing how little most sailors care about what goes on on shore.

BILLING. Very extraordinary.

DR. STOCKMANN. Sailors are like birds of passage; they feel equally at home in any latitude. And that is only an additional reason for our being all the more keen, Hovstad. Is there to be anything of public interest in tomorrow's *Messenger*?

HOVSTAD. Nothing about municipal affairs. But the day after tomorrow I was thinking of printing your article—

DR. STOCKMANN. Ah, devil take it—my article! Look here, that must wait a bit.

HOVSTAD.   Really? We had just got convenient space for it, and I thought it was just the opportune moment—

DR. STOCKMANN.   Yes, yes, very likely you are right; but it must wait all the same. I will explain to you later.

(PETRA *comes in from the hall, in hat and cloak and with a bundle of exercise books under her arm.*)

PETRA.   Good evening.

DR. STOCKMANN.   Good evening, Petra; come along.

(*Mutual greetings;* PETRA *takes off her things and puts them down on a chair by the door.*)

PETRA.   And you have all been sitting here enjoying yourselves, while I have been out slaving!

DR. STOCKMANN.   Well, come and enjoy yourself too!

BILLING.   May I mix a glass for you?

PETRA (*coming to the table*).   Thanks, I would rather do it; you always mix it too strong. But I forgot, father—I have a letter for you. (*Goes to the chair where she had laid her things.*)

DR. STOCKMANN.   A letter? From whom?

PETRA (*looking in her coat pocket*).   The postman gave it to me just as I was going out—

DR. STOCKMANN (*getting up and going to her*).   And you only give it to me now!

PETRA.   I really had not time to run up again. There it is!

DR. STOCKMANN (*seizing the letter*).   Let's see, let's see, child! (*Looks at the address.*) Yes, that's all right!

MRS. STOCKMANN.   Is it the one you have been expecting so anxiously, Thomas?

DR. STOCKMANN.   Yes, it is. I must go to my room now and—. Where shall I get a light, Katherine? Is there no lamp in my room again?

MRS. STOCKMANN.   Yes, your lamp is all ready lit on your desk.

DR. STOCKMANN.   Good, good. Excuse me for a moment—. (*Goes into his study.*)

PETRA.   What do you suppose it is, mother?

MRS. STOCKMANN.   I don't know; for the last day or two he has always been asking if the postman has not been.

BILLING.   Probably some country patient.

PETRA.   Poor old dad!—he will overwork himself soon. (*Mixes a glass for herself.*) There, that will taste good!

HOVSTAD.   Have you been teaching in the evening school again today?

PETRA (*sipping from her glass*).   Two hours.

BILLING.   And four hours of school in the morning—

PETRA.   Five hours.

MRS. STOCKMANN.   And you have still got exercises to correct, I see.

PETRA. A whole heap, yes.

HORSTER. You are pretty full up with work too, it seems to me.

PETRA. Yes—but that is good. One is so delightfully tired after it.

BILLING. Do you like that?

PETRA. Yes, because one sleeps so well then.

MORTEN. You must be dreadfully wicked, Petra.

PETRA. Wicked?

MORTEN. Yes, because you work so much. Mr. Rörlund says work is a punishment for our sins.

EJLIF. Pooh, what a duffer you are, to believe a thing like that!

MRS. STOCKMANN. Come, come, Ejlif!

BILLING (*laughing*). That's capital!

HOVSTAD. Don't you want to work as hard as that, Morten?

MORTEN. No, indeed I don't.

HOVSTAD. What do you want to be, then?

MORTEN. I should like best to be a Viking.

EJLIF. You would have to be a pagan then.

MORTEN. Well, I could become a pagan, couldn't I?

BILLING. I agree with you, Morten! My sentiments, exactly.

MRS. STOCKMANN (*signaling to him*). I am sure that is not true, Mr. Billing.

BILLING. Yes, I swear it is! I am a pagan, and I am proud of it. Believe me, before long we shall all be pagans.

MORTEN. And then we shall be allowed to do anything we like?

BILLING. Well, you see, Morten—.

MRS. STOCKMANN. You must go to your room now, boys; I am sure you have some lessons to learn for tomorrow.

EJLIF. I should like so much to stay a little longer—

MRS. STOCKMANN. No, no; away you go, both of you.

(*The boys say good-night and go into the room on the left.*)

HOVSTAD. Do you really think it can do the boys any harm to hear such things?

MRS. STOCKMANN. I don't know; but I don't like it.

PETRA. But you know, mother, I think you really are wrong about it.

MRS. STOCKMANN. Maybe, but I don't like it—not in our own home.

PETRA. There is so much falsehood both at home and at school. At home one must not speak, and at school we have to stand and tell lies to the children.

HORSTER. Tell lies?

PETRA. Yes, don't you suppose we have to teach them all sorts of things that we don't believe?

BILLING. That is perfectly true.

PETRA. If only I had the means I would start a school of my own, and it would be conducted on very different lines.

BILLING. Oh, bother the means—!

HORSTER. Well if you are thinking of that, Miss Stockmann, I shall be delighted to provide you with a schoolroom. The great big old house my father left me is standing almost empty; there is an immense dining-room downstairs—

PETRA (*laughing*). Thank you very much; but I am afraid nothing will come of it.

HOVSTAD. No, Miss Petra is much more likely to take to journalism, I expect. By the way, have you had time to do anything with that English story you promised to translate for us?

PETRA. No, not yet; but you shall have it in good time.

(DR. STOCKMANN *comes in from his room with an open letter in his hand.*)

DR. STOCKMANN (*waving the letter*). Well, now the town will have something new to talk about, I can tell you!

BILLING. Something new?

MRS. STOCKMANN. What is this?

DR. STOCKMANN. A great discovery, Katherine.

HOVSTAD. Really?

MRS. STOCKMANN. A discovery of yours?

DR. STOCKMANN. A discovery of mine. (*Walks up and down.*) Just let them come saying, as usual, that it is all fancy and a crazy man's imagination! But they will be careful what they say this time, I can tell you!

PETRA. But, father, tell us what it is.

DR. STOCKMANN. Yes, yes—only give me time, and you shall know all about it. If only I had Peter here now! It just shows how we men can go about forming our judgments, when in reality we are as blind as any moles—

HOVSTAD. What are you driving at, Doctor?

DR. STOCKMANN (*standing still by the table*). Isn't it the universal opinion that our town is a healthy spot?

HOVSTAD. Certainly.

DR. STOCKMANN. Quite an unusually healthy spot, in fact—a place that deserves to be recommended in the warmest possible manner either for invalids or for people who are well—

MRS. STOCKMANN. Yes, but my dear Thomas—

DR. STOCKMANN. And we have been recommending it and praising it—I have written and written, both in the *Messenger* and in pamphlets—

HOVSTAD. Well, what then?

DR. STOCKMANN. And the Baths—we have called them the "main artery of the town's life-blood," the "nerve-center of our town," and the devil knows what else—

BILLING. "The town's pulsating heart" was the expression I once used on an important occasion—

DR. STOCKMANN. Quite so. Well, do you know what they really are, these great, splendid, much praised Baths that have cost so much money—do you know what they are?

HOVSTAD. No, what are they?

MRS. STOCKMANN. Yes, what are they?

DR. STOCKMANN. The whole place is a pesthouse!

PETRA. The Baths, father?

MRS. STOCKMANN (*at the same time*). Our Baths!

HOVSTAD. But, Doctor—

BILLING. Absolutely incredible!

DR. STOCKMANN. The whole Bath establishment is a whited, poisoned sepulcher, I tell you—the gravest possible danger to the public health! All the nastiness up at Mölledal, all that stinking filth, is infecting the water in the conduit-pipes leading to the reservoir; and the same cursed, filthy poison oozes out on the shore too—

HORSTER. Where the bathing-place is?

DR. STOCKMANN. Just there.

HOVSTAD. How do you come to be so certain of all this, Doctor?

DR. STOCKMANN. I have investigated the matter most conscientiously. For a long time past I have suspected something of the kind. Last year we had some very strange cases of illness among the visitors—typhoid cases, and cases of gastric fever—

MRS. STOCKMANN. Yes, that is quite true.

DR. STOCKMANN. At the time, we supposed the visitors had been infected before they came; but later on, in the winter, I began to have a different opinion; and so I set myself to examine the water, as well as I could.

MRS. STOCKMANN. Then that is what you have been so busy with?

DR. STOCKMANN. Indeed I have been busy, Katherine. But here I had none of the necessary scientific apparatus; so I sent samples, both of the drinking-water and of the sea-water, up to the University, to have an accurate analysis made by a chemist.

HOVSTAD. And have you got that?

DR. STOCKMANN (*showing him the letter*). Here it is! It proves the presence of decomposing organic matter in the water—it is full of infusoria. The water is absolutely dangerous to use, either internally or externally.

MRS. STOCKMANN. What a mercy you discovered it in time.

DR. STOCKMANN. You may well say so.

HOVSTAD. And what do you propose to do now, Doctor?

DR. STOCKMANN. To see the matter put right—naturally.

HOVSTAD. Can that be done?

DR. STOCKMANN. It must be done. Otherwise the Baths will be absolutely useless and wasted. But we need not anticipate that; I have a very clear idea what we shall have to do.

MRS. STOCKMANN. But why have you kept this all so secret, dear?

DR. STOCKMANN. Do you suppose I was going to run about the town gossiping about it, before I had absolute proof? No, thank you. I am not such a fool.

PETRA. Still, you might have told us—

DR. STOCKMANN. Not a living soul. But tomorrow you may run round to the old Badger—

MRS. STOCKMANN. Oh, Thomas! Thomas!

DR. STOCKMANN. Well, to your grandfather, then. The old boy will have something to be astonished at! I know he thinks I am cracked—and there are lots of other people think so too, I have noticed. But now these good folks shall see—they shall just see—! (*Walks about, rubbing his hands.*) There will be a nice upset in the town, Katherine; you can't imagine what it will be. All the conduit-pipes will have to be relaid.

HOVSTAD (*getting up*). All the conduit-pipes—?

DR. STOCKMANN. Yes, of course. The intake is too low down; it will have to be lifted to a position much higher up.

PETRA. Then you were right after all.

DR. STOCKMANN. Ah, you remember, Petra—I wrote opposing the plans before the work was begun. But at that time no one would listen to me. Well, I am going to let them have it, now! Of course I have prepared a report for the Baths Committee; I have had it ready for a week, and was only waiting for this to come. (*Shows the letter.*) Now it shall go off at once. (*Goes into his room and comes back with some papers.*) Look at that! Four closely written sheets— and the letter shall go with them. Give me a bit of paper, Katherine— something to wrap them up in. That will do! Now give it to—to—(*stamps his foot*)—what the deuce is her name?—give it to the maid, and tell her to take it at once to the Mayor.

(MRS. STOCKMANN *takes the packet and goes out through the dining-room.*)

PETRA. What do you think uncle Peter will say, father?

DR. STOCKMANN. What is there for him to say? I should think he would be very glad that such an important truth has been brought to light.

HOVSTAD. Will you let me print a short note about your discovery in the *Messenger*?

DR. STOCKMANN. I shall be very much obliged if you will.

HOVSTAD. It is very desirable that the public should be informed of it without delay.

DR. STOCKMANN. Certainly.

MRS. STOCKMANN (*coming back*). She has just gone with it.

BILLING. Upon my soul, Doctor, you are going to be the foremost man in the town!

DR. STOCKMANN (*walking about happily*). Nonsense! As a matter of fact I have done nothing more than my duty. I have only made a lucky find— that's all. Still, all the same—

BILLING. Hovstad, don't you think the town ought to give Dr. Stockmann some sort of testimonial?

HOVSTAD. I will suggest it, anyway.

BILLING. And I will speak to Aslaksen about it.

DR. STOCKMANN. No, my good friends, don't let us have any of that nonsense. I won't hear of anything of the kind. And if the Baths Committee should think of voting me an increase of salary, I will not accept it. Do you hear, Katherine—I won't accept it.

MRS. STOCKMANN. You are quite right, Thomas.

PETRA (*lifting her glass*). Your health, father!

HOVSTAD *and* BILLING. Your health, Doctor! Good health!

HORSTER (*touches glasses with* DR. STOCKMANN). I hope it will bring you nothing but good luck.

DR. STOCKMANN. Thank you, thank you, my dear fellows! I feel tremendously happy! It is a splendid thing for a man to be able to feel that he has done a service to his native town and to his fellow-citizens. Hurrah, Katherine!

(*He puts his arms round her and whirls her round and round, while she protests with laughing cries. They all laugh, clap their hands and cheer the* DOCTOR. *The boys put their heads in at the door to see what is going on.*)

ACT II

SCENE. *The same. The door into the dining-room is shut. It is morning.* MRS. STOCKMANN, *with a sealed letter in her hand, comes in from the dining-room, goes to the door of the* DOCTOR'S *study and peeps in.*

MRS. STOCKMANN. Are you in, Thomas?

DR. STOCKMANN (*from within his room*). Yes, I have just come in. (*Comes into the room*) What is it?

MRS. STOCKMANN. A letter from your brother.

DR. STOCKMANN. Aha, let us see! (*Opens the letter and reads.*) "I return herewith the manuscript you sent me"—(*reads on in a low murmur.*) Hm!—

MRS. STOCKMANN. What does he say?

DR. STOCKMANN (*putting the papers in his pocket*). Oh, he only writes that he will come up here himself about midday.

MRS. STOCKMANN. Well, try and remember to be at home this time.

DR. STOCKMANN. That will be all right; I have got through all my morning visits.

MRS. STOCKMANN. I am extremely curious to know how he takes it.

DR. STOCKMANN. You will see he won't like it's having been I, and not he, that made the discovery.

MRS. STOCKMANN. Aren't you a little nervous about that?

DR. STOCKMANN. Oh, he really will be pleased enough, you know. But, at the same time, Peter is so confoundedly afraid of anyone's doing any service to the town except himself.

MRS. STOCKMANN. I will tell you what, Thomas—you should be good-natured, and share the credit of this with him. Couldn't you make out that it was he who set you on the scent of this discovery?

DR. STOCKMANN. I am quite willing. If only I can get the thing set right. I—

(MORTEN KIIL *puts his head in through the door leading from the hall, looks around in an inquiring manner and chuckles.*)

MORTEN KIIL (*slyly*). Is it—is it true?

MRS. STOCKMANN (*going to the door*). Father!—is it you?

DR. STOCKMANN. Ah, Mr. Kiil—good morning, good morning!

MRS. STOCKMANN. But come along in.

MORTEN KIIL. If it is true, I will; if not, I am off.

DR. STOCKMANN. If what is true?

MORTEN KIIL. This tale about the water-supply. Is it true?

DR. STOCKMANN. Certainly it is true. But how did you come to hear it?

MORTEN KIIL (*coming in*). Petra ran in on her way to the school—

DR. STOCKMANN. Did she?

MORTEN KIIL. Yes; and she declares that—. I thought she was only making a fool of me, but it isn't like Petra to do that.

DR. STOCKMANN. Of course not. How could you imagine such a thing!

MORTEN KIIL. Oh well, it is better never to trust anybody; you may find you have been made a fool of before you know where you are. But it is really true, all the same?

DR. STOCKMANN. You can depend upon it that it is true. Won't you sit down? (*Settles him on the couch.*) Isn't it a real bit of luck for the town—

MORTEN KIIL (*suppressing his laughter*). A bit of luck for the town?

DR. STOCKMANN. Yes, that I made the discovery in good time.

MORTEN KIIL (*as before*). Yes, yes, yes!—But I should never have thought you the sort of man to pull your own brother's leg like this!

DR. STOCKMANN. Pull his leg!

MRS. STOCKMANN. Really, father dear—

MORTEN KIIL (*resting his hands and his chin in the handle of his stick and winking slyly at the* DOCTOR). Let me see, what was the story? Some kind of beast that had got into the water-pipes, wasn't it?

DR. STOCKMANN. Infusoria—yes.

MORTEN KIIL. And a lot of these beasts had got in, according to Petra—a tremendous lot.

DR. STOCKMANN. Certainly; hundreds of thousands of them, probably.

MORTEN KIIL. But no one can see them—isn't that so?

DR. STOCKMANN. Yes; you can't see them.

MORTEN KIIL (*with a quiet chuckle*). Damme—it's the finest story I have ever heard!

DR. STOCKMANN. What do you mean?

MORTEN KIIL. But you will never get the Mayor to believe a thing like that.

DR. STOCKMANN. We shall see.

MORTEN KIIL. Do you think he will be fool enough to—?

DR. STOCKMANN. I hope the whole town will be fools enough.

MORTEN KIIL. The whole town! Well, it wouldn't be a bad thing. It would just serve them right and teach them a lesson. They think themselves so much cleverer than we old fellows. They hounded me out of the council; they did, I tell you—they hounded me out. Now they shall pay for it. You pull their legs too, Thomas!

DR. STOCKMANN. Really, I—

MORTEN KIIL. You pull their legs! (*Gets up.*) If you can work it so that the Mayor and his friends all swallow the same bait, I will give ten pounds to a charity—like a shot!

DR. STOCKMANN. That is very kind of you.

MORTEN KIIL. Yes, I haven't got much money to throw away, I can tell you; but if you can work this, I will give five pounds to a charity at Christmas.

(HOVSTAD *comes in by the hall door.*)

HOVSTAD. Good morning! (*Stops.*) Oh, I beg your pardon—

DR. STOCKMANN. Not at all; come in.

MORTEN KIIL (*with another chuckle*). Oho!—is he in this too?

HOVSTAD. What do you mean?

DR. STOCKMANN. Certainly he is.

MORTEN KIIL. I might have known it! It must get into the papers. You know how to do it, Thomas! Set your wits to work. Now I must go.

DR. STOCKMANN. Won't you stay a little while?

MORTEN KIIL. No, I must be off now. You keep up this game for all it is worth; you won't repent it, I'm damned if you will!

(*He goes out;* MRS. STOCKMANN *follows him into the hall.*)

DR. STOCKMANN (*laughing*). Just imagine—the old chap doesn't believe a word of all this about the water-supply.

HOVSTAD. Oh that was it, then?

DR. STOCKMANN. Yes, that was what we were talking about. Perhaps it is the same thing that brings you here?

HOVSTAD. Yes, it is. Can you spare me a few minutes, Doctor?

DR. STOCKMANN. As long as you like, my dear fellow.

HOVSTAD. Have you heard from the Mayor yet?

DR. STOCKMANN. Not yet. He is coming here later.

HOVSTAD. I have given the matter a great deal of thought since last night.

DR. STOCKMANN. Well?

HOVSTAD. From your point of view, as a doctor and a man of science, this affair of the water-supply is an isolated matter. I mean, you do not realize that it involves a great many other things.

DR. STOCKMANN. How, do you mean—let us sit down, my dear fellow. No, sit here on the couch. (HOVSTAD *sits down on the couch,* DR. STOCKMANN *on a chair on the other side of the table.*) Now then. You mean that—?

HOVSTAD. You said yesterday that the pollution of the water was due to impurities in the soil.

DR. STOCKMANN. Yes, unquestionably it is due to that poisonous morass up at Mölledal.

HOVSTAD. Begging your pardon, Doctor, I fancy it is due to quite another morass altogether.

DR. STOCKMANN. What morass?

HOVSTAD. The morass that the whole life of our town is built on and is rotting in.

DR. STOCKMANN. What the deuce are you driving at, Hovstad?

HOVSTAD. The whole of the town's interests have, little by little, got into the hands of a pack of officials.

DR. STOCKMANN. Oh, come!—they are not all officials.

HOVSTAD. No, but those that are not officials are at any rate the officials' friends and adherents; it is the wealthy folk, the old families in the town, that have got us entirely in their hands.

DR. STOCKMANN. Yes, but after all they are men of ability and knowledge.

HOVSTAD. Did they show any ability or knowledge when they laid the conduit-pipes where they are now?

DR. STOCKMANN. No, of course that was a great piece of stupidity on their part. But that is going to be set right now.

HOVSTAD. Do you think that will be all such plain sailing?

DR. STOCKMANN. Plain sailing or no, it has got to be done, anyway.

HOVSTAD. Yes, provided the press takes up the question.

DR. STOCKMANN. I don't think that will be necessary, my dear fellow, I am certain my brother—

HOVSTAD. Excuse me, doctor; I feel bound to tell you I am inclined to take the matter up.

DR. STOCKMANN. In the paper?

HOVSTAD. Yes. When I took over the *People's Messenger* my idea was to break up this ring of self-opinionated old fossils who had got hold of all the influence.

DR. STOCKMANN. But you know you told me yourself what the result had been; you nearly ruined your paper.

HOVSTAD. Yes, at the time we were obliged to climb down a peg or two, it is quite true; because there was a danger of the whole project of the Baths coming to nothing if they failed us. But now the scheme has been carried through, and we can dispense with these grand gentlemen.

DR. STOCKMANN. Dispense with them, yes; but we owe them a great debt of gratitude.

HOVSTAD. That shall be recognized ungrudgingly. But a journalist of my democratic tendencies cannot let such an opportunity as this slip. The bubble of official infallibility must be pricked. This superstition must be destroyed, like any other.

DR. STOCKMANN. I am whole-heartedly with you in that, Mr. Hovstad; if it is a superstition, away with it!

HOVSTAD. I should be very reluctant to bring the Mayor into it, because he is your brother. But I am sure you will agree with me that truth should be the first consideration.

DR. STOCKMANN. That goes without saying. (*With sudden emphasis.*) Yes, but—but—

HOVSTAD. You must not misjudge me. I am neither more self-interested nor more ambitious than most men.

DR. STOCKMANN. My dear fellow—who suggests anything of the kind?

HOVSTAD. I am of humble origin, as you know; and that has given me opportunities of knowing what is the most crying need in the humbler ranks of life. It is that they should be allowed some part in the direction of public affairs, Doctor. That is what will develop their faculties and intelligence and self-respect—

DR. STOCKMANN. I quite appreciate that.

HOVSTAD. Yes—and in my opinion a journalist incurs a heavy responsibility if he neglects a favorable opportunity of emancipating the masses—the humble and oppressed. I know well enough that in exalted circles I shall be called an agitator, and all that sort of thing; but they may call it what they like. If only my conscience doesn't reproach me, then—

DR. STOCKMANN. Quite right! Quite right, Mr. Hovstad. But all the same—devil take it! (*A knock is heard at the door.*) Come in!

(ASLAKSEN *appears at the door. He is poorly but decently dressed, in black, with a slightly crumpled white neckcloth; he wears gloves and has a felt hat in his hand.*)

ASLAKSEN (*bowing*). Excuse my taking the liberty, Doctor—

DR. STOCKMANN (*getting up*). Ah, it is you, Aslaksen!

ASLAKSEN. Yes, Doctor.

HOVSTAD (*standing up*). Is it me you want, Aslaksen?

ASLAKSEN. No; I didn't know I should find you here. No, it was the Doctor I—

DR. STOCKMANN. I am quite at your service. What is it?

ASLAKSEN. Is what I heard from Mr. Billing true, sir—that you mean to improve our water-supply?

DR. STOCKMANN. Yes, for the Baths.

ASLAKSEN. Quite so, I understand. Well, I have come to say that I will back that up by every means in my power.

HOVSTAD (*to the Doctor*). You see!

DR. STOCKMANN. I shall be very grateful to you, but—

ASLAKSEN. Because it may be no bad thing to have us small tradesmen at your back. We form, as it were, a compact majority in the town—if we choose. And it is always a good thing to have the majority with you, Doctor.

DR. STOCKMANN. That is undeniably true; but I confess I don't see why such unusual precautions should be necessary in this case. It seems to me that such a plain, straightforward thing—

ASLAKSEN. Oh, it may be very desirable, all the same. I know our local authorities so well; officials are not generally very ready to act on proposals that come from other people. That is why I think it would not be at all amiss if we made a little demonstration.

HOVSTAD. That's right.

DR. STOCKMANN. Demonstration, did you say? What on earth are you going to make a demonstration about?

ASLAKSEN. We shall proceed with the greatest moderation, Doctor. Moderation is always my aim; it is the greatest virtue in a citizen—at least, I think so.

DR. STOCKMANN. It is well known to be a characteristic of yours, Mr. Aslaksen.

ASLAKSEN. Yes, I think I may pride myself on that. And this matter of the water-supply is of the greatest importance to us small tradesmen. The Baths promise to be a regular gold-mine for the town. We shall all make our living out of them, especially those of us who are householders. That is why we will back up the project as strongly as possible. And as I am at present Chairman of the Householders' Association—

DR. STOCKMANN. Yes—?

ASLAKSEN. And, what is more, local secretary of the Temperance Society—you know sir, I suppose, that I am a worker in the temperance cause?

DR. STOCKMANN. Of course, of course.

ASLAKSEN. Well, you can understand that I come into contact with a great many people. And as I have the reputation of a temperate and law-abiding citizen—like yourself, Doctor—I have a certain influence in the town, a little bit of power, if I may be allowed to say so.

DR. STOCKMANN. I know that quite well, Mr. Aslaksen.

ASLAKSEN. So you see it would be an easy matter for me to set on foot some testimonial, if necessary?

DR. STOCKMANN. A testimonial?

ASLAKSEN. Yes, some kind of an address of thanks from the townsmen for your share in a matter of such importance to the community. I need scarcely say that it would have to be drawn up with the greatest regard to moderation, so as not to offend the authorities—who, after all, have the reins in their hands. If we pay strict attention to that, no one can take it amiss, I should think!

HOVSTAD. Well, and even supposing they didn't like it—

ASLAKSEN. No, no, no; there must be no discourtesy to the authorities, Mr. Hovstad. It is no use falling foul of those upon whom our welfare so closely depends. I have done that in my time, and no good ever comes of it. But no one can take exception to a reasonable and frank expression of a citizen's views.

DR. STOCKMANN (*shaking him by the hand*). I can't tell you, dear Mr. Aslaksen, how extremely pleased I am to find such hearty support among my fellow-citizens. I am delighted—delighted! Now, you will take a small glass of sherry, eh?

ASLAKSEN. No, thank you; I never drink alcohol of that kind.

DR. STOCKMANN. Well, what do you say to a glass of beer, then?

ASLAKSEN. Nor that either, thank you, Doctor. I never drink anything as early as this. I am going into town now to talk this over with one or two householders, and prepare the ground.

DR. STOCKMANN. It is tremendously kind of you, Mr. Aslaksen; but I really cannot understand the necessity for all these precautions. It seems to me that the thing should go of itself.

ASLAKSEN. The authorities are somewhat slow to move, Doctor. Far be it from me to seem to blame them—

HOVSTAD. We are going to stir them up in the paper tomorrow, Aslaksen.

ASLAKSEN. But not violently, I trust, Mr. Hovstad. Proceed with moderation, or you will do nothing with them. You may take my advice; I have gathered my experience in the school of life. Well, I must say good-bye, Doctor. You know now that we small tradesmen are at your back at all events, like a solid wall. You have the compact majority on your side, Doctor.

DR. STOCKMANN. I am very much obliged, dear Mr. Aslaksen. (*Shakes hands with him.*) Good-bye, good-bye.

ASLAKSEN. Are you going my way, towards the printing-office, Mr. Hovstad?

HOVSTAD. I will come later; I have something to settle up first.

ASLAKSEN. Very well.

(*Bows and goes out;* STOCKMANN *follows him into the hall.*)

HOVSTAD (*as* STOCKMANN *comes in again*). Well, what do you think of that, Doctor? Don't you think it is high time we stirred a little life into all this slackness and vacillation and cowardice?

DR. STOCKMANN. Are you referring to Aslaksen?

HOVSTAD. Yes, I am. He is one of those who are floundering in a bog—decent enough fellow though he may be, otherwise. And most of the people here are in just the same case—see-sawing and edging first to one side and then to the other, so overcome with caution and scruple that they never dare to take any decided step.

DR. STOCKMANN. Yes, but Aslaksen seemed to me so thoroughly well-intentioned.

HOVSTAD. There is one thing I esteem higher than that; and that is for a man to be self-reliant and sure of himself.

DR. STOCKMANN. I think you are perfectly right there.

HOVSTAD. That is why I want to seize this opportunity, and try if I cannot manage to put a little virility into these well-intentioned people for once. The idol of Authority must be shattered in this town. This gross and inexcusable blunder about the water-supply must be brought home to the mind of every municipal voter.

DR. STOCKMANN. Very well; if you are of opinion that it is for the good of the community, so be it. But not until I have had a talk with my brother.

HOVSTAD. Anyway, I will get a leading article ready; and if the Mayor refuses to take the matter up—

DR. STOCKMANN. How can you suppose such a thing possible?

HOVSTAD. It is conceivable. And in that case—

DR. STOCKMANN. In that case I promise you—. Look here, in that case you may print my report—every word of it.

HOVSTAD. May I? Have I your word for it?

DR. STOCKMANN (*giving him the MS.*). Here it is; take it with you. It can do no harm for you to read it through, and you can give it me back later on.

HOVSTAD. Good, good! That is what I will do. And now good-bye, Doctor.

DR. STOCKMANN. Good-bye, good-bye. You will see everything will run quite smoothly, Mr. Hovstad—quite smoothly.

HOVSTAD. Hm!—we shall see. (*Bows and goes out.*)

DR. STOCKMANN (*opens the dining-room door and looks in*). Katherine! Oh, you are back, Petra?

PETRA (*coming in*). Yes, I have just come from the school.

MRS. STOCKMANN (*coming in*). Has he not been here yet?

DR. STOCKMANN. Peter? No. But I have had a long talk with Hovstad. He is quite excited about my discovery. I find it has a much wider bearing than I at first imagined. And he has put his paper at my disposal if necessity should arise.

MRS. STOCKMANN. Do you think it will?

DR. STOCKMANN. Not for a moment. But at all events it makes me feel proud to know that I have the liberal-minded independent press on my side. Yes, and—just imagine—I have had a visit from the Chairman of the House-holders' Association!

MRS. STOCKMANN. Oh! What did he want?

DR. STOCKMANN. To offer me his support too. They will support me in a body if it should be necessary. Katherine—do you know what I have got behind me?

MRS. STOCKMANN. Behind you? No, what have you got behind you?

DR. STOCKMANN. The compact majority.

MRS. STOCKMANN. Really? Is that a good thing for you, Thomas?

DR. STOCKMANN. I should think it was a good thing. (*Walks up and down rubbing his hands.*) By Jove, it's a fine thing to feel this bond of brotherhood between oneself and one's fellow-citizens!

PETRA. And to be able to do so much that is good and useful, father!

DR. STOCKMANN. And for one's own native town into the bargain, my child!

MRS. STOCKMANN. That was a ring at the bell.

DR. STOCKMANN. It must be he, then. (*A knock is heard at the door.*) Come in!

PETER STOCKMANN (*comes in from the hall*). Good morning.

DR. STOCKMANN. Glad to see you, Peter!

MRS. STOCKMANN. Good morning, Peter. How are you?

PETER STOCKMANN. So so, thank you. (*To* DR. STOCKMANN.) I received from you yesterday, after office-hours, a report dealing with the condition of the water at the Baths.

DR. STOCKMANN. Yes. Have you read it?

PETER STOCKMANN. Yes, I have.

DR. STOCKMANN. And what have you to say to it?

PETER STOCKMANN (*with a sidelong glance*). Hm!—

MRS. STOCKMANN. Come along, Petra.

(*She and* PETRA *go into the room on the left.*)

PETER STOCKMANN (*after a pause*). Was it necessary to make all these investigations behind my back?

DR. STOCKMANN. Yes, because until I was absolutely certain about it—

PETER STOCKMANN. Then you mean that you are absolutely certain now?

DR. STOCKMANN. Surely you are convinced of that.

PETER STOCKMANN. Is it your intention to bring this document before the Baths Committee as a sort of official communication?

DR. STOCKMANN. Certainly. Something must be done in the matter— and that quickly.

PETER STOCKMANN. As usual, you employ violent expressions in your report. You say, amongst other things, that what we offer visitors in our Baths is a permanent supply of poison.

DR. STOCKMANN. Well, can you describe it any other way, Peter? Just think—water that is poisonous, whether you drink it or bathe in it! And this we offer to the poor sick folk who come to us trustfully and pay us at an exorbitant rate to be made well again!

PETER STOCKMANN. And your reasoning leads you to this conclusion, that we must build a sewer to draw off the alleged impurities from Mölledal and must relay the water-conduits.

DR. STOCKMANN. Yes. Do you see any other way out of it? I don't.

PETER STOCKMANN. I made a pretext this morning to go and see the town engineer, and, as if only half seriously, broached the subject of these proposals as a thing we might perhaps have to take under consideration some time later on.

DR. STOCKMANN. Some time later on!

PETER STOCKMANN. He smiled at what he considered to be my extravagance, naturally. Have you taken the trouble to consider what your proposed alterations would cost? According to the information I obtained, the expenses would probably mount up to fifteen or twenty thousand pounds.

DR. STOCKMANN. Would it cost so much?

PETER STOCKMANN. Yes; and the worst part of it would be that the work would take at least two years.

DR. STOCKMANN. Two years? Two whole years?

PETER STOCKMANN. At least. And what are we to do with the Baths in the meantime? Close them? Indeed we should be obliged to. And do you suppose any one would come near the place after it had got about that the water was dangerous?

DR. STOCKMANN. Yes, but, Peter, that is what it is.

PETER STOCKMANN. And all this at this juncture—just as the Baths are beginning to be known. There are other towns in the neighborhood with qualifications to attract visitors for bathing purposes. Don't you suppose they would immediately strain every nerve to divert the entire stream of strangers to themselves? Unquestionably they would; and then where should we be? We should probably have to abandon the whole thing, which has cost us so much money—and then you would have ruined your native town.

DR. STOCKMANN. I—should have ruined—!

PETER STOCKMANN. It is simply and solely through the Baths that the town has before it any future worth mentioning. You know that just as well as I.

DR. STOCKMANN. But what do you think ought to be done, then?

PETER STOCKMANN. Your report has not convinced me that the condition of the water at the Baths is as bad as you represent it to be.

DR. STOCKMANN. I tell you it is even worse!—or at all events it will be in summer, when the warm weather comes.

PETER STOCKMANN. As I said, I believe you exaggerate the matter considerably. A capable physician ought to know what measures to take—he ought to be capable of preventing injurious influences or of remedying them if they become obviously persistent.

DR. STOCKMANN. Well? What more?

PETER STOCKMAN. The water-supply for the Baths is now an established fact, and in consequence must be treated as such. But probably the Committee, at its discretion, will not be disinclined to consider the question of how far it might be possible to introduce certain improvements consistently with a reasonable expenditure.

DR. STOCKMANN. And do you suppose that I will have anything to do with such a piece of trickery as that?

PETER STOCKMANN. Trickery!!

DR. STOCKMANN. Yes, it would be a trick—a fraud, a lie, a downright crime towards the public, towards the whole community!

PETER STOCKMANN. I have not, as I remarked before, been able to convince myself that there is actually an imminent danger.

DR. STOCKMANN. You have! It is impossible that you should not be convinced. I have represented the facts absolutely truthfully and fairly. And you know it very well, Peter, only you won't acknowledge it. It was owing to your action that both the Baths and the water-conduits were built where they are; and that is what you won't acknowledge—that damnable blunder of yours. Pooh!—do you suppose I don't see through you?

PETER STOCKMANN. And even if that were true? If I perhaps guard my reputation somewhat anxiously, it is in the interests of the town. Without moral authority I am powerless to direct public affairs as seems, to my judgment, to be best for the common good. And on that account—and for various other reasons, too—it appears to me to be a matter of importance that your report should not be delivered to the Committee. In the interests of the public, you must withhold it. Then, later on, I will raise the question and we will do our best, privately; but nothing of this unfortunate affair—not a single word of it—must come to the ears of the public.

DR. STOCKMANN. I am afraid you will not be able to prevent that now, my dear Peter.

PETER STOCKMANN. It must and shall be prevented.

DR. STOCKMANN. It is no use, I tell you. There are too many people that know about it.

PETER STOCKMANN. That know about it? Who? Surely you don't mean those fellows on the *People's Messenger?*

DR. STOCKMANN. Yes, they know. The liberal-minded independent press is going to see that you do your duty.

PETER STOCKMANN (*after a short pause*). You are an extraordinarily independent man, Thomas. Have you given no thought to the consequences this may have for yourself?

DR. STOCKMANN. Consequences?—for me?

PETER STOCKMANN. For you and yours, yes.

DR. STOCKMANN. What the deuce do you mean?

PETER STOCKMANN. I believe I have always behaved in a brotherly way to you—have always been ready to oblige or to help you?

DR. STOCKMANN. Yes, you have, and I am grateful to you for it.

PETER STOCKMANN. There is no need. Indeed, to some extent I was forced to do so—for my own sake. I always hoped that, if I helped to improve your financial position, I should be able to keep some check on you.

DR. STOCKMANN. What!! Then it was only for your own sake—!

PETER STOCKMANN. Up to a certain point, yes. It is painful for a man in an official position to have his nearest relative compromising himself time after time.

DR. STOCKMANN. And do you consider that I do that?

PETER STOCKMANN. Yes, unfortunately, you do, without even being aware of it. You have a restless, pugnacious, rebellious disposition. And then there is that disastrous propensity of yours to want to write about every sort of possible and impossible thing. The moment an idea comes into your head, you must needs go and write a newspaper article or a whole pamphlet about it.

DR. STOCKMANN. Well, but is it not the duty of a citizen to let the public share in any new ideas he may have?

PETER STOCKMANN. Oh, the public doesn't require any new ideas. The public is best served by the good, old-established ideas it already has.

DR. STOCKMANN. And that is your honest opinion?

PETER STOCKMANN. Yes, and for once I must talk frankly to you. Hitherto I have tried to avoid doing so, because I know how irritable you are; but now I must tell you the truth, Thomas. You have no conception what an amount of harm you do yourself by your impetuosity. You complain of the authorities, you even complain of the government—you are always pulling them to pieces; you insist that you have been neglected and persecuted. But what else can such a cantankerous man as you expect?

DR. STOCKMANN. What next! Cantankerous, am I?

PETER STOCKMANN. Yes, Thomas, you are an extremely cantankerous man to work with—I know that to my cost. You disregard everything that you ought to have consideration for. You seem completely to forget that it is me you have to thank for your appointment here as medical officer to the Baths—

DR. STOCKMANN. I was entitled to it as a matter of course!—I and nobody else! I was the first person to see that the town could be made into a flourishing watering-place, and I was the only one who saw it at that time. I had to fight single-handed in support of the idea for many years; and I wrote and wrote—

PETER STOCKMANN. Undoubtedly. But things were not ripe for the scheme then—though, of course, you could not judge of that in your out-of-the-way corner up north. But as soon as the opportune moment came I—and the others—took the matter into our hands—

DR. STOCKMANN. Yes, and made this mess of all my beautiful plan. It is pretty obvious now what clever fellows you were!

PETER STOCKMANN. To my mind the whole thing only seems to mean that you are seeking another outlet for your combativeness. You want to pick a quarrel with your superiors—an old habit of yours. You cannot put up with any authority over you. You look askance at anyone who occupies a superior official position; you regard him as a personal enemy, and then any stick is good enough to beat him with. But now I have called your attention to the fact that the town's interests are at stake—and, incidentally, my own too. And therefore I must tell you, Thomas, that you will find me inexorable with regard to what I am about to require you to do.

DR. STOCKMANN. And what is that?

PETER STOCKMANN. As you have been so indiscreet as to speak of this delicate matter to outsiders, despite the fact that you ought to have treated it as entirely official and confidential, it is obviously impossible to hush it up now. All sorts of rumors will get about directly, and everybody who has a grudge against us will take care to embellish these rumors. So it will be necessary for you to refute them publicly.

DR. STOCKMANN. I! How? I don't understand.

PETER STOCKMANN. What we shall expect is that, after making further investigations, you will come to the conclusion that the matter is not by any means as dangerous or as critical as you imagined in the first instance.

DR. STOCKMANN. Oho!—so that is what you expect!

PETER STOCKMANN. And, what is more, we shall expect you to make public profession of your confidence in the Committee and in their readiness to consider fully and conscientiously what steps may be necessary to remedy any possible defects.

DR. STOCKMANN. But you will never be able to do that by patching and tinkering at it—never! Take my word for it, Peter; I mean what I say, as deliberately and emphatically as possible.

PETER STOCKMANN. As an officer under the Committee, you have no right to any individual opinion.

DR. STOCKMANN (*amazed*). No right?

PETER STOCKMANN. In your official capacity, no. As a private person, it is quite another matter. But as a subordinate member of the staff of the Baths, you have no right to express any opinion which runs contrary to that of your superiors.

DR. STOCKMANN. This is too much! I, a doctor, a man of science, have no right to—!

PETER STOCKMANN. The matter in hand is not simply a scientific one. It is a complicated matter and has its economic as well as its technical side.

DR. STOCKMANN. I don't care what it is! I intend to be free to express my opinion on any subject under the sun.

PETER STOCKMANN. As you please—but not on any subject concerning the Baths. That we forbid.

DR. STOCKMANN (*shouting*). You forbid—! You! A pack of—

PETER STOCKMANN. I forbid it—I, your chief; and if I forbid it, you have to obey.

DR. STOCKMANN (*controlling himself*). Peter—if you were not my brother—

PETRA (*throwing open the door*). Father, you shan't stand this!

MRS. STOCKMANN (*coming in after her*). Petra, Petra!

PETER STOCKMANN. Oh, so you have been eavesdropping.

MRS. STOCKMANN. You were talking so loud, we couldn't help—

PETRA. Yes, I was listening.

PETER STOCKMANN. Well, after all, I am very glad—

DR. STOCKMANN (*going up to him*). You were saying something about forbidding and obeying?

PETER STOCKMANN. You obliged me to take that tone with you.

DR. STOCKMANN. And so I am to give myself the lie, publicly?

PETER STOCKMANN. We consider it absolutely necessary that you should make some such public statement as I have asked for.

DR. STOCKMANN. And if I do not—obey?

PETER STOCKMANN. Then we shall publish a statement ourselves to reassure the public.

DR. STOCKMANN. Very well; but in that case I shall use my pen against you. I stick to what I have said; I will show that I am right and that you are wrong. And what will you do then?

PETER STOCKMANN. Then I shall not be able to prevent your being dismissed.

DR. STOCKMANN. What—?

PETRA. Father—dismissed!

MRS. STOCKMANN. Dismissed!

PETER STOCKMANN. Dismissed from the staff of the Baths. I shall be obliged to propose that you shall immediately be given notice, and shall not be allowed any further participation in the Baths' affairs.

DR. STOCKMANN. You would dare to do that!

PETER STOCKMANN. It is you that are playing the daring game.

PETRA. Uncle, that is a shameful way to treat a man like father!

MRS. STOCKMANN. Do hold your tongue, Petra!

PETER STOCKMANN (*looking at* PETRA). Oh, so we volunteer our opinions already, do we? Of course. (*To* MRS. STOCKMANN.) Katherine, I imagine you are the most sensible person in this house. Use any influence you may have over your husband, and make him see what this will entail for his family as well as—

DR. STOCKMANN. My family is my own concern and nobody else's!

PETER STOCKMANN. —for his own family, as I was saying, as well as for the town he lives in.

DR. STOCKMANN. It is I who have the real good of the town at heart! I want to lay bare the defects that sooner or later must come to the light of day. I will show whether I love my native town.

PETER STOCKMANN. You, who in your blind obstinacy want to cut off the most important source of the town's welfare?

DR. STOCKMANN. The source is poisoned, man! Are you mad? We are making our living by retailing filth and corruption! The whole of our flourishing municipal life derives its sustenance from a lie!

PETER STOCKMANN. All imagination— or something even worse. The man who can throw out such offensive insinuations about his native town must be an enemy of our community.

DR. STOCKMANN (*going up to him*). Do you dare to—!

MRS. STOCKMANN (*throwing herself between them*). Thomas!

PETRA (*catching her father by the arm*). Don't lose your temper, father!

PETER STOCKMANN. I will not expose myself to violence. Now you have had a warning; so reflect on what you owe to yourself and your family. Good-bye. (*Goes out.*)

DR. STOCKMANN (*walking up and down*). Am I to put up with such treatment as this? In my own house, Katherine! What do you think of that!

MRS. STOCKMANN. Indeed it is both shameful and absurd, Thomas—

PETRA. If only I could give uncle a piece of my mind—

DR. STOCKMANN. It is my own fault. I ought to have flown out at him long ago!—shown my teeth!—bitten! To hear him call me an enemy to our community! Me! I shall not take that lying down, upon my soul!

MRS. STOCKMANN. But, dear Thomas, your brother has power on his side—

DR. STOCKMANN. Yes, but I have right on mine, I tell you.

MRS. STOCKMANN. Oh yes, right—right. What is the use of having right on your side if you have not got might?

PETRA. Oh, mother—how can you say such a thing!

DR. STOCKMANN. Do you imagine that in a free country it is no use having right on your side? You are absurd, Katherine. Besides, haven't I got the liberal-minded, independent press to lead the way, and the compact majority behind me? That is might enough, I should think!

MRS. STOCKMANN. But, good heavens, Thomas, you don't mean to—?

DR. STOCKMANN. Don't mean to what?

MRS. STOCKMANN. To set yourself up in opposition to your brother.

DR. STOCKMANN. In God's name, what else do you suppose I should do but take my stand on right and truth?

PETRA. Yes, I was just going to say that.

MRS. STOCKMANN. But it won't do you any earthly good. If they won't do it, they won't.

DR. STOCKMANN. Oho, Katherine! Just give me time, and you will see how I will carry the war into their camp.

MRS. STOCKMANN. Yes, you carry the war into their camp, and you get your dismissal—that is what you will do.

DR. STOCKMANN. In any case I shall have done my duty towards the public—towards the community. I, who am called its enemy!

MRS. STOCKMANN. But towards your family, Thomas? Towards your own home! Do you think that is doing your duty towards those you have to provide for?

PETRA. Ah, don't think always first of us, mother.

MRS. STOCKMANN. Oh, it is easy for you to talk; you are able to shift for yourself, if need be. But remember the boys, Thomas; and think a little, too, of yourself, and of me—

DR. STOCKMANN. I think you are out of your senses, Katherine! If I were to be such a miserable coward as to go on my knees to Peter and his damned crew, do you suppose I should ever know an hour's peace of mind all my life afterwards?

MRS. STOCKMANN. I don't know anything about that; but God preserve us from the peace of mind we shall have, all the same, if you go on defying him! You will find yourself again without the means of subsistence, with no income to count upon. I should think we had had enough of that in the old days. Remember that, Thomas; think what that means.

DR. STOCKMANN (*collecting himself with a struggle and clenching his fist*). And this is what this slavery can bring upon a free, honorable man! Isn't it horrible, Katherine?

MRS. STOCKMANN. Yes, it is sinful to treat you so, it is perfectly true. But, good heavens, one has to put up with so much injustice in this world.—There are the boys, Thomas! Look at them! What is to become of them? Oh, no, no, you can never have the heart—.

(EJLIF *and* MORTEN *have come in while she was speaking, with their school books in their hands.*)

DR. STOCKMANN. The boys—! (*Recovers himself suddenly.*) No, even if the whole world goes to pieces, I will never bow my neck to this yoke! (*Goes towards his room.*)

MRS. STOCKMANN (*following him*). Thomas—what are you going to do!

DR. STOCKMANN (*at his door*). I mean to have the right to look my sons in the face when they are grown men. (*Goes into his room.*)

MRS. STOCKMANN (*bursting into tears*). God help us all!

PETRA. Father is splendid! He will not give in.

(*The boys look on in amazement;* PETRA *signs to them not to speak.*)

ACT III

SCENE. *The editorial office of the* People's Messenger. *The entrance door is on the left-hand side of the back wall; on the right-hand side is another door with glass panels through which the printing-room can be seen. Another door in the right-hand wall. In the middle of the room is a large table covered with paper, newspapers and books. In the foreground on the left a window, before which stand a desk and a high stool. There are a couple of easy chairs by the table, and other chairs standing along the wall. The room is dingy and uncomfortable; the furniture is old, the chairs stained and torn. In the printing-room the compositors are seen at work, and a printer is working a hand-press.* HOVSTAD *is sitting at the desk, writing.* BILLING *comes in from the right with* DR. STOCKMANN'S *manuscript in his hand.*

BILLING. Well, I must say!

HOVSTAD (*still writing*). Have you read it through?

BILLING (*laying the MS. on the desk*). Yes, indeed I have.

HOVSTAD. Don't you think the Doctor hits them pretty hard?

BILLING. Hard? Bless my soul, he's crushing! Every word falls like—how shall I put it?—like the blow of a sledgehammer.

HOVSTAD. Yes, but they are not the people to throw up the sponge at the first blow.

BILLING. That is true; and for that reason we must strike blow upon blow until the whole of this aristocracy tumbles to pieces. As I sat in there reading this, I almost seemed to see a revolution in being.

HOVSTAD (*turning round*). Hush!—Speak so Aslaksen cannot hear you.

BILLING (*lowering his voice*). Aslaksen is a chicken-hearted chap, a coward; there is nothing of the man in him. But this time you will insist on your own way, won't you? You will put the Doctor's article in?

HOVSTAD. Yes, and if the Mayor doesn't like it—

BILLING. That will be the devil of a nuisance.

HOVSTAD. Well, fortunately we can turn the situation to good account, whatever happens. If the Mayor will not fall in with the Doctor's project, he will have all the small tradesmen down on him—the whole of the Householders' Association and the rest of them. And if he does fall in with it, he will fall out with the whole crowd of large shareholders in the Baths, who up to now have been his most valuable supporters—

BILLING. Yes, because they will certainly have to fork out a pretty penny—

HOVSTAD. Yes, you may be sure they will. And in this way the ring will be broken up, you see, and then in every issue of the paper we will enlighten the public on the Mayor's incapability on one point and another, and make it clear that all the positions of trust in the town, the whole control of municipal affairs, ought to be put in the hands of the Liberals.

BILLING. That is perfectly true! I see it coming—I see it coming; we are on the threshold of a revolution!

(*A knock is heard at the door.*)

HOVSTAD. Hush! (*Calls out.*) Come in! (DR. STOCKMANN *comes in by the street door.* HOVSTAD *goes to meet him.*) Ah, it is you, Doctor! Well?

DR. STOCKMANN. You may set to work and print it, Mr. Hovstad!

HOVSTAD. Has it come to that, then?

BILLING. Hurrah!

DR. STOCKMANN. Yes, print away. Undoubtedly it has come to that. Now they must take what they get. There is going to be a fight in the town, Mr. Billing!

BILLING. War to the knife, I hope! We will get our knives to their throats, Doctor!

DR. STOCKMANN. This article is only a beginning. I have already got four or five more sketched out in my head. Where is Aslaksen?

BILLING (*calls into the printing-room*). Aslaksen, just come here for a minute!

HOVSTAD. Four or five more articles, did you say? On the same subject?

DR. STOCKMANN. No—far from it, my dear fellow. No, they are about quite another matter. But they all spring from the question of the water-supply and the drainage. One thing leads to another, you know. It is like beginning to pull down an old house, exactly.

BILLING. Upon my soul, it's true; you find you are not done till you have pulled all the old rubbish down.

ASLAKSEN (*coming in*). Pulled down? You are not thinking of pulling down the Baths surely, Doctor?

HOVSTAD. Far from it, don't be afraid.

DR. STOCKMANN. No, we meant something quite different. Well, what do you think of my article, Mr. Hovstad?

HOVSTAD. I think it is simply a masterpiece—

DR. STOCKMANN. Do you really think so? Well, I am very pleased, very pleased.

HOVSTAD. It is so clear and intelligible. One need have no special knowledge to understand the bearing of it. You will have every enlightened man on your side.

ASLAKSEN. And every prudent man too, I hope?

BILLING. The prudent and the imprudent—almost the whole town.

ASLAKSEN. In that case we may venture to print it.

DR. STOCKMANN. I should think so!

HOVSTAD. We will put it in tomorrow morning.

DR. STOCKMANN. Of course—you must not lose a single day. What I wanted to ask you, Mr. Aslaksen, was if you would supervise the printing of it yourself.

ASLAKSEN. With pleasure.

DR. STOCKMANN. Take care of it as if it were a treasure! No misprints— every word is important. I will look in again a little later; perhaps you will be able to let me see a proof. I can't tell you how eager I am to see it in print, and see it burst upon the public—

BILLING. Burst upon them—yes, like a flash of lightning!

DR. STOCKMANN. —and to have it submitted to the judgment of my intelligent fellow-townsmen. You cannot imagine what I have gone through today. I have been threatened first with one thing and then another; they have tried to rob me of my most elementary rights as a man—

BILLING. What! Your rights as a man!

DR. STOCKMANN. —they have tried to degrade me, to make a coward of me, to force me to put personal interests before my most sacred convictions—

BILLING. That is too much—I'm damned if it isn't.

HOVSTAD. Oh, you mustn't be surprised at anything from that quarter.

DR. STOCKMANN. Well, they will get the worst of it with me; they may assure themselves of that. I shall consider the *People's Messenger* my sheet-anchor now, and every single day I will bombard them with one article after another, like bomb-shells—

ASLAKSEN. Yes, but—

BILLING. Hurrah!—it is war, it is war!

DR. STOCKMANN. I shall smite them to the ground—I shall crush them—I shall break down all their defences, before the eyes of the honest public! That is what I shall do!

ASLAKSEN. Yes, but in moderation, Doctor—proceed with moderation—

BILLING. Not a bit of it, not a bit of it! Don't spare the dynamite!

DR. STOCKMANN. Because it is not merely a question of water-supply and drains now, you know. No—it is the whole of our social life that we have got to purify and disinfect—

BILLING. Spoken like a deliverer!

DR. STOCKMANN. All the incapables must be turned out, you understand—and that in every walk of life! Endless vistas have opened themselves to my mind's eye today. I cannot see it all quite clearly yet, but I shall in time. Young and vigorous standard-bearers—those are what we need and must seek, my friends; we must have new men in command at all our out-posts.

BILLING. Hear, hear!

DR. STOCKMANN. We only need to stand by one another, and it will all be perfectly easy. The revolution will be launched like a ship that runs smoothly off the stocks. Don't you think so?

HOVSTAD. For my part I think we have now a prospect of getting the municipal authority into the hands where it should lie.

ASLAKSEN. And if only we proceed with moderation, I cannot imagine that there will be any risk.

DR. STOCKMANN. Who the devil cares whether there is any risk or not! What I am doing, I am doing in the name of truth and for the sake of my conscience.

HOVSTAD. You are a man who deserves to be supported, Doctor.

ASLAKSEN. Yes, there is no denying that the Doctor is a true friend to the town—a real friend to the community, that he is.

BILLING. Take my word for it, Aslaksen, Dr. Stockmann is a friend of the people.

ASLAKSEN. I fancy the Householders' Association will make use of that expression before long.

DR. STOCKMANN (affected, grasps their hands). Thank you, thank you, my dear staunch friends. It is very refreshing to me to hear you say that; my brother called me something quite different. By Jove, he shall have it back, with interest! But now I must be off to see a poor devil—. I will come back, as I said. Keep a very careful eye on the manuscript, Aslaksen, and don't for worlds leave out any of my notes of exclamation! Rather put one or two more in! Capital, capital! Well, good-bye for the present—good-bye, good-bye!

(They show him to the door, and bow him out.)

HOVSTAD. He may prove an invaluably useful man to us.

ASLAKSEN. Yes, so long as he confines himself to this matter of the Baths. But if he goes farther afield, I don't think it would be advisable to follow him.

HOVSTAD. Hm!—that all depends—

BILLING. You are so infernally timid, Aslaksen!

ASLAKSEN. Timid? Yes, when it is a question of the local authorities, I am timid, Mr. Billing; it is a lesson I have learnt in the school of experience, let me tell you. But try me in higher politics, in matters that concern the government itself, and then see if I am timid.

BILLING. No, you aren't, I admit. But this is simply contradicting yourself.

ASLAKSEN. I am a man with a conscience, and that is the whole matter. If you attack the government, you don't do the community any harm, anyway;

these fellows pay no attention to attacks, you see—they go on just as they are, in spite of them. But *local* authorities are different; they *can* be turned out, and then perhaps you may get an ignorant lot into office who may do irreparable harm to the householders and everybody else.

HOVSTAD. But what of the education of citizens by self-government—don't you attach any importance to that?

ASLAKSEN. When a man has interests of his own to protect, he cannot think of everything, Mr. Hovstad.

HOVSTAD. Then I hope I shall never have interests of my own to protect!

BILLING. Hear, hear!

ASLAKSEN (*with a smile*). Hm! (*Points to the desk.*) Mr. Sheriff Stensgaard was your predecessor at that editorial desk.

BILLING (*spitting*). Bah! That turncoat.

HOVSTAD. I am not a weathercock—and never will be.

ASLAKSEN. A politician should never be too certain of anything, Mr. Hovstad. And as for you, Mr. Billing, I should think it is time for you to be taking in a reef or two in your sails, seeing that you are applying for the post of secretary to the Bench.

BILLING. I—!

HOVSTAD. Are you, Billing?

BILLING. Well, yes—but you must clearly understand I am doing it only to annoy the bigwigs.

ASLAKSEN. Anyhow, it is no business of mine. But if I am to be accused of timidity and of inconsistency in my principles, this is what I want to point out: my political past is an open book. I have never changed, except perhaps to become a little more moderate, you see. My heart is still with the people; but I don't deny that my reason has a certain bias towards the authorities— the local ones, I mean. (*Goes into the printing-room.*)

BILLING. Oughtn't we to try and get rid of him, Hovstad?

HOVSTAD. Do you know anyone else who will advance the money for our paper and printing bill?

BILLING. It is an infernal nuisance that we don't possess some capital to trade on.

HOVSTAD (*sitting down at his desk*). Yes, if we only had that, then—

BILLING. Suppose you were to apply to Dr. Stockmann?

HOVSTAD (*turning over some papers*). What is the use? He has got nothing.

BILLING. No, but he has got a warm man in the background, old Morten Kiil—"the Badger," as they call him.

HOVSTAD (*writing*). Are you so sure *he* has got anything?

BILLING. Good Lord, of course he has! And some of it must come to the Stockmanns. Most probably he will do something for the children, at all events.

HOVSTAD (*turning half round*). Are you counting on that?

BILLING. Counting on it? Of course I am not counting on anything.

HOVSTAD. That is right. And I should not count on the secretaryship to the Bench either, if I were you; for I can assure you—you won't get it.

BILLING. Do you think I am not quite aware of that? My object is precisely *not* to get it. A slight of that kind stimulates a man's fighting power—it is like getting a supply of fresh bile—and I am sure one needs that badly enough in a hole-and-corner place like this, where it is so seldom anything happens to stir one up.

HOVSTAD (*writing*). Quite so, quite so.

BILLING. Ah, I shall be heard of yet!—Now I shall go and write the appeal to the Householders' Association. (*Goes into the room on the right.*)

HOVSTAD (*sitting at his desk, biting his penholder, says slowly*). Hm!— that's it, is it? (*A knock is heard.*) Come in! (PETRA *comes in by the outer door.* HOVSTAD *gets up.*) What, you!—here?

PETRA. Yes, you must forgive me—

HOVSTAD (*pulling a chair forward*). Won't you sit down?

PETRA. No, thank you; I must go again in a moment.

HOVSTAD. Have you come with a message from your father, by any chance?

PETRA. No, I have come on my own account. (*Takes a book out of her coat pocket.*) Here is the English story.

HOVSTAD. Why have you brought it back?

PETRA. Because I am not going to translate it.

HOVSTAD. But you promised me faithfully—

PETRA. Yes, but then I had not read it. I don't suppose you have read it either?

HOVSTAD. No, you know quite well I don't understand English; but—

PETRA. Quite so. That is why I wanted to tell you that you must find something else. (*Lays the book on the table.*) You can't use this for the *People's Messenger.*

HOVSTAD. Why not?

PETRA. Because it conflicts with all your opinions.

HOVSTAD. Oh, for that matter—

PETRA. You don't understand me. The burden of this story is that there is a supernatural power that looks after the so-called good people in this world and makes everything happen for the best in their case—while all the so-called bad people are punished.

HOVSTAD. Well, but that is all right. That is just what our readers want.

PETRA. And are you going to be the one to give it to them? For myself, I do not believe a word of it. You know quite well that things do not happen so in reality.

HOVSTAD. You are perfectly right; but an editor cannot always act as he would prefer. He is often obliged to bow to the wishes of the public in unimportant matters. Politics are the most important thing in life—for a newspaper, anyway; and if I want to carry my public with me on the path that leads to liberty and progress, I must not frighten them away. If they find a moral tale of this sort in the serial at the bottom of the page, they will be all the more ready to read what is printed above it; they feel more secure, as it were.

PETRA. For shame! You would never go and set a snare like that for your readers; you are not a spider!

HOVSTAD (*smiling*). Thank you for having such a good opinion of me. No; as a matter of fact that is Billing's idea and not mine.

PETRA. Billing's!

HOVSTAD. Yes; anyway he propounded that theory here one day. And it is Billing who is so anxious to have that story in the paper; I don't know anything about the book.

PETRA. But how can Billing, with his emancipated views—

HOVSTAD. Oh, Billing is a many-sided man. He is applying for the post of secretary to the Bench, too, I hear.

PETRA. I don't believe it, Mr. Hovstad. How could he possibly bring himself to do such a thing?

HOVSTAD. Ah, you must ask him that.

PETRA. I should never have thought it of him.

HOVSTAD (*looking more closely at her*). No? Does it really surprise you so much?

PETRA. Yes. Or perhaps not altogether. Really, I don't quite know—

HOVSTAD. We journalists are not much worth, Miss Stockmann.

PETRA. Do you really mean that?

HOVSTAD. I think so sometimes.

PETRA. Yes, in the ordinary affairs of everyday life, perhaps; I can understand that. But now, when you have taken a weighty matter in hand—

HOVSTAD. This matter of your father's, you mean?

PETRA. Exactly. It seems to me that now you must feel you are a man worth more than most.

HOVSTAD. Yes, today I do feel something of that sort.

PETRA. Of course you do, don't you? It is a splendid vocation you have chosen—to smooth the way for the march of unappreciated truths, and new and courageous lines of thought. If it were nothing more than because you stand fearlessly in the open and take up the cause of an injured man—

HOVSTAD. Especially when that injured man is—ahem!—I don't rightly know how to—

PETRA When that man is so upright and so honest, you mean?

HOVSTAD (*more gently*). Especially when he is your father, I meant.

PETRA (*suddenly checked*). *That?*

HOVSTAD. Yes, Petra—Miss Petra.

PETRA. Is it *that*, that is first and foremost with you? Not the matter itself? Not the truth?—not my father's big generous heart?

HOVSTAD. Certainly—of course—that too.

PETRA. No, thank you; you have betrayed yourself, Mr. Hovstad, and now I shall never trust you again in anything.

HOVSTAD. Can you really take it so amiss in me that it is mostly for your sake—?

PETRA. What I am angry with you for, is for not having been honest with my father. You talked to him as if the truth and the good of the community were what lay nearest to your heart. You have made fools of both my father and me. You are not the man you made yourself out to be. And that I shall never forgive you—never!

HOVSTAD. You ought not to speak so bitterly, Miss Petra—least of all now.

PETRA. Why not now, especially?

HOVSTAD. Because your father cannot do without my help.

PETRA (*looking him up and down*). Are you that sort of man too? For shame!

HOVSTAD. No, no, I am not. This came upon me so unexpectedly—you must believe that.

PETRA. I know what to believe. Good-bye.

ASLAKSEN (*coming from the printing-room, hurriedly and with an air of mystery*). Damnation, Hovstad!—(*Sees* PETRA.) Oh, this is awkward—

PETRA. There is the book; you must give it to someone else. (*Goes toward the door.*)

HOVSTAD (*following her*). But, Miss Stockmann—

PETRA. Good-bye. (*Goes out.*)

ASLAKSEN. I say—Mr. Hovstad—

HOVSTAD. Well, well!—what is it?

ASLAKSEN. The Mayor is outside in the printing room.

HOVSTAD. The Mayor, did you say?

ASLAKSEN. Yes, he wants to speak to you. He came in by the back door—didn't want to be seen, you understand.

HOVSTAD. What can he want? Wait a bit—I will go myself. (*Goes to the door of the printing-room, opens it, bows and invites* PETER STOCKMANN *in.*) Just see, Aslaksen, that no one—

ASLAKSEN. Quite so. (*Goes into the printing room.*)

PETER STOCKMANN. You did not expect to see me here, Mr. Hovstad.

HOVSTAD. No, I confess I did not.

PETER STOCKMANN (*looking round*). You are very snug in here—very nice indeed.

HOVSTAD. Oh—

PETER STOCKMANN. And here I come, without any notice, to take up your time!

HOVSTAD. By all means, Mr. Mayor. I am at your service. But let me relieve you of your—(*Takes* STOCKMANN'S *hat and stick and puts them on a chair.*) Won't you sit down?

PETER STOCKMANN (*sitting down by the table*). Thank you. (HOVSTAD *sits down.*) I have had an extremely annoying experience today, Mr. Hovstad.

HOVSTAD. Really? Ah well, I expect with all the various business you have to attend to—

PETER STOCKMANN. The Medical Officer of the Baths is responsible for what happened today.

HOVSTAD. Indeed? The Doctor?

PETER STOCKMANN. He has addressed a kind of report to the Baths Committee on the subject of certain supposed defects in the Baths.

HOVSTAD. Has he indeed?

PETER STOCKMANN. Yes—has he not told you? I thought he said—

HOVSTAD. Ah, yes—it is true he did mention something about—

ASLAKSEN (coming from the printing-room). I ought to have that copy—

HOVSTAD (angrily). Ahem!—there it is on the desk.

ASLAKSEN (taking it). Right.

PETER STOCKMANN. But look there—that is the thing I was speaking of!

ASLAKSEN. Yes, that is the Doctor's article, Mr. Mayor.

HOVSTAD. Oh, is *that* what you were speaking about?

PETER STOCKMANN. Yes, that is it. What do you think of it?

HOVSTAD. Oh, I am only a layman—and I have only taken a very cursory glance at it.

PETER STOCKMANN. But you are going to print it?

HOVSTAD. I cannot very well refuse a distinguished man—

ASLAKSEN. I have nothing to do with editing the paper, Mr. Mayor.

PETER STOCKMANN. I understand.

ASLAKSEN. I merely print what is put into my hands.

PETER STOCKMANN. Quite so.

ASLAKSEN. And so I must— (Moves off toward the printing-room.)

PETER STOCKMANN No, but wait a moment, Mr. Aslaksen. You will allow me, Mr. Hovstad?

HOVSTAD. If you please, Mr. Mayor.

PETER STOCKMANN. You are a discreet and thoughtful man, Mr. Aslaksen.

ASLAKSEN. I am delighted to hear you think so, sir.

PETER STOCKMANN. And a man of very considerable influence.

ASLAKSEN. Chiefly among the small tradesmen, sir.

PETER STOCKMANN. The small tax-payers are the majority—here as everywhere else.

ASLAKSEN. That is true.

PETER STOCKMANN. And I have no doubt you know the general trend of opinion among them, don't you?

ASLAKSEN. Yes, I think I may say I do, Mr. Mayor.

PETER STOCKMANN. Yes. Well, since there is such a praiseworthy spirit of self-sacrifice among the less wealthy citizens of our town—

ASLAKSEN. What?

HOVSTAD. Self-sacrifice?

PETER STOCKMANN. It is pleasing evidence of a public-spirited feeling, extremely pleasing evidence. I might almost say I hardly expected it. But you have a closer knowledge of public opinion than I.

ASLAKSEN. But, Mr. Mayor—

PETER STOCKMANN. And indeed it is no small sacrifice that the town is going to make.

HOVSTAD. The town?

ASLAKSEN. But I don't understand. Is it the Baths—?

PETER STOCKMANN. At a provisional estimate, the alterations that the Medical Officer asserts to be desirable will cost somewhere about twenty thousand pounds.

ASLAKSEN. That is a lot of money, but—

PETER STOCKMANN. Of course it will be necessary to raise a municipal loan.

HOVSTAD (*getting up*). Surely you never mean that the town must pay—?

ASLAKSEN. Do you mean that it must come out of the municipal funds?—out of the ill-filled pockets of the small tradesmen?

PETER STOCKMANN. Well, my dear Mr. Aslaksen, where else is the money to come from?

ASLAKSEN. The gentlemen who own the Baths ought to provide that.

PETER STOCKMANN. The proprietors of the Baths are not in a position to incur any further expense.

ASLAKSEN. Is that absolutely certain, Mr. Mayor?

PETER STOCKMANN. I have satisified myself that it is so. If the town wants these very extensive alterations, it will have to pay for them.

ASLAKSEN. But, damn it all—I beg your pardon—this is quite another matter, Mr. Hovstad!

HOVSTAD. It is, indeed.

PETER STOCKMANN. The most fatal part of it is that we shall be obliged to shut the Baths for a couple of years.

HOVSTAD. Shut them? Shut them altogether?

ASLAKSEN. For two years?

PETER STOCKMANN. Yes, the work will take as long as that—at least.

ASLAKSEN. I'm damned if we will stand that, Mr. Mayor! What are we householders to live upon in the meantime?

PETER STOCKMANN. Unfortunately, that is an extremely difficult question to answer, Mr. Aslaksen. But what would you have us do? Do you suppose we shall have a single visitor in the town, if we go about proclaiming that our water is polluted, that we are living over a plague spot, that the entire town—

ASLAKSEN. And the whole thing is merely imagination?

PETER STOCKMANN. With the best will in the world, I have not been able to come to any other conclusion.

ASLAKSEN. Well then I must say it is absolutely unjustifiable of Dr. Stockmann—I beg your pardon, Mr. Mayor—

PETER STOCKMANN. What you say is lamentably true, Mr. Aslaksen. My brother has, unfortunately, always been a headstrong man.

ASLAKSEN. After this, do you mean to give him your support, Mr. Hovstad?

HOVSTAD. Can you suppose for a moment that I—?

PETER STOCKMANN. I have drawn up a short *résumé* of the situation as it appears from a reasonable man's point of view. In it I have indicated how certain possible defects might suitably be remedied without outrunning the resources of the Baths Committee.

HOVSTAD. Have you got it with you, Mr. Mayor?

PETER STOCKMANN (*fumbling in his pocket*). Yes, I brought it with me in case you should—

ASLAKSEN. Good Lord, there he is!

PETER STOCKMANN. Who? My brother?

HOVSTAD. Where? Where?

ASLAKSEN. He has just gone through the printing-room.

PETER STOCKMANN. How unlucky! I don't want to meet him here, and I had still several things to speak to you about.

HOVSTAD (*pointing to the door on the right*). Go in there for the present.

PETER STOCKMANN. But—?

HOVSTAD. You will only find Billing in there.

ASLAKSEN. Quick, quick, Mr. Mayor—he is just coming.

PETER STOCKMANN. Yes, very well; but see that you get rid of him quickly. (*Goes out through the door on the right, which* ASLAKSEN *opens for him and shuts after him.*)

HOVSTAD. Pretend to be doing something, Aslaksen.

(*Sits down and writes.* ASLAKSEN *begins foraging among a heap of newspapers that are lying on a chair.*)

DR. STOCKMANN (*coming in from the printing room*). Here I am again. (*Puts down his hat and stick.*)

HOVSTAD (*writing*). Already, Doctor? Hurry up with what we were speaking about, Aslaksen. We are very pressed for time today.

DR. STOCKMANN (*to* ASLAKSEN). No proof for me to see yet, I hear.

ASLAKSEN (*without turning round*). You couldn't expect it yet, Doctor.

DR. STOCKMANN. No, no; but I am impatient, as you can understand. I shall not know a moment's peace of mind till I see it in print.

HOVSTAD. Hm!—it will take a good while yet, won't it, Aslaksen?

ASLAKSEN. Yes, I am almost afraid it will.

DR. STOCKMANN. All right, my dear friends; I will come back. I do not mind coming back twice if necessary. A matter of such great importance—the welfare of the town at stake—it is no time to shirk trouble. (*Is just going, but stops and comes back.*) Look here—there is one thing more I want to speak to you about.

HOVSTAD. Excuse me, but could it not wait till some other time?

DR. STOCKMANN. I can tell you in half a dozen words. It is only this. When my article is read tomorrow and it is realized that I have been quietly working the whole winter for the welfare of the town—

HOVSTAD. Yes, but, Doctor—

DR. STOCKMANN. I know what you are going to say. You don't see how on earth it was any more than my duty—my obvious duty as a citizen. Of course it wasn't; I know that as well as you. But my fellow citizens, you know—! Good Lord, think of all the good souls who think so highly of me—!

ASLAKSEN. Yes, our townsfolk have had a very high opinion of you so far, Doctor.

DR. STOCKMANN. Yes, and that is just why I am afraid they—. Well, this is the point; when this reaches them, especially the poorer classes, and sounds in their ears like a summons to take the town's affairs into their own hands for the future—

HOVSTAD (*getting up*). Ahem! Doctor, I won't conceal from you the fact—

DR. STOCKMANN. Ah!—I knew there was something in the wind! But I won't hear a word of it. If anything of that sort is being set on foot—

HOVSTAD. Of what sort?

DR. STOCKMANN. Well, whatever it is—whether it is a demonstration in my honor, or a banquet, or a subscription list for some presentation to me—whatever it is, you must promise me solemnly and faithfully to put a stop to it. You too, Mr. Aslaksen; do you understand?

HOVSTAD. You must forgive me, Doctor, but sooner or later we must tell you the plain truth—

(*He is interrupted by the entrance of* MRS. STOCKMANN, *who comes in from the street door.*)

MRS. STOCKMANN (*seeing her husband*). Just as I thought!

HOVSTAD (*going towards her*). You too, Mrs. Stockmann?

DR. STOCKMANN. What on earth do *you* want here, Katherine?

MRS. STOCKMANN. I should think you know very well what I want.

HOVSTAD. Won't you sit down? Or perhaps—

MRS. STOCKMANN. No, thank you; don't trouble. And you must not be offended at my coming to fetch my husband; I am the mother of three children, you know.

DR. STOCKMANN. Nonsense!—we know all about that.

MRS. STOCKMANN. Well, one would not give you credit for much thought for your wife and children today; if you had had that, you would not have gone and dragged us all into misfortune.

DR. STOCKMANN. Are you out of your senses, Katherine! Because a man has a wife and children, is he not allowed to proclaim the truth—is he not to be allowed to be an actively useful citizen—is he not to be allowed to do a service to his native town!

MRS. STOCKMANN. Yes, Thomas—in reason.

ASLAKSEN. Just what I say. Moderation is everything.

MRS. STOCKMANN. And that is why you wrong us, Mr. Hovstad, in enticing my husband away from home and making a dupe of him in all this.

HOVSTAD. I certainly am making a dupe of no one—

DR. STOCKMANN. Making a dupe of me! Do you suppose *I* should allow myself to be duped!

MRS. STOCKMANN. It is just what you do. I know quite well you have more brains than anyone in the town, but you are extremely easily duped, Thomas. (*To* HOVSTAD) Please to realize that he loses his post at the Baths if you print what he has written—

ASLAKSEN. What!

HOVSTAD. Look here, Doctor—

DR. STOCKMANN (*laughing*). Ha—ha!—just let them try! No, no—they will take good care not to. I have got the compact majority behind me, let me tell you!

MRS. STOCKMANN. Yes, that is just the worst of it—your having any such horrid thing behind you.

DR. STOCKMANN. Rubbish, Katherine!—Go home and look after your house and leave me to look after the community. How can you be so afraid, when I am so confident and happy? (*Walks up and down, rubbing his hands.*) Truth and the People will win the fight, you may be certain! I see the whole of the broad-minded middle class marching like a victorious army—! (*Stops beside a chair.*) What the deuce is that lying there?

ASLAKSEN. Good Lord!

HOVSTAD. Ahem!

DR. STOCKMANN. Here we have the topmost pinnacle of authority! (*Takes the Mayor's official hat carefully between his finger-tips and holds it up in the air.*)

MRS. STOCKMANN. The Mayor's hat!

DR. STOCKMANN. And here is the staff of office too. How in the name of all that's wonderful—?

HOVSTAD. Well, you see—

DR. STOCKMANN. Oh, I understand. He has been here trying to talk you over. Ha—ha!—he made rather a mistake there! And as soon as he caught sight of me in the printing room—. (*Bursts out laughing.*) Did he run away, Mr. Aslaksen?

ASLAKSEN (*hurriedly*). Yes, he ran away, Doctor.

DR. STOCKMANN. Ran away without his stick or his—. Fiddlesticks! Peter doesn't run away and leave his belongings behind him. But what the deuce have you done with him? Ah!—in there, of course. Now you shall see, Katherine.

MRS. STOCKMANN. Thomas—please don't—!

ASLAKSEN. Don't be rash, Doctor.

(DR. STOCKMANN *has put on the Mayor's hat and taken his stick in his hand. He goes up to the door, opens it and stands with his hand to his hat at the salute.* PETER STOCKMANN *comes in, red with anger.* BILLING *follows him.*)

PETER STOCKMANN. What does this tomfoolery mean?

DR. STOCKMANN. Be respectful, my good Peter. I am the chief authority in the town now. (*Walks up and down.*)

MRS. STOCKMANN (*almost in tears*). Really, Thomas!

PETER STOCKMANN (*following him about*). Give me my hat and stick.

DR. STOCKMANN (*in the same tone as before*). If you are chief constable, let me tell you that I am the Mayor—I am the master of the whole town, please understand!

PETER STOCKMANN. Take off my hat, I tell you. Remember it is part of an official uniform.

DR. STOCKMANN. Pooh! Do you think the newly awakened lion-hearted people are going to be frightened by an official hat? There is going to be a revolution in the town tomorrow, let me tell you. You thought you could turn me out; but now I shall turn you out—turn you out of all your various offices. Do you think I cannot? Listen to me. I have triumphant social forces behind me. Hovstad and Billing will thunder in the *People's Messenger*, and Aslaksen will take the field at the head of the whole Householders' Association—

ASLAKSEN. That I won't, Doctor.

DR. STOCKMANN. Of course you will—

PETER STOCKMANN. Ah!—may I ask then if Mr. Hovstad intends to join this agitation?

HOVSTAD. No, Mr. Mayor.

ASLAKSEN. No, Mr. Hovstad is not such a fool as to go and ruin his paper and himself for the sake of an imaginary grievance.

DR. STOCKMANN (*looking round him*). What does this mean?

HOVSTAD. You have represented your case in a false light, Doctor, and therefore I am unable to give you my support.

BILLING. And after what the Mayor was so kind as to tell me just now, I—

DR. STOCKMANN. A false light! Leave that part of it to me. Only print my article; I am quite capable of defending it.

HOVSTAD. I am not going to print it. I cannot and will not and dare not print it.

DR. STOCKMANN. You dare not? What nonsense!—you are the editor; and an editor controls his paper, I suppose!

ASLAKSEN. No, it is the subscribers, Doctor.

PETER STOCKMANN. Fortunately, yes.

ASLAKSEN. It is public opinion—the enlightened public—householders and people of that kind; they control the newspapers.

DR. STOCKMANN (*composedly*). And I have all these influences against me?

ASLAKSEN. Yes, you have. It would mean the absolute ruin of the community if your article were to appear.

DR. STOCKMANN. Indeed.

PETER STOCKMANN. My hat and stick, if you please. (DR. STOCKMANN *takes off the hat and lays it on the table with the stick.* PETER STOCKMANN *takes them up.*) Your authority as Mayor has come to an untimely end.

DR. STOCKMANN. We have not got to the end yet. (*To* HOVSTAD.) Then it is quite impossible for you to print my article in the *People's Messenger*?

HOVSTAD. Quite impossible—out of regard for your family as well.

MRS. STOCKMANN. You need not concern yourself about his family, thank you, Mr. Hovstad.

PETER STOCKMANN (*taking a paper from his pocket*). It will be sufficient, for the guidance of the public, if this appears. It is an official statement. May I trouble you?

HOVSTAD (*taking the paper*). Certainly; I will see that it is printed.

DR. STOCKMANN. But not mine. Do you imagine that you can silence me and stifle the truth! You will not find it so easy as you suppose. Mr. Aslaksen, kindly take my manuscript at once and print it as a pamphlet—at my expense. I will have four hundred copies—no, five—six hundred.

ASLAKSEN. If you offered me its weight in gold, I could not lend my press for any such purpose, Doctor. It would be flying in the face of public opinion. You will not get it printed anywhere in the town.

DR. STOCKMANN. Then give it me back.

HOVSTAD (*giving him the MS.*). Here it is.

DR. STOCKMANN (*taking his hat and stick*). It shall be made public all the same. I will read it out at a mass meeting of the townspeople. All my fellow-citizens shall hear the voice of truth!

PETER STOCKMANN. You will not find any public body in the town that will give you the use of their hall for such a purpose.

ASLAKSEN. Not a single one, I am certain.

BILLING. No, I'm damned if you will find one.

MRS. STOCKMANN. But this is too shameful! Why should every one turn against you like that?

DR. STOCKMANN (*angrily*). I will tell you why. It is because all the men in this town are old women—like you; they all think of nothing but their families, and never of the community.

MRS. STOCKMANN (*putting her arm into his*). Then I will show them that an—an old woman can be a man for once. I am going to stand by you, Thomas!

DR. STOCKMANN. Bravely said, Katherine! It shall be made public—as I am a living soul! If I can't hire a hall, I shall hire a drum, and parade the town with it and read it at every street-corner.

PETER STOCKMANN. You are surely not such an arrant fool as that!

DR. STOCKMANN. Yes, I am.

ASLAKSEN. You won't find a single man in the whole town to go with you.

BILLING. No, I'm damned if you will.

MRS. STOCKMANN. Don't give in, Thomas. I will tell the boys to go with you.

DR. STOCKMANN. That is a splendid idea!

MRS. STOCKMANN. Morten will be delighted; and Ejlif will do whatever he does.

DR. STOCKMANN. Yes, and Petra!—and you too, Katherine!

MRS. STOCKMANN. No, I won't do that; but I will stand at the window and watch you, that's what I will do.

DR. STOCKMANN (*puts his arms round her and kisses her*). Thank you, my dear! Now you and I are going to try a fall, my fine gentlemen! I am going to see whether a pack of cowards can succeed in gagging a patriot who wants to purify society!

(*He and his wife go out by the street door.*)

PETER STOCKMANN (*shaking his head seriously*). Now he has sent *her* out of her senses, too.

ACT IV

SCENE. *A big old-fashioned room in* CAPTAIN HORSTER'S *house. At the back folding-doors, which are standing open, lead to an ante-room. Three windows in the left-hand wall. In the middle of the opposite wall a platform has been erected. On this is a small table with two candles, a water-bottle and glass, and a bell. The room is lit by lamps placed between the windows. In the foreground on the left there is a table with candles and a chair. To the right is a door and some chairs standing near it. The room is nearly filled with a crowd of townspeople of all sorts, a few women and schoolboys being amongst them. People are still streaming in from the back, and the room is soon filled.*

1ST CITIZEN (*meeting another*). Hullo, Lamstad! You here too?

2ND CITIZEN. I go to every public meeting, I do.

3RD CITIZEN. Brought your whistle too, I expect!

2ND CITIZEN. I should think so. Haven't you?

3RD CITIZEN. Rather! And old Evensen said he was going to bring a cow-horn, he did.

2ND CITIZEN. Good old Evensen!

(*Laughter among the crowd.*)

4TH CITIZEN (*coming up to them*). I say, tell me what is going on here tonight.

2ND CITIZEN. Dr. Stockmann is going to deliver an address attacking the Mayor.

4TH CITIZEN. But the Mayor is his brother.

1ST CITIZEN. That doesn't matter; Dr. Stockmann's not the chap to be afraid.

3RD CITIZEN. But he is in the wrong; it said so in the *People's Messenger*.

2ND CITIZEN. Yes, I expect he must be in the wrong this time, because neither the Householders' Association nor the Citizens' Club would lend him their hall for his meeting.

1ST CITIZEN. He couldn't even get the loan of the hall at the Baths.

2ND CITIZEN. No, I should think not.

A MAN (*in another part of the crowd*). I say—who are we to back up in this?

ANOTHER MAN (*beside him*). Watch Aslaksen, and do as he does.

BILLING (*pushing his way through the crowd, with a writing-case under his arm*). Excuse me, gentlemen—do you mind letting me through? I am reporting for the *People's Messenger*. Thank you very much! (*He sits down at the table on the left.*)

A WORKMAN. Who was that?

2ND WORKMAN. Don't you know him? It's Billing, who writes for Aslaksen's paper.

(CAPTAIN HORSTER *brings in* MRS. STOCKMANN *and* PETRA *through the door on the right.* EJLIF *and* MORTEN *follow them in.*)

HORSTER. I thought you might all sit here; you can slip out easily from here, if things get too lively.

MRS. STOCKMANN. Do you think there will be a disturbance?

HORSTER. One can never tell—with such a crowd. But sit down, and don't be uneasy.

MRS. STOCKMANN (*sitting down*). It was extremely kind of you to offer my husband the room.

HORSTER. Well, if nobody else would—

PETRA (*who has sat down beside her mother*). And it was a plucky thing to do, Captain Horster.

HORSTER. Oh, it is not such a great matter as all that.

(HOVSTAD *and* ASLAKSEN *make their way through the crowd.*)

ASLAKSEN (*going up to* HORSTER). Has the Doctor not come yet?

HORSTER. He is waiting in the next room.

(*Movement in the crowd by the door at the back.*)

HOVSTAD. Look—here comes the Mayor!

BILLING. Yes, I'm damned if he hasn't come after all!

(PETER STOCKMANN *makes his way gradually through the crowd, bows courteously and takes up a position by the wall on the left. Shortly afterwards* DR. STOCKMANN *comes in by the right-hand door. He is dressed in a black frock-coat, with a white tie. There is a little feeble applause, which is hushed down. Silence is obtained.*)

DR. STOCKMANN (*in an undertone*). How do you feel, Katherine?

MRS. STOCKMANN. All right, thank you. (*Lowering her voice.*) Be sure not to lose your temper, Thomas.

DR. STOCKMANN. Oh, I know how to control myself. (*Looks at his watch, steps on to the platform and bows.*) It is a quarter past—so I will begin. (*Takes his MS. out of his pocket.*)

ASLAKSEN. I think we ought to elect a chairman first.

DR. STOCKMANN. No, it is quite unnecessary.

SOME OF THE CROWD. Yes—yes!

PETER STOCKMANN. I certainly think, too, that we ought to have a chairman.

DR. STOCKMANN. But I have called this meeting to deliver a lecture, Peter.

PETER STOCKMANN. Dr. Stockmann's lecture may possibly lead to a considerable conflict of opinion.

VOICES IN THE CROWD. A chairman! A chairman!

HOVSTAD. The general wish of the meeting seems to be that a chairman should be elected.

DR. STOCKMANN (*restraining himself*). Very well—let the meeting have its way.

ASLAKSEN. Will the Mayor be good enough to undertake the task?

THREE MEN (*clapping their hands*). Bravo! Bravo!

PETER STOCKMANN. For various reasons, which you will easily understand, I must beg to be excused. But fortunately we have amongst us a man who I think will be acceptable to you all. I refer to the President of the Householders' Association, Mr. Aslaksen.

SEVERAL VOICES. Yes—Aslaksen! Bravo Aslaksen!

(DR. STOCKMANN *takes up his MS. and walks up and down the platform.*)

ASLAKSEN. Since my fellow-citizens choose to entrust me with this duty, I cannot refuse. (*Loud applause.* ASLAKSEN *mounts the platform.*)

BILLING (*writing*). "Mr. Aslaksen was elected with enthusiasm."

ASLAKSEN. And now, as I am in this position, I should like to say a few brief words. I am a quiet and peaceable man, who believes in discreet moderation, and—and—in moderate discretion. All my friends can bear witness to that.

SEVERAL VOICES. That's right! That's right, Aslaksen!

ASLAKSEN. I have learnt in the school of life and experience that moderation is the most valuable virtue a citizen can possess—

PETER STOCKMANN. Hear, hear!

ASLAKSEN. —And moreover that discretion and moderation are what enable a man to be of most service to the community. I would therefore suggest to our esteemed fellow citizen, who has called this meeting, that he should strive to keep strictly within the bounds of moderation.

A MAN (*by the door*). Three cheers for the Moderation Society!

A VOICE. Shame!

SEVERAL VOICES. Sh!—Sh!

ASLAKSEN. No interruptions, gentlemen, please! Does anyone wish to make any remarks?

PETER STOCKMANN. Mr. Chairman.

ASLAKSEN. The Mayor will address the meeting.

PETER STOCKMANN. In consideration of the close relationship in which, as you all know, I stand to the present Medical Officer of the Baths, I should have preferred not to speak this evening. But my official position with regard to the Baths and my solicitude for the vital interests of the town compel me to bring forward a motion. I venture to presume that there is not a single one of our citizens present who considers it desirable that unreliable and exaggerated accounts of the sanitary condition of the Baths and the town should be spread abroad.

SEVERAL VOICES. No, no! Certainly not! We protest against it!

PETER STOCKMANN. Therefore I should like to propose that the meeting should not permit the Medical Officer either to read or to comment on his proposed lecture.

DR. STOCKMANN (*impatiently*). Not permit—! What the devil—!

MRS. STOCKMANN (*coughing*). Ahem!—ahem!

DR. STOCKMANN (*collecting himself*). Very well. Go ahead!

PETER STOCKMANN. In my communication to the *People's Messenger*, I have put the essential facts before the public in such a way that every fair-minded citizen can easily form his own opinion. From it you will see that the main result of the Medical Officer's proposals—apart from their constituting a vote of censure on the leading men of the town—would be to saddle the ratepayers with an unnecessary expenditure of at least some thousands of pounds.

(*Sounds of disapproval among the audience, and some cat-calls.*)

ASLAKSEN (*ringing his bell*). Silence, please, gentlemen! I beg to support the Mayor's motion. I quite agree with him that there is something behind this agitation started by the Doctor. He talks about the Baths; but it is a revolution he is aiming at—he wants to get the administration of the town put into new hands. No one doubts the honesty of the Doctor's intentions—no one will suggest that there can be any two opinions as to that. I myself am a believer in self-government for the people, provided it does not fall too heavily on the ratepayers. But that would be the case here; and that is why I will see Dr. Stockmann damned—I beg your pardon—before I go with him in the matter. You can pay too dearly for a thing sometimes; that is my opinion.

(*Loud applause on all sides.*)

HOVSTAD. I, too, feel called upon to explain my position. Dr. Stockmann's agitation appeared to be gaining a certain amount of sympathy at first, so I supported it as impartially as I could. But presently we had reason to suspect that we had allowed ourselves to be misled by misrepresentation of the state of affairs—

DR. STOCKMANN. Misrepresentation—!

HOVSTAD. Well, let us say a not entirely trustworthy representation. The Mayor's statement has proved that. I hope no one here has any doubt as to my liberal principles; the attitude of the *People's Messenger* towards important political questions is well known to every one. But the advice of experienced and thoughtful men has convinced me that in purely local matters a newspaper ought to proceed with a certain caution.

ASLAKSEN. I entirely agree with the speaker.

HOVSTAD. And, in the matter before us, it is now an undoubted fact that Dr. Stockmann has public opinion against him. Now, what is an editor's first and most obvious duty, gentlemen? Is it not to work in harmony with his readers? Has he not received a sort of tacit mandate to work persistently and assiduously for the welfare of those whose opinions he represents? Or is it possible I am mistaken in that?

VOICES (*from the crowd*).   No, no! You are quite right!

HOVSTAD.   It has cost me a severe struggle to break with a man in whose house I have been lately a frequent guest—a man who till today has been able to pride himself on the undivided goodwill of his fellow-citizens—a man whose only, or at all events whose essential, failing is that he is swayed by his heart rather than his head.

A FEW SCATTERED VOICES.   That is true! Bravo, Stockmann!

HOVSTAD.   But my duty to the community obliged me to break with him. And there is another consideration that impels me to oppose him, and, as far as possible, to arrest him on the perilous course he has adopted; that is, consideration for his family—

DR. STOCKMANN.   Please stick to the water-supply and drainage!

HOVSTAD.   —consideration, I repeat, for his wife and his children for whom he has made no provision.

MORTEN.   Is that us, mother?

MRS. STOCKMANN.   Hush!

ASLAKSEN.   I will now put the Mayor's proposition to the vote.

DR. STOCKMANN.   There is no necessity! Tonight I have no intention of dealing with all that filth down at the Baths. No; I have something quite different to say to you.

PETER STOCKMANN (*aside*).   What is coming now?

A DRUNKEN MAN (*by the entrance door*).   I am a ratepayer! And therefore I have a right to speak too! And my entire—firm—inconceivable opinion is—

A NUMBER OF VOICES.   Be quiet, at the back there!

OTHERS.   He is drunk! Turn him out! (*They turn him out.*)

DR. STOCKMANN.   Am I allowed to speak?

ASLAKSEN (*ringing his bell*).   Dr. Stockmann will address the meeting.

DR. STOCKMANN.   I should like to have seen anyone, a few days ago, dare to attempt to silence me as has been done tonight! I would have defended my sacred rights as a man, like a lion! But now it is all one to me; I have something of even weightier importance to say to you.

(*The crowd presses nearer to him,* MORTEN KIIL *conspicuous among them.*)

DR. STOCKMANN (*continuing*).   I have thought and pondered a great deal, these last few days—pondered over such a variety of things that in the end my head seemed too full to hold them—

PETER STOCKMANN (*with a cough*).   Ahem!

DR. STOCKMANN.   —but I got them clear in my mind at last, and then I saw the whole situation lucidly. And that is why I am standing here tonight. I have a great revelation to make to you, my fellow-citizens! I will impart to you a discovery of a far wider scope than the trifling matter that our water-supply is poisoned and our medicinal Baths are standing on pestiferous soil.

A NUMBER OF VOICES (*shouting*). Don't talk about the Baths! We won't hear you! None of that!

DR. STOCKMANN. I have already told you that what I want to speak about is the great discovery I have made lately—the discovery that all the sources of our *moral* life are poisoned and that the whole fabric of our civic community is founded on the pestiferous soil of falsehood.

VOICES OF DISCONCERTED CITIZENS. What is that he says?

PETER STOCKMANN. Such an insinuation—!

ASLAKSEN (*with his hand on his bell*). I call upon the speaker to moderate his language.

DR. STOCKMANN. I have always loved my native town as a man only can love the home of his youthful days. I was not old when I went away from here; and exile, longing and memories cast, as it were, an additional halo over both the town and its inhabitants. (*Some clapping and applause.*) And there I stayed, for many years, in a horrible hole far away up north. When I came into contact with some of the people that lived scattered about among the rocks, I often thought it would have been more service to the poor half-starved creatures if a veterinary doctor has been sent up there, instead of a man like me. (*Murmurs among the crowd.*)

BILLING (*laying down his pen*). I'm damned if I have ever heard—!

HOVSTAD. It is an insult to a respectable population!

DR. STOCKMANN. Wait a bit! I do not think anyone will charge me with having forgotten my native town up there. I was like one of the eiderducks brooding on its nest, and what I hatched was—the plans for these Baths. (*Applause and protests.*) And then when fate at last decreed for me the great happiness of coming home again—I assure you, gentlemen, I thought I had nothing more in the world to wish for. Or rather, there was one thing I wished for—eagerly, untiringly, ardently—and that was to be able to be of service to my native town and the good of the community.

PETER STOCKMANN (*looking at the ceiling*). You chose a strange way of doing it—ahem!

DR. STOCKMANN. And so, with my eyes blinded to the real facts, I reveled in happiness. But yesterday morning—no, to be precise, it was yesterday afternoon—the eyes of my mind were opened wide, and the first thing I realized was the colossal stupidity of the authorities—.

(*Uproar, shouts and laughter. MRS. STOCKMANN coughs persistently.*)

PETER STOCKMANN. Mr. Chairman!

ASLAKSEN (*ringing his bell*). By virtue of my authority—!

DR. STOCKMANN. It is a petty thing to catch me up on a word, Mr. Aslaksen. What I mean is only that I got scent of the unbelievable piggishness our leading men had been responsible for down at the Baths. I can't stand leading men at any price!—I have had enough of such people in my time. They are like billy-goats in a young plantation; they do mischief everywhere. They stand in a free man's way, whichever way he turns, and what I should like best would be to see them exterminated like any other vermin—. (*Uproar.*)

PETER STOCKMANN. Mr. Chairman, can we allow such expressions to pass?

ASLAKSEN (*with his hand on his bell*). Doctor—!

DR. STOCKMANN. I cannot understand how it is that I have only now acquired a clear conception of what these gentry are, when I had almost daily before my eyes in this town such an excellent specimen of them—my brother Peter—slow-witted and hide-bound in prejudice—.

(*Laughter, uproar and hisses.* MRS. STOCKMANN *sits coughing assiduously.* ASLAKSEN *rings his bell violently.*)

THE DRUNKEN MAN (*who has got in again*). Is it me he is talking about? My name's Petersen, all right—but devil take me if I—

ANGRY VOICES. Turn out that drunken man! Turn him out. (*He is turned out again.*)

PETER STOCKMANN. Who was that person?

1ST CITIZEN. I don't know who he is, Mr. Mayor.

2ND CITIZEN. He doesn't belong here.

3RD CITIZEN. I expect he is a navvy from over at (*the rest is inaudible*).

ASLAKSEN. He had obviously had too much beer.—Proceed, Doctor; but please strive to be moderate in your language.

DR. STOCKMANN. Very well, gentlemen, I will say no more about our leading men. And if anyone imagines, from what I have just said, that my object is to attack these people this evening, he is wrong—absolutely wide of the mark. For I cherish the comforting conviction that these parasites—all these venerable relics of a dying school of thought—are most admirably paving the way for their own extinction; they need no doctor's help to hasten their end. Nor is it folk of that kind who constitute the most pressing danger to the community. It is not they who are most instrumental in poisoning the sources of our moral life and infecting the ground on which we stand. It is not they who are the most dangerous enemies of truth and freedom amongst us.

SHOUTS (*from all sides*). Who then? Who is it? Name! Name!

DR. STOCKMANN. You may depend upon it I shall name them! That is precisely the great discovery I made yesterday. (*Raises his voice.*) The most dangerous enemy of truth and freedom amongst us is the compact majority—yes, the damned compact Liberal majority—that is it! Now you know!

(*Tremendous uproar. Most of the crowd are shouting, stamping and hissing. Some of the older men among them exchange stolen glances and seem to be enjoying themselves.* MRS. STOCKMANN *gets up, looking anxious.* EJLIF *and* MORTEN *advance threateningly upon some schoolboys who are playing pranks.* ASLAKSEN *rings his bell and begs for silence.* HOVSTAD *and* BILLING *both talk at once, but are inaudible. At last quiet is restored.*)

ASLAKSEN. As chairman, I call upon the speaker to withdraw the ill-considered expressions he has just used.

DR. STOCKMANN. Never, Mr. Aslaksen! It is the majority in our community that denies me my freedom and seeks to prevent my speaking the truth.

HOVSTAD. The majority always has right on its side.

BILLING. And truth, by God!

DR. STOCKMANN. The majority *never* has right on its side. Never, I say! That is one of these social lies against which an independent, intelligent man must wage war. Who is it that constitute the majority of the population in a country? Is it the clever folk or the stupid? I don't imagine you will dispute the fact that at present the stupid people are in an absolutely overwhelming majority all the world over. But, good Lord!—you can never pretend that it is right that the stupid folk should govern the clever ones! (*Uproar and cries.*) Oh, yes—you can shout me down, I know! but you cannot answer me. The majority has *might* on its side—unfortunately; but *right* it has *not*. I am in the right—I and a few other scattered individuals. The minority is always in the right. (*Renewed uproar.*)

HOVSTAD. Aha!—so Dr. Stockmann has become an aristocrat since the day before yesterday!

DR. STOCKMANN. I have already said that I don't intend to waste a word on the puny, narrow-chested, short-winded crew whom we are leaving astern. Pulsating life no longer concerns itself with them. I am thinking of the few, the scattered few amongst us, who have absorbed new and vigorous truths. Such men stand, as it were, at the outposts, so far ahead that the compact majority has not yet been able to come up with them; and there they are fighting for truths that are too newly-born into the world of consciousness to have any considerable number of people on their side as yet.

HOVSTAD. So the Doctor is a revolutionary now!

DR. STOCKMANN. Good heavens—of course I am, Mr. Hovstad! I propose to raise a revolution against the lie that the majority has the monopoly of the truth. What sort of truths are they that the majority usually supports? They are truths that are of such advanced age that they are beginning to break up. And if a truth is as old as that, it is also in a fair way to become a lie, gentlemen. (*Laughter and mocking cries.*) Yes, believe me or not, as you like; but truths are by no means as long-lived as Methuselah—as some folk imagine. A normally constituted truth lives, let us say, as a rule seventeen or eighteen, or at most twenty years; seldom longer. But truths as aged as that are always worn frightfully thin, and nevertheless it is only then that the majority recognizes them and recommends them to the community as wholesome moral nourishment. There is no great nutritive value in that sort of fare, I can assure you; and, as a doctor, I ought to know. These "majority truths" are like last year's cured meat—like rancid, tainted ham; and they are the origin of the moral scurvy that is rampant in our communities.

ASLAKSEN. It appears to me that the speaker is wandering a long way from his subject.

PETER STOCKMANN. I quite agree with the Chairman.

DR. STOCKMANN. Have you gone clean out of your senses, Peter? I am sticking as closely to my subject as I can; for my subject is precisely this, that it is the masses, the majority—this infernal compact majority—that poisons the sources of our moral life and infects the ground we stand on.

HOVSTAD. And all this because the great, broad-minded majority of the people is prudent enough to show deference only to well-ascertained and well-approved truths.

DR. STOCKMANN. Ah, my good Mr. Hovstad, don't talk nonsense about well-ascertained truths! The truths of which the masses now approve are the very truths that the fighters at the outposts held to in the days of our grandfathers. We fighters at the outposts nowadays no longer approve of them; and I do not believe there is any other well-ascertained truth except this, that no community can live a healthy life if it is nourished only on such old marrowless truths.

HOVSTAD. But instead of standing there using vague generalities, it would be interesting if you would tell us what these old marrowless truths are, that we are nourished on. (*Applause from many quarters.*)

DR. STOCKMANN. Oh, I could give you a whole string of such abominations; but to begin with I will confine myself to one well-approved truth, which at bottom is a foul lie, but upon which nevertheless Mr. Hovstad and the *People's Messenger* and all the *Messenger's* supporters are nourished.

HOVSTAD. And that is—?

DR. STOCKMANN. That is, the doctrine you have inherited from your forefathers and proclaim thoughtlessly far and wide—the doctrine that the public, the crowd, the masses are the essential part of the population—that they constitute the People—that the common folk, the ignorant and incomplete element in the community, have the same right to pronounce judgment and to approve, to direct and to govern, as the isolated, intellectually superior personalities in it.

BILLING. Well, damn me if ever I—

HOVSTAD (*at the same time, shouting out*). Fellow-citizens, take good note of that!

A NUMBER OF VOICES (*angrily*). Oho!—we are not the People! Only the superior folks are to govern, are they!

A WORKMAN. Turn the fellow out, for talking such rubbish!

ANOTHER. Out with him!

ANOTHER (*calling out*). Blow your horn, Evensen! (*A horn is blown loudly, amidst hisses and an angry uproar.*)

DR. STOCKMANN (*when the noise has somewhat abated*). Be reasonable! Can't you stand hearing the voice of truth for once? I don't in the least expect you to agree with me all at once; but I must say I did expect Mr. Hovstad to admit I was right, when he had recovered his composure a little. He claims to be a freethinker—

VOICES (*in murmurs of astonishment*). Freethinker, did he say? Is Hovstad a freethinker?

HOVSTAD (*shouting*). Prove it, Dr. Stockmann! When have I said so in print?

DR. STOCKMANN (*reflecting*).   No, confound it, you are right!—you have never had the courage to. Well, I won't put you in a hole, Mr. Hovstad. Let us say it is I that am the freethinker, then. I am going to prove to you, scientifically, that the *People's Messenger* leads you by the nose in a shameful manner when it tells you that you—that the common people, the crowd, the masses are the real essence of the People. That is only a newspaper lie, I tell you! The common people are nothing more than the raw material of which a People is made. (*Groans, laughter and uproar.*) Well, isn't that the case? Isn't there an enormous difference between a well-bred and an ill-bred strain of animals? Take, for instance, a common barn-door hen. What sort of eating do you get from a shriveled-up old scrag of a fowl like that? Not much, do you! And what sort of eggs does it lay? A fairly good crow or a raven can lay pretty nearly as good an egg. But take a well-bred Spanish or Japanese hen, or a good pheasant or a turkey—then you will see the difference. Or take the case of dogs, with whom we humans are on such intimate terms. Think first of an ordinary common cur—I mean one of the horrible, coarse-haired, low-bred curs that do nothing but run about the streets and befoul the walls of the houses. Compare one of these curs with a poodle whose sires for many generations have been bred in a gentleman's house, where they have had the best of food and had the opportunity of hearing soft voices and music. Do you not think that the poodle's brain is developed to quite a different degree from that of the cur? Of course it is. It is puppies of well-bred poodles like that, that showmen train to do incredibly clever tricks—things that a common cur could never learn to do even if it stood on its head. (*Uproar and mocking cries.*)

A CITIZEN (*calls out*).   Are you going to make out we are dogs, now?

ANOTHER CITIZEN.   We are not animals, Doctor!

DR. STOCKMANN.   Yes, but bless my soul, we *are*, my friend! It is true we are the finest animals anyone could wish for; but, even amongst us, exceptionally fine animals are rare. There is a tremendous difference between poodle-men and cur-men. And the amusing part of it is, that Mr. Hovstad quite agrees with me as long as it is a question of four-footed animals—

HOVSTAD.   Yes, it is true enough as far as they are concerned.

DR. STOCKMANN.   Very well. But as soon as I extend the principle and apply it to two-legged animals, Mr. Hovstad stops short. He no longer dares to think independently, or to pursue his ideas to their logical conclusions; so he turns the whole theory upside down and proclaims in the *People's Messenger* that it is the barn-door hens and street curs that are the finest specimens in the menagerie. But that is always the way, as long as a man retains the traces of common origin and has not worked his way up to intellectual distinction.

HOVSTAD.   I lay no claim to any sort of distinction. I am the son of humble countryfolk, and I am proud that the stock I come from is rooted deep among the common people he insults.

VOICES.   Bravo, Hovstad! Bravo! Bravo!

DR. STOCKMANN.   The kind of common people I mean are not only to be found low down in the social scale; they crawl and swarm all around us—even in the highest social positions. You have only to look at your own fine, distinguished Mayor! My brother Peter is every bit as plebeian as anyone that walks in two shoes— (*Laughter and hisses.*)

PETER STOCKMANN. I protest against personal allusions of this kind.

DR. STOCKMANN (*imperturbably*). —and that, not because he is, like myself, descended from some old rascal of a pirate from Pomerania or thereabouts—because that is who we are descended from—

PETER STOCKMANN. An absurd legend. I deny it!

DR. STOCKMANN. —but because he thinks what his superiors think and holds the same opinions as they. People who do that are, intellectually speaking, common people; and that is why my magnificent brother Peter is in reality so very far from any distinction—and consequently also so far from being liberal-minded.

PETER STOCKMANN. Mr. Chairman—!

HOVSTAD. So it is only the distinguished men that are liberal-minded in this country? We are learning something quite new! (*Laughter.*)

DR. STOCKMANN. Yes, that is part of my new discovery too. And another part of it is that broad-mindedness is almost precisely the same thing as morality. That is why I maintain that it is absolutely inexcusable in the *People's Messenger* to proclaim, day in and day out, the false doctrine that it is the masses, the crowd, the compact majority that have the monopoly of broad-mindedness and morality—and that vice and corruption and every kind of intellectual depravity are the result of culture, just as all the filth that is draining into our Baths is the result of the tanneries up at Mölledal! (*Uproar and interruptions. DR. STOCKMANN is undisturbed, and goes on, carried away by his ardor, with a smile.*) And yet this same *People's Messenger* can go on preaching that the masses ought to be elevated to higher conditions of life! But, bless my soul, if the *Messenger's* teaching is to be depended upon, this very raising up the masses would mean nothing more or less than setting them straightway upon the paths of depravity! Happily the theory that culture demoralizes is only an old falsehood that our forefathers believed in and we have inherited. No, it is ignorance, poverty, ugly conditions of life that do the devil's work! In a house which does not get aired and swept every day—my wife Katherine maintains that the floor ought to be scrubbed as well, but that is a debatable question—in such a house, let me tell you, people will lose within two or three years the power of thinking or acting in a moral manner. Lack of oxygen weakens the conscience. And there must be a plentiful lack of oxygen in very many houses in this town, I should think, judging from the fact that the whole compact majority can be unconscientious enough to wish to build the town's prosperity on a quagmire of falsehood and deceit.

ASLAKSEN. We cannot allow such a grave accusation to be flung at a citizen community.

A CITIZEN. I move that the Chairman direct the speaker to sit down.

VOICES (*angrily*). Hear, hear! Quite right! Make him sit down!

DR. STOCKMANN (*losing his self-control*). Then I will go and shout the truth at every street corner! I will write it in other towns' newspapers! The whole country shall know what is going on here!

HOVSTAD. It almost seems as if Dr. Stockmann's intention were to ruin the town.

DR. STOCKMANN. Yes, my native town is so dear to me that I would rather ruin it than see it flourishing upon a lie.

ASLAKSEN. This is really serious.

(*Uproar and cat-calls.* MRS. STOCKMANN *coughs, but to no purpose; her husband does not listen to her any longer.*)

HOVSTAD (*shouting above the din*). A man must be a public enemy to wish to ruin a whole community!

DR. STOCKMANN (*with growing fervor*). What does the destruction of a community matter, if it lives on lies! It ought to be razed to the ground, I tell you! All who live by lies ought to be exterminated like vermin! You will end by infecting the whole country; you will bring about such a state of things that the whole country will deserve to be ruined. And if things come to that pass, I shall say from the bottom of my heart: Let the whole country perish, let all these people be exterminated!

VOICES (*from the crowd*). That is talking like an out-and-out enemy of the people!

BILLING. There sounded the voice of the people, by all that's holy!

THE WHOLE CROWD (*shouting*). Yes, yes! He is an enemy of the people! He hates his country! He hates his own people!

ASLAKSEN. Both as a citizen and as an individual, I am profoundly disturbed by what we have had to listen to. Dr. Stockmann has shown himself in a light I should never have dreamed of. I am unhappily obliged to subscribe to the opinion which I have just heard my estimable fellow-citizens utter; and I propose that we should give expression to that opinion in a resolution. I propose a resolution as follows: "This meeting declares that it considers Dr. Thomas Stockmann, Medical Officer of the Baths, to be an enemy of the people."

(*A storm of cheers and applause. A number of men surround the* DOCTOR *and hiss him.* MRS. STOCKMANN *and* PETRA *have got up from their seats.* MORTEN *and* EJLIF *are fighting the other schoolboys for hissing; some of their elders separate them.*)

DR. STOCKMAN (*to the men who are hissing him*). Oh, you fools! I tell you that—

ASLAKSEN (*ringing his bell*). We cannot hear you now, Doctor. A formal vote is about to be taken; but, out of regard for personal feelings, it shall be by ballot and not verbal. Have you any clean paper, Mr. Billing?

BILLING. I have both blue and white here.

ASLAKSEN (*going to him*). That will do nicely; we shall get on more quickly that way. Cut it up into small strips—yes, that's it. (*To the meeting.*) Blue means no; white means yes. I will come round myself and collect votes.

(PETER STOCKMANN *leaves the hall.* ASLAKSEN *and one or two others go round the room with the slips of paper in their hats.*)

1ST CITIZEN (*to* HOVSTAD).   I say, what has come to the Doctor? What are we to think of it?

HOVSTAD.   Oh, you know how headstrong he is.

2ND CITIZEN (*to* BILLING).   Billing, you go to their house—have you ever noticed if the fellow drinks?

BILLING.   Well I'm hanged if I know what to say. There are always spirits on the table when you go.

3RD CITIZEN.   I rather think he goes quite off his head sometimes.

1ST CITIZEN.   I wonder if there is any madness in his family?

BILLING.   I shouldn't wonder if there were.

4TH CITIZEN.   No, it is nothing more than sheer malice; he wants to get even with somebody for something or other.

BILLING.   Well certainly he suggested a rise in his salary on one occasion lately, and did not get it.

THE CITIZENS (*together*).   Ah!—then it is easy to understand how it is!

THE DRUNKEN MAN (*who has got amongst the audience again*).   I want a blue one, I do! And I want a white one too!

VOICES.   It's that drunken chap again! Turn him out!

MORTEN KIIL (*going up to* DR. STOCKMANN).   Well, Stockmann, do you see what these monkey tricks of yours lead to?

DR. STOCKMANN.   I have done my duty.

MORTEN KIIL.   What was that you said about the tanneries at Mölledal?

DR. STOCKMANN.   You heard well enough. I said they were the source of all the filth.

MORTEN KIIL.   My tannery too?

DR. STOCKMANN.   Unfortunately your tannery is by far the worst.

MORTEN KIIL.   Are you going to put that in the papers?

DR. STOCKMANN.   I shall conceal nothing.

MORTEN KIIL.   That may cost you dear, Stockmann. (*Goes out.*)

A STOUT MAN (*going up to* CAPTAIN HORSTER, *without taking any notice of the ladies*).   Well, Captain, so you lend your house to enemies of the people?

HORSTER.   I imagine I can do what I like with my own possessions, Mr. Vik.

THE STOUT MAN.   Then you can have no objection to my doing the same with mine.

HORSTER.   What do you mean, sir?

THE STOUT MAN.   You shall hear from me in the morning. (*Turns his back on him and moves off.*)

PETRA.   Was that not your owner, Captain Horster?

HORSTER.   Yes, that was Mr. Vik the ship-owner.

ASLAKSEN (*with the voting-papers in his hands, gets up on to the platform and rings his bell*). Gentlemen, allow me to announce the result. By the votes of every one here except one person—

A YOUNG MAN. That is the drunk chap!

ASLAKSEN. By the votes of every one here except a tipsy man, this meeting of citizens declares Dr. Thomas Stockmann to be an enemy of the people. (*Shouts and applause.*) Three cheers for our ancient and honorable citizen community! (*Renewed applause.*) Three cheers for our able and energetic Mayor, who has so loyally suppressed the promptings of family feeling! (*Cheers.*) The meeting is dissolved. (*Gets down.*)

BILLING. Three cheers for the Chairman!

THE WHOLE CROWD. Three cheers for Aslaksen! Hurrah!

DR. STOCKMANN. My hat and coat, Petra! Captain, have you room on your ship for passengers to the New World?

HORSTER. For you and yours we will make room, Doctor.

DR. STOCKMANN (*as PETRA helps him into his coat*). Good. Come, Katherine! Come boys!

MRS. STOCKMANN (*in an undertone*). Thomas, dear, let us go out by the back way.

DR. STOCKMANN. No back ways for me, Katherine. (*Raising his voice.*) You will hear more of this enemy of the people, before he shakes the dust off his shoes upon you! I am not so forgiving as a certain Person; I do not say: "I forgive you, for ye know not what ye do."

ASLAKSEN (*shouting*). That is a blasphemous comparison, Dr. Stockmann!

BILLING. It is, by God! It's dreadful for an earnest man to listen to.

A COARSE VOICE. Threatens us now, does he!

OTHER VOICES (*excitedly*). Let's go and break his windows! Duck him in the fjord!

ANOTHER VOICE. Blow your horn, Evensen! Pip, pip!

(*Horn-blowing, hisses and wild cries. DR. STOCKMANN goes out through the hall with his family, HORSTER elbowing a way for them.*)

THE WHOLE CROWD (*howling after them as they go*). Enemy of the People! Enemy of the People!

BILLING (*as he puts his papers together*). Well, I'm damned if I go and drink toddy with the Stockmanns tonight!

(*The crowd press towards the exit. The uproar continues outside; shouts of* "Enemy of the People!" *are heard from without.*)

ACT V

SCENE. DR. STOCKMANN'S *study. Bookcases, and cabinets containing specimens, line the walls. At the back is a door leading to the hall; in the foreground on the left, a door leading to the sitting-room. In the right-hand wall are two windows, of which all the panes are broken. The DOCTOR'S desk, littered with books and papers, stands in the middle of the room, which is in disorder. It is morning.* DR. STOCKMANN *in dressing-gown, slippers and a smoking-cap, is bending down and raking with an umbrella under one of the cabinets. After a little while he rakes out a stone.*

DR. STOCKMANN (*calling through the open sitting-room door*). Katherine, I have found another one.

MRS. STOCKMANN (*from the sitting-room*). Oh, you will find a lot more yet, I expect.

DR. STOCKMANN (*adding the stone to a heap of others on the table*). I shall treasure these stones as relics. Ejlif and Morten shall look at them every day, and when they are grown up they shall inherit them as heirlooms. (*Rakes about under a bookcase.*) Hasn't—what the deuce is her name—the girl, you know—hasn't she been to fetch the glazier yet?

MRS. STOCKMANN (*coming in*). Yes, but he said he didn't know if he would be able to come today.

DR. STOCKMANN. You will see he won't dare to come.

MRS. STOCKMANN. Well, that is just what Randine thought—that he didn't dare to, on account of the neighbors. (*Calls into the sitting-room.*) What is it you want, Randine? Give it to me. (*Goes in, and comes out again directly.*) Here is a letter for you, Thomas.

DR. STOCKMANN. Let me see it. (*Opens and reads it.*) Ah!—of course.

MRS. STOCKMANN. Who is it from?

DR. STOCKMANN. From the landlord. Notice to quit.

MRS. STOCKMANN. Is it possible? Such a nice man—

DR. STOCKMANN (*looking at the letter*). Does not dare do otherwise, he says. Doesn't like doing it, but dares not do otherwise—on account of his fellow-citizens—out of regard for public opinion. Is in a dependent position—dares not offend certain influential men—

MRS. STOCKMANN. There, you see, Thomas!

DR. STOCKMANN. Yes, yes, I see well enough; the whole lot of them in the town are cowards; not a man among them dares do anything for fear of the others. (*Throws the letter on to the table.*) But it doesn't matter to us, Katherine. We are going to sail away to the New World, and—

MRS. STOCKMANN. But, Thomas, are you sure we are well advised to take this step?

DR. STOCKMANN. Are you suggesting that I should stay here, where they have pilloried me as an enemy of the people—branded me—broken my windows! And just look here, Katherine—they have torn a great rent in my black trousers too!

MRS. STOCKMANN. Oh, dear—and they are the best pair you have got!

DR. STOCKMANN. You should never wear your best trousers when you go out to fight for freedom and truth. It is not that I care so much about the trousers, you know; you can always sew them up again for me. But that the common herd should dare to make this attack on me, as if they were my equals—that is what I cannot, for the life of me, swallow!

MRS. STOCKMANN. There is no doubt they have behaved very ill to you, Thomas; but is that sufficient reason for our leaving our native country for good and all?

DR. STOCKMANN. If we went to another town, do you suppose we should not find the common people just as insolent as they are here? Depend upon it, there is not much to choose between them. Oh, well, let the curs snap—that is not the worst part of it. The worst is that, from one end of this country to the other, every man is the slave of his Party. Although, as far as that goes, I daresay it is not much better in the free West either; the compact majority, and liberal public opinion, and all that infernal old bag of tricks are probably rampant there too. But there things are done on a larger scale, you see. They may kill you, but they won't put you to death by slow torture. They don't squeeze a free man's soul in a vice, as they do here. And, if need be, one can live in solitude. (*Walks up and down.*) If only I knew where there was a virgin forest or a small South Sea island for sale, cheap—

MRS. STOCKMANN. But think of the boys, Thomas.

DR. STOCKMANN (*standing still*). What a strange woman you are, Katherine! Would you prefer to have the boys grow up in a society like this? You saw for yourself last night that half the population are out of their minds; and if the other half have not lost their senses, it is because they are mere brutes, with no sense to lose.

MRS. STOCKMANN. But, Thomas dear, the imprudent things you said had something to do with it, you know.

DR. STOCKMANN. Well, isn't what I said perfectly true? Don't they turn every idea topsy-turvy? Don't they make a regular hotch-potch of right and wrong? Don't they say that the things I know are true, are lies? The craziest part of it all is the fact of these "liberals," men of full age, going about in crowds imagining that they are the broad-minded party! Did you ever hear anything like it, Katherine!

MRS. STOCKMANN. Yes, yes, it's mad enough of them, certainly; but— (PETRA *comes in from the sitting-room*). Back from school already?

PETRA. Yes. I have been given notice of dismissal.

MRS. STOCKMANN. Dismissal?

DR. STOCKMANN. You too?

PETRA. Mrs. Busk gave me my notice; so I thought it was best to go at once.

DR. STOCKMANN. You were perfectly right, too!

MRS. STOCKMANN. Who would have thought Mrs. Busk was a woman like that!

PETRA. Mrs. Busk isn't a bit like that, mother; I saw quite plainly how it hurt her to do it. But she didn't dare do otherwise, she said; and so I got my notice.

DR. STOCKMANN (*laughing and rubbing his hands*). She didn't dare do otherwise, either! It's delicious!

MRS. STOCKMANN. Well, after the dreadful scenes last night—

PETRA. It was not only that. Just listen to this, father!

DR. STOCKMANN. Well?

PETRA. Mrs. Busk showed me no less than three letters she received this morning—

DR. STOCKMANN. Anonymous, I suppose?

PETRA. Yes.

DR. STOCKMANN. Yes, because they didn't dare to risk signing their names, Katherine!

PETRA. And two of them were to the effect that a man who has been our guest here, was declaring last night at the Club that my views on various subjects are extremely emancipated—

DR. STOCKMANN. You did not deny that, I hope?

PETRA. No, you know I wouldn't. Mrs. Busk's own views are tolerably emancipated, when we are alone together; but now that this report about me is being spread, she dare not keep me on any longer.

MRS. STOCKMANN. And some one who had been a guest of ours! That shows you the return you get for your hospitality, Thomas!

DR. STOCKMANN. We won't live in such a disgusting hole any longer. Pack up as quickly as you can, Katherine; the sooner we can get away, the better.

MRS. STOCKMANN. Be quiet—I think I hear some one in the hall. See who it is, Petra.

PETRA (opening the door). Oh, it's you, Captain Horster! Do come in.

HORSTER (coming in). Good morning. I thought I would just come in and see how you were.

DR. STOCKMANN (shaking his hand). Thanks—that is really kind of you.

MRS. STOCKMANN. And thank you, too, for helping us through the crowd, Captain Horster.

PETRA. How did you manage to get home again?

HORSTER. Oh, somehow or other. I am fairly strong, and there is more sound than fury about these folk.

DR. STOCKMANN. Yes, isn't their swinish cowardice astonishing? Look here, I will show you something! There are all the stones they have thrown through my windows. Just look at them! I'm hanged if there are more than two decently large bits of hardstone in the whole heap; the rest are nothing but gravel—wretched little things. And yet they stood out there bawling and swearing that they would do me some violence; but as for doing anything— you don't see much of that in this town.

HORSTER. Just as well for you this time, Doctor!

DR. STOCKMANN. True enough. But it makes one angry all the same; because if some day it should be a question of a national fight in real earnest, you will see that public opinion will be in favor of taking to one's heels, and the compact majority will turn tail like a flock of sheep, Captain Horster. That is what is so mournful to think of; it gives me so much concern, that—. No, devil take it, it is ridiculous to care about it! They have called me an enemy of the people, so an enemy of the people let me be!

MRS. STOCKMANN. You will never be that, Thomas.

DR. STOCKMANN. Don't swear to that, Katherine. To be called an ugly name may have the same effect as a pin-scratch in the lung. And that hateful name—I can't get quit of it. It is sticking here in the pit of my stomach, eating into me like a corrosive acid. And no magnesia will remove it.

PETRA. Bah—you should only laugh at them, father.

HORSTER. They will change their minds some day, Doctor.

MRS. STOCKMANN. Yes, Thomas, as sure as you are standing here.

DR. STOCKMANN. Perhaps, when it is too late. Much good may it do them! They may wallow in their filth then and rue the day when they drove a patriot into exile. When do you sail, Captain Horster?

HORSTER. Hm!—that was just what I had come to speak about—

DR. STOCKMANN. Why, has anything gone wrong with the ship?

HORSTER. No; but what has happened is that I am not to sail in it.

PETRA. Do you mean that you have been dismissed from your command?

HORSTER (smiling). Yes, that's just it.

PETRA. You too.

MRS. STOCKMANN. There, you see, Thomas!

DR. STOCKMANN. And that for the truth's sake! Oh, if I had thought such a thing possible—

HORSTER. You mustn't take it to heart; I shall be sure to find a job with some ship-owner or other, elsewhere.

DR. STOCKMANN. And that is this man Vik—a wealthy man, independent of every one and everything—! Shame on him!

HORSTER. He is quite an excellent fellow otherwise; he told me himself he would willingly have kept me on, if only he had dared—

DR. STOCKMANN. But he didn't dare? No, of course not.

HORSTER. It is not such an easy matter, he said, for a party man—

DR. STOCKMANN. The worthy man spoke the truth. A party is like a sausage machine; it mashes up all sorts of heads together into the same mincemeat—fatheads and blockheads, all in one mash!

MRS. STOCKMANN. Come, come, Thomas dear!

PETRA (to HORSTER). If only you had not come home with us, things might not have come to this pass.

HORSTER. I do not regret it.

PETRA (holding out her hand to him). Thank you for that!

HORSTER (to DR. STOCKMANN). And so what I came to say was that if you are determined to go away, I have thought of another plan—

DR. STOCKMANN. That's splendid!—if only we can get away at once.

MRS. STOCKMANN. Hush—wasn't that some one knocking?

PETRA. That is uncle, surely.

DR. STOCKMANN. Aha! (Calls out.) Come in!

MRS. STOCKMANN. Dear Thomas, promise me definitely—

(PETER STOCKMANN comes in from the hall.)

PETER STOCKMANN. Oh, you are engaged. In that case, I will—

DR. STOCKMANN. No, no, come in.

PETER STOCKMANN. But I wanted to speak to you alone.

MRS. STOCKMANN. We will go into the sitting-room in the meanwhile.

HORSTER. And I will look in again later.

DR. STOCKMANN. No, go in there with them, Captain Horster; I want to hear more about—

HORSTER. Very well, I will wait, then. (*He follows* MRS. STOCKMANN *and* PETRA *into the sitting-room.*)

DR. STOCKMANN. I daresay you find it rather drafty here today. Put your hat on.

PETER STOCKMANN. Thank you, if I may. (*Does so.*) I think I caught cold last night; I stood and shivered—

DR. STOCKMANN. Really? I found it warm enough.

PETER STOCKMANN. I regret that it was not in my power to prevent those excesses last night.

DR. STOCKMANN. Have you anything particular to say to me besides that?

PETER STOCKMANN (*taking a big letter from his pocket*). I have this document for you, from the Baths Committee.

DR. STOCKMANN. My dismissal?

PETER STOCKMANN. Yes, dating from today. (*Lays the letter on the table.*) It gives us pain to do it; but, to speak frankly, we dared not do otherwise on account of public opinion.

DR. STOCKMANN (*smiling*). Dared not? I seem to have heard that word before, today.

PETER STOCKMANN. I must beg you to understand your position clearly. For the future you must not count on any practice whatever in the town.

DR. STOCKMANN. Devil take the practice! But why are you so sure of that?

PETER STOCKMANN. The Householders' Association is circulating a list from house to house. All right-minded citizens are being called upon to give up employing you; and I can assure you that not a single head of a family will risk refusing his signature. They simply dare not.

DR. STOCKMANN. No, no; I don't doubt it. But what then?

PETER STOCKMANN. If I might advise you, it would be best to leave the place for a little while—

DR. STOCKMANN. Yes, the propriety of leaving the place *has* occurred to me.

PETER STOCKMANN. Good. And then, when you have had six months to think things over, if, after mature consideration, you can persuade yourself to write a few words of regret, acknowledging your error—

DR. STOCKMANN. I might have my appointment restored to me, do you mean?

PETER STOCKMANN. Perhaps. It is not at all impossible.

DR. STOCKMANN. But what about public opinion, then? Surely you would not dare to do it on account of public feeling.

PETER STOCKMANN. Public opinion is an extremely mutable thing. And, to be quite candid with you, it is a matter of great importance to us to have some admission of that sort from you in writing.

DR. STOCKMANN. Oh, that's what you are after, is it! I will just trouble you to remember what I said to you lately about foxy tricks of that sort!

PETER STOCKMANN. Your position was quite different then. At that time you had reason to suppose you had the whole town at your back—

DR. STOCKMANN. Yes, and now I feel I have the whole town *on* my back—(*flaring up*) I would not do it if I had the devil and his dam on my back—! Never—never, I tell you!

PETER STOCKMANN. A man with a family has no right to behave as you do. You have no right to do it, Thomas.

DR. STOCKMANN. I have no right! There is only one single thing in the world a free man has no right to do. Do you know what that is?

PETER STOCKMANN. No.

DR. STOCKMANN. Of course you don't, but I will tell you. A free man has no right to soil himself with filth; he has no right to behave in a way that would justify his spitting in his own face.

PETER STOCKMANN. This sort of thing sounds extremely plausible, of course; and if there were no other explanation for your obstinacy—. But as it happens that there is—

DR. STOCKMANN. What do you mean?

PETER STOCKMANN. You understand very well what I mean. But, as your brother and as a man of discretion, I advise you not to build too much upon expectations and prospects that may so very easily fail you.

DR. STOCKMANN. What in the world is all this about?

PETER STOCKMANN. Do you really ask me to believe that you are ignorant of the terms of Mr. Kiil's will?

DR. STOCKMANN. I know that the small amount he possesses is to go to an institution for indigent old work-people. How does that concern me?

PETER STOCKMANN. In the first place, it is by no means a small amount that is in question. Mr. Kiil is a fairly wealthy man.

DR. STOCKMANN. I had no notion of that!

PETER STOCKMANN. Hm!—hadn't you really? Then I suppose you had no notion, either, that a considerable portion of his wealth will come to your children, you and your wife having a life-rent of the capital. Has he never told you so?

DR. STOCKMANN. Never, on my honor! Quite the reverse; he has consistently done nothing but fume at being so unconscionably heavily taxed. But are you perfectly certain of this, Peter?

PETER STOCKMANN. I have it from an absolutely reliable source.

DR. STOCKMANN. Then, thank God, Katherine is provided for—and the children too! I must tell her this at once— (*Calls out.*) Katherine, Katherine!

PETER STOCKMANN (*restraining him*). Hush, don't say a word yet!

MRS. STOCKMANN (*opening the door*). What is the matter?

DR. STOCKMANN. Oh, nothing, nothing; you can go back. (*She shuts the door.* DR. STOCKMANN *walks up and down in his excitement.*) Provided for!—Just think of it, we are all provided for! And for life! What a blessed feeling it is to know one is provided for!

PETER STOCKMANN. Yes, but that is just exactly what you are not. Mr. Kiil can alter his will any day he likes.

DR. STOCKMANN. But he won't do that, my dear Peter. The "Badger" is much too delighted at my attack on you and your wise friends.

PETER STOCKMANN (*starts and looks intently at him*). Ah, that throws a light on various things.

DR. STOCKMANN. What things?

PETER STOCKMANN. I see that the whole thing was a combined maneuver on your part and his. These violent, reckless attacks that you have made against the leading men of the town, under the pretence that it was in the name of truth—

DR. STOCKMANN. What about them?

PETER STOCKMANN. I see that they were nothing else than the stipulated price for that vindictive old man's will.

DR. STOCKMANN (*almost speechless*). Peter—you are the most disgusting plebeian I have ever met in all my life.

PETER STOCKMANN. All is over between us. Your dismissal is irrevocable—we have a weapon against you now. (*Goes out.*)

DR. STOCKMANN. For shame! For shame! (*Calls out.*) Katherine, you must have the floor scrubbed after him! Let— what's her name—devil take it, the girl who has always got soot on her nose—

MRS. STOCKMANN (*in the sitting-room*). Hush, Thomas, be quiet!

PETRA (*coming to the door*). Father, grandfather is here, asking if he may speak to you alone.

DR. STOCKMANN. Certainly he may. (*Going to the door*). Come in, Mr. Kiil. (MORTEN KIIL *comes in.* DR. STOCKMANN *shuts the door after him.*) What can I do for you? Won't you sit down?

MORTEN KIIL. I won't sit. (*Looks around.*) You look very comfortable here today, Thomas.

DR. STOCKMANN. Yes, don't we!

MORTEN KIIL. Very comfortable—plenty of fresh air. I should think you have got enough today of that oxygen you were talking about yesterday. Your conscience must be in splendid order today, I should think.

DR. STOCKMANN. It is.

MORTEN KIIL. So I should think. (*Taps his chest.*) Do you know what I have got here?

DR. STOCKMANN. A good conscience, too, I hope.

MORTEN KIIL. Bah!—No, it is something better than that. (*He takes a thick pocket-book from his breast-pocket, opens it, and displays a packet of papers.*)

DR. STOCKMANN (*looking at him in astonishment*). Shares in the Baths?

MORTEN KIIL. They were not difficult to get today.

DR. STOCKMANN. And you have been buying—?

MORTEN KIIL. As many as I could pay for.

DR. STOCKMANN. But, my dear Mr. Kiil—consider the state of the Baths' affairs!

MORTEN KIIL. If you behave like a reasonable man, you can soon set the Baths on their feet again.

DR. STOCKMANN. Well, you can see for yourself that I have done all I can, but—. They are all mad in this town!

MORTEN KIIL. You said yesterday that the worst of this pollution came from my tannery. If that is true, then my grandfather and my father before me, and I myself, for many years past, have been poisoning the town like three destroying angels. Do you think I am going to sit quiet under that reproach?

DR. STOCKMANN. Unfortunately, I am afraid you will have to.

MORTEN KIIL. No, thank you. I am jealous of my name and reputation. They call me "the Badger," I am told. A badger is a kind of pig, I believe; but I am not going to give them the right to call me that. I mean to live and die a clean man.

DR. STOCKMANN. And how are you going to set about it?

MORTEN KIIL. You shall cleanse me, Thomas.

DR. STOCKMANN. I!

MORTEN KIIL. Do you know what money I have bought these shares with? No, of course you can't know—but I will tell you. It is the money that Katherine and Petra and the boys will have when I am gone. Because I have been able to save a little bit after all, you know.

DR. STOCKMANN (*flaring up*). And you have gone and taken Katherine's money for *this!*

MORTEN KIIL. Yes, the whole of the money is invested in the Baths now. And now I just want to see whether you are quite stark, staring mad, Thomas! If you still make out that these animals and other nasty things of that sort come from my tannery, it will be exactly as if you were to flay broad strips of skin from Katherine's body, and Petra's, and the boys'; and no decent man would do that—unless he were mad.

DR. STOCKMANN (*walking up and down*). Yes, but I *am* mad; I *am* mad!

MORTEN KIIL. You cannot be so absurdly mad as all that, when it is a question of your wife and children.

DR. STOCKMANN (*standing still in front of him*). Why couldn't you consult me about it, before you went and bought all that trash?

MORTEN KIIL. What is done cannot be undone.

DR. STOCKMANN (*walks about uneasily*). If only I were not so certain about it—! But I am absolutely convinced that I am right.

MORTEN KIIL (*weighing the pocket-book in his hand*). If you stick to your mad idea, this won't be worth much, you know. (*Puts the pocket-book in his pocket.*)

DR. STOCKMANN. But, hang it all! it might be possible for science to discover some prophylactic, I should think—or some antidote of some kind—

MORTEN KIIL. To kill these animals, do you mean?

DR. STOCKMANN. Yes, or to make them innocuous.

MORTEN KIIL. Couldn't you try some rat's-bane?

DR. STOCKMANN. Don't talk nonsense! They all say it is only imagination, you know. Well, let it go at that! Let them have their own way about it! Haven't the ignorant, narrow-minded curs reviled me as an enemy of the people?—and haven't they been ready to tear the clothes off my back too?

MORTEN KIIL. And broken all your windows to pieces!

DR. STOCKMANN. And then there is my duty to my family. I must talk it over with Katherine; she is great on those things.

MORTEN KIIL. That is right; be guided by a reasonable woman's advice.

DR. STOCKMANN (advancing towards him). To think you could do such a preposterous thing! Risking Katherine's money in this way, and putting me in such a horribly painful dilemma! When I look at you, I think I see the devil himself—.

MORTEN KIIL. Then I had better go. But I must have an answer from you before two o'clock—yes or no. If it is no, the shares go to a charity, and that this very day.

DR. STOCKMANN. And what does Katherine get?

MORTEN KIIL. Not a halfpenny. (The door leading to the hall opens, and HOVSTAD and ASLAKSEN make their appearance.) Look at those two!

DR. STOCKMANN (staring at them). What the devil!—have you actually the face to come into my house?

HOVSTAD. Certainly.

ASLAKSEN. We have something to say to you, you see.

MORTEN KIIL (in a whisper). Yes or no—before two o'clock.

ASLAKSEN (glancing at HOVSTAD). Aha!

(MORTEN KIIL goes out.)

DR. STOCKMANN. Well, what do you want with me? Be brief.

HOVSTAD. I can quite understand that you are annoyed with us for our attitude at the meeting yesterday—

DR. STOCKMANN. Attitude, do you call it? Yes, it was a charming attitude! I call it weak, womanish—damnably shameful!

HOVSTAD. Call it what you like, we could not do otherwise.

DR. STOCKMANN. You dared not do otherwise—isn't that it?

HOVSTAD. Well, if you like to put it that way.

ASLAKSEN. But why did you not let us have word of it beforehand?—just a hint to Mr. Hovstad or to me?

DR. STOCKMANN. A hint? Of what?

ASLAKSEN. Of what was behind it all.

DR. STOCKMANN. I don't understand you in the least.

ASLAKSEN (with a confidential nod). Oh, yes, you do, Dr. Stockmann.

HOVSTAD. It is no good making a mystery of it any longer.

DR. STOCKMANN (looking first at one of them and then at the other). What the devil do you both mean?

ASLAKSEN. May I ask if your father-in-law is not going round the town buying up all the shares in the Baths?

DR. STOCKMANN. Yes, he has been buying Baths' shares today; but—

ASLAKSEN. It would have been more prudent to get some one else to do it—some one less nearly related to you.

HOVSTAD. And you should not have let your name appear in the affair. There was no need for anyone to know that the attack on the Baths came from you. You ought to have consulted me, Dr. Stockmann.

DR. STOCKMANN (*looks in front of him; then a light seems to dawn on him and he says in amazement*). Are such things conceivable? Are such things possible?

ASLAKSEN (*with a smile*). Evidently they are. But it is better to use a little *finesse*, you know.

HOVSTAD. And it is much better to have several persons in a thing of that sort; because the responsibility of each individual is lessened, when there are others with him.

DR. STOCKMANN (*composedly*). Come to the point, gentlemen. What do you want?

ASLAKSEN. Perhaps Mr. Hovstad had better—

HOVSTAD. No, you tell him, Aslaksen.

ASLAKSEN. Well, the fact is that, now we know the bearings of the whole affair, we think we might venture to put the *People's Messenger* at your disposal.

DR. STOCKMANN. Do you dare do that now? What about public opinion? Are you not afraid of a storm breaking upon our heads?

HOVSTAD. We will try to weather it.

ASLAKSEN. And you must be ready to go off quickly on a new tack, Doctor. As soon as your invective has done its work—

DR. STOCKMANN. Do you mean, as soon as my father-in-law and I have got hold of the shares at a low figure?

HOVSTAD. Your reasons for wishing to get the control of the Baths are mainly scientific, I take it.

DR. STOCKMANN. Of course; it was for scientific reasons that I persuaded the old "Badger" to stand in with me in the matter. So we will tinker at the conduit-pipes a little, and dig up a little bit of the shore, and it shan't cost the town a sixpence. That will be all right—eh?

HOVSTAD. I think so—if you have the *People's Messenger* behind you.

ASLAKSEN. The Press is a power in a free community, Doctor.

DR. STOCKMANN. Quite so. And so is public opinion. And you, Mr. Aslaksen—I suppose you will be answerable for the Householders' Association?

ASLAKSEN. Yes, and for the Temperance Society. You may rely on that.

DR. STOCKMANN. But, gentlemen—I really am ashamed to ask the question—but, what return do you—?

HOVSTAD. We should prefer to help you without any return whatever, believe me. But the *People's Messenger* is in rather a shaky condition; it doesn't go really well; and I should be very unwilling to suspend the paper now, when there is so much work to do here in the political way.

DR. STOCKMANN. Quite so; that would be a great trial to such a friend of the people as you are. (*Flares up.*) But I am an enemy of the people, remember! (*Walks about the room.*) Where have I put my stick? Where the devil is my stick?

HOVSTAD. What's that?

ASLAKSEN. Surely you never mean—?

DR. STOCKMANN (*standing still*). And suppose I don't give you a single penny of all I get out of it? Money is not very easy to get out of us rich folk, please to remember!

HOVSTAD. And you please to remember that this affair of the shares can be represented in two ways!

DR. STOCKMANN. Yes, and you are just the man to do it. If I don't come to the rescue of the *People's Messenger* you will certainly take an evil view of the affair; you will hunt me down, I can well imagine—pursue me—try to throttle me as a dog does a hare.

HOVSTAD. It is a natural law; every animal must fight for its own livelihood.

ASLAKSEN. And get its food where it can, you know.

DR. STOCKMANN (*walking about the room*). Then you go and look for yours in the gutter; because I am going to show you which is the strongest animal of us three! (*Finds an umbrella and brandishes it above his head.*) Ah, now—!

HOVSTAD. You are surely not going to use violence!

ASLAKSEN. Take care what you are doing with that umbrella.

DR. STOCKMANN. Out of the window with you, Mr. Hovstad!

HOVSTAD (*edging to the door*). Are you quite mad!

DR. STOCKMANN. Out of the window, Mr. Aslaksen! Jump, I tell you! You will have to do it, sooner or later.

ASLAKSEN (*running round the writing-table*). Moderation, Doctor—I am a delicate man—I can stand so little— (*Calls out.*) Help, help!

(MRS. STOCKMANN, PETRA *and* HORSTER *come in from the sitting-room.*)

MRS. STOCKMANN. Good gracious, Thomas! What is happening?

DR. STOCKMANN (*brandishing the umbrella*). Jump out, I tell you! Out into the gutter!

HOVSTAD. An assault on an unoffending man! I call you to witness, Captain Horster. (*Hurries out through the hall.*)

ASLAKSEN (*irresolutely*). If only I knew the way about here—. (*Steals out through the sitting-room.*)

MRS. STOCKMANN (*holding her husband back*). Control yourself, Thomas!

DR. STOCKMANN (*throwing down the umbrella*). Upon my soul, they have escaped after all.

MRS. STOCKMANN. What did they want you to do?

DR. STOCKMANN. I will tell you later on; I have something else to think about now. (*Goes to the table and writes something on a calling-card.*) Look there, Katherine; what is written there?

MRS. STOCKMANN. Three big No's; what does that mean?

DR. STOCKMANN. I will tell you that too, later on. (*Holds out the card to* PETRA.) There, Petra; tell sooty-face to run over to the "Badger's" with that, as quickly as she can. Hurry up!

(PETRA *takes the card and goes out to the hall.*)

DR. STOCKMANN. Well, I think I have had a visit from every one of the devil's messengers today! But now I am going to sharpen my pen till they can feel its point; I shall dip it in venom and gall; I shall hurl my inkpot at their heads!

MRS. STOCKMANN. Yes, but we are going away, you know, Thomas.

(PETRA *comes back.*)

DR. STOCKMANN. Well?

PETRA. She has gone with it.

DR. STOCKMANN. Good.—Going away, did you say? No, I'll be hanged if we are going away! We are going to stay where we are, Katherine!

PETRA. Stay here?

MRS. STOCKMANN. Here, in the town?

DR. STOCKMANN. Yes, here. This is the field of battle—this is where the fight will be. This is where I shall triumph! As soon as I have had my trousers sewn up I shall go out and look for another house. We must have a roof over our heads for the winter.

HORSTER. That you shall have in my house.

DR. STOCKMANN. Can I?

HORSTER. Yes, quite well. I have plenty of room, and I am almost never at home.

MRS. STOCKMANN. How good of you, Captain Horster!

PETRA. Thank you!

DR. STOCKMANN (*grasping his hand*). Thank you, thank you! That is one trouble over! Now I can set to work in earnest at once. There is an endless amount of things to look through here, Katherine! Luckily I shall have all my time at my disposal; because I have been dismissed from the Baths, you know.

MRS. STOCKMANN (*with a sigh*). Oh, yes, I expected that.

DR. STOCKMANN. And they want to take my practice away from me, too. Let them! I have got the poor people to fall back upon, anyway—those that don't pay anything; and, after all, they need me most, too. But, by Jove, they will have to listen to me; I shall preach to them in season and out of season, as it says somewhere.

MRS. STOCKMANN. But, dear Thomas, I should have thought events had showed you what use it is to preach.

DR. STOCKMANN. You are really ridiculous, Katherine. Do you want me to let myself be beaten off the field by public opinion and the compact majority and all that devilry? No, thank you! And what I want to do is so simple and clear and straightforward. I only want to drum into the heads of these curs the fact that the liberals are the most insidious enemies of freedom—that party programs strangle every young and vigorous truth—that considerations of expediency turn morality and justice upside down—and that they will end by making life here unbearable. Don't you think, Captain Horster, that I ought to be able to make people understand that?

HORSTER. Very likely; I don't know much about such things myself.

DR. STOCKMANN. Well, look here—I will explain! It is the party leaders that must be exterminated. A party leader is like a wolf, you see—like a voracious wolf. He requires a certain number of smaller victims to prey upon every year, if he is to live. Just look at Hovstad and Aslaksen! How many smaller victims have they not put an end to—or at any rate maimed and mangled until they are fit for nothing except to be householders or subscribers to the *People's Messenger!* (*Sits down on the edge of the table.*) Come here, Katherine—look how beautifully the sun shines today! And this lovely spring air I am drinking in!

MRS. STOCKMANN. Yes, if only we could live on sunshine and spring air, Thomas.

DR. STOCKMANN. Oh, you will have to pinch and save a bit—then we shall get along. That gives me very little concern. What is much worse is that I know of no one who is liberal-minded and high-minded enough to venture to take up my work after me.

PETRA. Don't think about that, father; you have plenty of time before you.—Hullo, here are the boys already!

(EJLIF *and* MORTEN *come in from the sitting-room.*)

MRS. STOCKMANN. Have you got a holiday?

MORTEN. No; but we were fighting with the other boys between lessons—

EJLIF. That isn't true; it was the other boys were fighting with us.

MORTEN. Well, and then Mr. Rörlund said we had better stay at home for a day or two.

DR. STOCKMANN (*snapping his fingers and getting up from the table*). I have it! I have it, by Jove! You shall never set foot in the school again!

THE BOYS. No more school!

MRS. STOCKMANN. But, Thomas—

DR. STOCKMANN. Never, I say. I will educate you myself; that is to say, you shan't learn a blessed thing—

MORTEN. Hooray!

DR. STOCKMANN. —but I will make liberal-minded and high-minded men of you. You must help me with that, Petra.

PETRA. Yes, father, you may be sure I will.

DR. STOCKMANN. And my school shall be in the room where they insulted me and called me an enemy of the people. But we are too few as we are; I must have at least twelve boys to begin with.

MRS. STOCKMANN. You will certainly never get them in this town.

DR. STOCKMANN. We shall. (*To the boys.*) Don't you know any street urchins—regular ragamuffins—?

MORTEN. Yes, father, I know lots!

DR. STOCKMANN. That's capital! Bring me some specimens of them. I am going to experiment with curs, just for once; there may be some exceptional heads amongst them.

MORTEN. And what are we going to do, when you have made liberal-minded and high-minded men of us?

DR. STOCKMANN. Then you shall drive all the wolves out of the country, my boys!

(EJLIF *looks rather doubtful about it;* MORTEN *jumps about crying* "Hurrah!")

MRS. STOCKMANN. Let us hope it won't be the wolves that will drive you out of the country, Thomas.

DR. STOCKMANN. Are you out of your mind, Katherine? Drive me out! Now—when I am the strongest man in the town!

MRS. STOCKMANN. The strongest—now!

DR. STOCKMANN. Yes, and I will go so far as to say that now I am the strongest man in the whole world.

MORTEN. I say!

DR. STOCKMANN (*lowering his voice*). Hush! You mustn't say anything about it yet; but I have made a great discovery.

MRS. STOCKMANN. Another one?

DR. STOCKMANN. Yes. (*Gathers them round him, and says confidentially*) It is this, let me tell you—that the strongest man in the world is he who stands most alone.

MRS. STOCKMANN (*smiling and shaking her head*). Oh, Thomas, Thomas!

PETRA (*encouragingly, as she grasps her father's hands*). Father!

QUESTIONS

1. Dr. Stockmann and his brother are early established as character foils. In what different ways are they contrasted? How does each help to bring out the character of the other?

2. Is Dr. Stockmann's desire to publish the truth about the Baths purely altruistic? Why is he so happy to learn, in Act I, that the Baths are polluted? Is he in any respect like his brother?

3. How astute is Dr. Stockmann in foreseeing the consequences of his discovery? in judging the characters of other people? How would you characterize him as a political man? Trace the stages of his political education. What does he learn in Act II? in Act III? in Act IV? in Act V? To what degree does he change during the course of the play?

4. Morten Kiil says, in Act II, "It is better never to trust anybody; you may find you have been made a fool of before you know where you are." In what respects are Kiil and Dr. Stockmann character foils? Who is shrewder? Who is more admirable?

5. Which of the following adjectives can be accurately applied to Dr. Stockmann's impromptu speech in Act IV: *courageous, intemperate, arrogant, foolish, large-minded, wise?* Support your answer.

6. What purpose is served by the characterization of Dr. Stockmann, in Act I, as a man who likes good things—roast beef, hot toddy, good company?

7. How are we to take Dr. Stockmann's discovery at the end of the play: "the strongest man in the world is he who stands most alone." In terms of the play, is it true?

8. It has been said that "Politics makes strange bedfellows." In this play, what are the respective alignments and relationships between Dr. Stockmann, Peter Stockmann, Hovstad and Billing, and Aslaksen (a) after Dr. Stockmann announces his discovery, (b) at the end of the play? What interests are represented by each of these men?

9. In Act III, Dr. Stockmann asks his wife, "Because a man has a wife and children is he not allowed to tell the truth?" The question poses a real moral dilemma. What answer does Peter Stockmann make to it? What answer to it is implied by the play? Is Dr. Stockmann the only character put under pressure by threats against another member of his family?

10. Evaluate, in terms of the action of the play, Dr. Stockmann's assertion that "The most dangerous enemy to truth and freedom . . . is the compact majority." What other assertions does he make about majorities? Is this play antidemocratic in theme? Why or why not?

11. Hovstad expresses at least three attitudes toward the function of a newspaper: (a) that "truth should be the first consideration" (Act II), (b) that a newspaper should carry the public "on the path that leads to liberty and progress" (Act III), and (c) that "an editor's first and most obvious duty" is "to work in harmony with his readers" (Act IV). In what order does Hovstad honor these three principles? In what order does Ibsen, as judged by the action of the play, rank them?

12. Of Dr. Stockmann's principal antagonists—Peter Stockmann, Hovstad, Billing, Aslaksen, Morton Kiil—which is the most powerful? Which is the second most powerful? Which is most corrupt? What are the chief characterizing qualities of each?

13. Where do Mrs. Stockmann's loyalties lie? Does she change during the course of the play? Is she more, or less, far-sighted than her husband?

14. Mark each of the following statements made by characters in the play as true or false. If the statement is false, explain whether its falseness springs from misjudgment, lack of self-knowledge, or an out-and-out lie: (a) DR. STOCK-MANN: "I shall smite them to the ground—I shall crush them—I shall break down all their defenses before the eyes of the honest public!" (Act III). (b) HOVSTAD: "I am not a weathercock—and never will be" (Act III). (c) BILLING (of his application for the post of secretary to the Bench): "You must clearly understand I am doing it only to annoy the big-wigs. . . . My object is precisely *not* to get it" (Act III). (d) HOVSTAD (of the idea that an editor is often obliged to bow to the wishes of the public in unimportant matters): "No; as a matter of fact, that is Billing's idea and not mine. . . .

And it is Billing who is so anxious to have that story in the paper" (Act III). (e) ASLAKSEN: "I have nothing to do with editing the paper, Mr. Mayor" (Act III). (f) PETER STOCKMANN: "The proprietors of the Baths are not in a position to incur any further expense" (Act III). (g) DR. STOCKMANN (in reply to his wife's injunction "Be sure not to lose your temper, Thomas"): "Oh, I know how to control myself" (Act IV). (h) PETER STOCKMANN: "In my communication to the *People's Messenger* I have put the essential facts before the public in such a way that every fair-minded citizen can easily form his own opinion" (Act IV).

15. What advantage does Ibsen's realistic technique have for his particular subject matter? How does he make clear that a character is speaking differently from what he thinks or feels? Or does he always? What would the effect on the tone of the play have been, had Ibsen used asides?

Tennessee Williams
THE GLASS MENAGERIE

CHARACTERS

AMANDA WINGFIELD, *the mother, a little woman of great but confused vitality clinging frantically to another time and place. Her characterization must be carefully created, not copied from type. She is not paranoiac, but her life is paranoia. There is much to admire in Amanda, and as much to love and pity as there is to laugh at. Certainly she has endurance and a kind of heroism, and though her foolishness makes her unwittingly cruel at times, there is tenderness in her slight person.*

LAURA WINGFIELD, *her daughter. Amanda, having failed to establish contact with reality, continues to live vitally in her illusions, but Laura's situation is even graver. A childhood illness has left her crippled, one leg slightly shorter than the other, and held in a brace. This defect need not be more than suggested on the stage. Stemming from this, Laura's separation increases till she is like a piece of her own glass collection, too exquisitely fragile to move from the shelf.*

TOM WINGFIELD, *her son and the narrator of the play. A poet with a job in a warehouse. His nature is not remorseless, but to escape from a trap he has to act without pity.*

JIM O'CONNOR, *the gentleman caller, a nice, ordinary, young man.*

SCENE. *An alley in St Louis.*

Part I. *Preparation for a gentleman caller.*
Part II. *The gentleman calls.*

Time: *Now and the Past.*

THE GLASS MENAGERIE First performed in 1944; developed from a short story, "Portrait of a Girl in Glass" (published later in *One Arm and Other Stories*). Tennessee Williams (1911–1983) was born Thomas Lanier Williams in Mississippi, the son of a traveling salesman. In 1918 the family moved to St. Louis when the father was made a sales manager of International Shoe Company. Here, while the family lived in a succession of rented apartments, Tom published his first story at 16, graduated from high school, attended the University of Missouri for three years, worked at a menial job in the shoe company (1932-1935), had a nervous breakdown, finished his education at Washington University and the University of Iowa. Adopting "Tennessee" as his writing name, he then embarked on a life which took him to Chicago, New Orleans, Los Angeles, Mexico City, New York, Key West, and other cities while he wrote steadily, supporting himself at odd jobs. *The Glass Menagerie*, his first commercial success, rescued him from penury. The play reflects his St. Louis years, although his real father (given to alcoholic excess) never disappeared from home; his sister (two years his elder) did have dates, was not crippled, and did not have a glass collection; a younger brother (eight years Tom's junior) does not appear; and "Miss Edwina" (Williams's mother and his guest at the first performance) has written, "The only resemblance I have to Amanda is that we both like jonquils."

SCENE I

The Wingfield apartment is in the rear of the building, one of those vast hive-like conglomerations of cellular living-units that flower as warty growths in overcrowded urban centers of lower middle-class population and are symptomatic of the impulse of this largest and fundamentally enslaved section of American society to avoid fluidity and differentiation and to exist and function as one interfused mass of automatism.

The apartment faces an alley and is entered by a fire-escape, a structure whose name is a touch of accidental poetic truth, for all of these huge buildings are always burning with the slow and implacable fires of human desperation. The fire-escape is part of what we see—that is, the landing of it and steps descending from it.

The scene is memory and is therefore nonrealistic. Memory takes a lot of poetic license. It omits some details; others are exaggerated, according to the emotional value of the articles it touches, for memory is seated predominantly in the heart. The interior is therefore rather dim and poetic.

At the rise of the curtain, the audience is faced with the dark, grim rear wall of the Wingfield tenement. This building is flanked on both sides by dark, narrow alleys which run into murky canyons of tangled clotheslines, garbage cans and the sinister latticework of neighboring fire-escapes. It is up and down these side alleys that exterior entrances and exits are made, during the play. At the end of TOM'S *opening commentary, the dark tenement wall slowly becomes transparent and reveals the interior of the ground floor Wingfield apartment.*

Nearest the audience is the living room, which also serves as a sleeping room for LAURA, *the sofa unfolding to make her bed. Just beyond, separated from the living room by a wide arch or second proscenium with transparent faded portieres (or second curtain), is the dining room. In an old-fashioned what-not in the living room are seen scores of transparent glass animals. A blown-up photograph of the father hangs on the wall of the living room to the left of the archway. It is the face of a very handsome young man in a doughboy's First World War cap. He is gallantly smiling, ineluctably smiling, as if to say, "I will be smiling forever."*

Also hanging on the wall, near the photograph, are a typewriter keyboard chart and a Gregg shorthand diagram. An upright typewriter on a small table stands beneath the charts.

The audience hears and sees the opening scene in the dining room through both the transparent fourth wall of the building and the transparent gauze portieres of the dining-room arch. It is during this revealing scene that the fourth wall slowly ascends, out of sight. This transparent exterior wall is not brought down again until the very end of the play, during TOM'S *final speech.*

The narrator is an undisguised convention of the play. He takes whatever license with dramatic convention as is convenient to his purposes.

TOM *enters, dressed as a merchant sailor, and strolls across the front of the stage to the fire-escape. There he stops and lights a cigarette. He addresses the audience.*

Tom. Yes, I have tricks in my pocket, I have things up my sleeve. But I am the opposite of a stage magician. He gives you illusion that has the appearance of truth. I give you truth in the pleasant disguise of illusion.

To begin with, I turn back time. I reverse it to that quaint period, the thirties, when the huge middle class of America was matriculating in a school for the blind. Their eyes had failed them, or they had failed their eyes, and so they were having their fingers pressed forcibly down on the fiery Braille alphabet of a dissolving economy.

In Spain there was revolution. Here there was only shouting and confusion. In Spain there was Guernica. Here there were disturbances of labor, sometimes pretty violent, in otherwise peaceful cities such as Chicago, Cleveland, Saint Louis . . . This is the social background of the play. (*Music.*)

The play is memory. Being a memory play, it is dimly lighted, it is sentimental, it is not realistic. In memory everything seems to happen to music. That explains the fiddle in the wings.

I am the narrator of the play, and also a character in it. The other characters are my mother, Amanda, my sister, Laura, and a gentleman caller who appears in the final scenes. He is the most realistic character in the play, being an emissary from a world of reality that we were somehow set apart from. But since I have a poet's weakness for symbols, I am using this character also as a symbol; he is the long delayed but always expected something that we live for.

There is a fifth character in the play who doesn't appear except in this larger-than-life-size photograph over the mantel. This is our father who left us a long time ago. He was a telephone man who fell in love with long distances; he gave up his job with the telephone company and skipped the light fantastic out of town . . .

The last we heard of him was a picture post-card from Mazatlan, on the Pacific coast of Mexico, containing a message of two words—"Hello— Good-bye!" and no address.

I think the rest of the play will explain itself . . .

(AMANDA'S *voice becomes audible through the portieres. He divides the portieres and enters the upstage area.* AMANDA *and* LAURA *are seated at a drop-leaf table. Eating is indicated by gestures without food or utensils.* AMANDA *faces the audience.* TOM *and* LAURA *are seated in profile. The interior has lit up softly and through the scrim we see* AMANDA *and* LAURA *seated at the table in the upstage area.*)

AMANDA (*calling*). Tom?

Tom. Yes, Mother.

AMANDA. We can't say grace until you come to the table!

Tom. Coming, Mother. (*He bows slightly and withdraws, reappearing a few moments later in his place at the table.*)

AMANDA (*to her son*). Honey, don't *push* with your *fingers*. If you have to push with something, the thing to push with is a crust of bread. And chew— chew! Animals have sections in their stomachs which enable them to digest food without mastication, but human beings are supposed to chew their food before they swallow it down. Eat food leisurely, son, and really enjoy it. A well-cooked meal has lots of delicate flavors that have to be held in the mouth for appreciation. So chew your food and give your salivary glands a chance to function!

(TOM *deliberately lays his imaginary fork down and pushes his chair back from the table.*)

TOM. I haven't enjoyed one bite of this dinner because of your constant directions on how to eat it. It's you that makes me rush through meals with your hawk-like attention to every bite I take. Sickening—spoils my appetite—all this discussion of—animals' secretion—salivary glands—mastication!

AMANDA (*lightly*). Temperament like a Metropolitan star! (*He rises and crosses downstage.*) You're not excused from the table.

TOM. I'm getting a cigarette.

AMANDA. You smoke too much.

(LAURA *rises.*)

LAURA. I'll bring in the blanc mange.

(*He remains standing with his cigarette by the portieres during the following.*)

AMANDA (*rising*). No, sister, no, sister—you be the lady this time and I'll be the darky.

LAURA. I'm already up.

AMANDA. Resume your seat, little sister—I want you to stay fresh and pretty—for gentlemen callers!

LAURA. I'm not expecting any gentlemen callers.

AMANDA (*crossing out to kitchenette. Airily*). Sometimes they come when they are least expected! Why, I remember one Sunday afternoon in Blue Mountain—(*enters kitchenette*).

TOM. I know what's coming!

LAURA. Yes. But let her tell it.

TOM. Again?

LAURA. She loves to tell it.

(AMANDA *returns with a bowl of dessert.*)

AMANDA. One Sunday afternoon in Blue Mountain—your mother received—*seventeen!*—gentlemen callers! Why, sometimes there weren't chairs enough to accommodate them all. We had to send the nigger over to bring in folding chairs from the parish house.

TOM (*remaining at portieres*). How did you entertain those gentlemen callers?

AMANDA. I understood the art of conversation!

TOM. I bet you could talk.

AMANDA. Girls in those days *knew* how to talk, I can tell you.

TOM. Yes?

AMANDA. They knew how to entertain their gentlemen callers. It wasn't enough for a girl to be possessed of a pretty face and a graceful figure— although I wasn't slighted in either respect. She also needed to have a nimble wit and a tongue to meet all occasions.

TOM. What did you talk about?

AMANDA. Things of importance going on in the world! Never anything coarse or common or vulgar. (*She addresses* TOM *as though he were seated in the vacant chair at the table though he remains by the portieres. He plays this scene as though he held the book.*) My callers were gentlemen—all! Among my callers were some of the most prominent young planters of the Mississippi Delta—planters and sons of planters!

(TOM *motions for music and a spot of light on* AMANDA. *Her eyes lift, her face glows, her voice becomes rich and elegiac.*)

There was young Champ Laughlin who later became vice-president of the Delta Planters Bank. Hadley Stevenson who was drowned in Moon Lake and left his widow one hundred and fifty thousand in Government bonds. There were the Cutrere brothers, Wesley and Bates. Bates was one of my bright particular beaux! He got in a quarrel with that wild Wainwright boy. They shot it out on the floor of Moon Lake Casino. Bates was shot through the stomach. Died in the ambulance on his way to Memphis. His widow was also well-provided for, came into eight or ten thousand acres, that's all. She married him on the rebound—never loved her—carried my picture on him the night he died! And there was that boy that every girl in the Delta had set her cap for! That beautiful, brilliant young Fitzhugh boy from Greene County!

TOM. What did he leave his widow?

AMANDA. He never married! Gracious, you talk as though all of my old admirers had turned up their toes to the daisies!

TOM. Isn't this the first you've mentioned that still survives?

AMANDA. That Fitzhugh boy went North and made a fortune—came to be known as the Wolf of Wall Street! He had the Midas touch, whatever he touched turned to gold! And I could have been Mrs. Duncan J. Fitzhugh, mind you! But—I picked your *father!*

LAURA (*rising*). Mother, let me clear the table.

AMANDA. No, dear, you go in front and study your typewriter chart. Or practice your shorthand a little. Stay fresh and pretty!—It's almost time for our gentlemen callers to start arriving. (*She flounces girlishly toward the kitch-enette.*) How many do you suppose we're going to entertain this afternoon?

(TOM *throws down the paper and jumps up with a groan.*)

LAURA (*alone in the dining room*). I don't believe we're going to receive any, Mother.

AMANDA (*reappearing, airily*). What? No one—not one? You must be joking! (LAURA *nervously echoes her laugh. She slips in a fugitive manner through the half-open portieres and draws them gently behind her. A shaft of very clear light is thrown on her face against the faded tapestry of the curtains. Music: "The Glass Menagerie"° under faintly. Lightly*) Not one gentleman caller? It can't be true! There must be a flood, there must have been a tornado!

LAURA. It isn't a flood, it's not a tornado, Mother. I'm just not popular like you were in Blue Mountain . . . (TOM *utters another groan.* LAURA *glances at him with a faint, apologetic smile. Her voice catching a little.*) Mother's afraid I'm going to be an old maid.

(*The scene dims out with "Glass Menagerie" music.*)

SCENE II

LAURA *is seated in the delicate ivory chair at the small claw-foot table. She wears a dress of soft violet material for a kimono—her hair tied back from her forehead with a ribbon. She is washing and polishing her collection of glass.* AMANDA *appears on the fire-escape steps. At the sound of her ascent,* LAURA *catches her breath, thrusts the bowl of ornaments away and seats herself stiffly before the diagram of the typewriter keyboard as though it held her spellbound. Something has happened to* AMANDA. *It is written in her face as she climbs to the landing: a look that is grim and hopeless and a little absurd. She has on one of those cheap or imitation velvety-looking cloth coats with imitation fur collar. Her hat is five or six years old, one of those dreadful cloche hats that were worn in the late twenties, and she is clasping an enormous black patent-leather pocketbook with nickel clasps and initials. This is her full-dress outfit, the one she usually wears to the D.A.R. Before entering she looks through the door. She purses her lips, opens her eyes very wide, rolls them upward and shakes her head. Then she slowly lets herself in the door. Seeing her mother's expression* LAURA *touches her lips with a nervous gesture.* LAURA. Hello, Mother, I was—

(*She makes a nervous gesture toward the chart on the wall.* AMANDA *leans against the shut door and stares at* LAURA *with a martyred look.*)

AMANDA. Deception? Deception? (*She slowly removes her hat and gloves, continuing the sweet suffering stare. She lets the hat and gloves fall on the floor—a bit of acting.*)

LAURA (*shakily*). How was the D.A.R. meeting? (AMANDA *slowly opens her purse and removes a dainty white handkerchief which she shakes out delicately and delicately touches to her lips and nostrils.*) Didn't you go to the D.A.R. meeting, Mother?

AMANDA (*faintly, almost inaudibly*). —No. —No. (*Then more forcibly.*) I did not have the strength—to go to the D.A.R. In fact, I did not have the

---

Music . . . : Music for the play, including "The Glass Menagerie" theme, was composed by Paul Bowles (1910-   ), American composer, novelist, and short story writer.

courage! I wanted to find a hole in the ground and hide myself in it forever! (*She crosses slowly to the wall and removes the diagram of the typewriter keyboard. She holds it in front of her for a second, staring at it sweetly and sorrowfully—then bites her lips and tears it in two pieces.*)

LAURA (*faintly*). Why did you do that, Mother? (AMANDA *repeats the same procedure with the chart of the Gregg Alphabet.*) Why are you—

AMANDA. Why? Why? How old are you, Laura?

LAURA. Mother, you know my age.

AMANDA. I thought that you were an adult; it seems that I was mistaken. (*She crosses slowly to the sofa and sinks down and stares at* LAURA.)

LAURA. Please don't stare at me, Mother.

(AMANDA *closes her eyes and lowers her head. There is a ten-second pause.*)

AMANDA. What are we going to do, what is going to become of us, what is the future?

(*There is another pause.*)

LAURA. Has something happened, Mother? (AMANDA *draws a long breath and takes out the handkerchief again. Dabbing process.*) Mother, has—something happened?

AMANDA. I'll be all right in a minute, I'm just bewildered— (*She hesitates*)—by life . . .

LAURA. Mother, I wish that you would tell me what's happened!

AMANDA. As you know, I was supposed to be inducted into my office at the D.A.R. this afternoon. But I stopped off at Rubicam's Business College to speak to your teachers about your having a cold and ask them what progress they thought you were making down there.

LAURA. Oh . . .

AMANDA. I went to the typing instructor and introduced myself as your mother. She didn't know who you were. Wingfield, she said. We don't have any such student enrolled at the school!

I assured her she did, that you had been going to classes since early in January.

"I wonder," she said, "if you could be talking about that terribly shy little girl who dropped out of school after only a few days' attendance?"

"No," I said, "Laura, my daughter, has been going to school every day for the past six weeks!"

"Excuse me," she said. She took the attendance book out and there was your name, unmistakably printed, and all the dates you were absent until they decided that you had dropped out of school.

I still said, "No, there must have been some mistake! There must have been some mix-up in the records!"

And she said, "No—I remember her perfectly now. Her hands shook so that she couldn't hit the right keys! The first time we gave a speed-test, she broke down completely—was sick at the stomach and almost had to be carried into the wash-room! After that morning she never showed up any more. We phoned the house but never got any answer"—While I was working at Famous and Barr, I suppose, demonstrating those—

Oh! (*She indicates a brassiere with her hands.*) I felt so weak I could barely keep on my feet! I had to sit down while they got me a glass of water! Fifty dollars' tuition, all of our plans—my hopes and ambitions for you—just gone up the spout, just gone up the spout like that. (LAURA *draws a long breath and gets awkwardly to her feet. She crosses to the victrola and winds it up.*)

What are you doing?

LAURA. Oh! (*She releases the handle and returns to her seat.*)

AMANDA. Laura, where have you been going when you've gone out pretending that you were going to business college?

LAURA. I've just been going out walking.

AMANDA. That's not true.

LAURA. It is. I just went walking.

AMANDA. Walking? Walking? In winter? Deliberately courting pneumonia in that light coat? Where did you walk to, Laura?

LAURA. All sorts of places—mostly in the park.

AMANDA. Even after you'd started catching that cold?

LAURA. It was the lesser of two evils, Mother. I couldn't go back up. I—threw up—on the floor!

AMANDA. From half past seven till after five every day you mean to tell me you walked around in the park, because you wanted to make me think that you were still going to Rubicam's Business College?

LAURA. It wasn't as bad as its sounds. I went inside places to get warmed up.

AMANDA. Inside where?

LAURA. I went in the art museum and the bird-houses at the Zoo. I visited the penguins every day! Sometimes I did without lunch and went to the movies. Lately I've been spending most of my afternoons in the Jewelbox, that big glass house where they raise the tropical flowers.

AMANDA. You did all this to deceive me, just for deception? (LAURA *looks down.*) Why?

LAURA. Mother, when you're disappointed, you get that awful suffering look on your face, like the picture of Jesus' mother in the museum!

AMANDA. Hush!

LAURA. I couldn't face it.

(*Pause. A whisper of strings.*)

AMANDA (*hopelessly fingering the huge pocketbook*). So what are we going to do the rest of our lives? Stay home and watch the parades go by? Amuse ourselves with the glass menagerie, darling? Eternally play those worn-out phonograph records your father left as a painful reminder of him? We won't have a business career—we've given that up because it gave us nervous indigestion! (*Laughs wearily.*) What is there left but dependency all our lives? I know so well what becomes of unmarried women who aren't prepared to occupy a position. I've seen such pitiful cases in the South—barely tolerated spinsters living upon the grudging patronage of sister's husband or brother's wife!—stuck away in some little mouse-trap of a room—encouraged by one in-law to visit another—little birdlike women without any nest—eating the crust of humility all their life!

Is that the future that we've mapped out for ourselves? I swear it's the only alternative I can think of! (*She pauses.*) It isn't a very pleasant alternative, is it? (*She pauses again.*) Of course—some girls *do* marry.

(LAURA *twists her hands nervously.*)

Haven't you ever liked some boy?

LAURA. Yes. I liked one once. (*Rises.*) I came across his picture a while ago.

AMANDA (*with some interest*). He gave you his picture?

LAURA. No, it's in the year-book.

AMANDA (*disappointed*). Oh—a high-school boy.

LAURA. Yes. His name was Jim. (LAURA *lifts the heavy annual from the claw-foot table.*) Here he is in *The Pirates of Penzance.*

AMANDA (*absently*). The what?

LAURA. The operetta the senior class put on. He had a wonderful voice and we sat across the aisle from each other Mondays, Wednesdays and Fridays in the Aud. Here he is with the silver cup for debating! See his grin?

AMANDA (*absently*). He must have had a jolly disposition.

LAURA. He used to call me—Blue Roses.

AMANDA. Why did he call you such a name as that?

LAURA. When I had that attack of pleurosis—he asked me what was the matter when I came back. I said pleurosis—he thought that I said Blue Roses! So that's what he always called me after that. Whenever he saw me, he'd holler, "Hello, Blue Roses!" I didn't care for the girl he went out with. Emily Meisenbach. Emily was the best-dressed girl at Soldan. She never struck me, though, as being sincere . . . It says in the Personal Section—they're engaged. That's—six years ago! They must be married by now.

AMANDA. Girls that aren't cut out for business careers usually wind up married to some nice man. (*Gets up with a spark of revival.*) Sister, that's what you'll do!

(LAURA *utters a startled, doubtful laugh. She reaches quickly for a piece of glass.*)

LAURA. But, Mother—

AMANDA. Yes? (*Crossing to photograph.*)

LAURA (*in a tone of frightened apology*). I'm—crippled!

AMANDA. Nonsense! Laura, I've told you never, never to use that word. Why, you're not crippled, you just have a little defect—hardly noticeable, even! When people have some slight disadvantage like that, they cultivate other things to make up for it—develop charm—and vivacity—and—*charm!* That's all you have to do! (*She turns again to the photograph.*) One thing your father had *plenty of*—was *charm!*

(TOM *motions to the fiddle in the wings. The scene fades out with music.*)

SCENE III

TOM *speaks from the fire-escape landing.*

TOM. After the fiasco at Rubicam's Business College, the idea of getting a gentleman caller for Laura began to play a more and more important part in Mother's calculations. It became an obsession. Like some archetype of the universal unconscious, the image of the gentleman caller haunted our small apartment . . .

An evening at home rarely passed without some allusion to this image, this specter, this hope . . . Even when he wasn't mentioned, his presence hung in Mother's preoccupied look and in my sister's frightened, apologetic manner—hung like a sentence passed upon the Wingfields!

Mother was a woman of action as well as words. She began to take logical steps in the planned direction. Late that winter and in the early spring— realizing that extra money would be needed to properly feather the nest and plume the bird—she conducted a vigorous campaign on the telephone, roping in subscribers to one of those magazines for matrons called *The Home-maker's Companion*, the type of journal that features the serialized sublimations of ladies of letters who think in terms of delicate cup-like breasts, slim, tapering waists, rich, creamy thighs, eyes like wood-smoke in autumn, fingers that soothe and caress like strains of music, bodies as powerful as Etruscan sculpture.

(AMANDA *enters with phone on long extension cord. She is spotted in the dim stage.*)

AMANDA. Ida Scott? This is Amanda Wingfield! We *missed* you at the D.A.R. last Monday! I said to myself: She's probably suffering with that sinus condition! How is that sinus condition?

Horrors! Heaven have mercy!—You're a Christian martyr, yes, that's what you are, a Christian martyr!

Well, I just now happened to notice that your subscription to the *Companion's* about to expire! Yes, it expires with the next issue, honey!—just when that wonderful new serial by Bessie Mae Hopper is getting off to such an exciting start. Oh, honey, it's something that you can't miss! You remember how *Gone with the Wind* took everybody by storm? You simply couldn't go out if you hadn't read it. All everybody *talked* was Scarlett O'Hara. Well, this is a book that critics already compare to *Gone with the Wind*. It's the

Gone with the Wind of the post-World War generation!—What?—Burning?—Oh, honey, don't let them burn, go take a look in the oven and I'll hold the wire! Heavens—I think she's hung up!

(*Before the stage is lighted, the violent voices of* TOM *and* AMANDA *are heard. They are quarreling behind the portieres. In front of them stands* LAURA *with clenched hands and panicky expression. A clear pool of light on her figure throughout this scene.*)

TOM. What in Christ's name am I—
AMANDA (*shrilly*). Don't you use that—
TOM. Supposed to do!
AMANDA. Expression! Not in my—
TOM. Ohhh!
AMANDA. Presence! Have you gone out of your senses?
TOM. I have, that's true, *driven* out!
AMANDA. What is the matter with you, you—big—big—IDIOT!
TOM. Look!—I've got *no thing,* no single thing—
AMANDA. Lower your voice!
TOM. In my life here that I can call my OWN! Everything is—
AMANDA. Stop that shouting!
TOM. Yesterday you confiscated my books! You had the nerve to—
AMANDA. I took that horrible novel back to the library—yes! That hideous book by that insane Mr. Lawrence.° (TOM *laughs wildly.*) I cannot control the output of diseased minds or people who cater to them—(TOM *laughs still more wildly.*) BUT I WON'T ALLOW SUCH FILTH BROUGHT INTO MY HOUSE! No, no, no, no, no!
TOM. House, house! Who pays rent on it, who makes a slave of himself to—
AMANDA (*fairly screeching*). Don't you DARE to—
TOM. No, no, *I* mustn't say things! *I've* got to just—
AMANDA. Let me tell you—
TOM. I don't want to hear any more!

(*He tears the portieres open. The upstage area is lit with a turgid smoky red glow.* AMANDA's *hair is in metal curlers and she wears a very old bathrobe, much too large for her slight figure, a relic of the faithless Mr. Wingfield. An upright typewriter and a wild disarray of manuscripts is on the drop-leaf table. The quarrel was probably precipitated by* AMANDA's *interruption of his creative labor. A chair lies overthrown on the floor. Their gesticulating shadows are cast on the ceiling by the fiery glow.*)

AMANDA. You *will* hear more, you—
TOM. No, I won't hear more, I'm going out!

Lawrence: D. H. Lawrence, author of "The Rocking-Horse Winner" (page 306), emphasized the force and importance of sexuality in human life in his novels.

AMANDA. You come right back in—

TOM. Out, out, out! Because I'm—

AMANDA. Come back here, Tom Wingfield! I'm not through talking to you!

TOM. Oh, go—

LAURA (*desperately*). —Tom!

AMANDA. You're going to listen, and no more insolence from you! I'm at the end of my patience!

(*He comes back toward her.*)

TOM. What do you think I'm at? Aren't I supposed to have any patience to reach the end of, Mother? I know, I know. It seems unimportant to you, what I'm *doing*—what I *want* to do—having a little *difference* between them! You don't think that—

AMANDA. I think you've been doing things that you're ashamed of. That's why you act like this. I don't believe that you go every night to the movies. Nobody goes to the movies night after night. Nobody in their right minds goes to the movies as often as you pretend to. People don't go to the movies at nearly midnight, and movies don't let out at two A.M. Come in stumbling. Muttering to yourself like a maniac! You get three hours' sleep and then go to work. Oh, I can picture the way you're doing down there. Moping, doping, because you're in no condition.

TOM (*wildly*). No, I'm in no condition!

AMANDA. What right have you got to jeopardize your job? Jeopardize the security of all of us? How do you think we'd manage if you were—

TOM. Listen! You think I'm crazy *about* the *warehouse?* (*He bends fiercely toward her slight figure.*) You think I'm in love with the Continental Shoemakers? You think I want to spend fifty-five *years* down there in that—*celotex interior!* with—*fluorescent—tubes!* Look! I'd rather somebody picked up a crowbar and battered out my brains—than go back mornings! I *go!* Every time you come in yelling that God damn *"Rise and Shine!" "Rise and Shine!"* I say to myself, "How *lucky dead* people are!" But I get up. I *go!* For sixty-five dollars a month I give up all that I dream of doing and being *ever!* And you say self—*self's* all I ever think of. Why, listen, if self is what I thought of, Mother, I'd be where he is—GONE! (*Pointing to father's picture.*) As far as the system of transportation reaches! (*He starts past her. She grabs his arm.*) Don't grab at me, Mother!

AMANDA. Where are you going?

TOM. I'm going to the *movies!*

AMANDA. I don't believe that lie!

TOM (*crouching toward her, overtowering her tiny figure. She backs away, gasping*). I'm going to opium dens! Yes, opium dens, dens of vice and criminals' hang-outs, Mother. I've joined the Hogan gang, I'm a hired assassin, I carry a tommy-gun in a violin case! I run a string of cat-houses in the Valley! They call me Killer, Killer Wingfield, I'm leading a double-life, a simple, honest warehouse worker by day, by night a dynamic *czar* of the *underworld,* *Mother.* I go to gambling casinos, I spin away fortunes on the roulette table! I wear a patch over one eye and a false mustache, sometimes I put on green whiskers. On those occasions they call me—*El Diablo!* Oh, I could tell you things to make you sleepless! My enemies plan to dynamite this place. They're going to blow us all sky-high some night! I'll be glad, very happy, and so will you! You'll go up, up on a broomstick, over Blue Mountain with seventeen gentlemen callers! You ugly—babbling old—*witch. . .*

(*He goes through a series of violent, clumsy movements, seizing his overcoat, lunging to the door, pulling it fiercely open. The women watch him, aghast. His arm catches in the sleeve of the coat as he struggles to pull it on. For a moment he is pinioned by the bulky garment. With an outraged groan he tears the coat off again, splitting the shoulder of it, and hurls it across the room. It strikes against the shelf of* LAURA'S *glass collection, there is a tinkle of shattering glass.* LAURA *cries out as if wounded. Music: "The Glass Menagerie."*)

LAURA (*shrilly*). *My glass!*—menagerie . . . (*She covers her face and turns away.*)

(*But* AMANDA *is still stunned and stupefied by the "ugly witch" so that she barely notices this occurrence. Now she recovers her speech.*)

AMANDA (*in an awful voice*). I won't speak to you—until you apologize!

(*She crosses through the portieres and draws them together behind her.* TOM *is left with* LAURA. LAURA *clings weakly to the mantel with her face averted.* TOM *stares at her stupidly for a moment. Then he crosses to shelf. Drops awkwardly on knees to collect the fallen glass, glancing at* LAURA *as if he would speak but couldn't. "The Glass Menagerie" steals in as the scene dims out.*)

SCENE IV

The interior of the apartment is dark. There is a faint light in the alley. A deep-voiced bell in a church is tolling the hour of five as the scene commences.

TOM *appears at the top of the alley. After each solemn boom of the bell in the tower, he shakes a little noise-maker or rattle as if to express the tiny spasm of man in contrast to the sustained power and dignity of the Almighty. This and the unsteadiness of his advance make it evident that he has been drinking. As he climbs the few steps to the fire-escape landing, light steals up inside.* LAURA *appears in night-dress, observing* TOM'S *empty bed in the front room.* TOM *fishes in his pockets for door-key, removing a motley assortment of articles in the search, including a perfect shower of movie-ticket stubs and an empty bottle. At last he finds the key, but just as he is about to insert it, it slips from his fingers. He strikes a match and crouches below the door.*

TOM (*bitterly*). One crack—and it falls through!

(LAURA *opens the door.*)

LAURA. Tom! Tom, what are you doing?

TOM. Looking for a door-key.

LAURA. Where have you been all this time?

TOM. I have been to the movies.

LAURA. All this time at the movies?

TOM. There was a very long program. There was a Garbo picture and a Mickey Mouse and a travelogue and a newsreel and a preview of coming attractions. And there was an organ solo and a collection for the milk-fund—simultaneously—which ended up in a terrible fight between a fat lady and an usher!

LAURA (*innocently*). Did you have to stay through everything?

TOM. Of course! And, oh, I forgot! There was a big stage show! The headliner on this stage show was Malvolio the Magician. He performed wonderful tricks, many of them, such as pouring water back and forth between pitchers. First it turned to wine and then it turned to beer and then it turned to whiskey. I know it was whiskey it finally turned into because he needed somebody to come up out of the audience to help him, and I came up—both shows! It was Kentucky Straight Bourbon. A very generous fellow, he gave souvenirs. (*He pulls from his back pocket a shimmering rainbow-colored scarf.*) He gave me this. This is his magic scarf. You can have it, Laura. You wave it over a canary cage and you get a bowl of goldfish. You wave it over the gold-fish bowl and they fly away canaries . . . But the wonderfullest trick of all was the coffin trick. We nailed him into a coffin and he got out of the coffin without removing one nail. (*He has come inside.*) There is a trick that would come in handy for me—get me out of this 2 by 4 situation! (*Flops onto bed and starts removing shoes.*)

LAURA. Tom—Shhh!

TOM. What're you shushing me for?

LAURA. You'll wake up Mother.

TOM. Goody, goody! Pay 'er back for all those "Rise an' Shines." (*Lies down, groaning.*) You know it don't take much intelligence to get yourself into a nailed-up coffin, Laura. But who in hell ever got himself out of one without removing one nail?

(*As if in answer, the father's grinning photograph lights up. Scene dims out.*)

(*Immediately following the church bell is heard striking six. At the sixth stroke the alarm clock goes off in* AMANDA'S *room, and after a few moments we hear her calling: "Rise and Shine! Rise and Shine! Laura, go tell your brother to rise and shine!"*)

TOM (*sitting up slowly*). I'll rise—but I won't shine.

(*The light increases.*)

AMANDA. Laura, tell your brother his coffee is ready.

(LAURA *slips into front room.*)

LAURA. Tom!—It's nearly seven. Don't make Mother nervous. (*He stares at her stupidly. Beseechingly*) Tom, speak to Mother this morning. Make up with her, apologize, speak to her!

TOM. She won't to me. It's her that started not speaking.

LAURA. If you just say you're sorry she'll start speaking.

TOM. Her not speaking—is that such a tragedy?

LAURA. Please—please!

AMANDA (*calling from kitchenette*). Laura, are you going to do what I asked you to do, or do I have to get dressed and go out myself?

LAURA. Going, going—soon as I get on my coat! (*She pulls on a shapeless felt hat with nervous, jerky movement, pleadingly glancing at* TOM. *Rushes awkwardly for coat. The coat is one of* AMANDA'S, *inaccurately made-over, the sleeves too short for* LAURA.) Butter and what else?

AMANDA (*entering upstage*). Just butter. Tell them to charge it.

LAURA. Mother, they make such faces when I do that.

AMANDA. Sticks and stones can break our bones, but the expression on Mr. Garfinkel's face won't harm us! Tell your brother his coffee is getting cold.

LAURA (*at door*). Do what I asked you, will you, will you, Tom?

(*He looks sullenly away.*)

AMANDA. Laura, go now or just don't go at all!

LAURA (*rushing out*). Going—going!

(*A second later she cries out.* TOM *springs up and crosses to door.* AMANDA *rushes anxiously in.* TOM *opens the door.*)

TOM. Laura?

LAURA. I'm all right. I slipped, but I'm all right.

AMANDA (*peering anxiously after her*). If anyone breaks a leg on those fire-escape steps, the landlord ought to be sued for every cent he possesses! (*She shuts door. Remembers she isn't speaking and returns to other room.*)

(*As* TOM *enters listlessly for his coffee, she turns her back to him and stands rigidly facing the window on the gloomy gray vault of the areaway. Its light on her face with its aged but childish features is cruelly sharp, satirical as a Daumier print.*

(*Music under: "Ave Maria."*)

(TOM *glances sheepishly but sullenly at her averted figure and slumps at the table. The coffee is scalding hot; he sips it and gasps and spits it back in the cup. At his gasp,* AMANDA *catches her breath and half turns. Then catches herself and turns back to window.* TOM *blows on his coffee, glancing sidewise at his mother. She clears her throat.* TOM *clears his. He starts to rise. Sinks back down again, scratches his head, clears his throat again.* AMANDA *coughs.* TOM *raises his cup in both hands to blow on it, his eyes staring over the rim of it at his mother for several moments. Then he slowly sets the cup down and awkwardly and hesitantly rises from the chair.*)

TOM (*hoarsely*). Mother. I—I apologize, Mother. (AMANDA *draws a quick, shuddering breath. Her face works grotesquely. She breaks into childlike tears.*) I'm sorry for what I said, for everything that I said, I didn't mean it.

AMANDA (*sobbingly.*) My devotion has made me a witch and so I make myself hateful to my children!

TOM. *No, you don't.*

AMANDA. I worry so much, don't sleep, it makes me nervous!

TOM (*gently*). I understand that.

AMANDA. I've had to put up a solitary battle all these years. But you're my right-hand bower! Don't fall down, don't fail!

TOM (*gently*). I try, Mother.

AMANDA (*with great enthusiasm*). Try and you will SUCCEED! (*The notion makes her breathless.*) Why, you—you're just *full* of natural endowments! Both of my children—they're *unusual* children! Don't you think I know it? I'm so—*proud!* Happy and—feel I've—so much to be thankful for but— Promise me one thing, Son!

TOM. What, Mother?

AMANDA. Promise, son, you'll—never be a drunkard!

TOM (*turns to her grinning*). I will never be a drunkard, Mother.

AMANDA. That's what frightened me so, that you'd be drinking! Eat a bowl of Purina!

TOM. Just coffee, Mother.

AMANDA. Shredded wheat biscuit?

TOM. No. No, Mother, just coffee.

AMANDA. You can't put in a day's work on an empty stomach. You've got ten minutes—don't gulp! Drinking too-hot liquids makes cancer of the stomach . . . Put cream in.

TOM. No, thank you.

AMANDA. To cool it.

TOM. No! No, thank you, I want it black.

AMANDA. I know, but it's not good for you. We have to do all that we can to build ourselves up. In these trying times we live in, all that we have to cling to is—each other . . . That's why it's so important to—Tom, I—I sent out your sister so I could discuss something with you. If you hadn't spoken I would have spoken to you. (*Sits down.*)

TOM (*gently*). What is it, Mother, that you want to discuss?

AMANDA. *Laura!*

(TOM *puts his cup down slowly. Music: "The Glass Menagerie."*)

TOM. —Oh.—Laura . . .

AMANDA (*touching his sleeve*). You know how Laura is. So quiet but— still water runs deep! She notices things and I think she—broods about them. (TOM *looks up.*) A few days ago I came in and she was crying.

TOM. What about?

AMANDA. You.

TOM. Me?

AMANDA. She has an idea that you're not happy here.

TOM. What gave her that idea?

AMANDA. What gives her any idea? However, you do act strangely. I—I'm not criticizing, understand *that!* I know your ambitions do not lie in the warehouse, that like everybody in the whole wide world—you've had to—make sacrifices, but—Tom—Tom—life's not easy, it calls for—Spartan endurance! There's so many things in my heart that I cannot describe to you! I've never told you but I—*loved* your father . . .

TOM (*gently*). I know that, Mother.

AMANDA. And you—when I see you taking after his ways! Staying out late—and—well, you *had* been drinking the night you were in that—terrifying condition! Laura says that you hate the apartment and that you go out nights to get away from it! Is that true, Tom?

TOM. No. You say there's so much in your heart that you can't describe to me. That's true of me, too. There's so much in my heart that I can't describe to *you!* So let's respect each other's—

AMANDA. But, why—*why*, Tom—are you always so *restless?* Where do you *go* to, nights?

TOM. I—go to the movies.

AMANDA. Why do you go to the movies so much, Tom?

TOM. I go to the movies because—I like adventure. Adventure is something I don't have much of at work, so I go to the movies.

AMANDA. But, Tom, you go to the movies *entirely* too *much!*

TOM. I like a lot of adventure.

(AMANDA *looks baffled, then hurt. As the familiar inquisition resumes he becomes hard and impatient again.* AMANDA *slips back into her querulous attitude toward him.*)

AMANDA. Most young men find adventure in their careers.

TOM. Then most young men are not employed in a warehouse.

AMANDA. The world is full of young men employed in warehouses and offices and factories.

TOM. Do all of them find adventure in their careers?

AMANDA. They do or they do without it! Not everybody has a craze for adventure.

TOM. Man is by instinct a lover, a hunter, a fighter, and none of those instincts are given much play at the warehouse!

AMANDA. Man is by instinct! Don't quote instinct to me! Instinct is something that people have got away from! It belongs to animals! Christian adults don't want it!

TOM. What do Christian adults want, then, Mother?

AMANDA. Superior things! Things of the mind and the spirit! Only animals have to satisfy instincts! Surely your aims are somewhat higher than theirs! Than monkeys—pigs—

TOM. I reckon they're not.

AMANDA. You're joking. However, that isn't what I wanted to discuss.

TOM (*rising*). I haven't much time.

AMANDA (*pushing his shoulders*). Sit down.

TOM. You want me to punch in red at the warehouse, Mother?

AMANDA. You have five minutes. I want to talk about Laura.

TOM. All right! What about Laura?

AMANDA. We have to be making some plans and provisions for her. She's older than you, two years, and nothing has happened. She just drifts along doing nothing. It frightens me terribly how she just drifts along.

TOM. I guess she's the type that people call home girls.

AMANDA. There's no such type, and if there is, it's a pity! That is unless the home is hers, with a husband!

TOM. What?

AMANDA. Oh, I can see the handwriting on the wall as plain as I see the nose in front of my face! It's terrifying! More and more you remind me of your father! He was out all hours without explanation!—Then *left! Good-bye!* And me with the bag to hold. I saw that letter you got from the Merchant Marine. I know what you're dreaming of. I'm not standing here blindfolded. (*She pauses.*) Very well, then. Then *do* it! But not till there's somebody to take your place.

TOM. What do you mean?

AMANDA. I mean that as soon as Laura has got somebody to take care of her, married, a home of her own, independent—why, then you'll be free to go wherever you please, on land, on sea, whichever way the wind blows you! But until that time you've got to look out for your sister. I don't say me because I'm old and don't matter! I say for your sister because she's young and dependent.

I put her in business college—a dismal failure! Frightened her so it made her sick at the stomach. I took her over to the Young People's League at the church. Another fiasco. She spoke to nobody, nobody spoke to her. Now all she does is fool with those pieces of glass and play those worn-out records. What kind of a life is that for a girl to lead?

TOM. What can I do about it?

AMANDA. Overcome selfishness! Self, self, self is all that you ever think of!

(TOM *springs up and crosses to get his coat. It is ugly and bulky. He pulls on a cap with earmuffs.*)

Where is your muffler? Put your wool muffler on!

(*He snatches it angrily from the closet and tosses it around his neck and pulls both ends tight.*)

Tom! I haven't said what I had in mind to ask you.

TOM. I'm too late to—

AMANDA (*catching his arm—very importunately. Then shyly.*) Down at the warehouse, aren't there some—nice young men?

TOM. No!

AMANDA. There *must* be—*some* . . .

TOM. Mother—(*Gesture.*)

AMANDA. Find out one that's clean-living—doesn't drink and—ask him out for sister!

TOM. What?

AMANDA. For *sister!* To *meet!* Get *acquainted!*

TOM (*stamping to door*). Oh, my go-osh!

AMANDA. Will you? (*He opens door. Imploringly.*) Will you? (*He starts down.*) Will you? Will you, dear?

TOM (*calling back*). YES!

(AMANDA *closes the door hesitantly and with a troubled but faintly hopeful expression.*)

(*Spot* AMANDA *at phone.*)

AMANDA. Ella Cartwright? This is Amanda Wingfield! How are you, honey?

How is that kidney condition? (*There is a five-second pause.*)

Horrors! (*There is another pause.*)

You're a Christian martyr, yes, honey, that's what you are, a Christian martyr! Well, I just now happened to notice in my little red book that your subscription to the *Companion* has just run out! I knew that you wouldn't want to miss out on the wonderful serial starting in this new issue. It's by Bessie Mae Hopper, the first thing she's written since *Honeymoon for Three.* Wasn't that a strange and interesting story? Well, this one is even lovelier, I believe. It has a sophisticated, society background. It's all about the horsey set on Long Island!

SCENE V

It is early dusk of a spring evening. Supper has just been finished in the Wingfield apartment. AMANDA *and* LAURA *in light-colored dresses are removing dishes from the table, in the upstage area, which is shadowy, their movements formalized almost as a dance or ritual, their moving forms as pale and silent as moths.* TOM, *in white shirt and trousers, rises from the table and crosses toward the fire-escape.*

AMANDA (*as he passes her*). Son, will you do me a favor?

TOM. What?

AMANDA. Comb your hair! You look so pretty when your hair is combed! (TOM *slouches on sofa with evening paper. Enormous caption "Franco Triumphs."*) There is only one respect in which I would like you to emulate your father.

TOM. What respect is that?

AMANDA. The care he always took of his appearance. He never allowed himself to look untidy. (*He throws down the paper and crosses to fire-escape.*) Where are you going?

TOM. I'm going out to smoke.

AMANDA. You smoke too much. A pack a day at fifteen cents a pack. How much would that amount to in a month? Thirty times fifteen is how much, Tom? Figure it out and you will be astounded at what you could save. Enough to give you a night-school course in accounting at Washington U! Just think what a wonderful thing that would be for you, Son!

TOM. I'd rather smoke. (*He steps out on landing, letting the screen door slam.*)

AMANDA (*sharply*). I know! That's the tragedy of it . . . (*Alone, she turns to look at her husband's picture.*)

(*Dance music: "All the World Is Waiting for the Sunrise!"*)

TOM (*to the audience*). Across the alley from us was the Paradise Dance Hall. On evenings in spring the windows and doors were open and the music came outdoors. Sometimes the lights were turned out except for a large glass sphere that hung from the ceiling. It would turn slowly about and filter the dusk with delicate rainbow colors. Then the orchestra played a waltz or a tango, something that had a slow and sensuous rhythm. Couples would come outside, to the relative privacy of the alley. You could see them kissing behind ash-pits and telephone poles. This was the compensation for lives that passed like mine, without any change or adventure. Adventure and change were imminent in this year. They were waiting around the corner for all these kids. Suspended in the mist over Berchtesgaden,° caught in the folds of Chamberlain's umbrella—° In Spain there was Guernica! ° But here there was only hot swing music and liquor, dance halls, bars, and movies, and sex that hung in the gloom like a chandelier and flooded the world with brief, deceptive rainbows . . . All the world was waiting for bombardments!

(AMANDA *turns from the picture and comes outside.*)

AMANDA (*sighing*). A fire-escape landing's a poor excuse for a porch. (*She spreads a newspaper on a step and sits down, gracefully and demurely as if she were settling into a swing on a Mississippi veranda.*) What are you looking at?

TOM. The moon.

AMANDA. Is there a moon this evening?

Berchtesgaden: Hitler's Bavarian summer retreat **Chamberlain's umbrella:** Neville Chamberlain, British prime minister (1937–1940), who always carried a furled umbrella, and whose name has become a symbol for appeasement, returned from a conference with Hitler in Munich in 1938 with a signed agreement which he proclaimed meant "Peace in our time." One year later, German troops invaded Poland, beginning World War II. **Guernica:** town in northern Spain destroyed during the Spanish Civil War, in 1937, by German bombers, in the first mass air attack on an urban community.

Tom. It's rising over Garfinkel's Delicatessen.

Amanda. So it is! A little silver slipper of a moon. Have you made a wish on it yet?

Tom. Um-hum.

Amanda. What did you wish for?

Tom. That's a secret.

Amanda. A secret, huh? Well, I won't tell mine either. I will be just as mysterious as you.

Tom. I bet I can guess what yours is.

Amanda. Is my head so transparent?

Tom. You're not a sphinx.

Amanda. No, I don't have secrets. I'll tell you what I wished for on the moon. Success and happiness for my precious children! I wish for that whenever there's a moon, and when there isn't a moon, I wish for it, too.

Tom. I thought perhaps you wished for a gentleman caller.

Amanda. Why do you say that?

Tom. Don't you remember asking me to fetch one?

Amanda. I remember suggesting that it would be nice for your sister if you brought home some nice young man from the warehouse. I think that I've made that suggestion more than once.

Tom. Yes, you have made it repeatedly.

Amanda. Well?

Tom. We are going to have one.

Amanda. *What?*

Tom. A gentleman caller!

(*The annunciation is celebrated with music.* Amanda *rises.*)

Amanda. You mean you have asked some nice young man to come over?

Tom. Yep. I've asked him to dinner.

Amanda. You really did?

Tom. I did!

Amanda. You did, and did he—*accept?*

Tom. He did!

Amanda. Well, well—well, well! That's—lovely!

Tom. I thought that you would be pleased.

Amanda. It's definite, then?

Tom. Very definite.

Amanda. Soon?

Tom. Very soon.

Amanda. For heaven's sake, stop putting on and tell me some things, will you?

Tom. What things do you want me to tell you?

Amanda. *Naturally* I would like to know when he's *coming!*

Tom. He's coming tomorrow.

Amanda. *Tomorrow?*

TOM. Yep. Tomorrow.

AMANDA. But, Tom!

TOM. Yes, Mother?

AMANDA. Tomorrow gives me no time!

TOM. Time for what?

AMANDA. Preparations! Why didn't you phone me at once, as soon as you asked him, the minute that he accepted? Then, don't you see, I could have been getting ready!

TOM. You don't have to make any fuss.

AMANDA. Oh, Tom, Tom, Tom, of course I have to make a fuss! I want things nice, not sloppy! Not thrown together. I'll certainly have to do some fast thinking, won't I?

TOM. I don't see why you have to think at all.

AMANDA. You just don't know. We can't have a gentleman caller in a pig-sty! All my wedding silver has to be polished, the monogrammed table linen ought to be laundered! The windows have to be washed and fresh curtains put up. And how about clothes? We have to *wear* something, don't we?

TOM. Mother, this boy is no one to make a fuss over!

AMANDA. Do you realize he's the first young man we've introduced to your sister?

It's terrible, dreadful, disgraceful that poor little sister has never received a single gentleman caller! Tom, come inside! (*She opens the screen door.*)

TOM. What for?

AMANDA. I want to ask you some things.

TOM. If you're going to make such a fuss, I'll call it off, I'll tell him not to come!

AMANDA. You certainly won't do anything of the kind. Nothing offends people worse than broken engagements. It simply means I'll have to work like a Turk! We won't be brilliant, but we will pass inspection. Come on inside. (TOM *follows, groaning.*) Sit down.

TOM. Any particular place you would like me to sit?

AMANDA. Thank heavens I've got the new sofa! I'm also making payments on a floor lamp I'll have sent out! And put the chintz covers on, they'll brighten things up! Of course I'd hoped to have these walls re-papered . . . What is the young man's name?

TOM. His name is O'Connor.

AMANDA. That, of course, means fish—tomorrow is Friday! I'll have that salmon loaf—with Durkee's dressing! What does he do? He works at the warehouse?

TOM. Of course! How else would I—

AMANDA. Tom, he—doesn't drink?

TOM. Why do you ask me that?

AMANDA. Your father *did!*

TOM. Don't get started on that!

AMANDA. He *does* drink, then?

TOM. Not that I know of!

AMANDA. Make sure, be certain! The last thing I want for my daughter's a boy who drinks!

TOM. Aren't you being a little bit premature? Mr. O'Connor has not yet appeared on the scene!

AMANDA. But will tomorrow. To meet your sister, and what do I know about his character? Nothing! Old maids are better off than wives of drunkards!

TOM. Oh, my God!

AMANDA. Be still!

TOM (*leaning foward to whisper*). Lots of fellows meet girls whom they don't marry!

AMANDA. Oh, talk sensibly, Tom—and don't be sarcastic! (*She has gotten a hairbrush.*)

TOM. What are you doing?

AMANDA. I'm brushing that cow-lick down! What is this young man's position at the warehouse?

TOM (*submitting grimly to the brush and the interrogation*). This young man's position is that of a shipping clerk, Mother.

AMANDA. Sounds to me like a fairly responsible job, the sort of a job *you* would be in if you just had more *get-up*. What is his salary? Have you any idea?

TOM. I would judge it to be approximately eighty-five dollars a month.

AMANDA. Well—not princely, but—

TOM. Twenty more than I make.

AMANDA. Yes, how well I know! But for a family man, eighty-five dollars a month is not much more than you can just get by on . . .

TOM. Yes, but Mr. O'Connor is not a family man.

AMANDA. He might be, mightn't he? Some time in the future?

TOM. I see. Plans and provisions.

AMANDA. You are the only young man that I know of who ignores the fact that the future becomes the present, the present the past, and the past turns into everlasting regret if you don't plan for it!

TOM. I will think that over and see what I can make of it.

AMANDA. Don't be supercilious with your mother! Tell me some more about this—what do you call him?

TOM. James D. O'Connor. The D. is for Delaney.

AMANDA. Irish on *both* sides! *Gracious!* And doesn't drink?

TOM. Shall I call him up and ask him right this minute?

AMANDA. The only way to find out about those things is to make discreet inquiries at the proper moment. When I was a girl in Blue Mountain and it was suspected that a young man drank, the girl whose attentions he had been receiving, if any girl *was*, would sometimes speak to the minister of his church, or rather her father would if her father was living, and sort of feel him out on the young man's character. That is the way such things are discreetly handled to keep a young woman from making a tragic mistake!

TOM. Then how did you happen to make a tragic mistake?

AMANDA. That innocent look of your father's had everyone fooled! He *smiled*—the world was *enchanted!* No girl can do worse than put herself at the mercy of a handsome appearance! I hope that Mr. O'Connor is not too good-looking.

TOM. No, he's not too good-looking. He's covered with freckles and hasn't too much of a nose.

AMANDA. He's not right-down homely, though?

TOM. Not right-down homely. Just medium homely, I'd say.

AMANDA. Character's what to look for in a man.

TOM. That's what I've always said, Mother.

AMANDA. You've never said anything of the kind and I suspect you would never give it a thought.

TOM. Don't be so suspicious of me.

AMANDA. At least I hope he's the type that's up and coming.

TOM. I think he really goes in for self-improvement.

AMANDA. What reason have you to think so?

TOM. He goes to night school.

AMANDA (*beaming*). Splendid! What does he do, I mean study?

TOM. Radio engineering and public speaking!

AMANDA. Then he has visions of being advanced in the world! Any young man who studies public speaking is aiming to have an executive job some day! And radio engineering? A thing for the future! Both of these facts are very illuminating. Those are the sort of things that a mother should know concerning any young man who comes to call on her daughter. Seriously or—not.

TOM. One little warning. He doesn't know about Laura. I didn't let on that we had dark ulterior motives. I just said, why don't you come and have dinner with us? He said okay and that was the whole conversation.

AMANDA. I bet it was! You're eloquent as an oyster. However, he'll know about Laura when he gets here. When he sees how lovely and sweet and pretty she is, he'll thank his lucky stars he was asked to dinner.

TOM. Mother, you mustn't expect too much of Laura.

AMANDA. What do you mean?

TOM. Laura seems all those things to you and me because she's ours and we love her. We don't even notice she's crippled any more.

AMANDA. Don't say crippled! You know that I never allow that word to be used!

TOM. But face facts, Mother. She is and— that's not all—

AMANDA. What do you mean "not all"?

TOM. Laura is very different from other girls.

AMANDA. I think the difference is all to her advantage.

TOM. Not quite all—in the eyes of others—strangers—she's terribly shy and lives in a world of her own and those things make her seem a little peculiar to people outside the house.

AMANDA. Don't say peculiar.

TOM. Face the facts. She is.

(*The dance-hall music changes to a tango that has a minor and somewhat ominous tone.*)

AMANDA. In what way is she peculiar—may I ask?

TOM (*gently*). She lives in a world of her own—a world of—little glass ornaments, Mother . . . (*Gets up.* AMANDA *remains holding brush, looking at him, troubled.*) She plays old phonograph records and—that's about all—(*He glances at himself in the mirror and crosses to door.*)

AMANDA (*sharply*). Where are you going?

TOM. I'm going to the movies. (*Out screen door.*)

AMANDA. Not to the movies, every night to the movies! (*Follows quickly to screen door.*) I don't believe you always go to the movies! (*He is gone.* AMANDA *looks worriedly after him for a moment. Then vitality and optimism return and she turns from the door, crossing to portieres.*) Laura! Laura!

(LAURA *answers from kitchenette.*)

LAURA. Yes, Mother.

AMANDA. Let those dishes go and come in front! (LAURA *appears with dish towel.* AMANDA *speaks to her gaily.*) Laura, come here and make a wish on the moon!

LAURA (*entering*). Moon—moon?

AMANDA. A little silver slipper of a moon. Look over your left shoulder, Laura, and make a wish!

(LAURA *looks faintly puzzled as if called out of sleep.* AMANDA *seizes her shoulders and turns her at an angle by the door.*)

LAURA. What shall I wish for, Mother?

AMANDA (*her voice trembling and her eyes suddenly filling with tears*). Happiness! Good fortune!

(*The sound of the violin rises and the stage dims out.*)

SCENE VI

TOM. And so the following evening I brought Jim home to dinner. I had known Jim slightly in high school. In high school Jim was a hero. He had tremendous Irish good nature and vitality with the scrubbed and polished look of white chinaware. He seemed to move in a continual spotlight. He was a star in basketball, captain of the debating club, president of the senior class and the glee club and he sang the male lead in the annual light operas. He was always running or bounding, never just walking. He seemed always at the point of defeating the law of gravity. He was shooting with such velocity through his adolescence that you would logically expect him to arrive at nothing short of the White House by the time he was thirty. But Jim apparently ran into more interference after his graduation from Soldan. His speed had definitely slowed. Six years after he left high school he was holding a job that wasn't much better than mine.

He was the only one at the warehouse with whom I was on friendly terms. I was valuable to him as someone who could remember his former glory, who had seen him win basketball games and the silver cup in debating. He knew of my secret practice of retiring to a cabinet of the washroom to work on poems when business was slack in the warehouse. He called me Shakespeare. And while the other boys in the warehouse regarded me with suspicious hostility, Jim took a humorous attitude toward me. Gradually his attitude affected the others, their hostility wore off and they also began to smile at me as people smile at an oddly fashioned dog who trots across their paths at some distance.

I knew that Jim and Laura had known each other at Soldan, and I had heard Laura speak admiringly of his voice. I didn't know if Jim remembered her or not. In high school Laura had been as unobtrusive as Jim had been astonishing. If he did remember Laura, it was not as my sister, for when I asked him to dinner, he grinned and said, "You know, Shakespeare, I never thought of you as having folks!"

He was about to discover that I did . . .

(*The light dims out on* TOM *and comes up in the Wingfield living room—a delicate lemony light. It is about five on a Friday evening of late spring which comes "scattering poems in the sky."*

(AMANDA *has worked like a Turk in preparation for the gentleman caller. The results are astonishing. The new floor lamp with its rose-silk shade is in place, a colored paper lantern conceals the broken light fixture in the ceiling, new billowing white curtains are at the windows, chintz covers are on chairs and sofa, a pair of new sofa pillows make their initial appearance. Open boxes and tissue paper are scattered on the floor.*

(LAURA *stands in the middle with lifted arms while* AMANDA *crouches before her, adjusting the hem of the new dress, devout and ritualistic. The dress is colored and designed by memory. The arrangement of* LAURA'S *hair is changed; it is softer and more becoming. A fragile, unearthly prettiness has come out in* LAURA: *she is like a piece of translucent glass touched by light, given a momentary radiance, not actual, not lasting.*)

AMANDA (*impatiently*). Why are you trembling?

LAURA. Mother, you've made me so nervous!

AMANDA. How have I made you nervous?

LAURA. By all this fuss! You make it seem so important!

AMANDA. I don't understand you, Laura. You couldn't be satisfied with just sitting home, and yet whenever I try to arrange something for you, you seem to resist it. (*She gets up.*) Now take a look at yourself. No, wait! Wait just a moment—I have an idea!

LAURA. What is it now?

(AMANDA *produces two powder puffs which she wraps in handkerchiefs and stuffs in* LAURA'S *bosom.*)

LAURA. Mother, what are you doing?
AMANDA. They call them "Gay Deceivers"!
LAURA. I won't wear them.
AMANDA. You will!
LAURA. Why should I?
AMANDA. Because, to be painfully honest, your chest is flat.
LAURA. You make it seem like we were setting a trap.
AMANDA. All pretty girls are a trap, a pretty trap, and men expect them to be. Now look at yourself, young lady. This is the prettiest you will ever be! (*She stands back to admire* LAURA.) I've got to fix myself now! You're going to be surprised by your mother's appearance! (*She crosses through portieres, humming gaily.*)

(LAURA *moves slowly to the long mirror and stares solemnly at herself. A wind blows the white curtains inward in a slow, graceful motion and with a faint, sorrowful sighing.*)

AMANDA (*from somewhere behind the portieres*). It isn't dark enough yet. (LAURA *turns slowly before the mirror with a troubled look.*)
AMANDA (*laughing, still not visible*). I'm going to show you something. I'm going to make a spectacular appearance!
LAURA. What is it, Mother?
AMANDA. Possess your soul in patience—you will see! Something I've resurrected from that old trunk! Styles haven't changed so terribly much after all . . . (*She parts the portieres.*) Now just look at your mother! (*She wears a girlish frock of yellowed voile with a blue silk sash. She carries a bunch of jonquils—the legend of her youth is nearly revived. Now she speaks feverishly.*) This is the dress in which I led the cotillion. Won the cakewalk twice at Sunset Hill, wore one spring to the Governor's ball in Jackson! See how I sashayed around the ballroom, Laura? (*She raises her skirt and does a mincing step around the room.*) I wore it on Sundays for my gentlemen callers! I had it on the day I met your father—I had malaria fever all that spring. The change of climate from East Tennessee to the Delta—weakened resistance—I had a little temperature all the time—not enough to be serious—just enough to make me restless and giddy!—Invitations poured in—parties all over the Delta!—"Stay in bed," said Mother, "you have fever!"—but I just wouldn't.—I took quinine but kept on going, going!—Evenings, dances!—Afternoons, long, long rides! Picnics—lovely!—So lovely, that country in May.—All lacy with dogwood, literally flooded with jonquils!—That was the spring I had the craze for jonquils. Jonquils became an absolute obsession. Mother said, "Honey, there's no more room for jonquils." And still I kept on bringing in more jonquils. Whenever, wherever I saw them, I'd say, "Stop!

Stop! I see jonquils!" I made the young men help me gather the jonquils! It was a joke, Amanda and her jonquils! Finally there were no more vases to hold them, every available space was filled with jonquils. No vases to hold them? All right, I'll hold them myself! And then I—(*She stops in front of the picture. Music.*) met your father! Malaria and jonquils and then—this—boy . . . (*She switches on the rose-colored lamp.*) I hope they get here before it starts to rain. (*She crosses upstage and places the jonquils in bowl on table.*) I gave your brother a little extra change so he and Mr. O'Connor could take the service car home.

LAURA (*with altered look*).   What did you say his name was?
AMANDA.   O'Connor.
LAURA.   What is his first name?
AMANDA.   I don't remember. Oh, yes, I do. It was—Jim!

(LAURA *sways slightly and catches hold of a chair.*)

LAURA (*faintly*).   Not—Jim!
AMANDA.   Yes, that was it, it was Jim! I've never known a Jim that wasn't nice!

(*The music becomes ominous.*)

LAURA.   Are you sure his name is Jim O'Connor?
AMANDA.   Yes. Why?
LAURA.   Is he the one that Tom used to know in high school?
AMANDA.   He didn't say so. I think he just got to know him at the warehouse.
LAURA.   There was a Jim O'Connor we both knew in high school— (*Then, with effort*) If that is the one that Tom is bringing to dinner—you'll have to excuse me, I won't come to the table.
AMANDA.   What sort of nonsense is this?
LAURA.   You asked me once if I'd ever liked a boy. Don't you remember I showed you this boy's picture?
AMANDA.   You mean the boy you showed me in the year book?
LAURA.   Yes, that boy.
AMANDA.   Laura, Laura, were you in love with that boy?
LAURA.   I don't know, Mother. All I know is I couldn't sit at the table if it was him!
AMANDA.   It won't be him! It isn't the least bit likely. But whether it is or not, you will come to the table. You will not be excused.
LAURA.   I'll have to be, Mother.
AMANDA.   I don't intend to humor your silliness, Laura. I've had too much from you and your brother, both! So just sit down and compose yourself till they come. Tom has forgotten his key so you'll have to let them in, when they arrive.
LAURA (*panicky*).   Oh, Mother—*you* answer the door!
AMANDA (*lightly*).   I'll be in the kitchen—busy!

LAURA. Oh, Mother, please answer the door, don't make me do it!

AMANDA (*crossing into kitchenette*). I've got to fix the dressing for the salmon. Fuss, fuss—silliness!—over a gentleman caller!

(*Door swings shut. LAURA is left alone. She utters a low moan and turns off the lamp—sits stiffly on the edge of the sofa, knotting her fingers together. TOM and JIM appear on the fire-escape steps and climb to landing. Hearing their approach, LAURA rises with a panicky gesture. She retreats to the portieres. The doorbell rings. LAURA catches her breath and touches her throat. Low drums sound.*)

AMANDA (*calling*). Laura, sweetheart! The door!

(LAURA *stares at it without moving.*)

JIM. I think we just beat the rain.

TOM. Uh-huh. (*He rings again, nervously.* JIM *whistles and fishes for a cigarette.*)

AMANDA (*very, very gaily*). Laura, that is your brother and Mr. O'Connor! Will you let them in, darling?

(LAURA *crosses toward kitchenette door.*)

LAURA (*breathlessly*). Mother—you go to the door!

(AMANDA *steps out of the kitchenette and stares furiously at* LAURA. *She points imperiously at the door.*)

LAURA. Please, please!

AMANDA (*in a fierce whisper*). What is the matter with you, you silly thing?

LAURA (*desperately*). Please, you answer it, *please!*

AMANDA. I told you I wasn't going to humor you, Laura. Why have you chosen this moment to lose your mind?

LAURA. Please, please, please, you go!

AMANDA. You'll have to go to the door because I can't!

LAURA (*despairingly*). I can't either!

AMANDA. *Why?*

LAURA. I'm *sick!*

AMANDA. I'm sick, too—of your nonsense! Why can't you and your brother be normal people? Fantastic whims and behavior.

(TOM *gives a long ring.*)

Preposterous goings on! Can you give me one reason—(*She calls out lyrically.*) COMING! JUST ONE SECOND!—why you should be afraid to open a door? Now you answer it, Laura!

LAURA. Oh, oh, oh . . . (*She returns through the portieres, darts to the victrola, winds it frantically and turns it on.*)

AMANDA. Laura Wingfield, you march right to that door!

LAURA. Yes—yes, Mother!

(*A faraway, scratchy rendition of "Dardanella" softens the air and gives her strength to move through it. She slips to the door and draws it cautiously open. TOM enters with the caller, JIM O'CONNOR.*)

TOM. Laura, this is Jim. Jim, this is my sister, Laura.

JIM (*stepping inside*). I didn't know that Shakespeare had a sister!

LAURA (*retreating stiff and trembling from the door*). How—how do you do?

JIM (*heartily extending his hand*). Okay!

(LAURA *touches it hesitantly with hers.*)

JIM. Your hand's *cold,* Laura!

LAURA. Yes, well—I've been playing the victrola . . .

JIM. Must have been playing classical music on it! You ought to play a little hot swing music to warm you up!

LAURA. Excuse me—I haven't finished playing the victrola . . . (*She turns awkwardly and hurries into the front room. She pauses a second by the victrola. Then she catches her breath and darts through the portieres like a frightened deer.*)

JIM (*grinning*). What was the matter?

TOM. Oh—with Laura? Laura is—terribly shy.

JIM. Shy, huh? It's unusual to meet a shy girl nowadays. I don't believe you ever mentioned you had a sister.

TOM. Well, now you know. I have one. Here is the *Post Dispatch.* You want a piece of it?

JIM. Uh-huh.

TOM. What piece? The comics?

JIM. Sports! (*Glances at it.*) Ole Dizzy Dean is on his bad behavior.

TOM (*uninterested*). Yeah? (*Lights a cigarette and crosses back to fire-escape door.*)

JIM. Where are *you* going?

TOM. I'm going out on the terrace.

JIM (*goes after him*). You know, Shakespeare—I'm going to sell you a bill of goods!

TOM. What goods?

JIM. A course I'm taking.

TOM. Huh?

JIM. In public speaking! You and me, we're not the warehouse type.

TOM. Thanks—that's good news. But what has public speaking got to do with it?

JIM. It fits you for—executive positions!

TOM. Awww.

JIM. I tell you it's done a helluva lot for me.

TOM. In what respect?

JIM. In every! Ask yourself what is the difference between you an' me and men in the office down front? Brains?—No!—Ability?—No! Then what? Just one little thing—

TOM. What is that one little thing?

JIM. Primarily it amounts to—social poise! Being able to square up to people and hold your own on any social level!

AMANDA (*from the kitchenette*). Tom?

TOM. Yes, Mother?

AMANDA. Is that you and Mr. O'Connor?

TOM. Yes, Mother.

AMANDA. Well, you just make yourselves comfortable in there.

TOM. Yes, Mother.

AMANDA. Ask Mr. O'Connor if he would like to wash his hands.

JIM. Aw, no—no—thank you—I took care of that at the warehouse. Tom—

TOM. Yes?

JIM. Mr. Mendoza was speaking to me about you.

TOM. Favorably?

JIM. What do you think?

TOM. Well—

JIM. You're going to be out of a job if you don't wake up.

TOM. I am waking up—

JIM. You show no signs.

TOM. The signs are interior. I'm planning to change. (*He leans over the rail speaking with quiet exhilaration. The incandescent marquees and signs of the first-run movie houses light his face from across the alley. He looks like a voyager.*) I'm right at the point of committing myself to a future that doesn't include the warehouse and Mr. Mendoza or even a night-school course in public speaking.

JIM. What are you gassing about?

TOM. I'm tired of the movies.

JIM. Movies!

TOM. Yes, movies! Look at them—(*A wave toward the marvels of Grand Avenue*) All of those glamorous people—having adventures—hogging it all, gobbling the whole thing up! You know what happens? People go to the *movies* instead of *moving!* Hollywood characters are supposed to have all the adventures for everybody in America, while everybody in America sits in a dark room and watches them have them! Yes, until there's a war. That's when adventure becomes available to the masses! *Everyone's* dish, not only Gable's! Then the people in the dark room come out of the dark room to have some adventures themselves—Goody, goody!—It's our turn now, to go to the South Sea Island—to make a safari—to be exotic, far-off!—But I'm not patient. I don't want to wait till then. I'm tired of the *movies* and I am *about* to *move!*

JIM (*incredulously*). Move?

TOM. Yes.

JIM. When?

TOM. Soon!

JIM. Where? Where?

(*The music seems to answer the question, while* TOM *thinks it over. He searches in his pockets.*)

TOM. I'm starting to boil inside. I know I seem dreamy, but inside—well, I'm boiling!—Whenever I pick up a shoe, I shudder a little thinking how short life is and what I am doing!—Whatever that means, I know it doesn't mean shoes—except as something to wear on a traveler's feet! (*Finds paper*) Look—

JIM. What?

TOM. I'm a member.

JIM (*reading*). The Union of Merchant Seamen.

TOM. I paid my dues this month, instead of the light bill.

JIM. You will regret it when they turn the lights off.

TOM. I won't be here.

JIM. How about your mother?

TOM. I'm like my father. The bastard son of a bastard! See how he grins? And he's been absent going on sixteen years!

JIM. You're just talking, you drip. How does your mother feel about it?

TOM. Shh!—Here comes Mother! Mother is not acquainted with my plans!

AMANDA (*coming through the portieres*). Where are you all?

TOM. On the terrace, Mother.

(*They start inside. She advances to them.* TOM *is distinctly shocked at her appearance. Even* JIM *blinks a little. He is making his first contact with girlish Southern vivacity and in spite of the night-school course in public speaking is somewhat thrown off the beam by the unexpected outlay of social charm. Certain responses are attempted by* JIM *but are swept aside by* AMANDA'S *gay laughter and chatter.* TOM *is embarrassed but after the first shock* JIM *reacts very warmly. He grins and chuckles, is altogether won over.*)

AMANDA (*coyly smiling, shaking her girlish ringlets*). Well, well, well, so this is Mr. O'Connor. Introductions entirely unnecessary. I've heard so much about you from my boy. I finally said to him, Tom—good gracious!—why don't you bring this paragon to supper? I'd like to meet this nice young man at the warehouse!—Instead of just hearing him sing your praises so much! I don't known why my son is so stand-offish—that's not Southern behavior! Let 's sit down and—I think we could stand a little more air in here! Tom, leave the door open. I felt a nice fresh breeze a moment ago. Where has it gone to? Mmm, so warm already! And not quite summer, even. We're going to burn up when summer really gets started. However, we're having—we're having a very light supper. I think light things are better fo' this time of year.

The same as light clothes are. Light clothes an' light food are what warm weather calls fo'. You know our blood gets so thick during th' winter—it takes a while fo' us to *adjust* ou'selves!—when the season changes . . . It's come so quick this year. I wasn't prepared. All of a sudden—heavens! Already summer!—I ran to the trunk an' pulled out this light dress—Terribly old! Historical almost! But feels so good—so good an' co-ol, y' know . . .

TOM. Mother—

AMANDA. Yes, honey?

TOM. How about—supper?

AMANDA. Honey, you go ask Sister if supper is ready! You know that Sister is in full charge of supper! Tell her you hungry boys are waiting for it. (*To* JIM.) Have you met Laura?

JIM. She—

AMANDA. Let you in? Oh, good, you've met already! It's rare for a girl as sweet an' pretty as Laura to be domestic! But Laura is, thank heavens, not only pretty but also very domestic. I'm not at all. I never was a bit. I never could make a thing but angel-food cake. Well, in the south we had so many servants. Gone, gone, gone. All vestige of gracious living! Gone completely! I wasn't prepared for what the future brought me. All of my gentlemen callers were sons of planters and so of course I assumed that I would be married to one and raise my family on a large piece of land with plenty of servants. But man proposes—and woman accepts the proposal!—To vary that old, old saying° a little bit—I married no planter! I married a man who worked for the telephone company!—That gallantly smiling gentleman over there! (*Points to the picture.*) A telephone man who— fell in love with long-distance!—Now he travels and I don't even know where!—But what am I going on for about my—tribulations? Tell me yours—I hope you don't have any! Tom?

TOM (*returning*). Yes, Mother?

AMANDA. Is supper nearly ready?

TOM. It looks to me like supper is on the table.

AMANDA. Let me look—(*She rises prettily and looks through portieres.*) Oh, lovely!—But where is Sister?

TOM. Laura is not feeling well and she says that she thinks she'd better not come to the table.

AMANDA. What?—Nonsense!—Laura? Oh, Laura!

LAURA (*off stage, faintly*). Yes, Mother.

AMANDA. Your really must come to the table. We won't be seated until you come to the table! Come in, Mr. O'Connor. You sit over there, and I'll—Laura? Laura Wingfield! You're keeping us waiting, honey! We can't say grace until you come to the table!

(*The kitchenette door is pushed weakly open and* LAURA *comes in. She is obviously quite faint, her lips trembling, her eyes wide and staring. She moves unsteadily toward the table. Outside a summer storm is coming abruptly. The*

---

old . . . saying: "Man proposes, but God disposes"

white curtains billow inward at the windows and there is a sorrowful murmur and deep blue dusk.

(LAURA *suddenly stumbles—she catches at a chair with a faint moan.*)

TOM. Laura!
AMANDA. Laura!

(*There is a clap of thunder.*)

(*Despairingly*) Why, Laura, you *are* sick, darling! Tom, help your sister into the living room, dear! Sit in the living room, Laura—rest on the sofa. Well! (*To* JIM *as* TOM *helps his sister to the sofa in the living room.*) Standing over the hot stove made her ill!—I told her that it was just too warm this evening, but—

(TOM *comes back to the table.*)

Is Laura all right now?
TOM. Yes.
AMANDA. What *is* that? Rain? A nice cool rain has come up! (*She gives the gentleman caller a frightened look.*) I think we may—have grace—now . . . (TOM *looks at her stupidly.*) Tom, honey—you say grace!
TOM. Oh . . . "For these and all thy mercies—"

(*They bow their heads,* AMANDA *stealing a nervous glance at* JIM. *In the living room* LAURA, *stretched on the sofa, clenches her hand to her lips, to hold back a shuddering sob.*)

God's Holy Name be praised—

(*The scene dims out.*)

SCENE VII

(*Half an hour later. Dinner is just being finished in the dining room.* LAURA *is still huddled upon the sofa, her feet drawn under her, her head resting on a pale blue pillow, her eyes wide and mysteriously watchful. The new floor lamp with its shade of rose-colored silk gives a soft, becoming light to her face, bringing out the fragile, unearthly prettiness which usually escapes attention. There is a steady murmur of rain, but it is slackening and soon stops; the air outside becomes pale and luminous as the moon breaks out. A moment after the curtain rises, the lights in both rooms flicker and go out.*)

JIM. Hey, there, Mr. Light Bulb!

(AMANDA *laughs nervously.*)

AMANDA. Where was Moses when the lights went out? Ha-ha. Do you know the answer to that one, Mr. O'Connor?
JIM. No, Ma'am, what's the answer?

AMANDA. In the dark! (JIM *laughs appreciatively*.) Everybody sit still. I'll light the candles. Isn't it lucky we have them on the table? Where's a match? Which of you gentlemen can provide a match?

JIM. Here.

AMANDA. Thank you, sir.

JIM. Not at all, Ma'am!

AMANDA. I guess the fuse has burnt out. Mr. O'Connor, can you tell a burnt-out fuse? I know I can't and Tom is a total loss when it comes to mechanics.

(*They rise from the table and go into the kitchenette, from where their voices are heard.*)

Oh, be careful you don't bump into something. We don't want our gentleman caller to break his neck. Now wouldn't that be a fine howdy-do?

JIM. Ha-ha! Where is the fuse-box?

AMANDA. Right here next to the stove. Can you see anything?

JIM. Just a minute.

AMANDA. Isn't electricity a mysterious thing? Wasn't it Benjamin Franklin who tied a key to a kite? We live in such a mysterious universe, don't we? Some people say that science clears up all the mysteries for us. In my opinion it only creates more! Have you found it yet?

JIM. No, Ma'am. All these fuses look okay to me.

AMANDA. Tom!

TOM. Yes, Mother?

AMANDA. That light bill I gave you several days ago. The one I told you we got the notices about?

TOM. Oh.—Yeah.

AMANDA. You didn't neglect to pay it by any chance?

TOM. Why, I—

AMANDA. Didn't! I might have known it!

JIM. Shakespeare probably wrote a poem on that light bill, Mrs. Wingfield.

AMANDA. I might have known better than to trust him with it! There's such a high price for negligence in this world!

JIM. Maybe the poem will win a ten-dollar prize.

AMANDA. We'll just have to spend the remainder of the evening in the nineteenth century, before Mr. Edison made the Mazda lamp!

JIM. Candlelight is my favorite kind of light.

AMANDA. That shows you're romantic! But that's no excuse for Tom. Well, we got through dinner. Very considerate of them to let us get through dinner before they plunged us into everlasting darkness, wasn't it, Mr. O'Connor?

JIM. Ha-ha!

AMANDA. Tom, as a penalty for your carelessness you can help me with the dishes.

JIM. Let me give you a hand.

AMANDA. Indeed you will not!

JIM. I ought to be good for something.

AMANDA. Good for something? (*Her tone is rhapsodic.*) You? Why, Mr. O'Connor nobody, *nobody's* given me this much entertainment in years—as you have!

JIM. Aw, now, Mrs. Wingfield!

AMANDA. I'm not exaggerating, not one bit! But Sister is all by her lonesome. You go keep her company in the parlor! I'll give you this lovely old candelabrum that used to be on the altar at the church of the Heavenly Rest. It was melted a little out of shape when the church burnt down. Lightning struck it one spring. Gypsy Jones was holding a revival at the time and he intimated that the church was destroyed because the Episcopalians gave card parties.

JIM. Ha-ha.

AMANDA. And how about you coaxing Sister to drink a little wine? I think it would be good for her! Can you carry both at once?

JIM. Sure. I'm Superman!

AMANDA. Now, Thomas, get into this apron!

(JIM *comes into the dining room, carrying the candelabrum, its candles lighted, in one hand and a glass of wine in the other. The door of the kitchenette swings closed on* AMANDA'S *gay laughter; the flickering light approaches the portieres.* LAURA *sits up nervously as he enters. Her speech at first is low and breathless from the almost intolerable strain of being alone with a stranger. At first, before* JIM'S *warmth overcomes her paralyzing shyness,* LAURA'S *voice is thin and breathless, as though she had just run up a steep flight of stairs.* JIM'S *attitude is gently humorous. While the incident is apparently unimportant, it is to* LAURA *the climax of her secret life.*)

JIM. Hello, there, Laura.

LAURA (*faintly*). Hello. (*She clears her throat.*)

JIM. How are you feeling now? Better?

LAURA. Yes. Yes, thank you.

JIM. This is for you. A little dandelion wine. (*He extends it toward her with extravagant gallantry.*)

LAURA. Thank you.

JIM. Drink it—but don't get drunk!

(*He laughs heartily.* LAURA *takes the glass uncertainly; laughs shyly.*)

Where shall I set the candles?

LAURA. Oh—oh, anywhere . . .

JIM. How about here on the floor? Any objections?

LAURA. No.

JIM. I'll spread a newspaper to catch the drippings. I like to sit on the floor. Mind if I do?

LAURA. Oh, no.

JIM. Give me a pillow?

LAURA. What?

JIM. A pillow!

LAURA. Oh . . . (*Hands him one quickly.*)

JIM. How about you? Don't you like to sit on the floor?

LAURA. Oh—yes.

JIM. Why don't you, then?

LAURA. I—will.

JIM. Take a pillow! (LAURA *does. Sits on the other side of the candelabrum.* JIM *crosses his legs and smiles engagingly at her.*) I can't hardly see you sitting way over there.

LAURA. I can—see you.

JIM. I know, but that's not fair, I'm in the limelight. (LAURA *moves her pillow closer.*) Good! Now I can see you! Comfortable?

LAURA. Yes.

JIM. So am I. Comfortable as a cow! Will you have some gum?

LAURA. No, thank you.

JIM. I think that I will indulge, with your permission. (*He musingly unwraps it and holds it up.*) Think of the fortune made by the guy that invented the first piece of chewing gum. Amazing, huh? The Wrigley Building is one of the sights of Chicago.—I saw it summer before last when I went up to the Century of Progress.° Did you take in the Century of Progress?

LAURA. No, I didn't.

JIM. Well, it was quite a wonderful exposition. What impressed me most was the Hall of Science. Gives you an idea of what the future will be in America, even more wonderful than the present time is! (*There is a pause.* JIM *smiles at her.*) Your brother tells me you're shy. Is that right, Laura?

LAURA. I—don't know.

JIM. I judge you to be an old-fashioned type of girl. Well, I think that's a pretty good type to be. Hope you don't think I'm being too personal—do you?

LAURA (*hastily, out of embarrassment*). I believe I *will* take a piece of gum, if you—don't mind. (*Clearing her throat.*) Mr. O'Connor, have you—kept up with your singing?

JIM. Singing? Me?

LAURA. Yes. I remember what a beautiful voice you had.

JIM. When did you hear me sing?

(*Voice off stage in the pause*
> O blow, ye winds, heigh-ho,
> A-roving I will go!
> I'm off to my love
> With a boxing glove—
> Ten thousand miles away!*)

Century of Progress: World's Fair in Chicago, 1933–34

JIM. You say you've heard me sing?

LAURA. Oh, yes! Yes, very often . . . I—don't suppose—you remember me—at all?

JIM (*smiling doubtfully*). You know I have an idea I've seen you before. I had that idea soon as you opened the door. It seemed almost like I was about to remember your name. But the name that I started to call you—wasn't a name! And so I stopped myself before I said it.

LAURA. Wasn't it—Blue Roses?

JIM (*springs up. Grinning*). Blue Roses!—My gosh, yes—Blue Roses! That's what I had on my tongue when you opened the door! Isn't it funny what tricks your memory plays? I didn't connect you with high school some-how or other. But that's where it was; it was high school. I didn't even know you were Shakespeare's sister! Gosh, I'm sorry.

LAURA. I didn't expect you to. You—barely knew me!

JIM. But we did have a speaking acquaintance, huh?

LAURA. Yes, we—spoke to each other.

JIM. When did you recognize me?

LAURA. Oh, right away!

JIM. Soon as I came in the door?

LAURA. When I heard your name I thought it was probably you. I knew that Tom used to know you a little in high school. So when you came in the door—well, then I was—sure.

JIM. Why didn't you *say* something, then?

LAURA (*breathlessly*). I didn't know what to say, I was—too surprised!

JIM. For goodness' sakes! You know, this sure is funny!

LAURA. Yes! Yes, isn't it, though . . .

JIM. Didn't we have a class in something together?

LAURA. Yes, we did.

JIM. What class was that?

LAURA. It was—singing—chorus!

JIM. Aw!

LAURA. I sat across the aisle from you in the Aud.

JIM. Aw.

LAURA. Mondays, Wednesdays and Fridays.

JIM. Now I remember—you always came in late.

LAURA. Yes, it was so hard for me getting upstairs. I had that brace on my leg—it clumped so loud!

JIM. I never heard any clumping.

LAURA (*wincing at the recollection*). To me it sounded like—thunder!

JIM. Well, well, well, I never even noticed.

LAURA. And everybody was seated before I came in. I had to walk in front of all those people. My seat was in the back row. I had to go clumping all the way up the aisle with everyone watching!

JIM. You shouldn't have been self-conscious.

LAURA. I know, but I was. It was always such a relief when the singing started.

JIM. Aw, yes, I've placed you now! I used to call you Blue Roses. How was it that I got started calling you that?

LAURA. I was out of school a little while with pleurosis. When I came back you asked me what was the matter. I said I had pleurosis—you thought I said Blue Roses. That's what you always called me after that!

JIM. I hope you didn't mind.

LAURA. Oh, no—I liked it. You see, I wasn't acquainted with many—people . . .

JIM. As I remember you sort of stuck by yourself.

LAURA. I—I—never have had much luck at—making friends.

JIM. I don't see why you wouldn't.

LAURA. Well, I—started out badly.

JIM. You mean being—

LAURA. Yes, it sort of—stood between me—

JIM. You shouldn't have let it!

LAURA. I know, but it did, and—

JIM. You were shy with people!

LAURA. I tried not to be but never could—

JIM. Overcome it?

LAURA. No, I—I never could!

JIM. I guess being shy is something you have to work out of kind of gradually.

LAURA (*sorrowfully*). Yes—I guess it—

JIM. Takes time!

LAURA. Yes—

JIM. People are not so dreadful when you know them. That's what you have to remember! And everybody has problems, not just you, but practically everybody has got some problems. You think of yourself as having the only problems, as being the only one who is disappointed. But just look around you and you will see lots of people as disappointed as you are. For instance, I hoped when I was going to high school that I would be further along at this time, six years later, than I am now— You remember that wonderful write-up I had in *The Torch?*

LAURA. Yes! (*She rises and crosses to table.*)

JIM. It said I was bound to succeed in anything I went into! (LAURA *returns with the annual.*) Holy Jeez! *The Torch!*

(*He accepts it reverently. They smile across it with mutual wonder.* LAURA *crouches beside him and they begin to turn through it.* LAURA'S *shyness is dissolving in his warmth.*)

LAURA. Here you are in *The Pirates of Penzance!*

JIM (*wistfully*). I sang the baritone lead in that operetta.

LAURA (*raptly*). So—*beautifully!*

JIM (*protesting*). Aw—

LAURA. Yes, yes—beautifully—beautifully!

JIM. You heard me?

LAURA. All three times!

JIM. No!

LAURA. Yes!

JIM. All three performances?

LAURA (*looking down*). Yes.

JIM. Why?

LAURA. I—wanted to ask you to—autograph my program.

JIM. Why didn't you ask me to?

LAURA. You were always surrounded by your own friends so much that I never had a chance to.

JIM. You should have just—

LAURA. Well, I—thought you might think I was—

JIM. Thought I might think you was—what?

LAURA. Oh—

JIM (*with reflective relish*). I was beleaguered by females in those days.

LAURA. You were terribly popular!

JIM. Yeah—

LAURA. You had such a—friendly way—

JIM. I was spoiled in high school.

LAURA. Everybody—liked you!

JIM. Including you?

LAURA. I—yes, I—I did, too—(*She gently closes the book in her lap.*)

JIM. Well, well, well!—Give me that program, Laura. (*She hands it to him. He signs it with a flourish.*) There you are—better late than never!

LAURA. Oh, I—what a—surprise!

JIM. My signature isn't worth very much right now. But some day—maybe—it will increase in value! Being disappointed is one thing and being discouraged is something else. I am disappointed but I am not discouraged. I'm twenty-three years old. How old are you?

LAURA. I'll be twenty-four in June.

JIM. That's not old age!

LAURA. No, but—

JIM. You finished high school?

LAURA (*with difficulty*). I didn't go back.

JIM. You mean you dropped out?

LAURA. I made bad grades in my final examinations. (*She rises and replaces the book and the program. Her voice is strained.*) How is—Emily Meisenbach getting along?

JIM. Oh, that kraut-head!

LAURA. Why do you call her that?

JIM. That's what she was.

LAURA. You're not still—going with her?

JIM. I never see her.

LAURA. It said in the Personal Section that you were—engaged!

JIM. I know, but I wasn't impressed by that—propaganda!

LAURA. It wasn't—the truth?

JIM. Only in Emily's optimistic opinion!

LAURA. Oh—

(JIM *lights a cigarette and leans indolently back on his elbows smiling at* LAURA *with a warmth and charm which lights her inwardly with altar candles. She remains by the table and turns in her hands a piece of glass to cover her tumult.*)

JIM (*after several reflective puffs on a cigarette*). What have you done since high school? (*She seems not to hear him.*) Huh? (LAURA *looks up.*) I said what have you done since high school, Laura?

LAURA. Nothing much.

JIM. You must have been doing something these six long years.

LAURA. Yes.

JIM. Well, then, such as what?

LAURA. I took a business course at business college—

JIM. How did that work out?

LAURA. Well, not very—well—I had to drop out, it gave me—indigestion—

(JIM *laughs gently.*)

JIM. What are you doing now?

LAURA. I don't do anything—much. Oh, please don't think I sit around doing nothing! My glass collection takes up a good deal of time. Glass is something you have to take good care of.

JIM. What did you say—about glass?

LAURA. Collection I said—I have one— (*She clears her throat and turns away again, acutely shy.*)

JIM (*abruptly*). You know what I judge to be the trouble with you? Inferiority complex! Know what that is? That's what they call it when someone low-rates himself! I understand it because I had it, too. Although my case was not so aggravated as yours seems to be. I had it until I took up public speaking, developed my voice, and learned that I had an aptitude for science. Before that time I never thought of myself as being outstanding in any way whatsoever! Now I've never made a regular study of it, but I have a friend who says I can analyze people better than doctors that make a profession of it. I don't claim that to be necessarily true, but I can sure guess a person's psychology, Laura! (*Takes out his gum.*) Excuse me, Laura. I always take it out when the flavor is gone. I'll use this scrap of paper to wrap it in. I know how it is to get it stuck on a shoe. Yep—that's what I judge to be your principal trouble. A lack of confidence in yourself as a person. You don't have the proper amount of faith in yourself. I'm basing that fact on a number of your remarks and also on certain observations I've made. For instance that clumping you thought was so awful in high school. You say that you even dreaded to walk into class. You see what you did? You dropped out of school, you gave up an education because of a clump, which as far as I know was practically non-existent! A little physical defect is what you have. Hardly noticeable even! Magnified thousands of times by imagination! You know what my strong advice to you is? Think of yourself as *superior* in some way!

LAURA. In what way would I think?

JIM. Why, man alive, Laura! Just look about you a little. What do you see? A world full of common people! All of 'em born and all of 'em going to die! Which of them has one-tenth of your good points! Or mine! Or anyone else's, as far as that goes—Gosh! Everybody excels in some one thing. Some in many! (*Unconsciously glances at himself in the mirror.*) All you've got to do is discover in *what!* Take me, for instance. (*He adjusts his tie at the mirror.*) My interest happens to lie in electro-dynamics. I'm taking a course in radio engineering at night school, Laura, on top of a fairly responsible job at the warehouse. I'm taking that course and studying public speaking.

LAURA. Ohhhh.

JIM. Because I believe in the future of television! (*Turning back to her.*) I wish to be ready to go up right along with it. Therefore I'm planning to get in on the ground floor. In fact I've already made the right connections and all that remains is for the industry itself to get under way! Full steam— (*His eyes are starry.*) *Knowledge—Zzzzzp! Money—Zzzzzzp!—Power!* That's the cycle democracy is built on! (*His attitude is convincingly dynamic.* LAURA *stares at him, even her shyness eclipsed in her absolute wonder. He suddenly grins.*) I guess you think I think a lot of myself!

LAURA. No—o-o-o, I—

JIM. Now how about you? Isn't there something you take more interest in than anything else?

LAURA. Well, I do—as I said—have my—glass collection—

(*A peal of girlish laughter from the kitchenette.*)

JIM. I'm not right sure I know what you're talking about. What kind of glass is it?

LAURA. Little articles of it, they're ornaments mostly! Most of them are little animals made out of glass, the tiniest little animals in the world. Mother calls them a glass menagerie! Here's an example of one, if you'd like to see it! This one is one of the oldest. It's nearly thirteen.

(*Music: "The Glass Menagerie." He stretches out his hand.*)

Oh, be careful—if you breathe, it breaks!

JIM. I'd better not take it. I'm pretty clumsy with things.

LAURA. Go on, I trust you with him! (*Places it in his palm.*) There now—you're holding him gently! Hold him over the light, he loves the light! You see how the light shines through him?

JIM. It sure does shine!

LAURA. I shouldn't be partial, but he is my favorite one.

JIM. What kind of a thing is this one supposed to be?

LAURA. Haven't you noticed the single horn on his forehead?

JIM. A unicorn, huh?

LAURA. Mmm-hmmm!

JIM. Unicorns, aren't they extinct in the modern world?

LAURA. I know!

JIM. Poor little fellow, he must feel sort of lonesome.

LAURA (*smiling*). Well, if he does he doesn't complain about it. He stays on a shelf with some horses that don't have horns and all of them seem to get along nicely together.

JIM. How do you know?.

LAURA (*lightly*). I haven't heard any arguments among them!

JIM (*grinning*). No arguments, huh? Well, that's a pretty good sign! Where shall I set him?

LAURA. Put him on the table. They all like a change of scenery once in a while!

JIM (*stretching*). Well, well, well, well—Look how big my shadow is when I stretch!

LAURA. Oh, oh, yes—it stretches across the ceiling!

JIM (*crossing to door*). I think it's stopped raining. (*Opens fire-escape door.*) Where does the music come from?

LAURA. From the Paradise Dance Hall across the alley.

JIM. How about cutting the rug a little, Miss Wingfield?

LAURA. Oh, I—

JIM. Or is your program filled up? Let me have a look at it. (*Grasps imaginary card*) Why, every dance is taken! I'll just have to scratch some out. (*Waltz music: "La Golondrina."*) Ahhh, a waltz! (*He executes some sweeping turns by himself then holds his arms toward* LAURA.)

LAURA (*breathlessly*). I—can't dance!

JIM. There you go, that inferiority stuff!

LAURA. I've never danced in my life!

JIM. Come on, try!

LAURA. Oh, but I'd step on you!

JIM. I'm not made out of glass.

LAURA. How—how—how do we start?

JIM. Just leave it to me. You hold your arms out a little.

LAURA. Like this?

JIM. A little bit higher. Right. Now don't tighten up, that's the main thing about it—relax.

LAURA (*laughing breathlessly*). It's hard not to.

JIM. Okay.

LAURA. I'm afraid you can't budge me.

JIM. What do you bet I can't? (*He swings her into motion.*)

LAURA. Goodness, yes, you can!

JIM. Let yourself go, now, Laura, just let yourself go.

LAURA. I'm—

JIM. Come on!

LAURA. Trying!

JIM. Not so stiff—Easy does it!

LAURA. I know but I'm—

JIM. Loosen th' backbone! There now, that's a lot better.

LAURA. Am I?

JIM. Lots, lots better! (*He moves her about the room in a clumsy waltz.*)

LAURA. Oh, my!

JIM. Ha-ha!

LAURA. Oh, my goodness!

JIM. Ha-ha-ha! (*They suddenly bump into the table. JIM stops.*) What did
we hit on?

LAURA. Table.

JIM. Did something fall off it? I think—

LAURA. Yes.

JIM. I hope that it wasn't the little glass horse with the horn!

LAURA. Yes.

JIM. Aw, aw, aw. Is it broken?

LAURA. Now it is just like all the other horses.

JIM. It's lost its—

LAURA. Horn! It doesn't matter. Maybe it's a blessing in disguise.

JIM. You'll never forgive me. I bet that was your favorite piece of glass.

LAURA. I don't have favorites much. It's no tragedy, Freckles. Glass
breaks so easily. No matter how careful you are. The traffic jars the shelves
and things fall off them.

JIM. Still I'm awfully sorry that I was the cause.

LAURA (*smiling*). I'll just imagine he had an operation. The horn was
removed to make him feel less—freakish! (*They both laugh.*) Now he will feel
more at home with the other horses, the ones that don't have horns . . .

JIM. Ha-ha, that's very funny! (*Suddenly serious.*) I'm glad to see that
you have a sense of humor. You know—you're—well—very different! Sur-
prisingly different from anyone else I know! (*His voice becomes soft and hesi-
tant with a genuine feeling.*) Do you mind me telling you that?

(LAURA *is abashed beyond speech.*)

I mean it in a nice way . . .

(LAURA *nods shyly, looking away.*)

You make me feel sort of—I don't know how to put it! I'm usually pretty
good at expressing things, but—this is something that I don't know how to
say!

(LAURA *touches her throat and clears it—turns the broken unicorn in her
hands. His voice becomes softer.*)

Has anyone ever told you that you were pretty?

(*Pause: music.* LAURA *looks up slowly, with wonder, and shakes her head.*)

Well, you are! In a very different way from anyone else. And all the nicer because of the difference, too. (*His voice becomes low and husky.* LAURA *turns away, nearly faint with the novelty of her emotions.*) I wish that you were my sister. I'd teach you to have some confidence in yourself. The different people are not like other people, but being different is nothing to be ashamed of. Because other people are not such wonderful people. They're one hundred times one thousand. You're one times one! They walk all over the earth. You just stay here. They're common as—weeds, but—you—well, you're—*Blue Roses!*

(*Music changes.*)

LAURA.   But blue is wrong for—roses . . .

JIM.   It's right for you!—You're—pretty!

LAURA.   In what respect am I pretty?

JIM.   In all respects—believe me! Your eyes—your hair—are pretty! Your hands are pretty! (*He catches hold of her hand.*) You think I'm making this up because I'm invited to dinner and have to be nice. Oh, I could do that! I could put on an act for you, Laura, and say lots of things without being very sincere. But this time I am. I'm talking to you sincerely. I happened to notice you had this inferiority complex that keeps you from feeling comfortable with people. Somebody needs to build your confidence up and make you proud instead of shy and turning away and—blushing—Somebody—ought to— Ought to—*kiss* you, Laura! (*His hand slips slowly up her arm to her shoulder. Music swells tumultuously. He suddenly turns her about and kisses her on the lips. When he releases her,* LAURA *sinks on the sofa with a bright, dazed look.* JIM *backs away and fishes in his pocket for a cigarette.*) Stumble-john!

(*He lights the cigarette, avoiding her look. There is a peal of girlish laughter from* AMANDA *in the kitchenette.* LAURA *slowly raises and opens her hand. It still contains the little broken glass animal. She looks at it with a tender, bewildered expression.*)

Stumble-john! I shouldn't have done that—That was way off the beam. You don't smoke, do you?

(*She looks up, smiling, not hearing the question. He sits beside her a little gingerly. She looks at him speechlessly—waiting. He coughs decorously and moves a little farther aside as he considers the situation and senses her feelings, dimly, with perturbation. He speaks gently.*)

Would you—care for a—mint?

(*She doesn't seem to hear him but her look grows brighter even.*)

Peppermint—Life-Saver? My pocket's a regular drug store—wherever I go . . . (*He pops a mint in his mouth. Then gulps and decides to make a clean breast of it. He speaks slowly and gingerly.*) Laura, you know, if I had a sister like you, I'd do the same thing as Tom. I'd bring out fellows and—introduce her to them. The right type of boys of a type to—appreciate her. Only— well—he made a mistake about me. Maybe I've got no call to be saying this. That may not have been the idea in having me over. But what if it was? There's nothing wrong about that. The only trouble is that in my case—I'm not in a situation to—do the right thing. I can't take down your number and say I'll phone. I can't call up next week and—ask for a date. I thought I had better explain the situation in case you—misunderstood it and—hurt your feelings . . .

(*Pause. Slowly, very slowly,* LAURA'S *look changes, her eyes returning slowly from his to the ornament in her palm.* AMANDA *utters another gay laugh in the kitchenette.*)

LAURA (*faintly*). You—won't—call again?

JIM. No, Laura, I can't. (*He rises from the sofa.*) As I was just explaining. I've—got strings on me. Laura, I've—been going steady! I go out all of the time with a girl named Betty. She's a home-girl like you, and Catholic, and Irish, and in a great many ways we—get along fine. I met her last summer on a moonlight boat trip up the river to Alton, on the *Majestic.* Well—right away from the start it was—love!

(LAURA *sways slightly forward and grips the arm of the sofa. He fails to notice, now enrapt in his own comfortable being.*)

Being in love has made a new man of me!

(*Leaning stiffly forward, clutching the arm of the sofa,* LAURA *struggles visibly with her storm. But* JIM *is oblivious, she is a long way off.*)

The power of love is really pretty tremendous! Love is something that— changes the whole world, Laura!

(*The storm abates a little and* LAURA *leans back. He notices her again.*)

It happened that Betty's aunt took sick, she got a wire and had to go to Centralia. So Tom—when he asked me to dinner—I naturally just accepted the invitation, not knowing that you—that he—that I—(*He stops awkwardly.*) Huh—I'm a stumble-john!

(*He flops back on the sofa. The holy candles in the altar of* LAURA'S *face have been snuffed out. There is a look of almost infinite desolation.* JIM *glances at her uneasily.*)

I wish that you would—say something.

(*She bites her lip which was trembling and then bravely smiles. She opens her hand again on the broken glass ornament. Then she gently takes his hand and raises it level with her own. She carefully places the unicorn in the palm of his hand, then pushes his fingers closed upon it.*)

What are you—doing that for? You want me to have him—Laura? (*She nods.*) What for?

LAURA. A—souvenir . . . (*She rises unsteadily and crouches beside the victrola to wind it up.*)

(*At this moment* AMANDA *rushes brightly back into the living room. She bears a pitcher of fruit punch in an old-fashioned cut-glass pitcher and a plate of macaroons. The plate has a gold border and poppies painted on it.*)

AMANDA. Well, well, well! Isn't the air delightful after the shower? I've made you children a little liquid refreshment.

(*She turns gaily to* JIM.) Jim, do you know that song about lemonade?

"Lemonade, lemonade
Made in the shade and stirred with a spade—
Good enough for any old maid!"

JIM (*uneasily*). Ha-ha! No—I never heard it.

AMANDA. Why, Laura! You look so serious!

JIM. We were having a serious conversation.

AMANDA. Good! Now you're better acquainted!

JIM (*uncertainly*). Ha-ha! Yes.

AMANDA. You modern young people are much more serious-minded than my generation. I was so gay as a girl!

JIM. You haven't changed, Mrs. Wingfield.

AMANDA. Tonight I'm rejuvenated! The gaiety of the occasion, Mr. O'Connor! (*She tosses her head with a peal of laughter. Spills lemonade.*) Oooo! I'm baptizing myself!

JIM. Here—let me—

AMANDA (*setting the pitcher down*). There now. I discovered we had some maraschino cherries. I dumped them in, juice and all!

JIM. You shouldn't have gone to that trouble, Mrs. Wingfield.

AMANDA. Trouble, trouble? Why, it was loads of fun! Didn't you hear me cutting up in the kitchen? I bet your ears were burning! I told Tom how outdone with him I was for keeping you to himself so long a time! He should have brought you over much, much sooner! Well, now that you've found your way, I want you to be a very frequent caller! Not just occasional but all the time. Oh, we're going to have a lot of gay times together! I see them coming! Mmm, just breathe that air! So fresh, and the moon's so pretty! I'll skip back out—I know where my place is when young folks are having a—serious conversation!

JIM. Oh, don't go out, Mrs. Wingfield. The fact of the matter is I've got to be going.

AMANDA. Going, now? You're joking! Why, it's only the shank of the evening, Mr. O'Connor!

JIM. Well, you know how it is.

AMANDA. You mean you're a young workingman and have to keep workingmen's hours. We'll let you off early tonight. But only on the condition that next time you stay later.

What's the best night for you? Isn't Saturday night the best night for you workingmen?

JIM. I have a couple of time-clocks to punch, Mrs. Wingfield. One at morning, another one at night!

AMANDA. My, but you *are* ambitious! You work at night, too?

JIM. No, Ma'am, not work but—Betty! (*He crosses deliberately to pick up his hat. The band at the Paradise Dance Hall goes into a tender waltz.*)

AMANDA. Betty? Betty? Who's—Betty!

(*There is an ominous cracking sound in the sky.*)

JIM. Oh, just a girl. The girl I go steady with! (*He smiles charmingly. The sky falls.*)

AMANDA (*a long-drawn exhalation*). Ohhhh . . . . Is it a serious romance, Mr. O'Connor?

JIM. We're going to be married the second Sunday in June.

AMANDA. Ohhhh—how nice! Tom didn't mention that you were engaged to be married.

JIM. The cat's not out of the bag at the warehouse yet. You know how they are. They call you Romeo and stuff like that. (*He stops at the oval mirror to put on his hat. He carefully shapes the brim and the crown to give a discreetly dashing effect.*)

It's been a wonderful evening, Mrs. Wingfield. I guess this is what they mean by Southern hospitality.

AMANDA. It really wasn't anything at all.

JIM. I hope it don't seem like I'm rushing off. But I promised Betty I'd pick her up at the Wabash depot, an' by the time I get my jalopy down there her train'll be in. Some women are pretty upset if you keep 'em waiting.

AMANDA. Yes, I know—The tyranny of women! (*Extends her hand.*) Good-bye, Mr. O'Connor. I wish you luck—and happiness—and success! All three of them, and so does Laura!—Don't you, Laura?

LAURA. Yes!

JIM (*taking her hand*). Good-bye, Laura. I'm certainly going to treasure that souvenir. And don't you forget the good advice I gave you. (*Raises his voice to a cheery shout.*) So long, Shakespeare! Thanks again, ladies—Good night!

(*He grins and ducks jauntily out. Still bravely grimacing,* AMANDA *closes the door on the gentleman caller. Then she turns back to the room with a puzzled expression. She and* LAURA *don't dare to face each other.* LAURA *crouches beside the victrola to wind it.*)

AMANDA (*faintly*). Things have a way of turning out so badly. I don't believe that I would play the victrola. Well, well—well—Our gentleman caller was engaged to be married! (*She raises her voice.*) Tom!

TOM (*from the kitchenette*). Yes, Mother?

AMANDA. Come in here a minute. I want to tell you something awfully funny.

TOM (*enters with macaroon and a glass of the lemonade*). Has the gentleman caller gotten away already?

AMANDA. The gentleman caller has made an early departure. What a wonderful joke you played on us!

TOM. How do you mean?

AMANDA. You didn't mention that he was engaged to be married.

TOM. Jim? Engaged?

AMANDA. That's what he just informed us.

TOM. I'll be jiggered! I didn't know about that.

AMANDA. That seems very peculiar.

TOM. What's peculiar about it?

AMANDA. Didn't you call him your best friend down at the warehouse?

TOM. He is, but how did I know?

AMANDA. It seems extremely peculiar that you wouldn't know your best friend was going to be married!

TOM. The warehouse is where I work, not where I know things about people!

AMANDA. You don't know things anywhere! You live in a dream; you manufacture illusions! (*He crosses to the door.*) Where are you going?

TOM. I'm going to the movies.

AMANDA. That's right, now that you've had us make such fools of ourselves. The effort, the preparations, all the expense! The new floor lamp, the rug, the clothes for Laura! All for what? To entertain some other girl's fiancé! Go to the movies, go! Don't think about us, a mother deserted, an unmarried sister who's crippled and has no job! Don't let anything interfere with your selfish pleasure! Just go, go, go—to the movies!

TOM. All right, I will! The more you shout about my selfishness to me the quicker I'll go, and I won't go to the movies!

AMANDA. Go, then! Then go to the moon—you selfish dreamer!

(TOM *smashes his glass on the floor. He plunges out on the fire-escape, slamming the door.* LAURA *screams in fright. The dance-hall music becomes louder.* TOM *goes to the rail and grips it desperately, lifting his face in the chill white moonlight penetrating the narrow abyss of the alley.*

(TOM's *closing speech is timed with what is happening inside the house. The interior scene is played as though viewed through soundproof glass.* AMANDA *appears to be making a comforting speech to* LAURA *who is huddled upon the sofa. Now that we cannot hear the mother's speech, her silliness is gone and she has dignity and tragic beauty.* LAURA's *dark hair hides her face until at the end of the speech she lifts it to smile at her mother.* AMANDA'S *gestures are slow and graceful, almost dance-like, as she comforts her daughter. At the end of her speech she glances a moment at the father's picture—then withdraws through the portieres. At the close of* TOM'S *speech,* LAURA *blows out the candles, ending the play.*)

TOM. I didn't go to the moon, I went much further—for time is the longest distance between two places—Not long after that I was fired for writing a poem on the lid of a shoe-box. I left Saint Louis. I descended the steps of this fire-escape for a last time and followed, from then on, in my father's footsteps, attempting to find in motion what was lost in space—I traveled around a great deal. The cities swept about me like dead leaves, leaves that were brightly colored but torn away from the branches. I would have stopped, but I was pursued by something. It always came upon me unawares, taking me altogether by surprise. Perhaps it was a familiar bit of music. Perhaps it was only a piece of transparent glass—Perhaps I am walking along a street at night, in some strange city, before I have found companions. I pass the lighted window of a shop where perfume is sold. The window is filled with pieces of colored glass, tiny transparent bottles in delicate colors, like bits of a shattered rainbow. Then all at once my sister touches my shoulder. I turn around and look into her eyes . . . Oh, Laura, Laura, I tried to leave you behind me, but I am more faithful than I intended to be! I reach for a cigarette, I cross the street, I run into the movies or a bar, I buy a drink, I speak to the nearest stranger—anything that can blow your candles out!

(LAURA *bends over the candles.*)

For nowadays the world is lit by lightning! Blow out your candles, Laura —and so good-bye . . .

(*She blows the candles out.*)

QUESTIONS

1. In presenting Scene I, the author says: "The scene is memory and is therefore nonrealistic." To whose memory does he refer? Why should memory be nonrealistic? List the different ways in which the play is nonrealistic. What, according to Tom in his opening speech, is the ultimate aim of this nonrealistic method of presentation?
2. How does the kind of language Tom uses as a narrator differ from that he uses as a character? What would happen to the play if Tom used the first kind of language throughout?
3. What is Tom's dilemma? Why is he always quarreling with his mother? What is his attitude toward Laura? Why does he finally leave? Does he ever resolve his dilemma?
4. What qualities possessed by Tom, and by him alone, make him the proper narrator of the play?

5. Laura is the pivotal character in the play, as evidenced by its title and by the fact that the main actions of the play revolve around her. What are the symptoms and causes of her mental condition? Can they all be traced to her physical defect? What qualities make her a sympathetic character? How does her relation with her mother differ from Tom's.

6. What symbolical meanings has Laura's glass menagerie? What, especially, is symbolized by the unicorn? How and why does her reaction to Jim's breaking the unicorn differ from her reaction to Tom's breaking several pieces at the end of Scene III? Why does she give the broken unicorn to Jim as a souvenir? What future do you predict for her? What symbolism has her blowing out the candles at the end of the play?

7. The author tells us (page 955) that "Amanda, having failed to establish contact with reality, continues to live vitally in her illusions." What part of this statement could be applied to Laura as well? What part could not? What are the chief instances in the play of Amanda's having lost "contact with reality"? What are her chief illusions? What are her strengths? How is she both cruel and tender with her children? What qualities has she in common with Jim, the gentleman caller? Why do you suppose her husband left her?

8. The author describes Jim O'Connor as "a nice, ordinary, young man" (page 955). Tom (in Scene I) describes him as "the most realistic character, being an emissary from that world of reality that we were set apart from." In what ways is Jim "nice"? In what ways is he "ordinary"? In what ways and in what sense is he more "realistic" than the Wingfields? Does this mean that he is without delusions? What would you predict for his future? Of what is he symbolic?

9. Account for Jim's treatment of Laura in Scene VII.

10. What trait do Laura, Amanda, and Tom all share, which makes Jim more realistic than they? Explain the dramatic irony in Amanda's remark to Tom, in their final dialogue, "You don't know things anywhere! You live in a dream; you manufacture illusions!"

11. What respective claims have Tom, Laura, and Amanda for being considered the protagonist of the play? For which character would it be most crucial to the success or failure of a production to obtain a highly accomplished actor or actress? Why?

12. The play is set in the 1930s. Of what significance are the many references throughout the play to its social and historical background? How are these larger events and the Wingfields' domestic lives related?

13. The play is divided into seven scenes. If you were to produce it with one intermission, where would you put the intermission? For what reasons?

Federico García Lorca

BLOOD WEDDING

CHARACTERS

THE BRIDEGROOM	THE BRIDE'S FATHER
THE BRIDEGROOM'S MOTHER	A SERVANT WOMAN
A NEIGHBOR WOMAN	YOUNG GIRLS
LEONARDO	YOUNG MEN
LEONARDO'S WIFE	OTHER WEDDING GUESTS
LEONARDO'S MOTHER-IN-LAW	WOODCUTTERS
THE BRIDE	THE MOON

ACT I

SCENE I

A room painted yellow.

BRIDEGROOM (*entering*). Mother.

MOTHER. What?

BRIDEGROOM. I'm going.

MOTHER. Where?

BRIDEGROOM. To the vineyard. (*He starts to go.*)

MOTHER. Wait.

BRIDEGROOM. You want something?

MOTHER. Your breakfast, son.

BRIDEGROOM. Forget it. I'll eat grapes. Give me the knife.

MOTHER. What for?

BRIDEGROOM (*laughing*). To cut the grapes with.

MOTHER (*muttering as she looks for the knife*). Knives, knives. Cursed be all knives, and the scoundrel who invented them.

BRIDEGROOM. Let's talk about something else.

MOTHER. And guns and pistols and the smallest little knife—and even hoes and pitchforks.

BRIDEGROOM. All right.

MOTHER. Everything that can slice a man's body. A handsome man, full

BLOOD WEDDING First performed in Madrid in 1933. English translation by James Graham-Lujan and Richard L. O'Connell. Federico García Lorca (1898–1936) was born near Granada in the region of southern Spain called Andalusia, the son of a prosperous landowner. Though he took a law degree at the University of Granada, his real interests were music, art, literature, and folklore, and he became widely known for his brilliant public readings of his poems and gypsy ballads. He combined his talents and interests when he turned his main energies to drama.

of young life, who goes out to the vineyards or to his own olive groves—his own because he's inherited them . . .

BRIDEGROOM (*lowering his head*). Be quiet.

MOTHER. . . . and then that man doesn't come back. Or if he does come back it's only for someone to cover him over with a palm leaf or a plate of rock salt so he won't bloat. I don't know how you dare carry a knife on your body—or how I let this serpent (*she takes a knife from a kitchen chest*) stay in the chest.

BRIDEGROOM. Have you had your say?

MOTHER. If I lived to be a hundred I'd talk of nothing else. First your father; to me he smelled like a carnation and I had him for barely three years. Then your brother. Oh, is it right—how can it be—that a small thing like a knife or a pistol can finish off a man—a bull of a man? No, I'll never be quiet. The months pass and the hopelessness of it stings in my eyes and even to the roots of my hair.

BRIDEGROOM (*forcefully*). Let's quit this talk!

MOTHER. No. No. Let's not quit this talk. Can anyone bring me your father back? Or your brother? Then there's the jail. What do they mean, jail? They eat there, smoke there, play music there! My dead men choking with weeds, silent, turning to dust. Two men like two beautiful flowers. The killers in jail, carefree, looking at the mountains.

BRIDEGROOM. Do you want me to go kill them?

MOTHER. No . . . If I talk about it it's because . . . Oh, how can I help talking about it, seeing you go out that door? It's . . . I don't like you to carry a knife. It's just that . . . that I wish you wouldn't go out to the fields.

BRIDEGROOM (*laughing*). Oh, come now!

MOTHER. I'd like it if you were a woman. Then you wouldn't be going out to the arroyo now and we'd both of us embroider flounces and little woolly dogs.

BRIDEGROOM (*he puts his arm around his mother and laughs*). Mother, what if I should take you with me to the vineyards?

MOTHER. What would an old lady do in the vineyards? Were you going to put me down under the young vines?

BRIDEGROOM (*lifting her in his arms*). Old lady, old lady—you little old, little old lady!

MOTHER. Your father, he used to take me. That's the way with men of good stock; good blood. Your grandfather left a son on every corner. That's what I like. Men, men; wheat, wheat.

BRIDEGROOM. And I, Mother?

MOTHER. You, what?

BRIDEGROOM. Do I need to tell you again?

MOTHER (*seriously*). Oh!

BRIDEGROOM. Do you think it's bad?

MOTHER. No.

BRIDEGROOM. Well, then?

MOTHER. I don't really know. Like this, suddenly, it always surprises me. I know the girl is good. Isn't she? Well behaved. Hard working. Kneads her bread, sews her skirts, but even so when I say her name I feel as though someone had hit me on the forehead with a rock.

BRIDEGROOM. Foolishness.

MOTHER. More than foolishness. I'll be left alone. Now only you are left me—I hate to see you go.

BRIDEGROOM. But you'll come with us.

MOTHER. No. I can't leave your father and brother here alone. I have to go to them every morning and if I go away it's possible one of the Félix family, one of the killers, might die—and they'd bury him next to ours. And that'll never happen! Oh, no! That'll never happen! Because I'd dig them out with my nails and, all by myself, crush them against the wall.

BRIDEGROOM (sternly). There you go again.

MOTHER. Forgive me. (pause) How long have you known her?

BRIDEGROOM. Three years. I've been able to buy the vineyard.

MOTHER. Three years. She used to have another sweetheart, didn't she?

BRIDEGROOM. I don't know. I don't think so. Girls have to look at what they'll marry.

MOTHER. Yes, I looked at nobody. I looked at your father, and when they killed him I looked at the wall in front of me. One woman with one man, and that's all.

BRIDEGROOM. You know my girl's good.

MOTHER. I don't doubt it. All the same, I'm sorry not to have known what her mother was like.

BRIDEGROOM. What difference does it make now?

MOTHER (looking at him). Son.

BRIDEGROOM. What is it?

MOTHER. That's true! You're right! When do you want me to ask for her?

BRIDEGROOM (happily). Does Sunday seem all right to you?

MOTHER (seriously). I'll take her the bronze earrings, they're very old—and you buy her . . .

BRIDEGROOM. You know more about that . . .

MOTHER. . . . you buy her some open-work stockings—and for you, two suits—three! I have no one but you now!

BRIDEGROOM. I'm going. Tomorrow I'll go see her.

MOTHER. Yes, yes—and see if you can make me happy with six grand-children—or as many as you want, since your father didn't live to give them to me.

BRIDEGROOM. The first-born for you!

MOTHER. Yes, but have some girls. I want to embroider and make lace, and be at peace.

BRIDEGROOM. I'm sure you'll love my wife.

MOTHER. I'll love her. (She starts to kiss him but changes her mind.) Go

on. You're too big now for kisses. Give them to your wife. (*Pause. To herself*)
When she is your wife.

BRIDEGROOM. I'm going.

MOTHER. And that land around the little mill—work it over. You've not
taken good care of it.

BRIDEGROOM. You're right. I will.

MOTHER. God keep you.

(*The son goes out. The* MOTHER *remains seated—her back to the door. A* NEIGH-
BOR WOMAN *with a 'kerchief on her head appears in the door.*)

Come in.

NEIGHBOR. How are you?

MOTHER. Just as you see me.

NEIGHBOR. I came down to the store and stopped in to see you. We live
so far away!

MOTHER. It's twenty years since I've been up to the top of the street.

NEIGHBOR. You're looking well.

MOTHER. You think so?

NEIGHBOR. Things happen. Two days ago they brought in my neighbor's son with both arms sliced off by the machine. (*She sits down.*)

MOTHER. Rafael?

NEIGHBOR. Yes. And there you have him. Many times I've thought your
son and mine are better off where they are—sleeping, resting—not running
the risk of being left helpless.

MOTHER. Hush. That's all just something thought up—but no consolation.

NEIGHBOR (*sighing*). Ay!

MOTHER (*sighing*). Ay!

(*Pause.*)

NEIGHBOR (*sadly*). Where's your son?

MOTHER. He went out.

NEIGHBOR. He finally bought the vineyard!

MOTHER. He was lucky.

NEIGHBOR. Now he'll get married.

MOTHER (*as though reminded of something, she draws her chair near the*
NEIGHBOR). Listen.

NEIGHBOR (*in a confidential manner*). Yes. What is it?

MOTHER. You know my son's sweetheart?

NEIGHBOR. A good girl!

MOTHER. Yes, but . . .

NEIGHBOR. But who knows her really well? There's nobody. She lives
out there alone with her father—so far away—fifteen miles from the nearest
house. But she's a good girl. Used to being alone.

MOTHER. And her mother?

NEIGHBOR. Her mother I *did* know. Beautiful. Her face glowed like a saint's—but *I* never liked her. She didn't love her husband.

MOTHER (*sternly*). Well, what a lot of things certain people know!

NEIGHBOR. I'm sorry. I didn't mean to offend—but it's true. Now, whether she was decent or not nobody said. That wasn't discussed. She was haughty.

MOTHER. There you go again!

NEIGHBOR. You asked me.

MOTHER. I wish no one knew anything about them—either the live one or the dead one—that they were like two thistles no one even names but cuts off at the right moment.

NEIGHBOR. You're right. Your son is worth a lot.

MOTHER. Yes—a lot. That's why I look after him. They told me the girl had a sweetheart some time ago.

NEIGHBOR. She was about fifteen. He's been married two years now—to a cousin of hers, as a matter of fact. But nobody remembers about their engagement.

MOTHER. How do you remember it?

NEIGHBOR. Oh, what questions you ask!

MOTHER. We like to know all about the things that hurt us. Who was the boy?

NEIGHBOR. Leonardo.

MOTHER. What Leonardo?

NEIGHBOR. Leonardo Félix.

MOTHER. Félix!

NEIGHBOR. Yes, but—how is Leonardo to blame for anything? He was eight years old when those things happened.

MOTHER. That's true. But I hear that name—Félix—and it's all the same. (*Muttering*) Félix, a slimy mouthful. (*She spits.*) It makes me spit—spit so I won't kill!

NEIGHBOR. Control yourself. What good will it do?

MOTHER. No good. But you see how it is.

NEIGHBOR. Don't get in the way of your son's happiness. Don't say anything to him. You're old. So am I. It's time for you and me to keep quiet.

MOTHER. I'll say nothing to him.

NEIGHBOR (*kissing her*). Nothing.

MOTHER (*calmly*). Such things . . . !

NEIGHBOR. I'm going. My men will soon be coming in from the fields.

MOTHER. Have you ever known such a hot sun?

NEIGHBOR. The children carrying water out to the reapers are black with it. Goodbye, woman.

MOTHER. Goodbye. (*The* MOTHER *starts toward the door at the left. Half-way there she stops and slowly crosses herself.*)

SCENE II

*A room painted rose with copperware and wreaths of common flowers. In the
center of the room is a table with a tablecloth. It is morning.*
LEONARDO'S MOTHER-IN-LAW *sits in one corner holding a child in her
arms and rocking it. His* WIFE *is in the other corner mending stockings.*

MOTHER-IN-LAW. Lullaby, my baby
    once there was a big horse
    who didn't like water.
    The water was black there
    under the branches.
    When it reached the bridge
    it stopped and it sang.
    Who can say, my baby,
    what the stream holds
    with its long tail
    in its green parlor?
WIFE (*softly*). Carnation, sleep and dream,
    the horse won't drink from the stream.
MOTHER-IN-LAW. My rose, asleep now lie,
    the horse is starting to cry.
    His poor hooves were bleeding,
    his long mane was frozen,
    and deep in his eyes
    stuck a silvery dagger.
    Down he went to the river,
    Oh, down he went down!
    And his blood was running,
    Oh, more than the water.
WIFE. Carnation, sleep and dream,
    the horse won't drink from the stream.
MOTHER-IN-LAW. My rose, asleep now lie,
    the horse is starting to cry.
WIFE. He never did touch
    the dank river shore
    though his muzzle was warm
    and with silvery flies.
    So, to the hard mountains
    he could only whinny
    just when the dead stream
    covered his throat.
    Ay-y-y, for the big horse
    who didn't like water!
    Ay-y-y, for the snow-wound
    big horse of the dawn!

MOTHER-IN-LAW. Don't come in! Stop him
   and close up the window
   with branches of dreams
   and a dream of branches.
WIFE. My baby is sleeping.
MOTHER-IN-LAW. My baby is quiet.
WIFE. Look, horse, my baby
   has him a pillow.
MOTHER-IN-LAW. His cradle is metal.
WIFE. His quilt a fine fabric.
MOTHER-IN-LAW. Lullaby, my baby.
WIFE. Ay-y-y, for the big horse
   who didn't like water!
MOTHER-IN-LAW. Don't come near, don't come in!
   Go away to the mountains
   and through the grey valleys,
   that's where your mare is.
WIFE (*looking at the baby*). My baby is sleeping.
MOTHER-IN-LAW. My baby is resting.
WIFE (*softly*). Carnation, sleep and dream,
   the horse won't drink from the stream.
MOTHER-IN-LAW (*getting up, very softly*).
   My rose, asleep now lie
   for the horse is starting to cry.

(*She carries the child out.* LEONARDO *enters.*)

LEONARDO. Where's the baby?
WIFE. He's sleeping.
LEONARDO. Yesterday he wasn't well. He cried during the night.
WIFE. Today he's like a dahlia. And you? Were you at the blacksmith's?
LEONARDO. I've just come from there. Would you believe it? For more
than two months he's been putting new shoes on the horse and they're always
coming off. As far as I can see he pulls them off on the stones.
WIFE. Couldn't it just be that you use him so much?
LEONARDO. No. I almost never use him.
WIFE. Yesterday the neighbors told me they'd seen you on the far side of
the plains.
LEONARDO. Who said that?
WIFE. The women who gather capers. It certainly surprised me. Was it
you?
LEONARDO. No. What would I be doing there, in that wasteland?
WIFE. That's what I said. But the horse was streaming sweat.
LEONARDO. Did you see him?
WIFE. No. Mother did.
LEONARDO. Is she with the baby?

WIFE. Yes. Do you want some lemonade?

LEONARDO. With good cold water.

WIFE. And then you didn't come to eat!

LEONARDO. I was with the wheat weighers. They always hold me up.

WIFE (*very tenderly, while she makes the lemonade*). Did they pay you a good price?

LEONARDO. Fair.

WIFE. I need a new dress and the baby a bonnet with ribbons.

LEONARDO (*getting up*). I'm going to take a look at him.

WIFE. Be careful. He's asleep.

MOTHER-IN-LAW (*coming in*). Well! Who's been racing the horse that way? He's down there, worn out, his eyes popping from their sockets as though he'd come from the ends of the earth.

LEONARDO (*acidly*). I have.

MOTHER-IN-LAW. Oh, excuse me! He's your horse.

WIFE (*timidly*). He was at the wheat buyers.

MOTHER-IN-LAW. He can burst for all of me!

(*She sits down. Pause.*)

WIFE. Your drink. Is it cold?

LEONARDO. Yes.

WIFE. Did you hear they're going to ask for my cousin?

LEONARDO. When?

WIFE. Tomorrow. The wedding will be within a month. I hope they're going to invite us.

LEONARDO (*gravely*). I don't know.

MOTHER-IN-LAW. His mother, I think, wasn't very happy about the match.

LEONARDO. Well, she may be right. She's a girl to be careful with.

WIFE. I don't like to have you thinking bad things about a good girl.

MOTHER-IN-LAW (*meaningfully*). If he does, it's because he knows her. Didn't you know he courted her for three years?

LEONARDO. But I left her. (*To his* WIFE.) Are you going to cry now? Quit that! (*He brusquely pulls her hands away from her face.*) Let's go see the baby.

(*They go in with their arms around each other. A* GIRL *appears. She is happy. She enters running.*)

GIRL. Señora.

MOTHER-IN-LAW. What is it?

GIRL. The groom came to the store and he's bought the best of everything they had.

MOTHER-IN-LAW. Was he alone?

GIRL. No. With his mother. Stern, tall. (*She imitates her.*) And such extravagance!

MOTHER-IN-LAW. They have money.

GIRL. And they bought some open-work stockings! Oh, such stockings! A woman's dream of stockings! Look: a swallow here (*she points to her ankle*), a ship here (*she points to her calf*), and here (*she points to her thigh*) a rose!

MOTHER-IN-LAW. Child!

GIRL. A rose with the seeds and the stem! Oh! All in silk.

MOTHER-IN-LAW. Two rich families are being brought together.

(LEONARDO *and his* WIFE *appear.*)

GIRL. I came to tell you what they're buying.

LEONARDO (*loudly*). We don't care.

WIFE. Leave her alone.

MOTHER-IN-LAW. Leonardo, it's not that important.

GIRL. Please excuse me. (*She leaves, weeping.*)

MOTHER-IN-LAW. Why do you always have to make trouble with people?

LEONARDO. I didn't ask for your opinion. (*He sits down.*)

MOTHER-IN-LAW. Very well.

(*Pause.*)

WIFE (*to* LEONARDO). What's the matter with you? What idea've you got boiling there inside your head? Don't leave me like this, not knowing anything.

LEONARDO. Stop that.

WIFE. No. I want you to look at me and tell me.

LEONARDO. Let me alone. (*He rises.*)

WIFE. Where are you going, love?

LEONARDO (*sharply*). Can't you shut up?

MOTHER-IN-LAW (*energetically, to her daughter*). Be quiet!

(LEONARDO *goes out.*)

The baby! (*She goes into the bedroom and comes out again with the baby in her arms. The* WIFE *has remained standing, unmoving.*)

MOTHER-IN-LAW. His poor hooves were bleeding,
    his long mane was frozen,
    and deep in his eyes
    stuck a silvery dagger.
    Down he went to the river,
    Oh, down he went down!
    And his blood was running,
    Oh, more than the water.

WIFE (*turning slowly, as though dreaming*).
    Carnation, sleep and dream,
    the horse is drinking from the stream.

MOTHER-IN-LAW. My rose, asleep now lie

the horse is starting to cry.

WIFE. Lullaby, my baby.

MOTHER-IN-LAW. Ay-y-y, for the big horse
  who didn't like water!

WIFE (*dramatically*). Don't come near, don't come in!
  Go away to the mountains!
  Ay-y-y, for the snow-wound,
  big horse of the dawn!

MOTHER-IN-LAW (*weeping*).
  My baby is sleeping . . .

WIFE (*weeping, as she slowly moves closer*).
  My baby is resting . . .

MOTHER-IN-LAW. Carnation, sleep and dream,
  the horse won't drink from the stream.

WIFE (*weeping, and leaning on the table*).
  My rose, asleep now lie,
  the horse is starting to cry.

SCENE III

Interior of the cave where the BRIDE *lives. At the back is a cross of large rose colored flowers. The round doors have lace curtains with rose colored ties. Around the walls, which are of a white and hard material, are round fans, blue jars, and little mirrors.*

SERVANT. Come right in . . .

(*She is very affable, full of humble hypocrisy. The* BRIDEGROOM *and his* MOTHER *enter. The* MOTHER *is dressed in black satin and wears a lace mantilla; the* BRIDEGROOM *in black corduroy with a great golden chain.*)

Won't you sit down? They'll be right here.

(*She leaves. The* MOTHER *and son are left sitting motionless as statues. Long pause.*)

MOTHER. Did you wear the watch?

BRIDEGROOM. Yes. (*He takes it out and looks at it.*)

MOTHER. We have to be back on time. How far away these people live!

BRIDEGROOM. But this is good land.

MOTHER. Good; but much too lonesome. A four-hour trip and not one house, not one tree.

BRIDEGROOM. This is the wasteland.

MOTHER. Your father would have covered it with trees.

BRIDEGROOM. Without water?

MOTHER. He would have found some. In the three years we were married he planted ten cherry trees, (*remembering*) those three walnut trees by the

mill, a whole vineyard and a plant called Jupiter which had scarlet flowers—
but it dried up.

(*Pause.*)

BRIDEGROOM (*referring to the* BRIDE). She must be dressing.

(*The* BRIDE'S FATHER *enters. He is very old, with shining white hair. His
head is bowed. The* MOTHER *and the* BRIDEGROOM *rise. They shake hands in
silence.*)

FATHER. Was it a long trip?
MOTHER. Four hours.

(*They sit down.*)

FATHER. You must have come the longest way.
MOTHER. I'm too old to come along the cliffs by the river.
BRIDEGROOM. She gets dizzy.

(*Pause.*)

FATHER. A good hemp harvest.
BRIDEGROOM. A really good one.
FATHER. When I was young this land didn't even grow hemp. We've had
to punish it, even weep over it, to make it give us anything useful.
MOTHER. But now it does. Don't complain. I'm not here to ask you for
anything.
FATHER (*smiling*). You're richer than I. Your vineyards are worth a for-
tune. Each young vine a silver coin. But—do you know?—what bothers me is
that our lands are separated. I like to have everything together. One thorn I
have in my heart, and that's the little orchard there, stuck in between my
fields—and they won't sell it to me for all the gold in the world.
BRIDEGROOM. That's the way it always is.
FATHER. If we could just take twenty teams of oxen and move your
vineyards over here, and put them down on the hillside, how happy I'd be!
MOTHER. But why?
FATHER. What's mine is hers and what's yours is his. That's why. Just to
see it all together. How beautiful it is to bring things together!
BRIDEGROOM. And it would be less work.
MOTHER. When I die, you could sell ours and buy here, right alongside.
FATHER. Sell, sell? Bah! Buy, my friend, buy everything. If I had had
sons I would have bought all this mountainside right up to the part with the
stream. It's not good land, but strong arms can make it good, and since no
people pass by, they don't steal your fruit and you can sleep in peace.

(*Pause.*)

MOTHER. You know what I'm here for.
FATHER. Yes.
MOTHER. And?

FATHER. It seems all right to me. They have talked it over.

MOTHER. My son has money and knows how to manage it.

FATHER. My daughter too.

MOTHER. My son is handsome. He's never known a woman. His good name cleaner than a sheet spread out in the sun.

FATHER. No need to tell you about my daughter. At three, when the morning star shines, she prepares the bread. She never talks: soft as wool, she embroiders all kinds of fancy work and she can cut a strong cord with her teeth.

MOTHER. God bless her house.

FATHER. May God bless it.

(*The* SERVANT *appears with two trays. One with drinks and the other with sweets.*)

MOTHER (*to the son*). When would you like the wedding?

BRIDEGROOM. Next Thursday.

FATHER. The day on which she'll be exactly twenty-two years old.

MOTHER. Twenty-two! My oldest son would be that age if he were alive. Warm and manly as he was, he'd be living now if men hadn't invented knives.

FATHER. One mustn't think about that.

MOTHER. Every minute. Always a hand on your breast.

FATHER. Thursday, then? Is that right?

BRIDEGROOM. That's right.

FATHER. You and I and the bridal couple will go in a carriage to the church which is very far from here; the wedding party on the carts and horses they'll bring with them.

MOTHER. Agreed.

(*The* SERVANT *passes through.*)

FATHER. Tell her she may come in now. (*To the* MOTHER.) I shall be much pleased if you like her.

(*The* BRIDE *appears. Her hands fall in a modest pose and her head is bowed.*)

MOTHER. Come here. Are you happy?

BRIDE. Yes, señora.

FATHER. You shouldn't be so solemn. After all, she's going to be your mother.

BRIDE. I'm happy. I've said "yes" because I wanted to.

MOTHER. Naturally. (*She takes her by the chin.*) Look at me.

FATHER. She resembles my wife in every way.

MOTHER. Yes? What a beautiful glance! Do you know what it is to be married, child?

BRIDE (*seriously*). I do.

MOTHER. A man, some children and a wall two yards thick for everything else.

BRIDEGROOM. Is anything else needed?

MOTHER. No. Just that you all live—that's it! Live long!

BRIDE. I'll know how to keep my word.

MOTHER. Here are some gifts for you.

BRIDE. Thank you.

FATHER. Shall we have something?

MOTHER. Nothing for me. (*To the son*) But you?

BRIDEGROOM. Yes, thank you.

(*He takes one sweet, the* BRIDE *another.*)

FATHER (*to the* BRIDEGROOM). Wine?

MOTHER. He doesn't touch it.

FATHER. All the better.

(*Pause. All are standing.*)

BRIDEGROOM (*to the* BRIDE). I'll come tomorrow.

BRIDE. What time?

BRIDEGROOM. Five.

BRIDE. I'll be waiting for you.

BRIDEGROOM. When I leave your side I feel a great emptiness, and something like a knot in my throat.

BRIDE. When you are my husband you won't have it any more.

BRIDEGROOM. That's what I tell myself.

MOTHER. Come. The sun doesn't wait. (*To the* FATHER) Are we agreed on everything?

FATHER. Agreed.

MOTHER (*to the* SERVANT). Goodbye, woman.

SERVANT. God go with you!

(*The* MOTHER *kisses the* BRIDE *and they begin to leave in silence.*)

MOTHER (*at the door*). Goodbye, daughter.

(*The* BRIDE *answers with her hand.*)

FATHER. I'll go out with you.

(*They leave.*)

SERVANT. I'm bursting to see the presents.

BRIDE (*sharply*). Stop that!

SERVANT. Oh, child, show them to me.

BRIDE. I don't want to.

SERVANT. At least the stockings. They say they're all open work. Please!

BRIDE. I said no.

SERVANT. Well, my Lord. All right then. It looks as if you didn't want to get married.

BRIDE (*biting her hand in anger*). Ay-y-y!

SERVANT. Child, child! What's the matter with you? Are you sorry to give up your queen's life? Don't think of bitter things. Have you any reason to? None. Let's look at the presents. (*She takes the box.*)

BRIDE (*holding her by the wrists*). Let go.

SERVANT. Ay-y-y, girl!

BRIDE. Let go, I said.

SERVANT. You're stronger than a man.

BRIDE. Haven't I done a man's work? I wish I were.

SERVANT. Don't talk like that.

BRIDE. Quiet, I said. Let's talk about something else.

(*The light is fading from the stage. Long pause.*)

SERVANT. Did you hear a horse last night?

BRIDE. What time?

SERVANT. Three.

BRIDE. It might have been a stray horse—from the herd.

SERVANT. No. It carried a rider.

BRIDE. How do you know?

SERVANT. Because I saw him. He was standing by your window. It shocked me greatly.

BRIDE. Maybe it was my fiancé. Sometimes he comes by at that time.

SERVANT. No.

BRIDE. You saw him?

SERVANT. Yes.

BRIDE. Who was it?

SERVANT. It was Leonardo.

BRIDE (*strongly*). Liar! You liar! Why should he come here?

SERVANT. He came.

BRIDE. Shut up! Shut your cursed mouth.

(*The sound of a horse is heard.*)

SERVANT (*at the window*). Look. Lean out. Was it Leonardo?

BRIDE. It was!

ACT II

SCENE I

The entrance hall of the BRIDE'S *house. A large door in the back. It is night. The* BRIDE *enters wearing ruffled white petticoats full of laces and embroidered bands, and a sleeveless white bodice. The* SERVANT *is dressed the same way.*

SERVANT. I'll finish combing your hair out here.

BRIDE. It's too warm to stay in there.

SERVANT. In this country it doesn't even cool off at dawn.

(*The* BRIDE *sits on a low chair and looks into a little hand mirror. The* SERVANT *combs her hair.*)

BRIDE. My mother came from a place with lots of trees—from a fertile country.

SERVANT. And she was so happy!

BRIDE. But she wasted away here.

SERVANT. Fate.

BRIDE. As we're all wasting away here. The very walls give off heat. Ay-y-y! Don't pull so hard.

SERVANT. I'm only trying to fix this wave better. I want it to fall over your forehead.

(*The* BRIDE *looks at herself in the mirror.*)

How beautiful you are! Ay-y-y! (*She kisses her passionately.*)

BRIDE (*seriously*). Keep right on combing.

SERVANT (*combing*). Oh, lucky you—going to put your arms around a man; and kiss him; and feel his weight.

BRIDE. Hush.

SERVANT. And the best part will be when you'll wake up and you'll feel him at your side and when he caresses your shoulders with his breath, like a little nightingale's feather.

BRIDE (*sternly*). Will you be quiet.

SERVANT. But, child! What *is* a wedding? A wedding is just that and nothing more. Is it the sweets—or the bouquets of flowers? No. It's a shining bed and a man and a woman.

BRIDE. But you shouldn't talk about it.

SERVANT. Oh, *that's* something else again. But fun enough too.

BRIDE. Or bitter enough.

SERVANT. I'm going to put the orange blossoms on from here to here, so the wreath will shine out on top of your hair. (*She tries on the sprigs of orange blossom.*)

BRIDE (*looking at herself in the mirror*). Give it to me. (*She takes the wreath, looks at it and lets her head fall in discouragement.*)

SERVANT. Now what's the matter?

BRIDE. Leave me alone.

SERVANT. This is no time for you to start feeling sad. (*Encouragingly*) Give me the wreath.

(*The* BRIDE *takes the wreath and hurls it away.*)

Child! You're just asking God to punish you, throwing the wreath on the floor like that. Raise your head! Don't you want to get married? Say it. You can still withdraw.

(*The* BRIDE *rises.*)

BRIDE. Storm clouds. A chill wind that cuts through my heart. Who hasn't felt it?

SERVANT. You love your sweetheart, don't you?

BRIDE. I love him.

SERVANT. Yes, yes. I'm sure you do.

BRIDE. But this is a very serious step.

SERVANT. You've got to take it.

BRIDE. I've already given my word.

SERVANT. I'll put on the wreath.

BRIDE (*she sits down*). Hurry. They should be arriving by now.

SERVANT. They've already been at least two hours on the way.

BRIDE. How far is it from here to the church?

SERVANT. Five leagues by the stream, but twice that by the road.

(*The* BRIDE *rises and the* SERVANT *grows excited as she looks at her.*)

SERVANT. Awake, O Bride, awaken,
   On your wedding morning waken!
   The world's rivers may all
   Bear along your bridal Crown!

BRIDE (*smiling*). Come now.

SERVANT (*enthusiastically kissing her and dancing around her*). Awake,
   with the fresh bouquet
   of flowering laurel.
   Awake,
   by the trunk and branch
   of the laurels!

(*The banging of the front door latch is heard.*)

BRIDE. Open the door! That must be the first guests.

(*She leaves. The* SERVANT *opens the door.*)

SERVANT (*in astonishment*). You!

LEONARDO. Yes, me. Good morning.

SERVANT. The first one!

LEONARDO. Wasn't I invited?

SERVANT. Yes.

LEONARDO. That's why I'm here.

SERVANT. Where's your wife?

LEONARDO. I came on my horse. She's coming by the road.

SERVANT. Didn't you meet anyone?

LEONARDO. I *passed* them on my horse.

SERVANT. You're going to kill that horse with so much racing.

LEONARDO. When he dies, he's dead!

(*Pause.*)

SERVANT. Sit down. Nobody's up yet.

LEONARDO. Where's the bride?

SERVANT. I'm just on my way to dress her.

LEONARDO. The bride! She ought to be happy!

SERVANT (*changing the subject*). How's the baby?

LEONARDO. What baby?

SERVANT. Your son.

LEONARDO (*remembering, as though in a dream*). Ah!

SERVANT. Are they bringing him?

LEONARDO. No.

(*Pause. Voices sing distantly.*)

VOICES. Awake, O Bride, awaken,
    On your wedding morning waken!

LEONARDO. Awake, O Bride, awaken,
    On your wedding morning waken!

SERVANT. It's the guests. They're still quite a way off.

LEONARDO. The bride's going to wear a big wreath, isn't she? But it ought not to be so large. One a little smaller would look better on her. Has the groom already brought her the orange blossom that must be worn on the breast?

BRIDE (*appearing, still in petticoats and wearing the wreath*). He brought it.

SERVANT (*sternly*). Don't come out like that.

BRIDE. What does it matter? (*Seriously*) Why do you ask if they brought the orange blossom? Do you have something in mind?

LEONARDO. Nothing. What would I have in mind? (*Drawing near her*) You, you know me; you know I don't. Tell me so. What have I ever meant to you? Open your memory, refresh it. But two oxen and an ugly little hut are almost nothing. That's the thorn.

BRIDE. What have you come here to do?

LEONARDO. To see your wedding.

BRIDE. Just as I saw yours!

LEONARDO. Tied up by you, done with your two hands. Oh, they can kill me but they can't spit on me. But even money, which shines so much, spits sometimes.

BRIDE. Liar!

LEONARDO. I don't want to talk. I'm hot-blooded and I don't want to shout so all these hills will hear me

BRIDE. My shouts would be louder.

SERVANT. You'll have to stop talking like this. (*To the* BRIDE) You don't have to talk about what's past. (*The* SERVANT *looks around uneasily at the doors.*)

BRIDE. She's right. I shouldn't even talk to you. But it offends me to the soul that you come here to watch me, and spy on my wedding, and ask about the orange blossom with something on your mind. Go and wait for your wife at the door.

LEONARDO. But, can't you and I even talk?

SERVANT (*with rage*). No! No, you can't talk.

LEONARDO. Ever since I got married I've been thinking night and day about whose fault it was, and every time I think about it, out comes a new fault to eat up the old one; but always there's a fault left!

BRIDE. A man with a horse knows a lot of things and can do a lot to ride roughshod over a girl stuck out in the desert. But I have my pride. And that's why I'm getting married. I'll lock myself in with my husband and then I'll have to love him above everyone else.

LEONARDO. Pride won't help you a bit. (*He draws near to her.*)

BRIDE. Don't come near me!

LEONARDO. To burn with desire and keep quiet about it is the greatest punishment we can bring on ourselves. What good was pride to me—and not seeing you, and letting you lie awake night after night? No good! It only served to bring the fire down on me! You think that time heals and walls hide things, but it isn't true, it isn't true! When things get that deep inside you there isn't anybody can change them.

BRIDE (*trembling*). I can't listen to you. I can't listen to your voice. It's as though I'd drunk a bottle of anise and fallen asleep wrapped in a quilt of roses. It pulls me along, and I know I'm drowning—but I go on down.

SERVANT (*seizing* LEONARDO *by the lapels*). You've got to go right now!

LEONARDO. This is the last time I'll ever talk to her. Don't you be afraid of anything.

BRIDE. And I know I'm crazy and I know my breast rots with longing; but here I am—calmed by hearing him, by just seeing him move his arms.

LEONARDO. I'd never be at peace if I didn't tell you these things. I got married. Now you get married.

SERVANT. But she *is* getting married!

(*Voices are heard singing, nearer.*).

VOICES.   Awake, O Bride, awaken,
         On your wedding morning waken!

BRIDE. Awake, O Bride, awaken.

(*She goes out, running toward her room.*)

SERVANT. The people are here now. (*To* LEONARDO) Don't you come near her again.

LEONARDO. Don't worry. (*He goes out to the left. Day begins to break.*)

FIRST GIRL (*entering*). Awake, O Bride, awaken,
         the morning you're to marry;
         sing round and dance round;
         balconies a wreath must carry.

VOICES. Bride, awaken!

SERVANT (*creating enthusiasm*). Awake,

with the green bouquet
of love in flower.
Awake,
by the trunk and the branch
of the laurels!

SECOND GIRL (*entering*). Awake,
with her long hair,
snowy sleeping gown,
patent leather boots with silver—
her forehead jasmines crown.

SERVANT. Oh, shepherdess,
the moon begins to shine!

FIRST GIRL. Oh, gallant,
leave your hat beneath the vine!

FIRST YOUNG MAN (*entering, holding his hat on high*).
Bride, awaken,
for over the fields
the wedding draws nigh
with trays heaped with dahlias
and cakes piled high.

VOICES. Bride, awaken!

SECOND GIRL. The bride
has set her white wreath in place
and the groom
ties it on with a golden lace.

SERVANT. By the orange tree,
sleepless the bride will be.

THIRD GIRL (*entering*). By the citron vine,
gifts from the groom will shine.

(*Three* GUESTS *come in.*)

FIRST YOUTH. Dove, awaken!
In the dawn
shadowy bells are shaken.

GUEST. The bride, the white bride
today a maiden,
tomorrow a wife.

FIRST GIRL. Dark one, come down
trailing the train of your silken gown.

GUEST. Little dark one, come down,
cold morning wears a dewy crown.

FIRST GUEST. Awaken, wife, awake,
orange blossoms the breezes shake.

SERVANT. A tree I would embroider her
with garnet sashes wound,

And on each sash a cupid,
with "Long Live" all around.

VOICES. Bride, awaken.

FIRST YOUTH. The morning you're to marry!

GUEST. The morning you're to marry
how elegant you'll seem;
worthy, mountain flower,
of a captain's dream.

FATHER (*entering*). A captain's wife
the groom will marry.
He comes with his oxen the treasure to carry!

THIRD GIRL. The groom
is like a flower of gold.
When he walks,
blossoms at his feet unfold.

SERVANT. Oh, my lucky girl!

SECOND YOUTH. Bride, awaken.

SERVANT. Oh, my elegant girl!

FIRST GIRL. Through the windows
hear the wedding shout.

SECOND GIRL. Let the bride come out.

FIRST GIRL. Come out, come out!

SERVANT. Let the bells
ring and ring out clear!

FIRST YOUTH. For here she comes!
For now she's near!

SERVANT. Like a bull, the wedding
is arising here!

(*The* BRIDE *appears. She wears a black dress in the style of 1900, with a bustle and large train covered with pleated gauzes and heavy laces. Upon her hair, brushed in a wave over her forehead, she wears an orange blossom wreath. Guitars sound. The* GIRLS *kiss the* BRIDE.)

THIRD GIRL. What scent did you put on your hair?

BRIDE (*laughing*). None at all.

SECOND GIRL (*looking at her dress*). This cloth is what you can't get.

FIRST YOUTH. Here's the groom!

BRIDEGROOM. Salud!

FIRST GIRL (*putting a flower behind his ear*). The groom
is like a flower of gold.

SECOND GIRL. Quiet breezes
from his eyes unfold.

(*The* GROOM *goes to the* BRIDE.)

BRIDE. Why did you put on those shoes?

BRIDEGROOM. They're gayer than the black ones.

LEONARDO'S WIFE (*entering and kissing the* BRIDE). Salud!

(*They all speak excitedly.*)

LEONARDO (*entering as one who performs a duty*).
    The morning you're to marry
    we give you a wreath to wear.

LEONARDO'S WIFE. So the fields may be made happy
    with the dew dropped from your hair!

MOTHER (*to the* FATHER). Are those people here, too?

FATHER. They're part of the family. Today is a day of forgiveness!

MOTHER. I'll put up with it, but I don't forgive.

BRIDEGROOM. With your wreath, it's a joy to look at you!

BRIDE. Let's go to the church quickly.

BRIDEGROOM. Are you in a hurry?

BRIDE. Yes. I want to be your wife right now so that I can be with you alone, not hearing any voice but yours.

BRIDEGROOM. That's what I want!

BRIDE. And not seeing any eyes but yours. And for you to hug me so hard, that even though my dead mother should call me, I wouldn't be able to draw away from you.

BRIDEGROOM. My arms are strong. I'll hug you for forty years without stopping.

BRIDE (*taking his arm, dramatically*). Forever!

FATHER. Quick now! Round up the teams and carts! The sun's already out.

MOTHER. And go along carefully! Let's hope nothing goes wrong.

(*The great door in the background opens.*)

SERVANT (*weeping*). As you set out from your house,
    oh, maiden white,
    remember you leave shining
    with a star's light.

FIRST GIRL. Clean of body, clean of clothes
    from her home to church she goes.

(*They start leaving.*)

SECOND GIRL. Now you leave your home
    for the church!

SERVANT. The wind sets flowers
    on the sands.

THIRD GIRL. Ah, the white maid!

SERVANT. Dark winds are the lace
    of her mantilla.

(*They leave. Guitars, castanets and tambourines are heard.* LEONARDO *and his* WIFE *are left alone.*)

WIFE. Let's go.
LEONARDO. Where?
WIFE. To the church. But not on your horse. You're coming with me.
LEONARDO. In the cart?
WIFE. Is there anything else?
LEONARDO. I'm not the kind of man to ride in a cart.
WIFE. Nor I the wife to go to a wedding without her husband. I can't stand any more of this!
LEONARDO. Neither can I!
WIFE. And why do you look at me that way? With a thorn in each eye.
LEONARDO. Let's go!
WIFE. I don't know what's happening. But I think, and I don't want to think. One thing I do know. I'm already cast off by you. But I have a son. And another coming. And so it goes. My mother's fate was the same. Well, I'm not moving from here.

(*Voices outside.*)

VOICES.   As you set out from your home
  and to the church go,
  remember you leave shining
  with a star's glow.
WIFE (*weeping*).   Remember you leave shining
  with a star's glow.
I left my house like that too. They could have stuffed the whole countryside in my mouth. I was that trusting.
LEONARDO (*rising*). Let's go!
WIFE. But you with me!
LEONARDO. Yes. (*pause*) Start moving!

(*They leave.*)

VOICES.   As you set out from your home
  and to the church go,
  remember you leave shining
  with a star's glow.

SCENE II

The exterior of the BRIDE'S *Cave Home, in white gray and cold blue tones. Large cactus trees. Shadowy and silver tones. Panoramas of light tan tablelands, everything hard like a landscape in popular ceramics.*

SERVANT (*arranging glasses and trays on a table*).

A-turning,
the wheel was a-turning
and the water was flowing,
for the wedding night comes.
May the branches part
and the moon be arrayed
at her white balcony rail.
(*In a loud voice*) Set out the tablecloths! (*In a pathetic voice*)
A-singing,
bride and groom were singing
and the water was flowing
for their wedding night comes.
Oh, rime-frost, flash!—
and almonds bitter
fill with honey!
(*In a loud voice*) Get the wine ready! (*In a poetic tone*)
Elegant girl,
most elegant in the world,
see the way the water is flowing,
for your wedding night comes.
Hold your skirts close in
under the bridegroom's wing
and never leave your house,
for the Bridegroom is a dove
with his breast a firebrand
and the fields wait for the whisper
of spurting blood.
A-turning
the wheel was a-turning
and the water was flowing
and your wedding night comes.
Oh, water, sparkle!

MOTHER (*entering*). At last!

FATHER. Are we the first ones?

SERVANT. No. Leonardo and his wife arrived a while ago. They drove like demons. His wife got here dead with fright. They made the trip as though they'd come on horseback.

FATHER. That one's looking for trouble. He's not of good blood.

MOTHER. What blood would you expect him to have? His whole family's blood. It comes down from his great grandfather, who started in killing, and it goes on down through the whole evil breed of knife wielding and false smiling men.

FATHER. Let's leave it at that!

SERVANT. But how can she leave it at that?

MOTHER. It hurts me to the tips of my veins. On the forehead of all of them I see only the hand with which they killed what was mine. Can you really see me? Don't I seem mad to you? Well, it's the madness of not having shrieked out all my breast needs to. Always in my breast there's a shriek standing tiptoe that I have to beat down and hold in under my shawls. But the dead are carried off and one has to keep still. And then, people find fault. (*She removes her shawl.*)

FATHER. Today's not the day for you to be remembering these things.

MOTHER. When the talk turns on it, I have to speak. And more so today. Because today I'm left alone in my house.

FATHER. But with the expectation of having someone with you.

MOTHER. That's my hope: grandchildren.

(*They sit down.*)

FATHER. I want them to have a lot of them. This land needs hands that aren't hired. There's a battle to be waged against weeds, the thistles, the big rocks that come from one doesn't know where. And those hands have to be the owner's, who chastises and dominates, who makes the seeds grow. Lots of sons are needed.

MOTHER. And some daughters! Men are like the wind! They're forced to handle weapons. Girls never go out into the street.

FATHER (*happily*). I think they'll have both.

MOTHER. My son will cover her well. He's of good seed. His father could have had many sons with me.

FATHER. What I'd like is to have all this happen in a day. So that right away they'd have two or three boys.

MOTHER. But it's not like that. It takes a long time. That's why it's so terrible to see one's own blood spilled out on the ground. A fountain that spurts for a minute, but costs us years. When I got to my son, he lay fallen in the middle of the street. I wet my hands with his blood and licked them with my tongue—because it was my blood. You don't know what that's like. In a glass and topaz shrine I'd put the earth moistened by his blood.

FATHER. Now you must hope. My daughter is wide-hipped and your son is strong.

MOTHER. That's why I'm hoping.

(*They rise.*)

FATHER. Get the wheat trays ready!

SERVANT. They're all ready.

LEONARDO'S WIFE (*entering*). May it be for the best!

MOTHER. Thank you.

LEONARDO. Is there going to be a celebration?

FATHER. A small one. People can't stay long.

SERVANT. Here they are!

(GUESTS *begin entering in gay groups. The* BRIDE *and* BRIDEGROOM *come in arm-in-arm.* LEONARDO *leaves.*)

BRIDEGROOM. There's never been a wedding with so many people!
BRIDE (*sullen*). Never.
FATHER. It was brilliant.
MOTHER. Whole branches of families came.
BRIDEGROOM. People who never went out of the house.
MOTHER. Your father sowed well, and now you're reaping it.
BRIDEGROOM. There were cousins of mine whom I no longer knew.
MOTHER. All the people from the seacoast.
BRIDEGROOM (*happily*). They were frightened of the horses.

(*They talk.*)

MOTHER (*to the* BRIDE). What are you thinking about?
BRIDE. I'm not thinking about anything.
MOTHER. Your blessings weigh heavily.

(*Guitars are heard.*)

BRIDE. Like lead.
MOTHER (*stern*). But they shouldn't weigh so. Happy as a dove you
ought to be.
BRIDE. Are you staying here tonight?
MOTHER. No. My house is empty.
BRIDE. You ought to stay!
FATHER (*to the* MOTHER). Look at the dance they're forming. Dances of
the far away seashore.

(LEONARDO *enters and sits down. His* WIFE *stands rigidly behind him.*)

MOTHER. They're my husband's cousins. Stiff as stones at dancing.
FATHER. It makes me happy to watch them. What a change for this
house! (*He leaves*).
BRIDEGROOM (*to the* BRIDE). Did you like the orange blossom?
BRIDE (*looks at him fixedly*). Yes.
BRIDEGROOM. It's all of wax. It will last forever. I'd like you to have had
them all over your dress.
BRIDE. No need of that.

(LEONARDO *goes off to the right.*)

FIRST GIRL. Let's go and take out your pins.
BRIDE (*to the* BRIDEGROOM). I'll be right back.
LEONARDO'S WIFE. I hope you'll be happy with my cousin!
BRIDEGROOM. I'm sure I will.
LEONARDO'S WIFE. The two of you here; never going out; building a
home. I wish I could live far away like this, too!
BRIDEGROOM. Why don't you buy land? The mountainside is cheap and
children grow up better.
LEONARDO'S WIFE. We don't have any money. And at the rate we're
going . . . !

BRIDEGROOM. Your husband is a good worker.

LEONARDO'S WIFE. Yes, but he likes to fly around too much; from one thing to another. He's not a patient man.

SERVANT. Aren't you having anything? I'm going to wrap some wine cakes for your mother. She likes them so much.

BRIDEGROOM. Put up three dozen for her.

LEONARDO'S WIFE. No, no. A half-dozen's enough for her!

BRIDEGROOM. But today's a day!

LEONARDO'S WIFE (*to the* SERVANT). Where's Leonardo?

BRIDEGROOM. He must be with the guests.

LEONARDO'S WIFE. I'm going to go see. (*She leaves.*)

SERVANT (*looking off at the dance*). That's beautiful there.

BRIDEGROOM. Aren't you dancing?

SERVANT. No one will ask me.

(*Two* GIRLS *pass across the back of the stage; during this whole scene the background should be an animated crossing of figures.*)

BRIDEGROOM (*happily*). They just don't know anything. Lively old girls like you dance better than the young ones.

SERVANT. Well! Are you tossing me a compliment, boy? What a family yours is! Men among men! As a little girl I saw your grandfather's wedding. What a figure! It seemed as if a mountain were getting married.

BRIDEGROOM. I'm not as tall.

SERVANT. But there's the same twinkle in your eye. Where's the girl?

BRIDEGROOM. Taking off her wreath.

SERVANT. Ah! Look. For midnight, since you won't be sleeping, I have prepared ham for you, and some large glasses of old wine. On the lower shelf of the cupboard. In case you need it.

BRIDEGROOM (*smiling*). I won't be eating at midnight.

SERVANT (*slyly*). If not you, maybe the bride. (*She leaves.*)

FIRST YOUTH (*entering*). You've got to come have a drink with us!

BRIDEGROOM. I'm waiting for the bride.

SECOND YOUTH. You'll have her at dawn!

FIRST YOUTH. That's when it's best!

SECOND YOUTH. Just for a minute.

BRIDEGROOM. Let's go.

(*They leave. Great excitement is heard. The* BRIDE *enters. From the opposite side two* GIRLS *come running to meet her.*)

FIRST GIRL. To whom did you give the first pin; me or this one?

BRIDE. I don't remember.

FIRST GIRL. To me, you gave it to me here.

SECOND GIRL. To me, in front of the altar.

BRIDE (*uneasily, with a great inner struggle*). I don't know anything about it.

FIRST GIRL. It's just that I wish you'd . . .

BRIDE (*interrupting*).   Nor do I care. I have a lot to think about.
SECOND GIRL.   Your pardon.

(LEONARDO *crosses at the rear of the stage.*)

BRIDE (*she sees* LEONARDO).   And this is an upsetting time.
FIRST GIRL.   We wouldn't know anything about that!
BRIDE.   You'll know about it when your time comes. This step is a very hard one to take.
FIRST GIRL.   Has she offended you?
BRIDE.   No. You must pardon me.
SECOND GIRL.   What for? But *both* the pins are good for getting married, aren't they?
BRIDE.   Both of them.
FIRST GIRL.   Maybe now one will get married before the other.
BRIDE.   Are you so eager?
SECOND GIRL (*shyly*).   Yes.
BRIDE.   Why?
FIRST GIRL.   Well . . .

(*She embraces the* SECOND GIRL. *Both go running off. The* BRIDEGROOM *comes in very slowly and embraces the* BRIDE *from behind.*)

BRIDE (*in sudden fright*).   Let go of me!
BRIDEGROOM.   Are you frightened of me?
BRIDE.   Ay-y-y! It's you?
BRIDEGROOM.   Who else would it be? (*pause*) Your father or me.
BRIDE.   That's true!
BRIDEGROOM.   Of course, your father would have hugged you more gently.
BRIDE (*darkly*).   Of course!
BRIDEGROOM (*embracing her strongly and a little bit brusquely*).   Because he's old.
BRIDE (*curtly*).   Let me go!
BRIDEGROOM.   Why? (*He lets her go.*)
BRIDE.   Well . . . the people. They can see us.

(*The* SERVANT *crosses at the back of the stage again without looking at the* BRIDE *and* BRIDEGROOM.)

BRIDEGROOM.   What of it? It's consecrated now.
BRIDE.   Yes, but let me be . . . Later.
BRIDEGROOM.   What's the matter with you? You look frightened!
BRIDE.   I'm all right. Don't go.

(LEONARDO'S WIFE *enters.*)

LEONARDO'S WIFE.   I don't mean to intrude . . .
BRIDEGROOM.   What is it?

LEONARDO'S WIFE. Did my husband come through here?

BRIDEGROOM. No.

LEONARDO'S WIFE. Because I can't find him, and his horse isn't in the stable either.

BRIDEGROOM (*happily*). He must be out racing it.

(*The* WIFE *leaves, troubled. The* SERVANT *enters.*)

SERVANT. Aren't you two proud and happy with so many good wishes?

BRIDEGROOM. I wish it were over with. The bride is a little tired.

SERVANT. That's no way to act, child.

BRIDE. It's as though I'd been struck on the head.

SERVANT. A bride from these mountains must be strong. (*To the* BRIDE-GROOM) You're the only one who can cure her, because she's yours. (*She goes running off.*)

BRIDEGROOM (*embracing the* BRIDE). Let's go dance a little. (*He kisses her.*)

BRIDE (*worried*). No. I'd like to stretch out on my bed a little.

BRIDEGROOM. I'll keep you company.

BRIDE. Never! With all these people here? What would they say? Let me be quiet for a moment.

BRIDEGROOM. Whatever you say! But don't be like that tonight!

BRIDE (*at the door*). I'll be better tonight.

BRIDEGROOM. That's what I want.

(*The* MOTHER *appears.*)

MOTHER. Son.

BRIDEGROOM. Where've you been?

MOTHER. Out there—in all that noise. Are you happy?

BRIDEGROOM. Yes.

MOTHER. Where's your wife?

BRIDEGROOM. Resting a little. It's a bad day for brides!

MOTHER. A bad day? The only good one. To me it was like coming into my own.

(*The* SERVANT *enters and goes toward the* BRIDE'S *room.*)

Like the breaking of new ground; the planting of new trees.

BRIDEGROOM. Are you going to leave?

MOTHER. Yes. I ought to be at home.

BRIDEGROOM. Alone.

MOTHER. Not alone. For my head is full of things: of men, and fights.

BRIDEGROOM. But now the fights are no longer fights.

(*The* SERVANT *enters quickly; she disappears at the rear of the stage, running.*)

MOTHER. While you live, you have to fight.

BRIDEGROOM. I'll always obey you!

MOTHER. Try to be loving with your wife, and if you see she's acting foolish or touchy, caress her in a way that will hurt her a little: a strong hug, a bite and then a soft kiss. Not so she'll be angry, but just so she'll feel you're the man, the boss, the one who gives orders. I learned that from your father. And since you don't have him, I have to be the one to tell you about these strong defenses.

BRIDEGROOM. I'll always do as you say.

FATHER (*entering*). Where's my daughter?

BRIDEGROOM. She's inside.

(*The* FATHER *goes to look for her.*)

FIRST GIRL. Get the bride and groom! We're going to dance a round!

FIRST YOUTH (*to the* BRIDEGROOM). You're going to lead it.

FATHER (*entering*). She's not there.

BRIDEGROOM. No?

FATHER. She must have gone up to the railing.

BRIDEGROOM. I'll go see! (*He leaves. A hubbub of excitement and guitars is heard.*)

FIRST GIRL. They've started it already! (*She leaves.*)

BRIDEGROOM (*entering*). She isn't there.

MOTHER (*uneasily*). Isn't she?

FATHER. But where could she have gone?

SERVANT (*entering*). But where's the girl, where is she?

MOTHER (*seriously*). That we don't know.

(*The* BRIDEGROOM *leaves. Three* GUESTS *enter.*)

FATHER (*dramatically*). But, isn't she in the dance?

SERVANT. She's not in the dance.

FATHER (*with a start*). There are a lot of people. Go look!

SERVANT. I've already looked.

FATHER (*tragically*). Then where is she?

BRIDEGROOM (*entering*). Nowhere. Not anywhere.

MOTHER (*to the* FATHER). What does this mean? Where is your daughter?

(LEONARDO'S WIFE *enters.*)

LEONARDO'S WIFE. They've run away! They've run away! She and Leonardo. On the horse. With their arms around each other, they rode off like a shooting star!

FATHER. That's not true! Not my daughter!

MOTHER. Yes, your daughter! Spawn of a wicked mother, and he, he too. But now she's my son's wife!

BRIDEGROOM (*entering*). Let's go after them! Who has a horse?

MOTHER. Who has a horse? Right away! Who has a horse? I'll give him all I have—my eyes, my tongue even . . .

VOICE. Here's one.

MOTHER (*to the* SON). Go! After them! (*He leaves with two young men.*) No. Don't go. Those people kill quickly and well . . . but yes, run, and I'll follow!

FATHER. It couldn't be my daughter. Perhaps she's thrown herself into the well.

MOTHER. Decent women throw themselves in water; not that one! But now she's my son's wife. Two groups. There are two groups here. (*They all enter.*) My family and yours. Everyone set out from here. Shake the dust from your heels! We'll go help my son. (*The people separate into two groups.*) For he has his family: his cousins from the sea, and all who came from inland. Out of here! On all roads. The hour of blood has come again. Two groups! You with yours and I with mine. After them! After them!

ACT III

SCENE I

A forest. It is nighttime. Great moist tree trunks. A dark atmosphere. Two violins are heard. Three WOODCUTTERS *enter.*

FIRST WOODCUTTER. And have they found them?

SECOND WOODCUTTER. No. But they're looking for them everywhere.

THIRD WOODCUTTER. They'll find them.

SECOND WOODCUTTER. Sh-h-h!

THIRD WOODCUTTER. What?

SECOND WOODCUTTER. They seem to be coming closer on all the roads at once.

FIRST WOODCUTTER. When the moon comes out they'll see them.

SECOND WOODCUTTER. They ought to let them go.

FIRST WOODCUTTER. The world is wide. Everybody can live in it.

THIRD WOODCUTTER. But they'll kill them.

SECOND WOODCUTTER. You have to follow your passion. They did right to run away.

FIRST WOODCUTTER. They were deceiving themselves but at the last blood was stronger.

THIRD WOODCUTTER. Blood!

FIRST WOODCUTTER. You have to follow the path of your blood.

SECOND WOODCUTTER. But blood that sees the light of day is drunk up by the earth.

FIRST WOODCUTTER. What of it? Better dead with the blood drained away than alive with it rotting.

THIRD WOODCUTTER. Hush!

FIRST WOODCUTTER. What? Do you hear something?

THIRD WOODCUTTER. I hear the crickets, the frogs, the night's ambush.

FIRST WOODCUTTER. But not the horse.

THIRD WOODCUTTER. No.

FIRST WOODCUTTER. By now he must be loving her.

SECOND WOODCUTTER. Her body for him; his body for her.

THIRD WOODCUTTER. They'll find them and they'll kill them.

FIRST WOODCUTTER. But by then they'll have mingled their bloods. They'll be like two empty jars, like two dry arroyos.

SECOND WOODCUTTER. There are many clouds and it would be easy for the moon not to come out.

THIRD WOODCUTTER. The bridegroom will find them with or without the moon. I saw him set out. Like a raging star. His face the color of ashes. He looked the fate of all his clan.

FIRST WOODCUTTER. His clan of dead men lying in the middle of the street.

SECOND WOODCUTTER. There you have it!

THIRD WOODCUTTER. You think they'll be able to break through the circle?

SECOND WOODCUTTER. It's hard to. There are knives and guns for ten leagues 'round.

THIRD WOODCUTTER. He's riding a good horse.

SECOND WOODCUTTER. But he's carrying a woman.

FIRST WOODCUTTER. We're close by now.

SECOND WOODCUTTER. A tree with forty branches. We'll soon cut it down.

THIRD WOODCUTTER. The moon's coming out now. Let's hurry.

(*From the left shines a brightness.*)

FIRST WOODCUTTER. O rising moon!
    Moon among the great leaves.

SECOND WOODCUTTER. Cover the blood with jasmines!

FIRST WOODCUTTER. O lonely moon!
    Moon among the great leaves.

SECOND WOODCUTTER. Silver on the bride's face.

THIRD WOODCUTTER. O evil moon!
    Leave for their love a branch in shadow.

FIRST WOODCUTTER. O sorrowing moon!
    Leave for their love a branch in shadow.

(*They go out. The* MOON *appears through the shining brightness at the left. The* MOON *is a young woodcutter with a white face. The stage takes on an intense blue radiance.*)

MOON. Round swan in the river
    and a cathedral's eye,
    false dawn on the leaves,
    they'll not escape; these things am I!
    Who is hiding? And who sobs

in the thornbrakes of the valley?
The moon sets a knife
abandoned in the air
which being a leaden threat
yearns to be blood's pain.
Let me in! I come freezing
down to walls and windows!
Open roofs, open breasts
where I may warm myself!
I'm cold! My ashes
of somnolent metals
seek the fire's crest
on mountains and streets.
But the snow carries me
upon its mottled back
and pools soak me
in their water, hard and cold.
But this night there will be
red blood for my cheeks,
and for the reeds that cluster
at the wide feet of the wind.
Let there be neither shadow nor bower,
and then they can't get away!
O let me enter a breast
where I may get warm!
A heart for me!
Warm! That will spurt
over the mountains of my chest;
let me come in, oh let me! (*To the branches*)
I want no shadows. My rays
must get in everywhere,
even among the dark trunks I want
the whisper of gleaming lights,
so that this night there will be
sweet blood for my cheeks,
and for the reeds that cluster
at the wide feet of the wind.
Who is hiding? Out, I say!
No! They will not get away!
I will light up the horse
with a fever bright as diamonds.

(*He disappears among the trunks, and the stage goes back to its dark lighting.
An* OLD WOMAN *comes out completely covered by thin green cloth. She is barefooted. Her face can barely be seen among the folds. This character does not
appear in the cast.*)

BEGGAR WOMAN. That moon's going away, just when they's near.
They won't get past here. The river's whisper
and the whispering tree trunks will muffle
the torn flight of their shrieks.
It has to be here, and soon. I'm worn out.
The coffins are ready, and white sheets
wait on the floor of the bedroom
for heavy bodies with torn throats.
Let not one bird awake, let the breeze,
gathering their moans in her skirt,
fly with them over black tree tops
or bury them in soft mud. (*Impatiently!*)
Oh, that moon! That moon!

(*The* MOON *appears. The intense blue light returns.*)

MOON. They're coming. One band through the ravine and the other
along the river. I'm going to light up the boulders. What do you need?
BEGGAR WOMAN. Nothing.
MOON. The wind blows hard now, with a double edge.
BEGGAR WOMAN. Light up the waistcoat and open the buttons; the
knives will know the path after that.
MOON. But let them be a long time a-dying. So the blood
will slide its delicate hissing between my fingers.
Look how my ashen valleys already are waking
in longing for this fountain of shuddering gushes!
BEGGAR WOMAN. Let's not let them get past the arroyo. Silence!
MOON. There they come! (*He goes. The stage is left dark.*)
BEGGAR WOMAN. Quick! Lots of light! Do you hear me? They can't get
away!

(*The* BRIDEGROOM *and the* FIRST YOUTH *enter. The* BEGGAR WOMAN *sits down and covers herself with her cloak.*)

BRIDEGROOM. This way.
FIRST YOUTH. You won't find them.
BRIDEGROOM (*angrily*). Yes, I'll find them.
FIRST YOUTH. I think they've taken another path.
BRIDEGROOM. No. Just a moment ago I felt the galloping.
FIRST YOUTH. It could have been another horse.
BRIDEGROOM (*intensely*). Listen to me. There's only one horse in the
whole world, and this one's it. Can't you understand that? If you're going to
follow me, follow me without talking.
FIRST YOUTH. It's only that I want to . . .
BRIDEGROOM. Be quiet! I'm sure of meeting them there. Do you see this
arm? Well, it's not my arm. It's my brother's arm, and my father's, and that of
all the dead ones in my family. And it has so much strength that it can pull

this tree up by the roots, if it wants to. And let's move on, because here I feel the clenched teeth of all my people in me so that I can't breathe easily.

BEGGAR WOMAN (*whining*). Ay-y-y!

FIRST YOUTH. Did you hear that?

BRIDEGROOM. You go that way and then circle back.

FIRST YOUTH. This is a hunt.

BRIDEGROOM. A hunt. The greatest hunt there is.

(*The* YOUTH *goes off. The* BRIDEGROOM *goes rapidly to the left and stumbles over the* BEGGAR WOMAN, *Death.*)

BEGGAR WOMAN. Ay-y-y!

BRIDEGROOM. What do you want?

BEGGAR WOMAN. I'm cold.

BRIDEGROOM. Which way are you going?

BEGGAR WOMAN (*always whining like a beggar*). Over there, far away . . .

BRIDEGROOM. Where are you from?

BEGGAR WOMAN. Over there . . . very far away.

BRIDEGROOM. Have you seen a man and a woman running away on a horse?

BEGGAR WOMAN (*awakening*). Wait a minute . . . (*She looks at him.*) Handsome young man. (*She rises.*) But you'd be much handsomer sleeping.

BRIDEGROOM. Tell me; answer me. Did you see them?

BEGGAR WOMAN. Wait a minute . . . What broad shoulders! How would you like to be laid out on them and not have to walk on the soles of your feet which are so small?

BRIDEGROOM (*shaking her*). I asked you if you saw them! Have they passed through here?

BEGGAR WOMAN (*energetically*). No. They haven't passed; but they're coming from the hill. Don't you hear them?

BRIDEGROOM. No.

BEGGAR WOMAN. Do you know the road?

BRIDEGROOM. I'll go, whatever it's like!

BEGGAR WOMAN. I'll go along with you. I know this country.

BRIDEGROOM (*impatiently*). Well, let's go! Which way?

BEGGAR WOMAN (*dramatically*). This way!

(*They go rapidly out. Two violins, which represent the forest, are heard distantly. The* WOODCUTTERS *return. They have their axes on their shoulders. They move slowly among the tree trunks.*)

FIRST WOODCUTTER. O rising death!
    Death among the great leaves.

SECOND WOODCUTTER. Don't open the gush of blood!

FIRST WOODCUTTER. O lonely death!
    Death among the dried leaves.

THIRD WOODCUTTER. Don't lay flowers over the wedding!
SECOND WOODCUTTER. O sad death!
> Leave for their love a green branch.
FIRST WOODCUTTER. O evil death!
> Leave for their love a branch of green!

(*They go out while they are talking.* LEONARDO *and the* BRIDE *appear.*)

LEONARDO. Hush!
BRIDE. From here I'll go on alone.
> You go now! I want you to turn back.
LEONARDO. Hush, I said!
BRIDE. With your teeth, with your hands, anyway you can,
> take from my clean throat
> the metal of this chain,
> and let me live forgotten
> back there in my house in the ground.
> And if you don't want to kill me
> as you would kill a tiny snake,
> set in my hands, a bride's hands,
> the barrel of your shotgun.
> Oh, what lamenting, what fire,
> sweeps upward through my head!
> What glass splinters are stuck in my tongue!
LEONARDO. We've taken the step now; hush!
> because they're close behind us,
> and I must take you with me.
BRIDE. Then it must be by force!
LEONARDO. By force? Who was it first
> went down the stairway?
BRIDE. I went down it.
LEONARDO. And who was it put
> a new bridle on the horse?
BRIDE. I myself did it. It's true.
LEONARDO. And whose were the hands
> strapped spurs to my boots?
BRIDE. The same hands, these that are yours,
> but which when they see you would like
> to break the blue branches
> and sunder the purl of your veins.
> I love you! I love you! But leave me!
> For if I were able to kill you
> I'd wrap you 'round in a shroud
> with the edges bordered in violets.
> Oh, what lamenting, what fire,
> sweeps upward through my head!

LEONARDO. What glass splinters are stuck in my tongue!
    Because I tried to forget you
    and put a wall of stone
    between your house and mine.
    It's true. You remember?
    And when I saw you in the distance
    I threw sand in my eyes.
    But I was riding a horse
    and the horse went straight to your door.
    And the silver pins of your wedding
    turned my red blood black.
    And in me our dream was choking
    my flesh with its poisoned weeds.
    Oh, it isn't my fault—
    the fault is the earth's—
    and this fragrance that you exhale
    from your breasts and your braids.
BRIDE. Oh, how untrue! I want
    from you neither bed nor food,
    yet there's not a minute each day
    that I don't want to be with you,
    because you drag me, and I come,
    then you tell me to go back
    and I follow you,
    like chaff blown on the breeze.
    I have left a good, honest man,
    and all his people,
    with the wedding feast half over
    and wearing my bridal wreath.
    But you are the one will be punished.
    and that I don't want to happen.
    Leave me alone now! You run away!
    There is no one who will defend you.
LEONARDO. The birds of early morning
    are calling among the trees.
    The night is dying
    on the stone's ridge.
    Let's go to a hidden corner
    where I may love you forever,
    for to me the people don't matter,
    nor the venom they throw on us. (*He embraces her strongly.*)
BRIDE. And I'll sleep at your feet,
    to watch over your dreams.
    Naked, looking over the fields,
    as though I were a bitch.

Because that's what I am! Oh, I look at you
and your beauty sears me.
LEONARDO. Fire is stirred by fire.
The same tiny flame
will kill two wheat heads together.
Let's go!
BRIDE. Where are you taking me?
LEONARDO. Where they cannot come,
these men who surround us.
Where I can look at you!
BRIDE (*sarcastically*). Carry me with you from fair to fair,
a shame to clean women,
so that people will see me
with my wedding sheets
on the breeze like banners.
LEONARDO. I, too, would want to leave you
if I thought as men should.
But wherever you go, I go.
You're the same. Take a step. Try.
Nails of moonlight have fused
my waist and your chains.

(*This whole scene is violent, full of great sensuality.*)

BRIDE. Listen!
LEONARDO.   They're coming.
BRIDE.   Run!
It's fitting that I should die here,
with water over my feet,
with thorns upon my head.
And fitting the leaves should mourn me,
a woman lost and virgin.
LEONARDO. Be quiet. Now they're appearing.
BRIDE.   Go now!
LEONARDO. Quiet. Don't let them hear us.

(*The* BRIDE *hesitates.*)

BRIDE. Both of us!
LEONARDO (*embracing her*).
                    Any way you want!
If they separate us, it will be
because I am dead.
BRIDE.   And I dead too.

(*They go out in each other's arms. The* MOON *appears very slowly. The stage takes on a strong blue light. The two violins are heard. Suddenly two long, ear-splitting shrieks are heard, and the music of the two violins is cut short. At the second shriek the* BEGGAR WOMAN *appears and stands with her back to the audience. She opens her cape and stands in the center of the stage like a great bird with immense wings. The* MOON *halts. The curtain comes down in absolute silence.*)

SCENE II

THE FINAL SCENE. *A white dwelling with arches and thick walls. To the right and left, are white stairs. At the back, a great arch and a wall of the same color. The floor also should be shining white. This simple dwelling should have the monumental feeling of a church. There should not be a single gray nor any shadow, not even what is necessary for perspective.*
    Two GIRLS *dressed in dark blue are winding a red skein.*

FIRST GIRL. Wool, red wool,
    what would you make?
SECOND GIRL. Oh, jasmine for dresses,
    fine wool like glass.
    At four o'clock born,
    at ten o'clock dead.
    A thread from this wool yarn,
    a chain 'round your feet
    a knot that will tighten
    the bitter white wreath.
LITTLE GIRL (*singing*). Were you at the wedding?
FIRST GIRL. No.
LITTLE GIRL. Well, neither was I!
    What could have happened
    'midst the shoots of the vineyards?
    What could have happened
    'neath the branch of the olive?
    What really happened
    that no one came back?
    Were you at the wedding?
SECOND GIRL. We told you once, no.
LITTLE GIRL (*leaving*). Well, neither was I!
SECOND GIRL. Wool, red wool,
    what would you sing?
FIRST GIRL. Their wounds turning waxen
    balm-myrtle for pain.
    Asleep in the morning,
    and watching at night.
LITTLE GIRL (*in the doorway*). And then, the thread stumbled
    on the flinty stones,
    but mountains, blue mountains,

are letting it pass.
Running, running, running,
and finally to come
to stick in a knife blade,
to take back the bread. (*She goes out.*)
SECOND GIRL. Wool, red wool,
what would you tell?
FIRST GIRL. The lover is silent,
crimson the groom,
at the still shoreline
I saw them laid out. (*She stops and looks at the skein.*)
LITTLE GIRL (*appearing in the doorway*). Running, running, running,
the thread runs to here.
All covered with clay
I feel them draw near.
Bodies stretched stiffly
in ivory sheets!

(*The* WIFE *and* MOTHER-IN-LAW *of* LEONARDO *appear. They are anguished.*)

FIRST GIRL. Are they coming yet?
MOTHER-IN-LAW (*harshly*). We don't know.
SECOND GIRL. What can you tell us about the wedding?
FIRST GIRL. Yes, tell me.
MOTHER-IN-LAW (*curtly*). Nothing.
LEONARDO'S WIFE. I want to go back and find out all about it.
MOTHER-IN-LAW (*sternly*). You, back to your house.
Brave and alone in your house.
To grow old and to weep.
But behind closed doors.
Never again. Neither dead nor alive.
We'll nail up our windows
and let rains and nights
fall on the bitter weeds.
LEONARDO'S WIFE.
What could have happened?
MOTHER-IN-LAW. It doesn't matter what.
Put a veil over your face.
Your children are yours,
that's all. On the bed
put a cross of ashes
where his pillow was. (*They go out.*)
BEGGAR WOMAN (*at the door*).
A crust of bread, little girls.
LITTLE GIRL. Go away!

(*The* Girls *huddle close together.*)

Beggar Woman. Why?
Little Girl. Because you whine; go away!
First Girl. Child!
Beggar Woman. I might have asked for your eyes! A cloud
    of birds is following me. Will you have one?
Little Girl. I want to get away from here!
Second Girl (*to the* Beggar Woman). Don't mind her!
First Girl. Did you come by the road through the arroyo?
Beggar Woman. I came that way!
First Girl (*timidly*). Can I ask you something?
Beggar Woman. I saw them: they'll be here soon; two torrents
    still at last, among the great boulders,
    two men at the horse's feet.
    Two dead men in the night's splendor. (*With pleasure*)
    Dead, yes, dead.
First Girl. Hush, old woman, hush!
Beggar Woman. Crushed flowers for eyes, and their teeth
    two fistfuls of hard-frozen snow.
    Both of them fell, and the Bride returns
    with bloodstains on her skirt and hair.
    And they come covered with two sheets
    carried on the shoulders of two tall boys.
    That's how it was; nothing more. What was fitting.
    Over the golden flower, dirty sand.

(*She goes. The* Girls *bow their heads and start going out rhythmically.*)

First Girl. Dirty sand.
Second Girl. Over the golden flower.
Little Girl. Over the golden flower
    they're bringing the dead from the arroyo.
    Dark the one,
    dark the other.
    What shadowy nightingale flies and weeps
    over the golden flower!

(*She goes. The stage is left empty. The* Mother *and a* Neighbor *woman appear. The* Neighbor *is weeping.*)

Mother. Hush.
Neighbor. I can't.
Mother. Hush, I said. (*At the door*) Is there nobody here? (*She puts her hands to her forehead.*) My son ought to answer me. But now my son is an armful of shriveled flowers. My son is a fading voice beyond the mountains now. (*With rage, to the* Neighbor) Will you shut up? I want no wailing in this

house. Your tears are only tears from your eyes, but when I'm alone mine will come—from the soles of my feet, from my roots—burning more than blood.

NEIGHBOR. You come to my house; don't you stay here.

MOTHER. I want to be here. Here. In peace. They're all dead now: and at midnight I'll sleep, sleep without terror of guns or knives. Other mothers will go to their windows, lashed by rain, to watch for their sons' faces. But not I. And of my dreams I'll make a cold ivory dove that will carry camellias of white frost to the graveyard. But no; not graveyard, not graveyard: the couch of earth, the bed that shelters them and rocks them in the sky. (*A woman dressed in black enters, goes toward the right, and there kneels. To the* NEIGHBOR) Take your hands from your face. We have terrible days ahead. I want to see no one. The earth and I. My grief and I. And these four walls. Ay-y-y! Ay-y-y! (*She sits down, overcome.*)

NEIGHBOR. Take pity on yourself!

MOTHER (*pushing back her hair*). I must be calm. (*She sits down.*) Because the neighbor women will come and I don't want them to see me so poor. So poor! A woman without even one son to hold to her lips.

(*The* BRIDE *appears. She is without her wreath and wears a black shawl.*)

NEIGHBOR (*with rage, seeing the* BRIDE). Where are you going?

BRIDE. I'm coming here.

MOTHER (*to the* NEIGHBOR). Who is it?

NEIGHBOR. Don't you recognize her?

MOTHER. That's why I asked who it was. Because I don't want to recognize her, so I won't sink my teeth in her throat. You snake! (*She moves wrathfully on the* BRIDE, *then stops. To the* NEIGHBOR) Look at her! There she is, and she's crying, while I stand here calmly and don't tear her eyes out. I don't understand myself. Can it be I didn't love my son? But, where's his good name? Where is it now? Where is it? (*She beats the* BRIDE, *who drops to the floor.*)

NEIGHBOR. For God's sake! (*She tries to separate them.*)

BRIDE (*to the* NEIGHBOR). Let her; I came here so she'd kill me and they'd take me away with them. (*To the* MOTHER) But not with her hands; with grappling hooks, with a sickle—and with force—until they break on my bones. Let her! I want her to know I'm clean, that I may be crazy, but that they can bury me without a single man ever having seen himself in the whiteness of my breasts.

MOTHER. Shut up, shut up; what do I care about that?

BRIDE. Because I ran away with the other one; I ran away! (*With anguish*) You would have gone, too. I was a woman burning with desire, full of sores inside and out, and your son was a little bit of water from which I hoped for children, land, health; but the other one was a dark river, choked with brush, that brought near me the undertone of its rushes and its whispered song. And I went along with your son who was like a little boy of cold water—and the other sent against me hundreds of birds who got in my way and left white frost on my wounds, my wounds of a poor withered woman, of a girl caressed by fire. I didn't want to; remember that! I didn't want to. Your son was my destiny and I have not betrayed him, but the other one's arm dragged me along like the pull of the sea, like the head toss of a mule, and he would have dragged me always, always, always—even if I were an old woman and all your son's sons held me by the hair!

(*A* NEIGHBOR *enters.*)

MOTHER. She is not to blame; nor am I! (*Sarcastically*) Who is, then? It's a delicate, lazy, sleepless woman who throws away an orange blossom wreath and goes looking for a piece of bed warmed by another woman!

BRIDE. Be still! Be still! Take your revenge on me; here I am! See how soft my throat is; it would be less work for you than cutting a dahlia in your garden. But never that! Clean, clean as a new-born little girl. And strong enough to prove it to you. Light the fire. Let's stick our hands in; you for your son, I, for my body. *You'll* draw yours out first.

(*Another* NEIGHBOR *enters.*)

MOTHER. But what does your good name matter to me? What does your death matter to me? What does anything about anything matter to me? Bléssed be the wheat stalks, because my sons are under them; bléssed be the rain, because it wets the face of the dead. Bléssed be God, who stretches us out together to rest.

(*Another* NEIGHBOR *enters.*)

BRIDE. Let me weep with you.
MOTHER. Weep. But at the door.

(*The* GIRL *enters. The* BRIDE *stays at the door. The* MOTHER *is at the center of the stage.*)

LEONARDO'S WIFE (*entering and going to the left*).
    He was a beautiful horseman,
    now he's a heap of snow.
    He rode to fairs and mountains
    and women's arms.
    Now, the night's dark moss
    crowns his forehead.
MOTHER. A sunflower to your mother,
    a mirror of the earth.
    Let them put on your breast
    the cross of bitter rosebay;
    and over you a sheet

of shining silk;
between your quiet hands
let water form its lament.

WIFE. Ay-y-y, four gallant boys
come with tired shoulders!

BRIDE. Ay-y-y, four gallant boys
carry death on high!

MOTHER. Neighbors.

LITTLE GIRL (*at the door*). They're bringing them now.

MOTHER. It's the same thing.
Always the cross, the cross.

WOMEN. Sweet nails,
cross adored,
sweet name
of Christ our Lord.

BRIDE.
May the cross protect both the quick and the dead.

MOTHER. Neighbors: with a knife,
with a little knife,
on their appointed day, between two and three,
these two men killed each other for love.
With a knife,
with a tiny knife
that barely fits the hand,
but that slides in clean
through the astonished flesh
and stops at the place
where trembles, enmeshed,
the dark root of a scream.

BRIDE. And this is a knife,
a tiny knife
that barely fits the hand;
fish without scales, without river,
so that on their appointed day, between two and three,
with this knife,
two men are left stiff,
with their lips turning yellow.

MOTHER. And it barely fits the hand
but it slides in clean
through the astonished flesh
and stops there, at the place
where trembles enmeshed
the dark root of a scream.

(*The* NEIGHBORS, *kneeling on the floor, sob.*)

QUESTIONS

1. Who is the protagonist of this tragedy—the mother? the bridegroom? Leonardo Félix? the bride? Why is only one of the characters given a name?
2. The external conflicts of the play are strong. In which characters are there also internal conflicts? What forces conflict in each? What are the two chief conflicting forces in the play? Does the play favor one force over the other?
3. Reconstruct the past history of Leonardo and the bride. Why did they not marry? Why did Leonardo marry someone else?
4. Reconstruct the past history of the bride's mother and father. Of what importance is this material to the play? Why is it included?
5. Explain the motivations in or attitudes toward the marriage of each of the following: the bridegroom's mother, the bride's father, the bride's servant, the bridegroom, the bride, Leonardo.
6. The setting of the play is a district in rural Spain. How much does the play reveal about the customs, mores, and culture of this society? What do you learn about its economy, family relationships, courtship and marriage customs, morality, and religious beliefs?
7. Where does the play place responsibility for the tragedy? What force or forces does the play assert to be dominant in human life? Could the tragedy have been averted?
8. The language of the play consists of prose dialogue, verse dialogue, and song. At what points is verse dialogue used? Why? What function is served by the songs? Are the three kinds of language sharply separated, or do they blend into each other? Compare the quality of the prose dialogue with that in *An Enemy of the People*. What function does language serve in each play?
9. Contrast the directions in this play regarding settings with those in *An Enemy of the People*. How do you explain the difference? What purpose do the settings serve in each play?
10. In Act II, Scene II, the wedding celebration, there is a great deal of coming and going, entering and exiting, by all the characters. Does this serve a utilitarian or a poetic purpose? Explain. Contrast with the use of exits and entrances in Act III of *An Enemy of the People*.
11. What function is served by the three woodcutters in Act III, Scene I? In what scenes do other characters serve a similar purpose?
12. Does the personification of the moon in Act III come as a shock? Why or why not? What would have happened to *An Enemy of the People* had a similar scene been introduced into it? Compare the use of the moon here with its use in *The Glass Menagerie*, Scene V.
13. In the scene in the forest, García Lorca directs the use of two violins. For what effect? Would background music be appropriate for Ibsen's play? Compare its use here and in *The Glass Menagerie*.
14. Why is the beggar woman not listed in the cast of characters? Since she is identified as death only in a stage direction, which the audience would not see, how is her role made clear? Could an audience identify it?
15. What symbolic meanings are suggested by each of the following? (a) the lullaby about the big horse (Act I, Scene II), (b) the fact that the bride lives in a cave house, (c) Leonardo's horse, (d) blood, (e) the moon, (f) the red skein (Act III, Scene 2).

16. Of the three plays in this section, two are translations (and the third *has* been translated into foreign languages). Considering the various kinds of language used in each play, which would you consider most subject to loss of impact by translation from its original language? Which least?
17. Rank the three plays on a scale from most realistic to least realistic and justify your ranking. Does any correlation exist between the method used in each play and its subject matter? Discuss.

3. Tragedy and Comedy

The two masks of drama—one with the corners of its mouth turned down, the other with the corners of its mouth turned up—are familiar everywhere. Derived from masks actually worn by the actors in ancient Greek plays, they symbolize two principal modes of drama. Indeed, just as life gravitates between tears and laughter, they seem to imply that all drama is divided between tragedy and comedy.

But drama is an ancient literary form; in its development from the beginnings to the present it has produced a rich variety of plays. Can all these plays be classified under two terms? If our answer to this question is Yes, we must define the terms very broadly. If our answer is No, then how many terms do we need, and where do we stop? Polonius, in *Hamlet,* says of a visiting troupe of players that they can act "tragedy, comedy, history, pastoral, pastoral-comical, historical-pastoral, tragical-historical, tragical-comical-historical-pastoral, scene individable, or poem unlimited." Like Polonius himself, his list seems ridiculous. Moreover, even if we adopted these terms, and more, could we be sure that they would accurately classify all plays or that a new play, written tomorrow, would not demand a totally new category?

The discussion that follows proceeds on four assumptions. First, perfect definitions and an airtight system of classification are impossible. There exist no views of tragedy and comedy that have not been challenged and no classification system that unequivocally provides for all examples. Second, it is quite unneccessary that we classify each play we read or see. The most important questions to ask about a play are not "Is this a tragedy?" or "Is this a comedy?" but "Does this play furnish an enjoyable, valid, and significant experience?" Third, the quality of experience furnished by a play may be partially dependent on our perception of its relationship to earlier literary forms, and therefore familiarity with traditional notions of tragedy and comedy is important for our understanding and appreciation of plays. Many of the conventions used in specific plays have been determined by the kind of play the author felt himself to be writing. Other plays have been written in deliberate defiance of these conventions. Fourth, whether or not tragedy and comedy be taken as the two all-inclusive dramatic modes, they are certainly, as symbolized by the masks, the two principal ones, and useful points, therefore, from which to begin discussion.

The popular distinctions between comedy and tragedy are fairly simple: comedy is funny; tragedy is sad. Comedy has a happy ending, tragedy an unhappy one. The typical ending for comedy is a marriage; the typical ending for tragedy is a death. There is some truth in these notions, but only some. Some plays called comedies make no attempt to be funny. Successful tragedies, though they involve suffering and sadness, do not leave the spectator depressed. Some funny plays have sad endings: they send the viewer away with a lump in the throat. A few plays usually classified as tragedies do not have unhappy endings but conclude with the protagonist's triumph. In short, the popular distinctions are unreliable. Though we need not entirely abandon them, we must take a more complex view. Let us begin with tragedy.

The first great theorist of dramatic art was Aristotle, whose discussion of tragedy in *Poetics* has dominated critical thought ever since. A very brief summary of Aristotle's view will be helpful.

A tragedy, so Aristotle wrote, is the imitation in dramatic form of an action that is serious and complete, with incidents arousing pity and fear wherewith it effects a catharsis of such emotions. The language used is pleasurable and throughout is appropriate to the situation in which it is used. The chief characters are noble personages ("better than ourselves," says Aristotle), and the actions they perform are noble actions. The plot involves a change in the protagonist's fortune, in which he falls from happiness to misery. The protagonist is not a perfectly good man nor yet a bad man; his misfortune is brought upon him not by vice and depravity but by some error of judgment. A good tragic plot has organic unity: the events follow not just *after* one another but *because* of one another. The best tragic plots involve a reversal (a change from one state of things within the play to its opposite) or a discovery (a change from ignorance to knowledge) or both.

In the account that follows, we will not attempt to delineate the boundaries of tragedy nor necessarily to describe it at its greatest. Instead, we will describe a common understanding of tragedy as a point of departure for further discussion. Nor shall we enter into the endless controversies over what Aristotle meant by "catharsis" or over which of his statements are meant to apply to all tragedies and which only to the best ones. The important thing is that Aristotle had important insights into the nature of some of the greatest tragedies and that, rightly or wrongly interpreted, his conceptions are the basis for a kind of archetypal notion of tragedy that has dominated critical thought. What are the central features of that archetype?

1. The tragic hero is a man of noble stature. He has a greatness about him. He is not an ordinary man but one of outstanding quality. In Greek and in Shakespearean tragedy, he is usually a prince or a king. We may, if we wish, set down this predilection of former times for kings as tragic heroes as an undemocratic prejudice that regarded some men to be of nobler "blood" than others—preeminent by virtue of their aristocratic birth. But it is only partially that. We may with equal validity regard the hero's kingship as the symbol rather than as the cause of his greatness. He is great not primarily by virtue of his kingship but by his possession of extraordinary powers, by qualities of passion or aspiration or nobility of mind. The tragic hero's kingship is also a symbol of his initial good fortune, the mark of his high position. If the hero's fall is to arouse in us the emotions of pity and fear, it must be a fall from a height.

2. Though the tragic hero is preeminently great, he is not perfect. Combined with his strength, there is a vulnerability. Aristotle says that his fall is caused by "some error of judgment," and probably he meant no more than that. Critical tradition, however, has frequently interpreted this error of judgment as a flaw in character—the so-called tragic flaw. With all his great qualities, the tragic hero may be afflicted with some fault of character such as inordinate ambition, quickness to anger, a tendency to jealousy, or overweening pride. Conversely, however, his vulnerability may result from an excess of virtue—a nobility of character that unfits him for life among ordinary mortals. But whatever it be—a fault of character, bad judgment, or excessive virtue—this vulnerability leads to his downfall.

3. The hero's downfall, therefore, is partially his own fault, the result

of his own free choice, not the result of pure accident or villainy or some overriding malignant fate. Accident, villainy, or fate may contribute to the downfall but only as cooperating agents: they are not alone responsible. The combination of the hero's greatness and his responsibility for his own downfall is what entitles us to describe his downfall as tragic rather than as merely pathetic. In common speech these two adjectives are often confused. If a father of ten children is accidentally killed at a street corner, the event, strictly speaking, is pathetic, not tragic. When a weak man succumbs to his weakness and comes to a bad end, the event should be called pathetic, not tragic. The tragic event involves a fall from greatness, brought about, at least partially, by the agent's free action.

4. Nevertheless, the hero's misfortune is not wholly deserved. The punishment exceeds the crime. We do not come away from tragedy with the feeling that "He got what he had coming to him" but rather with the sad sense of a waste of human potential. For what most impresses us about the tragic hero is not his weakness but his greatness. He is, in a sense, "larger than life," or, as Aristotle said, "better than ourselves." He reveals to us the dimensions of human possibility. He is a person mainly admirable, and his fall therefore fills us with pity and fear.

5. Yet the tragic fall is not pure loss. Though it may result in the protagonist's death, it involves, before his death, some increase in awareness, some gain in self-knowledge—as Aristotle puts it, some "discovery"—a change from ignorance to knowledge. On the level of plot, the discovery may be merely learning the truth about some fact or situation of which the protagonist was ignorant, but on the level of character it is accompanied or followed by a significant insight, a fuller self-knowledge, an increase not only in knowledge but in wisdom. Not unusually this increase in wisdom involves some sort of reconciliation with the universe or with the protagonist's situation. He exits not cursing his fate but accepting it and acknowledging that it is to some degree just.

6. Though it arouses solemn emotions—pity and fear, says Aristotle, but compassion and awe might be better terms—tragedy, when well performed, does not leave its audience in a state of depression. Though we cannot be sure what Aristotle meant by his term catharsis, some sort of emotional release at the end is a common experience of those who witness great tragedies on the stage. They have been greatly moved by pity, fear, and associated emotions, but they are not left emotionally beaten down or dejected. Instead, there may be a feeling almost of exhilaration. This feeling is a response to the tragic action. With the fall of the hero and his gain in wisdom or self-knowledge, there is, besides the appalling sense of human waste, a fresh recognition of human greatness, a sense that human

life has unrealized potentialities. Though the hero may be defeated, he at least has dared greatly, and he gains understanding from his defeat.

Is the comic mask laughing or smiling? The question is more important than may at first appear, for usually we laugh *at* someone but smile *with* someone. The laugh expresses recognition of some absurdity in human behavior; the smile expresses pleasure in someone's company or good fortune.

The comic mask may be interpreted both ways. Comedy, Northrop Frye has said, lies between satire and romance. Historically, there have been two chief kinds of comedy—scornful comedy and romantic comedy, laughing comedy and smiling comedy. Of the two, scornful or satiric comedy is the older and probably still the most dominant.

The most essential difference between tragedy and comedy, particularly scornful comedy, is in their depiction of human nature. Where tragedy emphasizes human greatness, comedy delineates human weakness. Where tragedy celebrates human freedom, comedy points up human limitation. Wherever human beings fail to measure up to their own resolutions or to their own self-conceptions, wherever they are guilty of hypocrisy, vanity, or folly, wherever they fly in the face of good sense and rational behavior, comedy exhibits their absurdity and invites us to laugh at them. Where tragedy tends to say, with Shakespeare's Hamlet, "What a piece of work is a man! how noble in reason! how infinite in faculty! in form and moving how express and admirable! in action how like an angel! in apprehension how like a god!" comedy says, with Shakespeare's Puck, "Lord, what fools these mortals be!"

Because comedy exposes human folly, its function is partly critical and corrective. Where tragedy challenges us with a vision of human possibility, comedy reveals to us a spectacle of human ridiculousness that it makes us want to avoid. No doubt, we should not exaggerate this function of comedy. We go to the theater primarily for enjoyment, not to receive lessons in personality or character development. Nevertheless, laughter may be educative at the same time that it is enjoyable. The comedies of Aristophanes and Molière, of Ben Jonson and Congreve, are, first of all, good fun, but, secondly, they are antidotes for human folly.

Romantic or smiling comedy, as opposed to scornful comedy, and as exemplified by many plays of Shakespeare—*As You Like It, Twelfth Night, Much Ado About Nothing, The Tempest,* for instance—puts its emphasis upon sympathetic rather than ridiculous characters. These characters—likeable, not given up to folly or vanity—are placed in various kinds of difficulties from which, at the end of the play, they are rescued, attaining their ends or having their good fortunes restored. Though different from the protagonists of scornful comedy, however, these characters are not the commanding or lofty figures that tragic heroes are. They are sensible and good rather than noble, aspiring, and grand. They do not strike us with awe as the tragic hero does. They do not so challengingly test the limits of human possibility. In short, they move in a smaller world. Romantic comedies, therefore, do not occupy a different universe from satric comedies; they simply lie at opposite sides of the same territory. The romantic comedy, moreover, though its protagonists are sympathetic, has usually a number of lesser characters whose folly is held up to ridicule. The satiric comedy, on the other hand, frequently has minor characters—often a pair of young lovers—who are sympathetic and likable. The difference between the two kinds of comedy may be only a matter of whether we laugh at the primary or at the secondary characters.

There are other differences between comedy and tragedy. The norms of comedy are primarily social. Where tragedy tends to isolate the tragic hero and emphasize his uniqueness, comedy puts its protagonists always in the midst of a group and emphasizes their commonness. Where the tragic hero possesses an overpowering individuality, so that his play is often named after him (for example, *Oedipus Rex, Othello*), the comic protagonist tends to be a type, and his play is often named for the type (for example, *The Misanthrope*). We judge the tragic hero by absolute moral standards, by how far he soars above society. We judge the comic protagonist by social standards, by how well he adjusts to society and conforms to the expectations of the group.

Finally, comic plots are less likely than tragic plots to exhibit the high degree of organic unity—of logical cause-and-effect progression—that Aristotle required of tragedy. Plausibility, in fact, is not usually the central characteristic of a comic plot. Unlikely coincidences, improbable disguises, mistaken identities—these are the stuff of which comedy is made; and, as long as they make us laugh and, at the same time, help to illuminate human nature and human folly, we need not greatly care. Not that plausibility is no longer important—only that other things are more important, and these other things are often achieved by the most outrageous violations of probability.

This is particularly true regarding the comic ending. Conventionally, comedies have a happy ending, but the emphasis here is on *conventionally*. The happy ending is, indeed, a *convention* of comedy, which is to say that a comedy ends happily because comedies end happily—that is the nature of the form—not necessarily because a happy ending is a plausible outcome of the events that have preceded. The greatest masters of comedy—Aristophanes, Shakespeare, Molière—have often been extremely arbitrary in the manner in which they achieved their endings. The accidental discovery of a lost will, rescue by an act of divine intervention (*deus ex machina*), the sudden reform of a mean-spirited person into a friendly person—such devices have been used by the greatest comic writers. And, even where the ending is achieved more plausibly, comedy asks us to forget for the time being that in actuality life has no endings, except for death. Marriage, which provides the ending for so many comedies, is really a beginning.

And now, though we do not wish to imitate the folly of Polonius, it is well that we learn two additional terms: melodrama and farce. In the two-part classification suggested by the two symbolic masks, melodrama belongs with tragedy and farce with comedy, but the differences are sufficient to make the two new terms useful.

MELODRAMA, like tragedy, attempts to arouse feelings of fear and pity, but it does so ordinarily through cruder means. The conflict is an oversimplified one between good and evil depicted in absolute terms. Plot is emphasized at the expense of characterization. Sensational incidents provide the staple of the plot. The young mother and her baby are evicted into a howling storm by the villain holding the mortgage. The heroine is tied to the railroad tracks as the express train approaches. Most important, good finally triumphs over evil, and the ending is happy. Typically, at the end, the hero marries the heroine; villainy is foiled or crushed. Melodrama may, of course, have different degrees of power and subtlety; it is not always as crude as its crudest examples. But, in it, moral issues are typically oversimplified, and good is finally triumphant. Melodrama does not provide the complex insights of tragedy. It is typically escapist rather than interpretive.

FARCE, more consistently than comedy, is aimed at arousing explosive laughter. But again the means are cruder. The conflicts are violent and usually at the physical level. Plot is emphasized at the expense of characterization, improbable situations and coincidence at the expense of articulated plot. Absurdity replaces plausibility. Coarse wit, practical jokes, and physical action are staples. Characters trip over benches, insult each other, run into walls, knock each other down, get into brawls. Performed with gusto, farce may be hilariously funny. Psychologically, it may boost our spirits and purge us of hostility and aggression. In content, however, like melodrama, it is escapist rather than interpretive.

Now we have four classifications—tragedy, comedy, melodrama, farce—the latter two as appendages of the former. But none of these classifications is rigid. They blend into each other and are incapable of exact definition. If we take them overseriously, the tragic mask may laugh, and the comic mask weep.

TOPIC FOR DISCUSSION

An Enemy of the People has been referred to, by at least one critic, as "a satiric comedy." Is this an accurate description? How does the play differ from comedy as popularly conceived? Does it have a happy ending? Is Dr. Stockmann the kind of hero you would most expect to find in satiric comedy, romantic comedy, or tragedy? Why?

Sophocles
OEDIPUS REX

The plots of Greek tragedies were based on legends with which Greek audiences were more or less familiar (as American audiences, for example, would be familiar with the major events in a historical play based on the life of Lincoln). These plays often owed much of their impact to the audience's previous knowledge of the characters and their fate, for it enabled the playwright to make powerful use of dramatic irony and allusion. Much of the audience's delight, in addition, came from seeing how the playwright worked out the details of the story. The purpose of this introductory note is therefore to supply such information as the play's first audiences might be presumed to have had.

Because of a prophecy that their new son would kill his father, Laius and Jocasta, King and Queen of Thebes, gave their infant to a shepherd with orders that he be left on a mountainside to die. The shepherd, however, after having pinned the babe's ankles together, took pity on him and gave him instead to a Corinthian shepherd. This shepherd in turn presented him to Polybus and Merope, King and Queen of Corinth, who, childless, adopted him as their own. The child was given the name Oedipus ("Swollen-foot") because of the injury to his ankles.

When grown to manhood at Polybus' court, Oedipus was accused by a drunken guest of not being his father's son. Though reassured by Polybus and Merope, he was still disturbed and traveled to consult the Delphic oracle. The oracle, without answering the question about his parentage, prophesied that Oedipus would kill his father and beget children by his mother. Horrified, resolved to avert this fate, Oedipus determined never to return to Corinth. Traveling from Delphi, he came to a place where three roads met and was ordered off the road by a man in a chariot. Blows were exchanged, and Oedipus killed the man and four of his attendants. Later, on the outskirts of Thebes, he encountered the Sphinx, a monster with the head of a woman, wings of an eagle, and body of a lion, which was terrorizing Thebes by slaying all who failed to answer its riddle ("What goes on four legs in the morning, two legs at noon, and three legs in the evening?"). When Oedipus correctly answered the riddle ("man, for he crawls as an infant, walks erect as a man, and uses a staff in old age"), the Sphinx destroyed herself. As a reward, Oedipus was named King of Thebes to replace the recently slain Laius and was given the hand of Jocasta in marriage. With her, he ruled Thebes successfully for some years and had four children—two sons and two daughters. Then the city was afflicted by a plague. It is at this point that the action of the play begins.

The play was first performed in Athens about 430 B.C. In the present version, prepared by Dudley Fitts and Robert Fitzgerald, the translators use spellings for the proper names that are closer to the original Greek than the more familiar Anglicized spellings used in this note. Sophocles (496?–406 B.C.), an active and devoted citizen of Athens during its democratic period, served as an elected general in an Athenian military expedition and held other posts of civic responsibility, but was most importantly its leading and most prolific playwright.

CHARACTERS

OEDIPUS, *King of Thebes, supposed son of Polybos and Meropê, King and Queen of Corinth*

IOKASTÊ, *wife of Oedipus and widow of the late King Laïos*

KREON, *brother of Iokastê, a prince of Thebes*

TEIRESIAS, *a blind seer who serves Apollo*

PRIEST

MESSENGER, *from Corinth*

SHEPHERD, *former servant of Laïos*

SECOND MESSENGER, *from the palace*

CHORUS OF THEBAN ELDERS

CHORAGOS, *leader of the Chorus*

ANTIGONE and ISMENE, *young daughters of Oedipus and Iokastê. They appear in the Éxodos but do not speak.*

SUPPLIANTS, GUARDS, SERVANTS

THE SCENE. *Before the palace of* OEDIPUS, *King of Thebes. A central door and two lateral doors open onto a platform which runs the length of the façade. On the platform, right and left, are altars; and three steps lead down into the* orchêstra, *or chorus-ground. At the beginning of the action these steps are crowded by suppliants who have brought branches and chaplets of olive leaves and who sit in various attitudes of despair.* OEDIPUS *enters.*

PROLOGUE

OEDIPUS.   My children, generations of the living
          In the line of Kadmos,° nursed at his ancient hearth:
          Why have you strewn yourselves before these altars
          In supplication, with your boughs and garlands?

---

2. Kadmos: founder of Thebes.

The breath of incense rises from the city   5
With a sound of prayer and lamentation.
                                        Children,
I would not have you speak through messengers,
And therefore I have come myself to hear you—
I, Oedipus, who bear the famous name.
(*To a* PRIEST) You, there, since you are eldest in the company,   10
Speak for them all, tell me what preys upon you,
Whether you come in dread, or crave some blessing:
Tell me, and never doubt that I will help you
In every way I can; I should be heartless
Were I not moved to find you suppliant here.   15
PRIEST.   Great Oedipus, O powerful king of Thebes!
    You see how all the ages of our people
    Cling to your altar steps: here are boys
    Who can barely stand alone, and here are priests
    By weight of age, as I am a priest of God,   20
    And young men chosen from those yet unmarried;
    As for the others, all that multitude,
    They wait with olive chaplets in the squares,
    At the two shrines of Pallas, and where Apollo
    Speaks in the glowing embers.
                                        Your own eyes   25
    Must tell you: Thebes is tossed on a murdering sea
    And can not lift her head from the death surge.
    A rust consumes the buds and fruits of the earth;
    The herds are sick; children die unborn,
    And labor is vain. The god of plague and pyre   30
    Raids like detestable lightning through the city,
    And all the house of Kadmos is laid waste,
    All emptied, and all darkened: Death alone
    Battens upon the misery of Thebes.

    You are not one of the immortal gods, we know;   35
    Yet we have come to you to make our prayer
    As to the man surest in mortal ways
    And wisest in the ways of God. You saved us
    From the Sphinx, that flinty singer, and the tribute
    We paid to her so long; yet you were never   40
    Better informed than we, nor could we teach you:
    A god's touch, it seems, enabled you to help us.

    Therefore, O mighty power, we turn to you:
    Find us our safety, find us a remedy,
    Whether by counsel of the gods or of men.   45
    A king of wisdom tested in the past

Can act in a time of troubles, and act well.
Noblest of men, restore
Life to your city! Think how all men call you
Liberator for your boldness long ago;   50
Ah, when your years of kingship are remembered,
Let them not say *We rose, but later fell*—
Keep the State from going down in the storm!
Once, years ago, with happy augury,
You brought us fortune; be the same again!   55
No man questions your power to rule the land:
But rule over men, not over a dead city!
Ships are only hulls, high walls are nothing,
When no life moves in the empty passageways.
OEDIPUS. Poor children! You may be sure I know   60
All that you longed for in your coming here.
I know that you are deathly sick; and yet,
Sick as you are, not one is as sick as I.
Each of you suffers in himself alone
His anguish, not another's; but my spirit   65
Groans for the city, for myself, for you.

I was not sleeping, you are not waking me.
No, I have been in tears for a long while
And in my restless thought walked many ways.
In all my search I found one remedy,   70
And I have adopted it: I have sent Kreon,
Son of Menoikeus, brother of the queen,
To Delphi, Apollo's place of revelation,
To learn there, if he can,
What act or pledge of mine may save the city.   75
I have counted the days, and now, this very day,
I am troubled, for he has overstayed his time.
What is he doing? He has been gone too long.
Yet whenever he comes back, I should do ill
Not to take any action the god orders.   80
PRIEST. It is a timely promise. At this instant
They tell me Kreon is here.
OEDIPUS.   O Lord Apollo!
May his news be fair as his face is radiant!
PRIEST. Good news, I gather! he is crowned with bay,
The chaplet is thick with berries.
OEDIPUS.   We shall soon know;   85
He is near enough to hear us now.

    (*Enter* KREON.)

                              O prince:
Brother: son of Menoikeus:

What answer do you bring us from the god?

KREON. A strong one. I can tell you, great afflictions
    Will turn out well, if they are taken well.   90

OEDIPUS. What was the oracle? These vague words
    Leave me still hanging between hope and fear.

KREON. Is it your pleasure to hear me with all these
    Gathered around us? I am prepared to speak,
    But should we not go in?

OEDIPUS.   Speak to them all,   95
    It is for them I suffer, more than for myself.

KREON. Then I will tell you what I heard at Delphi.
    In plain words
    The gods commands us to expel from the land of Thebes
    An old defilement we are sheltering.   100
    It is a deathly thing, beyond cure;
    We must not let it feed upon us longer.

OEDIPUS. What defilement? How shall we rid ourselves of it?

KREON. By exile or death, blood for blood. It was
    Murder that brought the plague-wind on the city.   105

OEDIPUS. Murder of whom? Surely the god has named him?

KREON. My lord: Laïos once ruled this land,
    Before you came to govern us.

OEDIPUS.   I know;
    I learned of him from others; I never saw him.

KREON. He was murdered; and Apollo commands us now   110
    To take revenge upon whoever killed him.

OEDIPUS. Upon whom? Where are they? Where shall we find a clue
    To solve that crime, after so many years?

KREON. Here in this land, he said. Search reveals
    Things that escape an inattentive man.   115

OEDIPUS. Tell me: Was Laïos murdered in his house,
    Or in the fields, or in some foreign country?

KREON. He said he planned to make a pilgrimage.
    He did not come home again.

OEDIPUS.   And was there no one,
    No witness, no companion, to tell what happened?   120

KREON. They were all killed but one, and he got away
    So frightened that he could remember one thing only.

OEDIPUS. What was that one thing? One may be the key
    To everything, if we resolve to use it.

KREON. He said that a band of highwaymen attacked them,   125
    Outnumbered them, and overwhelmed the king.

OEDIPUS. Strange, that a highwayman should be so daring—
    Unless some faction here bribed him to do it.

KREON. We thought of that. But after Laïos' death
    New troubles arose and we had no avenger.   130

OEDIPUS. What troubles could prevent your hunting down the killers?
KREON. The riddling Sphinx's song
  Made us deaf to all mysteries but her own.
OEDIPUS. Then once more I must bring what is dark to light.
  It is most fitting that Apollo shows,   135
  As you do, this compunction for the dead.
  You shall see how I stand by you, as I should,
  Avenging this country and the god as well,
  And not as though it were for some distant friend,
  But for my own sake, to be rid of evil.   140
  Whoever killed King Laïos might—who knows?—
  Lay violent hands even on me—and soon.
  I act for the murdered king in my own interest.

  Come, then, my children: leave the altar steps,
  Lift up your olive boughs!
                     One of you go   145
  And summon the people of Kadmos to gather here.
  I will do all that I can; you may tell them that.

  (*Exit a* PAGE.)

  So, with the help of God,
  We shall be saved—or else indeed we are lost.
PRIEST. Let us rise, children. It was for this we came,   150
  And now the king has promised it.
  Phoibos° has sent us an oracle; may he descend
  Himself to save us and drive out the plague.

  (*Exeunt* OEDIPUS *and* KREON *into the palace by the central door. The*
    PRIEST *and the* SUPPLIANTS *disperse right and left. After a short pause*
    the CHORUS *enters the orchêstra.*)

PÁRODOS°

STROPHE 1

CHORUS. What is God singing in his profound
  Delphi of gold and shadow?   155
  What oracle for Thebes, the sunwhipped city?
  Fear unjoints me, the roots of my heart tremble.

---

152. Phoibos: Apollo, god of light and truth. **Párodos:** The song or ode chanted by the
chorus on their entry. It is accompanied by dancing and music played on a flute. The chorus,
in this play, represents elders of the city of Thebes. They remain on stage (on a level lower
than the principal actors) for the remainder of the play. The choral odes and dances serve to
separate one scene from another (there was no curtain in Greek theater) as well as to

Now I remember, O Healer, your power, and wonder:
Will you send doom like a sudden cloud, or weave it
Like nightfall of the past?   160
Speak to me, tell me, O
Child of golden Hope, immortal Voice.

ANTISTROPHE 1

Let me pray to Athenê, the immortal daughter of Zeus,
And to Artemis her sister
Who keeps her famous throne in the market ring,   165
And to Apollo, archer from distant heaven—
O gods, descend! Like three streams leap against
The fires of our grief, the fires of darkness;
Be swift to bring us rest!
As in the old time from the brilliant house   170
Of air you stepped to save us, come again!

STROPHE 2

Now our afflictions have no end,
Now all our stricken host lies down
And no man fights off death with his mind;
The noble plowland bears no grain,   175
And groaning mothers can not bear—
See, how our lives like birds take wing,
Like sparks that fly when a fire soars,
To the shore of the god of evening.

ANTISTROPHE 2

The plague burns on, it is pitiless,   180
Though pallid children laden with death
Lie unwept in the stony ways,
And old gray women by every path
Flock to the strand about the altars
There to strike their breasts and cry   185
Worship of Phoibos in wailing prayers:
Be kind, God's golden child!

---

comment on the action, reinforce the emotion, and interpret the situation. The chorus also
performs dance movements during certain portions of the scenes themselves. *Strophe* and
antistrophe are terms denoting the movement and counter-movement of the chorus from
one side of their playing area to the other. When the chorus participates in dialogue with the
other characters, their lines are spoken by the Choragos, their leader.

There are no swords in this attack by fire,
No shields, but we are ringed with cries.
Send the besieger plunging from our homes   190
Into the vast sea-room of the Atlantic
Or into the waves that foam eastward of Thrace—
For the day ravages what the night spares—
Destroy our enemy, lord of the thunder!
Let him be riven by lightning from heaven!   195

ANTISTROPHE 3

Phoibos Apollo, stretch the sun's bowstring,
That golden cord, until it sing for us,
Flashing arrows in heaven!
                           Artemis, Huntress,
Race with flaring lights upon our mountains!
O scarlet god,° O golden-banded brow,   200
O Theban Bacchos in a storm of Maenads,

(*Enter* OEDIPUS, *center.*)

Whirl upon Death, that all the Undying hate!
Come with blinding torches, come in joy!

SCENE I

OEDIPUS. Is this your prayer? It may be answered. Come,
Listen to me, act as the crisis demands,   205
And you shall have relief from all these evils.

Until now I was a stranger to this tale,
As I had been a stranger to the crime.
Could I track down the murderer without a clue?
But now, friends,   210
As one who became a citizen after the murder,
I make this proclamation to all Thebans:
If any man knows by whose hand Laïos, son of Labdakos,
Met his death, I direct that man to tell me everything,
No matter what he fears for having so long withheld it.   215
Let it stand as promised that no further trouble
Will come to him, but he may leave the land in safety.

---

200. scarlet god: Bacchos, god of wine and revelry. The Maenads were his female attendants.

Moreover: If anyone knows the murderer to be foreign,
Let him not keep silent: he shall have his reward from me.
However, if he does conceal it; if any man   220
Fearing for his friend or for himself disobeys this edict,
Hear what I propose to do:

I solemnly forbid the people of this country,
Where power and throne are mine, ever to receive that man
Or speak to him, no matter who he is, or let him   225
Join in sacrifice, lustration, or in prayer.
I decree that he be driven from every house,
Being, as he is, corruption itself to us: the Delphic
Voice of Apollo has pronounced this revelation.
Thus I associate myself with the oracle   230
And take the side of the murdered king.

As for the criminal, I pray to God—
Whether it be a lurking thief, or one of a number—
I pray that that man's life be consumed in evil and wretchedness.
And as for me, this curse applies no less   235
If it should turn out that the culprit is my guest here,
Sharing my hearth.
                  You have heard the penalty.
I lay it on you now to attend to this
For my sake, for Apollo's, for the sick
Sterile city that heaven has abandoned.   240
Suppose the oracle had given you no command:
Should this defilement go uncleansed for ever?
You should have found the murderer: your king,
A noble king, had been destroyed!
                          Now I,
Having the power that he held before me,   245
Having his bed, begetting children there
Upon his wife, as he would have, had he lived—
Their son would have been my children's brother,
If Laïos had had luck in fatherhood!
(And now his bad fortune has struck him down)—   250
I say I take the son's part, just as though
I were his son, to press the fight for him
And see it won! I'll find the hand that brought
Death to Labdakos' and Polydoros' child,
Heir of Kadmos' and Agenor's line.°   255
And as for those who fail me,

___

255. **Labdakos, Polydoros, Kadmos, and Agenor:** father, grandfather, great-grandfather, and great-great-grandfather of Laïos.

May the gods deny them the fruit of the earth,
Fruit of the womb, and may they rot utterly!
Let them be wretched as we are wretched, and worse!

For you, for loyal Thebans, and for all   260
Who find my actions right, I pray the favor
Of justice, and of all the immortal gods.
CHORAGOS. Since I am under oath, my lord, I swear
I did not do the murder, I can not name
The murderer. Phoibos ordained the search;   265
Why did he not say who the culprit was?
OEDIPUS. An honest question. But no man in the world
Can make the gods do more than the gods will.
CHORAGOS. There is an alternative, I think—
OEDIPUS.   Tell me.
Any or all, you must not fail to tell me.   270
CHORAGOS. A lord clairvoyant to the lord Apollo,
As we all know, is the skilled Teiresias.
One might learn much about this from him, Oedipus.
OEDIPUS. I am not wasting time:
Kreon spoke of this, and I have sent for him—   275
Twice, in fact; it is strange that he is not here.
CHORAGOS. The other matter—that old report—seems useless.
OEDIPUS. What was that? I am interested in all reports.
CHORAGOS. The king was said to have been killed by highwaymen.
OEDIPUS. I know. But we have no witnesses to that.   280
CHORAGOS. If the killer can feel a particle of dread,
Your curse will bring him out of hiding!
OEDIPUS.   No.
The man who dared that act will fear no curse.

(*Enter the blind seer* TEIRESIAS, *led by a* PAGE.)

CHORAGOS. But there is one man who may detect the criminal.
This is Teiresias, this is the holy prophet   285
In whom, alone of all men, truth was born.
OEDIPUS. Teiresias: seer: student of mysteries,
Of all that's taught and all that no man tells,
Secrets of Heaven and secrets of the earth:
Blind though you are, you know the city lies   290
Sick with plague; and from this plague, my lord,
We find that you alone can guard or save us.

Possibly you did not hear the messengers?
Apollo, when we sent to him,
Sent us back word that this great pestilence   295
Would lift, but only if we established clearly

The identity of those who murdered Laïos.
They must be killed or exiled.

                                    Can you use
Birdflight° or any art of divination
To purify yourself, and Thebes, and me   300
From this contagion? We are in your hands.
There is no fairer duty
Than that of helping others in distress.

TEIRESIAS. How dreadful knowledge of the truth can be
When there's no help in truth! I knew this well,   305
But did not act on it: else I should not have come.

OEDIPUS. What is troubling you? Why are your eyes so cold?

TEIRESIAS. Let me go home. Bear your own fate, and I'll
Bear mine. It is better so: trust what I say.

OEDIPUS. What you say is ungracious and unhelpful   310
To your native country. Do not refuse to speak.

TEIRESIAS. When it comes to speech, your own is neither temperate
Nor opportune. I wish to be more prudent.

OEDIPUS. In God's name, we all beg you—

TEIRESIAS.   You are all ignorant.
No; I will never tell you what I know.   315
Now it is my misery; then, it would be yours.

OEDIPUS. What! You do know something, and will not tell us?
You would betray us all and wreck the State?

TEIRESIAS. I do not intend to torture myself, or you.
Why persist in asking? You will not persuade me.   320

OEDIPUS. What a wicked old man you are! You'd try a stone's
Patience! Out with it! Have you no feeling at all?

TEIRESIAS. You call me unfeeling. If you could only see
The nature of your own feelings . . .

OEDIPUS.   Why,
Who would not feel as I do? Who could endure   325
Your arrogance toward the city?

TEIRESIAS.   What does it matter?
Whether I speak or not, it is bound to come.

OEDIPUS. Then, if "it" is bound to come, you are bound to tell me.

TEIRESIAS. No, I will not go on. Rage as you please.

OEDIPUS. Rage? Why not!
                          And I'll tell you what I think: 330
You planned it, you had it done, you all but
Killed him with your own hands: if you had eyes,
I'd say the crime was yours, and yours alone.

___

299. Birdflight: Prophets predicted the future or divined the unknown by observing the
flight of birds.

TEIRESIAS. So? I charge you, then,
Abide by the proclamation you have made: 335
From this day forth
Never speak again to these men or to me;
You yourself are the pollution of this country.
OEDIPUS. You dare say that! Can you possibly think you have
Some way of going free, after such insolence?   340
TEIRESIAS. I have gone free. It is the truth sustains me.
OEDIPUS. Who taught you shamelessness? It was not your craft.
TEIRESIAS. You did. You made me speak. I did not want to.
OEDIPUS. Speak what? Let me hear it again more clearly.
TEIRESIAS. Was it not clear before? Are you tempting me?   345
OEDIPUS. I did not understand it. Say it again.
TEIRESIAS. I say that you are the murderer whom you seek.
OEDIPUS. Now twice you have spat out infamy. You'll pay for it!
TEIRESIAS. Would you care for more? Do you wish to be really angry?
OEDIPUS. Say what you will. Whatever you say is worthless.   350
TEIRESIAS. I say you live in hideous shame with those
Most dear to you. You can not see the evil.
OEDIPUS. Can you go on babbling like this for ever?
TEIRESIAS. I can, if there is power in truth.
OEDIPUS.   There is:
But not for you, not for you,   355
You sightless, witless, senseless, mad old man!
TEIRESIAS. You are the madman. There is no one here
Who will not curse you soon, as you curse me.
OEDIPUS. You child of total night! I would not touch you;
Neither would any man who sees the sun.   360
TEIRESIAS. True: it is not from you my fate will come.
That lies within Apollo's competence,
As it is his concern.
OEDIPUS.   Tell me, who made
These fine discoveries? Kreon? or someone else?
TEIRESIAS. Kreon is no threat. You weave your own doom.   365
OEDIPUS. Wealth, power, craft of statemanship!
Kingly position, everywhere admired!
What savage envy is stored up against these,
If Kreon, whom I trusted, Kreon my friend,
For this great office which the city once   370
Put in my hands unsought—if for this power
Kreon desires in secret to destroy me!

He has bought this decrepit fortune-teller, this
Collecter of dirty pennies, this prophet fraud—
Why, he is no more clairvoyant than I am!
                                        Tell us: 375

Has your mystic mummery ever approached the truth?
When that hellcat the Sphinx was performing here,
What help were you to these people?
Her magic was not for the first man who came along:
It demanded a real exorcist. Your birds— 380
What good were they? or the gods, for the matter of that?
But I came by,
Oedipus, the simple man, who knows nothing—
I thought it out for myself, no birds helped me!
And this is the man you think you can destroy, 385
That you may be close to Kreon when he's king!
Well, you and your friend Kreon, it seems to me,
Will suffer most. If you were not an old man,
You would have paid already for your plot.
CHORAGOS. We can not see that his words or yours 390
Have been spoken except in anger, Oedipus,
And of anger we have no need. How to accomplish
The god's will best: that is what most concerns us.
TEIRESIAS. You are a king. But where argument's concerned
I am your man, as much a king as you. 395
I am not your servant, but Apollo's.
I have no need of Kreon or Kreon's name.

Listen to me. You mock my blindness, do you?
But I say that you, with both your eyes, are blind:
You can not see the wretchedness of your life, 400
Nor in whose house you live, no, nor with whom.
Who are your father and mother? Can you tell me?
You do not even know the blind wrongs
That you have done them, on earth and in the world below.
But the double lash of your parents' curse will whip you 405
Out of this land some day, with only night
Upon your precious eyes.
Your cries then—where will they not be heard?
What fastness of Kithairon° will not echo them?
And that bridal-descant of yours—you'll know it then, 410
The song they sang when you came here to Thebes
And found your misguided berthing.
All this, and more, that you can not guess at now,
Will bring you to yourself among your children.

Be angry, then. Curse Kreon. Curse my words. 415
I tell you, no man that walks upon the earth
Shall be rooted out more horribly than you.

409. Kithairon: the mountain where Oedipus was taken to be exposed as an infant.

OEDIPUS. Am I to bear this from him?—Damnation
    Take you! Out of this place! Out of my sight!
TEIRESIAS. I would not have come at all if you had not asked me.   420
OEDIPUS. Could I have told that you'd talk nonsense, that
    You'd come here to make a fool of yourself, and of me?
TEIRESIAS. A fool? Your parents thought me sane enough.
OEDIPUS. My parents again!—Wait: who were my parents?
TEIRESIAS. This day will give you a father, and break your heart.   425
OEDIPUS. Your infantile riddles! Your damned abracadabra!
TEIRESIAS. You were a great man once at solving riddles.
OEDIPUS. Mock me with that if you like; you will find it true.
TEIRESIAS. It was true enough. It brought about your ruin.
OEDIPUS. But if it saved this town?
TEIRESIAS (to the PAGE).   Boy, give me your hand.   430
OEDIPUS. Yes, boy; lead him away.
                          —While you are here
    We can do nothing. Go; leave us in peace.
TEIRESIAS. I will go when I have said what I have to say.
    How can you hurt me? And I tell you again:
    The man you have been looking for all this time,   435
    The damned man, the murderer of Laïos,
    That man is in Thebes. To your mind he is foreign-born,
    But it will soon be shown that he is a Theban,
    A revelation that will fail to please.
                        A blind man,
    Who has his eyes now; a penniless man, who is rich now;   440
    And he will go tapping the strange earth with his staff.
    To the children with whom he lives now he will be
    Brother and father—the very same; to her
    Who bore him, son and husband—the very same
    Who came to his father's bed, wet with his father's blood.   445

    Enough. Go think that over.
    If later you find error in what I have said,
    You may say that I have no skill in prophecy.

(*Exit* TEIRESIAS, *led by his* PAGE. OEDIPUS *goes into the palace.*)

ODE I

STROPHE 1

CHORUS. The Delphic stone of prophecies
    Remembers ancient regicide   450
    And a still bloody hand.
    That killer's hour of flight has come.

He must be stronger than riderless
Coursers of untiring wind,
For the son° of Zeus armed with his father's thunder   455
Leaps in lightning after him;
And the Furies hold his track, the sad Furies.

ANTISTROPHE 1

Holy Parnassos'° peak of snow
Flashes and blinds that secret man,
That all shall hunt him down: 460
Though he may roam the forest shade
Like a bull gone wild from pasture
To rage through glooms of stone.
Doom comes down on him; flight will not avail him;
For the world's heart calls him desolate,   465
And the immortal voices follow, for ever follow.

STROPHE 2

But now a wilder thing is heard
From the old man skilled at hearing Fate in the wing-beat of a bird.
Bewildered as a blown bird, my soul hovers and can not find
Foothold in this debate, or any reason or rest of mind.   470
But no man ever brought—none can bring
Proof of strife between Thebes' royal house,
Labdakos' line, and the son of Polybos;
And never until now has any man brought word
Of Laïos' dark death staining Oedipus the King.   475

ANTISTROPHE 2

Divine Zeus and Apollo hold
Perfect intelligence alone of all tales ever told;
And well though this diviner works, he works in his own night;
No man can judge that rough unknown or trust in second sight,
For wisdom changes hands among the wise.   480
Shall I believe my great lord criminal
At a raging word that a blind old man let fall?
I saw him, when the carrion woman° faced him of old,
Prove his heroic mind. These evil words are lies.

---

455. **son:** Apollo. 458. **Parnassos:** mountain sacred to Apollo. 483. **woman:** the Sphinx.

SCENE II

KREON. Men of Thebes: 485
    I am told that heavy accusations
    Have been brought against me by King Oedipus.

    I am not the kind of man to bear this tamely.

    If in these present difficulties
    He holds me accountable for any harm to him   490
    Through anything I have said or done—why, then,
    I do not value life in this dishonor.
    It is not as though this rumor touched upon
    Some private indiscretion. The matter is grave.
    The fact is that I am being called disloyal   495
    To the State, to my fellow citizens, to my friends.
CHORAGOS. He may have spoken in anger, not from his mind.
KREON. But did you not hear him say I was the one
    Who seduced the old prophet into lying?
CHORAGOS. The thing was said; I do not know how seriously.   500
KREON. But you were watching him! Were his eyes steady?
    Did he look like a man in his right mind?
CHORAGOS.   I do not know.
    I can not judge the behavior of great men.
    But here is the king himself.

    (*Enter* OEDIPUS.)

OEDIPUS.   So you dared come back.
    Why? How brazen of you to come to my house,   505
    You murderer!
            Do you think I do not know
    That you plotted to kill me, plotted to steal my throne?
    Tell me, in God's name: am I coward, a fool,
    That you should dream you could accomplish this?
    A fool who could not see your slippery game?   510
    A coward, not to fight back when I saw it?
    You are the fool, Kreon, are you not? hoping
    Without support or friends to get a throne?
    Thrones may be won or bought: you could do neither.
KREON. Now listen to me. You have talked; let me talk, too. 515
    You can not judge unless you know the facts.
OEDIPUS. You speak well: there is one fact; but I find it hard
    To learn from the deadliest enemy I have.
KREON. That above all I must dispute with you.
OEDIPUS. That above all I will not hear you deny.   520

KREON. If you think there is anything good in being stubborn
  Against all reason, then I say you are wrong.
OEDIPUS. If you think a man can sin against his own kind
  And not be punished for it, I say you are mad.
KREON. I agree. But tell me: what have I done to you?   525
OEDIPUS. You advised me to send for that wizard, did you not?
KREON. I did. I should do it again.
OEDIPUS.   Very well. Now tell me:
  How long has it been since Laïos—
KREON.   What of Laïos?
OEDIPUS. Since he vanished in that onset by the road?
KREON. It was long ago, a long time.
OEDIPUS.   And this prophet,   530
  Was he practicing here then?
KREON.   He was; and with honor, as now.
OEDIPUS. Did he speak of me at that time?
KREON.   He never did,
  At least, not when I was present.
OEDIPUS.   But . . . the enquiry?
  I suppose you held one?
KREON.   We did, but we learned nothing.
OEDIPUS. Why did the prophet not speak against me then?   535
KREON. I do not know; and I am the kind of man
  Who holds his tongue when he has no facts to go on.
OEDIPUS. There's one fact that you know, and you could tell it.
KREON. What fact is that? If I know it, you shall have it.
OEDIPUS. If he were not involved with you, he could not say   540
  That it was I who murdered Laïos.
KREON. If he says that, you are the one that knows it!—
  But now it is my turn to question you.
OEDIPUS. Put your questions. I am no murderer.
KREON. First, then: You married my sister?
OEDIPUS.   I married your sister.   545
KREON. And you rule the kingdom equally with her?
OEDIPUS. Everything that she wants she has from me.
KREON. And I am the third, equal to both of you?
OEDIPUS. That is why I call you a bad friend.
KREON. No. Reason it out, as I have done.   550
  Think of this first: Would any sane man prefer
  Power, with all a king's anxieties,
  To that same power and the grace of sleep?
  Certainly not I.
  I have never longed for the king's power—only his rights.   555
  Would any wise man differ from me in this?

As matters stand, I have my way in everything
With your consent, and no responsibilities.
If I were king, I should be a slave to policy.
How could I desire a scepter more   560
Than what is now mine—untroubled influence?
No, I have not gone mad; I need no honors,
Except those with the perquisites I have now.
I am welcome everywhere; every man salutes me,
And those who want your favor seek my ear,   565
Since I know how to manage what they ask.
Should I exchange this ease for that anxiety?
Besides, no sober mind is treasonable.
I hate anarchy
And never would deal with any man who likes it.   570

Test what I have said. Go to the priestess
At Delphi, ask if I quoted her correctly.
And as for this other thing: if I am found
Guilty of treason with Teiresias,
Then sentence me to death. You have my word   575
It is a sentence I should cast my vote for—
But not without evidence!
                          You do wrong
When you take good men for bad, bad men for good.
A true friend thrown aside—why, life itself
Is not more precious!
                          In time you will know this well: 580
For time, and time alone, will show the just man,
Though scoundrels are discovered in a day.
CHORAGOS. This is well said, and a prudent man would ponder it.
    Judgments too quickly formed are dangerous.
OEDIPUS. But is he not quick in his duplicity?   585
    And shall I not be quick to parry him?
    Would you have me stand still, hold my peace, and let
    This man win everything, through my inaction?
KREON. And you want—what is it, then? To banish me?
OEDIPUS. No, not exile. It is your death I want,   590
    So that all the world may see what treason means.
KREON. You will persist, then? You will not believe me?
OEDIPUS. How can I believe you?
KREON.   Then you are a fool.
OEDIPUS. To save myself?
KREON.   In justice, think of me.
OEDIPUS. You are evil incarnate.

KREON.   But suppose that you are wrong?   595
OEDIPUS.   Still I must rule.
KREON.   But not if you rule badly.
OEDIPUS.   O city, city!
KREON.   It is my city, too!
CHORAGOS.   Now, my lords, be still. I see the queen,
   Iokastê, coming from her palace chambers;
   And it is time she came, for the sake of you both.   600
   This dreadful quarrel can be resolved through her.

(*Enter* IOKASTÊ.)

IOKASTÊ.   Poor foolish men, what wicked din is this?
   With Thebes sick to death, is it not shameful
   That you should rake some private quarrel up?
   (*To* OEDIPUS.) Come into the house.
                              —And you, Kreon, go now: 605
   Let us have no more of this tumult over nothing.
KREON.   Nothing? No, sister: what your husband plans for me
   Is one of two great evils: exile or death.
OEDIPUS.   He is right.
                     Why, woman I have caught him squarely
   Plotting against my life.
KREON.   No! Let me die   610
   Accurst if ever I have wished you harm!
IOKASTÊ.   Ah, believe it, Oedipus!
   In the name of the gods, respect this oath of his
   For my sake, for the sake of these people here!

STROPHE 1

CHORAGOS.   Open your mind to her, my lord. Be ruled by her, I
         beg you!   615
OEDIPUS.   What would you have me do?
CHORAGOS.   Respect Kreon's word. He has never spoken like a fool,
   And now he has sworn an oath.
OEDIPUS.   You know what you ask?
CHORAGOS.   I do.
OEDIPUS.   Speak on, then.
CHORAGOS.   A friend so sworn should not be baited so,
   In blind malice, and without final proof.   620
OEDIPUS.   You are aware, I hope, that what you say
   Means death for me, or exile at the least.

STROPHE 2

CHORAGOS. No, I swear by Helios, first in heaven!
                    May I die friendless and accurst,
                The worst of deaths, if ever I meant that!   625
                    It is the withering fields
                        That hurt my sick heart:
                    Must we bear all these ills,
                        And now your bad blood as well?
OEDIPUS. Then let him go. And let me die, if I must,   630
    Or be driven by him in shame from the land of Thebes.
    It is your unhappiness, and not his talk,
    That touches me.
                    As for him—
    Wherever he goes, hatred will follow him.
KREON. Ugly in yielding, as you were ugly in rage!   635
    Natures like yours chiefly torment themselves.
OEDIPUS. Can you not go? Can you not leave me?
KREON.   I can.
    You do not know me; but the city knows me,
    And in its eyes I am just, if not in yours. (*Exit* KREON.)

ANTISTROPHE 1

CHORAGOS. Lady Iokastê, did you not ask the King to go to his
        chambers?   640
IOKASTÊ. First tell me what has happened.
CHORAGOS. There was suspicion without evidence; yet it rankled
    As even false charges will.
IOKASTÊ. On both sides?
CHORAGOS.   On both.
IOKASTÊ.   But what was said?
CHORAGOS. Oh let it rest, let it be done with!
    Have we not suffered enough?   645
OEDIPUS. You see to what your decency has brought you:
    You have made difficulties where my heart saw none.

ANTISTROPHE 2

CHORAGOS. Oedipus, it is not once only I have told you—
                You must know I should count myself unwise
                To the point of madness, should I now forsake you—   650
                    You, under whose hand,
                        In the storm of another time,

>   Our dear land sailed out free.
>   But now stand fast at the helm!

IOKASTÊ. In God's name, Oedipus, inform your wife as well: 655
    Why are you so set in this hard anger?

OEDIPUS. I will tell you, for none of these men deserves
    My confidence as you do. It is Kreon's work,
    His treachery, his plotting against me.

IOKASTÊ. Go on, if you can make this clear to me.   660

OEDIPUS. He charges me with the murder of Laïos.

IOKASTÊ. Has he some knowledge? Or does he speak from hearsay?

OEDIPUS. He would not commit himself to such a charge,
    But he has brought in that damnable soothsayer
    To tell his story.

IOKASTÊ.   Set your mind at rest.   665
    If it is a question of soothsayers, I tell you
    That you will find no man whose craft gives knowledge
    Of the unknowable.
                    Here is my proof:
    An oracle was reported to Laïos once
    (I will not say from Phoibos himself, but from   670
    His appointed ministers, at any rate)
    That his doom would be death at the hands of his own son—
    His son, born of his flesh and of mine!

    Now, you remember the story: Laïos was killed
    By marauding strangers where three highways meet;   675
    But his child had not been three days in this world
    Before the king had pierced the baby's ankles
    And left him to die on a lonely mountainside.

    Thus, Apollo never caused that child
    To kill his father, and it was not Laïos' fate   680
    To die at the hands of his son, as he had feared.
    This is what prophets and prophecies are worth!
    Have no dread of them.
                 It is God himself
    Who can show us what he wills, in his own way.

OEDIPUS. How strange a shadowy memory crossed my mind,   685
    Just now while you were speaking; it chilled my heart.

IOKASTÊ. What do you mean? What memory do you speak of?

OEDIPUS. If I understand you, Laïos was killed
    At a place where three roads meet.

IOKASTÊ.   So it was said;
    We have no later story.

OEDIPUS.   Where did it happen?   690

IOKASTÊ. Phokis, it is called: at a place where the Theban Way

Divides into the roads toward Delphi and Daulia.
OEDIPUS. When?
IOKASTÊ.   We had the news not long before you came
    And proved the right to your succession here.
OEDIPUS. Ah, what net has God been weaving for me?   695
IOKASTÊ. Oedipus! Why does this trouble you?
OEDIPUS.   Do not ask me yet.
    First, tell me how Laïos looked, and tell me
    How old he was.
IOKASTÊ.   He was tall, his hair just touched
    With white; his form was not unlike your own.
OEDIPUS. I think that I myself may be accurst   700
    By my own ignorant edict.
IOKASTÊ.   You speak strangely.
    It makes me tremble to look at you, my king.
OEDIPUS. I am not sure that the blind man can not see.
    But I should know better if you were to tell me—
IOKASTÊ. Anything—though I dread to hear you ask it.   705
OEDIPUS. Was the king lightly escorted, or did he ride
    With a large company, as a ruler should?
IOKASTÊ. There were five men with him in all: one was a herald;
    And a single chariot, which he was driving.
OEDIPUS. Alas, that makes it plain enough!
                              But who—   710
    Who told you how it happened?
IOKASTÊ.   A household servant,
    The only one to escape.
OEDIPUS.   And is he still
    A servant of ours?
IOKASTÊ.   No; for when he came back at last
    And found you enthroned in the place of the dead king,
    He came to me, touched my hand with his, and begged   715
    That I would send him away to the frontier district
    Where only the shepherds go—
    As far away from the city as I could send him.
    I granted his prayer; for although the man was a slave,
    He had earned more than this favor at my hands.   720
OEDIPUS. Can he be called back quickly?
IOKASTÊ.   Easily.
    But why?
OEDIPUS.   I have taken too much upon myself
    Without enquiry; therefore I wish to consult him.
IOKASTÊ. Then he shall come.
                      But am I not one also
    To whom you might confide these fears of yours?   725

OEDIPUS. That is your right; it will not be denied you,
          Now least of all; for I have reached a pitch
          Of wild foreboding. Is there anyone
          To whom I should sooner speak?

          Polybos of Corinth is my father.   730
          My mother is a Dorian: Meropê.
          I grew up chief among the men of Corinth
          Until a strange thing happened—
          Not worth my passion, it may be, but strange.
          At a feast, a drunken man maundering in his cups   735
          Cries out that I am not my father's son!

          I contained myself that night, though I felt anger
          And a sinking heart. The next day I visited
          My father and mother, and questioned them. They stormed,
          Calling it all the slanderous rant of a fool;   740
          And this relieved me. Yet the suspicion
          Remained always aching in my mind;
          I knew there was talk; I could not rest;
          And finally, saying nothing to my parents,
          I went to the shrine at Delphi.   745

          The god dismissed my question without reply;
          He spoke of other things.
                              Some were clear,
          Full of wretchedness, dreadful, unbearable:
          As, that I should lie with my own mother, breed
          Children from whom all men would turn their eyes;   750
          And that I should be my father's murderer.

          I heard all this, and fled. And from that day
          Corinth to me was only in the stars
          Descending in that quarter of the sky,
          As I wandered farther and farther on my way   755
          To a land where I should never see the evil
          Sung by the oracle. And I came to this country
          Where, so you say, King Laïos was killed.

          I will tell you all that happened there, my lady.

          There were three highways   760
          Coming together at a place I passed;
          And there a herald came towards me, and a chariot
          Drawn by horses, with a man such as you describe
          Seated in it. The groom leading the horses
          Forced me off the road at his lord's command;   765
          But as this charioteer lurched over towards me

I struck him in my rage. The old man saw me
And brought his double goad down upon my head
As I came abreast.

              He was paid back, and more!
Swinging my club in this right hand I knocked him   770
Out of his car, and he rolled on the ground.

                             I killed him.

I killed them all.
Now if that stranger and Laïos were—kin,
Where is a man more miserable than I?
More hated by the gods? Citizen and alien alike   775
Must never shelter me or speak to me—
I must be shunned by all.

               And I myself
Pronounced this malediction upon myself!

Think of it: I have touched you with these hands,
These hands that killed your husband. What defilement!   780

Am I all evil, then? It must be so,
Since I must flee from Thebes, yet never again
See my own countrymen, my own country,
For fear of joining my mother in marriage
And killing Polybos, my father.

                     Ah,   785
If I was created so, born to this fate,
Who could deny the savagery of God?

O holy majesty of heavenly powers!
May I never see that day! Never!
Rather let me vanish from the race of men   790
Than know the abomination destined me!

CHORAGOS. We too, my lord, have felt dismay at this.
    But there is hope: you have yet to hear the shepherd.
OEDIPUS. Indeed, I fear no other hope is left me.
IOKASTÊ. What do you hope from him when he comes?
OEDIPUS.   This much: 795
    If his account of the murder tallies with yours,
    Then I am cleared.
IOKASTÊ.   What was it that I said
    Of such importance?
OEDIPUS.   Why, "marauders," you said,
    Killed the king, according to this man's story.
    If he maintains that still, if there were several,   800
    Clearly the guilt is not mine: I was alone.
    But if he says one man, singlehanded, did it,
    Then the evidence all points to me.

IOKASTÊ. You may be sure that he said there were several;
      And can he call back that story now? He can not.   805
      The whole city heard it as plainly as I.
      But suppose he alters some detail of it:
      He can not ever show that Laïos' death
      Fulfilled the oracle: for Apollo said
      My child was doomed to kill him; and my child—   810
      Poor baby!—it was my child that died first.

      No. From now on, where oracles are concerned,
      I would not waste a second thought on any.
OEDIPUS. You may be right.
                              But come: let someone go
      For the shepherd at once. This matter must be settled.   815
IOKASTÊ. I will send for him.
      I would not wish to cross you in anything,
      And surely not in this.—Let us go in.

      (*Exeunt into the palace.*)

ODE II

STROPHE 1

CHORUS. Let me be reverent in the ways of right,
      Lowly the paths I journey on;   820
      Let all my words and actions keep
      The laws of the pure universe
      From highest Heaven handed down.
      For Heaven is their bright nurse,
      Those generations of the realms of light;   825
      Ah, never of mortal kind were they begot,
      Nor are they slaves of memory, lost in sleep:
      Their Father is greater than Time, and ages not.

ANTISTROPHE 1

      The tyrant is a child of Pride
      Who drinks from his great sickening cup   830
      Recklessness and vanity,
      Until from his high crest headlong
      He plummets to the dust of hope.
      That strong man is not strong.
      But let no fair ambition be denied;   835
      May God protect the wrestler for the State
      In government, in comely policy,
      Who will fear God, and on His ordinance wait.

STROPHE 2

Haughtiness and the high hand of disdain
Tempt and outrage God's holy law; 840
And any mortal who dares hold
No immortal Power in awe
Will be caught up in a net of pain:
The price for which his levity is sold.
Let each man take due earnings, then, 845
And keep his hands from holy things,
And from blasphemy stand apart—
Else the crackling blast of heaven
Blows on his head, and on his desperate heart.
Though fools will honor impious men, 850
In their cities no tragic poet sings.

ANTISTROPHE 2

Shall we lose faith in Delphi's obscurities,
We who have heard the world's core
Discredited, and the sacred wood
Of Zeus at Elis praised no more? 855
The deeds and the strange prophecies
Must make a pattern yet to be understood.
Zeus, if indeed you are lord of all,
Throned in light over night and day,
Mirror this in your endless mind: 860
Our masters call the oracle
Words on the wind, and the Delphic vision blind!
Their hearts no longer know Apollo,
And reverence for the gods has died away.

SCENE III

Enter IOKASTÊ.

IOKASTÊ. Princes of Thebes, it has occurred to me 865
To visit the altars of the gods, bearing
These branches as a suppliant, and this incense.
Our king is not himself: his noble soul
Is overwrought with fantasies of dread,
Else he would consider 870
The new prophecies in the light of the old.
He will listen to any voice that speaks disaster,
And my advice goes for nothing.

(*She approaches the altar, right.*)

To you, then, Apollo,
Lycéan lord, since you are nearest, I turn in prayer.
Receive these offerings, and grant us deliverance   875
From defilement. Our hearts are heavy with fear
When we see our leader distracted, as helpless sailors
Are terrified by the confusion of their helmsman.

(*Enter* MESSENGER.)

MESSENGER. Friends, no doubt you can direct me:
Where shall I find the house of Oedipus,   880
Or, better still, where is the king himself?
CHORAGOS. It is this very place, stranger; he is inside.
This is his wife and mother of his children.
MESSENGER. I wish her happiness in a happy house,
Blest in all the fulfillment of her marriage.   885
IOKASTÊ. I wish as much for you: your courtesy
Deserves a like good fortune. But now, tell me:
Why have you come? What have you to say to us?
MESSENGER. Good news, my lady, for your house and your husband.
IOKASTÊ. What news? Who sent you here?
MESSENGER.   I am from Corinth.   890
The news I bring ought to mean joy for you,
Though it may be you will find some grief in it.
IOKASTÊ. What is it? How can it touch us in both ways?
MESSENGER. The word is that the people of the Isthmus
Intend to call Oedipus to be their king.   895
IOKASTÊ. But old King Polybos—is he not reigning still?
MESSENGER. No. Death holds him in his sepulchre.
IOKASTÊ. What are you saying? Polybos is dead?
MESSENGER. If I am not telling the truth, may I die myself.
IOKASTÊ (*to a* MAIDSERVANT). Go in, go quickly; tell this to
your master.   900
O riddlers of God's will, where are you now!
This was the man whom Oedipus, long ago,
Feared so, fled so, in dread of destroying him—
But it was another fate by which he died.

(*Enter* OEDIPUS, *center*.)

OEDIPUS. Dearest Iokastê, why have you sent for me?   905
IOKASTÊ. Listen to what this man says, and then tell me
What has become of the solemn prophecies.
OEDIPUS. Who is this man? What is his news for me?
IOKASTÊ. He has come from Corinth to announce your father's death!
OEDIPUS. Is it true, stranger? Tell me in your own words.   910
MESSENGER. I can not say it more clearly: the king is dead.

OEDIPUS. Was it by treason? Or by an attack of illness?
MESSENGER. A little thing brings old men to their rest.
OEDIPUS. It was sickness, then?
MESSENGER.   Yes, and his many years.
OEDIPUS. Ah!   915
   Why should a man respect the Pythian hearth,° or
   Give heed to the birds that jangle above his head?
   They prophesied that I should kill Polybos,
   Kill my own father; but he is dead and buried,
   And I am here—I never touched him, never,   920
   Unless he died of grief for my departure,
   And thus, in a sense, through me. No. Polybos
   Has packed the oracles off with him underground.
   They are empty words.
IOKASTÊ.   Had I not told you so?
OEDIPUS. You had; it was my faint heart that betrayed me.   925
IOKASTÊ. From now on never think of those things again.
OEDIPUS. And yet—must I not fear my mother's bed?
IOKASTÊ. Why should anyone in this world be afraid,
   Since Fate rules us and nothing can be foreseen?
   A man should live only for the present day.   930

   Have no more fear of sleeping with your mother:
   How many men, in dreams, have lain with their mothers!
   No reasonable man is troubled by such things.
OEDIPUS. That is true; only—
   If only my mother were not still alive!   935
   But she is alive. I can not help my dread.
IOKASTÊ. Yet this news of your father's death is wonderful.
OEDIPUS. Wonderful. But I fear the living woman.
MESSENGER. Tell me, who is this woman that you fear?
OEDIPUS. It is Meropê, man; the wife of King Polybos.   940
MESSENGER. Meropê? Why should you be afraid of her?
OEDIPUS. An oracle of the gods, a dreadful saying.
MESSENGER. Can you tell me about it or are you sworn to silence?
OEDIPUS. I can tell you, and I will.
   Apollo said through his prophet that I was the man   945
   Who should marry his own mother, shed his father's blood
   With his own hands. And so, for all these years
   I have kept clear of Corinth, and no harm has come—
   Though it would have been sweet to see my parents again.
MESSENGER. And is this the fear that drove you out of Corinth?   950
OEDIPUS. Would you have me kill my father?

916. Pythian hearth: Delphi.

MESSENGER.   As for that
   You must be reassured by the news I gave you.
OEDIPUS.   If you could reassure me, I would reward you.
MESSENGER.   I had that in mind, I will confess: I thought
   I could count on you when you returned to Corinth.   955
OEDIPUS.   No: I will never go near my parents again.
MESSENGER.   Ah, son, you still do not know what you are doing—
OEDIPUS.   What do you mean? In the name of God tell me!
MESSENGER.   —If these are your reasons for not going home.
OEDIPUS.   I tell you, I fear the oracle may come true.   960
MESSENGER.   And guilt may come upon you through your parents?
OEDIPUS.   That is the dread that is always in my heart.
MESSENGER.   Can you not see that all your fears are groundless?
OEDIPUS.   Groundless? Am I not my parents' son?
MESSENGER.   Polybos was not your father.
OEDIPUS.   Not my father?   965
MESSENGER.   No more your father than the man speaking to you.
OEDIPUS.   But you are nothing to me!
MESSENGER.   Neither was he.
OEDIPUS.   Then why did he call me son?
MESSENGER.   I will tell you:
   Long ago he had you from my hands, as a gift.
OEDIPUS.   Then how could he love me so, if I was not his?   970
MESSENGER.   He had no children, and his heart turned to you.
OEDIPUS.   What of you? Did you buy me? Did you find me by chance?
MESSENGER.   I came upon you in the woody vales of Kithairon.
OEDIPUS.   And what were you doing there?
MESSENGER.   Tending my flocks.
OEDIPUS.   A wandering sheperd?
MESSENGER.   But your savior, son, that day.   975
OEDIPUS.   From what did you save me?
MESSENGER.   Your ankles should tell you that.
OEDIPUS.   Ah, stranger, why do you speak of that childhood pain?
MESSENGER.   I pulled the skewer that pinned your feet together.
OEDIPUS.   I have had the mark as long as I can remember.
MESSENGER.   That was why you were given the name you bear.   980
OEDIPUS.   God! Was it my father or my mother who did it?
   Tell me!
MESSENGER.   I do not know. The man who gave you to me
   Can tell you better than I.
OEDIPUS.   It was not you that found me, but another?
MESSENGER.   It was another shepherd gave you to me.   985
OEDIPUS.   Who was he? Can you tell me who he was?
MESSENGER.   I think he was said to be one of Laïos' people.
OEDIPUS.   You mean the Laïos who was king here years ago?

MESSENGER. Yes; King Laïos; and the man was one of his herdsmen.

OEDIPUS. Is he still alive? Can I see him?

MESSENGER. These men here 990
Know best about such things.

OEDIPUS. Does anyone here
Know this shepherd that he is talking about?
Have you seen him in the fields, or in the town?
If you have, tell me. It is time things were made plain.

CHORAGOS. I think the man he means is that same shepherd 995
You have already asked to see. Iokastê perhaps
Could tell you something.

OEDIPUS. Do you know anything
About him, Lady? Is he the man we have summoned?
Is that the man this shepherd means?

IOKASTÊ. Why think of him?
Forget this herdsman. Forget it all. 1000
This talk is a waste of time.

OEDIPUS. How can you say that,
When the clues to my true birth are in my hands?

IOKASTÊ. For God's love, let us have no more questioning!
Is your life nothing to you?
My own is pain enough for me to bear. 1005

OEDIPUS. You need not worry. Suppose my mother a slave,
And born of slaves: no baseness can touch you.

IOKASTÊ. Listen to me, I beg you: do not do this thing!

OEDIPUS. I will not listen; the truth must be made known.

IOKASTÊ. Everything that I say is for your own good!

OEDIPUS. My own good 1010
Snaps my patience, then; I want none of it.

IOKASTÊ. You are fatally wrong! May you never learn who you are!

OEDIPUS. Go, one of you, and bring the shepherd here.
Let us leave this woman to brag of her royal name.

IOKASTÊ. Ah, miserable! 1015
That is the only word I have for you now.
That is the only word I can ever have. (*Exit into the palace.*)

CHORAGOS. Why has she left us, Oedipus? Why has she gone
In such a passion of sorrow? I fear this silence:
Something dreadful may come of it.

OEDIPUS. Let it come! 1020
However base my birth, I must know about it.
The Queen, like a woman, is perhaps ashamed
To think of my low origin. But I
Am a child of Luck; I can not be dishonored.
Luck is my mother; the passing months, my brothers, 1025
Have seen me rich and poor.

If this is so,
How could I wish that I were someone else?
How could I not be glad to know my birth?

ODE III

STROPHE

CHORUS. If ever the coming time were known
    To my heart's pondering,   1030
    Kithairon, now by Heaven I see the torches
    At the festival of the next full moon,
    And see the dance, and hear the choir sing
    A grace to your gentle shade:
    Mountain where Oedipus was found,   1035
    O mountain guard of a noble race!
    May the god° who heals us lend his aid,
    And let that glory come to pass
    For our king's cradling-ground.

ANTISTROPHE

    Of the nymphs that flower beyond the years,   1040
    Who bore you,° royal child,
    To Pan of the hills or the timberline Apollo,
    Cold in delight where the upland clears,
    Or Hermês for whom Kyllenê's heights are piled?
    Or flushed as evening cloud,   1045
    Great Dionysos, roamer of mountains,
    He—was it he who found you there,
    And caught you up in his own proud
    Arms from the sweet god-ravisher
    Who laughed by the Muses' fountains?   1050

SCENE IV

OEDIPUS. Sirs: though I do not know the man,
    I think I see him coming, this shepherd we want:
    He is old, like our friend here, and the men
    Bringing him seem to be servants of my house.
    But you can tell, if you have ever seen him.   1055

1037. god: Apollo. **1041. Who bore you:** The chorus is suggesting that perhaps Oedipus
is the son of one of the immortal nymphs and of a god—Pan, Apollo, Hermes, or Dionysos.
The "sweet god-ravisher" (line 1049) is the presumed mother.

(*Enter* SHEPHERD *escorted by* SERVANTS.)

CHORAGOS. I know him, he was Laïos' man. You can trust him.
OEDIPUS. Tell me first, you from Corinth: is this the shepherd
     We were discussing?
MESSENGER.   This is the very man.
OEDIPUS (*to* SHEPHERD). Come here. No, look at me. You must answer
     Everything I ask.—You belonged to Laïos?   1060
SHEPHERD. Yes: born his slave, brought up in his house.
OEDIPUS. Tell me: what kind of work did you do for him?
SHEPHERD. I was a shepherd of his, most of my life.
OEDIPUS. Where mainly did you go for pasturage?
SHEPHERD. Sometimes Kithairon, sometimes the hills near-by.   1065
OEDIPUS. Do you remember ever seeing this man out there?
SHEPHERD. What would he be doing there? This man?
OEDIPUS. This man standing here. Have you ever seen him before?
SHEPHERD. No. At least, not to my recollection.
MESSENGER. And that is not strange, my lord. But I'll refresh   1070
     His memory: he must remember when we two
     Spent three whole seasons together, March to September,
     On Kithairon or thereabouts. He had two flocks;
     I had one. Each autumn I'd drive mine home
     And he would go back with his to Laïos' sheepfold.—   1075
     Is this not true, just as I have described it?
SHEPHERD. True, yes; but it was all so long ago.
MESSENGER. Well, then: do you remember, back in those days,
     That you gave me a baby boy to bring up as my own?
SHEPHERD. What if I did? What are you trying to say?   1080
MESSENGER. King Oedipus was once that little child.
SHEPHERD. Damn you, hold your tongue!
OEDIPUS.   No more of that!
     It is your tongue needs watching, not this man's.
SHEPHERD. My king, my master, what is it I have done wrong?
OEDIPUS. You have not answered his question about the boy.   1085
SHEPHERD. He does not know . . . He is only making trouble . . .
OEDIPUS. Come, speak plainly, or it will go hard with you.
SHEPHERD. In God's name, do not torture an old man!
OEDIPUS. Come here, one of you; bind his arms behind him.
SHEPHERD. Unhappy king! What more do you wish to learn?   1090
OEDIPUS. Did you give this man the child he speaks of?
SHEPHERD.   I did.
     And I would to God I had died that very day.
OEDIPUS. You will die now unless you speak the truth.
SHEPHERD. Yet if I speak the truth, I am worse than dead.
OEDIPUS (*to* ATTENDANT). He intends to draw it out, apparently—   1095
SHEPHERD. No! I have told you already that I gave him the boy.

OEDIPUS. Where did you get him? From your house? From somewhere
 else?
SHEPHERD. Not from mine, no. A man gave him to me.
OEDIPUS. Is that man here? Whose house did he belong to?
SHEPHERD. For God's love, my king, do not ask me any more!   1100
OEDIPUS. You are a dead man if I have to ask you again.
SHEPHERD. Then . . . Then the child was from the palace of Laïos.
OEDIPUS. A slave child? or a child of his own line?
SHEPHERD. Ah, I am on the brink of dreadful speech!
OEDIPUS. And I of dreadful hearing. Yet I must hear.   1105
SHEPHERD. If you must be told, then . . .
          They said it was Laïos' child;
 But it is your wife who can tell you about that.
OEDIPUS. My wife!—Did she give it to you?
SHEPHERD.
           My lord, she did.
OEDIPUS. Do you know why?
SHEPHERD.
        I was told to get rid of it.
OEDIPUS. Oh heartless mother!
SHEPHERD.
        But in dread of prophecies . . . 1110
OEDIPUS. Tell me.
SHEPHERD.   It was said that the boy would kill his own father.
OEDIPUS. Then why did you give him over to this old man?
SHEPHERD. I pitied the baby, my king,
 And I thought that this man would take him far away
 To his own country.
       He saved him—but for what a fate! 1115
 For if you are what this man says you are,
 No man living is more wretched than Oedipus.
OEDIPUS. Ah God!
 It was true!
    All the prophecies!
        —Now,
 O Light, may I look on you for the last time! 1120
 I, Oedipus,
 Oedipus, damned in his birth, in his marriage damned,
 Damned in the blood he shed with his own hand! (*He rushes into the*
  palace.)

ODE IV

STROPHE 1

CHORUS. Alas for the seed of men.
 What measure shall I give these generations 1125
 That breathe on the void and are void
 And exist and do not exist?

Who bears more weight of joy
Than mass of sunlight shifting in images,
Or who shall make his thought stay on   1130
That down time drifts away?
Your splendor is all fallen.
O naked brow of wrath and tears,
O change of Oedipus!
I who saw your days call no man blest—   1135
Your great days like ghósts góne.

ANTISTROPHE 1

That mind was a strong bow.
Deep, how deep you drew it then, hard archer,
At a dim fearful range,
And brought dear glory down!   1140
You overcame the stranger°—
The virgin with her hooking lion claws—
And though death sang, stood like a tower
To make pale Thebes take heart.
Fortress against our sorrow!   1145
True king, giver of laws,
Majestic Oedipus!
No prince in Thebes had ever such renown,
No prince won such grace of power.

STROPHE 2

And now of all men ever known   1150
Most pitiful is this man's story:
His fortunes are most changed, his state
Fallen to a low slave's
Ground under bitter fate.
O Oedipus, most royal one!   1155
The great door° that expelled you to the light
Gave at night—ah, gave night to your glory:
As to the father, to the fathering son.
All understood too late.
How could that queen whom Laïos won,   1160
The garden that he harrowed at his height,
Be silent when that act was done?

1141. stranger: the Sphinx. **1156. door:** Iokastê's womb.

ANTISTROPHE 2

But all eyes fail before time's eye,
All actions come to justice there.
Though never willed, though far down the deep past,   1165
Your bed, your dread sirings,
Are brought to book at last.
Child by Laïos doomed to die,
Then doomed to lose that fortunate little death,
Would God you never took breath in this air   1170
That with my wailing lips I take to cry:
For I weep the world's outcast.
I was blind, and now I can tell why:
Asleep, for you had given ease of breath
To Thebes, while the false years went by.   1175

EXODOS°

Enter, from the palace, SECOND MESSENGER.

SECOND MESSENGER.   Elders of Thebes, most honored in this land,
What horrors are yours to see and hear, what weight
Of sorrow to be endured, if, true to your birth,
You venerate the line of Labdakos!
I think neither Istros nor Phasis, those great rivers,   1180
Could purify this place of all the evil
It shelters now, or soon must bring to light—
Evil not done unconsciously, but willed.

The greatest griefs are those we cause ourselves.
CHORAGOS.   Surely, friend, we have grief enough already;   1185
What new sorrow do you mean?
SECOND MESSENGER.   The queen is dead.
CHORAGOS.   O miserable queen! But at whose hand?
SECOND MESSENGER.   Her own.
The full horror of what happened you can not know,
For you did not see it; but I, who did, will tell you
As clearly as I can how she met her death.   1190

When she had left us,
In passionate silence, passing through the court,
She ran to her apartment in the house,
Her hair clutched by the fingers of both hands.
She closed the doors behind her; then, by that bed   1195

Exodos: final scene.

Where long ago the fatal son was conceived—
That son who should bring about his father's death—
We heard her call upon Laïos, dead so many years,
And heard her wail for the double fruit of her marriage,
A husband by her husband, children by her child.   1200

Exactly how she died I do not know:
For Oedipus burst in moaning and would not let us
Keep vigil to the end: it was by him
As he stormed about the room that our eyes were caught.
From one to another of us he went, begging a sword,   1205
Hunting the wife who was not his wife, the mother
Whose womb had carried his own children and himself.
I do not know: it was none of us aided him,
But surely one of the gods was in control!
For with a dreadful cry   1210
He hurled his weight, as though wrenched out of himself,
At the twin doors: the bolts gave, and he rushed in.
And there we saw her hanging, her body swaying
From the cruel cord she had noosed about her neck.
A great sob broke from him, heartbreaking to hear,   1215
As he loosed the rope and lowered her to the ground.

I would blot out from my mind what happened next!
For the king ripped from her gown the golden brooches
That were her ornament, and raised them, and plunged them down
Straight into his own eyeballs, crying, "No more,   1220
No more shall you look on the misery about me,
The horrors of my own doing! Too long you have known
The faces of those whom I should never have seen,
Too long been blind to those for whom I was searching!
From this hour, go in darkness!" And as he spoke,   1225
He struck at his eyes—not once, but many times;
And the blood spattered his beard,
Bursting from his ruined sockets like red hail.

So from the unhappiness of two this evil has sprung,
A curse on the man and woman alike. The old   1230
Happiness of the house of Labdakos
Was happiness enough: where is it today?
It is all wailing and ruin, disgrace, death—all
The misery of mankind that has a name—
And it is wholly and for ever theirs.   1235

CHORAGOS. Is he in agony still? Is there no rest for him?
SECOND MESSENGER. He is calling for someone to open the doors wide
   So that all the children of Kadmos may look upon

His father's murderer, his mother's—no,
I can not say it!
                    And then he will leave Thebes,   1240
Self-exiled, in order that the curse
Which he himself pronounced may depart from the house.
He is weak, and there is none to lead him,
So terrible is his suffering.
                    But you will see:
Look, the doors are opening; in a moment   1245
You will see a thing that would crush a heart of stone.

(*The central door is opened;* OEDIPUS, *blinded, is led in.*)

CHORAGOS. Dreadful indeed for men to see.
    Never have my own eyes
    Looked on a sight so full of fear.

    Oedipus!   1250
    What madness came upon you, what daemon
    Leaped on your life with heavier
    Punishment than a mortal man can bear?
    No: I can not even
    Look at you, poor ruined one.   1255
    And I would speak, question, ponder,
    If I were able. No.
    You make me shudder.
OEDIPUS. God. God.
    Is there a sorrow greater?   1260
    Where shall I find harbor in this world?
    My voice is hurled far on a dark wind.
    What has God done to me?
CHORAGOS. Too terrible to think of, or to see.

STROPHE 1

OEDIPUS. O cloud of night,   1265
    Never to be turned away: night coming on,
    I can not tell how: night like a shroud!
    My fair winds brought me here.
                    O God. Again
    The pain of the spikes where I had sight,
    The flooding pain   1270
    Of memory, never to be gouged out.
CHORAGOS. This is not strange.
    You suffer it all twice over, remorse in pain,
    Pain in remorse.

ANTISTROPHE 1

OEDIPUS. Ah dear friend 1275
  Are you faithful even yet, you alone?
  Are you still standing near me, will you stay here,
  Patient, to care for the blind?
                              The blind man!
  Yet even blind I know who it is attends me,
  By the voice's tone— 1280
  Though my new darkness hide the comforter.
CHORAGOS. Oh fearful act!
  What god was it drove you to rake black
  Night across your eyes?

STROPHE 2

OEDIPUS. Apollo. Apollo. Dear 1285
  Children, the god was Apollo.
  He brought my sick, sick fate upon me.
  But the blinding hand was my own!
  How could I bear to see
  When all my sight was horror everywhere? 1290
CHORAGOS. Everywhere; that is true.
OEDIPUS. And now what is left?
  Images? Love? A greeting even,
  Sweet to the senses? Is there anything?
  Ah, no, friends: lead me away. 1295
  Lead me away from Thebes.
                              Lead the great wreck
  And hell of Oedipus, whom the gods hate.
CHORAGOS. Your misery, you are not blind to that.
  Would God you had never found it out!

ANTISTROPHE 2

OEDIPUS. Death take the man who unbound 1300
  My feet on that hillside
  And delivered me from death to life! What life?
  If only I had died,
  This weight of monstrous doom
  Could not have dragged me and my darlings down. 1305
CHORAGOS. I would have wished the same.
OEDIPUS. Oh never to have come here
  With my father's blood upon me! Never
  To have been the man they call his mother's husband!

Oh accurst! Oh child of evil,   1310
To have entered that wretched bed—
                                   the selfsame one!
More primal than sin itself, this fell to me.
CHORAGOS.   I do not know what words to offer you.
You were better dead than alive and blind.
OEDIPUS.   Do not counsel me any more. This punishment   1315
That I have laid upon myself is just.
If I had eyes,
I do not know how I could bear the sight
Of my father, when I came to the house of Death,
Or my mother: for I have sinned against them both   1320
So vilely that I could not make my peace
By strangling my own life.
                              Or do you think my children,
Born as they were born, would be sweet to my eyes?
Ah never, never! Nor this town with its high walls,
Nor the holy images of the gods.
                                   For I,   1325
Thrice miserable!—Oedipus, noblest of all the line
Of Kadmos, have condemned myself to enjoy
These things no more, by my own malediction
Expelling that man whom the gods declared
To be a defilement in the house of Laïos.   1330
After exposing the rankness of my own guilt,
How could I look men frankly in the eyes?
No, I swear it,
If I could have stifled my hearing at its source,
I would have done it and made all this body   1335
A tight cell of misery, blank to light and sound:
So I should have been safe in my dark mind
Beyond external evil.
                    Ah Kithairon!
Why did you shelter me? When I was cast upon you,
Why did I not die? Then I should never   1340
Have shown the world my execrable birth.

Ah Polybos! Corinth, city that I believed
The ancient seat of my ancestors: how fair
I seemed, your child! And all the while this evil
Was cancerous within me!
                         For I am sick   1345
In my own being, sick in my origin.

O three roads, dark ravine, woodland and way
Where three roads met: you, drinking my father's blood,

My own blood, spilled by my own hand: can you remember
The unspeakable things I did there, and the things   1350
I went on from there to do?
                              O marriage, marriage!
The act that engendered me, and again the act
Performed by the son in the same bed—
                                       Ah, the net
Of incest, mingling fathers, brothers, sons,
With brides, wives, mothers: the last evil   1355
That can be known by men: no tongue can say
How evil!
          No. For the love of God, conceal me
Somewhere far from Thebes; or kill me; or hurl me
Into the sea, away from men's eyes for ever.

Come, lead me. You need not fear to touch me.   1360
Of all men, I alone can bear this guilt.

    (*Enter* KREON.)

CHORAGOS. Kreon is here now. As to what you ask,
    He may decide the course to take. He only
    Is left to protect the city in your place.
OEDIPUS. Alas, how can I speak to him? What right have I   1365
    To beg his courtesy whom I have deeply wronged?
KREON. I have not come to mock you, Oedipus,
    Or to reproach you, either.
        (*To* ATTENDANTS)   —You, standing there:
    If you have lost all respect for man's dignity,
    At least respect the flame of Lord Helios: 1370
    Do not allow this pollution to show itself
    Openly here, an affront to the earth
    And Heaven's rain and the light of day. No, take him
    Into the house as quickly as you can.
    For it is proper   1375
    That only the close kindred see his grief.
OEDIPUS. I pray you in God's name, since your courtesy
    Ignores my dark expectation, visiting
    With mercy this man of all men most execrable:
    Give me what I ask—for your good, not for mine.   1380
KREON. And what is it that you turn to me begging for?
OEDIPUS. Drive me out of this country as quickly as may be
    To a place where no human voice can ever greet me.
KREON. I should have done that before now—only,
    God's will had not been wholly revealed to me.   1385
OEDIPUS. But his command is plain: the parricide
    Must be destroyed. I am that evil man.

KREON. That is the sense of it, yes; but as things are,
  We had best discover clearly what is to be done.
OEDIPUS. You would learn more about a man like me?   1390
KREON. You are ready now to listen to the god.
OEDIPUS. I will listen. But it is to you
  That I must turn for help. I beg you, hear me.

  The woman in there—
  Give her whatever funeral you think proper: 1395
  She is your sister.
                    —But let me go, Kreon!
  Let me purge my father's Thebes of the pollution
  Of my living here, and go out to the wild hills,
  To Kithairon, that has won such fame with me,
  The tomb my mother and father appointed for me,   1400
  And let me die there, as they willed I should.
  And yet I know
  Death will not ever come to me through sickness
  Or in any natural way: I have been preserved
  For some unthinkable fate. But let that be.   1405

  As for my sons, you need not care for them.
  They are men, they will find some way to live.
  But my poor daughters, who have shared my table,
  Who never before have been parted from their father—
  Take care of them, Kreon; do this for me.   1410

  And will you let me touch them with my hands
  A last time, and let us weep together?
  Be kind, my lord,
  Great prince, be kind!
                      Could I but touch them,
  They would be mine again, as when I had my eyes.   1415

(*Enter* ANTIGONE *and* ISMENE, *attended.*)

  Ah, God!
  Is it my dearest children I hear weeping?
  Has Kreon pitied me and sent my daughters?
KREON. Yes, Oedipus: I knew that they were dear to you
  In the old days, and know you must love them still.   1420
OEDIPUS. May God bless you for this—and be a friendlier
  Guardian to you than he has been to me!

  Children, where are you?
  Come quickly to my hands: they are your brother's—
  Hands that have brought your father's once clear eyes   1425
  To this way of seeing—
                      Ah dearest ones,

I had neither sight nor knowledge then, your father
By the woman who was the source of his own life!
And I weep for you—having no strength to see you—,
I weep for you when I think of the bitterness   1430
That men will visit upon you all your lives.
What homes, what festivals can you attend
Without being forced to depart again in tears?
And when you come to marriageable age,
Where is the man, my daughters, who would dare   1435
Risk the bane that lies on all my children?
Is there any evil wanting? Your father killed
His father; sowed the womb of her who bore him;
Engendered you at the fount of his own existence!
That is what they will say of you.

                        Then, whom   1440
Can you ever marry? There are no bridegrooms for you,
And your lives must wither away in sterile dreaming.

O Kreon, son of Menoikeus!
You are the only father my daughters have,
Since we, their parents, are both of us gone for ever.   1445
They are your own blood: you will not let them
Fall into beggary and loneliness;
You will keep them from the miseries that are mine!
Take pity on them; see, they are only children,
Friendless except for you. Promise me this,   1450
Great prince, and give me your hand in token of it.

(KREON *clasps his right hand.*)

Children:
I could say much, if you could understand me,
But as it is, I have only this prayer for you:
Live where you can, be as happy as you can—   1455
Happier, please God, than God has made your father.

KREON. Enough. You have wept enough. Now go within.
OEDIPUS. I must; but it is hard.
KREON.   Time eases all things.
OEDIPUS. You know my mind, then?
KREON.   Say what you desire.
OEDIPUS. Send me from Thebes!
KREON.   God grant that I may!   1460
OEDIPUS. But since God hates me . . .
KREON.   No, he will grant your wish.
OEDIPUS. You promise?
KREON.   I can not speak beyond my knowledge.

OEDIPUS. Then lead me in.

KREON. Come now, and leave your children.

OEDIPUS. No! Do not take them from me!

KREON. Think no longer
That you are in command here, but rather think   1465
How, when you were, you served your own destruction.

(*Exeunt into the house all but the* CHORUS; *the* CHORAGOS *chants directly to the audience.*)

CHORAGOS. Men of Thebes: look upon Oedipus.

This is the king who solved the famous riddle
And towered up, most powerful of men.
No mortal eyes but looked on him with envy,   1470
Yet in the end ruin swept over him.

Let every man in mankind's frailty
Consider his last day; and let none
Presume on his good fortune until he find
Life, at his death, a memory without pain.   1475

QUESTIONS

1. The oracles had prophesied that Oedipus would kill his father and beget children by his mother. Is Oedipus therefore *made* to do these things? Is the play premised on the notion that Oedipus is bound or free—the puppet of fate or the creator of his own fate? Or some of each?

2. In what ways is Oedipus shown to be a person of extraordinary stature? Consider both his life before the play begins and his actions during the course of the play. What is Oedipus' primary motivation throughout the play? What characters try to dissuade him from pursuing that motivation? How do his subjects regard him?

3. What errors in judgment does Oedipus make? Are these errors grounded in weakness of character? If so, what are his weaknesses of character? (Do not answer this question too quickly. Respectable critics have differed sharply, not only over the identification of Oedipus' "flaw," but, indeed, over whether he has one.)

4. Is any common pattern of behavior exhibited in Oedipus' encounters with Laïos, with Teiresias, and with Kreon? Is there any justification for his anger with Teiresias? for his suspicion of Kreon? Why?

5. Oedipus' original question, "Who killed Laïos?" soon turns into the question "Who am I?" On the level of plot, the answer is "Son of Laïos and Iokastê, father's murderer, mother's husband." What is the answer at the level of character—that is, in a psychological or philosophical sense?

6. What philosophical issues are raised by Iokastê's judgment on the oracles (Scene II)? How does the chorus respond to her judgment? How does the play resolve these issues?

7. Why does Oedipus blind himself? Is this an act of weakness or of strength?

Why does he ask Kreon to drive him from Thebes? Does he feel that his fate has been just or unjust? Is his suffering, in fact, deserved? partially deserved? undeserved?

8. There is a good deal in the play about seeing and blindness. What purpose does this serve? How is Oedipus contrasted with Teiresias? How does Oedipus at the beginning of the play contrast with Oedipus at the end? Why is his blinding himself dramatically appropriate?

9. In what sense may Oedipus be regarded as a better man, though a less fortunate one, at the end of the play than at the beginning? What has he gained from his experience?

10. Some critics have suggested that Oedipus' answer to the Sphinx's riddle was incomplete—that the answer should have been not just man but Oedipus himself—and that Oedipus was as ignorant of the whole truth here as he is when he lays his curse in Scene I on the murderer of Laïos. Does this suggestion make sense? On how many legs does Oedipus walk at the end of the play?

11. If the answer to the Sphinx's riddle is not just man but Oedipus himself, may the answer to Oedipus' question "Who am I?" pertain not only to Oedipus but also to man, or at least to civilized Western man? What characteristics of Oedipus as an individual are also characteristics of man in the Western world? Is Sophocles writing only about Oedipus the king, or is he saying something about man's presumed place and his real place in the universe?

12. What purposes are served by the appearance of Antigone and Ismene in the Exodos?

13. What purposes does the chorus serve in the play? Whom does it speak for? Comment on the function of each of the four Odes.

14. What does the final speech of the Choragos tell us about human life?

15. A central formal feature of the play is its use of dramatic irony. Point out speeches by Oedipus, especially in the Prologue and Scene I, that have a different or a larger meaning for the audience than for Oedipus himself.

16. The plot of *Oedipus Rex* has been called one of the most perfect dramatic plots ever devised. Why is it admired? What are its outstanding characteristics?

William Shakespeare

OTHELLO

The Moor of Venice

CHARACTERS

DUKE OF VENICE
BRABANTIO, *a Senator*
OTHER SENATORS
GRATIANO, *brother to Brabantio*
LODOVICO, *kinsman to Brabantio*
OTHELLO, *a noble Moor in the service of the Venetian state*
CASSIO, *his lieutenant*
IAGO, *his ensign*
MONTANO, *Othello's predecessor in the government of Cyprus*
RODERIGO, *a Venetian gentleman*
CLOWN, *servant to Othello*
DESDEMONA, *daughter to Brabantio and wife to Othello*
EMILIA, *wife to Iago*
BIANCA, *mistress to Cassio*
SAILOR, MESSENGER, HERALD, OFFICERS, GENTLEMEN, MUSICIANS, *and* ATTENDANTS

OTHELLO, THE MOOR OF VENICE First performed in 1604. As was customary for Shakespeare and his contemporaries, the plot is not original but is derived from an Italian short story by Giambattista Giraldi Cinthio published in Venice in 1565. An English translation of Cinthio's story may be found in *The Moor of Venice: Cinthio's Tale and Shakespeare's Tragedy* by John Edward Taylor (London, 1855). The general historical background of the action is probably sometime between 1470 and 1522, a period when Venice, an independent city-state headed by a duke (or doge) elected by the heads of the noble families, was the strongest sea power of the Christian world and included Cyprus and Rhodes among its dominions. Its chief rival for power in the Mediterranean was the Turkish or Ottomite empire. Venetian law required that the commander-in-chief of its forces be an alien, not a Venetian citizen, to prevent political ambition from interfering with his duties. Othello, a black African of royal blood and a soldier of great experience, fulfills the qualifications. The events and characters of the play are fictional, and in any case Shakespeare was not overly concerned with historical accuracy.

William Shakespeare (1564-1616) was born in Stratford-on-Avon but went to London as a young man to make his fortune as an actor, playwright, and part-owner of the Globe Theater. He did not supervise the publication of his plays, and the two earliest printings of *Othello*—the quarto of 1622 and the folio of 1623—differ in various ways. Modern editors must rely on judgment and scholarship in reconciling the two to arrive at their texts. The version presented here is that of G. B. Harrison, from *Shakespeare: The Complete Works* (New York: Harcourt Brace Jovanovich, 1952). Selections from Harrison's notes are supplemented by those of the present editors.

ACT I

SCENE I. Venice. A street.

Enter RODERIGO *and* IAGO.

RODERIGO. Tush, never tell me! I take it much unkindly
    That thou, Iago, who hast had my purse
    As if the strings were thine, shouldst know of this.
IAGO. 'Sblood, but you will not hear me.
    If ever I did dream of such a matter,   5
    Abhor me.
RODERIGO. Thou told'st me thou didst hold him in thy hate.
IAGO. Despise me if I do not. Three great ones of the city,
    In personal suit to make me his Lieutenant,
    Off-capped to him. And, by the faith of man,   10
    I know my price, I am worth no worse a place.
    But he, as loving his own pride and purposes,
    Evades them, with a bombast circumstance
    Horribly stuffed with epithets of war.
    And, in conclusion,   15
    Nonsuits° my mediators, for, "Certes," says he,
    "I have already chose my officer."
    And what was he?
    Forsooth, a great arithmetician,°
    One Michael Cassio, a Florentine,   20
    A fellow almost damned in a fair wife,°
    That never set a squadron in the field,
    Nor the division of a battle knows
    More than a spinster, unless the bookish theoric,
    Wherein the toged Consuls° can propose   25
    As masterly as he—mere prattle without practice
    Is all his soldiership. But he, sir, had the election.
    And I, of whom his° eyes had seen the proof
    At Rhodes, at Cyprus, and on other grounds
    Christian and heathen, must be beleed° and calmed   30

---

16. Nonsuits: rejects the petition of.   **19. arithmetician:** Contemporary books on military tactics are full of elaborate diagrams and numerals to explain military formations. Cassio is a student of such books.   **21. almost . . . wife:** A much-disputed phrase. There is an Italian proverb, "You have married a fair wife? You are damned." If Iago has this in mind, he means by *almost* that Cassio is about to marry.   **25. toged Consuls:** senators in togas [Eds.].   **28. his:** Othello's [Eds.].   **30. beleed:** placed on the lee (or unfavorable) side.

By debitor and creditor. This countercaster,°
He, in good time,° must his Lieutenant be,
And I—God bless the mark!—his Moorship's Ancient.°
RODERIGO. By Heaven, I rather would have been his hangman.
IAGO. Why, there's no remedy. 'Tis the curse of service,   35
Preferment goes by letter and affection,
And not by old gradation,° where each second
Stood heir to the first. Now, sir, be judge yourself
Whether I in any just term am affined°
To love the Moor.
RODERIGO.   I would not follow him, then.   40
IAGO. Oh, sir, content you,
I follow him to serve my turn upon him.
We cannot all be masters, nor all masters
Cannot be truly followed. You shall mark
Many a duteous and knee-crooking knave   45
That doting on his own obsequious bondage
Wears out his time, much like his master's ass,
For naught but provender, and when he's old, cashiered.
Whip me such honest knaves. Others there are
Who, trimmed in forms and visages of duty,   50
Keep yet their hearts attending on themselves,
And throwing but shows of service on their lords
Do well thrive by them, and when they have lined their coats
Do themselves homage. These fellows have some soul,
And such a one do I profess myself. For, sir,   55
It is as sure as you are Roderigo,
Were I the Moor, I would not be Iago.
In following him, I follow but myself.
Heaven is my judge, not I for love and duty,
But seeming so, for my peculiar° end.   60
For when my outward action doth demonstrate
The native act and figure of my heart
In compliment extern, 'tis not long after
But I will wear my heart upon my sleeve
For daws to peck at. I am not what I am.   65
RODERIGO. What a full fortune does the thick-lips owe°
If he can carry 't thus!°

---

31. countercaster: calculator (repeating the idea of arithmetician). Counters were used in making calculations. **32. in . . . time:** A phrase expressing indignation. **33. Ancient:** ensign, the third officer in the company of which Othello is Captain and Cassio Lieutenant. **36–37. Preferment . . . gradation:** promotion comes through private recommendation and favoritism and not by order of seniority. **39. affined:** tied by affection. **60. peculiar:** personal [Eds.]. **66. owe:** own. **67. carry't thus:** i.e., bring off this marriage.

IAGO. Call up her father,
　Rouse him. Make after him, poison his delight,
　Proclaim him in the streets. Incense her kinsmen,
　And though he in a fertile climate dwell,　　　　　　　　　　70
　Plague him with flies. Though that his joy be joy,
　Yet throw such changes of vexation on 't
　As it may lose some color.
RODERIGO. Here is her father's house, I'll call aloud.
IAGO. Do, with like timorous° accent and dire yell　　　　　　75
　As when, by night and negligence, the fire
　Is spied in populous cities.
RODERIGO. What ho, Brabantio! Signior Brabantio, ho!
IAGO. Awake! What ho, Brabantio! Thieves! Thieves! Thieves!
　Look to your house, your daughter and your bags!°　　　　80
　Thieves! Thieves!

　(BRABANTIO *appears above, at a window.*)

BRABANTIO. What is the reason of this terrible summons?
　What is the matter there?
RODERIGO. Signior, is all your family within?
IAGO. Are your doors locked?
BRABANTIO. Why, wherefore ask you this?　　　85
IAGO. 'Zounds, sir, you're robbed. For shame, put on your gown,
　Your heart is burst, you have lost half your soul.
　Even now, now, very now, an old black ram
　Is tupping your white ewe. Arise, arise,
　Awake the snorting° citizens with the bell,　　　　　　　90
　Or else the Devil° will make a grandsire of you.
　Arise, I say.
BRABANTIO. What, have you lost your wits?
RODERIGO. Most reverend signior, do you know my voice?
BRABANTIO. Not I. What are you?
RODERIGO. My name is Roderigo.
BRABANTIO. The worser welcome.　　　95
　I have charged thee not to haunt about my doors.
　In honest plainness thou hast heard me say
　My daughter is not for thee, and now, in madness,
　Being full of supper and distempering draughts,
　Upon malicious bravery° dost thou come　　　　　　　100
　To start° my quiet.
RODERIGO. Sir, sir, sir—

---

75. timorous: terrifying. **80. bags:** moneybags. **90. snorting:** snoring. **91. Devil:**
The Devil in old pictures and woodcuts was represented as black. **100. bravery:** defiance. **101. start:** startle.

BRABANTIO.   But thou must needs be sure
My spirit and my place have in them power
To make this bitter to thee.
RODERIGO.   Patience, good sir.
BRABANTIO. What tell'st thou me of robbing? This is Venice,   105
My house is not a grange.°
RODERIGO.   Most grave Brabantio,
In simple and pure soul I come to you.
IAGO. 'Zounds, sir, you are one of those that will not serve God if the
Devil bid you. Because we come to do you service and you think we are
ruffians, you'll have your daughter covered with a Barbary° horse, you'll
have your nephews° neigh to you, you'll have coursers for cousins,°
and jennets° for germans.°   112
BRABANTIO. What profane wretch art thou?
IAGO. I am one, sir, that comes to tell you your daughter and the Moor
are now making the beast with two backs.
BRABANTIO. Thou art a villain.
IAGO.   You are—a Senator.
BRABANTIO. This thou shalt answer. I know thee, Roderigo.
RODERIGO. Sir, I will answer anything. But I beseech you
If 't be your pleasure and most wise consent,
As partly I find it is, that your fair daughter,   120
At this odd-even° and dull watch o' the night,
Transported with no worse nor better guard
But with a knave of common hire, a gondolier,
To the gross clasps of a lascivious Moor—
If this be known to you, and your allowance,°   125
We then have done you bold and saucy wrongs.
But if you know not this, my manners tell me
We have your wrong rebuke. Do not believe
That, from the sense of all civility,°
I thus would play and trifle with your reverence.   130
Your daughter, if you have not given her leave,
I say again, hath made a gross revolt,
Tying her duty, beauty, wit, and fortunes
In an extravagant° and wheeling° stranger
Of here and everywhere. Straight satisfy yourself.   135
If she be in her chamber or your house,
Let loose on me the justice of the state

---

106. **grange:** lonely farm. **110. Barbary:** Moorish. **111. nephews:** grandsons. **cousins:** near relations. **112. jennets:** Moorish ponies. **germans:** kinsmen. **121. odd-even:** about midnight. **125. your allowance:** by your permission. **129. from . . . civility:** contrary to all decency [Eds.]. **134. extravagant:** vagabond. **wheeling:** wandering.

For thus deluding you.

BRABANTIO.   Strike on the tinder,° ho!
Give me a taper!° Call up all my people!
This accident is not unlike my dream.   140
Belief of it oppresses me already.
Light, I say! Light!

(*Exit above.*)

IAGO.   Farewell, for I must leave you.
It seems not meet, nor wholesome to my place,°
To be produced—as if I stay I shall—
Against the Moor. For I do know the state,   145
However this may gall him with some check,
Cannot with safety cast° him. For he's embarked
With such loud reason to the Cyprus wars,
Which even now stand in act,° that, for their souls,
Another of his fathom they have none   150
To lead their business. In which regard,
Though I do hate him as I do Hell pains,
Yet for necessity of present life
I must show out a flag and sign of love,
Which is indeed but sign. That you shall surely find him,   155
Lead to the Sagittary° the raisèd search,
And there will I be with him. So farewell. (*Exit.*)

(*Enter, below,* BRABANTIO, *in his nightgown,° and* SERVANTS *with torches.*)

BRABANTIO.   It is too true an evil. Gone she is,
And what's to come of my despisèd time
Is naught but bitterness. Now, Roderigo,   160
Where didst thou see her? Oh, unhappy girl!
With the Moor, say'st thou? Who would be a father!
How didst thou know 'twas she? Oh, she deceives me
Past thought! What said she to you? Get more tapers.
Raise all my kindred. Are they married, think you?   165
RODERIGO.   Truly, I think they are.
BRABANTIO.   Oh Heaven! How got she out? Oh, treason of the blood!
Fathers, from hence trust not your daughters' minds
By what you see them act. Are there not charms°
By which the property° of youth and maidhood   170

---

138. tinder: the primitive method of making fire, used before the invention of matches. **139. taper:** candle. **143. place:** i.e., as Othello's officer. **147. cast:** dismiss from service. **149. stand in act:** are underway [Eds.]. **156. Sagittary:** presumably some inn in Venice. [Eds.] **157. s.d. nightgown:** dressing-gown [Eds.]. **169. charms:** magic spells. **170. property:** nature.

May be abused?° Have you not read, Roderigo,
Of some such thing?
RODERIGO.   Yes, sir, I have indeed.
BRABANTIO. Call up my brother.—Oh, would you had had her!—
Some one way, some another.—Do you know
Where we may apprehend her and the Moor?   175
RODERIGO. I think I can discover him, if you please
To get good guard and go along with me.
BRABANTIO. Pray you, lead on. At every house I'll call,
I may command° at most. Get weapons, ho!
And raise some special officers of night.   180
On, good Roderigo, I'll deserve your pains.° (*Exeunt.*)

SCENE II. Another street.

Enter OTHELLO, IAGO, *and* ATTENDANTS *with torches.*

IAGO. Though in the trade of war I have slain men,
Yet do I hold it very stuff o' the conscience
To do no contrivèd murder. I lack iniquity
Sometimes to do me service. Nine or ten times
I had thought to have yerked him° here under the ribs.   5
OTHELLO. 'Tis better as it is.
IAGO.   Nay, but he prated
And spoke such scurvy and provoking terms
Against your honor
That, with the little godliness I have,
I did full hard forbear him. But I pray you, sir,
Are you fast married? Be assured of this,   10
That the Magnifico is much beloved,
And hath in his effect a voice potential
As double as° the Duke's. He will divorce you,
Or put upon you what restraint and grievance   15
The law, with all his might to enforce it on,
Will give him cable.
OTHELLO.   Let him do his spite.
My services which I have done the signiory°
Shall out-tongue his complaints. 'Tis yet to know°—
Which, when I know that boasting is an honor,   20
I shall promulgate—I fetch my life and being
From men of royal siege,° and my demerits°

---

171. **abused:** deceived.   179. **command:** find supporters.   181. **deserve. . . pains:** reward your labor.   5. **yerked him:** stabbed Brabantio [Eds.].   13-14. **potential . . . as:**
twice as powerful as.   18. **signiory:** state of Venice.   19. **yet to know:** not widely known
[Eds.].   22. **siege:** rank [Eds.].   **demerits:** deserts.

May speak unbonneted to as proud a fortune
As this that I have reached. For know, Iago,
But that I love the gentle Desdemona,   25
I would not my unhoused° free condition
Put into circumscription and confine
For the sea's worth. But look! What lights come yond?

IAGO.   Those are the raisèd father and his friends.
You were best go in.

OTHELLO.   Not I, I must be found.   30
My parts, my title, and my perfect soul°
Shall manifest me rightly. Is it they?

IAGO.   By Janus, I think no.

(*Enter* CASSIO, *and certain* OFFICERS *with torches.*)

OTHELLO.   The servants of the Duke, and my Lieutenant.
The goodness of the night upon you, friends!   35
What is the news?

CASSIO.   The Duke does greet you, General,
And he requires your haste-posthaste appearance,
Even on the instant.

OTHELLO.   What is the matter, think you?

CASSIO.   Something from Cyprus, as I may divine.
It is a business of some heat. The galleys   40
Have sent a dozen sequent messengers
This very night at one another's heels,
And many of the consuls, raised and met,
Are at the Duke's already. You have been hotly called for
When, being not at your lodging to be found,   45
The Senate hath sent about three several° quests
To search you out.

OTHELLO.   'Tis well I am found by you.
I will but spend a word here in the house
And go with you. (*Exit.*)

CASSIO.   Ancient, what makes he here?

IAGO.   Faith, he tonight hath boarded a land carrack.°   50
If it prove lawful prize, he's made forever.

CASSIO.   I do not understand.

IAGO.   He's married.

CASSIO.   To who?

(*Re-enter* OTHELLO.)

IAGO.   Marry,° to—Come, Captain, will you go?

---

26. unhoused: unmarried.   **31. perfect soul:** clear conscience [Eds.].   **46. several:** separate.   **50. carrack:** large merchant ship.   **53. Marry:** a mild oath [Eds.].

OTHELLO.   Have with you.

CASSIO. Here comes another troop to seek for you.

IAGO. It is Brabantio. General, be advised,   55
  He comes to bad intent.

    (*Enter* BRABANTIO, RODERIGO, *and* OFFICERS *with torches and weapons.*)

OTHELLO.   Holloa! Stand there!

RODERIGO. Signior, it is the Moor.

BRABANTIO.   Down with him, thief!

    (*They draw on both sides.*)

IAGO. You, Roderigo! Come, sir, I am for you.

OTHELLO. Keep up° your bright swords, for the dew will rust them.
  Good signior, you shall more command with years   60
  Than with your weapons.

BRABANTIO. O thou foul thief, where hast thou stowed my daughter?
  Damned as thou art, thou hast enchanted her.
  For I'll refer me to all things of sense
  If she in chains of magic were not bound,   65
  Whether a maid so tender, fair, and happy,
  So opposite to marriage that she shunned
  The wealthy curlèd darlings of our nation,
  Would ever have, to incur a general mock,
  Run from her guardage° to the sooty bosom   70
  Of such a thing as thou, to fear, not to delight.
  Judge me the world if 'tis not gross in sense°
  That thou hast practiced on her with foul charms,
  Abused her delicate youth with drugs or minerals
  That weaken motion.° I'll have 't disputed on,°   75
  'Tis probable, and palpable to thinking.
  I therefore apprehend and do attach° thee
  For an abuser of the world, a practicer
  Of arts inhibited and out of warrant.°
  Lay hold upon him. If he do resist,   80
  Subdue him at his peril.

OTHELLO.   Hold your hands,
  Both you of my inclining and the rest.
  Were it my cue to fight, I should have known it
  Without a prompter. Where will you that I go
  To answer this your charge?

BRABANTIO.   To prison, till fit time   85

---

59. Keep up: sheathe. **70. guardage:** guardianship. **72. gross in sense:** obvious [Eds.]. **75. motion:** sense. **disputed on:** argued in the law courts. [Eds.]. **77. attach:** arrest. **79. inhibited . . . warrant:** forbidden and illegal [Eds.].

Of law and course of direct session
Call thee to answer.

OTHELLO.   What if I do obey?
How may the Duke be therewith satisfied,
Whose messengers are here about my side
Upon some present business of the state   90
To bring me to him?

FIRST OFFICER.   'Tis true, most worthy signior.
The Duke's in council, and your noble self
I am sure is sent for.

BRABANTIO.   How? The Duke in Council?
In this time of the night? Bring him away.
Mine's not an idle cause. The Duke himself,   95
Or any of my brothers of the state,
Cannot but feel this wrong as 'twere their own.
For if such actions may have passage free,
Bondslaves and pagans shall our statesmen be. (*Exeunt.*)

SCENE III. A council chamber.

The DUKE *and* SENATORS *sitting at a table,* OFFICERS *attending.*

DUKE.   There is no composition° in these news°
That gives them credit.

FIRST SENATOR.   Indeed they are disproportioned.
My letters say a hundred and seven galleys.

DUKE.   And mine, a hundred and forty.

SECOND SENATOR.   And mine, two hundred.
But though they jump not on a just account°—   5
As in these cases, where the aim reports,°
'Tis oft with difference—yet do they all confirm
A Turkish fleet, and bearing up to Cyprus.

DUKE.   Nay, it is possible enough to judgment.
I do not so secure me in the error,°   10
But the main article° I do approve
In fearful° sense.

SAILOR (*within*).   What ho! What ho! What ho!

FIRST OFFICER.   A messenger from the galleys.

(*Enter* SAILOR.)

---

1. composition: agreement. **news:** reports. **5. jump . . . account:** do not agree with an exact estimate. **6. aim reports:** i.e., intelligence reports of an enemy's intention often differ in the details. **10. I . . . error:** I do not consider myself free from danger, because the reports may not all be accurate. **11. main article:** general report. **12. fearful:** to be feared.

DUKE.   Now, what's the business?
SAILOR. The Turkish preparation makes for Rhodes.
      So was I bid report here to the state   15
      By Signior Angelo.
DUKE. How say you by this change?
FIRST SENATOR.   This cannot be,
      By no assay of reason. 'Tis a pageant
      To keep us in false gaze. When we consider
      The importancy of Cyprus to the Turk,   20
      And let ourselves again but understand
      That as it more concerns the Turk than Rhodes,
      So may he with more facile question bear it,°
      For that it stands not in such warlike brace
      But altogether lacks the abilities   25
      That Rhodes is dressed in—if we make thought of this,
      We must not think the Turk is so unskillful
      To leave that latest which concerns him first,
      Neglecting an attempt of ease and gain
      To wake and wage a danger profitless.   30
DUKE. Nay, in all confidence, he's not for Rhodes.
FIRST OFFICER. Here is more news.

      (*Enter a* MESSENGER.)

MESSENGER. The Ottomites,° Reverend and Gracious,
      Steering with due course toward the isle of Rhodes,
      Have there injointed° them with an after-fleet.°   35
FIRST SENATOR. Aye, so I thought. How many, as you guess?
MESSENGER. Of thirty sail. And now they do restem°
      Their backward course, bearing with frank appearance
      Their purposes toward Cyprus. Signior Montano,
      Your trusty and most valiant servitor,   40
      With his free duty recommends° you thus,
      And prays you to believe him.
DUKE. 'Tis certain then for Cyprus.
      Marcus Luccicos, is not he in town?
FIRST SENATOR. He's now in Florence.   45
DUKE. Write from us to him, post-posthaste dispatch.
FIRST SENATOR. Here comes Brabantio and the valiant Moor.

      (*Enter* BRABANTIO, OTHELLO, IAGO, RODERIGO, *and* OFFICERS.)

DUKE. Valiant Othello, we must straight employ you
      Against the general enemy Ottoman.

---

23. with . . . it: take it more easily. **33. Ottomites:** Turks. **35. injointed:** joined.
after-fleet: second fleet. **37. restem:** steer again. **41. recommends:** advises [Eds.].

(*To* BRABANTIO) I did not see you. Welcome, gentle signior,   50
We lacked your counsel and your help tonight.

BRABANTIO.   So did I yours. Good your Grace, pardon me,
Neither my place nor aught I heard of business
Hath raised me from my bed, nor doth the general care
Take hold on me. For my particular° grief   55
Is of so floodgate and o'erbearing nature
That it engluts and swallows other sorrows,
And it is still itself.

DUKE.   Why, what's the matter?

BRABANTIO.   My daughter! Oh, my daughter!

ALL.   Dead?

BRABANTIO.   Aye, to me.
She is abused, stol'n from me and corrupted   60
By spells and medicines bought of mountebanks.
For nature so preposterously to err,
Being not deficient, blind, or lame of sense,
Sans° witchcraft could not.

DUKE.   Whoe'er he be that in this foul proceeding   65
Hath thus beguiled your daughter of herself
And you of her, the bloody book of law
You shall yourself read in the bitter letter
After your own sense—yea, though our proper° son
Stood in your action.

BRABANTIO.   Humbly I thank your Grace.   70
Here is the man, this Moor, whom now, it seems,
Your special mandate for the state affairs
Hath hither brought.

ALL.   We are very sorry for 't.

DUKE (*to* OTHELLO).   What in your own part can you say to this?

BRABANTIO.   Nothing but this is so.   75

OTHELLO.   Most potent, grave, and reverend signiors,
My very noble and approved good masters,
That I have ta'en away this old man's daughter,
It is most true—true, I have married her.
The very head and front of my offending   80
Hath this extent, no more. Rude am I in my speech,
And little blest with the soft phrase of peace,
For since these arms of mine had seven years' pith
Till now some nine moons wasted, they have used
Their dearest action in the tented field;   85
And little of this great world can I speak,
More than pertains to feats of broil and battle,

---

55. particular: personal.   **64. Sans:** without.   **69. proper:** own.

And therefore little shall I grace my cause
In speaking for myself. Yet, by your gracious patience,
I will a round unvarnished tale° deliver   90
Of my whole course of love—what drugs, what charms,
What conjuration and what mighty magic—
For such proceeding I am charged withal—
I won his daughter.

BRABANTIO.   A maiden never bold,
Of spirit so still and quiet that her motion   95
Blushed at herself, and she—in spite of nature,
Of years, of country, credit,° everything—
To fall in love with what she feared to look on!
It is a judgment maimed and most imperfect
That will confess perfection so could err   100
Against all rules of nature, and must be driven
To find out practices of cunning Hell
Why this should be. I therefore vouch again
That with some mixtures powerful o'er the blood,
Or with some dram conjured to this effect,   105
He wrought upon her.

DUKE.   To vouch this is no proof
Without more certain and more overt test
Than these thin habits and poor likelihoods
Of modern seeming° do prefer against him.

FIRST SENATOR. But, Othello, speak.   110
Did you by indirect and forcèd courses
Subdue and poison this young maid's affections?
Or came it by request, and such fair question
As soul to soul affordeth?

OTHELLO.   I do beseech you
Send for the lady to the Sagittary,   115
And let her speak of me before her father.
If you do find me foul in her report,
The trust, the office I do hold of you,
Not only take away, but let your sentence
Even fall upon my life.

DUKE.   Fetch Desdemona hither.   120

OTHELLO. Ancient, conduct them, you best know the place.

(*Exeunt* IAGO *and* ATTENDANTS.)

And till she come, as truly as to Heaven
I do confess the vices of my blood,

---

90. round . . . tale: direct, unadorned account. **97. credit:** reputation. **108–09.
thin . . . seeming:** superficial, unlikely, and trivial suppositions [Eds.].

So justly to your grave ears I'll present
How I did thrive in this fair lady's love   125
And she in mine.
DUKE.   Say it, Othello.
OTHELLO.   Her father loved me, oft invited me,
Still° questioned me the story of my life
From year to year, the battles, sieges, fortunes,
That I have passed.   130
I ran it through, even from my boyish days
To the very moment that he bade me tell it.
Wherein I spake of most disastrous chances,
Of moving accidents by flood and field,
Of hairbreadth 'scapes i' the imminent deadly breach,   135
Of being taken by the insolent foe
And sold to slavery, of my redemption thence,
And portance in my travels' history.
Wherein of antres° vast and deserts idle,
Rough quarries, rocks, and hills whose heads touch heaven,   140
It was my hint to speak—such was the process.
And of the cannibals that each other eat,
The anthropophagi,° and men whose heads
Do grow beneath their shoulders. This to hear
Would Desdemona seriously incline.   145
But still the house affairs would draw her thence,
Which ever as she could with haste dispatch,
She'd come again, and with a greedy ear
Devour up my discourse. Which I observing,
Took once a pliant hour and found good means   150
To draw from her a prayer of earnest heart
That I would all my pilgrimage dilate,
Whereof by parcels she had something heard,
But not intentively. I did consent,
And often did beguile her of her tears   155
When I did speak of some distressful stroke
That my youth suffered. My story being done,
She gave me for my pains a world of sighs.
She swore, in faith, 'twas strange, 'twas passing strange,
'Twas pitiful, 'twas wondrous pitiful.   160
She wished she had not heard it, yet she wished
That Heaven had made her such a man. She thanked me,
And bade me, if I had a friend that loved her,
I should but teach him how to tell my story
And that would woo her. Upon this hint° I spake.   165

128. **Still:** always. **139. antres:** caves. **143. anthropophagi:** cannibals. **165. hint:**
opportunity [Eds.].

She loved me for the dangers I had passed,
And I loved her that she did pity them.
This only is the witchcraft I have used.
Here comes the lady, let her witness it.

(*Enter* DESDEMONA, IAGO, *and* ATTENDANTS.)

DUKE.   I think this tale would win my daughter too.   170
Good Brabantio,
Take up this mangled matter at the best.°
Men do their broken weapons rather use
Than their bare hands.
BRABANTIO.   I pray you hear her speak.
If she confess that she was half the wooer,   175
Destruction on my head if my bad blame
Light on the man! Come hither, gentle mistress.
Do you perceive in all this noble company
Where most you owe obedience?
DESDEMONA.   My noble father,
I do perceive here a divided duty.   180
To you I am bound for life and education,
My life and education both do learn me
How to respect you; you are the lord of duty,
I am hitherto your daughter. But here's my husband,
And so much duty as my mother showed   185
To you, preferring you before her father,
So much I challenge that I may profess
Due to the Moor my lord.
BRABANTIO.   God be with you! I have done.
Please it your Grace, on to the state affairs.
I had rather to adopt a child than get° it.   190
Come hither, Moor.
I here do give thee that with all my heart
Which, but thou hast already, with all my heart
I would keep from thee. For your sake, jewel,
I am glad at soul I have no other child,   195
For thy escape would teach me tyranny,
To hang clogs on them. I have done, my lord.
DUKE.   Let me speak like yourself, and lay a sentence°
Which, as a grise° or step, may help these lovers
Into your favor.   200
When remedies are past, the griefs are ended
By seeing the worst, which late on hopes depended.
To mourn a mischief that is past and gone

---

172. Take ... best: make the best settlement you can of this confused business.
190. get: beget. **198. sentence:** proverbial saying. **199. grise:** degree.

Is the next way to draw new mischief on.
What cannot be preserved when fortune takes,   205
Patience her injury a mockery makes.
The robbed that smiles steals something from the thief.
He robs himself that spends a bootless grief.
BRABANTIO.   So let the Turk of Cyprus us beguile,
We lose it not so long as we can smile.   210
He bears the sentence well that nothing bears
But the free comfort which from thence he hears.
But he bears both the sentence and the sorrow
That, to pay grief, must of poor patience borrow.
These sentences, to sugar or to gall,   215
Being strong on both sides, are equivocal.
But words are words. I never yet did hear
That the bruisèd heart was piercèd through the ear.
I humbly beseech you, proceed to the affairs of state.
DUKE.   The Turk with a most mighty preparation makes for Cyprus.
Othello, the fortitude of the place is best known to you, and though we
have there a substitute° of most allowed sufficiency, yet opinion, a sover-
eign mistress of effects, throws a more safer voice on you. You must
therefore be content to slubber° the gloss of your new fortunes with this
more stubborn and boisterous expedition.   225
OTHELLO.   The tyrant custom, most grave Senators,
Hath made the flinty and steel couch of war
My thrice-driven bed of down. I do agnize°
A natural and prompt alacrity
I find in hardness,° and do undertake   230
These present wars against the Ottomites.
Most humbly therefore bending to your state,
I crave fit disposition for my wife,
Due reference of place and exhibition,°
With such accommodation and besort°   235
As levels with her breeding.
DUKE.   If you please,
Be 't at her father's.
BRABANTIO.   I'll not have it so.
OTHELLO.   Nor I.
DESDEMONA.   Nor I. I would not there reside,
To put my father in impatient thoughts
By being in his eye. Most gracious Duke,   240
To my unfolding lend your prosperous° ear,

---

222. **substitute:** deputy commander. 224. **slubber:** tarnish. 228. **agnize:** confess. 230.
hardness: hardship. 234. **exhibition:** allowance. 235. **besort:** attendants. 241. **prosperous:** favorable.

And let me find a charter in your voice
   To assist my simpleness.
DUKE.   What would you, Desdemona?
DESDEMONA.   That I did love the Moor to live with him,   245
   My downright violence and storm of fortunes
   May trumpet to the world. My heart's subdued
   Even to the very quality° of my lord.
   I saw Othello's visage in his mind,
   And to his honors and his valiant parts°   250
   Did I my soul and fortunes consecrate.
   So that, dear lords, if I be left behind,
   A moth of peace, and he go to the war,
   The rites for which I love him are bereft me,
   And I a heavy interim shall support   255
   By his dear absence. Let me go with him.
OTHELLO.   Let her have your voices.
   Vouch with me, Heaven, I therefore beg it not
   To please the palate of my appetite,
   Nor to comply with heat—the young affects   260
   In me defunct°—and proper satisfaction,
   But to be free and bounteous to her mind.°
   And Heaven defend your good souls, that you think
   I will your serious and great business scant
   For she is with me. No, when light-winged toys   265
   Of feathered Cupid seel° with wanton dullness
   My speculative and officed instruments,°
   That my disports° corrupt and taint my business,
   Let housewives make a skillet of my helm,
   And all indign° and base adversities   270
   Make head against my estimation!°
DUKE.   Be it as you shall privately determine,
   Either for her stay or going. The affair cries haste,
   And speed must answer 't. You must hence tonight.
DESDEMONA.   Tonight, my lord?
DUKE.   This night.
OTHELLO.   With all my heart.   275
DUKE.   At nine i' the morning here we'll meet again.
   Othello, leave some officer behind,
   And he shall our commission bring to you,
   With such things else of quality and respect

248. **quality:** profession.   250. **parts:** qualities.   260–61. **young . . . defunct:** in me the
passion of youth is dead.   262. **to . . . mind:** Othello repeats Desdemona's claim that this
is a marriage of minds.   266. **seel:** close up.   267. **speculative . . . instruments:** powers
of sight and action; i.e., my efficiency as your general.   268. **disports:** amusements.   270.
indign: unworthy.   271. **estimation:** reputation.

As doth import you.

OTHELLO.   So please your Grace, my Ancient,   280
A man he is of honesty and trust.
To his conveyance I assign my wife,
With what else needful your good Grace shall think
To be sent after me.

DUKE.   Let it be so.
Good night to everyone. (*To* BRABANTIO) And, noble signior,   285
If virtue no delighted beauty lack,
Your son-in-law is far more fair than black.°

FIRST SENATOR.   Adieu, brave Moor. Use Desdemona well.

BRABANTIO.   Look to her, Moor, if thou hast eyes to see.
She has deceived her father, and may thee.   290

(*Exeunt* DUKE, SENATORS, OFFICERS, *etc.*)

OTHELLO.   My life upon her faith! Honest Iago,
My Desdemona must I leave to thee.
I prithee, let thy wife attend on her,
And bring them after in the best advantage.
Come, Desdemona, I have but an hour   295
Of love, of worldly matters and direction,
To spend with thee. We must obey the time.

(*Exeunt* OTHELLO *and* DESDEMONA.)

RODERIGO.   Iago!

IAGO.   What say'st thou, noble heart?

RODERIGO.   What will I do, thinkest thou?   300

IAGO.   Why, go to bed and sleep.

RODERIGO.   I will incontinently° drown myself.

IAGO.   If thou dost, I shall never love thee after. Why, thou silly gentleman!

RODERIGO.   It is silliness to live when to live is torment, and then have we a
prescription to die when death is our physician.   305

IAGO.   Oh, villainous! I have looked upon the world for four times seven
years, and since I could distinguish betwixt a benefit and an injury I never
found man that knew how to love himself. Ere I would say I would drown
myself for the love of a guinea hen, I would change my humanity with a
baboon.   310

RODERIGO.   What should I do? I confess it is my shame to be so fond, but it
is not in my virtue° to amend it.

IAGO.   Virtue! A fig! 'Tis in ourselves that we are thus or thus. Our bodies are
gardens, to the which our wills are gardeners. So that if we will plant
nettles or sow lettuce, set hyssop and weed up thyme, supply it with one

---

286–87. If . . . black: If worthiness is a beautiful thing in itself, your son-in-law, though
black, has beauty.   **302. incontinently:** immediately.   **312. virtue:** strength [Eds.].

gender of herbs or distract it with many, either to have it sterile with idleness or manured with industry—why, the power and corrigible° authority of this lies in our wills. If the balance of our lives had not one scale of reason to poise another of sensuality, the blood and baseness of our natures would conduct us to most preposterous conclusions. But we have reason to cool our raging motions, our carnal stings, our unbitted lusts, whereof I take this that you call love to be a sect or scion.°   322

RODERIGO. It cannot be.

IAGO. It is merely a lust of the blood and a permission of the will. Come, be a man! Drown thyself? Drown cats and blind puppies! I have professed me thy friend, and I confess me knit to thy deserving with cables of perdurable toughness. I could never better stead thee than now. Put money in thy purse, follow thou the wars, defeat thy favor with an usurped beard°— I say put money in thy purse. It cannot be that Desdemona should long continue her love to the Moor—put money in thy purse—nor he his to her. It was a violent commencement, and thou shalt see an answerable sequestration°—put but money in thy purse. These Moors are changeable in their wills.°—Fill thy purse with money. The food that to him now is as luscious as locusts shall be to him shortly as bitter as coloquintida. She must change for youth. When she is sated with his body, she will find the error of her choice. She must have change, she must—therefore put money in thy purse. If thou wilt needs damn thyself, do it a more delicate way than drowning. Make all the money thou canst.° If sanctimony and a frail vow betwixt an erring° barbarian and a supersubtle Venetian be not too hard for my wits and all the tribe of Hell, thou shalt enjoy her—therefore make money. A pox of drowning thyself! It is clean out of the way. Seek thou rather to be hanged in compassing thy joy than to be drowned and go without her.   343

RODERIGO. Wilt thou be fast to my hopes if I depend on the issue?

IAGO. Thou art sure of me. Go, make money. I have told thee often, and I retell thee again and again, I hate the Moor. My cause is hearted,° thine hath no less reason. Let us be conjunctive in our revenge against him. If thou canst cuckold him thou dost thyself a pleasure, me a sport. There are many events in the womb of time which will be delivered. Traverse, go, provide thy money. We will have more of this tomorrow. Adieu.   350

RODERIGO. Where shall we meet i' the morning?

IAGO. At my lodging.

RODERIGO. I'll be with thee betimes.

IAGO. Go to, farewell. Do you hear, Roderigo?

---

317. **corrigible:** correcting, directing. **322. sect or scion:** Both words mean a slip taken from a tree and planted to produce a new growth. **328–29. defeat . . . beard:** disguise your face by growing a beard. **332. answerable sequestration:** corresponding separation; i.e., reaction. **333. wills:** desires [Eds.]. **338. Make . . . canst:** turn all you can into ready cash. **339. erring:** vagabond. **346. hearted:** heartfelt.

RODERIGO. What say you?   355
IAGO. No more of drowning, do you hear?
RODERIGO. I am changed. I'll go sell all my land. (*Exit.*)
IAGO. Thus do I ever make my fool my purse,
    For I mine own gained knowledge should profane
    If I would time expend with such a snipe   360
    But for my sport and profit. I hate the Moor,
    And it is thought abroad that 'twixt my sheets
    He's done my office. I know not if 't be true,
    But I for mere suspicion in that kind
    Will do as if for surety. He holds me well,   365
    The better shall my purpose work on him.
    Cassio's a proper° man. Let me see now,
    To get his place, and to plume up° my will
    In double knavery—How, how?—Let's see.—
    After some time, to abuse Othello's ear   370
    That he is too familiar with his wife.
    He hath a person and a smooth dispose
    To be suspected,° framed to make women false.
    The Moor is of a free and open nature
    That thinks men honest that but seem to be so,   375
    And will as tenderly be led by the nose
    As asses are.
    I have 't. It is engendered. Hell and night
    Must bring this monstrous birth to the world's light. (*Exit.*)

ACT II

SCENE I. A seaport in Cyprus. An open place near the wharf.

Enter MONTANO *and two* GENTLEMEN.

MONTANO. What from the cape can you discern at sea?
FIRST GENTLEMAN. Nothing at all. It is a high-wrought flood.
    I cannot 'twixt the heaven and the main
    Descry a sail.
MONTANO. Methinks the wind hath spoke aloud at land,   5
    A fuller blast ne'er shook our battlements.
    If it hath ruffianed so upon the sea,
    What ribs of oak, when mountains melt on them,
    Can hold the mortise? What shall we hear of this?
SECOND GENTLEMAN. A segregation° of the Turkish fleet.   10

---

367. proper: handsome. **368. plume up:** glorify. **372–73. He . . . suspected:** an easy
way with him that is naturally suspected. **10.** segregation: separation.

For do but stand upon the foaming shore,
The chidden billow seems to pelt the clouds,
The wind-shaked surge, with high and monstrous mane,
Seems to cast water on the burning Bear,
And quench the guards of the ever-fixèd Pole.°   15
I never did like molestation view
On the enchafèd flood.
MONTANO.   If that the Turkish fleet
Be not ensheltered and embayed, they are drowned.
It is impossible to bear it out.

(*Enter a* THIRD GENTLEMAN.)

THIRD GENTLEMAN.   News, lads! Our wars are done.   20
The desperate tempest hath so banged the Turks
That their designment halts. A noble ship of Venice
Hath seen a grievous wreck and sufferance°
On most part of their fleet.
MONTANO.   How! Is this true?
THIRD GENTLEMAN.   The ship is here put in,   25
A Veronesa. Michael Cassio,
Lieutenant to the warlike Moor Othello,
Is come on shore, the Moor himself at sea,
And is in full commission here for Cyprus.
MONTANO.   I am glad on 't. 'Tis a worthy governor.   30
THIRD GENTLEMAN.   But this same Cassio, though he speak of comfort
Touching the Turkish loss, yet he looks sadly
And prays the Moor be safe, for they were parted
With foul and violent tempest.
MONTANO.   Pray Heavens he be,
For I have served him, and the man commands   35
Like a full soldier. Let's to the seaside, ho!
As well to see the vessel that's come in
As to throw out our eyes for brave Othello,
Even till we make the main and the aerial blue
An indistinct regard.
THIRD GENTLEMAN.   Come, let's do so.   40
For every minute is expectancy
Of more arrivance.

(*Enter* CASSIO.)

CASSIO.   Thanks, you the valiant of this warlike isle
That so approve the Moor! Oh, let the heavens
Give him defense against the elements,   45

14–15. cast . . . Pole: drown the constellations [Eds.].   23. sufferance: damage.

For I have lost him on a dangerous sea.

MONTANO. Is he well shipped?

CASSIO. His bark is stoutly timbered, and his pilot
Of very expert and approved allowance.
Therefore my hopes, not surfeited to death,　　　　　　　　　50
Stand in bold cure.

(*A cry within:* "A sail, a sail, a sail!" *Enter a* FOURTH GENTLEMAN.)

CASSIO. What noise?

FOURTH GENTLEMAN. The town is empty. On the brow o' the sea
Stand ranks of people, and they cry "A sail!"

CASSIO. My hopes do shape him for the governor.　　　　　　　55

(*Guns heard.*)

SECOND GENTLEMAN. They do discharge their shot of courtesy.
Our friends, at least.

CASSIO.　　　　　　　　　I pray you, sir, go forth,
And give us truth who 'tis that is arrived.

SECOND GENTLEMAN. I shall. (*Exit.*)

MONTANO. But, good Lieutenant, is your General wived?　　　60

CASSIO. Most fortunately. He hath achieved a maid
That paragons description and wild fame,
One that excels the quirks of blazoning pens
And in the essential vesture of creation
Does tire the ingener.°

(*Re-enter* SECOND GENTLEMAN.)

　　　　　　　　　　　How now! Who has put in?　　　　　65

SECOND GENTLEMAN. 'Tis one Iago, Ancient to the General.

CASSIO. He has had most favorable and happy speed.
Tempests themselves, high seas, and howling winds,
The guttered rocks, and congregated sands,
Traitors ensteeped to clog the guiltless keel,　　　　　　　70
As having sense of beauty, do omit
Their mortal° natures, letting go safely by
The divine Desdemona.

MONTANO.　　　　　　　　What is she?

CASSIO. She that I spake of, our great Captain's captain,
Left in the conduct of the bold Iago,　　　　　　　　　　75
Whose footing here anticipates our thoughts
A sennight's° speed. Great Jove, Othello guard,

63–65. One . . . ingener: one that is too good for the fancy phrases (*quirks*) of painting pens
(i.e., poets) and in her absolute perfection wearies the artist (i.e., the painter). **ingener:**
inventor. **72. mortal:** deadly. **77. sennight's:** week's.

And swell his sail with thine own powerful breath,
That he may bless this bay with his tall ship,
Make love's quick pants in Desdemona's arms,   80
Give renewed fire to our extinguished spirits,
And bring all Cyprus comfort.

(*Enter* DESDEMONA, EMILIA, IAGO, RODERIGO, *and* ATTENDANTS.)

                         Oh, behold,
The riches of the ship is come on shore!
Ye men of Cyprus, let her have your knees.
Hail to thee, lady! And the grace of Heaven,   85
Before, behind thee, and on every hand,
Enwheel thee round!
DESDEMONA.   I thank you, valiant Cassio.
What tidings can you tell me of my lord?
CASSIO. He is not yet arrived, nor know I aught
But that he's well and will be shortly here.   90
DESDEMONA. Oh, but I fear—How lost you company?
CASSIO. The great contention of the sea and skies
Parted our fellowship.—But hark! A sail.

(*A cry within:* "A sail, a sail!" *Guns heard.*)

SECOND GENTLEMAN. They give their greeting to the citadel.
This likewise is a friend.
CASSIO.   See for the news.   95

(*Exit* GENTLEMAN.)

Good Ancient, you are welcome. (*To* EMILIA) Welcome, mistress.
Let it not gall your patience, good Iago,
That I extend my manners. 'Tis my breeding
That gives me this bold show of courtesy. (*Kissing her.*)
IAGO. Sir, would she give you so much of her lips   100
As of her tongue she oft bestows on me,
You'd have enough.
DESDEMONA.   Alas, she has no speech.
IAGO. In faith, too much,
I find it still when I have list° to sleep.
Marry, before your ladyship, I grant,   105
She puts her tongue a little in her heart
And chides with thinking.
EMILIA. You have little cause to say so.
IAGO. Come on, come on. You are pictures° out of doors,
Bells° in your parlors, wildcats in your kitchens,   110

---

104. list: desire. **109. pictures:** i.e., painted and dumb. **110. Bells:** i.e., ever clacking.

Saints in your injuries,° devils being offended,
Players in your housewifery, and housewives in your beds.
DESDEMONA. Oh, fie upon thee, slanderer!
IAGO. Nay, it is true, or else I am a Turk.
You rise to play, and go to bed to work.   115
EMILIA. You shall not write my praise.
IAGO.   No, let me not.
DESDEMONA. What wouldst thou write of me if thou shouldst praise me?
IAGO. O gentle lady, do not put me to 't,
For I am nothing if not critical.
DESDEMONA. Come on, assay.°—There's one gone to the harbor?   120
IAGO. Aye, madam.
DESDEMONA (aside). I am not merry, but I do beguile
The thing I am by seeming otherwise.—
Come, how wouldst thou praise me?
IAGO. I am about it, but indeed my invention   125
Comes from my pate as birdlime does from frieze°—
It plucks out brains and all. But my Muse labors,
And thus she is delivered:
If she be fair and wise, fairness and wit,
The one's for use, the other useth it.   130
DESDEMONA. Well praised! How if she be black° and witty?
IAGO. If she be black, and thereto have a wit,
She'll find a white° that shall her blackness fit.
DESDEMONA. Worse and worse.
EMILIA. How if fair and foolish?   135
IAGO. She never yet was foolish that was fair,
For even her folly helped her to an heir.
DESDEMONA. These are old fond paradoxes to make fools laugh i' the ale-
house. What miserable praise hast thou for her that's foul and foolish?
IAGO. There's none so foul, and foolish thereunto,   140
But does foul pranks which fair and wise ones do.
DESDEMONA. Oh, heavy ignorance! Thou praisest the worst best. But what
praise couldst thou bestow on a deserving woman indeed, one that in
the authority of her merit did justly put on the vouch of very malice
itself?°   145
IAGO. She that was ever fair and never proud,
Had tongue at will° and yet was never loud,
Never lacked gold and yet went never gay,
Fled from her wish and yet said "Now I may";

111. Saints . . . injuries: saints when you hurt anyone else. 120. assay: try. 125–26.
my . . . frieze: my literary effort (*invention*) is as hard to pull out of my head as frieze
(cloth with a nap) stuck to birdlime. 131. black: brunette, dark-complexioned [Eds.].
133. white: with a pun on *wight* (l. 156), man, person. 143–45. one . . . itself:
one so deserving that even malice would declare her good. 147. tongue . . . will: a ready
flow of words.

She that, being angered, her revenge being nigh, 150
Bade her wrong stay and her displeasure fly;
She that in wisdom never was so frail
To change the cod's head for the salmon's tail;°
She that could think and ne'er disclose her mind,
See suitors following and not look behind; 155
She was a wight, if ever such wight were—

DESDEMONA. To do what?

IAGO. To suckle fools and chronicle small beer.°

DESDEMONA. Oh, most lame and impotent conclusion! Do not learn of him,
Emilia, though he be thy husband. How say you, Cassio? Is he not a most
profane and liberal° counselor? 161

CASSIO. He speaks home,° madam. You may relish him more in the soldier
than in the scholar.

IAGO (aside). He takes her by the palm. Aye, well said, whisper. With as little
a web as this will I ensnare as great a fly as Cassio. Aye, smile upon her,
do, I will gyve thee in thine own courtship.° You say true, 'tis so indeed.
If such tricks as these strip you out of your Lieutenantry, it had been
better you had not kissed your three fingers° so oft, which now again you
are most apt to play the sir° in. Very good, well kissed! An excellent
courtesy! 'Tis so indeed. Yet again your fingers to your lips? Would they
were clyster pipes° for your sake! (Trumpet within.) The Moor! I know his
trumpet. 172

CASSIO. 'Tis truly so.

DESDEMONA. Let's meet him and receive him.

CASSIO. Lo where he comes! 175

(Enter OTHELLO and ATTENDANTS.)

OTHELLO. O my fair warrior!°

DESDEMONA.   My dear Othello!

OTHELLO. It gives me wonder great as my content
To see you here before me. O my soul's joy!
If after every tempest come such calms,
May the winds blow till they have wakened death! 180
And let the laboring bark climb hills of seas
Olympus-high, and duck again as low
As Hell's from Heaven! If it were now to die,

---

153. To . . . tail: to prefer the tail end of a good thing to the head of a poor thing. 158.
suckle . . . beer: nurse babies and keep petty household accounts (i.e., even the best
woman belongs in the nursery and kitchen) [Eds.]. 161. liberal: gross. 162. home:
bluntly [Eds.]. 166. gyve . . . courtship: trap you with your own show of courtesy
[Eds.]. 168. kissed . . . fingers: a gesture of gallantry. 169. play the sir: act the fine
gentleman. 171. clyster pipes: an enema syringe. 176. warrior: because she is a soldier's wife.

'Twere now to be most happy, for I fear
My soul hath her content so absolute   185
That not another comfort like to this
Succeeds in unknown fate.
DESDEMONA.   The Heavens forbid
But that our loves and comforts should increase,
Even as our days do grow!
OTHELLO.   Amen to that, sweet powers!
I cannot speak enough of this content.   190
It stops me here,° it is too much of joy.
And this, and this, the greatest discords be (*Kissing her.*)
That e'er our hearts shall make!
IAGO (*aside*).   Oh, you are well tuned now,
But I'll set down the pegs° that make this music,
As honest as I am.
OTHELLO.   Come, let us to the castle.   195
News, friends! Our wars are done, the Turks are drowned.
How does my old acquaintance of this isle?
Honey, you shall be well desired in Cyprus,
I have found great love amongst them. O my sweet,
I prattle out of fashion, and I dote   200
In mine own comforts. I prithee, good Iago,
Go to the bay and disembark my coffers.°
Bring thou the master° to the citadel.
He is a good one, and his worthiness
Does challenge much respect. Come, Desdemona,   205
Once more well met at Cyprus.

(*Exeunt all but* IAGO *and* RODERIGO.)

IAGO. Do thou meet me presently at the harbor. Come hither. If thou beest
valiant—as they say base men being in love have then a nobility in their
natures more than is native to them—list me. The Lieutenant tonight
watches on the court of guard. First, I must tell thee this. Desdemona is
directly in love with him.   211
RODERIGO. With him! Why, 'tis not possible.
IAGO. Lay thy finger thus,° and let thy soul be instructed. Mark me with
what violence she first loved the Moor, but for bragging and telling her
fantastical lies. And will she love him still for prating? Let not thy discreet
heart think it. Her eye must be fed, and what delight shall she have to look
on the Devil? When the blood is made dull with the act of sport, there
should be, again to inflame it and to give satiety a fresh appetite, loveliness

191. here: i.e., in the heart. 194. set . . . pegs: i.e., make you sing out of tune. A stringed
instrument was tuned by the pegs. 202. coffers: trunks. 203. master: captain of the
ship. 213. thus: i.e., on the lips.

in favor,° sympathy in years, manners, and beauties, all which the Moor is defective in. Now, for want of these required conveniences, her delicate tenderness will find itself abused, begin to heave the gorge, disrelish and abhor the Moor. Very nature will instruct her in it and compel her to some second choice. Now, sir, this granted—as it is a most pregnant and unforced position°—who stands so eminently in the degree of this fortune as Cassio does? A knave very voluble, no further conscionable° than in putting on the mere form of civil and humane seeming° for the better compassing of his salt° and most hidden loose affection? Why, none, why, none. A slipper° and subtle knave, a finder-out of occasions, that has an eye can stamp and counterfeit advantages,° though true advantage never present itself. A devilish knave! Besides, the knave is handsome, young, and hath all those requisites in him that folly and green minds look after. A pestilent complete knave, and the woman hath found him already. 232

RODERIGO.   I cannot believe that in her. She's full of most blest condition.°

IAGO.   Blest fig's-end!° The wine she drinks is made of grapes. If she had been blest, she would never have loved the Moor. Blest pudding! Didst thou not see her paddle with the palm of his hand? Didst not mark that? 237

RODERIGO.   Yes, that I did, but that was but courtesy.

IAGO.   Lechery, by this hand, an index and obscure prologue to the history of lust and foul thoughts. They met so near with their lips that their breaths embraced together. Villainous thoughts, Roderigo! When these mutualities so marshal the way, hard at hand comes the master and main exercise, the incorporate° conclusion. Pish! But, sir, be you ruled by me. I have brought you from Venice. Watch you tonight. For the command, I'll lay't upon you. Cassio knows you not. I'll not be far from you. Do you find some occasion to anger Cassio, either by speaking too loud, or tainting° his discipline, or from what other course you please which the time shall more favorably minister. 248

RODERIGO.   Well.

IAGO.   Sir, he is rash and very sudden in choler,° and haply may strike at you. Provoke him, that he may, for even out of that will I cause these of Cyprus to mutiny, whose qualification shall come into no true taste again but by the displanting of Cassio. So shall you have a shorter journey to your desires by the means I shall then have to prefer° them, and the impediment most profitably removed without the which there were no expectation of our prosperity. 256

RODERIGO.   I will do this, if I can bring it to any opportunity.

---

219. favor: face. **223–24. pregnant . . . position:** very significant and probable argument. **225. no . . . conscionable:** who has no more conscience. **226. humane seeming:** courteous appearance. **227. salt:** lecherous. **228. slipper:** slippery. **229. stamp . . . advantages:** forge false opportunities. **233. condition:** disposition. **234. fig's-end:** nonsense [Eds.]. **243. incorporate:** bodily. **246. tainting:** disparaging. **250. choler:** anger. **254. prefer:** promote.

IAGO. I warrant thee. Meet me by and by at the citadel. I must fetch his necessaries ashore. Farewell.

RODERIGO. Adieu. (*Exit.*)   260

IAGO.   That Cassio loves her, I do well believe it.
That she loves him, 'tis apt and of great credit.°
The Moor, howbeit that I endure him not,
Is of a constant, loving, noble nature,
And I dare think he'll prove to Desdemona   265
A most dear husband. Now, I do love her too,
Not out of absolute lust, though peradventure
I stand accountant for as great a sin,
But partly led to diet° my revenge
For that I do suspect the lusty Moor   270
Hath leaped into my seat. The thought whereof
Doth like a poisonous mineral gnaw my inwards,
And nothing can or shall content my soul
Till I am evened with him, wife for wife.
Or failing so, yet that I put the Moor   275
At least into a jealousy so strong
That judgment cannot cure. Which thing to do,
If this poor trash of Venice, whom I trash
For his quick hunting,° stand the putting-on,
I'll have our Michael Cassio on the hip,   280
Abuse him to the Moor in the rank garb°—
For I fear Cassio with my nightcap too—
Make the Moor thank me, love me, and reward me
For making him egregiously an ass
And practicing upon his peace and quiet   285
Even to madness. 'Tis here, but yet confused.
Knavery's plain face is never seen till used. (*Exit.*)

SCENE II. A street.

Enter a HERALD with a proclamation, PEOPLE following.

HERALD.   It is Othello's pleasure, our noble and valiant General, that upon
certain tidings now arrived, importing the mere perdition° of the Turkish
fleet, every man put himself into triumph°—some to dance, some to make
bonfires, each man to what sport and revels his addiction leads him. For,
besides these beneficial news, it is the celebration of his nuptial. So much
was his pleasure should be proclaimed. All offices° are open, and there is

---

262. apt . . . credit: likely and very creditable. **269. diet:** feed. **278–79. trash . . .
hunting:** hold back from outrunning the pack [Eds.]. **281. rank garb:** gross manner; i.e.,
by accusing him of being Desdemona's lover. **2. mere perdition:** absolute destruction.
3. put . . . triumph: celebrate. **6. offices:** the kitchen and buttery—i.e., free food and
drink for all.

full liberty of feasting from this present hour of five till the bell have told eleven. Heaven bless the isle of Cyprus and our noble General Othello! (*Exeunt.*)

SCENE III. A hall in the castle.

Enter OTHELLO, DESDEMONA, CASSIO, *and* ATTENDANTS.

OTHELLO. Good Michael, look you to the guard tonight.
Let's teach ourselves that honorable stop,
Not to outsport discretion.°
CASSIO. Iago hath direction what to do,
But notwithstanding with my personal eye   5
Will I look to 't.
OTHELLO.   Iago is most honest.
Michael, good night. Tomorrow with your earliest
Let me have speech with you. (*To* DESDEMONA) Come, my dear love,
The purchase made, the fruits are to ensue—
That profit's yet to come 'tween me and you.   10
Good night.

(*Exeunt all but* CASSIO. *Enter* IAGO.)

CASSIO. Welcome, Iago. We must to the watch.
IAGO. Not this hour, Lieutenant, 'tis not yet ten o' the clock. Our General cast° us thus early for the love of his Desdemona, who let us not therefore blame. He hath not yet made wanton the night with her, and she is sport for Jove.   16
CASSIO. She's a most exquisite lady.
IAGO. And, I'll warrant her, full of game.
CASSIO. Indeed she's a most fresh and delicate creature.
IAGO. What an eye she has! Methinks it sounds a parley to provocation. 20
CASSIO. An inviting eye, and yet methinks right modest.
IAGO. And when she speaks, is it not an alarum to love?
CASSIO. She is indeed perfection.
IAGO. Well, happiness to their sheets! Come, Lieutenant, I have a stoup of wine, and here without are a brace of Cyprus gallants that would fain have a measure to the health of black Othello.   26
CASSIO. Not tonight, good Iago. I have very poor and unhappy brains for drinking. I could well wish courtesy would invent some other custom of entertainment.   29
IAGO. Oh, they are our friends. But one cup—I'll drink for you.
CASSIO. I have drunk but one cup tonight, and that was craftily qualified° too, and behold what innovation it makes here. I am unfortunate in the infirmity, and dare not task my weakness with any more.

---

3. outsport discretion: let the fun go too far.   **14. cast:** dismissed.   **31. qualified:** diluted [Eds.].

IAGO. What, man! 'Tis a night of revels. The gallants desire it.
CASSIO. Where are they? 35
IAGO. Here at the door. I pray you call them in.
CASSIO. I'll do 't, but it dislikes me. (*Exit.*)
IAGO. If I can fasten but one cup upon him,
  With that which he hath drunk tonight already,
  He'll be as full of quarrel and offense 40
  As my young mistress' dog. Now my sick fool Roderigo,
  Whom love hath turned almost the wrong side out,
  To Desdemona hath tonight caroused
  Potations pottle-deep, and he's to watch.
  Three lads of Cyprus, noble swelling spirits 45
  That hold their honors in a wary distance,°
  The very elements° of this warlike isle,
  Have I tonight flustered with flowing cups,
  And they watch too. Now, 'mongst this flock of drunkards,
  Am I to put our Cassio in some action 50
  That may offend the isle. But here they come.
  If consequence do but approve my dream,
  My boat sails freely, both with wind and stream.

  (*Re-enter* CASSIO, *with him* MONTANO *and* GENTLEMEN, SERVANTS *following with wine.*)

CASSIO. 'Fore God, they have given me a rouse already.
MONTANO. Good faith, a little one—not past a pint, as I am a soldier. 55
IAGO. Some wine, ho! (*Sings*)
        "And let me the cannikin clink, clink,
        And let me the cannikin clink.
          A soldier's a man,
          A life's but a span.° 60
        Why, then let a soldier drink."
  Some wine, boys!
CASSIO. 'Fore God, an excellent song.
IAGO. I learned it in England, where indeed they are most potent in potting.°
  Your Dane, your German, and your swag-bellied Hollander— Drink,
  ho!—are nothing to your English. 66
CASSIO. Is your Englishman so expert in his drinking?
IAGO. Why, he drinks you with facility your Dane dead drunk, he sweats not
  to overthrow your Almain,° he gives your Hollander a vomit° ere the
  next pottle can be filled. 70

---

46. hold . . . distance: are very sensitive about their honor [Eds.]. 47. very elements:
typical specimens. 60. span: lit., the measure between the thumb and little finger of the
outstretched hand; about 9 inches. 64. potting: drinking. 69. Almain: German. gives
. . . vomit: drinks as much as will make a Dutchman throw up.

CASSIO. To the health of our General!

MONTANO. I am for it, Lieutenant, and I'll do you justice.

IAGO. O sweet England! (*Sings*)

> "King Stephen was a worthy peer,
>> His breeches cost him but a crown.   75
> He held them sixpence all too dear,
>> With that he called the tailor lown.°

> "He was a wight of high renown,
>> And thou art but of low degree.
> 'Tis pride that pulls the country down.   80
>> Then take thine auld cloak about thee."

Some wine, ho!

CASSIO. Why, this is a more exquisite song than the other.

IAGO. Will you hear 't again?

CASSIO. No, for I hold him to be unworthy of his place that does those things. Well, God's above all, and there be souls must be saved and there be souls must not be saved.   87

IAGO. It's true, good Lieutenant.

CASSIO. For mine own part—no offense to the General, nor any man of quality—I hope to be saved.

IAGO. And so do I too, Lieutenant.   91

CASSIO. Aye, but, by your leave, not before me. The Lieutenant is to be saved before the Ancient. Let's have no more of this, let's to our affairs. God forgive us our sins! Gentlemen, let's look to our business. Do not think, gentlemen, I am drunk. This is my Ancient, this is my right hand and this is my left. I am not drunk now, I can stand well enough and speak well enough.   97

ALL. Excellent well.

CASSIO. Why, very well, then, you must not think then that I am drunk. (*Exit.*)

MONTANO. To the platform, masters. Come, let's set the watch.

IAGO. You see this fellow that is gone before.
He is a soldier fit to stand by Caesar
And give direction. And do but see his vice.
'Tis to his virtue a just equinox,
The one as long as the other. 'Tis pity of him.   105
I fear the trust Othello puts him in
On some odd time of his infirmity
Will shake this island.

MONTANO.   But is he often thus?

IAGO. 'Tis evermore the prologue to his sleep.

---

77. **lown:** lout.

He'll watch the horologe a double set,°   110
If drink rock not his cradle.
MONTANO.   It were well
The General were put in mind of it.
Perhaps he sees it not, or his good nature
Prizes the virtue that appears in Cassio
And looks not on his evils. Is not this true?   115

(*Enter* RODERIGO.)

IAGO (*aside to him*). How now, Roderigo! I pray you, after the Lieutenant. Go.

(*Exit* RODERIGO.)

MONTANO. And 'tis great pity that the noble Moor
Should hazard such a place as his own second
With one of an ingraft infirmity.   120
It were an honest action to say
So to the Moor.
IAGO.   Not I, for this fair island.
I do love Cassio well, and would do much
To cure him of this evil—But, hark! What noise?   124

(*A cry within:* "Help! Help!" *Re-enter* CASSIO, *driving in* RODERIGO.)

CASSIO. 'Zounds! You rogue! You rascal!
MONTANO.   What's the matter, Lieutenant?
CASSIO. A knave teach me my duty! But I'll beat the knave into a wicker bottle.
RODERIGO. Beat me!
CASSIO. Dost thou prate, rogue? (*Striking* RODERIGO.)
MONTANO. Nay, good Lieutenant (*staying him*),
                  I pray you sir, hold your hand.   131
CASSIO. Let me go, sir, or I'll knock you o'er the mazzard.°
MONTANO. Come, come, you're drunk.
CASSIO. Drunk!

(*They fight.*)

IAGO (*aside to* RODERIGO). Away, I say. Go out and cry a mutiny.   135

(*Exit* RODERIGO.)

Nay, good Lieutenant! God's will, gentlemen!
Help, ho!—Lieutenant—sir—Montano—sir—
Help, masters!—Here's a goodly watch indeed!

(*A bell rings.*)

---

110. **watch . . . set:** stay awake the clock twice round.   132. **mazzard:** head.

Who's that that rings the bell?—Diablo, ho!
The town will rise. God's will, Lieutenant, hold—   140
You will be shamed forever.

(*Re-enter* OTHELLO *and* ATTENDANTS.)

OTHELLO.   What is the matter here?
MONTANO. 'Zounds, I bleed still, I am hurt to the death. (*Faints*)
OTHELLO. Hold, for your lives!
IAGO. Hold, ho! Lieutenant—sir—Montano—gentlemen—
   Have you forgot all sense of place and duty?   145
   Hold! The General speaks to you. Hold, hold, for shame!
OTHELLO. Why, how now, ho! From whence ariseth this?
   Are we turned Turks, and to ourselves do that
   Which Heaven hath forbid the Ottomites?
   For Christian shame, put by this barbarous brawl.   150
   He that stirs next to carve for his own rage
   Holds his soul light, he dies upon his motion.
   Silence that dreadful bell. It frights the isle
   From her propriety. What is the matter, masters?
   Honest Iago, that look'st dead with grieving,   155
   Speak, who began this? On thy love, I charge thee.
IAGO. I do not know. Friends all but now, even now,
   In quarter and in terms like bride and groom
   Devesting them for bed. And then, but now,
   As if some planet had unwitted men,   160
   Swords out, and tilting one at other's breast
   In opposition bloody. I cannot speak
   Any beginning to this peevish odds,
   And would in action glorious I had lost
   Those legs that brought me to a part of it!   165
OTHELLO. How comes it, Michael, you are thus forgot?°
CASSIO. I pray you, pardon me, I cannot speak.
OTHELLO. Worthy Montano, you were wont be civil.
   The gravity and stillness of your youth
   The world hath noted, and your name is great   170
   In mouths of wisest censure.° What's the matter
   That you unlace your reputation thus
   And spend your rich opinion° for the name
   Of a night brawler? Give me answer to it.
MONTANO. Worthy Othello, I am hurt to danger.   175
   Your officer, Iago, can inform you—

---

166. are . . . forgot: have so forgotten yourself. **171. censure:** judgment. **173. opinion:**
reputation [Eds.].

While I spare speech, which something now offends me—
Of all that I do know. Nor know I aught
By me that's said or done amiss this night,
Unless self-charity° be sometimes a vice,   180
And to defend ourselves it be a sin
When violence assails us.

OTHELLO.   Now, by Heaven,
My blood begins my safer guides to rule,
And passion, having my best judgment collied,°
Assays to lead the way. If I once stir,   185
Or do but lift this arm, the best of you
Shall sink in my rebuke. Give me to know
How this foul rout began, who set it on,
And he that is approved° in this offense,
Though he had twinned with me, both at a birth,   190
Shall lose me. What! In a town of war,
Yet wild, the people's hearts brimful of fear,
To manage private and domestic quarrel,
In night, and on the court and guard of safety!
'Tis monstrous. Iago, who began 't?   195

MONTANO.   If partially affined, or leagued in office,
Thou dost deliver more or less than truth,
Thou art no soldier.

IAGO.   Touch me not so near.
I had rather have this tongue cut from my mouth
Than it should do offense to Michael Cassio.   200
Yet I persuade myself to speak the truth
Shall nothing wrong him. Thus it is, General.
Montano and myself being in speech,
There comes a fellow crying out for help,
And Cassio following him with determined sword   205
To execute upon him. Sir, this gentleman
Steps in to Cassio and entreats his pause.
Myself the crying fellow did pursue
Lest by his clamor—as it so fell out—
The town might fall in fright. He, swift of foot,   210
Outran my purpose, and I returned the rather
For that I heard the clink and fall of swords,
And Cassio high in oath, which till tonight
I ne'er might say before. When I came back—
For this was brief—I found them close together,   215
At blow and thrust, even as again they were
When you yourself did part them.

---

180. self-charity: love for oneself.   **184. collied:** darkened.   **189. approved:** proved guilty.

More of this matter cannot I report.
But men are men, the best sometimes forget.
Though Cassio did some little wrong to him,   220
As men in rage strike those that wish them best,
Yet surely Cassio, I believe, received
From him that fled some strange indignity,
Which patience could not pass.
OTHELLO.   I know, Iago,
Thy honesty and love doth mince this matter,   225
Making it light to Cassio. Cassio, I love thee,
But never more be officer of mine.

(*Re-enter* DESDEMONA, *attended.*)

Look, if my gentle love be not raised up!
I'll make thee an example.
DESDEMONA.   What's the matter?
OTHELLO. All's well now, sweeting. Come away to bed.   230
(*To* MONTANO, *who is led off*)
Sir, for your hurts, myself will be your surgeon.
Lead him off.
Iago, look with care about the town,
And silence those whom this vile brawl distracted.
Come, Desdemona. 'Tis the soldiers' life   235
To have their balmy slumbers waked with strife.

(*Exeunt all but* IAGO *and* CASSIO.)

IAGO. What, are you hurt, Lieutenant?
CASSIO. Aye, past all surgery.
IAGO. Marry, Heaven forbid!
CASSIO. Reputation, reputation, reputation! Oh, I have lost my reputation! I
have lost the immortal part of myself, and what remains is bestial. My
reputation, Iago, my reputation!   242
IAGO. As I am an honest man, I thought you had received some bodily
wound. There is more sense in that than in reputation. Reputation is an
idle and most false imposition, oft got without merit and lost without
deserving. You have lost no reputation at all unless you repute yourself
such a loser. What, man! There are ways to recover the General again.
You are but now cast in his mood,° a punishment more in policy° than in
malice—even so as one would beat his offenseless dog to affright an
imperious lion.° Sue to him again and he's yours.   250
CASSIO. I will rather sue to be despised than to deceive so good a commander

---

248. cast . . . mood: dismissed because he is in a bad mood. **in policy:** i.e., because he
must appear to be angry before the Cypriots. **249–50. even . . . lion:** a proverb meaning
that when the lion sees the dog beaten, he will know what is coming to him.

with so slight, so drunken, and so indiscreet an officer. Drunk? And speak parrot?° And squabble? Swagger? Swear? And discourse fustian° with one's own shadow? O thou invisible spirit of wine, if thou hast no name to be known by, let us call thee devil! 255

IAGO. What was he that you followed with your sword? What had he done to you?

CASSIO. I know not.

IAGO. Is 't possible?

CASSIO. I remember a mass of things, but nothing distinctly—a quarrel, but nothing wherefore. Oh God, that men should put an enemy in their mouths to steal away their brains! That we should, with joy, pleasance, revel, and applause, transform ourselves into beasts! 263

IAGO. Why, but you are now well enough. How came you thus recovered?

CASSIO. It hath pleased the devil drunkenness to give place to the devil wrath. One unperfectness shows me another, to make me frankly despise myself. 267

IAGO. Come, you are too severe a moraler. As the time, the place, and the condition of this country stands, I could heartily wish this had not be-fallen. But since it is as it is, mend it for your own good. 270

CASSIO. I will ask him for my place again, he shall tell me I am a drunkard! Had I as many mouths as Hydra, such an answer would stop them all. To be now a sensible man, by and by a fool, and presently a beast! Oh, strange! Every inordinate cup is unblest, and the ingredient is a devil.

IAGO. Come, come, good wine is a good familiar creature, if it be well used. Exclaim no more against it. And, good Lieutenant, I think you think I love you. 277

CASSIO. I have well approved it, sir. I drunk!

IAGO. You or any man living may be drunk at some time, man. I'll tell you what you shall do. Our General's wife is now the General. I may say so in this respect, for that he hath devoted and given up himself to the contem-plation, mark, and denotement of her parts and graces. Confess yourself freely to her, importune her help to put you in your place again. She is of so free, so kind, so apt, so blessed a disposition, she holds it a vice in her goodness not to do more than she is requested. This broken joint between you and her husband entreat her to splinter° and, my fortunes against any lay° worth naming, this crack of your love shall grow stronger than it was before. 288

CASSIO. You advise me well.

IAGO. I protest, in the sincerity of love and honest kindness.

CASSIO. I think it freely, and betimes in the morning I will beseech the virtuous Desdemona to undertake for me. I am desperate of my fortunes if they check me here. 293

IAGO. You are in the right. Good night, Lieutenant, I must to the watch.

253. speak parrot: babble. **fustian:** nonsense. **286. splinter:** put in splints. **287. lay:** bet.

CASSIO. Good night, honest Iago. (*Exit.*)

IAGO. And what's he then that says I play the villain?   296
When this advice is free I give and honest,
Probal° to thinking, and indeed the course
To win the Moor again? For 'tis most easy
The inclining Desdemona to subdue   300
In any honest suit. She's framed as fruitful
As the free elements. And then for her
To win the Moor, were 't to renounce his baptism,
All seals and symbols of redeemèd sin,
His soul is so enfettered to her love   305
That she may make, unmake, do what she list,
Even as her appetite shall play the god
With his weak function.° How am I then a villain
To counsel Cassio to this parallel course,
Directly to his good? Divinity of Hell!   310
When devils will the blackest sins put on,
They do suggest at first with heavenly shows,
As I do now. For whiles this honest fool
Plies Desdemona to repair his fortunes,
And she for him pleads strongly to the Moor,   315
I'll pour this pestilence into his ear,
That she repeals° him for her body's lust
And by how much she strives to do him good,
She shall undo her credit with the Moor.
So will I turn her virtue into pitch,   320
And out of her own goodness make the net
That shall enmesh them all.

(*Enter* RODERIGO.)

                              How now, Roderigo!   322

RODERIGO. I do follow here in the chase, not like a hound that hunts but one
that fills up the cry. My money is almost spent, I have been tonight
exceedingly well cudgeled, and I think the issue will be I shall have so
much experience for my pains and so, with no money at all and a little
more wit, return again to Venice.   327

IAGO. How poor are they that have not patience!
What wound did ever heal but by degrees?
Thou know'st we work by wit and not by witchcraft,   330
And wit depends on dilatory Time.
Does 't not go well? Cassio hath beaten thee,
And thou by that small hurt hast cashiered Cassio.
Though other things grow fair against the sun,

---

298. Probal: probable.   **308. function:** mental faculties [Eds.].   **317. repeals:** calls back.

Yet fruits that blossom first will first be ripe. 335
Content thyself awhile. By the mass, 'tis morning.
Pleasure and action make the hours seem short.
Retire thee, go where thou art billeted.
Away, I say. Thou shalt know more hereafter.
Nay, get thee gone.

(*Exit* RODERIGO.)

            Two things are to be done: 340
My wife must move for Cassio to her mistress,
I'll set her on,
Myself the while to draw the Moor apart
And bring him jump° when he may Cassio find
Soliciting his wife. Aye, that's the way. 345
Dull not device by coldness and delay. (*Exit.*)

ACT III

SCENE I. Before the castle.

Enter CASSIO *and some* MUSICIANS.

CASSIO. Masters, play here, I will content your pains°—
  Something that's brief, and bid "Good morrow, General."°

(*Music. Enter* CLOWN.)

CLOWN. Why, masters, have your instruments been in Naples, that
  they speak i' the nose thus?
FIRST MUSICIAN. How, sir, how? 5
CLOWN. Are these, I pray you, wind instruments?
FIRST MUSICIAN. Aye, marry are they, sir.
CLOWN. Oh, thereby hangs a tail.
FIRST MUSICIAN. Whereby hangs a tale, sir?
CLOWN. Marry, sir, by many a wind instrument that I know. But, masters,
  here's money for you. And the General so likes your music that he desires
  you, for love's sake, to make no more noise with it. 12
FIRST MUSICIAN. Well, sir, we will not.
CLOWN. If you have any music that may not be heard, to 't again. But,
  as they say, to hear music the General does not greatly care. 15
FIRST MUSICIAN. We have none such, sir.

---

344. **jump:** at the moment. **1. content . . . pains:** reward your labor. **2. bid . . . General:** It was a common custom to play or sing a song beneath the bedroom window of a distinguished guest or of a newly wedded couple on the morning after their wedding night.

CLOWN. Then put up your pipes in your bag, for I'll away. Go, vanish into air, away!

(*Exeunt* MUSICIANS.)

CASSIO. Dost thou hear, my honest friend?
CLOWN. No, I hear not your honest friend, I hear you.   20
CASSIO. Prithee keep up thy quillets.° There's a poor piece of gold for thee. If the gentlewoman that attends the General's wife be stirring, tell her there's one Cassio entreats her a little favor of speech. Wilt thou do this?
CLOWN. She is stirring, sir. If she will stir hither, I shall seem to notify unto her.   25
CASSIO. Do, good my friend.

(*Exit* CLOWN. *Enter* IAGO.)

In happy time, Iago.
IAGO. You have not been abed, then?
CASSIO. Why, no, the day had broke
Before we parted. I have made bold, Iago,
To send in to your wife. My suit to her   30
Is that she will to virtuous Desdemona
Procure me some access.
IAGO.   I'll send her to you presently,
And I'll devise a mean to draw the Moor
Out of the way, that your convérse and business
May be more free.   35
CASSIO. I humbly thank you for 't.

(*Exit* IAGO.)

I never knew
A Florentine more kind and honest.

(*Enter* EMILIA.)

EMILIA. Good morrow, good Lieutenant. I am sorry
For your displeasure, but all will sure be well.
The General and his wife are talking of it,   40
And she speaks for you stoutly. The Moor replies
That he you hurt is of great fame in Cyprus
And great affinity,° and that in wholesome wisdom
He might not but refuse you. But he protests he loves you,
And needs no other suitor but his likings   45
To take the safest occasion by the front
To bring you in again.

---

21. keep . . . quillets: put away your wisecracks. **43. affinity:** kindred.

CASSIO.   Yet I beseech you
If you think fit, or that it may be done,
Give me advantage of some brief discourse
With Desdemona alone.
EMILIA.   Pray you, come in.   50
I will bestow you where you shall have time
To speak your bosom freely.
CASSIO.   I am much bound to you.

(*Exeunt.*)

SCENE II. *A room in the castle.*

Enter OTHELLO, IAGO, *and* GENTLEMEN.

OTHELLO.   These letters give, Iago, to the pilot,
And by him do my duties to the Senate.
That done, I will be walking on the works.°
Repair there to me.
IAGO.   Well, my good lord, I'll do 't.
OTHELLO.   This fortification, gentlemen, shall we see 't?   5
GENTLEMEN. We'll wait upon your lordship.

(*Exeunt.*)

SCENE III. *The garden of the castle.*

Enter DESDEMONA, CASSIO, *and* EMILIA.

DESDEMONA.   Be thou assured, good Cassio, I will do
All my abilities in thy behalf.
EMILIA.   Good madam, do. I warrant it grieves my husband
As if the case were his.
DESDEMONA.   Oh, that's an honest fellow. Do not doubt, Cassio,   5
But I will have my lord and you again
As friendly as you were.
CASSIO.   Bounteous madam,
Whatever shall become of Michael Cassio,
He's never anything but your true servant.
DESDEMONA.   I know 't. I thank you. You do love my lord.   10
You have known him long, and be you well assured
He shall in strangeness stand no farther off
Than in a politic distance.°

---

3. works: fortifications.   **12–13. He . . . distance:** i.e., his apparent coldness to you shall
only be so much as his official position demands for reasons of policy.

CASSIO.   Aye, but lady,
   That policy may either last so long,
   Or feed upon such nice and waterish diet,   15
   Or breed itself so out of circumstance,
   That, I being absent and my place supplied,
   My General will forget my love and service.
DESDEMONA.   Do not doubt° that. Before Emilia here
   I give thee warrant of thy place. Assure thee,   20
   If I do vow a friendship, I'll perform it
   To the last article. My lord shall never rest.
   I'll watch him tame and talk him out of patience,
   His bed shall seem a school, his board a shrift.°
   I'll intermingle every thing he does   25
   With Cassio's suit. Therefore be merry, Cassio,
   For thy solicitor shall rather die
   Than give thy cause away.

   (*Enter* OTHELLO *and* IAGO, *at a distance.*)

EMILIA.   Madam, here comes my lord.
CASSIO.   Madam, I'll take my leave.   30
DESDEMONA.   Nay, stay and hear me speak.
CASSIO.   Madam, not now. I am very ill at ease,
   Unfit for mine own purposes.
DESDEMONA.   Well, do your discretion.

   (*Exit* CASSIO.)

IAGO.   Ha! I like not that.   35
OTHELLO.   What dost thou say?
IAGO.   Nothing, my lord. Or if—I know not what.
OTHELLO.   Was not that Cassio parted from my wife?
IAGO.   Cassio, my lord! No, sure, I cannot think it,
   That he would steal away so guilty-like,   40
   Seeing you coming.
OTHELLO.   I do believe 'twas he.
DESDEMONA.   How now, my lord!
   I have been talking with a suitor here,
   A man that languishes in your displeasure.
OTHELLO.   Who is 't you mean?   45
DESDEMONA.   Why, your Lieutenant, Cassio. Good my lord,
   If I have any grace or power to move you,
   His present reconciliation take.°

---

19. doubt: fear.   **24. shrift:** place of confession [Eds.].   **48. His . . . take:** accept his immediate apology and forgive him.

For if he be not one that truly loves you,
That errs in ignorance and not in cunning,   50
I have no judgment in an honest face.
I prithee call him back.
OTHELLO.   Went he hence now?
DESDEMONA. Aye, sooth, so humbled
    That he hath left part of his grief with me,
    To suffer with him. Good love, call him back.   55
OTHELLO. Not now, sweet Desdemona, some other time.
DESDEMONA. But shall 't be shortly?
OTHELLO.   The sooner, sweet, for you.
DESDEMONA. Shall 't be tonight at supper?
OTHELLO.   No, not tonight.
DESDEMONA. Tomorrow dinner then?
OTHELLO.   I shall not dine at home.
    I meet the captains at the citadel.   60
DESDEMONA. Why, then tomorrow night or Tuesday morn,
    On Tuesday noon, or night, on Wednesday morn.
    I prithee name the time, but let it not
    Exceed three days. In faith, he's penitent,
    And yet his trespass, in our common reason—   65
    Save that, they say, the wars must make examples
    Out of their best—is not almost° a fault
    To incur a private check.° When shall he come?
    Tell me, Othello. I wonder in my soul
    What you would ask me that I should deny,   70
    Or stand so mammering° on. What! Michael Cassio,
    That came a-wooing with you, and so many a time
    When I have spoke of you dispraisingly
    Hath ta'en your part—to have so much to do
    To bring him in! Trust me, I could do much—   75
OTHELLO. Prithee, no more. Let him come when he will.
    I will deny thee nothing.
DESDEMONA.   Why, this is not a boon.
    'Tis as I should entreat you wear your gloves,
    Or feed on nourishing dishes, or keep you warm,
    Or sue to you to do a peculiar profit   80
    To your own person. Nay, when I have a suit
    Wherein I mean to touch your love indeed,
    It shall be full of poise and difficult weight,
    And fearful to be granted.
OTHELLO.   I will deny thee nothing.
    Whereon I do beseech thee grant me this,   85

---

67. not almost: hardly. **68. check:** rebuke. **71. mammering:** hesitating.

To leave me but a little to myself.

DESDEMONA.　Shall I deny you? No. Farewell, my lord.

OTHELLO.　Farewell, my Desdemona. I'll come to thee straight.

DESDEMONA.　Emilia, come. Be as your fancies teach you.
　　Whate'er you be, I am obedient. 90

(*Exeunt* DESDEMONA *and* EMILIA.)

OTHELLO.　Excellent wretch! Perdition catch my soul
　　But I do love thee! And when I love thee not,
　　Chaos is come again.

IAGO.　My noble lord—

OTHELLO.　　　　　　What dost thou say, Iago?

IAGO.　Did Michael Cassio, when you wooed my lady, 95
　　Know of your love?

OTHELLO.　He did, from first to last. Why dost thou ask?

IAGO.　But for a satisfaction of my thought,
　　No further harm.

OTHELLO.　　　　　Why of thy thought, Iago?

IAGO.　I did not think he had been acquainted with her. 100

OTHELLO.　Oh yes, and went between us very oft.

IAGO.　Indeed!

OTHELLO.　Indeed! Aye, indeed. Discern'st thou aught in that?
　　Is he not honest?

IAGO.　　　　　Honest, my lord!

OTHELLO.　　　　　　　　　Honest! Aye, honest.

IAGO.　My lord, for aught I know.

OTHELLO.　　　　　　　What dost thou think? 105

IAGO.　Think, my lord!

OTHELLO.　Think, my lord! By Heaven, he echoes me
　　As if there were some monster in his thought
　　Too hideous to be shown. Thou dost mean something.
　　I heard thee say even now thou likedst not that 110
　　When Cassio left my wife. What didst not like?
　　And when I told thee he was of my counsel
　　In my whole course of wooing, thou criedst "Indeed!"
　　And didst contract and purse thy brow together
　　As if thou then hadst shut up in thy brain 115
　　Some horrible conceit. If thou dost love me,
　　Show me thy thought.

IAGO.　My lord, you know I love you.

OTHELLO.　　　　　　　　I think thou dost,
　　And for I know thou'rt full of love and honesty
　　And weigh'st thy words before thou givest them breath, 120
　　Therefore these stops of thine fright me the more.
　　For such things in a false disloyal knave

Are tricks of custom, but in a man that's just
They're close delations,° working from the heart,
That passion cannot rule.
IAGO.   For Michael Cassio,   125
    I dare be sworn I think that he is honest.
OTHELLO. I think so too.
IAGO.   Men should be what they seem,
    Or those that be not, would they might seem none!°
OTHELLO. Certain, men should be what they seem.
IAGO. Why, then I think Cassio's an honest man.   130
OTHELLO. Nay, yet there's more in this.
    I prithee speak to me as to thy thinkings,
    As thou dost ruminate, and give thy worst of thoughts
    The worst of words.
IAGO.   Good my lord, pardon me.
    Though I am bound to every act of duty,   135
    I am not bound to that all slaves are free to.
    Utter my thoughts? Why, say they are vile and false,
    As where's that palace whereinto foul things
    Sometimes intrude not? Who has a breast so pure
    But some uncleanly apprehensions   140
    Keep leets° and law days, and in session sit
    With meditations lawful?
OTHELLO. Thou dost conspire against thy friend, Iago,
    If thou but think'st him wronged and makest his ear
    A stranger to thy thoughts.
IAGO.   I do beseech you—   145
    Though I perchance am vicious in my guess,
    As, I confess, it is my nature's plague
    To spy into abuses, and oft my jealousy°
    Shapes faults that are not—that your wisdom yet,
    From one that so imperfectly conceits,°   150
    Would take no notice, nor build yourself a trouble
    Out of his scattering and unsure observance.°
    It were not for your quiet nor your good,
    Nor for my manhood, honesty, or wisdom,
    To let you know my thoughts.
OTHELLO.   What dost thou mean?   155
IAGO. Good name in man and woman, dear my lord,
    Is the immediate jewel of their souls.
    Who steals my purse steals trash—'tis something, nothing,

---

124. **close delations:** concealed accusations. **128. seem none:** i.e., not seem to be honest
men. **141. leets:** courts. **148. jealousy:** suspicion. **150. conceits:** conceives. **152. observance:** observation.

'Twas mine, 'tis his, and has been slave to thousands—
But he that filches from me my good name   160
Robs me of that which not enriches him
And makes me poor indeed.
OTHELLO. By Heaven, I'll know thy thoughts.
IAGO. You cannot, if my heart were in your hand,
Nor shall not, whilst 'tis in my custody.   165
OTHELLO. Ha!
IAGO.   Oh, beware, my lord, of jealousy.
It is the green-eyed monster which doth mock
The meat it feeds on. That cuckold lives in bliss
Who, certain of his fate, loves not his wronger.°
But, oh, what damnèd minutes tells he o'er   170
Who dotes, yet doubts, suspects, yet strongly loves!
OTHELLO. Oh misery!
IAGO. Poor and content is rich, and rich enough,
But riches fineless° is as poor as winter
To him that ever fears he shall be poor.   175
Good God, the souls of all my tribe defend
From jealousy!
OTHELLO.   Why, why is this?
Think'st thou I'd make a life of jealousy,
To follow still the changes of the moon
With fresh suspicions? No, to be once in doubt   180
Is once to be resolved.° Exchange me for a goat
When I shall turn the business of my soul
To such exsufflicate° and blown surmises,
Matching thy inference.° 'Tis not to make me jealous
To say my wife is fair, feeds well, loves company,   185
Is free of speech, sings, plays, and dances well.
Where virtue is, these are more virtuous.
Nor from mine own weak merits will I draw
The smallest fear or doubt of her revolt,
For she had eyes, and chose me. No, Iago,   190
I'll see before I doubt, when I doubt, prove,
And on the proof, there is no more but this—
Away at once with love or jealousy!
IAGO. I am glad of it, for now I shall have reason
To show the love and duty that I bear you   195

168–69. That . . . wronger: i.e., the cuckold who hates his wife and knows her falseness is not tormented by suspicious jealousy. **174. fineless:** limitless. **180–81. to . . . resolved:** whenever I find myself in doubt I at once seek out the truth. **182–84. When . . . inference:** when I shall allow that which concerns me most dearly to be influenced by such trifling suggestions as yours. **exsufflicate:** blown up like a bubble.

With franker spirit. Therefore, as I am bound,
Receive it from me. I speak not yet of proof.
Look to your wife. Observe her well with Cassio.
Wear your eye thus, not jealous nor secure.°
I would not have your free and noble nature   200
Out of self-bounty° be abused. Look to 't.
I know our country disposition well.
In Venice° they do let Heaven see the pranks
They dare not show their husbands. Their best conscience
Is not to leave 't undone, but keep 't unknown.   205

OTHELLO.   Dost thou say so?

IAGO.   She did deceive her father, marrying you,
And when she seemed to shake and fear your looks,
She loved them most.

OTHELLO.   And so she did.

IAGO.   Why, go to, then.
She that so young could give out such a seeming   210
To seel° her father's eyes up close as oak—
He thought 'twas witchcraft—but I am much to blame.
I humbly do beseech you of your pardon
For too much loving you.

OTHELLO.   I am bound to thee forever.

IAGO.   I see this hath a little dashed your spirits.   215

OTHELLO.   Not a jot, not a jot.

IAGO.   I' faith, I fear it has.
I hope you will consider what is spoke
Comes from my love. But I do see you're moved.
I am to pray you not to strain my speech
To grosser issues nor to larger reach   220
Than to suspicion.

OTHELLO.   I will not.

IAGO.   Should you do so, my lord,
My speech should fall into such vile success
As my thoughts aim not at. Cassio's my worthy friend.—
My lord, I see you're moved.

OTHELLO.   No, not much moved.   225
I do not think but Desdemona's honest.°

IAGO.   Long live she so! And long live you to think so!

OTHELLO.   And yet, how nature erring from itself—

---

199. secure: overconfident   **201. self-bounty:** natural goodness.   **203. In Venice:** Venice was notorious for its loose women; the Venetian courtesans were among the sights of Europe and were much commented upon by travelers.   **211. seel:** blind.   **226. honest:** When applied to Desdemona, "honest" means "chaste," but applied to Iago it has the modern meaning of "open and sincere."

IAGO. Aye, there's the point. As—to be bold with you—
　　Not to affect° many proposèd matches　　　　　　　　　230
　　Of her own clime, complexion, and degree,
　　Whereto we see in all things nature tends°—
　　Foh! One may smell in such a will most rank,°
　　Foul disproportion, thoughts unnatural.
　　But pardon me. I do not in position　　　　　　　　　235
　　Distinctly speak of her, though I may fear
　　Her will, recoiling to her better judgment,
　　May fall to match° you with her country forms,°
　　And happily° repent.
OTHELLO.　　　　　　　　Farewell, farewell.
　　If more thou dost perceive, let me know more.　　　　　240
　　Set on thy wife to observe. Leave me, Iago.
IAGO (going). My lord, I take my leave.
OTHELLO. Why did I marry? This honest creature doubtless
　　Sees and knows more, much more, than he unfolds.
IAGO (returning). My lord, I would I might entreat your honor　245
　　To scan this thing no further. Leave it to time.
　　Though it be fit that Cassio have his place,
　　For sure he fills it up with great ability,
　　Yet if you please to hold him off awhile,
　　You shall by that perceive him and his means.　　　　250
　　Note if your lady strain his entertainment°
　　With any strong or vehement importunity—
　　Much will be seen in that. In the meantime,
　　Let me be thought too busy in my fears—
　　As worthy cause I have to fear I am—　　　　　　　　255
　　And hold her free, I do beseech your Honor.
OTHELLO. Fear not my government.°
IAGO. I once more take my leave. (Exit.)
OTHELLO. This fellow's of exceeding honesty,
　　And knows all qualities, with a learned spirit,　　　　260
　　Of human dealings. If I do prove her haggard,°
　　Though that her jesses were my dear heartstrings,
　　I'd whistle her off and let her down the wind
　　To prey at fortune.° Haply, for° I am black

---

230. affect: be inclined to. **232. in . . . tends:** i.e., a woman naturally marries a man of her own country, color, and rank. **233. will . . . rank:** desire most lustful. **238. match:** compare. **country forms:** the appearance of her countrymen; i.e., white men. **239. happily:** haply, by chance. **251. strain . . . entertainment:** urge you to receive him. **257. government:** self-control. **261–64. If . . . fortune:** Othello keeps up the imagery of falconry throughout. He means: If I find that she is wild, I'll whistle her off the game and let her go where she will, for she's not worth keeping. **haggard:** a wild hawk. **jesses:** the straps attached to a hawk's legs. **264. Haply, for:** Perhaps, because [Eds.].

And have not those soft parts of conversation 265
That chamberers° have, or for I am declined
Into the vale of years—yet that's not much—
She's gone, I am abused, and my relief
Must be to loathe her. Oh, curse of marriage,
That we can call these delicate creatures ours, 270
And not their appetites! I had rather be a toad
And live upon the vapor of a dungeon
Than keep a corner in the thing I love
For others' uses. Yet, 'tis the plague of great ones,
Prerogatived are they less than the base. 275
'Tis destiny unshunnable, like death.
Even then this forkèd plague° is fated to us
When we do quicken.° Desdemona comes.

(*Re-enter* DESDEMONA *and* EMILIA.)

If she be false, oh, then Heaven mocks itself!
I'll not believe 't.
DESDEMONA.   How now, my dear Othello! 280
Your dinner, and the generous° islanders
By you invited, do attend your presence.
OTHELLO. I am to blame.
DESDEMONA.   Why do you speak so faintly?
Are you not well?
OTHELLO. I have a pain upon my forehead here. 285
DESDEMONA. Faith, that's with watching,° 'twill away again.
Let me but bind it hard, within this hour
It will be well.
OTHELLO.   Your napkin° is too little,

(*He puts the handkerchief from him, and she drops it.*)

Let it alone. Come, I'll go in with you.
DESDEMONA. I am very sorry that you are not well. 290

(*Exeunt* OTHELLO *and* DESDEMONA.)

EMILIA. I am glad I have found this napkin.
This was her first remembrance from the Moor.
My wayward° husband hath a hundred times
Wooed me to steal it, but she so loves the token,
For he conjured° her she should ever keep it, 295
That she reserves it evermore about her

---

266. **chamberers:** playboys. 277. **forkèd plague:** i.e., to be a cuckold. 278. **quicken:** stir in our mother's womb. 281. **generous:** noble. 286. **watching:** lack of sleep. 288. **napkin:** handkerchief. 293. **wayward:** unaccountable. 295. **conjured:** begged with an oath.

To kiss and talk to. I'll have the work ta'en out,°
And give 't Iago. What he will do with it
Heaven knows, not I.
I nothing know, but for his fantasy.°   300

(*Re-enter* IAGO.)

IAGO. How now! What do you here alone?
EMILIA. Do not you chide, I have a thing for you.
IAGO. A thing for me? It is a common thing—
EMILIA. Ha!
IAGO. To have a foolish wife.   305
EMILIA. Oh, is that all? What will you give me now
  For that same handkerchief?
IAGO.   What handkerchief?
EMILIA. What handkerchief!
  Why, that the Moor first gave to Desdemona,
  That which so often you did bid me steal.   310
IAGO. Hast stol'n it from her?
EMILIA. No, faith, she let it drop by negligence,
  And, to the advantage, I being here took 't up.
  Look, here it is.
IAGO. A good wench. Give it me.
EMILIA. What will you do with 't, that you have been so earnest   315
  To have me filch it?
IAGO (*snatching it*).   Why, what's that to you?
EMILIA. If 't be not for some purpose of import,
  Give 't me again. Poor lady, she'll run mad
  When she shall lack it.   320
IAGO. Be not acknown on 't,° I have use for it.
  Go, leave me.

(*Exit* EMILIA.)

I will in Cassio's lodging lose this napkin,
And let him find it. Trifles light as air
Are to the jealous confirmations strong   325
As proofs of Holy Writ. This may do something.
The Moor already changes with my poison.
Dangerous conceits° are in their natures poisons,
Which at the first are scarce found to distaste,
But, with a little, act upon the blood,   330
Burn like the mines of sulphur. I did say so.°

---

297. work . . . out: pattern copied. **300. fantasy:** whim. **321. Be . . .'t:** know nothing about it. **328. conceits:** ideas [Eds.]. **331. I . . . so:** As Iago says this, Othello is seen approaching, with all the signs of his agitation outwardly visible.

Look where he comes!

(*Re-enter* OTHELLO.)

Not poppy,° nor mandragora,°

Nor all the drowsy syrups of the world,
Shall ever medicine thee to that sweet sleep
Which thou owedst° yesterday,

OTHELLO. Ha! Ha! False to me?   335
IAGO. Why, how now, General! No more of that.
OTHELLO. Avaunt! Be gone! Thou hast set me on the rack.
    I swear 'tis better to be much abused
    Than but to know 't a little.
IAGO.   How now, my lord!
OTHELLO. What sense had I of her stol'n hours of lust?   340
    I saw 't not, thought it not, it harmed not me.
    I slept the next night well, was free and merry.
    I found not Cassio's kisses on her lips.
    He that is robbed, not wanting° what is stol'n,
    Let him not know 't and he's not robbed at all.   345
IAGO. I am sorry to hear this.
OTHELLO. I had been happy if the general camp,
    Pioners° and all, had tasted her sweet body,
    So I had nothing known. Oh, now forever
    Farewell the tranquil mind! Farewell content!   350
    Farewell the plumèd troop and the big wars
    That make ambition virtue! Oh, farewell,
    Farewell the neighing steed and the shrill trump,
    The spirit-stirring drum, the ear-piercing fife,
    The royal banner, and all quality,   355
    Pride, pomp, and circumstance of glorious war!
    And, O you mortal engines,° whose rude throats
    The immortal Jove's dread clamors counterfeit,
    Farewell! Othello's occupation's gone!
IAGO. Is 't possible, my lord?   360
OTHELLO. Villain, be sure thou prove my love a whore,
    Be sure of it, give me the ocular proof.
    Or by the worth of man's eternal soul,
    Thou hadst been better have been born a dog
    Than answer my waked wrath!
IAGO.   Is 't come to this?   365
OTHELLO. Make me to see 't, or at the least so prove it

---

332. **poppy:** opium. **mandragora:** called also mandrake, a root used as a drug to bring sleep. **335. owedst:** owned. **344. wanting:** missing. **348. Pioners:** pioneers, the lowest type of soldier. **357. mortal engines:** deadly cannon.

That the probation° bear no hinge nor loop
To hang a doubt on, or woe upon thy life!

IAGO. My noble lord—

OTHELLO.   If thou dost slander her and torture me,   370
Never pray more, abandon all remorse.°
On horror's head horrors accumulate,
Do deeds to make Heaven weep, all earth amazed,
For nothing canst thou to damnation add
Greater than that.

IAGO.   Oh, grace! Oh, Heaven defend me!   375
Are you a man? Have you a soul or sense?
God be wi' you, take mine office. O wretched fool,
That livest to make thine honesty a vice!
O monstrous world! Take note, take note, O world,
To be direct and honest is not safe.   380
I thank you for this profit, and from hence
I'll love no friend, sith° love breeds such offense.

OTHELLO.   Nay, stay. Thou shouldst be honest.

IAGO.   I should be wise, for honesty's a fool,
And loses that it works for.

OTHELLO.   By the world,   385
I think my wife be honest, and think she is not.
I think that thou art just, and think thou art not.
I'll have some proof. Her name, that was as fresh
As Dian's° visage, is now begrimed and black
As mine own face. If there be cords, or knives,   390
Poison, or fire, or suffocating streams,
I'll not endure it. Would I were satisfied!

IAGO.   I see, sir, you are eaten up with passion.
I do repent me that I put it to you.
You would be satisfied?

OTHELLO.   Would! Nay, I will.   395

IAGO.   And may, but, how? How satisfied, my lord?
Would you, the supervisor,° grossly gape on?
Behold her topped?

OTHELLO.   Death and damnation! Oh!

IAGO.   It were a tedious difficulty, I think,
To bring them to that prospect. Damn them then,   400
If ever mortal eyes do see them bolster°
More than their own! What then? How then?
What shall I say? Where's satisfaction?
It is impossible you should see this,

---

367. probation: proof.   **371. remorse:** pity.   **382. sith:** since.   **389. Dian:** Diana, goddess
of chastity.   **397. supervisor:** looker-on.   **401. bolster:** sleep together.

Were they as prime° as goats, as hot as monkeys,   405
As salt° as wolves in pride,° and fools as gross
As ignorance made drunk. But yet I say
If imputation° and strong circumstances,
Which lead directly to the door of truth,
Will give you satisfaction, you may have 't.   410
OTHELLO.   Give me a living reason she's disloyal.
IAGO.   I do not like the office.
But sith I am entered in this cause so far,
Pricked to 't by foolish honesty and love,
I will go on. I lay with Cassio lately,   415
And being troubled with a raging tooth,
I could not sleep.
There are a kind of men so loose of soul
That in their sleeps will mutter their affairs.
One of this kind is Cassio.   420
In sleep I heard him say "Sweet Desdemona,
Let us be wary, let us hide our loves."
And then, sir, would he gripe° and wring my hand,
Cry "O sweet creature!" and then kiss me hard,
As if he plucked up kisses by the roots   425
That grew upon my lips. Then laid his leg
Over my thigh, and sighed and kissed, and then
Cried "Cursed fate that gave thee to the Moor!"
OTHELLO.   Oh, monstrous! Monstrous!
IAGO.   Nay, this was but his dream.
OTHELLO.   But this denoted a foregone conclusion.   430
'Tis a shrewd doubt,° though it be but a dream.
IAGO.   And this may help to thicken other proofs
That do demonstrate thinly.
OTHELLO.   I'll tear her all to pieces.
IAGO.   Nay, but be wise. Yet we see nothing done.
She may be honest yet. Tell me this: 435
Have you not sometimes seen a handkerchief
Spotted with strawberries in your wife's hand?
OTHELLO.   I gave her such a one, 'twas my first gift.
IAGO.   I know not that. But such a handkerchief—
I am sure it was your wife's—did I today   440
See Cassio wipe his beard with.
OTHELLO.   If it be that—
IAGO.   If it be that, or any that was hers,
It speaks against her with the other proofs.

---

405. prime: lustful.   **406. salt:** eager.   **pride:** in heat.   **408. imputation:** probability.
423. gripe: grip.   **431. shrewd doubt:** bitter suspicion.

OTHELLO. Oh, that the slave had forty thousand lives!
One is too poor, too weak, for my revenge.   445
Now do I see 'tis true. Look here, Iago,
All my fond love thus do I blow to Heaven—
'Tis gone.
Arise, black Vengeance, from thy hollow cell!
Yield up, O Love, thy crown and hearted throne   450
To tyrannous hate! Swell, bosom, with thy fraught,°
For 'tis of aspics'° tongues!
IAGO.   Yet be content.
OTHELLO. Oh, blood, blood, blood!
IAGO. Patience, I say. Your mind perhaps may change.
OTHELLO. Never, Iago. Like to the Pontic Sea,   455
Whose icy current and compulsive course
Ne'er feels retiring ebb but keeps due on
To the Propontic and the Hellespont;
Even so my bloody thoughts, with violent pace,
Shall ne'er look back, ne'er ebb to humble love,   460
Till that a capable° and wide revenge
Swallow them up. Now, by yond marble Heaven,
In the due reverence of a sacred vow (*Kneels.*)
I here engage my words.
IAGO.   Do not rise yet. (*Kneels.*)
Witness, you ever burning lights above,   465
You elements that clip° us round about,
Witness that here Iago doth give up
The execution of his wit,° hands, heart,
To wronged Othello's service! Let him command,
And to obey shall be in me remorse,°   470
What bloody business ever.

(*They rise.*)

OTHELLO.   I greet thy love,
Not with vain thanks, but with acceptance bounteous,
And will upon the instant put thee to 't.
Within these three days let me hear thee say
That Cassio's not alive.   475
IAGO. My friend is dead. 'Tis done at your request.
But let her live.
OTHELLO. Damn her, lewd minx! Oh, damn her!
Come, go with me apart. I will withdraw,
To furnish me with some swift means of death   480

---

451. **fraught:** freight.   452. **aspics':** asps'.   461. **capable:** comprehensive.   466. **clip:**
embrace.   468. **wit:** mind [Eds.].   470. **remorse:** solemn obligation.

For the fair devil. Now art thou my Lieutenant.
IAGO. I am your own forever.

(*Exeunt.*)

SCENE IV. *Before the castle.*

Enter DESDEMONA, EMILIA, *and* CLOWN.

DESDEMONA. Do you know, sirrah, where Lieutenant Cassio lies?
CLOWN. I dare not say he lies anywhere.
DESDEMONA. Why, man?
CLOWN. He's a soldier, and for one to say a soldier lies is stabbing.
DESDEMONA. Go to. Where lodges he?   5
CLOWN. To tell you where he lodges is to tell you where I lie.
DESDEMONA. Can anything be made of this?
CLOWN. I know not where he lodges, and for me to devise a lodging, and say
    he lies here or he lies there, were to lie in mine own throat.
DESDEMONA. Can you inquire him out and be edified by report?°   10
CLOWN. I will catechize the world for him; that is, make questions and by
    them answer.
DESDEMONA. Seek him, bid him come hither. Tell him I have moved my
    lord on his behalf and hope all will be well.
CLOWN. To do this is within the compass of man's wit, and therefore I will
    attempt the doing it. (*Exit.*)   16
DESDEMONA. Where should I lose that handkerchief, Emilia?
EMILIA. I know not, madam.
DESDEMONA. Believe me, I had rather have lost my purse
    Full of crusados. And, but my noble Moor   20
    Is true of mind and made of no such baseness
    As jealous creatures are, it were enough
    To put him to ill thinking.
EMILIA.   Is he not jealous?
DESDEMONA. Who, he? I think the sun where he was born
    Drew all such humors from him.
EMILIA.   Look where he comes.   25
DESDEMONA. I will not leave him now till Cassio
    Be called to him.

(*Enter* OTHELLO.)

                    How is 't with you, my lord?
OTHELLO. Well, my good lady. (*Aside*) Oh, hardness to dissemble!
    How do you, Desdemona?

___

10. edified . . . report: enlightened by the information. Desdemona speaks with mock
pomposity.

DESDEMONA.   Well, my good lord.
OTHELLO.   Give me your hand. This hand is moist,° my lady.   30
DESDEMONA.   It yet has felt no age nor known no sorrow.
OTHELLO.   This argues fruitfulness and liberal heart.
    Hot, hot, and moist—this hand of yours requires
    A sequester from liberty, fasting and prayer,
    Much castigation, exercise devout.   35
    For here's a young and sweating devil here,
    That commonly rebels. 'Tis a good hand,
    A frank one.
DESDEMONA.   You may indeed say so,
    For 'twas that hand that gave away my heart.
OTHELLO.   A liberal° hand. The hearts of old gave hands,   40
    But our new heraldry is hands, not hearts.°
DESDEMONA.   I cannot speak of this. Come now, your promise.
OTHELLO.   What promise, chuck?°
DESDEMONA.   I have sent to bid Cassio come speak with you.
OTHELLO.   I have a salt and sorry rheum offends me.   45
    Lend me thy handkerchief.
DESDEMONA.   Here, my lord.
OTHELLO.   That which I gave you.
DESDEMONA.   I have it not about me.
OTHELLO.   Not?
DESDEMONA.   No indeed, my lord.
OTHELLO.   That's a fault. That handkerchief
    Did an Egyptian to my mother give.   50
    She was a charmer, and could almost read
    The thoughts of people. She told her while she kept it
    'Twould make her amiable and subdue my father
    Entirely to her love, but if she lost it
    Or made a gift of it, my father's eye   55
    Should hold her loathèd and his spirits should hunt
    After new fancies. She dying gave it me,
    And bid me, when my fate would have me wive,
    To give it her. I did so. And take heed on 't,
    Make it a darling like your precious eye.   60
    To lose 't or give 't away were such perdition
    As nothing else could match.
DESDEMONA.   Is 't possible?

---

30. moist: a hot moist palm was believed to show desire.   **40. liberal:** overgenerous.
40–41. The . . . hearts: once love and deeds went together, but now it is all deeds (i.e.,
faithlessness) and no love.   **43. chuck:** a term of affection, but not the kind of word with
which a person of Othello's dignity would normally address his wife. He is beginning to
treat her with contemptuous familiarity.

OTHELLO. 'Tis true. There's magic in the web of it.
A sibyl that had numbered in the world
The sun to course two hundred compasses   65
In her prophetic fury sewed the work.
The worms were hallowed that did breed the silk,
And it was dyed in mummy which the skillful
Conserved° of maiden's hearts.
DESDEMONA.   Indeed! Is 't true?
OTHELLO. Most veritable, therefore look to 't well.   70
DESDEMONA. Then would to God that I had never seen 't.
OTHELLO. Ha! Wherefore?
DESDEMONA. Why do you speak so startlingly and rash?
OTHELLO. Is 't lost? Is 't gone? Speak, is it out o' the way?
DESDEMONA. Heaven bless us!   75
OTHELLO. Say you?
DESDEMONA. It is not lost, but what an if it were?
OTHELLO. How!
DESDEMONA. I say it is not lost.
OTHELLO.   Fetch 't, let me see it.
DESDEMONA. Why, so I can, sir, but I will not now.   80
This is a trick to put me from my suit.
Pray you let Cassio be received again.
OTHELLO. Fetch me the handkerchief. My mind misgives.
DESDEMONA. Come, come,
You'll never meet a more sufficient man.   85
OTHELLO. The handkerchief!
DESDEMONA.   I pray talk me of Cassio.
OTHELLO. The handkerchief!
DESDEMONA.   A man that all his time
Hath founded his good fortunes on your love,
Shared dangers with you—
OTHELLO. The handkerchief!   90
DESDEMONA. In sooth, you are to blame.
OTHELLO. Away! (*Exit.*)
EMILIA. Is not this man jealous?
DESDEMONA. I ne'er saw this before.
Sure there's some wonder in this handkerchief.   95
I am most unhappy in the loss of it.
EMILIA. 'Tis not a year or two shows us a man.°
They are all but stomachs and we all but food.
They eat us hungerly, and when they are full
They belch us. Look you, Cassio and my husband.   100

---

69. Conserved: prepared.   **97. 'Tis . . . man:** it does not take a couple of years to discover the nature of a man; i.e., he soon shows his real nature.

(Enter CASSIO *and* IAGO.)

IAGO.   There is no other way, 'tis she must do 't.
    And, lo, the happiness!° Go and impórtune her.
DESDEMONA.   How now, good Cassio! What's the news with you?
CASSIO.   Madam, my former suit. I do beseech you
    That by your virtuous means I may again   105
    Exist, and be a member of his love
    Whom I with all the office of my heart
    Entirely honor. I would not be delayed.
    If my offense be of such mortal kind
    That nor my service past nor present sorrows   110
    Nor purposed merit in futurity
    Can ransom me into his love again,
    But to know so must be my benefit.
    So shall I clothe me in a forced content
    And shut myself up in some other course   115
    To Fortune's alms.
DESDEMONA.   Alas, thrice-gentle Cassio!
    My advocation° is not now in tune.
    My lord is not my lord, nor should I know him
    Were he in favor° as in humor altered.
    So help me every spirit sanctified,   120
    As I have spoken for you all my best
    And stood within the blank° of his displeasure
    For my free speech! You must awhile be patient.
    What I can do I will, and more I will
    Than for myself I dare. Let that suffice you.   125
IAGO.   Is my lord angry?
EMILIA.   He went hence but now,
    And certainly in strange unquietness.
IAGO.   Can he be angry? I have seen the cannon
    When it hath blown his ranks into the air,
    And, like the Devil, from his very arm   130
    Puffed his own brother, and can he be angry?
    Something of moment then. I will go meet him.
    There's matter in 't indeed if he be angry.
DESDEMONA.   I prithee do so. *(Exit* IAGO.)
                   Something sure of state,
    Either from Venice, or some unhatched practice   135
    Made demonstrable° here in Cyprus to him,

---

102. **And . . . happiness:** what good luck, here she is.   117. **advocation:** advocacy.   119.
favor: face [Eds.].   122. **blank:** aim.   135–36. **unhatched . . . demonstrable:** some
plot, not yet matured, which has been revealed.

Hath puddled his clear spirit. And in such cases
Men's natures wrangle with inferior things,
Though great ones are their object. 'Tis even so,
For let our finger ache and it indues   140
Our other healthful members even to that sense
Of pain. Nay, we must think men are not gods,
Nor of them look for such observancy
As fits the bridal.° Beshrew me much, Emilia,
I was, unhandsome warrior° as I am,   145
Arraigning his unkindness with my soul,
But now I find I had suborned the witness,°
And he's indicted falsely.
EMILIA.   Pray Heaven it be state matters, as you think,
And no conception nor no jealous toy°   150
Concerning you.
DESDEMONA.   Alas the day, I never gave him cause!
EMILIA.   But jealous souls will not be answered so.
They are not ever jealous for the cause,
But jealous for they are jealous. 'Tis a monster   155
Begot upon itself, born on itself.
DESDEMONA.   Heaven keep that monster from Othello's mind!
EMILIA.   Lady, amen.
DESDEMONA.   I will go seek him. Cassio, walk hereabout.
If I do find him fit, I'll move your suit,   160
And seek to effect it to my uttermost.
CASSIO.   I humbly thank your ladyship.

(*Exeunt* DESDEMONA *and* EMILIA. *Enter* BIANCA.)

BIANCA.   Save you, friend Cassio!
CASSIO.   What make you from home?
How is it with you, my most fair Bianca?
I' faith, sweet love, I was coming to your house.   165
BIANCA.   And I was going to your lodging, Cassio.
What, keep a week away? Seven days and nights?
Eightscore eight hours? And lovers' absent hours,
More tedious than the dial eightscore times?
Oh, weary reckoning!
CASSIO.   Pardon me, Bianca.   170
I have this while with leaden thoughts been pressed,
But I shall in a more continuate time

---

144. **bridal:** honeymoon.   145. **unhandsome warrior:** clumsy soldier. Desdemona continually thinks of herself as Othello's companion in arms. Cf. I.iii.248 ff.   147. **suborned
. . . witness:** corrupted the evidence; i.e., misunderstood his behavior [Eds.].   150. **jealous
toy:** silly suspicion.

Strike off this score of absence. Sweet Bianca,
(*Giving her* DESDEMONA'S *handkerchief*)
Take me this work out.
BIANCA.   O Cassio, whence came this?
This is some token from a newer friend.   175
To the felt absence now I feel a cause.
Is 't come to this? Well, well.
CASSIO.   Go to, woman!
Throw your vile guesses in the Devil's teeth,
From whence you have them. You are jealous now
That this is from some mistress, some remembrance.   180
No, by my faith, Bianca.
BIANCA.   Why, whose is it?
CASSIO.   I know not, sweet. I found it in my chamber.
I like the work well. Ere it be demanded—
As like enough it will—I'd have it copied.
Take it, and do 't, and leave me for this time.   185
BIANCA.   Leave you! Wherefore?
CASSIO.   I do attend here on the General,
And think it no addition,° nor my wish
To have him see me womaned.°
BIANCA.   Why, I pray you?
CASSIO.   Not that I love you not.
BIANCA.   But that you do not love me.   190
I pray you bring me on the way a little,
And say if I shall see you soon at night.
CASSIO.   'Tis but a little way that I can bring you,
For I attend here. But I'll see you soon.
BIANCA.   'Tis very good, I must be circumstanced.°   195

(*Exeunt.*)

ACT IV

SCENE I. Cyprus. Before the castle.

Enter OTHELLO *and* IAGO.

IAGO.   Will you think so?
OTHELLO.   Think so, Iago!
IAGO.   What,
To kiss in private?
OTHELLO.   An unauthorized kiss.

---

188. **addition:** honor.   189. **womaned:** with a girl.   195. **circumstanced:** put off.

IAGO. Or to be naked with her friend in bed
     An hour or more, not meaning any harm?
OTHELLO. Naked in bed, Iago, and not mean harm!   5
     It is hypocrisy against the Devil.
     They that mean virtuously and yet do so,
     The Devil their virtue tempts and they tempt Heaven.
IAGO. So they do nothing, 'tis a venial° slip.
     But if I give my wife a handkerchief—   10
OTHELLO What then?
IAGO. Why, then, 'tis hers, my lord, and being hers,
     She may, I think, bestow 't on any man.
OTHELLO. She is protectress of her honor too.
     May she give that?   15
IAGO. Her honor is an essence that's not seen.
     They have it very oft that have it not.
     But for the handkerchief—
OTHELLO. By Heaven, I would most gladly have forgot it.
     Thou said'st—oh, it comes o'er my memory,   20
     As doth the raven o'er the infected house
     Boding to all°—he had my handkerchief.
IAGO. Aye, what of that?
OTHELLO.   That's not so good now.
IAGO.   What
     If I had said I had seen him do you wrong?
     Or heard him say—as knaves be such abroad,   25
     Who having, by their own importunate suit,
     Or voluntary dotage of some mistress,
     Convincèd or supplied° them, cannot choose
     But they must blab—
OTHELLO.   Hath he said anything?
IAGO. He hath, my lord, but be you well assured,   30
     No more than he'll unswear.
OTHELLO.   What hath he said?
IAGO. Faith, that he did— I know not what he did.
OTHELLO. What? What?
IAGO. Lie—
OTHELLO. With her?
IAGO.   With her, on her, what you will. 34
OTHELLO. Lie° with her! Lie on her!—We say lie on her when they belie
     her.—Lie with her! 'Zounds, that's fulsome!° Handkerchief—confes-

---

9. venial: pardonable. **21-22. As doth the raven . . . all:** as an evil omen (such as a raven
overhead) brings evil tidings to all who live in a plague-infested house [Eds.]. **28. Con-
vincèd or supplied:** overcome or satisfied their desires. **35-41. Lie . . . devil:** Othello
breaks into incoherent muttering before he falls down in a fit.

sions—handkerchief!—To confess, and be hanged for his labor. First to
be hanged, and then to confess. I tremble at it. Nature would not invest
herself in such shadowing passion without some instruction.° It is not
words that shake me thus. Pish! Noses, ears, and lips. Is 't possible?—
Confess?—Handkerchief?—Oh, devil! (*Falls in a trance.*)   41
IAGO. Work on,
   My medicine, work! Thus credulous fools are caught,
   And many worthy and chaste dames even thus,
   All guiltless, meet reproach. What ho! My lord!   45
   My lord, I say! Othello!

(*Enter* CASSIO.)

How now, Cassio!

CASSIO. What's the matter?
IAGO. My lord is fall'n into an epilepsy.
   This is his second fit, he had one yesterday.
CASSIO. Rub him about the temples.
IAGO.   No, forbear,   50
   The lethargy° must have his quiet course.
   If not, he foams at mouth and by and by
   Breaks out to savage madness. Look, he stirs.
   Do you withdraw yourself a little while,
   He will recover straight. When he is gone,   55
   I would on great occasion speak with you.

(*Exit* CASSIO.)

How is it, General? Have you not hurt your head?°
OTHELLO. Dost thou mock me?
IAGO.   I mock you! No, by Heaven.
   Would you would bear your fortune like a man!
OTHELLO. A hornèd man's a monster and a beast.   60
IAGO. There's many a beast, then, in a populous city,
   And many a civil monster.
OTHELLO. Did he confess it?
IAGO.   Good sir, be a man.
   Think every bearded fellow that's but yoked°
   May draw with you.° There's millions now alive   65
   That nightly lie in those unproper beds

---

36. fulsome: disgusting. **38–39. Nature . . . instruction:** nature would not fill me with
such overwhelming emotion unless there was some cause. **51. lethargy:** epileptic
fit. **57. Have . . . head:** With brutal cynicism Iago asks whether Othello is suffering from
cuckold's headache. **64. yoked:** married. **65. draw . . . you:** be your yoke fellow.

Which they dare swear peculiar.° Your case is better.
Oh, 'tis the spite of Hell, the Fiend's arch-mock,
To lip° a wanton in a secure couch°
And to suppose her chaste! No, let me know,   70
And knowing what I am, I know what she shall be.
OTHELLO.   Oh, thou art wise, 'tis certain.
IAGO.   Stand you awhile apart,
Confine yourself but in a patient list.°
Whilst you were here o'erwhelmèd with your grief—
A passion most unsuiting such a man—   75
Cassio came hither. I shifted him away,
And laid good 'scuse upon your ecstasy,°
Bade him anon return and here speak with me,
The which he promised. Do but encave yourself,
And mark the fleers, the gibes, and notable scorns,   80
That dwell in every region of his face.
For I will make him tell the tale anew,
Where, how, how oft, how long ago, and when
He hath and is again to cope° your wife.
I say but mark his gesture. Marry, patience,   85
Or I shall say you are all in all in spleen,
And nothing of a man.
OTHELLO.   Dost thou hear, Iago?
I will be found most cunning in my patience,
But—dost thou hear?—most bloody.
IAGO.   That's not amiss,
But yet keep time in all. Will you withdraw?   90

(OTHELLO *retires.*)

Now will I question Cassio of Bianca,
A housewife° that by selling her desires
Buys herself bread and clothes. It is a creature
That dotes on Cassio, as 'tis the strumpet's plague
To beguile many and be beguiled by one.   95
He, when he hears of her, cannot refrain
From the excess of laughter. Here he comes.

(*Re-enter* CASSIO.)

As he shall smile, Othello shall go mad,
And his unbookish° jealousy must construe

66–67. That . . . peculiar: that lie nightly in beds which they believe are their own but
which others have shared.   **69. lip:** kiss.   **secure couch:** lit., a carefree bed; i.e., a bed
which has been used by the wife's lover, but secretly.   **73. patient list:** confines of patience.   **77. ecstasy:** fit.   **84. cope:** encounter.   **92. housewife:** hussy.   **99. unbookish:**
unlearned.

Poor Cassio's smiles, gestures, and light behavior   100
Quite in the wrong. How do you now, Lieutenant?
CASSIO. The worser that you give me the addition°
Whose want even kills me.
IAGO. Ply Desdemona well, and you are sure on 't.
Now, if this suit lay in Bianca's power,   105
How quickly should you speed!
CASSIO.   Alas, poor caitiff!°
OTHELLO. Look how he laughs already!
IAGO. I never knew a woman love man so.
CASSIO. Alas, poor rogue! I think, i' faith, she loves me.
OTHELLO. Now he denies it faintly and laughs it out.   110
IAGO. Do you hear, Cassio?
OTHELLO.   Now he impórtunes him
To tell it o'er. Go to. Well said, well said.
IAGO. She gives it out that you shall marry her.
Do you intend it?
CASSIO. Ha, ha, ha!   115
OTHELLO. Do you triumph, Roman?° Do you triumph?
CASSIO. I marry her! What, a customer!° I prithee bear some charity to my
wit. Do not think it so unwholesome. Ha, ha, ha!
OTHELLO. So, so, so, so. They laugh that win.
IAGO. Faith, the cry goes that you shall marry her.   120
CASSIO. Prithee say true.
IAGO. I am a very villain else.
OTHELLO. Have you scored° me? Well.
CASSIO. This is the monkey's own giving out. She is persuaded I will marry
her out of her own love and flattery, not out of my promise.   125
OTHELLO. Iago beckons me, now he begins the story.
CASSIO. She was here even now. She haunts me in every place. I was the
other day talking on the sea bank with certain Venetians, and thither
comes the bauble, and, by this hand, she falls me thus about my
neck—   130
OTHELLO. Crying "O dear Cassio!" as it were. His gesture imports it.
CASSIO. So hangs and lolls and weeps upon me, so hales and pulls me. Ha,
ha, ha!
OTHELLO. Now he tells how she plucked him to my chamber. Oh, I see that
nose of yours, but not that dog I shall throw it to.   135
CASSIO. Well, I must leave her company.
IAGO. Before me!° Look where she comes.

---

102. **addition:** title (Lieutenant) which he has lost. 106. **caitiff:** wretch. 116. **triumph, Roman:** The word "triumph" suggests "Roman" because the Romans celebrated their victories with triumphs, elaborate shows, and processions. 117. **customer:** harlot. 123. **scored:** marked, as with a blow from a whip. 137. **Before me:** by my soul.

CASSIO. 'Tis such another fitchew!° Marry, a perfumed one.

(*Enter* BIANCA.)

What do you mean by this haunting of me?

BIANCA. Let the Devil and his dam haunt you! What did you mean by that same handkerchief you gave me even now? I was a fine fool to take it. I must take out the work? A likely piece of work, that you should find it in your chamber and not know who left it there! This is some minx's token, and I must take out the work? There, give it your hobbyhorse. Wheresoever you had it, I'll take out no work on 't.   145

CASSIO. How now, my sweet Bianca! How now! How now!

OTHELLO. By Heaven, that should be my handkerchief!

BIANCA. An° you'll come to supper tonight, you may. An you will not, come when you are next prepared for. (*Exit.*)

IAGO. After her, after her.   150

CASSIO. Faith, I must, she'll rail i' the street else.

IAGO. Will you sup there?

CASSIO. Faith, I intend so.

IAGO. Well, I may chance to see you, for I would very fain speak with you.   155

CASSIO. Prithee, come, will you?

IAGO. Go to. Say no more.

(*Exit* CASSIO.)

OTHELLO (*advancing*). How shall I murder him, Iago?

IAGO. Did you perceive how he laughed at his vice?

OTHELLO. Oh, Iago!   160

IAGO. And did you see the handkerchief?

OTHELLO. Was that mine?

IAGO. Yours, by this hand. And to see how he prizes the foolish woman your wife! She gave it him, and he hath given it his whore.

OTHELLO. I would have him nine years a-killing. A fine woman! A fair woman! A sweet woman!   166

IAGO. Nay, you must forget that.

OTHELLO. Aye, let her rot, and perish, and be damned tonight, for she shall not live. No, my heart is turned to stone, I strike it and it hurts my hand. Oh, the world hath not a sweeter creature. She might lie by an emperor's side, and command him tasks.   171

IAGO. Nay, that's not your way.°

OTHELLO. Hang her! I do but say what she is, so delicate with her needle, an admirable musician—oh, she will sing the savageness out of a bear—of so high and plenteous wit and invention—   175

IAGO. She's the worse for all this.

OTHELLO Oh, a thousand thousand times. And then, of so gentle a condition!

138. fitchew: polecat.   **148. An:** if.   **172. Nay . . . way:** i.e., don't get soft thoughts about her.

IAGO.   Aye, too gentle.

OTHELLO.   Nay, that's certain. But yet the pity of it, Iago! O Iago, the pity of it, Iago!   180

IAGO.   If you are so fond over her iniquity, give her patent to offend, for if it touch not you, it comes near nobody.

OTHELLO.   I will chop her into messes.° Cuckold me!

IAGO.   Oh, 'tis foul in her.

OTHELLO.   With mine officer!   185

IAGO.   That's fouler.

OTHELLO.   Get me some poison, Iago, this night. I'll not expostulate with her, lest her body and beauty unprovide my mind again. This night, Iago.

IAGO.   Do it not with poison, strangle her in her bed, even the bed she hath contaminated.   191

OTHELLO.   Good, good. The justice of it pleases. Very good.

IAGO.   And for Cassio, let me be his undertaker.°
    You shall hear more by midnight.

OTHELLO.   Excellent good. (*A trumpet within.*) What trumpet is that same?

IAGO.   Something from Venice, sure. 'Tis Lodovico   195
    Come from the Duke. And see, your wife is with him.

(*Enter* LODOVICO, DESDEMONA, *and* ATTENDANTS.)

LODOVICO.   God save the worthy General!

OTHELLO.   With all my heart, sir.

LODOVICO.   The Duke and Senators of Venice greet you. (*Gives him a letter.*)

OTHELLO.   I kiss the instrument of their pleasures. (*Opens the letter, and reads.*)   200

DESDEMONA.   And what's the news, good Cousin Lodovico?

IAGO.   I am very glad to see you, signior.
    Welcome to Cyprus.

LODOVICO.   I thank you. How does Lieutenant Cassio?

IAGO.   Lives, sir.   205

DESDEMONA.   Cousin, there's fall'n between him and my lord
    An unkind breach, but you shall make all well.

OTHELLO.   Are you sure of that?

DESDEMONA.   My lord?

OTHELLO (*reads*).   "This fail you not to do, as you will—"   210

LODOVICO.   He did not call, he's busy in the paper.
    Is there division 'twixt my lord and Cassio?

DESDEMONA.   A most unhappy one. I would do much
    To atone° them, for the love I bear to Cassio.

OTHELLO.   Fire and brimstone!

---

183. **messes:** mincemeat [Eds.].   193. **be . . . undertaker:** undertake to manage his business. In Shakespeare's plays the word does *not* mean "mortician."   214. **atone:** reconcile.

DESDEMONA.   My lord?
OTHELLO.   Are you wise?°   215
DESDEMONA. What, is he angry?
LODOVICO.   Maybe the letter moved him,
　　For, as I think, they do command him home,
　　Deputing Cassio in his government.
DESDEMONA. By my troth, I am glad on 't.
OTHELLO.   Indeed!
DESDEMONA.   My lord?
OTHELLO. I am glad to see you mad.
DESDEMONA.   Why, sweet Othello?   220
OTHELLO. Devil! (*Striking her.*)
DESDEMONA. I have not deserved this.
LODOVICO. My lord, this would not be believed in Venice
　　Though I should swear I saw 't. 'Tis very much.
　　Make her amends, she weeps.
OTHELLO.   O devil, devil!   225
　　If that the earth could teem with a woman's tears,
　　Each drop she falls would prove a crocodile.°
　　Out of my sight!
DESDEMONA.   I will not stay to offend you. (*Going.*)
LODOVICO. Truly, an obedient lady.
　　I do beseech your lordship, call her back.   230
OTHELLO. Mistress!
DESDEMONA. My lord?
OTHELLO. What would you with her, sir?
LODOVICO.   Who, I, my lord?
OTHELLO. Aye, you did wish that I would make her turn.
　　Sir, she can turn and turn, and yet go on   235
　　And turn again. And she can weep, sir, weep.
　　And she's obedient, as you say, obedient,
　　Very obedient.—Proceed you in your tears—
　　Concerning this, sir—oh, well-painted passion!°—
　　I am commanded home.—Get you away.   240
　　I'll send for you anon.—Sir, I obey the mandate,
　　And will return to Venice.—Hence, avaunt!

　　(*Exit* DESDEMONA.)

　　Cassio shall have my place. And, sir, tonight,
　　I do entreat that we may sup together.

---

215. Are . . . wise: i.e., in saying you bear love to Cassio. **226–227. If . . . crocodile:** If the earth could breed from woman's tears, each tear that she lets fall would become a crocodile. It was believed that the crocodile would cry and sob to attract the sympathetic passer-by, who was then snapped up. **239. passion:** emotion [Eds.].

You are welcome, sir, to Cyprus.—Goats and monkeys! (*Exit.*)   245
LODOVICO. Is this the noble Moor whom our full Senate
  Call all-in-all sufficient? This the nature
  Whom passion could not shake? Whose solid virtue
  The shot of accident nor dart of chance
  Could neither graze nor pierce?
IAGO.   He is much changed.   250
LODOVICO. Are his wits safe? Is he not light of brain?
IAGO. He's that he is. I may not breathe my censure°
  What he might be. If what he might he is not,
  I would to Heaven he were!
LODOVICO.   What, strike his wife!
IAGO. Faith, that was not so well, yet would I knew   255
  That stroke would prove the worst!
LODOVICO.   Is it his use?
  Or did the letters work upon his blood,
  And new-create this fault?
IAGO.   Alas, alas!
  It is not honesty in me to speak
  What I have seen and known. You shall observe him,   260
  And his own courses will denote him so
  That I may save my speech. Do but go after,
  And mark how he continues.
LODOVICO. I am sorry that I am deceived in him.

  (*Exeunt.*)

SCENE II. *A room in the castle.*

  Enter OTHELLO *and* EMILIA.

OTHELLO. You have seen nothing, then?
EMILIA. Nor ever heard, nor ever did suspect.
OTHELLO. Yes, you have seen Cassio and she together.
EMILIA. But then I saw no harm, and then I heard
  Each syllable that breath made up between them.   5
OTHELLO. What, did they never whisper?
EMILIA.   Never, my lord.
OTHELLO. Nor send you out o' the way?
EMILIA. Never.
OTHELLO. To fetch her fan, her gloves, her mask, nor nothing?
EMILIA. Never, my lord.   10
OTHELLO. That's strange.
EMILIA. I durst, my lord, to wager she is honest,

---

252. **censure:** opinion [Eds.].

Lay down my soul at stake. If you think other,
Remove your thought, it doth abuse your bosom.
If any wretch have put this in your head,   15
Let Heaven requite it with the serpent's curse!
For if she be not honest, chaste, and true,
There's no man happy, the purest of their wives
Is foul as slander.
OTHELLO.   Bid her come hither. Go.

(*Exit* EMILIA.)

She says enough. Yet she's a simple bawd   20
That cannot say as much. This is a subtle whore,
A closet lock and key of villainous secrets.
And yet she'll kneel and pray, I have seen her do 't.

(*Enter* DESDEMONA *with* EMILIA.)

DESDEMONA.   My lord, what is your will?
OTHELLO.   Pray, chuck, come hither.
DESDEMONA.   What is your pleasure?
OTHELLO.   Let me see your eyes.   25
     Look in my face.
DESDEMONA.   What horrible fancy's this?
OTHELLO (*to* EMILIA).   Some of your function,° mistress.
     Leave procreants alone and shut the door,
     Cough, or cry hem, if anybody come.
     Your mystery,° your mystery. Nay, dispatch.   30

(*Exit* EMILIA.)

DESDEMONA.   Upon my knees, what doth your speech import?
     I understand a fury in your words,
     But not the words.
OTHELLO.   Why, what art thou?
DESDEMONA.   Your wife, my lord, your true and loyal wife.
OTHELLO.   Come, swear it, damn thyself,   35
     Lest, being like one of Heaven,° the devils themselves
     Should fear to seize thee. Therefore be double-damned.
     Swear thou art honest.
DESDEMONA.   Heaven doth truly know it.
OTHELLO.   Heaven truly knows that thou art false as Hell.
DESDEMONA.   To whom, my lord? With whom? How am I false?   40
OTHELLO.   O Desdemona! Away! Away! Away!

---

27. Some . . . function: get about your business; i.e., prostitution. Othello pretends that
Emilia is keeper of a brothel and Desdemona one of the women.   **30. mystery:** profession.   **36. being . . . Heaven:** because you look like an angel.

DESDEMONA. Alas the heavy day! Why do you weep!
　　Am I the motive of these tears, my lord?
　　If haply you my father do suspect
　　An instrument of this your calling-back,　　　　　　　　45
　　Lay not your blame on me. If you have lost him,
　　Why, I have lost him too.
OTHELLO.　　　　　　　　　Had it pleased Heaven
　　To try me with affliction, had they rained
　　All kinds of sores and shames on my bare head,
　　Steeped me in poverty to the very lips,　　　　　　　　50
　　Given to captivity me and my utmost hopes,
　　I should have found in some place of my soul
　　A drop of patience. But, alas, to make me
　　A fixèd figure for the time of scorn
　　To point his slow unmoving finger at!　　　　　　　　55
　　Yet could I bear that too, well, very well.
　　But there where I have garnered up my heart,
　　Where either I must live or bear no life,
　　The fountain from the which my current runs
　　Or else dries up—to be discarded thence!　　　　　　60
　　Or keep it as a cistern for foul toads
　　To knot and gender in! Turn thy complexion there,
　　Patience, thou young and rose-lipped cherubin—
　　Aye, there, look grim as Hell!
DESDEMONA. I hope my noble lord esteems me honest.　　65
OTHELLO. Oh, aye, as summer flies are in the shambles,°
　　That quicken even with blowing.° O thou weed,
　　Who art so lovely fair and smell'st so sweet
　　That the sense aches at thee, would thou hadst ne'er been born!
DESDEMONA. Alas, what ignorant sin have I committed?　　70
OTHELLO. Was this fair paper,° this most goodly book,
　　Made to write "whore" upon? What committed!
　　Committed! O thou public commoner!°
　　I should make very forges of my cheeks
　　That would to cinders burn up modesty　　　　　　　75
　　Did I but speak thy deeds. What committed!
　　Heaven stops the nose at it, and the moon winks.
　　The bawdy wind, that kisses all it meets,
　　Is hushed within the hollow mine of earth
　　And will not hear it. What committed!　　　　　　　80
　　Impudent strumpet!

---

66. shambles: slaughterhouse. **67. quicken . . . blowing:** come to life as soon as the eggs are laid. **71. fair paper:** i.e., her white body. **73. public commoner:** one who offers herself to all comers.

DESDEMONA.   By Heaven, you do me wrong.
OTHELLO. Are not you a strumpet?
DESDEMONA.   No, as I am a Christian.
    If to preserve this vessel for my lord
    From any other foul unlawful touch
    Be not to be a strumpet, I am none.   85
OTHELLO. What, not a whore?
DESDEMONA.   No, as I shall be saved.
OTHELLO. Is 't possible?
DESDEMONA. Oh, Heaven forgive us!
OTHELLO.   I cry you mercy, then.
    I took you for that cunning whore of Venice
    That married with Othello. (*Raising his voice*) You mistress,   90
    That have the office opposite to Saint Peter,
    And keep the gate of Hell!

(*Re-enter* EMILIA.)

                         You, you, aye, you!
    We have done our course, there's money for your pains.
    I pray you turn the key, and keep our counsel. (*Exit.*)
EMILIA. Alas, what does this gentleman conceive?   95
    How do you, madam? How do you, my good lady?
DESDEMONA. Faith, half-asleep.
EMILIA. Good madam, what's the matter with my lord?
DESDEMONA. With who?
EMILIA. Why, with my lord, madam.   100
DESDEMONA. Who is thy lord?
EMILIA.   He that is yours, sweet lady.
DESDEMONA. I have none. Do not talk to me, Emilia.
    I cannot weep, nor answer have I none
    But what should go by water.° Prithee tonight
    Lay on my bed my wedding sheets. Remember,   105
    And call thy husband hither.
EMILIA.   Here's a change indeed! (*Exit.*)
DESDEMONA. 'Tis meet I should be used so, very meet.
    How have I been behaved that he might stick
    The small'st opinion on my least misuse?°

(*Re-enter* EMILIA *with* IAGO.)

IAGO. What is your pleasure, madam? How is 't with you?   110
DESDEMONA. I cannot tell. Those that do teach young babes
    Do it with gentle means and easy tasks.
    He might have chid me so, for, in good faith,

104. go . . . water: be expressed in tears.   109. misuse: mistake.

I am a child to chiding.

IAGO.   What's the matter, lady?

EMILIA. Alas, Iago, my lord hath so bewhored her,   115
   Thrown such despite and heavy terms upon her,
   As true hearts cannot bear.

DESDEMONA. Am I that name, Iago?

IAGO.   What name, fair lady?

DESDEMONA. Such as she says my lord did say I was.

EMILIA. He called her whore. A beggar in his drink   120
   Could not have laid such terms upon his callet.°

IAGO. Why did he so?

DESDEMONA. I do not know. I am sure I am none such.

IAGO. Do not weep, do not weep. Alas the day!

EMILIA. Hath she forsook so many noble matches,   125
   Her father and her country and her friends,
   To be called whore? Would it not make one weep?

DESDEMONA. It is my wretched fortune.

IAGO.   Beshrew him for 't!
   How comes this trick upon him?

DESDEMONA.   Nay, Heaven doth know.

EMILIA. I will be hanged if some eternal villain,   130
   Some busy and insinuating rogue,
   Some cogging, cozening slave, to get some office,
   Have not devised this slander. I'll be hanged else.

IAGO. Fie, there is no such man, it is impossible.

DESDEMONA. If any such there be, Heaven pardon him!   135

EMILIA. A halter pardon him! And Hell gnaw his bones!
   Why should he call her whore? Who keeps her company?
   What place? What time? What form? What likelihood?
   The Moor's abused by some most villainous knave,
   Some base notorious knave, some scurvy fellow.   140
   O Heaven, that such companions° Thou'dst unfold,°
   And put in every honest hand a whip
   To lash the rascals naked through the world
   Even from the east to the west!

IAGO.   Speak withindoor.°

EMILIA. Oh, fie upon them! Some such squire he was   145
   That turned your wit the seamy side without,
   And made you to suspect me with the Moor.

IAGO. You are a fool. Go to.°

DESDEMONA.   O good Iago,
   What shall I do to win my lord again?

---

121. callet: slut [Eds.]. **141. companions:** low creatures. **unfold:** bring to light. **144. Speak withindoor:** don't shout so loud that all the street will hear you. **148. Go to:** an expression of derision.

Good friend, go to him, for, by this light of Heaven,   150
I know not how I lost him. Here I kneel.
If e'er my will did trespass 'gainst his love
Either in discourse of thought or actual deed,
Or that mine eyes, mine ears, or any sense
Delighted them in any other form,   155
Or that I do not yet,° and ever did,
And ever will, though he do shake me off
To beggarly divorcement, love him dearly,
Comfort forswear me! Unkindness may do much,
And his unkindness may defeat my life,   160
But never taint my love. I cannot say "whore,"
It doth abhor me now I speak the word.
To do the act that might the addition° earn
Not the world's mass of vanity° could make me.

IAGO.   I pray you be content, 'tis but his humor.   165
The business of the state does him offense,
And he does chide with you.

DESDEMONA.   If 'twere no other—

IAGO.   'Tis but so, I warrant. (*Trumpets within.*)
Hark how these instruments summon to supper!
The messengers of Venice stay the meat.°   170
Go in, and weep not, all things shall be well.

(*Exeunt* DESDEMONA *and* EMILIA. *Enter* RODERIGO.)

How now, Roderigo!

RODERIGO.   I do not find that thou dealest justly with me.

IAGO.   What in the contrary?

RODERIGO.   Every day thou daffest me with some device, Iago, and rather, as
it seems to me now, keepest from me all conveniency than suppliest
me with the least advantage of hope. I will indeed no longer endure it, nor
am I yet persuaded to put up in peace what already I have foolishly
suffered.   179

IAGO.   Will you hear me, Roderigo?

RODERIGO.   Faith, I have heard too much, for your words and performances
are no kin together.

IAGO.   You charge me most unjustly.

RODERIGO.   With naught but truth. I have wasted myself out of my means.
The jewels you have had from me to deliver to Desdemona would half
have corrupted a votarist.° You have told me she hath received them, and
returned me expectations and comforts of sudden respect and acquaintance, but I find none.   188

---

156. yet: still [Eds.].   **163. addition:** title.   **164. vanity:** i.e., riches.   **170. meat:** serving
of supper.   **186. votarist:** nun.

IAGO. Well, go to, very well.

RODERIGO. Very well! Go to! I cannot go to, man, nor 'tis not very well. By
this hand, I say 'tis very scurvy, and begin to find myself fopped in it.

IAGO. Very well. 192

RODERIGO. I tell you 'tis not very well. I will make myself known to
Desdemona. If she will return me my jewels, I will give over my suit and
repent my unlawful solicitation. If not, assure yourself I will seek satisfaction of you. 196

IAGO. You have said now.°

RODERIGO. Aye, and said nothing but what I protest intendment of doing.

IAGO. Why, now I see there's mettle in thee, and even from this instant do
build on thee a better opinion than ever before. Give me thy hand,
Roderigo. Thou hast taken against me a most just exception, but yet I
protest I have dealt most directly in thy affair. 202

RODERIGO. It hath not appeared.

IAGO. I grant indeed it hath not appeared, and your suspicion is not without
wit and judgment. But, Roderigo, if thou hast that in thee indeed which I
have greater reason to believe now than ever—I mean purpose, courage,
and valor—this night show it. If thou the next night following enjoy
not Desdemona, take me from this world with treachery and devise en-
gines° for my life. 209

RODERIGO. Well, what is it? Is it within reason and compass?

IAGO. Sir, there is especial commission come from Venice to depute Cassio
in Othello's place.

RODERIGO. Is that true? Why, then Othello and Desdemona return again to
Venice. 214

IAGO. Oh, no. He goes into Mauritania, and takes away with him the fair
Desdemona, unless his abode be lingered here by some accident, wherein
none can be so determinate as the removing of Cassio.

RODERIGO. How do you mean, "removing of" him? 218

IAGO. Why, by making him uncapable of Othello's place, knocking out his
brains.

RODERIGO. And that you would have me to do?

IAGO. Aye, if you dare do yourself a profit and a right. He sups tonight with
a harlotry,° and thither will I go to him. He knows not yet of his honorable fortune. If you will watch his going thence, which I will fashion to
fall out between twelve and one, you may take him at your pleasure. I will
be near to second your attempt, and he shall fall between us. Come, stand
not amazed at it, but go along with me. I will show you such a necessity in
his death that you shall think yourself bound to put it on him. It is now
high suppertime and the night grows to waste. About it.

RODERIGO. I will hear further reason for this. 230

___

197. You . . . now: or in modern slang, "Oh yeah." 208–209. engines: instruments of
torture. 223. harlotry: harlot.

IAGO. And you shall be satisfied.

(*Exeunt.*)

SCENE III. *Another room in the castle.*

Enter OTHELLO, LODOVICO, DESDEMONA, EMILIA, *and* ATTENDANTS.

LODOVICO. I do beseech you, sir, trouble yourself no further.
OTHELLO. Oh, pardon me, 'twill do me good to walk.
LODOVICO. Madam, good night. I humbly thank your ladyship.
DESDEMONA. Your Honor is most welcome.
OTHELLO.   Will you walk, sir?
    Oh—Desdemona—   5
DESDEMONA. My lord?
OTHELLO. Get you to bed on the instant, I will be returned forthwith.
    Dismiss your attendant there. Look it be done.
DESDEMONA. I will, my lord.

(*Exeunt* OTHELLO, LODOVICO, *and* ATTENDANTS.)

EMILIA. How goes it now? He looks gentler than he did.   10
DESDEMONA. He says he will return incontinent.°
    He hath commanded me to go to bed,
    And bade me to dismiss you.
EMILIA.   Dismiss me!
DESDEMONA. It was his bidding, therefore, good Emilia,
    Give me my nightly wearing, and adieu.   15
    We must not now displease him.
EMILIA. I would you had never seen him!
DESDEMONA. So would not I. My love doth so approve him
    That even his stubbornness, his checks, his frowns—
    Prithee, unpin me—have grace and favor in them.   20
EMILIA. I have laid those sheets you bade me on the bed.
DESDEMONA. All's one. Good faith, how foolish are our minds!
    If I do die before thee, prithee shroud me
    In one of those same sheets.
EMILIA.   Come, come, you talk.
DESDEMONA. My mother had a maid called Barbary.   25
    She was in love, and he she loved proved mad
    And did forsake her. She had a song of "willow"°—
    An old thing 'twas, but it expressed her fortune,
    And she died singing it. That song tonight
    Will not go from my mind. I have much to do   30
    But to go hang my head all at one side

11. **incontinent:** immediately. 27. **willow:** the emblem of the forlorn lover.

And sing it like poor Barbary. Prithee, dispatch.

EMILIA. Shall I go fetch your nightgown?

DESDEMONA.   No, unpin me here.
This Lodovico is a proper man.

EMILIA. A very handsome man.   35

DESDEMONA. He speaks well.

EMILIA. I know a lady in Venice would have walked barefoot to Palestine for a touch of his nether lip.

DESDEMONA (*singing*).
    "The poor soul sat sighing by a sycamore tree,
        Sing all a green willow.   40
    Her hand on her bosom, her head on her knee,
        Sing willow, willow, willow.
    The fresh streams ran by her, and murmured her moans,
        Sing willow, willow, willow.
    Her salt tears fell from her, and softened the stones—"   45
Lay by these—(*singing*)
    "Sing willow, willow, willow,"
Prithee, hie thee, he'll come anon.—(*singing*)
    "Sing all a green willow must be my garland.
    Let nobody blame him, his scorn I approve—"   50
Nay, that's not next. Hark! Who is 't that knocks?

EMILIA. It's the wind.

DESDEMONA (*singing*).
    "I called my love false love, but what said he then?
        Sing willow, willow, willow.
    If I court moe° women, you'll couch with moe men."   55
So get thee gone, good night. Mine eyes do itch.
Doth that bode weeping?

EMILIA.   'Tis neither here nor there.

DESDEMONA. I have heard it said so. Oh, these men, these men!
Dost thou in conscience think—tell me, Emilia—
That there be women do abuse their husbands   60
In such gross kind?

EMILIA.   There be some such, no question.

DESDEMONA. Wouldst thou do such a deed for all the world?

EMILIA. Why, would not you?

DESDEMONA.   No, by this heavenly light!

EMILIA. Nor I neither by this heavenly light.
I might do 't as well i' the dark.   65

DESDEMONA. Wouldst thou do such a deed for all the world?

EMILIA. The world's a huge thing. It is a great price
For a small vice.

---

55. moe: more.

DESDEMONA.   In troth, I think thou wouldst not.
EMILIA.   In troth, I think I should, and undo 't when I had done. Marry, I
   would not do such a thing for a joint ring,° nor for measures of lawn,° nor
   for gowns, petticoats, nor caps, nor any petty exhibition;° but for the
   whole world—why, who would not make her husband a cuckold to make
   him a monarch? I should venture Purgatory for 't.   73
DESDEMONA.   Beshrew me if I would do such a wrong for the whole
   world.
EMILIA.   Why, the wrong is but a wrong i' the world, and having the world
   for your labor, 'tis a wrong in your own world and you might quickly
   make it right.   78
DESDEMONA.   I do not think there is any such woman.
EMILIA.   Yes, a dozen, and as many to the vantage as would store the world
   they played for.
   But I do think it is their husbands' faults
   If wives do fall. Say that they slack their duties
   And pour our treasures into foreign laps,
   Or else break out in peevish jealousies,   85
   Throwing restraint upon us, or say they strike us,
   Or scant our former having in despite,°
   Why, we have galls,° and though we have some grace,
   Yet have we some revenge. Let husbands know
   Their wives have sense like them. They see and smell   90
   And have their palates both for sweet and sour,
   As husbands have. What is it that they do
   When they change us for others? Is it sport?
   I think it is. And doth affection breed it?
   I think it doth. Is 't frailty that thus errs?   95
   It is so too. And have not we affections,
   Desires for sport, and frailty, as men have?
   Then let them use us well. Else let them know
   The ills we do, their ills instruct us so.
DESDEMONA.   Good night, good night. Heaven me such uses send,   100
   Not to pick bad from bad, but by bad mend! (*Exeunt.*)

ACT V

SCENE I. Cyprus. A street

Enter IAGO *and* RODERIGO.

IAGO.   Here, stand behind this bulk, straight will he come.
   Wear thy good rapier bare, and put it home.
   Quick, quick, fear nothing, I'll be at thy elbow.

---

70. joint ring: ring made in two pieces, a lover's gift. **measures of lawn:** lengths of
finest linen [Eds.]. **71. petty exhibition:** small allowance of money. **87. scant . . . despite:** for spite cut down our allowance. **88. galls:** bile, the cause of bitterness.

It makes us, or it mars us. Think on that,
And fix most firm they resolution.   5
RODERIGO. Be near at hand, I may miscarry in 't.
IAGO. Here, at thy hand. Be bold, and take thy stand. (*Retires.*)
RODERIGO. I have no great devotion to the deed,
And yet he hath given me satisfying reasons.
'Tis but a man gone. Forth, my sword. He dies.   10
IAGO. I have rubbed this young quat° almost to the sense,°
And he grows angry. Now, whether he kill Cassio,
Or Cassio him, or each do kill the other,
Every way makes my gain. Live Roderigo,°
He calls me to a restitution large   15
Of gold and jewels that I bobbed from him
As gifts to Desdemona.
It must not be. If Cassio do remain,
He hath a daily beauty in his life
That makes me ugly,° and besides, the Moor   20
May unfold me to him. There stand I in much peril.
No, he must die. Be 't so. I hear him coming.

(*Enter* CASSIO.)

RODERIGO. I know his gait, 'tis he. Villain, thou diest! (*Makes a pass at*
    CASSIO.)
CASSIO. That thrust had been mine enemy indeed
But that my coat is better than thou know'st.   25
I will make proof of thine. (*Draws, and wounds* RODERIGO.)
RODERIGO.   Oh, I am slain!

(IAGO *from behind wounds* CASSIO *in the leg, and exit.*)

CASSIO. I am maimed for ever. Help, ho! Murder! Murder! (*Falls.*)

(*Enter* OTHELLO.)

OTHELLO. The voice of Cassio. Iago keeps his word.
RODERIGO. Oh, villain that I am!
OTHELLO.   It is even so.
CASSIO. Oh, help, ho! Light! A surgeon!   30
OTHELLO. 'Tis he. O brave Iago, honest and just,
That hast such noble sense of thy friend's wrong!
Thou teachest me. Minion,° your dear friend lies dead,
And your unblest fate hies. Strumpet, I come!
Forth of my heart those charms, thine eyes, are blotted.   35
Thy bed lust-stained shall with lust's blood be spotted. (*Exit.*)

---

11. **quat:** pimple. **sense:** quick. **14. Live Roderigo:** If Roderigo lives [Eds.]. **19–20. He
. . . ugly:** by comparison with him I am a poor thing. Iago is conscious of his lack
of social graces. **33. Minion:** darling, in a bad sense.

(Enter LODOVICO *and* GRATIANO.)

CASSIO. What ho! No watch?° No passage?° Murder! Murder!
GRATIANO. 'Tis some mischance, the cry is very direful.
CASSIO. Oh, help!
LODOVICO. Hark!   40
RODERIGO. Oh, wretched villain!
LODOVICO. Two or three groan. It is a heavy° night.
    These may be counterfeits. Let's think 't unsafe
    To come in to the cry without more help.
RODERIGO. Nobody come? Then shall I bleed to death.   45
LODOVICO. Hark!

    (Re-enter IAGO, *with a light.)*

GRATIANO. Here's one comes in his shirt, with light and weapons.
IAGO. Who's there? Whose noise is this that cries on murder?
LODOVICO. We do not know.
IAGO.   Did not you hear a cry?
CASSIO. Here, here! For Heaven's sake, help me!
IAGO.   What's the matter?   50
GRATIANO. This is Othello's Ancient, as I take it.
LODOVICO. The same indeed, a very valiant fellow.
IAGO. What are you here that cry so grievously?
CASSIO. Iago? Oh, I am spoiled, undone by villains! Give me some help.
IAGO. Oh me, Lieutenant! What villains have done this?   55
CASSIO. I think that one of them is hereabout,
    And cannot make away.
IAGO.   Oh, treacherous villains!
    (To LODOVICO *and* GRATIANO) What are you there?
    Come in and give some help.
RODERIGO.   Oh, help me here!
CASSIO. That's one of them.
IAGO.   Oh, murderous slave! Oh, villain!   60
    (Stabs RODERIGO.)
RODERIGO. Oh, damned Iago! Oh, inhuman dog!
IAGO. Kill men i' the dark! Where be these bloody thieves?
    How silent is this town! Ho! Murder! Murder!
    What may you be? Are you of good or evil?
LODOVICO. As you shall prove us, praise us.   65
IAGO. Signior Lodovico?
LODOVICO. He, sir.
IAGO. I cry you mercy. Here's Cassio hurt by villains.
GRATIANO. Cassio!

---

37. watch: police. **No passage:** nobody passing. **42. heavy:** thick.

IAGO. How is 't, brother? 70
CASSIO. My leg is cut in two.
IAGO. Marry, Heaven forbid!
Light, gentlemen. I'll bind it with my shirt.

(*Enter* BIANCA.)

BIANCA. What is the matter, ho? Who is 't that cried?
IAGO. Who is 't that cried!
BIANCA. Oh, my dear Cassio! My sweet Cassio! 75
Oh, Cassio, Cassio, Cassio!
IAGO. Oh, notable strumpet! Cassio, may you suspect
Who they should be that have thus mangled you?
CASSIO. No.
GRATIANO. I am sorry to find you thus. I have been to seek you. 80
IAGO. Lend me a garter. So. Oh, for a chair,
To bear him easily hence!
BIANCA. Alas, he faints! Oh, Cassio, Cassio, Cassio!
IAGO. Gentlemen all, I do suspect this trash
To be a party in this injury. 85
Patience awhile, good Cassio. Come, come,
Lend me a light. Know we this face or no?
Alas, my friend and my dear countryman
Roderigo? No—yes, sure. Oh Heaven! Roderigo.
GRATIANO. What, of Venice? 90
IAGO. Even he, sir. Did you know him?
GRATIANO. Know him! Aye.
IAGO. Signior Gratiano? I cry you gentle pardon.
These bloody accidents must excuse my manners,
That so neglected you.
GRATIANO. I am glad to see you.
IAGO. How do you, Cassio? Oh, a chair, a chair! 95
GRATIANO. Roderigo!
IAGO. He, he, 'tis he. (*A chair brought in*) Oh, that's well said, the chair.
Some good man bear him carefully from hence.
I'll fetch the General's surgeon. (*To* BIANCA) For you, mistress,
Save you your labor. He that lies slain here, Cassio, 100
Was my dear friend. What malice was between you?
CASSIO. None in the world, nor do I know the man.
IAGO (*to* BIANCA). What, look you pale? Oh, bear him out o' the air.

(CASSIO *and* RODERIGO *are borne off.*)

Stay you, good gentlemen. Look you pale, mistress?
Do you perceive the gastness of her eye? 105
Nay, if you stare, we shall hear more anon.
Behold her well, I pray you look upon her.

Do you see, gentlemen? Nay, guiltiness will speak,
Though tongues were out of use.

(*Enter* EMILIA.)

EMILIA. 'Las, what's the matter? What's the matter, husband?   110
IAGO. Cassio hath here been set on in the dark
    By Roderigo, and fellows that are 'scaped.
    He's almost slain, and Roderigo dead.
EMILIA. Alas, good gentlemen! Alas, good Cassio!
IAGO. This is the fruit of whoring. Prithee, Emilia,   115
    Go know of Cassio where he supped tonight.
    What, do you shake at that?
BIANCA. He supped at my house, but I therefore shake not.
IAGO. Oh, did he so? I charge you, go with me.
EMILIA. Fie, fie upon thee, strumpet!   120
BIANCA. I am no strumpet, but of life as honest
    As you that thus abuse me.
EMILIA.   As I! Foh! Fie upon thee!
IAGO. Kind gentlemen, let's go see poor Cassio dressed.°
    Come, mistress, you must tell's another tale.
    Emilia, run you to the citadel,   125
    And tell my lord and lady what hath happed!
    Will you go on afore? I pray. (*Aside*) This is the night
    That either makes me or fordoes me quite.

(*Exeunt.*)

SCENE II. *A bedchamber in the castle.* DESDEMONA *in bed asleep, a light
    burning.*

Enter OTHELLO.

OTHELLO. It is the cause,° it is the cause, my soul.
    Let me not name it to you, you chaste stars!
    It is the cause. Yet I'll not shed her blood,
    Nor scar that whiter skin of hers than snow
    And smooth as monumental alabaster.   5
    Yet she must die, else she'll betray more men.
    Put out the light, and then put out the light.
    If I quench thee, thou flaming minister,°
    I can again thy former light restore,

---

123. **dressed:** i.e., his wound dressed.   **1. It . . . cause:** The meaning of the opening lines
of this speech has been much discussed. The *cause* is Desdemona's supposed faithlessness;
Othello, at this moment, sees himself as embodied vengeance, the avenger of man betrayed
by woman. **8. minister:** servant.

Should I repent me. But once put out thy light,   10
Thou cunning'st° pattern of excelling nature,
I know not where is that Promethean heat
That can thy light relume. When I have plucked the rose,
I cannot give it vital growth again,
It needs must wither. I'll smell it on the tree. (*Kissing her*)   15
Ah, balmy breath, that dost almost persuade
Justice to break her sword! One more, one more.
Be thus when thou art dead, and I will kill thee,
And love thee after. One more, and this the last.
So sweet was ne'er so fatal. I must weep,   20
But they are cruel tears. This sorrow's heavenly,
It strikes where it doth love. She wakes.
DESDEMONA. Who's there? Othello?
OTHELLO.   Aye, Desdemona.
DESDEMONA. Will you come to bed, my lord?
OTHELLO. Have you prayed tonight, Desdemona?
DESDEMONA.   Aye, my lord.   25
OTHELLO. If you bethink yourself of any crime
    Unreconciled as yet to Heaven and grace,
    Solicit for it straight.
DESDEMONA. Alas, my lord, what may you mean by that?
OTHELLO. Well, do it, and be brief. I will walk by.   30
    I would not kill thy unprepared spirit.
    No, Heaven forfend! I would not kill thy soul.
DESDEMONA. Talk you of killing?
OTHELLO.   Aye, I do.
DESDEMONA.   Then Heaven
    Have mercy on me!
OTHELLO.   Amen, with all my heart!
DESDEMONA. If you say so, I hope you will not kill me.   35
OTHELLO. Hum!
DESDEMONA. And yet I fear you, for you are fatal then
    When your eyes roll so. Why I should fear I know not,
    Since guiltiness I know not, but yet I feel I fear.
OTHELLO. Think on thy sins.
DESDEMONA.   They are loves I bear to you.   40
OTHELLO. Aye, and for that thou diest.
DESDEMONA. That death's unnatural that kills for loving.
    Alas, why gnaw you so your nether lip?
    Some bloody passion shakes your very frame.
    These are portents, but yet I hope, I hope,   45
    They do not point on me.

11. **cunning'st:** most skillfully made.

OTHELLO. Peace, and be still!

DESDEMONA. I will so. What's the matter?

OTHELLO. That handkerchief which I so loved and gave thee
Thou gavest to Cassio.

DESDEMONA. No, by my life and soul!
Send for the man, and ask him.

OTHELLO. Sweet soul, take heed, 50
Take heed of perjury, thou art on thy deathbed.

DESDEMONA. Aye, but not yet to die.

OTHELLO. Yes, presently.°
Therefore confess thee freely of thy sin,
For to deny each article with oath
Cannot remove nor choke the strong conception 55
That I do groan withal. Thou art to die.

DESDEMONA. Then Lord have mercy on me!

OTHELLO. I say amen.

DESDEMONA. And have you mercy too! I never did
Offend you in my life, never loved Cassio
But with such general warranty of Heaven 60
As I might love. I never gave him token.

OTHELLO. By Heaven, I saw my handkerchief in 's hand.
O perjured woman! Thou dost stone° my heart,
And makest me call what I intend to do
A murder, which I thought a sacrifice. 65
I saw the handkerchief.

DESDEMONA. He found it, then,
I never gave it him. Send for him hither.
Let him confess a truth.

OTHELLO. He hath confessed.

DESDEMONA. What, my lord?

OTHELLO. That he hath used thee.

DESDEMONA. How? Unlawfully?

OTHELLO. Aye. 70

DESDEMONA. He will not say so.

OTHELLO. No, his mouth is stopped.
Honest Iago hath ta'en order for 't.

DESDEMONA. Oh, my fear interprets! What, is he dead?

OTHELLO. Had all his hairs been lives, my great revenge
Had stomach for them all. 75

DESDEMONA. Alas, he is betrayed, and I undone!

OTHELLO. Out, strumpet! Weep'st thou for him to my face?

DESDEMONA. Oh, banish me, my lord, but kill me not!

OTHELLO. Down, strumpet!

52. **presently:** at once. 63. **stone:** turn to stone.

DESDEMONA. Kill me tomorrow, let me live tonight!   80
OTHELLO. Nay, if you strive—
DESDEMONA. But half an hour!
OTHELLO.   Being done, there is no pause.
DESDEMONA. But while I say one prayer!
OTHELLO.   It is too late. (*He stifles her.*)
EMILIA (*within*). My lord, my lord! What ho! My lord, my lord!
OTHELLO. What noise is this? Not dead? Not yet quite dead?   85
   I that am cruel am yet merciful,
   I would not have thee linger in thy pain.
   So, so.
EMILIA (*within*). What ho! My lord, my lord!
OTHELLO.   Who's there?
EMILIA (*within*). Oh, good my lord, I would speak a word with you!
OTHELLO. Yes, 'tis Emilia. By and by. She's dead.   90
   'Tis like she comes to speak of Cassio's death.
   The noise was here. Ha! No more moving?
   Still as the grave. Shall she come in? Were 't good?
   I think she stirs again. No. What's best to do?
   If she come in, she'll sure speak to my wife.   95
   My wife! My wife! What wife? I have no wife.
   Oh, insupportable! Oh, heavy hour!
   Methinks it should be now a huge eclipse
   Of sun and moon, and that the affrighted globe
   Should yawn° at alteration.
EMILIA (*within*).   I do beseech you   100
   That I may speak with you, O good my lord!
OTHELLO. I had forgot thee. Oh, come in, Emilia.
   Soft, by and by. Let me the curtains° draw.
   What art thou? (*Unlocks the door.*)

   (*Enter* EMILIA.)

           What's the matter with thee now?
EMILIA. Oh, my good lord, yonder's foul murders done!   105
OTHELLO. What, now?
EMILIA. But now, my lord.
OTHELLO. It is the very error of the moon.
   She comes more nearer earth than she was wont
   And makes men mad.   110
EMILIA. Cassio, my lord, hath killed a young Venetian
   Called Roderigo.
OTHELLO.   Roderigo killed!
   And Cassio killed!

---

100. yawn: split open in an earthquake [Eds.]. **103. curtains:** i.e., of the bed.

EMILIA. No, Cassio is not killed.

OTHELLO. Not Cassio killed! Then murder's out of tune,
And sweet revenge grows harsh. 115

DESDEMONA. Oh, falsely, falsely murdered!

EMILIA. Alas, what cry is that?

OTHELLO. That! What?

EMILIA. Out and alas! That was my lady's voice.
Help! Help, ho! Help! O lady, speak again!
Sweet Desdemona! O sweet mistress, speak! 120

DESDEMONA. A guiltless death I die.

EMILIA. Oh, who hath done this deed?

DESDEMONA. Nobody, I myself. Farewell.
Commend me to my kind lord. Oh, farewell! (*Dies.*)

OTHELLO. Why, how should she be murdered?

EMILIA. Alas, who knows? 125

OTHELLO. You heard her say herself it was not I.

EMILIA. She said so. I must needs report the truth.

OTHELLO. She's like a liar gone to burning Hell.
'Twas I that killed her.

EMILIA. Oh, the more angel she,
And you the blacker devil! 130

OTHELLO. She turned to folly, and she was a whore.

EMILIA. Thou dost belie her, and thou art a devil.

OTHELLO. She was false as water.

EMILIA. Thou art rash as fire to say
That she was false. Oh, she was heavenly true!

OTHELLO. Cassio did top her, ask thy husband else. 135
Oh, I were damned beneath all depth in Hell
But that I did proceed upon just grounds
To this extremity. Thy husband knew it all.

EMILIA. My husband!

OTHELLO. Thy husband. 140

EMILIA. That she was false to wedlock?

OTHELLO. Aye, with Cassio. Nay, had she been true,
If Heaven would make me such another world
Of one entire and perfect chrysolite,
I'd not have sold her for it.

EMILIA. My husband! 145

OTHELLO. Aye, 'twas he that told me first.
An honest man he is, and hates the slime
That sticks on filthy deeds.

EMILIA. My husband!

OTHELLO. What needs this iteration, woman? I say thy husband.

EMILIA. Oh, mistress, villainy hath made mocks with love! 150
My husband say that she was false!

OTHELLO. He, woman.

I say thy husband. Dost understand the word?
My friend, thy husband, honest, honest Iago.
EMILIA. If he say so, may his pernicious soul
  Rot half a grain a day! He lies to the heart.   155
  She was too fond of her most filthy bargain.
OTHELLO. Ha!
EMILIA. Do thy worst.
  This deed of thine is no more worthy Heaven
  Than thou wast worthy her.
OTHELLO.   Peace, you were best.   160
EMILIA. Thou hast not half that power to do me harm
  As I have to be hurt. O gull! O dolt!
  As ignorant as dirt! Thou hast done a deed—
  I care not for thy sword, I'll make thee known,
  Though I lost twenty lives. Help! Help, ho! Help!   165
  The Moor hath killed my mistress! Murder! Murder!

(*Enter* MONTANO, GRATIANO, IAGO, *and others.*)

MONTANA. What is the matter? How now, General!
EMILIA. Oh, are you come, Iago? You have done well,
  That men must lay their murders on your neck.
GRATIANO. What is the matter?   170
EMILIA. Disprove this villain, if thou be'st a man.
  He says thou told'st him that his wife was false.
  I know thou didst not, thou'rt not such a villain.
  Speak, for my heart is full.
IAGO. I told him what I thought, and told no more   175
  Than what he found himself was apt and true.
EMILIA. But did you ever tell him she was false?
IAGO. I did.
EMILIA. You told a lie, an odious, damnèd lie,
  Upon my soul, a lie, a wicked lie!   180
  She false with Cassio! Did you say with Cassio?
IAGO. With Cassio, mistress. Go to, charm your tongue.°
EMILIA. I will not charm my tongue, I am bound to speak.
  My mistress here lies murdered in her bed.
ALL. Oh, Heavens forfend!   185
EMILIA. And your reports have set the murder on.
OTHELLO. Nay, stare not, masters. It is true indeed.
GRATIANO. 'Tis a strange truth.
MONTANO. Oh, monstrous act!
EMILIA.   Villainy, villainy, villainy!
  I think upon 't. I think I smell 't. Oh, villainy!   190

182. charm . . . tongue: be silent.

I thought so then. I'll kill myself for grief.
Oh, villainy, villainy!

IAGO. What, are you mad? I charge you, get you home.

EMILIA. Good gentlemen, let me have leave to speak.
'Tis proper I obey him, but not now.   195
Perchance, Iago, I will ne'er go home.

OTHELLO. Oh! Oh! Oh! (*Falling on the bed*).

EMILIA.   Nay, lay thee down and roar,
For thou hast killed the sweetest innocent
That e'er did lift up eye.

OTHELLO (*rising*).   Oh, she was foul!
I scarce did know you, Uncle. There lies your niece,   200
Whose breath indeed these hands have newly stopped.
I know this act shows horrible and grim.

GRATIANO. Poor Desdemona! I am glad thy father's dead.
Thy match was mortal to him, and pure grief
Shore his old thread in twain. Did he live now,   205
This sight would make him do a desperate turn—
Yea, curse his better angel from his side,
And fall to reprobation.°

OTHELLO. 'Tis pitiful, but yet Iago knows
That she with Cassio hath the act of shame   210
A thousand times committed. Cassio confessed it.
And she did gratify his amorous works
With that recognizance and pledge of love
Which I first gave her, I saw it in his hand.
It was a handkerchief, an antique token   215
My father gave my mother.

EMILIA. Oh, Heaven! Oh, heavenly powers!

IAGO. 'Zounds! Hold your peace.

EMILIA.   'Twill out, 'twill out. I peace!
No, I will speak as liberal as the north.°
Let Heaven and men and devils, let them all,   220
All, all, cry shame against me, yet I'll speak.

IAGO. Be wise, and get you home.

EMILIA.   I will not.

(IAGO *offers to stab* EMILIA.)

GRATIANO.   Fie!
Your sword upon a woman!

EMILIA. O thou dull Moor! That handkerchief thou speak'st of
I found by fortune and did give my husband,   225

---

208. reprobation: damnation; i.e., by self-murder.   **219. liberal . . . north:** as freely as
the north wind, which is loud and bitter.

For often with a solemn earnestness,
More than indeed belonged to such a trifle,
He begged of me to steal it.
IAGO.   Villainous whore!
EMILIA.   She give it Cassio! No, alas, I found it,
And I did give 't my husband.
IAGO.   Filth, thou liest!   230
EMILIA.   By Heaven, I do not, I do not, gentlemen.
Oh, murderous coxcomb! What should such a fool
Do with so good a wife!
OTHELLO.   Are there no stones° in Heaven
But what serve for the thunder? Precious villain!

(*He runs at* IAGO. IAGO, *from behind, stabs* EMILIA, *and exit.*)

GRATIANO.   The woman falls. Sure, he hath killed his wife.   235
EMILIA.   Aye, aye. Oh, lay me by my mistress' side.
GRATIANO.   He's gone, but his wife's killed.
MONTANO.   'Tis a notorious villain. Take you this weapon,
Which I have here recovered from the Moor.
Come, guard the door without, let him not pass,   240
But kill him rather. I'll after that same villain,
For 'tis a damnèd slave.

(*Exeunt all but* OTHELLO *and* EMILIA.)

OTHELLO.   I am not valiant neither,
But every puny whipster gets my sword.
But why should honor outlive honesty?
Let it go all.
EMILIA.   What did thy song bode, lady?   245
Hark, canst thou hear me? I will play the swan,
And die in music. (*Singing.*)
                         "Willow, willow, willow."
Moor, she was chaste. She loved thee, cruel Moor,
So come my soul to bliss as I speak true.
So speaking as I think, I die, I die (*Dies.*)   250
OTHELLO.   I have another weapon in this chamber.
It is a sword of Spain, the ice brook's temper.—
Oh, here it is. Uncle, I must come forth.
GRATIANO (*within*).   If thou attempt it, it will cost thee dear.
Thou hast no weapon, and perforce must suffer.   255
OTHELLO.   Look in upon me then, and speak with me,
Or, naked° as I am, I will assault thee.

(*Re-enter* GRATIANO.)

233. **stones:** thunderbolts.   257. **naked:** unarmed.

GRATIANO. What is the matter?

OTHELLO.   Behold, I have a weapon,
   A better never did itself sustain
   Upon a soldier's thigh. I have seen the day   260
   That with this little arm and this good sword
   I have made my way through more impediments
   Than twenty times your stop. But, oh, vain boast!
   Who can control his fate? 'Tis not so now.
   Be not afraid, though you do see me weaponed.   265
   Here is my journey's end, here is my butt°
   And very sea mark of my utmost sail.
   Do you go back dismayed? 'Tis a lost fear.
   Man but a rush° against Othello's breast,
   And he retires. Where should Othello go?   270
   Now, how dost thou look now? O ill-starred wench!
   Pale as thy smock! When we shall meet at compt,°
   This look of thine will hurl my soul from Heaven
   And fiends will snatch at it. Cold, cold, my girl!
   Even like thy chastity. Oh, cursèd slave!   275
   Whip me, ye devils,
   From the possession of this heavenly sight!
   Blow me about in winds! Roast me in sulphur!
   Wash me in steep-down gulfs of liquid fire!
   O Desdemona! Desdemona! Dead!   280
   Oh! Oh! Oh!

(*Enter* LODOVICO, MONTANO, CASSIO *carried in a chair, and* OFFICERS
   with IAGO, *prisoner.*)

LODOVICO. Where is this rash and most unfortunate man?

OTHELLO. That's he that was Othello. Here I am.

LODOVICO. Where is that viper? Bring the villain forth.

OTHELLO. I look down toward his feet,° but that's a fable.   285
   If that thou be'st a devil, I cannot kill thee. (*Wounds* IAGO.)

LODOVICO. Wrench his sword from him.

IAGO.   I bleed, sir, but not killed.

OTHELLO. I am not sorry neither. I'd have thee live,
   For, in my sense, 'tis happiness to die.

LODOVICO. O thou Othello, that wert once so good,   290
   Fall'n in the practice° of a damnèd slave,
   What shall be said to thee?

OTHELLO.   Why, anything.

---

266. butt: aim. **269. Man . . . rush:** attack with only a reed. **272. compt:** account; i.e.,
the Day of Judgment. **285. toward . . . feet:** i.e., to see if he has the cloven hoof of a
devil. **291. Fall'n . . . practice:** destroyed by the plotting.

An honorable murderer, if you will,
For naught did I in hate, but all in honor.
LODOVICO. This wretch hath part confessed his villainy.   295
Did you and he consent in Cassio's death?
OTHELLO. Aye.
CASSIO. Dear General, I never gave you cause.
OTHELLO. I do believe it, and I ask your pardon.
Will you, I pray, demand that demi-devil   300
Why he hath thus ensnared my soul and body?
IAGO. Demand me nothing. What you know, you know.
From this time forth I never will speak word.
LODOVICO. What, not to pray?
GRATIANO.   Torments will ope your lips.
OTHELLO. Well, thou dost best.   305
LODOVICO. Sir, you shall understand what hath befall'n,
Which, as I think, you know not. Here is a letter
Found in the pocket of the slain Roderigo,
And here another. The one of them imports
The death of Cassio to be undertook   310
By Roderigo.
OTHELLO. Oh, villain!
CASSIO.   Most heathenish and most gross!
LODOVICO. Now here's another discontented paper,
Found in his pocket too. And this, it seems,
Roderigo meant to have sent this damnèd villain   315
But that, belike, Iago in the interim
Came in and satisfied him.
OTHELLO.   Oh, the pernicious caitiff!
How came you, Cassio, by that handkerchief
That was my wife's?
CASSIO.   I found it in my chamber.
And he himself confessed but even now   320
That there he dropped it for a special purpose
Which wrought to his desire.
OTHELLO.   O fool! Fool! Fool!
CASSIO. There is besides in Roderigo's letter
How he upbraids Iago, that he made him
Brave° me upon the watch, whereon it came   325
That I was cast.° And even but now he spake
After long seeming dead, Iago hurt him,
Iago set him on.
LODOVICO. You must forsake this room, and go with us.
Your power and your command is taken off,   330

325. **Brave:** insult.   326. **cast:** dismissed.

And Cassio rules in Cyprus. For this slave,
If there be any cunning cruelty
That can torment him much and hold him long,°
It shall be his. You shall close prisoner rest
Till that the nature of your fault be known   335
To the Venetian state. Come, bring away.
OTHELLO. Soft you, a word or two before you go.
I have done the state some service, and they know 't.
No more of that. I pray you, in your letters,
When you shall these unlucky deeds relate,   340
Speak of me as I am, nothing extenuate,
Nor set down aught in malice. Then must you speak
Of one that loved not wisely but too well;
Of one not easily jealous, but, being wrought,
Perplexed in the extreme; of one whose hand,   345
Like the base Indian, threw a pearl away
Richer than all his tribe; of one whose subdued eyes,
Albeit unusèd to the melting mood,
Drop tears as fast as the Arabian trees
Their medicinal gum. Set you down this,   350
And say besides that in Aleppo once,
Where a malignant and a turbaned Turk
Beat a Venetian and traduced the state,
I took by the throat the circumcisèd dog
And smote him, thus. (*Stabs himself.*)   355
LODOVICO. Oh, bloody period!
GRATIANO.   All that's spoke is marred.
OTHELLO. I kissed thee ere I killed thee. No way but this,
Killing myself, to die upon a kiss. (*Falls on the bed, and dies.*)
CASSIO. This did I fear, but thought he had no weapon,
For he was great of heart.
LODOVICO (*to* IAGO).   O Spartan° dog,   360
More fell° than anguish, hunger, or the sea!
Look on the tragic loading of this bed:
This is thy work. The object poisons sight,
Let it be hid.° Gratiano, keep the house,
And seize upon the fortunes of the Moor,   365
For they succeed on you. To you, Lord Governor,
Remains the censure of this hellish villain,
The time, the place, the torture.

---

333. long: i.e., in dying. **360. Spartan:** i.e., hardhearted. **361. fell:** cruel. **364. Let . . .
hid:** At these words the curtains are closed across the inner stage (or chamber, if this scene
was acted aloft), concealing all three bodies.

Oh, enforce it!
Myself will straight aboard, and to the state   370
This heavy act with heavy heart relate. (*Exeunt.*)

QUESTIONS

1. In what ways is Othello, in the first two acts, shown to be a person of extraordinary quality?
2. Is Othello a person jealous "by nature"? Does he show any disposition to jealousy in the first two acts? What does he say about himself in his final soliloquy? (There has been much critical controversy over the psychological probability of Othello's being roused so quickly to such a high pitch of jealousy in Act III. Some have explained it by attributing a predisposition to jealousy in Othello; others have attributed it to the almost superhuman Machiavellian cleverness of Iago, which would have taken in any husband. In general, however, Shakespeare was less interested in psychological consistency and the subtle tracing of motivation—which are modern interests—than he was in theatrical effectiveness and the orchestration of emotions. Perhaps the question we should properly ask is not "How probable is Othello's jealousy?" but "How vital and effective has Shakespeare rendered it?")
3. Who is more naturally suspicious of human nature—Othello or Iago?
4. Is something of Othello's nobility manifested even in the scale of his jealousy? How does he respond to his conviction that Desdemona has been unfaithful to him? Would a lesser man have responded in the same way? Why or why not?
5. How does Othello's final speech reestablish his greatness?
6. What are Iago's motivations in his actions toward Othello, Cassio, and Roderigo? What is his philosophy? How does his technique of handling Roderigo differ from his technique in handling Othello and Cassio? Why?
7. In rousing Othello's suspicions against Desdemona (III, iii) Iago uses the same technique, in part, that he had used with Othello in inculpating Cassio (II, iii) and that he later uses with Lodovico in inculpating Othello (IV, ii). What is this technique? Why is it effective? How does he change his tactics in the opening of IV, i?
8. What opinions of Iago, before his exposure, are expressed by Othello, Desdemona, Cassio, and Lodovico? Is Othello the only one taken in by him? Does his own wife think him capable of villainy?
9. Though Othello is the protagonist, the majority of the soliloquies and asides are given to Iago. Why?
10. The difference between Othello and Desdemona that Iago plays on most is that of color, and, reading the play today, we may be tempted to see the play as being centrally about race relations. However, only one other character, besides Othello, makes much of this difference in color. Which one? Is this character sympathetically portrayed? What attitude toward Othello himself, and his marriage, is taken by the Duke, Cassio, Lodovico, Emilia, Desdemona herself? What differences between Othello and Desdemona,

besides color, are used by Iago to undermine Othello's confidence in Desdemona's fidelity? What differences does Othello himself take into account?

11. What are Desdemona's principal character traits? In what ways are she and Emilia character foils? Is she entirely discreet in pleading Cassio's case to Othello? Why or why not? Why does she lie about the handkerchief (III, iv)?

12. Like Sophocles in *Oedipus Rex*, Shakespeare makes extensive use of dramatic irony in this play. Point out effective examples.

13. Unlike *Oedipus Rex*, *Othello* utilizes comedy. For what purposes is it used? What larger difference in effect between *Othello* and *Oedipus Rex* does this use of comedy contribute to?

14. Find several occasions when chance and coincidence are involved in the plot (for example, Bianca's entry in IV, i). How important are these to the development of the plot? To what extent do they *cause* subsequent events to happen?

15. As much responsible as any other quality for the original popularity and continued vitality of *Othello* is its poetry. What are some of the prominent characteristics of that poetry (language, imagery, rhythm)? What speeches are particularly memorable or effective? Though most of the play is written in blank verse, some passages are written in rhymed iambic pentameter couplets and others in prose. Can you suggest any reasons for Shakespeare's use of these other mediums?

16. How would the effect of the play have been different if Othello had died *before* discovering Desdemona's innocence?

Molière

THE MISANTHROPE

CHARACTERS

ALCESTE, *in love with Célimène*
PHILINTE, *Alceste's friend*
ORONTE, *in love with Célimène*
CÉLIMÈNE, *Alceste's beloved*
ELIANTE, *Célimène's cousin*
ARSINOÉ, *a friend of Célimène's*

ACASTE }
CLITANDRE } *marquesses*
BASQUE, *Célimène's servant*
A GUARD *of the Marshalsea*
DUBOIS, *Alceste's valet*

The scene throughout is in Célimène's house at Paris.

ACT I

SCENE I

PHILINTE. Now, what's got into you?
ALCESTE (*seated*).   Kindly leave me alone.
PHILINTE. Come, come, what is it? This lugubrious tone . . .
ALCESTE. Leave me, I said; you spoil my solitude.
PHILINTE. Oh, listen to me, now, and don't be rude.
ALCESTE. I choose to be rude, Sir, and to be hard of hearing.   5
PHILINTE. These ugly moods of yours are not endearing;
    Friends though we are, I really must insist . . .
ALCESTE (*abruptly rising*). Friends? Friends, you say? Well, cross
    me off your list.
    I've been your friend till now, as you well know;
    But after what I saw a moment ago   10
    I tell you flatly that our ways must part.
    I wish no place in a dishonest heart.
PHILINTE. Why, what have I done, Alceste? Is this quite just?
ALCESTE. My God, you ought to die of self-disgust.

THE MISANTHROPE First performed, in Paris, in 1666, during the reign of the Sun King, Louis XIV, a time in social and aristocratic circles when great emphasis was placed on elegance in dress, manners, and taste. Translated by Richard Wilbur. Molière (1622–1673) was born Jean-Baptiste Poquelin in Paris and was given excellent schooling by his father, a successful upholsterer employed by the court. He took "Molière" as his stage-name when, at the age of twenty-one, he joined a traveling group of players. The rest of his life was spent in the theater as actor, manager, and author. Though twice sent to prison for debts, and often in trouble with the civil authorities for his writing, he enjoyed a certain amount of royal favor after his establishment in Paris in 1658.

I call your conduct inexcusable, Sir,   15
And every man of honor will concur.
I see you almost hug a man to death,
Exclaim for joy until you're out of breath,
And supplement these loving demonstrations
With endless offers, vows, and protestations;   20
Then when I ask you "Who was that?" I find
That you can barely bring his name to mind!
Once the man's back is turned, you cease to love him,
And speak with absolute indifference of him!
By God, I say it's base and scandalous   25
To falsify the heart's affections thus;
If I caught myself behaving in such a way,
I'd hang myself for shame, without delay.

PHILINTE.   It hardly seems a hanging matter to me;
I hope that you will take it graciously   30
If I extend myself a slight reprieve,
And live a little longer, by your leave.

ALCESTE.   How dare you joke about a crime so grave?

PHILINTE.   What crime? How else are people to behave?

ALCESTE.   I'd have them be sincere, and never part   35
With any word that isn't from the heart.

PHILINTE.   When someone greets us with a show of pleasure,
It's but polite to give him equal measure,
Return his love the best that we know how,
And trade him offer for offer, vow for vow.   40

ALCESTE.   No, no, this formula you'd have me follow,
However fashionable, is false and hollow,
And I despise the frenzied operations
Of all these barterers of protestations,
These lavishers of meaningless embraces,   45
These utterers of obliging commonplaces,
Who court and flatter everyone on earth
And praise the fool no less than the man of worth.
Should you rejoice that someone fondles you,
Offers his love and service, swears to be true,   50
And fills your ears with praises of your name,
When to the first damned fop he'll say the same?
No, no: no self-respecting heart would dream
Of prizing so promiscuous an esteem;
However high the praise, there's nothing worse   55
Than sharing honors with the universe.
Esteem is founded on comparison:
To honor all men is to honor none.
Since you embrace this indiscriminate vice,

Your friendship comes at far too cheap a price;   60
    I spurn the easy tribute of a heart
    Which will not set the worthy man apart:
    I choose, Sir, to be chosen; and in fine,
    The friend of mankind is no friend of mine.
PHILINTE. But in polite society, custom decrees   65
    That we show certain outward courtesies . . .
ALCESTE. Ah, no! we should condemn with all our force
    Such false and artificial intercourse.
    Let men behave like men; let them display
    Their inmost hearts in everything they say;   70
    Let the heart speak, and let our sentiments
    Not mask themselves in silly compliments.
PHILINTE. In certain cases it would be uncouth
    And most absurd to speak the naked truth;
    With all respect for your exalted notions,   75
    It's often best to veil one's true emotions.
    Wouldn't the social fabric come undone
    If we were wholly frank with everyone?
    Suppose you met with someone you couldn't bear;
    Would you inform him of it then and there?   80
ALCESTE. Yes.
PHILINTE.   Then you'd tell old Emilie it's pathetic
    The way she daubs her features with cosmetic
    And plays the gay coquette at sixty-four?
ALCESTE. I would.
PHILINTE.   And you'd call Dorilas a bore,
    And tell him every ear at court is lame   85
    From hearing him brag about his noble name?
ALCESTE. Precisely.
PHILINTE.   Ah, you're joking.
ALCESTE.   *Au contraire:*°
    In this regard there's none I'd choose to spare.
    All are corrupt; there's nothing to be seen
    In court or town but aggravates my spleen.   90
    I fall into deep gloom and melancholy
    When I survey the scene of human folly,
    Finding on every hand base flattery,
    Injustice, fraud, self-interest, treachery . . .
    Ah, it's too much; mankind has grown so base,   95
    I mean to break with the whole human race.
PHILINTE. This philosophic rage is a bit extreme;
    You've no idea how comical you seem;

---

87. *Au contraire:* On the contrary

Indeed, we're like those brothers in the play
Called *School for Husbands,* one of whom was prey . . .°   100
ALCESTE.   Enough, now! None of your stupid similes.
PHILINTE.   Then let's have no more tirades, if you please.
The world won't change, whatever you say or do;
And since plain speaking means so much to you,
I'll tell you plainly that by being frank   105
You've earned the reputation of a crank,
And that you're thought ridiculous when you rage
And rant against the manners of the age.
ALCESTE.   So much the better; just what I wish to hear.
No news could be more grateful to my ear.   110
All men are so detestable in my eyes,
I should be sorry if they thought me wise.
PHILINTE.   Your hatred's very sweeping, is it not?
ALCESTE.   Quite right: I hate the whole degraded lot.
PHILINTE.   Must all poor human creatures be embraced,   115
Without distinction, by your vast distaste?
Even in these bad times, there are surely a few . . .
ALCESTE.   No, I include all men in one dim view:
Some men I hate for being rogues; the others
I hate because they treat the rogues like brothers,   120
And, lacking a virtuous scorn for what is vile,
Receive the villain with a complaisant smile.
Notice how tolerant people choose to be
Toward that bold rascal who's at law with me.
His social polish can't conceal his nature;   125
One sees at once that he's a treacherous creature;
No one could possibly be taken in
By those soft speeches and that sugary grin.
The whole world knows the shady means by which
The low-brow's grown so powerful and rich,   130
And risen to a rank so bright and high
That virtue can but blush, and merit sigh.
Whenever his name comes up in conversation,
None will defend his wretched reputation;
Call him knave, liar, scoundrel, and all the rest,   135
Each head will nod, and no one will protest.
And yet his smirk is seen in every house,

---

100. School . . . prey: *School for Husbands* is an earlier play by Molière. The chief
characters are two brothers, one of whom, puritanical and suspicious, mistrusts the fashions
and customs of the world, shuts up his ward and fiancée to keep her from infection by them,
and is outwitted and betrayed by her. The other, more amiable and easy going, allows his
ward a free rein and is rewarded with her love.

He's greeted everywhere with smiles and bows,
And when there's any honor that can be got
By pulling strings, he'll get it, like as not.   140
My God! It chills my heart to see the ways
Men come to terms with evil nowadays;
Sometimes, I swear, I'm moved to flee and find
Some desert land unfouled by humankind.

PHILINTE. Come, let's forget the follies of the times   145
And pardon mankind for its petty crimes;
Let's have an end of rantings and of railings,
And show some leniency toward human failings.
This world requires a pliant rectitude;
Too stern a virtue makes one stiff and rude;   150
Good sense views all extremes with detestation,
And bids us to be noble in moderation.
The rigid virtues of the ancient days
Are not for us; they jar with all our ways
And ask of us too lofty a perfection.   155
Wise men accept their times without objection,
And there's no greater folly, if you ask me,
Than trying to reform society.
Like you, I see each day a hundred and one
Unhandsome deeds that might be better done,   160
But still, for all the faults that meet my view,
I'm never known to storm and rave like you.
I take men as they are, or let them be,
And teach my soul to bear their frailty;
And whether in court or town, whatever the scene,   165
My phlegm's as philosophic as your spleen.

ALCESTE. This phlegm which you so eloquently commend,
Does nothing ever rile it up, my friend?
Suppose some man you trust should treacherously
Conspire to rob you of your property,   170
And do his best to wreck your reputation?
Wouldn't you feel a certain indignation?

PHILINTE. Why, no. These faults of which you complain
Are part of human nature, I maintain,
And it's no more a matter for disgust   175
That men are knavish, selfish and unjust,
Than that the vulture dines upon the dead,
And wolves are furious, and apes ill-bred.

ALCESTE. Shall I see myself betrayed, robbed, torn to bits,
And not . . . Oh, let's be still and rest our wits.   180
Enough of reasoning, now. I've had my fill.

PHILINTE. Indeed, you would do well, Sir, to be still.

Rage less at your opponent, and give some thought
To how you'll win this lawsuit that he's brought.
ALCESTE. I assure you I'll do nothing of the sort.   185
PHILINTE. Then who will plead your case before the court?
ALCESTE. Reason and right and justice will plead for me.
PHILINTE. Oh, Lord. What judges do you plan to see?
ALCESTE. Why, none. The justice of my cause is clear.
PHILINTE. Of course, man; but there's politics to fear . . .   190
ALCESTE. No, I refuse to lift a hand. That's flat.
    I'm either right, or wrong.
PHILINTE.   Don't count on that.
ALCESTE. No, I'll do nothing.
PHILINTE.   Your enemy's influence
    Is great, you know . . .
ALCESTE.   That makes no difference.
PHILINTE. It will; you'll see.
ALCESTE   Must honor bow to guile?   195
    If so, I shall be proud to lose the trial.
PHILINTE. Oh, really . . .
ALCESTE.   I'll discover by this case
    Whether or not men are sufficiently base
    And impudent and villainous and perverse
    To do me wrong before the universe.   200
PHILINTE. What a man!
ALCESTE.   Oh, I could wish, whatever the cost,
    Just for the beauty of it, that my trial were lost.
PHILINTE. If people heard you talking so, Alceste,
    They'd split their sides. Your name would be a jest.
ALCESTE. So much the worse for jesters.
PHILINTE.   May I enquire   205
    Whether this rectitude you so admire,
    And these hard virtues you're enamored of
    Are qualities of the lady whom you love?
    It much surprises me that you, who seem
    To view mankind with furious disesteem,   210
    Have yet found something to enchant your eyes
    Amidst a species which you so despise.
    And what is more amazing, I'm afraid,
    Is the most curious choice your heart has made.
    The honest Eliante is fond of you,   215
    Arsinoé, the prude, admires you too;
    And yet your spirit's been perversely led
    To choose the flighty Célimène instead,
    Whose brittle malice and coquettish ways
    So typify the manners of our days.   220

How is it that the traits you most abhor
Are bearable in this lady you adore?
Are you so blind with love that you can't find them?
Or do you contrive, in her case, not to mind them?
ALCESTE. My love for that young widow's not the kind   225
  That can't perceive defects; no, I'm not blind.
  I see her faults, despite my ardent love,
  And all I see I fervently reprove.
  And yet I'm weak; for all her falsity,
  That woman knows the art of pleasing me,   230
  And though I never cease complaining of her,
  I swear I cannot manage not to love her.
  Her charm outweighs her faults; I can but aim
  To cleanse her spirit in my love's pure flame.
PHILINTE. That's no small task; I wish you all success.   235
  You think then that she loves you?
ALCESTE.   Heavens, yes!
  I wouldn't love her did she not love me.
PHILINTE. Well, if her taste for you is plain to see,
  Why do these rivals cause you such despair?
ALCESTE. True love, Sir, is possessive, and cannot bear   240
  To share with all the world. I'm here today
  To tell her she must send that mob away.
PHILINTE. If I were you, and had your choice to make,
  Eliante, her cousin, would be the one I'd take;
  That honest heart, which cares for you alone,   245
  Would harmonize far better with your own.
ALCESTE. True, true: each day my reason tells me so;
  But reason doesn't rule in love, you know.
PHILINTE. I fear some bitter sorrow is in store;
  This love . . .

SCENE II°

ORONTE (*to* ALCESTE). The servants told me at the door   250
  That Eliante and Célimène were out,
  But when I heard, dear Sir, that you were about,
  I came to say, without exaggeration,
  That I hold you in the vastest admiration,
  And that it's always been my dearest desire   255

Scene II: In English and in most modern plays, a scene is a continuous section of the action in one setting, and acts are not usually divided into scenes unless there is a shift in setting or a shift in time. In older French drama, however, a scene is any portion of the play involving one group of characters, and a new scene begins, without interruption of the action, whenever any important character enters or exits.

To be the friend of one I so admire.
I hope to see my love of merit requited,
And you and I in friendship's bond united.
I'm sure you won't refuse—if I may be frank—
A friend of my devotedness—and rank. (*During this speech of* ORONTE'S,
ALCESTE *is abstracted, and seems unaware that he is being spoken to. He
only breaks off his reverie when* ORONTE *says*)
It was for you, if you please, that my words were intended.   261
ALCESTE. For me, Sir?
ORONTE.   Yes, for you. You're not offended?
ALCESTE. By no means. But this much surprises me . . .
   The honor comes most unexpectedly . . .
ORONTE. My high regard should not astonish you;   265
   The whole world feels the same. It is your due.
ALCESTE. Sir . . .
ORONTE.   Why, in all the State there isn't one
   Can match your merits; they shine, Sir, like the sun.
ALCESTE. Sir . . .
ORONTE.   You are higher in my estimation
   Than all that's most illustrious in the nation.   270
ALCESTE. Sir . . .
ORONTE.   If I lie, may heaven strike me dead!
   To show you that I mean what I have said,
   Permit me, Sir, to embrace you most sincerely,
   And swear that I will prize our friendship dearly.
   Give me your hand. And now, Sir, if you choose,   275
   We'll make our vows.
ALCESTE.   Sir . . .
ORONTE.   What! You refuse?
ALCESTE. Sir, it's a very great honor you extend:
   But friendship is a sacred thing, my friend;
   It would be profanation to bestow
   The name of friend on one you hardly know.   280
   All parts are better played when well-rehearsed;
   Let's put off friendship, and get acquainted first.
   We may discover it would be unwise
   To try to make our natures harmonize.
ORONTE. By heaven! You're sagacious to the core;   285
   This speech has made me admire you even more.
   Let time, then, bring us closer day by day;
   Meanwhile, I shall be yours in every way.
   If, for example, there should be anything
   You wish at court, I'll mention it to the King.   290
   I have his ear, of course; it's quite well known
   That I am much in favor with the throne.
   In short, I am your servant. And now, dear friend,

Since you have such fine judgment, I intend
To please you, if I can, with a small sonnet   295
I wrote not long ago. Please comment on it,
And tell me whether I ought to publish it.
ALCESTE. You must excuse me, Sir; I'm hardly fit
To judge such matters.
ORONTE.   Why not?
ALCESTE.   I am, I fear,
Inclined to be unfashionably sincere.   300
ORONTE. Just what I ask; I'd take no satisfaction
In anything but your sincere reaction.
I beg you not to dream of being kind.
ALCESTE. Since you desire it, Sir, I'll speak my mind.
ORONTE. *Sonnet.* It's a sonnet . . . *Hope* . . . The poem's addressed   305
To a lady who wakened hopes within my breast.
Hope . . . this is not the pompous sort of thing,
Just modest little verses, with a tender ring.
ALCESTE. Well, we shall see.
ORONTE.   *Hope* . . . I'm anxious to hear
Whether the style seems properly smooth and clear,   310
And whether the choice of words is good or bad.
ALCESTE. We'll see, we'll see.
ORONTE.   Perhaps I ought to add
That it took me only a quarter-hour to write it.
ALCESTE. The time's irrelevant, Sir: kindly recite it.
ORONTE (*reading*). Hope comforts us awhile, 'tis true,   315
              Lulling our cares with careless laughter,
              And yet such joy is full of rue,
              My Phyllis, if nothing follows after.
PHILINTE. I'm charmed by this already; the style's delightful.
ALCESTE (*sotto voce, to* PHILINTE). How can you say that? Why, the thing is
    frightful.   320
ORONTE.   Your fair face smiled on me awhile,
              But was it kindness so to enchant me?
              'Twould have been fairer not to smile,
              If hope was all you meant to grant me.
PHILINTE. What a clever thought! How handsomely you phrase it!   325
ALCESTE (*sotto voce, to* PHILINTE). You know the thing is trash. How dare
    you praise it?
ORONTE.   If it's to be my passion's fate
              Thus everlastingly to wait,
              Then death will come to set me free:
              For death is fairer than the fair;   330
              Phyllis, to hope is to despair
              When one must hope eternally.
PHILINTE. The close is exquisite—full of feeling and grace.

ALCESTE (*sotto voce, aside*).   Oh, blast the close; you'd better close your face
    Before you send your lying soul to hell.   335
PHILINTE.   I can't remember a poem I've liked so well.
ALCESTE (*sotto voce, aside*).   Good Lord!
ORONTE (*to* PHILINTE).   I fear you're flattering me a bit.
PHILINTE.   Oh, no!
ALCESTE (*sotto voce, aside*).   What else d'you call it, you hypocrite?
ORONTE (*to* ALCESTE).   But you, Sir, keep your promise now: don't shrink
    From telling me sincerely what you think.   340
ALCESTE.   Sir, these are delicate matters; we all desire
    To be told that we've the true poetic fire.
    But once, to one whose name I shall not mention,
    I said, regarding some verse of his invention,
    That gentlemen should rigorously control   345
    That itch to write which often afflicts the soul;
    That one should curb the heady inclination
    To publicize one's little avocation;
    And that in showing off one's works of art
    One often plays a very clownish part.   350
ORONTE.   Are you suggesting in a devious way
    That I ought not . . .
ALCESTE.   Oh, that I do not say.
    Further, I told him that no fault is worse
    Than that of writing frigid, lifeless verse,
    And that the merest whisper of such a shame   355
    Suffices to destroy a man's good name.
ORONTE.   D'you mean to say my sonnet's dull and trite?
ALCESTE.   I don't say that. But I went on to cite
    Numerous cases of once-respected men
    Who came to grief by taking up the pen.   360
ORONTE.   And am I like them? Do I write so poorly?
ALCESTE.   I don't say that. But I told this person, "Surely
    You're under no necessity to compose;
    Why you should wish to publish, heaven knows.
    There's no excuse for printing tedious rot   365
    Unless one writes for bread, as you do not.
    Resist temptation, then, I beg of you;
    Conceal your pastimes from the public view;
    And don't give up, on any provocation,
    Your present high and courtly reputation,   370
    To purchase at a greedy printer's shop
    The name of silly author and scribbling fop."
    These were the points I tried to make him see.
ORONTE.   I sense that they are also aimed at me;
    But now—about my sonnet—I'd like to be told . . .   375

ALCESTE.   Frankly, that sonnet should be pigeonholed.
You've chosen the worst models to imitate.
The style's unnatural. Let me illustrate:

> For example, Your fair face smiled on me awhile,
> Followed by, 'Twould have been fairer not to smile!   380
> Or this: such joy is full of rue;
> Or this: For death is fairer than the fair;
> Or, Phyllis, to hope is to despair
>   When one must hope eternally!

This artificial style, that's all the fashion,   385
Has neither taste, nor honesty, nor passion;
It's nothing but a sort of wordy play,
And nature never spoke in such a way.
What, in this shallow age, is not debased?
Our fathers, though less refined, had better taste;   390
I'd barter all that men admire today
For one old love-song I shall try to say:

> If the King had given me for my own
> Paris, his citadel,
> And I for that must leave alone   395
> Her whom I love so well,
> I'd say then to the Crown,
> Take back your glittering town;
> My darling is more fair, I swear,
> My darling is more fair.   400

The rhyme's not rich, the style is rough and old,
But don't you see that it's the purest gold
Beside the tinsel nonsense now preferred,
And that there's passion in its every word?

> If the King had given me for my own   405
> Paris, his citadel,
> And I for that must leave alone
> Her whom I love so well,
> I'd say then to the Crown,
> Take back your glittering town;   410
> My darling is more fair, I swear,
> My darling is more fair.

There speaks a loving heart. (*To* PHILINTE) You're laughing, eh?
Laugh on, my precious wit. Whatever you say,
I hold that song's worth all the bibelots   415
That people hail today with ah's and oh's.
ORONTE.   And I maintain my sonnet's very good.

ALCESTE. It's not at all surprising that you should.
    You have your reasons; permit me to have mine
    For thinking that you cannot write a line.   420
ORONTE. Others have praised my sonnet to the skies.
ALCESTE. I lack their art of telling pleasant lies.
ORONTE. You seem to think you've got no end of wit.
ALCESTE. To praise your verse, I'd need still more of it.
ORONTE. I'm not in need of your approval, Sir.   425
ALCESTE. That's good; you couldn't have it if you were.
ORONTE. Come now, I'll lend you the subject of my sonnet;
    I'd like to see you try to improve upon it.
ALCESTE. I might, by chance, write something just as shoddy;
    But then I wouldn't show it to everybody.   430
ORONTE. You're most opinionated and conceited.
ALCESTE. Go find your flatterers, and be better treated.
ORONTE. Look here, my little fellow, pray watch your tone.
ALCESTE. My great big fellow, you'd better watch your own.
PHILINTE (*stepping between them*). Oh, please, please, gentlemen!
    This will never do.   435
ORONTE. The fault is mine, and I leave the field to you.
    I am your servant, Sir, in every way.
ALCESTE. And I, Sir, am your most abject valet.

SCENE III

PHILINTE. Well, as you see, sincerity in excess
    Can get you into a very pretty mess;   440
    Oronte was hungry for appreciation . . .
ALCESTE. Don't speak to me.
PHILINTE.   What?
ALCESTE.   No more conversation.
PHILINTE. Really, now . . .
ALCESTE.   Leave me alone.
PHILINTE.   If I . . .
ALCESTE.   Out of my sight!
PHILINTE. But what . . .
ALCESTE.   I won't listen.
PHILINTE.   But . . .
ALCESTE.   Silence!
PHILINTE.   Now, is it polite . . .
ALCESTE. By heaven, I've had enough. Don't follow me.   445
PHILINTE. Ah, you're just joking. I'll keep you company.

ACT II

SCENE I

ALCESTE. Shall I speak plainly, Madam? I confess
    Your conduct gives me infinite distress,
    And my resentment's grown too hot to smother.
    Soon, I foresee, we'll break with one another.
    If I said otherwise, I should deceive you;   5
    Sooner or later, I shall be forced to leave you,
    And if I swore that we shall never part,
    I should misread the omens of my heart.
CÉLIMÈNE. You kindly saw me home, it would appear,
    So as to pour invectives in my ear.   10
ALCESTE. I've no desire to quarrel. But I deplore
    Your inability to shut the door
    On all these suitors who beset you so.
    There's what annoys me, if you care to know.
CÉLIMÈNE. Is it my fault that all these men pursue me?   15
    Am I to blame if they're attracted to me?
    And when they gently beg an audience,
    Ought I to take a stick and drive them hence?
ALCESTE. Madam, there's no necessity for a stick;
    A less responsive heart would do the trick.   20
    Of your attractiveness I don't complain;
    But those your charms attract, you then detain
    By a most melting and receptive manner,
    And so enlist their hearts beneath your banner.
    It's the agreeable hopes which you excite   25
    That keep these lovers round you day and night;
    Were they less liberally smiled upon,
    That sighing troop would very soon be gone.
    But tell me, Madam, why it is that lately
    This man Clitandre interests you so greatly?   30
    Because of what high merits do you deem
    Him worthy of the honor of your esteem?
    Is it that your admiring glances linger
    On the splendidly long nail of his little finger?
    Or do you share the general deep respect   35
    For the blond wig he chooses to affect?
    Are you in love with his embroidered hose?
    Do you adore his ribbons and his bows?
    Or is it that this paragon bewitches
    Your tasteful eye with his vast German breeches?   40

Perhaps his giggle, or his falsetto voice,
Makes him the latest gallant of your choice?
CÉLIMÈNE. You're much mistaken to resent him so.
Why I put up with him you surely know:
My lawsuit's very shortly to be tried,   45
And I must have his influence on my side.
ALCESTE. Then lose your lawsuit, Madam, or let it drop;
Don't torture me by humoring such a fop.
CÉLIMÈNE. You're jealous of the whole world, Sir.
ALCESTE.   That's true,
Since the whole world is well-received by you.   50
CÉLIMÈNE. That my good nature is so unconfined
Should serve to pacify your jealous mind;
Were I to smile on one, and scorn the rest,
Then you might have some cause to be distressed.
ALCESTE. Well, if I mustn't be jealous, tell me, then,   55
Just how I'm better treated than other men.
CÉLIMÈNE. You know you have my love. Will that not do?
ALCESTE. What proof have I that what you say is true?
CÉLIMÈNE. I would expect, Sir, that my having said it
Might give the statement a sufficient credit.   60
ALCESTE. But how can I be sure that you don't tell
The selfsame thing to other men as well?
CÉLIMÈNE. What a gallant speech! How flattering to me!
What a sweet creature you make me out to be!
Well then, to save you from the pangs of doubt,   65
All that I've said I hereby cancel out;
Now, none but yourself shall make a monkey of you:
Are you content?
ALCESTE.   Why, why am I doomed to love you?
I swear that I shall bless the blissful hour
When this poor heart's no longer in your power!   70
I make no secret of it: I've done my best
To exorcise this passion from my breast;
But thus far all in vain; it will not go;
It's for my sins that I must love you so.
CÉLIMÈNE. Your love for me is matchless, Sir; that's clear.   75
ALCESTE. Indeed, in all the world it has no peer;
Words can't describe the nature of my passion,
And no man ever loved in such a fashion.
CÉLIMÈNE. Yes, it's a brand-new fashion, I agree:
You show your love by castigating me,   80
And all your speeches are enraged and rude.
I've never been so furiously wooed.
ALCESTE. Yet you could calm that fury, if you chose.

Come, shall we bring our quarrels to a close?
Let's speak with open hearts, then, and begin . . .   85

SCENE II

CÉLIMÈNE. What is it?
BASQUE.   Acaste is here.
CÉLIMÈNE.   Well, send him in.

SCENE III

ALCESTE. What! Shall we never be alone at all?
    You're always ready to receive a call,
    And you can't bear, for ten ticks of the clock,
    Not to keep open house for all who knock.   90
CÉLIMÈNE. I couldn't refuse him: he'd be most put out.
ALCESTE. Surely that's not worth worrying about.
CÉLIMÈNE. Acaste would never forgive me if he guessed
    That I consider him a dreadful pest.
ALCESTE. If he's a pest, why bother with him then?   95
CÉLIMÈNE. Heavens! One can't antagonize such men;
    Why, they're the chartered gossips of the court,
    And have a say in things of every sort.
    One must receive them, and be full of charm;
    They're no great help, but they can do you harm,   100
    And though your influence be ever so great,
    They're hardly the best people to alienate.
ALCESTE. I see, dear lady, that you could make a case
    For putting up with the whole human race;
    These friendships that you calculate so nicely . . .   105

SCENE IV

BASQUE. Madam, Clitandre is here as well.
ALCESTE.   Precisely.
CÉLIMÈNE. Where are you going?
ALCESTE.   Elsewhere.
CÉLIMÈNE.   Stay.
ALCESTE.   No, no.
CÉLIMÈNE. Stay, Sir.
ALCESTE.   I can't.
CÉLIMÈNE.   I wish it.
ALCESTE.   No, I must go.
    I beg you, Madam, not to press the matter;
    You know I have no taste for idle chatter.   110

CÉLIMÈNE. Stay: I command you.
ALCESTE.   No, I cannot stay.
CÉLIMÈNE. Very well; you have my leave to go away.

SCENE V

ELIANTE (*to* CÉLIMÈNE). The Marquesses have kindly come to call.
    Were they announced?
CÉLIMÈNE.   Yes. Basque, bring chairs for all. (BASQUE *pro-*
    vides the chairs, and exits. To ALCESTE)
    You haven't gone?
ALCESTE.   No; and I shan't depart   115
    Till you decide who's foremost in your heart.
CÉLIMÈNE. Oh, hush.
ALCESTE.   It's time to choose; take them or me.
CÉLIMÈNE. You're mad.
ALCESTE.   I'm not, as you shall shortly see.
CÉLIMÈNE. Oh?
ALCESTE.   You'll decide.
CÉLIMÈNE.   You're joking now, dear friend.
ALCESTE. No, no; you'll choose; my patience is at an end.   120
CLITANDRE. Madam, I come from court, where poor Cléonte
    Behaved like a perfect fool, as is his wont.
    Has he no friend to counsel him, I wonder,
    And teach him less unerringly to blunder?
CÉLIMÈNE. It's true, the man's a most accomplished dunce;   125
    His gauche behavior charms the eye at once;
    And every time one sees him, on my word,
    His manner's grown a trifle more absurd.
ACASTE. Speaking of dunces, I've just now conversed
    With old Damon, who's one of the very worst;   130
    I stood a lifetime in the broiling sun
    Before his dreary monologue was done.
CÉLIMÈNE. Oh, he's a wondrous talker, and has the power
    To tell you nothing hour after hour:
    If, by mistake, he ever came to the point,   135
    The shock would put his jawbone out of joint.
ELIANTE (*to* PHILINTE). The conversation takes its usual turn,
    And all our dear friends' ears will shortly burn.
CLITANDRE. Timante's a character, Madam.
CÉLIMÈNE.   Isn't he, though?
    A man of mystery from top to toe,   140
    Who moves about in a romantic mist
    On secret missions which do not exist.
    His talk is full of eyebrows and grimaces;

How tired one gets of his momentous faces;
He's always whispering something confidential   145
Which turns out to be quite inconsequential;
Nothing's too slight for him to mystify;
He even whispers when he says "good-by."
ACASTE. Tell us about Géralde.
CÉLIMÈNE.   That tiresome ass.
He mixes only with the titled class,   150
And fawns on dukes and princes, and is bored
With anyone who's not at least a lord.
The man's obsessed with rank, and his discourses
Are all of hounds and carriages and horses;
He uses Christian names with all the great,   155
And the word Milord, with him, is out of date.
CLITANDRE. He's very taken with Bélise, I hear.
CÉLIMÈNE. She is the dreariest company, poor dear.
Whenever she comes to call, I grope about
To find some topic which will draw her out,   160
But, owing to her dry and faint replies,
The conversation wilts, and droops, and dies.
In vain one hopes to animate her face
By mentioning the ultimate commonplace;
But sun or shower, even hail or frost   165
Are matters she can instantly exhaust.
Meanwhile her visit, painful though it is,
Drags on and on through mute eternities,
And though you ask the time, and yawn, and yawn,
She sits there like a stone and won't be gone.   170
ACASTE. Now for Adraste.
CÉLIMÈNE.   Oh, that conceited elf
Has a gigantic passion for himself;
He rails against the court, and cannot bear it
That none will recognize his hidden merit;
All honors given to others give offense   175
To his imaginary excellence.
CLITANDRE. What about young Cléon? His house, they say,
Is full of the best society, night and day.
CÉLIMÈNE. His cook has made him popular, not he:
It's Cléon's table that people come to see.   180
ELIANTE. He gives a splendid dinner, you must admit.
CÉLIMÈNE. But must he serve himself along with it?
For my taste, he's a most insipid dish
Whose presence sours the wine and spoils the fish.
PHILINTE. Damis, his uncle, is admired no end.   185
What's your opinion, Madam?

CÉLIMÈNE.   Why, he's my friend.

PHILINTE.   He seems a decent fellow, and rather clever.

CÉLIMÈNE.   He works too hard at cleverness, however.

> I hate to see him sweat and struggle so
> To fill his conversation with bons mots.   190
> Since he's decided to become a wit
> His taste's so pure that nothing pleases it;
> He scolds at all the latest books and plays,
> Thinking that wit must never stoop to praise,
> That finding fault's a sign of intellect,   195
> That all appreciation is abject,
> And that by damning everything in sight
> One shows oneself in a distinguished light.
> He's scornful even of our conversations:
> Their trivial nature sorely tries his patience;   200
> He folds his arms, and stands above the battle,
> And listens sadly to our childish prattle.

ACASTE.   Wonderful, Madam! You've hit him off precisely.

CLITANDRE.   No one can sketch a character so nicely.

ALCESTE.   How bravely, Sirs, you cut and thrust at all   205

> These absent fools, till one by one they fall:
> But let one come in sight, and you'll at once
> Embrace the man you lately called a dunce,
> Telling him in a tone sincere and fervent
> How proud you are to be his humble servant.   210

CLITANDRE.   Why pick on us? Madame's been speaking, Sir,

> And you should quarrel, if you must, with her.

ALCESTE.   No, no, by God, the fault is yours, because

> You lead her on with laughter and applause,
> And make her think that she's the more delightful   215
> The more her talk is scandalous and spiteful.
> Oh, she would stoop to malice far, far less
> If no such claque approved her cleverness.
> It's flatterers like you whose foolish praise
> Nourishes all the vices of these days.   220

PHILINTE.   But why protest when someone ridicules

> Those you'd condemn, yourself, as knaves or fools?

CÉLIMÈNE.   Why, Sir? Because he loves to make a fuss.

> You don't expect him to agree with us,
> When there's an opportunity to express   225
> His heaven-sent spirit of contrariness?
> What other people think, he can't abide;
> Whatever they say, he's on the other side;
> He lives in deadly terror of agreeing;
> 'Twould make him seem an ordinary being.   230

Indeed, he's so in love with contradiction,
He'll turn against his most profound conviction
And with a furious eloquence deplore it,
If only someone else is speaking for it.

ALCESTE. Go on, dear lady, mock me as you please;   235
You have your audience in ecstasies.

PHILINTE. But what she says is true: you have a way
Of bridling at whatever people say;
Whether they praise or blame, your angry spirit
Is equally unsatisfied to hear it.   240

ALCESTE. Men, Sir, are always wrong, and that's the reason
That righteous anger's never out of season;
All that I hear in all their conversation
Is flattering praise or reckless condemnation.

CÉLIMÈNE. But . . .

ALCESTE.   No, no, Madam, I am forced to state   245
That you have pleasures which I deprecate,
And that these others, here, are much to blame
For nourishing the faults which are your shame.

CLITANDRE. I shan't defend myself, Sir; but I vow
I'd thought this lady faultless until now.   250

ACASTE. I see her charms and graces, which are many;
But as for faults, I've never noticed any.

ALCESTE. I see them, Sir; and rather than ignore them,
I strenuously criticize her for them.
The more one loves, the more one should object   255
To every blemish, every least defect.
Were I this lady, I would soon get rid
Of lovers who approved of all I did,
And by their slack indulgence and applause
Endorsed my follies and excused my flaws.   260

CÉLIMÈNE. If all hearts beat according to your measure,
The dawn of love would be the end of pleasure;
And love would find its perfect consummation
In ecstasies of rage and reprobation.

ELIANTE. Love, as a rule, affects men otherwise,   265
And lovers rarely love to criticize.
They see their lady as a charming blur,
And find all things commendable in her.
If she has any blemish, fault, or shame,
They will redeem it by a pleasing name.   270
The pale-faced lady's lily-white, perforce;
The swarthy one's a sweet brunette, of course;
The spindly lady has a slender grace;
The fat one has a most majestic pace;

The plain one, with her dress in disarray,   275
They classify as *beauté négligée;*°
The hulking one's a goddess in their eyes,
The dwarf, a concentrate of Paradise;
The haughty lady has a noble mind;
The mean one's witty, and the dull one's kind;   280
The chatterbox has liveliness and verve,
The mute one has a virtuous reserve.
So lovers manage, in their passion's cause,
To love their ladies even for their flaws.
ALCESTE. But I still say. . .
CÉLIMÈNE.   I think it would be nice   285
To stroll around the gallery once or twice.
What! You're not going, Sirs?
CLITANDRE *and* ACASTE.   No, Madam, no.
ALCESTE. You seem to be in terror lest they go.
Do what you will, Sirs; leave, or linger on,
But I shan't go till after you are gone.   290
ACASTE. I'm free to linger, unless I should perceive
Madame is tired, and wishes me to leave.
CLITANDRE. And as for me, I needn't go today
Until the hour of the King's *coucher.*°
CÉLIMÈNE (*to* ALCESTE). You're joking, surely?
ALCESTE.   Not in the least; we'll see
Whether you'd rather part with them, or me.   296

SCENE VI

BASQUE (*to* ALCESTE).   Sir, there's a fellow here who bids me state
That he must see you, and that it can't wait.
ALCESTE. Tell him that I have no such pressing affairs.
BASQUE. It's a long tailcoat that this fellow wears,   300
With gold all over.
CÉLIMÈNE (*to* ALCESTE).   You'd best go down and see.
Or—have him enter.

SCENE VII

ALCESTE (*confronting the guard*). Well, what do you want with me?
Come in, Sir.
GUARD.   I've a word, Sir, for your ear.
ALCESTE. Speak it aloud, Sir; I shall strive to hear.

276. beauté négligé: careless beauty
294. coucher: bedtime (the King's going-to-bed was a ceremonial occasion)

GUARD. The Marshals have instructed me to say   305
  You must report to them without delay.
ALCESTE. Who? Me, Sir?
GUARD.   Yes, Sir; you.
ALCESTE.   But what do they want?
PHILINTE (*to* ALCESTE). To scotch your silly quarrel with Oronte.
CÉLIMÈNE (*to* PHILINTE). What quarrel?
PHILINTE.   Oronte and he have fallen out
  Over some verse he spoke his mind about;   310
  The Marshals wish to arbitrate the matter.
ALCESTE. Never shall I equivocate or flatter!
PHILINTE. You'd best obey their summons; come, let's go.
ALCESTE. How can they mend our quarrel, I'd like to know?
  Am I to make a cowardly retraction,   315
  And praise those jingles to his satisfaction?
  I'll not recant; I've judged that sonnet rightly.
  It's bad.
PHILINTE. But you might say so more politely. . . .
ALCESTE. I'll not back down; his verses make me sick.
PHILINTE. If only you could be more politic!   320
  But come, let's go.
ALCESTE.   I'll go, but I won't unsay
  A single word.
PHILINTE.   Well, let's be on our way.
ALCESTE. Till I am ordered by my lord the King
  To praise that poem, I shall say the thing
  Is scandalous, by God, and that the poet   325
  Ought to be hanged for having the nerve to show it. (*To* CLITANDRE *and*
  ACASTE, *who are laughing*)
  By heaven, Sirs, I really didn't know
  That I was being humorous.
CÉLIMÈNE.   Go, Sir, go;
  Settle your business.
ALCESTE.   I shall, and when I'm through,
  I shall return to settle things with you.   330

ACT III

SCENE I

CLITANDRE. Dear Marquess, how contented you appear;
  All things delight you, nothing mars your cheer.
  Can you, in perfect honesty, declare
  That you've a right to be so debonair?
ACASTE. By Jove, when I survey myself, I find   5

No cause whatever for distress of mind.
I'm young and rich; I can in modesty
Lay claim to an exalted pedigree;
And owing to my name and my condition
I shall not want for honors and position. 10
Then as to courage, that most precious trait,
I seem to have it, as was proved of late
Upon the field of honor, where my bearing,
They say, was very cool and rather daring.
I've wit, of course; and taste in such perfection 15
That I can judge without the least reflection,
And at the theater, which is my delight,
Can make or break a play on opening night,
And lead the crowd in hisses or bravos,
And generally be known as one who knows. 20
I'm clever, handsome, gracefully polite;
My waist is small, my teeth are strong and white;
As for my dress, the world's astonished eyes
Assure me that I bear away the prize.
I find myself in favor everywhere, 25
Honored by men, and worshiped by the fair;
And since these things are so, it seems to me
I'm justified in my complacency.
CLITANDRE. Well, if so many ladies hold you dear,
Why do you press a hopeless courtship here? 30
ACASTE. Hopeless, you say? I'm not the sort of fool
That likes his ladies difficult and cool.
Men who are awkward, shy, and peasantish
May pine for heartless beauties, if they wish,
Grovel before them, bear their cruelties, 35
Woo them with tears and sighs and bended knees,
And hope by dogged faithfulness to gain
What their poor merits never could obtain.
For men like me, however, it makes no sense
To love on trust, and foot the whole expense. 40
Whatever any lady's merits be,
I think, thank God, that I'm as choice as she;
That if my heart is kind enough to burn
For her, she owes me something in return;
And that in any proper love affair 45
The partners must invest an equal share.
CLITANDRE. You think, then, that our hostess favors you?
ACASTE. I've reason to believe that that is true.
CLITANDRE. How did you come to such a mad conclusion?
You're blind, dear fellow. This is sheer delusion. 50

ACASTE. All right, then: I'm deluded and I'm blind.
CLITANDRE. Whatever put the notion in your mind?
ACASTE. Delusion.
CLITANDRE. What persuades you that you're right?
ACASTE. I'm blind.
CLITANDRE. But have you any proofs to cite?
ACASTE. I tell you I'm deluded.
CLITANDRE. Have you, then,   55
   Received some secret pledge from Célimène?
ACASTE. Oh, no: she scorns me.
CLITANDRE. Tell me the truth, I beg.
ACASTE. She just can't bear me.
CLITANDRE. Ah, don't pull my leg.
   Tell me what hope she's given you, I pray.
ACASTE. I'm hopeless, and it's you who win the day.   60
   She hates me thoroughly, and I'm so vexed
   I mean to hang myself on Tuesday next.
CLITANDRE. Dear Marquess, let us have an armistice
   And make a treaty. What do you say to this?
   If ever one of us can plainly prove   65
   That Célimène encourages his love,
   The other must abandon hope, and yield,
   And leave him in possession of the field.
ACASTE. Now, there's a bargain that appeals to me;
   With all my heart, dear Marquess, I agree.   70
   But hush.

SCENE II

CÉLIMÈNE. Still here?
CLITANDRE. 'Twas love that stayed our feet.
CÉLIMÈNE. I think I heard a carriage in the street.
   Whose is it? D'you know?

SCENE III

BASQUE. Arsinoé is here,
   Madame.
CÉLIMÈNE. Arsinoé, you say? Oh, dear.
BASQUE. Eliante is entertaining her below.   75
CÉLIMÈNE. What brings the creature here, I'd like to know?
ACASTE. They say she's dreadfully prudish, but in fact
   I think her piety. . .
CÉLIMÈNE. It's all an act.
   At heart she's worldly, and her poor success

In snaring men explains her prudishness.   80
It breaks her heart to see the beaux and gallants
Engrossed by other women's charms and talents,
And so she's always in a jealous rage
Against the faulty standards of the age.
She lets the world believe that she's a prude   85
To justify her loveless solitude,
And strives to put a brand of moral shame
On all the graces that she cannot claim.
But still she'd love a lover; and Alceste
Appears to be the one she'd love the best.   90
His visits here are poison to her pride;
She seems to think I've lured him from her side;
And everywhere, at court or in the town,
The spiteful, envious woman runs me down.
In short, she's just as stupid as can be,   95
Vicious and arrogant in the last degree,
And. . .

SCENE IV

CÉLIMÈNE. Ah! What happy chance has brought you here?
   I've thought about you ever so much, my dear.
ARSINOÉ. I've come to tell you something you should know.
CÉLIMÈNE. How good of you to think of doing so!   100
   (CLITANDRE and ACASTE go out, laughing.)

SCENE V

ARSINOÉ. It's just as well those gentlemen didn't tarry.
CÉLIMÈNE. Shall we sit down?
ARSINOÉ.   That won't be necessary.
   Madam, the flame of friendship ought to burn
   Brightest in matters of the most concern,
   And as there's nothing which concerns us more   105
   Than honor, I have hastened to your door
   To bring you, as your friend, some information
   About the status of your reputation.
   I visited, last night, some virtuous folk,
   And, quite by chance, it was of you they spoke;   110
   There was, I fear, no tendency to praise
   Your light behavior and your dashing ways.
   The quantity of gentlemen you see
   And your by now notorious coquetry
   Were both so vehemently criticized   115

By everyone, that I was much surprised.
Of course, I needn't tell you where I stood;
I came to your defense as best I could,
Assured them you were harmless, and declared
Your soul was absolutely unimpaired.   120
But there are some things, you must realize,
One can't excuse, however hard one tries,
And I was forced at last into conceding
That your behavior, Madam, is misleading,
That it makes a bad impression, giving rise   125
To ugly gossip and obscene surmise,
And that if you were more *overtly* good,
You wouldn't be so much misunderstood.
Not that I think you've been unchaste—no! no!
The saints preserve me from a thought so low!   130
But mere good conscience never did suffice:
One must avoid the outward show of vice.
Madam, you're too intelligent, I'm sure,
To think my motives anything but pure
In offering you this counsel—which I do   135
Out of a zealous interest in you.
CÉLIMÈNE. Madam, I haven't taken you amiss;
I'm very much obliged to you for this;
And I'll at once discharge the obligation
By telling you about *your* reputation.   140
You've been so friendly as to let me know
What certain people say of me, and so
I mean to follow your benign example
By offering you a somewhat similar sample.
The other day, I went to an affair   145
And found some most distinguished people there
Discussing piety, both false and true.
The conversation soon came round to you.
Alas! Your prudery and bustling zeal
Appeared to have a very slight appeal.   150
Your affectation of a grave demeanor,
Your endless talk of virtue and of honor,
The aptitude of your suspicious mind
For finding sin where there is none to find,
Your towering self-esteem, that pitying face   155
With which you contemplate the human race,
Your sermonizings and your sharp aspersions
On people's pure and innocent diversions—
All these were mentioned, Madam, and, in fact,
Were roundly and concertedly attacked.   160

"What good," they said, "are all these outward shows,
When everything belies her pious pose?
She prays incessantly; but then, they say,
She beats her maids and cheats them of their pay;
She shows her zeal in every holy place,   165
But still she's vain enough to paint her face;
She holds that naked statues are immoral,
But with a naked *man* she'd have no quarrel."
Of course, I said to everybody there
That they were being viciously unfair;   170
But still they were disposed to criticize you,
And all agreed that someone should advise you
To leave the morals of the world alone,
And worry rather more about your own.
They felt that one's self-knowledge should be great   175
Before one thinks of setting others straight;
That one should learn the art of living well
Before one threatens other men with hell,
And that the Church is best equipped, no doubt,
To guide our souls and root our vices out.   180
Madam, you're too intelligent, I'm sure,
To think my motives anything but pure
In offering you this counsel—which I do
Out of a zealous interest in you.
ARSINOÉ. I dared not hope for gratitude, but I   185
Did not expect so acid a reply;
I judge, since you've been so extremely tart,
That my good counsel pierced you to the heart.
CÉLIMÈNE. Far from it, Madam. Indeed, it seems to me
We ought to trade advice more frequently.   190
One's vision of oneself is so defective
That it would be an excellent corrective.
If you are willing, Madam, let's arrange
Shortly to have another frank exchange
In which we'll tell each other, *entre nous,*°   195
What you've heard tell of me, and I of you.
ARSINOÉ. Oh, people never censure you, my dear;
It's me they criticize. Or so I hear.
CÉLIMÈNE. Madam, I think we either blame or praise
According to our taste and length of days.   200
There is a time of life for coquetry,
And there's a season, too, for prudery.
When all one's charms are gone, it is, I'm sure,

195. *entre nous:* between ourselves

Good strategy to be devout and pure:
It makes one seem a little less forsaken. 205
Some day, perhaps, I'll take the road you've taken:
Time brings all things. But I have time aplenty,
And see no cause to be a prude at twenty.
ARSINOÉ.   You give your age in such a gloating tone
That one would think I was an ancient crone; 210
We're not so far apart, in sober truth,
That you can mock me with a boast of youth!
Madam, you baffle me. I wish I knew
What moves you to provoke me as you do.
CÉLIMÈNE.   For my part, Madam, I should like to know 215
Why you abuse me everywhere you go.
Is it my fault, dear lady, that your hand
Is not, alas, in very great demand?
If men admire me, if they pay me court
And daily make me offers of the sort 220
You'd dearly love to have them make to you,
How can I help it? What would you have me do?
If what you want is lovers, please feel free
To take as many as you can from me.
ARSINOÉ.   Oh, come. D'you think the world is losing sleep 225
Over that flock of lovers which you keep,
Or that we find it difficult to guess
What price you pay for their devotedness?
Surely you don't expect us to suppose
Mere merit could attract so many beaux? 230
It's not your virtue that they're dazzled by;
Nor is it virtuous love for which they sigh.
You're fooling no one, Madam; the world's not blind;
There's many a lady heaven has designed
To call men's noblest, tenderest feelings out, 235
Who has no lovers dogging her about;
From which it's plain that lovers nowadays
Must be acquired in bold and shameless ways,
And only pay one court for such reward
As modesty and virtue can't afford. 240
Then don't be quite so puffed up, if you please,
About your tawdry little victories;
Try, if you can, to be a shade less vain,
And treat the world with somewhat less disdain.
If one were envious of your amours, 245
One soon could have a following like yours;
Lovers are no great trouble to collect
If one prefers them to one's self-respect.

CÉLIMÈNE. Collect them then, my dear; I'd love to see
    You demonstrate that charming theory;   250
    Who knows, you might . . .
ARSINOÉ.   Now, Madam, that will do;
    It's time to end this trying interview.
    My coach is late in coming to your door,
    Or I'd have taken leave of you before.
CÉLIMÈNE. Oh, please don't feel that you must rush away;   255
    I'd be delighted, Madam, if you'd stay.
    However, lest my conversation bore you,
    Let me provide some better company for you;
    This gentleman, who comes most apropos,
    Will please you more than I could do, I know.   260

SCENE VI

CÉLIMÈNE. Alceste, I have a little note to write
    Which simply must go out before tonight;
    Please entertain *Madame;* I'm sure that she
    Will overlook my incivility.

SCENE VII

ARSINOÉ. Well, Sir, our hostess graciously contrives   265
    For us to chat until my coach arrives;
    And I shall be forever in her debt
    For granting me this little tête-á-tête.
    We women very rightly give our hearts
    To men of noble character and parts,   270
    And your especial merits, dear Alceste,
    Have roused the deepest sympathy in my breast.
    Oh, how I wish they had sufficient sense
    At court, to recognize your excellence!
    They wrong you greatly, Sir. How it must hurt you   275
    Never to be rewarded for your virtue!
ALCESTE. Why, Madam, what cause have I to feel aggrieved?
    What great and brilliant thing have I achieved?
    What service have I rendered to the King
    That I should look to him for anything?   280
ARSINOÉ. Not everyone who's honored by the State
    Has done great services. A man must wait
    Till time and fortune offer him the chance.
    Your merit, Sir, is obvious at a glance,
    And . . .
ALCESTE.   Ah, forget my merit; I'm not neglected.   285

The court, I think, can hardly be expected
To mine men's souls for merit, and unearth
Our hidden virtues and our secret worth.
ARSINOÉ. *Some* virtues, though, are far too bright to hide;
    Yours are acknowledged, Sir, on every side. 290
    Indeed, I've heard you warmly praised of late
    By persons of considerable weight.
ALCESTE. This fawning age has praise for everyone,
    And all distinctions, Madam, are undone.
    All things have equal honor nowadays, 295
    And no one should be gratified by praise.
    To be admired, one only need exist,
    And every lackey's on the honors list.
ARSINOÉ. I only wish, Sir, that you had your eye
    On some position at court, however high; 300
    You'd only have to hint at such a notion
    For me to set the proper wheels in motion;
    I've certain friendships I'd be glad to use
    To get you any office you might choose.
ALCESTE. Madam, I fear that any such ambition 305
    Is wholly foreign to my disposition.
    The soul God gave me isn't of the sort
    That prospers in the weather of a court.
    It's all too obvious that I don't possess
    The virtues necessary for success. 310
    My one great talent is for speaking plain;
    I've never learned to flatter or to feign;
    And anyone so stupidly sincere
    Had best not seek a courtier's career.
    Outside the court, I know, one must dispense 315
    With honors, privilege, and influence;
    But still one gains the right, foregoing these,
    Not to be tortured by the wish to please.
    One needn't live in dread of snubs and slights,
    Nor praise the verse that every idiot writes, 320
    Nor humor silly Marquesses, nor bestow
    Politic sighs on Madam So-and-so.
ARSINOÉ. Forget the court, then; let the matter rest.
    But I've another cause to be distressed
    About your present situation, Sir. 325
    It's to your love affair that I refer.
    She whom you love, and who pretends to love you,
    Is, I regret to say, unworthy of you.
ALCESTE. Why, Madam! Can you seriously intend
    To make so grave a charge against your friend? 330

ARSINOÉ. Alas, I must. I've stood aside too long
   And let that lady do you grievous wrong;
   But now my debt to conscience shall be paid:
   I tell you that your love has been betrayed.
ALCESTE. I thank you, Madam; you're extremely kind.   335
   Such words are soothing to a lover's mind.
ARSINOÉ. Yes, though she *is* my friend, I say again
   You're very much too good for Célimène.
   She's wantonly misled you from the start.
ALCESTE. You may be right; who knows another's heart?   340
   But ask yourself if it's the part of charity
   To shake my soul with doubts of her sincerity.
ARSINOÉ. Well if you'd rather be a dupe than doubt her,
   That's your affair. I'll say no more about her.
ALCESTE. Madam, you know that doubt and vague suspicion   345
   Are painful to a man in my position;
   It's most unkind to worry me this way
   Unless you've some real proof of what you say.
ARSINOÉ. Sir, say no more: all doubt shall be removed,
   And all that I've been saying shall be proved.   350
   You've only to escort me home, and there
   We'll look into the heart of this affair.
   I've ocular evidence which will persuade you
   Beyond a doubt, that Célimène's betrayed you.
   Then, if you're saddened by that revelation,   355
   Perhaps I can provide some consolation.

ACT IV

SCENE I

PHILINTE. Madam, he acted like a stubborn child;
   I thought they never would be reconciled;
   In vain we reasoned, threatened, and appealed;
   He stood his ground and simply would not yield.
   The Marshals, I feel sure, have never heard   5
   An argument so splendidly absurd.
   "No, gentlemen," said he, "I'll not retract.
   His verse is bad: extremely bad, in fact.
   Surely it does the man no harm to know it.
   Does it disgrace him, not to be a poet?   10
   A gentleman may be respected still,
   Whether he writes a sonnet well or ill.
   That I dislike his verse should not offend him;
   In all that touches honor, I commend him;

He's noble, brave, and virtuous—but I fear 15
He can't in truth be called a sonneteer.
I'll gladly praise his wardrobe; I'll endorse
His dancing, or the way he sits a horse;
But, gentlemen, I cannot praise his rhyme.
In fact, it ought to be a capital crime 20
For anyone so sadly unendowed
To write a sonnet, and read the thing aloud."
At length he fell into a gentler mood
And, striking a concessive attitude,
He paid Oronte the following courtesies: 25
"Sir, I regret that I'm so hard to please,
And I'm profoundly sorry that your lyric
Failed to provoke me to a panegyric."
After these curious words, the two embraced,
And then the hearing was adjourned—in haste. 30
ELIANTE. His conduct has been very singular lately;
Still, I confess that I respect him greatly.
The honesty in which he takes such pride
Has—to my mind—its noble, heroic side.
In this false age, such candor seems outrageous; 35
But I could wish that it were more contagious.
PHILINTE. What most intrigues me in our friend Alceste
Is the grand passion that rages in his breast.
The sullen humors he's compounded of
Should not, I think, dispose his heart to love; 40
But since they do, it puzzles me still more
That he should choose your cousin to adore.
ELIANTE. It does, indeed, belie the theory
That love is born of gentle sympathy,
And that the tender passion must be based 45
On sweet accords of temper and of taste.
PHILINTE. Does she return his love, do you suppose?
ELIANTE. Ah, that's a difficult question, Sir. Who knows?
How can we judge the truth of her devotion?
Her heart's a stranger to its own emotion. 50
Sometimes it thinks it loves, when no love's there;
At other times it loves quite unaware.
PHILINTE. I rather think Alceste is in for more
Distress and sorrow than he's bargained for;
Were he of my mind, Madam, his affection 55
Would turn in quite a different direction,
And we would see him more responsive to
The kind regard which he receives from you.
ELIANTE. Sir, I believe in frankness, and I'm inclined,

In matters of the heart, to speak my mind.   60
I don't oppose his love for her; indeed,
I hope with all my heart that he'll succeed,
And were it in my power, I'd rejoice
In giving him the lady of his choice.
But if, as happens frequently enough   65
In love affairs, he meets with a rebuff—
If Célimène should grant some rival's suit—
I'd gladly play the role of substitute;
Nor would his tender speeches please me less
Because they'd once been made without success.   70
PHILINTE. Well, Madam, as for me, I don't oppose
Your hopes in this affair; and heaven knows
That in my conversations with the man
I plead your cause as often as I can.
But if those two should marry, and so remove   75
All chance that he will offer you his love,
Then I'll declare my own, and hope to see
Your gracious favor pass from him to me.
In short, should you be cheated of Alceste,
I'd be most happy to be second best.   80
ELIANTE. Philinte, you're teasing.
PHILINTE.   Ah, Madam, never fear;
No words of mine were ever so sincere,
And I shall live in fretful expectation
Till I can make a fuller declaration.

SCENE II

ALCESTE. Avenge me, Madam! I must have satisfaction,   85
Or this great wrong will drive me to distraction!
ELIANTE. Why, what's the matter? What's upset you so?
ALCESTE. Madam, I've had a mortal, mortal blow.
If Chaos repossessed the universe,
I swear I'd not be shaken any worse.   90
I'm ruined . . . I can say no more . . . My soul . . .
ELIANTE. Do try, Sir, to regain your self-control.
ALCESTE. Just heaven! Why were so much beauty and grace
Bestowed on one so vicious and so base?
ELIANTE. Once more, Sir, tell us . . .
ALCESTE.   My world has gone to wrack; 95
I'm— I'm betrayed; she's stabbed me in the back:
Yes, Célimène (who would have thought it of her?)
Is false to me, and has another lover.
ELIANTE. Are you quite certain? Can you prove these things?

PHILINTE. Lovers are prey to wild imaginings   100
    And jealous fancies. No doubt there's some mistake . . .
ALCESTE. Mind your own business, Sir, for heaven's sake.
    (*To* ELIANTE) Madam, I have the proof that you demand
    Here in my pocket, penned by her own hand.
    Yes, all the shameful evidence one could want   105
    Lies in this letter written to Oronte—
    Oronte! whom I felt sure she couldn't love,
    And hardly bothered to be jealous of.
PHILINTE. Still, in a letter, appearances may deceive;
    This may not be so bad as you believe.   110
ALCESTE. Once more I beg you, Sir, to let me be;
    Tend to your own affairs; leave mine to me.
ELIANTE. Compose yourself; this anguish that you feel . . .
ALCESTE. Is something, Madam, you alone can heal.
    My outraged heart, beside itself with grief,   115
    Appeals to you for comfort and relief.
    Avenge me on your cousin, whose unjust
    And faithless nature has deceived my trust;
    Avenge a crime your pure soul must detest.
ELIANTE. But how, Sir?
ALCESTE.   Madam, this heart within my breast   120
    Is yours; pray take it; redeem my heart from her,
    And so avenge me on my torturer.
    Let her be punished by the fond emotion,
    The ardent love, the bottomless devotion,
    The faithful worship which this heart of mine   125
    Will offer up to yours as to a shrine.
ELIANTE. You have my sympathy, Sir, in all you suffer;
    Nor do I scorn the noble heart you offer;
    But I suspect you'll soon be mollified,
    And this desire for vengeance will subside.   130
    When some beloved hand has done us wrong
    We thirst for retribution—but not for long;
    However dark the deed that she's committed,
    A lovely culprit's very soon acquitted.
    Nothing's so stormy as an injured lover,   135
    And yet no storm so quickly passes over.
ALCESTE. No, Madam, no—this is no lovers' spat;
    I'll not forgive her; it's gone too far for that;
    My mind's made up; I'll kill myself before
    I waste my hopes upon her any more.   140
    Ah, here she is. My wrath intensifies.
    I shall confront her with her tricks and lies,
    And crush her utterly, and bring you then
    A heart no longer slave to Célimène.

SCENE III

ALCESTE (*aside*). Sweet heaven, help me to control my passion.   145
CÉLIMÈNE (*aside, to* ALCESTE). Oh, Lord. Why stand there staring in that
    fashion?
    And what d'you mean by those dramatic sighs,
    And that malignant glitter in your eyes?
ALCESTE. I mean that sins which cause the blood to freeze
    Look innocent beside your treacheries;   150
    That nothing Hell's or Heaven's wrath could do
    Ever produced so bad a thing as you.
CÉLIMÈNE. Your compliments were always sweet and pretty.
ALCESTE. Madam, it's not the moment to be witty.
    No, blush and hang your head; you've ample reason,   155
    Since I've the fullest evidence of your treason.
    Ah, this is what my sad heart prophesied;
    Now all my anxious fears are verified;
    My dark suspicion and my gloomy doubt
    Divined the truth, and now the truth is out.   160
    For all your trickery, I was not deceived;
    It was my bitter stars that I believed.
    But don't imagine that you'll go scot-free;
    You shan't misuse me with impunity.
    I know that love's irrational and blind;   165
    I know the heart's not subject to the mind,
    And can't be reasoned into beating faster;
    I know each soul is free to choose its master;
    Therefore had you but spoken from the heart,
    Rejecting my attentions from the start,   170
    I'd have no grievance, or at any rate
    I could complain of nothing but my fate.
    Ah, but so falsely to encourage me—
    That was a treason and a treachery
    For which you cannot suffer too severely,   175
    And you shall pay for that behavior dearly.
    Yes, now I have no pity, not a shred;
    My temper's out of hand; I've lost my head;
    Shocked by the knowledge of your double-dealings,
    My reason can't restrain my savage feelings;   180
    A righteous wrath deprives me of my senses,
    And I won't answer for the consequences.
CÉLIMÈNE. What does this outburst mean? Will you please explain?
    Have you, by any chance, gone quite insane?
ALCESTE. Yes, yes, I went insane the day I fell   185
    A victim to your black and fatal spell,

Thinking to meet with some sincerity
Among the treacherous charms that beckoned me.
CÉLIMÈNE. Pooh. Of what treachery can you complain?
ALCESTE. How sly you are, how cleverly you feign! 190
But you'll not victimize me any more.
Look: here's a document you've seen before.
This evidence, which I acquired today,
Leaves you, I think, without a thing to say.
CÉLIMÈNE. Is this what sent you into such a fit? 195
ALCESTE. You should be blushing at the sight of it.
CÉLIMÈNE. Ought I to blush? I truly don't see why.
ALCESTE. Ah, now you're being bold as well as sly;
Since there's no signature, perhaps you'll claim . . .
CÉLIMÈNE. I wrote it, whether or not it bears my name. 200
ALCESTE. And you can view with equanimity
This proof of your disloyalty to me!
CÉLIMÈNE. Oh, don't be so outrageous and extreme.
ALCESTE. You take this matter lightly, it would seem.
Was it no wrong to me, no shame to you, 205
That you should send Oronte this billet-doux?
CÉLIMÈNE. Oronte! Who said it was for him?
ALCESTE. Why, those
Who brought me this example of your prose.
But what's the difference? If you wrote the letter
To someone else, it pleases me no better. 210
My grievance and your guilt remain the same.
CÉLIMÈNE. But need you rage, and need I blush for shame,
If this was written to a *woman* friend?
ALCESTE. Ah! Most ingenious. I'm impressed no end;
And after that incredible evasion 215
Your guilt is clear. I need no more persuasion.
How dare you try so clumsy a deception?
D'you think I'm wholly wanting in perception?
Come, come, let's see how brazenly you'll try
To bolster up so palpable a lie: 220
Kindly construe this ardent closing section
As nothing more than sisterly affection!
Here, let me read it. Tell me, if you dare to,
That this is for a woman . . .
CÉLIMÈNE. I don't care to.
What right have you to badger and berate me, 225
And so highhandedly interrogate me?
ALCESTE. Now, don't be angry; all I ask of you
Is that you justify a phrase or two . . .
CÉLIMÈNE. No, I shall not. I utterly refuse,

And you may take those phrases as you choose.   230
ALCESTE.   Just show me how this letter could be meant
   For a woman's eyes, and I shall be content.
CÉLIMÈNE.   No, no, it's for Oronte; you're perfectly right.
   I welcome his attentions with delight,
   I prize his character and his intellect,   235
   And everything is just as you suspect.
   Come, do your worst now; give your rage free rein;
   But kindly cease to bicker and complain.
ALCESTE (aside).   Good God! Could anything be more inhuman?
   Was ever a heart so mangled by a woman?   240
   When I complain of how she has betrayed me,
   She bridles, and commences to upbraid me!
   She tries my tortured patience to the limit;
   She won't deny her guilt; she glories in it!
   And yet my heart's too faint and cowardly   245
   To break these chains of passion, and be free,
   To scorn her as it should, and rise above
   This unrewarded, mad, and bitter love.
   (To CÉLIMÈNE) Ah, traitress, in how confident a fashion
   You take advantage of my helpless passion,   250
   And use my weakness for your faithless charms
   To make me once again throw down my arms!
   But do at least deny this black transgression;
   Take back that mocking and perverse confession;
   Defend this letter and your innocence,   255
   And I, poor fool, will aid in your defense.
   Pretend, pretend, that you are just and true,
   And I shall make myself believe in you.
CÉLIMÈNE.   Oh, stop it. Don't be such a jealous dunce,
   Or I shall leave off loving you at once.   260
   Just why should I pretend? What could impel me
   To stoop so low as that? And kindly tell me
   Why, if I loved another, I shouldn't merely
   Inform you of it, simply and sincerely!
   I've told you where you stand, and that admission   265
   Should altogether clear me of suspicion;
   After so generous a guarantee,
   What right have you to harbor doubts of me?
   Since women are (from natural reticence)
   Reluctant to declare their sentiments,   270
   And since the honor of our sex requires
   That we conceal our amorous desires,
   Ought any man for whom such laws are broken
   To question what the oracle has spoken?

Should he not rather feel an obligation   275
    To trust that most obliging declaration?
    Enough, now. Your suspicions quite disgust me;
    Why should I love a man who doesn't trust me?
    I cannot understand why I continue,
    Fool that I am, to take an interest in you.   280
    I ought to choose a man less prone to doubt,
    And give you something to be vexed about.
ALCESTE. Ah, what a poor enchanted fool I am;
    These gentle words, no doubt, were all a sham;
    But destiny requires me to entrust   285
    My happiness to you, and so I must.
    I'll love you to the bitter end, and see
    How false and treacherous you dare to be.
CÉLIMÈNE. No, you don't really love me as you ought.
ALCESTE. I love you more than can be said or thought;   290
    Indeed, I wish you were in such distress
    That I might show my deep devotedness.
    Yes, I could wish that you were wretchedly poor,
    Unloved, uncherished, utterly obscure;
    That fate had set you down upon the earth   295
    Without possessions, rank, or gentle birth;
    Then, by the offer of my heart, I might
    Repair the great injustice of your plight;
    I'd raise you from the dust, and proudly prove
    The purity and vastness of my love.   300
CÉLIMÈNE. This is a strange benevolence indeed!
    God grant that I may never be in need . . .
    Ah, here's Monsieur Dubois, in quaint disguise.

SCENE IV

ALCESTE. Well, why this costume? Why those frightened eyes?
    What ails you?
DUBOIS.   Well, Sir, things are most mysterious.   305
ALCESTE. What do you mean?
DUBOIS.   I fear they're very serious.
ALCESTE. What?
DUBOIS.   Shall I speak more loudly?
ALCESTE.   Yes; speak out.
DUBOIS. Isn't there someone here, Sir?
ALCESTE.   Speak, you lout!
    Stop wasting time.
DUBOIS.   Sir, we must slip away.
ALCESTE. How's that?

DUBOIS.   We must decamp without delay.   310
ALCESTE. Explain yourself.
DUBOIS.   I tell you we must fly.
ALCESTE. What for?
DUBOIS.   We mustn't pause to say good-by.
ALCESTE. Now what d'you mean by all of this, you clown?
DUBOIS. I mean, Sir, that we've got to leave this town.
ALCESTE. I'll tear you limb from limb and joint from joint   315
    If you don't come more quickly to the point.
DUBOIS. Well, Sir, today a man in a black suit,
    Who wore a black and ugly scowl to boot,
    Left us a document scrawled in such a hand
    As even Satan couldn't understand.   320
    It bears upon your lawsuit, I don't doubt;
    But all hell's devils couldn't make it out.
ALCESTE. Well, well, go on. What then? I fail to see
    How this event obliges us to flee.
DUBOIS. Well, Sir: an hour later, hardly more,   325
    A gentleman who's often called before
    Came looking for you in an anxious way.
    Not finding you, he asked me to convey
    (Knowing I could be trusted with the same)
    The following message . . . Now, what *was* his name?   330
ALCESTE. Forget his name, you idiot. What did he say?
DUBOIS. Well, it was one of your friends, Sir, anyway.
    He warned you to begone, and he suggested
    That if you stay, you may well be arrested.
ALCESTE. What? Nothing more specific? Think, man, think!   335
DUBOIS. No, Sir. He had me bring him pen and ink,
    And dashed you off a letter which, I'm sure,
    Will render things distinctly less obscure.
ALCESTE. Well—let me have it!
CÉLIMÈNE.   What *is* this all about?
ALCESTE. God knows; but I have hopes of finding out.   340
    How long am I to wait, you blitherer?
DUBOIS (*after a protracted search for the letter*). I must have left it on
    your table, Sir.
ALCESTE. I ought to . . .
CÉLIMÈNE.   No, no, keep your self-control;
    Go find out what's behind his rigmarole.
ALCESTE. It seems that fate, no matter what I do,   345
    Has sworn that I may not converse with you;
    But, Madam, pray permit your faithful lover
    To try once more before the day is over.

ACT V

SCENE I

ALCESTE. No, it's too much. My mind's made up, I tell you.
PHILINTE. Why should this blow, however hard, compel you . . .
ALCESTE. No, no, don't waste your breath in argument;
 Nothing you say will alter my intent;
 This age is vile, and I've made up my mind   5
 To have no further commerce with mankind.
 Did not truth, honor, decency, and the laws
 Oppose my enemy and approve my cause?
 My claims were justified in all men's sight;
 I put my trust in equity and right;   10
 Yet, to my horror and the world's disgrace,
 Justice is mocked, and I have lost my case!
 A scoundrel whose dishonesty is notorious
 Emerges from another lie victorious!
 Honor and right condone his brazen fraud,   15
 While rectitude and decency applaud!
 Before his smirking face, the truth stands charmed,
 And virtue conquered, and the law disarmed!
 His crime is sanctioned by a court decree!
 And not content with what he's done to me,   20
 The dog now seeks to ruin me by stating
 That I composed a book now circulating,
 A book so wholly criminal and vicious
 That even to speak its title is seditious!
 Meanwhile Oronte, my rival, lends his credit   25
 To the same libelous tale, and helps to spread it!
 Oronte! a man of honor and of rank,
 With whom I've been entirely fair and frank;
 Who sought me out and forced me, willy-nilly,
 To judge some verse I found extremely silly;   30
 And who, because I properly refused
 To flatter him, or see the truth abused,
 Abets my enemy in a rotten slander!
 There's the reward of honesty and candor!
 The man will hate me to the end of time   35
 For failing to commend his wretched rhyme!
 And not this man alone, but all humanity
 Do what they do from interest and vanity;
 They prate of honor, truth, and righteousness,
 But lie, betray, and swindle nonetheless.   40
 Come then: man's villainy is too much to bear;

Let's leave this jungle and this jackal's lair.
Yes! treacherous and savage race of men,
You shall not look upon my face again.
PHILINTE. Oh, don't rush into exile prematurely;   45
Things aren't as dreadful as you make them, surely.
It's rather obvious, since you're still at large,
That people don't believe your enemy's charge.
Indeed, his tale's so patently untrue
That it may do more harm to him than you.   50
ALCESTE. Nothing could do that scoundrel any harm:
His frank corruption is his greatest charm,
And, far from hurting him, a further shame
Would only serve to magnify his name.
PHILINTE. In any case, his bald prevarication   55
Has done no injury to your reputation,
And you may feel secure in that regard.
As for your lawsuit, it should not be hard
To have the case reopened, and contest
This judgment . . .
ALCESTE.   No, no, let the verdict rest.   60
Whatever cruel penalty it may bring,
I wouldn't have it changed for anything.
It shows the times' injustice with such clarity
That I shall pass it down to our posterity
As a great proof and signal demonstration   65
Of the black wickedness of this generation.
It may cost twenty thousand francs; but I
Shall pay their twenty thousand, and gain thereby
The right to storm and rage at human evil,
And send the race of mankind to the devil.   70
PHILINTE. Listen to me . . .
ALCESTE.   Why? What can you possibly say?
Don't argue, Sir; your labor's thrown away.
Do you propose to offer lame excuses
For men's behavior and the times' abuses?
PHILINTE. No, all you say I'll readily concede: 75
This is a low, dishonest age indeed;
Nothing but trickery prospers nowadays,
And people ought to mend their shabby ways.
Yes, man's a beastly creature; but must we then
Abandon the society of men?   80
Here in the world, each human frailty
Provides occasion for philosophy,
And that is virtue's noblest exercise;
If honesty shone forth from all men's eyes,

If every heart were frank and kind and just,   85
    What could our virtues do but gather dust
    (Since their employment is to help us bear
    The villainies of men without despair)?
    A heart well-armed with virtue can endure . . .
ALCESTE. Sir, you're a matchless reasoner, to be sure;   90
    Your words are fine and full of cogency;
    But don't waste time and eloquence on me.
    My reason bids me go, for my own good.
    My tongue won't lie and flatter as it should;
    God knows what frankness it might next commit,   95
    And what I'd suffer on account of it.
    Pray let me wait for Célimène's return
    In peace and quiet. I shall shortly learn,
    By her response to what I have in view,
    Whether her love for me is feigned or true.   100
PHILINTE. Till then, let's visit Eliante upstairs.
ALCESTE. No, I am too weighed down with somber cares.
    Go to her, do; and leave me with my gloom
    Here in the darkened corner of this room.
PHILINTE. Why, that's no sort of company, my friend;   105
    I'll see if Eliante will not descend.

SCENE II

ORONTE. Yes, Madam, if you wish me to remain
    Your true and ardent lover, you must deign
    To give me some more positive assurance.
    All this suspense is quite beyond endurance.   110
    If your heart shares the sweet desires of mine,
    Show me as much by some convincing sign;
    And here's the sign I urgently suggest:
    That you no longer tolerate Alceste,
    But sacrifice him to my love, and sever   115
    All your relations with the man forever.
CÉLIMÈNE. Why do you suddenly dislike him so?
    You praised him to the skies not long ago.
ORONTE. Madam, that's not the point. I'm here to find
    Which way your tender feelings are inclined.   120
    Choose, if you please, between Alceste and me,
    And I shall stay or go accordingly.
ALCESTE (*emerging from the corner*). Yes, Madam, choose; this
      gentleman's demand
    Is wholly just, and I support his stand.
    I too am true and ardent; I too am here   125

To ask you that you make your feelings clear.
No more delays, now; no equivocation;
The time has come to make your declaration.
ORONTE. Sir, I've no wish in any way to be
    An obstacle to your felicity.   130
ALCESTE. Sir, I've no wish to share her heart with you;
    That may sound jealous, but at least it's true.
ORONTE. If, weighing us, she leans in your direction. . .
ALCESTE. If she regards you with the least affection. . .
ORONTE. I swear I'll yield her to you there and then.   135
ALCESTE. I swear I'll never see her face again.
ORONTE. Now, Madam, tell us what we've come to hear.
ALCESTE. Madam, speak openly and have no fear.
ORONTE. Just say which one is to remain your lover.
ALCESTE. Just name one name, and it will all be over.   140
ORONTE. What! Is it possible that you're undecided?
ALCESTE. What! Can your feelings possibly be divided?
CÉLIMÈNE. Enough: this inquisition's gone too far:
    How utterly unreasonable you are!
    Not that I couldn't make the choice with ease;   145
    My heart has no conflicting sympathies;
    I know full well which one of you I favor,
    And you'd not see me hesitate or waver.
    But how can you expect me to reveal
    So cruelly and bluntly what I feel?   150
    I think it altogether too unpleasant
    To choose between two men when both are present;
    One's heart has means more subtle and more kind
    Of letting its affections be divined,
    Nor need one be uncharitably plain   155
    To let a lover know he loves in vain.
ORONTE. No, no, speak plainly; I for one can stand it.
    I beg you to be frank.
ALCESTE.   And I demand it.
    The simple truth is what I wish to know,
    And there's no need for softening the blow.   160
    You've made an art of pleasing everyone,
    But now your days of coquetry are done:
    You have no choice now, Madam, but to choose,
    For I'll know what to think if you refuse;
    I'll take your silence for a clear admission   165
    That I'm entitled to my worst suspicion.
ORONTE. I thank you for this ultimatum, Sir,
    And I may say I heartily concur.
CÉLIMÈNE. Really, this foolishness is very wearing:
    Must you be so unjust and overbearing?   170

Haven't I told you why I must demur?
Ah, here's Eliante; I'll put the case to her.

SCENE III

CÉLIMÈNE. Cousin, I'm being persecuted here
By these two persons, who, it would appear,
Will not be satisfied till I confess   175
Which one I love the more, and which the less,
And tell the latter to his face that he
Is henceforth banished from my company.
Tell me, has ever such a thing been done?
ELIANTE. You'd best not turn to me; I'm not the one   180
To back you in a matter of this kind:
I'm all for those who frankly speak their mind.
ORONTE. Madam, you'll search in vain for a defender.
ALCESTE. You're beaten, Madam, and may as well surrender.
ORONTE. Speak, speak, you must; and end this awful strain.   185
ALCESTE. Or don't, and your position will be plain.
ORONTE. A single word will close this painful scene.
ALCESTE. But if you're silent, I'll know what you mean.

SCENE IV

ACASTE (to CÉLIMÈNE). Madam, with all due deference, we two
Have come to pick a little bone with you.   190
CLITANDRE (to ORONTE and ALCESTE). I'm glad you're present, Sirs; as
you'll soon learn,
Our business here is also your concern.
ARSINOÉ (to CÉLIMÈNE). Madam, I visit you so soon again
Only because of these two gentlemen,
Who came to me indignant and aggrieved   195
About a crime too base to be believed.
Knowing your virtue, having such confidence in it,
I couldn't think you guilty for a minute,
In spite of all their telling evidence;
And, rising above our little difference,   200
I've hastened here in friendship's name to see
You clear yourself of this great calumny.
ACASTE. Yes, Madam, let us see with what composure
You'll manage to respond to this disclosure.
You lately sent Clitandre this tender note.   205
CLITANDRE. And this one, for Acaste, you also wrote.
ACASTE (to ORONTE and ALCESTE). You'll recognize this writing, Sirs,
I think;
The lady is so free with pen and ink

That you must know it all too well, I fear.
But listen: this is something you should hear.   210

"How absurd you are to condemn my lightheartedness in society, and
to accuse me of being happiest in the company of others. Nothing could
be more unjust; and if you do not come to me instantly and beg pardon for
saying such a thing, I shall never forgive you as long as I live. Our big
bumbling friend the Viscount . . ."   215

What a shame that he's not here.

"Our big bumbling friend the Viscount, whose name stands first in
your complaint, is hardly a man to my taste; and ever since the day I
watched him spend three-quarters of an hour spitting into a well, so as to
make circles in the water, I have been unable to think highly of him. As
for the little Marquess . . ."   221

In all modesty, gentlemen, that is I.

"As for the little Marquess, who sat squeezing my hand for such a
long while yesterday, I find him in all respects the most trifling creature
alive; and the only things of value about him are his cape and his sword.
As for the man with the green ribbons . . ."   226

(*To* ALCESTE) It's your turn now, Sir.

"As for the man with the green ribbons, he amuses me now and then
with his bluntness and his bearish ill-humor; but there are many times
indeed when I think him the greatest bore in the world. And as for the
sonneteer . . ."   231

(*To* ORONTE) Here's your helping.

"And as for the sonneteer, who has taken it into his head to be witty,
and insists on being an author in the teeth of opinion, I simply cannot be
bothered to listen to him, and his prose wearies me quite as much as his
poetry. Be assured that I am not always so well-entertained as you suppose; that I long for your company, more than I dare to say, at all these
entertainments to which people drag me; and that the presence of those
one loves is true and perfect seasoning to all one's pleasures." 239

CLITANDRE. And now for me.

"Clitandre, whom you mention, and who so pesters me with his saccharine speeches, is the last man on earth for whom I could feel any
affection. He is quite mad to suppose that I love him, and so are you, to
doubt that you are loved. Do come to your senses; exchange your suppositions for his; and visit me as often as possible, to help me bear the annoyance of his unwelcome attentions."   246

It's a sweet character that these letters show,

And what to call it, Madam, you well know.
Enough. We're off to make the world acquainted
With this sublime self-portrait that you've painted.   250
ACASTE. Madam, I'll make you no farewell oration;
No, you're not worthy of my indignation.
Far choicer hearts than yours, as you'll discover,
Would like this little Marquess for a lover.

SCENE V

ORONTE. So! After all those loving letters you wrote,   255
You turn on me like this, and cut my throat!
And your dissembling, faithless heart, I find,
Has pledged itself by turns to all mankind!
How blind I've been! But now I clearly see;
I thank you, Madam, for enlightening me.   260
My heart is mine once more, and I'm content;
The loss of it shall be your punishment.
(*To* ALCESTE) Sir, she is yours; I'll seek no more to stand
Between your wishes and this lady's hand.

SCENE VI

ARSINOÉ (*to* CÉLIMÈNE). Madam, I'm forced to speak. I'm far too
stirred   265
To keep my counsel, after what I've heard.
I'm shocked and staggered by your want of morals.
It's not my way to mix in others' quarrels;
But really, when this fine and noble spirit,
This man of honor and surpassing merit,   270
Laid down the offering of his heart before you,
How *could* you . . .
ALCESTE.   Madam, permit me, I implore you,
To represent myself in this debate.
Don't bother, please, to be my advocate.
My heart, in any case, could not afford   275
To give your services their due reward;
And if I chose, for consolation's sake,
Some other lady, t'would not be you I'd take.
ARSINOÉ. What makes you think you could, Sir? And how dare you
Imply that I've been trying to ensnare you?   280
If you can for a moment entertain
Such flattering fancies, you're extremely vain.
I'm not so interested as you suppose
In Célimène's discarded gigolos.

Get rid of that absurd illusion, do.   285
Women like me are not for such as you.
Stay with this creature, to whom you're so attached;
I've never seen two people better matched.

SCENE VII

ALCESTE (*to* CÉLIMÈNE). Well, I've been still throughout this exposé,
   Till everyone but me has said his say.   290
   Come, have I shown sufficient self-restraint?
   And may I now . . .
CÉLIMÈNE.   Yes, make your just complaint.
   Reproach me freely, call me what you will;
   You've every right to say I've used you ill.
   I've wronged you, I confess it; and in my shame   295
   I'll make no effort to escape the blame.
   The anger of those others I could despise;
   My guilt toward you I sadly recognize.
   Your wrath is wholly justified, I fear;
   I know how culpable I must appear,   300
   I know all things bespeak my treachery,
   And that, in short, you've grounds for hating me.
   Do so; I give you leave.
ALCESTE.   Ah, traitress—how,
   How should I cease to love you, even now?
   Though mind and will were passionately bent   305
   On hating you, my heart would not consent.
   (*To* ELIANTE *and* PHILINTE) Be witness to my madness, both of you;
   See what infatuation drives one to;
   But wait; my folly's only just begun,
   And I shall prove to you before I'm done   310
   How strange the human heart is, and how far
   From rational we sorry creatures are.
   (*To* CÉLIMÈNE) Woman, I'm willing to forget your shame,
   And clothe your treacheries in a sweeter name;
   I'll call them youthful errors, instead of crimes,   315
   And lay the blame on these corrupting times.
   My one condition is that you agree
   To share my chosen fate, and fly with me
   To that wild, trackless solitary place
   In which I shall forget the human race.   320
   Only by such a course can you atone
   For those atrocious letters; by that alone
   Can you remove my present horror of you,
   And make it possible for me to love you.

CÉLIMÈNE. What! *I* renounce the world at my young age,   325
    And die of boredom in some hermitage?
ALCESTE. Ah, if you really loved me as you ought,
    You wouldn't give the world a moment's thought;
    Must you have me, and all the world beside?
CÉLIMÈNE. Alas, at twenty one is terrified   330
    Of solitude. I fear I lack the force
    And depth of soul to take so stern a course.
    But if my hand in marriage will content you,
    Why, there's a plan which I might well consent to,
    And . . .
ALCESTE.   No, I detest you now. I could excuse   335
    Everything else, but since you thus refuse
    To love me wholly, as a wife should do,
    And see the world in me, as I in you,
    Go! I reject your hand, and disenthrall
    My heart from your enchantments, once for all.   340

SCENE VIII

ALCESTE (*to* ELIANTE). Madam, your virtuous beauty has no peer,
    Of all this world, you only are sincere;
    I've long esteemed you highly, as you know;
    Permit me ever to esteem you so,
    And if I do not now request your hand,   345
    Forgive me, Madam, and try to understand.
    I feel unworthy of it; I sense that fate
    Does not intend me for the married state,
    That I should do you wrong by offering you
    My shattered heart's unhappy residue,   350
    And that in short . . .
ELIANTE.   Your argument's well taken:
    Nor need you fear that I shall feel forsaken.
    Were I to offer him this hand of mine,
    Your friend Philinte, I think, would not decline.
PHILINTE. Ah, Madam, that's my heart's most cherished goal,   355
    For which I'd gladly give my life and soul.
ALCESTE (*to* ELIANTE *and* PHILINTE). May you be true to all you
      now profess,
    And so deserve unending happiness.
    Meanwhile, betrayed and wronged in everything,
    I'll flee this bitter world where vice is king,   360
    And seek some spot unpeopled and apart
    Where I'll be free to have an honest heart.
PHILINTE. Come, Madam, let's do everything we can
    To change the mind of this unhappy man.

QUESTIONS

1. How does the argument between Alceste and Philinte in the opening scene state the play's major thematic conflict? Which of the two philosophies expressed is the more idealistic? Which more realistic? Is either or are both of them extreme?

2. What are the attitudes of Célimène, Eliante, and Arsinoé toward Alceste? Do they respect him? Why or why not?

3. *The Misanthrope* is generally acknowledged to be one of the world's greatest comedies, but, at the same time, it is an atypical one, both in its hero and in its ending. In what ways does Alceste approach the stature of a tragic hero? In what way is the ending unlike a comic ending?

4. Alceste is in conflict with social convention, with social injustice, and with Célimène. Does he discriminate between them as to their relative importance? Discuss.

5. Are there any indications in the opening scene that the motivations behind Alceste's hatred of social convention are not as unmixed as he thinks them?

6. Alceste declares himself not blind to Célimène's faults. Is he blind in any way about his relationship with Célimène? If so, what does his blindness spring from?

7. What do Alceste's reasons for refusing to appeal his law suit (Act V, Scene i) and his wish that Célimène were "Unloved, uncherished, utterly obscure" so that he might raise her "from the dust" (Act IV, Scene iii) tell us about his character?

8. What are Célimène's good qualities? What are her bad ones? In what ways are she and Alceste foils? Might Célimène have been redeemed had Alceste been able to accept her without taking her from society?

9. How is the gossip session between Acaste, Clitandre, and Célimène (Act II, Scene v) a double-edged satire? Which of Célimène's satirical portraits is the finest? How accurate is Célimène's portrait of Alceste himself?

10. Which is the more scathingly satirized—Alceste, or the society in which he lives? Why?

11. What character in the play most nearly represents a desirable norm of social behavior? Why?

12. What characteristics keep Alceste from being a tragic hero? What keeps the ending from being a tragic ending?

13. The verse form used by Richard Wilbur in translating Molière's play is quite different from that used by Shakespeare in *Othello*. Describe the differences. What relation is there between the poetic style of each play and its subject matter?

14. Compare *The Misanthrope* and *An Enemy of the People* as plays dealing with conflict between an individual and his society. How are the characters of Alceste and Dr. Stockmann similar? How are they different? Which is portrayed by his creator with the greater sympathy? Why?

15. Are politeness and hypocrisy the same thing? If not, distinguish between them.

Tom Stoppard

PROFESSIONAL FOUL

A Play for Television

CHARACTERS

ANDERSON	CAPTAIN (MAN 6)	MRS HOLLAR
MCKENDRICK	POLICEMAN (MAN 1)	SACHA (*ten years old*)
CHETWYN	POLICEMAN (MAN 2)	GRAYSON
HOLLAR	POLICEMAN (MAN 3)	CHAMBERLAIN
BROADBENT	POLICEMAN (MAN 4)	FRENCHMAN
CRISP	POLICEMAN (MAN 5)	CHAIRMAN
STONE		

CLERK, LIFT OPERATORS, CONCIERGES,
INTERPRETERS, CUSTOMS, POLICE, *etc.*

1. INTERIOR: AIRPLANE IN FLIGHT

The tourist class cabin of a passenger jet.
We are mainly concerned with two passengers. ANDERSON *is an Oxbridge°*
don, a professor. He is middle-aged, or more. He is sitting in an aisle seat, on the
left as we look down the gangway towards the tail. MCKENDRICK *is also in an*
aisle seat, but across the gangway and one row nearer the tail. MCKENDRICK *is*
about forty. He is also a don, but where ANDERSON *gives a somewhat fastidious*
impression, MCKENDRICK *is a rougher sort of diamond.*

MCKENDRICK *is sitting in the first row of smokers' seats, and* ANDERSON *in*
the last row of the non-smokers' seats looking aft. The plane is by no means full.

PROFESSIONAL FOUL   First shown (on BBC TV) in 1977. Soon after World War II, Czechoslovakia, once a democratic state, came under tight control of its Communist Party. During the so-called "Prague Spring" of 1968, however, under the leadership of Alexander Dubček, there occurred a lifting of censorship and other liberal reforms, crushed when five Warsaw Pact countries (Russia, East Germany, Poland, Hungary, Bulgaria) invaded the country, ousted Dubček, and replaced him with Gustav Husak, who quickly reestablished rigid totalitarian controls.—To keep from adding to the verbal misunderstandings of which this play is full, American readers should keep in mind that football to all Europeans is the sport Americans call soccer. Tom Stoppard was born in Czechoslovakia in 1937, and from 1939 to 1946 lived with his family in Singapore and India before settling in England. After British schooling he became at seventeen a newspaper reporter and at twenty-nine, with *Rosencrantz and Guildenstern Are Dead,* a successful playwright. *Professional Foul* was written after a trip to Prague in 1977, where he met several dissident actors and playwrights, one of whom was arrested shortly after his return. He is dedicated to the activities of Amnesty International (see note, page 1283). His work is celebrated for its brilliance of language, and his commitment to verbal play has led him to call himself "a bounced Czech."

Oxbridge: a term signifying Oxford and/or Cambridge

The three seats across the aisle from ANDERSON *are vacant. The seat next to* ANDERSON *on his right is also vacant but the seat beyond that, by the window, accommodates a* SLEEPING MAN. *On the vacant seat between* ANDERSON *and the* SLEEPING MAN *is lying a sex magazine of the* Penthouse *type. The magazine, however, is as yet face down. The passengers are coming to the end of a meal. They have trays of food in front of them.*

McKENDRICK *puts down his fork and lights a cigarette.* ANDERSON *dabs at his mouth with his napkin and puts it down. He glances around casually and notes the magazine next to him. He notes the* SLEEPING MAN. McKENDRICK *has a briefcase on the seat next to him, and from this he takes a glossy brochure. In fact, this is quite an elaborate publication associated with a philosophical congress. The cover of this program is seen to read: "Colloquium Philosophicum Prague 77."* ANDERSON *slides out from under his lunch tray a brochure identical to* McKENDRICK's. *He glances at it for a mere moment and loses interest. He turns his attention back to the magazine on the seat. He turns the magazine over and notes the naked woman on the cover. He picks the magazine up, with a further glance at the* SLEEPING MAN, *and opens it to a spread of color photographs. Consciously or unconsciously he is holding the brochure in such a way as to provide a shield for the magazine.* McKENDRICK *casually glancing round, sees the twin to his own brochure.*

McKENDRICK. Snap.
(ANDERSON *looks up guiltily.*)
ANDERSON. Ah . . .

(ANDERSON *closes the magazine and slides it face-up under his lunch tray.* McKENDRICK's *manner is extrovert. Almost breezy.* ANDERSON's *manner is a little vague.*)

McKENDRICK. I wasn't sure it was you. Not a very good likeness.
ANDERSON. I assure you this is how I look.
McKENDRICK. I mean your photograph. (*He flips his brochure open. It contains small photographs and pen portraits of various men and women who are in fact to be speakers at the colloquium.*) The photograph is younger.
ANDERSON. It must be an old photograph.

(McKENDRICK *gets up and comes to sit in the empty seat across the aisle from* ANDERSON.)

McKENDRICK (*changing seats*). Bill McKendrick.
ANDERSON. How odd.
McKENDRICK. Is it?
ANDERSON. Young therefore old. Old therefore young. Only odd at first glance.
McKENDRICK. Oh yes.

(ANDERSON *takes a notebook, with pencil attached, from his pocket and writes in it as he speaks.*)

ANDERSON. The second glance is known as linguistic analysis. A lot of chaps pointing out that we don't always mean what we say, even when we manage to say what we mean. Personally I'm quite prepared to believe it. (*He finishes writing and closes the notebook. He glances uneasily out of the window.*) Have you noticed the way the wings keep *wagging?* I try to look away and think of something else but I am drawn back irresistibly . . . I wouldn't be nervous about flying if the wings didn't wag. Solid steel. Thick as a bank safe. Flexing like tree branches. It's not natural. There is a coldness around my heart as though I'd seen your cigarette smoke knock against the ceiling and break in two like a bread stick. By the way, that is a non-smoking seat.

McKENDRICK. Sorry

(McKENDRICK *stubs out his cigarette.* ANDERSON *puts his notebook back into his pocket.*)

ANDERSON. Yes, I like to collect little curiosities for the language chaps. It's like handing round a bag of licorice allsorts. They're terribly grateful. (*A thought strikes him.*) Oh, you're not a language chap yourself?

(*The question seems to surprise* McKENDRICK, *and amuse him.*)

McKENDRICK. No. I'm McKendrick.
ANDERSON. You'll be giving a paper?
McKENDRICK. Yes. Nothing new, actually. More of a summing-up of my corner. My usual thing, you know. . . ? (McKENDRICK *is fishing but* AN-DERSON *doesn't seem to notice.*)

ANDERSON. Jolly good.
McKENDRICK. Perhaps you've come across some of my stuff. . . ?

(ANDERSON *now wakes up to the situation and is contrite.*)

ANDERSON. Clearly that is a reasonable expectation. I *am* sorry. I'm sure I know your name. I don't read the philosophical journals as much as I should, and hardly ever go to these international bunfights. No time nowadays. They shouldn't call us professors. It's more like being the faculty almoner.

McKENDRICK. At least my paper will be new to you. We are the only English, actually singing for our supper, I mean. I expect there'll be a few others going for the free trip and the social life. In fact, I see we've got one on board. At the back. (McKENDRICK *jerks his head towards the back of the plane.* ANDERSON *turns round to look. The object of attention is* CHETWYN, *asleep in the back row, on the aisle.* CHETWYN *is younger than* McKENDRICK *and altogether frailer and neater.* ANDERSON *squints down the plane at* CHETWYN.) Do you know Prague?

ANDERSON (*warily*). Not personally. I know the name. (*Then he wakes up to that.*) Oh, *Prague.* Sorry. No, I've never been there. (*Small pause.*) Or have I? I got an honorary degree at Bratislava once. We changed planes in

Prague. (*Pause.*) It might have been Vienna actually. (*Pause. He looks at the window.*) Wag, wag.

McKENDRICK. It's Andrew Chetwyn. Do you know him?

ANDERSON (*warily*). Not personally.

McKENDRICK. I don't know him *personally*. Do you know his line at all?

ANDERSON. Not as such.

McKENDRICK (*suspiciously*). Have you *heard* of him?

ANDERSON. No. In a word.

McKENDRICK. Oh. He's been quite public recently.

ANDERSON. He's an ethics chap is he?

McKENDRICK. His line is that Aristotle got it more or less right, and St Augustine brought it up to date.

ANDERSON. I can see that that might make him conspicuous.

McKENDRICK. Oh, it's not *that*. I mean politics. Letters to *The Times* about persecuted professors with unpronounceable names. I'm surprised the Czechs gave him a visa.

ANDERSON. There are some rather dubious things happening in Czechoslovakia. Ethically.

McKENDRICK. Oh yes. No doubt.

ANDERSON. We must not try to pretend otherwise.

McKENDRICK. Oh quite. I mean I don't. My work is pretty political. I mean by implication, of course. As yours is. I'm looking forward to hearing you.

ANDERSON. Thank you. I'm sure your paper will be very interesting too.

McKENDRICK. As a matter of fact I think there's a lot of juice left in the fictions problem.

ANDERSON. Is that what you're speaking on?

McKENDRICK. No—you are.

ANDERSON. Oh, am I? (*He looks in his brochure briefly.*) So I am.

McKENDRICK. "Ethical Fictions as Ethical Foundations."

ANDERSON. Yes. To tell you the truth I have an ulterior motive for coming to Czechoslovakia at this time. I'm being a tiny bit naughty.

McKENDRICK. Naughty?

ANDERSON. Unethical. Well, I am being paid for by the Czech government, after all.

McKENDRICK. And what . . . ?

ANDERSON. I don't think I'm going to tell you. You see, if I tell you I make you a co-conspirator whether or not you would have wished to be one. Ethically I should give you the opportunity of choosing to be one or not.

McKENDRICK. Then why don't you give me the opportunity?

ANDERSON. I can't without telling you. An impasse.

(McKENDRICK *is already putting two and two together and cannot hide his curiosity.*)

MCKENDRICK. Look . . . Professor Anderson . . . if it's political in any way I'd really be very interested.

ANDERSON. Why, are you a politics chap?

MCKENDRICK. One is naturally interested in what is happening in these places. And I have an academic interest—my field is the philosophical assumptions of social science.

ANDERSON. How fascinating. What is that exactly?

MCKENDRICK (*slightly hurt*). Perhaps my paper tomorrow afternoon will give you a fair idea.

ANDERSON (*mortified*). Tomorrow afternoon? I say, what rotten luck. That's exactly when I have to play truant. I *am* sorry.

MCKENDRICK (*coldly*). That's all right.

ANDERSON. I expect they'll have copies.

MCKENDRICK. I expect so.

ANDERSON. The science of social philosophy, eh?

MCKENDRICK (*brusquely*). More or less.

ANDERSON (*with polite interest*). McCarthy.

MCKENDRICK. McKendrick.

ANDERSON. And how are things at . . . er . . .

MCKENDRICK. Stoke.

ANDERSON (*enthusiastically*). *Stoke!* An excellent university, I believe.

MCKENDRICK. You know perfectly well you wouldn't be seen dead in it.

(ANDERSON *considers this.*)

ANDERSON. Even if that were true, my being seen dead in a place has never so far as I know been thought a condition of its excellence.

(MCKENDRICK *despite himself laughs, though somewhat bitterly.*)

MCKENDRICK. Very good. (*An* AIR HOSTESS *is walking down the aisle removing people's lunch trays. She removes* ANDERSON'*s tray, revealing the cover of the sexy magazine, in the middle of* MCKENDRICK'*s next speech and passes down the aisle.*) Wit and paradox. Verbal felicity. An occupation for gentlemen. A higher civilization alive and well in the older universities. I see you like tits and bums, by the way.

ANDERSON (*embarrassed*). Ah . . .

(*The turning of tables cheers* MCKENDRICK *up considerably.*)

MCKENDRICK. They won't let you in with that you know. You'll have to hide it.

ANDERSON. As a matter of fact it doesn't belong to me.

MCKENDRICK. Western decadence you see. Marxists are a terrible lot of prudes. I can say that because I'm a bit that way myself.

ANDERSON. You surprise me.

MCKENDRICK. Mind you, when I say I'm a Marxist . . .

ANDERSON. Oh, I see.

MCKENDRICK. . . . I don't mean I'm an apologist for everything done in the name of Marxism.

ANDERSON. No, no, quite. There's nothing anti-socialist about it. Quite the reverse. The rich have always had it to themselves.

MCKENDRICK. On the contrary. That's why I'd be really very interested in any extra-curricular activities which might be going. I have an open mind about it.

ANDERSON (*his wires crossed*). Oh, yes, indeed, so have I.

MCKENDRICK. I sail pretty close to the wind, Marx-wise.

ANDERSON. Mind you, it's an odd thing but travel broadens the mind in a way that the proverbialist didn't quite intend. It's only at airports and railway stations that one finds in oneself a curiosity about er—er—erotica, um, girly magazines.

(MCKENDRICK *realizes that they've had their wires crossed.*)

MCKENDRICK. Perhaps you've come across some of my articles.

ANDERSON (*amazed and fascinated*). You mean you write for—? (*He pulls himself up and together.*) Oh—your—er articles—I'm afraid as I explained I'm not very good at keeping up with the philosophical. . . .

(MCKENDRICK *has gone back to his former seat to fish about in his briefcase. He emerges with another girly magazine and hands it along the aisle to* ANDERSON.)

MCKENDRICK. I've got one here. Page sixty-one. The Science Fiction short story. Not a bad life. Science Fiction and sex. And, of course, the philosophical assumptions of social science.

ANDERSON (*faintly*). Thank you very much.

MCKENDRICK. Keep it by all means. (ANDERSON *cautiously thumbs through pages of naked women.*) I wonder if there'll be any decent women?

2. INTERIOR: HOTEL LOBBY. PRAGUE

We are near the reception desk. ANDERSON, MCKENDRICK *and* CHETWYN *have just arrived together. Perhaps with other people. Their luggage consists only of small overnight suitcases and briefcases.* MCKENDRICK *is at the desk half-way through his negotiations. The lobby ought to be rather large, with lifts, etc. It should be large enough to make inconspicuous a* MAN *who is carefully watching the three Englishmen. This* MAN *is aged thirty-five or younger. He is poorly dressed, but not tramp-like. His name is* PAVEL HOLLAR. *The lobby contains other people and a poorly equipped newsstand. We catch up with* ANDERSON *talking to* CHETWYN.

ANDERSON (*enthusiastically*). *Birmingham!* Excellent university. Some very good people.

(*The desk* CLERK *comes to the counter where* MCKENDRICK *is first in the queue. The* CLERK *and other Czech people in this script obviously speak with an accent but there is no attempt here to reproduce it.*)

CLERK. Third floor. Dr McKendrick.

MCKENDRICK. Only of philosophy.

CLERK. Your baggage is there?

MCKENDRICK (*hastily*). Oh, I'll see to that. Can I have the key, please?

CLERK. Third floor. Dr Anderson. Ninth floor. A letter for you. (*The* CLERK *gives* ANDERSON *a sealed envelope and also a key.* ANDERSON *seems to have been expecting the letter. He thanks the* CLERK *and takes it.*) Dr Chetwyn. Ninth floor.

(*The three philosophers walk towards the lifts.* PAVEL *watches them go. When they reach the lift* ANDERSON *glances round and sees two men some way off across the lobby, perhaps at the newsstand. These men are called* CRISP *and* BROADBENT. CRISP *looks very young, he is twenty-two. He wears a very smart, slightly flashy suit and tie.* BROADBENT *is balding but young, in his thirties. He wears flannels and a blazer.* CRISP *is quite small.* BROADBENT *is big and heavy. But both look fit.*)

ANDERSON. I say, look who's over there . . . Broadbent and Crisp.

(*The lift now opens before them.* ANDERSON *goes in showing his key to the middle-aged* WOMAN *in charge of the lift.* MCKENDRICK *and* CHETWYN *do likewise. Over this:*)

CHETWYN. Who? (*He sees them and recognizes them.*) Oh yes.

MCKENDRICK (*sees them*). Who?

CHETWYN. Crisp and Broadbent. They must be staying here too.

MCKENDRICK. Crisp? Broadbent? That kid over by the newsstand?

ANDERSON. That's Crisp.

MCKENDRICK. My God, they get younger all the time.

(*The lift doors close. Inside the lift.*)

ANDERSON. Crisp is twenty-two. Broadbent is past his peak but Crisp is the next genius in my opinion.

MCKENDRICK. Do you know him?

ANDERSON. Not personally. I've been watching him for a couple of years.

CHETWYN. He's Newcastle, isn't he?

ANDERSON. Yes.

MCKENDRICK. I've never heard of him. What's his role there?

ANDERSON. He's what used to be called left wing. Broadbent's in the center. He's an opportunist more than anything.

(*The lift has stopped at the third floor.*)

(*To* MCKENDRICK.) This is you—see you later.

(McKENDRICK *steps out of the lift and looks round.*)

McKENDRICK. Do you think the rooms are bugged?

(*The lift doors shut him off. Inside the lift.* ANDERSON *and* CHETWYN *ride up in silence for a few moments.*)

ANDERSON. What was it Aristotle said about the higher you go the further you fall . . . ?

CHETWYN. He was talking about tragic heroes. (*The lift stops at the ninth floor.* ANDERSON *and* CHETWYN *leave the lift.*) I'm this way. There's a restaurant downstairs. The menu is very limited but it's all right.

ANDERSON. You've been here before?

CHETWYN. Yes. Perhaps see you later then, sir. (CHETWYN *goes down a corridor away from* ANDERSON'*s corridor.*)

ANDERSON (*to himself*). Sir? (ANDERSON *follows the arrow towards his own room number.*)

3. INTERIOR: ANDERSON'S HOTEL ROOM

The room contains a bed, a wardrobe, a chest. A telephone. A bathroom containing a bath leads off through a door. ANDERSON *is unpacking. He puts some clothes into a drawer and closes it. His suitcase is open on the bed.* ANDERSON *turns his attention to his briefcase and brings out* McKENDRICK'*s magazine. He looks round wondering what to do with it. There is a knock on the door.* ANDERSON *tosses the girly magazine into his suitcase and closes the case. He goes to open the door. The caller is* PAVEL HOLLAR.

ANDERSON. Yes?

HOLLAR. I am Pavel Hollar.

ANDERSON. Yes?

HOLLAR. Professor Anderson. (HOLLAR *is Czech and speaks with an accent.*)

ANDERSON. Hollar? Oh, heavens, yes. How extraordinary. Come in.

HOLLAR. Thank you. I'm sorry to—

ANDERSON. No, no—what a pleasant surprise. I've only just arrived as you can see. Sit where you can. How are you? What are you doing? You live in Prague?

HOLLAR. Oh yes.

(ANDERSON *closes the door.*)

ANDERSON. Well, well. Well, well, well, well. How are you? Must be ten years.

HOLLAR. Yes. It is ten. I took my degree in sixty-seven.

ANDERSON. You got a decent degree, too, didn't you?

HOLLAR. Yes, I got a first.

ANDERSON. Of course you did. Well done, well done. Are you still in philosophy?

HOLLAR. No, unfortunately.

ANDERSON. Ah. What are you doing now?

HOLLAR. I am a what do you say—a cleaner.

ANDERSON (*with intelligent interest*). A cleaner? What is that?

HOLLAR (*surprised*). Cleaning. Washing. With a brush and a bucket. I am a cleaner at the bus station.

ANDERSON. You wash buses?

HOLLAR. No, not buses—the lavatories, the floors where people walk and so on.

ANDERSON. Oh. I see. You're a *cleaner*.

HOLLAR. Yes.

(*Pause.*)

ANDERSON. Are you married now, or anything?

HOLLAR. Yes. I married. She was almost my fiancée when I went to England. Irma. She is a country girl. No English. No philosophy. We have a son who is Sacha. That is Alexander.

ANDERSON. I see.

HOLLAR. And Mrs Anderson?

ANDERSON. She died. Did you meet her ever?

HOLLAR. No.

ANDERSON (*pause*). I don't know what to say.

HOLLAR. Did she die recently?

ANDERSON. No, I mean—a cleaner.

HOLLAR. I had one year graduate research. My doctorate studies were on certain connections with Thomas Paine and Locke.° But then, since sixty-nine. . . .

ANDERSON. Cleaning lavatories.

HOLLAR. First I was in a bakery. Later on construction, building houses. Many other things. It is the way it is for many people.

ANDERSON. Is it all right for you to be here talking to me?

HOLLAR. Of course. Why not? You are my old professor. (HOLLAR *is carrying a bag or briefcase. He puts this down and opens it.*) I have something here. (*From the bag he takes out the sort of envelope which would contain about thirty type-written foolscap pages. He also takes out a child's "magic eraser" pad, the sort of pad on which one scratches a message and then slides it out to erase it.*) You understand these things of course?

ANDERSON (*nonplussed*). Er . . .

Paine and Locke: The political ideas of the English philosopher John Locke (1632–1704) formed the basis of the thinking expressed in the American Declaration of Independence, and the writings of the English political theorist Thomas Paine (1737–1809) did much to encourage the American revolution. Both men were champions of political freedom and "natural rights."

HOLLAR (*smiling*). Of course. (HOLLAR *demonstrates the pad briefly, then writes on the pad while Anderson watches.*)

ANDERSON (*stares at him*). To England?

(HOLLAR *abandons the use of the pad, and whispers in* ANDERSON'*s ear.*)

HOLLAR. Excuse me. (HOLLAR *goes to the door and opens it for* ANDERSON. HOLLAR *carries his envelope but leaves his bag in the room.* ANDERSON *goes out of the door baffled.* HOLLAR *follows him. They walk a few paces down the corridor.*) Thank you. It is better to be careful.

ANDERSON. Why? You don't seriously suggest that my room is bugged?

HOLLAR. It is better to assume it.

ANDERSON. Why? (*Just then the door of the room next to* ANDERSON'*s opens and a* MAN *comes out. He is about forty and wears a dark rather shapeless suit. He glances at* ANDERSON *and* HOLLAR. *And then walks off in the opposite direction towards the lifts and passes out of sight.* HOLLAR *and* ANDERSON *instinctively pause until the* MAN *has gone.*) I hope you're not getting me into trouble.

HOLLAR. I hope not. I don't think so. I have friends in trouble.

ANDERSON. I know, it's dreadful—but . . . well, what is it?

(HOLLAR *indicates his envelope.*)

HOLLAR. My doctoral thesis. It is mainly theoretical. Only ten thousand words, but very formally arranged.

ANDERSON. My goodness . . . ten years in the writing.

HOLLAR. No. I wrote it this month—when I heard of this congress here and you coming. I decided. Everyday in the night.

ANDERSON. Of course. I'd be very happy to read it.

HOLLAR. It is in Czech.

ANDERSON. Oh . . . well . . . ?

HOLLAR. I'm afraid so. But Peter Volkansky—he was with me, you remember—we came together in sixty-three—

ANDERSON. Oh yes—Volkansky—yes, I do remember him. He never came back here.

HOLLAR. No. He didn't come back. He was a realist.

ANDERSON. He's at Reading or somewhere like that.

HOLLAR. Lyster.

ANDERSON. Leicester. Exactly. Are you in touch with him?

HOLLAR. A little. He will translate it and try to have it published in English. If it's good. I think it is good.

ANDERSON. But can't you publish it in Czech? . . . (*This catches up on him and he shakes his head.*) Oh, Hollar . . . now, you know, really, I'm a guest of the government here.

HOLLAR. They would not search you.

ANDERSON. That's not the point. I'm sorry . . . I mean it would be bad manners, wouldn't it?

HOLLAR. Bad manners?

ANDERSON. I know it sounds rather lame. But ethics and manners are interestingly related. The history of human calumny is largely a series of breaches of good manners. . . . (*Pause.*) Perhaps if I said correct behavior it wouldn't sound so ridiculous. You do see what I mean. I am sorry. . . . Look, can we go back . . . I ought to unpack.

HOLLAR. My thesis is about correct behavior.

ANDERSON. Oh yes?

HOLLAR. Here you know, individual correctness is defined by what is correct for the State.

ANDERSON. Yes, I know.

HOLLAR. I ask how collective right can have meaning by itself. I ask where it comes from, the idea of a collective ethic.

ANDERSON. Yes.

HOLLAR. I reply, it comes from the individual. One man's dealings with another man.

ANDERSON. Yes.

HOLLAR. The collective ethic can only be the individual ethic writ big.

ANDERSON. Writ large.

HOLLAR. Writ large, precisely. The ethics of the State must be judged against the fundamental ethic of the individual. The human being, not the citizen. I conclude there is an obligation, a human responsibility, to fight against the State correctness. Unfortunately that is not a safe conclusion.

ANDERSON. Quite. The difficulty arises when one asks oneself how the *individual* ethic can have any meaning by itself. Where does *that* come from? In what sense is it intelligible, for example, to say that a man has certain inherent, individual rights? It is much easier to understand how a community of individuals can decide to give each other certain rights. These rights may or may not include, for example, the right to publish something. In that situation, the individual ethic would flow from the collective ethic, just as the State says it does. (*Pause.*) I only mean it is a question you would have to deal with.

HOLLAR. I mean, it is not safe for me.

ANDERSON (*still misunderstanding*). Well yes, but for example, you could say that such an arrangement between a man and the State is a sort of contract, and it is the essence of a contract that both parties enter into it freely. And you have not entered into it freely. I mean, that would be one line of attack.

HOLLAR. It is not the main line. You see, to me the idea of an inherent right is intelligible. I believe that we have such rights, and they are paramount.

ANDERSON. Yes, I see you do, but how do you justify the assertion?

HOLLAR. I observe. I observe my son for example.

ANDERSON. Your son?

HOLLAR. For example.

(*Pause.*)

ANDERSON. Look, there's no need to stand out here. There's . . . no point. I was going to have a bath and change . . . meeting some of my colleagues later. . . . (ANDERSON *moves to go but* HOLLAR *stops him with a touch on the arm.*)

HOLLAR. I am not a famous dissident. A writer, a scientist. . . .

ANDERSON. No.

HOLLAR. If I am picked up—on the way home, let us say—there is no fuss. A cleaner. I will be one of hundreds. It's all right. In the end it must change. But I have something to say—that is all. If I leave my statement behind, then it's O.K. You understand?

ANDERSON. Perhaps the correct thing for me to have done is not to have accepted their invitation to speak here. But I did accept it. It is a contract, as it were, freely entered into. And having accepted their hospitality I cannot in all conscience start smuggling. . . . It's just not ethical.

HOLLAR. But if you didn't know you were smuggling it—

ANDERSON. Smuggling entails knowledge.

HOLLAR. If I hid my thesis in your luggage, for instance.

ANDERSON. That's childish. Also, you could be getting me into trouble, and your quarrel is not with me. Your action would be unethical on your own terms—one man's dealings with another man. I am sorry. (ANDERSON *goes back towards his door, which* HOLLAR *had left ajar.* HOLLAR *follows him.*)

HOLLAR. No, it is I who must apologize. The man next door, is he one of your group?

ANDERSON. No. I don't know him. (ANDERSON *opens his bedroom door. He turns as if to say good-bye.*)

HOLLAR. My bag.

ANDERSON. Oh yes.

(HOLLAR *follows* ANDERSON *into the room.*)

HOLLAR. You will have a bath . . . ?

ANDERSON. I thought I would.

(HOLLAR *turns into the bathroom.* ANDERSON *stays in the bedroom, surprised. He hears the bath water being turned on. The bath water makes a rush of sound.* ANDERSON *enters the bathroom and sees* HOLLAR *sitting on the edge of the bath. Interior bathroom.*)

HOLLAR (*quietly*). I have not yet made a copy.

ANDERSON (*loudly*). What?

(HOLLAR *goes up to* ANDERSON *and speaks close to* ANDERSON's *ear. The bath taps make a loud background noise.*)

HOLLAR. I have not yet made a copy. I have a bad feeling about carrying this home. (*He indicates his envelope.*) I did not expect to take it away. I ask a favor. (*Smiles.*) Ethical.

ANDERSON (*quietly now*). What is it?

HOLLAR. Let me leave this here and you can bring it to my apartment tomorrow—I have a safe place for it there. (HOLLAR *takes a piece of paper and a pencil from his pocket and starts writing his address in capital letters.*)

ANDERSON. But you know my time here is very crowded—(*Then he gives in.*) Do you live nearby?

HOLLAR. It is not far. I have written my address. (HOLLAR *gives* ANDERSON *the paper.*)

ANDERSON (*forgetting to be quiet*). Do you seriously—(HOLLAR *quietens* ANDERSON.) Do you seriously expect to be searched on the way home?

HOLLAR. I don't know, but it is better to be careful. I wrote a letter to Mr Husak. Also some other things. So sometimes they follow me.

ANDERSON. But you weren't worried about bringing the thesis with you.

HOLLAR. No. If anybody watches me they want to know what books *you* give *me*.

ANDERSON. I see. Yes, all right, Hollar. I'll bring it tomorrow.

HOLLAR. Please don't leave it in your room when you go to eat. Take your briefcase.

(*They go back into the bedroom.* ANDERSON *puts* HOLLAR *'s envelope into his briefcase.*)

(*Normal voice*) So perhaps you will come and meet my wife.

ANDERSON. Yes. Should I telephone?

HOLLAR. Unfortunately my telephone is removed. I am home all day. Saturday.

ANDERSON. Oh yes.

HOLLAR. Good-bye.

ANDERSON. Good-bye.

(HOLLAR *goes to the door carrying his bag.*)

HOLLAR. I forgot—welcome to Prague.

(HOLLAR *leaves closing the door.* ANDERSON *stands still for a few moments. Then he hears footsteps approaching down the corridor. The footsteps appear to stop outside his room. But then the door to the next room is opened and the unseen man enters the room next door and loudly closes the door behind him.*)

4. INTERIOR: ANDERSON'S ROOM. MORNING

Close-up of the colloquium brochure. It is lying on ANDERSON *'s table. Then* ANDERSON *picks it up. His dress and appearance, and the light outside the window, tell us that it is morning. Dressed to go out,* ANDERSON *picks up his briefcase and leaves the room. In the corridor he walks towards the lifts. At the lifts he finds* CRISP *waiting.* ANDERSON *stands next to* CRISP *silently for a few moments.*

ANDERSON. Good morning. (*Pause.*) Mr Crisp . . . my name is Anderson. I'm a very great admirer of yours.

CRISP (*chewing gum*). Oh . . . ta.°
ANDERSON. Good luck this afternoon.
CRISP. Thanks. Bloody useless, the lifts in this place.
ANDERSON. Are you all staying in this hotel?

(CRISP *doesn't seem to hear this.* CRISP *sees* BROADBENT *emerging from a room.* BROADBENT *carries a zipped bag,* CRISP *has a similar bag.*)

CRISP (*shouts*). Here you are, Roy—it's waiting for you.

(BROADBENT *arrives.*)

ANDERSON. Good morning. Good luck this afternoon.
BROADBENT. Right. Thanks. Are you over for the match?
ANDERSON. Yes. Well, partly. I've got my ticket. (ANDERSON *takes out of his pocket the envelope he received from the hotel* CLERK *and shows it.*)
CRISP (*quietly*). You didn't pull her, then?
BROADBENT. No chance.
CRISP. They don't trust you, do they?
BROADBENT. Well, they're right, aren't they? Remember Milan.
CRISP (*laughing*). Yeah—(*The bell sounds to indicate that the lift is arriving.*) About bloody time.
ANDERSON. I see from yesterday's paper that they've brought in Jirasek for Vladislav.
BROADBENT. Yes, that's right. Six foot eight, they say.
ANDERSON. He's not very good in the air unless he's got lots of space.

(BROADBENT *looks at him curiously. The lift doors open and the three of them get in. There is no one else in the lift except the female* OPERATOR. *Interior lift.*)

BROADBENT. You've seen him, have you?
ANDERSON. I've seen him twice. In the UFA Cup a few seasons ago. . . . I happened to be in Berlin for the Hegel Colloquium, er, bunfight. And then last season I was in Bratislava to receive an honorary degree.
CRISP. Tap his ankles for him. Teach him to be six foot eight.
BROADBENT. Leave off—(*He nods at the lift* OPERATOR.) You never know, do you?
CRISP. Yeah, maybe the lift's bugged.
ANDERSON. He scored both times from the same move, and came close twice more—
BROADBENT. Oh yes?
(*Pause.*)
ANDERSON (*in a rush*). I realize it's none of my business—I mean you may think I'm an absolute ass, but—(*Pause.*)
Look, if Halas takes a corner he's going to make it short—almost certainly—

ta: thank you

push it back to Deml or Kautsky, who pulls the defence out. Jirasek hangs about for the chip to the far post. They'll do the same thing from a set piece.° Three or four times in the same match. *Really.* Short corners and free kicks. (*The lift stops at the third floor.* BROADBENT *and* CRISP *are staring at* ANDERSON.)
(*Lamely.*) Anyway, that's why they've brought Jirasek back, in my opinion.

(*The lift doors open and* MCKENDRICK *gets in.* MCKENDRICK's *manner is breezy and bright.*)

MCKENDRICK. Good morning! You've got together then?
ANDERSON. A colleague. Mr McKendrick . . .
MCKENDRICK. You're Crisp. (*He takes* CRISP's *hand and shakes it.*) Bill McKendrick. I hear you're doing some very interesting work in Newcastle. Great stuff. I still like to think of myself as a bit of a left-winger at Stoke. Of course, my stuff is largely empirical—I leave epistemological questions to the scholastics—eh, Anderson? (*He pokes* ANDERSON *in the ribs.*)
ANDERSON. McKendrick . . .
BROADBENT. Did you say *Stoke?*

(*The lift arrives at the ground floor.*)

MCKENDRICK (*to* BROADBENT). We've met, haven't we? Your face is familiar . . .

(BROADBENT, CRISP *and* MCKENDRICK *in close attendance leave the lift.* ANDERSON *is slow on the uptake but follows.*)

ANDERSON. McKendrick—?
MCKENDRICK (*prattling*). There's a choice of open forums tonight— neo-Hegelians, or Quinian neo-Positivists. Which do you fancy? Pity Quine couldn't be here. And Hegel° for that matter. (MCKENDRICK *laughs brazenly in the lobby.* BROADBENT *and* CRISP *eye him warily.* ANDERSON *winces.*)

5. INTERIOR: THE COLLOQUIUM

The general idea is that a lot of philosophers sit in a sort of theater while on stage one of their number reads a paper from behind a lectern, with a CHAIRMAN *in attendance behind him. The set up however is quite complicated. To one side are three glassed-in booths, each one containing "simultaneous interpreters." These interpreters have earphones and microphones. They also have a copy of the*

Look . . . set piece: In the tactic described, the Czechs are in control of the ball at their opponents' end of the field. Either during play action or from "a set piece" (where the Czechs are awarded a free kick from the corner of the field), Halas kicks the ball to a nearby teammate, who, after drawing the opponents' defenders toward him, gives the ball a short but high kick to the extremely tall Jirasek, who, near the far side of the goal, "heads" it in.
Quine . . . Hegel: The American philosopher Quine, born in 1908, was living. The German philosopher Hegel (1770–1831) was dead.

lecture being given. One of these interpreters is translating into Czech, another into French, another into German. The audience is furnished either with ear-phones or with those hand-held phones which are issued in theaters sometimes. Each of these phones can tune into any of the three interpreters depending upon the language of the listener. For our purposes it is better to have hand-held phones.

It is important to the play, specifically to a later scene when ANDERSON *is talking, that the hall and the audience should be substantial.*

At the moment ANDERSON *is in the audience, sitting next to* McKENDRICK. McKENDRICK *is still discomforted.* CHETWYN *is elsewhere in the audience. We begin however with a large close-up of the speaker who is an American called* STONE. *After the first sentence or two of* STONE's *speech, the camera will ac-quaint us with the situation. At different points during* STONE's *speech, there is conversation between* ANDERSON *and* McKENDRICK. *In this script, these conver-sations are placed immediately after that part of* STONE's *speech which they will cover. This applies also to any other interpolations. Obviously,* STONE *does not pause to let these other things in.*

STONE.   The confusion which often arises from the ambiguity of ordi-nary language raises special problems for a logical language. This is especially so when the ambiguity is not casual and inadvertent—but when it's contrived. In fact, the limitations of a logical language are likely to appear when we ask ourselves whether it can accommodate a literature, or whether poetry can be reduced to a logical language. It is here that deliberate ambiguity for effect makes problems.

ANDERSON.   Perfectly understandable mistake.

STONE.   Nor must we confuse ambiguity, furthermore, with mere synonymity. When we say that a politician ran for office that is not an ambig-uous statement, it is merely an instance of a word having different applica-tions, literal, idiomatic and so on.

McKENDRICK.   I said I knew his face.

ANDERSON.   Match of the Day.°

STONE.   The intent is clear in each application. The show ran well on Broadway. Native Dancer° ran well at Kentucky, and so on. (*In the audience a Frenchman expresses dismay and bewilderment as his earphones give a literal translation of "a native dancer" running at Kentucky. Likewise a German listener has the same problem.*) And what about this word "Well"? Again, it is applied as a qualifier with various intent—the show ran for a long time, the horse ran fast, and so on.

McKENDRICK.   So this pressing engagement of yours is a football match.

ANDERSON.   A World Cup qualifier is not just a football match.

STONE.   Again, there is no problem here so long as these variations are what I propose to call reliable. "You eat well" says Mary to John, "You cook

Match of the Day: a popular BBC TV sports program
Native Dancer: an American race horse, winner of the Preakness and the Belmont Stakes in 1953 but not of the Kentucky Derby

well" says John to Mary. We know that when Mary says "You *eat* well" she does not mean that John eats *skillfully*. Just as we know that when John says "You cook well" he does not mean that Mary cooks *abundantly*.

ANDERSON. But I'm sorry about missing your paper, I really am.

STONE. I say that we know this, but I mean only that our general experience indicates it. The qualifier takes its meaning from the contextual force of the verb it qualifies. But it is the mark of a sound theory that it should take account not merely of our general experience, but also of the particular experience, and not merely of the particular experience but also of the unique experience, and not merely of the unique experience but also of the hypothetical experience. It is when we consider the world of *possibilities,* hypothetical experience, that we get closer to ambiguity. "You cook well" says John to Mary. "You eat well" says Mary to John.

MCKENDRICK. Do you ever wonder whether all this is worthwhile?

ANDERSON. No.

MCKENDRICK. I know what you mean.

(CHETWYN *is twisting the knob on his translation phone, to try all this out in different languages. He is clearly bored. He looks at his watch.*)

STONE. No problems there. But I ask you to imagine a competition when what is being judged is table manners.

(*Insert* FRENCH INTERPRETER's *box—interior.*)

INTERPRETER. . . . bonne tenue á table . . .

STONE. John enters this competition and afterwards Mary says, "Well, you certainly ate well!" Now Mary seems to be saying that John ate *skillfully—with refinement.* And again, I ask you to imagine a competition where the amount of food eaten is taken into account along with refinement of table manners. *Now* Mary says to John, "Well, you didn't eat very well, but at least you ate well."

INTERPRETER. Alors, vous n'avez pas bien mangé . . . mais . . .

(*All* INTREPRETERS *baffled by this.*)

STONE. Now clearly there is no way to tell whether Mary means that John ate abundantly but clumsily, or that John ate frugally but elegantly. Here we have a genuine ambiguity. To restate Mary's sentence in a logical language we would have to ask her what she meant.

MCKENDRICK. By the way, I've got you a copy of my paper.

ANDERSON. Oh, many thanks.

MCKENDRICK. It's not a long paper. You could read it comfortably during half-time. (MCKENDRICK *gives* ANDERSON *his paper.*)

STONE. But this is to assume that Mary exists. Let us say she is a fictitious character in a story I have written. Very well, you say to me, the author, "What did Mary mean?" Well I might reply—"I don't know what she meant. Her ambiguity makes the necessary point of my story." And here I think the idea of a logical language which can *only* be unambiguous, breaks down.

(ANDERSON *opens his briefcase and puts* McKENDRICK'S *paper into it. He fingers* HOLLAR'S *envelope and broods over it.* STONE *has concluded. He sits down to applause. The* CHAIRMAN, *who has been sitting behind him has stood up.*)

ANDERSON. I'm going to make a discreet exit—I've got a call to make before the match. (ANDERSON *stands up.*)
CHAIRMAN. Yes—Professor Anderson I think . . . ?

(ANDERSON *is caught like a rabbit in the headlights.* McKENDRICK *enjoys his predicament and becomes interested in how* ANDERSON *will deal with it.*)

ANDERSON. Ah . . . I would only like to offer Professor Stone the observation that language is not the only level of human communication, and perhaps not the most important level. Whereof we cannot speak, thereof we are by no means silent. (McKENDRICK *smiles "Bravo."*) Verbal language is a technical refinement of our capacity for communication, rather than the *fons et origo*° of that capacity. The likelihood is that language develops in an *ad hoc* way,° so there is no reason to expect its development to be logical. (*A thought strikes him.*) The importance of language is overrated. It allows me and Professor Stone to show off a bit, and it is very useful for communicating detail—but the important truths are simple and monolithic. The essentials of a given situation speak for themselves, and language is as capable of obscuring the truth as of revealing it. Thank you. (ANDERSON *edges his way out towards the door.*)
CHAIRMAN (*uncertainly*). Professor Stone . . .
STONE. Well, what was the question?

6. EXTERIOR: FRONT DOOR OF THE HOLLAR APARTMENT

The apartment is one of two half-way up a large old building. The stairwell is dirty and uncared for. The HOLLAR *front door is on a landing, and the front door of another flat is across the landing. Stairs go up and down.* ANDERSON *comes up the stairs and finds the right number on the door and rings the bell. He is carrying his briefcase. All the men in this scene are Czech plainclothes* POLICE-MEN. *They will be identified in this text merely by number.* MAN 3 *is the one in charge.* MAN 1 *comes to the door.*

ANDERSON. I'm looking for Mr Hollar.

(MAN 1 *shakes his head. He looks behind him.* MAN 2 *comes to the door.*)

MAN 2 (*in Czech*). Yes? Who are you?
ANDERSON. English? Um. Parlez-vous français? Er. Spreckanzydoitch?
MAN 2 (*in German*). Deutsch? Ein Bischen.°

---

fons et origo: fount and origin
in an *ad hoc* way: to meet special needs or situations
Ein Bischen: a bit

ANDERSON. Actually I don't. Does Mr Hollar live here? Apartment Hollar?

(MAN 2 *speaks to somebody behind him.*)

MAN 2 (*in Czech*). An Englishman. Do you know him?

(MRS HOLLAR *comes to the door. She is about the same age as* HOLLAR.)

ANDERSON. Mrs Hollar? (MRS HOLLAR *nods.*) Is your husband here? Pavel . . .

MRS HOLLAR (*in Czech*). Pavel is arrested.

(*Inside, behind the door,* MAN 3 *is heard shouting, in Czech.*)

MAN 3 (*not seen*). What's going on there? (MAN 3 *comes to the door.*)

ANDERSON. I am looking for Mr Hollar. I am a friend from England. His Professor. My name is Anderson.

MAN 3 (*in English*). Not here. (*In Czech to* MRS HOLLAR.) He says he is a friend of your husband. Anderson.

ANDERSON. He was my student.

(MRS HOLLAR *calls out.*)

MAN 3 (*in Czech*). Shut up.

ANDERSON. Student. Philosophy.

(MRS HOLLAR *calls out.*)

MAN 3. Shut up.

(MAN 3 *and* MAN 2 *come out of the flat on to the landing, closing the door behind them.*)

ANDERSON. I just came to see him. Just to say hello. For a minute. I have a taxi waiting. Taxi.

MAN 3. Taxi.

ANDERSON. Yes, I can't stay.

MAN 3 (*in English*). Moment. O.K.

ANDERSON. I can't stay. (MAN 3 *rings the bell of the adjacent flat. A rather scared woman opens the door.* MAN 3 *asks, in Czech, to use the phone.* MAN 3 *goes inside the other flat.* ANDERSON *begins to realize the situation.*) Well, look, if you don't mind—I'm on my way to—an engagement . . .

MAN 2 (*in Czech*). Stay here.

(*Pause.* ANDERSON *looks at his watch. Then from inside the flat* MRS HOLLAR *is shouting in Czech.*)

MRS HOLLAR (*unseen*). I'm entitled to a witness of my choice.

(*The door is opened violently and immediately slammed.* ANDERSON *becomes agitated.*)

ANDERSON. What's going on in there?

MAN 2 (*in Czech*). Stay here, he won't be a minute.

(ANDERSON *can hear* MRS HOLLAR *shouting.*)

ANDERSON. Now look here—(ANDERSON *rings the doorbell. The door is opened by* MAN 4.) I demand to speak to Mrs Hollar.

(*Upstairs and downstairs doors are opening and people are shouting, in Czech* "What's going on?" *And so on. There is also shouting from inside the flat.* MAN 2 *shouts up and down the staircase, in Czech.*)

MAN 2 (*in Czech*). Go inside!

ANDERSON. Now look here, I am the J.S. Mill Professor of Ethics° at the University of Cambridge and I demand that I am allowed to leave or to telephone the British Ambassador!

MAN 4 (*in Czech*). Bring him inside.

MAN 2 (*in Czech*). In. (*He pushes* ANDERSON *into the flat. Interior flat. The hallway. Inside it is apparent that the front door leads to more than one flat. Off the very small dirty hall there is a kitchen, a lavatory and two other doors, not counting the door to the* HOLLAR *rooms.*)

MAN 4 (*in Czech*). Stay with him.

(The HOLLAR *interior door is opened from inside by* MRS HOLLAR.)

MRS HOLLAR (*in Czech*). If he's my witness he's allowed in here.

MAN 4 (*in Czech*). Go inside—he's not your witness. (MAN 4 *pushes* MRS HOLLAR *inside and closes the door from within. This leaves* ANDERSON *and* MAN 2 *in the little hall. Another door now opens, and a small girl, poorly dressed, looks round it. She is jerked back out of sight by someone and the door is pulled closed. The* HOLLAR *door is flung open again, by* MRS HOLLAR.)

MRS HOLLAR (*in Czech*). I want this door open.

MAN 2 (*in Czech*). Leave it open then. He'll be back in a minute.

(MAN 4 *disappears back inside the flat.* MRS HOLLAR *is heard.*)

MRS HOLLAR (*unseen; in Czech*). Bastards.

(ANDERSON *stands in the hallway. He can hear* MRS HOLLAR *starting to cry.* ANDERSON *looks completely out of his depth.*)

ANDERSON. My God. . . .

(*Then the doorbell rings.* MAN 2 *opens it to let in* MAN 3.)

MAN 2 (*in Czech*). We had to come in to shut her up.

MAN 3 (*in Czech*). Well, he's coming over. (*In English to* ANDERSON.) Captain coming. Speak English.

J. S. Mill Professor of Ethics: Anderson holds an endowed chair named after John Stuart Mill (1806–1873), English philosopher and author of *On Liberty,* one of the great justifications of individual human freedoms.

ANDERSON. I would like to telephone the British Ambassador.

MAN 3 (*in English*). O.K. Captain coming.

ANDERSON. How long will he be? I have an appointment. (*He looks at his watch.*) Yes, by God! I do have an engagement and it starts in half an hour—

MAN 3 (*in English*). Please.

(*A lavatory flushes. From the other interior door an* OLD MAN *comes out.* MAN 3 *nods curtly at the* OLD MAN. *The* OLD MAN *shuffles by looking at* ANDERSON. MAN 3 *becomes uneasy at being in the traffic. He decides to bring* ANDERSON *inside the flat. He does so.*

(*Interior:* HOLLAR'S *room. There are two connecting rooms. Beyond this room is a door leading to a bedroom. This door is open. The rooms seem full of people. The rooms are small and shabby. They are being thoroughly searched, and obviously have been in this process for hours. The searchers do not spoil or destroy anything. There are no torn cushions or anything like that. However, the floor of the first room is almost covered in books. The bookcases which line perhaps two of the walls are empty. The rug could be rolled up, and there could be one or two floorboards up.*

(MAN 1 *is going through the books, leafing through each one and looking along the spine. He is starting to put books back on the shelves one by one.* MAN 5 *has emptied drawers of their contents and is going through a pile of papers.* MRS HOLLAR *stands in the doorway between the two rooms. Beyond her* MAN 2 *can be seen searching.* [MAN 4 *is out of sight in the bedroom.*] MAN 3 *indicates a chair on which* ANDERSON *should sit.* ANDERSON *sits putting his briefcase on the floor by his feet. He looks around. He sees a clock showing 2.35.*

(*Mix to clock showing 2.55.*

(ANDERSON *is where he was.* MAN 1 *is still on the books.* MAN 5 *is still looking through papers.* MAN 3 *is examining the inside of a radio set. Voices are heard faintly on the stairs. There is a man remonstrating. A woman's voice too. The doorbell rings.*

(MAN 3 *leaves the room, closing the door.* ANDERSON *hears him go to the front door. There is some conversation. The front door closes again and* MAN 3 *re-enters the room.*)

MAN 3 (*in English to* ANDERSON). Taxi.

ANDERSON. Oh—I forgot him. Dear me.

MAN 3. O.K.

ANDERSON. I must pay him. (ANDERSON *takes out his wallet.* MAN 3 *takes it from him without snatching.*)

MAN 3. O.K. (MAN 3 *looks through the wallet.*)

ANDERSON. Give that back— (*Furious.*) Now, you listen to me—this has gone on quite long enough—I demand—to be allowed to leave. . . .

(ANDERSON *has stood up.* MAN 3 *gently pushes him back into the chair. In* ANDERSON'S *wallet* MAN 3 *finds his envelope and discovers the football ticket. He puts it back. He looks sympathetically at* ANDERSON.)

MAN 3 (*in Czech*). The old boy's got a ticket for the England match. No wonder he's furious. (*He gives the wallet back to* ANDERSON. *In English.*) Taxi O.K. No money. He go. Football no good.

ANDERSON. Serve me right.

MAN 5 (*in Czech*). It's on the radio. Let him have it on.

(MAN 3 *returns to the radio and turns it on.* MRS HOLLAR *enters quickly from the bedroom and turns it off.*)

MRS HOLLAR (*in Czech*). That's my radio.

MAN 3 (*in Czech*). Your friend wants to listen to the match.

(MRS HOLLAR *looks at* ANDERSON. *She turns the radio on. The radio is talking about the match which is just about to begin.*)

MAN 3 (*in English*). Is good. O.K.?

(ANDERSON, *listening, realizes that the radio is listing the names of the English team. Then the match begins. Mix to the same situation about half an hour later. The radio is still on.* MAN 1 *is still on the books. He has put aside three or four English books.* MAN 5 *has disappeared.* MAN 2 *is sorting out the fluff from a carpet sweeper.* MAN 4 *is standing on a chair examining the inside of a ventilation grating.* ANDERSON *gets up off his chair and starts to walk towards the bedroom. The three* MEN *in the room look up but don't stop him.* ANDERSON *enters the bedroom.*

(*Interior bedroom.* MAN 3 *is going through pockets in a wardrobe.* MAN 5 *is looking under floorboards.* MRS HOLLAR *is sitting on the bed watching them.*)

ANDERSON. It's half-past three. I demand to be allowed to leave or to telephone the British—

MAN 3. Please—too slow.

ANDERSON. I demand to leave—

MAN 3. O.K. Who wins football?

ANDERSON (*pause*). No score.

(*The doorbell goes.* MAN 3 *goes into the other room and to the door.* ANDERSON *follows him as far as the other room. On the way through* MAN 3 *signals to turn off the radio.* MAN 2 *turns off the radio.* MRS HOLLAR *comes in and turns the radio on.*)

MRS HOLLAR (*in Czech*). Show me where it says I can't listen to my own radio.

(MAN 3 *returns from the front door with* MAN 6. MAN 6 *enters the room.*)

MAN 6 (*in Czech*). I said don't let him leave—I didn't say bring him inside. (*To* ANDERSON *in English.*) Professor Anderson? I'm sorry your friend Mr Hollar has got himself into trouble.

ANDERSON. Thank Christ—now listen to me—I am a professor of philosophy. I am a guest of the Czechoslovakian government. I might almost say an honored guest. I have been invited to speak at the Colloquium in Prague.

My connections in England reach up to the highest in the land—

MAN 6.   Do you know the Queen?

ANDERSON.   Certainly. (*But he has rushed into that.*) No, I do not know the Queen—but I speak the truth when I say that I am personally acquainted with two members of the government, one of whom has been to my house, and I assure you that unless I am allowed to leave this building immediately there is going to be a major incident about the way my liberty has been impeded by your men. I do not know what they are doing here, I do not care what they are doing here—

MAN 6.   Excuse me. Professor. There is some mistake. I thought you were here as a friend of the Hollar family.

ANDERSON.   I know Pavel Hollar, certainly.

MAN 6.   Absolutely. You are here as a friend, at Mrs Hollar's request.

ANDERSON.   I just dropped in to—what do you mean?

MAN 6.   Mr Hollar unfortunately has been arrested for a serious crime against the State. It is usual for the home of an accused person to be searched for evidence, and so on. I am sure the same thing happens in your country. Well, under our law Mrs Hollar is entitled to have a friendly witness present during the search. To be frank she is entitled to two witnesses. So if, for example, an expensive vase is broken by mistake, and the police claim it was broken before, it will not just be her word against theirs. And so on. I think you will agree that's fair.

ANDERSON.   Well?

MAN 6.   Well, my understanding is that she asked you to be her witness. (*In Czech to* MRS HOLLAR.) Did you ask him to be your witness?

MRS HOLLAR (*in Czech*).   Yes, I did.

MAN 6 (*in English to* ANDERSON).   Yes. Exactly so. (*Pause.*) You are Mr Hollar's friend, aren't you?

ANDERSON.   I taught him in Cambridge after he left Czechoslovakia.

MAN 6.   A brave man.

ANDERSON.   Yes . . . a change of language . . . and culture . . .

MAN 6.   He walked across a minefield. In 1962. Brave.

ANDERSON.   Perhaps he was simply desperate.

MAN 6.   Perhaps a little ungrateful. The State, you know, educated him, fed him, for eighteen years. "Thank you very much—good-bye."

ANDERSON.   Well he came back, in the Spring of sixty-eight.

MAN 6.   Oh yes.

ANDERSON.   A miscalculation.

MAN 6.   How do you mean?

ANDERSON.   Well, really . . . there are a lot of things wrong in England but it is still not "a serious crime against the State" to put forward a philosophical view which does not find favor with the Government.

MAN 6.   Professor . . . Hollar is charged with currency offences. There is a black market in hard currency. It is illegal. We do not have laws about philosophy. He is an ordinary criminal.

(Pause. The radio commentary has continued softly. But in this pause it changes pitch. It is clear to ANDERSON, *and to us, that something particular has occurred in the match.* MAN 6 *is listening.)*

(in English.) Penalty. *(He listens for a moment.)* For us, I'm afraid.

ANDERSON. Yes, I can hear.

(This is because it is clear from the crowd noise that it's a penalty for the home side. MAN 6 *listens again.)*

MAN 6 *(in English)*. Broadbent—a bad tackle when Deml had a certain goal . . . a what you call it?—a necessary foul.

ANDERSON. A professional foul.°

MAN 6. Yes. *(On the radio the goal is scored. This is perfectly clear from the crowd reaction.)* Not good for you. *(*MAN 6 *turns off the radio. Pause.* MAN 6 *considers* ANDERSON.*)* So you have had a philosophical discussion with Hollar.

ANDERSON. I believe you implied that I was free to go. *(He stands up.)* I am quite sure you know that Hollar visited me at my hotel last night. It was a social call, which I was returning when I walked into this. And furthermore, I understood nothing about being a witness—I was prevented from leaving. I only came to say hello, and meet Pavel's wife, on my way to the football—

MAN 6 *(with surprise)*. So you came to Czechoslovakia to go to the football match, Professor?

(This rattles ANDERSON.*)*

ANDERSON. Certainly not. Well, the afternoon of the Colloquium was devoted to—well, it was not a condition of my invitation that I should attend all the sessions. *(Pause.)* I was invited to *speak*, not to listen. I am speaking tomorrow morning.

MAN 6. Why should I know Hollar visited you at the hotel?

ANDERSON. He told me he was often followed.

MAN 6. Well, when a man is known to be engaged in meeting foreigners to buy currency—

ANDERSON. I don't believe any of that—he was being harassed because of his letter to Husak—

MAN 6. A letter to President Husak? What sort of letter?

ANDERSON *(flustered)*. Your people knew about it—

MAN 6. It is not a crime to write to the President—

ANDERSON. No doubt that depends on what is written.

MAN 6. You mean he wrote some kind of slander?

ANDERSON *(heatedly)*. I insist on leaving now.

MAN 6. Of course. You know, your taxi driver has made a complaint against you.

---

professional foul: Broadbent, in order to prevent an almost certain goal, has committed an intentional foul against Deml by sliding into him from behind. The tactic proves unsuccessful, however, for the Czechs are awarded a free penalty kick and score on it. The incident is described again on pages 1269 and 1276.

ANDERSON. What are you talking about?

MAN 6. He never got paid.

ANDERSON. Yes, I'm sorry but—

MAN 6. You are not to blame. My officer told him to go.

ANDERSON. Yes, that's right.

MAN 6. Still, he is very unhappy. You told him you would be five minutes you were delivering something—

ANDERSON. How could I have told him that? I don't speak Czech.

MAN 6. You showed him five on your watch, and you did all the things people do when they talk to each other without a language. He was quite certain you were delivering something in your briefcase.

(*Pause.*)

ANDERSON. Yes. All right. But it was not money.

MAN 6. Of course not. You are not a criminal.

ANDERSON. Quite so. I promised to bring Pavel one or two of the Colloquium papers. He naturally has an interest in philosophy and I assume it is not illegal.

MAN 6. Naturally not. Then you won't mind showing me. (ANDERSON *hesitates then opens the briefcase and takes out* MCKENDRICK'*s paper and his own and passes them over.* MAN 6 *takes them and reads their English titles.*) "Ethical Fictions as Ethical Foundations" . . . "Philosophy and the Catastrophe Theory." (MAN 6 *gives the papers back to* ANDERSON.)

MAN 6. You wish to go to the football match? You will see twenty minutes, perhaps more.

ANDERSON. No. I'm going back to the university, to the Colloquium.

MRS HOLLAR (*in Czech*). Is he leaving?

MAN 6. Mrs Hollar would like you to remain.

ANDERSON (*to* MRS HOLLAR). No, I'm sorry. (*A thought strikes him.*) If you spoke to the taxi driver you would have known perfectly well I was going to the England match.

(MAN 6 *doesn't reply to this either in word or expression.* ANDERSON *closes his briefcase. The doorbell rings and* MAN 3 *goes to open the door. From the bedroom* MAN 5 *enters with a small parcel wrapped in old newspaper.*)

MAN 5 (*in Czech*). I found this, Chief, under the floorboards. (MAN 5 *gives the parcel to* MAN 6 *who unwraps it to reveal a bundle of American dollars.* MRS HOLLAR *watches this with disbelief and there is an outburst.*)

MRS HOLLAR (*in Czech*). He's lying! (*To* ANDERSON.) It's a lie—

(*The door reopens for* MAN 3. SACHA HOLLAR, *aged ten, comes in with him. He is rather a tough little boy. He runs across to his mother, who is crying and shouting, and embraces her. It is rather as though he were a small adult comforting her.*)

ANDERSON. Oh my God . . . Mrs Hollar . . . (ANDERSON, *out of his depth and afraid, decides abruptly to leave and does so.* MAN 3 *isn't sure whether to let him go but* MAN 6 *nods at him and* ANDERSON *leaves.*)

7. INTERIOR: HOTEL CORRIDOR. EVENING

ANDERSON *approaches his room. He is worn out. When he gets to his door and fumbles with his key he realizes that he can hear a voice in the room next door to his. He puts his ear to this other door.*

GRAYSON (*inside*). Yes, a new top for the running piece—O.K.—Prague, Saturday. (GRAYSON *speaks not particularly slowly but with great deliberation enunciating every consonant and splitting syllables up where necessary for clarity. He is, of course, dictating to a fast typist.*) There'll be Czechs bouncing in the streets of Prague tonight as bankruptcy stares English football in the face, stop, new par.

(ANDERSON *knocks on the door.*)

(*Inside.*) It's open! (ANDERSON *opens the door and looks into the room. Interior room. It is of course a room very like* ANDERSON'S *own room, if not identical. Its occupant, the man we had seen leave the room earlier, is* GRAYSON, *a sports reporter from England. He is on the telephone as* ANDERSON *cautiously enters the room.*) Make no mistake, comma, the four-goal credit which these slick Slovaks netted here this afternoon will keep them in the black through the second leg of the World Cup Eliminator at Wembley next month, stop. New par— (*To* ANDERSON.) Yes? (*Into phone.*) You can bank on it.

ANDERSON. I'm next door.

GRAYSON (*into phone*). —bank on it. New par—(*To* ANDERSON.) Look, can you come back? (*Into phone.*) But for some determined saving by third-choice Jim Bart in the injury hyphen jinxed England goal, we would have been overdrawn by four more when the books were closed, stop. Maybe Napoleon was wrong when he said we were a nation of shopkeepers, stop. Today England looked like a nation of goalkeepers, stop. Davey, Petherbridge, and Shell all made saves on the line. New par.

ANDERSON. Do you mind if I listen—I missed the match.

(GRAYSON *waves him to a chair.* ANDERSON *sits on a chair next to a door which is in fact a connecting door into the next room. Not* ANDERSON'S *own room but the room on the other side of* GRAYSON'S *room.*)

GRAYSON (*into phone*). Dickenson and Pratt were mostly left standing by Wolker, with a W, and Deml, D dog, E Edward, M mother, L London—who could go round the halls as a telepathy act, stop. Only Crisp looked as if he had a future outside Madame Tussaud's°—a.u.d.s.—stop. He laid on the two best chances, comma, both wasted by Pratt who skied one and stubbed his toe on the other, stop. Crisp's, apostrophe s. comment from where I was sitting looked salt and vinegar flavored . . .

(ANDERSON *has become aware that another voice is cutting in from the next room. The door between the two rooms is not quite closed. During* GRAYSON'S *last speech* ANDERSON *gently pushes open the door and looks behind him and realizes*

Madame Tussaud's: a famous wax museum in London

that a colleague of GRAYSON's *is also dictating in the next room.* ANDERSON *stands up and looks into the next room and is drawn into it by the rival report. This room belongs to* CHAMBERLAIN. *Interior:* CHAMBERLAIN's *room.* CHAMBERLAIN *on phone.*)

CHAMBERLAIN. Wilson, who would like to be thought the big bad man of the English defence merely looked slow-footed and slow-witted stop. Deml—D.E.M. mother L.—Deml got round him five times on the trot, bracket, literally, close bracket, using the same swerve, comma, making Wilson look elephantine in everything but memory, stop. On the fifth occasion there was nothing to prevent Deml scoring except what Broadbent took it on himself to do, which was to scythe Deml down from behind, stop. Halas scored from the penalty, stop. (ANDERSON *sighs and sits down on the equivalent chair in* CHAMBERLAIN's *room.* CHAMBERLAIN *sees him.*) Can I help you—?

ANDERSON. Sorry—I'm from next door.

CHAMBERLAIN (*into phone*). New paragraph—(*To* ANDERSON.) I won't be long—(*Into phone.*) This goal emboldened the Czechs to move Bartok, like the composer, forward and risk the consequences, stop. Ten minutes later, just before half time, comma, he was the man left over to collect a short corner from Halas and it was his chip which Jirasek rose to meet for a simple goal at the far post—

ANDERSON. I knew it!

(CHAMBERLAIN *turns to look at him.*)

CHAMBERLAIN (*into phone*). New paragraph. As with tragic opera, things got worse after the interval . . .

(ANDERSON *has stood up to leave. He leaves through* GRAYSON's *room.* GRAYSON *is on the phone saying:*)

GRAYSON (*into the phone*). . . . Jirasek, unmarked at the far post, flapped into the air like a great stork, and rising a yard higher than Bart's outstretched hands, he put Czechoslovakia on the road to victory.

(ANDERSON *leaves the room without looking at* GRAYSON *or being noticed.*)

8. INTERIOR: HOTEL DINING ROOM

The cut is to gay Czech music. The dining room has a stage. A small group of Czech musicians and singers in the tourist version of peasant costume is performing. It is evening. At one of the tables STONE, *the American, and a* FRENCHMAN *are sitting next to each other and sharing the table are* ANDERSON, MCKENDRICK, *and* CHETWYN. *The three of them are, for different reasons, subdued.* STONE *is unsubdued. They are reaching the end of the meal.*

STONE. Hell's bells. Don't you understand English? When I say to you, "Tell me what you mean," you can only reply, "I would wish to say so and so." "Never mind what you would wish to say," I reply. "Tell me what you *mean*."

FRENCHMAN. Mais oui, but if you ask me in French, you must say, "Qu'est-ce que vous voulez dire?"—"What is that which you wish to say?" Naturellement, it is in order for me to reply, "Je veux dire etcetera."

STONE (*excitedly*). But you are making *my* point—don't you see?

McKENDRICK. What do you think the chances are of meeting a free and easy woman in a place like this?

STONE. I *can't* ask you in French.

McKENDRICK. I don't mean free, necessarily.

FRENCHMAN. Pourquoi non? Qu'est-ce que vous voulez dire? Voilà!— now I have asked you.

CHETWYN. You don't often see goose on an English menu. (CHETWYN *is the last to finish his main course. They have all eaten the main course. There are drinks and cups of coffee on the table.*)

STONE. The French have no verb meaning "I mean."

CHETWYN. Why's that I wonder.

STONE. They just don't.

CHETWYN. People are always eating goose in Dickens.

McKENDRICK. Do you think it will be safe?

FRENCHMAN. Par exemple. Je vous dis, "Qu'est-ce que vous voulez dire?"

McKENDRICK. I mean one wouldn't want to be photographed through a two-way mirror.

STONE. I don't want to ask you what you would wish to say. I want to ask you what you *mean*. Let's assume there is a difference.

ANDERSON. We do have goose liver. What do they do with the rest of the goose?

STONE. Now assume that you say one but mean the other.

FRENCHMAN. Je dis quelque chose, mais je veux dire—

STONE. Right.

McKENDRICK (*to* STONE). Excuse me, Brad.

STONE. Yes?

McKENDRICK. You eat well but you're a lousy eater.

(*This is a fair comment.* STONE *has spoken with his mouth full of bread, cake, coffee, etc., and he is generally messy about it.* STONE *smiles forgivingly but hardly pauses.*)

STONE. Excuse us.

FRENCHMAN. A bientôt. (STONE *and the* FRENCHMAN *get up to leave.*)

STONE (*leaving*). You see, what you've got is an incorrect statement which when corrected looks like itself.

(*There is a pause.*)

McKENDRICK. Did you have a chance to read my paper?

ANDERSON. I only had time to glance at it. I look forward to reading it carefully.

CHETWYN. I read it.

ANDERSON. Weren't you there for it?

MCKENDRICK. No, he sloped off for the afternoon.

ANDERSON. Well, you sly devil, Chetwyn. I bet you had a depressing afternoon. It makes the heart sick, doesn't it?

CHETWYN. Yes, it does rather. We don't know we've been born.

MCKENDRICK. He wasn't at the football match.

CHETWYN. Oh—is that where you were?

ANDERSON. No, I got distracted.

MCKENDRICK. He's being mysterious. I think it's a woman.

ANDERSON (*to* CHETWYN). What were you doing?

CHETWYN. I was meeting some friends.

MCKENDRICK. He's being mysterious. I don't think it's a woman.

CHETWYN. I have friends here, that's all.

ANDERSON (*to* MCKENDRICK). Was your paper well received?

MCKENDRICK. No. They didn't get it. I could tell from the questions that there'd been some kind of communications failure.

ANDERSON. The translation phones?

MCKENDRICK. No, no—they simply didn't understand the line of argument. Most of them had never heard of catastrophe theory, so they weren't ready for what is admittedly an audacious application of it.

ANDERSON. I must admit I'm not absolutely clear about it.

MCKENDRICK. It's like a reverse gear—no—it's like a breaking point. The mistake that people make is, they think a moral principle is indefinitely extendible, that it holds good for any situation, a straight line cutting across the graph of our actual situation—here you are, you see—(*He uses a knife to score a line in front of him straight across the table cloth, left to right in front of him.*) "Morality" down there; running parallel to "Immorality" up here—(*He scores a parallel-line.*)—and never the twain shall meet. They think that is what a principle means.

ANDERSON. And isn't it?

MCKENDRICK. No. The two lines are on the same plane. (*He holds out his flat hand, palm down, above the scored lines.*) They're the edges of the same plane—it's in three dimensions, you see—and if you twist the plane in a certain way, into what we call the catastrophe curve, you get a model of the sort of behavior we find in the real world. There's a point—the catastrophe point—where your progress along one line of behavior jumps you into the opposite line; the principle reverses itself at the point where a rational man would abandon it.

CHETWYN. Then it's not a principle.

MCKENDRICK. There aren't any principles in your sense. There are only a lot of principled people trying to behave as if there were.

ANDERSON. That's the same thing, surely.

MCKENDRICK. You're a worse case than Chetwyn and his primitive Greeks. At least he has the excuse of *believing* in goodness and beauty. You know they're fictions but you're so hung up on them you want to treat them as if they were God-given absolutes.

ANDERSON. I don't see how else they would have any practical value—

McKENDRICK. So you end up using a moral principle as your excuse for acting against a moral interest. It's a sort of funk—

(ANDERSON, *under pressure, slams his cup back on to its saucer in a very uncharacteristic and surprising way. His anger is all the more alarming for that.*)

ANDERSON. You make your points altogether too easily, McKendrick. What need have you of moral courage when your principles reverse themselves so conveniently?

McKENDRICK. All right! I've gone too far. As usual. Sorry. Let's talk about something else. There's quite an attractive woman hanging about outside, loitering in the vestibule. (*The dining room door offers a view of the lobby.*) Do you think it is a trap? My wife said to me—now, Bill, don't do anything daft, you know what you're like, if a blonde knocked on your door with the top three buttons of her police uniform undone and asked for a cup of sugar you'd convince yourself she was a bus conductress brewing up in the next room.

ANDERSON (*chastened*). I'm sorry . . . you're right up to a point. There would be no moral dilemmas if moral principles worked in straight lines and never crossed each other. One meets test situations which have troubled much cleverer men than us.

CHETWYN. A good rule, I find, is to try them out on men much *less* clever than us. I often ask my son what *he* thinks.

ANDERSON. Your son?

CHETWYN. Yes. He's eight.

McKENDRICK. She's definitely glancing this way—seriously, do you think one could chat her up?

(ANDERSON *turns round to look through the door and we see now that the woman is* MRS HOLLAR.)

ANDERSON. Excuse me. (*He gets up and starts to leave but then comes back immediately and takes his briefcase from under the table and then leaves. We stay with the table.* McKENDRICK *watches* ANDERSON *meet* MRS HOLLAR *and shake her hand and they disappear.*)

McKENDRICK. Bloody hell, it *was* a woman. Crafty old beggar.

9. EXTERIOR: STREET. NIGHT

ANDERSON *and* MRS HOLLAR *walking. A park. A park bench.* SACHA HOLLAR *sitting on the bench.* ANDERSON *and* MRS HOLLAR *arrive.*

MRS HOLLAR (*in Czech*). Here he is. (*To* ANDERSON.) Sacha. (*In Czech.*) Thank him for coming.

SACHA. She is saying thank you that you come.

MRS HOLLAR (*in Czech*). We're sorry to bother him.

SACHA. She is saying sorry for the trouble.

ANDERSON. No, no, I am sorry about . . . everything. Do you learn English at school?

SACHA. Yes. I am learning English two years. With my father also.

ANDERSON. You are very good.

SACHA. Not good. You are a friend of my father. Thank you.

ANDERSON. I'm afraid I've done nothing.

SACHA. You have his writing?

ANDERSON. His thesis? Yes. It's in here. (*He indicates his briefcase.*)

SACHA (*in Czech*). It's all right, he's still got it.

(MRS HOLLAR *nods.*)

MRS HOLLAR (*in Czech*). Tell him I didn't know who he was today.

SACHA. My mother is not knowing who you are, tomorrow at the apartment.

ANDERSON. Today.

SACHA. Today. Pardon. So she is saying, "Come here! Come here! Come inside the apartment!" Because she is not knowing. My father is not telling her. He is telling me only.

ANDERSON. I see. What did he tell you?

SACHA. He will go see his friend the English professor. He is taking the writing.

ANDERSON. I see. Did he return home last night?

SACHA. No. He is arrested outside hotel. Then in the night they come to make search.

ANDERSON. Had they been there all night?

SACHA. At eleven o'clock they are coming. They search twenty hours.

ANDERSON. My God.

SACHA. In morning I go to Bartolomesskaya to be seeing him.

MRS HOLLAR (*explains*). Police.

SACHA. But I am not seeing him. They say go home. I am waiting. Then I am going home. Then I am seeing you.

ANDERSON. What were they looking for?

SACHA (*shrugs*). Western books. Also my father is writing things. Letters, politics, philosophy. They find nothing. Some English books they don't like but really nothing. But the dollars, of course, they pretend to find.

(MRS HOLLAR *hears the word dollars.*)

MRS HOLLAR (*in Czech*). Tell him the dollars were put there by the police.

SACHA. Not my father's dollars. He is having no moneys.

ANDERSON. Yes. I know.

SACHA. They must arrest him for dollars because he does nothing. No bad things. He is signing something. So they are making trouble.

ANDERSON. Yes.

MRS HOLLAR (*in Czech*). Tell him about Jan.

SACHA. You must give back my father's thesis. Not now. The next days. My mother cannot take it.

ANDERSON. He asked me to take it to England.

SACHA. Not possible now. But thank you.

ANDERSON. He asked me to take it.

SACHA. Not possible. Now they search you, I think. At the airport. Because they are seeing you coming to the apartment and you have too much contact. Maybe they are seeing us now. (ANDERSON *looks around him.*) Is possible.

ANDERSON (*uncomfortably*). I ought to tell you . . . (*Quickly.*) I came to the apartment to give the thesis back. I refused him. But he was afraid he might be stopped—I thought he just meant searched, not arrested—

SACHA. Too quick—too quick—

(*Pause.*)

ANDERSON. What do you want me to do?

SACHA. My father's friend—he is coming to Philosophy Congress today.

ANDERSON. Tomorrow.

SACHA. Yes tomorrow. You give him the writing. Is called Jan. Is O.K. Good friend.

(ANDERSON *nods.*)

ANDERSON. Jan.

SACHA (*in Czech*). He'll bring it to the university hall for Jan tomorrow. (SACHA *stands up.*) We go home now.

(MRS HOLLAR *gets up and shakes hands with* ANDERSON.)

ANDERSON. I'm sorry . . . What will happen to him?

MRS HOLLAR (*in Czech*). What was that?

SACHA (*in Czech*). He wants to know what will happen to Daddy.

MRS HOLLAR. Ruzyne.

SACHA. That is the prison. Ruzyne.

(*Pause.*)

ANDERSON. I will, of course, try to help in England. I'll write letters. The Czech Ambassador . . . I have friends, too, in our government— (ANDERSON *realizes that the boy has started to cry. He is specially taken aback because he has been talking to him like an adult.*) Now listen—I am personally friendly with important people—the Minister of Education— people like that.

MRS HOLLAR (*in Czech but to* ANDERSON). Please help Pavel—

ANDERSON. Mrs Hollar—I will do everything I can for him. (*He watches* MRS HOLLAR *and* SACHA *walk away into the dark.*)

10. INTERIOR: ANDERSON'S ROOM. NIGHT

ANDERSON *is lying fully dressed on the bed. His eyes open. Only light from the window. There are faint voices from* GRAYSON'S *room. After a while* ANDERSON *gets up and leaves his room and knocks on* GRAYSON'S *door.*
Exterior GRAYSON'S *room.* GRAYSON *opens his door.*

GRAYSON. Oh hello. Sorry, are we making too much noise?

ANDERSON. No, it's all right, but I heard you were still up and I wondered if I could ask a favor of you. I wonder if I could borrow your typewriter.

GRAYSON. My typewriter?

ANDERSON. Yes.

GRAYSON. Well, I'm leaving in the morning.

ANDERSON. I'll let you have it back first thing. I'm leaving on the afternoon plane myself.

GRAYSON. Oh—all right then.

ANDERSON. That's most kind.

(*During the above the voices from the room have been semi-audible.* MCKENDRICK'S *voice, rather drunk, but articulate, is heard.*)

MCKENDRICK (*his voice only, heard underneath the above dialogue*). Now, listen to me, I'm a professional philosopher. You'll do well to listen to what I have to say.

ANDERSON. That sounds as if you've got McKendrick in there.

GRAYSON. Oh—is he one of yours?

ANDERSON. I wouldn't put it like that.

GRAYSON. He's getting as tight as a tick.

ANDERSON. Yes.

GRAYSON. You couldn't collect him, could you? He's going to get clouted in a minute.

ANDERSON. Go ahead and clout him, if you like.

GRAYSON. It's not me. It's Broadbent and a couple of the lads. Your pal sort of latched on to us in the bar. He really ought to be getting home.

ANDERSON. I'll see what I can do. (ANDERSON *follows* GRAYSON *into the room.*)

MCKENDRICK. How can you expect the kids to be little gentlemen when their heroes behave like yobs—answer me that—no—you haven't answered my question—if you've got yobs on the fields you're going to have yobs on the terraces. °

(*Interior:* GRAYSON'S *room.* MCKENDRICK *is the only person standing up. He is holding court, with a bottle of whiskey in one hand and his glass in the*

on the terraces: in the stands

other. Around this small room are BROADBENT, CRISP, CHAMBERLAIN, *and perhaps one or two members of the England squad. Signs of a bottle party.*)

GRAYSON (*closing his door*). I thought philosophers were quiet, studious sort of people.

ANDERSON. Well, some of us are.

McKENDRICK (*shouts*). Anderson! You're the very man I want to see! We're having a philosophical discussion about the yob ethics of professional footballers—

BROADBENT. You want to watch it, mate.

McKENDRICK. Roy here is sensitive because he gave away a penalty today, by a deliberate foul. To stop a certain goal he hacked a chap down. After all, a penalty might be saved and broken legs are quite rare—(BROADBENT *stands up but* McKENDRICK *pacifies him with a gesture*) it's perfectly all right—you were adopting the utilitarian values of the game, for the good of the team, for England! But I'm not talking about particular acts of expediency. No, I'm talking about the whole *ethos*.

ANDERSON. McKendrick, don't you think it's about time we retired?

McKENDRICK (*ignoring him*). Now, I've played soccer for years. Years and *years*. I played soccer from the age of *eight* until I was *thirteen*. At which point I went to a rugger school. Even so, Tommy here will tell you that I still consider myself something of a left winger. (*This is to* CRISP.) Sorry about that business in the lift, by the way, Tommy. Well, one thing I remember clearly from my years and *years* of soccer is that if two players go for a ball which then goes into touch,° there's never any doubt *among those players* which of them touched the ball last. I can't remember one occasion in all those years and *years* when the player who touched the ball last didn't realize it. So, what I want to know *is*—why is it that on Match of the Day, every time the bloody ball goes into touch, *both* players claim the throw-in for their own side? I merely ask for information. Is it because they are very, very stupid or is it because a dishonest advantage is as welcome as an honest one?

CHAMBERLAIN. Well, look, it's been a long evening, old chap—

ANDERSON. Tomorrow is another day, McKendrick.

McKENDRICK. Tomorrow, in my experience, is usually the same day. Have a drink—

ANDERSON. No thank you.

McKENDRICK. Here's a question for anthropologists. Name me a tribe which organizes itself into teams for sporting encounters and greets every score against their opponents with paroxysms of childish glee, whooping, dancing and embracing in an ecstasy of crowing self-congratulation in the very midst of their disconsolate fellows?—Who are these primitives who pile all their responses into the immediate sensation, unaware or uncaring of the

---

into touch: out of bounds

long undulations of life's fortunes? Yes, you've got it! (*He chants the Match of the Day signature tune.*) It's the yob-of-the-month competition, entries on a postcard please. But the question is—is it because they're working class, or is it because financial greed has corrupted them? Or is it both?

ANDERSON. McKendrick, you are being offensive.

McKENDRICK. Anderson is one of life's cricketers. Clap, clap. (*He claps in a well-bred sort of way and puts on a well-bred voice.*) Well played, sir. Bad luck, old chap. The comparison with cricket may suggest to you that yob ethics are working class. (BROADBENT *comes up to* McKENDRICK *and pushes him against the wall.* McKENDRICK *is completely unconcerned, escapes and continues without pause.*) But you would be quite wrong. Let me refer you to a typical rugby team of Welsh miners. A score is acknowledged with pride but with restraint, the scorer himself composing his features into an expressionless mask lest he might be suspected of exulting in his opponents' misfortune—my God, it does the heart good, doesn't it? I conclude that yob ethics are caused by financial greed.

ANDERSON. Don't be such as ass.

(McKENDRICK *takes this as an intellectual objection.*)

McKENDRICK. You think it's the adulation, perhaps? (*To* CRISP.) Is it the adulation, Tommy, which has corrupted you?

CRISP. What's he flaming on about?

CHAMBERLAIN. Well I think it's time for my shut-eye.

CRISP. No, I want to know what he's saying about me. He's giving me the needle.

ANDERSON (*to* McKENDRICK). May I remind you that you profess to be something of a pragmatist yourself in matters of ethics—

McKENDRICK. Ah yes—I see—you think that because I don't believe in reliable signposts on the yellow brick road to rainbowland,° you think I'm a bit of a yob myself—the swift kick in the kneecap on the way up the academic ladder—the Roy Broadbent of Stoke—(*To* BROADBENT.) Stoke's my team, you know.

BROADBENT. Will you tell this stupid bugger his philosophy is getting up my nostrils.

GRAYSON. You're not making much sense, old boy.

McKENDRICK. Ah! Grayson here has a fine logical mind. He has put his finger on the flaw in my argument, namely that the reason footballers are yobs may be nothing to do with being working class, or with financial greed, or with adulation, or even with being footballers. It may be simply that football attracts a certain kind of person, namely yobs—

yellow brick road to rainbowland: In L. Frank Baum's famous children's book (and the musical made from it) there is a yellow brick road to Oz, a fabulous city.

(*This is as far as he gets when* BROADBENT *smashes him in the face.* McKENDRICK *drops.*)

CRISP. Good on you, Roy.

(ANDERSON *goes to* McKENDRICK *who is flat on the floor.*)

ANDERSON. McKendrick . . .
CHAMBERLAIN. Well, I'm going to bed. (CHAMBERLAIN *goes through the connecting door into his own room and closes the door.*)
BROADBENT. He can't say that sort of thing and get away with it.
GRAYSON. Where's his room?
ANDERSON. On the third floor.
GRAYSON. Bloody hell.
CRISP. He's waking up.
BROADBENT. He's all right.
ANDERSON. Come on, McKendrick. (*They all lift* McKENDRICK *to his feet.* McKENDRICK *makes no protest. He's just about able to walk.*) I'll take him down in the lift. (*He sees the typewriter in its case and says to* GRAYSON.) I'll come back for the typewriter. (*He leads* McKENDRICK *towards the door.*)
McKENDRICK (*mutters*). All right. I went too far. Let's talk about something else. (*But* McKENDRICK *keeps walking or staggering.* ANDERSON *opens* GRAYSON'*s door.*)
BROADBENT. Here. That bloody Jirasek. Just like you said.
ANDERSON. Yes.
BROADBENT. They don't teach you nothing at that place then.
ANDERSON. No. (ANDERSON *helps* McKENDRICK *out and closes the door.*)

11. THE COLLOQUIUM

ANDERSON *comes to the lectern. There is a Czech* CHAIRMAN *behind him.* CHETWYN *is in the audience but* McKENDRICK *is not. We arrive as* ANDERSON *approaches the microphone.* ANDERSON *lays a sheaf of typewritten paper on the lectern.*

ANDERSON. I propose in this paper to take up a problem which many have taken up before me, namely the conflict between the rights of individuals and the rights of the community. I will be making a distinction between rights and rules.
(*We note that the* CHAIRMAN, *listening politely and intently, is suddenly puzzled. He himself has some papers and from these he extracts one, which is in fact the official copy of* ANDERSON'*s official paper. He starts looking at it. It doesn't take him long to satisfy himself that* ANDERSON *is giving a different paper. These things happen while* ANDERSON *speaks. At the same time the three* INTERPRETERS *in their booths, while speaking into their microphones as* ANDERSON *speaks, are*

also in some difficulty because they have copies of ANDERSON's *official paper.*)
I will seek to show that rules, in so far as they are related to rights, are a
secondary and consequential elaboration of primary rights, and I will be
associating rules generally with communities and rights generally with individuals. I will seek to show that a conflict between the two is generally a
pseudo-conflict arising out of one side or the other pressing a pseudo-right.
Although claiming priority for rights over rules—where they are in conflict—I will be defining rights as fictions acting as incentives to the adoption
of practical values; and I will further propose that although these rights are
fictions there is an obligation to treat them as if they were truths; and further,
that although this obligation can be shown to be based on values which are
based on fictions, there is an obligation to treat *that* obligation as though it
were based on truth; and so on *ad infinitum.*

(*At this point the* CHAIRMAN *interrupts him.*)

CHAIRMAN. Pardon me—Professor—this is not your paper—
ANDERSON. In what sense? I am indisputably giving it.
CHAIRMAN. But it is not the paper you were invited to give.
ANDERSON. I wasn't invited to give a particular paper.
CHAIRMAN. You offered one.
ANDERSON. That's true.
CHAIRMAN. But this is not it.
ANDERSON. No. I changed my mind.
CHAIRMAN. But it is irregular.
ANDERSON. I didn't realize it mattered.
CHAIRMAN. It is a discourtesy.
ANDERSON (*taken aback*).   Bad manners? I am sorry.
CHAIRMAN. You cannot give this paper. We do not have copies.
ANDERSON. Do you mean that philosophical papers require some sort of
clearance?
CHAIRMAN. The interpreters cannot work without copies.
ANDERSON. Don't worry. It is not a technical paper. I will speak a little
slower if you like. (ANDERSON *turns back to the microphone.*) If we decline to
define rights as fictions, albeit with the force of truths, there are only two
senses in which humans could be said to have rights. Firstly, humans might
be said to have certain rights if they had collectively and mutually agreed to
give each other these rights. This would merely mean that humanity is a
rather large club with club rules, but it is not what is generally meant by
human rights. It is not what Locke meant, and it is not what the American
Founding Fathers meant when, taking the hint from Locke, they held certain
rights to be unalienable—among them, life, liberty and the pursuit of happiness. The early Americans claimed these as the endowment of God—which is
the *second* sense in which humans might be said to have rights. This is a view
more encouraged in some communities than in others. I do not wish to dwell

on it here except to say that it *is* a view and not a deduction, and that I do not hold it myself.

What strikes us is the consensus about an individual's rights put forward both by those who invoke God's authority and by those who invoke no authority at all other than their own idea of what is fair and sensible. The first Article of the American Constitution, guaranteeing freedom of religious observance, of expression, of the press, and of assembly, is closely echoed by Articles 28 and 32 of the no less admirable Constitution of Czechoslovakia, our generous hosts on this occasion. Likewise, protection from invasion of privacy, from unreasonable search and from interference with letters and correspondence guaranteed to the American people by Article 4 is likewise guaranteed to the Czech people by Article 31.

(*The* CHAIRMAN, *who has been more and more uncomfortable, leaves the stage at this point. He goes into the "wings." At some distance from* ANDERSON, *but still just in earshot of* ANDERSON, *i.e. one can hear* ANDERSON's *words clearly if faintly, is a telephone. Perhaps in a stage manager's office. We go with the* CHAIRMAN *but we can still hear* ANDERSON.)

Is such a consensus remarkable? Not at all. If there is a God, we his creations would doubtless subscribe to his values. And if there is not a God, he, our creation, would undoubtedly be credited with values which we think to be fair and sensible. But what is fairness? What is sense? What are these values which we take to be self-evident? And why are they values?

12. INTERIOR: McKENDRICK'S ROOM

McKENDRICK *is fully dressed and coming round from a severe hangover. His room is untidier than* ANDERSON's. *Clothes are strewn about. His suitcase, half full, is open. His briefcase is also in evidence.* McKENDRICK *looks at his watch, but it has stopped. He goes to the telephone and dials.*

13. INTERIOR: ANDERSON'S ROOM

The phone starts to ring. The camera pulls back from the phone and we see that there are two men in the room, plainclothes POLICEMEN, *searching the room. They look at the phone but only for a moment, and while it rings they continue quietly. They search the room very discreetly. We see one carefully slide open a drawer and we cut away.*

14. THE COLLOQUIUM

We have returned to ANDERSON's *paper. There is no* CHAIRMAN *on stage.*

ANDERSON. Ethics were once regarded as a sort of monument, a ghostly Eiffel Tower constructed of Platonic entities like honesty, loyalty, fairness, and so on, all bolted together and consistent with each other, harmoniously stressed so as to keep the edifice standing up: an ideal against which we measured our behavior. The tower has long been demolished. In our own time linguistic philosophy proposes that the notion of, say, justice has no existence outside the ways in which we choose to employ the word, and indeed *consists* only of the way in which we employ it. In other words, that ethics are not the inspiration of our behavior but merely the creation of our utterances.

(*Over the latter part of this we have gone back to the* CHAIRMAN *who is on the telephone. The* CHAIRMAN *is doing little talking and some listening.*)

And yet common observation shows us that this view demands qualification. A small child who cries "that's not fair" when punished for something done by his brother or sister is apparently appealing to an idea of justice which is, for want of a better word, natural. And we must see that natural justice, however illusory, does inspire many people's behavior much of the time. As an ethical utterance it seems to be an attempt to define a sense of rightness which is not simply derived from some other utterance elsewhere.

(*We cut now to a backstage area, but* ANDERSON's *voice is continuous, heard through the sort of P.A. system which one finds backstage at theaters. The* CHAIRMAN *hurries along the corridor, seeking, and now finding a uniformed "*FIRE-MAN,*" a backstage official. During this* ANDERSON *speaks.*)

Now a philosopher exploring the difficult terrain of right and wrong should not be over-impressed by the argument "a child would know the difference." But when, let us say, we are being persuaded that it is ethical to put someone in prison for reading or writing the wrong books, it is well to be reminded that you can persuade a man to believe almost anything provided he is clever enough, but it is much more difficult to persuade someone less clever. There is a sense of right and wrong which precedes utterance. It is individually experienced and it concerns one person's dealings with another person. From this experience we have built a system of ethics which is the sum of individual acts of recognition of individual right.

(*During this we have returned to* ANDERSON *in person. And at this point the* CHAIRMAN *re-enters the stage and goes and sits in his chair.* ANDERSON *continues, ignoring him.*)

If this is so, the implications are serious for a collective or State ethic which finds itself in conflict with individual rights, and seeks, in the name of the people, to impose its values on the very individuals who comprise the State. The illogic of this maneuver is an embarrassment to totalitarian systems. An attempt is sometimes made to answer it by consigning the whole argument to "bourgeois logic," which is a concept no easier to grasp than bourgeois physics or bourgeois astronomy. No, the fallacy must lie elsewhere—

(*At this point loud bells, electric bells, ring. The fire alarm. The* CHAIRMAN *leaps up and shouts.*)

CHAIRMAN (*in Czech*). Don't panic! There appears to be a fire. Please leave the hall in an orderly manner. (*In English.*) Fire! Please leave quietly!

(*The philosophers get to their feet and start heading for the exit.* ANDERSON *calmly gathers his papers up and leaves the stage.*)

15. INTERIOR: AIRPORT

People leaving the country have to go through a baggage check. There are at least three separate but adjacent benches at which customs men and women search the baggage of travelers. The situation here is as follows: At the first bench CHETWYN *is in mid-search. At the second bench* ANDERSON *is in mid-search. At the third bench a traveler is in mid-search. There is a short queue of people waiting for each bench. The leading man in the queue waiting for the third bench is* MCKENDRICK. *The search at this third bench is cursory. However,* ANDERSON *is being searched very thoroughly. We begin on* ANDERSON. *We have not yet noted* CHETWYN.

At ANDERSON'*s bench a uniformed customs* WOMAN *is examining the contents of his suitcase, helped by a uniformed customs* MAN. *At the same time a plainclothes* POLICEMAN *is very carefully searching everything in* ANDERSON'*s briefcase. We see the customs* MAN *take a cellophane wrapped box of chocolates from* ANDERSON'*s case. He strips off the cellophane and looks at the chocolates and then he digs down to look at the second layer of chocolates.* ANDERSON *watches this with amazement. The chocolate box is closed and put back in the case. Meanwhile a nest of wooden dolls, the kind in which one doll fits inside another, is reduced to its components.*

The camera moves to find MCKENDRICK *arriving at the third desk. There is no plainclothes man there. The customs* OFFICER *there opens his briefcase and flips, in a rather cursory way, through* MCKENDRICK'*s papers. He asks* MCKENDRICK *to open his case. He digs about for a moment in* MCKENDRICK'*s case.*

Back at ANDERSON'*s bench the plainclothes* MAN *is taking* ANDERSON'*s wallet from* ANDERSON'*s hand. He goes through every piece of paper in the wallet.*

We go back to MCKENDRICK'*s bench to find* MCKENDRICK *closing his case and being moved on.* MCKENDRICK *turns round to* ANDERSON *to speak.*

MCKENDRICK. You picked the wrong queue, old man. Russian roulette. And Chetwyn.

(*We now discover* CHETWYN, *who is going through a similar search to* ANDERSON'*s. He has a plainclothes* MAN *too. This* MAN *is looking down the spine of a book from* CHETWYN'*s suitcase. We now return to* ANDERSON'*s bench. We find that the customs* MAN *has discovered a suspicious bulge in the zipped compartment on the underside of the lid of* ANDERSON'*s suitcase.* ANDERSON'*s face tells us that he has a spasm of anxiety. The bulge suggests something about the size of* HOLLAR'*s envelope. The customs* MAN *zips open the compartment and extracts the copy of* MCKENDRICK'*s girly magazine.* ANDERSON *is embarrassed. We return to* CHETWYN, *whose briefcase is being searched paper by paper. The customs* OFFICIAL *searching his suitcase finds a laundered shirt, nicely ironed and folded. He opens the shirt up and discovers about half a dozen sheets of writing-paper, thin paper with typewriting on it. Also a photograph of a man. The plainclothes* MAN *joins the customs* OFFICIAL *and he starts looking at these pieces of paper. He looks up at* CHETWYN, *whose face has gone white.*)

The plane is taxiing.
MCKENDRICK *and* ANDERSON *are sitting together.*
MCKENDRICK *looks shocked.*

MCKENDRICK. Silly bugger. Honestly.
ANDERSON. It's all right—they'll put him on the next plane.
MCKENDRICK. To Siberia.
ANDERSON. No, no, don't be ridiculous. It wouldn't look well for them, would it? All the publicity. I don't think there's anything in Czech law about being in possession of letters to Amnesty International° and the U.N. and that sort of thing. They couldn't treat Chetwyn as though he were a Czech national anyway.
MCKENDRICK. Very unpleasant for him though.
ANDERSON. Yes.
MCKENDRICK. He took a big risk.
ANDERSON. Yes.
MCKENDRICK. I wouldn't do it. Would you?
ANDERSON. No. He should have known he'd be searched.
MCKENDRICK. Why did they search you?
ANDERSON. They thought I might have something.
MCKENDRICK. Did you have anything?
ANDERSON. I did in a way.
MCKENDRICK. What was it?
ANDERSON. A thesis. Apparently rather slanderous from the State's point of view.
MCKENDRICK. Where did you hide it?
ANDERSON. In your briefcase.

(Pause.)

MCKENDRICK. You what?
ANDERSON. Last night. I'm afraid I reversed a principle.

(MCKENDRICK *opens his briefcase and finds* HOLLAR'S *envelope.* ANDERSON *takes it from him.* MCKENDRICK *is furious.*)

MCKENDRICK. You utter bastard.
ANDERSON. I thought you would approve.
MCKENDRICK. Don't get clever with me. (*He relapses, shaking.*) Jesus. It's not quite playing the game is it?
ANDERSON. No, I suppose not. But they were very unlikely to search *you.*
MCKENDRICK. That's not the bloody point.

Amnesty International: a London-based organization which keeps track of political prisoners and works for their release

ANDERSON. I thought it was. But you could be right. Ethics is a very complicated business. That's why they have these congresses.

(*The plane picks up speed on the runway towards take-off.*)

QUESTIONS

1. Professor Stone's paper (Scene 5) deals with the "confusion which often arises from the ambiguity of ordinary language." Much of the comedy of this play arises from the constant flow of such confusions. Cite examples. When Professor Anderson rises to leave after Stone's paper, he remarks that language is only one form of human communication. How has he just illustrated that nonverbal acts can also be a source of confusion?
2. Professor Anderson is the protagonist—one might even say the hero—of the play. How and where is his intellectual brilliance demonstrated? What is his principal motivation at the beginning of the play? How, where, and why does it change? How do Professors Chetwyn and McKendrick, in opposite ways, provide foils for his character?
3. Though perhaps the hero of the play, Anderson is a comic hero. Why? How are his human limitations displayed, especially in Scene 1?
4. To what extent is Anderson's paper at the colloquium (Scenes 11, 14) different from that which he had originally planned? What ideas have been contributed to it by Pavel Hollar in Scene 3? by Chetwyn in Scene 8? by his own sudden thought on leaving the meeting in Scene 5?
5. Explain the connection between (a) McKendrick's "catastrophe theory" (pages 1271–72), Broadbent's "professional foul" (pages 1266, 1269, 1276), and Anderson's hiding Hollar's thesis in McKendrick's briefcase. Might McKendrick's theory be described as a version of the idea that "The end justifies the means"? Compare Anderson's "foul" with Broadbent's as regards the nature of the end, the nature of the means, and the probability that the means will achieve the end desired. How does each stand up under McKendrick's observation, leveled against the English team in Scene 10 and against Anderson in Scene 16, that "it's not quite playing the game"?
6. Why is McKendrick so upset by Anderson's "professional foul" when it exemplifies his own theory? Give a full account of McKendrick's character, beliefs, and motivations. How do they compare with Anderson's?
7. How does Professor Stone compare with the other professors in the play?
8. The play has a surprise ending. Is it adequately prepared for by preceding action and dialogue? Does it contribute to or distract from the theme of the play? Does it justify itself?
9. Is this play closer to satiric ("scornful") comedy, or to romantic ("smiling") comedy?
10. How much of the discussion in "The Nature of Drama" (pages 837–40) must be qualified in discussing a play for television? What advantages has television as a medium? What disadvantages? How would this play have to be changed if presented in a theater? Choose one of the first seven scenes of the play and either (a) rewrite it for stage performance, or (b) describe exactly what in it would need to be changed and why.

Plays for
Further Reading

Anton Chekhov

THE CHERRY ORCHARD

A Comedy in Four Acts

CHARACTERS

RANEVSKAYA, LYUBOV [LYUBA] ANDREYEVNA, *a widowed landowner returning home from Paris to her Russian estate*
ANYA, *her daughter, age 17*
VARYA [VARVARA MIKHAILOVNA], *her adopted daughter, age 24*
GAYEV, LEONID [LYONYA] ANDREYEVICH [ANDREICH], *Madame Ranevskaya's brother, age 51*
LOPAKHIN, YERMOLAI ALEKSEYEVICH [ALEKSEYICH, ALEKSEICH], *a businessman*
TROFIMOV, PYOTR [PETYA] SERGEYEVICH [SERGEICH], *a student in his late twenties, tutor of Madame Ranevskaya's late son Grisha*
SEMYONOV-PISHCHIK, BORIS BORISOVICH, *a landowner*
CHARLOTTA IVANOVNA, *Anya's governess*
YEPIKHODOV, SEMYON PANTELEYEVICH [PANTELEICH], *a clerk on the estate*
DUNYASHA [AVDOTYA FEDOROVNA or FYODOROVNA] *a maidservant*
FIRS [NIKOLAYEVICH], *an old manservant, age 87*
YASHA, *a young footman*
A STRANGER; THE STATIONMASTER; A POST-OFFICE CLERK; GUESTS; SERVANTS

(Characters are listed here with nicknames and short forms of names that occur in the text. For an explanation of Russian names, see p. 471.)

The action takes place on Madame Ranevskaya's estate.

ACT I

A room that is still called the nursery. One of the doors leads into ANYA's room. Dawn; the sun will soon rise. It is May, the cherry trees are in bloom, but

THE CHERRY ORCHARD First performed in Moscow in 1904. Translated by Ann Dunnigan. At the turn of the century Russia was in transition from a semi-feudal monarchy to a modern state, and the aristocratic landowners were losing out economically to a rising business class. Various attempts at political and social reform during the preceding half-century included the freeing of the serfs in 1861, the establishment of local self-government councils in the sixties and seventies, the abolition of the poll tax in 1887, and throughout the period increasing educational opportunities at all levels—yet, in the census of 1897 for example, 74 percent of the citizens were still illiterate. Like the character Lopakhin, Anton Chekhov (1860-1904)—also author of the story "In Exile" (page 464)—was the grandson of a serf and the son of a small shopkeeper, but had made enough money from his writing to buy a small country estate near Moscow in 1892.

it is cold in the orchard; there is a morning frost. The windows in the room are closed. Enter DUNYASHA *with a candle, and* LOPAKHIN *with a book in his hand.*

LOPAKHIN. The train is in, thank God. What time is it?

DUNYASHA. Nearly two. (*Blows out the candle.*) It's already light.

LOPAKHIN. How late is the train, anyway? A couple of hours at least. (*Yawns and stretches.*) I'm a fine one! What a fool I've made of myself! Came here on purpose to meet them at the station, and then overslept. . . . Fell asleep in the chair. It's annoying. . . . You might have waked me.

DUNYASHA. I thought you had gone. (*Listens.*) They're coming now, I think!

LOPAKHIN (*listens*). No . . . they've got to get the luggage and one thing and another. (*Pause*) Lyubov Andreyevna has lived abroad for five years, I don't know what she's like now. . . . She's a fine person. Sweet-tempered, simple. I remember when I was a boy of fifteen, my late father—he had a shop in the village then—gave me a punch in the face and made my nose bleed. . . . We had come into the yard here for some reason or other, and he'd had a drop too much. Lyubov Andreyevna—I remember as if it were yesterday—still young, and so slender, led me to the washstand in this very room, the nursery. "Don't cry, little peasant," she said, "it will heal in time for your wedding. . . ." (*Pause*) Little peasant . . . my father was a peasant, it's true, and here I am in a white waistcoat and tan shoes. Like a pig in a pastry shop. . . . I may be rich, I've made a lot of money, but if you think about it, analyze it, I'm a peasant through and through. (*Turning pages of the book*) Here I've been reading this book, and I didn't understand a thing. Fell asleep over it. (*Pause*)

DUNYASHA. The dogs didn't sleep all night: they can tell that their masters are coming.

LOPAKHIN. What's the matter with you, Dunyasha, you're so . . .

DUNYASHA. My hands are trembling. I'm going to faint.

LOPAKHIN. You're much too delicate, Dunyasha. You dress like a lady, and do your hair like one, too. It's not right. You should know your place.

(*Enter* YEPIKHODOV *with a bouquet; he wears a jacket and highly polished boots that squeak loudly. He drops the flowers as he comes in.*)

YEPIKHODOV (*picking up the flowers*). Here, the gardener sent these. He says you're to put them in the dining room. (*Hands the bouquet to* DUNYASHA.)

LOPAKHIN. And bring me some kvas.°

DUNYASHA. Yes, sir. (*Goes out.*)

YEPIKHODOV. There's a frost this morning—three degrees—and the cherry trees are in bloom. I cannot approve of our climate. (*Sighs.*) I cannot. Our climate is not exactly conducive. And now, Yermolai Alekseyevich, permit me to append: the day before yesterday I bought myself a pair of boots,

kvas: homemade beer

which, I venture to assure you, squeak so that it's quite infeasible. What should I grease them with?

LOPAKHIN. Leave me alone. You make me tired.

YEPIKHODOV. Every day some misfortune happens to me. But I don't complain, I'm used to it, I even smile.

(DUNYASHA *enters, serves* LOPAKHIN *the kvas.*)

YEPIKHODOV. I'm going. (*Stumbles over a chair and upsets it.*) There! (*As if in triumph.*) Now you see, excuse the expression . . . the sort of circumstance, incidentally. . . . It's really quite remarkable! (*Goes out.*)

DUNYASHA. You know, Yermolai Alekseyich, I have to confess that Yepikhodov has proposed to me.

LOPAKHIN. Ah!

DUNYASHA. And I simply don't know. . . . He's a quiet man, but sometimes, when he starts talking, you can't understand a thing he says. It's nice, and full of feeling, only it doesn't make sense. I sort of like him. He's madly in love with me. But he's an unlucky fellow: every day something happens to him. They tease him about it around here; they call him Two-and-twenty Troubles.

LOPAKHIN (*listening*). I think I hear them coming . . .

DUNYASHA. They're coming! What's the matter with me? I'm cold all over.

LOPAKHIN. They're really coming. Let's go and meet them. Will she recognize me? It's five years since we've seen each other.

DUNYASHA (*agitated*). I'll faint this very minute . . . oh, I'm going to faint!

(*Two carriages are heard driving up to the house.* LOPAKHIN *and* DUNYASHA *go out quickly. The stage is empty. There is a hubbub in the adjoining rooms.* FIRS *hurriedly crosses the stage leaning on a stick. He has been to meet* LYUBOV ANDREYEVNA *and wears old-fashioned livery and a high hat. He mutters something to himself, not a word of which can be understood. The noise offstage grows louder and louder. A voice:* "Let's go through here. . . ." *Enter* LYUBOV ANDREYEVNA, ANYA, CHARLOTTA IVANOVNA *with a little dog on a chain, all in traveling dress;* VARYA *wearing a coat and kerchief;* GAYEV, SEMYONOV-PISHCHIK, LOPAKHIN, DUNYASHA *with a bundle and parasol; servants with luggage—all walk through the room.*)

ANYA. Let's go this way. Do you remember, Mama, what room this is?

LYUBOV ANDREYEVNA (*joyfully, through tears*). The nursery!

VARYA. How cold it is! My hands are numb. (*To* LYUBOV ANDREYEVNA) Your rooms, both the white one and the violet one, are just as you left them, Mama.

LYUBOV ANDREYEVNA. The nursery . . . my dear, lovely nursery. . . . I used to sleep here when I was little. . . . (*Weeps.*) And now, like a child, I . . .

(*Kisses her brother,* VARYA, *then her brother again.*) Varya hasn't changed; she still looks like a nun. And I recognized Dunyasha. . . . (*Kisses* DUNYASHA.)

GAYEV. The train was two hours late. How's that? What kind of management is that?

CHARLOTTA (*to* PISHCHIK). My dog even eats nuts.

PISHCHIK (*amazed*). Think of that now!

(*They all go out except* ANYA *and* DUNYASHA.)

DUNYASHA. We've been waiting and waiting for you. . . . (*Takes off* ANYA'*s coat and hat.*)

ANYA. I didn't sleep for four nights on the road . . . now I feel cold.

DUNYASHA. It was Lent when you went away, there was snow and frost then, but now? My darling! (*Laughs and kisses her.*) I've waited so long for you, my joy, my precious . . . I must tell you at once, I can't wait another minute. . . .

ANYA (*listlessly*). What now?

DUNYASHA. The clerk, Yepikhodov, proposed to me just after Easter.

ANYA. You always talk about the same thing. . . . (*Straightening her hair*) I've lost all my hairpins. . . . (*She is so exhausted she can hardly stand.*)

DUNYASHA. I really don't know what to think. He loves me—he loves me so!

ANYA (*looking through the door into her room, tenderly*). My room, my windows . . . it's just as though I'd never been away. I am home! Tomorrow morning I'll get up and run into the orchard. . . . Oh, if I could only sleep! I didn't sleep during the entire journey, I was so tormented by anxiety.

DUNYASHA. Pyotr Sergeich arrived the day before yesterday.

ANYA (*joyfully*). Petya!

DUNYASHA. He's asleep in the bathhouse, he's staying there. "I'm afraid of being in the way," he said. (*Looks at her pocket watch.*) I ought to wake him up, but Varvara Mikhailovna told me not to. "Don't you wake him," she said.

(*Enter* VARYA *with a bunch of keys. As household manager, she carries keys to all the cupboards and storage rooms.*)

VARYA. Dunyasha, coffee, quickly . . . Mama's asking for coffee.

DUNYASHA. This very minute. (*Goes out.*)

VARYA. Thank God, you've come! You're home again. (*Caressing her*) My little darling has come back! My pretty one is here!

ANYA. I've been through so much.

VARYA. I can imagine.

ANYA. I left in Holy Week, it was cold then. Charlotta never stopped talking and doing her conjuring tricks the entire journey. Why did you saddle me with Charlotta?

VARYA. You couldn't have traveled alone, darling. At seventeen!

ANYA. When we arrived in Paris, it was cold, snowing. My French is awful. . . . Mama was living on the fifth floor, and when I got there, she had all sorts of Frenchmen and ladies with her, and an old priest with a little book, and it was full of smoke, dismal. Suddenly I felt sorry for Mama, so sorry. I took her head in my arms and held her close and couldn't let her go. Afterward she kept hugging me and crying. . . .

VARYA (*through her tears*). Don't talk about it, don't talk about it. . . .

ANYA. She had already sold her villa near Mentone,° and she had nothing left, nothing. And I hadn't so much as a kopeck left, we barely managed to get there. But Mama doesn't understand! When we had dinner in a station restaurant, she always ordered the most expensive dishes and tipped each of the waiters a ruble. Charlotta is the same. And Yasha also ordered a dinner, it was simply awful. You know, Yasha is Mama's footman; we brought him with us.

VARYA. I saw the rogue.

ANYA. Well, how are things? Have you paid the interest?

VARYA. How could we?

ANYA. Oh, my God, my God!

VARYA. In August the estate will be put up for sale.

ANYA. My God!

(LOPAKHIN *peeps in at the door and moo's like a cow.*)

LOPAKHIN. Moo-o-o! (*Disappears.*)

VARYA (*through her tears*). What I couldn't do to him! (*Shakes her fist.*)

ANYA (*embracing* VARYA, *softly*). Varya, has he proposed to you? (VARYA *shakes her head.*) But he loves you. . . . Why don't you come to an understanding, what are you waiting for?

VARYA. I don't think anything will ever come of it. He's too busy, he has no time for me . . . he doesn't even notice me. I've washed my hands of him, it makes me miserable to see him. . . . Everyone talks of our wedding, they all congratulate me, and actually there's nothing to it—it's all like a dream. . . . (*In a different tone*) You have a brooch like a bee.

ANYA (*sadly*). Mama bought it. (*Goes into her own room; speaks gaily, like a child.*) In Paris I went up in a balloon!

VARYA. My darling is home! My pretty one has come back!

(DUNYASHA *has come in with the coffeepot and prepares coffee.*)

VARYA (*stands at the door of* ANYA*'s room*). You know, darling, all day long I'm busy looking after the house, but I keep dreaming. If we could marry you to a rich man I'd be at peace. I could go into a hermitage, then to Kiev, to Moscow, and from one holy place to another. . . . I'd go on and on. What a blessing!

ANYA. The birds are singing in the orchard. What time is it?

Mentone: town on the Mediterranean coast of France

VARYA. It must be after two. Time you were asleep, darling. (*Goes into* ANYA *'s room.*) What a blessing!

(YASHA *enters with a lap robe and a traveling bag.*)

YASHA (*crosses the stage mincingly*). May one go through here?

DUNYASHA. A person would hardly recognize you, Yasha. Your stay abroad has done wonders for you.

YASHA. Hm. . . . And who are you?

DUNYASHA. When you left here I was only that high—(*indicating with her hand*). I'm Dunyasha, Fyodor Kozoyedov's daughter. You don't remember!

YASHA. Hm. . . . A little cucumber! (*Looks around, then embraces her; she cries out and drops a saucer. He quickly goes out.*)

VARYA (*in a tone of annoyance, from the doorway*). What's going on here?

DUNYASHA (*tearfully*). I broke a saucer.

VARYA. That's good luck.

ANYA. We ought to prepare Mama: Petya is here. . . .

VARYA. I gave orders not to wake him.

ANYA (*pensively*). Six years ago Father died, and a month later brother Grisha drowned in the river . . . a pretty little seven-year-old boy. Mama couldn't bear it and went away . . . went without looking back. . . . (*Shudders.*) How I understand her, if she only knew! (*Pause*) And Petya Trofimov was Grisha's tutor, he may remind her. . . .

(*Enter* FIRS *wearing a jacket and a white waistcoat.*)

FIRS (*goes to the coffeepot, anxiously*). The mistress will have her coffee here. (*Puts on white gloves.*) Is the coffee ready? (*To* DUNYASHA, *sternly*) You! Where's the cream?

DUNYASHA. Oh, my goodness! (*Quickly goes out.*)

FIRS (*fussing over the coffeepot*). Ah, what an addlepate! (*Mutters to himself.*) They've come back from Paris. . . . The master used to go to Paris . . . by carriage. . . . (*Laughs.*)

VARYA. What is it, Firs?

FIRS. If you please? (*Joyfully*) My mistress has come home! At last! Now I can die. . . . (*Weeps with joy.*)

(*Enter* LYUBOV ANDREYEVNA, GAYEV, *and* SEMYONOV-PISHCHIK, *the last wearing a sleeveless peasant coat of fine cloth and full trousers.* GAYEV, *as he comes in, goes through the motions of playing billiards.*)

LYUBOV ANDREYEVNA. How does it go? Let's see if I can remember . . . cue ball into the corner! Double the rail to center table.

GAYEV. Cut shot into the corner! There was a time, sister, when you and I used to sleep here in this very room, and now I'm fifty-one, strange as it may seem. . . .

LOPAKHIN. Yes, time passes.

GAYEV. How's that?

LOPAKHIN. Time, I say, passes.

GAYEV. It smells of patchouli° here.

ANYA. I'm going to bed. Good night, Mama. (*Kisses her mother.*)

LYUBOV ANDREYEVNA. My precious child. (*Kisses her hands.*) Are you glad to be home? I still feel dazed.

ANYA. Good night, Uncle.

GAYEV (*kisses her face and hands*). God bless you. How like your mother you are! (*To his sister*) At her age you were exactly like her, Lyuba.

(ANYA *shakes hands with* LOPAKHIN *and* PISHCHIK *and goes out, closing the door after her.*)

LYUBOV ANDREYEVNA. She's exhausted.

PISHCHIK. Must have been a long journey.

VARYA. Well, gentlemen? It's after two, high time you were going.

LYUBOV ANDREYEVNA (*laughs*). You haven't changed, Varya. (*Draws* VARYA *to her and kisses her.*) I'll just drink my coffee and then we'll all go. (*FIRS places a cushion under her feet.*) Thank you, my dear. I've got used to coffee. I drink it day and night. Thanks, dear old man. (*Kisses him.*)

VARYA. I'd better see if all the luggage has been brought in.

LYUBOV ANDREYEVNA. Is this really me sitting here? (*Laughs.*) I feel like jumping about and waving my arms. (*Buries her face in her hands.*) What if it's only a dream! God knows I love my country, love it dearly. I couldn't look out the train window, I was crying so! (*Through tears*) But I must drink my coffee. Thank you, Firs, thank you, my dear old friend. I'm so glad you're still alive.

FIRS. The day before yesterday.

GAYEV. He's hard of hearing.

LOPAKHIN. I must go now, I'm leaving for Kharkov about five o'clock. It's so annoying! I wanted to have a good look at you, and have a talk. You're as splendid as ever.

PISHCHIK (*breathing heavily*). Even more beautiful. . . . Dressed like a Parisienne. . . . There goes my wagon, all four wheels!°

LOPAKHIN. Your brother here, Leonid Andreich, says I'm a boor, a moneygrubber, but I don't mind. Let him talk. All I want is that you should trust me as you used to, and that your wonderful, touching eyes should look at me as they did then. Merciful God! My father was one of your father's serfs, and your grandfather's, but you yourself did so much for me once, that I've forgotten all that and love you as if you were my own kin—more than my kin.

LYUBOV ANDREYEVNA. I can't sit still, I simply cannot. (*Jumps up and*

patchouli: a perfume
There goes . . . wheels!: proverbial saying, meaning "I can't help falling for her!"

walks about the room in great excitement.) I cannot bear this joy. . . . Laugh at me, I'm silly. . . . My dear little bookcase . . . (*Kisses bookcase.*) my little table . . .

GAYEV.   Nurse died while you were away.

LYUBOV ANDREYEVNA (*sits down and drinks coffee*).   Yes, God rest her soul. They wrote me.

GAYEV.   And Anastasy is dead. Petrushka Kosoi left me and is now with the police inspector in town. (*Takes a box of hard candies from his pocket and begins to suck one.*)

PISHCHIK.   My daughter, Dashenka . . . sends her regards . . .

LOPAKHIN.   I wish I could tell you something very pleasant and cheering. (*Glances at his watch.*) I must go directly, there's no time to talk, but . . . well, I'll say it in a couple of words. As you know, the cherry orchard is to be sold to pay your debts. The auction is set for August twenty-second, but you need not worry, my dear, you can sleep in peace, there is a way out. This is my plan. Now, please listen! Your estate is only twenty versts° from town, the railway runs close by, and if the cherry orchard and the land along the river were cut up into lots and leased for summer cottages, you'd have, at the very least, an income of twenty-five thousand a year.

GAYEV.   Excuse me, what nonsense!

LYUBOV ANDREYEVNA.   I don't quite understand you, Yermolai Alekseich.

LOPAKHIN.   You will get, at the very least, twenty-five rubles a year for a two-and-a-half-acre lot, and if you advertise now, I guarantee you won't have a single plot of ground left by autumn, everything will be snapped up. In short, I congratulate you, you are saved. The site is splendid, the river is deep. Only, of course, the ground must be cleared . . . you must tear down all the old outbuildings, for instance, and this house, which is worthless, cut down the old cherry orchard——

LYUBOV ANDREYEVNA.   Cut it down? Forgive me, my dear, but you don't know what you are talking about. If there is one thing in the whole province that is interesting, not to say remarkable, it's our cherry orchard.

LOPAKHIN.   The only remarkable thing about this orchard is that it is very big. There's a crop of cherries every other year, and then you can't get rid of them, nobody buys them.

GAYEV.   This orchard is even mentioned in the *Encyclopedia.*

LOPAKHIN (*glancing at his watch*).   If we don't think of something and come to a decision, on the twenty-second of August the cherry orchard, and the entire estate, will be sold at auction. Make up your minds! There is no other way out, I swear to you. None whatsoever.

FIRS.   In the old days, forty or fifty years ago, the cherries were dried, soaked, marinated, and made into jam, and they used to——

GAYEV.   Be quiet, Firs.

FIRS.   And they used to send cartloads of dried cherries to Moscow and

twenty versts: about thirteen miles

Kharkov. And that brought in money! The dried cherries were soft and juicy in those days, sweet, fragrant. . . . They had a method then . . .

LYUBOV ANDREYEVNA. And what has become of that method now?

FIRS. Forgotten. Nobody remembers. . . .

PISHCHIK. How was it in Paris? What's it like there? Did you eat frogs?

LYUBOV ANDREYEVNA. I ate crocodiles.

PISHCHIK. Think of that now!

LOPAKHIN. There used to be only the gentry and the peasants living in the country, but now these summer people have appeared. All the towns, even the smallest ones, are surrounded by summer cottages. And it is safe to say that in another twenty years these people will multiply enormously. Now the summer resident only drinks tea on his porch, but it may well be that he'll take to cultivating his acre, and then your cherry orchard will be a happy, rich, luxuriant——

GAYEV (*indignantly*). What nonsense!

(*Enter* VARYA *and* YASHA.)

VARYA. There are two telegrams for you, Mama. (*Picks out a key and with a jingling sound opens an old-fashioned bookcase.*) Here they are.

LYUBOV ANDREYEVNA. From Paris. (*Tears up the telegrams without reading them.*) That's all over. . . .

GAYEV. Do you know, Lyuba, how old this bookcase is? A week ago I pulled out the bottom drawer, and what do I see? Some figures burnt into it. The bookcase was made exactly a hundred years ago. What do you think of that? Eh? We could have celebrated its jubilee. It's an inanimate object, but nevertheless, for all that, it's a bookcase.

PISHCHIK. A hundred years . . . think of that now!

GAYEV. Yes . . . that is something. . . . (*Feeling the bookcase*) Dear, honored bookcase, I salute thy existence, which for over one hundred years has served the glorious ideals of goodness and justice; thy silent appeal to fruitful endeavor, unflagging in the course of a hundred years, tearfully sustaining through generations of our family, courage and faith in a better future, and fostering in us ideals of goodness and social consciousness. . . .

(*A pause*)

LOPAKHIN. Yes . . .

LYUBOV ANDREYEVNA. You are the same as ever, Lyonya.

GAYEV (*somewhat embarrassed*). Carom into the corner, cut shot to center table.

LOPAKHIN (*looks at his watch*). Well, time for me to go.

YASHA (*hands medicine to* LYUBOV ANDREYEVNA). Perhaps you will take your pills now.

PISHCHIK. Don't take medicaments, dearest lady, they do neither harm nor good. Let me have them, honored lady. (*Takes the pill box, shakes the pills into his hand, blows on them, puts them into his mouth, and washes them down with kvas.*) There!

Lyubov Andreyevna (*alarmed*). Why you must be mad!

Pishchik. I've taken all the pills.

Lopakhin. What a glutton!

(*Everyone laughs.*)

Firs. The gentleman stayed with us during Holy Week . . . ate half a bucket of pickles. . . . (*Mumbles.*)

Lyubov Andreyevna. What is he saying?

Varya. He's been muttering like that for three years now. We've grown used to it.

Yasha. He's in his dotage.

(Charlotta Ivanovna, *very thin, tightly laced, in a white dress with a lorgnette at her belt, crosses the stage.*)

Lopakhin. Forgive me, Charlotta Ivanovna, I haven't had a chance to say how do you do to you. (*Tries to kiss her hand.*)

Charlotta (*pulls her hand away*). If I permit you to kiss my hand you'll be wanting to kiss my elbow next, then my shoulder.

Lopakhin. I have no luck today. (*Everyone laughs.*) Charlotta Ivanovna, show us a trick!

Lyubov Andreyevna. Charlotta, show us a trick!

Charlotta. No. I want to sleep. (*Goes out.*)

Lopakhin. In three weeks we'll meet again. (*Kisses* Lyubov Andreyevna*'s hand.*) Good-bye till then. Time to go. (*To* Gayev) Goodbye. (*Kisses* Pishchik.) Good-bye. (*Shakes hands with* Varya, *then with* Firs *and* Yasha.) I don't feel like going. (*To* Lyubov Andreyevna) If you make up your mind about the summer cottages and come to a decision, let me know; I'll get you a loan of fifty thousand or so. Think it over seriously.

Varya (*angrily*). Oh, why don't you go!

Lopakhin. I'm going. I'm going. (*Goes out.*)

Gayev. Boor. Oh, pardon. Varya's going to marry him, he's Varya's young man.

Varya. Uncle dear, you talk too much.

Lyubov Andreyevna. Well, Varya, I shall be very glad. He's a good man.

Pishchik. A man, I must truly say . . . most worthy. . . . And my Dashenka . . . says, too, that . . . says all sorts of things. (*Snores but wakes up at once.*) In any case, honored lady, oblige me . . . a loan of two hundred and forty rubles . . . tomorrow the interest on my mortgage is due. . . .

Varya (*in alarm*). We have nothing, nothing at all!

Lyubov Andreyevna. I really haven't any money.

Pishchik. It'll turn up. (*Laughs.*) I never lose hope. Just when I thought everything was lost, that I was done for, lo and behold—the railway line ran through my land . . . and they paid me for it. And before you know it, something else will turn up, if not today—tomorrow. . . . Dashenka will win two hundred thousand . . . she's got a lottery ticket.

Lyubov Andreyevna. The coffee is finished, we can go to bed.

FIRS (*brushing* GAYEV *'s clothes, admonishingly*). You've put on the wrong trousers again. What am I to do with you?

VARYA (*softly*). Anya's asleep. (*Quietly opens the window.*) The sun has risen, it's no longer cold. Look, Mama dear, what wonderful trees! Oh, Lord, the air! The starlings are singing!

GAYEV (*opens another window*). The orchard is all white. You haven't forgotten, Lyuba? That long avenue there that runs straight—straight as a stretched-out strap; it gleams on moonlight nights. Remember? You've not forgotten?

LYUBOV ANDREYEVNA (*looking out the window at the orchard*). Oh, my childhood, my innocence! I used to sleep in this nursery, I looked out from here into the orchard, happiness awoke with me each morning, it was just as it is now, nothing has changed. (*Laughing with joy*) All, all white! Oh, my orchard! After the dark, rainy autumn and the cold winter, you are young again, full of happiness, the heavenly angels have not forsaken you. . . . If I could cast off this heavy stone weighing on my breast and shoulders, if I could forget my past!

GAYEV. Yes, and the orchard will be sold for our debts, strange as it may seem. . . .

LYUBOV ANDREYEVNA. Look, our dead mother walks in the orchard . . . in a white dress! (*Laughs with joy.*) It is she!

GAYEV. Where?

VARYA. God be with you, Mama dear.

LYUBOV ANDREYEVNA. There's no one there, I just imagined it. To the right, as you turn to the summerhouse, a slender white sapling is bent over . . . it looks like a woman.

(*Enter* TROFIMOV *wearing a shabby student's uniform and spectacles.*)

LYUBOV ANDREYEVNA. What a wonderful orchard! The white masses of blossoms, the blue sky——

TROFIMOV. Lyubov Andreyevna! (*She looks around at him.*) I only want to pay my respects, then I'll go at once. (*Kisses her hand ardently.*) I was told to wait until morning, but I hadn't the patience.

(LYUBOV ANDREYEVNA *looks at him, puzzled.*)

VARYA (*through tears*). This is Petya Trofimov.

TROFIMOV. Petya Trofimov, I was Grisha's tutor. . . . Can I have changed so much?

(LYUBOV ANDREYEVNA *embraces him, quietly weeping.*)

GAYEV (*embarrassed*). There, there, Lyuba.

VARYA (*crying*). Didn't I tell you, Petya, to wait till tomorrow?

LYUBOV ANDREYEVNA. My Grisha . . . my little boy . . . Grisha . . . my son. . . .

VARYA. What can we do, Mama dear? It's God's will.

TROFIMOV (*gently, through tears*). Don't, don't. . . .

LYUBOV ANDREYEVNA (*quietly weeping*). My little boy dead, drowned. . . . Why? Why, my friend? (*In a lower voice*) Anya is sleeping in there, and I'm talking loudly . . . making all this noise. . . . But Petya, why do you look so bad? Why have you grown so old?

TROFIMOV. A peasant woman in the train called me a mangy gentleman.

LYUBOV ANDREYEVNA. You were just a boy then, a charming little student, and now your hair is thin—and spectacles! Is it possible you are still a student? (*Goes toward the door.*)

TROFIMOV. I shall probably be an eternal student.

LYUBOV ANDREYEVNA (*kisses her brother, then* VARYA). Now, go to bed. . . . You've grown older too, Leonid.

PISHCHIK (*follows her*). Well, seems to be time to sleep. . . . Oh, my gout! I'm staying the night. Lyubov Andreyevna, my soul, tomorrow morning . . . two hundred and forty rubles. . . .

GAYEV. He keeps at it.

PISHCHIK. Two hundred and forty rubles . . . to pay the interest on my mortgage.

LYUBOV ANDREYEVNA. I have no money, my friend.

PISHCHIK. My dear, I'll pay it back. . . . It's a trifling sum.

LYUBOV ANDREYEVNA. Well, all right, Leonid will give it to you. . . . Give it to him, Leonid.

GAYEV. Me give it to him! . . . Hold out your pocket!

LYUBOV ANDREYEVNA. It can't be helped, give it to him. . . . He needs it. . . . He'll pay it back.

(LYUBOV ANDREYEVNA, TROFIMOV, PISHCHIK, *and* FIRS *go out.* GAYEV, VARYA, *and* YASHA *remain.*)

GAYEV. My sister hasn't yet lost her habit of squandering money. (*To* YASHA) Go away, my good fellow, you smell of the henhouse.

YASHA (*with a smirk*). And you, Leonid Andreyevich, are just the same as ever.

GAYEV. How's that? (*To* VARYA) What did he say?

VARYA. Your mother has come from the village; she's been sitting in the servants' room since yesterday, waiting to see you. . . .

YASHA. Let her wait, for God's sake!

VARYA. Aren't you ashamed?

YASHA. A lot I need her! She could have come tomorrow. (*Goes out.*)

VARYA. Mama's the same as ever, she hasn't changed a bit. She'd give away everything, if she could.

GAYEV. Yes. . . . (*A pause*) If a great many remedies are suggested for a disease, it means that the disease is incurable. I keep thinking, racking my brains, I have many remedies, a great many, and that means, in effect, that I have none. It would be good to receive a legacy from someone, good to marry our Anya to a very rich man, good to go to Yaroslavl° and try our luck with our aunt, the Countess. She is very, very rich, you know.

VARYA (*crying*). If only God would help us!

GAYEV. Stop bawling. Auntie's very rich, but she doesn't like us. In the first place, sister married a lawyer, not a nobleman . . . (ANYA *appears in the doorway.*) She married beneath her, and it cannot be said that she has conducted herself very virtuously. She is good, kind, charming, and I love her dearly, but no matter how much you allow for extenuating circumstances, you must admit she leads a sinful life. You feel it in her slightest movement.

VARYA (*in a whisper*). Anya is standing in the doorway.

GAYEV. What? (*Pause*) Funny, something got into my right eye . . . I can't see very well. And Thursday, when I was in the district court . . .

(ANYA *enters.*)

VARYA. Why aren't you asleep, Anya?

ANYA. I can't get to sleep. I just can't.

GAYEV. My little one! (*Kisses* ANYA's *face and hands.*) My child. . . . (*Through tears*) You are not my niece, you are my angel, you are everything to me. Believe me, believe . . .

ANYA. I believe you, Uncle. Everyone loves you and respects you, but, Uncle dear, you must keep quiet, just keep quiet. What were you saying just now about my mother, about your own sister? What made you say that?

GAYEV. Yes, yes. . . . (*Covers his face with her hand.*) Really, it's awful! My God! God help me! And today I made a speech to the bookcase . . . so stupid! And it was only when I had finished that I realized it was stupid.

VARYA. It's true, Uncle dear, you ought to keep quiet. Just don't talk, that's all.

ANYA. If you could keep from talking, it would make things easier for you, too.

GAYEV. I'll be quiet. (*Kisses* ANYA's *and* VARYA's *hands.*) I'll be quiet. Only this is about business. On Thursday I was in the district court, well, a group of us gathered together and began talking about one thing and another, this and that, and it seems it might be possible to arrange a loan on a promissory note to pay the interest at the bank.

VARYA. If only God would help us!

GAYEV. On Tuesday I'll go and talk it over again. (*To* VARYA) Stop bawling. (*To* ANYA) Your mama will talk to Lopakhin; he, of course, will not refuse her. . . . And as soon as you've rested, you will go to Yaroslavl to the Countess, your great-aunt. In that way we shall be working from three directions—and our business is in the hat. We'll pay the interest, I'm certain of it. . . . (*Puts a candy in his mouth.*) On my honor, I'll swear by anything you like, the estate shall not be sold. (*Excitedly*) By my happiness, I swear it! Here's my hand on it, call me a worthless, dishonorable man if I let it come to auction! I swear by my whole being!

Yaroslavl: old Russian town on the Volga River

ANYA (*a calm mood returns to her, she is happy*). How good you are, Uncle, how clever! (*Embraces him.*) Now I am at peace! I'm at peace! I'm happy!

(*Enter* FIRS.)

FIRS (*reproachfully*). Leonid Andreich, have you no fear of God? When are you going to bed?

GAYEV. Presently, presently. Go away, Firs. I'll . . . all right, I'll undress myself. Well, children, bye-bye. . . . Details tomorrow, and now go to sleep. (*Kisses* ANYA *and* VARYA.) I am a man of the eighties.° . . . They don't think much of that period today, nevertheless, I can say that in the course of my life I have suffered not a little for my convictions. It is not for nothing that the peasant loves me. You have to know the peasant! You have to know from what——

ANYA. There you go again, Uncle!

VARYA. Uncle dear, do be quiet.

FIRS (*angrily*). Leonid Andreich!

GAYEV. I'm coming, I'm coming. . . . Go to bed. A clean double rail shot to center table. . . . (*Goes out;* FIRS *hobbles after him.*)

ANYA. I'm at peace now. I would rather not go to Yaroslavl, I don't like my great-aunt, but still, I'm at peace, thanks to Uncle. (*She sits down.*)

VARYA. We must get some sleep. I'm going now. Oh, something unpleasant happened while you were away. In the old servants' quarters, as you know, there are only the old people: Yefimushka, Polya, Yevstignei, and, of course, Karp. They began letting in all sorts of rogues to spend the night—I didn't say anything. But then I heard they'd been spreading a rumor that I'd given an order for them to be fed nothing but dried peas. Out of stinginess, you see. . . . It was all Yevstignei's doing. . . . Very well, I think, if that's how it is, you just wait. I send for Yevstignei . . . (*yawning*) he comes. . . . "How is it, Yevstignei," I say, "that you could be such a fool. . . ." (*Looks at* ANYA.) She's fallen asleep. (*Takes her by the arm.*) Come to your little bed. . . . Come along. (*Leading her*) My little darling fell asleep. Come. . . . (*They go.*)

(*In the distance, beyond the orchard, a shepherd is playing on a reed pipe.* TROFIMOV *crosses the stage and, seeing* VARYA *and* ANYA, *stops.*)

VARYA. Sh! She's asleep . . . asleep. . . . Come along, darling.

ANYA (*softly, half-asleep*). I'm so tired. . . . Those bells . . . Uncle . . . dear . . . Mama and Uncle . . .

VARYA. Come, darling, come along. (*They go into* ANYA's *room.*)

TROFIMOV (*deeply moved*). My sunshine! My spring!

man of the eighties: Gayev is probably taking credit for involvement in the altruistic "era of small deeds" when the gentry encouraged peasants' efforts to participate in local self-government and to improve public health, education and local economies. Looking backward from the end of the century, the eighties seemed a time of gradual, peaceful change, in contrast to the more fervent revolutionary movements that preceded the decade, or those following it that were to culminate in the 1905 revolution the year after Chekhov's death.

ACT II

A meadow. An old, lopsided, long-abandoned little chapel; near it a well, large stones that apparently were once tombstones, and an old bench. A road to the GAYEV *manor house can be seen. On one side, where the cherry orchard begins, tall poplars loom. In the distance a row of telegraph poles, and far, far away, on the horizon, the faint outline of a large town, which is visible only in very fine, clear weather. The sun will soon set.* CHARLOTTA, YASHA, *and* DUNYASHA *are sitting on the bench;* YEPIKHODOV *stands near playing something sad on the guitar. They are all lost in thought.* CHARLOTTA *wears an old forage cap; she has taken a gun from her shoulder and is adjusting the buckle on the sling.*

CHARLOTTA (*reflectively*). I haven't got a real passport, I don't know how old I am, but it always seems to me that I'm quite young. When I was a little girl, my father and mother used to travel from one fair to another giving performances—very good ones. And I did the *salto mortale*° and all sorts of tricks. Then when Papa and Mama died, a German lady took me to live with her and began teaching me. Good. I grew up and became a governess. But where I come from and who I am—I do not know. . . . Who my parents were—perhaps they weren't even married—I don't know. (*Takes a cucumber out of her pocket and eats it.*) I don't know anything. (*Pause*) One wants so much to talk, but there isn't anyone to talk to . . . I have no one.

YEPIKHODOV (*plays the guitar and sings*). "What care I for the clamorous world, what's friend or foe to me?" . . . How pleasant it is to play a mandolin!

DUNYASHA. That's a guitar, not a mandolin. (*Looks at herself in a hand mirror and powders her face.*)

YEPIKHODOV. To a madman, in love, it is a mandolin. . . . (*Sings.*) "Would that the heart were warmed by the flame of requited love . . ."

(YASHA *joins in.*)

CHARLOTTA. How horribly these people sing! . . . Pfui! Like jackals!

DUNYASHA (*to* YASHA). Really, how fortunate to have been abroad!

YASHA. Yes, to be sure. I cannot but agree with you there. (*Yawns, then lights a cigar.*)

YEPIKHODOV. It stands to reason. Abroad everything has long since been fully constituted.

YASHA. Obviously.

YEPIKHODOV. I am a cultivated man, I read all sorts of remarkable books, but I am in no way able to make out my own inclinations, what it is I really want, whether, strictly speaking, to live or to shoot myself; nevertheless, I always carry a revolver on me. Here it is. (*Shows revolver.*)

CHARLOTTA. Finished. Now I'm going. (*Slings the gun over her shoulder.*) You're a very clever man, Yepikhodov, and quite terrifying; women must be mad about you. Brrr! (*Starts to go.*) These clever people are all so stupid,

salto mortale: Italian, "leap of death," an acrobatic trick

there's no one for me to talk to. . . . Alone, always alone, I have no one . . . and who I am, and why I am, nobody knows. . . . (*Goes out unhurriedly*.)

YEPIKHODOV. Strictly speaking, all else aside, I must state regarding myself, that fate treats me unmercifully, as a storm does a small ship. If, let us assume, I am mistaken, then why, to mention a single instance, do I wake up this morning, and there on my chest see a spider of terrifying magnitude? . . . Like that (*Indicates with both hands*). And likewise, I take up some kvas to quench my thirst, and there see something in the highest degree unseemly, like a cockroach. (*Pause*) Have you read Buckle?° (*Pause*) If I may trouble you, Avdotya Fedorovna, I should like to have a word or two with you.

DUNYASHA. Go ahead.

YEPIKHODOV. I prefer to speak with you alone. . . . (*Sighs.*)

DUNYASHA (*embarrassed*). Very well . . . only first bring me my little cape . . . you'll find it by the cupboard. . . . It's rather damp here. . . .

YEPIKHODOV. Certainly, ma'am . . . I'll fetch it, ma'am. . . . Now I know what to do with my revolver. . . . (*Takes the guitar and goes off playing it.*)

YASHA. Two-and-twenty Troubles! Between ourselves, a stupid fellow. (*Yawns.*)

DUNYASHA. God forbid that he should shoot himself. (*Pause*) I've grown so anxious, I'm always worried. I was only a little girl when I was taken into the master's house, and now I'm quite unused to the simple life, and my hands are white as can be, just like a lady's. I've become so delicate, so tender and ladylike, I'm afraid of everything. . . . Frightfully so. And, Yasha, if you deceive me, I just don't know what will become of my nerves.

YASHA (*kisses her*). You little cucumber! Of course, a girl should never forget herself. What I dislike above everything is when a girl doesn't conduct herself properly.

DUNYASHA. I'm passionately in love with you; you're educated, you can discuss anything. (*Pause*)

YASHA (*yawns*). Yes. . . . As I see it, it's like this: if a girl loves somebody, that means she's immoral. (*Pause*) Very pleasant smoking a cigar in the open air. . . . (*Listens.*) Someone's coming this way. . . . It's the masters. (DUNYASHA *impulsively embraces him.*) You go home, as if you'd been to the river to bathe; take the path, otherwise they'll see you and suspect me of having a rendezvous with you. I can't endure that sort of thing.

DUNYASHA (*with a little cough*). My head is beginning to ache from your cigar. . . . (*Goes out.*)

(YASHA *remains, sitting near the chapel.* LYUBOV ANDREYEVNA, GAYEV, *and* LOPAKHIN *enter.*)

LOPAKHIN. You must make up your mind once and for all—time won't stand still. The question, after all, is quite simple. Do you agree to lease the

---

Buckle: Henry Thomas Buckle, English historian (1821–1862)

land for summer cottages or not? Answer in one word: yes or no? Only one word!

LYUBOV ANDREYEVNA. Who is it that smokes those disgusting cigars out here? (*Sits down.*)

GAYEV. Now that the railway line is so near, it's made things convenient. (*Sits down.*) We went to town and had lunch . . . cue ball to the center! I feel like going to the house first and playing a game.

LYUBOV ANDREYEVNA. Later.

LOPAKHIN. Just one word! (*Imploringly*) Do give me an answer!

GAYEV (*yawning*). How's that?

LYUBOV ANDREYEVNA (*looks into her purse*). Yesterday I had a lot of money, and today there's hardly any left. My poor Varya tries to economize by feeding everyone milk soup, and in the kitchen the old people get nothing but dried peas, while I squander money foolishly. . . . (*Drops the purse, scattering gold coins.*) There they go. . . . (*Vexed*)

YASHA. Allow me, I'll pick them up in an instant. (*Picks up the money.*)

LYUBOV ANDREYEVNA. Please do, Yasha. And why did I go to town for lunch? . . . That miserable restaurant of yours with its music, and tablecloths smelling of soap. . . . Why drink so much, Lyonya? Why eat so much? Why talk so much? Today in the restaurant again you talked too much, and it was all so pointless. About the seventies, about the decadents.° And to whom? Talking to waiters about the decadents!

LOPAKHIN. Yes.

GAYEV (*waving his hand*). I'm incorrigible, that's evident. . . . (*Irritably to* YASHA) Why do you keep twirling about in front of me?

YASHA (*laughs*). I can't help laughing when I hear your voice.

GAYEV (*to his sister*). Either he or I——

LYUBOV ANDREYEVNA. Go away, Yasha, run along.

YASHA (*hands* LYUBOV ANDREYEVNA *her purse*). I'm going, right away. (*Hardly able to contain his laughter.*) This very instant. . . . (*Goes out.*)

LOPAKHIN. That rich man, Deriganov, is prepared to buy the estate. They say he's coming to the auction himself.

LYUBOV ANDREYEVNA. Where did you hear that?

LOPAKHIN. That's what they're saying in town.

LYUBOV ANDREYEVNA. Our aunt in Yaroslavl promised to send us something, but when and how much, no one knows.

LOPAKHIN. How much do you think she'll send? A hundred thousand? Two hundred?

LYUBOV ANDREYEVNA. Oh . . . ten or fifteen thousand, and we'll be thankful for that.

LOPAKHIN. Forgive me, but I have never seen such frivolous, such queer, unbusinesslike people as you, my friends. You are told in plain language that your estate is to be sold, and it's as though you don't understand it.

LYUBOV ANDREYEVNA. But what are we to do? Tell us what to do.

decadents: writers and painters of the symbolist movement

LOPAKHIN. I tell you every day. Every day I say the same thing. Both the cherry orchard and the land must be leased for summer cottages, and it must be done now, as quickly as possible—the auction is close at hand. Try to understand! Once you definitely decide on the cottages, you can raise as much money as you like, and then you are saved.

LYUBOV ANDREYEVNA. Cottages, summer people—forgive me, but it's so vulgar.

GAYEV. I agree with you, absolutely.

LOPAKHIN. I'll either burst into tears, start shouting, or fall into a faint! I can't stand it! You've worn me out! (*To* GAYEV) You're an old woman!

GAYEV. How's that?

LOPAKHIN. An old woman! (*Starts to go.*)

LYUBOV ANDREYEVNA (*alarmed*). No, don't go, stay, my dear. I beg you. Perhaps we'll think of something!

LOPAKHIN. What is there to think of?

LYUBOV ANDREYEVNA. Don't go away, please. With you here it's more cheerful somehow. . . . (*Pause*) I keep expecting something to happen, like the house caving in on us.

GAYEV (*in deep thought*). Double rail shot into the corner. . . . Cross table to the center. . . .

LYUBOV ANDREYEVNA. We have sinned so much. . . .

LOPAKHIN. What sins could you have——

GAYEV (*puts a candy into his mouth*). They say I've eaten up my entire fortune in candies. . . . (*Laughs.*)

LYUBOV ANDREYEVNA. Oh, my sins. . . . I've always squandered money recklessly, like a madwoman, and I married a man who did nothing but amass debts. My husband died from champagne—he drank terribly—then, to my sorrow, I fell in love with another man, lived with him, and just at that time—that was my first punishment, a blow on the head—my little boy was drowned . . . here in the river. And I went abroad, went away for good, never to return, never to see this river. . . . I closed my eyes and ran, beside myself, and *he* after me . . . callously, without pity. I bought a villa near Mentone, because he fell ill there, and for three years I had no rest, day or night. The sick man wore me out, my soul dried up. Then last year, when the villa was sold to pay my debts, I went to Paris, and there he stripped me of everything, and left me for another woman; I tried to poison myself. . . . So stupid, so shameful. . . . And suddenly I felt a longing for Russia, for my own country, for my little girl. . . . (*Wipes away her tears.*) Lord, Lord, be merciful, forgive my sins! Don't punish me any more! (*Takes a telegram out of her pocket.*) This came today from Paris. . . . He asks my forgiveness, begs me to return. . . . (*Tears up telegram.*) Do I hear music? (*Listens.*)

GAYEV. That's our famous Jewish band. You remember, four violins, a flute and double bass.

LYUBOV ANDREYEVNA. It's still in existence? We ought to send for them some time and give a party.

LOPAKHIN (*listens*). I don't hear anything. . . . (*Sings softly.*) "The Germans, for pay, will turn Russians into Frenchmen, they say." (*Laughs.*) What a play I saw yesterday at the theater—very funny!

LYUBOV ANDREYEVNA. There was probably nothing funny about it. Instead of going to see plays you ought to look at yourselves a little more often. How drab your lives are, how full of futile talk!

LOPAKHIN. That's true. I must say, this life of ours is stupid. . . . (*Pause*) My father was a peasant, an idiot; he understood nothing, taught me nothing; all he did was beat me when he was drunk, and always with a stick. As a matter of fact, I'm as big a blockhead and idiot as he was. I never learned anything, my handwriting's disgusting, I write like a pig—I'm ashamed to have people see it.

LYUBOV ANDREYEVNA. You ought to get married, my friend.

LOPAKHIN. Yes . . . that's true.

LYUBOV ANDREYEVNA. To our Varya. She's a nice girl.

LOPAKHIN. Yes.

LYUBOV ANDREYEVNA. She's a girl who comes from simple people, works all day long, but the main thing is she loves you. Besides, you've liked her for a long time now.

LOPAKHIN. Well? I've nothing against it. . . . She's a good girl. (*Pause*)

GAYEV. I've been offered a place in the bank. Six thousand a year. . . . Have you heard?

LYUBOV ANDREYEVNA. How could you! You stay where you are. . . .

(FIRS *enters carrying an overcoat.*)

FIRS (*to* GAYEV). If you please, sir, put this on, it's damp.

GAYEV (*puts on the overcoat*). You're a pest, old man.

FIRS. Never mind. . . . You went off this morning without telling me. (*Looks him over.*)

LYUBOV ANDREYEVNA. How you have aged, Firs!

FIRS. What do you wish, madam?

LOPAKHIN. She says you've grown very old!

FIRS. I've lived a long time. They were arranging a marriage for me before your papa was born. . . . (*Laughs.*) I was already head footman when the Emancipation° came. At that time I wouldn't consent to my freedom, I stayed with the masters. . . . (*Pause*) I remember, everyone was happy, but what they were happy about, they themselves didn't know.

LOPAKHIN. It was better in the old days. At least they flogged them.

FIRS (*not hearing*). Of course. The peasants kept to the masters, the masters kept to the peasants; but now they have all gone their own ways, you can't tell about anything.

GAYEV. Be quiet, Firs. Tomorrow I must go to town. I've been promised an introduction to a certain general who might let us have a loan.

LOPAKHIN. Nothing will come of it. And you can rest assured, you won't even pay the interest.

Emancipation: the emancipation of the serfs, 1861

LYUBOV ANDREYEVNA. He's raving. There is no such general.

(*Enter* TROFIMOV, ANYA, *and* VARYA.)

GAYEV. Here come our young people.

ANYA. There's Mama.

LYUBOV ANDREYEVNA (*tenderly*). Come, come along, my darlings. (*Embraces* ANYA *and* VARYA.) If you only knew how I love you both! Sit here beside me—there, like that.

(*They all sit down.*)

LOPAKHIN. Our eternal student is always with the young ladies.

TROFIMOV. That's none of your business.

LOPAKHIN. He'll soon be fifty, but he's still a student.

TROFIMOV. Drop your stupid jokes.

LOPAKHIN. What are you so angry about, you queer fellow?

TROFIMOV. Just leave me alone.

LOPAKHIN (*laughs*). Let me ask you something: what do you make of me?

TROFIMOV. My idea of you, Yermolai Alekseich, is this: you're a rich man, you will soon be a millionaire. Just as the beast of prey, which devours everything that crosses its path, is necessary in the metabolic process, so are you necessary.

(*Everyone laughs.*)

VARYA. Petya, you'd better tell us something about the planets.

LYUBOV ANDREYEVNA. No, let's go on with yesterday's conversation.

TROFIMOV. What was it about?

GAYEV. About the proud man.

TROFIMOV. We talked a long time yesterday, but we didn't get anywhere. In the proud man, in your sense of the word, there's something mystical. And you may be right from your point of view, but if you look at it simply, without being abstruse, why even talk about pride? Is there any sense in it if, physiologically, man is poorly constructed, if, in the vast majority of cases, he is coarse, ignorant, and profoundly unhappy? We should stop admiring ourselves. We should just work, and that's all.

GAYEV. You die, anyway.

TROFIMOV. Who knows? And what does it mean—to die? It may be that man has a hundred senses, and at his death only the five that are known to us perish, and the other ninety-five go on living.

LYUBOV ANDREYEVNA. How clever you are, Petya!

LOPAKHIN (*ironically*). Terribly clever!

TROFIMOV. Mankind goes forward, perfecting its powers. Everything that is now unattainable will someday be comprehensible and within our grasp, only we must work, and help with all our might those who are seeking the truth. So far, among us here in Russia, only a very few work. The great majority of the intelligentsia that I know seek nothing, do nothing, and as yet are incapable of work. They call themselves the intelligentsia, yet they belittle their servants, treat the peasants like animals, are wretched students, never read anything serious, and do absolutely nothing; they only talk about science and know very little about art. They all look serious, have grim expressions, speak of weighty matters, and philosophize; and meanwhile anyone can see that the workers eat abominably, sleep without pillows, thirty or forty to a room, and everywhere there are bedbugs, stench, dampness, and immorality. . . . It's obvious that all our fine talk is merely to delude ourselves and others. Show me the day nurseries they are talking about—and where are the reading rooms? They only write about them in novels, but in reality they don't exist. There is nothing but filth, vulgarity, asiaticism. . . . I'm afraid of those very serious countenances, I don't like them, I'm afraid of serious conversations. We'd do better to remain silent.

LOPAKHIN. You know, I get up before five in the morning, and I work from morning to night; now, I'm always handling money, my own and other people's, and I see what people around me are like. You have only to start doing something to find out how few honest, decent people there are. Sometimes, when I can't sleep, I think: "Lord, Thou gavest us vast forests, boundless fields, broad horizons, and living in their midst we ourselves ought truly to be giants. . . ."

LYUBOV ANDREYEVNA. Now you want giants! They're good only in fairy tales, otherwise they're frightening.

(YEPIKHODOV *crosses at the rear of the stage, playing the guitar.*)

LYUBOV ANDREYEVNA (*pensively*). There goes Yepikhodov . . .
ANYA (*pensively*). There goes Yepikhodov . . .
GAYEV. The sun has set, ladies and gentlemen.
TROFIMOV. Yes.
GAYEV (*in a low voice, as though reciting*). Oh, Nature, wondrous Nature, you shine with eternal radiance, beautiful and indifferent; you, whom we call mother, unite within yourself both life and death, giving life and taking it away. . . .
VARYA (*beseechingly*). Uncle dear!
ANYA. Uncle, you're doing it again!
TROFIMOV. You'd better cue ball into the center.
GAYEV. I'll be silent, silent.

(*All sit lost in thought. The silence is broken only by the subdued muttering of* FIRS. *Suddenly a distant sound is heard, as if from the sky, like the sound of a snapped string*° *mournfully dying away.*)

LYUBOV ANDREYEVNA. What was that?
LOPAKHIN. I don't know. Somewhere far off in a mine shaft a bucket's broken loose. But somewhere very far away.
GAYEV. It might be a bird of some sort . . . like a heron.

°**string:** The sound indicated is that of a breaking string from a musical instrument such as a harp.

TROFIMOV. Or an owl . . .

LYUBOV ANDREYEVNA (*shudders*). It's unpleasant somehow. . . . (*Pause*)

FIRS. The same thing happened before the troubles: an owl hooted and the samovar hissed continually.

GAYEV. Before what troubles?

FIRS. Before the Emancipation.

LYUBOV ANDREYEVNA. Come along, my friends, let us go, evening is falling. (*To* ANYA) There are tears in your eyes—what is it, my little one?

(*Embraces her.*)

ANYA. It's all right, Mama. It's nothing.

TROFIMOV. Someone is coming.

(*A* STRANGER *appears wearing a shabby white forage cap and an overcoat. He is slightly drunk.*)

STRANGER. Permit me to inquire, can I go straight through here to the station?

GAYEV. You can. Follow the road.

STRANGER. I am deeply grateful to you. (*Coughs.*) Splendid weather. . . . (*Reciting*) "My brother, my suffering brother . . . come to the Volga, whose groans"° . . . (*To* VARYA) Mademoiselle, will you oblige a hungry Russian with thirty kopecks?

(VARYA, *frightened, cries out.*)

LOPAKHIN (*angrily*). There's a limit to everything.

LYUBOV ANDREYEVNA (*panic-stricken*). Here you are—take this. . . . (*Fumbles in her purse.*) I have no silver. . . . Never mind, here's a gold piece for you. . .

STRANGER. I am deeply grateful to you. (*Goes off.*)

(*Laughter*)

VARYA (*frightened*). I'm leaving . . . I'm leaving. . . . Oh, Mama, dear, there's nothing in the house for the servants to eat, and you give him a gold piece!

LYUBOV ANDREYEVNA. What's to be done with such a silly creature? When we get home I'll give you all I've got. Yermolai Alekseyevich, you'll lend me some more!

LOPAKHIN. At your service.

LYUBOV ANDREYEVNA. Come, my friends, it's time to go. Oh, Varya, we have definitely made a match for you. Congratulations!

VARYA (*through tears*). Mama, that's not something to joke about.

"My brother . . . groans": The quoted phrases are from two Russian poems with contrasting contexts; the first poem expresses love overcoming evil, the second compares the moans of suffering people to the sounds of the Volga River.

LOPAKHIN. "Aurelia,° get thee to a nunnery . . .."

GAYEV. Look, my hands are trembling: it's a long time since I've played a game of billiards.

LOPAKHIN. "Aurelia, O Nymph, in thy orisons, be all my sins remember'd!"

LYUBOV ANDREYEVNA. Let us go, my friends, it will soon be suppertime.

VARYA. He frightened me. My heart is simply pounding.

LOPAKHIN. Let me remind you, ladies and gentlemen: on the twenty-second of August the cherry orchard is to be sold. Think about that!—Think!

(*All go out except* TROFIMOV *and* ANYA.)

ANYA (*laughs*). My thanks to the stranger for frightening Varya, now we are alone.

TROFIMOV. Varya is so afraid we might suddenly fall in love with each other that she hasn't left us alone for days. With her narrow mind she can't understand that we are above love. To avoid the petty and the illusory, which prevent our being free and happy—that is the aim and meaning of life. Forward! We are moving irresistibly toward the bright star that burns in the distance! Forward! Do not fall behind, friends!

ANYA (*clasping her hands*). How well you talk! (*Pause*) It's marvelous here today!

TROFIMOV. Yes, the weather is wonderful.

ANYA. What have you done to me, Petya, that I no longer love the cherry orchard as I used to? I loved it so tenderly, it seemed to me there was no better place on earth than our orchard.

TROFIMOV. All Russia is our orchard. It is a great and beautiful land, and there are many wonderful places in it. (*Pause*) Just think, Anya: your grandfather, and your great-grandfather, and all your ancestors were serf-owners, possessors of living souls. Don't you see that from every cherry tree, from every leaf and trunk, human beings are peering out at you? Don't you hear their voices? To possess living souls—that has corrupted all of you, those who lived before and you who are living now, so that your mother, you, your uncle, no longer perceive that you are living in debt, at someone else's expense, at the expense of those whom you wouldn't allow to cross your threshold. . . . We are at least two hundred years behind the times, we have as yet absolutely nothing, we have no definite attitude toward the past, we only philosophize, complain of boredom, or drink vodka. Yet it's quite clear that to begin to live we must first atone for the past, be done with it, and we can atone for it only by suffering, only by extraordinary, unceasing labor. Understand this, Anya.

ANYA. The house we live in hasn't really been ours for a long time, and I shall leave it, I give you my word.

Aurelia: Lopakhin's error for "Ophelia" as he alludes to the "nunnery scene" in *Hamlet* (III.i)

TROFIMOV. If you have the keys of the household, throw them into the well and go. Be as free as the wind.

ANYA (*in ecstasy*). How well you put that!

TROFIMOV. Believe me, Anya, believe me! I am not yet thirty, I am young, still a student, but I have already been through so much! As soon as winter comes, I am hungry, sick, worried, poor as a beggar, and—where has not fate driven me! Where have I not been? And yet always, every minute of the day and night, my soul was filled with inexplicable premonitions. I have a premonition of happiness, Anya, I can see it . . .

ANYA. The moon is rising.

(YEPIKHODOV *is heard playing the same melancholy song on the guitar. The moon rises. Somewhere near the poplars* VARYA *is looking for* ANYA *and calling:* "Anya, where are you?")

TROFIMOV. Yes, the moon is rising. (*Pause*) There it is—happiness . . . it's coming, nearer and nearer, I can hear its footsteps. And if we do not see it, if we do not recognize it, what does it matter? Others will see it.

VARYA'S VOICE. Anya! Where are you?

TROFIMOV. That Varya again! (*Angrily*) It's revolting!

ANYA. Well? Let's go down to the river. It's lovely there.

TROFIMOV. Come on. (*They go.*)

VARYA'S VOICE. Anya! Anya!

ACT III

The drawing room, separated by an arch from the ballroom. The chandelier is lighted. The Jewish band that was mentioned in Act II is heard playing in the hall. It is evening. In the ballroom they are dancing a grand rond. The voice of SEMYONOV-PISHCHIK: *"Promenade à une paire!" They all enter the drawing room:* PISCHICK *and* CHARLOTTA IVANOVNA *are the first couple,* TROFIMOV *and* LYUBOV ANDREYEVNA *the second,* ANYA *and the* POST-OFFICE CLERK *the third,* VARYA *and the* STATIONMASTER *the fourth, etc.* VARYA, *quietly weeping, dries her tears as she dances.* DUNYASHA *is in the last couple. As they cross the drawing room* PISHCHIK *calls: "Grand rond, balancez!" and "Les cavaliers à genoux et remercier vos dames!"* FIRS, *wearing a dress coat, brings in a tray with seltzer water.* PISHCHIK *and* TROFIMOV *come into the drawing room.*

PISHCHIK. I'm a full-blooded man, I've already had two strokes, and dancing's hard work for me, but as they say, "If you run with the pack, you can bark or not, but at least wag your tail." At that, I'm as strong as a horse. My late father—quite a joker he was, God rest his soul—used to say, talking about our origins, that the ancient line of Semyonov-Pishchik was descended from the very horse that Caligula° had seated in the Senate. . . . (*Sits down.*)

Caligula: first century A.D. emperor who appointed his favorite horse to the Roman Senate

But the trouble is—no money! A hungry dog believes in nothing but meat. . . . (*Snores but wakes up at once.*) It's the same with me—I can think of nothing but money. . . .

TROFIMOV. You know, there really is something equine about your figure.

PISHCHIK. Well, a horse is a fine animal. . . . You can sell a horse.

(*There is the sound of a billiard game in the next room. VARYA appears in the archway.*)

TROFIMOV (*teasing her*). Madame Lopakhina! Madame Lopakhina!

VARYA (*angrily*). Mangy gentleman!

TROFIMOV. Yes, I am a mangy gentleman, and proud of it!

VARYA (*reflecting bitterly*). Here we've hired musicians, and what are we going to pay them with? (*Goes out.*)

TROFIMOV (*to PISHCHIK*). If the energy you have expended in the course of your life trying to find money to pay interest had gone into something else, ultimately, you might very well have turned the world upside down.

PISHCHIK. Nietzsche . . . the philosopher . . . the greatest, most renowned . . . a man of tremendous intellect . . . says in his works that it is possible to forge banknotes.

TROFIMOV. And have you read Nietzsche?

PISHCHIK. Well . . . Dashenka told me. I'm in such a state now that I'm just about ready for forging. . . . The day after tomorrow I have to pay three hundred and ten rubles . . . I've got a hundred and thirty. . . . (*Feels in his pocket, grows alarmed.*) The money is gone! I've lost the money! (*Tearfully*) Where is my money? (*Joyfully*) Here it is, inside the lining. . . . I'm all in a sweat. . . .

(LYUBOV ANDREYEVNA *and* CHARLOTTA IVANOVNA *come in.*)

LYUBOV ANDREYEVNA (*humming a* Lezginka°). Why does Leonid take so long? What is he doing in town? (*To* DUNYASHA) Dunyasha, offer the musicians some tea.

TROFIMOV. In all probability, the auction didn't take place.

LYUBOV ANDREYEVNA. It was the wrong time to have the musicians, the wrong time to give a dance. . . . Well, never mind. . . . (*Sits down and hums softly.*)

CHARLOTTA (*gives* PISHCHIK *a deck of cards*). Here's a deck of cards for you. Think of a card.

PISHCHIK. I've thought of one.

CHARLOTTA. Now shuffle the pack. Very good. And now, my dear Mr. Pishchik, hand it to me. *Ein, zwei, drei!*° Now look for it—it's in your side pocket.

Lezginka: Caucasian dance tune
Ein, zwei, drei: German, "One, two, three"

PISHCHIK (*takes the card out of his side pocket*). The eight of spades—absolutely right! (*Amazed*) Think of that, now!

CHARLOTTA (*holding the deck of cards in the palm of her hand, to* TROFIMOV). Quickly, tell me, which card is on top?

TROFIMOV. What? Well, the queen of spades.

CHARLOTTA. Right! (*To* PISHCHIK) Now which card is on top?

PISHCHIK. The ace of hearts.

CHARLOTTA. Right! (*Claps her hands and the deck of cards disappears.*) What lovely weather we're having today! (*A mysterious feminine voice, which seems to come from under the floor, answers her:* "Oh, yes, splendid weather, madam.") You are so nice, you're my ideal. . . . (*The voice:* "And I am very fond of you, too, madam.")

STATIONMASTER (*applauding*). Bravo, Madame Ventriloquist!

PISHCHIK (*amazed*). Think of that, now! Most enchanting Charlotta Ivanova . . . I am simply in love with you. . . .

CHARLOTTA. In love? (*Shrugs her shoulders.*) Is it possible that you can love? *Guter Mensch, aber schlechter Musikant.°*

TROFIMOV (*claps* PISHCHIK *on the shoulder*). You old horse, you!

CHARLOTTA. Attention, please! One more trick. (*Takes a lap robe from a chair.*) Here's a very fine lap robe; I should like to sell it. (*Shakes it out.*) Doesn't anyone want to buy it?

PISHCHIK (*amazed*). Think of that, now!

CHARLOTTA. *Ein, zwei, drei!* (*Quickly raises the lap robe; behind it stands* ANYA, *who curtseys, runs to her mother, embraces her, and runs back into the ballroom amid the general enthusiasm.*)

LYUBOV ANDREYEVNA (*applauding*). Bravo, bravo!

CHARLOTTA. Once again! *Ein, zwei, drei.* (*Raises the lap robe; behind it stands* VARYA, *who bows.*)

PISHCHIK (*amazed*). Think of that, now!

CHARLOTTA. The end! (*Throws the robe at* PISHCHIK, *makes a curtsey, and runs out of the room.*)

PISHCHIK (*hurries after her*). The minx! . . . What a woman! What a woman! (*Goes out.*)

LYUBOV ANDREYEVNA. And Leonid still not here. What he is doing in town so long, I do not understand! It must be all over by now. Either the estate is sold, or the auction didn't take place—but why keep us in suspense so long!

VARYA (*trying to comfort her*). Uncle has bought it, I am certain of that.

TROFIMOV (*mockingly*). Yes.

VARYA. Great-aunt sent him power of attorney to buy it in her name and transfer the debt. She's doing it for Anya's sake. And I am sure, with God's help, Uncle will buy it.

LYUBOV ANDREYEVNA. Our great-aunt in Yaroslavl sent fifteen thousand to buy the estate in her name—she doesn't trust us—but that's not even

Guter Mensch, aber schlechter Musikant: German, "A good man, but a poor musician"

enough to pay the interest. (*Covers her face with her hands.*) Today my fate will be decided, my fate . . .

TROFIMOV (*teasing* VARYA). Madame Lopakhina!

VARYA (*angrily*). Eternal student! Twice already you've been expelled from the university.

LYUBOV ANDREYEVNA. Why are you so cross, Varya? If he teases you about Lopakhin, what of it? Go ahead and marry Lopakhin if you want to. He's a nice man, he's interesting. And if you don't want to, don't. Nobody's forcing you, my pet.

VARYA. To be frank, Mama dear, I regard this matter seriously. He is a good man, I like him.

LYUBOV ANDREYEVNA. Then marry him. I don't know what you're waiting for!

VARYA. Mama, I can't propose to him myself. For the last two years everyone's been talking to me about him; everyone talks, but he is either silent or he jokes. I understand. He's getting rich, he's absorbed in business, he has no time for me. If I had some money, no matter how little, if it were only a hundred rubles, I'd drop everything and go far away. I'd go into a nunnery.

TROFIMOV. A blessing!

VARYA (*to* TROFIMOV). A student ought to be intelligent! (*In a gentle tone, tearfully*) How homely you have grown, Petya, how old! (*To* LYUBOV ANDREYEVNA, *no longer crying*) It's just that I cannot live without work, Mama. I must be doing something every minute.

(YASHA *enters.*)

YASHA (*barely able to suppress his laughter*). Yepikhodov has broken a billiard cue! (*Goes out.*)

VARYA. But why is Yepikhodov here? Who gave him permission to play billiards? I don't understand these people. . . . (*Goes out.*)

LYUBOV ANDREYEVNA. Don't tease her, Petya. You can see she's unhappy enough without that.

TROFIMOV. She's much too zealous, always meddling in other people's affairs. All summer long she's given Anya and me no peace—afraid a romance might develop. What business is it of hers? Besides, I've given no occasion for it, I am far removed from such banality. We are above love!

LYUBOV ANDREYEVNA. And I suppose I am beneath love. (*In great agitation*) Why isn't Leonid here? If only I knew whether the estate had been sold or not! The disaster seems to me so incredible that I don't even know what to think. I'm lost. . . . I could scream this very instant . . . I could do something foolish. Save me, Petya. Talk to me, say something. . . .

TROFIMOV. Whether or not the estate is sold today—does it really matter? That's all done with long ago; there's no turning back, the path is overgrown. Be calm, my dear. One must not deceive oneself; at least once in one's life one ought to look the truth straight in the eye.

LYUBOV ANDREYEVNA. What truth? You can see where there is truth and where there isn't, but I seem to have lost my sight, I see nothing. You boldly settle all the important problems, but tell me, my dear boy, isn't it because you are young and have not yet had to suffer for a single one of your problems? You boldly look ahead, but isn't it because you neither see nor expect anything dreadful, since life is still hidden from your young eyes? You're bolder, more honest, deeper than we are, but think about it, be just a little bit magnanimous, and spare me. You see, I was born here, my mother and father lived here, and my grandfather. I love this house, without the cherry orchard my life has no meaning for me, and if it must be sold, then sell me with the orchard. . . . (*Embraces* TROFIMOV *and kisses him on the forehead.*) And my son was drowned here. . . . (*Weeps.*) Have pity on me, you good, kind man.

TROFIMOV. You know I feel for you with all my heart.

LYUBOV ANDREYEVNA. But that should have been said differently, quite differently. . . . (*Takes out her handkerchief and a telegram falls to the floor.*) My heart is heavy today, you can't imagine. It's so noisy here, my soul quivers at every sound, I tremble all over, and yet I can't go to my room. When I am alone the silence frightens me. Don't condemn me, Petya . . . I love you as if you were my own. I would gladly let you marry Anya, I swear it, only you must study, my dear, you must get your degree. You do nothing, fate simply tosses you from place to place—it's so strange. . . . Isn't that true? Isn't it? And you must do something about your beard, to make it grow somehow. . . . (*Laughs.*) You're so funny!

TROFIMOV (*picks up the telegram*). I have no desire to be an Adonis.

LYUBOV ANDREYEVNA. That's a telegram from Paris. I get them every day. One yesterday, one today. That wild man has fallen ill again, he's in trouble again. . . . He begs my forgiveness, implores me to come, and really, I ought to go to Paris to be near him. Your face is stern, Petya, but what can one do, my dear? What am I to do? He is ill, he's alone and unhappy, and who will look after him there, who will keep him from making mistakes, who will give him his medicine on time? And why hide it or keep silent, I love him, that's clear. I love him, love him. . . . It's a millstone round my neck, I'm sinking to the bottom with it, but I love that stone, I cannot live without it. (*Presses* TROFIMOV's *hand.*) Don't think badly of me, Petya, and don't say anything to me, don't say anything. . . .

TROFIMOV (*through tears*). For God's sake, forgive my frankness: you know that he robbed you!

LYUBOV ANDREYEVNA. No, no, no, you mustn't say such things! (*Covers her ears.*)

TROFIMOV. But he's a scoundrel! You're the only one who doesn't know it! He's a petty scoundrel, a nonentity——

LYUBOV ANDREYEVNA (*angry, but controlling herself*). You are twenty-six or twenty-seven years old, but you're still a schoolboy!

TROFIMOV. That may be!

LYUBOV ANDREYEVNA. You should be a man, at your age you ought to understand those who love. And you ought to be in love yourself. (*Angrily*)

Yes, yes! It's not purity with you, it's simply prudery, you're a ridiculous crank, a freak——

TROFIMOV (*horrified*). What is she saying!

LYUBOV ANDREYEVNA. "I am above love!" You're not above love, you're just an addlepate, as Firs would say. Not to have a mistress at your age!

TROFIMOV (*in horror*). This is awful! What is she saying! . . . . (*Goes quickly toward the ballroom.*) This is awful . . . I can't . . . I won't stay here. . . . (*Goes out, but immediately returns.*) All is over between us! (*Goes out to the hall.*)

LYUBOV ANDREYEVNA (*calls after him*). Petya, wait! You absurd creature, I was joking! Petya!

(*In the hall there is the sound of someone running quickly downstairs and suddenly falling with a crash. ANYA and VARYA scream, but a moment later laughter is heard.*)

LYUBOV ANDREYEVNA. What was that?

(ANYA *runs in.*)

ANYA (*laughing*). Petya fell down the stairs! (*Runs out.*)

LYUBOV ANDREYEVNA. What a funny boy that Petya is!

(*The STATIONMASTER stands in the middle of the ballroom and recites A. Tolstoy's "The Sinner." Everyone listens to him, but he has no sooner spoken a few lines than the sound of a waltz is heard from the hall and the recitation is broken off. They all dance. TROFIMOV, ANYA, VARYA, and LYUBOV ANDREYEVNA come in from the hall.*)

LYUBOV ANDREYEVNA. Come, Petya . . . come, you pure soul . . . please, forgive me. . . . Let's dance. . . . (*They dance.*)

(ANYA *and* VARYA *dance.* FIRS *comes in, puts his stick by the side door.* YASHA *also comes into the drawing room and watches the dancers.*)

YASHA. What is it, grandpa?

FIRS. I don't feel well. In the old days we used to have generals, barons, admirals, dancing at our balls, but now we send for the post-office clerk and the stationmaster, and even they are none too eager to come. Somehow I've grown weak. The late master, their grandfather, dosed everyone with sealing wax, no matter what ailed them. I've been taking sealing wax every day for twenty years or more; maybe that's what's kept me alive.

YASHA. You bore me, grandpa. (*Yawns.*) High time you croaked.

FIRS. Ah, you . . . addlepate! (*Mumbles.*)

(TROFIMOV *and* LYUBOV ANDREYEVNA *dance from the ballroom into the drawing room.*)

LYUBOV ANDREYEVNA. *Merci.* I'll sit down a while. (*Sits.*) I'm tired.

(ANYA *comes in.*)

ANYA (*excitedly*). There was a man in the kitchen just now saying that the cherry orchard was sold today.

LYUBOV ANDREYEVNA. Sold to whom?

ANYA. He didn't say. He's gone. (*Dances with* TROFIMOV; *they go into the ballroom.*)

YASHA. That was just some old man babbling. A stranger.

FIRS. Leonid Andreich is not back yet, still hasn't come. And he's wearing the light, between-seasons overcoat; like enough he'll catch cold. Ah, when they're young they're green.

LYUBOV ANDREYEVNA. This is killing me. Yasha, go and find out who it was sold to.

YASHA. But that old man left long ago. (*Laughs.*)

LYUBOV ANDREYEVNA (*slightly annoyed*). Well, what are you laughing at? What are you so happy about?

YASHA. That Yepikhodov is very funny! Hopeless! Two-and-twenty Troubles.

LYUBOV ANDREYEVNA. Firs, if the estate is sold, where will you go?

FIRS. Wherever you tell me to go, I'll go.

LYUBOV ANDREYEVNA. Why do you look like that? Aren't you well? You ought to go to bed.

FIRS. Yes . . . (*With a smirk.*) Go to bed, and without me who will serve, who will see to things? I'm the only one in the whole house.

YASHA (*to* LYUBOV ANDREYEVNA). Lyubov Andreyevna! Permit me to make a request, be so kind! If you go back to Paris again, do me the favor of taking me with you. It is positively impossible for me to stay here. (*Looking around, then in a low voice*) There's no need to say it, you can see for yourself, it's an uncivilized country, the people have no morals, and the boredom! The food they give us in the kitchen is unmentionable, and besides, there's this Firs who keeps walking about mumbling all sorts of inappropriate things. Take me with you, be so kind!

(*Enter* PISHCHIK.)

PISHCHIK. May I have the pleasure of a waltz with you, fairest lady? (LYUBOV ANDREYEVNA *goes with him.*) I really must borrow a hundred and eighty rubles from you, my charmer . . . I really must. . . . (*Dancing.*) Just a hundred and eighty rubles. . . . (*They pass into the ballroom.*)

YASHA (*softly sings*). "Wilt thou know my soul's unrest . . ."

(*In the ballroom a figure in a gray top hat and checked trousers is jumping about, waving its arms; there are shouts of* "Bravo, Charlotta Ivanovna!")

DUNYASHA (*stopping to powder her face*). The young mistress told me to dance—there are lots of gentlemen and not enough ladies—but dancing makes me dizzy, and my heart begins to thump. Firs Nikolayevich, the post-office clerk just said something to me that took my breath away.

(The music grows more subdued.)

FIRS. What did he say to you?

DUNYASHA. "You," he said, "are like a flower."

YASHA (*yawns*). What ignorance. . . . (*Goes out.*)

DUNYASHA. Like a flower. . . . I'm such a delicate girl, I just adore tender words.

FIRS. You'll get your head turned.

(Enter YEPIKHODOV.)

YEPIKHODOV. Avdotya Fyodorovna, you are not desirous of seeing me . . . I might almost be some sort of insect. (*Sighs.*) Ah, life!

DUNYASHA. What is it you want?

YEPIKHODOV. Indubitably, you may be right. (*Sighs.*) But, of course, if one looks at it from a point of view, then, if I may so express myself, and you will forgive my frankness, you have completely reduced me to a state of mind. I know of my fate, every day some misfortune befalls me, but I have long since grown accustomed to that; I look upon my fate with a smile. But you gave me your word, and although I——

DUNYASHA. Please, we'll talk about it later, but leave me in peace now. Just now I'm dreaming. . . . (*Plays with her fan.*)

YEPIKHODOV. Every day a misfortune, and yet, if I may so express myself, I merely smile, I even laugh.

(VARYA enters from the ballroom.)

VARYA. Are you still here, Semyon? What a disrespectful man you are, really! (*To* DUNYASHA) Run along, Dunyasha. (*To* YEPIKHODOV) First you play billiards and break a cue, then you wander about the drawing room as though you were a guest.

YEPIKHODOV. You cannot, if I may express myself, penalize me.

VARYA. I am not penalizing you, I'm telling you. You do nothing but wander from one place to another, and you don't do your work. We keep a clerk, but for what, I don't know.

YEPIKHODOV (*offended*). Whether I work, or wander about, or eat, or play billiards, these are matters to be discussed only by persons of discernment, and my elders.

VARYA. You dare say that to me! (*Flaring up*) You dare? You mean to say I have no discernment? Get out of here! This instant!

YEPIKHODOV (*intimidated*). I beg you to express yourself in a more delicate manner.

VARYA (*beside herself*). Get out, this very instant! Get out! (*He goes to the door, she follows him.*) Two-and-twenty Troubles! Don't let me set eyes on you again!

YEPIKHODOV (*goes out, his voice is heard behind the door*). I shall lodge a complaint against you!

VARYA. Oh, you're coming back? (*Seizes the stick left near the door by* FIRS). Come, come on. . . . Come, I'll show you. . . . Ah, so you're coming, are you? Then take that—(*Swings the stick just as* LOPAKHIN *enters.*)

LOPAKHIN. Thank you kindly.

VARYA (*angrily and mockingly*). I beg your pardon.

LOPAKHIN. Not at all. I humbly thank you for your charming reception.

VARYA. Don't mention it. (*Walks away, then looks back and gently asks.*) I didn't hurt you, did I?

LOPAKHIN. No, it's nothing. A huge bump coming up, that's all.

(*Voices in the ballroom:* "Lopakhin has come! Yermolai Alekseich!" PISHCHIK *enters.*)

PISHCHIK. As I live and breathe! (*Kisses* LOPAKHIN.) There is a whiff of cognac about you, dear soul. And we've been making merry here, too.

(*Enter* LYUBOV ANDREYEVNA.)

LYUBOV ANDREYEVNA. Is that you, Yermolai Alekseich? What kept you so long? Where's Leonid?

LOPAKHIN. Leonid Andreich arrived with me, he's coming . . .

LYUBOV ANDREYEVNA (*agitated*). Well, what happened? Did the sale take place? Tell me!

LOPAKHIN (*embarrassed, fearing to reveal his joy*). The auction was over by four o'clock. . . . We missed the train, had to wait till half past nine. (*Sighing heavily*) Ugh! My head is swimming. . . .

(*Enter* GAYEV; *he carries his purchases in one hand and wipes away his tears with the other.*)

LYUBOV ANDREYEVNA. Lyonya, what happened? Well, Lyonya? (*Impatiently, through tears*) Be quick, for God's sake!

GAYEV (*not answering her, simply waves his hand. To* FIRS, *weeping*). Here, take these. . . . There's anchovies, Kerch herrings. . . . I haven't eaten anything all day. . . . What I have been through! (*The click of billiard balls is heard through the open door to the billiard room, and* YASHA's *voice:* "Seven and eighteen!" GAYEV's *expression changes, he is no longer weeping.*) I'm terribly tired. Firs, help me change. (*Goes through the ballroom to his own room, followed by* FIRS.)

PISHCHIK. What happened at the auction? Come on, tell us!

LYUBOV ANDREYEVNA. Is the cherry orchard sold?

LOPAKHIN. It's sold.

LYUBOV ANDREYEVNA. Who bought it?

LOPAKHIN. I bought it. (*Pause*)

(LYUBOV ANDREYEVNA *is overcome; she would fall to the floor if it were not for the chair and table near which she stands.* VARYA *takes the keys from her belt and throws them on the floor in the middle of the drawing room and goes out.*)

LOPAKHIN. I bought it! Kindly wait a moment, ladies and gentlemen, my head is swimming, I can't talk. . . . (*Laughs.*) We arrived at the auction, Deriganov was already there. Leonid Andreich had only fifteen thousand, and straight off Deriganov bid thirty thousand over and above the mortgage. I saw how the land lay, so I got into the fight and bid forty. He bid forty-five. I bid fifty-five. In other words, he kept raising it by five thousand, and I by ten. Well, it finally came to an end. I bid ninety thousand above the mortgage, and it was knocked down to me. The cherry orchard is now mine! Mine! (*Laughs uproariously.*) Lord! God in heaven! The cherry orchard is mine! Tell me I'm drunk, out of my mind, that I imagine it. . . . (*Stamps his feet.*) Don't laugh at me! If my father and my grandfather could only rise from their graves and see all that has happened, how their Yermolai, their beaten, half-literate Yermolai, who used to run about barefoot in winter, how that same Yermolai has bought an estate, the most beautiful estate in the whole world! I bought the estate where my father and grandfather were slaves, where they weren't even allowed in the kitchen. I'm asleep, this is just some dream of mine, it only seems to be. . . . It's the fruit of your imagination, hidden in the darkness of uncertainty. . . . (*Picks up the keys, smiling tenderly.*) She threw down the keys, wants to show that she's not mistress here any more. . . . (*Jingles the keys.*) Well, no matter. (*The orchestra is heard tuning up.*) Hey, musicians, play, I want to hear you! Come on, everybody, and see how Yermolai Lopakhin will lay the ax to the cherry orchard, how the trees will fall to the ground! We're going to build summer cottages, and our grandsons and great-grandsons will see a new life here. . . . Music! Strike up!

(*The orchestra plays.* LYUBOV ANDREYEVNA *sinks into a chair and weeps bitterly.*)

LOPAKHIN (*reproachfully*). Why didn't you listen to me, why? My poor friend, there's no turning back now. (*With tears*) Oh, if only all this could be over quickly, if somehow our discordant, unhappy life could be changed!

PISHCHIK (*takes him by the arm; speaks in an undertone*). She's crying. Let's go into the ballroom, let her be alone. . . . Come on. . . . (*Leads him into the ballroom*).

LOPAKHIN. What's happened? Musicians, play so I can hear you! Let everything be as I want it! (*Ironically*) Here comes the new master, owner of the cherry orchard! (*Accidentally bumps into a little table, almost upsetting the candelabrum.*) I can pay for everything! (*Goes out with* PISHCHIK.)

(*There is no one left in either the drawing room or the ballroom except* LYUBOV ANDREYEVNA, *who sits huddled up and weeping bitterly. The music plays softly.* ANYA *and* TROFIMOV *enter hurriedly.* ANYA *goes to her mother and kneels before her.* TROFIMOV *remains in the doorway of the ballroom.*)

ANYA. Mama! . . . Mama, you're crying! Dear, kind, good Mama, my beautiful one, I love you . . . I bless you. The cherry orchard is sold, it's gone, that's true, true, but don't cry, Mama, life is still before you, you still have your good, pure soul. . . . Come with me, come, darling, we'll go away from here! . . . We'll plant a new orchard, more luxuriant than this one. You will see it and understand; and joy, quiet, deep joy, will sink into your soul, like the evening sun, and you will smile, Mama! Come, darling, let us go. . . .

ACT IV

The scene is the same as Act I. There are neither curtains on the windows nor pictures on the walls, and only a little furniture piled up in one corner, as if for sale. There is a sense of emptiness. Near the outer door, at the rear of the stage, suitcases, traveling bags, etc., are piled up. Through the open door on the left the voices of VARYA *and* ANYA *can be heard.* LOPAKHIN *stands waiting.* YASHA *is holding a tray with little glasses of champagne. In the hall,* YEPIKHODOV *is tying up a box. Off stage, at the rear, there is a hum of voices. It is the peasants who have come to say good-bye.* GAYEV's *voice:* "Thanks, brothers, thank you."

YASHA. The peasants have come to say good-bye. In my opinion, Yermolai Alekseich, peasants are good-natured, but they don't know much.

(*The hum subsides.* LYUBOV ANDREYEVNA *enters from the hall with* GAYEV. *She is not crying, but she is pale, her face twitches, and she cannot speak.*)

GAYEV. You gave them your purse, Lyuba. That won't do! That won't do!

LYUBOV ANDREYEVNA. I couldn't help it! I couldn't help it! (*They both go out.*)

LOPAKHIN (*in the doorway, calls after them*). Please, do me the honor of having a little glass at parting. I didn't think of bringing champagne from town, and at the station I found only one bottle. Please! What's the matter, friends, don't you want any? (*Walks away from the door.*) If I'd known that, I wouldn't have bought it. Well, then I won't drink any either. (YASHA *carefully sets the tray down on a chair.*) At least you have a glass, Yasha.

YASHA. To those who are departing! Good luck! (*Drinks.*) This champagne is not the real stuff, I can assure you.

LOPAKHIN. Eight rubles a bottle. (*Pause*) It's devilish cold in here.

YASHA. They didn't light the stoves today; it doesn't matter, since we're leaving. (*Laughs.*)

LOPAKHIN. Why are you laughing?

YASHA. Because I'm pleased.

LOPAKHIN. It's October, yet it's sunny and still outside, like summer. Good for building. (*Looks at his watch, then calls through the door.*) Bear in mind, ladies and gentlemen, only forty-six minutes till train time! That means leaving for the station in twenty minutes. Better hurry up!

(TROFIMOV *enters from outside wearing an overcoat.*)

TROFIMOV. Seems to me it's time to start. The carriages are at the door.

What the devil has become of my rubbers? They're lost. (*Calls through the door.*) Anya, my rubbers are not here. I can't find them.

LOPAKHIN. I've got to go to Kharkov. I'm taking the same train you are. I'm going to spend the winter in Kharkov. I've been hanging around here with you, and I'm sick and tired of loafing. I can't live without work, I don't know what to do with my hands; they dangle in some strange way, as if they didn't belong to me.

TROFIMOV. We'll soon be gone, then you can take up your useful labors again.

LOPAKHIN. Here, have a little drink.

TROFIMOV. No, I don't want any.

LOPAKHIN. So you're off for Moscow?

TROFIMOV. Yes, I'll see them into town, and tomorrow I'll go to Moscow.

LOPAKHIN. Yes. . . . Well, I expect the professors haven't been giving any lectures: they're waiting for you to come!

TROFIMOV. That's none of your business.

LOPAKHIN. How many years is it you've been studying at the university?

TROFIMOV. Can't you think of something new? That's stale and flat. (*Looks for his rubbers.*) You know, we'll probably never see each other again, so allow me to give you one piece of advice at parting: don't wave your arms about! Get out of that habit—of arm waving. And another thing, building cottages and counting on the summer residents in time becoming independent farmers—that's just another form of arm-waving. Well, when all's said and done, I'm fond of you anyway. You have fine, delicate fingers, like an artist; you have a fine delicate soul.

LOPAKHIN (*embraces him*). Good-bye, my dear fellow. Thank you for everything. Let me give you some money for the journey, if you need it.

TROFIMOV. What for? I don't need it.

LOPAKHIN. But you haven't any!

TROFIMOV. I have. Thank you. I got some money for a translation. Here it is in my pocket. (*Anxiously*) But where are my rubbers?

VARYA (*from the next room*). Here, take the nasty things! (*Flings a pair of rubbers onto the stage.*)

TROFIMOV. What are you so cross about, Varya? Hm. . . . But these are not my rubbers.

LOPAKHIN. In the spring I sowed three thousand acres of poppies,° and now I've made forty thousand rubles clear. And when my poppies were in bloom, what a picture it was! So, I'm telling you, I've made forty thousand, which means I'm offering you a loan because I can afford to. Why turn up your nose? I'm a peasant—I speak bluntly.

TROFIMOV. Your father was a peasant, mine was a pharmacist—which proves absolutely nothing. (LOPAKHIN *takes out his wallet.*) No, don't—even if

poppies: cultivated for their seeds for cooking purposes you gave me two hundred thousand I wouldn't take it. I'm a free man. And everything that is valued so highly and held so dear by all of you, rich and poor alike, has not the slightest power over me—it's like a feather floating in the air. I can get along without you, I can pass you by, I'm strong and proud. Mankind is advancing toward the highest truth, the highest happiness attainable on earth, and I am in the front ranks!

LOPAKHIN. Will you get there?

TROFIMOV. I'll get there. (*Pause*) I'll either get there or I'll show others the way to get there.

(*The sound of axes chopping down trees is heard in the distance.*)

LOPAKHIN. Well, good-bye, my dear fellow. It's time to go. We turn up our noses at one another, but life goes on just the same. When I work for a long time without stopping, my mind is easier, and it seems to me that I, too, know why I exist. But how many there are in Russia, brother, who exist nobody knows why. Well, it doesn't matter, that's not what makes the wheels go round. They say Leonid Andreich has taken a position in the bank, six thousand a year. . . . Only, of course, he won't stick it out, he's too lazy. . . .

ANYA (*in the doorway*). Mama asks you not to start cutting down the cherry orchard until she's gone.

TROFIMOV. Yes, really, not to have had the tact . . . (*Goes out through the hall.*)

LOPAKHIN. Right away, right away. . . . Ach, what people. . . . (*Follows* TROFIMOV *out.*)

ANYA. Has Firs been taken to the hospital?

YASHA. I told them this morning. They must have taken him.

ANYA (*to* YEPIKHODOV, *who is crossing the room*). Semyon Panteleich, please find out if Firs has been taken to the hospital.

YASHA (*offended*). I told Yegor this morning. Why ask a dozen times?

YEPIKHODOV. It is my conclusive opinion that the venerable Firs is beyond repair; it's time he was gathered to his fathers. And I can only envy him. (*Puts a suitcase down on a hatbox and crushes it.*) There you are! Of course! I knew it! (*Goes out.*)

YASHA (*mockingly*). Two-and-twenty Troubles!

VARYA (*through the door*). Has Firs been taken to the hospital?

ANYA. Yes, he has.

VARYA. Then why didn't they take the letter to the doctor?

ANYA. We must send it on after them. . . . (*Goes out.*)

VARYA (*from the adjoining room*). Where is Yasha? Tell him his mother has come to say good-bye to him.

YASHA (*waves his hand*). They really try my patience.

(DUNYASHA *has been fussing with the luggage; now that* YASHA *is alone she goes up to him.*)

DUNYASHA. You might give me one little look, Yasha. You're going away . . . leaving me. . . . (*Cries and throws herself on his neck.*)

YASHA. What's there to cry about? (*Drinks champagne.*) In six days I'll be in Paris again. Tomorrow we'll take the express, off we go, and that's the last you'll see of us. I can hardly believe it. *Vive la France!* This place is not for me, I can't live here. . . . It can't be helped. I've had enough of this ignorance—I'm fed up with it. (*Drinks champagne.*) What are you crying for? Behave yourself properly, then you won't cry.

DUNYASHA (*looks into a small mirror and powders her face*). Send me a letter from Paris. You know, I loved you, Yasha, how I loved you! I'm such a tender creature, Yasha!

YASHA. Here they come. (*Busies himself with the luggage, humming softly.*)

(*Enter* LYUBOV ANDREYEVNA, GAYEV, CHARLOTTA IVANOVNA.)

GAYEV. We ought to be leaving. There's not much time now. (*Looks at* YASHA.) Who smells of herring?

LYUBOV ANDREYEVNA. In about ten minutes we should be getting into the carriages. (*Glances around the room.*) Good-bye, dear house, old grandfather. Winter will pass, spring will come, and you will no longer be here, they will tear you down. How much these walls have seen! (*Kisses her daughter warmly.*) My treasure, you are radiant, your eyes are sparkling like two diamonds. Are you glad? Very?

ANYA. Very! A new life is beginning, Mama!

GAYEV (*cheerfully*). Yes, indeed, everything is all right now. Before the cherry orchard was sold we were all worried and miserable, but afterward, when the question was finally settled once and for all, everybody calmed down and felt quite cheerful. . . . I'm in a bank now, a financier . . . cue ball into the center . . . and you, Lyuba, say what you like, you look better, no doubt about it.

LYUBOV ANDREYEVNA. Yes. My nerves are better, that's true. (*Her hat and coat are handed to her.*) I sleep well. Carry out my things, Yasha, it's time. (*To* ANYA) My little girl, we shall see each other soon. . . . I shall go to Paris and live there on the money your great-aunt sent to buy the estate—long live Auntie!—but that money won't last long.

ANYA. You'll come back soon, Mama, soon . . . won't you? I'll study hard and pass my high-school examinations, and then I can work and help you. We'll read all sorts of books together, Mama. . . . Won't we? (*Kisses her mother's hand.*) We'll read in the autumn evenings, we'll read lots of books, and a new and wonderful world will open up before us. . . . (*Dreaming*) Mama, come back. . . .

LYUBOV ANDREYEVNA. I'll come, my precious. (*Embraces her.*)

(*Enter* LOPAKHIN. CHARLOTTA IVANOVNA *is softly humming a song.*)

GAYEV. Happy Charlotta: she's singing!

CHARLOTTA (*picks up a bundle and holds it like a baby in swaddling clothes*). Bye, baby, bye. . . . (*A baby's crying is heard,* "Wah! Wah!") Be quiet, my darling, my dear little boy. ("Wah! Wah!") I'm so sorry for you! (*Throws the bundle down.*) You will find me a position, won't you? I can't go on like this.

LOPAKHIN.   We'll find something, Charlotta Ivanovna, don't worry.

GAYEV.   Everyone is leaving us, Varya's going away . . . all of a sudden nobody needs us.

CHARLOTTA.   I have nowhere to go in town. I must go away. (*Hums.*) It doesn't matter . . .

(*Enter* PISHCHIK.)

LOPAKHIN.   Nature's wonder!

PISHCHIK (*panting*).   Ugh! Let me catch my breath. . . . I'm exhausted. . . . My esteemed friends. . . . Give me some water. . . .

GAYEV.   After money, I suppose? Excuse me, I'm fleeing from temptation. . . . (*Goes out.*)

PISHCHIK.   It's a long time since I've been to see you . . . fairest lady. . . . (*To* LOPAKHIN) So you're here. . . . Glad to see you, you intellectual giant. . . . Here . . . take it . . . four hundred rubles . . . I still owe you eight hundred and forty . . .

LOPAKHIN (*shrugs his shoulders in bewilderment*).   I must be dreaming. . . . Where did you get it?

PISHCHIK.   Wait . . . I'm hot. . . . A most extraordinary event. Some Englishmen came to my place and discovered some kind of white clay on my land. (*To* LYUBOV ANDREYEVNA) And four hundred for you . . . fairest, most wonderful lady. . . . (*Hands her the money.*) The rest later. (*Takes a drink of water.*) Just now a young man in the train was saying that a certain . . . great philosopher recommends jumping off roofs. . . . "Jump!" he says, and therein lies the whole problem. (*In amazement*) Think of that, now! . . . Water!

LOPAKHIN.   Who are those Englishmen?

PISHCHIK.   I leased them the tract of land with the clay on it for twenty-four years. . . . And now, excuse me, I have no time . . . I must be trotting along . . . I'm going to Znoikov's . . . to Kardamanov's . . . I owe everybody. (*Drinks.*) Keep well . . . I'll drop in on Thursday . . .

LYUBOV ANDREYEVNA.   We're just moving into town, and tomorrow I go abroad . . .

PISHCHIK.   What? (*Alarmed*) Why into town? That's why I see the furniture . . . suitcases. . . . Well, never mind. . . . (*Through tears*) Never mind. . . . Men of the greatest intellect, those Englishmen. . . . Never mind. . . . Be happy. . . . God will help you. . . . Never mind. . . . Everything in this world comes to an end. . . . (*Kisses* LYUBOV ANDREYEVNA's *hand.*) And should the news reach you that my end has come, just remember this old horse, and say: "There once lived a certain Semyonov-Pishchik, God rest his soul." . . . Splendid weather. . . . Yes. . . . (*Goes out greatly discon-*

certed, but immediately returns and speaks from the doorway.) Dashenka sends her regards. (*Goes out.*)

LYUBOV ANDREYEVNA. Now we can go. I am leaving with two things on my mind. First—that Firs is sick. (*Looks at her watch.*) We still have about five minutes. . . .

ANYA. Mama, Firs has already been taken to the hospital. Yasha sent him there this morning.

LYUBOV ANDREYEVNA. My second concern is Varya. She's used to getting up early and working, and now, with no work to do, she's like a fish out of water. She's grown pale and thin, and cries all the time, poor girl. . . . (*Pause*) You know very well, Yermolai Alekseich, that I dreamed of marrying her to you, and everything pointed to your getting married. (*Whispers to* ANYA, *who nods to* CHARLOTTA, *and they both go out.*) She loves you, you are fond of her, and I don't know—I don't know why it is you seem to avoid each other. I can't understand it!

LOPAKHIN. To tell you the truth, I don't understand it myself. The whole thing is strange, somehow. . . . If there's still time, I'm ready right now. . . . Let's finish it up—and *basta,*° but without you I feel I'll never be able to propose to her.

LYUBOV ANDREYEVNA. Splendid! After all, it only takes a minute. I'll call her in at once. . . .

LOPAKHIN. And we even have the champagne. (*Looks at the glasses.*) Empty! Somebody's already drunk it. (YASHA *coughs.*) That's what you call lapping it up.

LYUBOV ANDREYEVNA (*animatedly*). Splendid! We'll leave you. . . . Yasha, *allez!*° I'll call her. . . . (*At the door*) Varya, leave everything and come here. Come! (*Goes out with* YASHA.)

LOPAKHIN (*looking at his watch*). Yes. . . . (*Pause*)

(*Behind the door there is smothered laughter and whispering; finally* VARYA *enters.*)

VARYA (*looking over the luggage for a long time*). Strange, I can't seem to find it . . .

LOPAKHIN. What are you looking for?

VARYA. I packed it myself, and I can't remember . . . (*Pause*)

LOPAKHIN. Where are you going now, Varya Mikhailovna?

VARYA. I? To the Ragulins'. . . . I've agreed to go there to look after the house . . . as a sort of housekeeper.

LOPAKHIN. At Yashnevo? That would be about seventy versts from here. (*Pause*) Well, life in this house has come to an end. . . .

VARYA (*examining the luggage*). Where can it be? . . . Perhaps I put it in the trunk. . . . Yes, life in this house has come to an end . . . there'll be no more . . .

basta: Italian, "enough"
allez!: French, "Let's go!"

LOPAKHIN. And I'm off for Kharkov . . . by the next train. I have a lot to do. I'm leaving Yepikhodov here . . . I've taken him on.

VARYA. Really!

LOPAKHIN. Last year at this time it was already snowing, if you remember, but now it's still and sunny. It's cold though. . . . About three degrees of frost.

VARYA. I haven't looked. (*Pause*) And besides, our thermometer's broken. (*Pause*)

(*A voice from the yard calls:* "Yermolai Alekseich!")

LOPAKHIN (*as if he had been waiting for a long time for the call*). Coming! (*Goes out quickly.*)

(VARYA *sits on the floor, lays her head on a bundle of clothes, and quietly sobs. The door opens and* LYUBOV ANDREYEVNA *enters cautiously.*)

LYUBOV ANDREYEVNA. Well? (*Pause*) We must be going.

VARYA (*no longer crying, dries her eyes*). Yes, it's time, Mama dear. I can get to the Ragulins' today, if only we don't miss the train.

LYUBOV ANDREYEVNA (*in the doorway*). Anya, put your things on!

(*Enter* ANYA, *then* GAYEV *and* CHARLOTTA IVANOVNA. GAYEV *wears a warm overcoat with a hood. The servants and coachmen come in.* YEPIKHODOV *bustles about the luggage.*)

LYUBOV ANDREYEVNA. Now we can be on our way.

ANYA (*joyfully*). On our way!

GAYEV. My friends, my dear, cherished friends! Leaving this house forever, can I pass over in silence, can I refrain from giving utterance, as we say farewell, to those feelings that now fill my whole being——

ANYA (*imploringly*). Uncle!

VARYA. Uncle dear, don't!

GAYEV (*forlornly*). Double the rail off the white to center table . . . yellow into the side pocket. . . . I'll be quiet. . . .

(*Enter* TROFIMOV, *then* LOPAKHIN.)

TROFIMOV. Well, ladies and gentlemen, it's time to go!

LOPAKHIN. Yepikhodov, my coat!

LYUBOV ANDREYEVNA. I'll sit here just one more minute. It's as though I had never before seen what the walls of this house were like, what the ceilings were like, and now I look at them hungrily, with such tender love . . .

GAYEV. I remember when I was six years old, sitting on this window sill on Whitsunday, watching my father going to church . . .

LYUBOV ANDREYEVNA. Have they taken all the things?

LOPAKHIN. Everything, I think. (*Puts on his overcoat.*) Yepikhodov, see that everything is in order.

YEPIKHODOV (*in a hoarse voice*). Rest assured, Yermolai Alekseich!

LOPAKHIN. What's the matter with your voice?

YEPIKHODOV. Just drank some water . . . must have swallowed something.

YASHA (*contemptuously*). What ignorance!

LYUBOV ANDREYEVNA. When we go—there won't be a soul left here. . . .

LOPAKHIN. Till spring.

VARYA (*pulls an umbrella out of a bundle as though she were going to hit someone;* LOPAKHIN *pretends to be frightened*). Why are you—I never thought of such a thing!

TROFIMOV. Ladies and gentlemen, let's get into the carriages—it's time now! The train will soon be in!

VARYA. Petya, there they are—your rubbers, by the suitcase. (*Tearfully*) And what dirty old things they are!

TROFIMOV (*putting on his rubbers*). Let's go, ladies and gentlemen!

GAYEV (*extremely upset, afraid of bursting into tears*). The train . . . the station. . . . Cross table to the center, double the rail . . . on the white into the corner.

LYUBOV ANDREYEVNA. Let us go!

GAYEV. Are we all here? No one in there? (*Locks the side door on the left.*) There are some things stored in there, we must lock up. Let's go!

ANYA. Good-bye, house! Good-bye, old life!

TROFIMOV. Hail to the new life! (*Goes out with* ANYA.)

(VARYA *looks around the room and slowly goes out.* YASHA *and* CHARLOTTA *with her dog go out.*)

LOPAKHIN. And so, till spring. Come along, my friends. . . . Till we meet! (*Goes out.*)

(LYUBOV ANDREYEVNA *and* GAYEV *are left alone. As though they had been waiting for this, they fall onto each other's necks and break into quiet, restrained sobs, afraid of being heard.*)

GAYEV (*in despair*). My sister, my sister. . . .

LYUBOV ANDREYEVNA. Oh, my dear, sweet, lovely orchard! . . . My life, my youth, my happiness, good-bye! . . . Good-bye!

ANYA'S VOICE (*gaily calling*). Mama!

TROFIMOV'S VOICE (*gay and excited*). Aa-oo!

LYUBOV ANDREYEVNA. One last look at these walls, these windows. . . . Mother loved to walk about in this room. . . .

GAYEV. My sister, my sister!

ANYA'S VOICE. Mama!

TROFIMOV'S VOICE. Aa-oo!

LYUBOV ANDREYEVNA. We're coming! (*They go out.*)

(*The stage is empty. There is the sound of doors being locked, then of the carriages driving away. It grows quiet. In the stillness there is the dull thud of an ax on a tree, a forlorn, melancholy sound. Footsteps are heard. From the door on the right* FIRS *appears. He is dressed as always in a jacket and white waistcoat, and wears slippers. He is ill.*)

FIRS (*goes to the door and tries the handle*).   Locked. They have gone. . . .
(*Sits down on the sofa.*) They've forgotten me . . . Never mind . . . I'll sit here
awhile. . . . I expect Leonid Andreich hasn't put on his fur coat and has gone
off in his overcoat. (*Sighs anxiously.*) And I didn't see to it. . . . When they're
young, they're green! (*Mumbles something which cannot be understood.*) I'll lie
down awhile. . . . There's no strength left in you, nothing's left, nothing. . . .
Ach, you . . . addlepate! (*Lies motionless.*)

(*A distant sound is heard that seems to come from the sky, the sound of a
snapped string mournfully dying away. A stillness falls, and nothing is heard but
the thud of the ax on a tree far away in the orchard.*)

Arthur Miller
DEATH OF A SALESMAN
Certain Private Conversations in Two Acts and a Requiem

CHARACTERS

WILLY LOMAN	CHARLEY, *a neighbor*
LINDA, *his wife*	BERNARD, *Charley's son*
BIFF ⎱ *his sons*	JENNY, *Charley's secretary*
HAPPY ⎰	STANLEY, *a waiter*
UNCLE BEN, *his older brother*	MISS FORSYTHE ⎱ *young women*
HOWARD WAGNER, *his employer*	LETTA ⎰
THE WOMAN	

The action takes place in Willy Loman's house and yard and in various places he visits in the New York and Boston of today.

ACT I

A melody is heard, played upon a flute. It is small and fine, telling of grass and trees and the horizon. The curtain rises.

Before us is the Salesman's house. We are aware of towering, angular shapes behind it, surrounding it on all sides. Only the blue light of the sky falls upon the house and forestage; the surrounding area shows an angry glow of orange. As more light appears, we see a solid vault of apartment houses around the small, fragile-seeming home. An air of the dream clings to the place, a dream rising out of reality. The kitchen at center seems actual enough, for there is a kitchen table with three chairs, and a refrigerator. But no other fixtures are seen. At the back of the kitchen there is a draped entrance, which leads to the living-room. To the right of the kitchen, on a level raised two feet, is a bedroom furnished only with a brass bedstead and a straight chair. On a shelf over the bed a silver athletic trophy stands. A window opens onto the apartment house at the side.

Behind the kitchen, on a level raised six and a half feet, is the boys' bedroom, at present barely visible. Two beds are dimly seen, and at the back of the room a dormer window. (This bedroom is above the unseen living-room.) At the left a stairway curves up to it from the kitchen.

DEATH OF A SALESMAN First performed in 1949. Arthur Miller was born in 1915 in New York City, the son of a well-to-do Jewish manufacturer whose financial losses in the depression forced a move to Brooklyn in 1929. Here Miller graduated from high school and worked in an automobile parts warehouse for two years before entering the University of Michigan, where he won three drama prizes. After graduation in 1938, he returned to Brooklyn, married, and fathered a son and daughter. *Death of a Salesman* was his third Broadway play.

The entire setting is wholly, or, in some places, partially transparent. The roof-line of the house is one-dimensional; under and over it we see the apartment buildings. Before the house lies an apron, curving beyond the forestage into the orchestra. This forward area serves as the back yard as well as the locale of all WILLY's *imaginings and of his city scenes. Whenever the action is in the present the actors observe the imaginary wall-lines, entering the house only through its door at the left. But in the scenes of the past these boundaries are broken, and characters enter or leave a room by stepping "through" a wall onto the forestage.*

From the right, WILLY LOMAN, *the Salesman, enters, carrying two large sample cases. The flute plays on. He hears but is not aware of it. He is past sixty years of age, dressed quietly. Even as he crosses the stage to the doorway of the house, his exhaustion is apparent. He unlocks the door, comes into the kitchen, and thankfully lets his burden down, feeling the soreness of his palms. A word-sigh escapes his lips—it might be "Oh, boy, oh, boy." He closes the door, then carries his cases out into the living-room, through the draped kitchen doorway.*

LINDA, *his wife, has stirred in her bed at the right. She gets out and puts on a robe, listening. Most often jovial, she has developed an iron repression of her exceptions to* WILLY's *behavior—she more than loves him, she admires him, as though his mercurial nature, his temper, his massive dreams and little cruelties, served her only as sharp reminders of the turbulent longings within him, longings which she shares but lacks the temperament to utter and follow to their end.*

LINDA (*hearing* WILLY *outside the bedroom, calls with some trepidation*). Willy!

WILLY. It's all right. I came back.

LINDA. Why? What happened? (*Slight pause*) Did something happen, Willy?

WILLY. No, nothing happened.

LINDA. You didn't smash the car, did you?

WILLY (*with casual irritation*). I said nothing happened. Didn't you hear me?

LINDA. Don't you feel well?

WILLY. I'm tired to the death. (*The flute has faded away. He sits on the bed beside her, a little numb.*) I couldn't make it. I just couldn't make it, Linda.

LINDA (*very carefully, delicately*). Where were you all day? You look terrible.

WILLY. I got as far as a little above Yonkers. I stopped for a cup of coffee. Maybe it was the coffee.

LINDA. What?

WILLY (*after a pause*). I suddenly couldn't drive any more. The car kept going off onto the shoulder, y'know?

LINDA (*helpfully*). Oh. Maybe it was the steering again. I don't think Angelo knows the Studebaker.

WILLY. No, it's me, it's me. Suddenly I realize I'm goin' sixty miles an hour and I don't remember the last five minutes. I'm—I can't seem to—keep my mind to it.

LINDA. Maybe it's your glasses. You never went for your new glasses.

WILLY. No, I see everything. I came back ten miles an hour. It took me nearly four hours from Yonkers.

LINDA (*resigned*). Well, you'll just have to take a rest, Willy, you can't continue this way.

WILLY. I just got back from Florida.

LINDA. But you didn't rest your mind. Your mind is overactive, and the mind is what counts, dear.

WILLY. I'll start out in the morning. Maybe I'll feel better in the morning. (*She is taking off his shoes.*) These goddam arch supports are killing me.

LINDA. Take an aspirin. Should I get you an aspirin? It'll soothe you.

WILLY (*with wonder*). I was driving along, you understand? And I was fine. I was even observing the scenery. You can imagine, me looking at scenery, on the road every week of my life. But it's so beautiful up there, Linda, the trees are so thick, and the sun is warm. I opened the windshield and just let the warm air bathe over me. And then all of a sudden I'm goin' off the road! I'm tellin' ya, I absolutely forgot I was driving. If I'd've gone the other way over the white line I might've killed somebody. So I went on again—and five minutes later I'm dreamin' again, and I nearly—(*He presses two fingers against his eyes.*) I have such thoughts, I have such strange thoughts.

LINDA. Willy, dear. Talk to them again. There's no reason why you can't work in New York.

WILLY. They don't need me in New York. I'm the New England man. I'm vital in New England.

LINDA. But you're sixty years old. They can't expect you to keep traveling every week.

WILLY. I'll have to send a wire to Portland. I'm supposed to see Brown and Morrison tomorrow morning at ten o'clock to show the line. Goddammit, I could sell them! (*He starts putting on his jacket.*)

LINDA (*taking the jacket from him*). Why don't you go down to the place tomorrow and tell Howard you've simply got to work in New York? You're too accommodating, dear.

WILLY. If old man Wagner was alive I'd a been in charge of New York now! That man was a prince, he was a masterful man. But that boy of his, that Howard, he don't appreciate. When I went north the first time, the Wagner Company didn't know where New England was!

LINDA. Why don't you tell those things to Howard, dear?

WILLY (*encouraged*). I will, I definitely will. Is there any cheese?

LINDA. I'll make you a sandwich.

WILLY. No, go to sleep. I'll take some milk. I'll be up right away. The boys in?

LINDA. They're sleeping. Happy took Biff on a date tonight.

WILLY (*interested*). That so?

LINDA. It was so nice to see them shaving together, one behind the other, in the bathroom. And going out together. You notice? The whole house smells of shaving lotion.

WILLY. Figure it out. Work a lifetime to pay off a house. You finally own it, and there's nobody to live in it.

LINDA. Well, dear, life is a casting off. It's always that way.

WILLY. No, no, some people—some people accomplish something. Did Biff say anything after I went this morning?

LINDA. You shouldn't have criticized him, Willy, especially after he just got off the train. You mustn't lose your temper with him.

WILLY. When the hell did I lose my temper? I simply asked him if he was making any money. Is that a criticism?

LINDA. But, dear, how could he make any money?

WILLY (*worried and angered*). There's such an undercurrent in him. He became a moody man. Did he apologize when I left this morning?

LINDA. He was crestfallen, Willy. You know how he admires you. I think if he finds himself, then you'll both be happier and not fight any more.

WILLY. How can he find himself on a farm? Is that a life? A farmhand? In the beginning, when he was young, I thought, well, a young man, it's good for him to tramp around, take a lot of different jobs. But it's more than ten years now and he has yet to make thirty-five dollars a week!

LINDA. He's finding himself, Willy.

WILLY. Not finding yourself at the age of thirty-four is a disgrace!

LINDA. Shh!

WILLY. The trouble is he's lazy, goddammit!

LINDA. Willy, please!

WILLY. Biff is a lazy bum!

LINDA. They're sleeping. Get something to eat. Go on down.

WILLY. Why did he come home? I would like to know what brought him home.

LINDA. I don't know. I think he's still lost, Willy. I think he's very lost.

WILLY. Biff Loman is lost. In the greatest country in the world a young man with such—personal attractiveness, gets lost. And such a hard worker. There's one thing about Biff—he's not lazy.

LINDA. Never.

WILLY (*with pity and resolve*). I'll see him in the morning; I'll have a nice talk with him. I'll get him a job selling. He could be big in no time. My God! Remember how they used to follow him around in high school? When he smiled at one of them their faces lit up. When he walked down the street . . . (*He loses himself in reminiscences.*)

LINDA (*trying to bring him out of it*). Willy, dear, I got a new kind of American-type cheese today. It's whipped.

WILLY. Why do you get American when I like Swiss?

LINDA. I just thought you'd like a change—

WILLY. I don't want a change! I want Swiss cheese. Why am I always being contradicted?

LINDA (*with a covering laugh*). I thought it would be a surprise.

WILLY. Why don't you open a window in here, for God's sake?

LINDA (*with infinite patience*). They're all open, dear.

WILLY. The way they boxed us in here. Bricks and windows, windows and bricks.

LINDA. We should've bought the land next door.

WILLY. The street is lined with cars. There's not a breath of fresh air in the neighborhood. The grass don't grow any more, you can't raise a carrot in the back yard. They should've had a law against apartment houses. Remember those two beautiful elm trees out there? When I and Biff hung the swing between them?

LINDA. Yeah, like being a million miles from the city.

WILLY. They should've arrested the builder for cutting those down. They massacred the neighborhood. (*Lost*) More and more I think of those days, Linda. This time of year it was lilac and wisteria. And then the peonies would come out, and the daffodils. What fragrance in this room!

LINDA. Well, after all, people had to move somewhere.

WILLY. No, there's more people now.

LINDA. I don't think there's more people. I think—

WILLY. There's more people! That's what's ruining this country! Population is getting out of control. The competition is maddening! Smell the stink from that apartment house! And another one on the other side . . . How can they whip cheese?

(*On* WILLY's *last line, Biff and Happy raise themselves up in their beds, listening.*)

LINDA. Go down, try it. And be quiet.

WILLY (*turning to* LINDA, *guiltily*). You're not worried about me, are you, sweetheart?

BIFF. What's the matter?

HAPPY. Listen!

LINDA. You've got too much on the ball to worry about.

WILLY. You're my foundation and my support, Linda.

LINDA. Just try to relax, dear. You make mountains out of molehills.

WILLY. I won't fight with him any more. If he wants to go back to Texas, let him go.

LINDA. He'll find his way.

WILLY. Sure. Certain men just don't get started till later in life. Like Thomas Edison, I think. Or B. F. Goodrich. One of them was deaf. (*He starts for the bedroom doorway.*) I'll put my money on Biff.

LINDA. And Willy—if it's warm Sunday we'll drive in the country. And we'll open the windshield, and take lunch.

WILLY. No, the windshields don't open on the new cars.

LINDA. But you opened it today.

WILLY. Me? I didn't. (*He stops.*) Now isn't that peculiar! Isn't that a remarkable—(*He breaks off in amazement and fright as the flute is heard distantly.*)

LINDA. What, darling?

WILLY. That is the most remarkable thing.

LINDA. What, dear?

WILLY. I was thinking of the Chevvy. (*Slight pause*) Nineteen twenty-eight . . . when I had that red Chevvy—(*Breaks off*) That's funny? I coulda sworn I was driving that Chevvy today.

LINDA. Well, that's nothing. Something must've reminded you.

WILLY. Remarkable. Ts. Remember those days? The way Biff used to simonize that car? The dealer refused to believe there was eighty thousand miles on it. (*He shakes his head.*) Heh! (*To* LINDA) Close your eyes, I'll be right up. (*He walks out of the bedroom.*)

HAPPY (*to* BIFF). Jesus, maybe he smashed up the car again!

LINDA (*calling after* WILLY). Be careful on the stairs, dear! The cheese is on the middle shelf! (*She turns, goes over to the bed, takes his jacket, and goes out of the bedroom.*)

(*Light has risen on the boys' room. Unseen,* WILLY *is heard talking to himself,* "Eighty-thousand miles," *and a little laugh.* BIFF *gets out of bed, comes downstage a bit, and stands attentively.* BIFF *is two years older than his brother* HAPPY, *well built, but in these days bears a worn air and seems less self-assured. He has succeeded less, and his dreams are stronger and less acceptable than* HAPPY's. HAPPY *is tall, powerfully made. Sexuality is like a visible color on him, or a scent that many women have discovered. He, like his brother, is lost, but in a different way, for he has never allowed himself to turn his face toward defeat and is thus more confused and hard-skinned, although seemingly more content.*)

HAPPY (*getting out of bed*). He's going to get his license taken away if he keeps that up. I'm getting nervous about him, y'know, Biff?

BIFF. His eyes are going.

HAPPY. No, I've driven with him. He sees all right. He just doesn't keep his mind on it. I drove into the city with him last week. He stops at a green light and then it turns red and he goes. (*He laughs.*)

BIFF. Maybe he's color-blind.

HAPPY. Pop? Why he's got the finest eye for color in the business. You know that.

BIFF (*sitting down on his bed*). I'm going to sleep.

HAPPY. You're not still sour on Dad, are you, Biff?

BIFF. He's all right, I guess.

WILLY (*underneath them, in the living-room*). Yes, sir, eighty thousand miles—eighty-two thousand!

BIFF. You smoking?

HAPPY (*holding out a pack of cigarettes*). Want one?

BIFF (*taking a cigarette*). I can never sleep when I smell it.

WILLY. What a simonizing job, heh!

HAPPY (*with deep sentiment*). Funny, Biff, y'know? Us sleeping in here again? The old beds. (*He pats his bed affectionately.*) All the talk that went across those two beds, huh? Our whole lives.

BIFF. Yeah. Lotta dreams and plans.

HAPPY (*with a deep and masculine laugh*). About five hundred women would like to know what was said in this room.

(*They share a soft laugh.*)

BIFF. Remember that big Betsy something—what the hell was her name—over on Bushwick Avenue?

HAPPY (*combing his hair*). With the collie dog!

BIFF. That's the one. I got you in there, remember?

HAPPY. Yeah, that was my first time—I think. Boy, there was a pig! (*They laugh, almost crudely.*) You taught me everything I know about women. Don't forget that.

BIFF. I bet you forgot how bashful you used to be. Especially with girls.

HAPPY. Oh, I still am, Biff.

BIFF. Oh, go on.

HAPPY. I just control it, that's all. I think I got less bashful and you got more so. What happened, Biff? Where's the old humor, the old confidence? (*He shakes* BIFF's *knee.* BIFF *gets up and moves restlessly about the room.*) What's the matter?

BIFF. Why does Dad mock me all the time?

HAPPY. He's not mocking you, he—

BIFF. Everything I say there's a twist of mockery on his face. I can't get near him.

HAPPY. He just wants you to make good, that's all. I wanted to talk to you about Dad for a long time, Biff. Something's—happening to him. He—talks to himself.

BIFF. I noticed that this morning. But he always mumbled.

HAPPY. But not so noticeable. It got so embarrassing I sent him to Florida. And you know something? Most of the time he's talking to you.

BIFF. What's he say about me?

HAPPY. I can't make it out.

BIFF. What's he say about me?

HAPPY. I think the fact that you're not settled, that you're still kind of up in the air . . .

BIFF. There's one or two other things depressing him, Happy.

HAPPY. What do you mean?

BIFF. Never mind. Just don't lay it all to me.

HAPPY. But I think if you just got started—I mean—is there any future for you out there?

BIFF. I'll tell ya, Hap, I don't know what the future is. I don't know—what I'm supposed to want.

HAPPY. What do you mean?

BIFF. Well, I spent six or seven years after high school trying to work myself up. Shipping clerk, salesman, business of one kind or another. And it's a measly manner of existence. To get on that subway on the hot mornings in summer. To devote your whole life to keeping stock, or making phone calls, or selling or buying. To suffer fifty weeks of the year for the sake of a two-week vacation, when all you really desire is to be outdoors, with your shirt off. And always to have to get ahead of the next fella. And still—that's how you build a future.

HAPPY. Well, you really enjoy it on a farm? Are you content out there?

BIFF (*with rising agitation*). Hap, I've had twenty or thirty different kinds of jobs since I left home before the war, and it always turns out the same. I just realized it lately. In Nebraska when I herded cattle, and the Dakotas, and Arizona, and now in Texas. It's why I came home now, I guess, because I realized it. This farm I work on, it's spring there now, see? And they've got about fifteen new colts. There's nothing more inspiring or—beautiful than the sight of a mare and a new colt. And it's cool there now, see? Texas is cool now, and it's spring. And whenever spring comes to where I am, I suddenly get the feeling, my God, I'm not gettin' anywhere! What the hell am I doing, playing around with horses, twenty-eight dollars a week! I'm thirty-four years old, I oughta be makin' my future. That's when I come running home. And now, I get here, and I don't know what to do with myself. (*After a pause*) I've always made a point of not wasting my life, and everytime I come back here I know that all I've done is to waste my life.

HAPPY. You're a poet, you know that, Biff? You're a—you're an idealist!

BIFF. No, I'm mixed up very bad. Maybe I oughta get married. Maybe I oughta get stuck into something. Maybe that's my trouble. I'm like a boy. I'm not married, I'm not in business, I just—I'm like a boy. Are you content, Hap? You're a success, aren't you? Are you content?

HAPPY. Hell, no!

BIFF. Why? You're making money, aren't you?

HAPPY (*moving about with energy, expressiveness*). All I can do now is wait for the merchandise manager to die. And suppose I get to be merchandise manager? He's a good friend of mine, and he just built a terrific estate on Long Island. And he lived there about two months and sold it, and now he's building another one. He can't enjoy it once it's finished. And I know that's just what I would do. I don't know what the hell I'm workin' for. Sometimes I sit in my apartment—all alone. And I think of the rent I'm paying. And it's crazy. But then, it's what I always wanted. My own apartment, a car, and plenty of women. And still, goddammit, I'm lonely.

BIFF (*with enthusiasm*). Listen, why don't you come out West with me?

HAPPY. You and I, heh?

BIFF. Sure, maybe we could buy a ranch. Raise cattle, use our muscles. Men built like we are should be working out in the open.

HAPPY (*avidly*). The Loman Brothers, heh?

BIFF (*with vast affection*). Sure, we'd be known all over the counties!

HAPPY (*enthralled*). That's what I dream about, Biff. Sometimes I want to just rip my clothes off in the middle of the store and outbox that goddam merchandise manager. I mean I can outbox, outrun, and outlift anybody in that store, and I have to take orders from those common, petty sons-of-bitches till I can't stand it any more.

BIFF. I'm tellin' you, kid, if you were with me I'd be happy out there.

HAPPY (*enthused*). See, Biff, everybody around me is so false that I'm constantly lowering my ideals . . .

BIFF. Baby, together we'd stand up for one another, we'd have someone to trust.

HAPPY. If I were around you—

BIFF. Hap, the trouble is we weren't brought up to grub for money. I don't know how to do it.

HAPPY. Neither can I!

BIFF. Then let's go!

HAPPY. The only thing is—what can you make out there?

BIFF. But look at your friend. Builds an estate and then hasn't the peace of mind to live in it.

HAPPY. Yeah, but when he walks into the store the waves part in front of him. That's fifty-two thousand dollars a year coming through the revolving door, and I got more in my pinky finger than he's got in his head.

BIFF. Yeah, but you just said—

HAPPY. I gotta show some of those pompous, self-important executives over there that Hap Loman can make the grade. I want to walk into the store the way he walks in. Then I'll go with you, Biff. We'll be together yet, I swear. But take those two we had tonight. Now weren't they gorgeous creatures?

BIFF. Yeah, yeah, most gorgeous I've had in years.

HAPPY. I get that any time I want, Biff. Whenever I feel disgusted. The only trouble is, it gets like bowling or something. I just keep knockin' them over and it doesn't mean anything. You still run around a lot?

BIFF. Naa. I'd like to find a girl—steady, somebody with substance.

HAPPY. That's what I long for.

BIFF. Go on! You'd never come home.

HAPPY. I would! Somebody with character, with resistance! Like Mom, y'know? You're gonna call me a bastard when I tell you this. That girl Charlotte I was with tonight is engaged to be married in five weeks. (*He tries on his new hat.*)

BIFF. No kiddin'!

HAPPY. Sure, the guy's in line for the vice-presidency of the store. I don't know what gets into me, maybe I just have an overdeveloped sense of competition or something, but I went and ruined her, and furthermore I can't get rid of her. And he's the third executive I've done that to. Isn't that a crummy characteristic? And to top it all, I go to their weddings! (*Indignantly, but laughing*) Like I'm not supposed to take bribes. Manufacturers offer me a hundred-dollar bill now and then to throw an order their way. You know how honest I am, but it's like this girl, see. I hate myself for it. Because I don't want the girl, and, still, I take it and—I love it!

BIFF. Let's go to sleep.

HAPPY. I guess we didn't settle anything, heh?

BIFF. I just got one idea that I think I'm going to try.

HAPPY. What's that?

BIFF. Remember Bill Oliver?

HAPPY. Sure, Oliver is very big now. You want to work for him again?

BIFF. No, but when I quit he said something to me. He put his arm on my shoulder, and he said, "Biff, if you ever need anything, come to me."

HAPPY. I remember that. That sounds good.

BIFF. I think I'll go to see him. If I could get ten thousand or even seven or eight thousand dollars I could buy a beautiful ranch.

HAPPY. I bet he'd back you. 'Cause he thought highly of you, Biff. I mean, they all do. You're well liked, Biff. That's why I say to come back here, and we both have the apartment. And I'm tellin' you, Biff, any babe you want . . .

BIFF. No, with a ranch I could do the work I like and still be something. I just wonder though. I wonder if Oliver still thinks I stole that carton of basketballs.

HAPPY. Oh, he probably forgot that long ago. It's almost ten years. You're too sensitive. Anyway, he didn't really fire you.

BIFF. Well, I think he was going to. I think that's why I quit. I was never sure whether he knew or not. I know he thought the world of me, though. I was the only one he'd let lock up the place.

WILLY (*below*). You gonna wash the engine, Biff?

HAPPY. Shh!

(BIFF *looks at* HAPPY, *who is gazing down, listening.* WILLY *is mumbling in the parlor.*)

HAPPY. You hear that?

(*They listen.* WILLY *laughs warmly.*)

BIFF (*growing angry*). Doesn't he know Mom can hear that?

WILLY. Don't get your sweater dirty, Biff!

(*A look of pain crosses* BIFF'S *face.*)

HAPPY. Isn't that terrible? Don't leave again, will you? You'll find a job here. You gotta stick around. I don't know what to do about him, it's getting embarrassing.

WILLY. What a simonizing job!

BIFF. Mom's hearing that!

WILLY. No kiddin', Biff, you got a date? Wonderful!

HAPPY. Go on to sleep. But talk to him in the morning, will you?

BIFF (*reluctantly getting into bed*). With her in the house. Brother!

HAPPY (*getting into bed*). I wish you'd have a good talk with him.

(*The light on their room begins to fade.*)

BIFF (*to himself in bed*). That selfish, stupid . . .
HAPPY. Sh . . . Sleep, Biff.

(*Their light is out. Well before they have finished speaking,* WILLY'*s form is dimly seen below in the darkened kitchen. He opens the refrigerator, searches in there, and takes out a bottle of milk. The apartment houses are fading out, and the entire house and surroundings become covered with leaves. Music insinuates itself as the leaves appear.*)

WILLY. Just wanna be careful with those girls, Biff, that's all. Don't make any promises. No promises of any kind. Because a girl, y'know, they always believe what you tell 'em, and you're very young, Biff, you're too young to be talking seriously to girls.

(*Light rises on the kitchen.* WILLY, *talking, shuts the refrigerator door and comes downstage to the kitchen table. He pours milk into a glass. He is totally immersed in himself, smiling faintly.*)

WILLY. Too young entirely, Biff. You want to watch your schooling first. Then when you're all set, there'll be plenty of girls for a boy like you. (*He smiles broadly at a kitchen chair.*) That so? The girls pay for you? (*He laughs.*) Boy, you must really be makin' a hit.

(WILLY *is gradually addressing—physically—a point offstage, speaking through the wall of the kitchen, and his voice has been rising in volume to that of a normal conversation.*)

WILLY. I been wondering why you polish the car so careful. Ha! Don't leave the hubcaps, boys. Get the chamois to the hubcaps. Happy, use newspaper on the windows, it's the easiest thing. Show him how to do it, Biff! You see, Happy? Pad it up, use it like a pad. That's it, that's it, good work. You're doin' all right, Hap. (*He pauses, then nods in approbation for a few seconds, then looks upward.*) Biff, first thing we gotta do when we get time is clip that big branch over the house. Afraid it's gonna fall in a storm and hit the roof. Tell you what. We get a rope and sling her around, and then we climb up there with a couple of saws and take her down. Soon as you finish the car, boys, I wanna see ya. I got a surprise for you, boys.
BIFF (*offstage*). Whatta ya got, Dad?
WILLY. No, you finish first. Never leave a job till you're finished—remember that. (*Looking toward the "big trees"*) Biff, up in Albany I saw a beautiful hammock. I think I'll buy it next trip, and we'll hang it right between those two elms. Wouldn't that be something? Just swingin' there under those branches. Boy, that would be . . .

(YOUNG BIFF *and* YOUNG HAPPY *appear from the direction* WILLY *was addressing.* HAPPY *carries rags and a pail of water.* BIFF, *wearing a sweater with a block "S," carries a football.*)

BIFF (*pointing in the direction of the car offstage*). How's that, Pop, professional?

WILLY. Terrific. Terrific job, boys. Good work, Biff.

HAPPY. Where's the surprise, Pop?

WILLY. In the back seat of the car.

HAPPY. Boy! (*He runs off.*)

BIFF. What is it, Dad? Tell me, what'd you buy?

WILLY (*laughing, cuffs him*). Never mind, something I want you to have.

BIFF (*turns and starts off*). What is it, Hap?

HAPPY (*offstage*). It's a punching bag!

BIFF. Oh, Pop!

WILLY. It's got Gene Tunney's signature on it!

(HAPPY *runs onstage with a punching bag.*)

BIFF. Gee, how'd you know we wanted a punching bag?

WILLY. Well, it's the finest thing for the timing.

HAPPY (*lies down on his back and pedals with his feet*). I'm losing weight, you notice, Pop?

WILLY (*to* HAPPY). Jumping rope is good too.

BIFF. Did you see the new football I got?

WILLY (*examining the ball*). Where'd you get a new ball?

BIFF. The coach told me to practice my passing.

WILLY. That so? And he gave you the ball, heh?

BIFF. Well, I borrowed it from the locker room. (*He laughs confidentially.*)

WILLY (*laughing with him at the theft*). I want you to return that.

HAPPY. I told you he wouldn't like it!

BIFF (*angrily*). Well, I'm bringing it back!

WILLY (*stopping the incipient argument, to* HAPPY). Sure, he's gotta practice with a regulation ball, doesn't he? (*To* BIFF) Coach'll probably congratulate you on your initiative!

BIFF. Oh, he keeps congratulating my initiative all the time, Pop.

WILLY. That's because he likes you. If somebody else took that ball there'd be an uproar. So what's the report, boys, what's the report?

BIFF. Where'd you go this time, Dad? Gee, we were lonesome for you.

WILLY (*pleased, puts an arm around each boy and they come down to the apron*). Lonesome, heh?

BIFF. Missed you every minute.

WILLY. Don't say? Tell you a secret, boys. Don't breathe it to a soul. Someday I'll have my own business, and I'll never have to leave home any more.

HAPPY. Like Uncle Charley, heh?

WILLY. Bigger than Uncle Charley! Because Charley is not—liked. He's liked, but he's not—well liked.

BIFF. Where'd you go this time, Dad?

WILLY. Well, I got on the road, and I went north to Providence. Met the Mayor.

BIFF. The Mayor of Providence!

WILLY. He was sitting in the hotel lobby.

BIFF. What'd he say?

WILLY. He said, "Morning!" And I said, "You got a fine city here, Mayor." And then he had coffee with me. And then I went to Waterbury. Waterbury is a fine city. Big clock city, the famous Waterbury clock. Sold a nice bill there. And then Boston—Boston is the cradle of the Revolution. A fine city. And a couple of other towns in Mass., and on to Portland and Bangor and straight home!

BIFF. Gee, I'd love to go with you sometime, Dad.

WILLY. Soon as summer comes.

HAPPY. Promise?

WILLY. You and Hap and I, and I'll show you all the towns. America is full of beautiful towns and fine, upstanding people. And they know me, boys, they know me up and down New England. The finest people. And when I bring you fellas up, there'll be open sesame for all of us, 'cause one thing, boys: I have friends. I can park my car in any street in New England, and the cops protect it like their own. This summer, heh?

BIFF *and* HAPPY (*together*). Yeah! You bet!

WILLY. We'll take our bathing suits.

HAPPY. We'll carry your bags, Pop!

WILLY. Oh, won't that be something! Me comin' into the Boston stores with you boys carryin' my bags. What a sensation!

(BIFF *is prancing around, practicing passing the ball.*)

WILLY. You nervous, Biff, about the game?

BIFF. Not if you're gonna be there.

WILLY. What do they say about you in school, now that they made you captain?

HAPPY. There's a crowd of girls behind him everytime the classes change.

BIFF (*taking* WILLY's *hand*). This Saturday, Pop, this Saturday—just for you, I'm going to break through for a touchdown.

HAPPY. You're supposed to pass.

BIFF. I'm takin' one play for Pop. You watch me, Pop, and when I take off my helmet, that means I'm breakin' out. Then you watch me crash through that line!

WILLY (*kisses* BIFF). Oh, wait'll I tell this in Boston!

(BERNARD *enters in knickers. He is younger than* BIFF, *earnest and loyal, a worried boy.*)

BERNARD. Biff, where are you? You're supposed to study with me today.

WILLY. Hey, looka Bernard. What're you lookin' so anemic about, Bernard?

BERNARD. He's gotta study, Uncle Willy. He's got Regents° next week.

HAPPY (*tauntingly, spinning* BERNARD *around*). Let's box, Bernard!

BERNARD. Biff! (*He gets away from* HAPPY.) Listen, Biff, I heard Mr. Birnbaum say that if you don't start studyin' math he's gonna flunk you, and you won't graduate. I heard him!

WILLY. You better study with him, Biff. Go ahead now.

BERNARD. I heard him!

BIFF. Oh, Pop, you didn't see my sneakers! (*He holds up a foot for* WILLY *to look at.*)

WILLY. Hey, that's a beautiful job of printing!

BERNARD (*wiping his glasses*). Just because he printed University of Virginia on his sneakers doesn't mean they've got to graduate him. Uncle Willy!

WILLY (*angrily*). What're you talking about? With scholarships to three universities they're gonna flunk him?

BERNARD. But I heard Mr. Birnbaum say—

WILLY. Don't be a pest, Bernard! (*To his boys*) What an anemic!

BERNARD. Okay, I'm waiting for you in my house, Biff.

(BERNARD *goes off. The* LOMANS *laugh.*)

WILLY. Bernard is not well liked, is he?

BIFF. He's liked, but he's not well liked.

HAPPY. That's right, Pop.

WILLY. That's just what I mean. Bernard can get the best marks in school, y'understand, but when he gets out in the business world, y'understand, you are going to be five times ahead of him. That's why I thank Almighty God you're both built like Adonises. Because the man who makes an appearance in the business world, the man who creates personal interest, is the man who gets ahead. Be liked and you will never want. You take me, for instance. I never have to wait in line to see a buyer. "Willy Loman is here!" That's all they have to know, and I go right through.

BIFF. Did you knock them dead, Pop?

WILLY. Knocked 'em cold in Providence, slaughtered 'em in Boston.

HAPPY (*on his back, pedaling again*). I'm losing weight, you notice, Pop?

(LINDA *enters, as of old, a ribbon in her hair, carrying a basket of washing.*)

LINDA (*with youthful energy*). Hello, dear!

WILLY. Sweetheart!

LINDA. How'd the Chevvy run?

WILLY. Chevrolet, Linda, is the greatest car ever built. (*To the* BOYS) Since when do you let your mother carry wash up the stairs?

Regents: a statewide proficiency examination administered in New York high schools

BIFF. Grab hold there, boy!

HAPPY. Where to, Mom?

LINDA. Hang them up on the line. And you better go down to your friends, Biff. The cellar is full of boys. They don't know what to do with themselves.

BIFF. Ah, when Pop comes home they can wait!

WILLY (*laughs appreciatively*). You better go down and tell them what to do, Biff.

BIFF. I think I'll have them sweep out the furnace room.

WILLY. Good work, Biff.

BIFF (*goes through wall-line of kitchen to doorway at back and calls down*). Fellas! Everybody sweep out the furnace room! I'll be right down!

VOICES. All right! Okay, Biff.

BIFF. George and Sam and Frank, come out back! We're hangin' up the wash! Come on, Hap, on the double! (*He and* HAPPY *carry out the basket.*)

LINDA. The way they obey him!

WILLY. Well, that's training, the training. I'm tellin' you, I was sellin' thousands and thousands, but I had to come home.

LINDA. Oh, the whole block'll be at that game. Did you sell anything?

WILLY. I did five hundred gross in Providence and seven hundred gross in Boston.

LINDA. No! Wait a minute, I've got a pencil. (*She pulls pencil and paper out of her apron pocket.*) That makes your commission . . . Two hundred—my God! Two hundred and twelve dollars!

WILLY. Well, I didn't figure it yet, but . . .

LINDA. How much did you do?

WILLY. Well, I—I did—about a hundred and eighty gross in Providence. Well no—it came to—roughly two hundred gross on the whole trip.

LINDA (*without hesitation*). Two hundred gross. That's . . . (*She figures.*)

WILLY. The trouble was that three of the stores were half closed for inventory in Boston. Otherwise I woulda broke records.

LINDA. Well, it makes seventy dollars and some pennies. That's very good.

WILLY. What do we owe?

LINDA. Well, on the first there's sixteen dollars on the refrigerator—

WILLY. Why sixteen?

LINDA. Well, the fan belt broke, so it was a dollar eighty.

WILLY. But it's brand new.

LINDA. Well, the man said that's the way it is. Till they work themselves in, y'know.

(*They move through the wall-line into the kitchen.*)

WILLY. I hope we didn't get stuck on that machine.

LINDA. They got the biggest ads of any of them!

WILLY. I know, it's a fine machine. What else?

LINDA. Well, there's nine-sixty for the washing machine. And for the vacuum cleaner there's three and a half due on the fifteenth. Then the roof, you got twenty-one dollars remaining.

WILLY. It don't leak, does it?

LINDA. No, they did a wonderful job. Then you owe Frank for the carburetor.

WILLY. I'm not going to pay that man! That goddam Chevrolet, they ought to prohibit the manufacture of that car!

LINDA. Well, you owe him three and a half. And odds and ends, comes to around a hundred and twenty dollars by the fifteenth.

WILLY. A hundred and twenty dollars! My God, if business don't pick up I don't know what I'm gonna do!

LINDA. Well, next week you'll do better.

WILLY. Oh, I'll knock 'em dead next week. I'll go to Hartford. I'm very well liked in Hartford. You know, the trouble is, Linda, people don't seem to take to me.

(*They move onto the forestage.*)

LINDA. Oh, don't be foolish.

WILLY. I know it when I walk in. They seem to laugh at me.

LINDA. Why? Why would they laugh at you? Don't talk that way, Willy.

(WILLY *moves to the edge of the stage.* LINDA *goes into the kitchen and starts to darn stockings.*)

WILLY. I don't know the reason for it, but they just pass me by. I'm not noticed.

LINDA. But you're doing wonderful, dear. You're making seventy to a hundred dollars a week.

WILLY. But I gotta be at it ten, twelve hours a day. Other men—I don't know—they do it easier. I don't know why—I can't stop myself—I talk too much. A man oughta come in with a few words. One thing about Charley. He's a man of few words, and they respect him.

LINDA. You don't talk too much, you're just lively.

WILLY (*smiling*). Well, I figure, what the hell, life is short, a couple of jokes. (*To himself*) I joke too much! (*The smile goes.*)

LINDA. Why? You're—

WILLY. I'm fat. I'm very—foolish to look at, Linda. I didn't tell you, but Christmas time I happened to be calling on F. H. Stewarts, and a salesman I know, as I was going in to see the buyer I heard him say something about—walrus. And I—I cracked him right across the face. I won't take that. I simply will not take that. But they do laugh at me. I know that.

LINDA. Darling . . .

WILLY. I gotta overcome it. I know I gotta overcome it. I'm not dressing to advantage, maybe.

LINDA. Willy, darling, you're the handsomest man in the world—

WILLY. Oh, no, Linda.

LINDA. To me you are. (*Slight pause*) The handsomest.

(*From the darkness is heard the laughter of a woman.* WILLY *doesn't turn to it, but it continues through* LINDA'S *lines.*)

LINDA. And the boys, Willy. Few men are idolized by their children the way you are.

(*Music is heard as behind a scrim, to the left of the house,* THE WOMAN, *dimly seen, is dressing.*)

WILLY (*with great feeling*). You're the best there is, Linda, you're a pal, you know that? On the road—on the road I want to grab you sometimes and just kiss the life outa you.

(*The laughter is loud now, and he moves into a brightening area at the left, where* THE WOMAN *has come from behind the scrim and is standing, putting on her hat, looking into a "mirror" and laughing.*)

WILLY. 'Cause I get so lonely—especially when business is bad and there's nobody to talk to. I get the feeling that I'll never sell anything again, that I won't make a living for you, or a business, a business for the boys. (*He talks through* THE WOMAN's *subsiding laughter;* THE WOMAN *primps at the "mirror."*) There's so much I want to make for—

THE WOMAN. Me? You didn't make me, Willy. I picked you.

WILLY (*pleased*). You picked me?

THE WOMAN (*who is quite proper-looking,* WILLY's *age*). I did. I've been sitting at that desk watching all the salesmen go by, day in, day out. But you've got such a sense of humor, and we do have such a good time together, don't we?

WILLY. Sure, sure. (*He takes her in his arms.*) Why do you have to go now?

THE WOMAN. It's two o'clock . . .

WILLY. No, come on in! (*He pulls her.*)

THE WOMAN. . . . my sisters'll be scandalized. When'll you be back?

WILLY. Oh, two weeks about. Will you come up again?

THE WOMAN. Sure thing. You do make me laugh. It's good for me. (*She squeezes his arm, kisses him.*) And I think you're a wonderful man.

WILLY. You picked me, heh?

THE WOMAN. Sure. Because you're so sweet. And such a kidder.

WILLY. Well, I'll see you next time I'm in Boston.

THE WOMAN. I'll put you right through to the buyers.

WILLY (*slapping her bottom*). Right. Well, bottoms up!

THE WOMAN (*slaps him gently and laughs*). You just kill me, Willy. (*He suddenly grabs her and kisses her roughly.*) You kill me. And thanks for the stockings. I love a lot of stockings. Well, good night.

WILLY. Good night. And keep your pores open!

THE WOMAN. Oh, Willy!

(THE WOMAN *bursts out laughing, and* LINDA's *laughter blends in.* THE WOMAN *disappears into the dark. Now the area at the kitchen table brightens.* LINDA *is sitting where she was at the kitchen table, but now is mending a pair of her silk stockings.*)

LINDA. You are, Willy. The handsomest man. You've got no reason to feel that—

WILLY (*coming out of* THE WOMAN's *dimming area and going over to* LINDA). I'll make it all up to you, Linda, I'll—

LINDA. There's nothing to make up, dear. You're doing fine, better than—

WILLY (*noticing her mending*). What's that?

LINDA. Just mending my stockings. They're so expensive—

WILLY (*angrily, taking them from her*). I won't have you mending stockings in this house! Now throw them out!

(LINDA *puts the stockings in her pocket.*)

BERNARD (*entering on the run*). Where is he? If he doesn't study!

WILLY (*moving to the forestage, with great agitation*). You'll give him the answers!

BERNARD. I do, but I can't on a Regents! That's a state exam! They're liable to arrest me!

WILLY. Where is he? I'll whip him, I'll whip him!

LINDA. And he'd better give back that football, Willy, it's not nice.

WILLY. Biff! Where is he? Why is he taking everything?

LINDA. He's too rough with the girls, Willy. All the mothers are afraid of him!

WILLY. I'll whip him!

BERNARD. He's driving the car without a license!

(THE WOMAN's *laugh is heard.*)

WILLY. Shut up!

LINDA. All the mothers—

WILLY. Shut up!

BERNARD (*backing quietly away and out*). Mr. Birnbaum says he's stuck up.

WILLY. Get outa here!

BERNARD. If he doesn't buckle down he'll flunk math! (*He goes off.*)

LINDA. He's right, Willy, you've gotta—

WILLY (*exploding at her*). There's nothing the matter with him! You want him to be a worm like Bernard? He's got spirit, personality . . .

(*As he speaks,* LINDA, *almost in tears, exits into the living-room.* WILLY *is alone in the kitchen, wilting and staring. The leaves are gone. It is night again, and the apartment houses look down from behind.*)

WILLY. Loaded with it. Loaded! What is he stealing? He's giving it back, isn't he? Why is he stealing? What did I tell him? I never in my life told him anything but decent things.

(HAPPY *in pajamas has come down the stairs;* WILLY *suddenly becomes aware of* HAPPY's *presence.*)

HAPPY. Let's go now, come on.

WILLY (*sitting down at the kitchen table*). Huh! Why did she have to wax the floors herself? Everytime she waxes the floors she keels over. She knows that!

HAPPY. Shh! Take it easy. What brought you back tonight?

WILLY. I got an awful scare. Nearly hit a kid in Yonkers. God! Why didn't I go to Alaska with my brother Ben that time! Ben! That man was a genius, that man was success incarnate! What a mistake! He begged me to go.

HAPPY. Well, there's no use in—

WILLY. You guys! There was a man started with the clothes on his back and ended up with diamond mines!

HAPPY. Boy, someday I'd like to know how he did it.

WILLY. What's the mystery? The man knew what he wanted and went out and got it! Walked into a jungle, and comes out, the age of twenty-one, and he's rich! The world is an oyster, but you don't crack it open on a mattress.

HAPPY. Pop, I told you I'm gonna retire you for life.

WILLY. You'll retire me for life on seventy goddam dollars a week? And your women and your car and your apartment, and you'll retire me for life! Christ's sake, I couldn't get past Yonkers today! Where are you guys, where are you? The woods are burning! I can't drive a car!

(CHARLEY *has appeared in the doorway. He is a large man, slow of speech, laconic, immovable. In all he says, despite what he says, there is pity, and, now, trepidation. He has a robe over pajamas, slippers on his feet. He enters the kitchen.*)

CHARLEY. Everything all right?

HAPPY. Yeah, Charley, everything's . . .

WILLY. What's the matter?

CHARLEY. I heard some noise. I thought something happened. Can't we do something about the walls? You sneeze in here, and in my house hats blow off.

HAPPY. Let's go to bed, Dad. Come on.

(CHARLEY *signals to* HAPPY *to go.*)

WILLY. You go ahead, I'm not tired at the moment.

HAPPY (*to* WILLY). Take it easy, huh? (*He exits.*)

WILLY. What're you doin' up?

CHARLEY (*sitting down at the kitchen table opposite* WILLY). Couldn't sleep good. I had a heartburn.

WILLY. Well, you don't know how to eat.

CHARLEY. I eat with my mouth.

WILLY. No, you're ignorant. You gotta know about vitamins and things like that.

CHARLEY. Come on, let's shoot. Tire you out a little.

WILLY (*hesitantly*). All right. You got cards?

CHARLEY (*taking a deck from his pocket*). Yeah, I got them. Someplace. What is it with those vitamins?

WILLY (*dealing*). They build up your bones. Chemistry.

CHARLEY. Yeah, but there's no bones in a heartburn.

WILLY. What are you talkin' about? Do you know the first thing about it?

CHARLEY. Don't get insulted.

WILLY. Don't talk about something you don't know anything about.

(*They are playing. Pause.*)

CHARLEY. What're you doin' home?

WILLY. A little trouble with the car.

CHARLEY. Oh. (*Pause*) I'd like to take a trip to California.

WILLY. Don't say.

CHARLEY. You want a job?

WILLY. I got a job, I told you that. (*After a slight pause*) What the hell are you offering me a job for?

CHARLEY. Don't get insulted.

WILLY. Don't insult me.

CHARLEY. I don't see no sense in it. You don't have to go on this way.

WILLY. I got a good job. (*Slight pause*) What do you keep comin' in here for?

CHARLEY. You want me to go?

WILLY (*after a pause, withering*). I can't understand it. He's going back to Texas again. What the hell is that?

CHARLEY. Let him go.

WILLY. I got nothin' to give him, Charley, I'm clean, I'm clean.

CHARLEY. He won't starve. None a them starve. Forget about him.

WILLY. Then what have I got to remember?

CHARLEY. You take it too hard. To hell with it. When a deposit bottle is broken you don't get your nickel back.

WILLY. That's easy enough for you to say.

CHARLEY. That ain't easy for me to say.

WILLY. Did you see the ceiling I put up in the living room?

CHARLEY. Yeah, that's a piece of work. To put up a ceiling is a mystery to me. How do you do it?

WILLY. What's the difference?

CHARLEY. Well, talk about it.

WILLY. You gonna put up a ceiling?

CHARLEY. How could I put up a ceiling?

WILLY. Then what the hell are you bothering me for?

CHARLEY. You're insulted again.

WILLY. A man who can't handle tools is not a man. You're disgusting.

CHARLEY. Don't call me disgusting, Willy

(UNCLE BEN, *carrying a valise and an umbrella, enters the forestage from around the right corner of the house. He is a stolid man, in his sixties, with a mustache and an authoritative air. He is utterly certain of his destiny, and there is an aura of far places about him. He enters exactly as* WILLY *speaks.*)

WILLY. I'm getting awfully tired, Ben.

(BEN*'s music is heard.* BEN *looks around at everything.*)

CHARLEY. Good, keep playing; you'll sleep better. Did you call me Ben?

(BEN *looks at his watch.*)

WILLY. That's funny. For a second there you reminded me of my brother Ben.

BEN. I only have a few minutes.

(*He strolls, inspecting the place.* WILLY *and* CHARLEY *continue playing.*)

CHARLEY. You never heard from him again, heh? Since that time?

WILLY. Didn't Linda tell you? Couple of weeks ago we got a letter from his wife in Africa. He died.

CHARLEY. That so.

BEN (*chuckling*). So this is Brooklyn, eh?

CHARLEY. Maybe you're in for some of his money.

WILLY. Naa, he had seven sons. There's just one opportunity I had with that man . . .

BEN. I must make a train, William. There are several properties I'm looking at in Alaska.

WILLY. Sure, sure! If I'd gone with him to Alaska that time, everything would've been totally different.

CHARLEY. Go on, you'd froze to death up there.

WILLY. What're you talking about?

BEN. Opportunity is tremendous in Alaska, William. Surprised you're not up there.

WILLY. Sure, tremendous.

CHARLEY. Heh?

WILLY. There was the only man I ever met who knew the answers.

CHARLEY. Who?

BEN. How are you all?

WILLY (*taking a pot, smiling*). Fine, fine.

CHARLEY. Pretty sharp tonight.

BEN. Is Mother living with you?

WILLY. No, she died a long time ago.

CHARLEY. Who?

BEN. That's too bad. Fine specimen of a lady, Mother.

WILLY (*to* CHARLEY). Heh?

BEN. I'd hoped to see the old girl.

CHARLEY. Who died?

BEN. Heard anything from Father, have you?

WILLY (*unnerved*). What do you mean, who died?

CHARLEY (*taking a pot*). What're you talkin' about?

BEN (*looking at his watch*). William, it's half-past eight!

WILLY (*as though to dispel his confusion he angrily stops* CHARLEY'*s hand*). That's my build!

CHARLEY. I put the ace—

WILLY. If you don't know how to play the game I'm not gonna throw my money away on you!

CHARLEY (*rising*). It was my ace, for God's sake!

WILLY. I'm through, I'm through!

BEN. When did Mother die?

WILLY. Long ago. Since the beginning you never knew how to play cards.

CHARLEY (*picks up the cards and goes to the door*). All right! Next time I'll bring a deck with five aces.

WILLY. I don't play that kind of game!

CHARLEY (*turning to him*). You ought to be ashamed of yourself!

WILLY. Yeah?

CHARLEY. Yeah! (*He goes out.*)

WILLY (*slamming the door after him*). Ignoramus!

BEN (*as* WILLY *comes toward him through the wall-line of the kitchen*). So you're William.

WILLY (*shaking* BEN'*s hand*). Ben! I've been waiting for you so long! What's the answer? How did you do it?

BEN. Oh, there's a story in that.

(LINDA *enters the forestage, as of old, carrying the wash basket.*)

LINDA. Is this Ben?

BEN (*gallantly*). How do you do, my dear.

LINDA. Where've you been all these years? Willy's always wondered why you—

WILLY (*pulling* BEN *away from her impatiently*). Where is Dad? Didn't you follow him? How did you get started?

BEN. Well, I don't know how much you remember.

WILLY. Well, I was just a baby, of course, only three or four years old—

BEN. Three years and eleven months.

WILLY. What a memory, Ben!

BEN. I have many enterprises, William, and I have never kept books.

WILLY. I remember I was sitting under the wagon in—was it Nebraska?

BEN. It was South Dakota, and I gave you a bunch of wild flowers.

WILLY. I remember you walking away down some open road.

BEN (*laughing*). I was going to find Father in Alaska.

WILLY. Where is he?

BEN. At that age I had a very faulty view of geography, William. I discovered after a few days that I was heading due south, so instead of Alaska, I ended up in Africa.

LINDA. Africa!

WILLY. The Gold Coast!

BEN. Principally diamond mines.

LINDA. Diamond mines!

BEN. Yes, my dear. But I've only a few minutes—

WILLY. No! Boys! Boys! (YOUNG BIFF *and* HAPPY *appear.*) Listen to this. This is your Uncle Ben, a great man! Tell my boys, Ben!

BEN. Why, boys, when I was seventeen I walked into the jungle, and when I was twenty-one I walked out. (*He laughs.*) And by God I was rich.

WILLY (*to the boys*). You see what I been talking about? The greatest things can happen!

BEN (*glancing at his watch*). I have an appointment in Ketchikan Tuesday week.

WILLY. No, Ben! Please tell about Dad. I want my boys to hear. I want them to know the kind of stock they spring from. All I remember is a man with a big beard, and I was in Mamma's lap, sitting around a fire, and some kind of high music.

BEN. His flute. He played the flute.

WILLY. Sure, the flute, that's right!

(*New music is heard, a high, rollicking tune.*)

BEN. Father was a very great and a very wild-hearted man. We would start in Boston, and he'd toss the whole family into the wagon, and then he'd drive the team right across the country; through Ohio, and Indiana, Michigan, Illinois, and all the Western states. And we'd stop in the towns and sell the flutes that he'd made on the way. Great inventor, Father. With one gadget he made more in a week than a man like you could make in a lifetime.

WILLY. That's just the way I'm bringing them up, Ben—rugged, well liked, all-around.

BEN. Yeah? (*To* BIFF) Hit that, boy—hard as you can. (*He pounds his stomach.*)

BIFF. Oh, no, sir!

BEN (*taking boxing stance*). Come on, get to me! (*He laughs.*)

WILLY. Go to it, Biff! Go ahead, show him!

BIFF. Okay! (*He cocks his fists and starts in.*)

LINDA (*to* WILLY). Why must he fight, dear?

BEN (*sparring with* BIFF). Good boy! Good boy!

WILLY. How's that, Ben, heh?

HAPPY. Give him the left, Biff!

LINDA. Why are you fighting?

BEN. Good boy! (*Suddenly comes in, trips* BIFF, *and stands over him, the point of his umbrella poised over* BIFF's *eye.*)

LINDA. Look out, Biff!

BIFF. Gee!

BEN (*patting* BIFF's *knee*). Never fight fair with a stranger, boy. You'll never get out of the jungle that way. (*Taking* LINDA's *hand and bowing*) It was an honor and a pleasure to meet you, Linda.

LINDA (*withdrawing her hand coldly, frightened*). Have a nice—trip.

BEN (*to* WILLY). And good luck with your—what do you do?

WILLY. Selling.

BEN. Yes. Well . . . (*He raises his hand in farewell to all.*)

WILLY. No, Ben, I don't want you to think . . . (*He takes* BEN's *arm to show him.*) It's Brooklyn, I know, but we hunt too.

BEN. Really, now.

WILLY. Oh, sure, there's snakes and rabbits and—that's why I moved out here. Why, Biff can fell any one of these trees in no time! Boys! Go right over to where they're building the apartment house and get some sand. We're gonna rebuild the entire front stoop right now! Watch this, Ben!

BIFF. Yes, sir! On the double, Hap!

HAPPY (*as he and* BIFF *run off*). I lost weight, Pop, you notice?

(CHARLEY *enters in knickers, even before the boys are gone.*)

CHARLEY. Listen, if they steal any more from that building the watchman'll put the cops on them!

LINDA (to WILLY). Don't let Biff . . .

(BEN *laughs lustily.*)

WILLY. You shoulda seen the lumber they brought home last week. At least a dozen six-by-tens worth all kinds a money.

CHARLEY. Listen, if that watchman—

WILLY. I gave them hell, understand. But I got a couple of fearless characters there.

CHARLEY. Willy, the jails are full of fearless characters.

BEN (*clapping* WILLY *on the back, with a laugh at* CHARLEY). And the stock exchange, friend!

WILLY (*joining in* BEN's *laughter*). Where are the rest of your pants?

CHARLEY. My wife bought them.

WILLY. Now all you need is a golf club and you can go upstairs and go to sleep. (*To* BEN) Great athlete! Between him and his son Bernard they can't hammer a nail!

BERNARD (*rushing in*). The watchman's chasing Biff!

WILLY (*angrily*). Shut up! He's not stealing anything!

LINDA (*alarmed, hurrying off left*). Where is he? Biff, dear! (*She exits.*)

WILLY (*moving toward the left, away from* BEN). There's nothing wrong. What's the matter with you?

BEN. Nervy boy. Good!

WILLY (*laughing*). Oh, nerves of iron, that Biff!

CHARLEY. Don't know what it is. My New England man comes back and he's bleedin', they murdered him up there.

WILLY. It's contacts, Charley, I got important contacts!

CHARLEY (*sarcastically*). Glad to hear it, Willy. Come in later, we'll shoot a little casino. I'll take some of your Portland money. (*He laughs at* WILLY *and exits.*)

WILLY (*turning to* BEN). Business is bad, it's murderous. But not for me, of course.

BEN. I'll stop by on my way back to Africa.

WILLY (*longingly*). Can't you stay a few days? You're just what I need, Ben, because I—I have a fine position here, but I—well, Dad left when I was such a baby and I never had a chance to talk to him and I still feel—kind of temporary about myself.

BEN. I'll be late for my train.

(*They are at opposite ends of the stage.*)

WILLY. Ben, my boys—can't we talk? They'd go into the jaws of hell for me, but I—

BEN. William, you're being first-rate with your boys. Outstanding, manly chaps!

WILLY (*hanging on to his words*). Oh, Ben, that's good to hear! Because sometimes I'm afraid that I'm not teaching them the right kind of— Ben, how should I teach them?

BEN (*giving great weight to each word, and with a certain vicious audacity*). William, when I walked into the jungle, I was seventeen. When I walked out I was twenty-one. And, by God, I was rich! (*He goes off into darkness around the right corner of the house.*)

WILLY. . . . was rich! That's just the spirit I want to imbue them with! To walk into a jungle! I was right! I was right! I was right!

(BEN *is gone, but* WILLY *is still speaking to him as* LINDA, *in nightgown and robe, enters the kitchen, glances around for* WILLY, *then goes to the door of the house, looks out and sees him. Comes down to his left. He looks at her.*)

LINDA. Willy, dear? Willy?

WILLY. I was right!

LINDA. Did you have some cheese? (*He can't answer.*) It's very late, darling. Come to bed, heh?

WILLY (*looking straight up*). Gotta break your neck to see a star in this yard.

LINDA. You coming in?

WILLY. Whatever happened to that diamond watch fob? Remember? When Ben came from Africa that time? Didn't he give me a watch fob with a diamond in it?

LINDA. You pawned it, dear. Twelve, thirteen years ago. For Biff's radio correspondence course.

WILLY. Gee, that was a beautiful thing. I'll take a walk.

LINDA. But you're in your slippers.

WILLY (*starting to go around the house at the left*). I was right! I was! (*Half to* LINDA, *as he goes, shaking his head*) What a man! There was a man worth talking to. I was right!

LINDA (*calling after* WILLY). But in your slippers, Willy!

(WILLY *is almost gone when* BIFF, *in his pajamas, comes down the stairs and enters the kitchen.*)

BIFF. What is he doing out there?

LINDA. Sh!

BIFF. God Almighty, Mom, how long has he been doing this?

LINDA. Don't, he'll hear you.

BIFF. What the hell is the matter with him?

LINDA. It'll pass by morning.

BIFF. Shouldn't we do anything?

LINDA. Oh, my dear, you should do a lot of things, but there's nothing to do, so go to sleep.

(HAPPY *comes down the stairs and sits on the steps.*)

HAPPY. I never heard him so loud, Mom.

LINDA. Well, come around more often; you'll hear him. (*She sits down at the table and mends the lining of* WILLY's *jacket.*)

BIFF. Why didn't you ever write me about this, Mom?

LINDA. How would I write to you? For over three months you had no address.

BIFF. I was on the move. But you know I thought of you all the time. You know that, don't you, pal?

LINDA. I know, dear, I know. But he likes to have a letter. Just to know that there's still a possibility for better things.

BIFF. He's not like this all the time, is he?

LINDA. It's when you come home he's always the worst.

BIFF. When I come home?

LINDA. When you write you're coming, he's all smiles, and talks about the future, and—he's just wonderful. And then the closer you seem to come, the more shaky he gets, and then, by the time you get here, he's arguing, and he seems angry at you. I think it's just that maybe he can't bring himself to—to open up to you. Why are you so hateful to each other? Why is that?

BIFF (*evasively*). I'm not hateful, Mom.

LINDA. But you no sooner come in the door than you're fighting!

BIFF. I don't know why. I mean to change. I'm tryin', Mom, you understand?

LINDA. Are you home to stay now?

BIFF. I don't know. I want to look around, see what's doin'.

LINDA. Biff, you can't look around all your life, can you?

BIFF. I just can't take hold, Mom. I can't take hold of some kind of a life.

LINDA. Biff, a man is not a bird to come and go with the springtime.

BIFF. Your hair . . . (*He touches her hair.*) Your hair got so gray.

LINDA. Oh, it's been gray since you were in high school. I just stopped dyeing it, that's all.

BIFF. Dye it again, will ya? I don't want my pal looking old. (*He smiles.*)

LINDA. You're such a boy! You think you can go away for a year and . . . You've got to get it into your head now that one day you'll knock on this door and there'll be strange people here—

BIFF. What are you talking about? You're not even sixty, Mom.

LINDA. But what about your father?

BIFF (*lamely*). Well, I meant him, too.

HAPPY. He admires Pop.

LINDA. Biff, dear, if you don't have any feeling for him, then you can't have any feeling for me.

BIFF. Sure I can, Mom.

LINDA. No. You can't just come to see me, because I love him. (*With a threat, but only a threat, of tears*) He's the dearest man in the world to me, and I won't have anyone making him feel unwanted and low and blue. You've got to make up your mind now, darling, there's no leeway any more. Either he's your father and you pay him that respect, or else you're not to come here. I know he's not easy to get along with—nobody knows that better than me—but . . .

WILLY (*from the left, with a laugh*). Hey, hey, Biffo!

BIFF (*starting to go out after* WILLY). What the hell is the matter with him?

(HAPPY *stops him.*)

LINDA. Don't—don't go near him!

BIFF. Stop making excuses for him! He always, always wiped the floor with you. Never had an ounce of respect for you.

HAPPY. He's always had respect for—

BIFF. What the hell do you know about it?

HAPPY (*surlily*). Just don't call him crazy!

BIFF. He's got no character—Charley wouldn't do this. Not in his own house—spewing out that vomit from his mind.

HAPPY. Charley never had to cope with what he's got to.

BIFF. People are worse off than Willy Loman. Believe me, I've seen them.

LINDA. Then make Charley your father, Biff. You can't do that, can you? I don't say he's a great man. Willy Loman never made a lot of money. His name was never in the paper. He's not the finest character that ever lived. But he's a human being, and a terrible thing is happening to him. So attention must be paid. He's not to be allowed to fall into his grave like an old dog. Attention, attention must be finally paid to such a person. You called him crazy—

BIFF. I didn't mean—

LINDA. No, a lot of people think he's lost his—balance. But you don't have to be very smart to know what his trouble is. The man is exhausted.

HAPPY. Sure!

LINDA. A small man can be just as exhausted as a great man. He works for a company thirty-six years this March, opens up unheard-of territories to their trademark, and now in his old age they take his salary away.

HAPPY (*indignantly*). I didn't know that, Mom.

LINDA. You never asked, my dear! Now that you get your spending money someplace else you don't trouble your mind with him.

HAPPY. But I gave you money last—

LINDA. Christmas time, fifty dollars! To fix the hot water it cost ninety-seven fifty! For five weeks he's been on straight commission, like a beginner, an unknown!

BIFF. Those ungrateful bastards!

LINDA. Are they any worse than his sons? When he brought them business, when he was young, they were glad to see him. But now his old friends, the old buyers that loved him so and always found some order to hand him in a pinch—they're all dead, retired. He used to be able to make six, seven calls a day in Boston. Now he takes his valises out of the car and puts them back and takes them out again and he's exhausted. Instead of walking he talks now. He drives seven hundred miles, and when he gets there no one knows him any more, no one welcomes him. And what goes through a man's mind, driving seven hundred miles home without having earned a cent? Why shouldn't he talk to himself? Why? When he has to go to Charley and borrow fifty dollars a week and pretend to me that it's his pay? How long can that go on? How long? You see what I'm sitting here and waiting for? And you tell me he has no character? The man who never worked a day but for your benefit? When does he get the medal for that? Is this his reward—to turn around at the age of sixty-three and find his sons, who he loved better than his life, one a philandering bum—

HAPPY. Mom!

LINDA. That's all you are, my baby! (*To* BIFF) And you! What happened to the love you had for him? You were such pals! How you used to talk to him on the phone every night! How lonely he was till he could come home to you!

BIFF. All right, Mom, I'll live here in my room, and I'll get a job. I'll keep away from him, that's all.

LINDA. No, Biff. You can't stay here and fight all the time.

BIFF. He threw me out of this house, remember that.

LINDA. Why did he do that? I never knew why.

BIFF. Because I know he's a fake and he doesn't like anybody around who knows!

LINDA. Why a fake? In what way? What do you mean?

BIFF. Just don't lay it all at my feet. It's between me and him—that's all I have to say. I'll chip in from now on. He'll settle for half my pay check. He'll be all right. I'm going to bed. (*He starts for the stairs.*)

LINDA. He won't be all right.

BIFF (*turning on the stairs, furiously*). I hate this city and I'll stay here. Now what do you want?

LINDA. He's dying, Biff.

(HAPPY *turns quickly to her, shocked.*)

BIFF (*after a pause*). Why is he dying?

LINDA. He's been trying to kill himself.

BIFF (*with great horror*). How?

LINDA. I live from day to day.

BIFF. What're you talking about?

LINDA. Remember I wrote you that he smashed up the car again? In February?

BIFF. Well?

LINDA. The insurance inspector came. He said that they have evidence. That all these accidents in the last year—weren't—weren't—accidents.

HAPPY. How can they tell that? That's a lie.

LINDA. It seems there's a woman . . . (*She takes a breath as*)

⎰BIFF (*sharply but contained*). What woman?

⎱LINDA (*simultaneously*). . . . and this woman . . .

LINDA. What?

BIFF. Nothing. Go ahead.

LINDA. What did you say?

BIFF. Nothing. I just said what woman?

HAPPY. What about her?

LINDA. Well, it seems she was walking down the road and saw his car. She says that he wasn't driving fast at all, and that he didn't skid. She says he came to that little bridge, and then deliberately smashed into the railing, and it was only the shallowness of the water that saved him.

BIFF. Oh, no, he probably just fell asleep again.

LINDA. I don't think he fell asleep.

BIFF. Why not?

LINDA. Last month . . . (*With great difficulty*) Oh, boys, it's so hard to say a thing like this! He's just a big stupid man to you, but I tell you there's more good in him than in many other people. (*She chokes, wipes her eyes.*) I was looking for a fuse. The lights blew out, and I went down the cellar. And behind the fuse box—it happened to fall out—was a length of rubber pipe—just short.

HAPPY. No kidding?

LINDA. There's a little attachment on the end of it. I knew right away. And sure enough, on the bottom of the water heater there's a new little nipple on the gas pipe.

HAPPY (*angrily*). That—jerk.

BIFF. Did you have it taken off?

LINDA. I'm—I'm ashamed to. How can I mention it to him? Every day I go down and take away that little rubber pipe. But, when he comes home, I put it back where it was. How can I insult him that way? I don't know what to do. I live from day to day, boys. I tell you, I know every thought in his mind. It sounds so old-fashioned and silly, but I tell you he put his whole life into you and you've turned your backs on him. (*She is bent over in the chair, weeping, her face in her hands.*) Biff, I swear to God! Biff, his life is in your hands!

HAPPY (*to* BIFF). How do you like that damned fool!

BIFF (*kissing her*). All right, pal, all right. It's all settled now. I've been remiss. I know that, Mom. But now I'll stay, and I swear to you, I'll apply myself. (*Kneeling in front of her, in a fever of self-reproach*) It's just—you see, Mom, I don't fit in business. Not that I won't try. I'll try, and I'll make good.

HAPPY. Sure you will. The trouble with you in business was you never tried to please people.

BIFF. I know, I—

HAPPY. Like when you worked for Harrison's. Bob Harrison said you were tops, and then you go and do some damn fool thing like whistling whole songs in the elevator like a comedian.

BIFF (*against* HAPPY). So what? I like to whistle sometimes.

HAPPY. You don't raise a guy to a responsible job who whistles in the elevator!

LINDA. Well, don't argue about it now.

HAPPY. Like when you'd go off and swim in the middle of the day instead of taking the line around.

BIFF (*his resentment rising*). Well, don't you run off? You take off sometimes, don't you? On a nice summer day?

HAPPY. Yeah, but I cover myself!

LINDA. Boys!

HAPPY. If I'm going to take a fade the boss can call any number where I'm supposed to be and they'll swear to him that I just left. I'll tell you something that I hate to say, Biff, but in the business world some of them think you're crazy.

BIFF (*angered*). Screw the business world!

HAPPY. All right, screw it! Great, but cover yourself!

LINDA. Hap, Hap!

BIFF. I don't care what they think! They've laughed at Dad for years, and you know why? Because we don't belong in this nuthouse of a city! We should be mixing cement on some open plain, or—or carpenters. A carpenter is allowed to whistle!

(WILLY *walks in from the entrance of the house, at left.*)

WILLY. Even your grandfather was better than a carpenter. (*Pause. They watch him.*) You never grew up. Bernard does not whistle in the elevator, I assure you.

BIFF (*as though to laugh* WILLY *out of it*). Yeah, but you do, Pop.

WILLY. I never in my life whistled in an elevator! And who in the business world thinks I'm crazy?

BIFF. I didn't mean it like that, Pop. Now don't make a whole thing out of it, will ya?

WILLY. Go back to the West! Be a carpenter, a cowboy, enjoy yourself!

LINDA. Willy, he was just saying—

WILLY. I heard what he said!

HAPPY (*trying to quiet* WILLY). Hey, Pop, come on now . . .

WILLY (*continuing over* HAPPY'*s line*). They laugh at me, heh? Go to Filene's, go to the Hub, go to Slattery's, Boston. Call out the name Willy Loman and see what happens! Big shot!

BIFF. All right, Pop.

WILLY. Big!

BIFF. All right!

WILLY. Why do you always insult me?

BIFF. I didn't say a word. (*To* LINDA) Did I say a word?

LINDA. He didn't say anything, Willy.

WILLY (*going to the doorway of the living room*). All right, good night, good night.

LINDA. Willy, dear, he just decided . . .

WILLY (*to* BIFF). If you get tired hanging around tomorrow, paint the ceiling I put up in the living room.

BIFF. I'm leaving early tomorrow.

HAPPY. He's going to see Bill Oliver, Pop.

WILLY (*interestedly*). Oliver? For what?

BIFF (*with reserve, but trying, trying*). He always said he'd stake me. I'd like to go into business, so maybe I can take him up on it.

LINDA. Isn't that wonderful?

WILLY. Don't interrupt. What's wonderful about it? There's fifty men in the City of New York who'd stake him. (*To* BIFF) Sporting goods?

BIFF. I guess so. I know something about it and—

WILLY. He knows something about it! You know sporting goods better than Spalding, for God's sake! How much is he giving you?

BIFF. I don't know, I didn't even see him yet, but—

WILLY. Then what're you talkin' about?

BIFF (*getting angry*). Well, all I said was I'm gonna see him, that's all!

WILLY (*turning away*). Ah, you're counting your chickens again.

BIFF (*starting left for the stairs*). Oh, Jesus, I'm going to sleep!

WILLY (*calling after him*). Don't curse in this house!

BIFF (*turning*). Since when did you get so clean?

HAPPY (*trying to stop them*). Wait a . . .

WILLY. Don't use that language to me! I won't have it!

HAPPY (*grabbing* BIFF, *shouts*). Wait a minute! I got an idea. I got a feasible idea. Come here, Biff, let's talk this over now, let's talk some sense here. When I was down in Florida last time, I thought of a great idea to sell sporting goods. It just came back to me. You and I, Biff—we have a line, the Loman Line. We train a couple of weeks, and put on a couple of exhibitions, see?

WILLY. That's an idea!

HAPPY. Wait! We form two basketball teams, see? Two water-polo teams. We play each other. It's a million dollars' worth of publicity. Two brothers, see? The Loman Brothers. Displays in the Royal Palms—all the hotels. And banners over the ring and the basketball court: "Loman Brothers." Baby, we could sell sporting goods!

WILLY. That is a one-million-dollar idea!

LINDA. Marvelous!

BIFF. I'm in great shape as far as that's concerned.

HAPPY. And the beauty of it is, Biff, it wouldn't be like a business. We'd be out playin' ball again . . .

BIFF (*enthused*). Yeah, that's . . .

WILLY. Million-dollar . . .

HAPPY. And you wouldn't get fed up with it, Biff. It'd be the family again. There'd be the old honor, and comradeship, and if you wanted to go off for a swim or somethin'—well, you'd do it! Without some smart cooky gettin' up ahead of you!

WILLY. Lick the world! You guys together could absolutely lick the civilized world.

BIFF. I'll see Oliver tomorrow. Hap, if we could work that out . . .

LINDA. Maybe things are beginning to——

WILLY (*wildly enthused, to* LINDA). Stop interrupting! (*To* BIFF) But don't wear sport jacket and slacks when you see Oliver.

BIFF. No, I'll—

WILLY. A business suit, and talk as little as possible, and don't crack any jokes.

BIFF. He did like me. Always liked me.

LINDA. He loved you!

WILLY (*to* LINDA). Will you stop! (*To* BIFF) Walk in very serious. You are not applying for a boy's job. Money is to pass. Be quiet, fine, and serious. Everybody likes a kidder, but nobody lends him money.

HAPPY. I'll try to get some myself, Biff. I'm sure I can.

WILLY. I see great things for you kids, I think your troubles are over. But remember, start big and you'll end big. Ask for fifteen. How much you gonna ask for?

BIFF. Gee, I don't know—

WILLY. And don't say "Gee." "Gee" is a boy's word. A man walking in for fifteen thousand dollars does not say "Gee!"

BIFF. Ten, I think, would be top though.

WILLY. Don't be so modest. You always started too low. Walk in with a big laugh. Don't look worried. Start off with a couple of your good stories to lighten things up. It's not what you say, it's how you say it—because personality always wins the day.

LINDA. Oliver always thought the highest of him—

WILLY. Will you let me talk?

BIFF. Don't yell at her, Pop, will ya?

WILLY (*angrily*). I was talking, wasn't I?

BIFF. I don't like you yelling at her all the time, and I'm tellin' you, that's all.

WILLY. What're you, takin' over this house?

LINDA. Willy—

WILLY (*turning on her*). Don't take his side all the time, goddammit!

BIFF (*furiously*). Stop yelling at her!

WILLY (*suddenly pulling on his cheek, beaten down, guilt ridden*). Give my best to Bill Oliver—he may remember me. (*He exits through the living-room doorway.*)

LINDA (*her voice subdued*). What'd you have to start that for? (BIFF *turns away.*) You see how sweet he was as soon as you talked hopefully? (*She goes over to* BIFF.) Come up and say good night to him. Don't let him go to bed that way.

HAPPY. Come on, Biff, let's buck him up.

LINDA. Please, dear. Just say good night. It takes so little to make him happy. Come. (*She goes through the living-room doorway, calling upstairs from within the living-room.*) Your pajamas are hanging in the bathroom, Willy!

HAPPY (*looking toward where* LINDA *went out*). What a woman! They broke the mold when they made her. You know that, Biff?

BIFF. He's off salary. My God, working on commission!

HAPPY. Well, let's face it: he's no hot-shot selling man. Except that sometimes, you have to admit, he's a sweet personality.

BIFF (*decidedly*). Lend me ten bucks, will ya? I want to buy some new ties.

HAPPY. I'll take you to a place I know. Beautiful stuff. Wear one of my striped shirts tomorrow.

BIFF. She got gray. Mom got awful old. Gee, I'm gonna go in to Oliver tomorrow and knock him for a—

HAPPY. Come on up. Tell that to Dad. Let's give him a whirl. Come on.

BIFF (*steamed up*). You know, with ten thousand bucks, boy!

HAPPY (*as they go into the living-room*). That's the talk, Biff, that's the first time I've heard the old confidence out of you! (*From within the living-room, fading off*) You're gonna live with me, kid, and any babe you want just say the word . . . (*The last lines are hardly heard. They are mounting the stairs to their parents' bedroom.*)

LINDA (*entering her bedroom and addressing* WILLY, *who is in the bathroom. She is straightening the bed for him*). Can you do anything about the shower? It drips.

WILLY (*from the bathroom*). All of a sudden everything falls to pieces! Goddam plumbing, oughta be sued, those people. I hardly finished putting it in and the thing . . . (*His words rumble off.*)

LINDA. I'm just wondering if Oliver will remember him. You think he might?

WILLY (*coming out of the bathroom in his pajamas*). Remember him? What's the matter with you, you crazy? If he'd've stayed with Oliver he'd be on top by now! Wait'll Oliver gets a look at him. You don't know the average caliber any more. The average young man today—(*he is getting into bed*)—is got a caliber of zero. Greatest thing in the world for him was to bum around.

(BIFF *and* HAPPY *enter the bedroom. Slight pause.*)

WILLY (*stops short, looking at* BIFF). Glad to hear it, boy.

HAPPY. He wanted to say good night to you, sport.

WILLY (*to* BIFF). Yeah. Knock him dead, boy. What'd you want to tell me?

BIFF. Just take it easy, Pop. Good night. (*He turns to go.*)

WILLY (*unable to resist*). And if anything falls off the desk while you're talking to him—like a package or something—don't you pick it up. They have office boys for that.

LINDA. I'll make a big breakfast—

WILLY. Will you let me finish? (*To* BIFF) Tell him you were in the business in the West. Not farm work.

BIFF. All right, Dad.

LINDA. I think everything—

WILLY (*going right through her speech*). And don't undersell yourself. No less than fifteen thousand dollars.

BIFF (*unable to bear him*). Okay. Good night, Mom. (*He starts moving.*)

WILLY. Because you got a greatness in you, Biff, remember that. You got all kinds of greatness . . .

(*He lies back, exhausted.* BIFF *walks out.*)

LINDA (*calling after* BIFF). Sleep well, darling!

HAPPY. I'm gonna get married, Mom. I wanted to tell you.

LINDA. Go to sleep, dear.

HAPPY (*going*). I just wanted to tell you.

WILLY. Keep up the good work. (HAPPY *exits.*) God . . . remember that Ebbets Field game? The championship of the city?

LINDA. Just rest. Should I sing to you?

WILLY. Yeah. Sing to me. (LINDA *hums a soft lullaby.*) When that team came out—he was the tallest, remember?

LINDA. Oh, yes. And in gold.

(BIFF *enters the darkened kitchen, takes a cigarette, and leaves the house. He comes downstage into a golden pool of light. He smokes, staring at the night.*)

WILLY. Like a young god. Hercules—something like that. And the sun, the sun all around him. Remember how he waved to me? Right up from the field, with the representatives of three colleges standing by? And the buyers I brought, and the cheers when he came out—Loman, Loman, Loman! God Almighty, he'll be great yet. A star like that, magnificent, can never really fade away!

(*The light on* WILLY *is fading. The gas heater begins to glow through the kitchen wall, near the stairs, a blue flame beneath red coils.*)

LINDA (*timidly*). Willy dear, what has he got against you?

WILLY. I'm so tired. Don't talk any more.

(BIFF *slowly returns to the kitchen. He stops, stares toward the heater.*)

LINDA. Will you ask Howard to let you work in New York?

WILLY. First thing in the morning. Everything'll be all right.

(BIFF *reaches behind the heater and draws out a length of rubber tubing. He is horrified and turns his head toward* WILLY'*s room, still dimly lit, from which the strains of* LINDA'*s desperate but monotonous humming rise.*)

WILLY (*staring through the window into the moonlight*). Gee, look at the moon moving between the buildings!

(BIFF *wraps the tubing around his hand and quickly goes up the stairs.*)

ACT II

Music is heard, gay and bright. The curtain rises as the music fades away. WILLY, *in shirt sleeves, is sitting at the kitchen table, sipping coffee, his hat in his lap.* LINDA *is filling his cup when she can.*

WILLY. Wonderful coffee. Meal in itself.

LINDA. Can I make you some eggs?

WILLY. No. Take a breath.

LINDA. You look so rested, dear.

WILLY. I slept like a dead one. First time in months. Imagine, sleeping till ten on a Tuesday morning. Boys left nice and early, heh?

LINDA. They were out of here by eight o'clock.

WILLY. Good work!

LINDA. It was so thrilling to see them leaving together. I can't get over the shaving lotion in this house!

WILLY (*smiling*). Mmm—

LINDA. Biff was very changed this morning. His whole attitude seemed to be hopeful. He couldn't wait to get downtown to see Oliver.

WILLY. He's heading for a change. There's no question, there simply are certain men that take longer to get—solidified. How did he dress?

LINDA. His blue suit. He's so handsome in that suit. He could be a— anything in that suit!

(WILLY *gets up from the table.* LINDA *holds his jacket for him.*)

WILLY. There's no question, no question at all. Gee, on the way home tonight I'd like to buy some seeds.

LINDA (*laughing*). That'd be wonderful. But not enough sun gets back there. Nothing'll grow any more.

WILLY. You wait, kid, before it's all over we're gonna get a little place out in the country, and I'll raise some vegetables, a couple of chickens . . .

LINDA. You'll do it yet, dear.

(WILLY *walks out of his jacket.* LINDA *follows him.*)

WILLY. And they'll get married, and come for a weekend. I'd build a little guest house. 'Cause I got so many fine tools, all I'd need would be a little lumber and some peace of mind.

LINDA (*joyfully*). I sewed the lining . . .

WILLY. I would build two guest houses, so they'd both come. Did he decide how much he's going to ask Oliver for?

LINDA (*getting him into the jacket*). He didn't mention it, but I imagine ten or fifteen thousand. You going to talk to Howard today?

WILLY. Yeah. I'll put it to him straight and simple. He'll just have to take me off the road.

LINDA. And, Willy, don't forget to ask for a little advance, because we've got the insurance premium. It's the grace period now.

WILLY. That's a hundred . . . ?

LINDA. A hundred and eight, sixty-eight. Because we're a little short again.

WILLY. Why are we short?

LINDA. Well, you had the motor job on the car . . .

WILLY. That goddam Studebaker!

LINDA. And you got one more payment on the refrigerator . . .

WILLY. But it just broke again!

LINDA. Well, it's old, dear.

WILLY. I told you we should've bought a well-advertised machine. Charley bought a General Electric and it's twenty years old and it's still good, that son-of-a-bitch.

LINDA. But, Willy—

WILLY. Whoever heard of a Hastings refrigerator? Once in my life I would like to own something outright before it's broken! I'm always in a race with the junkyard! I just finished paying for the car and it's on its last legs. The refrigerator consumes belts like a goddam maniac. They time those things. They time them so when you finally paid for them, they're used up.

LINDA (*buttoning up his jacket as he unbuttons it*). All told, about two hundred dollars would carry us, dear. But that includes the last payment on the mortgage. After this payment, Willy, the house belongs to us.

WILLY. It's twenty-five years!

LINDA. Biff was nine years old when we bought it.

WILLY. Well, that's a great thing. To weather a twenty-five year mortgage is—

LINDA. It's an accomplishment.

WILLY. All the cement, lumber, the reconstruction I put in this house! There ain't a crack to be found in it any more.

LINDA. Well, it served its purpose.

WILLY. What purpose? Some stranger'll come along, move in, and that's that. If only Biff would take this house, and raise a family . . . (*He starts to go.*) Good-by, I'm late.

LINDA (*suddenly remembering*). Oh, I forgot! You're supposed to meet them for dinner.

WILLY. Me?

LINDA. At Frank's Chop House on Forty-eighth near Sixth Avenue.

WILLY. Is that so! How about you?

LINDA. No, just the three of you. They're gonna blow you to a big meal!

WILLY. Don't say! Who thought of that?

LINDA. Biff came to me this morning, Willy, and he said, "Tell Dad, we want to blow him to a big meal." Be there six o'clock. You and your two boys are going to have dinner.

WILLY. Gee whiz! That's really somethin'. I'm gonna knock Howard for a loop, kid. I'll get an advance, and I'll come home with a New York job. Goddammit, now I'm gonna do it!

LINDA. Oh, that's the spirit, Willy!

WILLY. I will never get behind a wheel the rest of my life!

LINDA. It's changing, Willy, I can feel it changing!

WILLY. Beyond a question. G'by, I'm late. (*He starts to go again.*)

LINDA (*calling after him as she runs to the kitchen table for a handkerchief*). You got your glasses?

WILLY (*feels for them, then comes back in*). Yeah, yeah, got my glasses.

LINDA (*giving him the handkerchief*). And a handkerchief.

WILLY. Yeah, handkerchief.

LINDA. And your saccharine?

WILLY. Yeah, my saccharine.

LINDA. Be careful on the subway stairs.

(*She kisses him, and a silk stocking is seen hanging from her hand.* WILLY *notices it.*)

WILLY. Will you stop mending stockings? At least while I'm in the house. It gets me nervous. I can't tell you. Please.

(LINDA *hides the stocking in her hand as she follows* WILLY *across the forestage in front of the house.*)

LINDA. Remember, Frank's Chop House.

WILLY (*passing the apron*). Maybe beets would grow out there.

LINDA (*laughing*). But you tried so many times.

WILLY. Yeah. Well, don't work hard today. (*He disappears around the right corner of the house.*)

LINDA. Be careful!

(*As* WILLY *vanishes,* LINDA *waves to him. Suddenly the phone rings. She runs across the stage and into the kitchen and lifts it.*)

LINDA. Hello? Oh Biff! I'm so glad you called, I just . . . Yes, sure, I just told him. Yes, he'll be there for dinner at six o'clock, I didn't forget. Listen, I was just dying to tell you. You know that little rubber pipe I told you about? That he connected to the gas heater? I finally decided to go down the cellar this morning and take it away and destroy it. But it's gone! Imagine? He took it away himself, it isn't there! (*She listens.*) When? Oh, then you took it. Oh—nothing, it's just that I'd hoped he'd taken it away himself. Oh, I'm not worried, darling, because this morning he left in such high spirits, it was like the old days! I'm not afraid any more. Did Mr. Oliver see you? . . . Well, you wait there then. And make a nice impression on him, darling. Just don't perspire too much before you see him. And have a nice time with Dad. He may have big news too! . . . That's right, a New York job. And be sweet to him tonight, dear. Be loving to him. Because he's only a little boat looking for a harbor. (*She is trembling with sorrow and joy.*) Oh, that's wonderful, Biff, you'll save his life. Thanks, darling. Just put your arm around him when he comes into the restaurant. Give him a smile. That's the boy . . . Good-by, dear . . . You got your comb? . . . That's fine. Good-by, Biff dear.

(*In the middle of her speech,* HOWARD WAGNER, *thirty-six, wheels on a small typewriter table on which is a wire-recording machine and proceeds to plug it in. This is on the left forestage. Light slowly fades on* LINDA *as it rises on* HOWARD. HOWARD *is intent on threading the machine and only glances over his shoulder as* WILLY *appears.*)

WILLY. Pst! Pst!

HOWARD. Hello, Willy, come in.

WILLY. Like to have a little talk with you, Howard.

HOWARD. Sorry to keep you waiting. I'll be with you in a minute.

WILLY. What's that, Howard?

HOWARD. Didn't you ever see one of these? Wire recorder.

WILLY. Oh. Can we talk a minute?

HOWARD. Records things. Just got delivery yesterday. Been driving me crazy, the most terrific machine I ever saw in my life. I was up all night with it.

WILLY. What do you do with it?

HOWARD. I bought it for dictation, but you can do anything with it. Listen to this. I had it home last night. Listen to what I picked up. The first one is my daughter. Get this. (*He flicks the switch and "Roll Out the Barrel" is heard being whistled.*) Listen to that kid whistle.

WILLY. That is lifelike, isn't it?

HOWARD. Seven years old. Get that tone.

WILLY. Ts, ts. Like to ask a little favor of you . . .

(*The whistling breaks off, and the voice of* HOWARD's *daughter is heard.*)

HIS DAUGHTER. "Now you, Daddy."

HOWARD. She's crazy for me! (*Again the same song is whistled.*) That's me! Ha! (*He winks.*)

WILLY. You're very good!

(*The whistling breaks off again. The machine runs silent for a moment.*)

HOWARD. Sh! Get this now, this is my son.

HIS SON. "The capital of Alabama is Montgomery; the capital of Arizona is Phoenix; the capital of Arkansas is Little Rock; the capital of California is Sacramento . . ." (*and on, and on*).

HOWARD (*holding up five fingers*). Five years old, Willy!

WILLY. He'll make an announcer some day!

HIS SON (*continuing*). "The capital . . ."

HOWARD. Get that—alphabetical order! (*The machine breaks off suddenly.*) Wait a minute. The maid kicked the plug out.

WILLY. It certainly is a—

HOWARD. Sh, for God's sake!

HIS SON. "It's nine o'clock, Bulova watch time. So I have to go to sleep."

WILLY. That really is—

HOWARD. Wait a minute! The next is my wife.

(*They wait.*)

HOWARD'S VOICE. "Go on, say something." (*Pause*) "Well, you gonna talk?"

HIS WIFE. "I can't think of anything."

HOWARD'S VOICE. "Well, talk—it's turning."

HIS WIFE (*shyly, beaten*). "Hello." (*Silence*) "Oh, Howard, I can't talk into this . . ."

HOWARD (*snapping the machine off*). That was my wife.

WILLY. That is a wonderful machine. Can we—

HOWARD. I tell you, Willy, I'm gonna take my camera, and my bandsaw, and all my hobbies, and out they go. This is the most fascinating relaxation I ever found.

WILLY. I think I'll get one myself.

HOWARD. Sure, they're only a hundred and a half. You can't do without it. Supposing you wanna hear Jack Benny, see? But you can't be at home at that hour. So you tell the maid to turn the radio on when Jack Benny comes on, and this automatically goes on with the radio . . .

WILLY. And when you come home you . . .

HOWARD. You can come home twelve o'clock, one o'clock, any time you like, and you get yourself a Coke and sit yourself down, throw the switch, and there's Jack Benny's program in the middle of the night!

WILLY. I'm definitely going to get one. Because lots of time I'm on the road, and I think to myself, what I must be missing on the radio!

HOWARD. Don't you have a radio in the car?

WILLY. Well, yeah, but who ever thinks of turning it on?

HOWARD. Say, aren't you supposed to be in Boston?

WILLY. That's what I want to talk to you about, Howard. You got a minute? (*He draws a chair in from the wing.*)

HOWARD. What happened? What're you doing here?

WILLY. Well . . .

HOWARD. You didn't crack up again, did you?

WILLY. Oh, no. No . . .

HOWARD. Geez, you had me worried there for a minute. What's the trouble?

WILLY. Well, tell you the truth, Howard. I've come to the decision that I'd rather not travel any more.

HOWARD. Not travel! Well, what'll you do?

WILLY. Remember, Christmas time, when you had the party here? You said you'd try to think of some spot for me here in town.

HOWARD. With us?

WILLY. Well, sure.

HOWARD. Oh, yeah, yeah. I remember. Well, I couldn't think of anything for you, Willy.

WILLY. I tell ya, Howard. The kids are all grown up, y'know. I don't need much any more. If I could take home—well, sixty-five dollars a week, I could swing it.

HOWARD. Yeah, but Willy, see I—

WILLY. I tell ya why, Howard. Speaking frankly and between the two of us, y'know—I'm just a little tired.

HOWARD. Oh, I could understand that, Willy. But you're a road man, Willy, and we do a road business. We've only got a half-dozen salesmen on the floor here.

WILLY. God knows, Howard, I never asked a favor of any man. But I was with the firm when your father used to carry you in here in his arms.

HOWARD. I know that, Willy, but—

WILLY. Your father came to me the day you were born and asked me what I thought of the name of Howard, may he rest in peace.

HOWARD. I appreciate that, Willy, but there just is no spot here for you. If I had a spot I'd slam you right in, but I just don't have a single solitary spot.

(*He looks for his lighter.* WILLY *has picked it up and gives it to him. Pause.*)

WILLY (*with increasing anger*). Howard, all I need to set my table is fifty dollars a week.

HOWARD. But where am I going to put you, kid?

WILLY. Look, it isn't a question of whether I can sell merchandise, is it?

HOWARD. No, but it's a business, kid, and everybody's gotta pull his own weight.

WILLY (*desperately*). Just let me tell you a story, Howard—

HOWARD. 'Cause you gotta admit, business is business.

WILLY (*angrily*). Business is definitely business, but just listen for a minute. You don't understand this. When I was a boy—eighteen, nineteen—I was already on the road. And there was a question in my mind as to whether selling had a future for me. Because in those days I had a yearning to go to Alaska. See, there were three gold strikes in one month in Alaska, and I felt like going out. Just for the ride, you might say.

HOWARD (*barely interested*). Don't say.

WILLY. Oh, yeah, my father lived many years in Alaska. He was an adventurous man. We've got quite a little streak of self-reliance in our family. I thought I'd go out with my older brother and try to locate him, and maybe settle in the North with the old man. And I was almost decided to go, when I met a salesman in the Parker House. His name was Dave Singleman. And he was eighty-four years old, and he'd drummed merchandise in thirty-one states. And old Dave, he'd go up to his room, y'understand, put on his green velvet slippers—I'll never forget—and pick up his phone and call the buyers, and without ever leaving his room, at the age of eighty-four, he made his living. And when I saw that, I realized that selling was the greatest career a man could want. 'Cause what could be more satisfying than to be able to go, at the age of eighty-four, into twenty or thirty different cities, and pick up a phone, and be remembered and loved and helped by so many different people? Do you know? when he died—and by the way he died the death of a salesman, in his green velvet slippers in the smoker of the New York, New Haven and Hartford, going into Boston—when he died, hundreds of salesmen and buyers were at his funeral. Things were sad on a lotta trains for months after that. (*He stands up.* HOWARD *has not looked at him.*) In those days there was personality in it, Howard. There was respect, and comradeship, and gratitude in it. Today, it's all cut and dried, and there's no chance for bringing friendship to bear—or personality. You see what I mean? They don't know me any more.

HOWARD (*moving away, to the right*). That's just the thing, Willy.

WILLY. If I had forty dollars a week—that's all I'd need. Forty dollars, Howard.

HOWARD. Kid, I can't take blood from a stone, I—

WILLY (*desperation is on him now*). Howard, the year Al Smith° was nominated, your father came to me and—

HOWARD (*starting to go off*). I've got to see some people, kid.

WILLY (*stopping him*). I'm talking about your father! There were promises made across this desk! You mustn't tell me you've got people to see—I put thirty-four years into this firm, Howard, and now I can't pay my insurance! You can't eat the orange and throw the peel away—a man is not a piece of fruit! (*After a pause*) Now pay attention. Your father—in 1928 I had a big year. I averaged a hundred and seventy dollars a week in commissions.

HOWARD (*impatiently*). Now, Willy, you never averaged—

WILLY (*banging his hand on the desk*). I averaged a hundred and seventy dollars a week in the year of 1928! And your father came to me—or rather, I was in the office here—it was right over this desk—and he put his hand on my shoulder—

HOWARD (*getting up*). You'll have to excuse me, Willy, I gotta see some people. Pull yourself together. (*Going out*) I'll be back in a little while.

(*On* HOWARD's *exit, the light on his chair grows very bright and strange.*)

WILLY. Pull myself together! What the hell did I say to him? My God, I was yelling at him! How could I! (WILLY *breaks off, staring at the light, which occupies the chair, animating it. He approaches this chair, standing across the desk from it.*) Frank, Frank, don't you remember what you told me that time? How you put your hand on my shoulder, and Frank . . . (*He leans on the desk and as he speaks the dead man's name he accidentally switches on the recorder, and instantly*)

HOWARD's SON. ". . . of New York is Albany. The capital of Ohio is Cincinnati, the capital of Rhode island is . . ." (*The recitation continues.*)

WILLY (*leaping away with fright, shouting*). Ha! Howard! Howard! Howard!

HOWARD (*rushing in*). What happened?

WILLY (*pointing at the machine, which continues nasally, childishly, with the capital cities*). Shut it off! Shut it off!

HOWARD (*pulling the plug out*). Look, Willy . . .

WILLY (*pressing his hands to his eyes*). I gotta get myself some coffee. I'll get some coffee . . .

(WILLY *starts to walk out.* HOWARD *stops him.*)

HOWARD (*rolling up the cord*). Willy, look . . .

WILLY. I'll go to Boston.

HOWARD. Willy, you can't go to Boston for us.

WILLY. Why can't I go?

Al Smith: A four-term governor of New York, Al Smith was the Democratic nominee for President in 1928, but lost to Herbert Hoover.

HOWARD. I don't want you to represent us. I've been meaning to tell you for a long time now.

WILLY. Howard, are you firing me?

HOWARD. I think you need a good long rest, Willy.

WILLY. Howard—

HOWARD. And when you feel better, come back, and we'll see if we can work something out.

WILLY. But I gotta earn money, Howard. I'm in no position to—

HOWARD. Where are your sons? Why don't your sons give you a hand?

WILLY. They're working on a very big deal.

HOWARD. This is no time for false pride, Willy. You go to your sons and you tell them that you're tired. You've got two great boys, haven't you?

WILLY. Oh, no question, no question, but in the meantime . . .

HOWARD. Then that's that, heh?

WILLY. All right, I'll go to Boston tomorrow.

HOWARD. No, no.

WILLY. I can't throw myself on my sons. I'm not a cripple!

HOWARD. Look, kid, I'm busy this morning.

WILLY (*grasping* HOWARD*'s arm*). Howard, you've got to let me go to Boston!

HOWARD (*hard, keeping himself under control*). I've got a line of people to see this morning. Sit down, take five minutes, and pull yourself together, and then go home, will ya? I need the office, Willy. (*He starts to go, turns, remembering the recorder, starts to push off the table holding the recorder.*) Oh, yeah. Whenever you can this week, stop by and drop off the samples. You'll feel better, Willy, and then come back and we'll talk. Pull yourself together, kid, there's people outside.

(HOWARD *exits, pushing the table off left.* WILLY *stares into space, exhausted. Now the music is heard*—BEN's *music*—*first distantly, then closer, closer. As* WILLY *speaks,* BEN *enters from the right. He carries valise and umbrella.*)

WILLY. Oh, Ben, how did you do it? What is the answer? Did you wind up the Alaska deal already?

BEN. Doesn't take much time if you know what you're doing. Just a short business trip. Boarding ship in an hour. Wanted to say good-by.

WILLY. Ben, I've got to talk to you.

BEN (*glancing at his watch*). Haven't the time, William.

WILLY (*crossing the apron to* BEN). Ben, nothing's working out. I don't know what to do.

BEN. Now look here, William. I've bought timberland in Alaska and I need a man to look after things for me.

WILLY. God, timberland! Me and my boys in those grand outdoors!

BEN. You've a new continent at your doorstep, William. Get out of these cities, they're full of talk and time payments and courts of law. Screw on your fists and you can fight for a fortune up there.

WILLY. Yes, yes! Linda, Linda!

(LINDA *enters as of old, with the wash.*)

LINDA. Oh, you're back?

BEN. I haven't much time.

WILLY. No, wait! Linda, he's got a proposition for me in Alaska.

LINDA. But you've got—(*To* BEN) He's got a beautiful job here.

WILLY. But in Alaska, kid, I could—

LINDA. You're doing well enough, Willy!

BEN (*to* LINDA). Enough for what, my dear?

LINDA (*frightened of* BEN *and angry at him*). Don't say those things to him! Enough to be happy right here, right now. (*To* WILLY, *while* BEN *laughs*) Why must everybody conquer the world? You're well liked, and the boys love you, and someday—(*to* BEN)—why, old man Wagner told him just the other day that if he keeps it up he'll be a member of the firm, didn't he, Willy?

WILLY. Sure, sure. I am building something with this firm, Ben, and if a man is building something he must be on the right track, mustn't he?

BEN. What are you building? Lay your hand on it. Where is it?

WILLY (*hesitantly*). That's true, Linda, there's nothing.

LINDA. Why? (*To* BEN) There's a man eighty-four years old—

WILLY. That's right, Ben, that's right. When I look at that man I say, what is there to worry about?

BEN. Bah!

WILLY. It's true, Ben. All he has to do is go into any city, pick up the phone, and he's making his living and you know why?

BEN (*picking up his valise*). I've got to go.

WILLY (*holding* BEN *back*). Look at this boy!

(BIFF, *in his high school sweater, enters carrying suitcase.* HAPPY *carries* BIFF's *shoulder guards, gold helmet, and football pants.*)

WILLY. Without a penny to his name, three great universities are begging for him, and from there the sky's the limit, because it's not what you do, Ben. It's who you know and the smile on your face! It's contacts, Ben, contacts! The whole wealth of Alaska passes over the lunch table at the Commodore Hotel, and that's the wonder, the wonder of this country, that a man can end with diamonds here on the basis of being liked! (*He turns to* BIFF) And that's why when you get out on that field today, it's important. Because thousands of people will be rooting for you and loving you. (*To* BEN, *who has again begun to leave*) And Ben! when he walks into a business office his name will sound out like a bell and all the doors will open to him! I've seen it, Ben, I've seen it a thousand times! You can't feel it with your hand like timber, but it's there!

BEN. Good-by, William.

WILLY. Ben, am I right? Don't you think I'm right? I value your advice.

BEN. There's a new continent at your doorstep, William. You could walk out rich. Rich! (*He is gone.*)

WILLY. We'll do it here, Ben! You hear me? We're gonna do it here!

(YOUNG BERNARD *rushes in. The gay music of the boys is heard*).

BERNARD. Oh, gee, I was afraid you left already!

WILLY. Why? What time is it?

BERNARD. It's half-past one!

WILLY. Well, come on, everybody! Ebbets Field° next stop! Where's the pennants? (*He rushes through the wall-line of the kitchen and out into the living-room.*)

LINDA (*to* BIFF). Did you pack fresh underwear?

BIFF (*who has been limbering up*). I want to go!

BERNARD. Biff, I'm carrying your helmet, ain't I?

HAPPY. No, I'm carrying the helmet.

BERNARD. Oh, Biff, you promised me.

HAPPY. I'm carrying the helmet.

BERNARD. How am I going to get in the locker room?

LINDA. Let him carry the shoulder guards. (*She puts her coat and hat on in the kitchen.*)

BERNARD. Can I, Biff? 'Cause I told everybody I'm going to be in the locker room.

HAPPY. In Ebbets Field it's the clubhouse.

BERNARD. I meant the clubhouse, Biff!

HAPPY. Biff!

BIFF (*grandly, after a slight pause*). Let him carry the shoulder guards.

HAPPY (*as he gives* BERNARD *the shoulder guards*). Stay close to us now.

(WILLY *rushes in with the pennants.*)

WILLY (*handing them out*). Everybody wave when Biff comes out on the field. (HAPPY *and* BERNARD *run off.*) You set now, boy?

(*The music has died away.*)

BIFF. Ready to go, Pop. Every muscle is ready.

WILLY (*at the edge of the apron*). You realize what this means?

BIFF. That's right, Pop.

WILLY (*feeling* BIFF'S *muscles*). You're comin' home this afternoon captain of the All-Scholastic Championship Team of the City of New York.

BIFF. I got it, Pop. And remember, pal, when I take off my helmet, that touchdown is for you.

WILLY. Let's go! (*He is starting out, with his arm around* BIFF, *when* CHARLEY *enters, as of old, in knickers.*) I got no room for you, Charley.

CHARLEY. Room? For what?

WILLY. In the car.

Ebbets Field: a baseball stadium, the home of the Brooklyn Dodgers, torn down in 1960. Because it was used primarily for baseball, its locker rooms were called clubhouses.

CHARLEY. You goin' for a ride? I wanted to shoot some casino.

WILLY (*furiously*). Casino! (*Incredulously*) Don't you realize what today is?

LINDA. Oh, he knows, Willy. He's just kidding you.

WILLY. That's nothing to kid about!

CHARLEY. No, Linda, what's goin' on?

LINDA. He's playing in Ebbets Field.

CHARLEY. Baseball in this weather?

WILLY. Don't talk to him. Come on, come on! (*He is pushing them out.*)

CHARLEY. Wait a minute, didn't you hear the news?

WILLY. What?

CHARLEY. Don't you listen to the radio? Ebbets Field just blew up.

WILLY. You go to hell! (CHARLEY *laughs. Pushing them out*) Come on, come on! We're late.

CHARLEY (*as they go*). Knock a homer, Biff, knock a homer!

WILLY (*the last to leave, turning to* CHARLEY). I don't think that was funny, Charley. This is the greatest day of his life.

CHARLEY. Willy, when are you going to grow up?

WILLY. Yeah, heh? When this game is over, Charley, you'll be laughing out the other side of your face. They'll be calling him another Red Grange.° Twenty-five thousand a year.

CHARLEY (*kidding*). Is that so?

WILLY. Yeah, that's so.

CHARLEY. Well, then, I'm sorry, Willy. But tell me something.

WILLY. What?

CHARLEY. Who is Red Grange?

WILLY. Put up your hands. Goddam you, put up your hands!

(CHARLEY, *chuckling, shakes his head and walks away, around the left corner of the stage.* WILLY *follows him. The music rises to a mocking frenzy.*)

WILLY. Who the hell do you think you are, better than everybody else? You don't know everything, you big, ignorant, stupid . . . Put up your hands!

(*Light rises, on the right side of the forestage, on a small table in the reception room of* CHARLEY's *office. Traffic sounds are heard.* BERNARD, *now mature, sits whistling to himself. A pair of tennis rackets and an overnight bag are on the floor beside him.*)

WILLY (*offstage*). What are you walking away for? Don't walk away! If you're going to say something say it to my face! I know you laugh at me behind my back. You'll laugh out of the other side of your goddam face after this game. Touchdown! Touchdown! Eighty thousand people! Touchdown! Right between the goal posts.

Red Grange: famous All-American running back at the University of Illinois (1923–25)

(BERNARD *is a quiet, earnest, but self-assured young man.* WILLY'S *voice is coming from right upstage now.* BERNARD *lowers his feet off the table and listens.* JENNY, *his father's secretary, enters.*)

JENNY (*distressed*). Say, Bernard, will you go out in the hall?

BERNARD. What is that noise? Who is it?

JENNY. Mr. Loman. He just got off the elevator.

BERNARD (*getting up*). Who's he arguing with?

JENNY. Nobody. There's nobody with him. I can't deal with him any more, and your father gets all upset everytime he comes. I've got a lot of typing to do, and your father's waiting to sign it. Will you see him?

WILLY (*entering*). Touchdown! Touch—(*He sees* JENNY.) Jenny, Jenny, good to see you. How're ya? Workin'? Or still honest?

JENNY. Fine. How've you been feeling?

WILLY. Not much any more, Jenny. Ha, Ha! (*He is surprised to see the rackets.*)

BERNARD. Hello, Uncle Willy.

WILLY (*almost shocked*). Bernard! Well, look who's here! (*He comes quickly, guiltily, to* BERNARD *and warmly shakes his hand.*)

BERNARD. How are you? Good to see you.

WILLY. What are you doing here?

BERNARD. Oh, just stopped by to see Pop. Get off my feet till my train leaves. I'm going to Washington in a few minutes.

WILLY. Is he in?

BERNARD. Yes, he's in his office with the accountant. Sit down.

WILLY (*sitting down*). What're you going to do in Washington?

BERNARD. Oh, just a case I've got there, Willy.

WILLY. That so? (*Indicating the rackets*) You going to play tennis there?

BERNARD. I'm staying with a friend who's got a court.

WILLY. Don't say. His own tennis court. Must be fine people, I bet.

BERNARD. They are, very nice. Dad tells me Biff's in town.

WILLY (*with a big smile*). Yeah, Biff's in. Working on a very big deal, Bernard.

BERNARD. What's Biff doing?

WILLY. Well, he's been doing very big things in the West. But he decided to establish himself here. Very big. We're having dinner. Did I hear your wife had a boy?

BERNARD. That's right. Our second.

WILLY. Two boys! What do you know!

BERNARD. What kind of a deal has Biff got?

WILLY. Well, Bill Oliver—very big sporting goods man—he wants Biff very badly. Called him in from the West. Long distance, carte blanche, special deliveries. Your friends have their own private tennis court?

BERNARD. You still with the old firm, Willy?

WILLY (*after a pause*). I'm—I'm overjoyed to see how you made the grade, Bernard, overjoyed. It's an encouraging thing to see a young man really—really—Looks very good for Biff—very—(*He breaks off, then*) Bernard—(*He is so full of emotion, he breaks off again.*)

BERNARD. What is it, Willy?

WILLY (*small and alone*). What—what's the secret?

BERNARD. What secret?

WILLY. How—how did you? Why didn't he ever catch on?

BERNARD. I wouldn't know that, Willy.

WILLY (*confidentially, desperately*). You were his friend, his boyhood friend. There's something I don't understand about it. His life ended after that Ebbets Field game. From the age of seventeen nothing good ever happened to him.

BERNARD. He never trained himself for anything.

WILLY. But he did, he did. After high school he took so many correspondence courses. Radio mechanics; television; God knows what, and never made the slightest mark.

BERNARD (*taking off his glasses*). Willy, do you want to talk candidly?

WILLY (*rising, faces* BERNARD). I regard you as a very brilliant man, Bernard. I value your advice.

BERNARD. Oh, the hell with the advice, Willy. I couldn't advise you. There's just one thing I've always wanted to ask you. When he was supposed to graduate, and the math teacher flunked him—

WILLY. Oh, that son-of-a-bitch ruined his life.

BERNARD. Yeah, but, Willy, all he had to do was go to summer school and make up that subject.

WILLY. That's right, that's right.

BERNARD. Did you tell him not to go to summer school?

WILLY. Me? I begged him to go. I ordered him to go!

BERNARD. Then why wouldn't he go?

WILLY. Why? Why! Bernard, that question has been trailing me like a ghost for the last fifteen years. He flunked the subject, and laid down and died like a hammer hit him!

BERNARD. Take it easy, kid.

WILLY. Let me talk to you—I got nobody to talk to. Bernard, Bernard, was it my fault? Y'see? It keeps going around in my mind, maybe I did something to him. I got nothing to give him.

BERNARD. Don't take it so hard.

WILLY. Why did he lay down? What is the story there? You were his friend!

BERNARD. Willy, I remember, it was June, and our grades came out. And he'd flunked math.

WILLY. That son-of-a-bitch!

BERNARD. No, it wasn't right then. Biff just got very angry, I remember, and he was ready to enroll in summer school.

WILLY (*surprised*). He was?

BERNARD. He wasn't beaten by it at all. But then, Willy, he disappeared from the block for almost a month. And I got the idea that he'd gone up to New England to see you. Did he have a talk with you then?

(WILLY *stares in silence.*)

BERNARD. Willy?

WILLY (*with a strong edge of resentment in his voice*). Yeah, he came to Boston. What about it?

BERNARD. Well, just that when he came back—I'll never forget this, it always mystifies me. Because I thought so well of Biff, even though he'd always taken advantage of me. I loved him, Willy, y'know? And he came back after that month and took his sneakers—remember those sneakers with "University of Virginia" printed on them? He was so proud of those, wore them every day. And he took them down in the cellar, and burned them up in the furnace. We had a fist fight. It lasted at least half an hour. Just the two of us, punching each other down the cellar, and crying right through it. I've often thought of how strange it was that I knew he'd given up his life. What happened in Boston, Willy?

(WILLY *looks at him as at an intruder.*)

BERNARD. I just bring it up because you asked me.

WILLY (*angrily*). Nothing. What do you mean, "What happened?" What's that got to do with anything?

BERNARD. Well, don't get sore.

WILLY. What are you trying to do, blame it on me? If a boy lays down is that my fault?

BERNARD. Now, Willy, don't get—

WILLY. Well, don't—don't talk to me that way! What does that mean, "What happened?"

(CHARLEY *enters. He is in his vest, and he carries a bottle of bourbon.*)

CHARLEY. Hey, you're going to miss that train. (*He waves the bottle.*)

BERNARD. Yeah, I'm going. (*He takes the bottle.*) Thanks, Pop. (*He picks up his rackets and bag.*) Good-by, Willy, and don't worry about it. You know, "If at first you don't succeed . . ."

WILLY. Yes, I believe in that.

BERNARD. But sometimes, Willy, it's better for a man just to walk away.

WILLY. Walk away?

BERNARD. That's right.

WILLY. But if you can't walk away?

BERNARD (*after a slight pause*). I guess that's when it's tough. (*Extending his hand*) Good-by, Willy.

WILLY (*shaking BERNARD's hand*). Good-by, boy.

CHARLEY (*an arm on BERNARD's shoulder*). How do you like this kid? Gonna argue a case in front of the Supreme Court.

BERNARD (*protesting*). Pop!
WILLY (*genuinely shocked, pained, and happy*). No! The Supreme Court!
BERNARD. I gotta run. 'By Dad!
CHARLEY. Knock 'em dead, Bernard!

(BERNARD *goes off.*)

WILLY (*as* CHARLEY *takes out his wallet*). The Supreme Court! And he didn't even mention it!
CHARLEY (*counting out money on the desk*). He don't have to—he's gonna do it.
WILLY. And you never told him what to do, did you? You never took any interest in him.
CHARLEY. My salvation is that I never took any interest in anything. There's some money—fifty dollars. I got an accountant inside.
WILLY. Charley, look . . . (*With difficulty*) I got my insurance to pay. If you can manage it—I need a hundred and ten dollars.

(CHARLEY *doesn't reply for a moment; merely stops moving.*)

WILLY. I'd draw it from my bank but Linda would know, and I . . .
CHARLEY. Sit down, Willy.
WILLY (*moving toward the chair*). I'm keeping an account of everything, remember. I'll pay every penny back. (*He sits.*)
CHARLEY. Now listen to me, Willy.
WILLY. I want you to know I appreciate . . .
CHARLEY (*sitting down on the table*). Willy, what're you doin'? What the hell is goin' on in your head?
WILLY. Why? I'm simply . . .
CHARLEY. I offered you a job. You can make fifty dollars a week. And I won't send you on the road.
WILLY. I've got a job.
CHARLEY. Without pay? What kind of a job is a job without pay? (*He rises.*) Now, look, kid, enough is enough. I'm no genius but I know when I'm being insulted.
WILLY. Insulted!
CHARLEY. Why don't you want to work for me?
WILLY. What's the matter with you? I've got a job.
CHARLEY. Then what're you walkin' in here every week for?
WILLY (*getting up*). Well, if you don't want me to walk in here—
CHARLEY. I am offering you a job.
WILLY. I don't want your goddam job!
CHARLEY. When the hell are you going to grow up?
WILLY (*furiously*). You big ignoramus, if you say that to me again I'll rap you one! I don't care how big you are! (*He's ready to fight.*)

(*Pause*)

CHARLEY (*kindly, going to him*). How much do you need, Willy?

WILLY. Charley, I'm strapped. I'm strapped. I don't know what to do. I was just fired.

CHARLEY. Howard fired you?

WILLY. That snotnose. Imagine that? I named him. I named him Howard.

CHARLEY. Willy, when're you gonna realize that them things don't mean anything? You named him Howard, but you can't sell that. The only thing you got in this world is what you can sell. And the funny thing is that you're a salesman, and you don't know that.

WILLY. I've always tried to think otherwise, I guess. I always felt that if a man was impressive, and well liked, that nothing—

CHARLEY. Why must everybody like you? Who liked J. P. Morgan? Was he impressive? In a Turkish bath he'd look like a butcher. But with his pockets on he was very well liked. Now listen, Willy, I know you don't like me, and nobody can say I'm in love with you, but I'll give you a job because—just for the hell of it, put it that way. Now what do you say?

WILLY. I—I just can't work for you, Charley.

CHARLEY. What're you, jealous of me?

WILLY. I can't work for you, that's all, don't ask me why.

CHARLEY (*angered, takes out more bills*). You been jealous of me all your life, you damned fool! Here, pay your insurance. (*He puts the money in* WILLY'*s hand.*)

WILLY. I'm keeping strict accounts.

CHARLEY. I've got some work to do. Take care of yourself. And pay your insurance.

WILLY (*moving to the right*). Funny, y'know? After all the highways, and the trains, and the appointments, and the years, you end up worth more dead than alive.

CHARLEY. Willy, nobody's worth nothin' dead. (*After a slight pause*) Did you hear what I said? (WILLY *stands still, dreaming.*) Willy!

WILLY. Apologize to Bernard for me when you see him. I didn't mean to argue with him. He's a fine boy. They're all fine boys, and they'll end up big—all of them. Someday they'll all play tennis together. Wish me luck, Charley. He saw Bill Oliver today.

CHARLEY. Good luck.

WILLY (*on the verge of tears*). Charley, you're the only friend I got. Isn't that a remarkable thing? (*He goes out.*)

CHARLEY. Jesus!

(CHARLEY *stares after him a moment and follows. All light blacks out. Suddenly raucous music is heard, and a red glow rises behind the screen at right.* STANLEY, *a young waiter, appears, carrying a table, followed by* HAPPY, *who is carrying two chairs.*)

STANLEY (*putting the table down*). That's all right, Mr. Loman, I can handle it myself. (*He turns and takes the chairs from* HAPPY *and places them at the table.*)

HAPPY (*glancing around*). Oh, this is better.

STANLEY. Sure, in the front there you're in the middle of all kinds a noise. Whenever you got a party, Mr. Loman, you just tell me and I'll put you back here. Y'know, there's a lotta people they don't like it private, because when they go out they like to see a lotta action around them because they're sick and tired to stay in the house by theirself. But I know you, you ain't from Hackensack. You know what I mean?

HAPPY (*sitting down*). So how's it coming, Stanley?

STANLEY. Ah, it's a dog's life. I only wish during the war they'd a took me in the Army. I coulda been dead by now.

HAPPY. My brother's back, Stanley.

STANLEY. Oh, he come back, heh? From the Far West.

HAPPY. Yeah, big cattle man, my brother, so treat him right. And my father's coming too.

STANLEY. Oh, your father too!

HAPPY. You got a couple of nice lobsters?

STANLEY. Hundred per cent, big.

HAPPY. I want them with the claws.

STANLEY. Don't worry, I don't give you no mice. (HAPPY *laughs.*) How about some wine? It'll put a head on the meal.

HAPPY. No. You remember, Stanley, that recipe I brought you from overseas? With the champagne in it?

STANLEY. Oh, yeah, sure. I still got it tacked up yet in the kitchen. But that'll have to cost a buck apiece anyways.

HAPPY. That's all right.

STANLEY. What'd you, hit a number or somethin'?

HAPPY. No, it's a little celebration. My brother is—I think he pulled off a big deal today. I think we're going into business together.

STANLEY. Great! That's the best for you. Because a family business, you know what I mean?—that's the best.

HAPPY. That's what I think.

STANLEY. 'Cause what's the difference? Somebody steals? It's in the family. Know what I mean? (*Sotto voce*) Like this bartender here. The boss is goin' crazy what kinda leak he's got in the cash register. You put it in but it don't come out.

HAPPY (*raising his head*). Sh!

STANLEY. What?

HAPPY. You notice I wasn't lookin' right or left, was I?

STANLEY. No.

HAPPY. And my eyes are closed.

STANLEY. So what's the—?

HAPPY. Strudel's comin'.

STANLEY (*catching on, looks around*). Ah, no, there's no—

(*He breaks off as a furred, lavishly dressed girl enters and sits at the next table. Both follow her with their eyes.*)

STANLEY. Geez, how'd ya know?

HAPPY. I got radar or something. (*Staring directly at her profile*) Oooooooo . . . Stanley.

STANLEY. I think that's for you, Mr. Loman.

HAPPY. Look at that mouth. Oh, God. And the binoculars.

STANLEY. Geez, you got a life, Mr. Loman.

HAPPY. Wait on her.

STANLEY (*going to the* GIRL'S *table*). Would you like a menu, ma'am?

GIRL. I'm expecting someone, but I'd like a—

HAPPY. Why don't you bring her—excuse me, miss, do you mind? I sell champagne, and I'd like you to try my brand. Bring her a champagne, Stanley.

GIRL. That's awfully nice of you.

HAPPY. Don't mention it. It's all company money. (*He laughs.*)

GIRL. That's a charming product to be selling, isn't it?

HAPPY. Oh, gets to be like everything else. Selling is selling, y'know.

GIRL. I suppose.

HAPPY. You don't happen to sell, do you?

GIRL. No, I don't sell.

HAPPY. Would you object to a compliment from a stranger? You ought to be on a magazine cover.

GIRL (*looking at him a little archly*). I have been.

(STANLEY *comes in with a glass of champagne.*)

HAPPY. What'd I say before, Stanley? You see? She's a cover girl.

STANLEY. Oh, I could see, I could see.

HAPPY (*to the* GIRL). What magazine?

GIRL. Oh, a lot of them. (*She takes the drink.*) Thank you.

HAPPY. You know what they say in France, don't you? "Champagne is the drink of the complexion"—Hya, Biff!

(BIFF *has entered and sits with* HAPPY.)

BIFF. Hello, kid. Sorry I'm late.

HAPPY. I just got here. Uh, Miss—?

GIRL. Forsythe.

HAPPY. Miss Forsythe, this is my brother.

BIFF. Is Dad here?

HAPPY. His name is Biff? You might've heard of him. Great football player.

GIRL. Really? What team?

HAPPY. Are you familiar with football?

GIRL. No, I'm afraid I'm not.

HAPPY. Biff is quarterback with the New York Giants.

GIRL. Well, that is nice, isn't it? (*She drinks.*)

HAPPY. Good health.

GIRL. I'm happy to meet you.

HAPPY. That's my name. Hap. It's really Harold, but at West Point they called me Happy.

GIRL (*now really impressed*). Oh, I see. How do you do? (*She turns her profile.*)

BIFF. Isn't Dad coming?

HAPPY. You want her?

BIFF. Oh, I could never make that.

HAPPY. I remember the time that idea would never come into your head. Where's the old confidence, Biff?

BIFF. I just saw Oliver—

HAPPY. Wait a minute. I've got to see that old confidence again. Do you want her? She's on call.

BIFF. Oh, no. (*He turns to look at the* GIRL.)

HAPPY. I'm telling you. Watch this. (*Turning to the* GIRL) Honey? (*She turns to him.*) Are you busy?

GIRL. Well, I am . . . but I could make a phone call.

HAPPY. Do that, will you, honey? And see if you can get a friend. We'll be here for a while. Biff is one of the greatest football players in the country.

GIRL (*standing up*). Well, I'm certainly happy to meet you.

HAPPY. Come back soon.

GIRL. I'll try.

HAPPY. Don't try, honey, try hard.

(*The* GIRL *exits.* STANLEY *follows, shaking his head in bewildered admiration.*)

HAPPY. Isn't that a shame now? A beautiful girl like that? That's why I can't get married. There's not a good woman in a thousand. New York is loaded with them, kid!

BIFF. Hap, look—

HAPPY. I told you she was on call!

BIFF (*strangely unnerved*). Cut it out, will ya? I want to say something to you.

HAPPY. Did you see Oliver?

BIFF. I saw him all right. Now look, I want to tell Dad a couple of things and I want you to help me.

HAPPY. What? Is he going to back you?

BIFF. Are you crazy? You're out of your goddam head, you know that?

HAPPY. Why? What happened?

BIFF (*breathlessly*). I did a terrible thing today, Hap. It's been the strangest day I ever went through. I'm all numb, I swear.

HAPPY. You mean he wouldn't see you?

BIFF. Well, I waited for six hours for him, see? All day. Kept sending my name in. Even tried to date his secretary so she'd get me to him, but no soap.

HAPPY. Because you're not showin' the old confidence, Biff. He remembered you, didn't he?

BIFF (*stopping* HAPPY *with a gesture*). Finally, about five o'clock, he comes out. Didn't remember who I was or anything. I felt like such an idiot, Hap.

HAPPY. Did you tell him my Florida idea?

BIFF. He walked away. I saw him for one minute. I got so mad I could've torn the walls down! How the hell did I ever get the idea I was a salesman there? I even believed myself that I'd been a salesman for him! And then he gave me one look and—I realized what a ridiculous lie my whole life has been! We've been talking in a dream for fifteen years. I was a shipping clerk.

HAPPY. What'd you do?

BIFF (*with great tension and wonder*). Well, he left, see. And the secretary went out. I was all alone in the waiting-room. I don't know what came over me, Hap. The next thing I know I'm in his office—paneled walls, everything. I can't explain it. I—Hap, I took his fountain pen.

HAPPY. Geez, did he catch you?

BIFF. I ran out. I ran down all eleven flights. I ran and ran and ran.

HAPPY. That was an awful dumb—what'd you do that for?

BIFF (*agonized*). I don't know, I just—wanted to take something, I don't know. You gotta help me, Hap, I'm gonna tell Pop.

HAPPY. You crazy? What for?

BIFF. Hap, he's got to understand that I'm not the man somebody lends that kind of money to. He thinks I've been spiting him all these years and it's eating him up.

HAPPY. That's just it. You tell him something nice.

BIFF. I can't.

HAPPY. Say you got a lunch date with Oliver tomorrow.

BIFF. So what do I do tomorrow?

HAPPY. You leave the house tomorrow and come back at night and say Oliver is thinking it over. And he thinks it over for a couple of weeks, and gradually it fades away and nobody's the worse.

BIFF. But it'll go on forever!

HAPPY. Dad is never so happy as when he's looking forward to something!

(WILLY *enters*.)

HAPPY. Hello, scout!

WILLY. Gee, I haven't been here in years!

(STANLEY *has followed* WILLY *in and sets a chair for him.* STANLEY *starts off but* HAPPY *stops him.*)

HAPPY. Stanley!

(STANLEY *stands by, waiting for an order.*)

BIFF (*going to* WILLY *with guilt, as to an invalid*). Sit down, Pop. You want a drink?

WILLY. Sure, I don't mind.

BIFF. Let's get a load on.

WILLY. You look worried.

BIFF. N-no. (*To* STANLEY) Scotch all around. Make it doubles.

STANLEY. Doubles, right. (*He goes.*)

WILLY. You had a couple already, didn't you?

BIFF. Just a couple, yeah.

WILLY. Well, what happened, boy? (*Nodding affirmatively, with a smile*) Everything go all right?

BIFF (*takes a breath, then reaches out and grasps* WILLY's *hand*). Pal . . . (*He is smiling bravely, and* WILLY *is smiling too.*) I had an experience today.

HAPPY. Terrific, Pop.

WILLY. That so? What happened?

BIFF (*high, slightly alcoholic, above the earth*). I'm going to tell you everything from first to last. It's been a strange day. (*Silence. He looks around, composes himself as best he can, but his breath keeps breaking the rhythm of his voice.*) I had to wait quite a while for him, and—

WILLY. Oliver?

BIFF. Yeah, Oliver. All day, as a matter of cold fact. And a lot of— instances—facts, Pop, facts about my life came back to me. Who was it, Pop? Who ever said I was a salesman with Oliver?

WILLY. Well, you were.

BIFF. No, Dad, I was a shipping clerk.

WILLY. But you were practically—

BIFF (*with determination*). Dad, I don't know who said it first, but I was never a salesman for Bill Oliver.

WILLY. What're you talking about?

BIFF. Let's hold on to the facts tonight, Pop. We're not going to get anywhere bullin' around. I was a shipping clerk.

WILLY (*angrily*). All right, now listen to me—

BIFF. Why don't you let me finish?

WILLY. I'm not interested in stories about the past or any crap of that kind because the woods are burning, boys, you understand? There's a big blaze going on all around. I was fired today.

BIFF (*shocked*). How could you be?

WILLY. I was fired, and I'm looking for a little good news to tell your mother, because the woman has waited and the woman has suffered. The gist of it is that I haven't got a story left in my head, Biff. So don't give me a lecture about facts and aspects. I am not interested. Now what've you got to say to me?

(STANLEY *enters with three drinks. They wait until he leaves.*)

WILLY. Did you see Oliver?

BIFF. Jesus, Dad!

WILLY. You mean you didn't go up there?

HAPPY. Sure he went up there.

BIFF. I did. I—saw him. How could they fire you?

WILLY (*on the edge of his chair*). What kind of a welcome did he give you?

BIFF. He won't even let you work on commission?

WILLY. I'm out! (*Driving*) So tell me, he gave you a warm welcome?

HAPPY. Sure, Pop, sure!

BIFF (*driven*). Well, it was kind of—

WILLY. I was wondering if he'd remember you. (*To* HAPPY) Imagine, man doesn't see him for ten, twelve years and gives him that kind of a welcome!

HAPPY. Damn right!

BIFF (*trying to return to the offensive*). Pop look—

WILLY. You know why he remembered you, don't you? Because you impressed him in those days.

BIFF. Let's talk quietly and get this down to the facts, huh?

WILLY (*as though* BIFF *had been interrupting*). Well, what happened? It's great news, Biff. Did he take you into his office or'd you talk in the waiting-room?

BIFF. Well, he came in, see, and—

WILLY (*with a big smile*). What'd he say? Betcha he threw his arm around you.

BIFF. Well, he kinda—

WILLY. He's a fine man. (*To* HAPPY) Very hard man to see, y'know.

HAPPY (*agreeing*). Oh, I know.

WILLY (*to* BIFF). Is that where you had the drinks?

BIFF. Yeah, he gave me a couple of—no, no!

HAPPY (*cutting in*). He told him my Florida idea.

WILLY. Don't interrupt. (*To* BIFF) How'd he react to the Florida idea?

BIFF. Dad, will you give me a minute to explain?

WILLY. I've been waiting for you to explain since I sat down here! What happened? He took you into his office and what?

BIFF. Well—I talked. And—and he listened, see.

WILLY. Famous for the way he listens, y'know. What was his answer?

BIFF. His answer was—(*He breaks off, suddenly angry.*) Dad, you're not letting me tell you what I want to tell you!

WILLY (*accusing, angered*). You didn't see him, did you?

BIFF. I did see him!

WILLY. What'd you insult him or something? You insulted him, didn't you?

BIFF. Listen, will you let me out of it, will you just let me out of it!

HAPPY. What the hell!

WILLY. Tell me what happened!

BIFF (*to* HAPPY). I can't talk to him!

(*A single trumpet note jars the ear. The light of green leaves stains the house, which holds the air of night and a dream.* YOUNG BERNARD *enters and knocks on the door of the house.*)

YOUNG BERNARD (*frantically*). Mrs. Loman, Mrs. Loman!
HAPPY. Tell him what happened!
BIFF (*to* HAPPY). Shut up and leave me alone!
WILLY. No, no! You had to go and flunk math!
BIFF. What math? What're you talking about?
YOUNG BERNARD. Mrs. Loman, Mrs. Loman!

(LINDA *appears in the house, as of old.*)

WILLY (*wildly*). Math, math, math!
BIFF. Take it easy, Pop!
YOUNG BERNARD. Mrs. Loman!
WILLY (*furiously*). If you hadn't flunked you'd've been set by now!
BIFF. Now, look, I'm gonna tell you what happened, and you're going to listen to me.
YOUNG BERNARD. Mrs. Loman!
BIFF. I waited six hours—
HAPPY. What the hell are you saying?
BIFF. I kept sending in my name but he wouldn't see me. So finally he . . . (*He continues unheard as light fades low on the restaurant.*)
YOUNG BERNARD. Biff flunked math!
LINDA. No!
YOUNG BERNARD. Birnbaum flunked him! They won't graduate him!
LINDA. But they have to. He's gotta go to the university. Where is he? Biff! Biff!
YOUNG BERNARD. No, he left. He went to Grand Central.
LINDA. Grand—You mean he went to Boston!
YOUNG BERNARD. Is Uncle Willy in Boston?
LINDA. Oh, maybe Willy can talk to the teacher. Oh, the poor, poor boy!

(*Light on house area snaps out.*)

BIFF (*at the table, now audible, holding up a gold fountain pen*). . . . so I'm washed up with Oliver, you understand? Are you listening to me?
WILLY (*at a loss*). Yeah, sure. If you hadn't flunked—
BIFF. Flunked what? What're you talking about?
WILLY. Don't blame everything on me! I didn't flunk math—you did! What pen?
HAPPY. That was awful dumb, Biff, a pen like that is worth—
WILLY (*seeing the pen for the first time*). You took Oliver's pen?
BIFF (*weakening*). Dad, I just explained it to you.
WILLY. You stole Bill Oliver's fountain pen!

BIFF. I didn't exactly steal it! That's just what I've been explaining to you!

HAPPY. He had it in his hand and just then Oliver walked in, so he got nervous and stuck it in his pocket!

WILLY. My God, Biff!

BIFF. I never intended to do it, Dad!

OPERATOR'S VOICE. Standish Arms, good evening!

WILLY (*shouting*). I'm not in my room!

BIFF (*frightened*). Dad, what's the matter? (*He and* HAPPY *stand up.*)

OPERATOR. Ringing Mr. Loman for you!

WILLY. I'm not there, stop it!

BIFF (*horrified, gets down on one knee before* WILLY). Dad, I'll make good, I'll make good. (WILLY *tries to get to his feet.* BIFF *holds him down.*) Sit down now.

WILLY. No, you're no good, you're no good for anything.

BIFF. I am, Dad, I'll find something else, you understand? Now don't worry about anything. (*He holds up* WILLY's *face.*) Talk to me, Dad.

OPERATOR. Mr. Loman does not answer. Shall I page him?

WILLY (*attempting to stand, as though to rush and silence the* OPERATOR). No, no, no!

HAPPY. He'll strike something, Pop.

WILLY. No, no . . .

BIFF (*desperately, standing over* WILLY). Pop, listen! Listen to me! I'm telling you something good. Oliver talked to his partner about the Florida idea. You listening? He—he talked to his partner, and he came to me . . . I'm going to be all right, you hear? Dad, listen to me, he said it was just a question of the amount!

WILLY. Then you . . . got it?

HAPPY. He's gonna be terrific, Pop!

WILLY (*trying to stand*). Then you got it, haven't you? You got it! You got it!

BIFF (*agonized, holds* WILLY *down*). No, no. Look, Pop. I'm supposed to have lunch with them tomorrow. I'm just telling you this so you'll know that I can still make an impression, Pop. And I'll make good somewhere, but I can't go tomorrow, see?

WILLY. Why not? You simply—

BIFF. But the pen, Pop!

WILLY. You give it to him and tell him it was an oversight!

HAPPY. Sure, have lunch tomorrow!

BIFF. I can't say that—

WILLY. You were doing a crossword puzzle and accidentally used his pen!

BIFF. Listen, kid, I took those balls years ago, now I walk in with his fountain pen? That clinches it, don't you see? I can't face him like that! I'll try elsewhere.

PAGE'S VOICE. Paging Mr. Loman!

WILLY. Don't you want to be anything?

BIFF. Pop, how can I go back?

WILLY. You don't want to be anything, is that what's behind it?

BIFF (*now angry at* WILLY *for not crediting his sympathy*). Don't take it that way! You think it was easy walking into that office after what I'd done to him? A team of horses couldn't have dragged me back to Bill Oliver!

WILLY. Then why'd you go?

BIFF. Why did I go? Why did I go! Look at you! Look at what's become of you!

(*Off left,* THE WOMAN *laughs.*)

WILLY. Biff, you're going to go to that lunch tomorrow, or—

BIFF. I can't go. I've got no appointment!

HAPPY. Biff, for . . . !

WILLY. Are you spiting me?

BIFF. Don't take it that way! Goddammit!

WILLY (*strikes* BIFF *and falters away from the table*). You rotten little louse! Are you spiting me?

THE WOMAN. Someone's at the door, Willy!

BIFF. I'm no good, can't you see what I am?

HAPPY (*separating them*). Hey, you're in a restaurant! Now cut it out, both of you! (*The* GIRLS *enter.*) Hello, girls, sit down.

(THE WOMAN *laughs, off left.*)

MISS FORSYTHE. I guess we might as well. This is Letta.

THE WOMAN. Willy, are you going to wake up?

BIFF (*ignoring* WILLY). How're ya, miss, sit down. What do you drink?

MISS FORSYTHE. Letta might not be able to stay long.

LETTA. I gotta get up very early tomorrow. I got jury duty. I'm so excited! Were you fellows ever on a jury?

BIFF. No, but I been in front of them! (*The* GIRLS *laugh.*) This is my father.

LETTA. Isn't he cute? Sit down with us, Pop.

HAPPY. Sit him down, Biff!

BIFF (*going to him*). Come on, slugger, drink us under the table. To hell with it! Come on, sit down, pal.

(*On* BIFF'S *last insistence,* WILLY *is about to sit.*)

THE WOMAN (*now urgently*). Willy, are you going to answer the door!

(THE WOMAN'S *call pulls* WILLY *back. He starts right, befuddled.*)

BIFF. Hey, where are you going?

WILLY. Open the door.

BIFF. The door?

WILLY. The washroom . . . the door . . . where's the door?

BIFF (*leading* WILLY *to the left*). Just go straight down.

(WILLY *moves left.*)

THE WOMAN. Willy, Willy, are you going to get up, get up, get up, get up?

(WILLY *exits left.*)

LETTA. I think it's sweet you bring your daddy along.

MISS FORSYTHE. Oh, he isn't really your father!

BIFF (*at left, turning to her resentfully*). Miss Forsythe, you've just seen a prince walk by. A fine, troubled prince. A hard-working, unappreciated prince. A pal, you understand? A good companion. Always for his boys.

LETTA. That's so sweet.

HAPPY. Well, girls, what's the program? We're wasting time. Come on, Biff. Gather round. Where would you like to go?

BIFF. Why don't you do something for him?

HAPPY. Me!

BIFF. Don't you give a damn for him, Hap?

HAPPY. What're you talking about? I'm the one who—

BIFF. I sense it, you don't give a good goddam about him. (*He takes the rolled-up hose from his pocket and puts it on the table in front of* HAPPY.) Look what I found in the cellar, for Christ's sake. How can you bear to let it go on?

HAPPY. Me? Who goes away? Who runs off and—

BIFF. Yeah, but he doesn't mean anything to you. You could help him—I can't! Don't you understand what I'm talking about? He's going to kill himself, don't you know that?

HAPPY. Don't I know it! Me!

BIFF. Hap, help him! Jesus . . . help him . . . Help me, help me, I can't bear to look at his face! (*Ready to weep, he hurries out, up right.*)

HAPPY (*starting after him*). Where are you going?

MISS FORSYTHE. What's he so mad about?

HAPPY. Come on, girls, we'll catch up with him.

MISS FORSYTHE (*as* HAPPY *pushes her out*). Say, I don't like that temper of his!

HAPPY. He's just a little overstrung, he'll be all right!

WILLY (*off left, as* THE WOMAN *laughs*). Don't answer! Don't answer!

LETTA. Don't you want to tell your father—

HAPPY. No, that's not my father. He's just a guy. Come on, we'll catch Biff, and, honey, we're going to paint this town! Stanley, where's the check! Hey, Stanley!

(*They exit.* STANLEY *looks toward left.*)

STANLEY (*calling to* HAPPY *indignantly*). Mr. Loman! Mr. Loman!

(STANLEY *picks up a chair and follows them off. Knocking is heard off left.* THE WOMAN *enters, laughing.* WILLY *follows her. She is in a black slip; he is buttoning his shirt. Raw, sensuous music accompanies their speech.*)

WILLY. Will you stop laughing? Will you stop?

THE WOMAN. Aren't you going to answer the door? He'll wake the whole hotel.

WILLY. I'm not expecting anybody.

THE WOMAN. Whyn't you have another drink, honey, and stop being so damn self-centered?

WILLY. I'm so lonely.

THE WOMAN. You know you ruined me, Willy? From now on, whenever you come to the office, I'll see that you go right through to the buyers. No waiting at my desk any more, Willy. You ruined me.

WILLY. That's nice of you to say that.

THE WOMAN. Gee, you are self-centered! Why so sad? You are the saddest, self-centeredest soul I ever did see-saw. (*She laughs. He kisses her.*) Come on inside, drummer boy. It's silly to be dressing in the middle of the night. (*As knocking is heard*) Aren't you going to answer the door?

WILLY. They're knocking on the wrong door.

THE WOMAN. But I felt the knocking. And he heard us talking in here. Maybe the hotel's on fire!

WILLY (*his terror rising*). It's a mistake.

THE WOMAN. Then tell him to go away!

WILLY. There's nobody there.

THE WOMAN. It's getting on my nerves, Willy. There's somebody standing out there and it's getting on my nerves!

WILLY (*pushing her away from him*). All right, stay in the bathroom here, and don't come out. I think there's a law in Massachusetts about it, so don't come out. It may be that new room clerk. He looked very mean. So don't come out. It's a mistake, there's no fire.

(*The knocking is heard again. He takes a few steps away from her, and she vanishes into the wing. The light follows him, and now he is facing* YOUNG BIFF, *who carries a suitcase.* BIFF *steps toward him. The music is gone.*)

BIFF. Why didn't you answer?

WILLY. Biff! What are you doing in Boston?

BIFF. Why didn't you answer? I've been knocking for five minutes, I called you on the phone—

WILLY. I just heard you. I was in the bathroom and had the door shut. Did anything happen home?

BIFF. Dad—I let you down.

WILLY. What do you mean?

BIFF. Dad . . .

WILLY. Biffo, what's this about? (*Putting his arm around* BIFF) Come on, let's go downstairs and get you a malted.

BIFF. Dad, I flunked math.

WILLY. Not for the term?

BIFF. The term. I haven't got enough credits to graduate.

WILLY. You mean to say Bernard wouldn't give you the answers?

BIFF. He did, he tried, but I only got a sixty-one.

WILLY. And they wouldn't give you four points.

BIFF. Birnbaum refused absolutely. I begged him, Pop, but he won't give me those points. You gotta talk to him before they close the school. Because if he saw the kind of man you are, and you just talked to him in your way, I'm sure he'd come through for me. The class came right before practice, see, and I didn't go enough. Would you talk to him? He'd like you, Pop. You know the way you could talk.

WILLY. You're on. We'll drive right back.

BIFF. Oh, Dad, good work! I'm sure he'll change it for you!

WILLY. Go downstairs and tell the clerk I'm checkin' out. Go right down.

BIFF. Yes, sir! See, the reason he hates me, Pop—one day he was late for class so I got up at the blackboard and imitated him. I crossed my eyes and talked with a lithp.

WILLY (*laughing*). You did? The kids like it?

BIFF. They nearly died laughing!

WILLY. Yeah? What'd you do?

BIFF. The thquare root of thixthy twee is . . . (WILLY *bursts out laughing;* BIFF *joins him.*) And in the middle of it he walked in!

(WILLY *laughs and* THE WOMAN *joins in off-stage.*)

WILLY (*without hesitation*). Hurry downstairs and—

BIFF. Somebody in there?

WILLY. No, that was next door.

(THE WOMAN *laughs offstage.*)

BIFF. Somebody got in your bathroom!

WILLY. No, it's the next room, there's a party—

THE WOMAN (*enters, laughing. She lisps this*). Can I come in? There's something in the bathtub, Willy, and it's moving!

(WILLY *looks at* BIFF, *who is staring open-mouthed and horrified at* THE WOMAN.)

WILLY. Ah—you better go back to your room. They must be finished painting by now. They're painting her room so I let her take a shower here. Go back, go back . . . (*He pushes her.*)

THE WOMAN (*resisting*). But I've got to get dressed, Willy, I can't—

WILLY. Get out of here! Go back, go back . . . (*Suddenly striving for the ordinary*) This is Miss Francis, Biff, she's a buyer. They're painting her room. Go back, Miss Francis, go back . . .

THE WOMAN. But my clothes, I can't go out naked in the hall!

WILLY (*pushing her offstage*). Get outa here! Go back, go back!

(BIFF *slowly sits down on his suitcase as the argument continues offstage.*)

THE WOMAN. Where's my stockings? You promised me stockings, Willy!

WILLY. I have no stockings here!

THE WOMAN. You had two boxes of size nine sheers for me, and I want them!

WILLY. Here, for God's sake, will you get outa here!

THE WOMAN (*enters holding a box of stockings*). I just hope there's nobody in the hall. That's all I hope. (*To* BIFF) Are you football or baseball?

BIFF. Football.

THE WOMAN (*angry, humiliated*). That's me too. G'night. (*She snatches her clothes from* WILLY *and walks out.*)

WILLY (*after a pause*). Well, better get going. I want to get to the school first thing in the morning. Get my suits out of the closet. I'll get my valise. (BIFF *doesn't move.*) What's the matter? (BIFF *remains motionless, tears falling.*) She's a buyer. Buys for J. H. Simmons. She lives down the hall—they're painting. You don't imagine—(*He breaks off. After a pause*) Now listen, pal, she's just a buyer. She sees merchandise in her room and they have to keep it looking just so . . . (*Pause. Assuming command*) All right, get my suits. (BIFF *doesn't move.*) Now stop crying and do as I say. I gave you an order. Biff, I gave you an order! Is that what you do when I give you an order? How dare you cry! (*Putting his arm around* BIFF) Now look, Biff, when you grow up you'll understand about these things. You mustn't—you mustn't overemphasize a thing like this. I'll see Birnbaum first thing.in the morning.

BIFF. Never mind.

WILLY (*getting down beside* BIFF). Never mind! He's going to give you those points. I'll see to it.

BIFF. He wouldn't listen to you.

WILLY. He certainly will listen to me. You need those points for the U. of Virginia.

BIFF. I'm not going there.

WILLY. Heh? If I can't get him to change that mark you'll make it up in summer school. You've got all summer to—

BIFF (*his weeping breaking from him*). Dad . . .

WILLY (*infected by it*). Oh, my boy . . .

BIFF. Dad . . .

WILLY. She's nothing to me, Biff. I was lonely, I was terribly lonely.

BIFF. You—you gave her Mama's stockings! (*His tears break through qnd he rises to go.*)

WILLY (*grabbing for* BIFF). I gave you an order!

BIFF. Don't touch me, you—liar!

WILLY. Apologize for that!

BIFF. You fake! You phony little fake! You fake! (*Overcome, he turns quickly and weeping fully goes out with his suitcase.* WILLY *is left on the floor on his knees.*)

WILLY. I gave you an order! Biff, come back here or I'll beat you! Come back here! I'll whip you!

(STANLEY *comes quickly in from the right and stands in front of* WILLY.)

WILLY (*shouts at* STANLEY). I gave you an order . . .

STANLEY. Hey, let's pick it up, pick it up, Mr. Loman. (*He helps* WILLY *to his feet.*) Your boys left with the chippies. They said they'll see you home.

(*A second waiter watches some distance away.*)

WILLY. But we were supposed to have dinner together.

(*Music is heard,* WILLY's *theme.*)

STANLEY. Can you make it?

WILLY. I'll—sure. I can make it. (*Suddenly concerned about his clothes*) Do I—I look all right?

STANLEY. Sure, you look all right. (*He flicks a speck off* WILLY's *lapel.*)

WILLY. Here—here's a dollar.

STANLEY. Oh, your son paid me. It's all right.

WILLY (*putting it in* STANLEY's *hand*). No, take it. You're a good boy.

STANLEY. Oh, no, you don't have to . . .

WILLY. Here's some more, I don't need it any more. (*After a slight pause*) Tell me—is there a seed store in the neighborhood?

STANLEY. Seeds? You mean like to plant?

(*As* WILLY *turns,* STANLEY *slips the money back into his jacket pocket.*)

WILLY. Yes. Carrots, peas . . .

STANLEY. Well, there's hardware stores on Sixth Avenue, but it may be too late now.

WILLY (*anxiously*). Oh, I'd better hurry. I've got to get some seeds. (*He starts off to the right.*) I've got to get some seeds, right away. Nothing's planted. I don't have a thing in the ground.

(WILLY *hurries out as the light goes down.* STANLEY *moves over to the right after him, watches him off. The other waiter has been staring at* WILLY.)

STANLEY (*to the waiter*). Well, whatta you looking at?

(*The waiter picks up the chairs and moves off right.* STANLEY *takes the table and follows him. The light fades on this area. There is a long pause, the sound of the flute coming over. The light gradually rises on the kitchen, which is empty.* HAPPY *appears at the door of the house, followed by* BIFF. HAPPY *is carrying a large bunch of long-stemmed roses. He enters the kitchen, looks around for*

LINDA. *Not seeing her, he turns to* BIFF, *who is just outside the house door, and makes a gesture with his hands, indicating "Not here, I guess." He looks into the living-room and freezes. Inside,* LINDA, *unseen, is seated,* WILLY's *coat on her lap. She rises ominously and quietly and moves toward* HAPPY, *who backs up into the kitchen, afraid.*)

HAPPY.   Hey, what're you doing up? (LINDA *says nothing but moves toward him implacably.*) Where's Pop? (*He keeps backing to the right, and now* LINDA *is in full view in the doorway to the living-room.*) Is he sleeping?
LINDA.   Where were you?
HAPPY (*trying to laugh it off*).   We met two girls, Mom, very fine types. Here, we brought you some flowers. (*Offering them to her*) Put them in your room, Ma.

(*She knocks them to the floor at* BIFF's *feet. He has now come inside and closed the door behind him. She stares at* BIFF, *silent.*)

HAPPY.   Now what'd you do that for? Mom, I want you to have some flowers—
LINDA (*cutting* HAPPY *off, violently to* BIFF).   Don't you care whether he lives or dies?
HAPPY (*going to the stairs*).   Come upstairs, Biff.
BIFF (*with a flare of disgust, to* HAPPY).   Go away from me! (*To* LINDA) What do you mean, lives or dies? Nobody's dying around here, pal.
LINDA.   Get out of my sight! Get out of here!
BIFF.   I wanna see the boss.
LINDA.   You're not to go near him!
BIFF.   Where is he? (*He moves into the living-room and* LINDA *follows.*)
LINDA (*shouting after* BIFF).   You invite him to dinner. He looks forward to it all day—(BIFF *appears in his parents' bedroom, looks around, and exits*)— and then you desert him there. There's no stranger you'd do that to!
HAPPY.   Why? He had a swell time with us. Listen, when I—(LINDA *comes back into the kitchen*)—desert him I hope I don't outlive the day!
LINDA.   Get out of here!
HAPPY.   Now look, Mom . . .
LINDA.   Did you have to go to women tonight? You and your lousy rotten whores!

(BIFF *re-enters the kitchen.*)

HAPPY.   Mom, all we did was follow Biff around trying to cheer him up! (*To* BIFF) Boy, what a night you gave me!
LINDA.   Get out of here, both of you, and don't come back! I don't want you tormenting him any more. Go on now, get your things together! (*To* BIFF) You can sleep in his apartment. (*She starts to pick up the flowers and stops herself.*) Pick up this stuff, I'm not your maid any more. Pick it up, you bum, you!

(HAPPY *turns his back to her in refusal.* BIFF *slowly moves over and gets down on his knees, picking up the flowers.*)

LINDA. You're a pair of animals! Not one, not another living soul would have had the cruelty to walk out on that man in a restaurant!

BIFF (*not looking at her*). Is that what he said?

LINDA. He didn't have to say anything. He was so humiliated he nearly limped when he came in.

HAPPY. But, Mom, he had a great time with us—

BIFF (*cutting him off violently*). Shut up!

(*Without another word,* HAPPY *goes upstairs.*)

LINDA. You! You didn't even go in to see if he was all right!

BIFF (*still on the floor in front of* LINDA, *the flowers in his hand; with self-loathing*). No. Didn't. Didn't do a damned thing. How do you like that, heh? Left him babbling in a toilet.

LINDA. You louse. You . . .

BIFF. Now you hit it on the nose! (*He gets up, throws the flowers in the wastebasket.*) The scum of the earth, and you're looking at him!

LINDA. Get out of here!

BIFF. I gotta talk to the boss, Mom. Where is he?

LINDA. You're not going near him. Get out of this house!

BIFF (*with absolute assurance, determination*). No. We're gonna have an abrupt conversation, him and me.

LINDA. You're not talking to him!

(*Hammering is heard from outside the house, off right.* BIFF *turns toward the noise.*)

LINDA (*suddenly pleading*). Will you please leave him alone?

BIFF. What's he doing out there?

LINDA. He's planting the garden!

BIFF (*quietly*). Now? Oh, my God!

(BIFF *moves outside,* LINDA *following. The light dies down on them and comes up on the center of the apron as* WILLY *walks into it. He is carrying a flashlight, a hoe, and a handful of seed packets. He raps the top of the hoe sharply to fix it firmly, and then moves to the left, measuring off the distance with his foot. He holds the flashlight to look at the seed packets, reading off the instructions. He is in the blue of night.*)

WILLY. Carrots . . . quarter-inch apart. Rows . . . one-foot rows. (*He measures it off.*) One foot. (*He puts down a package and measures off.*) Beets. (*He puts down another package and measures again.*) Lettuce. (*He reads the package, puts it down.*) One foot—(*He breaks off as* BEN *appears at the right and moves slowly down to him.*) What a proposition, ts, ts. Terrific, terrific. 'Cause she's suffered, Ben, the woman has suffered. You understand me? A man can't go out the way he came in. Ben, a man has got to add up to something. You can't, you can't—(BEN *moves toward him as though to interrupt.*) You gotta consider, now. Don't answer so quick. Remember, it's a guaranteed twenty-thousand-dollar proposition. Now look, Ben, I want you to go through the ins and outs of this thing with me. I've got nobody to talk to, Ben, and the woman has suffered, you hear me?

BEN (*standing still, considering*). What's the proposition?

WILLY. It's twenty thousand dollars on the barrelhead. Guaranteed, gilt-edged, you understand?

BEN. You don't want to make a fool of yourself. They might not honor the policy.

WILLY. How can they dare refuse? Didn't I work like a coolie to meet every premium on the nose? And now they don't pay off? Impossible!

BEN. It's called a cowardly thing, William.

WILLY. Why? Does it take more guts to stand here the rest of my life ringing up a zero?

BEN (*yielding*). That's a point, William. (*He moves, thinking, turns.*) And twenty thousand—that *is* something one can feel with the hand, it is there.

WILLY (*now assured, with rising power*). Oh, Ben, that's the whole beauty of it! I can see it like a diamond shining in the dark, hard and rough, that I can pick up and touch in my hand. Not like—like an appointment! This would not be another damned-fool appointment, Ben, and it changes all the aspects. Because he thinks I'm nothing, see, and so he spites me. But the funeral—(*Straightening up*) Ben, that funeral will be massive! They'll come from Maine, Massachusetts, Vermont, New Hampshire! All the old-timers with the strange license plates—that boy will be thunder-struck, Ben, because he never realized—I am known! Rhode Island, New York, New Jersey—I am known, Ben, and he'll see it with his eyes once and for all. He'll see what I am, Ben! He's in for a shock, that boy!

BEN (*coming down to the edge of the garden*). He'll call you a coward.

WILLY (*suddenly fearful*). No, that would be terrible.

BEN. Yes. And a damned fool.

WILLY. No, no, he mustn't, I won't have that! (*He is broken and desperate.*)

BEN. He'll hate you, William.

(*The gay music of the boys is heard.*)

WILLY. Oh, Ben, how do we get back to all the great times? Used to be so full of light, and comradeship, the sleigh-riding in winter and the ruddiness on his cheeks. And always some kind of good news coming up, always something nice coming up ahead. And never let me carry the valises in the house, and simonizing, simonizing that little red car! Why, why can't I give him something and not have him hate me?

BEN. Let me think about it. (*He glances at his watch.*) I still have a little time. Remarkable proposition, but you've got to be sure you're not making a fool of yourself.

(BEN *drifts off upstage and goes out of sight.* BIFF *comes down from the left.*)

WILLY (*suddenly conscious of* BIFF, *turns and looks up at him, then begins picking up the packages of seeds in confusion*).   Where the hell is that seed? (*Indignantly*) You can't see nothing out here! They boxed in the whole goddam neighborhood!

BIFF.   There are people all around here. Don't you realize that?

WILLY.   I'm busy. Don't bother me.

BIFF (*taking the hoe from* WILLY).   I'm saying good-by to you, Pop. (WILLY *looks at him, silent, unable to move.*) I'm not coming back any more.

WILLY.   You're not going to see Oliver tomorrow?

BIFF.   I've got no appointment, Dad.

WILLY.   He put his arms around you, and you've got no appointment?

BIFF.   Pop, get this now, will you? Every time I've left it's been a fight that sent me out of here. Today I realized something about myself and I tried to explain it to you and I—I think I'm just not smart enough to make any sense out of it for you. To hell with whose fault it is or anything like that. (*He takes* WILLY's *arm.*) Let's just wrap it up, heh? Come on in, we'll tell Mom. (*He gently tries to pull* WILLY *to left.*)

WILLY (*frozen, immobile, with guilt in his voice*).   No, I don't want to see her.

BIFF.   Come on!

(*He pulls again, and* WILLY *tries to pull away.*)

WILLY (*highly nervous*).   No, no, I don't want to see her.

BIFF (*tries to look into* WILLY's *face, as if to find the answer there.*)   Why don't you want to see her?

WILLY (*more harshly now*).   Don't bother me, will you?

BIFF.   What do you mean, you don't want to see her? You don't want them calling you yellow do you? This isn't your fault; it's me, I'm a bum. Now come inside! (WILLY *strains to get away.*) Did you hear what I said to you?

(WILLY *pulls away and quickly goes by himself into the house.* BIFF *follows.*)

LINDA (*to* WILLY).   Did you plant, dear?

BIFF (*at the door, to* LINDA).   All right, we had it out. I'm going and I'm not writing any more.

LINDA (*going to* WILLY *in the kitchen*).   I think that's the best way, dear. 'Cause there's no use drawing it out, you'll just never get along.

(WILLY *does not respond.*)

BIFF.   People ask where I am and what I'm doing, you don't know, and you don't care. That way it'll be off your mind and you can start brightening up again. All right? That clears it, doesn't it? (WILLY *is silent, and* BIFF *goes to him.*) You gonna wish me luck, scout? (*He extends his hand.*) What do you say?

LINDA. Shake his hand, Willy.

WILLY (*turning to her, seething with hurt*). There's no necessity to mention the pen at all, y'know.

BIFF (*gently*). I've got no appointment, Dad.

WILLY (*erupting fiercely*). He put his arm around . . . ?

BIFF. Dad, you're never going to see what I am, so what's the use of arguing? If I strike oil I'll send you a check. Meantime forget I'm alive.

WILLY (*to* LINDA). Spite, see?

BIFF. Shake hands, Dad.

WILLY. Not my hand.

BIFF. I was hoping not to go this way.

WILLY. Well, this is the way you're going. Good-by.

(BIFF *looks at him a moment, then turns sharply and goes to the stairs.*)

WILLY (*stops him with*). May you rot in hell if you leave this house!

BIFF (*turning*). Exactly what is it that you want from me?

WILLY. I want you to know, on the train, in the mountains, in the valleys, wherever you go, that you cut down your life for spite!

BIFF. No, no.

WILLY. Spite, spite, is the word of your undoing! And when you're down and out, remember what did it. When you're rotting somewhere beside the railroad tracks, remember, and don't you dare blame it on me!

BIFF. I'm not blaming it on you!

WILLY. I won't take the rap for this, you hear?

(HAPPY *comes down the stairs and stands on the bottom step, watching.*)

BIFF. That's just what I'm telling you!

WILLY (*sinking into a chair at the table, with full accusation*). You're trying to put a knife in me—don't think I don't know what you're doing!

BIFF. All right, phony! Then let's lay it on the line. (*He whips the rubber tube out of his pocket and puts it on the table.*)

HAPPY. You crazy—

LINDA. Biff! (*She moves to grab the hose, but* BIFF *holds it down with his hand.*)

BIFF. Leave it there! Don't move it!

WILLY (*not looking at it*). What is that?

BIFF. You know goddam well what that is.

WILLY (*caged, wanting to escape*). I never saw that.

BIFF. You saw it. The mice didn't bring it into the cellar! What is this supposed to do, make a hero out of you? This supposed to make me sorry for you?

WILLY. Never heard of it.

BIFF. There'll be no pity for you, you hear it? No pity!

WILLY (*to* LINDA). You hear the spite!

BIFF. No, you're going to hear the truth—what you are and what I am!

LINDA. Stop it!

WILLY. Spite!

HAPPY (*coming down toward* BIFF). You cut it out now!

BIFF (*to* HAPPY). The man don't know who we are! The man is gonna know! (*To* WILLY) We never told the truth for ten minutes in this house!

HAPPY. We always told the truth!

BIFF (*turning on him*). You big blow, are you the assistant buyer? You're one of two assistants to the assistant, aren't you?

HAPPY. Well, I'm practically—

BIFF. You're practically full of it! We all are! And I'm through with it. (*To* WILLY) Now hear this, Willy, this is me.

WILLY. I know you!

BIFF. You know why I had no address for three months? I stole a suit in Kansas City and I was in jail. (*To* LINDA, *who is sobbing*) Stop crying. I'm through with it.

(LINDA *turns away from them, her hands covering her face.*)

WILLY. I suppose that's my fault!

BIFF. I stole myself out of every good job since high school!

WILLY. And whose fault is that?

BIFF. And I never got anywhere because you blew me so full of hot air I could never stand taking orders from anybody! That's whose fault it is!

WILLY. I hear that!

LINDA. Don't, Biff!

BIFF. It's goddam time you heard that! I had to be boss big shot in two weeks, and I'm through with it!

WILLY. Then hang yourself! For spite, hang yourself!

BIFF. No! Nobody's hanging himself, Willy! I ran down eleven flights with a pen in my hand today. And suddenly I stopped, you hear me? And in the middle of that office building, do you hear this? I stopped in the middle of that building and I saw—the sky. I saw the things that I love in this world. The work and the food and time to sit and smoke. And I looked at the pen and said to myself, what the hell am I grabbing this for? Why am I trying to become what I don't want to be? What am I doing in an office, making a contemptuous, begging fool of myself, when all I want is out there, waiting for me the minute I say I know who I am! Why can't I say that, Willy?

(*He tries to make* WILLY *face him, but* WILLY *pulls away and moves to the left.*)

WILLY (*with hatred, threateningly*). The door of your life is wide open!

BIFF. Pop! I'm a dime a dozen, and so are you!

WILLY (*turning on him now in an uncontrolled outburst*). I am not a dime a dozen! I am Willy Loman, and you are Biff Loman!

(BIFF *starts for* WILLY, *but is blocked by* HAPPY. *In his fury,* BIFF *seems on the verge of attacking his father.*)

BIFF. I am not a leader of men, Willy, and neither are you. You were never anything but a hard-working drummer who landed in the ash can like all the rest of them! I'm one dollar an hour, Willy! I tried seven states and couldn't raise it. A buck an hour! Do you gather my meaning? I'm not bringing home any prizes any more, and you're going to stop waiting for me to bring them home!

WILLY (*directly to* BIFF). You vengeful, spiteful mutt!

(BIFF *breaks from* HAPPY. WILLY, *in fright, starts up the stairs.* BIFF *grabs him.*)

BIFF (*at the peak of his fury*). Pop, I'm nothing! I'm nothing, Pop. Can't you understand that? There's no spite in it any more. I'm just what I am, that's all.

(BIFF's *fury has spent itself, and he breaks down, sobbing, holding on to* WILLY, *who dumbly fumbles for* BIFF's *face.*)

WILLY (*astonished*). What're you doing? What're you doing? (*To* LINDA) Why is he crying?

BIFF (*crying, broken*). Will you let me go, for Christ's sake? Will you take that phony dream and burn it before something happens? (*Struggling to contain himself, he pulls away and moves to the stairs.*) I'll go in the morning. Put him—put him to bed. (*Exhausted,* BIFF *moves up the stairs to his room.*)

WILLY (*after a long pause, astonished, elevated*). Isn't that—isn't that remarkable? Biff—he likes me!

LINDA. He loves you, Willy!

HAPPY (*deeply moved*). Always did, Pop.

WILLY. Oh, Biff! (*Staring wildly*) He cried! Cried to me. (*He is choking with his love, and now cries out his promise.*) That boy—that boy is going to be magnificent!

(BEN *appears in the light just outside the kitchen.*)

BEN. Yes, outstanding, with twenty thousand behind him.

LINDA (*sensing the racing of his mind, fearfully, carefully*). Now come to bed, Willy. It's all settled now.

WILLY (*finding it difficult not to rush out of the house*). Yes, we'll sleep. Come on. Go to sleep, Hap.

BEN. And it does take a great kind of a man to crack the jungle.

(*In accents of dread,* BEN's *idyllic music starts up.*)

HAPPY (*his arm around* LINDA). I'm getting married, Pop, don't forget it. I'm changing everything. I'm gonna run that department before the year is up. You'll see, Mom. (*He kisses her.*)

BEN. The jungle is dark but full of diamonds, Willy.

(WILLY *turns, moves, listening to* BEN.)

LINDA. Be good. You're both good boys, just act that way, that's all.

HAPPY. 'Night, Pop. (*He goes upstairs.*)

LINDA (*to* WILLY). Come, dear.

BEN (*with greater force*). One must go in to fetch a diamond out.

WILLY (*to* LINDA, *as he moves slowly along the edge of the kitchen, toward the door*). I just want to get settled down, Linda. Let me sit alone for a little.

LINDA (*almost uttering her fear*). I want you upstairs.

WILLY (*taking her in his arms*). In a few minutes, Linda. I couldn't sleep right now. Go on, you look awful tired. (*He kisses her.*)

BEN. Not like an appointment at all. A diamond is rough and hard to the touch.

WILLY. Go on now. I'll be right up.

LINDA. I think this is the only way, Willy.

WILLY. Sure, it's the best thing.

BEN. Best thing!

WILLY. The only way. Everything is gonna be—go on, kid, get to bed. You look so tired.

LINDA. Come right up.

WILLY. Two minutes.

(LINDA *goes into the living-room, then reappears in her bedroom.* WILLY *moves just outside the kitchen door.*)

WILLY. Loves me. (*Wonderingly*) Always loved me. Isn't that a remarkable thing? Ben, he'll worship me for it!

BEN (*with promise*). It's dark there, but full of diamonds.

WILLY. Can you imagine that magnificence with twenty thousand dollars in his pocket?

LINDA (*calling from her room*). Willy! Come up!

WILLY (*calling into the kitchen*). Yes, Yes. Coming! It's very smart, you realize that, don't you, sweetheart? Even Ben sees it. I gotta go, baby. 'By! 'By! (*Going over to* BEN, *almost dancing*) Imagine? When the mail comes he'll be ahead of Bernard again!

BEN. A perfect proposition all around.

WILLY. Did you see how he cried to me? Oh, if I could kiss him, Ben!

BEN. Time, William, time!

WILLY. Oh, Ben, I always knew one way or another we were gonna make it, Biff and I!

BEN (*looking at his watch*). The boat. We'll be late. (*He moves slowly off into the darkness.*)

WILLY (*elegiacally, turning to the house*). Now when you kick off, boy, I want a seventy-yard boot, and get right down the field under the ball, and when you hit, hit low and hit hard, because it's important, boy. (*He swings around and faces the audience.*) There's all kinds of important people in the stands, and the first thing you know . . . (*Suddenly realizing he is alone*) Ben! Ben, where do I . . . ? (*He makes a sudden movement of search.*) Ben, how do I . . . ?

LINDA (*calling*). Willy, you coming up?

WILLY (*uttering a gasp of fear, whirling about as if to quiet her*). Sh! (*He turns around as if to find his way; sounds, faces, voices, seem to be swarming in upon him and he flicks at them, crying*) Sh! Sh! (*Suddenly music, faint and high, stops him. It rises in intensity, almost to an unbearable scream. He goes up and down on his toes, and rushes off around the house.*) Shhh!

LINDA. Willy?

(*There is no answer. LINDA waits. BIFF gets up off his bed. He is still in his clothes. HAPPY sits up. BIFF stands listening.*)

LINDA (*with real fear*). Willy, answer me! Willy!

(*There is the sound of a car starting and moving away at full speed.*)

LINDA. No!

BIFF (*rushing down the stairs*). Pop!

(*As the car speeds off, the music crashes down in a frenzy of sound, which becomes the soft pulsation of a single cello string. BIFF slowly returns to his bedroom. He and HAPPY gravely don their jackets. LINDA slowly walks out of her room. The music has developed into a dead march. The leaves of day are appearing over everything. CHARLEY and BERNARD, somberly dressed, appear and knock on the kitchen door. BIFF and HAPPY slowly descend the stairs to the kitchen as CHARLEY and BERNARD enter. All stop a moment when LINDA, in clothes of mourning, bearing a little bunch of roses, comes through the draped doorway into the kitchen. She goes to CHARLEY and takes his arm. Now all move toward the audience, through the wall-line of the kitchen. At the limit of the apron, LINDA lays down the flowers, kneels, and sits back on her heels. All stare down at the grave.*)

REQUIEM

CHARLEY. It's getting dark, Linda.

(*LINDA doesn't react. She stares at the grave.*)

BIFF. How about it, Mom? Better get some rest, heh? They'll be closing the gate soon.

(*LINDA makes no move. Pause.*)

HAPPY (*deeply angered*). He had no right to do that. There was no necessity for it. We would've helped him.

CHARLEY (*grunting*). Hmmm.

BIFF. Come along, Mom.

LINDA. Why didn't anybody come?

CHARLEY. It was a very nice funeral.

LINDA. But where are all the people he knew? Maybe they blame him.

CHARLEY. Naa. It's a rough world, Linda. They wouldn't blame him.

LINDA. I can't understand it. At this time especially. First time in thirty-five years we were just about free and clear. He only needed a little salary. He was even finished with the dentist.

CHARLEY. No man only needs a little salary.

LINDA. I can't understand it.

BIFF. There were a lot of nice days. When he'd come home from a trip; or on Sundays, making the stoop; finishing the cellar; putting on the new porch; when he built the extra bathroom; and put up the garage. You know something, Charley, there's more of him in that front stoop than in all the sales he ever made.

CHARLEY. Yeah. He was a happy man with a batch of cement.

LINDA. He was so wonderful with his hands.

BIFF. He had the wrong dreams. All, all, wrong.

HAPPY (*almost ready to fight* BIFF). Don't say that!

BIFF. He never knew who he was.

CHARLEY (*stopping* HAPPY'*s movement and reply. To* BIFF). Nobody dast blame this man. You don't understand: Willy was a salesman. And for a salesman, there is no rock bottom to the life. He don't put a bolt to a nut, he don't tell you the law or give you medicine. He's a man way out there in the blue, riding on a smile and a shoestring. And when they start not smiling back—that's an earthquake. And then you get yourself a couple of spots on your hat, and you're finished. Nobody dast blame this man. A salesman is got to dream, boy. It comes with the territory.

BIFF. Charley, the man didn't know who he was.

HAPPY (*infuriated*). Don't say that!

BIFF. Why don't you come with me, Happy?

HAPPY. I'm not licked that easily. I'm staying right in this city, and I'm gonna beat this racket! (*He looks at* BIFF, *his chin set.*) The Loman Brothers!

BIFF. I know who I am, kid.

HAPPY. All right, boy. I'm gonna show you and everybody else that Willy Loman did not die in vain. He had a good dream. It's the only dream you can have—to come out number-one man. He fought it out here, and this is where I'm gonna win it for him.

BIFF (*with a hopeless glance at* HAPPY, *bends toward his mother*). Let's go, Mom.

LINDA. I'll be with you in a minute. Go on, Charley. (*He hesitates.*) I want to, just for a minute. I never had a chance to say good-by.

(CHARLEY *moves away, followed by* HAPPY. BIFF *remains a slight distance up and left of* LINDA. *She sits there, summoning herself. The flute begins, not far away, playing behind her speech.*)

LINDA. Forgive me, dear. I can't cry. I don't know what it is, but I can't cry. I don't understand it. Why did you ever do that? Help me, Willy, I can't cry. It seems to me that you're just on another trip. I keep expecting you. Willy, dear, I can't cry. Why did you do it? I search and search and I search, and I can't understand it, Willy. I made the last payment on the house today. Today, dear. And there'll be nobody home. (*A sob rises in her throat.*) We're free and clear. (*Sobbing more fully, released*) We're free. (BIFF *comes slowly toward her.*) We're free . . . We're free . . .

(BIFF *lifts her to her feet and moves out up right with her in his arms.* LINDA *sobs quietly.* BERNARD *and* CHARLEY *come together and follow them, followed by* HAPPY. *Only the music of the flute is left on the darkening stage as over the house the hard towers of the apartment buildings rise into sharp focus, and the curtain falls.*)

Appendix 1: Writing about Literature

Writing about Literature

I. WHY WRITE ABOUT LITERATURE?

Written assignments in a literature class have two purposes: (1) to give you additional practice in writing clearly and persuasively, and (2) to deepen your understanding of literary works by making you read and think about a few works more searchingly than you might otherwise do. But these two purposes are private. To be successful, your paper must have a public purpose as well: it should be written to enlighten others besides yourself. Even if no one else ever reads your paper, you should never treat it as a private note to your instructor. You should write every paper as if it were intended for publication.

II. FOR WHOM DO YOU WRITE?

The audience for whom you write will govern both the content and expression of your paper. You need to know something about its backgrounds—national, racial, social, religious—and be able to make intelligent guesses about its knowledge, interests, and previous reading. In writing about George Herbert's "Redemption" (page 598) for a Hindu audience, you would need to include explanations of Christian belief and biblical stories that would be unnecessary for a western European or American audience. In presenting Graham Greene's "The Destructors" (page 49) and John Galsworthy's "The Japanese Quince" (page 61), your editors have felt it necessary to provide information (in footnotes) that would not be needed by an English audience. But the most crucial question about audience is, *Has it read the work you are writing about?* The book reviewer in your Sunday paper generally writes about a newly published book which his audience has not read. A reviewer's purpose is to let readers know something of what the book is about and to give them some notion of whether they will enjoy or profit from reading it. At an opposite extreme, the scholar writing in a specialized scholarly journal can generally assume an audience that *has* read the work, that has a knowledge of previous interpretations of the work, and that is familiar with other works in its period or genre. The scholar's purpose, not infrequently, is to persuade this audience that some new information or some new way of looking at the work appreciably deepens or alters its meaning or significance.

Clearly, two essays written for such different audiences and with such different purposes will differ considerably in content, organization, and style. The book reviewer reviewing a novel will give the reader a general idea of its plot while being careful not to reveal the outcome. The scholar will assume that readers already know the plot and will have no compunction about discussing its outcome. The reviewer will try to write interestingly and engagingly about the novel and to persuade readers that he has valid grounds for his opinion of its worth, but his manner will generally be informal. The scholar is more interested in presenting a cogent argument, logically arranged, and solidly based on evidence. He will be more formal, and may use critical terms and refer to related works that would be unfamiliar to nonspecialized readers. In documentation the two essays will be quite different. The reviewer's only documentation is normally the identification of the novel's title, author, publisher, and price at the top of the review. For other information and opinions he hopes readers will rely on his own intelligence, knowledge, and judgment. The scholar, on the other hand, may furnish an elaborate array of footnotes allowing readers to verify the accuracy or basis of any important part of his argument. He expects to be challenged, and sees to it that all parts of his argument are buttressed.

Between these two extremes—the generalized, local newspaper audience and the specialized, perhaps international scholarly audience—stretches a wide spectrum of other audiences differing in levels of intellectual sophistication and in degrees of specialized literary knowledge. However, the professional writer always has a fairly good notion of whom he is writing for. The newspaper reviewer, often an employee of the paper for which he writes, knows that his audience constitutes that portion of the paper's readers with enough interest in books to glance at the weekly book section, and he knows also that the readers of the *Denver Post* differ from those of the *Village Voice* or the *Christian Science Monitor*. The scholarly writer generally knows to what journal he will submit his article when it is completed, and to what other journals he may send it if the first does not accept it. He may modify his article for the audience of the second journal.

For whom, then, should *you* write? Unless your instructor stipulates (or you request) a different audience, the best plan is to assume that you are writing for the other members of your class. Pretend that your class publishes a journal of which it also constitutes the readership. Your instructor is the editor and determines editorial policy. If you write on a work that has been assigned for class reading, you assume that your audience is familiar with it. (This kind of paper is generally of most educational value, for it is most open to challenge and class discussion, and places on you a heavier

III.1.

burden of proof.) If you compare an assigned work with one that has not been assigned, you must judge what portion of your audience is familiar with the unassigned work, and proceed accordingly. If the unassigned story were A. Conan Doyle's "The Adventure of the Speckled Band," you would probably not need to explain that "Sherlock Holmes is a detective" and that "Dr. Watson is his friend," for you can assume that *this* audience, through movies, TV, or reading, is familiar with these characters; but you could not assume familiarity with this particular story. You know that, as members of the same class, your readers have certain backgrounds and interests in common and are at comparable levels of education. Anything you know about your audience may be important for how you write your paper and what you put in it.

III. CHOOSING A TOPIC

As editor of this imaginary publication, your instructor is responsible for the nature of its contents. He may be very specific in his assignments, or he may be very general, inviting you to submit a paper on any subject within a broadly defined area. He will also have editorial policies concerning length of papers, preparation of manuscript, and deadlines for submission (all of which should be meticulously heeded). Your instructor may further specify whether he wants the paper to be entirely the work of your own critical thinking, or whether it is to be an investigative assignment—that is, one involving research into what other writers have written concerning your subject and using their findings, where relevant, to help you reach your own conclusions.

For convenience let us consider the kinds of paper you might write under four categories: (1) papers that focus on a single literary work; (2) papers of comparison and contrast; (3) papers on a number of works by a single author; and (4) papers on a number of works having some feature other than authorship in common.

1. Papers that Focus on a Single Literary Work

If your assignment is a specific one (Who is the central character in Lardner's story "Haircut"? Who are the speakers, and in what order do they speak, in Auden's poem "O what is that sound"? Which character is the stronger—Mrs. X or Miss Y—in Strindberg's play?), your task is clear-cut. You have only to read the selection carefully (probably more than once), formulate your answer, and support it with corroborating evidence from within the text as cogently and convincingly as possible. In order to convince your readers that your answer is the best one, you will need to examine and account for apparently contrary evidence as well as clearly supportive; otherwise your readers, reluctant to change their minds, will simply point to "important points" that you have "overlooked."

Specific questions like these, when they are central to the work considered and may be a matter of dispute, make excellent topics for papers. You may discover them for yourself when you disagree with a classmate about the interpretation of a story or poem. The study questions following the selections in this anthology frequently suggest topics of this kind.

If your assignment is more general, and if you are given some choice as to what story, poem, or play you write on, it is usually best to choose one you enjoyed, whether or not you entirely understood it. (You are more likely to write a good paper on a selection you liked than on one you disliked, and you should arrive at a fuller understanding of it while thinking through your paper.) You must then decide what kind of paper you will write, and this will be related to the length and kind of selection you have chosen and the amount of space at your disposal. Probably your paper will be either an *explication* or an *analysis*.

An *explication* (literally, an "unfolding") has been defined as "an examination of a work of literature for a knowledge of each part, for the relations of these parts to each other, and for their relations to the whole."* It is a detailed elucidation of a work, sometimes line by line or word by word, which is interested not only in *what* that work means but in *how* it means what it means. It thus considers all relevant aspects of a work—speaker or point-of-view, connotative words and double meanings, images, figurative language, allusions, form, structure, sound, rhythm—and discusses, if not all of these, at least the most important. (There is no such thing as exhausting the meanings and the ways to those meanings in a really rich piece of literature, and the explicator must settle for something less than completeness.) Explication follows from what we sometimes call "close reading"—looking at a piece of writing, as it were, through a magnifying glass.

Clearly, the kinds of literature for which *an* explication is appropriate are limited. First, the work must be rich enough to repay the kind of close attention demanded. One would not think of explicating "Thirty days hath September" (unless for purposes of parody), for it has no meanings that need elucidation and no "art" worthy of comment. Second, the work must be short enough to be encompassed in a relatively brief discussion. A thorough explication of *Othello* would be longer than the play itself and would tire the patience of the most dogged reader. Explications work best with short poems. (Sonnets like Shakespeare's "That time of year" and Frost's "Design" almost beg for explication.) Explication may also be sometimes appropriate for passages in long poems, as, for example, the lines spoken by Macbeth after the death of his wife (page 632) or the "sonnet" from *Romeo and Juliet* (page 729), and occasionally for exceptionally rich or crucial passages of prose, perhaps the final paragraphs of stories like "Defender of the Faith," "Paul's Case," or "Miss Brill." But explication as a critical form should perhaps be separated from explication as a method. Whenever

* George Arms, "A Note on Explication," *Western Review*, 15 (Autumn 1950), 57.

one elucidates even a small part of a literary work by a close examination that relates it to the whole, he is essentially explicating (unfolding). If one points out the double meaning in the title of "The Most Dangerous Game" as it relates to that story's action, he is explicating the title.

For an example of explication, see "A Study of Reading Habits," page 1432. The text of this book uses the explicative method frequently, but has no pure examples of explication. The discussion of "You, Andrew Marvell" (pages 595–96) comes close to being an explication, and might be considered one if it had included answers to the study questions and one or two other matters.

The list of questions suggested in the Exercise on page 537 should be helpful to you in writing an explication of a poem. Not all the questions will be applicable to every poem, and you need not answer all those that are applicable, but you should consider those that are central and important for the poem you have chosen.

An *analysis* (literally a "breaking-up" or separation of something into its constituent parts), instead of trying to examine all parts of a work in relation to the whole, selects *one* aspect or element or part to examine in relation to the whole. Clearly, an analysis is a better approach to longer works and to prose works than is an explication. A literary work may be usefully approached through almost any of its elements—point of view, characterization, plot, setting, symbolism, structure, and the like—so long as you relate this element to the central meaning or the whole. (An analysis of meter is meaningless unless it shows how meter serves the meaning.) The list of General Questions for Analysis and Evaluation on page 338 suggests various approaches that might be taken to a story, play, or narrative poem; the list on page 537 may suggest approaches to poems and verse plays. As always, it is important to choose a topic appropriate to the space available. "Characterization in Flannery O'Connor's 'Greenleaf' " is too large a topic to be usefully treated in a few pages, but a character analysis of Mrs. May or of her two sons might fit the space neatly. For an example of an analysis, see "The Function of the Loveladys in 'That Evening Sun,' " page 1436).

2. Papers of Comparison and Contrast

The comparison and contrast of two stories, poems, or plays having one or more features in common may be an illuminating exercise, because the similarities highlight the differences, or vice versa, and thus lead to a better understanding not only of both pieces but of literary processes in general. The selections chosen may be similar in plot but different in theme, similar in subject but different in tone, similar in theme but different in literary value, or, conversely, different in plot but similar in theme, different in subject but similar in tone, and so on. In writing such a paper, it is usually best to decide first whether the similarities or the differences are most significant, begin with a brief summary of the less significant, then concentrate on the more significant.*

3. Papers on a Number of Works by a Single Author

Most readers when they discover a story or poem they particularly like, look for other works by the same author. The paper which focuses on a single author rather than a single work is the natural corollary of such an interest. The most common concern in a paper of this type is to identify the characteristics that make this author different from other authors and therefore of particular interest to the writer. What are the author's characteristic subjects, settings, or themes? With what kinds of life does he characteristically deal? What are his preferred literary forms? What tones does he favor? Is he ironic, witty, serious, comic, tragic? Is the author's vision directed principally inward or outward? In short, what configuration of patterns makes his fingerprints unique? Your paper may consider several or one of these questions.†

A more ambitious type of paper on a single author examines his work for signs of development. The attitudes which any person, especially an author, takes towards his world, may change as he passes from adolescence to adulthood to old age. So also may the author's means of expressing them. Though some writers are remarkably consistent throughout their careers in outlook and expression, others manifest surprising changes. What are the differences between early Yeats, middle Yeats, and late Yeats? To write such a paper, you must have accurate information about the dates when works were written, and the works must be read in chronological order. When you have mastered the differences, you may be able to illustrate them through close examination of two or three stories, plays, or poems—one for each stage.

---

*A number of selections in this collection have been "paired" to encourage just this kind of study: "The Most Dangerous Game" and "The Child by Tiger" in chapter 1 of the fiction section; "The Storm" and "That Evening Sun," "The Catbird Seat" and "The Drunkard," "A Christmas Memory" and "God Rest You Merry, Gentlemen" in chapter 7; "A Municipal Report" and "A Jury of Her Peers," "Spotted Horses" and "Mule in the Yard" in chapter 9; in the poetry section "Ulysses" and "Curiosity," "Dust of Snow" and "Soft Snow" in chapter 6; "A Red, Red Rose" and "The Rose Family," "The Unknown Citizen" and "Departmental" in chapter 7; "Barter" and "Stopping by Woods on a Snowy Evening," "Song" and "Dirge," "To a Waterfowl" and "Design," "what if a much of a which of a wind" and "when serpents bargain for the right to squirm." "The Caged Skylark" and "Aubade" in chapter 9; "The Villain" and "Apparently with no surprise," "The Telephone" and "Love in Brooklyn," "One dignity delays for all" and "Apparently with no surprise," "Crossing the Bar" and "The Oxen" in chapter 10; "Had I the Choice" and "The Aim Was Song" in chapter 11; "Boot and Saddle" and "Night of Spring" in chapter 13; and nine pairs of poems in chapter 15.

†Emily Dickinson, A. E. Housman, and Robert Frost are represented in this anthology by a sufficient number of poems to support such a paper without turning to outside sources.

When readers become particularly interested in the works of a particular author, they may develop a curiosity about his life as well. This is a legitimate interest, and, if there is sufficient space and your editor permits it, you may want to incorporate biographical information into your paper. If so, however, three *caveats* should be heeded. First, your main interest should be in the literature itself: the biographical material should be subordinated to and used in service of your examination of the work. In general, discuss only those aspects of the author's life which bear directly on the work: biography should not be used as "filler." Second, you should be extremely cautious about identifying an event in a work with an event in the life of the author. Almost never is a story, poem, or play an exact transcription of its author's experience. The author fictionalizes himself in putting himself into a work of imagination. If you consider that even in an autobiography, where the author's purpose is to give an accurate account of his life, he must select from the vast complexity of his experience those experiences he chooses to report, that his memory of past events may be defective, and that at best he presents them from his own point of view—as *he* saw them, not as others saw them—in short, when one realizes that even autobiography cannot be an absolutely reliable transcription of historical fact, one should be more fully prepared not to expect such an equation in a work whose object is imaginative truth. Third, you must document the sources of your information about the author's life (see pages 1421–28).

4. Papers on a Number of Works with Some Feature in Common Other than Authorship

Papers on works by various authors which have some feature in common—subject, form, setting, point of view, and the like—where the purpose is to discover different ways that different works may use or regard that common feature, are often illuminating. Probably the most familiar paper of this type is the one which treats works having a similar thematic concern (love, war, religious belief or doubt, art, adolescence, initiation, maturity, old age, death, parents and children, racial conflict, social injustice). But a paper may also examine particular forms of literature, for example, the Italian sonnet, the dramatic monologue, the short story with an unreliable narrator. Topics of this kind may be further limited by time or place or number—four attitudes toward death, Elizabethan love lyrics, poetry of the Viet Nam war, the use of the chorus in three Greek tragedies.

IV. PROVING YOUR POINT

In writing about literature, your object generally is to convince your readers that your understanding of a work is valid and important and to lead them to share that understanding. When writing about other subjects, it may be appropriate to persuade your readers through various rhetorical means—through eloquent diction, devices of suspense, analogies, personal anecdotes, and the like. But readers of essays about literature usually look for "proof." They want you to show them *how* the work, or the element you are discussing, does what you claim it does. Like the scientist who requires proof of the sort that he can duplicate in his own laboratory, readers of criticism want access to the process of inference, analysis, and deduction that has led to your conclusions, so that they may respond as you have done.

To provide this proof is no easy task, for it depends on your own mastery of reading and of writing. You must understand what a work means and what its effects are; you must be able to point out precisely how it communicates that meaning and how it achieves those effects; and you must be able to present your experience clearly and directly. When you have spent considerable time in coming to understand and respond to a work of literature, it may become so familiar that it seems self-evident to you, and you will need to "back off" sufficiently to be able to put yourself in your readers' position—they may have vague feelings about the work ("I like it" or "It moves me deeply"), without knowing what it is that produced those feelings. It is your job to refine and define away the vagueness.

Some forms of "proof" rarely do the job. Precision does not result from explaining a metaphor metaphorically ("When William Whitehead calls love the 'pleasing plague' the reader is reminded of taking bitter-tasting medicine"). Nor can you prove anything about a work by hypothesizing about what it might have been if it did not contain what it does ("If Desdemona had not lost her handkerchief, Othello would never have murdered her"—this is equivalent to saying "If the play were not what it is, it would not be what it is"). Your own personal experiences will rarely help your readers ("Drifting helplessly at sea for a week when our engine and radio were out of commission was like Madame Ranevskaya's hopelessness as she loses her cherry orchard"). Even your personal history of coming to understand a literary work will seldom help, though you present it in more general terms ("The opening of *Othello* at first confuses the reader because the marriage of Othello and Desdemona is not revealed until near the end of the first scene"). Just as in formal logic argument by analogy is not regarded as valid, so in critical discourse analogies are usually unconvincing ("Desdemona's ignorance about adultery is like a child's inability to balance a checkbook"). These strategies all have in common the looseness and vagueness of trying to define something by saying what it is not, or what it is like, rather than dealing with what it *is*.

"Proof" in writing about literature is primarily an exercise in strict definition. The Whitehead phrase quoted above derives its feeling from the paradoxical linking of pleasure to pain or disease, as a representation of the conflicting emotions of the lover. To provide an appropriate definition of the effect of the phrase, you would need to identify the figure of speech as oxymoron, and to investigate the way in which love can simultaneously

V.

inflict pain and give pleasure, and you might find it useful to point to the alliteration that so closely ties these opposites together. Obviously comparing this kind of proof to that required by science is inexact, since what you are doing is reminding your readers, or perhaps informing them, of feelings that are associated with language, not of the properties of chemical compounds. Furthermore, a scientific proof is incomplete if it does not present every step in a process. If that requirement were placed on literary analysis, a critical essay would be interminable, since there is always a little more to be said about any interpretive point. So, rather than attempting to prove every point that you make, you will be expected to demonstrate that your *method* of analysis is valid by providing persuasive proof of your major point or points. If you have shown that your handling of a major point is sound, your readers will tend to trust your judgment on lesser matters.

V. WRITING THE PAPER

The general procedures for writing a good paper on literature are much the same as the procedures for writing a good paper on any subject.

1. As soon as possible after receiving the assignment, read carefully and thoughtfully the literary materials on which it is based, mulling over the problem to be solved or—if the assignment is general—a good choice of subject, sidelining or underlining important passages with a pencil if the book is your own,* and jotting down notes. If possible, read the material more than once.

2. Then, rather than proceeding directly to the writing of the paper, put the materials aside for several days and let them steep in your mind. The advantage of this is that your unconscious mind, if you have truly placed the problem in it, will continue to work on the problem while you are engaged in other activities, indeed even while you are asleep. Repeated investigations into the psychology of creativity have shown that great solutions to scientific and artistic problems frequently occur while the scientist or artist is thinking of something else; the answer pops into his mind as if out of nowhere but really out of the hidden recesses of his mind where it has been quietly incubating. Whether this apparent "miracle" happens to you or not, it is probable that you will have more ideas when you sit down to write after a period of incubation than you will if you try to write your paper immediately after reading the materials.

3. When you are ready to write (allow yourself as long an incubation period as possible, but also allow ample time for writing, looking things up, revising, copying your revision, and correcting your final copy), jot down a list of the ideas you have, select connecting ideas relevant to your problem or to a single acceptable subject, and formulate a thesis statement that will

---

*If you use a library book, make notes of the page or line numbers of such passages so that you can readily find them again.

clearly express in one sentence what you wish to say about that subject. Make a rough outline, rearranging your ideas in the order that will best support your thesis. Do they make a coherent case? Have you left out anything necessary to demonstrate your thesis? If so, add it in the proper place. Then begin to write, using your rough outline as a guide. Write this first draft as swiftly as possible, not bothering about sentence structure, grammar, diction, spelling, or verification of sources. Concentrate on putting on paper what is in your head and on your outline without interrupting the flow of thought for any other purpose. If alternative ways of expressing a thought occur to you, put down both for a later decision. Nothing is more unprofitable than staring at a blank sheet of paper, chewing a pencil, wondering, "How shall I begin?" Just begin. Get something down on paper. Like any newborn creature, it may look awful. It can be licked into shape later.

4. Once you have something on paper, it is much easier to see what should be done with it. The next step is to revise. Does your paper proceed from an introductory paragraph which either defines the problem to be solved or states your thesis, through a series of logically arranged paragraphs which advance toward a solution of the problem or demonstrate your thesis, to a final paragraph which either solves the problem or sums up and restates your thesis but in somewhat different words? If not, analyze the difficulty. Do the paragraphs need reorganization or amplification? Are more examples needed? Does the thesis itself need modification? Make whatever adjustments are necessary for a logical and convincing demonstration. This may require a rewriting of the paper. Or it may call only for a few strike-outs, insertions, and circlings with arrows showing that a sentence or paragraph should be shifted from one place to another.

5. Having revised your paper for the logic, coherence, and completeness of its argument, your next step is to revise it for effectiveness of expression. Do this slowly and carefully. How many words can you cut out without loss of meaning? Are your sentences constructed for maximum force and economy? Are they correctly punctuated? Do the pronouns have clear antecedents? Do the verbs agree with their subjects? Are the tenses consistent? Have you chosen the most exact words and spelled them correctly? Now is the time to use the dictionary, to verify quotations and other references, and to supply whatever documentation is needed. A conscientious writer may put a paper through several revisions.

6. After all is in order, write or type your final copy, being sure to follow the editorial policies of your instructor for the submission of manuscripts.

7. Read over your final copy slowly and carefully, and correct any mistakes (omissions, repetitions, typographical errors) you may have made in copying from your draft. This final step—too often omitted from haste or fatigue—is extremely important, and may make the difference between an "A" or a "C" paper, or between a "C" paper and an "F." It is easy to

VI.

make careless mistakes in copying; but your editor should not be counted on to recognize the difference between a copying error and one of ignorance. Moreover, the smallest error may utterly destroy the sense of what you have written: omission of a "not" may make your paper say the exact opposite of what you meant it to say. Few editors require or want you to recopy or retype a whole page of your paper at this stage. It is enough to make neat corrections in ink on the paper itself.

VI. INTRODUCING QUOTATIONS

In writing about literature it is often desirable, sometimes imperative, to quote from the work under discussion. Quoted material is needed (a) to provide essential evidence in support of your argument, and (b) to set before your reader any passage that you are going to examine in detail. It will also keep your reader in contact with the text and allow you to use felicitous phrasing from the text to enhance your own presentation. You must, however, be careful not to overquote. If a paper consists of more than 20 percent quotation, it loses the appearance of closely knit argument and seems instead merely a collection of strung-together quotations like clothes hung out on a line to dry. Avoid, especially, unnecessary use of long quotations. Readers tend to skip them. Consider carefully whether the material presented may not be more economically presented by paraphrase, or whether the quotation, if judged necessary, may not be effectively shortened by ellipsis (see Q9 below). Readers faced with a long quotation may reasonably expect you to examine it in some detail; that is, the longer your quotation, the more you should do with it. As with every other aspect of good writing, the amount of quotation one uses is a matter of intelligence and tact and cannot be decreed. Effective use of quotation is an art.

Principles and "Rules"

There is no national legislative body that establishes laws governing the formal aspects of quoting, documenting, or any other aspect of writing. The only "rules" are the editorial policies of the publisher to whom you submit your work. Nevertheless, broad areas of agreement exist, and the following instructions will apply to most situations. Your instructor will tell you where his own editorial policies differ. The examples are drawn from pages 1189–92 of this book.

Q1. If the quotation is short (roughly, less than sixty words of prose; not more than two lines of verse), put it in quotation marks and introduce it directly into the text of your essay.

```
        Othello, before stabbing himself, reminds his listen-
a       ers, "I have done the state some service, and they
b       know't." He speaks of himself as "one that loved not
c       wisely but too well" and compares himself to "the base
        Indian" who "threw a pearl away / Richer than all his
        tribe" (V.ii.338-47).
```

Q2. If the quotation is long (roughly more than sixty words of prose; two lines or more of verse), indent it, begin it on a new line (and end it on its own line), single-space it, and write it *without quotation marks*. (Since the indentation, single-spacing, etc., signal a quotation, the use of quotation marks would be redundant.)

```
        In the final scene, convinced that Desdemona is en-
        tirely innocent and having decided to kill himself,
        Othello says to his auditors:

a                       I pray you, in your letters,
            When you shall these unlucky deeds relate,
            Speak of me as I am, nothing extenuate,
            Nor set down aught in malice.    (V.ii.339-42)

        He speaks of himself as

b                       one whose hand,
            Like the base Indian, threw a pearl away
            Richer than all his tribe.    (V.ii.345-47)
```

The two boxed examples illustrate (1) the "run-in" quotation, where the quotation is "run in" with the writer's own text, and (2) the "set-off" or "block" quotation, where the quotation is separated from the writer's text. Definitions of "short" and "long" are variable and differ with editorial policy; more than two lines of verse may be "run in" if the lines are very short. Block quotations in prose should be indented five spaces; block quotations in verse are centered on the page.

Q3. In quoting verse, it is extremely important to preserve the line arrangement of the original, for the verse line is a rhythmical unit and thus affects its meaning. When more than one line of verse is "run in," the lines are separated by a slanting diagonal (or slash), and capitalization after the first line follows that of the original. (See Q1.c. above.)

Q4. In general, sentences containing quotation are punctuated as they would be if there were no quotation. In Q1.a. above, a comma precedes the quoted sentence as it would if there were no quotation marks. In Q2.a., a colon precedes the quoted sentence because it is long and complex. In Q1.b., Q1.c., and Q2.b., there is no punctuation at all before the quotations. Do not put punctuation before a quotation unless it is otherwise called for.

Q5. Your quotation must combine with its introduction to make a grammatically correct sentence. The normal processes of grammar and syntax, like the normal processes of punctuation, are unaffected by quotation. Subjects must agree with their verbs, verbs must be consistent in tense, pronouns must have their normal relation with antecedents.

WRONG   Othello says, "One that loved not wisely but too
        well."

(Incomplete sentence)

RIGHT   Othello speaks of himself as "one that loved not
        wisely but too well."

WRONG   Othello asks his auditors to "speak of me
        as I am."

(The pronouns "me" and "I" do not agree in person with their antecedent.)

RIGHT   Othello bids his auditors,

            Speak of me as I am, nothing extenuate,
            Nor set down aught in malice. Then must you
                speak
            Of one that loved not wisely but too well.

WRONG   Othello says that "I have done the state some
        service" (V.ii.338).

(Incorrect mixture of direct and indirect quotation)

RIGHT   Othello says, "I have done the state some
        service."

WRONG   Othello says that he "have done the state some
        service."

(Subject and verb of subordinate clause lack agreement.)

RIGHT   Othello says that he has "done the state some
service."

Q6. Your introduction must supply enough context to make the quotation meaningful. Be careful that all pronouns in the quotation have clearly identifiable antecedents.

WRONG   In the final speech of the play, Lodovico says,
"Look on the tragic loading of this bed: / This is
thy work." (V.ii.362–63).

(Whose work?)

RIGHT   In the final speech of the play, Lodovico says to
Iago, "Look on the tragic loading of this bed: /
This is thy work."

Q7. The words within your quotation marks must be quoted *exactly* from the original.

WRONG   Though Iago bids his wife to "hold her peace,"
Emilia declares, "I will speak as liberally as
the north wind" (V.ii.218–19).

Q8. It is permissible to insert or supply words in a quotation *if* you enclose them within brackets. Brackets (parentheses with square corners) are used to indicate *editorial* changes or additions. If parentheses were used, the reader might interpret the enclosed material as *authorial* (as part of the quotation). Since brackets do not appear on most typewriters, you may have to put them in with pen or pencil. Avoid excessive use of brackets: they have a pedantic air. Find other solutions. Often paraphrase will serve as well as quotation.

CORRECT   Though Iago bids his wife to "hold [her]
peace," Emilia declares, "I will speak as
liberal[ly] as the north [wind]" (V.ii.218–19).

BETTER   Though Iago bids his wife to hold her peace,
Emilia declares that she will speak as liberally
as the north wind.

VI.

Notice that a word within brackets can either replace a word in the original (as in the substitution of "her" for "your" above) or be added to explain or complete the original (as with "-ly" and "wind" above). Since a reader understands that brackets signal either substitutions or additions, it is superfluous to include words that have been substituted for.

WRONG   Iago bids his wife to "hold your [her] peace."

Your sentences, including bracketed words, must read as if there were no brackets.

RIGHT   After Iago's treachery has been completely exposed, Lodovico tells Othello:

> You must forsake this room, and go with us.
> Your power and command is taken off,
> And Cassio rules in Cyprus. For this slave [Iago],
> If there be any cunning cruelty
> That can torment him much and hold him long,
> It shall be his.   (V.ii.329–34)

Q9. It is permissible to omit words from quoted material, but *only if* the omission is indicated. Three spaced periods are used to indicate the omission (technically known as an ellipsis). If there are four periods, one is the normal period at the end of a sentence, the other three indicate the ellipsis.

The statement just concluded, if quoted, might be shortened in the following way: "It is permissible to omit words . . . *if* the omission is indicated. Three spaced periods are used to indicate the omission. . . . If there are four periods, one is the normal period at the end of a sentence."

In quoting poetry, the omission of a whole stanza, or of a number of lines, or even one line, may be indicated, if desired, by supplying a whole line of spaced periods:

Othello begins and ends his last speech before stabbing

himself with reminders of his loyalty to Venice:

> Soft you, a word or two before you go.
> I have done the state some service, and they know't.
> .   .   .   .
>   in Aleppo once,
> Where a malignant and a turbaned Turk
> Beat a Venetian and traduced the state,
> I took by the throat the circumcisèd dog
> and smote him.   (V.ii.337–55)

Q10. The only exceptions to the rule about *exact* quotation (Q7) are that the initial letter and final mark of punctuation may be adjusted to fit the requirements of the sentence containing the quotation, and that double quotes, if they occur within a run-in quotation, should be reduced to single quotes. In Q1.a., a quotation ending with a comma in the original has been concluded with a period instead. In Q2.b., a semicolon at the end of the original quotation has been replaced by a period. In Q8 (the "correct" example), the capital letter of "Hold your peace" has been reduced to lower case, and the period after "peace" has been replaced by a comma. In the following example, a lower case initial letter has been capitalized and double quotes (for a quotation within a quotation) have been reduced to single quotes:

```
In her dying speech, Emilia asks her dead mistress,
"Canst thou hear me? I will play the swan, / And die in
music. 'Willow, willow, willow'" (V.ii.246-47).
```

Q11. At the conclusion of a run-in quotation, commas and periods are conventionally placed *within* quotation marks; semicolons and colons are placed outside. (The convention is based on appearance, not on logic.) Question marks and exclamation points are placed inside if they belong to the quoted sentence, outside if they belong to your sentence. (This is logic.) Special rules apply when the quotation is followed by parenthetical documentation (see PD4, page 1425). The following examples are all correct:

```
"I am not valiant neither," says Othello (V.ii.242).
Othello says, "I am not valiant neither."
Othello says, "I am not valiant neither"; but we know, of
    course, that he is valiant.
"Who can control his fate?" cries Othello (V.ii.264).
Does Shakespeare endorse Othello's implication that no one
    "can control his fate"?
```

VII. DOCUMENTATION

Documentation is the process of identifying the sources of materials used in your paper. The sources are of two kinds: primary and secondary. *Primary* sources are materials written by the author being studied, and may be confined to the single work being discussed. *Secondary* sources are materials by other writers about the author or work being discussed, or materials having some bearing on that work. Documentation serves two purposes:

(1) it enables your reader to locate and check any material he may think you have misinterpreted; (2) it enables you to make proper acknowledgment of information, ideas, opinions, or phraseology that are not your own. Documentation may be given (a) in the text of your essay; (b) in parentheses placed within the text of your essay; (c) in footnotes placed at the bottom of the page or collected at the end of your essay; or (d) in some combination of these.

1. Textual Documentation

Every literary essay contains textual documentation. A title like "Dramatic Irony in *Oedipus Rex*" identifies the play which will furnish the main materials in a paper. A paragraph beginning "In scene II . . ." locates more specifically the source of what follows. An informally documented essay is one which relies on textual documentation exclusively. Perhaps the majority of articles published in newspapers and periodicals with wide circulation are of this kind. Informal documentation works best for essays written on a single short work, without use of secondary sources, for readers without great scholarly expectations. A first-rate paper might be written on John Galsworthy's "The Japanese Quince" using only textual documentation. The author's name and the title of the story mentioned somewhere near the beginning of the essay, plus a few phrases like "In the opening paragraph" or "When Mr. Nilson first sees Mr. Tandram" or "At the story's conclusion" would provide all the documentation needed for this audience. The story is short enough that the reader can easily locate any detail within it. If the essay is intended for our hypothetical journal published by your literature class (all of whose members are using the same anthology), its readers can readily locate the story. But the informal method, although less appropriate, can also be used for more complex subjects, and can even accommodate secondary sources with phrases like "As Herman Ould points out, in his biography of Galsworthy. . ."

Principles and "Rules"

TD1. Enclose titles of short stories, articles, and poems (unless they are book-length) in quotation marks; underline titles of plays, magazines, newspapers, and books. Do not underline or put the title of your own paper in quotation marks. The general principle is that titles of separate publications are underlined; titles of selections or parts of books are put within quotation marks. Plays, like *Othello* and *Oedipus Rex,* though part of *this* book, are elsewhere published separately and should be underlined. Underlining, in manuscripts, is equivalent to italics in printed matter.

TD2. Capitalize the first word and all important words in titles. Do not capitalize articles, prepositions, and conjunctions except when they begin the title ("The Child by Tiger," *An Enemy of the People*).

TD3. When the title above a poem is identical with its first line or a major part of its first line, there is a strong presumption that the poet left the poem untitled and the editor or anthologist has used the first line or part of it to serve as a title. In such a case you may *use* the first line as a title, but should not *refer* to it as a title (Don't write: "The poet's repetition of his title in his first line emphasizes . . ."). In using it as a title, capitalize only those words which are capitalized in the first line. (In this book, since the titles above the poems are in capitals throughout, you can make the distinction only by consulting the table of contents or the index.)

TD4. Never use page numbers in the body of your discussion, for a page is not a constituent part of a story, poem, or play. You may refer in your discussion to paragraphs, sections, stanzas, lines, acts, or scenes, as appropriate, but use page numbers *only* in parenthetical or footnote documentation where a specific edition of the work has been named.

TD5. Spell out numerical references when they precede the unit they refer to; use numbers when they follow the unit (the fifth act, or act V; the second paragraph, or paragraph 2; the fourth line, or line 4; the tenth stanza, or stanza 10). Use the first of these alternative forms sparingly, and only with small numbers. Never write "In the thirty-fourth and thirty-fifth lines . . . ," for to do so is to waste good space and irritate your reader; write "In lines 34–35 . . ."

2. Parenthetical Documentation

Parenthetical documentation makes possible fuller and more precise accreditation without a forbidding apparatus of footnotes. With a full-length play like Arthur Miller's *Death of a Salesman*, a phrase like "midway through Act I" is insufficient to allow the reader to locate the passage easily. This can be done by giving a page number, within parentheses, after the passage cited. But the reader needs to know also what book or edition the page number refers to, so this information must be supplied the first time such a citation is made, or possibly the first time the play is mentioned. In this first citation full publishing details should be given, but parenthetical documentation should supplement textual documentation; that is, information provided in the text of your essay should not be repeated within the parentheses. For the readers of our hypothetical class journal, the first reference in a paper on Miller's play might look like this:

In Arthur Miller's <u>Death of a Salesman</u> (reprinted in Laurence Perrine, <u>Literature</u>: <u>Structure</u>, <u>Sound</u>, <u>and</u> <u>Sense</u>,

4th ed., New York: Harcourt Brace Jovanovich, 1983, pp.

1328—1403), the playwright examines . . .

In subsequent references, only the page number need be given:

Biff blames his failure on his father: "I never got any-

where because you blew me so full of hot air I could never

stand taking orders from anybody! That's whose fault it

is!" (p. 1398).

Parenthetical documentation works best for papers using relatively few sources, chiefly primary.

Principles and "Rules"

PD1. For the first citation to a selection from a book, give the author's name; the title of the selection; the name of the book from which it is taken; the editor (preceded by the abbreviation *ed.* for "edited by") or the translator (preceded by the abbreviation *trans.* for "translated by"); the edition (designated by an Arabic number) if there has been more than one; the city of publication (the first given will suffice if there is more than one); the publisher (this may be given in shortened form, dropping words like "Co.," "and Sons," "Inc.," "The," and so on); the date of publication (if none is given on the title page, use the most recent copyright date on the back of the title page); and the page number (using the abbreviation *p.* for page and *pp.* for pages). Do not, however, repeat parenthetically documentation already given textually. The following example correctly combines textual with parenthetical documentation:

In "The Mountain," Frost has a New England farmer say

that "all the fun's in how you say a thing" (<u>The</u> <u>Poetry</u>

<u>of</u> <u>Robert</u> <u>Frost</u>, ed. Edward Connery Lathem, New York:

Holt, Rinehart and Winston, 1969, p. 44).

PD2. For your principal primary source, after the first reference, only a page number is required. For long poems, however, it may be more useful, if easily available, to give line numbers (using the abbreviations *l.* for line and *ll.* for lines), or the stanza number, rather than the page number. If the poem is short, line numbers are unnecessary and should be omitted. For plays in verse also, citation by line number (preceded by act and scene number) will often be more useful than by page, for example, *Othello* (V.ii.269).

PD3. Documentation for run-in quotations always follows the quotation marks. If the quotation ends with a period, remove it to the end of the documentation. If it ends with an exclamation point or question mark, leave it, but put a period after the documentation as well. The following examples are from *Othello*:

```
"She was false as water" (V.ii.133).
"Alas, what cry is that?" (V.ii.116).
```

PD4. With block quotations, parenthetical documentation follows the last mark of punctuation without further punctuation except for the parentheses:

```
Help! Help, ho! Help! O lady, speak again!
Sweet Desdemona! O sweet mistress, speak! (V.ii.119–20)
```

PD5. Avoid cluttering your paper with excessive documentation. When possible, use one note to cover a series of short quotations. (See example, Q1). Remember that short poems need no parenthetical documentation at all after the first reference. Do not document well-known sayings or proverbs that you use for stylistic purposes and which form no part of the substance of your investigation.

PD6. It is customary in a formal paper to document all quoted materials. Do not, however, fall victim to the too frequent delusion that *only* quotations need documentation. The first purpose of documentation (see page 1422) implies that any major or possibly controversial assertion concerning interpretation may need documentation. If you declare that the turning point in a long story occurs with an apparently minor event, it may be more important for the reader to have a page number for that event than for any quotation from the story. Judgment must be exercised. You cannot and should not provide page numbers for every detail of a story; but neither should you think that you have necessarily done your duty if you merely document all quotations.

3. Footnote Documentation

Documentation by footnotes, or by notes collected at the end of your paper (more properly called endnotes), is the best form for a paper drawing on a large variety of sources, especially if many of them are secondary. In short, it is the most appropriate form of documentation for the investigative or "research" paper. Because footnotes and endnotes are separated from the material annotated, the material and the notes need to be numbered to establish their connection. The use of footnote or endnote documentation, however, does not require the abandonment of parenthetical documentation. It is highly desirable to have no more footnotes than necessary, and one way to reduce their number is to continue the use of parenthetical annotation for any primary source which is frequently cited. If your paper is on *Othello*, your first reference to it should be footnoted and should include all publication details. Further references should be parenthetical and should not be assigned a number. Never think that any editor will be favorably impressed by the number of footnotes your paper has. An editor may be impressed by the number and quality of the sources you use, but *not* by the number of footnotes.

Principles and "Rules"

The following instructions cover only the most general situations. For the dozens of more special situations that can occur, consult a manual on research papers. In a pinch, fall back on principle. The note is there to be of service to your readers. Do whatever will most help them. The "rules" or conventions of footnoting are themselves devised, by providing uniformity, to serve this end.

FD1. Number the notes consecutively throughout your paper. In your text place the footnote number at the end of the material referred to, after the final punctuation, and slightly raised above the line. The note itself should begin with its number, slightly raised above the line. If you use true footnotes, placed at the bottom of the page, single-space each note, but double-space between notes.

FD2. Unless your instructor requires the notes to be placed at the foot of the page, place them at the end of your essay and begin them on a new page headed "Notes." (For a paper whose final appearance will be typed or handwritten, it is more convenient for the reader to have them at the bottom of the page, but much more difficult for the writer, who must gauge how much space to leave. For a paper which will be set up in type, it is easier for the printer to have them as endnotes even when they will appear as footnotes.) Endnotes should be double-spaced throughout.

FD3. Treat each note as a small paragraph. Indent it as for a paragraph, begin it with a capital letter, and end it with a period.

FD4. For the first full entry referring to a book, use the same form described for parenthetical documentation (see PD1), but put city, publisher, and date in parentheses:

⁴H. D. F. Kitto, <u>Greek</u> <u>Tragedy</u> (London: Methuen, 1950), p. 138.

FD5. For a periodical article, the first footnote takes this form: first, the author of the article; second, the title of the article in quotation marks; third, the title of the journal underlined; fourth, the volume number in Arabic numerals (even if the periodical itself uses Roman numerals); fifth, the date, in parentheses, of the issue in which the article appears; sixth, the page numbers.

⁵P. J. Yarrow, "A Reconsideration of Alceste," <u>French</u> <u>Studies</u>, 13 (October 1959), 314–29.

FD6. If further references to a secondary source are made, use a shortened form for subsequent footnotes:

⁶Kitto, p. 140.
 or
⁶Kitto, <u>Greek</u> <u>Tragedy</u>, p. 140.

⁷Yarrow, p. 324.
 or
⁷Yarrow, "Alceste," p. 324.

FD7. Notice that no punctuation precedes parentheses in the examples given. Parentheses are never preceded by other marks of punctuation in a sentence or in footnotes, because parenthetical material is always an explanation or modification of what has gone before, not of what comes after.

FD8. Authors' names, whether in parenthetical notes or footnotes, should be in their normal order, first name first, last name last. The only reason for ever putting a last name first is that it occurs in an alphabetical list or is on a form that is to be filed alphabetically.

FD9. With secondary sources it is frequently more important to footnote unquoted material than quoted material. The second important purpose of documentation (page 1422) is to give due acknowledgment for information, ideas, insights, or phraseology that is not your own. The presence of quotation marks at least acknowledges the use of someone else's words, though without indicating whose. The use of someone else's ideas or insights in your own words, since it does not require quotation marks, makes an even heavier demand for acknowledgment either in text or footnote. Though you need not document matters of common knowledge, your use without acknowledgment of material that is uniquely someone else's is not only dishonest but illegal, and could result in penalties ranging from an

VIII.1./2.

F on the paper through expulsion from school to a term in jail, depending on the magnitude of the offense.

VIII. GRAMMAR, PUNCTUATION, AND USAGE: SPECIAL PROBLEMS

1. Grammar

G1. In discussing the action of a literary work, rely primarily on the present tense (even though the work itself uses the past), keeping the past, future, and perfect tenses available for prior or subsequent actions; for example, "When Mrs. May imagines that the bull may have gored Greenleaf and killed him, and thinks of this as 'the perfect ending' for a story she has been telling her friends, the situation is highly ironical, for she does not guess that the bull will cause her own death."

G2. Do not let pronouns refer to nouns in the possessive case. Antecedents of pronouns should always hold a strong grammatical position: a possessive is a mere modifier, like an adjective.

WRONG   In Shakespeare's play <u>Othello</u>, he writes

(Antecedent of "he" is in possessive case.)

RIGHT   In his play <u>Othello</u>, Shakespeare writes

(Antecedent of "his" is the subject of the sentence.)

G3. When a quotation is used as a noun phrase, be careful to integrate it into your sentence structure.

WRONG   The aimless boredom of the women in "Prufrock" is expressed by "come and go."

RIGHT   The aimless boredom of the women in "Prufrock" is expressed by the phrase "come and go."

2. Punctuation

P1. Do not set off restrictive appositives with commas. A "restrictive" appositive is one necessary to the meaning of the sentence; a "nonrestrictive" appositive could be left out without changing the meaning.

WRONG   In his book, <u>A Boy's Will</u>, Robert Frost . . .

(Without the title we do not know which of Frost's books

is referred to. As punctuated, the sentence falsely implies that Frost wrote only one book.)

RIGHT In his book <u>A Boy's Will</u>, Robert Frost . . .

RIGHT In his first book, <u>A Boy's Will</u>, Robert Frost . . .

(The adjective "first" identifies the book. The title simply supplies additional information and could be omitted without changing the meaning.)

P2. Words used simply as words should be either underlined or put in quotation marks.

WRONG The sixth word in "The Road Not Taken" is yellow.

(This statement is false; all the words in the poem are black.)

RIGHT The sixth word in "The Road Not Taken" is

"yellow."

Since the word "yellow" is quoted from the poem, it has here been put in quotation marks. However, if you list a series of words from the poem, you may prefer underlining for the sake of appearance. Whichever system you choose, be consistent throughout your paper.

3. Usage

U1. Though accepted usage changes with time and the distinctions between the following pairs of words are fading, many instructors will bless you if you try to preserve them.

convince, persuade *Convince* pertains to belief (conviction); *persuade* pertains to either action or belief. The following sentences observe the distinction. "In 'To His Coy Mistress' the speaker tries to persuade a young woman to sleep with him." "In 'To His Coy Mistress' the speaker tries to convince a young woman that she has nothing to lose by sleeping with him." "I persuaded him to have another drink though he was convinced he ought not to."

disinterested, uninterested A disinterested judge is one who has no "stake" or personal interest in the outcome of a case and who can therefore judge fairly; an uninterested judge goes to sleep on the bench. A good judge is interested in the case but disinterested in its outcome. An uninterested reader finds reading boring. A disinterested reader? Perhaps one who can enjoy a good book whatever its subject matter.

imply, infer   A writer or speaker implies; a reader or listener infers. An implication is a meaning hinted at but not stated outright. An inference is a conclusion drawn from evidence not complete enough for proof. If you imply that I am a snob, I may infer that you do not like me.

sensuous, sensual   *Sensuous* normally pertains to the finer senses, *sensual* to the appetites. Good poetry is sensuous: it appeals through the imagination to the senses. A voluptuous woman or a succulent pot roast makes a sensual appeal which stirs a desire for possession.

quote, quotation   *Quote* was originally used only as a verb. Today the use of "single quotes" and "double quotes" in reference to quotation marks is almost universally accepted; but, although the use of "quote" for "quotation" is common in informal speech, it is still unacceptable in formal writing. —Note also that quoting is an act performed by the writer about literature, not by the writer of literature.

WRONG   Shakespeare's famous quotation "To be or not to
　　　　 be" . . .

RIGHT   The famous quotation from Shakespeare, "To be or
　　　　 not to be" . . .

RIGHT   Shakespeare's famous line "To be or not to
　　　　 be" . . .

BETTER   Hamlet's famous line "To be or not to be" . . .

BEST   Probably the most-quoted line by Shakespeare is
　　　　 Hamlet's "To be or not to be". . .

U2.   Other words and phrases to be avoided:

center around   A geometrical impossibility. A story may perhaps center *on* a certain feature, but to make it center *around* that feature is to make the hub surround the wheel.

lifestyle   An over-used neologism, especially inappropriate for use with older literature.

keeper who knuckles under to the bad guys. He therefore has turned to a more powerful means of escape, one which protects him from dwelling on what he knows about himself: drunkenness. His final words are memorable--so "unpoetical" in a traditional sense, so poetically effective in characterizing this speaker. "Get stewed," he tells himself. "Books are a load of crap."

It would be a serious mistake to identify the speaker of the poem, or his attitudes or his language, with the poet. Poets, writers of books themselves, do not think that "Books are a load of crap." Philip Larkin, moreover, an English poet and a graduate of Oxford, is and has been for years a university librarian (James Vinson, ed., Contemporary Poets, 3d ed., New York: St. Martin's Press, 1980, p. 877). "A Study of Reading Habits" is both dramatic and ironic. It presents a first-person speaker who has been unable to cope with the reality of his life in any of its stages and has therefore turned toward various means of escaping it. His confessions reveal a progressive deterioration of values (from good to evil to sodden indifference) and a decline in reading tastes (from adventure stories to prurient sexual novels to none) which reflects his downward slide.

Comments

The title of this paper is enclosed in quotation marks because the writer has used the title of the poem for the title of his paper. The paper uses textual and parenthetical but no footnote documentation. Line numbers for quotations from the poem are not supplied, because the poem is too short to require them: they would serve no useful purpose. Notice that in quoting from stanza 1, the writer has changed the phrase "ruining my eyes" to fit his own syntax, but has indicated the alteration by putting the changed word within brackets. The paper is written for an American audience; if it had been written for an English audience the writer would not

what the author was trying to say was The implication of this expression is that the author failed to say what he meant, and its use puts you in the patronizing position of implying that you could have done a much better job of it. To which the only proper rejoinder is "If you're so smart, why ain't you famous?"

Others suggested by your instructor:

_____ _____

_____ _____

_____ _____

_____ _____

_____ _____

_____ _____

_____ _____

_____ _____

_____ _____

_____ _____

_____ _____

_____ _____

_____ _____

IX. A SAMPLE EXPLICATION

"A STUDY OF READING HABITS"

The first noteworthy feature of Philip Larkin's "A Study of Reading Habits" (Laurence Perrine, <u>Literature</u>: <u>Structure</u>, <u>Sound</u>, <u>and Sense</u>, 4th ed., New York: Harcourt Brace Jovanovich, 1983, p. 544) is the ironic discrepancy between the formal language of its title and the colloquial, slangy, even vulgar language of the poem itself. The title by its tone implies a formal sociological research paper, possibly one which samples a cross section of a population and draws conclusions about people's reading. The poem presents, instead, the confessions of one man whose attitudes toward reading have progressively deteriorated to the point where books seem to him "a load of crap." Its real subject, moreover, is not his reading habits but the revelation of life and character they provide.

The poem is patterned in three stanzas having an identical rime scheme (<u>abcbac</u>) and the same basic meter (iambic-anapestic trimeter). This formal division of the poem corresponds to the internal structure of meaning, for the three stanzas present the speaker at three stages of his life: as schoolboy, adolescent, and adult. The chronological progression is signaled in the first lines of the stanzas by the words "When," "Later," and "now." The "now" is the present out of which he speaks, recalling the two earlier periods.

The boy he remembers in stanza 1 was unhappy, both in his home and, even more so, at school. Perhaps small and bullied by bigger boys, probably an indifferent student, making poor grades, and scolded by teachers, he found a partial escape from his miseries through reading. The books he [...] of action and adventure, pitting good guys against [...] full of physical conflict, and ending with the good [...] torious—enabled him to construct a fantasy life in w[...] identified with the virtuous hero and in his imaginatic[...] up villains twice his size, thus reversing the situation [...] his real life.

In stanza 2 the speaker recalls his adolescence, when his dreams were of sexual rather than muscular prowess. True to the prediction of "ruining [his] eyes" in stanza 1, he had to wear spectacles which he describes hyperbolically as "inch-thick"—a further detriment to his social life. To compensate for his lack of success with girls, he envisioned himself as a Dracula-figure with cloak and fangs, enjoying a series of sexual triumphs. His reading continued to feed his fantasy life, but, instead of identifying with the virtuous hero, he identified with the glamorous, sexually ruthless villain. The poet puns on the word "ripping" (the speaker "had ripping times in the dark"), implying both the British slang meaning of "splendid" and the violence of the rapist who rips the clothes off his victim and of the murderous "Jack the Ripper."

In stanza 3 the speaker, now a young adult, confesses that he no longer reads much. His accumulated experience of personal failure and his long familiarity with his shortcom[...] ings have made it impossible for him to identify, even in [...] tasy, with the strong virtuous hero or the viciously po[...] villain. He can no longer hide from himself the truth [...] resembles more closely the weak secondary charac[...] escapist tales he picks up. He recognizes h[...] dependable dude who fails the heroine, o[...]

have needed to explain that "ripping" is British slang or to have made it a point that the poet is English. The paper is documented for an audience using this textbook. If it were directed toward a wider audience, the writer would want to refer for his text of the poem not to a textbook or anthology but to the volume of Larkin's containing this poem (*The Whitsun Weddings*, London: Faber and Faber, 1964, p. 31). Also, he would probably wish to include the poet's name in his title: Philip Larkin's "A Study of Reading Habits" (or) An Examination of Larkin's "A Study of Reading Habits."

X.

X. A SAMPLE ANALYSIS

THE FUNCTION OF THE LOVELADYS IN "THAT EVENING SUN"

At the very climax of "That Evening Sun"—the point at which Nancy's terror passes from frantic efforts to protect herself against the murderous revenge of her husband into terrified conviction that he will slay her that night no matter what precautions she takes—more than nine-tenths of the way through the story—Faulkner introduces three new characters. Nancy has just told the children's father for the third time, "When yawl go home, I gone," but now adds, "Anyway, I got my coffin money saved up with Mr. Lovelady." Quentin explains:

> Mr. Lovelady was a short, dirty man who collected the Negro insurance, coming around to the cabins or kitchens every Saturday, to collect fifteen cents. He and his wife lived at the hotel. One morning his wife committed suicide. They had a child, a little girl. He and the child went away. After a week or two he came back alone. We would see him going along the lanes and the back streets on Saturday mornings.[1]

Why does Faulkner introduce this apparent digression? Was it really necessary that Nancy name the man she has her burial money saved up with? In any case, why does not Faulkner stop after Quentin's first dozen words? What has Mr. Lovelady's domestic situation to do with Nancy's fear or with the theme of the story?

Quentin's explanation raises more questions than it answers. Why did Mrs. Lovelady commit suicide? What happened

[1] Laurence Perrine, Literature: Structure, Sound, and Sense, 4th ed. (New York: Harcourt Brace Jovanovich, 1983), p. 266. All subsequent page numbers refer to this text.

to the child? We are told of Mr. Lovelady only that he is "a short, dirty man" who collects the Negro insurance. He was short when they married, so this hardly explains his wife's suicide. That he washes infrequently is sufficient cause for marital conflict but hardly for suicide. The remaining possibility is that her act was related to her husband's business. I confess I know nothing personally about Negro insurance. Fortunately, however, we have already read in this course two stories containing white insurance agents who deal with blacks. In "The Child by Tiger" Ben Pounders, who boasts of putting the first shot into Dick Prosser, is described as having a ferret face, a furtive eye, and a mongrel mouth, and is identified as "the collector of usurious lendings to the blacks" (p. 38). In "Greenleaf" Mrs. May's son Scofield is in insurance. Mrs. May "would not have minded his selling insurance if he had sold a nicer kind but he sold the kind that only Negroes buy. . . . He said there was more money in nigger-insurance than any other kind, and before company he . . . would shout, 'Mama don't like to hear me say it but I'm the best nigger-insurance salesman in this county!'" (pp. 224–25). From these accounts it is clear that "Negro insurance" is a blatant form of economic exploitation of blacks by whites. After his wife's suicide Mr. Lovelady apparently found their child an inconvenience and preferred to give her up rather than give up his trade. One other feature of Quentin's account may be significant. Mr. Lovelady is "a short, dirty man" whose wife commits suicide. Jesus is "a short black man" (p. 255) with a "dirty"-looking razor scar (p. 256) whose wife attempts suicide. If this parallel is intentional, its significance must be sought in an examination of the relationship between Nancy and Jesus.

X.

    "That Evening Sun" is the story of a black woman's
terror that she will be murdered by her husband for having
been made pregnant by a white man whom she has served as a
prostitute. She has ambivalent feelings toward her actions.
On the one hand, she feels victimized by the white world and
powerless to have done other than she has done. "I ain't
nothing but a nigger," she says. "It ain't none of my
fault" (p. 257). On the other hand, she feels guilty of having wronged her husband. "I reckon it belong to me. I
reckon what I going to get ain't no more than mine" (p. 266).
She knows what she would want to do if she found Jesus unfaithful to her (p. 258), and she naturally thinks that
Jesus, a violent man, has similar feelings toward her infi-
delity to him. Real cause for fear, heightened by guilt, thus
towers in Nancy into incapacitating terror and tumbles finally into resignation. The end of the story leaves Nancy in
her cabin, the door open, waiting for the death she is sure
will come. The lamp is brightly lit, and the fire blazing,
for she's "scaired for it to happen in the dark" (p. 266),
and she is making "the sound that was not singing and not
unsinging" which is expressive of her fear (p. 267).

    But if Nancy's terror occupies the forefront of "That
Evening Sun," the background is occupied by racial conflict,
economic exploitation, and the brutal treatment of blacks
by whites. All power in the town is concentrated in the hands
of the whites. They own the big houses, manage the banks,
control the courts, run the jails. Mr. Stovall's use of Nancy's body three times without payment is a clear case of sexual and economic exploitation. When Nancy presses for payment, the town marshal lets Stovall knock her down and kick
her teeth out before restraining him. Mr. Stovall is <u>not</u>

arrested for assault and battery. Nancy is put in jail, presumably for prostitution. When she tries to hang herself, the jailer cuts her down, whips her, and beats her. There is obvious truth in Nancy's attitude, "I ain't nothing but a nigger. It ain't my fault." It is Jesus, however, who most eloquently sums up the black predicament. "I can't hang around white man's kitchen. But white man can hang around mine. White man can come in my house, but I can't stop him. When white man want to come in my house, I ain't got no house . . ." (p. 256). Though Jesus' speech is general, he has in mind not only Mr. Jason, but also Mr. Stovall. When Stovall comes in, Jesus "ain't got no house." Jesus' "house" here represents both his home and Nancy's womb.

Mention of Mr. Jason[2] reminds us that, besides Mr. and Mrs. Lovelady, and Nancy and Jesus, the story includes a third married couple. Mr. Jason is the kindest and most decent white in the story, though even he can be guilty of insensitivity, as when he tells Nancy that Jesus "probably got another wife by now and forgot all about you" (p. 258). Mr. Jason's wife treats blacks as creatures of small importance. When her husband proposes to walk Nancy home on the first night of Nancy's terror, she protests, "You'll leave me alone, to take Nancy home? Is her safety more precious to you than mine?" When he insists he won't be gone long, and the children beg to go too, she says, "Jason!" "She was speaking to Father," Quentin explains. "You could tell that by the way she said the name. Like she believed that all day Father had been trying to think of doing the thing she wouldn't like the most, and that she knew all the time that

---

[2]Jason is his first name. His last name is not mentioned in the story.

after a while he would think of it" (p. 257). Though Mr.
Jason overrules his wife on this occasion, he accommodates
her the next time she complains (p. 258), and a pallet is
fixed for Nancy in the kitchen. But on the night of Nancy's
biggest terror, Mr. Jason completely capitulates to his
wife. With Dilsey well, Nancy is no longer needed at the
house. Deprived of its protection, Nancy is sure that this is
the night Jesus is going to kill her. She begs the children,
"Go ask your maw to let me stay here tonight." When the
mother answers, "I can't have Negroes sleeping in the bedrooms," a discussion follows between the mother and the father. Mr. Jason apparently proposes that at least he walk
Nancy back home. "I must wait here alone in this big
house," she persists, "while you take a Negro woman home."
"You know that I am not lying outside with a razor," he
replies. But the upshot is that Caddy is sent to the kitchen
with the message, "Father said for you to go home and lock
the door, and you'll be all right" (pp. 260–61).

     It is now time to return to the question concerning Mr.
and Mrs. Lovelady. What the story presents us with, we see,
is three married couples—one black and two white—in each of
which conflict is generated or exacerbated by the relationship of one of the pair with a person or persons of the opposite color. Mr. Jason tries to protect Nancy from her fears
but cannot do so without upsetting his neurotic wife. Nancy
is made pregnant by a white man and lives in terror that her
husband will cut her throat. Mr. Lovelady collects insurance
money from the blacks, and his wife commits suicide. Though
the story is centrally concerned with racial conflict and the
ruthless exploitation of the blacks by whites, what it says
through the three married couples is that the white attitude

toward blacks creates conflict not only <u>between</u> the races but
<u>within</u> each race. The whites cannot exploit the blacks with-
out damaging themselves. The inclusion of Mr. and Mrs. Lovelady in the story is necessary to complete and to underscore
this point.

Comments

This analysis is written for our hypothetical class journal, as the reference to two stories "already read in this course" shows. If it were written
for a more general audience, the writer would have to eliminate the overly
personal confession of knowing nothing about Negro insurance and present
more solid evidence of what this business entails (or entailed at the time of
the story), but for *this* audience the two stories work nicely. Notice that on
two occasions, once in the third paragraph, and once in the fifth, the writer
supplies page references where there is no quotation, assuming (quite
rightly) that the reader might want to check this point. Notice also that
when he uses a string of quotations all from the same episode (most notably
in the latter half of the fifth paragraph), he gives a note only after the last of
them. Notice also the punctuation of quotation within quotation in the
passage about "Greenleaf."

Appendix 2: The Source of Othello

The "Tale of the Moor of Venice" was the seventh novella in the third decade of the Hecatommithi *(Hundred Tales) by Gianbattista Giraldi Cinthio, Venice, 1565. It is possible that Shakespeare read the story in an English version that has not survived.*

There once lived in Venice a Moor, who was very valiant, and of a handsome person; and having given proofs in war of great skill and prudence, he was highly esteemed by the Signoria of the Republic, who in rewarding deeds of valour advanced the interests of the State.

It happened that a virtuous lady, of marvellous beauty, named Disdemona, fell in love with the Moor, moved thereto by his valour; and he, vanquished by the beauty and the noble character of Disdemona, returned her love; and their affection was so mutual, that, although the parents of the lady strove all they could to induce her to take another husband, she consented to marry the Moor; and they lived in such harmony and peace in Venice, that no word ever passed between that was not affectionate and kind.

Now it happened at this time that the Signoria of Venice made a change in the troops whom they used to maintain in Cyprus, and they appointed the Moor commander of the soldiers whom they despatched thither. Joyful as was the Moor at the honour proffered him—such dignity being only conferred on men of noble rank and well-tried faith, and who had displayed bravery in arms—yet his pleasure was lessened when he reflected on the length and dangers of the voyage, fearing that Disdemona would be pained at his absence. But Disdemona, who had no other happiness in the world than the Moor, and who rejoiced to witness the testimony of his valour her husband had received from so powerful and noble a Republic, was all impatient that he should embark with his troops, and longed to accompany him

THE SOURCE OF OTHELLO   From *The Moore of Venice: Cinthio's Tale and Shakespere's Tragedy* by John Edward Taylor (London: Chapman and Hall, 1855).

to so honourable a post. And all the more it vexed her to see the Moor so troubled; and not knowing what could be the reason, one day, when they were at dinner, she said to him, "How is it, O Moor, that when so honourable a post has been conferred on you by the Signoria, you are thus melancholy?"

The Moor answered Disdemona, "My pleasure at the honour I have received is disturbed by the love I bear you; for I see that of necessity one of two things must happen; either I take you with me, to encounter the perils of the sea, or, to save you from this danger, I must leave you here in Venice. The first could not be otherwise than serious to me, for all the toil you would have to bear, and every danger that might befall you, would cause me extreme anxiety and pain. Yet, were I to leave you behind me, I should be hateful to myself, since in parting from you I should part from my own life."

Disdemona, on hearing this, replied, "My husband, what thoughts are these that wander through your mind? Why let such things disturb you? I will accompany you whithersoe'er you go, were it to pass through fire, as now to cross the water in a safe and well-provided ship: if indeed there are toils and perils to encounter, I will share them with you. And in truth I should think you loved me little, were you to leave me here in Venice, denying me to bear you company, or could believe that I would liefer bide in safety here, than share the dangers that await you. Prepare then for the voyage, with all the readiness which the dignity of the post you hold deserves."

The Moor, in the fulness of his joy, threw his arms around his wife's neck, and with an affectionate and tender kiss exclaimed, "God keep you long in such love, dear wife!" Then speedily donning his armour, and having prepared everything for his expedition, he embarked on board the galley, with his wife and all his troops; and setting sail, they pursued their voyage, and with a perfectly tranquil sea arrived safely at Cyprus.

Now amongst the soldiery there was an Ensign, a man of handsome figure, but of the most depraved nature in the world. This man was in great favour with the Moor, who had not the slightest idea of his wickedness; for despite the malice lurking in his heart, he cloaked with proud and valourous speech, and with a specious presence, the villainy of his soul, with such art, that he was to all outward show another Hector or Achilles. This man had likewise taken with him his wife to Cyprus, a young, and fair, and virtuous lady; and being of Italian birth, she was much loved by Disdemona, who spent the greater part of every day with her.

In the same Company there was a certain Captain of a troop, to whom the Moor was much affectioned. And Disdemona, for this cause, knowing how much her husband valued him, showed him proofs of the greatest kindness, which was all very grateful to the Moor. Now the wicked Ensign, regardless of the faith that he had pledged his wife, no less than of the friendship, fidelity, and obligation which he owed the Moor, fell passionately in love with Disdemona, and bent all his thoughts to achieve his conquest; yet he dared not to declare his passion openly, fearing that, should the Moor perceive it, he would at once kill him. He therefore sought in various ways, and with secret guile, to betray his passion to the lady. But she, whose every wish was centred in the Moor, had no thought for this Ensign more than for any other man; and all the means he tried to gain her love, had no more effect than if he had not tried them. But the Ensign imagined that the cause of his ill success was that Disdemona loved the Captain of the troop; and he pondered how to remove him from her sight. The love which he had borne the lady now changed into the bitterest hate; and, having failed in his purposes, he devoted all his thoughts to plot the death of the Captain of the troop, and to divert the affection of the Moor from Disdemona. After revolving in his mind various schemes, all alike wicked, he at length resolved to accuse her of unfaithfulness to her husband, and to represent the Captain as her paramour. But knowing the singular love the Moor bore to Disdemona, and the friendship which he had for the Captain, he was well aware that, unless he practised an artful fraud upon the Moor, it were impossible to make him give ear to either accusation: wherefore he resolved to wait, until time and circumstance should open a path for him to engage in his foul project.

Not long afterwards, it happened that the Captain, having drawn his sword upon a soldier of the guard, and struck him, the Moor deprived him of his rank; whereat Disdemona was deeply grieved, and endeavoured again and again to reconcile her husband to the man. This the Moor told to the wicked Ensign, and how his wife importuned him so much about the Captain, that he feared he should be forced at last to receive him back to service. Upon this hint the Ensign resolved to act, and began to work his web of intrigue; "Perchance," said he, "the lady Disdemona may have good reason to look kindly on him."

"And wherefore?" said the Moor.

"Nay, I would not step 'twixt man and wife," replied the Ensign; "but let your eyes be witness to themselves."

In vain the Moor went on to question the officer—he would proceed no further; nevertheless his words left a sharp stinging thorn in the Moor's heart, who could think of nothing else, trying to guess their meaning, and lost in melancholy. And one day, when his wife had been endeavouring to pacify his anger toward the Captain, and praying him not to be unmindful of ancient services and friendship, for one small fault, especially since peace had been made between the Captain and the soldier he had struck, the Moor was angered, and exclaimed "Great cause have you, Disdemona, to care so anxiously about this man! Is he a brother, or your kinsman, that he should be so near your heart?"

The lady, with all gentleness and humility, replied, "Be not angered, my dear lord; I have no other cause to bid me speak, than sorrow that I see you lose so dear a friend as, by your own words, this Captain has been to you: nor has he done so grave a fault, that you should bear him so much enmity. Nay, but you Moors are of so hot a nature, that every little trifle moves you to anger and revenge."

Still more enraged at these words, the Moor replied, "I could bring proofs—by heaven it mocks belief! but for the wrongs I have endured, revenge must satisfy my wrath."

Disdemona, in astonishment and fright, seeing her husband's anger kindled against her, so contrary to his wont, said humbly and with timidity, "None save a good intent has led me thus to speak with you, my lord; but to give cause no longer for offence, I'll never speak a word more on the subject."

The Moor, observing the earnestness with which his wife again pleaded for the Captain, began to guess the meaning of the Ensign's words; and in deep melancholy he went to seek that villain, and induce him to speak more openly of what he knew. Then the Ensign, who was bent upon injuring the unhappy lady, after feigning at first great reluctance to say aught that might displease the Moor, at length pretended to yield to his entreaties, and said, "I can't deny, it pains me to the soul to be thus forced to say what needs must be more hard to hear than any other grief; but since you will it so, and that the regard I owe your honour compels me to confess the truth, I will no longer refuse to satisfy your questions and my duty. Know then, that for no other reason is your lady vext to see the Captain in disfavour, than for the pleasure that she has in his company whenever he comes to your house, and all the more since she has taken an aversion to your blackness."

These words went straight to the Moor's heart; but in order to hear more (now that he believed true all that the Ensign had told him), he replied, with a fierce glance, "By heavens, I scarce can hold this hand from plucking out that tongue of thine, so bold, which dares to speak such slander of my wife!"

"Captain," replied the Ensign, "I looked for such reward, for these my faithful offices—none else; but since my duty, and the jealous care I bear your honour, have carried me thus far, I do repeat, so stands the truth, as you have heard it from these lips: and if the lady Disdemona hath, with a false show of love for you, blinded your eyes to what you should have seen, this is no argument but that I speak the truth. Nay, this same Captain told it me himself, like one whose happiness is incomplete until he can declare it to another: and, but that I feared your anger, I should have given him, when he told it me, his merited reward, and slain him. But since informing you, of what concerns more you than any other man, brings me so undeserved a recompense, would I had held my peace, since silence might have spared me your displeasure."

Then the Moor, burning with indignation and anguish, said, "Make thou these eyes self-witnesses of what thou tell'st, or on thy life I'll make thee wish thou hadst been born without a tongue."

"An easy task it would have been," replied the villain, "when he was used to visit at your house; but now, that you have banished him, not for just cause, but for more frivolous pretext, it will be hard to prove the truth. Still I do not forgo the hope, to make you witness of that which you will not credit from my lips."

Thus they parted. The wretched Moor, struck to the heart as by a barbed dart, returned to his home, and awaited the day when the Ensign should disclose to him the truth which was to make him miserable to the end of his days. But the evil-minded Ensign was, on his part, not less troubled by the chastity which he knew the lady Disdemona observed inviolate; and it seemed to him impossible to discover a means of making the Moor believe what he had falsely told him; and turning the matter over in his thoughts, in various ways, the villain resolved on a new deed of guilt.

Disdemona often used to go, as I have already said, to visit the Ensign's wife, and remained with her a good part of the day. Now the Ensign observed, that she carried about with her a handkerchief, which he knew the Moor had given her, finely embroidered in the Moorish fashion, and which was precious to Disdemona, nor less so to the Moor. Then he conceived the plan, of taking this kerchief from her secretly, and thus laying the snare for her final ruin. The Ensign had a little daughter, a child three years of age who was much loved by Disdemona; and one day, when the unhappy lady had gone to pay a visit at the house of this vile man, he took the little child up in his arms, and carried her to Disdemona, who took her, and pressed her to her bosom; whilst at the same instant this traitor, who had extreme dexterity of hand, drew the kerchief from her sash so cunningly, that she did not notice him, and overjoyed he took his leave of her.

Disdemona, ignorant of what had happened, returned home, and, busied with other thoughts, forgot the handkerchief. But a few days afterwards looking for it, and not finding it, she was in alarm, lest the Moor should ask her for it, as he oft was wont to do. Meanwhile the wicked Ensign, seizing a fit opportunity, went to the Captain of the troop, and with crafty malice left the handkerchief at the head of his bed, without his discovering the trick; until the following morning, when, in his getting out of bed, the handkerchief fell upon the floor, and he set his foot upon it. And not being able to imagine how it had come into his house, knowing that it belonged to Disdemona, he resolved to give it her; and waiting until the Moor had gone from home, he went to the back door, and knocked. It seemed as if fate conspired with the Ensign to work the death of the unhappy Disdemona. Just at that time the Moor returned home, and hearing a knocking at the back door, he went to the window, and in a rage exclaimed, "Who knocks there?" The Captain, hearing the Moor's voice, and fearing lest he should come downstairs and attack him, took to flight without answering a word. The Moor went down, and opening the door, hastened into the street, and looked about, but in vain. Then returning into the house, in great anger, he demanded of his wife who it was that had knocked at the door. Disdemona replied, as was true, that she did not know: but the Moor said, "It seemed to me the Captain."

"I know not," answered Disdemona, "whether it was he, or another person."

The Moor restrained his fury, great as it was, wishing to do nothing before consulting the Ensign, to whom he hastened instantly, and told him all that had passed, praying him to gather from the Captain all he could respecting the affair. The Ensign, overjoyed at the occurrence, promised the Moor to do as he requested; and one day he took occasion to speak with the Captain, when the Moor was so placed that he could see and hear them as they conversed. And whilst talking to him of every other subject than of Disdemona, he kept laughing all the time aloud; and feigning astonishment, he made various movements with his head and hands, as if listening to some tale of marvel. As soon as the Moor saw the Captain depart, he went up to the Ensign, to hear what he had said to him. And the Ensign, after long entreaty, at length said, "He has hidden from me nothing, and has told me that he has been used to visit your wife whenever you went from home, and that on the last occasion she gave him this handkerchief, which you presented to her when you married her."

The Moor thanked the Ensign, and it seemed now clear to him that, should he find Disdemona not to have the handkerchief, it was all true that the Ensign had told to him. One day, therefore, after dinner, in conversation with his wife on various subjects, he asked her for the kerchief. The unhappy lady, who had been in great fear of this, grew red as fire at this demand; and to hide the scarlet of her cheeks, which was closely noted by the Moor, she ran to a chest, and pretended to seek the handkerchief: and after hunting for it a long time, she said, "I know not how it is—I cannot find it—can you perchance have taken it?"

"If I had taken it," said the Moor, "why should I ask it of you? but you will look better another time."

On leaving the room, the Moor fell to meditating how he should put his wife to death, and likewise the Captain of the troop, so that their death should not be laid to his charge. And as he ruminated over this day and night, he could not prevent his wife's observing that he was not the same toward her as he had been wont; and she said to him again and again, "What is the matter? what troubles you? how comes it that you, who were the most light-hearted man in the world, are now so melancholy?"

The Moor feigned various reasons in reply to his wife's questioning, but she was not satisfied; and, although conscious that she had given the Moor no cause, by act or deed, to be so troubled, yet she feared that he might have grown wearied of her; and she would say to the Ensign's wife, "I know not what to say of the Moor; he used to be all love toward me; but within these few days he has become another man; and much I fear, that I shall prove a warning to young girls not to marry against the wishes of their parents, and that the Italian ladies may learn from me not to wed a man whom nature and habitude of life estrange from us. But as I know the Moor is on such terms of friendship with your husband, and communicates to him all his affairs, I pray you, if you have heard from him aught that you may tell me of, fail not to befriend me." And as she said this, she wept bitterly.

The Ensign's wife, who knew the whole truth (her husband wishing to make use of her to compass the death of Disdemona), but could never consent to such a project, dared not, from fear of her husband, disclose a single circumstance: all she said was, "Beware lest you give any cause of suspicion to your husband, and show to him by every means your fidelity and love."

"Indeed I do so," replied Disdemona; "but it is all of no avail."

Meanwhile the Moor sought in every way to convince himself of what he fain would have found untrue; and he prayed the Ensign to contrive that he might see the handkerchief in the possession of the Captain. This was a difficult matter to the wicked Ensign, nevertheless he promised to use every means to satisfy the Moor of the truth of what he said.

Now the Captain had a wife at home, who worked the most marvellous embroidery upon lawn; and seeing the handkerchief which belonged to the Moor's wife, she resolved, before it was returned to her, to work one like it. As she was engaged in this task, the Ensign observed her standing at a window, where she could be seen by all passers-by in the street; and he pointed her out to the Moor, who was now perfectly convinced of his wife's guilt. Then he arranged with the Ensign to slay Disdemona, and the Captain of the troop, treating them as it seemed they both deserved. And the Moor prayed the Ensign that he would kill the Captain, promising eternal gratitude to him. But the Ensign at first refused to undertake so dangerous a task, the Captain being a man of equal skill and courage; until at length, after much entreating, and being richly paid, the Moor prevailed on him to promise to attempt the deed.

Having formed this resolution, the Ensign, going out one dark night, sword in hand, met the Captain, on his way to visit a courtesan, and struck him a blow on his right thigh, which cut off his leg, and felled him to the earth. Then the Ensign was on the point of putting an end to his life, when the Captain, who was a courageous man, and used to the sight of blood and death, drew his sword, and, wounded as he was, kept on his defence, exclaiming with a loud voice, "I'm murdered!" Thereupon the Ensign, hearing the people come running up, with some of the soldiers who were lodged thereabouts, took to his heels, to escape being caught; then turning about again, he joined the crowd, petending to have been attracted by the noise. And when he saw the Captain's leg cut off, he judged that, if not already dead, the blow must at all events end his life; and whilst in his heart he was rejoiced at this, he yet feigned to compassionate the Captain as he had been his brother.

The next morning the tidings of this affair spread through the whole city, and reached the ears of Disdemona; whereat she, who was kind-hearted and little dreamed that any ill would betide her, evinced the greatest grief at the calamity. This served but to confirm the Moor's suspicions, and he went to seek for the Ensign, and said to him. "Do you know, that my wife is in such grief at the Captain's accident, that she is well-nigh gone mad."

"And what could you expect, seeing he is her very soul?" replied the Ensign.

"Ay, soul forsooth!" exclaimed the Moor; "I'll draw the soul from out her body: call me no man, if that I fail to shut the world upon this wretch."

Then they consulted of one means and another—poison and daggers—to kill poor Disdemona, but could resolve on nothing. At length the Ensign said, "A plan comes to my mind, which will give you satisfaction, and raise cause for no suspicion—it is this: the house in which you live is very old, and the ceiling of your chamber has many cracks; I propose we take a stocking, filled with sand, and beat Disdemona with it till she dies; thus will her body bear no signs of violence. When she is dead, we can pull down a portion of the ceiling, and thus make it seem as if a rafter falling on her head had killed the lady. Suspicion can not rest on you, since all men will impute her death to accident."

This cruel counsel pleased the Moor, and he only waited for a fitting time to execute the plot. One night, when he and Disdemona had retired to bed, the Ensign, whom the Moor had concealed in a closet which opened into the chamber, raised a noise in the closet, according to a concerted plan; whereat the Moor said to his wife, "Did you not hear that noise?"

"Indeed I heard it." she replied.

"Rise," said the Moor, "and see what 'tis."

The unhappy Disdemona rose from bed, and the instant she approached the closet, out rushed the Ensign, and being strong and of stout nerve, he beat her cruelly with the bag of sand across her back; upon which Disdemona fell to the ground, scarce able to draw her breath: but with the little voice she had left, she called upon the Moor for aid. But the Moor, leaping from bed, exclaimed, "Thou wickedest of women, thus has thy falseness found its just reward—the recompense to wives, who counterfeiting love, place horns upon their husbands' brows."

The wretched lady, hearing these words, and feeling that she was near her end (for the Ensign had given her another blow), appealed to the justice of Heaven, since justice here had failed her, in proof of her fidelity and truth; and as she was thus calling Heaven to witness, the wicked Ensign inflicted a third blow, under which she sank lifeless on the floor.

Then the Ensign and the Moor, laying Disdemona on the bed, and wounding her head, pulled down part of the ceiling of the chamber, as they had arranged; whereupon the Moor began to call aloud for help, exclaiming that the house was falling. Hearing this uproar, the neighbors all came running up, and there found Disdemona lying dead beneath a rafter—a sight which, from the good life of that poor lady, did fill all hearts with sorrow.

On the following day Disdemona was buried, followed to the grave by the universal grief of the people. But Heaven, the just regarder of all hearts, willed not that so wicked a deed should go unpunished. Ere long the Moor, whom Disdemona had loved more than her own life, began to feel such sorrow at her loss, that he went wandering about, as one bereft of reason, searching in every part of the house. And reflecting in his thoughts that the Ensign had been the cause that he had lost, with Disdemona, all joy in life, he conceived so deep a hatred to that wicked man, he could not bear to set eyes on him; and had it not been for his fear of the inviolable justice of the Signoria of Venice, he would have slain him openly. But being unable to do this with safety, he deprived him of his rank, and would not allow him to remain in his Company; whereat such an enmity arose between the two, that no greater or more deadly can be imagined.

The Ensign, that wickedest of all bad men, now turned his thoughts to injuring the Moor; and seeking out the Captain, whose wound was by this time healed, and who went about with a wooden leg, in place of the one that had been cut off, he said to him, "'Tis time you should be avenged for your lost limb; and if you will come with me to Venice, I'll tell you who the malefactor is, whom I dare not mention to you here, for many reasons, and I will bring you proofs."

The Captain of the troop, whose anger returned fiercely, but without knowing why, thanked the Ensign, and went with him to Venice. On arriving there, the Ensign told him that it was the Moor who had cut off his leg, on account of the suspicion he had formed of Disdemona's conduct with him; and for that reason he had slain her, and then spread the report that the ceiling had fallen and killed her. Upon hearing which, the Captain accused the Moor to the Signoria, both of having cut off his leg and killed his wife, and called the Ensign to witness the truth of what he said. The Ensign declared both charges to be true, for that the Moor had disclosed to him the whole plot, and had tried to persuade him to perpetrate both crimes; and that having afterwards killed his wife, out of jealousy he had conceived, he had narrated to him the manner in which he had perpetrated her death.

The Signoria of Venice, when they heard of the cruelty inflicted by a barbarian upon a lady of their city, commanded that the Moor's arms should be pinioned in Cyprus, and he be brought to Venice, where with many tortures they sought to draw from him the truth. But the Moor, bearing with unyielding courage all the torment, denied the whole charge so resolutely, that no confession could be drawn from him. But although, by his constancy and firmness, he escaped death, he was, after being confined for several days in prison, condemned to perpetual banishment, in which he was eventually slain by the kinsfolk of Disdemona, as he merited. The Ensign returned to his own country, and following up his wonted

what the author was trying to say was   The implication of this expression is
that the author failed to say what he meant, and its use puts you in the
patronizing position of implying that you could have done a much
better job of it. To which the only proper rejoinder is "If you're so
smart, why ain't you famous?"

Others suggested by your instructor:

_____   _____

_____   _____

_____   _____

_____   _____

_____   _____

_____   _____

_____   _____

_____   _____

_____   _____

_____   _____

_____   _____

_____   _____

_____   _____

IX. A SAMPLE EXPLICATION

"A STUDY OF READING HABITS"

The first noteworthy feature of Philip Larkin's "A Study of Reading Habits" (Laurence Perrine, Literature: Structure, Sound, and Sense, 4th ed., New York: Harcourt Brace Jovanovich, 1983, p. 544) is the ironic discrepancy between the formal language of its title and the colloquial, slangy, even vulgar language of the poem itself. The title by its tone implies a formal sociological research paper, possibly one which samples a cross section of a population and draws conclusions about people's reading. The poem presents, instead, the confessions of one man whose attitudes toward reading have progressively deteriorated to the point where books seem to him "a load of crap." Its real subject, moreover, is not his reading habits but the revelation of life and character they provide.

The poem is patterned in three stanzas having an identical rime scheme (abcbac) and the same basic meter (iambic-anapestic trimeter). This formal division of the poem corresponds to the internal structure of meaning, for the three stanzas present the speaker at three stages of his life: as schoolboy, adolescent, and adult. The chronological progression is signaled in the first lines of the stanzas by the words "When," "Later," and "now." The "now" is the present out of which he speaks, recalling the two earlier periods.

The boy he remembers in stanza 1 was unhappy, both in his home and, even more so, at school. Perhaps small and bullied by bigger boys, probably an indifferent student, making poor grades, and scolded by teachers, he found a partial escape from his miseries through reading. The books he read—tales of action and adventure, pitting good guys against bad guys, full of physical conflict, and ending with the good guy victorious—enabled him to construct a fantasy life in which he identified with the virtuous hero and in his imagination beat up villains twice his size, thus reversing the situation of his real life.

In stanza 2 the speaker recalls his adolescence, when his dreams were of sexual rather than muscular prowess. True to the prediction of "ruining [his] eyes" in stanza 1, he had to wear spectacles which he describes hyperbolically as "inch-thick"—a further detriment to his social life. To compensate for his lack of success with girls, he envisioned himself as a Dracula-figure with cloak and fangs, enjoying a series of sexual triumphs. His reading continued to feed his fantasy life, but, instead of identifying with the virtuous hero, he identified with the glamorous, sexually ruthless villain. The poet puns on the word "ripping" (the speaker "had ripping times in the dark"), implying both the British slang meaning of "splendid" and the violence of the rapist who rips the clothes off his victim and of the murderous "Jack the Ripper."

In stanza 3 the speaker, now a young adult, confesses that he no longer reads much. His accumulated experience of personal failure and his long familiarity with his shortcomings have made it impossible for him to identify, even in fantasy, with the strong virtuous hero or the viciously potent villain. He can no longer hide from himself the truth that he resembles more closely the weak secondary characters of the escapist tales he picks up. He recognizes himself in the undependable dude who fails the heroine, or the cowardly storekeeper who knuckles under to the bad guys. He therefore has turned to a more powerful means of escape, one which protects him from dwelling on what he knows about himself: drunkenness. His final words are memorable—so "unpoetical" in a traditional sense, so poetically effective in characterizing this speaker. "Get stewed," he tells himself. "Books are a load of crap."

It would be a serious mistake to identify the speaker of the poem, or his attitudes or his language, with the poet. Poets, writers of books themselves, do not think that "Books are a load of crap." Philip Larkin, moreover, an English poet and a graduate of Oxford, is and has been for years a university librarian (James Vinson, ed., Contemporary Poets, 3d ed., New York: St. Martin's Press, 1980, p. 877). "A Study of Reading Habits" is both dramatic and ironic. It presents a first-person speaker who has been unable to cope with the reality of his life in any of its stages and has therefore turned toward various means of escaping it. His confessions reveal a progressive deterioration of values (from good to evil to sodden indifference) and a decline in reading tastes (from adventure stories to prurient sexual novels to none) which reflects his downward slide.

Comments

The title of this paper is enclosed in quotation marks because the writer has used the title of the poem for the title of his paper. The paper uses textual and parenthetical but no footnote documentation. Line numbers for quotations from the poem are not supplied, because the poem is too short to require them: they would serve no useful purpose. Notice that in quoting from stanza 1, the writer has changed the phrase "ruining my eyes" to fit his own syntax, but has indicated the alteration by putting the changed word within brackets. The paper is written for an American audience; if it had been written for an English audience the writer would not

villainy, he accused one of his companions of having sought to persuade him to kill an enemy of his, who was a man of noble rank; whereupon this person was arrested, and put to the torture; but when he denied the truth of what his accuser had declared, the Ensign himself was likewise tortured, to make him prove the truth of his accusation; and he was tortured so that his body ruptured, upon which he was removed from prison and taken home, where he died a miserable death. Thus did Heaven avenge the innocence of Disdemona; and all these events were narrated by the Ensign's wife, who was privy to the whole, after his death, as I have told them here.

Glossary of Fictional Terms

Page numbers refer to discussion in the text, which in most but not all cases is fuller than that in the glossary.

Antagonist. Any force in a story that is in conflict with the *protagonist*. An antagonist may be another person, an aspect of the physical or social environment, or a destructive element in the protagonist's own nature. See *Conflict.* 42–43

Artistic unity. That condition of a successful literary work whereby all its elements work together for the achievement of its central purpose. In an artistically unified work nothing is included that is irrelevant to the central purpose, nothing is omitted that is essential to it, and the parts are arranged in the most effective order for the achievement of that purpose. 47, 240–41, 335–37

Chance. The occurrence of an event that has no apparent cause in antecedent events or in predisposition of character. 47–48

Character. (1) Any of the persons involved in a story (sense 1). (2) The distinguishing moral qualities and personal traits of *a character* (sense 2). 65–69

    Flat character. A *character* (sense 1) whose *character* (sense 2) is summed up in one or two traits. 67–68

    Round character. A *character* (sense 1) whose *character* (sense 2) is complex and many-sided. 67–68

    Stock character. A stereotyped character: one whose nature is familiar to us from prototypes in previous fiction. 68–69

Static character. A character who is the same sort of person at the end of a story as he was at the beginning. 69

Developing (or *dynamic*) *character.* A *character* (sense 1) who during the course of a story undergoes a permanent change in some aspect of his *character* (sense 2) or outlook. 69

Climax. The turning point or high point in a plot. 48

Coincidence. The chance concurrence of two events having a peculiar correspondence between them. 47–48

Commercial fiction. Fiction written to meet the taste of a wide popular audience and relying usually on tested formulas for satisfying such taste. 6

Conflict. A clash of actions, desires, ideas, or goals in the plot of a story. Conflict may exist between the main character and some other person or persons (man against man), between the main character and some external force—physical nature, society, or "fate" (man against environment), or between the main character and some destructive element in his own nature (man against himself). 42–43

Denouement. That portion of a plot that reveals the final outcome of its conflicts or the solution of its mysteries.

Deus ex machina ("god from the machine"). The resolution of a plot by use of a highly improbable chance or coincidence (so named from the practice of some Greek dramatists of having a god descend from heaven—in the theater by means of a stage machine—to rescue the protagonist from an impossible situation at the last possible minute). 47

Developing character. See *Character.*

Dilemma. A situation in which a character must choose between two courses of action, both undesirable. 43–44

Direct presentation of character. That method of characterization in which the author, by exposition or analysis, tells us directly what a character is like, or has someone else in the story do so. 66–67

Dramatic irony. See *Irony.*

Dramatic point of view. See *Point of view.*

Dramatization. The presentation of character or of emotion through the speech or action of characters rather than through exposition, analysis, or description by the author. See *Indirect presentation.* 67, 242–43

Dynamic character. See *Character.*

Editorializing. Writing that departs from the narrative or dramatic mode and instructs the reader how to think or feel about the events of a story or the behavior of a character. 243

Escape literature. Literature written purely for entertainment, with little or no attempt to provide insights into the true nature of human life or behavior. 3–8

Falling action. That segment of the plot that comes between the climax and the conclusion. 48

Fantasy. A kind of fiction that pictures creatures or events beyond the boundaries of known reality. 304–06

First person point of view. See *Point of view.*

Flat character. See *Character.*

Happy ending. An ending in which events turn out well for a sympathetic protagonist. 45–46

Indeterminate ending. An ending in which the central problem or conflict is left unresolved. 46–47

Indirect presentation of character. That method of characterization in which the author shows us a character in action, compelling us to infer what he is like from what he says or does. 66–67

Interpretive literature. Literature that attempts to provide valid insights into the nature of human life or behavior. 3–8

Irony. A situation, or a use of language, involving some kind of incongruity or discrepancy. 201–04. Three kinds of irony are distinguished in this book:

Verbal irony. A figure of speech in which what is said is the opposite of what is meant. 201–02

Dramatic irony. An incongruity or discrepancy between what a character says or thinks and what the reader knows to be true (or between what a character perceives and what the author intends the reader to perceive). 202–03

Irony of situation. A situation in which there is an incongruity between appearance and reality, or between expectation and fulfillment, or between the actual situation and what would seem appropriate. 203–04

Limited omniscient point of view. See *Point of view.*

Moral. A rule of conduct or maxim for living expressed or implied as the "point" of a literary work. Compare *Theme.* 107–08

Motivation. The incentives or goals that, in combination with the inherent natures of characters, cause them to behave as they do. In poor fiction actions may be unmotivated, insufficiently motivated, or implausibly motivated. 67

Mystery. An unusual set of circumstances for which the reader craves an explanation, used to create suspense. 43–44

Objective point of view. See *Point of view.*

Omniscient point of view. See *Point of view.*

Plot. The sequence of incidents or events of which a story is composed. 41–49

Plot manipulation. A situation in which an author gives his plot a twist or turn unjustified by preceding action or by the characters involved. 47

Poeticizing. Writing that uses immoderately heightened or distended language to sway the reader's feelings. 243

Point of view. The angle of vision from which a story is told. 161–67. The four basic points of view are as follows:

Omniscient point of view: The author tells the story, using the third person; he knows all and is free to tell us anything, including what the characters are thinking or feeling and why they act as they do. 162–63

Limited omniscient point of view: The author tells the story, using the third person, but limits himself to a complete knowledge of one character in the story and tells us only what that one character thinks, feels, sees, or hears. 163–64

First person point of view: The story is told by one of its characters, using the first person. 164–65

Objective (or *Dramatic*) *point of view:* The author tells the story, using the third person, but limits himself to reporting what his characters say or do; he does not interpret their behavior or tell us their private thoughts or feelings. 165–66

Protagonist. The central character in a story. 42

Quality fiction. Fiction that rejects tested formulas in an attempt to give a fresh interpretation of life. 6

Rising action. That development of plot in a story that precedes and leads up to the climax. 48

Round character. See *Character.*

Sentimentality. Unmerited or contrived tender feeling; that quality in a story that elicits or seeks to elicit tears through an oversimplification or falsification of reality. 242–44

Setting. The context in time and place in which the action of a story occurs.

Static character. See *Character.*

Stock character. See *Character.*

Surprise. An unexpected turn in the development of a plot. 45

Surprise ending. A completely unexpected revelation or turn of plot at the conclusion of a story. 45

Suspense. That quality in a story that makes the reader eager to discover what happens next and how it will end. 43–45

Symbol (*literary*). Something that means *more* than what it is; an object, person, situation, or action that in addition to its literal meaning suggests other meanings as well. 196–201

Theme.   The central idea or unifying generalization implied or stated by a literary work.   105–12

Unhappy ending.   An ending that turns out unhappily for a sympathetic protagonist.   45–46

Verbal irony.   See *Irony.*

Glossary of Poetic Terms

The definitions in this glossary sometimes repeat and sometimes differ in language from those in the text. Where they differ, the intention is to give a fuller sense of the term's meaning by allowing the reader a double perspective on it. Page numbers refer to discussion in the text, which in most but not all cases is fuller than that in the glossary.

Accent. In this book, the same as *stress.* A syllable given more prominence in pronunciation than its neighbors is said to be accented. 680–81

Allegory. A narrative or description having a second meaning beneath the surface one. 597–99

Alliteration. The repetition at close intervals of the initial consonant sounds of accented syllables or important words (for example, *m*ap-*m*oon, *k*ill-*c*ode, *p*reach-ap*p*rove). Important words and accented syllables beginning with vowels may also be said to alliterate with each other inasmuch as they all have the same lack of an initial consonant sound (for example, "*In*ebri*a*te of *a*ir am *I*"). 668–69, 670–71, 672

Allusion. A reference, explicit or implicit, to something in previous literature or history. (The term is reserved by some writers for implicit references only, such as those in "On His Blindness," 633, and "In the Garden," 639; but the distinction between the two kinds of reference is not always clear-cut.) 629–32

Anapest. A metrical foot consisting of two unaccented syllables followed by one accented syllable (for example, ŭn-dĕr-stānd). 682, 689

Anapestic meter. A meter in which a majority of the feet are anapests. (But see *Triple meter.*) 682, 690

Apostrophe. A figure of speech in which someone absent or dead or something nonhuman is addressed as if it were alive and present and could reply. 574–76

Approximate rime (also known as *imperfect rime, near rime, slant rime,* or *oblique rime*). A term used for words in a riming pattern that have some kind of sound correspondence but are not perfect rimes. See *Rime*. Approximate rimes occur occasionally in patterns where most of the rimes are perfect (for example, arrayed-said in "Richard Cory," 553), and sometimes are used systematically in place of perfect rime (for example, "Mr. Z," 625). 669, 670–71

Assonance. The repetition at close intervals of the vowel sounds of accented syllables or important words (for example, h*a*t-r*a*n-*a*mber, v*ei*n-m*a*de). 668–69, 670–71

Aubade. A poem about dawn; a morning love song; or a poem about the parting of lovers at dawn. 563, 576, 648

Ballad. A fairly short narrative poem written in a songlike stanza form. Examples: "O what is that sound," 542; "Farewell to barn and stack and tree," 658; "Edward," 731; "La Belle Dame sans Merci," 801. Also see *Folk ballad.*

Blank verse. Unrimed iambic pentameter. 691

Cacophony. A harsh, discordant, unpleasant-sounding choice and arrangement of sounds. 703–04

Caesura. See *Grammatical pause* and *Rhetorical pause.*

Connotation. What a word suggests beyond its basic definition; a word's overtones of meaning. 546–51

Consonance. The repetition at close intervals of the final consonant sounds of accented syllables or important words (for example, boo*k*-plaque-thi*ck*er). 668–69, 670–71

Continuous form. That form of a poem in which the lines follow each other without formal grouping, the only breaks being dictated by units of meaning. 717–18

Couplet. Two successive lines, usually in the same meter, linked by rime. 691 (Exercise 2), 722

Dactyl. A metrical foot consisting of one accented syllable followed by two unaccented syllables (for examples, mēr-rĭ-lȳ). 682

Dactylic meter. A meter in which a majority of the feet are dactyls. (But see *Triple meter.*) 682, 690

Denotation. The basic definition or dictionary meaning of a word. 546–51

Didactic poetry. Poetry having as a primary purpose to teach or preach. 739

Dimeter. A metrical line containing two feet. 682

Dipodic foot. The basic foot of *dipodic verse,* consisting (when complete) of an unaccented syllable, a lightly accented syllable, an unaccented syllable, and a heavily accented syllable, in that succession. However, dipodic verse accommodates a tremendous amount of variety, as shown by the examples in the text. 697

Dipodic verse. A meter in which there is a perceptible alternation between light and heavy stresses. See *Dipodic foot.* 697

Double rime. A rime in which the repeated vowel is in the second last syllable of the words involved (for example, politely-rightly-spritely); one form of *feminine rime.* 677 (Question 5)

Dramatic framework. The situation, whether actual or fictional, realistic or fanciful, in which an author places his or her characters in order to express the theme. 536-37

Dramatic irony. See *Irony.*

Duple meter. A meter in which a majority of the feet contain two syllables. Iambic and trochaic are both duple meters. 682

Elegy. A poem, usually formal, sustained, and meditative, expressing sorrow or lamentation over the death of someone loved or esteemed by the poet. 659, 660 (Question 2)

End rime. Rimes that occur at the ends of lines. 669

End-stopped line. A line that ends with a natural speech pause, usually marked by punctuation. 691

English (or Shakespearean) sonnet. A sonnet riming *ababcdcdefefgg*. Its content or structure ideally parallels the rime scheme, falling into three coordinate quatrains and a concluding couplet; but it is often structured, like the Italian sonnet, into octave and sestet, the principal break in thought coming at the end of the eighth line. 722-23, 723 (Exercise 3)

Euphony. A smooth, pleasant-sounding choice and arrangement of sounds. 703-04

Expected rhythm. The metrical expectation set up by the basic meter of a poem. 688

Extended figure (also known as *sustained figure*). A figure of speech (usually metaphor, simile, personification, or apostrophe) sustained or developed through a considerable number of lines or through a whole poem. 581

Feminine rime. A rime in which the repeated accented vowel is in either the second or third last syllable of the words involved (for example, ceiling-appealing; hurrying-scurrying). 669, 677 (Question 5)

Figurative language. Language employing figures of speech; language that cannot be taken literally or only literally. 570-80, 589-99, 609-17

Figure of speech. Broadly, any way of saying something other than the ordinary way; more narrowly (and for the purposes of this book) a way of saying one thing and meaning another. 570-80, 589-99, 609-17

Fixed form. Any form of poem in which the length and pattern are prescribed by previous usage or tradition, such as *sonnet, limerick, villanelle, haiku, sestina,* and so on. 720-23

Folk ballad. A narrative poem designed to be sung, composed by an anonymous author, and transmitted orally for years or generations before being written down. It has usually undergone modification through the process of oral transmission. "Edward," 731.

Foot The basic unit used in the scansion or measurement of verse. A foot usually contains one accented syllable and one or two unaccented syllables, but the *monosyllabic foot*, the *spondaic foot* (*spondee*), and the *dipodic foot* are all modifications of this principle. 681–82, 697

Form. The external pattern or shape of a poem, describable without reference to its content, as *continuous form, stanzaic form, fixed form* (and their varieties), *free verse*, and *syllabic verse*. 690, 717–24, 727. See *Structure.*

Free verse. Non-metrical verse. Poetry written in free verse is arranged in lines, may be more or less rhythmical, but has no fixed metrical pattern or expectation. 690

Grammatical pause (also known as *caesura*). A pause introduced into the reading of a line by a mark of punctuation. Grammatical pauses do not affect scansion. 688

Haiku. A three-line poem, Japanese in origin, narrowly conceived of as a fixed form in which the lines contain respectively 5, 7, and 5 syllables (in American practice this requirement is frequently dispensed with). Haiku are generally concerned with some aspect of nature and present a single image or two juxtaposed images without comment, relying on suggestion rather than on explicit statement to communicate their meaning. 727

Heard rhythm. The actual rhythm of a metrical poem as we hear it when it is read naturally. The heard rhythm mostly conforms to but sometimes departs from or modifies the *expected rhythm.* 688

Heptameter. A metrical line containing seven feet. 682

Hexameter. A metrical line containing six feet. 682

Hyperbole. See *Overstatement.*

Iamb. A metrical foot consisting of one unaccented syllable followed by one accented syllable (for example, rĕ-hēarse). 682

Iambic meter. A meter in which the majority of feet are iambs. The most common English meter. 682, 689

Iambic-anapestic meter. A meter which freely mixes iambs and anapests, and in which it might be difficult to determine which foot prevails without actually counting. 690

Imagery. The representation through language of sense experience. 560–63

Internal rime. A rime in which one or both of the rime-words occur *within* the line. 669

Irony. A situation, or a use of language, involving some kind of incongruity or discrepancey. 614. Three kinds of irony are distinguished in this book:

Verbal irony. A figure of speech in which what is meant is the opposite of what is said. 612–14

Dramatic irony. A device by which the author implies a different meaning from that intended by the speaker (or by *a* speaker) in a literary work. 615–16

Irony of situation (or *situational irony*). A situation in which there is an incongruity between actual circumstances and those that would seem appropriate or between what is anticipated and what actually comes to pass.

Italian (or *Petrarchan*) *sonnet*. A sonnet consisting of an octave riming *abbaabba* and of a sestet using any arrangement of two or three additional rimes, such as *cdcdcd* or *cdecde*. 721-22, 723 (Exercise 3)

Limerick. A fixed form consisting of five lines of anapestic meter, the first two trimeter, the next two dimeter, the last line trimeter, riming *aabba*; used exclusively for humorous or nonsense verse. 720-21, 724-25

Masculine rime (also known as *single rime*). A rime in which the repeated accented vowel sound is in the final syllable of the words involved (for example, dance-pants, scald-recalled). 669, 677 (Question 5)

Metaphor. A figure of speech in which an implicit comparison is made between two things essentially unlike. It may take one of four forms: (1) that in which the literal term and the figurative term are both *named;* (2) that in which the literal term is *named* and the figurative term *implied;* (3) that in which the literal term is *implied* and the figurative term *named;* (4) that in which both the literal and the figurative terms are *implied*. 671-74, 578-79

Meter. Regularized rhythm; an arrangement of language in which the accents occur at apparently equal intervals in time. 680-91

Metonymy. A figure of speech in which some significant aspect or detail of an experience is used to represent the whole experience. In this book the single term *metonymy* is used for what are sometimes distinguished as two separate figures: *synecdoche* (the use of the part for the whole) and *metonymy* (the use of something closely related for the thing actually meant). 576-78

Metrical pause. A pause that supplies the place of an expected accented syllable. Unlike *grammatical* and *rhetorical pauses*, metrical pauses affect scansion. 697-98

Monometer. A metrical line containing one foot. 682

Monosyllabic foot. A foot consisting of a single accented syllable (for example, shīne).

Octameter. A metrical line containing eight feet. 682

Octave. (1) An eight-line stanza. (2) The first eight lines of a sonnet, especially one structured in the manner of an Italian sonnet. 721

Onomatopoeia. The use of words that supposedly mimic their meaning in their sound (for example, boom, click, plop). 701

Onomatopoetic language. Language employing *onomatopoeia*.

Overstatement (or *hyperbole*). A figure of speech in which exaggeration is used in the service of truth. 610-12

Oxymoron. A compact paradox, one in which two successive words apparently contradict each other. 694

Paradox. A statement or situation containing apparently contradictory or incompatible elements. 609–10

Paradoxical situation. A situation containing apparently but not actually incompatible elements. The celebration of a fifth birthday anniversary by a twenty-year-old man is paradoxical but explainable if the man was born on February 29. The Christian doctrines that Christ was born of a virgin and is both God and man are, for a Christian believer, paradoxes (that is, apparently impossible but true). 609

Paradoxical statement (or *verbal paradox*). A figure of speech in which an apparently self-contradictory statement is nevertheless found to be true. 609–10

Paraphrase. A restatement of the content of a poem designed to make its *prose meaning* as clear as possible. 639

Pentameter. A metrical line containing five feet. 682

Personification. A figure of speech in which human attributes are given to an animal, an object, or a concept. 574–76

Petrarchan sonnet. See *Italian sonnet.*

Phonetic intensive. A word whose sound, by an obscure process, to some degree suggests its meaning. As differentiated from *onomatopoetic* words, the meanings of phonetic intensives do not refer to sounds. 701–02

Prose. Non-metrical language; the opposite of *verse.* 680–81

Prose meaning. That part of a poem's *total meaning* that can be separated out and expressed through paraphrase. 640–43

Prose poem. Usually a short composition having the intentions of poetry but written in prose rather than verse. 691

Quatrain. (1) A four-line stanza. (2) A four-line division of a sonnet marked off by its rime scheme. 716

Refrain. A repeated word, phrase, line, or group of lines, normally at some fixed position in a poem written in stanzaic form. 670, 672 (Exercise), 720

Rhetorical pause (also known as *caesura*). A natural pause, unmarked by punctuation, introduced into the reading of a line by its phrasing or syntax. Rhetorical pauses do not affect scansion. 688

Rhetorical poetry. Poetry using artificially eloquent language, that is, language too high-flown for its occasion and unfaithful to the full complexity of human experience. 739

Rhythm. Any wavelike recurrence of motion or sound. 680–81

Rime (or *rhyme*). The repetition of the accented vowel sound and all succeeding sounds in important or importantly positioned words (for example, old-cold, vane-reign, court-report, order-recorder). The above definition applies to *perfect rime* and assumes that the accented vowel sounds involved are preceded by differing consonant sounds. If the preceding consonant sound is the same (for example, manse-romance, style-stile), or if there is no preceding consonant sound in either word (for example, aisle-isle, alter-altar), or if the same word is repeated in the riming position (for example, hill-hill), the words are called *identical rimes*. Both *perfect rimes* and *identical rimes* are to be distinguished from *approximate rimes*. 669, 670

Rime scheme. Any fixed pattern of rimes characterizing a whole poem or its stanzas. 720

Run-on line. A line which has no natural speech pause at its end, allowing the sense to flow uninterruptedly into the succeeding line. 691

Sarcasm. Bitter or cutting speech; speech intended by its speaker to give pain to the person addressed. 612-613

Satire. A kind of literature that ridicules human folly or vice with the purpose of bringing about reform or of keeping others from falling into similar folly or vice. 612-13

Scansion. The process of measuring verse, that is, of marking accented and unaccented syllables, dividing the lines into feet, identifying the metrical pattern, and noting significant variations from that pattern. 682

Sentimental poetry. Poetry aimed primarily at stimulating the emotions rather than at communicating experience honestly and freshly. 738-39

Sestet. (1) A six-line stanza. (2) The last six lines of a sonnet structured on the Italian model. 721

Sestina. A complex fixed form of six six-line stanzas plus an *envoi* (or *envoy*), using the same six end-words throughout but repeated in a different order in each stanza. 731 (Question 6)

Shakespearean sonnet. See *English sonnet.*

Simile. A figure of speech in which an explicit comparison is made between two things essentially unlike. The comparison is made explicit by the use of some such word or phrase as *like, as, than, similar to, resembles,* or *seems.* 571

Single rime. See *Masculine rime.*

Situational irony. See *Irony.*

Sonnet. A fixed form of fourteen lines, normally iambic pentameter, with a rime scheme conforming to or approximating one of two main types—the *Italian* or the *English.* 721-24

Spondee. A metrical foot consisting of two syllables equally or almost equally accented (for example, trūe-blūe). 682

Stanza. A group of lines whose metrical pattern (and usually its rime scheme as well) is repeated throughout a poem. 682, 718-20

Stanzaic form. The form taken by a poem when it is written in a series of units having the same number of lines and usually other characteristics in common, such as metrical pattern or rime scheme. 718-20

Stress. In this book, the same as *Accent.* But see 681 (footnote).

Structure. The internal organization of a poem's content. See *Form.*

Sustained figure. See *Extended figure.*

Syllabic verse. Verse measured by the number of syllables rather than the number of feet per line. 727 (Question 4). Also see *Haiku.*

Symbol. A figure of speech in which something (object, person, situation, or action) means more than what it is. A symbol, in other words, may be read both literally and metaphorically. 589-97, 599 (Exercise)

Synecdoche. A figure of speech in which a part is used for the whole. In this book it is subsumed under the term *Metonymy.* 576-78

Terza rima. See 723 (Exercise 2).

Tetrameter. A metrical line containing four feet. 682

Theme. The central idea of a literary work. 539

Tone. The writer's or speaker's attitude toward his subject, his audience, or himself; the emotional coloring, or emotional meaning, of a work. 652-56

Total meaning. The total experience communicated by a poem. It includes all those dimensions of experience by which a poem communicates—sensuous, emotional, imaginative, and intellectual—and it can be communicated in no other words than those of the poem itself. 640-43

Trimeter. A metrical line containing three feet. 682

Triple meter. A meter in which a majority of the feet contain three syllables. (Actually, if more than 25 percent of the feet in a poem are triple, its effect is more triple than duple, and it ought perhaps to be referred to as triple meter.) Anapestic and dactylic are both triple meter. 682

Triple rime. A rime in which the repeated accented vowel sound is in the third last syllable of the words involved (for example, gainfully-disdainfully); one form of *feminine rime.* 677 (Question 5)

Trochaic meter. A meter in which the majority of feet are trochees. 682

Trochee. A metrical foot consisting of one accented syllable followed by one unaccented syllable (for example, bār-tĕr). 682

Understatement. A figure of speech that consists of saying less than one means, or of saying what one means with less force than the occasion warrants. 610-12

Verbal irony. See *Irony.*

Verse. Metrical language; the opposite of *prose.* 680-81

Villanelle. See 723 (Exercise 1).

Glossary of Dramatic Terms

This glossary is brief because most of the terms important for drama have already been defined either in the Glossary of Fictional Terms or in the Glossary of Poetic Terms. Page numbers after the terms here defined refer to discussion in the text, which in most cases but not all is fuller than that in the glossary.

Absurd, Drama of the.   A type of drama, allied to comedy, radically non-realistic in both content and presentation, that emphasizes the absurdity, emptiness, or meaninglessness of life.   875–76, 880

Aside.   A brief speech in which a character turns from the person he is addressing to speak directly to the audience; a dramatic device for letting the audience know what he is really thinking or feeling as opposed to what he pretends to think or feel.   838

Catharsis.   A term used by Aristotle to describe some sort of emotional release experienced by the audience at the end of a successful tragedy.   1052–53, 1054–55

Chorus.   A group of actors speaking or chanting in unison, often while going through the steps of an elaborate formalized dance; a characteristic device of Greek drama for conveying communal or group emotion.   879

Comedy.   A type of drama, opposed to tragedy, having usually a happy ending, and emphasizing human limitation rather than human greatness.   1052, 1055–58

Scornful comedy.   A type of comedy whose main purpose is to expose and ridicule human folly, vanity, or hypocrisy.   1055

Romantic comedy.   A type of comedy whose likable and sensible main characters are placed in difficulties from which they are rescued at the end of the play, either attaining their ends or having their good fortunes restored.   1055–56

Dramatic convention. Any dramatic device which, though it departs from reality, is implicitly accepted by author and audience as a means of representing reality. 879–80

Farce. A type of drama related to comedy but emphasizing improbable situations, violent conflicts, physical action, and coarse wit over characterization or articulated plot. 1057

Melodrama. A type of drama related to tragedy but featuring sensational incidents, emphasizing plot at the expense of characterization, relying on cruder conflicts (virtuous protagonist versus villainous antagonist), and having a happy ending in which good triumphs over evil. 1057

Narrator. In drama a character, found in some plays, who, speaking directly to the audience, introduces the action and provides a string of commentary between the dramatic scenes. He may or may not be a major character in the action itself. 879

Nonrealistic drama. Drama that, in content, presentation, or both, departs markedly from fidelity to the outward appearances of life. 877–81

Playwright. A maker of plays. 838

Realistic drama. Drama that attempts, in content and in presentation, to preserve the illusion of actual, everyday life. 877–81

Romantic comedy. See *Comedy.*

Scornful comedy. See *Comedy.*

Soliloquy. A speech in which a character, alone on the stage, addresses himself; a soliloquy is a "thinking out loud," a dramatic means of letting an audience know a character's thoughts and feelings. 838

Tragedy. A type of drama, opposed to comedy, in which the protagonist, a person of unusual moral or intellectual stature or outstanding abilities, suffers a fall in fortune because of some error of judgment, excessive virtue, or flaw in his nature. 1051–55, 1056

MCKNIGHT MALMAR "The Storm" reprinted by permission of Curtis Brown, Ltd. Copyright © 1944, 1972 by McKnight Malmar.

KATHERINE MANSFIELD "Miss Brill" copyright 1922 by Alfred A. Knopf, Inc. and renewed 1950 by John Middleton Murry. Reprinted from *The Short Stories of Katherine Mansfield* by permission of the publisher.

ALICE MUNRO "An Ounce of Cure" from *Dance of the Happy Shades and Other Stories* by Alice Munro. Reprinted by permission of McGraw-Hill Ryerson Limited.

FLANNERY O'CONNOR "Greenleaf" from *Everything That Rises Must Converge* by Flannery O'Connor. Copyright © 1956, 1965 by the Estate of Mary Flannery O'Connor.

FRANK O'CONNOR "The Drunkard" copyright 1951 by Frank O'Connor. Reprinted from *Collected Stories*, by Frank O'Connor, by permission of Alfred A. Knopf, Inc.

KATHERINE ANNE PORTER "Rope" copyright, 1930, 1958, by Katherine Anne Porter. Reprinted from her volume *Flowering Judas and Other Stories* by permission of Harcourt Brace Jovanovich, Inc.

PHILIP ROTH "Defender of the Faith" from *Goodbye, Columbus* by Philip Roth. Copyright © 1959 by Philip Roth. Reprinted by permission of Houghton Mifflin Company.

JAMES THURBER "The Catbird Seat" copyright © 1945 James Thurber. Copyright © 1973 Helen W. Thurber and Rosemary T. Sauers. From *The Thurber Carnival*, published by Harper & Row.

LEO TOLSTOY "The Death of Ivan Ilych" from *The Death of Ivan Ilych and Other Stories* by Leo Tolstoy, translated by Louise and Aylmer Maude. Reprinted by permission of Oxford University Press.

ALICE WALKER "To Hell with Dying" copyright © 1967 by Alice Walker. Reprinted from her volume *In Love & Trouble: Stories of Black Women* by permission of Harcourt Brace Jovanovich, Inc.

EUDORA WELTY "Death of a Traveling Salesman" from *A Curtain of Green and Other Stories*, copyright, 1941, 1969 by Eudora Welty. Reprinted by permission of Harcourt Brace Jovanovich, Inc.

THOMAS WOLFE "The Child by Tiger" from *The Web and the Rock* by Thomas Wolfe. Copyright 1937 by Maxwell Perkins; renewed 1965 by Paul Gitlin, C. T. A., Administrator of the Estate of Thomas Wolfe. Reprinted by permission of Harper & Row, Publishers, Inc. This version originally appeared in the *Saturday Evening Post*.

POETRY

LEONARD ADAME "Black and White" from *American Poetry Review*, Vol. 6, No. 3, May/June 1977, by permission of the author.

SAMUEL ALLEN "To Satch" from *American Negro Poetry* by Samuel Allen. Reprinted by permission of the author.

KINGSLEY AMIS "The Last War" from *A Case of Samples* by Kingsley Amis. Reprinted by permission of A.D. Peters & Co. Ltd.

MARGARET ATWOOD "Landcrab" from *Field #22*, Spring 1980, by permission of *Field* Magazine.

W. H. AUDEN "O where are you going?" copyright 1934 and renewed 1962 by W. H. Auden. "That night when joy began" and "O what is that sound" copyright 1937 and renewed 1965 by W. H. Auden. "Musee des Beaux Arts" and "The Unknown Citizen" copyright 1940 and renewed 1968 by W. H. Auden. Reprinted from *Collected*

SARA TEASDALE "Barter" reprinted with permission of Macmillan Publishing Co., Inc. from *Collected Poems* by Sara Teasdale. Copyright 1917 by Macmillan Publishing Co., Inc., renewed 1945 by Mamie T. Whaless.

DYLAN THOMAS "Poem in October," "Do not go gentle into that good night," and "Fern Hill" from *The Poems of Dylan Thomas*. Copyright 1946 by New Directions Publishing Corporation, copyright 1952 by Dylan Thomas. Reprinted by permission of New Directions Publishing Corporation, J. M. Dent & Sons Ltd., and the Trustees of the Copyrights of the late Dylan Thomas.

EDWARD THOMAS "The Owl" is reprinted from *Collected Poems* of Edward Thomas, by permission of W. W. Norton & Company, Inc. Copyright 1974 by Faber and Faber Ltd.

JOHN UPDIKE "Winter Ocean" copyright © 1960 by John Updike. Reprinted from *Telephone Poles and Other Poems*, by John Updike, by permission of Alfred A. Knopf, Inc.

HENRY VAN DYKE "America for Me" from *The Poems of Henry van Dyke* by Henry van Dyke. Copyright 1911 Charles Scribner's Sons; copyright renewed. Reprinted by permission of the publisher.

DAVID WAGONER "Being Herded Past the Prison's Honor Farm" from *In Broken Country: Poems* by David Wagoner. Copyright © 1979 by David Wagoner. First Appeared in *Poetry*, January, 1979. By permission of Little, Brown and Company in association with Atlantic Monthly Press.

JOHN WAKEMAN "Love in Brooklyn" first appeared in *Poetry*. Copyright © 1980 by the Modern Poetry Association, Reprinted by permission of the Editor of *Poetry* and the author.

DEREK WALCOTT "The Virgins" from *Seagrapes* by Derek Walcott. Copyright © 1971, 1973, 1974, 1975, 1976 by Derek Walcott. Reprinted by permission of Farrar, Straus and Giroux, Inc.

ROBERT PENN WARREN "Boy Wandering in Simms' Valley" copyright © 1977 by Robert Penn Warren. Reprinted from *Now and Then: Poems 1976–1978*, by Robert Penn Warren, by permission of Random House, Inc.

JOHN HALL WHEELOCK "Earth" from *The Gardener and Other Poems* by John Hall Wheelock. Copyright © 1961 John Hall Wheelock. Reprinted by permission of Charles Scribner's Sons.

RICHARD WILBUR "The Mill" from *Things of This World* © 1956 by Richard Wilbur. Reprinted by permission of Harcourt Brace Jovanovich, Inc. "A Hole in the Floor" © 1961 by Richard Wilbur. Reprinted from his volume *Advice to a Prophet and Other Poems* by permission of Harcourt Brace Jovanovich, Inc. First published in *The New Yorker*. "A Late Aubade" © 1968 by Richard Wilbur. Reprinted from his volume *Walking to Sleep: New Poems and Translations* by permission of Harcourt Brace Jovanovich, Inc. First published in the *New Yorker*.

WILLIAM CARLOS WILLIAMS "The Dance" from *Collected Later Poems* by William Carlos Williams. Copyright 1944 by William Carlos Williams. "The Red Wheelbarrow" from *Collected Earlier Poems* by William Carlos Williams. Copyright 1938 by New Directions Publishing Corporation. Both poems reprinted by permission of New Directions Publishing Corporation.

WILLIAM BUTLER YEATS "Leda and the Swan" and "Sailing to Byzantium" copyright 1928 by Macmillan Publishing Co., Inc., renewed 1956 by Georgie Yeats; "Down by the Salley Gardens" copyright 1906 by Macmillan Publishing Co., Inc., renewed 1934

William Butler Yeats; "The Coming of Wisdom with Time, copyright 1912 by Mac-millan Publishing Co., Inc., renewed 1940 by Bertha Georgie Yeats; "The Wild Swans at Coole" copyright 1919 by Macmillan Publishing Co., Inc., renewed 1947 by Bertha Georgie Yeats; "The Second Coming" copyright 1924 by Macmillan Publish-ing Co., Inc., renewed 1952 by Bertha Georgie Yeats. Reprinted from *The Collected Poems of W. B. Yeats* by permission of Macmillan Publishing Co., Inc., M. B. Yeats, Anne Yeats, and Macmillan London Ltd.

DRAMA

EDWARD ALBEE   *The Sandbox* reprinted by permission of Coward-McCann & Geohegan, Inc. from *The Sandbox* by Edward Albee. Copyright © 1960 by Edward Albee. *The Sandbox* is the sole property of the author and is fully protected by copyright. It may not be acted either by professionals or amateurs without written consent. Public read-ings, radio and television broadcasts likewise are forbidden. All inquiries concerning these rights should be addressed to the William Morris Agency, 1350 Avenue of the Americas, New York, N.Y. 10019.

ANTON CHEKHOV   *The Cherry Orchard* from *Chekhov: The Major Plays*, a new translation by Ann Dunnigan. Copyright © 1964 by Ann Dunnigan. Reprinted by arrangement with The New American Library, Inc., New York, N.Y.

FEDERICO GARCIA LORCA   *Blood Wedding* from *Three Tragedies* by Federico García Lorca, translated by James Graham-Lujan and Richard O'Connell. Copyright © 1941 by Charles Scribner's Sons, © 1963 by New Directions Publishing Corporation. Re-printed by permission of New Directions.

ARTHUR MILLER   *Death of a Salesman*. Copyright 1949 by Arthur Miller. Copyright re-newed 1977 by Arthur Miller. Reprinted by permission of Viking Penguin Inc. Cau-tion: This play in its printed form is designed for the reading public only. All dramatic rights in it are fully protected by copyright, and no public or private performance—professional or amateur—may be given without the written permission of the author and the payment of royalty. As the courts have also ruled that the public reading of a play constitutes a public performance, no such reading may be given except under the conditions stated above. Communication should be addressed to the author's repre-sentative, Ashley Famous Agency, Inc., 1301 Avenue of the Americas, New York, N.Y. 10019.

MOLIÈRE   *The Misanthrope* by Molière translated by Richard Wilbur, copyright © 1954, 1955, by Richard Wilbur. Reprinted by permission of Harcourt Brace Jovanovich, Inc. Caution: Professionals and amateurs are hereby warned that this translation, being fully protected under the copyright laws of the United States of America, the British Empire, including the Dominion of Canada, and all other countries which are signatories to the Universal Copyright Convention and the International Copyright Union, are subject to royalty. All rights, including professional, amateur, motion picture, recitation, lecturing, public reading, radio broadcasting, and television, are strictly reserved. Particular emphasis is laid on the question of readings, permission for which must be secured from the author's agent in writing. Inquiries on profes-sional rights (except for amateur rights) should be addressed to Mr. Gilbert Parker, Curtis Brown, Ltd., 60 East 56th Street, New York, N.Y. 10022. The amateur acting rights are controlled exclusively by the Dramatists Play Service, Inc., 440 Park Ave-nue South, New York, N.Y. 10016. No amateur performance of the play may be given without obtaining in advance the written permission of the Dramatists Play Service, Inc., and paying the requisite fee.

Index of Authors, Titles, and First Lines

Authors' names appear in capitals, titles of selections in italics, and first lines of poems in roman type. Numbers in roman type indicate the page of a selection, and italic numbers indicate discussion of the selection.